A People & A Nation

A PEOPLE
& A NATION

A History of The United States

BRIEF TENTH EDITION

Mary Beth Norton
Cornell University

Jane Kamensky
Brandeis University

Carol Sheriff
College of William and Mary

David W. Blight
Yale University

Howard P. Chudacoff
Brown University

Fredrik Logevall
Cornell University

Beth Bailey
Temple University

Debra Michals
Merrimack College

CENGAGE
Learning·

Australia • Brazil • Japan • Korea • Mexico • Singapore • Spain • United Kingdom • United States

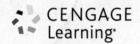
CENGAGE
Learning·

A People and A Nation, **Brief Tenth Edition**
Mary Beth Norton, Jane Kamensky,
Carol Sheriff, David W. Blight,
Howard P. Chudacoff, Fredrik Logevall,
Beth Bailey, Debra Michals

Product Director: Suzanne Jeans

Senior Product Manager: Ann West

Content Developer: Lauren Floyd

Associate Content Developer:
   Megan Chrisman

Product Assistant: Liz Fraser

Senior Media Developer: Laura Hildebrand

Marketing Manager: Valerie Hartman

Market Development Manager:
   Kyle Zimmerman

Senior Content Project Manager: Jane Lee

Senior Art Director: Cate Rickard Barr

Manufacturing Planner: Sandee Milewski

Senior Rights Acquisition Specialist:
   Jennifer Meyer Dare

Production Service:
   Integra Software Services

Cover Designer: Dutton & Sherman Design

Cover Image: Mora, Francis Luis
   (1874–1940). *Subway Evening News,* 1914.
   Museum of the City of New York, New
   York, NY, USA. Photo Credit: © Museum
   of the City of New York/The Art Archive
   at Art Resource, NY.

Compositor: Integra Software Services

For product information and technology assistance, contact us at
Cengage Learning Customer & Sales Support, 1-800-354-9706

For permission to use material from this text or product,
submit all requests online at **www.cengage.com/permissions.**
Further permissions questions can be emailed to
permissionrequest@cengage.com.

Library of Congress Control Number: 2013944018

Student Edition:

ISBN-13: 978-1-285-43084-3

ISBN-10: 1-285-43084-0

Cengage Learning
200 First Stamford Place, 4th Floor
Stamford, CT 06902
USA

Cengage Learning is a leading provider of customized learning solutions
with office locations around the globe, including Singapore, the United
Kingdom, Australia, Mexico, Brazil and Japan. Locate your local office at
international.cengage.com/region.

Cengage Learning products are represented in Canada by Nelson
Education, Ltd.

For your course and learning solutions, visit **www.cengage.com.**

Purchase any of our products at your local college store or at our
preferred online store **www.cengagebrain.com.**

Instructors: Please visit **login.cengage.com** and log in to access
instructor-specific resources.

Printed in Canada
2 3 4 5 6 7 17 16 15 14

Brief Contents

v

Contents

Features

FIGURES

TABLES

Preface

Published originally in 1982, *A People and A Nation* was the first U.S. history survey textbook to move beyond a political history to tell the story of the nation's people—the story of *all* its people—as well. That commitment remains. Our text encompasses the diversity of America's people, the changing texture of their everyday lives, and the country's political narrative. But as historical questions have evolved over the years and new authors have joined the textbook team, we have asked new questions about "a people" and "a nation." The *A People* and *A Nation* that appear in the book's title are neither timeless nor stable. European colonists and the land's indigenous inhabitants did not belong to this "nation" or work to create it, and Americans have struggled over the shape and meaning of their nation since its very beginning. The people about whom we write thought of themselves in various ways that changed over time. Thus we emphasize not only the ongoing diversity of the nation's people, but their struggles, through time, over who belongs to that "people" and on what terms.

In the tenth edition, we emphasize the changing global and transnational contexts within which the American colonies and the United States have acted. We discuss the ways that an evolving market economy shaped the nation and the possibilities for its different peoples. We show how the meaning of personal, regional, and familial identity changes over time, and we find the nation's history in the contact and collision of its peoples. We think about the role of the state and the expanding reach of the federal government; we emphasize historical contests between federal power and local authority. We examine the consequences of America's expansion and rise to unprecedented world power. And we focus on the meaning of democracy and equality in American history, most particularly in tales of Americans' struggles for equal rights and social justice.

About *A People and A Nation,* Brief

This brief tenth edition, as with earlier brief editions, aims to preserve the integrity of the complete work—along with its unique approach—while condensing it. This edition reflects the scholarship, readability, and comprehensiveness of the full-length version. It also maintains the integration of social, cultural, political, economic, and foreign relations history that has been a hallmark of *A People and A Nation.*

Dr. Debra Michals has worked with us again, along with Dr. Robert Heinrich, to ensure that the changes in content and organization incorporated in the full-length tenth edition were retained in the condensation. The authors attained reductions by paring down details rather than deleting entire sections. The brief tenth edition thus contains fewer statistics, fewer quotations, and fewer examples than the unabridged edition. The brief edition also includes more pedagogy than the unabridged edition: each main heading has a marginal question to give students a preview of the key topics covered. These questions are answered at the end of the chapter in the "Chapter Review." Throughout the chapters, students get assistance from key terms that are boldfaced in the text and defined in the margins.

What's New in This Edition

A primary goal of the revision of *APAN* 10e was to streamline coverage, reducing the number of chapters and so making the book easier to use in an academic semester. The Brief edition follows this new chapter organization and is built on *A People and A Nation*'s hallmark themes, giving increased attention to the global perspective on American history that has characterized the book since its first edition. From the "Atlantic world" context of European colonies in North and South America to the discussion of international terrorism, the authors have incorporated the most recent globally oriented scholarship throughout the volume. We have stressed the incorporation of different peoples into the United States through territorial acquisition as well as through immigration. At the same time, we have integrated the discussion of such diversity into our narrative so as not to artificially isolate any group from the mainstream.

Chapter-by-Chapter Changes

We reduced the number of chapters in the complete book by four—two in each volume. We achieved this reduction by taking a hard look at the areas where the same topics were covered in multiple chapters or where combining material in new ways allowed us to explain historical events more clearly. The list that follows indicates where content has been combined or reworked and which chapter in the ninth edition that content corresponds to (where there has been a change in chapter number). Other chapter-by-chapter changes and additions (including new scholarship) are outlined below as well.

1. **Three Old Worlds Create a New, 1492–1600**
   - New chapter opening vignette on Doña Marina establishes a major theme of cross-cultural communication and miscommunication
   - Increased emphasis on a world in motion: the circulation of goods, peoples, ideas, and money around the Atlantic basin, with new content on African history and the African diaspora
   - New Visualizing the Past, "Naming America"
   - New Legacy for A People and A Nation, "Revitalizing Native Languages"

2. **Europeans Colonize North America, 1600–1650**
   - Chapter-opening vignette reshaped to emphasize the growth of slavery, which receives increased attention in the chapter
   - Expanded coverage of the "sugar revolution" in the Caribbean colonies, their economic importance to Europe, and their role in the growth of new world slavery
   - New Legacy for A People and A Nation, "'Modern' Families"
   - New map, "Caribbean Colonies ca. 1700" (Map 2.2), offers more detail on the economically central colonies of the English, French, Spanish, and Dutch Caribbean

3. **North America in the Atlantic World, 1650–1720**
   - New chapter-opening vignette on the "Indian Kings"
   - Revised and increased coverage of Atlantic slavery, with new statistical foundation in the authoritative Trans-Atlantic Slave Trade Database
   - New Visualizing the Past, "The Pine Tree Shilling"

- Revised map, "The Anglo-American Colonies in the Early Eighteenth Century" (Map 3.1), with increased attention to England's non-mainland colonies
- Revised map, "Atlantic Trade Routes" (Map 3.2)

4. Becoming America? 1720–1760

- New chapter-opening vignette on the 1744 progress of Dr. Hamilton through the colonies
- New central problem framed: are Britain's North American colonies becoming more like or more unlike Britain in the mid-eighteenth century?
- Increased coverage of imperial warfare, including the capture and subsequent return of Louisbourg by colonial troops fighting for Britain
- New Figure 4.1, showing the origins of immigrants to North America in the eighteenth century; shows increasing ethnic diversity of the colonies and overwhelming dominance of African forced migration
- New Figure 4.2, showing the value of exports and imports by colony, demonstrating the economic dominance of Britain's Caribbean possessions

5. The Ends of Empire, 1754–1774

- Combines material from the ninth edition's Chapters 4 , 5, and 6
- New chapter-opening vignette on Boston's "Day of General Rejoicing," celebrating Britain's capture of Quebec
- Increased attention to the *dis*unity of the British colonies on the eve of revolution
- New coverage of slavery and emergent antislavery in the context of the imperial crisis
- New section, "The Unsettled Backcountry," pulls together material fragmented across three chapters in earlier editions and extends discussion of the Regulator movement in the Carolinas
- New Links to the World, "Writing and Stationery Supplies," tied to the Stamp Act protests
- New Visualizing the Past, "Phillis Wheatley, Enslaved Poet in the Cradle of Liberty"
- Revised map, "Colonial Resistance to the Stamp Act" (Map 5.3), showing more locations in continental North America and the Caribbean where the Stamp Act inspired crowd actions

6. American Revolutions, 1775–1783

- Combines material from the ninth edition's Chapters 6 and 7
- New chapter-opening vignette on Mohawk leader Konwatsitsiaenni (Molly Brant) establishes the Revolution as a multisided, multicausal conflict featuring multiple perspectives
- Expands coverage of loyalists, black and white, and neutrals
- New treatment of the Revolution as a global war
- New focus on the logic behind British tactics in prosecuting the American war, and on the relationship between war aims in the Caribbean and the shape of the conflict in North America
- New section on funding the Revolution, including the hyperinflation of the Continental dollar
- New concluding section on the ambivalent endings of the conflict for Britons and Americans in the new United States

7. **Forging a Nation, 1783–1800**
   - Combines material from the ninth edition's Chapters 7 and 8
   - New chapter-opening vignette on the journey to freedom of former slave Harry Washington, which took him from George Washington's Mount Vernon to Halifax to Sierra Leone
   - Introduces new concept of the "revolutionary settlement," which continues in subsequent chapters: winning of the War of Independence marks one formal revolution in American society; the "settlement" of the revolution between 1783 and 1815 involved numerous other contests. Stresses tensions between the broad promises of the Declaration and the bounded world of American citizenship, and the extent to which domestic political and economic visions are forged among other nations, especially Britain and France, but also Iroquoia
   - Expanded coverage of the role of culture and the arts in the creation of a national identity to encompass a highly pluralistic and divided society

8. **Defining the Nation, 1801–1823**
   - Combines material from the ninth edition's Chapters 9, 11, and 12
   - New section on religious revivals
   - Material on early abolitionism and colonization has been moved here from the ninth edition's Chapter 12, which allows us to consider its southern as well as its northern manifestations
   - Includes material on preindustrial farms, preindustrial artisans, and early industrialization from the ninth edition's Chapter 11, which allows us to consider southern as well as northern aspects of these topics
   - Reorganizes some material so that it now more closely follows a chronological order (e.g., the Missouri Compromise of 1820 now comes before the Monroe Doctrine of 1823)
   - New Links to the World, "Emigration to Liberia"

9. **The Rise of the South, 1815–1860**
   - Chapter 10 in the ninth edition
   - Adds new material to reflect recent scholarship on slavery and capitalism

10. **The Restless North, 1815–1860**
    - Combines material from the ninth edition's Chapters 11 and 12
    - Material on religion, reform, engineering and science, utopianism, and post-1820s abolitionism and the Liberty Party has been moved to this chapter
    - Visualizing the Past, "Engaging Children," has been moved here from the ninth edition's Chapter 12

11. **The Contested West, 1815–1860**
    - Chapter 13 in the ninth edition
    - Adds section on "War of a Thousand Deserts" (southwestern borderlands warfare), helping to set the stage for war with Mexico in Chapter 12

12. **Politics and the Fate of the Union, 1824–1859**
    - Combines material from the ninth edition's Chapters 12 and 14
    - New chapter-opening vignette on Harriet Beecher Stowe's *Uncle Tom's Cabin*
    - Includes section on "The Politics of Territorial Expansion" from the ninth edition's Chapter 13

- Now ends with John Brown's raid on Harpers Ferry in 1859
- New Legacy for A People and A Nation, "Coalition Politics"

13. Transforming Fire: The Civil War, 1860–1865
- Chapter 15 in the ninth edition
- Chapter now begins with the election of 1860, secession, and Fort Sumter
- Updates death numbers for the Civil War

14. Reconstruction: An Unfinished Revolution, 1865–1877
- Chapter 16 in the ninth edition
- New material reflects recent scholarship on southerners' dependence on the state for goods and services well after the traditional end of Reconstruction

15. The Ecology of the West and South, 1865–1900
- Combines material from the ninth edition's Chapters 17 and 20
- New chapter-opening vignette on Nannie Stillwell Jackson's diary entries about everyday life in rural Arkansas in the late nineteenth century
- New theme of ecology (interactions between humans and the environment)
- New and expanded coverage of the South from the ninth edition's Chapter 20

16. Building Factories, Building Cities, 1877–1920
- Combines material from the ninth edition's Chapters 18 and 19
- New chapter-opening vignette on Coney Island
- Streamlines and reorganizes material

17. Gilded Age Politics, 1877–1900
- Chapter 20 in the ninth edition
- New chapter-opening vignette on William Graham Sumner, champion of individual liberties
- New content on influence of police power (government intervention), especially at state and local levels, to balance traditional interpretations that the Gilded Age was an era of laissez-faire

18. The Progressive Era, 1895–1920
- Chapter 21 in the ninth edition
- Expanded and reorganized material on foreign influences
- New Links to the World, "Toynbee Hall, London"

19. The Quest for Empire, 1865–1914
- Chapter 22 in the ninth edition
- Tightens some sections and adds new material to reflect recent scholarship

20. Americans in the Great War, 1914–1920
- Chapter 23 in the ninth edition

21. The New Era, 1920–1929
- Combines material from the ninth edition's Chapters 24 and 26
- Reorganized to integrate economic expansion abroad

22. The Great Depression and the New Deal, 1929–1939
- Combines material from the ninth edition's Chapters 25 and 26

- Integrates material on the international causes and effects of the Great Depression, better situating the United States in the global economic crisis and growing global struggles
- Incorporates the section "The Approach of War" from the ninth edition's Chapter 26, newly connecting 1930s foreign policy to the domestic economic crisis Tightens domestic sections and eliminates some detail

23. The Second World War at Home and Abroad, 1939–1945

- Combines material from the ninth edition's Chapters 26 and 27
- New chapter-opening vignette on Hawai'i and the Pearl Harbor attack
- Includes material leading up to America's entry into the war, showing more clearly that America's role did not begin when Japan attacked Pearl Harbor
- Condenses coverage of the war into a single chapter

24. The Cold War and American Globalism, 1945–1961

- Chapter 28 in the ninth edition
- Provides new detail pertaining to Eisenhower's Cold War, in particular relating to the Third World
- Updates the map, "The Rise of the Third World: Newly Independent Nations Since 1943" (Map 24.3)

25. America at Midcentury, 1945–1960

- Chapter 29 in the ninth edition
- Expands discussion of the role of popular opinion in the civil rights struggle
- Adds an emphasis on how African American leaders focused on the international context in their ongoing struggle for social justice and civil rights
- Provides new comparative statistics on family life
- Revises discussion of the GI Bill

26. The Tumultuous Sixties, 1960–1968

- Chapter 30 in the ninth edition
- Reorganizes the section on "Liberalism and the Great Society"
- Provides new information on the growth of federal spending

27. A Pivotal Era, 1969–1980

- Chapter 31 in the ninth edition
- New chapter title conveys significant reinterpretation based on recent scholarship
- New section titled "Rights, Liberation, and Nationalism" incorporates and recasts material from the ninth edition's "The New Politics of Identity" and "The Women's Movement and Gay Liberation"
- Emphasizes the growing importance of marketplace solutions and development of debates about government regulation and the marketplace, as well as giving greater attention to government deficits—to help students understand the historical origins of current political debates
- Revises and reorganizes discussion of affirmative action to reflect recent scholarship
- Clarifies explanation of the causes of economic crises
- Emphasizes the original bipartisan support for the ERA
- Includes new comments on Nixon's domestic role

28. Conservatism Revived, 1980–1992

- Chapter 32 in the ninth edition
- Significantly revises and reorganizes previous material to show the broader social forces/shifts that helped to forge the new conservative coalition, in keeping with current scholarship
- Gives more attention to regulation and the economy
- Provides new material on the role and tactics of ACT UP
- Reorganizes the section on "The End of the Cold War and Global Disorder" to clarify the role of the George Bush (Sr.) administration and the relationship between international and domestic material

29. Into the Global Millennium: America Since 1992

- Chapter 33 in the ninth edition
- Tightens and reorganizes domestic material on the 1990s; replaces "Violence and Anger in American Society" with "Domestic Terrorism"
- New section on "Violence, Crime, and Incarceration" draws on recent scholarship on mass incarceration and its impact on American society, including discussion of gun violence
- Updates information on demographics, population diversity and race/ethnicity, immigration, health, and the changing American family in "Americans in the New Millennium"
- Substantially adds to treatment of the war in Afghanistan and significantly revises Iraq War treatment, including the drawdown of U.S. troops
- Includes a new section on the death of bin Laden
- Adds information about the election of 2012, Obama's first term, congressional deadlock and partisan conflict, the tea party, Obamacare, and DADT
- Discusses tensions with Iran under Obama, and foreign policy in the 2012
- New Visualizing the Past, "American War Dead"
- New Legacy for A People and A Nation, "Twitter Revolution"
- Updated figures, tables, and maps

Chapter Features: Legacies, Links to the World, and Visualizing the Past

The features in *A People and A Nation, Brief,* tenth edition, illustrate key themes of the text and give students alternative ways to experience historical content.

Legacy for A People and A Nation features appear toward the end of each chapter and offer compelling and timely answers to students who question the relevance of historical study by exploring the historical roots of contemporary topics. New Legacies in this edition include "Revitalizing Native Languages," "'Modern' Families," "Coalition Politics," and "Twitter Revolution."

Links to the World examine ties between America (and Americans) and the rest of the world. These brief essays detail the often little-known connections between developments here and abroad, vividly demonstrating that the geographical region that is now the United States has never been isolated from other peoples and countries. Essay topics range broadly over economic, political, social, technological, medical, and cultural history, and the feature appears near relevant discussions in each chapter. This edition includes new Links on emigration to Liberia and on Toynbee Hall, London. Each Link feature highlights global interconnections with unusual and lively examples that will both intrigue and inform students.

Visualizing the Past offers striking images along with brief discussions intended to help students analyze the images as historical sources and to understand how visual materials can reveal aspects of America's story that otherwise might remain unknown. New to this edition are features about the naming of America, the pine tree shilling, and poet Phillis Wheatley.

A People and A Nation Versions and Platforms

A People and A Nation is available in a number of different versions and formats, so you can choose the learning experience that works best for you and your students. The options include downloadable and online ebooks, Aplia™ online homework, and MindTap™, a personalized, fully online digital learning platform with ebook and homework all in one place. In addition, a number of useful teaching and learning aids are available to help you with course management/presentation and students with course review and self-testing. These supplements have been created with the diverse needs of today's students and instructors in mind.

CengageBrain eBook. An easy-to-use ebook version of *A People & A Nation, Brief* is available for purchase in its entirety or as individual chapters at www.Cengage Brain.com. This ebook has the same look and pagination as the printed text and is fully searchable, easy to navigate, and accessible online or offline. Students can also purchase the full ebook from our partner, CourseSmart, at www.CourseSmart.com.

MindTap Reader **for** *A People and A Nation, Brief* is an interactive ebook specifically designed for the ways in which students assimilate content and media assets in online—and often mobile—reading environments. MindTap Reader combines thoughtful navigation, advanced student annotation support, and a high level of instructor-driven personalization through the placement of online documents and media assets. These features create an engaging reading experience for today's learners. The MindTap Reader eBook is available inside MindTap and Aplia online products. (See below.)

MindTap™: The Personal Learning Experience. MindTap for *A People and A Nation, Brief* is a personalized, online digital learning platform providing students with the full content from the book and related interactive assignments—and instructors a choice in the configuration of coursework and curriculum enhancement. Through a carefully designed chapter-based Learning Path, students work their way through the content in each chapter, aided by dynamic author videos, reading in the ebook (MindTap Reader), robust Aplia™ assignments built around the text content, primary sources, and maps and frequent Check Your Understanding quizzes. A set of web applications known as MindApps helps students in many aspects of their learning and range from ReadSpeaker (which reads the text out loud), to Kaltura (which allows instructors to insert online video and audio into the ebook), to ConnectYard (which allows instructors to create digital "yards" through social media—all without "friending" their students). To learn more, ask your Cengage Learning sales representative to demo it for you—or go to www.Cengage.com/MindTap.

Aplia™ is an online homework product that improves comprehension and outcomes by increasing student effort and engagement. Founded by a professor to enhance his own courses, Aplia provides automatically graded assignments with detailed, immediate explanations on every question. The assignments developed for *A People & A Nation* address the major concepts in each chapter and are designed to promote critical thinking. Question types include questions built around animated maps, primary sources such as newspaper extracts and cartoons, or imagined scenarios, like engaging in a conversation with Benjamin Franklin; images, video clips, and audio clips are incorporated into many of the questions. More in-depth primary source question sets built around larger topics, such as "Native American and European Encounters" or "The Cultural Cold War," promote deeper analysis of historical evidence. Students get immediate feedback on their work (not only what they got right or wrong, but *why*), and they can choose to see another set of related questions if they want to practice further. A searchable **MindTap Reader ebook** is available inside the course as well, for easy reference. Aplia's simple-to-use course management interface allows instructors to post announcements, upload course materials, host student discussions, e-mail students, and manage the gradebook. Personalized support from a knowledgeable and friendly support team also offers assistance in customizing assignments to the instructor's course schedule. For a more comprehensive, all-in-one course solution, Aplia assignments may be found within the MindTap Personal Learning platform (see previous page). To learn more, ask your Cengage Learning sales representative to provide a demo—or view a specific demo for this book at www.aplia.com.

Instructor Resources

Instructor Companion Site. Instructors will find here all the tools they need to teach a rich and successful U.S. history survey course. The protected teaching materials include the *Instructor's Resource Manual*, a set of customizable Microsoft® PowerPoint® lecture slides, and a set of customizable Microsoft® PowerPoint® image slides, including all of the images (photos, art, and maps) from the text. Also included is Cognero®, a flexible, online testing system that allows you to author, edit, and manage test bank content for *A People and A Nation, Brief.* You can create multiple test versions instantly and deliver them through your LMS from your classroom, or wherever you may be, with no special installations or downloads required. The test items include multiple-choice, identification, geography, and essay questions. Go to login.cengage.com to access this site.

eInstructor's Resource Manual. This manual (found on the Instructor Companion site), authored by Chad William Timm of Grand View University, contains a set of learning objectives, a comprehensive chapter outline, ideas for classroom activities, discussion questions, suggested paper topics, and a lecture supplement for each chapter in *A People and A Nation, Brief.*

Student Resources

cengagebrain.com. Save your students time and money. Direct them to www.cengagebrain.com for choice in formats and savings and a better chance to succeed in class. Students have the freedom to purchase à la carte exactly what they need when they need it. Students can purchase or rent their text or purchase access to a downloadable ebook version of *A People and A Nation, Brief.* eAudio modules from *The History Handbook,* or other useful study tools.

Companion Website. The *A People & A Nation, Brief* Student Companion website, available on CengageBrain.com, offers a variety of free learning materials to help students review content and prepare for class and tests. These materials include flashcards, primary source links, and quizzes for self-testing.

Additional Resources

Reader Program

Cengage Learning publishes a number of readers, some devoted exclusively to primary or secondary sources, and others combining primary and secondary sources—all designed to guide students through the process of historical inquiry. Visit www.cengage.com/history for a complete list of readers or ask your sales representative to recommend a reader that would work well for your specific needs.

CourseReader

Cengage Learning's CourseReader lets instructors create a customized electronic reader in minutes. Instructors can choose exactly what their students will be assigned by searching or browsing Cengage Learning's extensive document database. Sources include hundreds of historical documents, images, and media, plus literary essays that can add additional interest and insight to a primary source assignment. Or instructors can start with the "Editor's Choice" collection created for *A People and A Nation*—and then update it to suit their particular needs. Each source comes with all the pedagogical tools needed to provide a full learning experience, including a descriptive headnote that puts the reading into context as well as critical thinking and multiple-choice questions designed to reinforce key points. Contact your local Cengage Learning sales representative for more information and packaging options.

Rand McNally Atlas of American History, 2e

This comprehensive atlas features more than eighty maps, with new content covering global perspectives, including events in the Middle East from 1945 to 2005, as well as population trends in the United States and around the world. Additional maps document voyages of discovery; the settling of the colonies; major U.S. military engagements, including the American Revolution and World Wars I and II; and sources of immigrations, ethnic populations, and patterns of economic change.

Custom Options

Nobody knows your students like you, so why not give them a text tailored to their needs? Cengage Learning offers custom solutions for your course—whether it's making a small modification to *A People and A Nation, Brief* to match your syllabus or combining multiple sources to create something truly unique. You can pick and choose chapters, include your own material, and add additional map exercises along with the Rand McNally Atlas (including questions developed around the maps in the atlas) to create a text that fits the way you teach. Ensure that your students get the most out of their textbook dollar by giving them exactly what they need. Contact your Cengage Learning representative to explore custom solutions for your course.

Acknowledgments

The authors would like to thank David Farber and John Hannigan for their assistance with the preparation of this edition.

We also want to thank the many instructors who have adopted *A People and A Nation* over the years and whose syllabi provided powerful insights leading to the tenth edition's chapter reduction. Also, we have been very grateful for the comments from the historian reviewers who read drafts of our chapters. Their suggestions, corrections, and pleas helped guide us through this momentous revision. We could not include all of their recommendations, but the book is better for our having heeded most of their advice. We heartily thank:

Sara Alpern, Texas A&M University
Mary Axelson, Colorado Mountain College
Friederike Baer, Temple University
Jennifer Bertolet, The George Washington University
Troy Bickham, Texas A&M University
Robert Bionaz, Chicago State University
Victoria Bynum, Texas State University, San Marcos
Randall Couch, Tulane University
Julie Courtwright, Iowa State University
Anthony Edmonds, Ball State University
Mario Fenyo, Bowie State University
Judy Gordon-Omelka, Friends University
Kathleen Gorman, Minnesota State University, Mankato
Michael Harkins, Harper College
Walter Hixson, University of Akron
B.T. Huntley, Front Range Community College
Edith Macdonald, University of Central Florida
Thomas Martin, Sinclair Community College
Allison McNeese, Mount Mercy College
David Montgomery, North Central Michigan College
Steve O'Brien, Bridgewater State College
Paul O'Hara, Xavier University
John Putman, San Diego State University
Thomas Roy, University of Oklahoma
Manfred Silva, El Paso Community College
Laurie Sprankle, Community College of Allegheny County
Michael Thompson, University of Tennessee at Chattanooga
Chad Timm, Grand View University
Jose Torre, College at Brockport, SUNY
Michael Vollbach, Oakland Community College
Kenneth Watras, Paradise Valley Community College
Jeffrey Williams, Northern Kentucky University

The authors thank the helpful Cengage people who designed, edited, produced, and nourished this book. Many thanks to Ann West, senior sponsoring editor; Margaret McAndrew Beasley, senior development editor; Megan Chrisman, associate content developer; Pembroke Herbert, photo researcher; Charlotte Miller, art editor; and Jane Lee, senior content project manager.

M. B. N.

J. K.

C. S.

D. B.

H. C.

F. L.

B. B.

D. M.

About the Authors

Mary Beth Norton

Born in Ann Arbor, Michigan, Mary Beth Norton received her BA from the University of Michigan (1964) and her PhD from Harvard University (1969). She is the Mary Donlon Alger Professor of American History at Cornell University. Her dissertation won the Allan Nevins Prize. She has written *The British-Americans* (1972); *Liberty's Daughters* (1980, 1996); *Founding Mothers & Fathers* (1996), which was one of three finalists for the 1997 Pulitzer Prize in History; and *In the Devil's Snare* (2002), one of five finalists for the 2003 *L.A. Times* Book Prize in History and won the English-Speaking Union's Ambassador Book Award in American Studies for 2003. Her most recent book is *Separated by Their Sex* (2011). She has coedited three volumes on American women's history. She was also general editor of the *American Historical Association's Guide to Historical Literature* (1995). Her articles have appeared in such journals as the *American Historical Review, William and Mary Quarterly*, and *Journal of Women's History*. Mary Beth has served as president of the Berkshire Conference of Women Historians, as vice president for research of the American Historical Association, and as a presidential appointee to the National Council on the Humanities. She has appeared on Book TV, the History and Discovery Channels, PBS, and NBC as a commentator on early American history, and she has lectured frequently to high school teachers. She has received four honorary degrees and is an elected member of both the American Academy of Arts and Sciences and the American Philosophical Society. She has held fellowships from the National Endowment for the Humanities; the Guggenheim, Rockefeller, and Starr Foundations; and the Henry E. Huntington Library. In 2005–2006, she was the Pitt Professor of American History and Institutions at the University of Cambridge and Newnham College.

Jane Kamensky

Born in New York City, Jane Kamensky earned her BA (1985) and PhD (1993) from Yale University. She is now Harry S Truman Professor of American Civilization at Brandeis University, where she has taught since 1993 and has won two university-wide teaching prizes. She is the author of *The Exchange Artist: A Tale of High-Flying Speculation and America's First Banking Collapse* (2008), a finalist for the 2009 George Washington Book Prize; *Governing the Tongue: The Politics of Speech in Early New England* (1997); and *The Colonial Mosaic: American Women, 1600–1760* (1995); and coeditor of *The Oxford Handbook of the American Revolution* (2012). With Jill Lepore, she is the coauthor of the historical novel *Blindspot* (2008), a *New York Times* editor's choice and *Boston Globe* bestseller. In 1999, she and Lepore also cofounded *Common-place* (www.common-place.org), which remains a leading online journal of early American history and life. Jane has also served on the editorial boards of the *American Historical Review*, the *Journal of American History*, and the *Journal of the Early Republic*; as well as on the Council of the American Antiquarian Society and the Executive Board of the Organization of American Historians. Called on frequently as an adviser to public history projects, she has appeared on PBS, C-SPAN, the History Channel, and NPR, among other media outlets. Jane has won numerous major grants and fellowships to support her scholarship. In 2007–2008, a grant from the Andrew W. Mellon Foundation allowed her to pursue advanced training in art history at the Courtauld Institute of Art in London. Her next book, a history of painting and politics in the age of revolution, centered on the life of John Singleton Copley, will be published by W. W. Norton.

Carol Sheriff

Born in Washington, D.C., and raised in Bethesda, Maryland, Carol Sheriff received her BA from Wesleyan University (1985) and her PhD from Yale University (1993). Since 1993, she has taught history at the College of William and Mary, where she has won the Thomas Jefferson Teaching Award; the Alumni Teaching Fellowship Award; the University Professorship for Teaching Excellence; The Class of 2013 Distinguished Professorship for Excellence in Scholarship, Teaching, and Service; and the Arts and Sciences Award for Teaching Excellence. Her publications include *The Artificial River: The Erie Canal and the Paradox of Progress* (1996), which won the Dixon Ryan Fox Award from the New York State Historical Association and the Award for Excellence in Research from the New York State Archives; and *A People at War: Civilians and Soldiers in America's Civil War, 1854–1877* (with Scott Reynolds Nelson, 2007). In 2012, she won the John T. Hubbell Prize from *Civil War History* for her article on the state-commissioned Virginia history textbooks of the 1950s, and the controversies their portrayals of the Civil War era provoked in ensuing decades. Carol has written sections of a teaching manual for the New York State history curriculum, given presentations at Teaching American History grant projects, consulted on an exhibit for the Rochester Museum and Science Center, and appeared in The History Channel's Modern Marvels show on the Erie Canal, and she is engaged in several public-history projects marking the sesquicentennial of the Civil War. At William and Mary, she teaches the U.S. history survey as well as upper-level classes on the Early Republic, the Civil War Era, and the American West.

David W. Blight

Born in Flint, Michigan, David W. Blight received his BA from Michigan State University (1971) and his PhD from the University of Wisconsin (1985). He is now professor of history and director of the Gilder Lehrman Center for the Study of Slavery, Resistance, and Abolition at Yale University and will be Pitt Professor of American History and Institutions at the University of Cambridge in the United Kingdom, 2013–2014. For the first seven years of his career, David was a public high school teacher in Flint. He has written *Frederick Douglass's Civil War* (1989) and *Race and Reunion: The Civil War in American Memory, 1863–1915* (2000). His most recent books are *American Oracle: The Civil War in the Civil Rights Era* (2011) and *A Slave No More: The Emancipation of John Washington and Wallace Turnage* (2007), and he is currently writing a new full biography of Frederick Douglass. His edited works include *When This Cruel War Is Over: The Civil War Letters of Charles Harvey Brewster* (1992), *Narrative of the Life of Frederick Douglass* (1993), W. E. B. Du Bois, *The Souls of Black Folk* (with Robert Gooding Williams, 1997), *Union and Emancipation* (with Brooks Simpson, 1997), and *Caleb Bingham, The Columbian Orator* (1997). David's essays have appeared in the *Journal of American History* and *Civil War History,* among others. A consultant to several documentary films, David appeared in the 1998 PBS series, *Africans in America.* In 2012, he was elected to the American Academy of Arts and Sciences, and he is currently serving on the Executive Board of the Organization of American Historians. David also teaches summer seminars for secondary school teachers, as well as for park rangers and historians of the National Park Service. His book, *Race and Reunion: The Civil War in American Memory, 1863–1915* (2000), received many honors in 2002, including the Bancroft Prize, Abraham Lincoln Prize, and the Frederick Douglass Prize. From the Organization of American Historians, he has received the Merle Curti Prize in Social History, the Merle Curti Prize in Intellectual History, the Ellis Hawley Prize in Political History, and the James Rawley Prize in Race Relations.

Howard P. Chudacoff

Howard P. Chudacoff, the George L. Littlefield Professor of American History and Professor of Urban Studies at Brown University, was born in Omaha, Nebraska. He earned his AB (1965) and PhD (1969) from the University of Chicago. He has written *Mobile Americans* (1972), *How Old Are You?* (1989), *The Age of the Bachelor* (1999), *The Evolution of American Urban Society* (with Judith Smith, 2004), and *Children at Play: An American History* (2007). His current book project is *Game Changers: Major Turning Points in the History of Intercollegiate Athletics.* He has also coedited with Peter Baldwin *Major Problems in American Urban History* (2004). His articles have appeared in such journals as the *Journal of Family History, Reviews in American History,* and *Journal of American History.* At Brown University, Howard has cochaired the American Civilization Program and chaired the Department of History, and serves as Brown's faculty representative to the NCAA. He has also served on the board of directors of the Urban History Association and the editorial board of *The National Journal of Play.* The National Endowment for the Humanities, Ford Foundation, and Rockefeller Foundation have given him awards to advance his scholarship.

Fredrik Logevall

A native of Stockholm, Sweden, Fredrik Logevall is John S. Knight Professor of International Studies and Professor of History at Cornell University, where he serves as vice provost and as director of the Mario Einaudi Center for International Studies. He received his BA from Simon Fraser University (1986) and his PhD from Yale University (1993). His most recent book is *Embers of War: The Fall of an Empire and the Making of America's Vietnam* (2012), which won the Pulitzer Prize in History and the Francis Parkman Prize, and which was named a best book of the year by the *Washington Post* and the *Christian Science Monitor.* His other publications include *Choosing War* (1999), which won three prizes, including the Warren F. Kuehl Book Prize from the Society for Historians of American Foreign Relations (SHAFR); *America's Cold War: The Politics of Insecurity* (with Campbell Craig; 2009); *The Origins of the Vietnam War* (2001); *Terrorism and 9/11: A Reader* (2002); and, as coeditor, *The First Vietnam War: Colonial Conflict and Cold War Crisis* (2007); and *Nixon and the World: American Foreign Relations, 1969–1977* (2008). Fred is a past recipient of the Stuart L. Bernath article, book, and lecture prizes from SHAFR, and a past member of the Cornell University Press faculty board. He serves on numerous editorial advisory boards and is coeditor of the book series, "From Indochina to Vietnam: Revolution and War in a Global Perspective" (University of California Press).

Beth Bailey

Born in Atlanta, Georgia, Beth Bailey received her BA from Northwestern University (1979) and her PhD from the University of Chicago (1986). She is now a professor of history at Temple University. Her research and teaching fields include war and society and the U.S. military, American cultural history (nineteenth and twentieth centuries), popular culture, and gender and sexuality. Beth served as the coordinating author for this edition of *A People and A Nation*. She is the author, most recently, of *America's Army: Making the All-Volunteer Force* (2009). Her other publications include *From Front Porch to Back Seat: Courtship in 20th Century America* (1988), a historical analysis of conventions governing the courtship of heterosexual youth; *The First Strange Place: The Alchemy of Race and Sex in WWII Hawaii* (with David Farber, 1992), which analyzes cultural contact among Americans in wartime Hawai'i; *Sex in the Heartland* (1999), a social and cultural history of the post–WWII "sexual revolution"; and *The Columbia Companion to America in the 1960s* (with David Farber, 2001). She is also coeditor of *A History of Our Time* (with William Chafe and Harvard Sitkoff, 6th ed., 2002; 7th ed., 2007; 8th ed., 2011). Beth has served as a consultant and/or on-screen expert for numerous television documentaries developed for PBS and The History Channel. She has received grants or fellowships from the ACLS, the NEH, and the Woodrow Wilson International Center for Scholars, and was named the Ann Whitney Olin scholar at Barnard College, Columbia University, where she was the director of the American Studies Program, and Regents Lecturer at the University of New Mexico. She has been a visiting scholar at Saitama University, Japan; at the University of Paris Diderot; and at Trinity College at the University of Melbourne, and a senior Fulbright lecturer in Indonesia. She teaches courses on sexuality and gender and war and American culture.

Debra Michals

Born in Boston, Massachusetts, Debra Michals received her BS from Boston University (1984) and her PhD from New York University (2002). She is an instructor of women's history and women's and gender studies at Merrimack College, where in 2008 she also served as acting chair of the Women's and Gender Studies Program. In 2013, Debra coauthored a permanent exhibit for the National Women's History Museum entitled "From Ideas to Independence: A Century of Entrepreneurial Women" (http://entrepreneurs.nwhm.org/). She is currently completing a book on the emergence of women entrepreneurs and the growing number of female breadwinners since World War II, and she has also begun research for a book about gender and modern fatherhood. Debra has been a visiting scholar to Northeastern University (2003), and served as the Acting Associate Director of Women's Studies at New York University (1994–1996), where she helped obtain and administer a Ford Foundation Grant in Women's and Area Studies and earned the university's President's Leadership Service Award. She has contributed to several anthologies, including *Sisterhood Is Forever* (2003); *Image Nation: American Countercultures in the 1960s and '70s* (2002); and *Reading Women's Lives* (2003), as well as the encyclopedia *Notable American Women* (2004). Debra has served as a consultant/editor for The History Channel and has written for the *History Channel Magazine*. She was the content director for The Women's Museum: An Institute for the Future (1998–2000), a consultant to the Elizabeth Cady Stanton Trust, and currently sits on the advisory board for the International Museum of Women. In addition to her own research, Debra is a frequent editor and adviser for scholarly books and pedagogical materials on U.S. history.

Three Old Worlds Create a New

1

1492–1600

A generation after Columbus crossed the Atlantic, a Spanish soldier named Hernán Cortés traded words with the ruler of the Aztec empire. Motecuhzoma II was among the most powerful men in the Americas. Thousands of loyal courtiers accompanied him to the gates of Tenochtitlán, the capital, one of the largest cities in the world. Cortés, his Spanish troops, and their native allies approached on horseback. The conquistador and the Aztec ruler bowed to each other, and spoke. "Montezuma bade him welcome," recalled Bernal Díaz del Castillo, a soldier on the expedition. "We have come to your house in Mexico as friends," Cortés told his host.

This mixture of ceremony, half-truths, and outright lies was among the first exchanges between two great civilizations from two sides of a great ocean. It was not an easy conversation to have. Motecuhzoma spoke Nahuatl; Cortés spoke Spanish. (The Spanish could not even pronounce the Aztec emperor's name, garbling "Motecuhzoma" as "Montezuma.") But in fact the conversation between Cortés and Motecuhzoma was not a dialogue but a three-way exchange. As Bernal Díaz explains, Cortés addressed the Aztec emperor "through the mouth of Doña Marina."

Who was Doña Marina? Born to Nahuatl-speaking nobles around the year 1500, she grew up at the margins of Aztec and Maya territories. As a child, she was either stolen from her family or given by them to indigenous slave traders. She wound up in the Gulf Coast town of Tabasco. In 1519, the leaders of Tabasco gave Marina to Cortés as one of many offerings they hoped would persuade the Spanish to continue west, into the heart of their enemies' territory. Marina learned Spanish quickly, and her fluency proved vital to the success of the Spaniards' expedition.

Marina was a young woman in whom worlds met and mingled. The Spanish signaled their respect by addressing her as "Doña," meaning lady. Nahuatl speakers rendered *Marina* as *Malintzin*, using the suffix *–tzin* to denote her high status. Spaniards stumbled over the Nahuatl *Malinztin* and often called her *La Malinche*: a triple name, from a double mistranslation.

The legacy of Doña Marina/Malintzin/La Malinche remains as ambiguous as her name. Her fluency helped the invaders to

Link to Bernal Díaz, *The
Conquest of New Spain*,
in English

triumph—a catastrophe for the Aztecs and other indigenous peoples. Their descendants consider Doña Marina their foremother and their betrayer, at once a victim and a perpetrator of the Spanish conquest. Marina continues to embody the ambiguities of colonial history, in which power was shifting and contested, and much was lost in translation.

For thousands of years before 1492, human societies in the Americas developed in isolation from the rest of the world. That isolation ended in the Christian fifteenth century. As Europeans sought treasure and trade, peoples from two sides of the globe came into regular contact for the first time. Their interactions involved curiosity and confusion, trade and theft, enslavement and endurance. The history of the colonies that became the United States must be seen in this context of European exploration and exploitation, of native resistance, and of African enslavement and survival. In the Americas of the fifteenth and sixteenth centuries, three old worlds came together to produce a new.

The continents that European sailors reached in the late fifteenth century had their own histories, internal struggles that the intruders sometimes exploited and often ignored. The indigenous residents of what came to be called *the Americas* were the world's most skillful plant breeders; they developed crops more nutritious and productive than those grown in Europe, Asia, or Africa. They had invented systems of writing and mathematics. As in Europe, their societies rose and fell as leaders succeeded or failed. But the arrival of Europeans altered the Americans' struggles with one another.

After 1400, European nations tried to acquire valuable colonies and trading posts worldwide. Initially interested in Asia and Africa, Europeans eventually focused mostly on the Americas. Their designs changed the course of history on four continents.

As you read this chapter, keep the following questions in mind:

- **What were the key characteristics of the three worlds that met in the Americas?**

- **What impacts did their encounter have on each of them?**

- **What were the crucial initial developments in that encounter?**

American Societies

What led to the development of major North American civilizations in the centuries before Europeans arrived?

Human beings originated on the continent of Africa, where humanlike remains about 3 million years old have been found in what is now Ethiopia. Over many millennia, the growing population dispersed to the other continents. Because the climate was then far colder than it is now, much of the earth's water was concentrated in huge rivers of ice called glaciers. Sea levels were lower, and landmasses covered a larger

Chronology

12,000–10,000 BCE	Paleo-Indians migrate from Asia to North America across the Beringia land bridge
7000 BCE	Cultivation of food crops begins in America
ca. 2000 BCE	Olmec civilization appears
ca. 300–600 CE	Height of influence of Teotihuacán
ca. 600–900 CE	Classic Mayan civilization
1000 CE	Ancient Pueblos build settlements in modern states of Arizona and New Mexico
1001	Norse establish settlement in "Vinland"
1050–1250	Height of influence of Cahokia Prevalence of Mississippian culture in modern midwestern and south-eastern United States
14th century	Aztec rise to power
1450s–80s	Portuguese colonize islands in the Mediterranean Atlantic
1477	Marco Polo's *Travels* describes China
1492	Columbus reaches Bahamas
1494	Treaty of Tordesillas divides land claims in Africa, India, and South America between Spain and Portugal
1497	Cabot reaches North America
1513	Ponce de León explores Florida
1518–30	Smallpox epidemic devastates Indian population of West Indies and Central and South America
1519	Cortés invades Mexico
1521	Aztec Empire falls to Spaniards
1524	Verrazzano sails along Atlantic coast of North America
1534–35	Cartier explores St. Lawrence River
1539–42	De Soto explores southeastern North America
1540–42	Coronado explores southwestern North America
1587–90	Raleigh's Roanoke colony vanishes
1588	Harriot publishes *A Briefe and True Report of the New Found Land of Virginia*

proportion of the earth's surface. Scholars long believed the earliest inhabitants of the Americas crossed a land bridge known as Beringia (at the site of the Bering Strait) approximately 12,000 to 14,000 years ago. Yet new archaeological discoveries suggest that parts of the Americas may have been settled much earlier, possibly in three successive waves beginning roughly 30,000 years ago. About 12,500 years ago, when the climate warmed and sea levels rose, Americans were separated from the connected continents of Asia, Africa, and Europe.

Ancient America

The first Americans, called **Paleo-Indians**, were nomadic hunters of game and gatherers of wild plants. They spread throughout North and South America, probably as bands of extended families. By about 11,500 years ago, the Paleo-Indians were making fine stone projectile points, which they attached to wooden spears and used to kill and butcher bison (buffalo), woolly mammoths, and other large mammals. As the Ice Age ended and the human population increased, all the large American mammals except the bison disappeared.

Consequently, by approximately nine thousand years ago, the residents of what is now central Mexico began to cultivate food crops, especially maize (corn), squash, beans, avocados, and peppers. In the Andes Mountains of South America, people started to grow potatoes. As knowledge of agricultural techniques improved, vegetables and maize proved a more reliable source of food than hunting and gathering.

Paleo-Indians The earliest peoples of the Americas.

Most Paleo-Indians started to stay longer in one place, so that they could tend fields regularly. Some established permanent settlements; others moved several times a year. They used controlled burning to clear forests, which created cultivable lands by killing trees and fertilizing the soil with ashes, and also opened meadows that attracted deer and other wildlife. Although they traded such items as shells, flint, salt, and copper, no society became dependent on another group for items vital to its survival.

Wherever agriculture dominated, complex civilizations flourished. Assured of steady supplies of food, such societies could accumulate wealth, trade with other groups, produce ornamental objects, and create elaborate rituals and ceremonies. In North America, the successful cultivation of nutritious crops seems to have led to the growth and development of all the major civilizations: first the large city-states of Mesoamerica (modern Mexico and Guatemala) and then the urban clusters known collectively as the Mississippian culture (in the present-day United States). Each reached its height of population and influence only after achieving success in agriculture. Each later collapsed after reaching the limits of its food supply.

Mesoamerican Civilizations

Scholars know little about the first major Mesoamerican civilization, the Olmecs, who about four thousand years ago lived in cities near the Gulf of Mexico. The Mayas and Teotihuacán, which developed approximately two thousand years later, are better recorded. Teotihuacán, founded in the Valley of Mexico about 300 BCE (Before the Common Era), became one of the largest urban areas in the world, housing perhaps 100,000 people in the fifth century CE (Common Era). Teotihuacán's commercial network extended hundreds of miles. Pilgrims traveled long distances to visit Teotihuacán's pyramids and the great temple of Quetzalcoatl—the feathered serpent, primary god of central Mexico.

On the Yucatan Peninsula, in today's eastern Mexico, the Mayas built urban centers containing tall pyramids and temples, studied astronomy, and created an elaborate writing system. Their city-states engaged in near-constant battle with one another. Warfare and an inadequate food supply caused the collapse of the most powerful cities by 900 CE, ending the classic era of Mayan civilization.

Pueblos and Mississippians

Ancient native societies in what is now the United States learned to grow maize, squash, and beans from Mesoamericans. The Hohokam, Mogollon, and ancient Pueblo peoples of the modern states of Arizona and New Mexico subsisted by combining hunting and gathering with agriculture in an arid region. Hohokam villagers constructed extensive irrigation systems. Between 900 and 1150 CE, Chaco Canyon, at the junction of perhaps four hundred miles of roads, served as a major trading and processing center for turquoise. Yet the sparse and unpredictable rainfall caused the Chacoans to migrate to other sites.

Almost simultaneously, the unrelated Mississippian culture flourished in what is now the midwestern and southeastern United States. Relying largely on maize, squash, nuts, pumpkins, and venison, the Mississippians lived in hierarchically organized settlements. Their largest urban center was the **City of the Sun** (now called Cahokia), near modern St. Louis. Located on rich farmland near the confluence of the Illinois, Missouri, and Mississippi rivers, Cahokia, like Teotihuacán and

City of the Sun (Cahokia)
Area located near modern St. Louis, Missouri, where about twenty thousand people inhabited a metropolitan area.

Chaco Canyon, served as a focal point for religion and trade. At its peak (in the eleventh and twelfth centuries CE), the City of the Sun covered more than five square miles and had a population of about twenty thousand—small by Mesoamerican standards but larger than London in the same era.

The sun-worshipping Cahokians developed an accurate calendar, and the tallest of the city's 120 pyramids, today called Monks Mound, remains the largest earthwork in the Americas. Yet following 1250 CE, the city was abandoned. Archaeologists believe that climate change and the degradation of the environment, caused by overpopulation and the destruction of nearby forests, contributed to its collapse.

Aztecs

Far to the South, the Aztecs (also called Mexicas) migrated into the Valley of Mexico during the twelfth century CE. Their chronicles record that their primary deity, Huitzilopochtli—a war god represented by an eagle—directed them to establish their capital on an island where they saw an eagle eating a serpent, the symbol of Quetzalcoatl. That island city became Tenochtitlán, the nerve center of a rigidly stratified society composed of warriors, merchants, priests, common folk, and slaves.

The Aztecs conquered their neighbors, forcing them to pay tribute in textiles, gold, foodstuffs, and humans who could be sacrificed to Huitzilopochtli. In the Aztec year Ten Rabbit (the Christian 1502), at the coronation of Motecuhzoma II, thousands of people were sacrificed by having their still-beating hearts torn from their bodies.

North America in 1492

What were the gender dimensions of labor in native cultures?

Over the centuries, the Americans who lived north of Mexico adapted their once-similar ways of life to very different climates and terrains, thus creating the diverse culture areas (ways of subsistence) that the Europeans encountered (see Map 1.1). Scholars often delineate such culture areas by language group (such as Algonquian or Iroquoian). Bands that lived in environments not suited to agriculture followed a nomadic lifestyle typified by the Paiutes and Shoshones, who inhabited the Great Basin (now Nevada and Utah). Because finding sufficient food was difficult, such hunter-gatherer bands were small, usually composed of one or more related families. The men hunted small animals, and women gathered seeds and berries.

In more favorable environments, larger groups, like the Chinooks who lived near the seacoasts of present-day Washington and Oregon, combined agriculture with gathering, hunting, and fishing. Residents of the interior (for example, the Arikaras of the Missouri River valley) hunted large animals while also cultivating maize, squash, and beans. The peoples of what is now eastern Canada and the northeastern United States also combined hunting, fishing, and agriculture. They used controlled fires both to open land for cultivation and to assist in hunting.

Trade routes linked distant peoples. For instance, hoe and spade blades manufactured from stone mined in modern southern Illinois have been found as far northeast as Lake Erie and as far west as the Plains. Commercial and other interactions among disparate groups speaking different languages were aided by the universally understood symbol of friendship—the calumet, a feathered tobacco

MAP 1.1

Native Cultures of North America

The natives of the North American continent effectively used the resources of the regions in which they lived. As this map shows, coastal groups relied on fishing, residents of fertile areas engaged in agriculture, and other peoples employed hunting (often combined with gathering) as a primary mode of subsistence. Source: Copyright © Cengage Learning 2015

pipe offered to strangers at initial encounters. Across the continent, native groups sought alliances and waged war against their enemies when diplomacy failed.

Gendered Division of Labor

Societies that relied on hunting large animals, such as deer and buffalo, assigned that task to men, allotting food preparation and clothing production to women. Agricultural societies assigned work in divergent ways. The Pueblo peoples defined agricultural labor as men's work. In the east, peoples speaking Algonquian, Iroquoian, and Muskogean languages allocated most agricultural chores to women, although men cleared the land.

Everywhere in North America, women cared for young children, while older youths learned adult skills from their same-sex parent. Children had a great deal of

Collection of Mary Beth Norton

Jacques Le Moyne, an artist accompanying the French settlement in Florida in the 1560s (see page 31), produced some of the first European images of North American peoples. His depiction of native agricultural practices shows the gendered division of labor: men breaking up the ground with fishbone hoes before women drop seeds into the holes. But Le Moyne's version of the scene cannot be accepted uncritically: unable to abandon a European view of proper farming methods, he erroneously drew plowed furrows in the soil.

freedom. Young people commonly chose their own marital partners, and in most societies couples could easily divorce. Infants and toddlers nursed until the age of two or even longer, and taboos prevented couples from having sexual intercourse during that period.

Social Organization

Southwestern and eastern agricultural peoples also lived in villages, sometimes with a thousand or more inhabitants. The Pueblos resided in multistory buildings constructed on terraces along the sides of cliffs or other easily defended sites. Northern Iroquois villages (in modern New York State) were composed of large, rectangular, bark-covered structures, or longhouses; the name Haudenosaunee, which the Iroquois called themselves, means "People of the Longhouse." In the present-day southeastern United States, Muskogeans and southern Algonquians lived in large thatch houses.

In all the agricultural societies, each dwelling housed an extended family defined matrilineally (through a female line of descent). Mothers, their married daughters, and their daughters' husbands and children all lived together. Matrilineal descent did not imply matriarchy, or the wielding of power by women, but rather denoted kinship and linked extended families into clans. The nomadic bands of the Prairies and Great Plains, by contrast, were most often related patrilineally (through the male line).

War and Politics

Long before Europeans arrived, residents of the continent fought one another for control of hunting and fishing territories, fertile agricultural lands, or the sources of essential items, such as salt (for preserving meat) and flint (for making knives and arrowheads). Native warriors protected by wooden armor engaged in face-to-face combat, since their clubs and throwing spears were effective only at close quarters. They began to shoot arrows from behind trees only when they confronted European guns. War captives were sometimes enslaved, but slavery was never an important source of labor in pre-Columbian America.

Political structures varied considerably. Among Pueblos, the village council, composed of ten to thirty men, was the highest political authority; no larger organization connected multiple villages. The Iroquois had an elaborate hierarchy incorporating villages into nations and nations into a confederation. A council of representatives from each nation made crucial decisions of war and peace. Women more often assumed leadership roles among agricultural peoples. Female sachems (rulers) led Algonquian villages in what is now Massachusetts, but women never became heads of hunting bands. Iroquois women did not become chiefs, yet clan matrons exercised political power, including the power to start and stop wars.

Religion

All the continent's native peoples were polytheistic, worshipping a multitude of gods. The major deities of agricultural peoples like the Pueblos and Muskogeans were associated with cultivation, and their festivals centered on planting and harvest. The most important gods of hunters like those living on the Great Plains were associated with animals, and their major festivals were related to hunting.

A wide variety of cultures, comprising more than 10 million people who spoke over one thousand languages, inhabited America north of Mexico when Europeans arrived. They did not consider themselves one people or "Americans," nor did they think of uniting to repel the invaders who washed up on their shores beginning in 1492.

African Societies

What were the chief characteristics of West African societies in the fifteenth century?

Fifteenth-century Africa, like America, housed a variety of cultures with complex histories of their own. In the north, along the Mediterranean Sea, lived the Berbers, who were Muslims—followers of the Islamic religion. On the east coast of Africa, Muslim city-states traded with India, the Moluccas (part of modern Indonesia), and China. Sustained contact and intermarriage among Arabs and Africans created the Swahili language and culture. Through the East African city-states passed the Spice Route, the conduit of waterborne commerce between the eastern

Mediterranean and East Asia; the rest followed the Silk Road, the long land route across Central Asia.

South of the Mediterranean coast in the African interior lie the great Saharan and Libyan deserts. The introduction of the camel in the fifth century CE made long-distance travel possible, and as Islam expanded after the ninth century, commerce controlled by Muslim merchants helped to spread similar religious and cultural ideas. Below the deserts, the continent is divided between tropical rain forests (along the coasts) and grassy plains (in the interior). South of the Gulf of Guinea, the grassy landscape came to be dominated by Bantu-speaking peoples, who left their homeland in modern Nigeria about two thousand years ago.

West Africa (Guinea)

West Africa was a land of tropical forests and savanna grasslands where fishing, cattle herding, and agriculture had supported the inhabitants for at least ten thousand years before Europeans arrived. The northern region of West Africa, or Upper Guinea, was heavily influenced by Mediterranean Islamic culture. Trade via camel caravans between Upper Guinea and the Muslim Mediterranean connected sub-Saharan Africa to Europe and West Asia. Africans sold ivory, gold, and slaves to northern merchants to obtain salt, dates, silk, and cotton cloth.

Upper Guinea runs northeast-southwest from Cape Verde to Cape Palmas. The people of its northernmost region, the so-called Rice Coast (present-day Gambia, Senegal, and Guinea), fished and cultivated rice in coastal swamplands. The Grain Coast, to the south, was thinly populated and had only one good harbor (modern Freetown, Sierra Leone). Its inhabitants farmed and raised livestock.

In Lower Guinea, south and east of Cape Palmas, most Africans were farmers who practiced traditional religions, rather than Islam. They believed spirits inhabited particular places, and they developed rituals intended to ensure good harvests. Individual villages composed of kin groups were linked into hierarchical kingdoms. At the time of initial European contact, decentralized political and social authority characterized the region.

Complementary Gender Roles

In the societies of West Africa, as in those of the Americas, men and women pursued different tasks. In general, both sexes shared agricultural duties. Men also hunted, managed livestock, and fished. Women were responsible for child care, food preparation, manufacture, and trade. They managed the local and regional networks through which families, villages, and small kingdoms exchanged goods.

Lower Guinea had similar social systems organized according to what anthropologists have called the dual-sex principle. Each sex handled its own affairs: male political and religious leaders governed men, and females ruled women. Many West African societies practiced polygyny (one man's having several wives, each of whom lived separately with her children). Thus, few adults lived permanently in marital households, but the dual-sex system ensured that they were monitored by their own sex.

Throughout Guinea, both women and men served as heads of the cults and secret societies that directed the spiritual life of the villages. Young women were initiated into the Sandé cult, young men into Poro. Neither cult was allowed to reveal its secrets to the opposite sex. Unlike some of their Native American contemporaries, West African women rarely held formal power over men. Yet female religious leaders did govern other members of their sex, enforcing conformity to accepted norms of behavior and overseeing their spiritual well-being.

Slavery in Guinea

West African law recognized individual and communal landownership, but men seeking wealth needed laborers—wives, children, or slaves—who could work the land. West Africans enslaved for life were therefore central elements of the economy. Enslavement was sometimes used to punish criminals, but more often slaves were enemy captives or people who voluntarily enslaved themselves or their children to pay debts. Slaveholders had a right to the products of their bondspeople's labor, although slave status did not always descend to the next generation. Some slaves were held as chattel; others could engage in trade, retaining a portion of their profits; and still others achieved prominent political or military positions. All, however, could be traded at any time.

West Africans, then, were agricultural peoples accustomed to a relatively egalitarian relationship between the sexes. Carried as captives to the Americas, they became essential to transplanted European societies that used their labor but had little respect for their cultures.

European Societies

What were the motives behind fifteenth- and sixteenth-century European explorations?

In the fifteenth century, Europeans, too, were agricultural peoples. Split into numerous small, warring countries, the continent of Europe was divided linguistically, politically, and economically. Yet the daily lives of ordinary people exhibited many similarities. In most European societies, a few families wielded autocratic power over the majority. Although Europeans were not subjected to perpetual slavery, Christian doctrine permitted the enslavement of "heathens" (non-Christians), and some Europeans' freedom was restricted by serfdom, which tied them to the land or to specific owners. In short, Europe's kingdoms resembled those of Africa or Mesoamerica but differed greatly from the more egalitarian societies found in America north of Mexico.

Gender, Work, Politics, and Religion

Most Europeans, like Africans and Americans, lived in small villages. European farmers, called peasants, owned or leased separate landholdings, but they worked the fields communally. Men did most of the fieldwork; women helped at planting and harvesting. In some regions men concentrated on herding livestock while women cared for children, prepared and preserved food, milked cows, and kept poultry. A woman married to a city artisan or storekeeper might assist her husband in business. Because Europeans kept domesticated animals for meat, hunting had little economic importance.

Men dominated all areas of life in Europe. A few women—notably Queen Elizabeth I of England—achieved power by birthright, but most were excluded from positions of authority. European women also held inferior social, religious, and economic positions, yet they wielded power over children and servants.

Christianity was the dominant European religion. In the West, authority rested in the Catholic Church, based in Rome. Although Europeans were nominally Catholic, many adhered to local belief systems that the church deemed heretical. Still, Europe's Christian nations from the twelfth century on publicly united in a goal of driving nonbelievers (especially Muslims) not only from the European continent but also from the holy city of Jerusalem, triggering wars known as the Crusades. Nevertheless, in the fifteenth century, Muslims dominated the commerce and geography of the Mediterranean, especially after they conquered Constantinople (capital of the Christian Byzantine empire) in 1453.

Effects of Plague and Warfare

When the fifteenth century began, European nations were recovering from the devastating Black Death epidemic, which traders seem to have brought from China in 1346. The disease recurred with severity in the 1360s and 1370s, and the best estimate is that one-third of Europe's people died from the epidemic. A precipitous economic decline followed—as did social, political, and religious disruption.

As plague ravaged the population, England and France waged the Hundred Years' War (1337–1453), initiated because English monarchs claimed the French throne. The war interrupted overland trade routes connecting England and Antwerp (in modern Belgium) to Venice, and thence to India and China. Needing a new way to reach their northern trading partners, eastern Mediterranean merchants forged a maritime route to Antwerp. Using a triangular, or lateen, sail (rather than then-standard square rigging) improved the maneuverability of ships, enabling vessels to sail out of the Mediterranean and north around the European coast. Maritime navigation also improved through the acquisition of a Chinese invention, the compass, and the perfection of instruments like the astrolabe and the quadrant, which allowed sailors to estimate their latitude by measuring the relationship of the sun, moon, or certain stars to the horizon.

Political and Technological Change

After the Hundred Years' War, European monarchs consolidated their political power and raised revenues by taxing an already hard-pressed peasantry. The military struggle

De Agostini Picture Library / G. Dagli Orti / The Bridgeman Art Library

Daily life in early sixteenth-century Portugal, as illustrated in a manuscript prayer book. At top a prosperous family shares a meal being served by an African slave. Other scenes show male laborers clearing land and hunting birds (left) and chopping wood (right), while at bottom a woman plants seeds in a prepared bed and in the top background female servants work in the kitchen.

inspired new pride in national identity, which eclipsed regional and dynastic loyalties. In England, Henry VII in 1485 founded the Tudor dynasty and began uniting a divided land. Most successful were Ferdinand of Aragón and Isabella of Castile, the Catholic monarchs of Spain. In 1492, they defeated the Muslims who had lived in Spain and Portugal for centuries, and expelled all Jews and Muslims from their domain.

movable type Type in which each character is cast on a separate piece of metal.

printing press A machine that transfers lettering or images by contact with various forms of inked surface onto paper or similar material fed into it in various ways.

The fifteenth century also brought technological change to Europe. **Movable type** and the **printing press**, invented in Germany in the 1450s, made information more accessible, creating a market for books about fabled lands across the sea. The most important such works were Ptolemy's *Geography,* a description of the known world written in ancient times, first published in 1475; and Marco Polo's *Travels*, published in 1477. The *Travels* recounted a Venetian merchant's adventures in thirteenth-century China and described that nation as bordered on the east by an ocean. The book led many Europeans to believe they could reach China by sea. A transoceanic route would allow Europeans to circumvent the Muslim and Venetian merchants who controlled their access to Asian goods.

Motives for Exploration

In the fifteenth and sixteenth centuries, European countries craved easy access to African and Asian goods—silk, dyes, perfumes, jewels, sugar, gold, and especially spices, which were desirable for seasoning food and as possible medicines. The allure of pepper, cinnamon, and cloves stemmed largely from their rarity, extraordinary cost, and mysterious origins. Acquiring these products directly would improve a nation's balance of trade and its standing relative to other countries.

A concern for spreading Christianity around the world supplemented economic motives. Fifteenth-century Europeans saw no conflict between material and spiritual goals. Explorers and colonizers sought to convert "heathen" peoples while at the same time establishing direct trade with Africa, China, India, and the Moluccas.

Early European Explorations

What sailing innovation ultimately facilitated the widespread exploration of the Atlantic and Pacific?

To establish that trade, European mariners first had to explore the oceans. Seafarers needed not just maneuverable vessels and navigational aids but also knowledge of the sea, its currents, and its winds. But where would Atlantic breezes carry their square-rigged ships, which needed the wind directly behind the vessel?

Sailing the Mediterranean Atlantic

Europeans learned the answer to this question in the Mediterranean Atlantic, the expanse of ocean located south and west of Spain and bounded by the Azores (on the west) and the Canaries (on the south), with the Madeiras in their midst. Europeans reached all three sets of islands during the fourteenth century. Sailing to the Canaries from Europe was easy, because strong Northeast Trade Winds blow southward along the Iberian and African coastlines. The voyage took about a week.

The Iberian sailor attempting to return home, however, faced winds that blew directly at him. Instead of waiting for the wind to change, mariners developed a new technique: sailing "around the wind." That meant sailing as directly against the wind as was possible without changing course. In the Mediterranean Atlantic, a mariner would head northwest into the open ocean, until—weeks later—he reached the winds that would carry him home, the so-called Westerlies. This solution became the key to successful exploration of both the Atlantic and the Pacific oceans.

Islands of the Mediterranean Atlantic

During the fifteenth century, Iberian seamen regularly visited the three island groups. The uninhabited Azores were soon settled by Portuguese migrants, who raised wheat for sale in Europe and sold livestock to passing sailors. By the 1450s Portuguese colonists who settled the uninhabited Madeiras were employing slaves (probably Jews and Muslims brought from Iberia) to grow sugar for export. By the 1470s, Madeira had developed a colonial **plantation** economy. For the first time in history, a region was settled explicitly to cultivate a valuable crop to be sold elsewhere. Because the work was so backbreaking, only a supply of enslaved laborers (who could not quit) could ensure the system's success.

plantation A large-scale agricultural enterprise growing commercial crops and usually employing coerced or slave labor.

The Canaries had indigenous residents—the Guanche people, who traded animal skins and dyes with Europeans. After 1402, the French, Portuguese, and Spanish sporadically attacked the islands. The Guanches resisted but were weakened by European diseases. The seven islands eventually fell to Europeans who then carried off Guanches as slaves to the Madeiras or Iberia. Spain conquered the last island in 1496 and devoted it to sugar plantations.

Portuguese Trading Posts in Africa

Other Europeans viewed the Mediterranean Atlantic islands as stepping-stones to Africa. In 1415, Portugal seized control of Ceuta, a Muslim city in North Africa. Prince Henry the Navigator, son of King John I of Portugal, dispatched ships southward along the African coast, attempting to discover an oceanic route to Asia. But not until after Prince Henry's death did Bartholomew Dias round the southern tip of Africa (1488) and Vasco da Gama finally reach India (1498).

Although West African states successfully resisted European penetration of the interior, they let Portugal establish coastal trading posts. The African kingdoms charged traders rent and levied duties on imports. The Portuguese profited by transporting African gold, ivory, and slaves to Europe. By bargaining with African masters to purchase slaves and carrying those bondspeople to Iberia, the Portuguese introduced black slavery into Europe.

Lessons of Early Colonization

Portugal's success grew after it colonized São Tomé, located in the Gulf of Guinea, in the 1480s. With Madeira at its sugar-producing capacity, São Tomé proved an ideal new locale for raising the valuable crop. Planters imported slaves to work in the cane fields, creating the first economy based primarily on the bondage of black Africans.

By the 1490s, Europeans had learned three key lessons of colonization in the Mediterranean Atlantic. First, they learned how to transplant crops and livestock to exotic locations. Second, they discovered that the native peoples of those lands could be conquered or exploited. Third, they developed a model of plantation slavery. The stage was set for a pivotal moment in world history.

Voyages of Columbus, Cabot, and Their Successors

What three themes in Columbus's log about his explorations would come to mark much of the future settlement of Europeans in the Americas?

Christopher Columbus
Italian explorer who claimed the island of San Salvador in the Bahamas for the king and queen of Spain.

Christopher Columbus understood the lessons of the Mediterranean Atlantic. Born in 1451 in the Italian city-state of Genoa, this largely self-educated son of a wool merchant was by the 1490s an experienced sailor and mapmaker. Drawn to Portugal and its islands, he sailed to the Portuguese outpost on Africa's Gold Coast, where he became obsessed with gold and witnessed the economic potential of the slave trade.

Like all accomplished seafarers, Columbus knew the world was round. But he thought that China lay only three thousand miles from Europe's southern coast. Thus, he argued, it would be easier to reach Asia by sailing west. Experts scoffed, accurately predicting that the two continents lay twelve thousand miles apart. When Columbus in 1484 asked the Portuguese rulers to back his plan to sail west to Asia, they rejected what appeared to be a crazy scheme.

Columbus's Voyage

Jealous of Portugal's successes in Africa, Ferdinand and Isabella of Spain agreed to finance most of the risky voyage—Columbus himself would have to pay a quarter of the costs—in part because they hoped the profits would pay for a new expedition to conquer Muslim-held Jerusalem. On August 3, 1492, Columbus set sail from the Spanish port of Palos in command of three ships—the *Pinta*, the *Niña*, and the *Santa Maria*.

On October 12, the vessels found land approximately where Columbus thought Cipangu (Japan) was located (see Map 1.2). He and his men anchored off an island in the Bahamas, called Guanahaní by its inhabitants. Columbus claimed the territory for Spain and renamed Guanahaní San Salvador. Later, he explored the islands now known as Cuba and Hispaniola, which the native Taíno people called Colba and Bohío. Because he thought he had reached the East Indies (the Spice Islands), Columbus referred to the inhabitants as "Indians." The Taínos thought the Europeans had come from the sky, and crowds gathered to meet and exchange gifts with Columbus.

Columbus's Observations

Three themes predominate in Columbus's log. First, he insistently asked the Taínos where he could find gold, pearls, and spices. His informants replied (via signs) that such products could be obtained on other islands or on the mainland. He came to mistrust such answers, noting, "they will tell me anything I want to hear."

Second, Columbus wrote of the strange and beautiful plants and animals. His interest was not only aesthetic. "I believe that there are many plants and trees

MAP 1.2

European Explorations in America

In the century following Columbus's voyages, European adventurers explored the coasts and parts of the interior of North and South America.

Source: Copyright © Cengage Learning 2015

here that could be worth a lot in Spain for use as dyes, spices, and medicines," he observed, adding that he was carrying home samples for experts to examine.

Included in his cargo of curiosities were some of the islands' human residents, whom Columbus also evaluated as resources to answer European needs. The Taínos were, he said, handsome, gentle, and friendly, though they told him of the fierce Caniba (today called Caribs) who lived on other islands, raided their villages, and ate some captives (hence today's word *cannibal*). Columbus saw the Taínos as likely converts to Catholicism as well as "good and skilled servants."

Columbus made three more voyages, exploring most of the major Caribbean islands and sailing along the coasts of Central and South America. Until the day he died, in 1506 at the age of fifty-five, he believed he had reached Asia.

Others knew better. The Florentine merchant Amerigo Vespucci, who explored the South American coast in 1499, was the first to publish that a new continent had been discovered. By then, Spain, Portugal, and Pope Alexander VI had signed the Treaty of Tordesillas (1494), confirming Portugal's dominance in Africa—and later Brazil—in exchange for Spanish preeminence in the rest of the Western Hemisphere.

Link to the journal of Christopher Columbus

Link to Christopher Columbus's letter to the king and queen of Spain

Visualizing THE PAST

Naming America

In 1507, German cartographer Martin Waldseemüller created the first map to label the newly discovered landmass on the western side of the Atlantic Ocean as "America." He named the continent after Amerigo Vespucci, the Italian explorer who realized he had reached a "new world" rather than islands off the coast of Asia. Waldseemüller's map appeared in a short book called *Cosmographiae Introductio*, or *Introduction to Cosmography*—the study of the known world. The world he illustrated was both familiar and new. The sun revolved around the earth, as scholars had believed for a millennium. Yet the voyages of Columbus, Vespucci, and others had reconfigured the globe.

When the twelve sheets of Waldseemüller's map are put together, the image stretches nearly five by eight feet. One of the largest printed maps ever then produced, it includes an astonishing level of detail. What symbols indicate European territorial claims in America and Africa? Why might Africa be shown as the center of the known world?

Waldseemüller map

Library of Congress

African peoples

Library of Congress

America

Library of Congress

Norse and Other Northern Voyagers

Five hundred years before Columbus, about the year 1001, a **Norse** expedition under Leif Ericsson sailed to North America across the Davis Strait, which separated Greenland from Baffin Island (located northeast of Hudson Bay; see Map 1.1) by just 200 nautical miles. They settled at a site they named "**Vinland**," but attacks by local residents forced them out after just a few years. In the 1960s, archaeologists determined that the Norse had established an outpost at what is now L'Anse aux Meadows, Newfoundland. Vinland was probably located farther south.

Norse Also known as Vikings, they were a warrior culture from Scandinavia.

Vinland The site of the first known attempt at European settlement in the Americas.

John Cabot's Explorations

The European generally credited with "discovering" North America is Zuan Cabboto, known today as **John Cabot**. Cabot brought to Europe the first formal knowledge of the northern continental coastline and claimed the land for England. Like Columbus, Cabot was a master mariner from the Italian city-state of Genoa; the two men probably knew each other. Calculating that England—which traded with Asia only through intermediaries—would be eager to sponsor exploratory voyages, he gained financial backing from King Henry VII. He set sail from Bristol in May 1497, reaching North America about a month later. After exploring the coast of modern Newfoundland for a month, Cabot rode the Westerlies back to England, arriving in fifteen days.

John Cabot Italian explorer who established English claims to the New World

The voyages of Columbus, Cabot, and their successors brought the Eastern and Western Hemispheres together. Portuguese explorer Pedro Álvares Cabral reached Brazil in 1500; John Cabot's son Sebastian arrived in North America in 1507; France financed Giovanni da Verrazzano in 1524 and Jacques Cartier in 1534; and in 1609 and 1610, Henry Hudson explored the North American coast for the Dutch West India Company (see Map 1.2). All were searching primarily for an easy water route to the riches of Asia—the legendary, nonexistent "Northwest Passage" through the Americas. But in a sign of what was to come, Verrazzano observed that "the [American] countryside is, in fact, full of promise and deserves to be developed for itself."

Spanish Exploration and Conquest

What model of colonization did Spain establish that other nations would later attempt to follow?

Only Spain began colonization immediately. On his second voyage in 1493, Columbus brought to Hispaniola seventeen ships loaded with twelve hundred men, seeds, plants, livestock, chickens, and dogs—as well as microbes, rats, and weeds. The settlement he named Isabela (in the modern Dominican Republic) and its successors became the staging area for the Spanish invasion of America.

Cortés and Other Explorers

At first, Spanish explorers fanned out around the Caribbean basin. In 1513, Juan Ponce de León reached Florida, and Vasco Núñez de Balboa crossed the Isthmus of Panama to the Pacific Ocean, followed by Pánfilo de Narváez and others who traced the coast of the Gulf of Mexico. In the 1530s and 1540s, **conquistadors** explored other regions claimed by Spain: Francisco

conquistadors Spanish conquerors or adventurers in the Americas.

Vásquez de Coronado journeyed through the southwestern portion of what is now the United States, while Hernán de Soto explored the Southeast. Francisco Pizarro, who ventured into western South America, acquired the richest silver mines in the world by conquering the Incas. But the most important conquistador was Hernán Cortés. In 1519, he led a force of roughly six hundred men from Cuba to the Mexican mainland to search for rumored wealthy cities.

Capture of Tenochtitlán

As he traveled toward the Aztec capital, Cortés, speaking through Doña Marina and other interpreters, recruited peoples whom the Aztecs had long subjugated. The Spaniards' strange beasts and noisy weapons awed their new allies. Yet the Spaniards, too, were awed. Years later, Bernal Díaz del Castillo recalled his first sight of Tenochtitlán, built on islands in Lake Texcoco: "We were amazed … on account of the great towers and cues [temples] and buildings rising from the water, and all built of masonry."

The Spaniards also brought smallpox to Tenochtitlán. The disease peaked in 1520, fatally weakening Tenochtitlán's defenders. Largely as a consequence, Tenochtitlán surrendered in 1521, and the Spaniards built Mexico City on its site. Cortés and his men seized a treasure of gold and silver. Thus, the Spanish monarchs controlled the richest, most extensive empire Europe had known since ancient Rome.

Spanish Colonization

Spain established the model of colonization that other countries later imitated, a model with three major elements. First, the Crown sought tight control over the colonies, imposing a hierarchical government that allowed little autonomy to American jurisdictions. That control included carefully vetting prospective emigrants and limiting their number. The Crown insisted that colonists import all their manufactured goods from Spain. Roman Catholic priests attempted to ensure colonists' conformity with orthodox religious views.

Second, men comprised most of the first colonists. Although some Spanish women later immigrated to America, the men took primarily Indian—and, later, African—women as their wives or concubines, a development usually encouraged by colonial administrators. They thereby began creating the racially mixed population that characterizes much of Latin America today.

Third, the colonies' wealth was based on the exploitation of the native population and slaves from Africa. Spaniards took over the role once assumed by native leaders who had exacted labor and tribute from their subjects. Cortés established the **encomienda system**, which granted Indian villages to conquistadors as a reward for their services, thus legalizing slavery in all but name.

encomienda system
Grants by the Spanish which awarded Indian labor to wealthy colonists.

In 1542, after criticism from colonial priest Bartolomé de las Casas, the monarch formulated a new code of laws forbidding the conquerors from enslaving Indians while still allowing them to collect money and goods from tributary villages. These laws, combined with the declining Indian population, led the *encomenderos* to import kidnapped Africans as their controlled labor force. They employed Indians and Africans primarily in gold and silver mines, on sugar plantations, and on huge ranches. African slavery was more common on the larger Caribbean islands than on the mainland.

Snark/Art Resource, NY

An image from the Codex Azcatitlan, an account of the Aztec (Mexica) people's history from their arrival in the Valley of Mexico through the conquest by Cortés. Printed European-style in the late sixteenth century—that is, about seven decades after the conquest—the codex nonetheless presents a native viewpoint on the cataclysmic events. Here Cortés and his men are preceded by Malinche, his interpreter and mistress, and followed by their native allies bearing food supplies. Also in the crowd is Cortés's black slave.

Many demoralized residents of Mesoamerica accepted the Christian religion brought to New Spain by Franciscan and Dominican friars—men who had joined religious orders bound by vows of poverty and celibacy. Spaniards leveled cities, constructing cathedrals and monasteries on sites once occupied by Aztec, Incan, and Mayan temples. Indians were exposed to European customs and religious rituals designed to assimilate Catholic and pagan beliefs. Friars juxtaposed the cult of the Virgin Mary with that of the corn goddess, and the Indians melded aspects of their worldview with Christianity, in a process anthropologists call *syncretism*. Thousands of Indians embraced Catholicism, at least partly because it was the religion of their new rulers.

Gold, Silver, and Spain's Decline

The new world's gold and silver, initially a boon, ultimately brought about the decline of Spain as a major power. China, a huge country with silver coinage, gobbled up about half of the total output of new world mines. In the 1570s, the Spanish dispatched silver-laden galleons annually from Acapulco (on Mexico's west coast) to trade at their new settlement at Manila, in the Philippines. This gave Spaniards easy access to luxury Chinese goods such as silk and Asian spices.

The influx of wealth led to rapid inflation, which caused Spanish products to be overpriced in international markets and imported goods to become cheaper in Spain. The Spanish textile industry collapsed. The seemingly endless income from American colonies also emboldened Spanish monarchs to spend lavishly on wars against the Dutch and the English. Late sixteenth- and early seventeenth-century monarchs repudiated the state debt, wreaking havoc on the nation's finances.

When the South American gold and silver mines faltered in the mid-seventeenth century, Spain's economy crumbled, and the nation lost much of its international importance.

The Columbian Exchange

What were the results of contact between native populations and European settlers and explorers?

Columbian Exchange
The widespread exchange of animals, plants, germs, and peoples between Europe, Africa, and the Americas.

A mutual transfer of diseases, plants, and animals (called the **Columbian Exchange** by historian Alfred Crosby; see Map 1.3) resulted from the European voyages of the fifteenth and sixteenth centuries and from Spanish colonization. Many large mammals, such as cattle and horses, were native to the connected continents of Europe, Asia, and Africa, but not the Americas. The Americas' vegetable crops—particularly maize, beans, squash, cassava, and potatoes—were more nutritious and produced higher yields than Europe's and Africa's wheat, millet, and rye. Native peoples learned to raise and consume European livestock, and Europeans and Africans planted and ate American crops. (About three-fifths of all crops cultivated in the world today were first grown in the Americas.) The diets of all peoples were enriched, helping the world's population to double over the next three hundred years. Increased population in Europe fueled further waves of settler colonists, keeping the exchange in motion.

MAP 1.3
Major Items in the Columbian Exchange
As European adventurers traversed the world in the fifteenth and sixteenth centuries, they initiated the "Columbian Exchange" of plants, animals, and diseases. These events changed the lives of the peoples of the world forever, bringing new foods and new pestilence to both sides of the Atlantic. Source: Copyright © Cengage Learning 2015

Smallpox and Other Diseases

Diseases carried from Europe and Africa devastated the Americas. Indians fell victim to microbes that had long infested other continents, killing hundreds of thousands but also leaving survivors with some immunity. When Columbus landed on Hispaniola in 1492, approximately half a million people resided there. Fifty years later, there were fewer than two thousand native inhabitants.

Although measles, typhus, influenza, malaria, and other illnesses severely afflicted the native peoples, the greatest killer was smallpox. Historians estimate that the long-term effects of the alien microorganisms could have reduced the pre-contact American population by as much as 90 percent. Large numbers of deaths further disrupted societies already undergoing severe strains caused by colonization, rendering native peoples more vulnerable to droughts, crop failures, and European invaders.

Even far to the north, where smaller American populations encountered only a few Europeans, disease ravaged the countryside. A great epidemic, probably viral hepatitis, swept through the villages along the coast north of Cape Cod from 1616 to 1618. Again, the mortality rate may have been as high as 90 percent. Just a few years after this dramatic depopulation of the area, English colonists were able to establish settlements virtually unopposed. Disease made a powerful if accidental ally.

The Americans, though, probably gave the Europeans syphilis, a virulent sexually transmitted disease. The first recorded European case occurred in 1493 in Spain, shortly after Columbus's return from the Caribbean. Carried by soldiers, sailors, and prostitutes, it spread quickly through Europe and Asia, reaching China by 1505.

Sugar, Horses, and Tobacco

The exchange of three commodities had significant impacts on Europe and the Americas. European demand for sugar led Columbus to take Canary Island sugar canes to Hispaniola in 1493. By the 1520s, Greater Antilles plantations worked by African slaves regularly shipped sugar to Spain. Half a century later, Portugal's Brazil colony (founded 1532) was producing sugar for the European market on an even larger scale. After 1640, sugar cultivation became the crucial component of English and French colonization in the Caribbean.

Through trade and theft, horses—which, like sugar, were brought to America by Columbus in 1493—spread among the peoples of the Great Plains by 1750. Lakotas, Comanches, and Crows, among others, used horses for transportation and hunting, calculated their wealth in number of horses owned, and waged war on horseback. After acquiring horses, these Indians' mode of subsistence shifted from hunting combined with gathering and agriculture, to one focused almost wholly on hunting buffalo.

In America, Europeans encountered tobacco, which at first they believed was medicinal. Smoking and chewing the "Indian weed" became a fad in Europe in the sixteenth century. Despite the efforts of King James I of England, who in 1604 pronounced smoking "hatefull to the Nose, harmfull to the brain, [and] dangerous to the Lungs," tobacco's popularity soared.

Maize

Mesoamericans believed that maize was a gift from Quetzalcoatl. Cherokees told of an old woman whose blood produced the prized stalks after her grandson buried her body in a field. For the Abenakis, the crop began when a beautiful maiden ordered a youth to drag her by the hair through a burned-over field. The long hair turned into silk, the flower on corn stalks. Both tales' symbolic association of corn and women supports archaeologists' recent suggestion that—in eastern North America at least—female plant breeders substantially improved the productivity of maize.

Sacred to the Indians who grew it, maize was a major dietary staple. They dried the kernels; ground into meal, maize was cooked as a mush or baked as flat cakes, the forerunners of modern tortillas. Although European invaders initially disdained maize, they soon learned it could be cultivated in a wide variety of conditions. So Europeans, too, came to rely on corn, growing it in their American settlements and their homelands.

Maize cultivation spread to Asia and Africa. Today, China is second only to the United States in corn production. In Africa, corn is grown more widely than any other crop. Still, the United States produces over 40 percent of the world's corn, and it is the nation's largest crop. More than half of American corn is consumed by livestock. Much of the rest is processed into syrup, which sweetens carbonated beverages and candies, or into ethanol, a gasoline additive that reduces both pollution and dependence on fossil fuels. Of the ten thousand products in a modern American grocery store, about one-fourth rely on corn.

Today, this crop provides one-fifth of all the calories consumed by the earth's peoples. The gift of Quetzalcoatl has linked the globe.

The LuEsther T. Mertz Library, NYBG / Art Resource, NY

The earliest known European drawing of maize, the American plant that was to have such an extraordinary impact on the entire world.

Europeans in North America

Europeans were initially more interested in exploiting North America's natural resources than in establishing colonies. John Cabot had reported that fish were plentiful near Newfoundland, so French, Spanish, Basque, and Portuguese sailors rushed to take advantage. In the early 1570s, the English joined the Newfoundland fishery. England became dominant in the region, which by the end of the sixteenth century was the focal point of a European commerce more valuable than that with the Gulf of Mexico.

How did England's rivalry with Spain shape its North American colonization efforts during the sixteenth century?

Trade Among Indians and Europeans

Fishermen quickly realized they could increase profits by exchanging cloth and metal goods, such as pots and knives, for native trappers' beaver pelts, used to make fashionable hats in Europe. Initially, Europeans traded from ships sailing along the coast, but later male adventurers set up outposts on the mainland.

Indians similarly desired European goods that could make their lives easier and establish their tribal superiority. Some bands concentrated so completely on trapping for the European market that they abandoned their traditional economies and became partially dependent on others for food. The intensive trade in pelts also had serious ecological consequences. In some regions, beavers were wiped out. The disappearance of their dams led to soil erosion, which later increased when European settlers cleared forests for farmland.

Contest Between Spain and England

The English watched enviously as Spain was enriched by its American possessions. In the mid-sixteenth century, English "sea dogs" like John Hawkins and Sir Francis Drake raided Spanish treasure fleets sailing home from the Caribbean. Their actions helped foment a war that in 1588 culminated in the defeat of a huge Spanish invasion force—the Armada—off the English coast. English leaders started to consider planting colonies in the Western Hemisphere, thereby gaining better access to trade goods while preventing their enemy from dominating the Americas. By the late sixteenth century, world maps designated vast territories "New Spain" and "New France." The glaring absence of a region called "New England" would have been a sore spot for Queen Elizabeth I and her courtiers.

Encouraging the queen to fund increased exploration was Richard Hakluyt, an English clergyman. He translated and published numerous accounts of discoveries, insisting on England's preeminent claim to North America. In *Divers Voyages* (1582) and especially *Principall Navigations* (1589), he argued for the benefits of English colonization.

The first English colonial planners hoped to reproduce Spanish successes by dispatching to America men who would exploit the native peoples for their own and their nation's benefit. A group that included Sir Walter Raleigh promoted a scheme to establish outposts that could trade with the Indians and serve as bases for attacks on Spain's possessions. Queen Elizabeth authorized Raleigh to colonize North America.

A watercolor by John White, an artist with Raleigh's second preliminary expedition (and who later was governor of the ill-fated 1587 colony). He identified his subjects as the wife and daughter of the chief of Pomeioc, a village near Roanoke. Note the woman's elaborate tattoos and the fact that the daughter carries an Elizabethan doll, obviously given to her by one of the Englishmen.

Link to Thomas Harriot's "The Algonquian Peoples of the Atlantic Coast" from *A Briefe and True Report* …

Roanoke

After two preliminary expeditions, in 1587 Raleigh sent 118 colonists to the territory that tens of thousands of native peoples called Ossomocomuck. Raleigh renamed it Virginia, after Elizabeth, the "Virgin Queen." The group established a settlement on Roanoke Island, in what is now North Carolina. But in August 1590, resupply ships found the colonists had vanished, leaving only the word *Croatoan* (the name of a nearby island as well as one of the area's powerful native groups) carved on a tree. Tree-ring studies show that the North Carolina coast experienced a severe drought between 1587 and 1589, which could have led colonists to abandon Roanoke.

England's first effort at planting a permanent settlement on the North American coast failed, as had earlier ventures by Portugal on Cape Breton Island (early 1520s), Spain in modern Georgia (mid 1520s), and France in South Carolina and northern Florida (1560s). All three enterprises collapsed because of the hostility of neighboring peoples and colonists' inability to be self-sustaining in foodstuffs.

Harriot's Briefe and True Report

The reasons for such failings become clear in Thomas Harriot's *A Briefe and True Report of the New Found Land of Virginia*, published in 1588. Harriot, a noted scientist who sailed with the second of the preliminary voyages to Roanoke, revealed that, although the explorers depended on nearby villagers for food, they antagonized their neighbors by killing some of them for what Harriot admitted were unjustifiable reasons.

Harriot advised later colonizers to deal more humanely with native peoples. But his book also reveals why that advice would rarely be followed. *A Briefe and True Report* examined the possibilities for economic development in America, stressing three points: the availability of valuable commodities, the potential profitability of American products, and the relative ease of manipulating the native population.

Harriot's *Briefe and True Report* depicted a bountiful land full of opportunities for quick profit. The native people residing there would, he thought, "in a short time be brought to civilitie" through conversion or conquest—if they did not die from disease. But European dominance of North America never was fully achieved, in the sense Harriot and his compatriots intended.

Revitalizing Native Languages

If knowledge is power, then language is power. Words make us human, and languages carry the DNA of cultures. From one generation to the next, humans use language as a tool to maintain the distinct identities of individuals and groups. Like peoples, languages evolve, and they are fragile. Their lives depend upon the regular nourishment that new speakers provide.

On the eve of European contact, continental North America was home to the speakers of as many as 1,200 distinct tongues, grouped into over a dozen major language families. (For comparison, linguists sort the languages of Europe into just four main families.) Over the last five centuries, many of those languages— a crucial part of the biodiversity of humankind—have been silenced by the violence of colonialism, by dispersal and disease, by informal pressures to assimilate to increasingly dominant European cultures, and by formal campaigns to suppress their usage. Today an estimated 139 native languages are spoken in the United States; the fluent speakers of perhaps 70 of these tongues are elderly, leaving those languages at risk.

Since the 1970s, however, a native language revitalization movement has grown in strength and visibility across the United States. Cultural survival activists have created immersion schools and nests, language camps, computer programs, even video games to preserve and transmit indigenous languages. Such efforts have trained many fluent speakers of languages once endangered, such as Hawai'ian, for example: in 1984, there were fewer than thirty fluent speakers of Ōlelo Hawai'i under the age of twelve. Today, there are tens of thousands.

One of the most extraordinary language reclamation programs instructs students in Wôpanâak, the Algonquian-family language of the Wampanoag nation of Massachusetts. Founded in 1993 by Jessie Little Doe Baird (Mashpee) and the late Helen Manning, the Wôpanâak Language Reclamation Project (WLRP) faced formidable obstacles: although Wôpanâak was the first indigenous American language to be expressed in alphabetic characters, its last speakers had died in the mid-nineteenth century. Using a range of documents— including sermons and scripture printed in Wôpanâak in the seventeenth century by English missionaries, and colonial land records using the language well into the eighteenth—the WLRP has created a dictionary of over 11,000 words, as well as first- and second-language curricula, an apprenticeship program, and immersion camps. A young Mashpee girl fluent in Wôpanâak and English is the language's first native speaker in seven generations. A Wôpanâak-immersion elementary school is scheduled to open in 2015.

Summary

Initial contact among Europeans, Africans, and Americans began in the fourteenth century, when Portuguese sailors first explored the Mediterranean Atlantic and the West African coast. Those seamen established commercial ties that brought African slaves first to Iberia and then to the islands the Europeans conquered. The Mediterranean Atlantic and its island sugar plantations nurtured the ambitions of mariners. Except for the Spanish, early explorers regarded the Americas primarily as a barrier keeping them from an oceanic route to the riches of China and the Moluccas. European fishermen were the first to realize that the northern coasts had valuable fish and furs.

The Aztecs experienced hunger after Cortés's invasion, and their great temples fell as Spaniards used their stones (and Indian laborers) to construct cathedrals.

The conquerors coerced natives and, later, enslaved Africans to till the fields, mine the precious metals, and herd the livestock that earned immense profits.

The first contacts of old world and new devastated the Western Hemisphere's native inhabitants. European diseases killed millions; European livestock, along with other imported animals and plants, forever modified the environment. Europe, too, was changed: American foodstuffs improved nutrition, and American gold and silver first enriched, then ruined, the Spanish economy.

A century after Columbus landed, many fewer people resided in North America than had lived there in 1491. And the people who did live there—Indian, African, and European—together made a world that was indeed new, a world engaged in the unprecedented process of combining religions, economies, ways of life, and political systems that had developed separately for millennia.

Chapter Review

American Societies

What led to the development of major North American civilizations in the centuries before Europeans arrived?

Agricultural success facilitated the rise of North American civilizations in the era before Europeans arrived. After the Ice Age ended and the prevalence of large mammals decreased, many native peoples in what is now central Mexico about 9000 years ago shifted from hunting to cultivating food crops for survival, including maize (corn), squash, beans, avocados, and peppers. As agricultural methods improved, vegetables became a reliable and nutritious food source, and native people established more permanent settlements. Early Americans began developing trade, accumulating wealth, creating elaborate cultural ceremonies and rituals, and building urban centers. But food supply was so keenly linked to a civilization's success that the first large city-states of Meso-america and Mississippian culture ultimately collapsed when food sources became scarce.

North America in 1492

What were the gender dimensions of labor in native cultures?

Like Europeans, Native American societies assigned various tasks and responsibilities to members along gender lines. Native societies that were predominantly hunting assigned women to making food and clothing and carrying their families' possessions whenever they moved. Agricultural peoples had different patterns of the gendered division of labor; some, like the Pueblos, defined farming as men's work, while others, like the Algonquian, Iroquoian, and Muskogean, gave women most agricultural chores, and men hunted and cleared the land. Women just about everywhere raised children, gathered wild foods, and prepared all of what people ate. Agricultural families were defined matrilineally, through the female line of descent, and women assumed more leadership roles than in nomadic hunter peoples. They rarely became chiefs, but older Iroquois women chose chiefs and could start or stop wars.

African Societies

What were the chief characteristics of West African societies in the fifteenth century?

People in West Africa made their living fishing, cattle herding, or farming, depending on where they lived. Those in Upper Guinea fished and grew rice; those in Lower Guinea farmed. Upper Guinea was also the region's overland trade link to Europe and Asia. Islamic culture influenced life in Upper Guinea, while people in the lower region practiced more traditional religions. Like other cultures around the world, West Africans designated tasks according to gender, although their roles were seen as complementary. Both sexes farmed; men hunted and managed livestock and fished, while women cared for children, prepared the food, and managed trade networks. In Lower Guinea, male political and religious leaders ruled men, while women ruled women. Polygyny was common throughout West Africa. So was slavery. In West Africa, a person could be enslaved for committing a crime, to repay debts, or as an enemy's captive, but slave status did not automatically transfer to the next generation, and some slaves could engage in trade and keep some of the profits or rise to important military or political positions.

European Societies

What were the motives behind fifteenth- and sixteenth-century European explorations?

The driving force behind early European explorations was the quest for a transoceanic trade route—the Northwest Passage—that would provide direct access to desirable African and Asian goods such as silks, dyes, jewels, sugar, gold, and spices. If such a route existed, it would allow northern Europeans to bypass the Muslim and Venetian merchants who served as middlemen for these items. Rulers also believed that the more they controlled access to these much-desired products, the better their nation's standing would be relative to other countries. Another, secondary motivation was to spread Christianity and convert those they considered to be heathen peoples.

Early European Explorations

What sailing innovation ultimately facilitated the widespread exploration of the Atlantic and Pacific?

The new technique of "sailing around the wind" made travel faster and less arduous for Atlantic explorers, which ultimately made them increasingly inclined to take on such expeditions. While sailors would travel with the wind in one direction, returning home had previously meant rowing against the wind or waiting for the wind to change, so trips back across the Atlantic were difficult and took weeks longer. But sailing around the wind sped up the journey; when mariners met with a difficult wind, they would now literally sail around it until they could find a wind that would easily and quickly carry them on their way. The same technique could be applied elsewhere under similar conditions; consequently, more and more mariners set out to explore the Atlantic and Pacific.

Voyages of Columbus, Cabot, and Their Successors

What three themes in Columbus's log about his explorations would come to mark much of the future settlement of Europeans in the Americas?

First, Columbus's log notes his quest for gold and other riches. Second, he wrote that the region's resources could be exploited to generate profits for his host country of Spain. In particular, he described the vast potential value of the dyes, spices, and medicines that could be made from plants found in the Americas. Third, Columbus wrote that the inhabitants could be easily converted to Catholicism and remade into servants. His and other explorers' discoveries inspired further exploration by European nations, though for most, colonization would lag for generations.

Spanish Exploration and Conquest

What model of colonization did Spain establish that other nations would later attempt to follow?

Spain developed a model of colonization in the Americas based on three key concepts. First, Spain's monarchy maintained firm control over its colonies with virtually no autonomy granted to American colonies. Second, men made up the majority of early colonists, taking first Indian, and later African, women as wives or concubines. Third, the development of the colonies and the exploitation of their resources were based on exploiting native people and African slaves as labor.

The Columbian Exchange

What were the results of contact between native populations and European settlers and explorers?

Native Americans and Europeans exchanged diseases, plants, and animals when they came into contact in North and South America in the fifteenth and sixteenth centuries. Native American vegetable crops were more nutritious than those in Europe and Africa, while Europeans brought livestock that helped enrich Indians' diets, too. The Spanish also brought horses to their American territories, which aided the shift in native society of the Great Plains from hunting combined with some farming and gathering, to almost exclusively hunting buffalo as the main form of subsistence. Europeans brought many diseases, from typhus to malaria to hepatitis, all of which devastated tribal populations, but none as much as smallpox. Europeans, meanwhile, acquired syphilis from Native Americans, which was debilitating, but not usually fatal.

Europeans in North America

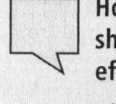 **How did England's rivalry with Spain shape its North American colonization efforts during the sixteenth century?**

The English recognized that Spain gained great riches from its American possessions. English sea dogs, such as John Hawkins and Sir Francis Drake, began to raid Spanish treasure ships as they returned to Europe from the Caribbean. These raids led to a war in 1588 in which the English defeated the Spanish Armada. After this victory, the English looked to start new colonies in America in order to gain better access to trade goods and to blunt Spanish influence in the Western Hemisphere.

Suggestions for Further Reading

David Abulafia, *The Discovery of Mankind: Atlantic Encounters in the Age of Columbus* (2008)

Alfred W. Crosby, *The Columbian Exchange: Biological and Cultural Consequences of 1492* (1972)

John H. Elliott, *Empires of the Atlantic World: Britain and Spain in America, 1492–1830* (2006)

Alison Games, *The Web of Empire: English Cosmopolitans in an Age of Expansion, 1560–1660* (2008)

James Horn, *A Kingdom Strange: The Brief and Tragic History of the Lost Colony of Roanoke* (2010)

Peter C. Mancall, *Hakluyt's Promise: An Elizabethan's Obsession for an English America* (2007)

Charles C. Mann, *1491: New Revelations of the Americas Before Columbus* (2005); *1493: Uncovering the New World Columbus Created* (2011)

Samuel Eliot Morison, *The European Discovery of America: The Southern Voyages, A.D. 1492–1616* (1974); *The Northern Voyages, A.D. 1500–1600* (1971)

Daniel K. Richter, *Before the Revolution: America's Ancient Pasts* (2011)

John K. Thornton, *Africa and Africans in the Making of the Atlantic World, 1400–1680* (1992)

Europeans Colonize North America

1600–1650

C aptain William Rudyerd seemed like the sort of man any colony in the Americas would prize, so when his older brother urged the planners of the new settlement to appoint him as its muster master general, they agreed. A veteran of wars on the European continent, Rudyerd followed the new dissenting English faith, as did the planners and many of the settlers. Those who mocked these zealous Protestants called them "Puritans."

At first, Rudyerd proved to be a vigorous soldier who worked hard to train the new colony's settlers to defend themselves from attack. But he also quarreled continually with those who failed to show him respect as a gentleman of noble birth. And he was no kinder to those who worked his new land. He beat a servant named Floud, whom scurvy had weakened. When Floud complained to the authorities, Rudyerd had him tied to a tree and whipped. Some weeks later, Floud died.

Such conflicts occurred in all the Anglo-American settlements. But in this colony the disputes were especially dangerous. Rudyerd lived on Providence Island, an isolated Puritan outpost off the coast of modern Nicaragua.

Providence Island, founded by Puritan adventurers in 1630—the same year as Massachusetts Bay—was designed as an English beachhead in the tropics. Labor shortages plagued the colony from the beginning. Planters wanted to grow and export tobacco, so they brought poor young people—mostly men—from London and the countryside, paying their passage across the ocean in exchange for a set number of years in service. But too few migrants took the bait. Those who did, when they didn't die of ill treatment or hunger or disease, eventually became free—demanding rather than supplying labor.

There were other bound laborers on Providence Island from the beginning, too: black slaves, brought from Africa via Bermuda. As the colony's servant troubles increased, the Puritan planters came to rely increasingly on slaves, bound to service in perpetuity. By the end of the decade, there were several hundred

The Caribbean
Sugar Cultivation

LEGACY FOR A PEOPLE AND A NATION
"Modern" Families

SUMMARY

bondsmen and bondswomen on Providence Island—more Africans than English.

Despite adopting slavery, the Providence Island planters failed to establish a viable economy in a volatile region. In the end, the colony's desperate attempts to prosper by serving as a base for English privateers caused its downfall. In May 1641, a fleet of seven Spanish ships carrying two thousand soldiers captured the island.

By then, Spain no longer predominated in the Americas. France, the Netherlands, and England all had permanent colonies in North America by the 1640s. Like the conquistadors, French and Dutch merchants and planters hoped to make a quick profit and then perhaps return to their homelands.

Unlike other Europeans, most English colonists came to America intending to stay. When they succeeded, they permanently displaced native populations. In the area that came to be known as New England, settler-colonists arrived in family groups. They re-created the European agricultural economy and family life to an extent impossible in colonies where single men predominated, as they did in the colonies of the Chesapeake region and the Caribbean, which focused on the large-scale production of cash crops for export.

English settlers prospered only after adapting to the alien environment. They had to learn to grow such unfamiliar American crops as maize and squash. They also had to develop extensive trading relationships with native peoples and with other English and European colonies. Needing field laborers, they first used English indentured servants. But like the Providence Islanders, they soon imported African slaves. The early history of England's America is best understood as a series of complex negotiations among European, African, and American peoples.

As you read this chapter, keep the following questions in mind:

- **Why did different groups come to the Americas? Which people came by choice, and which were forced to migrate?**

- **How did different native peoples react to their presence?**

- **In what ways did the English colonies in North America and the Caribbean differ, and in what ways were they alike?**

Chronology

1558	Elizabeth I becomes queen of England
1565	Founding of St. Augustine (Florida), oldest permanent European settlement in present-day United States
1598	Oñate conquers Pueblos in New Mexico for Spain
1603	James I becomes king of England
1607	Jamestown founded, first permanent English settlement in North America
1608	Quebec founded by the French
1610	Santa Fe, New Mexico, founded by the Spanish
1614	Fort Orange (Albany) founded by the Dutch
1619	Virginia House of Burgesses established, first representative assembly in the English colonies
1620	Plymouth colony founded, first permanent English settlement in New England
1622	Powhatan Confederacy rebels against Virginia
1624	Dutch settle on Manhattan Island (New Amsterdam)
	James I revokes Virginia Company's charter
	St. Kitt's founded, England's first Caribbean colony
1625	Charles I becomes king of England
1627	English colonize Barbados
1630	Massachusetts Bay colony founded
1634	Maryland founded
1636	Roger Williams expelled from Massachusetts Bay, founds Providence, Rhode Island
	Connecticut founded
1637	Pequot War in New England
1638	Anne Hutchinson expelled from Massachusetts Bay
1642	Montreal founded by the French
1646	Treaty ends hostilities between Virginia and Powhatan Confederacy

Spanish, French, and Dutch North America

How did the Jesuits' treatment of Native Americans differ from that of explorers and other settlers?

Spaniards established the first permanent European settlement within the boundaries of the modern United States, but others had tried previously. Twice in the 1560s Huguenots (French Protestants) escaping persecution planted colonies on the south Atlantic coast. A passing ship rescued the starving survivors of the first colony, located in present-day South Carolina. The second, near modern Jacksonville, Florida, was destroyed in 1565 by a Spanish expedition commanded by Pedro Menéndez de Avilés. Menéndez set up a fortified outpost named St. Augustine—now the oldest continuously inhabited European settlement in the United States.

The local Guale and Timucua nations initially allied themselves with the Spanish and welcomed Franciscan friars into their villages, but they soon resisted the imposition of Spanish authority. Still, the Franciscans offered the Indians spiritual solace for the diseases and troubles besetting them after the Europeans' invasion, and eventually gained numerous converts at missions that stretched westward across Florida and northward into the islands along the Atlantic coast.

New Mexico

In 1598, more than thirty years after the founding of St. Augustine, Juan de Oñate, a Mexican-born adventurer whose *mestiza* wife descended from both Cortés and Motecuhzoma, led about five hundred soldiers and settlers to New Mexico seeking riches. The Pueblo peoples greeted them cordially. But when the Spaniards used torture, murder, and rape to extort supplies from the villagers, the residents of Acoma killed several soldiers, including Oñate's nephew. The invaders responded ferociously, killing more than eight hundred people and capturing the remainder. All captives above the age of twelve were enslaved for twenty years, and men older than twenty-five had one foot amputated. Horrified, the other Pueblo villages surrendered.

Oñate's bloody victory proved illusory. New Mexico held little wealth and was too far from the Pacific to protect Spanish sea-lanes. The Spanish maintained a small military outpost and a few Christian missions in the area, with the capital at Santa Fe (founded 1610). As in regions to the south, Spanish leaders were granted *encomiendas,* giving them control over Pueblo villagers' labor. In the absence of mines or fertile agricultural lands, however, such grants yielded small profit.

Quebec and Montreal   The French focused on the area that Jacques Cartier had explored in the 1530s. They tried to establish permanent bases along Canada's Atlantic coast but failed until 1605, when they founded Port Royal. In 1608, Samuel de Champlain set up a trading post at an interior site that the Iroquois called Stadacona. Champlain renamed it Quebec. It was the most defensible spot in the St. Lawrence River valley, a stronghold that controlled access to the continent's heartland. In 1642, the French established a second post, Montreal, at the falls of the St. Lawrence, a place the Indians knew as Hochelaga.

The new posts quickly took over the lucrative trade in beaver pelts (see Table 2.1). The colony's leaders granted land along the river to wealthy *seigneurs*

TABLE 2.1   The Founding of Permanent European Colonies in North America, 1565–1638

Colony	Founder(s)	Date	Basis of Economy
Florida	Pedro Menéndez de Avilés	1565	Farming
New Mexico	Juan de Oñate	1598	Livestock
Virginia	Virginia Co.	1607	Tobacco
New France	France	1608	Fur trading
Bermuda	English sailors	1609	Tobacco, ship-building
New Netherland	Dutch West India Co.	1614	Fur trading
Plymouth	Separatists	1620	Farming, fishing
Maine	Sir Ferdinando Gorges	1622	Fishing
St. Kitts, Barbados, et al.	European immigrants	1624	Sugar
Massachusetts Bay	Massachusetts Bay Company	1630	Farming, fishing, fur trading
Maryland	Cecilius Calvert	1634	Tobacco
Rhode Island	Roger Williams	1636	Farming
Connecticut	Thomas Hooker	1636	Farming, fur trading
New Haven	Massachusetts migrants	1638	Farming
New Hampshire	Massachusetts migrants	1638	Farming, fishing

(nobles), who imported tenants to work their farms. Only a few Europeans resided in New France; most were men, some of whom married Indian women. More than twenty-five years after its founding, Quebec had just sixty-four resident families, along with traders and soldiers. Northern New France never grew much beyond the river valley between Quebec and Montreal (see Map 2.1).

Jesuit Missions in New France

French missionaries of the Society of Jesus (Jesuits), a Roman Catholic order dedicated to converting nonbelievers to Christianity, first arrived in Quebec in 1625. The Jesuits, whom the Indians called Black Robes, tried to persuade indigenous peoples to live near French settlements and adopt European agricultural methods. When that effort failed, they attempted to introduce Catholicism without insisting that Indians fundamentally alter their traditions. The Black Robes learned Indian languages and traveled to remote regions, where they lived among the Huron, Iroquois, and Abenaki peoples.

Jesuits sought to undermine the authority of traditional religious leaders. Immune to smallpox (having survived it already), they explained epidemics as God's punishment for sin, their arguments aided by the ineffectiveness of traditional remedies against the pestilence. Jesuits predicted eclipses and amazed villagers by communicating with each other over long distances through marks on paper. The Indians' desire to harness the power of literacy made them receptive to the missionaries.

Jesuits slowly gained thousands of converts. Catholicism offered women the inspiring role model of the Virgin Mary, personified in Montreal and Quebec by Ursuline nuns who ministered to Indian women and children. Many converts cast off native customs allowing premarital sex and easy divorce, which Catholic doctrine prohibited. In the late 1670s, one convert, a young Mohawk named Kateri Tekakwitha, inspired thousands with her celibacy and other ascetic devotional practices. Known as "the Lily of the Mohawks," her grave was said to be the site of miracles. In October 2012, the Roman Catholic Church made her the first Native American saint.

If they embraced some Christian doctrine, most native converts resisted strict European child-rearing methods. Jesuits recognized that such aspects of native culture could be compatible with Christianity. Their conversion efforts were further aided by their lack of interest in labor tribute or land.

New Netherland

In 1614, five years after Henry Hudson explored the river that now bears his name, his sponsor, the Dutch West India Company, established an outpost (Fort Orange) at present-day Albany, New York. The Dutch sought beaver pelts, and their presence so close to Quebec threatened France's regional domination. The Netherlands, the world's dominant commercial power, sought trade rather than colonization. Thus **New Netherland** remained small. The colony's southern anchor was **New Amsterdam**, founded in 1624 on Manhattan Island.

New Netherland was a small outpost of a vast commercial empire that extended to Africa, Brazil, and modern-day Indonesia. Autocratic directors-general ruled the colony, and settlers felt little loyalty to their nominal leaders. Few migrants

New Netherland Dutch colony in America.

New Amsterdam Dutch colony that would become New York.

MAP 2.1

European Settlements and Indian Tribes in Eastern North America, 1650

The few European settlements established in the East before 1650 were widely scattered, hugging the shores of the Atlantic Ocean and the banks of its major rivers. By contrast, America's native inhabitants controlled the vast interior expanse of the continent, and Spaniards had begun to move into the West. Source: Copyright © Cengage Learning 2015

Acoma Pueblo

Today, as in the late sixteenth century when it was captured by the Spanish, the Acoma Pueblo sits high atop an isolated mesa. The Ancient Pueblo selected the location, 365 feet above the valley floor, because they could easily defend it. Building the complex was a massive undertaking. Its rooms alone required over forty tons of sandstone to be cut from the surrounding cliffs and pulled up the mesa. Much of the labor was likely provided by other natives enslaved by the Ancient Pueblos. The buildings for which they gave their labor and their lives endured; some structures dating to the eleventh century still stand in the middle of the village.

In addition to making construction difficult, situating the city so high above the plains created problems with water supply. To this day there is no source of water in the village. Acoma's residents had to carry water up a steep set of stairs cut into the mesa's side (today there is an almost equally steep road). The women of Acoma were and are accomplished potters. Some pots, like the one shown here, were designed with a low center of gravity. How would that design help women to reach the top of the mesa with much-needed water? How would they carry such pots?

© Kevin Fleming/CORBIS

Acoma Pueblo today. The village is now used primarily for ritual purposes; few people reside there permanently, because all water must be trucked in.

Richard A. Cooke/CORBIS

A pot designed for carrying water to the top of the mesa.

arrived; as late as the mid-1660s, New Netherland had only about five thousand European inhabitants. Some were Swedes and Finns in the former colony of New Sweden (founded in 1638 on the Delaware River; see Map 2.1), which the Dutch seized in 1655.

Indian allies of New France and New Netherland clashed partly because of fur-trade rivalries. In the 1640s the Iroquois, who traded chiefly with the Dutch and lived in modern upstate New York, warred with the Huron, who traded primarily with the French and lived in present-day Ontario. With guns supplied by the Dutch, the Iroquois virtually exterminated the Huron, whose population had been decimated by smallpox. The Iroquois thus established themselves as a major force in the region.

England's America

What two developments prompted England to consider North American colonization in the early seventeenth century?

The failure of Raleigh's Roanoke colony ended English efforts to settle North America for nearly two decades. When the English decided in 1606 to try once more, they found success using a model unlike those of Spain, France, or the Netherlands. England sent large numbers of men and women to establish agriculturally based colonies on the mainland. Two major developments prompted approximately 200,000 ordinary English men and women to move to North America in the seventeenth century.

Social and Economic Change

The first development was the onset of dramatic social and economic change. In the 150-year period after 1530, largely due to the importation of American crops, England's population doubled. Those additional people competed for food, clothing, and other goods, which led to inflation. The increased number of workers caused a simultaneous fall in wages, and many laborers fell into poverty. When landowners raised rents, seized lands that peasants had long used in common (enclosure), or combined smallholdings into large units, they displaced their tenants. England's cities swelled to bursting. Approximately 75,000 people lived in London in 1550. A century later, nearly 400,000 people packed its narrow alleys and cramped buildings.

As "masterless men"—the landless and homeless—crowded the streets, officials came to believe that colonies in North America could siphon off what they viewed as England's "surplus population." Similarly, many ordinary people decided they could improve their circumstances by migrating to the new world.

English Reformation

The sixteenth century also witnessed a religious transformation that eventually led many English dissenters to leave. In 1533 Henry VIII, wanting a male heir and infatuated with Anne Boleyn, asked the pope to annul his nearly twenty-year marriage to the Spanish-born Catherine of Aragón. When the pope refused, Henry founded the Church of England and—with Parliament's concurrence—proclaimed himself its head.

At first, the Church of England differed little from Catholicism. Under Henry's daughter, Elizabeth I (child of his second marriage, to Anne Boleyn), though, new currents of religious belief dramatically affected England's recently established church.

These currents constituted the **Protestant Reformation**, led by Martin Luther, a German monk, and **Jean Calvin**, a French cleric and lawyer. Challenging the Catholic doctrine that priests were intermediaries between laypeople and God, Luther and Calvin insisted that people could interpret the Bible for themselves. Both rejected Catholic rituals and elaborate church hierarchy. They also asserted that the key to salvation was faith in God, rather than the Catholic combination of faith and good works. Calvin went further, stressing the need for total submission to God's will.

Protestant Reformation
Split of reformers from Roman Catholic church; triggered by Martin Luther.

Jean Calvin Early Protestant theologian who believed in "predestination."

Puritans, Separatists, and Presbyterians

During the long reign of Elizabeth I (1558–1603), Calvin's ideas gained influence in England, Wales, and especially Scotland. (In Ireland, Catholicism remained dominant.) The Scottish church eventually adopted Presbyterianism, which eliminated bishops and placed religious authority in bodies of clerics and laymen called presbyteries. By the late sixteenth century, though, many Calvinists—including those called Puritans (because they wanted to purify the church), or Separatists (because they wanted to leave it entirely)—believed that reformers in England and Scotland had not gone far enough. Henry had simplified the church hierarchy, and the Scots had altered it; Puritans and Separatists wanted to abolish it. Henry and the Scots had subordinated the church to the state; the dissenters wanted a church free from political interference. The established churches of England and Scotland continued to encompass all residents of the realm. Calvinists wanted to confine church membership to those God had chosen for salvation.

Paradoxically, dissenters insisted that people could not know if they were "saved." Mere mortals could not comprehend or affect their predestination to heaven or hell. Thus, pious Calvinists confronted serious dilemmas: if the saved (or "elect") could not be identified with certainty, how could proper churches be constituted? And if you could not alter fate, why attend church or respect civil law? Calvinists admitted that their judgments about church membership only approximated God's unknowable decisions. They reasoned that God gave the elect the ability to accept salvation and to lead a moral life. Though good works would not earn you a place in heaven, pious behavior might signal that you belonged there.

Stuart Monarchs

Elizabeth I's Stuart successors, her cousin James I (1603–1625) and his son Charles I (1625–1649), exhibited little tolerance for Calvinists (see Table 2.2). As Scots, they also had little respect for the traditions of representative government that had developed in England. James I publicly declared the divine right of kings, the notion that a monarch's power came directly from God and that his subjects had a duty to obey him.

Both James I and Charles I wanted to enforce religious conformity. Because Calvinists—and remaining Catholics in England and Scotland—challenged many important precepts of the Church of England, the Stuart monarchs authorized the

TABLE 2.2 Tudor and Stuart Monarchs of England, 1509–1649

Monarch	Reign	Relation to Predecessor
Henry VIII	1509–1547	Son
Edward VI	1547–1553	Son
Mary I	1553–1558	Half-sister
Elizabeth I	1558–1603	Half-sister
James I	1603–1625	Cousin
Charles I	1625–1649	Son

removal of dissenting clergymen. In the 1620s and 1630s, some Puritans, Separatists, Presbyterians, and Catholics decided to move to America, where they hoped to practice their beliefs freely. Some fled to avoid arrest and imprisonment.

The Founding of Virginia

How did English cultural traditions clash with those of Native Americans in Virginia?

The impetus for England's first permanent colony in the Western Hemisphere was both religious and economic. The newly militant English Protestants wanted to combat "popery" at home and in the Americas. Accordingly, in 1606, a group of merchants and wealthy gentry—some of them aligned with religious reformers—obtained a royal charter for the Virginia Company, organized as a **joint-stock company**. Such forerunners of modern corporations pooled the resources of many small investors through stock sales. Although Virginia Company investors anticipated great profits, neither settlement the company established—one in Maine that collapsed within a year, and **Jamestown**—earned much.

joint-stock company Business corporation that amasses capital through sales of stock to investors.

Jamestown First successful English colony, established in 1607.

Jamestown and Tsenacommacah

In 1607, the Virginia Company dispatched 108 men and boys to a region near Chesapeake Bay called Tsenacommacah by its native inhabitants. That May, the colonists established a settlement called Jamestown on a swampy peninsula in a river they also named for their monarch. The colonists fell victim to dissension and disease. The gentlemen and soldiers at Jamestown expected to rely on local Indians for food and tribute, yet the residents of Tsenacommacah refused to cooperate. Moreover, the settlers arrived in the midst of a severe drought. The arrival of hundreds more colonists over the next several years only added to the pressure on scarce resources.

The weroance (chief) of Tsenacommacah, Powhatan, had inherited rule over six Algonquian villages and later controlled some twenty-five others (see Map 2.1). Late in 1607, Powhatan tentatively agreed to an alliance negotiated by colonial leader Captain **John Smith**. In exchange for foodstuffs, Powhatan wanted guns, hatchets, and swords, which would give him a technological advantage over his enemies.

John Smith Colonial leader of Jamestown who established order, good relations with Indians.

The fragile relationship soon foundered on mutual mistrust. The weroance relocated his primary village in early 1609 to a place the newcomers could not access easily. Without Powhatan's assistance, Jamestown experienced a "starving time" (winter 1609–1610). Hundreds perished and at least one survivor resorted to digging up corpses for food. When spring came, barely 60 of the 500 colonists who had come to Jamestown remained alive. They left on a newly arrived ship, but en route up the James River encountered ships carrying a new governor, additional settlers, and supplies, so they returned to Jamestown.

Link to John Smith's description of the "starving time" in Jamestown

To gain the upper hand with the Indians, the settlers in 1613 kidnapped Powhatan's daughter, Pocahontas. In captivity, she converted to Christianity and married a colonist, John Rolfe. Their union initiated a period of peace between the English and her people. Funded by the Virginia Company, she and Rolfe sailed to England to promote the colony. Pocahontas died at Gravesend in 1616, leaving an infant son who returned to Virginia as a young adult.

Algonquian and English Cultural Differences

English settlers and Algonquian natives focused on their cultural differences, although both groups held deep religious beliefs, subsisted primarily through agriculture, accepted social and political hierarchy, and observed well-defined gender roles. English men regarded Indian men as lazy because they did not cultivate crops and spent their time hunting (a sport, not work, in English eyes). Indian men thought English men effeminate because they did the "woman's work" of cultivation. English political and military leaders tended to rule autocratically, whereas Algonquian leaders (even Powhatan) had more limited authority.

Furthermore, Algonquian and English concepts of property differed. Most Algonquian villages held their land communally. Land could not be bought or sold outright, although certain rights to use it (for example, for hunting or fishing) could be transferred. Enclosures in the previous century had made English villagers accustomed to individual farms. The English also refused to accept Indians' claims to traditional hunting territories, insisting that only cultivated land could be owned or occupied. Ownership of such "unclaimed" property, the English believed, lay with the English monarchy, whose flag **John Cabot** had planted in North America in 1497.

John Cabot Italian explorer who established English claims to North America.

The English believed in the superiority of their civilization, and they expected native peoples to adopt English customs and to convert to Christianity. They showed little respect for the Indians when they believed English interests were at stake, as was demonstrated once the settlers found a salable commodity.

Tobacco Cultivation

That commodity was tobacco. In 1611, John Rolfe planted seeds of a variety from the Spanish Caribbean, which was superior to the strain Indians grew. Nine years later, Virginians exported 40,000 pounds of cured leaves; by the late 1620s, annual shipments had jumped to 1.5 million pounds.

Tobacco cultivation made Virginia prosper and altered life for everyone. It required abundant land because a field could produce only about three good crops before it had to lie fallow for several years to regain its fertility. Virginians therefore established farms along both sides of the James River at some distance from one another—a settlement pattern convenient for tobacco cultivation but dangerous for defense.

Opechancanough's Rebellion

Opechancanough, Powhatan's brother and successor, watched the English colonists' expansion and their attempts to convert natives to Christianity. Recognizing the danger, he launched attacks along the James River on March 22, 1622. By day's end, 347 English colonists (about one-quarter of the population) lay dead. Only a warning from two Christian converts saved Jamestown from destruction.

Reinforced by shipments of migrants and arms from England, the settlers repeatedly attacked Opechancanough's villages. A peace treaty was signed in 1632, but in April 1644 the elderly Opechancanough assaulted the invaders one last time. In 1646, survivors of the Powhatan Confederacy formally subordinated themselves to England.

End of Virginia Company

The 1622 assault killed the Virginia Company, which had remained unprofitable due to internal corruption and the heavy costs of settlement. But before its demise, the company developed two precedent-setting policies. First, to attract settlers, it established the "headright" system in 1617. Every new arrival paying his or her own way was promised fifty acres; those who financed the passage of others received similar headrights. To English farmers who owned little or no land, the headright system offered a powerful incentive to move to Virginia. To wealthy gentry, it promised the possibility of vast agricultural enterprises. Two years later, the company authorized the landowning men of the major Virginia settlements to elect representatives to an assembly called the **House of Burgesses**. Just as they had at home, English landholders expected to elect members of Parliament and control local governments.

House of Burgesses First elected representative legislature in North America that first met in 1619.

When James I revoked the charter in 1624, transforming Virginia into a royal colony, he continued the company's headright policy but abolished the assembly. Virginians protested, and by 1629 the House of Burgesses was functioning again. The colonists successfully insisted on governing themselves; thus, the political structure of England's American possessions differed from that of the Spanish, Dutch, and French colonies.

Life in the Chesapeake

What were the myths and realities of indentured servitude in the Chesapeake?

By the 1630s, tobacco was the chief source of revenue in Virginia and in the second English Chesapeake colony: Maryland. Given by Charles I to George Calvert, first Lord Baltimore, as a personal possession (proprietorship), Maryland was colonized in 1634. (Virginia and Maryland border Chesapeake Bay—see Map 2.1—and are referred to collectively as "the Chesapeake.") The Calvert family intended the colony as a haven for their persecuted fellow Catholics. Cecilius Calvert, second Lord Baltimore, became the first colonizer to offer freedom of religion to all Christian settlers, codified in Maryland's Act of Religious Toleration (1649). In everything but religion, the two Chesapeake colonies resembled each other.

Demand for Laborers

Above all else, successful Chesapeake farms required workers. Powhatans, their numbers reduced by war and disease, could not supply such needs. Nor were enslaved Africans widely available: traders could more easily and profitably sell slaves to Caribbean planters. By 1650, only about seven hundred blacks lived in Virginia and Maryland.

At first, Chesapeake tobacco farmers looked primarily to England to supply their labor needs. The headright system (which Maryland also adopted) allowed a tobacco planter to obtain both land and labor by importing English workers. He could use his profits to pay for the passage of more workers, thereby gaining more land, and even movement into the ranks of the emerging planter gentry.

Male laborers, along with a few women, immigrated to America as **indentured servants**, paying their passage by contracting to work from four to seven years. Indentured servants accounted for 75 to 85 percent of the approximately 130,000 English immigrants to Virginia and Maryland during the seventeenth century.

Males between the ages of fifteen and twenty-four composed roughly three-quarters of the servants; only one immigrant in five or six was female. Most of these young men came from farming or laboring families.

indentured servants
Young men and women, usually unemployed and poor, who were given free passage to America, plus basic needs such as food, shelter, and clothing, in exchange for labor, usually for four to seven years.

Conditions of Servitude

From a distance at least, the Chesapeake seemed to offer such people chances for advancement unavailable in England. Servants who fulfilled the terms of their indenture earned "freedom dues" of clothes, tools, livestock, corn, tobacco, and sometimes even land. Yet servants typically worked six days a week, ten to fourteen hours a day—often in starvation conditions—in a disease-riddled semitropical climate.

Servants faced severe penalties for running away. But laws did require masters to supply servants with sufficient food, clothing, and shelter, and they were not to be beaten excessively. Cruelly treated servants could turn to the courts, sometimes winning verdicts that transferred them to more humane masters or released them from their indentures.

Servants and their owners alike first had to survive the process the colonists called "seasoning," a bout with disease (probably malaria) that usually occurred during their first Chesapeake summer. About 40 percent of male servants did not survive long enough to become freedmen. Young men of twenty-two who successfully weathered their seasoning could expect to live only another twenty years.

For those who survived, the opportunities for advancement were real. Until the late seventeenth century, former servants often became independent farmers ("freeholders"). But in the 1670s, tobacco prices entered a fifty-year period of stagnation and decline, while good land grew scarce and expensive. In 1681, Maryland dropped its requirement that servants receive land as part of their freedom dues, forcing many freed servants to live as wage laborers or tenant farmers. By 1700, the Chesapeake was no longer the land of opportunity it once had been.

Standard of Living

Life in the early Chesapeake was hard for everyone, regardless of sex or status. The imbalanced sex ratio

Age and Sex Composition

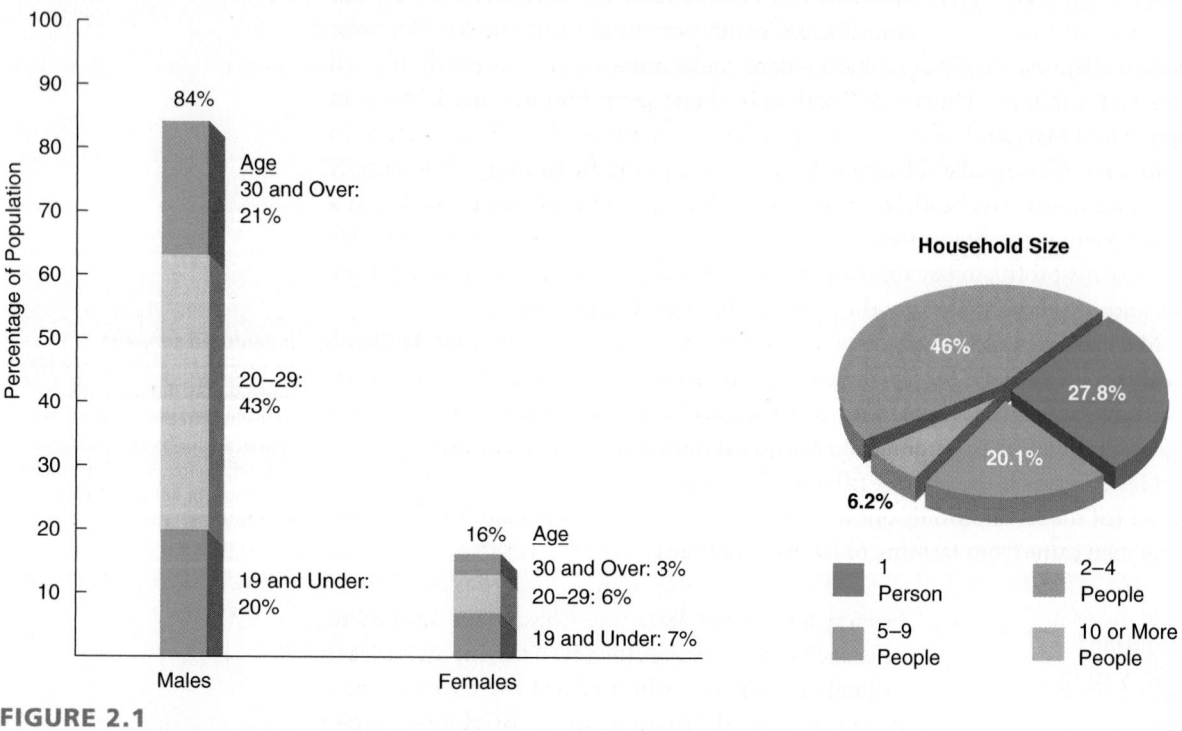

FIGURE 2.1
Population of Virginia, 1625

The only detailed census taken in the English mainland North American colonies during the seventeenth century was prepared in Virginia in 1625. It listed a total of 1,218 people, constituting 309 "households" and living in 278 dwellings—so some houses contained more than one family. The chart shows, on the left, the proportionate age and gender distribution of the 765 individuals for whom full information was recorded, and, on the right, the percentage variation in the sizes of the 309 households. The approximately 42 percent of the residents of the colony who were servants were concentrated in 30 percent of the households. Nearly 70 percent of the households had no servants at all.

(Source: Wells, Robert V., *The Population of the British Colonies in America Before 1776.* © 1975 Princeton University Press, 2003 renewed PUP. Reprinted by permission of Princeton University Press.)

(see Figure 2.1), the incidence of servitude, and the high rates of mortality combined to produce small and fragile households.

Farmers (and sometimes their wives) toiled in the fields alongside servants. Because hogs needed little tending, Chesapeake households subsisted mainly on pork and corn, a filling but not nutritious diet. Families supplemented with fish, wildfowl, and vegetables they grew in small gardens. The difficulty of preserving food for winter consumption magnified the health problems caused by epidemic disease.

Few households had many possessions beyond farm implements, bedding, and basic cooking and eating utensils. Ramshackle houses commonly had just one or two rooms. Rather than making clothing or tools, families imported them from England.

Chesapeake Politics

Throughout the seventeenth century, immigrants made up a majority of the Chesapeake population. Most members of Virginia's House of Burgesses and

Maryland's House of Delegates (established in 1635) were immigrants; they also dominated the governor's council, which simultaneously served as the highest court, part of the legislature, and executive adviser to the governor. A native-born ruling elite emerged only in the early eighteenth century.

In the seventeenth-century Chesapeake, most property-owning white males could vote, and they chose as their legislators (burgesses) the local elites who seemed to be their natural leaders. But because most such men were immigrants lacking strong ties to one another or to the region, the assemblies remained unstable and contentious.

The Founding of New England

What were John Winthrop's expectations for the Massachusetts Bay Company colony?

Economic and religious motives also drew people to New England. Environmental factors and the Puritans' organization of the New England colonies meant that the northern settlements developed very differently from their southern counterparts.

Contrasting Regional Demographic Patterns

Royal bureaucrats in late 1634 ordered port officials in London to collect information on travelers departing for the colonies. The records for 1635 document the departure of 53 vessels—20 to Virginia, 17 to New England, 8 to Barbados, 5 to St. Christopher, 2 to Bermuda, and 1 to Providence Island. Almost 5,000 people sailed on those ships—2,000 for Virginia, about 1,200 for New England, and the rest for island destinations. Nearly three-fifths of the passengers were between 15 and 24 years old.

But among those bound for New England, such youths constituted less than one-third of the total. Whereas women made up 14 percent of those headed to Virginia, they were almost 40 percent of New England–bound passengers. New England migrants often traveled in family groups and with others from the same towns. They also brought more goods and livestock with them than their Chesapeake counterparts.

Contrasting Regional Religious Patterns

Puritan congregations became key institutions in colonial New England, whereas spread-out settlement patterns made it difficult to organize a church in the Chesapeake. Not until the 1690s did the Church of England plant deeper roots in Virginia; by then, it had also replaced Catholicism as the established church in Maryland.

In both New England and the Chesapeake, religion affected the lives of pious Calvinists who were expected to reassess the state of their souls regularly. Because even the most pious could never be certain they were among the elect, anxiety troubled them. This anxiety lent a special intensity to their beliefs and to their concern with proper behavior—their own and that of others.

Separatists

Separatists who thought the Church of England too corrupt to be salvaged became the first religious dissenters to move to New England. In 1609, a Separatist congregation relocated to Leiden, in the Netherlands, where they found freedom of worship but also toleration of religions and behaviors they abhorred. Hoping to isolate themselves from worldly temptations, these people, known today as Pilgrims, received permission from the Virginia Company to colonize the northern part of its territory.

In September 1620, more than one hundred people, only thirty of them Separatists, set sail from England on the *Mayflower*. In November, they landed on Cape Cod, farther north than intended. They moved across Massachusetts Bay to a fine harbor (named **Plymouth** by John Smith, who had visited it in 1614) and into the empty dwellings of a Pawutuxet village whose inhabitants had died in the epidemic of 1616–1618.

Plymouth Colony established by Pilgrims in Massachusetts.

Mayflower Compact Agreement signed by *Mayflower* passengers to establish order in their new settlement.

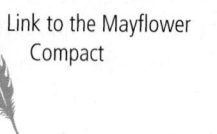

Link to the Mayflower Compact

Pilgrims and Pokanokets

Because they landed outside the jurisdiction of the Virginia Company, some non-Separatists questioned the authority of the colony's leaders. In response, the **Mayflower Compact**, signed in November 1620 on shipboard, established a "Civil Body Politic" as a temporary substitute for a charter. Male settlers elected a governor and made decisions at town meetings. Later, Plymouth created an assembly to which landowning male settlers elected representatives.

Only half of the *Mayflower*'s passengers lived until spring. Survivors owed much to the Pokanokets (a branch of the Wampanoags) who controlled the area. Pokanoket villages had suffered terrible losses in the recent epidemic, so to protect themselves from the powerful Narragansetts of the southern New England coast, the Pokanokets allied themselves with the newcomers. In the spring of 1621, their leader or sachem, Massasoit, agreed to a treaty, and the Pokanokets supplied the settlers with foodstuffs. The colonists also relied on Tisquantum (or Squanto), a Pawutuxet who served as a conduit between native peoples and Europeans. Captured by fishermen in the early 1610s and taken to Europe, Tisquantum had learned to speak English. He returned to find that the epidemic had wiped out his village. Caught between worlds, Tisquantum became the settlers' interpreter and a source of information about the environment.

Massachusetts Bay Company

Before the 1620s ended, another group of Puritans (Congregationalists, who hoped to reform the Church of England from within) launched the colonial enterprise that would come to dominate New England. Charles I, who became king in 1625, attempted to suppress Puritan practices. Some Congregationalist merchants, concerned about their long-term prospects in England, dispatched colonists to Cape Ann (north of Cape Cod) in 1628. The following year, the merchants obtained a royal charter, constituting themselves as the Massachusetts Bay Company.

The new joint-stock company quickly attracted Puritans who feared they no longer would be able to practice their religion freely in their homeland. They looked toward New England, where they could handle their affairs—secular and religious—as they pleased.

Turkeys

Near the end of their first year in North America, the Plymouth colonists held a traditional English feast to celebrate the harvest. Famously, they invited Massasoit's Pokanokets, and they probably consumed turkey. But why was this bird, originally from America and enjoyed at Thanksgiving today, named for a region of the then–Ottoman Empire? The native peoples of the Americas had named the fowl in their own languages; Aztecs, for example, called a male bird *huexoloti* and a female *totolin*.

When Columbus carried the birds back to Spain after his first voyage, the Iberian Peninsula was a focal point for Mediterranean commerce, and Spanish mariners sailed frequently to the Middle East. One Spanish vessel took some *huexoloti* and *totolin* to the Ottoman Empire. There, farmers familiar with distant Asian relatives of the bird improved the breed, ultimately producing a plumper, tamer version. By the end of the century "turkeys" were widely consumed throughout the British Isles.

When Thomas Harriot in his 1588 *Briefe and True Report* mentioned the wild North American version of the birds, he termed them "Turkie cockes and Turkie hennes." He failed to give the names native peoples used because these birds were not new to his audience.

Jamestown and Plymouth settlers recognized the birds in their new homelands as relatives of the fowls they had consumed in England. But they regarded the wild American birds as inferior since they ravaged young crops and were viewed as pests. So the settlers in both Virginia and New England soon imported English turkeys to raise for meat.

Were the "turkeys" consumed at the so-called First Thanksgiving the wild American birds or the tame Ottoman-English variety? No matter; that they were termed "turkeys" linked these fowls of American origin to the Mediterranean, Europe, and the Middle East as a prime example of animals in the Columbian Exchange.

Victoria & Albert Museum; London; UK/The Bridgeman Art Library

Turkeys from the Americas quickly traveled around the world, as is illustrated by this Mughal painting from the Islamic empire in India. The local artist Ustad Mansur painted a "turkey-cock" brought to the emperor Jahangir in 1612 from Goa—a Portuguese enclave on the west coast of the Indian subcontinent. Presumably the turkey had been transported from the Iberian Peninsula to that European outpost, whence the fowl made its way to Jahangir's court—where it was immortalized by an artist to whom it was an unusual sight.

The South part of New-England, as it is Planted this yeare, 1634.

William Wood, "The South Part of New-England, as it is Planted This Yeare," 1634, from *New England Prospect*/Picture Research Consultants & Archives

William Wood's "The South Part of New-England," which appeared in his book New Englands Prospect *(London, 1634),* was the first printed map of the region by an Englishman who had settled there. English place names—the Charles River, Elizabeth Isle, Cape Ann, New Ipswich—dot the map, illustrating the colonists' desire to remake the territory in the image of their homeland. But Wood also records many Algonquian place names—including Massachusetts Bay itself—reminding the viewer of the power of local native groups and their proximity to English settlement.

Link to John Winthrop's "A Model of Christian Charity"

Governor John Winthrop

In October 1629, the Massachusetts Bay Company elected **John Winthrop**, a member of the lesser English gentry, as its governor. Winthrop organized the initial segment of the great Puritan migration. In 1630, more than one thousand English men and women moved to Massachusetts—most of them to Boston. By 1643, nearly twenty thousand more had followed.

Caught up in the currents of European utopian thought, the colony's backers envisioned a utopia across the ocean—a new Jerusalem. Some time before the colonists embarked, Winthrop set down his expectations for the new colony in an essay called "Christian Charitie." Winthrop stressed the communal nature of the colonists' endeavor. Differences in status or wealth—though retained—would not imply differences in worth. On the contrary, God had planned the world so that "every man might have need of others, and from hence they might be all knit more nearly together in the bond of brotherly affection." In New England, Winthrop warned, "we shall be as a city upon a hill, the eyes of all people are upon us." If the Puritan experiment failed, "the Lord will surely break out in wrath against us."

Winthrop's essay became famous two centuries later. In 1838, one of his descendants published it for the first time, under its now-familiar title, "A Model of Christian Charity," recasting the discourse as a sermon preached en route to New England, and a parable about uniquely American virtues.

Covenant Ideal

The Puritans expressed their communal ideal in the doctrine of the covenant. They believed God had made a contract with them when they were chosen for the special mission to America. In turn, they covenanted with one another to work together. Founders of churches, towns, and even colonies in Anglo America often drafted documents setting forth the principles on which their institutions would be based. The Pilgrims' Mayflower Compact was a covenant, as was the Fundamental Orders of Connecticut (1639), which defined the basic law for the settlements along the Connecticut River valley.

The leaders of Massachusetts Bay likewise transformed their joint-stock company charter into the basis for a covenanted community based on mutual consent. They gradually changed the General Court—the company's small governing body—into a colonial legislature. They also granted the status of freeman, or voting member, to property-owning adult male church members. Less than two decades after its founding, the colony had a functioning system of self-government composed of a governor and a two-house legislature.

New England Towns

In Massachusetts groups of men—often from the same English village—applied for grants of land on which to establish towns (novel governance units that did not exist in England). The grantees copied the villages from whence they had come. First, they laid out lots for houses and a church. Then they gave each family parcels of land around the town center, reserving the best and largest plots for the most distinguished residents, including the minister. The "lower sort" received smaller and less desirable allotments. Still, every man and even a few single women obtained land.

Town centers developed quickly, evolving in three distinct ways. Isolated agricultural settlements in the interior tried to sustain Winthrop's vision of community life based on diversified family farms. Coastal towns, like Boston and Salem, became bustling seaports. And commercialized agricultural towns grew up in the Connecticut River valley, where easy water transportation enabled farmers to sell surplus goods.

Pequot War and Its Aftermath

Migration into the Connecticut Valley ended the Puritans' relative freedom from clashes with nearby Indians. Relocating under the direction of their minister, Thomas Hooker, their new settlements were within the territory of the powerful Pequot nation.

Pequot War Clash in 1637 that resulted as English colonists moved to settle in the Connecticut Valley on land inhabited by the Pequot Indians. The colonists were victorious and took over the Indians' land.

The arrival of English settlers ended the Pequots' monopoly over regional trading networks. Clashes between Pequots and English colonists had begun earlier, but the establishment of settlements in the Connecticut Valley moved them toward war. After two English traders were killed (not by Pequots), the English raided a Pequot village. In return, Pequots attacked Wethersfield, Connecticut, in April 1637, killing nine and capturing two. The following month, Englishmen and their Narragansett allies burned the main Pequot town on the Mystic River, slaughtering at least four hundred Pequots, mostly women and children, and enslaving the survivors.

For the next four decades, New England Indians accommodated themselves to the European invasion. They traded with the newcomers and sometimes worked for them, but they resisted incorporation into English society. The one European practice they consistently adopted was keeping livestock, for domesticated animals provided excellent sources of meat once hunting territories became English farms and wild game disappeared.

Missionary Activities

Only a few Massachusetts clerics, most notably John Eliot and Thomas Mayhew, seriously undertook missionary work among the Algonquin. Eliot insisted that converts farm the land in English fashion, take English names, and discard a wide range of their own customs. He met with little success. Only eleven hundred

Indians (out of many thousands) lived in the fourteen "Praying Towns" he established, and just 10 percent of the town residents had been baptized.

The missions in New France were more successful. Puritan services lacked Catholicism's beautiful ceremonies and special appeal for women, and Calvinists could not promise believers a heavenly afterlife. Yet on the island of Martha's Vineyard, Thomas Mayhew converted many Indians to Calvinist Christianity by allowing Wampanoag Christians to lead traditional lives and by training their men as ministers.

What attracted Indians to such religious ideas? Many must have turned to European religion to cope with the dramatic changes the intruders had wrought. The combination of disease, alcohol, new trading patterns, and loss of territory disrupted customary ways of life. Shamans had little success restoring traditional ways. Many natives must have concluded that the Europeans' ideas could help them survive.

Life in New England

What was the impact of religion on colonial life in New England?

New England's colonizers lived differently than their Algonquian neighbors and Chesapeake counterparts. Algonquian bands usually moved four or five times each year to maximize their environment. In spring, women planted the fields, but once crops were established, they gathered wild foods while men hunted and fished. Villagers returned to their fields for harvest, separated again for fall hunting, and wintered together in a sheltered spot.

English people lived year-round in the same location. Household furnishings and house sizes resembled those in the Chesapeake, but New Englanders' houses were sturdier. Their diets were also more varied. They replowed fields, employing manure as fertilizer rather than clearing new fields every few years. They fenced croplands to keep out the cattle, sheep, and hogs that were their chief meat sources.

Cradle, from Barnstable or Yarmouth, Massachusetts, 1665-85 (red oak & white pine), American School, (17th century)/Historic New England, Boston, Massachusetts, USA/The Bridgeman Art Library

Cradles like this one, made by a joiner living in the English plantations on Cape Cod in the third quarter of the seventeenth century, would have seen a lot of use in New England, where an even ratio of male to female settlers, early marriages, and relatively long life expectancies meant that large families—of five or more surviving children—quickly became the norm.

New England Families   Because Puritans often moved to America in family groups, the age range in early New England was wide; and because many more women migrated to New England than to the tobacco colonies, the population could immediately begin to reproduce itself. New England was also healthier. Where Chesapeake population patterns gave rise to few, mostly small families, New England families were numerous, large, and long-lived. Most men married; immigrant women married young (at age twenty, on the average); and marriages lasted longer and produced more children, who were more likely to live to maturity. New England women could anticipate raising five to seven healthy children.

The presence of so many children, combined with Puritans' stress on reading the Bible, led to concern for education. Schooling in the spread-out Chesapeake was haphazard. Living in towns, New Englanders could establish small schools. Whereas early Chesapeake parents commonly died before their children married, New England parents exercised much control over their adult offspring. Young men needed acreage from their fathers before they could marry. Daughters, too, needed a dowry of household goods supplied by their parents. These needs sometimes led to conflict between the generations.

Labor in a New Land

Early New England farms produced chiefly for subsistence and local sale; the region's climate generally did not support the production of staple crops. Family labor was the norm. Sons took up the callings of their fathers, and daughters, their mothers.

The prevalence of family labor should not blind us to the presence of slavery in New England. As the planters of Providence Island demonstrated, Puritan principles did not rule out chattel slavery. John Winthrop kept a Narragansett man and his wife as slaves; upon his death, he bequeathed them to one of his sons. One Salem captain, William Pierce, sold a consignment of captured Pequots in the Caribbean and used the proceeds to buy African slaves.

Like cotton, tobacco, and salt, African men, women, and children were Atlantic commodities, bought and sold in ports around the ocean's rim. By mid-century, roughly four hundred people of African descent lived in New England, the great majority enslaved. Their number hovered around two in every hundred New Englanders for most of the colonial era, with higher concentrations in seaports like Boston and, later, Newport, Rhode Island. In 1650, the scale of New England's black population, and the legal status of those forced migrants, closely resembled that of the Chesapeake.

Impact of Religion

Puritans controlled the governments of the early northern colonies. In Massachusetts Bay and New Haven, church membership was a prerequisite for voting. All the early English colonies, north and south, taxed residents to build churches and pay ministers' salaries, but only New England based criminal codes on the Old Testament. New Englanders were required to attend religious services. Their leaders also believed the state was obliged to support the one true church—theirs.

Puritan legal codes dwelled heavily on moral conduct. Laws forbade drunkenness, card playing, dancing, or even cursing—yet the frequency of such offenses demonstrates that New Englanders regularly engaged in these banned activities. Couples who had sex before marriage (as revealed by the birth of a baby less than nine months after their wedding) faced fines and public humiliation. Nonetheless, roughly one bride in ten was pregnant. Sodomy, usually defined as sex between men, was punishable by death. Yet only two men were executed for the crime in the seventeenth century.

It is easy to think of the Puritans as killjoys and hypocrites, as many people did at the time. But New England's social conservatism stemmed from its radical views on the nature of true religion and its relationship to just government. A central irony of Puritan dissent—and a central dilemma of the early New England colonies—was that their godly experiment attracted people more radical than the colonies' leaders. New England preachers and magistrates refused to grant freedom of worship to those who held different beliefs.

Roger Williams A minister who advocated complete separation of church and state and religious toleration.

| Roger Williams |

Roger Williams, a young minister trained at Cambridge, England, migrated to Massachusetts in 1631. Williams preached that the Massachusetts Bay Company had no right to land already occupied by Indians, that church and state should be separate, and that Puritans should not impose their ideas on others.

Called before the General Court in October 1635, Williams refused to retract his claim that the colony's churches were "full of Antichristian pol[l]ution," among other statements. Fearful that his beliefs tended to anarchy, the magistrates banished him from the colony. When soldiers came to escort him to a ship back to England, they discovered that he had fled.

Williams trekked through the hard winter of 1636 to the head of Narragansett Bay, where he founded the town of Providence on land he obtained from the Narragansetts and Wampanoags. Providence and other towns in what became Rhode Island tolerated all faiths, including Judaism, and became a haven for other dissenters.

Anne Hutchinson Dissenter feared not only for her theology but also because she challenged gender roles; banished from Massachusetts.

| Anne Hutchinson |

A skilled medical practitioner popular with the women of Boston, **Anne Hutchinson** greatly admired John Cotton, a minister who emphasized the covenant of grace, or God's free gift of salvation. (By contrast, most Puritan clerics stressed the need for believers to engage in good works in preparation to receive God's grace.) Hutchinson held religious meetings in her home. Proclaiming that the faithful could communicate directly with God, she questioned the importance of the institutional church and its ministers. Such ideas—along with Hutchinson's model of female authority—threatened Puritan orthodoxy.

In November 1637, officials charged her with maligning the colony's ministers. After two days of holding her own in debate during her trial, she boldly declared that God had spoken to her directly. That assertion ensured her banishment. The clergy also excommunicated her. "You have stepped out of your place," one preacher told her; "you have rather been a Husband than a Wife and a preacher than a Hearer; and a Magistrate than a Subject." Civil authorities exiled Hutchinson, her family, and some of her followers to Rhode Island in 1638.

The Caribbean

What made the Caribbean islands initially desirable for colonization?

New England and the Chesapeake often dominate histories of colonial America. But if we look forward from the seventeenth century instead of backward from 1776, or if we imagine ourselves in the countinghouses of London rather than the meetinghouses of Boston, New England and the Chesapeake recede in importance, and the Caribbean looms large. In many respects, the island colonies of the West Indies lay at the center of what Europeans meant by "America."

France, the Netherlands, and England collided repeatedly in the Caribbean. The Spanish concentrated their colonization efforts on the Greater Antilles—Cuba, Hispaniola, Jamaica, and Puerto Rico. The tiny islands Spain ignored attracted other European powers seeking bases from which to attack Spanish ships loaded with American gold and silver.

England was the first northern European nation to establish a permanent foothold in the smaller Caribbean islands (the Lesser Antilles), colonizing St. Christopher (St. Kitts) in 1624, then later other islands, such as Barbados (1627), Providence (1630), and Antigua (1632). France colonized Guadeloupe and Martinique, and the Dutch gained control of tiny St. Eustatius (strategically located near St. Christopher). Like Providence Island, many colonies changed hands during the seventeenth century. For example, the English drove the Spanish out of Jamaica in 1655, and the French soon thereafter took over half of Hispaniola, creating the colony of St. Domingue (modern Haiti).

MAP 2.2
Caribbean Colonies ca. 1700

English, Spanish, French, Dutch, and other European powers fought for territory in the Caribbean basin throughout the colonial period. At stake were prized shipping routes and the high value of the cash crops produced on the islands, especially sugar, which brought in far more revenue than any other colonial product. Sugar demanded a huge labor force, and so the Caribbean was also the center of the transatlantic slave trade. Many of the enslaved people in mainland English North America were first brought in chains to Jamaica or Barbados. Source: Copyright © Cengage Learning 2015

Sugar Cultivation

Beginning in the 1630s, what historians call a "sugar revolution" remade the West Indies and changed the center of gravity in England's America. Entering Europe in substantial quantities at approximately the same time as coffee and tea—stimulating, addictive, and bitter Asian drinks—sugar quickly became crucial to the European diet. By 1700, the English were consuming four pounds of sugar per person each year—a figure that would more than quadruple by the end of the century.

The first sugar grown in the West Indies reached Spain in 1517. By the 1530s, some thirty-four sugar mills operated on the island of Hispaniola alone. These were factory-like complexes staffed by round-the-clock workforces. The work was backbreaking, even lethal. The island's sugar was processed by large numbers of enslaved Africans—perhaps 25,000 of them by 1550.

By 1600, Brazil had come to dominate the West Indies sugar trade. Connections between Portuguese planters there and the Portuguese merchants who controlled the slaving forts of Angola gave Brazilian sugar growers a competitive advantage. Eager to seize that advantage for themselves, the Dutch conquered both ends of this supply chain in the 1630s.

©Topham/The Image Works

First printed in 1657, Richard Ligon's map of Barbados depicts the colony in the midst of its transition to a sugar-growing monoculture. English plantations line the island's Leeward Coast. At the top left corner of the map, a planter on horseback fires his musket at two African runaways. Ligon had seen such cruelty firsthand, and he wrote about it in his True and Exact History of Barbados.

"Modern" Families

Since the late twentieth century, "family values" has been a catchphrase in American politics. Organizations such as Focus on the Family and the American Family Association (both founded by Christian evangelicals in 1977) lobby Washington to protect so-called traditional families from what they see as the modern plagues of premarital sex, fatherless households, and easy divorce. But not much about the "traditional" American family is in fact traditional. In many ways, the families created by seventeenth-century English migrants to the Chesapeake look remarkably modern.

English women were scarce in early Virginia and Maryland. In the first decades of colonization, men outnumbered women by as much as six to one; by mid-century, there were still as many as three male settlers for every female. Young women who made the journey typically migrated as indentured servants. By law, they could not marry during that time; masters did not want to lose working hands to pregnancy. Roughly one in five servant women became pregnant while under indenture nonetheless. Marriage itself could be informally contracted. With few ministers around to solemnize their vows, some couples simply declared themselves wed—or, on occasion, divorced.

Women in the Chesapeake had their pick of husbands. But indenture delayed marriage, and the region's high rates of endemic disease meant that families were easily broken. Only one marriage in three lasted as long as a decade before a spouse died—typically the man. Widows remarried quickly, often within a few months of a husband's death. Men planned for this eventuality, giving their wives an unusual degree of control over their property and their children.

What did early Chesapeake families look like, then? With two or three children, they were smaller than American families in the post–World War II era. Households formed when parents remarried and combined the remnants of previous families and so included a motley array of blood kin and step-kin. Children routinely grew up with orphaned cousins, half-siblings, and stepparents.

As the region's demography slowly stabilized, these decidedly modern households of English descent began to police family boundaries more zealously—especially as African slaves were brought to the Chesapeake. Those boundaries, too, were modern innovations, not time-honored traditions. Then as now, new worlds made extraordinary demands on families, and tradition was a luxury few could afford.

The English colonizers of Barbados discovered in the early 1640s that the island's soil and climate were ideal for cultivating sugar cane. In the 1640s and 1650s, Barbadian tobacco growers and other small farmers sold out to sugar planters, who amassed enormous landholdings. The sugar planters staffed their fields and furnaces with large gangs of bound laborers—African slaves, English and Irish servants, Portuguese convicts—any man who could be bought and worked for six or eight years, till sugar used him up.

But as the Atlantic trade in Africans grew cheaper and more efficient, race-based slavery came to prevail. By the last quarter of the seventeenth century, 175 large planters, each of whom owned more than 100 acres and 60 slaves, controlled the economy of Barbados, which, like the West Indies more broadly, had become a slave society. The island's English population fell from 30,000 in the 1640s to less than 20,000 in 1680, while the number of the enslaved rose from 6,000 to more than 46,000. By then, Barbados had become the most valuable colony in English America. Its sugar exports were worth more than all of the exports from the rest of English America—*combined.*

Summary

B y the mid-seventeenth century, Europeans had come to North America and the Caribbean to stay, indelibly altering not only their own lives but also those of native peoples. Europeans killed Indians with weapons and diseases and had varying success in converting them to Christianity. Indigenous peoples taught Europeans to eat new foods and recognize—however reluctantly—other cultures. The prosperity and survival of many of the European colonies depended on the cultivation of American crops (maize and tobacco) and an Asian crop (sugar), thus attesting to the importance of post-Columbian ecological exchange.

To a greater extent than their European counterparts, the English transferred the society and politics of their homeland to a new environment. Their sheer numbers, coupled with their hunger for vast quantities of land, brought them into conflict with their Indian neighbors. New England and the Chesapeake differed in the structure of their populations, the nature of their economies, their settlement patterns, and their religious culture. Yet they resembled each other in the conflicts their expansion engendered, and in their tentative experiments with the use of slave labor. In years to come, both regions would become embroiled in increasingly fierce rivalries besetting the European powers

Chapter Review

Spanish, French, and Dutch North America

> **How did the Jesuits' treatment of Native Americans differ from that of explorers and other settlers?**

Spanish and other settlers typically sought to dominate the native populations, controlling their labor and often enslaving them, sometimes through the use of violence. The French Jesuits who settled New France (Montreal and Quebec) initially tried to convert Indians to Christianity and convince them to farm in the European style. When that failed, missionaries introduced Catholicism without insisting that Indians abandon their traditions. Missionaries learned Indian languages and lived among potential converts, and while they tried to undermine the authority of shamans, Jesuits also recognized the compatibility of some aspects of native culture with Christianity. This somewhat flexible approach, combined with their lack of interest in land or tribute, made at least some Indians receptive to conversion.

England's America

> **What two developments prompted England to consider North American colonization in the early seventeenth century?**

First, dramatic population growth in England, partly as a result of more nutritious foods of American origin, increased competition for food, clothing, shelter, and jobs. That, in turn, spurred inflation; wages also fell. Some profited, but those at the lower end of the socioeconomic spectrum—those with little or no land—lapsed into poverty and homelessness. Cities became overcrowded, leading officials to see colonizing North America as a way to reduce England's "surplus" population and related woes. Others hoped to improve their lot in the land-rich colonies. Second, the Protestant Reformation sparked new forms of Christianity that diverged from the Church of England, and while Elizabeth I tolerated such dissent, her successors, the Stuart monarchs, did not. Ultimately, seeking to practice freely their religious beliefs (and avoid imprisonment), some English Puritans, Separatists, and Catholics fled to America.

The Founding of Virginia

How did English cultural traditions clash with those of Native Americans in Virginia?

While both were religious, Englishmen considered Indian men lazy because they let women cultivate crops while they hunted, which the English regarded as a sport and not work. Native Americans thought Englishmen were effeminate because they farmed, which Indians considered women's work. English political and military leaders tended to rule autocratically, whereas Algonquian leaders had more limited authority. Most importantly, where the English believed in individual farms and private landownership, the Algonquians held land communally as a village.

Life in the Chesapeake

What were the myths and realities of indentured servitude in the Chesapeake?

Chesapeake tobacco farmers filled their extensive demand for labor with indentured servants from England—typically young men who worked for four to seven years in exchange for their passage. Indentured servitude for these young men represented a chance at upward mobility. Most gained "freedom dues" at the completion of their contract, including clothes, tools, livestock, casks of corn and tobacco, and sometimes land. But they worked long hours, six or seven days a week, doing intense physical labor in hot climates. Masters could discipline or sell them, and if indentured servants fled, they faced extreme penalties, although some did win verdicts against cruel masters calling for their transfer or release from indenture. Exposure to disease combined with intense labor so that only 60 percent of indentured men lived to become freedmen, and many who did lived only another twenty years.

The Founding of New England

What were John Winthrop's expectations for the Massachusetts Bay Company colony?

First elected governor in 1629, John Winthrop was instrumental in organizing the first Puritan migration from England to the colony. In his essay "Christian Charitie," Winthrop called for the new colony to serve as a moral and spiritual example for the rest of the world, a "city upon a hill." He urged colonists of varying ranks to work together, to mediate status differences, and to unite around their communal interests. He envisioned a true commonwealth, where people put the common good ahead of their own and were governed by Christian brotherhood.

Life in New England

What was the impact of religion on colonial life in New England?

Although Puritans fled England to practice their faith freely in New England, they offered no such freedom of worship to those who dissented from their beliefs. Puritans controlled the government in many early northern colonies and made Congregationalism the only recognized religion, with church membership and voting rights linked. Colonists were punished with fines or whippings for missing religious services. In addition, strict behavioral codes meant colonists were tried for drunkenness, card playing, dancing, or idleness. Couples who had sex during their engagement were fined and publicly humiliated. People who behaved in ways that today would be called homosexual were sometimes executed. Dissenters such as Roger Williams or Anne Hutchinson, who challenged Puritan orthodoxy, were tried and banished—Williams founded Providence, Rhode Island, based on religious tolerance and was subsequently joined by Hutchinson. Beyond challenging church authority, Hutchinson violated gender norms by preaching.

The Caribbean

What made the Caribbean islands initially desirable for colonization?

European colonizers had different reasons for being drawn to the Caribbean islands. Spain, which focused on larger islands, saw them as offering the potential for greater wealth with less effort than smaller islands might. Other countries saw the smaller islands as a base to attack Spanish vessels transporting gold, silver, and other valuable commodities from the Americas. The second reason for settling on the smaller islands was sugar cultivation. Sugar was in high demand in Europe, particularly since the sweetener improved the taste of coffee and tea and provided a sweet, yet quick, energy boost.

Suggestions for Further Reading

Richard S. Dunn, *Sugar and Slaves: The Rise of the Planter Class in the English West Indies, 1624–1713* (1972)

Alison Games, *Migration and the Origins of the English Atlantic World* (1999)

David D. Hall, *A Reforming People: Puritanism and the Transformation of Public Life in New England* (2011)

Jane Kamensky, *Governing the Tongue: The Politics of Speech in Early New England* (1997)

Karen O. Kupperman, *The Jamestown Project* (2007)

C. S. Manegold, *Ten Hills Farm: The Forgotten History of Slavery in the North* (2010)

Mary Beth Norton, *Founding Mothers & Fathers: Gendered Power and the Forming of American Society* (1996)

Stephan Palmié and Francisco Scarano, eds., *The Caribbean: A History of the Region and Its Peoples* (2011)

Christopher L. Tomlins, *Freedom Bound: Law, Labor, and Civic Identity in Colonizing English America, 1580–1865* (2010)

David J. Weber, *The Spanish Frontier in North America* (1992)

North America in the Atlantic World

3

1650–1720

Their journey began in Mohawk country, where western New York met eastern Iroquoia. As European settlements in the region grew in size and power, each of the four men had sought a new birth under the Christian God. Tejonihokarawa, from the Wolf Clan, became Hendrick. Sagayenkwaraton, whose Mohawk name meant Vanishing Smoke, would be called Brant. Onigoheriago was baptized John. Etowaucum, a Mohican, took the name Nicholas. If they found solace in their adopted faith, they also found in the English new allies against old enemies.

Now, during Queen Anne's War—part of England's decades-long struggle to wrest the heart of North America from the French—those new English allies tapped the four Christian Indians for a diplomatic mission. Hendrick, Brant, John, Nicholas, and their retinue traveled overland from Albany to Boston. At Boston's Long Wharf, they boarded one of the vessels that regularly sailed the Atlantic, carrying English manufactures to New England and returning east loaded with timbers, fish, and furs. Six weeks later, after what they called "a long and tedious Voyage," the delegation arrived in London.

In the teeming metropolis, the go-betweens were groomed for their task. Scarlet cloaks trimmed in gold replaced their blankets. Their feet were encased in soft yellow slippers and their long hair tucked beneath turbans. They were given grand new titles to match their elaborate costumes: the four men became Indian Kings.

Finally, on the morning of April 19, 1710, they arrived at St. James Palace. The diplomats presented Queen Anne—ruler of Scotland and England, newly unified as Great Britain—with gifts of wampum, pledged their help against "her Enemies the *French*," and asked her to commit more men and materiel to prosecute the war at the western edges of her dominion.

The Four Indian Kings stayed in London for two weeks, making a royal progress. They sat for state portraits that would hang in Kensington Palace; they dined with dukes and admirals; they watched plays and cockfights. Crowds trailed them everywhere, and thousands more read about them in the newspapers. Before

57

they left, the Four Kings sailed down the Thames to Greenwich, where they toured the dockyards that made the ships that were knitting together the Crown's growing blue water empire.

Hendrick, Brant, John, and Nicholas were hardly the first Native Americans to cross the Atlantic, but the Four Indian Kings came as tributaries from a *new* new world. England's tentative plantations overseas had become an empire. Oceangoing vessels now crisscrossed the globe, carrying European goods to America and Africa, Africans to the Americas, Caribbean sugar to New England and Europe, and New England fish and wood products (and occasionally Indian slaves) to the Caribbean. The North American colonies expanded their territorial claims and diversified their economies after the mid-seventeenth century. Mohawk country was closer to the British metropolis than ever before.

Three developments shaped life in the mainland English colonies between 1650 and 1720: escalating conflicts with Indians and with other European colonies; the expansion of slavery; and changes in the colonies' relationships with England.

The explosive growth of the slave trade significantly altered the Anglo-American economy. At first involving primarily Indians and already enslaved Africans from the Caribbean, the trade soon came to focus on men and women kidnapped in Africa and brought directly to the Americas. The large influx of West African slaves expanded agricultural productivity, fueled the international trading system, and dramatically reshaped colonial society.

The burgeoning North American economy attracted new attention from English administrators. After 1660, London bureaucrats attempted to supervise the American settlements to ensure that the mother country benefited from their economic growth.

As English settlements expanded, they came into conflict not only with powerful Indian nations but also with the Dutch, the Spanish, and especially the French. By 1720, war—between Europeans and Indians, among Europeans, and among Indians allied with different colonial powers—had become an all-too-familiar feature of American life. The people and products of the North American colonies had become integral to the world trading system and enmeshed in its conflicts.

As you read this chapter, keep the following questions in mind:

- **What were the consequences of the transatlantic slave trade in North America and Africa?**
- **How did English policy toward the colonies change from 1650 to 1720?**
- **What were the causes and results of new friction between Europeans and native peoples?**

The Growth of Anglo-American Settlements

Why did New York's development lag behind that of other British colonies in the seventeenth century?

Between 1642 and 1646, civil war between supporters of King Charles I and the Puritan-dominated Parliament engulfed England. Parliament triumphed, leading to the execution of the king in 1649 and interim rule by the parliamentary army's leader, Oliver Cromwell, during the so-called Commonwealth period. But after Cromwell's death, Parliament restored

Chronology

1642–46	English Civil War
1649	Charles I executed
1651	First Navigation Act passed to regulate colonial trade
1660	Stuarts (Charles II) restored to throne
1663	Carolina chartered
1664	English conquer New Netherland; New York founded
	New Jersey established
1672	England's Royal African Company chartered; becomes largest single slave-trading enterprise
1675–76	Bacon's Rebellion disrupts Virginia government; Jamestown destroyed
1675–78	King Philip's War devastates New England
1680–1700	Pueblo revolt temporarily drives Spaniards from New Mexico
1681	Pennsylvania chartered
1685	James II becomes king
1686–88	Dominion of New England established, superseding charters of colonies from Maine to New Jersey
1688–89	James II deposed in Glorious Revolution; William and Mary ascend English throne
1689	Glorious Revolution in America; Massachusetts, New York, and Maryland overthrow royal governors
1688–99	King William's War fought on northern New England frontier
1691	New Massachusetts charter issued
1692	Witchcraft crisis in Salem; nineteen people hanged
	Earthquake ravages Port Royal, Jamaica
1696	Board of Trade and Plantations established to coordinate English colonial administration
	Vice-admiralty courts established in America
1701	Iroquois Confederacy adopts neutrality policy toward France and England
1702–13	Queen Anne's War fought by French and English
1710	Four "Indian Kings" visit London
1711–13	Tuscarora War (North Carolina) leads to capture or migration of most Tuscaroras
1715	Yamasee War nearly destroys South Carolina

the monarchy once Charles I's son and heir, Charles II, agreed to restrictions on his authority (see Table 3.1).

The Restoration, as the period following the coronation of Charles II was known, transformed the British empire. Assuming the throne in 1660, the new king rewarded nobles and other supporters with vast tracts of land on the North American continent and in the West Indies. The colonies thereby established six of the thirteen polities that eventually would form the United States—New York, New Jersey, Pennsylvania (including Delaware), and North and South Carolina (see Map 3.1)—as

TABLE 3.1 Restored Stuart Monarchs of England, 1660–1714

Monarch	Reign	Relation to Predecessor
Charles II	1660–1685	Son
James II	1685–1688	Brother
Mary	1688–1694	Daughter
William	1688–1702	Son-in-law
Anne	1702–1714	Sister, Sister-in-law

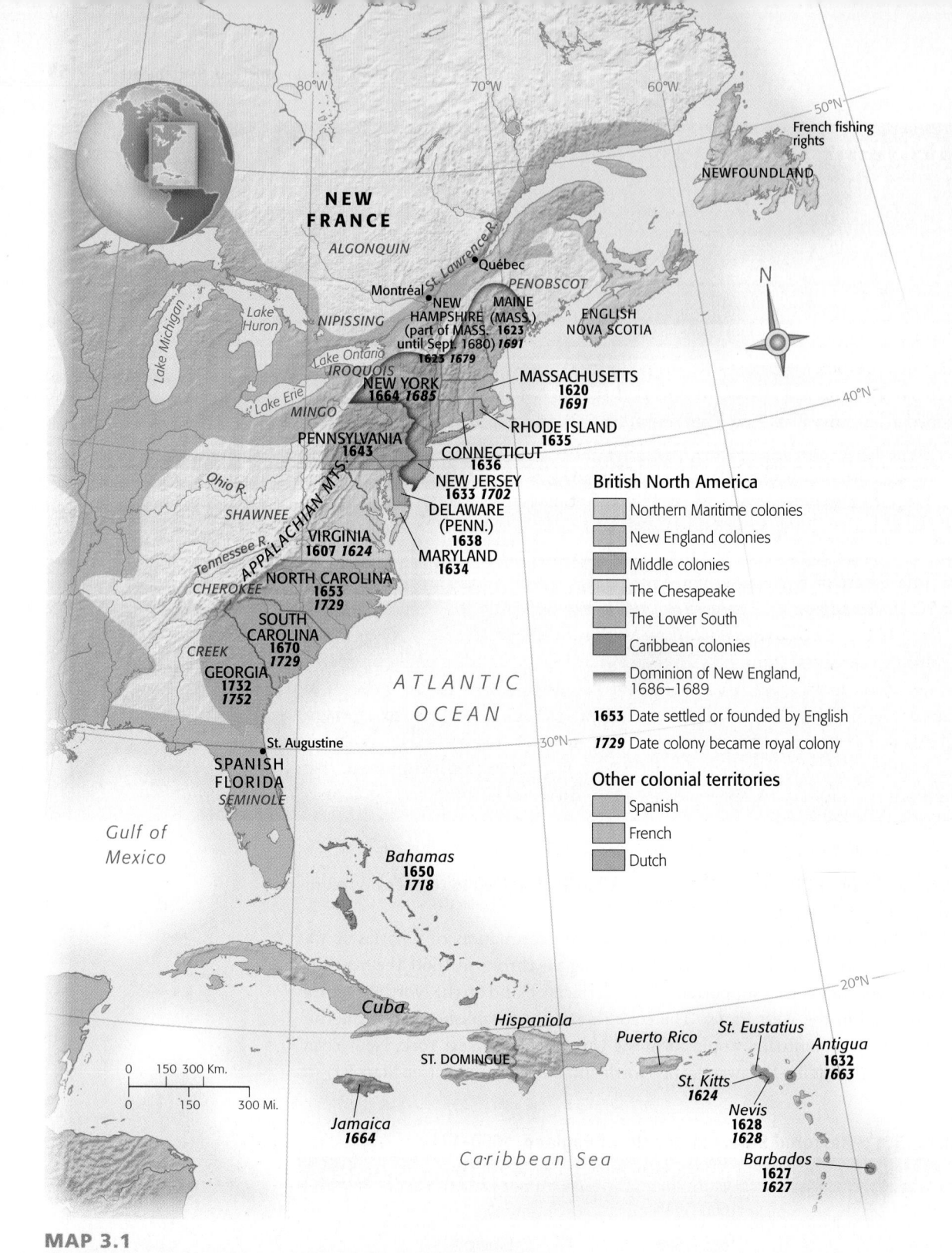

MAP 3.1

The Anglo-American Colonies in the Early Eighteenth Century

By the early eighteenth century, the English colonies nominally dominated the Atlantic coastline of North America. But the colonies' formal boundary lines are deceiving because the western reaches of each colony were still largely unfamiliar to Europeans and because much of the land was still inhabited by Native Americans. Source: Copyright © Cengage Learning 2015 well as Jamaica, the richest of the thirteen colonies that would remain loyal to the Crown. Collectively, these became known as the Restoration colonies.

New York

In 1664, Charles II deeded the region between the Connecticut and Delaware rivers, including the Hudson Valley and Long Island, to his younger brother James, the duke of York. That the Dutch had settled there mattered little. In August, James's warships anchored off Manhattan Island, demanding New Netherland's surrender. The colony complied without resistance. Although in 1672 the Netherlands briefly retook the colony, the Dutch permanently ceded it in 1674.

In New Netherland, James acquired a heterogeneous possession, which he renamed after himself, as New York (see Table 3.2). In 1664, a significant minority of English people (mostly Puritan New Englanders on Long Island) already lived there, along with the Dutch, Algonquians, Mohawks, Mohicans, Iroquois, Africans, Germans, Scandinavians, and a smattering of other Europeans. In addition, the Dutch West India Company had imported slaves into the colony. At the time of the English conquest, almost one-fifth of Manhattan's approximately fifteen hundred inhabitants were of African descent. Slaves then made up a higher proportion of New York's urban population than of the Chesapeake's rural people.

James's representatives moved cautiously in establishing English authority over this diverse population. The Duke's Laws, a 1665 legal code, applied solely to the English settlements on Long Island and was only later extended to the entire colony. James initially allowed Dutch residents to maintain their local government, land titles, and customary legal practices. Each town could choose which church (Dutch Reformed, Congregational, or Anglican) to support with its taxes. But James distrusted legislative bodies, and not until 1683 did he agree to the colonists' requests for an elected legislature.

The duke did not promote migration, so the colony's population grew slowly, barely reaching eighteen thousand by 1698. Until the second decade of the eighteenth century, Manhattan remained a commercial backwater within the orbit of Boston.

New Jersey

In 1664, the duke of York regranted the land between the Hudson and Delaware rivers—East and West Jersey—to his friends Sir George Carteret and John

TABLE 3.2 The Founding of English Colonies in North America and the West Indies, 1655–1681

Colony	Founder(s)	Date	Basis of Economy
Jamaica	Oliver Cromwell, Charles II	1655/1661	Cacao, indigo, beef, sugar
New York (formerly New Netherland)	James, duke of York	1664	Farming, fur trading
New Jersey	Sir George Carteret, John Lord Berkeley	1664	Farming
North Carolina	Carolina proprietors	1665	Tobacco, forest products
South Carolina	Carolina proprietors	1670	Rice, indigo
Pennsylvania (incl. Delaware)	William Penn	1681	Farming

Lord Berkeley. The Jersey proprietors quickly attracted settlers, promising generous land grants, limited freedom of religion, and—without authorization from the Crown—a representative assembly. Many Puritan New Englanders migrated to the Jerseys, along with Barbadians, Dutch New Yorkers, and eventually Scots. By 1726, New Jersey had 32,500 inhabitants, only 8,000 fewer than New York.

Within twenty years, members of the Society of Friends, also called **Quakers**, purchased Carteret's share (West Jersey) and portions of Berkeley's (East Jersey). Quakers rejected earthly and religious hierarchies. With no formally trained clergy, the small radical sect allowed men and women to speak in meetings and become "public Friends" who traveled throughout the Atlantic world to preach God's word. Authorities did not welcome the Quakers' radical egalitarianism, and Friends encountered persecution everywhere.

Quakers Members of a religious sect that embraced egalitarianism and rejected traditional religious hierarchies. They believed that the Holy Spirit or the "inner light" could inspire every soul.

Pennsylvania

In 1681, Charles II granted the region between Maryland and New York to his friend **William Penn**, a prominent Quaker. Penn held the colony as a personal proprietorship, one that earned profits for his descendants until the American Revolution. But Penn also saw his province as a haven for persecuted coreligionists. In widely distributed promotional tracts printed in German, French, and Dutch, Penn touted fertile land available to all comers on liberal terms. He promised to tolerate all religions—although only Christian men could vote—and to establish a representative assembly. He guaranteed such legal protections as the right to bail and trial by jury, prized and ancient rights known throughout England's American realm as "English liberties."

William Penn The proprietor of the last unallocated tract of American territory at the king's disposal, which would become Pennsylvania.

By mid-1683, more than three thousand people—among them Welsh, Irish, Dutch, and Germans—had moved to Pennsylvania. Within five years the population reached twelve thousand. Philadelphia, sited on the easily navigable Delaware River, drew merchants and artisans from throughout the English-speaking world. Pennsylvania's plentiful and fertile lands enabled its residents to export surplus flour and other foodstuffs to the West Indies. Practically overnight Philadelphia acquired more than two thousand citizens and challenged Boston's commercial dominance.

Penn attempted to treat native peoples fairly. He learned the language of the Delawares (or Lenapes), from whom he purchased land to sell to European settlers. Penn also established strict trade regulations and forbade the sale of alcohol to Indians. Yet the same toleration that attracted Tuscarora, Shawnee, and Miami peoples to Pennsylvania also brought non-Quaker Europeans—Scots-Irish (Irish Protestants), Germans, and Swiss—who clashed repeatedly over land with the Indians.

Carolina

The southernmost proprietary colony, granted by Charles II in 1663, stretched from the southern boundary of Virginia to Spanish Florida. Strategically, a successful English settlement there would prevent Spaniards from pushing farther north. The fertile, semitropical land also promised to yield valuable figs, olives, wines, and silk. The proprietors named their new province Carolina in honor of Charles (whose Latin name was Carolus). The "Fundamental Constitutions of Carolina," which they asked the political philosopher John Locke to draft, outlined

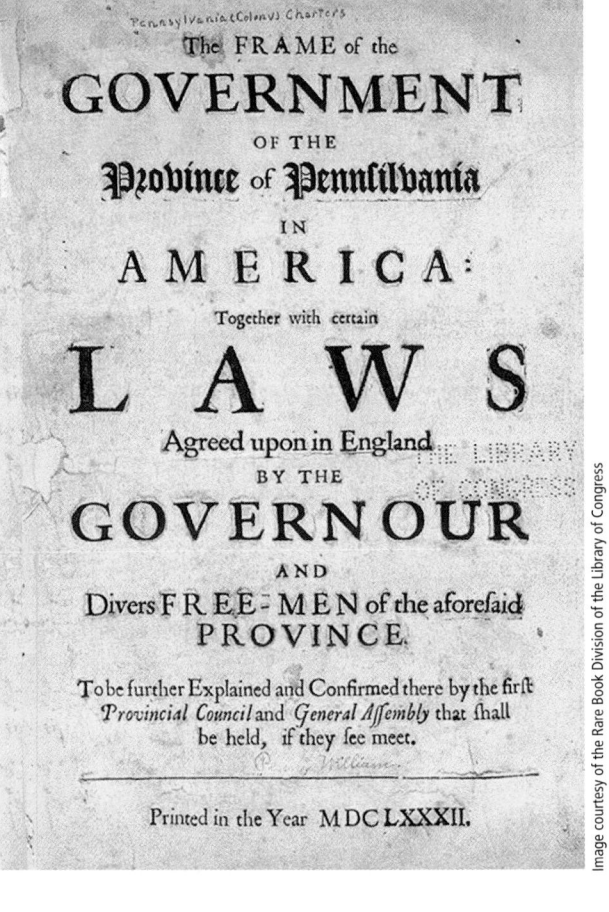

William Penn, later the proprietor of Pennsylvania, as he looked during his youth in Ireland. In numerous pamphlets (right) printed in the late seventeenth century, Penn spread the word about his new colony to thousands of readers in England and its other colonial possessions.

a colony governed by landholding aristocrats and characterized by a structured distribution of political and economic power.

But Carolina failed to follow this plan. Instead, it quickly developed two distinct population centers, which in 1729 split into separate colonies under royal rule. Virginia planters settled the Albemarle region that became North Carolina. They established an economy based on cultivating tobacco and exporting forest products. The other population center, which eventually formed the core of South Carolina, developed at Charles Town, founded in 1670. Many of its early residents migrated from Barbados, where land was increasingly consolidated as the sugar revolution advanced.

Carolina settlers raised corn and cattle, which they sold to Caribbean planters to feed their slaves. They also depended on trade with nearby Indians for commodities they could sell elsewhere, especially deerskins and enslaved Indians. Before 1715, Carolinians exported an estimated thirty thousand to fifty thousand Indian slaves.

Jamaica

Like Carolina, Jamaica absorbed numerous migrants from Barbados in the late seventeenth century. First colonized by Spain in 1494, the enormous island— at nearly 4,500 square miles, it is twenty-six times the size of Barbados—was still thinly settled when English troops seized it in 1655. Intended as a base from which to plunder Spanish treasure ships, the English garrison fared poorly at first. After the Restoration, however, powerful merchants in London convinced Charles II to convert Jamaica to a royal colony. In those early years, Jamaica was a haven for privateers, transported convicts, and smugglers.

But for all its anarchic tendencies, the colony soon began to grow and even flourish. A census taken in 1673 put Jamaica's population at 17,272, more than ten times what it had been when the English captured it. More than half the inhabitants—some 9,504—were enslaved Africans. As the sugar revolution took hold in Jamaica, the number of slaves soared, reaching 55,000—more than eight times the number of white settlers—by 1713. The enslaved rebelled frequently; six organized revolts rocked the colony before 1693. In the mid-eighteenth century, Jamaica's slave rebellions evolved into full-scale wars.

Jamaica proved as profitable as it was volatile, however. Nowhere was the combustible mixture more visible than in the provincial English boomtown of Port Royal. By 1680, it had nearly three thousand inhabitants. Wealthy planters, privateers, and the merchants lived in opulent brick houses, while their slaves crowded into huts. Taverns and brothels lined the wharves. Those who thought of Port Royal as a new world Sodom saw divine justice when, in 1692, an earthquake buried the city and hundreds of its inhabitants beneath the sea. A devastating fire ravaged the remainder eleven years later.

Yet Port Royal, no less than Boston, and Jamaica, no less than Pennsylvania, epitomized British America. The island recovered from the heavy blows of the late seventeenth century. On the eve of the American Revolution, Jamaica was the most valuable British colony, if not the economic capital of the Anglo-Atlantic world.

Chesapeake

The English Civil War retarded the development of the earlier English settlements. Struggles between supporters of the king and Parliament caused military clashes in Maryland and political upheavals in Virginia in the 1640s. But once the war ended and immigration resumed, the colonies again expanded. Tobacco growers imported increasing numbers of English indentured servants as farms developed into plantations.

Chesapeake tobacco planters continued to acquire small numbers of enslaved workers. At first, almost all came from a population that historian Ira Berlin has termed "Atlantic creoles": people (sometimes of mixed race) who came from other European settlements in the Atlantic world, primarily Iberian outposts. Not all the Atlantic creoles who came to the Chesapeake were bondspeople; some were free or indentured. With their arrival, the Chesapeake became what Berlin calls a "society with slaves," where slavery coexisted with other labor systems.

New England

Migration to New England essentially ceased when the Civil War began in 1642. While English Puritans were challenging the king and then governing England as a commonwealth, they had little incentive to leave their homeland. Yet the Puritan colonies' population grew dramatically by natural increase. By the 1670s, New England's population had more than tripled to approximately seventy thousand, which placed pressure on available land. Colonial settlement spread far into the

The Pine Tree Shilling

The early settlers of Massachusetts shipped most of the coins they had brought with them back across the Atlantic, to pay for goods imported from England and Europe. With money always in short supply, they conducted local and regional trade with tokens including musket balls and wampum, the clamshell beads Algonquian and Iroquois peoples prized for ceremonial exchanges. But in the 1640s, the value of wampum collapsed, just as Bostonians entered Caribbean trade.

Long-distance commerce demanded a circulating medium whose value held stable across space and time. That meant coins made from precious metal, whose weight governed their worth. Trade brought silver coins to New England from the Spanish mines at Potosí, but they were often shaved or debased—worth less than their face value. So in 1652, Massachusetts began to mint its own higher-quality coins. Mint master John Hull, a staunch Puritan, designed them without a human face, since the Bible's commandments forbade the worship of graven images. For the usual king's profile, he substituted a tall pine tree.

When Charles II was restored to the throne, he began to question colonial laws that departed from English norms. In 1665, his royal commissioners directed Massachusetts to close its mint. By minting money, Boston was acting like a city-state; the Crown would have it behave like a colony. Yet Massachusetts kept producing silver shillings until the colony's charter was revoked in the late 1680s. What did the pine tree signify in Atlantic commerce? How did the colonists identify themselves on the shilling?

Pine Tree Shilling front

Pine Tree Shilling back

interior of Massachusetts and Connecticut, and many later generations migrated to other colonies to find sufficient farmland. Others learned such skills as blacksmithing or carpentry to support themselves in the growing towns. By 1680, some 4,500 people lived in Boston, which was becoming a genuine city.

New Englanders who remained in the small, yet densely populated and intensely fractious older communities experienced a range of social tensions. Men and women frequently sued their neighbors for slander, debt, and other offenses. After 1650, accusations of witchcraft—roughly 100 in all before 1690—landed suspects in courtrooms across the region. But few of the accused, most of whom were middle-aged women, were convicted, and fewer still were executed.

Colonial Political Structures

By the last quarter of the seventeenth century, almost all the Anglo-American colonies had well-established political and judicial structures. In New England, property-holding men or the legislature elected the governors; in other regions, the king or the proprietor appointed such leaders. A council, elected or appointed, advised the governor and served as the upper house of the legislature. Each colony had a judiciary with local justices of the peace, county courts, and, usually, an appeals court composed of the councilors. Most colonies had local governing bodies as well.

A Decade of Imperial Crises: The 1670s

How did settlers' interests collide with those of Native Americans?

Between 1670 and 1680, New France, New Mexico, New England, and Virginia experienced bitter conflicts as their interests collided with those of America's original inhabitants.

New France and the Iroquois

In the mid-1670s Louis de Buade de Frontenac, the governor-general of Canada, decided to expand New France's reach south and west to establish a trade route to Mexico and to gain direct control of the fur trade. Accordingly, he encouraged the explorations of Father Jacques Marquette, Louis Jolliet, and René-Robert Cavelier de La Salle in the Great Lakes and Mississippi valley regions. Frontenac's goal, however, led to conflict with the powerful Iroquois Confederacy, composed of five Indian nations—the Mohawks, Oneidas, Onondagas, Cayugas, and Senecas. (In 1722, the Tuscaroras became the sixth.)

Link to letter from Father Marquette describing some interactions with Indians

Before the arrival of Europeans, the Iroquois waged wars primarily to acquire captives to replenish their population. Foreigners brought ravaging disease as early as 1633, intensifying the need for captives. The Europeans' presence also created an economic motive for warfare: the desire to dominate the fur trade and to gain unimpeded access to imported goods. Bloody conflict with the Huron in the 1640s initiated a series of conflicts with other Indians known as the **Beaver Wars**, in which the Iroquois fought to control the peltry trade. Iroquois warriors raided other villages for pelts or attacked Indians carrying furs to European outposts. Then the Iroquois traded that booty for European blankets, knives, guns, alcohol, and other items.

Beaver Wars Series of conflicts between the Hurons (and other Indians) and Iroquois in a quest for pelts.

As Iroquois dominance grew, beginning in the mid-1670s, the French repeatedly attacked, seeing the Iroquois as a threat to France's plans to trade with western Indians. Although in 1677 New Yorkers and the Iroquois established a formal alliance known as the Covenant Chain, the English offered little beyond weapons to their trading partners. Without much aid, the Confederacy held its own and even expanded, enabling it in 1701 to negotiate neutrality treaties with France and other Indians. For the next half-century, the Iroquois maintained their power through trade and diplomacy rather than warfare. The mission of the "Indian Kings" to London belonged to this diplomatic tradition.

Pueblo Peoples and Spaniards

In New Mexico, too, events of the 1670s led to a crisis with long-term consequences. Under Spanish domination, the Pueblo peoples had added Christianity to their beliefs while retaining traditional rituals. But as decades passed, Franciscans adopted increasingly violent tactics to eliminate the native religion. Priests and secular colonists who held *encomiendas* placed heavy labor demands on the people, who were also suffering from Apache raids and food shortages. In 1680, the Pueblos revolted under the leadership of **Popé**, a respected shaman, driving the Spaniards out of New Mexico. Although Spain restored its authority by 1700, Spanish governors now stressed cooperation with the Pueblos. The **Pueblo Revolt of 1680** constituted the most successful and longest-sustained Indian resistance movement in colonial North America.

Popé Leader of the Pueblo Revolt against Spanish in 1680.

Pueblo Revolt of 1680 The most successful Indian uprising in American history. Pueblo Indians rebelled against Spanish authority and drove the Spanish from their New Mexico settlements.

King Philip's War

In the more densely settled English colonies, hostilities developed over land. By the early 1670s, the growing settlements in southern New England surrounded Wampanoag ancestral lands on Narragansett Bay. The local chief, Metacom—whom the English called "King Philip"—was troubled by the impact of European culture on his land and people. Philip led attacks on nearby communities in June 1675. Other Algonquian peoples, among them Nipmucks and Narragansetts, joined King Philip's forces. In the fall, they attacked settlements in the northern Connecticut River valley; the war spread to Maine when the Abenakis entered the conflict. In 1676, the Indian allies devastated villages like Lancaster, and even attacked Plymouth and Providence. Altogether, the native alliance wholly or partially destroyed twenty-seven of ninety-two towns and attacked forty others, pushing the line of English settlement back toward the coast.

King Philip's War Major war between Indians and New England settlers.

In summer 1676, the Indian coalition ran short of food and ammunition. On June 12, the Mohawks—ancient Iroquois enemies of New England Algonquians—devastated a major Wampanoag encampment while most of the warriors were away attacking an English town. After King Philip was shot to death that August, the southern alliance crumbled. But fighting on the Maine frontier continued for another two years until the English and Abenakis agreed to end the conflict in 1678.

After the war, hundreds of Wampanoags, Nipmucks, Narragansetts, and Abenakis were captured and sold into slavery; many more died of starvation and disease. New Englanders had broken the power of the southern coastal tribes. Thereafter the southern Indians lived in small clusters, subordinated to the colonists and often working as servants or sailors. Only on the island of Martha's Vineyard did Christian Wampanoags (who had not participated in the war) preserve their cultural identity.

The settlers paid a terrible price for their victory: an estimated one-tenth of New England's adult male population was killed or wounded. Proportional to population, it was the most lethal conflict in American history. The colonists' heavy losses also caused many Puritans to wonder if God had turned against them. New Englanders did not fully rebuild abandoned interior towns for another three decades, and not until the American Revolution did the region's per capita income again reach pre-1675 levels.

Bacon's Rebellion
Uprising that resulted from many conflicts, among them mounting land shortage and settlers' desires for Indian lands.

Link to Nathaniel Bacon's Declaration in the Name of the People

Bacon's Rebellion

Conflict over land simultaneously wracked Virginia. In the early 1670s, ex-servants unable to acquire land greedily eyed the territory reserved by treaty for Virginia's natives. Governor William Berkeley resisted starting a war to further the aims of backcountry settlers. Dissatisfied colonists then rallied behind a recent immigrant, the gentleman Nathaniel Bacon, who shared their frustration that all the desirable land had been claimed. Using as a pretext the July 1675 killing of an indentured servant by Doeg Indians, Bacon and his followers attacked the Doegs and the more powerful Susquehannocks. In retaliation, Susquehannocks raided outlying farms early in 1676.

The governor declared Bacon and his men outlaws. During the chaotic summer of 1676, Bacon alternately pursued Indians and battled the governor. In September, Bacon's forces burned Jamestown to the ground. But when Bacon died of dysentery the following month, the rebellion collapsed. Even so, a new treaty signed in 1677 opened much of the disputed territory to settlement. The end of Bacon's Rebellion thus pushed most of Virginia's Indians west beyond the Appalachians.

The Atlantic Trading System

How was slavery at the center of the expanding trade network between Europe and the colonies?

In the 1670s and 1680s, the prosperity of the Chesapeake rested on tobacco, which depended on an ample labor supply. But fewer English men and women proved willing to indenture themselves. Population pressures had eased in England, and the Restoration colonies and Caribbean sugar boom gave migrants other settlement options. Furthermore, fluctuating tobacco prices and land scarcity made the Chesapeake less appealing. Wealthy Chesapeake planters found the answer to their labor problem in the Caribbean sugar islands, where Dutch, French, English, and Spanish planters purchased African slaves.

Why African Slavery?

Slavery had been practiced in Europe and Islamic lands for centuries. European Christians justified enslaving heathen peoples in religious terms, arguing that slavery might lead to conversion. Muslims, too, enslaved infidels and imported black African bondspeople into North Africa and the Middle East. Others believed that prisoners of war could be enslaved. Consequently, when Portuguese mariners encountered African societies holding slaves, they purchased bondspeople. From the 1440s on, Portugal imported large numbers of slaves into the Iberian Peninsula.

English people had few moral qualms about enslaving other humans. Slavery was sanctioned in the Bible and widely practiced by contemporaries. Yet colonists did not inherit the law and culture of slavery fully formed. Instead, they fashioned the institution of bondage and concepts of "race" to suit their economic and social needs. The 1670 Virginia law that first tried to define which people could be enslaved declared, "all servants not being christians imported into this colony by shipping shal be slaves for their lives." Such awkward, nonracial phrasing reveals that Anglo-American settlers had not yet fully developed the meaning of *race* or the category of *slave*.

Atlantic Slave Trade

North American mainland planters could not have obtained bondspeople without the rapid development of an Atlantic trading system. Although this elaborate system has been called the triangular trade, people and products did not move across the ocean in easily diagrammed patterns (see Map 3.2).

Chesapeake tobacco and Caribbean and Brazilian sugar were shipped to Europe, where they were in demand. The profits paid for African laborers and European manufactured goods. The African coastal rulers took payment for slaves in European manufactures and East Indian textiles. Europeans purchased slaves from Africa for resale in their colonies and acquired sugar and tobacco from America, in exchange dispatching their manufactures everywhere.

European nations fought bitterly to control the Atlantic trade. The Portuguese dominated at first, but were supplanted by the Dutch in the 1630s. Between 1652 and 1674, England and the Netherlands fought three wars—conflicts over naval supremacy that largely centered on the slave trade. The Dutch lost out to the English, who controlled the trade through the Royal African Company, chartered by Charles II in 1672. The company maintained seventeen forts and trading posts, dispatched to West Africa hundreds of ships carrying English goods, and transported thousands of slaves to the Caribbean colonies. Some of its agents made fortunes, yet even before the company's monopoly expired in 1712, independent traders carried most of the Africans imported into the colonies. In the fifty years beginning in 1676, British and American ships transported an estimated 689,600 captured Africans, more than 177,000 of them in vessels owned by the Royal African Company.

Colonial Williamsburg Foundation. Museum Purchase.

By the middle of the eighteenth century, American tobacco had become closely associated with African slavery. An English woodcut advertising tobacco from the York River in Virginia accordingly depicted not a Chesapeake planter but rather an African, shown with a hoe in one hand and a pipe in the other. Usually, of course, slaves would not have smoked the high-quality tobacco produced for export, although they were allowed to cultivate small crops for their own use.

West Africa and the Slave Trade

Most of the enslaved people carried to North America originated in West Africa. Some came from the Rice Coast and Grain Coast, but even more had resided in the Gold Coast, Slave Coast, and the Bight of Biafra (modern Nigeria) and Angola. Certain coastal rulers—for instance, the Adja kings of the Slave Coast—allowed the establishment of permanent slave-trading posts in their territories. Such rulers controlled Europeans' access to bound laborers and simultaneously controlled inland Africans' access to desirable trade goods.

The slave trade affected West African nations unevenly. It helped to create such powerful eighteenth-century kingdoms as Dahomey and Asante (formed from the Akan States), while rulers in parts of Upper Guinea, especially modern Gambia and Senegal, largely resisted involvement with the trade. Traffic in slaves destroyed smaller polities and disrupted traditional economic patterns. Agricultural production intensified, especially in rice-growing areas, to supply hundreds of slave ships with foodstuffs. Because prisoners of war constituted the bulk of the exported slaves, some nations initiated conflicts specifically to acquire valuable captives.

MAP 3.2
Atlantic Trade Routes

By the late seventeenth century, an elaborate trade network linked the countries and colonies bordering the Atlantic Ocean. The most valuable commodities exchanged were enslaved people and the products of slave labor. Source: Copyright © Cengage Learning 2015

Atlas Blaeu van der Hem

In the fifteenth century, Portuguese explorers renamed the town of Elmina—a trading village on the coast of present-day Ghana—after the gold they exported from the site. (El mina means "the mine.") The construction of the massive fort or "castle" depicted in this watercolor began in 1482. At first, its primary purpose was to protect the precious metal trade along what Europeans called Africa's Gold Coast. But during the seventeenth century, enslaved Africans became the primary exports of ports like Elmina, which the Dutch acquired in 1637. Captive men, women, and children were held in the fortress's dungeons before beginning the long voyage to the Americas. The fort's export gate, facing the sea, came to be known as the Door of No Return.

New England and the Caribbean

New England had a complex relationship to the trading system. The region produced only one item England wanted: tall trees to serve as masts for sailing vessels. To buy English manufactures, New Englanders depended on profits earned in the Caribbean. The Caribbean colonies lacked precisely the items that New England produced: cheap corn and salted fish to feed slaves, and wood for barrels. By the late 1640s, decades before the Chesapeake economy became dependent on *production* by slaves, New England's commerce rested on *consumption* by slaves and owners.

Slaving Voyages

Tying the system together was the voyage (commonly called the **middle passage**) that brought Africans to the Americas. Brought aboard in small groups, drawn from many inland nations, speaking diverse languages, an average of 300 men, women, and children comprised what slave merchants called a "full complement" of human merchandise, though voyages transporting 400 or 500 Africans were not uncommon, and cargoes exceeding 600 were not unheard of.

On shipboard, men were shackled in pairs in the hold except for periods of exercise on deck. Women and children were usually allowed to move around, and to work at such assigned tasks as food preparation and cleaning. Many resisted enslavement by refusing to eat, jumping overboard, or joining in revolts, which rarely succeeded. Their communal singing and drumming, reported by numerous observers, must have lifted their spirits and forged solidarity. But conditions were hellish, as captains packed captives into holds that were hot, crowded, and reeking with smells from vomit and the "necessary tubs."

middle passage The brutal and often fatal journey of slaves from Africa to America.

Links TO THE WORLD

Exotic Beverages

American and European demand for tea (from China), coffee (from Arabia), chocolate (from Mesoamerica), and rum (distilled from sugar, which also sweetened the bitter taste of the other three) helped to reshape the world economy after the mid-seventeenth century. Approximately two-thirds of the people who migrated across the Atlantic before 1776 were involved—primarily as slaves—in the production of tobacco, calico, and these four drinks. As they moved from luxury to necessity, the exotic beverages had a profound impact on custom and culture.

Each beverage had its own pattern of consumption. Chocolate, brought to Spain from Mexico, became the preferred drink of aristocrats, who took it hot, at intimate gatherings. Coffee became the morning beverage of English and colonial businessmen, who praised it for keeping drinkers sober and focused. Coffee was served in new public coffeehouses, patronized chiefly by men. The English called them "penny universities";

government leaders thought coffeehouses were nurseries of subversion. The first coffeehouse opened in London in the 1660s; Boston had several by the 1690s. By the mid-eighteenth century, though, tea—consumed in the afternoon at tea tables presided over by women—had supplanted coffee in England and America. Where tea embodied genteel status and polite conversation, rum was imbibed by free working people.

The American colonies played a vital role in the production, distribution, and consumption of these beverages. Chocolate originated in America, and cacao plantations in the tropics multiplied to meet the rising demand. Coffee and tea were avidly consumed in the colonies. And rum involved Americans in every phase of its production and consumption. The sugar grown on Caribbean plantations was transported to the mainland in barrels and ships made from North American wood. There the syrup was turned into rum at 140 distilleries. Americans drank an estimated four gallons per person each year. Much of the rest they transported to Africa, where the rum purchased more slaves, beginning the cycle again.

The frontispiece of Peter Muguet, Tractatus De Poto Caphe, Chinesium The et de Chocolata, *1685. Muguet's treatise visually linked the three hot, exotic beverages recently introduced to Europeans. The drinks are consumed by representatives of the cultures in which they originated: a turbaned Turk (with coffeepot in the foreground), a Chinese man (with teapot on the table), and an Indian drinking from a hollowed, handled gourd (with a chocolate pot and ladle on the floor in front of him).*

Library of Congress

The traumatic voyage brought heavy fatalities to captives and crew. An average of 10 to 20 percent of the newly enslaved died en route. Another 20 percent or so died either before the ships left Africa or shortly after their arrival in the Americas. Merchants tallied lost lives in pounds sterling. Sailors also died at high rates—one in four or five—chiefly through exposure to diseases.

Slavery in North America and the Caribbean

What skills did African slaves bring to America that proved vital to the development of colonial South Carolina?

Barbados, America's first "slave society" (an economy wholly dependent on enslavement), spawned others. As the island's population expanded, about 40 percent of the early English residents dispersed to other colonies. Migrants carried their laws, commercial contacts, and slaveholding practices with them. A large proportion of the first Africans imported into North America came via Barbados. In addition to the many Barbadians who settled in Carolina, others moved to the southern regions of Virginia, New Jersey, and New England.

African Enslavement in the Chesapeake

Newly arrived Africans in the Chesapeake tended to be assigned to outlying parts of plantations (called quarters) until they learned some English and the routines of American tobacco cultivation. Mostly men, they lived in groups of ten to fifteen workers housed together in one or two buildings and supervised by an Anglo-American overseer. Each man was expected to cultivate about two acres of tobacco a year. Their lives must have been filled with toil and loneliness, for few spoke the same language, and all worked six days a week. Many used their Sunday off to cultivate their own gardens or to hunt or fish to supplement their meager diet. Only rarely could they form families because of the scarcity of women.

Slaves usually cost about two and a half times as much as indentured servants, but they supplied a lifetime of service, assuming they survived—which large numbers did not. Planters with enough money could acquire slaves and accumulate greater wealth, whereas the less affluent could not even afford indentured servants. The introduction of large numbers of Africans into the Chesapeake therefore widened the gap between rich and poor planters in Anglo-American society.

So many Africans were imported into Virginia and Maryland that by 1710 people of African descent composed one-fifth of the population. Even so, a decade later American-born slaves outnumbered their African-born counterparts in the Chesapeake, a trend that continued thereafter.

Link to Colonial Virginia Laws Pertaining to Slaves and Servants

African Enslavement in South Carolina

Africans came with their owners from Barbados to South Carolina in 1670, composing one-quarter to one-third of the colony's early population. The Barbadian slave owners quickly discovered that African-born slaves had skills well suited to South Carolina's semitropical environment. African-style dugout canoes became the chief means of transportation in the colony. Fishing nets copied from African models proved efficient. Africans also adapted their cattle herding techniques. Because meat and hides were early exports, Africans contributed to South Carolina's prosperity.

In 1693, as slavery was taking firm root in South Carolina, officials in Spanish Florida began offering freedom to runaways who would convert to Catholicism. Over the years, hundreds of South Carolina fugitives took advantage of the offer, although not all won their liberty.

After 1700, South Carolinians started to import slaves directly from Africa. From about 1710 until midcentury, the African-born constituted a majority of the enslaved population in the colony, and by 1750, bondspeople composed a majority of its residents. The similarity of the South Carolinian and West African environments, coupled with the substantial African-born population, ensured the survival of more aspects of West African culture than elsewhere on the North American mainland. Only in South Carolina did enslaved parents continue to give their children African names; only there did a dialect develop that combined English words with terms from Wolof, Bambara, and other African languages. (Known as Gullah, it has survived to the present day in isolated areas.) African skills remained useful, so techniques lost in other regions when the migrant generation died were instead passed down to the migrants' children.

Rice and Indigo

Slave importation coincided with the successful introduction of rice in South Carolina. English people knew nothing about producing rice, but captives taken from Africa's Rice Coast had long worked with the crop.

On rice plantations, which were far larger than Chesapeake tobacco quarters, every field worker was expected to cultivate three to four acres a year. Most were female because many enslaved men were assigned to jobs like blacksmithing or carpentry. Planters also expected slaves to grow part of their own food. By the early eighteenth century, a "task" system of predefined work assignments prevailed. After bondspeople had finished their set tasks for the day, they could rest or work their own garden plots or undertake other projects. One scholar has suggested that the **task system** resulted from negotiations between slaves familiar with rice cultivation and masters who needed their expertise.

task system Each slave had a daily or weekly quota of tasks to complete.

Developers of South Carolina's second cash crop also used the task system and drew on slaves' specialized skills. Indigo, the only source of blue dye for the growing English textile industry, was much prized. In the early 1740s, Eliza Lucas, a young woman born in Antigua, drew on the knowledge of slaves and overseers from the West Indies and developed planting and processing techniques for the precious commodity.

Indian Enslavement in North and South Carolina

In 1708, Indian bondspeople accounted for as much as 14 percent of the South Carolina population. The trade in Indian slaves began when the Westos (originally known as the Eries), migrated south from the Great Lakes region in the mid-1650s, after the Beaver Wars. The Westos raided Spain's lightly defended Florida missions and sold Indian captives to Virginians. The Carolina proprietors monopolized trade with the Westos, which infuriated settlers shut out of the commerce in slaves and deerskins.

Carolina planters secretly financed attacks on the Westos, wiping them out by 1682. Southeastern Indians reacted to such slave raids—continued by other native peoples after the defeat of the Westos—by trying to protect themselves through subordination to the English or Spanish, or by coalescing into new, larger political units, such as those known later as Creeks, Chickasaws, or Cherokees.

At first, the Carolinians did not clash with neighboring Indians. But in 1711 the Tuscaroras, an Iroquoian people, attacked a Swiss-German settlement at New Bern, North Carolina, which had expropriated their lands, which ignited the **Tuscarora War**. South Carolinians and their Indian allies then combined to defeat the Tuscaroras in a bloody war. Afterward, more than a thousand Tuscaroras were enslaved. The remainder migrated northward and joined the Iroquois Confederacy.

Tuscarora War War in the Carolinas from 1711 through 1713 that pitted Tuscarora Indians against colonists and their Indian allies.

Four years later, the Yamasees, who had helped Carolina to conquer the Tuscaroras, enlisted the Creeks and other Muskogean peoples to attack outlying English settlements. The Yamasee-Creek offensive was thwarted only when reinforcements arrived from the north, colonists hastily armed their African slaves, and Cherokees joined the fight. After the war, Carolina's involvement in the Indian slave trade ceased, because the Creeks, Yamasees, and Tuscaroras had all moved away for self-protection. The native peoples who remained were able to rebuild their strength, for they were no longer subjected to slavers' raids.

Enslavement in the North

Atlantic creoles from the Caribbean and native peoples from the Carolinas and Florida, along with Indians enslaved for crime or debt, composed the bound laborers in the northern mainland colonies. Some bondspeople resided in urban areas, especially New York. Yet even in the North most bondspeople worked in the countryside on farms and large estates. Some bondsmen toiled in new rural enterprises, such as ironworks, alongside hired laborers and indentured servants. Slavery made its most dramatic contribution to the northern economy at one remove, through the West Indies provision trade. But although relatively few northern colonists owned slaves, some individual slaveholders benefited directly from the institution and wanted to preserve it.

NEGROES, TO BE SOLD

A Parcel of young able bodied Negro Men, one of whom is a Cooper by Trade, two Negroes Wenches, and likewise two Girls, one of 12 Years old, and the other 16, the latter a good Seemſtreſs, and can be well recommended.

The Granger Collection, NYC

This advertisement for a sale of slaves of African descent appeared in the New York Journal *in 1768. The expertise of two of the people described would have appealed to urban buyers: a cooper would have been useful to a barrelmaker or shipper, and the seamstress might have attracted attention from dressmakers. The other bondspeople mentioned could have been purchased by people who wanted house servants or laborers.*

Slave Resistance

As slavery grew, so too did slaves' resistance. Usually resistance took the form of work slowdown or escape, but occasionally bondspeople planned rebellions. Seven times before 1713, the English Caribbean experienced major revolts involving at least fifty slaves and causing the deaths of both whites and blacks.

The first slave revolt in the mainland English colonies occurred in New York in 1712. The rebels set a fire and then ambushed those who tried to put it out, killing eight and wounding another twelve. Some rebels committed suicide to avoid capture; of those caught and tried, eighteen were tortured and executed. Their decapitated bodies were left to rot outdoors as a warning to others.

Forging and Testing the Bonds of Empire

How did mercantilism benefit some colonies economically and hurt others?

English officials seeking new sources of revenue focused on the expanding Atlantic trade in slaves and the products of slave labor. Parliament and the Stuart monarchs drafted laws to harness the proceeds of the trade for the mother country.

Colonies Into Empire

Like other European nations, England based its commercial policy on *mercantilism*, the theory that viewed the economic world as a collection of countries whose governments competed for shares of a finite amount of wealth. What one nation gained, another lost. Each nation sought economic self-sufficiency while maintaining a favorable balance of trade by exporting more than it imported. Colonies played an important role, supplying the mother country with valuable raw materials and serving as a market for the parent country's manufactured goods.

Parliament's Navigation Acts—passed between 1651 and 1673—established three principles of mercantilist theory. First, only English or colonial merchants could legally trade in the colonies. Second, certain valuable American products could be sold only in the mother country or in other English colonies. At first, these "enumerated" commodities included wool, sugar, tobacco, indigo, ginger, and dyes; later acts added rice, naval stores (masts, spars, pitch, tar, and turpentine), copper, and furs. Third, foreign goods destined for sale in the colonies had to be shipped through England, paying English import duties. Years later, new laws established a fourth principle: the colonies could not export items that competed with English manufactures.

These laws adversely affected Chesapeake planters who could not seek foreign markets for their staple crops. The statutes initially helped English Caribbean sugar producers by driving Brazilian sugar out of the home market, but later prevented English planters from selling sugar elsewhere. Others benefited. The laws stimulated the creation of a lucrative shipbuilding industry in New England. And the northern and middle colonies produced many unenumerated goods—fish, flour, meat and livestock, and barrel staves—that could be traded directly to the French, Spanish, or Dutch Caribbean islands if carried in English or American ships.

Mercantilism and Navigation Acts

English authorities soon learned that enforcing mercantilist legislation would be difficult. Smuggling was widespread, and colonial officials often looked the other way when illegally imported goods were sold.

Because American juries tended to favor local smugglers, Parliament in 1696 established American vice-admiralty courts, which operated without juries and adjudicated violations of the Navigation Acts.

The Navigation Acts imposed regulations on Americans' international trade, but by the early 1680s the mainland colonies had become accustomed to a considerable degree of political autonomy. Massachusetts, Plymouth, Connecticut, and Rhode Island operated as independent entities, subject neither to the direct authority of the king nor to a proprietor. Virginia was a royal colony and New Hampshire (1679) and New York (1685) gained that status, but all other mainland settlements were proprietorships, over which the Crown exercised little control. In the English colonies, free adult men who owned property expected to have a voice in their governments, especially in decisions concerning taxation.

James II, who became king in 1685, and his successors sought to tighten the reins of government and reduce the colonies' political autonomy. English officials targeted New England, which they saw as a hotbed of smuggling. Moreover, Puritans denied freedom of religion to non-Congregationalists and maintained laws incompatible with English practice. The charters of all the colonies from New Jersey to Maine were revoked, and a royal Dominion of New England was established in 1686. (For the boundaries of the Dominion, see Map 3.1) Sir Edmund Andros, the Dominion's governor, had immense power: Parliament dissolved the assemblies, and Andros needed only the consent of an appointed council to make laws and levy taxes.

Glorious Revolution in America

New Englanders had endured Andros's **autocratic** rule for more than two years when they learned that James II's power was crumbling. The king had angered his subjects by levying taxes without parliamentary approval and by converting to Catholicism. In April 1689, Boston's leaders jailed Andros and his associates. The following month, they received news of the bloodless coup known as the Glorious Revolution, in which James had been replaced in late 1688 by his daughter Mary and her husband, the Dutch prince William of Orange.

autocratic Absolute or dictatorial rule.

The Glorious Revolution affirmed the supremacy of Protestantism and Parliament. The new monarchs acceded to Parliament's Declaration of Rights "vindicating and asserting their ancient rights and liberties," which confirmed citizens' entitlement to free elections, fair trials, and petition, and specified that no monarch could ignore acts of Parliament on issues of taxation and defense. In 1776, the American Declaration of Independence would borrow heavily from Parliament's 1689 Declaration of Rights.

Link to the 1689 English Bill of Rights

Across the mainland colonies, the Glorious Revolution inspired revolt. In Maryland, the Protestant Association overturned the government of the Catholic proprietor, and in New York a militia officer of German origin, Jacob Leisler, assumed control of the government.

But like James II, William and Mary believed England should exercise tighter control over its unruly American possessions. Consequently, only the Maryland rebellion received royal sanction, primarily because of its anti-Catholic thrust. In New York, Leisler was hanged for treason. Massachusetts became a royal colony with an appointed governor. Its new 1691 charter eliminated the religious test for voting and office holding. A parish of the Church of England appeared in Boston. The **"city upon a hill"** as John Winthrop had envisioned it, had fallen.

"city upon a hill" John Winthrop's vision of the Puritan settlement in New England as a model for the world.

King William's War

A war with the French and their Algonquian allies compounded New England's difficulties. After King Louis XIV of France allied himself with the deposed James II, England declared war on France in 1689. (This war is today known as the Nine Years' War, but the colonists called it King William's War.) Even before war broke out in Europe, Anglo-Americans and Abenakis clashed over settlements in Maine that colonists had reoccupied after the 1678 truce. Abenaki attacks wholly or partially destroyed several towns, and colonial expeditions against Montreal and Quebec in 1690 failed. The Peace of Ryswick (1697) formally ended the war in Europe but failed to bring much respite to North America's northern frontiers.

The 1692 Witchcraft Crisis

For eight months in 1692, witchcraft accusations spread through Essex County, Massachusetts, a heavily populated area directly threatened by the Indian attacks to the north. Before the outbreak ended, fourteen women and five men were hanged, one man was pressed to death with heavy stones, fifty-four people confessed to being witches, and more than 140 suspects were jailed. The worst phase of the crisis concluded when the governor dissolved the special court established to try the accused. During the final trials, which took place in regular courts, judges and juries discounted so-called spectral evidence, offered by witnesses who claimed to be afflicted by witches in the form of specters. Almost all the defendants were acquitted, and the governor quickly reprieved the few found guilty. If frontier warfare and political turmoil had created an environment where witch fears could become epidemic, the imposition of a new imperial order on the colony helped to cure the plague.

Link to Ann Putnam's Confession

New Imperial Measures

In 1696, England created the fifteen-member Board of Trade and Plantations, the chief government organ concerned with the American colonies. The board gathered information, reviewed Crown appointments in America, scrutinized colonial legislation, supervised trade policies, and advised ministries on colonial issues. Still, it had no enforcement powers. Although the Board of Trade improved colonial administration, supervision of the American provinces remained decentralized and haphazard.

Most colonists resented English "placemen" who arrived to implement the policies of king and Parliament, but they adjusted to their demands and to the restrictions imposed by the Navigation Acts. They fought another of Europe's wars—the War of the Spanish Succession, called Queen Anne's War in the colonies—from 1702 to 1713.

Colonists who allied with the royal government received patronage in the form of offices and land grants and composed "court parties" that supported English officials. Others, who were either less fortunate in their friends or defended colonial autonomy, made up the opposition, or "country" interest.

Americans of African Descent

People of African descent composed only a tiny proportion of the population of the mainland North American colonies before 1650. But the rise of southern economies based largely on the enslavement of Africans, coupled with the widespread employment of enslaved Africans in northern colonies, dramatically altered the American population. By 1775, some 280,000 Africans had been imported into the territory that later became the United States; they and their descendants constituted about 20 percent of the population at that time.

According to the 2010 census, 13.6 percent of the American people now claim descent from African ancestors. Because the legal importation of African slaves ended in 1808, and because the United States attracted relatively few voluntary migrants from Africa until the twentieth century, most of today's African Americans have colonial ancestors—a claim few Americans of European descent can make.

The modern African American population includes people with many different skin colors, reflecting a long history of interracial sexual relationships (both coerced and voluntary). African Americans have had children with Europeans and Indians since the colonial period; more recently, they have intermarried with Asian and Latino immigrants. In part, the mingling of different peoples of color resulted from state laws that for centuries forbade legal marriages between Americans of European descent and those of other races. In 1967, the Supreme Court ruled in *Loving v. Virginia* that such laws violated the rights to due process and equal protection enshrined in the Fourteenth Amendment to the U.S. Constitution.

In the year 2000, the census for the first time recognized the children of interracial unions by allowing Americans to define themselves as members of more than one race. By 2010, the number of black Americans identifying as mixed race had reached 3.1 million, increasing at a higher rate than those identifying as black alone.

Beginning in the late twentieth century, the number of black Americans whose origins lie in modern Africa increased substantially. In 2005, the annual number of voluntary migrants from Africa to the United States passed the number of Africans brought to this country against their will during any of the peak years of the slave trade. No historic figure better represents this emerging face of black America than Barack Hussein Obama II. In 2008, this Hawai'ian-born son of a man from Kenya and a woman from Kansas became the forty-fourth president of the United States.

Summary

The years from 1650 to 1720 established economic and political patterns that would structure subsequent changes in mainland colonial society. England's first attempt to regulate colonial trade, the Navigation Act of 1651, was quickly followed by others. By 1720, the essential elements of the imperial administrative structure that would govern the English colonies until 1775 had been put in place.

In 1650, just two isolated centers of English population, New England and the Chesapeake, existed along the seaboard, along with the Dutch New Netherland. In 1720, nearly the entire East Coast of North America was in English hands, and Indian control east of the Appalachian Mountains had largely been broken by warfare. West of the mountains, Iroquois power reigned. What had been an immigrant population was now mostly American-born, except for the African-born people in South

Carolina and the Chesapeake; economies originally based on trade in fur and skins had become more complex and more closely linked with the mother country; and political structures had become more uniform. Yet at the same time the adoption of large-scale slavery and cash crop agriculture in the Chesapeake, the Carolinas, and the West Indies differentiated these true slave societies from the colonies to the north.

Yet the economies of the northern colonies also rested on profits from the Atlantic trading system, the key element of which was traffic in slaves. New England sold foodstuffs and wood products to the West Indies. Pennsylvania and New York, too, found in the Caribbean a ready market for their livestock, grains, and flour. Atlantic slavery drove all the English colonial economies in these years. The West Indies colonies, especially Barbados and Jamaica, were the empire's economic engine. In 1720, their exports to Britain—chiefly 705,000 tons of sugar—were worth more than double what the combined mainland colonies produced.

Spanish settlements in America north of Mexico remained largely centered on Florida missions and on New Mexican military outposts (*presidios*) and missions during these years. The French had explored the Mississippi Valley but had not yet planted many settlements in the Great Lakes or the west. Both nations' colonists depended on indigenous people's labor and goodwill. Yet the Spanish and French presence to the south and west of the English settlements ensured future conflicts among the European powers in North America.

Chapter Review

The Growth of Anglo-American Settlements

> **Why did New York's development lag behind that of other British colonies in the seventeenth century?**

Granted to James the duke of York in 1664, New York remained a shadow of Boston until well into the 1720s largely because James, unlike William Penn of Pennsylvania and other proprietors, did not encourage migration with offers of land grants and religious freedom to would-be colonists. Instead, migrants traveled to New Jersey and Pennsylvania. In addition James refused a legislative assembly—which many English colonists wanted—until 1683.

A Decade of Imperial Crises: The 1670s

> **How did settlers' interests collide with those of Native Americans?**

Settlers' and Native Americans' interests clashed in two pivotal areas: control of trade and desire for more land. New France and the Iroquois Confederacy clashed over control of the valuable fur trade, which the Iroquois had fought hard to attain. Bitter battles and attacks lasted for twenty years, before culminating in a neutrality treaty. Similarly, in the densely settled New England colonies in the 1670s, hostilities developed as Wampanoags led by King Philip felt threatened by the Anglo-American communities that surrounded their territory. And in Virginia Nathaniel Bacon and his followers also focused on seizing desirable interior land from Indians, ultimately attacking them and pushing them farther west.

The Atlantic Trading System

> **How was slavery at the center of the expanding trade network between Europe and the colonies?**

First, the Chesapeake developed around tobacco farming, which required a vast supply of workers. Fewer English workers were available as population pressures in England eased and Restoration colonies offered land and other opportunities to would-be settlers. Tobacco growers instead turned to slave labor, as did other plantation colonies, thereby expanding the sale and transport of slaves. In addition, commodities produced by slave labor helped boost exports and trade networks, while the need to feed and clothe slaves stimulated new business opportunities for other colonies. New England, for example, profited by selling foodstuffs to feed slaves. The slave trade itself created a global economic network and tensions among European nations seeking to control the lucrative trade.

Slavery in North America and the Caribbean

 What skills did African slaves bring to America that proved vital to the development of colonial South Carolina?

African-born slaves had several skills that were crucial to the economic development of South Carolina. From a similarly semitropical climate, these slaves adapted dugout canoes from their homeland to create a key means of transportation in the many rivers of the Carolinas. Their fishing nets also proved more efficient. African cattle herding techniques aided in producing the meat and hides that were an early export from the region. Some slaves, particularly women, also knew how to cultivate rice, which was rapidly becoming a staple crop in South Carolina. The area's other cash crop—indigo (the only source of blue dye for the growing English textile industry)—similarly drew on the knowledge of slaves transported to South Carolina from the Caribbean, where indigo plantations flourished.

Forging and Testing the Bonds of Empire

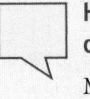 **How did mercantilism benefit some colonies economically and hurt others?**

Mercantilism was grounded in the notion that the world contained a finite amount of wealth, and that if one nation gained, another had to lose. For England, that meant controlling colonial trade and development in ways that benefited the mother country. England passed the Navigation Acts between 1651 and 1673, which allowed only English merchants to trade in the colonies, permitted certain American products to be sold only to England or other English colonies, and required foreign goods bound for the colonies to be shipped through England so it could collect related duties. Later, England additionally prevented colonists from exporting anything that competed with English goods. For Chesapeake planters, these policies had a negative effect, preventing them from selling staple crops in foreign markets. English sugar producers in the Caribbean were initially helped, as their Brazilian competitors were driven from the market, but later suffered when they were prevented from selling their sugar elsewhere. New England benefited from the emergence of a lucrative shipbuilding industry, while the northern and middle colonies gained from trading goods not included in the Navigation Acts such as fish, flour, meat, livestock, and barrels.

Suggestions for Further Reading

Ned Blackhawk, *Violence Over the Land: Indians and Empires in the Early American West* (2006)

David Eltis and David Richardson, *Atlas of the Transatlantic Slave Trade* (2010)

Alan Gallay, *The Indian Slave Trade: The Rise of the English Empire in the American South, 1670–1717* (2002)

Eric Hinderaker, *The Two Hendricks: Untangling a Mohawk Mystery* (2010)

Andrew Knaut, *The Pueblo Revolt of 1680* (1995)

Jill Lepore, *The Name of War: King Philip's War and the Origins of American Identity* (1998)

Edmund S. Morgan, *American Slavery, American Freedom: The Ordeal of Colonial Virginia* (1975)

Mary Beth Norton, *In the Devil's Snare: The Salem Witchcraft Crisis of 1692* (2002)

Marcus Rediker, *The Slave Ship: A Human History* (2007)

Stephanie E. Smallwood, *Saltwater Slavery: A Middle Passage From Africa to American Diaspora* (2007)

Owen Stanwood, *The Empire Reformed: English America in the Age of the Glorious Revolution* (2011)

Becoming America?

1720–1760

4

D r. Alexander Hamilton was a learned man. The son of a theologian, he studied medicine at the University of Edinburgh, which boasted the best medical school in the world. But if Edinburgh was crowded with genius, it was hardly brimming with opportunity. In 1739, Hamilton lit out for the colonies, settling in Annapolis, where his older brother preached.

Dr. Hamilton quickly established himself among the town's elite, but like many migrants to the Chesapeake, he sickened in the climate. He thought travel might improve his health. In May 1744, he and a slave named Dromo set off on a four-month tour of the countryside from Maryland to Maine. An avid reader of polite literature including the new books called *novels* then flooding British presses, the doctor recorded his impressions in a journal to which he gave the Latin title *Itinerarium*.

The diversity of the colonists astonished Hamilton. In one Philadelphia tavern, he dined with "Scots, English, Dutch, Germans, and Irish; there were Roman Catholicks, Church [of England] men, Presbyterians, Quakers, Newlightmen, Methodists, Seventh day men, Moravians, Anabaptists, and one Jew," all talking politics, while a "knott of Quakers" debated the price of flour. He met rich planters from Jamaica, Antigua, and Barbados. He saw Africans everywhere. In Boston, he watched "a parade of Indian chiefs." Their leader, the Mohawk sachem Hendrick Theyanoguin, urged the assembled natives to "brighten the chain with the English, our friends, and take up the hatchet against the French, our enemies."

Hendrick, Hamilton wrote, was a "bold, intrepid fellow." In Scotland, a better man commanded deference from his inferiors. Here, there was little respect on offer. He and Dromo watched "a boxing match between a master and his servant," who had called the master a "shitten elf." These "infant countrys of America" bred "aggrandized upstarts," Hamilton wrote. About the "different ranks of men in polite nations" they knew little, and cared less.

But for all their "nastiness, impudence, and rusticity," there was a strange worldliness about "the American providences."

Farmers' wives wore fine imported cloth, and tradesmen talked philosophy. Hamilton viewed botanical engravings in rural Maryland and a plaster copy of the Venus de Medici in Boston. He drank tea in every hamlet, coffee in every town, and rum at every crossroads. Always, there was talk of international politics, especially "the dreaded French war"—King George's War—that once again drew the raw edges of the empire into the maelstrom of European rivalries.

As many travelers to North America in the eighteenth century noticed, they did things differently in the colonies. People didn't stay within their stations. Property was held more widely, and opinions voiced more readily, in more languages, than anywhere in Europe. After 1720, a massive migration of European and African peoples changed the North American landscape. Ethnic diversity became especially pronounced in the cities. The British colonies south of New England drew the largest number of newcomers, whose arrival swelled the population, altered political balances, and introduced new religious sects. Unwilling immigrants (slaves and transported convicts) likewise clustered in the middle and southern colonies. The rough equality Hamilton witnessed among whites was everywhere built upon the bondage of Africans and their descendants.

This polyglot population hardly resembled the places from which its peoples had been drawn. But in some ways, the America Hamilton encountered was more British than ever. A flood of European and especially British goods allowed genteel and middling folks to fashion themselves in the image of fashionable Britons. Educated colonists participated in transatlantic intellectual life. Yet most colonists, whether free or enslaved, worked with their hands daily from dawn to dark. The social and economic distance among different ranks of Anglo-Americans had widened noticeably.

In 1720, much of North America remained under Indian control. Four decades later, indigenous peoples still dominated the interior, yet their lives had been indelibly altered by the expansion of European settlements. France extended its reach from the St. Lawrence to the Gulf of Mexico. Spanish outposts spread east and west from a New Mexican heartland. The British colonies stretched from the Atlantic coast to the Appalachian Mountains, where they threatened French and Indian claims. North America's resources were worth fighting for, and as European conflicts crossed the Atlantic once again during the 1740s (see Table 4.1 on page 104), many colonists in British North America defended King George II's empire against other nations jockeying for control of the continent.

As you read this chapter, keep the following questions in mind:

- **What were the effects of demographic, geographic, and economic changes on Europeans, Africans, and Indian nations alike?**

- **What were the key elements of eighteenth-century provincial cultures?**

- **In what ways was North America becoming less like Britain at midcentury? In what ways were colonists *more* British than before?**

Chronology

1690	Locke's *Essay Concerning Human Understanding* published, a key example of Enlightenment thought
1718	New Orleans founded in French Louisiana
1721–22	Smallpox epidemic in Boston leads to first widespread adoption of inoculation in America
1732	Founding of Georgia
1733	Printer John Peter Zenger tried for and acquitted of "seditious libel" in New York
1737	"Walking Purchase" of Delaware and Shawnee lands in Pennsylvania
1739	Stono Rebellion (South Carolina)
	George Whitefield arrives in America; Great Awakening broadens
1739–48	King George's War affects American economies
1740s	Black population of the Chesapeake begins to grow by natural increase
1741	New York City "conspiracy" reflects whites' continuing fears of slave revolts
1745	Fall of Louisbourg to New England troops; returned to France in 1748
1751	Franklin's *Experiments and Observations on Electricity* published, important American contribution to Enlightenment science
1760–75	Peak of eighteenth-century European and African migration to English colonies

Geographic Expansion and Ethnic Diversity

What spurred population growth in the British colonies in the thirty years before 1775?

In the mid-eighteenth century, dramatic population growth, along with geographic expansion, characterized the British mainland colonies. In 1700, only about 250,000 European Americans and African Americans resided in the colonies. Thirty years later, that number had more than doubled, reaching 2.5 million by 1775.

Migration from Scotland, Ireland, England, Germany, and especially Africa contributed to the growth, but most of the gain stemmed from natural increase. Once the difficult early decades of settlement had passed, the population of Britain's mainland colonies doubled approximately every twenty-five years. A chief cause of this growth was women's youthful age at first marriage (early twenties for Euro-Americans, late teens for African Americans). Married women became pregnant every two to three years and normally bore five to ten children. Since the colonies, especially those north of Virginia, were relatively healthful places to live, a large proportion of children who survived infancy reached maturity and began families of their own. The result was a young, rapidly growing population; about half the people in Anglo America were under sixteen years old in 1775. (By contrast, less than one-quarter of the U.S. population is currently under sixteen.)

Spanish and French Territorial Expansion

British North America's growing population was sandwiched between the Atlantic coast (on the east) and Appalachian Mountains (on the west). By contrast, Spanish and French territories expanded across the continent while their populations increased only modestly. Nevertheless, French and Spanish geographic expansion had far-reaching effects on native peoples.

Venturing into the Mississippi Valley in the early eighteenth century, the French and Spanish encountered powerful Indian nations like the Quapaws,

Osages, and Caddos. A few Europeans—priests, soldiers, farmers, traders, ranchers—met native peoples who wanted access to manufactured goods, and who accordingly sought friendly relations. The Spanish and French invaders had to adapt to Indian diplomatic and cultural practices. French officials, for example, often complained of being forced to endure lengthy calumet ceremonies; Spaniards, unaccustomed to involving women in diplomacy, had to accede to Texas Indians' use of female representatives. The European nations established neighboring outposts in the lower Mississippi region in 1716—the French at Natchitoches (west of the Mississippi), the Spaniards at nearby Los Adaes (see Map 4.1). France had already settled Biloxi Bay (in the modern state of Mississippi) in 1699, and strengthened its presence near the Gulf of Mexico by establishing New Orleans in 1718.

Spaniards focused first on Texas (establishing San Antonio in 1718), and later on the region they called Alta (upper) California. After learning that Russians were planning to colonize the region, they sent expeditions north from their missions in Baja California. From a base at San Diego, where the Franciscan Junipero Serra set up the first mission in Alta California in 1769, they traveled to Monterey Bay. There, in 1770, they claimed Alta California for Spain. Over the next decades, they established presidios and missions along the coast from modern San Francisco to San Diego.

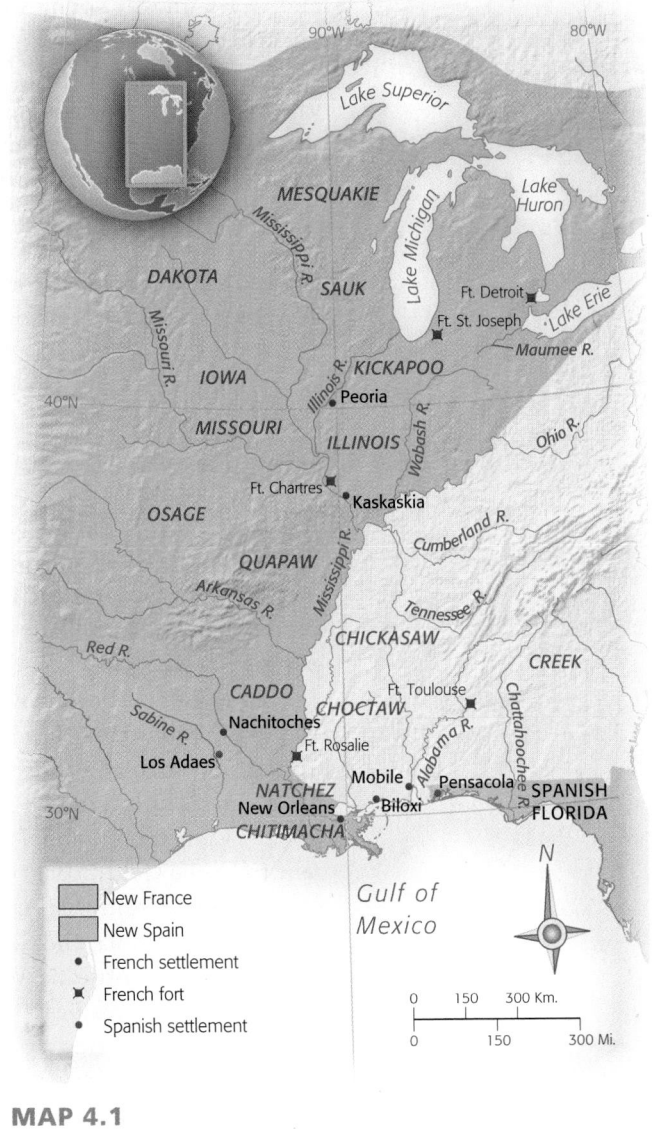

MAP 4.1
Louisiana, ca. 1720

By 1720, French forts and settlements dotted the Mississippi River and its tributaries in the interior of North America. Two isolated Spanish outposts were situated near the Gulf of Mexico. Source: Copyright © Cengage Learning 2015

France and the Mississippi

French settlements north of New Orleans served as the glue of empire. *Coureurs de bois* (literally, "forest runners") used rivers and lakes to carry goods between Quebec and the new Louisiana territory. Indians traded furs and hides for guns, ammunition, and other items. The population of the largest French settlements, known collectively as *le pays de Illinois* ("the Illinois country"), never totaled much above three thousand.

French expansion reshaped native alliances elsewhere. For example, the equestrian Comanches of the Plains, now able to trade with the French, no longer needed Spanish goods—or their previous allies, the Utes. Deprived of powerful partners, the Utes negotiated peace with New Mexico in 1752. Once enslaved by Spaniards, Utes enslaved Paiutes and other nonequestrian peoples. They exchanged hides and slaves—mostly young women—for horses and metal goods until the end of Spanish rule in the region.

In French officials' minds, Louisiana's paramount goals were protection of the valuable Caribbean islands and prevention of Spanish and British expansion. But the profit-seeking farmers and Indian traders who settled there demanded slaves from the French government. In 1719 officials acquiesced, dispatching more than six thousand Africans, mostly from Senegal, over the next decade. Yet Louisiana's residents never developed a successful plantation economy. They did raise some tobacco and indigo, which, along with skins and hides obtained from the Indians, composed the colony's major exports.

Involuntary Migrants from Africa

Elsewhere in the Americas, slavery took hold more firmly during the eighteenth century. In all, more Africans than Europeans came to the Americas, the majority of them as slaves and about half between 1700 and 1800. Most were transported to Brazil or the Caribbean, primarily in British or Portuguese vessels. The estimated 280,000 people imported before 1780 into the region that became the United States amounted to less than 3 percent of the approximately 12.3 million enslaved people brought to the Americas during the existence of slavery.

Link to Alexander Falconbridge, *The African Slave Trade* (1788)

Slaves came from many different ethnic groups and regions of Africa (see Map 4.2). More than 40 percent embarked from West Central Africa (modern Congo and Angola), nearly 20 percent from the Bight of Benin (modern Togo, Benin, and southwestern Nigeria), about 13 percent from the Bight of Biafra (today's Cameroon, Gabon, and southeastern Nigeria), and approximately 9 percent from the Gold Coast (modern Ghana and neighboring countries). Smaller numbers came from East Africa, the Windward Coast, and the Rice Coast (modern Senegal, Gambia, and Sierra Leone). Thousands, possibly tens of thousands, of these enslaved Africans were Muslims. Some were literate in Arabic, and some came from noble families.

Standard slave-trading practice, in which a vessel loaded its human cargo at one port and sold it in another, meant that people from the same broad area tended to arrive in the Americas together. That tendency was heightened by planter partiality for particular ethnic groups. Virginians, for example, purchased primarily Igbos from the Bight of Biafra, whereas South Carolinians and Georgians selected Senegambians and people from West Central Africa. Rice planters' desire to purchase Senegambians, who cultivated rice in their homeland, is easily explained, but historians disagree about the reasons underlying the other preferences.

Especially after 1740, American-born people of African descent came to dominate the mainland enslaved population because of natural increase. Although about 40 percent of the Africans were male, women and children together composed a majority of slave imports; planters valued girls and women for their reproductive and productive capacities. All the colonies passed laws to ensure that the children of enslaved women were born into slavery. A planter who owned adult female slaves could engineer the growth of his labor force without additional major purchases of workers.

MAP 4.2

Major Origins and Destinations of Africans Enslaved in the Americas

As this schematic map shows, enslaved Africans were drawn from many regions of western Africa (with some coming from the interior of the continent) and were shipped to areas throughout the Americas. Source: Copyright © Cengage Learning 2015

Newcomers from Europe

About 350,000 Europeans moved to mainland British North America between 1700 and 1780, most of them after 1730. Influenced by mercantilist thought, British authorities had come to regard a large, industrious population at home as an asset. Thus, they discouraged emigration, except for the deportation of such "undesirables" as vagabonds and Jacobite rebels (supporters of the deposed Stuart monarchs). Instead, they recruited German and French Protestants to the colonies by offering free land, religious toleration, and, after 1740, relaxed citizenship (naturalization) requirements.

The most successful migrants came well prepared, having learned from earlier arrivals that land and resources were abundant, but that they would need capital. Penniless bound laborers, who constituted approximately 40 percent of the newcomers, did less well.

Worst off were the 50,000 or so migrants who arrived as convicted felons sentenced to transportation for two to fourteen years. Typically unskilled and perhaps one-third female, they were dispatched most often to Maryland to work in tobacco fields, as ironworkers, or as household servants.

Visualizing THE PAST

Slaves' Symbolic Resistance

Although revolts and escapes have been the focus of many studies of enslaved Africans' resistance to bondage, archaeological finds from the mid-eighteenth century such as those illustrated here reveal important aspects of slaves' personal lives and other forms of resistance. The set of objects found in Annapolis constitutes a *minkisi,* or West African spiritual bundle. Africans and African Americans placed such bundles of objects, each with a symbolic meaning (for example, bent nails reflected the power of fire), under hearths or sills to direct the spirits who entered houses through doors or chimneys. The *minkisi's* primary purpose was to protect bondspeople from the power of their masters—for example, by preventing the breakup of a family. The statue of a man was uncovered in an enslaved blacksmith's quarters. It too reflects resistance, but of a different sort: the quiet rebellion of a talented craftsman who used his master's iron and his own time and skill to create a remarkable object. What can we learn about enslaved people's lives from such artifacts as these, even though the illiterate bondspeople left no written records?

Artifact found in an excavation in Alexandria, Virginia.

A minkisi *from the eighteenth century found under the floor of the Charles Carroll house in Annapolis, Maryland.*

Scots-Irish, Scots, and Germans

One of the largest groups of immigrants—about 143,000—came from Ireland or Scotland, largely as families. About 66,000 Scots-Irish, descendants of Presbyterian Scots who had settled in the north of Ireland during the seventeenth century, joined some 35,000 people who came to America from Scotland (see Figure 4.1). Another 42,000 Protestants and Catholics migrated from southern Ireland. High rents, poor harvests, and religious discrimination (in Ireland) combined to push people from their homelands.

Irish immigrants usually landed in Philadelphia or New Castle, Delaware. Many moved into the Pennsylvania backcountry. Later migrants moved to the backcountry of Maryland, Virginia, and the Carolinas, where they squatted on land belonging to Indians, land speculators, or colonial governments. They gained a reputation for lawlessness, drinking, and fighting.

Migrants from Germany and German-speaking areas of Switzerland numbered about 85,000 between 1730 and 1755. They, too, usually came in family groups and landed in Philadelphia. Like earlier English indentured servants, many paid for their passage by contracting to work as servants for a specified period. Germans tended to settle together when they could. Many moved west into Pennsylvania and then south into the backcountry of Maryland and Virginia. Others landed in Charles Town and settled in the Carolina interior. The Germans belonged to a

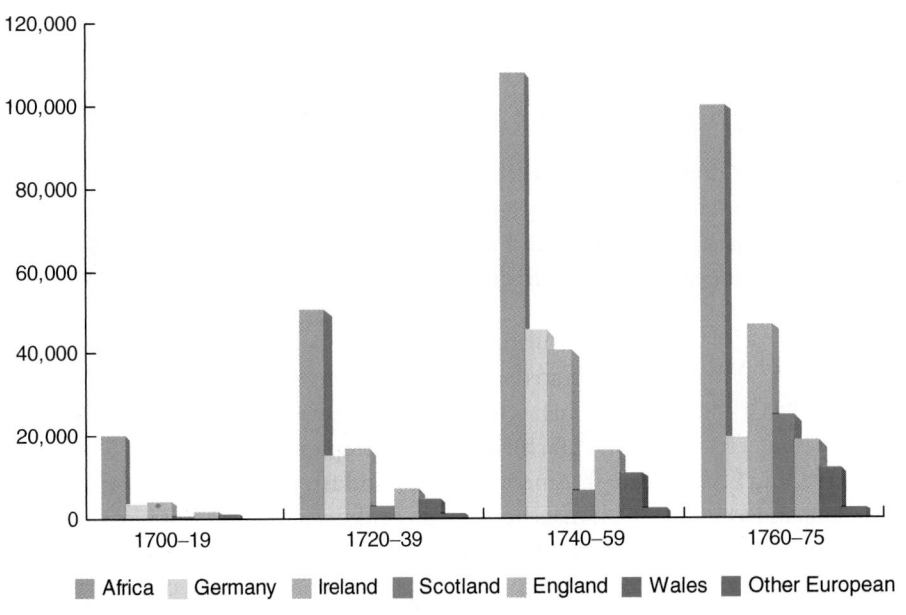

FIGURE 4.1

Atlantic Origins of Migrants to Thirteen Mainland Colonies of British North America, 1700–1775

Immigrants from Ireland, Scotland, and Germany significantly outnumbered those from England throughout the eighteenth century. But as this figure shows, forced migrants from Africa comprised by far the largest number of new arrivals in the mainland British colonies. In the Caribbean colonies, the pattern would be yet more pronounced.

(Source for European numbers: Aaron Fogelman, "Migrations to the Thirteen British North American Colonies, 1700–1775: New Estimates," *The Journal of Interdisciplinary History,* vol. 22, no. 4 (Spring 1992), pp. 691–709. Source for African numbers: The Trans-Atlantic Slave Trade Database, available online at: http://www.slavevoyages.org. Accessed August 1, 2012.)

variety of Protestant sects—primarily Lutheran, German Reformed, and Moravian—and added to the religious diversity of Pennsylvania.

The most concentrated period of colonial immigration fell between 1760 and 1775, when more than 125,000 free migrants and 100,000 enslaved people arrived—nearly 10 percent of the population of British North America. Late-arriving free immigrants had to crowd into the cities or move to the edges of settlement; land elsewhere was occupied (see Map 4.3).

Maintaining Ethnic and Religious Identities

These migration patterns made British North America one of the most diverse places on earth. How readily migrants assimilated into Anglo-American culture depended on patterns of settlement, group size, and migrants' cultural ties. The French Protestants (**Huguenots**) who migrated to Charles Town or New York City were unable to sustain their language or their religious practices for more than two generations, whereas Huguenots who settled in the Hudson Valley remained recognizably French and Calvinist for a century. Small groups of colonial Jews maintained a distinct identity wherever they settled. In places like New York City, Newport, Savannah, and Kingston, Jamaica, they established synagogues and worked actively to preserve their faith and culture. Larger groups of migrants (Germans, Irish, and Scots) found it easier to sustain European ways.

Huguenots French Calvinist dissenters from that country's dominant Catholicism.

Economic Growth and Development in British America

How were the colonies' economic fates increasingly linked to world markets?

The dramatic increase in the population of British America caused colonial economies to grow. By contrast, New Spain's northern borderlands stagnated, and of France's American possessions, only the Caribbean islands flourished.

Commerce and Manufacturing

In British North America, the rising population generated ever-greater demand for goods and services, fueling the development of small-scale colonial manufacturing and a complex network of internal trade. Iron making became British America's largest industry, with production surpassing England's by 1775. Colonists built roads, bridges, mills, and stores to serve new settlements. A lively coastal trade developed; by the late 1760s, more than half of the vessels leaving Boston sailed to other mainland colonies. The colonies no longer wholly depended on European goods.

Settlers' prosperity nevertheless depended heavily on overseas demand for tobacco, rice, indigo, fish, and timber products. Selling such items earned the colonists the credit they needed to buy English and European goods. Between 1700 and 1775, colonists' purchases of British manufactures increased from 5 percent to 25 percent of Britain's total exports. But when British demand for American products slowed, the colonists' income and purchasing power dropped, leading to economic downswings.

Wealth and Poverty

Despite fluctuations, the American economy grew during the eighteenth century. That growth produced better standards of living for all property-owning Americans. Early in the century, as the price of British manufactures fell, more households acquired amenities such as chairs and earthenware dishes. Diet also improved as trade brought more varied foodstuffs. After 1750, luxury items could be found in the homes of the wealthy, and the "middling sort" imported English ceramics. Even the poorest property owners had better household goods.

While wealthy Americans improved their position relative to other colonists, new arrivals had less opportunity for advancement than their predecessors. Even so, few free settlers in rural areas (where about 95 percent of the colonists lived) appear to have been truly poor. By 1750, at least two-thirds of rural householders owned their own land.

City Life

Nowhere was the maturation of the colonial economy more evident than in the port cities of British North America. By 1760, Boston (with a population around 15,600), New York (18,000), and fast-growing Philadelphia (nearly 24,000) had become provincial British cities on the scale of Bristol and Liverpool. Unlike rural colonists, city dwellers purchased their food and wood. They lived by the clock rather than the sun, and men's jobs frequently took them away from their households.

Early American cities also saw growing extremes of wealth and poverty. By the last quarter of the eighteenth century, some of the largest merchant families—such as the Hancocks in Boston—had amassed fortunes their forebears could not have imagined. Yet roughly one-fifth of Philadelphia's workforce was enslaved, and blacks comprised nearly 15 percent of the population of New York City. White or black, the families of urban laborers lived on the edge of destitution.

Even some of the poorest city people—common sailors, prostitutes—had extensive contact with worlds far beyond their homes. By 1760,

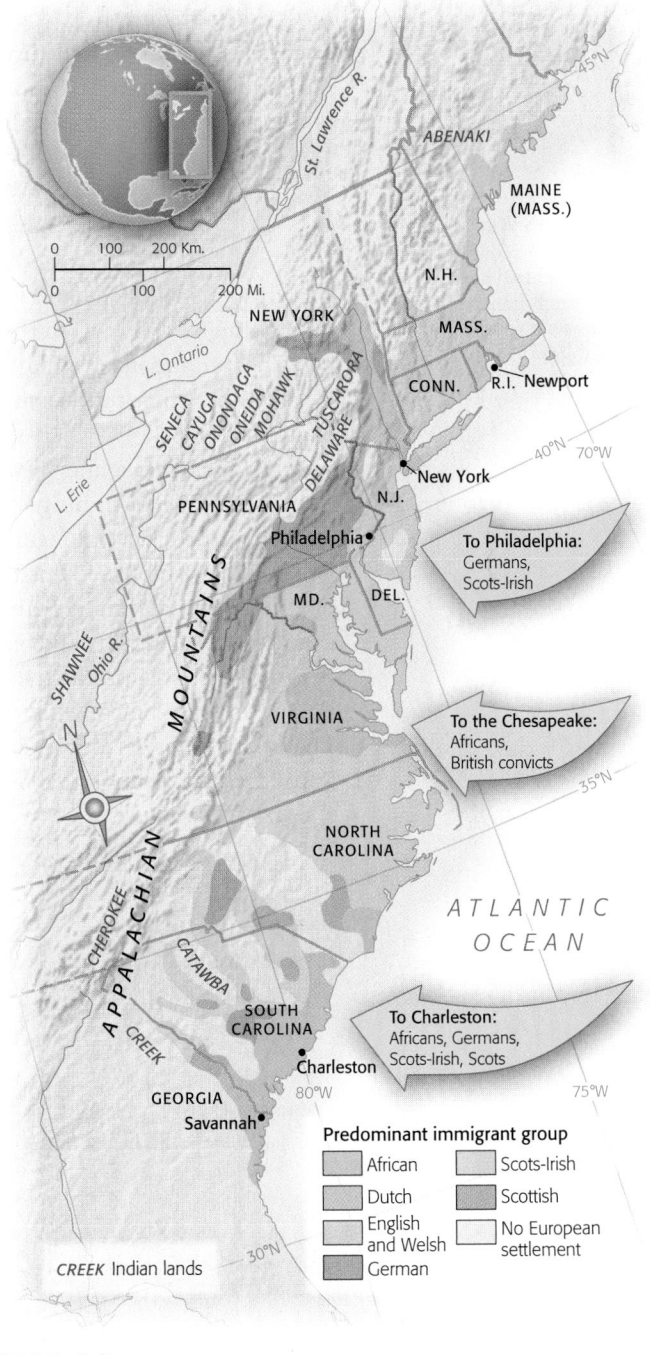

MAP 4.3

Non-English Ethnic Groups in the British Colonies, ca. 1775

Non-African immigrants arriving in the years after 1720 were pushed to the peripheries of settlement, as is shown by these maps. Scottish, Scots-Irish, French, and German newcomers had to move to the frontiers. The Dutch remained where they had originally settled in the seventeenth century. Africans were concentrated in coastal plantation regions.

Source: Copyright © Cengage Learning 2015

most substantial towns had at least one weekly newspaper. The press offered the latest "advices from London" (usually two to three months old), news from other colonies, and local reports. Newspapers were available (and often read aloud) at taverns and coffeehouses, so people who could not afford or read them could learn the news.

King George's War Also known as the War of Austrian Succession, started out as a conflict between Britain and Spain, but then escalated when France sided with Spain.

Regional Economies

Within this overall picture, broad regional patterns emerged, heightened by **King George's War**, also called the War of the Austrian Succession (1739–1748). The war created strong demand for ships and sailors, thus invigorating the economy of New England. But when the shipbuilding boom ended, the economy stagnated.

The war and its aftermath brought prosperity to the middle colonies and the Chesapeake, where fertile soil and a long growing season produced an abundance of grain. After 1748, when several poor harvests in Europe caused flour prices to rise, Philadelphia and New York took the lead in the foodstuffs trade. In the Chesapeake, the beginnings of grain cultivation changed settlement patterns by encouraging the development of port towns (like Baltimore) where merchants and shipbuilders established businesses to handle the new trade.

In South Carolina, rice and indigo fields were periodically devastated by hurricanes, causing hardship and bankruptcies. Yet after 1730, when Parliament removed rice from the list of products enumerated by the Navigation Acts, South Carolinians prospered by trading directly with Europe. The outbreak of war disrupted that trade. The colony entered a depression that did not end until the 1760s. Overall, though, South Carolina experienced rapid economic growth. By the time of the Revolution,

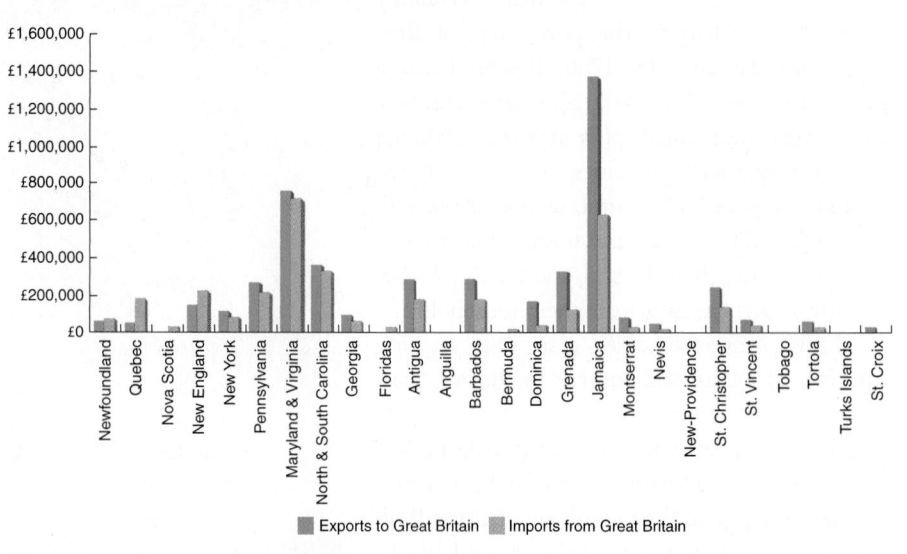

FIGURE 4.2

Trade Revenue from the British Colonies in 1769

As this figure shows, the different regions of the British mainland colonies had distinct trading patterns with Britain. New England imported more than it exported; much of its export trade was with the Caribbean. The exports of the Chesapeake colonies (especially tobacco) and the Carolinas (rice and indigo) were more significant, but the value of sugar from Jamaica dwarfed the produce of all the other British colonies.

(Source: David MacPherson, *Annals of Commerce, Manufactures, Fisheries and Navigation, with Brief Notices of the Arts and Sciences Connected with them, Containing the Commercial Transactions of the British Empire and Other Countries* (1805), volume III, p. 495.)

its freeholders had the highest average wealth in continental Anglo America, though the wealth of Barbadian and Jamaican planters dwarfed even theirs.

The newest British settlement, Georgia, was chartered in 1732 as a haven for English debtors released from prison. Its founder, **James Oglethorpe**, envisioned Georgia as a garrison whose farmers would defend the southern flank of English settlement against Spanish Florida. To ensure that all adult men could serve as the colony's armed protectors, Georgia's charter prohibited slavery. But Carolina rice planters won the removal of the restriction in 1751. Thereafter, Georgia developed into a rice-planting slave society.

James Oglethorpe Founder of Georgia colony.

"Oeconomical" Households: Families, Production, and Reproduction

How did European American families differ from those of Indians or African Americans?

Throughout the colonial era and well into the nineteenth century, the household was the basic unit of economic production, and economic production was the overriding concern of American families. Indeed, the Greek word *oikos*, meaning "household," is also the root of the English word *economy*. Seventeenth-century English writers often used *oeconomie* to discuss household and family matters. Families constituted the chief mechanisms for both production and consumption, yet family forms and structures varied widely.

Indian and Mixed-Race Families

Once Europeans established dominance in any region, Indians there could no longer pursue traditional modes of subsistence. That led to unusual family structures as well as new economic strategies. In New England, Algonquian husbands and wives often could not live together, for adults supported themselves by working separately (perhaps wives as domestic servants, husbands as sailors). Some native women married African American men, unions encouraged by sexual imbalances in both populations. And in New Mexico, detribalized Navajos, Pueblos, Paiutes, and Apaches employed as servants by Spanish settlers clustered in small borderlands towns. Known as *genizaros,* they lost contact with Indian cultures, instead living on the fringes of Latino society.

Wherever the population contained relatively few European women, sexual liaisons occurred between European men and Indian women. The resulting mixed-race people, whom Spanish colonists called *mestizos* and French settlers designated *métis,* often served as go-betweens, navigating the intersection of two cultures. In New France and the Anglo-American backcountry, many of the children of such families became Native American leaders. By contrast, in the Spanish borderlands, the offspring of Europeans and *genizaros* were considered inferior. Often denied legal marriage, they bore generations of "illegitimate" children of various racial mixtures, giving rise in Latino society to multiple labels describing precise degrees of skin color.

European American Families

Eighteenth-century Anglo-Americans referred to all the people who occupied one household (including servants or slaves) as a family. In 1790, the average home in the United States contained 5.7 free people. Few included grandparents or other extended kin. The head of the household represented it to the outside world, voting in elections, managing the finances, and holding legal authority over the rest of the family—his wife, children, and servants or slaves. In the eyes of the law, wives were *femes covert*, their personhood "covered" by their husbands.

In English, French, and Spanish America, the vast majority of European families supported themselves through farming and raising livestock. Household tasks were allocated by sex. The mistress took responsibility for what Anglo-Americans called "indoor affairs." She and her female helpers prepared food, cleaned the house, and washed and made clothing. Women's work—often performed while pregnant, nursing, or sometimes both—was unremitting.

The husband and his male helpers, responsible for "outdoor affairs," planted and cultivated fields, built fences, chopped wood, harvested and marketed crops, tended livestock, and butchered cattle and hogs. Farmwork was so extensive that no married couple could do it alone. If childless, they hired servants or purchased slaves.

African American Families

Most African American families lived as components of European American households. More than 95 percent of colonial African Americans were held in bondage. In South Carolina, a majority of the population was of African descent; in Georgia, about half; and in the Chesapeake, 40 percent. Portions of the Carolina low country were nearly 90 percent African American by 1790.

In the North, the scarcity of other blacks made it difficult for bondspeople to form households. In the Chesapeake, men and women who regarded themselves as married (slaves could not legally wed) frequently lived in different quarters or on different plantations. On large Carolina and Georgia rice plantations, enslaved couples usually lived together and accumulated property by working for themselves after completing daily "tasks." Everywhere, slave family ties were forged against the threat of separation by sale.

Forms of Resistance

Because all British colonies permitted slavery, bondspeople had few options for escaping servitude other than fleeing to Florida, where the Spanish offered protection. Some recently arrived Africans stole boats or ran off to join the Indians or establish independent communities. Others made their way to cities like Philadelphia, where they might melt into small communities of free black laborers and artisans.

Among American-born slaves, family ties strongly affected the decision to "steal" oneself by running away. Many owners therefore kept families together for practical reasons. Most escaped slaves advertised in the newspapers were young men; it was harder for women with children to escape.

Although colonial slaves rarely rebelled collectively, they resisted in other ways. Bondspeople rejected owners' attempts to commandeer their labor on Sundays without compensation. Links among families also helped to ameliorate the uncertainties of existence under slavery. If parents and children were separated by sale, other relatives helped with child rearing.

Most slave families carved out some autonomy, especially in their working and spiritual lives, and particularly in the Lower South. Some African Americans preserved traditional beliefs or Islamic faith. Others converted to Christianity (often retaining some African elements), comforted by the Bible's promise that all would be free and equal in heaven. Slaves in South Carolina and Georgia jealously guarded their customary ability to control their time after completing their "tasks." On Chesapeake tobacco plantations, slaves planted their own gardens, trapped, and fished to supplement their minimal diet. Late in the century, some Chesapeake planters began to hire slaves out to others, often allowing the workers to keep a small part of their earnings.

Provincial Cultures

How did rituals function in colonial America?

The early American household was a nursery of culture, a term with many, sometimes competing definitions. When anthropologists speak of culture, they typically mean the customs and rituals that define a community—its folkways, in other words. Where folkways belong to the many, learned or "high" culture—art, literature, philosophy, and science—may be the realm of the few. Yet folkways interact with the life of the mind, and cultures are always plural. In some respects, diverse, increasingly stratified North American cultures grew more British as the colonies became more fully integrated provinces of empire. But in other ways, as Dr. Hamilton learned, the ragged outer margins of the British realm fashioned very distinctive cultures indeed.

Oral Cultures

Most people in North America were illiterate. Those who could read often could not write. Parents, older siblings, or widows who needed extra income taught youngsters to read; middling boys and genteel girls might learn to write in private schools. Few Americans other than some Anglican missionaries tried to instruct enslaved children; masters feared literate slaves, who could forge documents to pass as free. And few Indian converts learned European literacy skills.

Thus, the everyday cultures of colonial North America were primarily oral and—at least through the first half of the eighteenth century—intensely local. Household and public rituals served as the chief means through which the colonists forged cultural identities and navigated the boundaries among them.

Rituals on the "Middle Ground"

Particularly important rituals developed on what the historian Richard White has termed the "middle ground"—the psychological and geographical space in which Indians and Europeans encountered each other, primarily via trade or warfare.

When Europeans sought to trade with Indians, they encountered indigenous systems of exchange that stressed gift giving rather than buying and selling. Successful bargaining required French and English traders to present Indians with gifts (cloth, rum, gunpowder, and other goods) before negotiating for pelts and skins. Only after those gifts were reciprocated could formal trading proceed.

Civic Rituals

Ceremonial occasions reinforced identities within as well as boundaries between cultures. New England governments proclaimed days of thanksgiving (for good harvests, military victories, and other "providences") and days of fasting and prayer (to lament war, drought, or epidemic). Everyone was expected to participate. Because able-bodied men between the ages of sixteen and sixty were required to serve in local militias, monthly musters also brought townsfolk together.

In the Chesapeake, widely spaced farms meant that communities came together less frequently. Ritual life centered on court and election days. When the county court met, men came to file lawsuits, appear as witnesses, or serve as jurors. Court attendance provided civic education; men watched to learn what their neighbors expected of them. Elections served a similar purpose, for property-holding men voted in public. An election official, often flanked by the candidates for office, called each man forward to declare his preference. The gentleman for whom the ballot was cast would then thank the voter. Later, the candidates treated their supporters to rum.

Throughout colonial North America, the punishment of criminals reminded the community of proper behavioral standards. Public hangings and whippings, along with orders to sit in the stocks, expressed a community's outrage and restored harmony.

Museum of Fine Arts, Boston. Gift of Joseph W.R. Rogers and Mary C. Rogers. Photograph© 2008 Museum of Fine Arts, Boston

Elizabeth Murray, the subject of this 1769 painting by John Singleton Copley, was the wife of James Smith, a wealthy rum distiller. Her fashionable dress and pose would seem to mark her as a lady of leisure, yet both before and during her marriage this Scottish immigrant ran a successful dry goods shop in Boston. She thus simultaneously catered to and participated in the new culture of consumption.

Rituals of Consumption

By 1770, Anglo-Americans spent roughly one-quarter of their household budgets on consumer goods. Since similar British imports flooded shop counters from Maine to Georgia, such purchases established cultural links among the residents of North America, creating what historians have termed "an empire of goods."

Seventeenth-century settlers had acquired necessities by bartering with neighbors or ordering from a home-country merchant. By the middle of the eighteenth century, specialized shops proliferated in colonial towns and cities. Colonists would take time to "go shopping," a novel and pleasurable leisure activity. Buyers confronted a dazzling array of possibilities and fashioned their identities by choosing among them. Some historians have termed this shift a "consumer revolution."

The purchase of an object—for example, a mirror or some beautiful imported fabric—initiated a series of consumption rituals. Consumers proudly deployed their purchases (and thus their status and taste): hanging the mirror prominently on a wall, sewing the fabric into a special piece of clothing. A prosperous man might hire an artist to paint his family using imported objects and wearing fine clothing, thereby creating a pictorial record to be admired and passed down as a kind of cultural inheritance.

Poor and rural people similarly took pleasure even in inexpensive purchases. Backcountry storekeepers accepted bartered goods; one Virginia woman traded hens and chickens for a pewter dish. Slaves exchanged cotton they grew in their free time for ribbons and hats.

Tea and Madeira

Tea drinking, a consumption ritual largely controlled by women, played an important role throughout Anglo America. Households with aspirations to genteel status purchased pots, cups, strainers, sugar tongs, even special tables. Tea provided a focal point for socializing and, because of its cost, served as a marker of cosmopolitan status. Poor households consumed tea as well, but without the fancy equipment used by their better-off neighbors.

Madeira wine, imported from the Portuguese islands, had also become a favored drink of the elite by 1770. Serving the wine required specialized accoutrements and elaborate ceremony; purchasing it involved considerable expense. In 1784, one Philadelphia merchant's spending on Madeira and other exotic liquors equaled the combined annual budgets of two artisan families.

Polite and Learned Culture

Wealthy colonists spent their money ostentatiously. They built large brick homes of the neoclassical style newly fashionable in England, with columns, symmetrical floor plans, and an array of specialized rooms.

Andre Jenny/Alamy

Built in 1730, William Byrd's grand home, which he called Westover, reflects the genteel aspirations of a new generation of British Americans. Byrd, one of Virginia's wealthiest planters, had spent time in London, and he designed his James River plantation according to the most current English tastes, with an emphasis on symmetry and a highly theatrical entrance. Byrd's diaries reveal the uneasy combination of cosmopolitan refinement and slaveholding barbarism that marked the daily lives of elites in the southern colonies.

The grandest houses in the colonies would barely have qualified as outbuildings of England's great country houses, yet they were far more elaborate than the homes of earlier settlers. Sufficiently well-off to enjoy "leisure" time (a first for North America), genteel Euro-Americans also cultivated polite manners, adopting stylized forms of address and paying attention to "proper" comportment.

Although the effects of accumulated wealth were most pronounced in British America, elite families in New Mexico, Louisiana, and Quebec also fashioned genteel cultures that distinguished them from the "lesser sort." One historian has termed these processes "the refinement of America."

Refined gentlemen prided themselves not only on their possessions, but also on their education and on their intellectual connections to Europe. Many had been tutored by private teachers; some attended college. (Harvard, the first colonial college, founded in 1636, was joined by William and Mary in 1693, Yale in 1701, and later by several others, including Princeton in 1747.) By the 1740s, aspiring colonial gentlemen regularly traveled to London and Edinburgh to complete their educations in law or medicine, and to Italy to become connoisseurs of art and antiquities.

American women were largely excluded from advanced education, with the exception of devout women who joined nunneries in Canada or Louisiana. Instead, genteel daughters perfected womanly accomplishments like French (rather than Latin), needlework, and musicianship. Even relatively educated women including John Adams's wife Abigail and Benjamin Franklin's sister Jane bemoaned their scant learning and poor spelling.

Yet women, like men, were part of a burgeoning world of print in Anglo America. There were more than a thousand private libraries in seventeenth-century Virginia. In Boston, the Mather family's collection numbered several thousand titles by 1700. Booksellers in cities and towns offered a wide selection of titles imported from England and an increasing number printed in the colonies. The number of newspapers grew rapidly as well, from three journals in 1720 to 31 in 1770. Those who could not afford to buy newspapers perused them in coffeehouses, and those who could not afford to buy books might read them in new civic institutions called libraries. Benjamin Franklin, a candle-maker's son who made his living as a printer, founded the Library Company of Philadelphia, the first subscription library in North America, in 1731.

The Enlightenment

Spreading through travel and print and polite conversation, the intellectual currents known as the **Enlightenment** deeply affected American provincials. Around 1650, some European thinkers began to analyze nature to determine the laws governing the universe. They conducted experiments to discover general principles underlying phenomena like the motions of planets. Enlightenment philosophers sought knowledge through reason and challenged previously unquestioned assumptions. **John Locke**'s *Essay Concerning Human Understanding* (1690), for example, disputed the notion that human beings are born imprinted with innate ideas. All knowledge, Locke asserted, derives from observations.

The Enlightenment supplied educated Europeans and Americans with a common vocabulary and a unified worldview, one that insisted the enlightened eighteenth century was better, and wiser, than ages past. A prime example of America's

Enlightenment Intellectual revolution that elevated reason, science, and logic.

John Locke British philosopher and major Enlightenment thinker; known for his emphasis on the power of human reasoning.

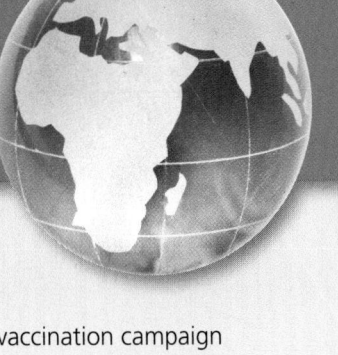

Smallpox Inoculation

Smallpox, the world's greatest killer of human beings, repeatedly ravaged North American colonists and Indians. Thus, when the vessel *Seahorse* arrived in Boston from the Caribbean in April 1721 carrying smallpox-infected passengers, authorities quarantined the ship. But it was too late: smallpox escaped into the city, and by June several dozen were afflicted.

The Reverend Cotton Mather, a member of London's Royal Society (an Enlightenment organization), had read years earlier of a medical technique unknown to Europeans but widely employed in North Africa and the Middle East. Called inoculation, it involved taking pus from the pustules (or poxes) of an infected person and inserting it into a small cut on the arm of a healthy individual. With luck, that person would experience a mild case of smallpox, followed by lifetime immunity. Mather's interest was further piqued by his slave, Onesimus, a North African who had been inoculated as a youth and who described the procedure in detail.

Mather promoted inoculation as a solution to the smallpox epidemic, but nearly all the city's doctors ridiculed his ideas. Mather won only one major convert, Zabdiel Boylston, a physician and apothecary. The two men inoculated their own children and about two hundred others, despite bitter opposition. After the epidemic ended, Bostonians could see the results: of those inoculated, just 3 percent had died; among the thousands who took the disease "in the natural way," mortality was 15 percent. Even Mather's most vocal opponents thereafter supported inoculation.

Thus, through transatlantic links forged by the Enlightenment and enslavement, American colonists learned how to combat the deadliest disease.

Today, thanks to a successful vaccination campaign by the World Health Organization, smallpox has been eradicated.

An Historical

ACCOUNT

OF THE

SMALL-POX

INOCULATED

IN

NEW ENGLAND,

Upon all Sorts of Perfons, *Whites, Blacks,* and of all Ages and Conftitutions.

With fome Account of the Nature of the Infection in the NATURAL and INOCULATED Way, and their different Effects on HUMAN BODIES.

With fome fhort DIRECTIONS to the UNEXPERIENCED in this Method of Practice.

Humbly dedicated to her Royal Highnefs the Princefs of WALES, by *Zabdiel Boylfton,* Phyfician.

LONDON:
Printed for S. CHANDLER, *at the* Crofs-Keys *in the* Poultry. M. DCC. XXVI.

Several years after he and Cotton Mather combated a Boston smallpox epidemic by employing inoculation, Zabdiel Boylston published this pamphlet in London to spread the news of their success. The dedication to the Princess of Wales was designed to indicate the royal family's support of the procedure.

participation in the Enlightenment was **Benjamin Franklin**, who retired from his successful printing business in 1748 at age forty-two, thereafter devoting himself to scientific experimentation and public service. His *Experiments and Observations on Electricity* (1751) established the terminology and basic theory of electricity still used today.

Enlightenment rationalism affected politics as well. Locke's *Two Treatises of Government* (1691) and works by French and Scottish philosophers challenged a

Benjamin Franklin American who embodied Enlightenment ideas.

divinely sanctioned, hierarchical political order originating in the power of fathers over families. Men created governments and so could alter them, Locke declared. A ruler who broke the social contract and failed to protect people's rights could legitimately be ousted—peacefully or violently. Enlightenment theorists proclaimed that God's natural laws governed even monarchs. The rough and tumble political philosophy Dr. Hamilton found on his 1744 journey through the colonies offers evidence of a vernacular Enlightenment bubbling up from the lower orders as well.

A Changing Religious Culture

What was the social and political impact of the Great Awakening?

Religious observance was perhaps the most pervasive facet of eighteenth-century provincial culture. In Congregational (Puritan) churches, church leaders assigned seating to reflect standing in the community. By midcentury, wealthy men and their wives sat in privately owned pews; children, servants, slaves, and the less fortunate still sat in sex-segregated fashion in the rear, sides, or balcony of the church. Seating in Virginia's Church of England parishes also mirrored the local status hierarchy. By contrast, Quaker meetinghouses in Pennsylvania and elsewhere used an egalitarian but sex-segregated seating system.

The religious culture of the colonies began to change significantly in the mid-eighteenth century. From the mid-1730s through the 1760s, waves of revivalism—today known as the First **Great Awakening**—swept over British America, especially New England (1735–1745) and Virginia (1750s–1760s). Orthodox Calvinists sought to combat Enlightenment rationalism, which denied innate human depravity. Simultaneously, the uncertainty accompanying King George's War made colonists receptive to **evangelists'** messages.

Great Awakening Protestant revival movement that emphasized each person's urgent need for salvation by God.

evangelist A preacher or minister who enthusiastically promotes the Christian gospels.

America's revivals began in New England. In the mid-1730s, the Reverend Jonathan Edwards, a preacher and theologian in Northampton, Massachusetts, gained new youthful followers with the Calvinist message that sinners could attain salvation only by recognizing their depraved nature and surrendering completely to God's will. Parishioners of both sexes experienced an emotional release from sin, which came to be seen as a moment of conversion, a new birth.

Link to excerpts from Jonathan Edwards' "A Faithful Narrative of the Surprising Work of God, in the Conversion of Many Hundred Souls, in Northampton...."

George Whitefield English preacher who toured the colonies and played a major role in the Great Awakening.

George Whitefield

Such ecstatic conversions remained isolated until 1739, when **George Whitefield**, an Anglican clergyman already celebrated for leading revivals in Britain, crossed the Atlantic. For fifteen months, he toured the British colonies, concentrating his efforts in the major cities. One historian has termed Whitefield "the first modern celebrity" because of his skillful self-promotion. Everywhere he traveled, his fame preceded him. Thousands of free and enslaved folk turned out to listen—and to experience conversion. Whitefield's tour created new interconnections among far-flung colonies.

Established clerics initially welcomed Whitefield and his American-born imitators. Soon, however, many concluded that the "revived" religion challenged their approach to doctrine and practice. They disliked the emotional style of the revivalists, whose itinerancy also disrupted normal patterns of church attendance.

Particularly troublesome to the orthodox were the female exhorters who publicly proclaimed their right to expound God's word.

Impact of the Awakening

Opposition to the Awakening splintered congregations. "Old Lights"—orthodox clerics and their followers—engaged in bitter disputes with "New Light" evangelicals. American Protestantism fragmented further as Congregationalists and Presbyterians split into factions, and as new evangelical sects—Methodists and Baptists—gained adherents. Paradoxically, the proliferation of distinct denominations eventually fostered a willingness to tolerate religious pluralism. Where no sect could monopolize orthodoxy, denominations had to coexist if they were to exist at all.

The Awakening challenged traditional modes of thought. Revivalists' emphasis on emotion over learning undermined received wisdom about society and politics as well as religion. Some New Lights defended the rights of people to dissent from a community consensus, thereby challenging one of the fundamental tenets of colonial political life.

Virginia Baptists

The egalitarian themes of the Awakening tended to attract ordinary folk and repel the elite. By the 1760s, Baptists had gained a secure foothold in Virginia;

George Whitefield preaching, Collet, John (c.1725–80)/Private Collection/The Bridgeman Art Library

This painting by John Collet shows the charismatic evangelist George Whitefield preaching out of doors in Britain, but the same scene would have been repeated many times in the colonies, especially after the clergy of established churches denied him access to their pulpits, deeming him too radical for their liking. Note the swooning woman in the foreground; women were reputed to be especially susceptible to Whitefield's message. Is the worker offering him a mug of ale derisively or devotedly? The answer is not clear, except that the gesture underscores the diversity of Whitefield's audience—not all were genteel or middling folk.

inevitably, their beliefs and behavior clashed with the refined lifestyle of the plantation gentry.

Strikingly, almost all Virginia Baptist congregations included free and enslaved members, and some had African American majorities. Church rules applied equally to all members; interracial sexual relationships, divorce, and adultery were proscribed for all. In addition, congregations forbade masters' breaking up slave couples through sale. Yet it is easy to overstate the racial egalitarianism of Virginia evangelicals and the attractiveness of the new sects to black members. Masters censured for abusing their slaves were quickly readmitted, and African Americans totaled only 1 percent of southern evangelicals.

The Great Awakening had important social and political consequences. In some ways, the evangelicals were profoundly conservative, preaching an old-style theology. In other respects, the revivalists were recognizably modern, using the techniques of Atlantic commerce, and calling into question habitual modes of behavior in the **secular** as well as the religious realm.

secular Not specifically relating to religion or to a religious body.

Stability and Crisis at Midcentury

What were the myths and realities of colonial assemblies?

The Great Awakening points to the unsettled nature of provincial life in the mid-eighteenth century. A number of other crises—ethnic, racial, economic, and military—exposed lines of fracture within North America's diverse society. In the 1740s and 1750s, Britain expanded its claims to North American territory and to the obligations of provincials. At the same time, Anglo-American colonists felt more strongly entitled to the liberties of British subjects. And Britain and France alike came to see North America as increasingly central to their economic, diplomatic, and military strategies in Europe.

Colonial Political Orders

Men from genteel families dominated political structures, for voters (free male property holders) tended to defer to their "betters" on election days. These political leaders sought to increase the powers of elected assemblies relative to the powers of governors and other appointed officials. Assemblies began to claim privileges associated with the British House of Commons, such as initiating tax legislation and controlling the militia. Assemblies also influenced Crown appointees by threatening to withhold their salaries.

To win hotly contested elections, New York's leaders began competing openly for votes. Yet in 1735, the colony's government imprisoned newspaper editor **John Peter Zenger**, who had too vigorously criticized its actions. Defending Zenger against the charge of "seditious libel," his lawyer argued that the truth could not be defamatory, thus helping to establish a free-press principle later found in American law.

John Peter Zenger Central figure in a trial that opened the way for freedom of the press.

Assemblymen saw themselves as thwarting encroachments on colonists' British liberties—for example, by preventing governors from imposing oppressive taxes. By midcentury, they often compared the structure of their governments to Britain's mixed polity, equating their governors with the monarch, their councils with the aristocracy, and their assemblies with Britain's House of Commons. But Anglo-Americans increasingly viewed royal governors and appointed councils as potential threats to colonial ways of life. Many colonists saw the assemblies as the people's protectors. In reality, however, colonial assemblies, often controlled by dominant families, rarely responded to poorer constituents' concerns.

At midcentury, the political structures that had stabilized in a period of relative calm confronted a series of crises. Significantly, these upheavals demonstrated that the political accommodations forged in the aftermath of the **Glorious Revolution** had become inadequate to govern Britain's American empire.

Glorious Revolution Overthrow of James II in favor of William and Mary.

Stono Rebellion A slave uprising in 1739 in South Carolina.

Slave Rebellions and Internal Disorder

Early on Sunday, September 9, 1739, about twenty enslaved men, most likely Catholics from Kongo, gathered near the Stono River south of Charles Town. September fell in the midst of South Carolina's rice harvest (and thus at a time of great pressure for male Africans), and September 8 was, to Catholics, the birthday of the Virgin Mary. Seizing guns and ammunition, the rebels killed storekeepers and nearby planter families. Joined by other local bondsmen, they then headed toward Florida in hopes of finding refuge. That afternoon, however, a troop of militia attacked the fugitives, who numbered about a hundred, killing some and dispersing the rest. The colony quickly captured and executed the survivors, but rumors about escaped renegades haunted the colony for years.

News of the **Stono Rebellion** reverberated far beyond South Carolina. The press frequently reported on slave uprisings in the West Indies, but on the mainland, where slaves did not so vastly outnumber their masters, such an organized revolt was remarkable, and terrifying. Throughout British America, laws governing the behavior of African Americans were stiffened after Stono. In New York City, which had witnessed the first mainland slave revolt in 1712, the news from the South, coupled with fears of Spain generated by the outbreak of King George's War, set off a reign of terror in 1741. Thirty-one blacks and four whites were executed—gruesomely—for allegedly plotting a slave uprising under the guidance of a Spanish priest. The Stono Rebellion and the New York "conspiracy" confirmed Anglo-Americans' deepest fears about the dangers of slaveholding and revealed the assemblies' inability to prevent internal disorder.

A JOURNAL OF THE PROCEEDINGS IN The Detection of the Conspiracy FORMED BY Some *White* People, in Conjunction with *Negro* and other *Slaves*, FOR Burning the City of NEW-YORK in AMERICA, And Murdering the Inhabitants.

Daniel Horsmanden played a leading role in the prosecution of alleged conspirators who had so terrified white inhabitants of New York City in 1741. He expected many buyers for his Journal of the Proceedings in the Detection of the Conspiracy, *an exacting and often sensationalist account of the trials that had resulted in the execution of thirty-five people, thirteen of whom were burned at the stake. But by 1744, public opinion had begun to turn against the trials, which some compared to the Salem witchcraft hysteria. Horsmanden was mocked in the newspapers, and in 1748 the* Journal's *printer slashed its price, noting, "as he has been a considerable Loser by printing that Book, he proposes to sell 'em very cheap."*

European Rivalries in North America

In addition to their internal divisions, Britain's mainland colonies were surrounded by hostile, or potentially hostile, neighbors: Indians everywhere, the Spanish in Florida and along the Gulf coast, the French along the rivers and lakes that stretched from the St. Lawrence to the Mississippi. The Spanish posed little direct threat; the French were another matter. In none of the three Anglo-French wars fought between 1689 and 1748 was Britain able to shake France's hold on the American frontier (see Table 4.1 and Map 5.1).

The Fall of Louisbourg

In the North American theater of King George's War, hostilities largely played out along the northern border between British and French America. The massive French fortress at Louisbourg, on Cape Breton Island, quickly became the largest French town on the continent, with more than 4,000 settlers and some 1,500 soldiers. Privateers based at Louisbourg regularly menaced New England merchants and fishermen. In 1744, William Shirley, the royal governor of Massachusetts, hatched a scheme to seize the fort for the Crown.

Many thought Shirley's plan to conquer Louisbourg foolhardy, but in June 1745, after a two-month-long siege, the fort fell to ragtag regiments of some 4,000 colonial soldiers, most of them from Massachusetts. But when the war ended in 1748, Britain returned the fortress to France in exchange for concessions in India and the Low Countries, the imperial priorities of the moment. Massachusetts was left with staggering debt, hundreds of new widows and orphans, and needy soldiers crippled in the futile fight.

The Ohio Country

By the time King George's War ended, the crucible of North America's imperial rivalries could be found farther south, in lands west of the Appalachians and

TABLE 4.1   The Colonial Wars, 1689–1763

American Name	European Name	Dates	Participants	American Sites	Dispute
King William's War	Nine Years' War	1689–97	England, Holland versus France, Spain	New England, New York, Canada	French power
Queen Anne's War	War of Spanish Succession	1702–13	England, Holland, Austria versus France, Spain	Florida, New England	Throne of Spain
King George's War	War of Austrian Succession	1739–48	England, Holland, Austria versus France, Spain, Prussia	West Indies, New England, Canada	Throne of Austria
French and Indian War	Seven Years' War	1756–63	England versus France, Spain	Ohio Country, Canada	Possession of Ohio Country

east of the Mississippi that came to be known as the Ohio Country. The trouble started in the 1730s, as Anglo-American traders pushed west and challenged French power beyond the Appalachians. French officials' fear of British incursions increased when the Delawares and Shawnees ceded large tracts of land to Pennsylvania. In 1737, two sons of William Penn and their Iroquois allies persuaded the Delawares to sell off as much land as a man could walk in a day and a half. Then the Pennsylvania negotiators sent trained runners down prepared trails to multiply the acreage. Delawares derided the deceitful Walking Purchase as "ye Running Walk." The agreements reached by the Penn family and the Iroquois ignored the claims of both the local Indians and Scots-Irish and German squatters, all of whom were told to move. Disgruntled Delawares and Shawnees migrated west, where they joined other displaced eastern Indians who nursed similar grievances.

Claimed by both Virginia and Pennsylvania, the region to which they migrated was coveted by wealthy Virginians. In 1745, a group of land speculators organized as the Ohio Company of Virginia received a grant of nearly a third of a million acres from the House of Burgesses. The company's agents established trading posts in the crucial area where the Allegheny and Monongahela rivers join to form the Ohio. But that region was also strategically vital to the French, because the Ohio River offered access by water to French posts along the Mississippi. By the early 1750s, Pennsylvania fur traders, Ohio Company representatives, the French military, Scots-Irish and German squatters, Iroquois, Delawares, and Shawnees all jostled for position in the region.

Iroquois Neutrality   Maintaining the policy of neutrality they developed in 1701, the Iroquois Confederacy manipulated the European rivals and consolidated their control over the vast regions north of Virginia and south of the Great Lakes. During Queen Anne's War and again in King George's War, they refused to commit warriors exclusively to either side, and so were showered with gifts by both. Conflict with Cherokees and Catawbas in the South gave young Iroquois warriors combat experience and replenished their population with new captives. They also cultivated peaceful relationships with Pennsylvania and Virginia; their role in treaties like the Walking Purchase furthered Iroquois domination of the Shawnees and Delawares. And they forged friendly ties with French-allied Algonquians of the Great Lakes region. But even the Iroquois could not fully control the Ohio Country, and by the late 1750s, conflict there would spread to Europe, and then around the globe.

When he traveled the colonies in 1744, Dr. Hamilton never once referred to the people who lived there as *Americans*. Nor did colonial settlers much use that term at the time. But after King George's War, and especially after the next and most convulsive of the century's Anglo-French wars, colonists began increasingly to imagine themselves as a group with shared and distinct concerns. Colonial writers began occasionally to refer to "Americans," "American colonists," or "continentals." These newly labeled Americans continued to pledge their allegiance to Britain, but some of them began to wonder whether Parliament and the Crown understood their needs and their rights.

"Self-Made Men"

American culture celebrates the "self-made man" (always someone explicitly *male*) of humble origins who gains wealth or prominence through extraordinary effort. Those most commonly cited include the nineteenth-century businessmen Andrew Carnegie (once a poor immigrant from Scotland) and John D. Rockefeller (born on a hardscrabble farm in upstate New York).

The first exemplars of this tradition lived in the eighteenth century. Benjamin Franklin's *Autobiography* chronicled his method for achieving success after beginning life as the seventeenth child of a Boston candle-maker. From such humble origins Franklin became a wealthy, influential man active in science, politics, education, and diplomacy. Yet Franklin's tale is rivaled by that of a slave who became one of the eighteenth century's leading antislavery activists. He acquired literacy, purchased his freedom, married a wealthy Englishwoman, and published a popular autobiography that predated Franklin's. His first master called him Gustavus Vassa, but when publishing his *Interesting Narrative* in 1789, he called himself Olaudah Equiano.

In that *Narrative*, Equiano said he was born in Africa in 1745, kidnapped at age eleven, and transported to Barbados and then to Virginia, where a British naval officer purchased him. For years, scholars have relied on that account for its insights into the middle passage. But evidence recently uncovered by Vincent Carretta, although confirming much of Equiano's autobiography, shows that Equiano twice identified his birthplace as Carolina and was three to five years younger than he claimed. Carretta speculates that the *Narrative* gained part of its credibility from Equiano's African birth and that admitting his real age would have raised questions about the account of his early life.

Equiano, or Vassa, thus truly "made himself," just as Benjamin Franklin and many others have done. (Franklin tended to omit, rather than alter, inconvenient parts of his personal history—for example, his illegitimate son and his ownership of slaves.) Equiano used information undoubtedly gleaned from acquaintances who *had* experienced the middle passage to craft an accurate depiction of its horrors. In the process, he became one of the first Americans to explicitly remake himself.

Summary

The decades before 1760 transformed North America. French and Spanish settlements expanded, and newcomers from Germany, Scotland, Ireland, and Africa brought their languages, customs, and religions with them to the British colonies. European immigrants were concentrated in the growing cities and in the backcountry, while most enslaved migrants from Africa lived and worked within one hundred miles of the Atlantic coast. In many areas of the colonial South, 50 to 90 percent of the population was of African origin. In the West Indies, the enslaved black majority was far larger.

The economic life of Europe's mainland North American colonies proceeded simultaneously on local and transatlantic levels. On the farms, plantations, and ranches where most colonists resided, arduous labor dominated people's lives while providing goods for consumption and sale. Simultaneously, an international trade network affected colonial economies. The wars fought by European nations during the eighteenth century created new opportunities for overseas sales and disrupted traditional markets. The fortunate few who reaped the profits of international commerce comprised the wealthy class of merchants and landowners who dominated colonial life.

A century and a half after European peoples first settled in North America, the colonies mixed diverse European, American, and African traditions into a novel cultural blend. Yet at the same time, colonists continued to identify themselves as French, Spanish, or British rather than as Americans. That did not change in the West Indies, Canada, Louisiana, or in the Spanish territory, but in the 1760s some Anglo-Americans began to realize that their interests did not necessarily coincide with those of Great Britain.

Chapter Review

Geographic Expansion and Ethnic Diversity

What spurred population growth in the British colonies in the thirty years before 1775?

Immigration—particularly of Scots-Irish and Germans—contributed to the population growth among European Americans, but the largest single factor was natural increase (live births). Once the difficult years of early settlement passed and the sex ratio evened out in the South, the population doubled every twenty-five years. Natural increase also boosted the African American enslaved population after 1740, and in some regions the slave population was further augmented by new imports of enslaved people.

Economic Growth and Development in British America

How were the colonies' economic fates increasingly linked to world markets?

As colonies became more entwined in overseas trade, their fortunes were increasingly tied to the ups and downs of those economies. Although colonists developed small-scale manufacturing and broader trade networks to meet increased local demand for goods and services, they nonetheless required external markets for their products—tobacco, rice, indigo, fish, and timber. They used the money made from these items to purchase European and English imports. If demand for American goods fell, so did colonists' income, causing economic downturns. The outbreak of King George's War, for example, increased overseas demand for grain grown in the Chesapeake and led tobacco farmers to convert more of their acreage to the crop, while New England suffered when the shipbuilding boom of the war years ended.

"Oeconomical" Households: Families, Production, and Reproduction

How did European American families differ from those of Indians or African Americans?

Anglo Americans used the word "family" to describe everyone in a household: parents, children, extended kin, and slaves. Families typically supported themselves by farming, with each member assigned a task according to gender norms. (Women did indoor work and related tasks; men did outdoor work.) After contact, extended kin became more important to Native families, particularly as they were decimated by disease. Shortages of European women in French and Spanish colonies led to increased intermarriages, with children raised in Indian villages rather than among settlers. Most African Americans were enslaved, and their families subsumed under European American households. In the Chesapeake, slaves couples who considered themselves married (despite laws prohibiting slave marriage) often lived apart, in different quarters or plantations, with children residing with mothers. On large Carolina and Georgia rice plantations, enslaved couples usually lived together and accumulated property by working for themselves after completing daily "tasks." All slave families could be destroyed by sale at any time.

Provincial Cultures

> **How did rituals function in colonial America?**

Cultural rituals played a central role in colonial life, both to create community and to reinforce social status. Civic rituals generated community involvement and revealed the behavior communities expected of their members. In New England, everyone was required to participate in official holidays or local militia musters; in the Chesapeake, rituals centered on court or election days; and public punishment of criminals throughout North America was designed to reinforce behavioral standards. Even simple rituals, such as tea-drinking, reinforced gender norms and distinctions of wealth and status. Colonists adapted rituals to facilitate trade with Indians, who had vastly different customs. Europeans seeking to trade with Indians engaged in the gift-giving system typical of native cultures before trade could begin.

A Changing Religious Culture

> **What was the social and political impact of the Great Awakening?**

Socially, the Great Awakening challenged traditional norms and patterns. A few women, for example, began to claim a right to preach, and Protestant denominations further split into the "Old Lights"—who followed traditional teachings and ministers—and the "New Light" evangelicals. While initially sparking animosity, ultimately the rise of new denominations promoted greater tolerance for religious diversity. The Great Awakening's egalitarianism also challenged the colonial tradition of deference, in which people knew their place and respected their so-called "betters." New Lights attracted ordinary people as followers and preachers and argued that the world was divided into the saved and the damned without respect to gender, age, or status.

Stability and Crisis at Midcentury

> **What were the myths and realities of colonial assemblies?**

Anglo-American assemblymen believed they safeguarded colonists' liberties from encroachments by the British government, such as oppressive taxation. Regarding Britain's appointed councils and governors as potential threats, colonists looked to assemblies as their protectors. In truth, elite, wealthy families dominated the assemblies and paid little regard to poorer constituents' concerns, nor did they reapportion themselves so that new settlements would gain representatives, which angered backcountry residents and non-English immigrants.

Suggestions for Further Reading

Richard R. Beeman, *The Varieties of Political Experience in Eighteenth-Century America* (2004)

William E. Burns, *Science and Technology in Colonial America* (2005)

Richard Bushman, *The Refinement of America: Persons, Houses, Cities* (1992)

Kathleen DuVal, *The Native Ground: Indians and Colonists in the Heart of the Continent* (2006)

Ellen Hartigan-O'Connor, *The Ties That* Buy: *Women and Commerce in Revolutionary America* (2009)

Rhys Isaac, *The Transformation of Virginia, 1740–1790* (1982)

Jill Lepore, *New York Burning: Liberty, Slavery, and Conspiracy in Eighteenth-Century Manhattan* (2005)

Paul W. Mapp, *The Elusive West and the Contest for Empire, 1713–1763* (2011)

Harry S. Stout, *The Divine Dramatist: George Whitefield and the Rise of Modern Evangelicalism* (1991)

David Waldstreicher, *Runaway America: Benjamin Franklin, Slavery, and the American Revolution* (2004)

The Ends of Empire

5

1754–1774

A spectacular victory demanded a stirring celebration, and the capture of Quebec from the French in September 1759 was indeed a spectacular victory. When news of this latest British triumph reached Boston, in October, town fathers proclaimed a "Day of general Rejoicing." Church bells started ringing at dawn and pealed through the day. Troops paraded down King Street, pausing to blast "Rejoicing Fires" from their muskets. As night fell, a feast for the eyes joined the sounds of celebration. Public buildings blazed with candlelight. The hills surrounding the town glowed with "large bonfires formed in a pyramidal manner." An "abundance of extraordinary Fire-Works were play'd off in almost every Street," the *Boston Gazette* reported. In the seaport's lanes and alleys, "Persons of all Ranks" joined in the revelry.

Boston's "Rejoicing" was "the greatest ever known an universal Joy," the *Gazette* declared. As word of Britain's stunning victory spread through the colonies in the waning days of 1759, similar festivities took place across Anglo America.

The celebratory mood would not last. Within months, the war in North America would be over, and the wartime business boom would go bust. By the end of the 1760s, many provincials would come to suspect King George II's grandson, George III, had turned tyrant. From Nova Scotia to Antigua, protestors against the Crown's new taxes—taxes designed to pay for costly British victories like the one at Quebec—would flood the streets. But the inhabitants of Anglo America knew none of this in the fall of 1759. Proud subjects living on the western edge of His Majesty's empire, they had little reason to anticipate that "this country" would ever be anything but British.

The American Revolution required a thorough transformation in consciousness: a shift of political allegiance from Britain to a polity that was called, at first, the United Colonies. "The Revolution was effected before the war commenced," John Adams later wrote. The true Revolution was not the war, he said, but a fundamental change "in the minds and hearts of the people."

Between 1760 and 1775, huge numbers of ordinary Americans transferred their obligations and affections from their mother country to their sister colonies. Yet Adams spoke of a singular Revolution, when in fact there were many. Rich and poor, free and enslaved, indigenous and European, urban and rural, mainland and Caribbean, even male and female Americans experienced the era's upheavals differently.

In the 1750s, a series of events began to draw colonists' attention from domestic matters to their relations with Great Britain. It started with the conflict in which Britain captured Quebec: the Seven Years' War. Britain's overwhelming victory dramatically altered the balance of power in North America. Anglo-Americans no longer had to fear the French, who were ousted from the continent, or the Spanish, who were ejected from Florida. Indians, who had become expert at playing European powers against one another, found one of their major diplomatic tools blunted.

The victory also transformed Great Britain's colonial policy. Britain's massive war-related debt needed to be paid. Parliament saw the colonies as the chief beneficiaries of British success, and for the first time imposed revenue-raising taxes on the North American territories, in addition to the customs duties that had long regulated trade. That decision exposed differences in the political thinking of Britons in mainland America and Britons in the home islands and the West Indies—differences long obscured by a shared political vocabulary centered on English liberties.

During the 1760s and early 1770s, a broad coalition of the residents of Anglo America, men and women alike, resisted the new tax levies and attempts by British officials to tighten their control over provincial governments. They laid aside old antagonisms to coordinate responses to the new measures, and they slowly began to reorient their political thinking. As late as the summer of 1774, though, most continued to seek a solution within the framework of the empire.

As you read this chapter, keep the following questions in mind:

- **What were the causes and consequences of the Seven Years' War?**

- **What British policies did Americans protest, and what theories and strategies did they develop to support those protests?**

- **Why did the Tea Act of 1773 dramatically heighten tensions between the mainland colonies and Great Britain?**

Chronology

1754	Albany Congress fails to forge colonial unity
	George Washington defeated at Fort Necessity, Pennsylvania
1755	Braddock's army routed in Pennsylvania
1756	Britain declares war on France; Seven Years' War officially begins
1759	British take Quebec
1760	American phase of war ends with British capture of Montreal
	George III becomes king
1763	Treaty of Paris ends Seven Years' War
	Pontiac's allies attack forts and settlements in American West
	Proclamation of 1763 attempts to close land west of Appalachians to settlement
1764	Sugar Act lays new duties on molasses, tightens customs regulations
	Currency Act outlaws colonial paper money
1765	Stamp Act requires stamps on all printed materials in colonies
	Sons of Liberty forms
1765–66	Hudson River land riots pit tenants and squatters against large landlords
1766	Parliament repeals Stamp Act
	Declaratory Act insists that Parliament can tax the colonies
1767	Townshend Acts lay duties on trade within the empire, send new officials to America
1767–69	Regulator movement (South Carolina) tries to establish order in backcountry
1768–70	Townshend duties resisted; boycotts and protests divide merchants and urban artisans
1770	Townshend duties repealed except for tea tax
	Boston Massacre: five colonial rioters killed by British regulars
1771	North Carolina Regulators defeated by eastern militia; six executed for treason
1772	Boston Committee of Correspondence formed
1773	Tea Act aids East India Company, spurs protest in Boston
1774	Coercive Acts punish Boston and Massachusetts
	Quebec Act reforms government of Quebec
	"Lord Dunmore's War" between Shawnees and backcountry settlers in Virginia
	First Continental Congress convenes in Philadelphia, adopts Articles of Association
1774–75	Provincial conventions replace collapsing colonial governments

From the Ohio Country to Global War

What was at stake in the Seven Years' War?

In the early 1750s, British officials drafted plans better to coordinate what one writer called "the Interior Government" of their American territories. Imperial reformers were concerned because the disunity of the colonies made it hard to construct an effective bulwark against the French, who were once again on the march in the continent's interior. The unchecked incursions of backcountry traders and squatters had alienated native allies vital to the British colonies' defense. In the summer of 1753, as the French erected a chain of forts in the Ohio Country, the Mohawk leader Hendrick Theyanoguin declared the Covenant Chain binding his people to the English broken. When news of the Iroquois breakdown and the French buildup reached London, the Board of Trade directed the colonies to assemble in conference and bury the hatchet.

This engraving, labeled "The brave old Hendrick, the Great Sachem or Chief of the Mohawk Indians...now in Alliance with & Subject to the King of Great Britain," was sold in London in late 1755, just after the war chief Hendrick Theyanoguin died fighting for the British at the Battle of Lake George. Though he holds a hatchet and a wampum belt, Hendrick wears a fine English-style coat edged with gold braid, and elegant ruffled linens. This costume matches the finery Alexander Hamilton described when he saw Hendrick parade through the streets of Boston a decade before. (See Chapter 4)

Albany Congress

In response to the board's instructions, twenty-five delegates from the seven northern and middle colonies and more than two hundred Indians from the Six Nations of the Iroquois Confederacy gathered in Albany, New York, in June 1754. The colonists sought to forge a stronger alliance with the Iroquois and to coordinate plans for intercolonial defense. They failed on both counts. Hendrick's Mohawks renewed their support for the British, but the rest of the Iroquois nations reaffirmed their neutrality policy. The colonists, too, remained divided. Connecticut land speculators battled the Pennsylvania proprietors; New England commissioners refused funds to defend western New York; New York's delegates fought even among themselves.

Before they dispersed in July, the Congress endorsed the Plan of Union crafted by Pennsylvania's Benjamin Franklin. The plan proposed the creation of an elected intercolonial legislature with the power to tax and outlined strategies for a common defense. It met with quick and universal rejection in the provincial legislatures, which wanted to safeguard their autonomy more than their citizens.

While the Albany Congress deliberated, the war had already begun. In the fall of 1753, Governor Robert Dinwiddie of Virginia had dispatched a small militia troop to build a palisade at the forks of the Ohio River. Reinforcements quickly followed. When a substantial French force arrived the following April, the Virginia militia surrendered. The French then constructed Fort Duquesne. Learning of the confrontation, the inexperienced young major who commanded more Virginia reinforcements

Benjamin Franklin published this cartoon, labeled "Join, or Die," in his newspaper, The Pennsylvania Gazette, in May 1754. The woodcut depicts the British provinces from South Carolina to New England as segments of a snake that had perished because of its violent division. The cartoon promoted Franklin's Plan of Union, which would have created an intercolonial legislature. Though the Albany Congress endorsed the plan, it was roundly rejected by the legislatures of those colonies that considered it.

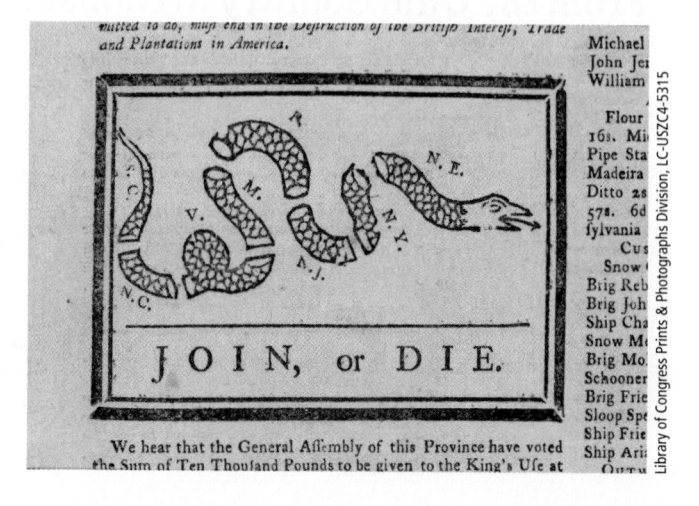

soon engaged a French detachment. Hoping to start a war that would force the British to defend the Ohio Country against the French, Tanaghrisson, the leader of the major's Ohio Indian scouts, murdered the French commander. Pursuing French troops then trapped the Virginians and their Indian allies in the crudely built Fort Necessity at Great Meadows, Pennsylvania. After a day-long battle during which more than one-third of his men were killed or wounded, twenty-two-year-old Major George Washington surrendered on July 3, 1754.

Seven Years' War

Tanaghrisson's attack, and Washington's blunder, ignited what became the first global war—a testament to the increasing centrality of North America in European nations' struggles for dominance. The fighting at the forks of the Ohio helped to reinvigorate a conflict between Austria and Prussia that sent European nations scrambling for allies. Eventually England, Hanover, and Prussia lined up against France, Austria, and Russia, joined by Sweden, Saxony, and, later, Spain.

Seven Years' War Major French-English conflict that was the first worldwide war.

The war began disastrously for the British. In July 1755, French and Indian warriors attacked Major General Edward Braddock's troops as they prepared for a renewed assault on Fort Duquesne. Braddock was killed and his forces decimated. Many Ohio Indians subsequently joined the French. Delaware warriors repeatedly attacked the Pennsylvania frontier for two more years. Settlers felt betrayed because the Indians attacking them had once been (one observer noted) "familiars at their houses [who] eat drank cursed and swore together were even intimate play mates."

Britain declared war on France in 1756, thus formally beginning the Seven Years' War. Even before then, Britons and New Englanders feared that France would try to retake Nova Scotia, where most of the population was descended from seventeenth-century French settlers who had intermarried with local M'ikmaqs. Afraid that the approximately twelve thousand settlers, known as Acadians, would abandon their posture of neutrality, British commanders in 1755 forced about seven thousand of them from their homeland—the first large-scale modern deportation, now called ethnic cleansing. Ships crammed with Acadians sailed to each mainland colony. Many families were separated, some forever. After 1763, the survivors relocated: some returned to Canada, others traveled to France or its Caribbean colonies. Many settled in Louisiana, where they became known as Cajuns (derived from *Acadian*).

British officers met with scant success coercing the colonies to supply men and materiel to the army. When William Pitt, the Member of Parliament placed in charge of the Crown's war effort in 1757, agreed to reimburse the colonies' wartime expenditures and placed recruitment in local hands, he gained greater American support. Even so, Virginia's burgesses appropriated more funds to defend against slave insurrections than to fight the French and Indians. Many colonial militiamen served, not always happily, alongside equally large numbers of red-coated regulars from Britain.

Eventually, Pitt's strategy turned the tide. In July 1758, British forces recaptured the fortress at Louisbourg, thus severing the major French supply artery down the St. Lawrence River. In the fall, the Delawares and Shawnees accepted British peace overtures, and the French abandoned Fort Duquesne. Then, in September 1759,

MAP 5.1

European Settlements and Indians, 1754

By 1754, Europeans had expanded the limits of the English colonies to the eastern slopes of the Appalachian Mountains. Few independent Indian nations still existed in the East, but beyond the mountains they controlled the countryside. Only a few widely scattered English and French forts maintained the Europeans' presence there. Source: Copyright © Cengage Learning 2015

MAP 5.2
European Claims in North America
The dramatic results of the British victory in the Seven Years' (French and Indian) War are vividly demonstrated in these maps, which depict the abandonment of French claims to the mainland after the Treaty of Paris in 1763. Source: Copyright © Cengage Learning 2015

General James Wolfe's forces defeated the French and took Quebec. A year later, the British captured Montreal, and the American phase of the war ended.

In the **Treaty of Paris** (1763), France surrendered to Britain its major North American holdings (excepting New Orleans), as well as several Caribbean islands, its slave-trading posts in Senegambia, and all of its possessions in India. Spain, an ally of France toward war's end, gave Florida to the victors. France ceded Louisiana west of the Mississippi to Spain, in partial compensation for its ally's losses elsewhere (see Map 5.2).

Treaty of Paris Treaty by which France ceded most of its holdings to Great Britain and some smaller amounts to Spain.

1763: A Turning Point

Indigenous peoples of the interior first felt the impact of Britain's victory. After Britain gained the upper hand in the American theater of war in 1758, the Creeks and Cherokees lost their ability to force concessions by threatening to turn to France or Spain. In desperation, and in retaliation for British atrocities, Cherokees attacked the Carolina and Virginia frontiers in 1760. Though initially victorious, the Indians were defeated the following year. Late in 1761, a treaty allowed the construction of British forts in their territories and opened a large tract to European settlement.

How did colonists' ideas about government differ from those of the British in the 1760s?

Neolin and Pontiac

In the Ohio Country, the Ottawas, Chippewas, and Potawatomis reacted angrily when Great Britain, no longer facing French competition, raised prices on trade goods and ended traditional gift-giving practices. As settlers surged into the Monongahela and Susquehanna valleys, a shaman named Neolin (also known as the Delaware Prophet) urged Indians to oppose European incursions on their lands and cultures. Contending that Indians were destroying themselves through dependence on European goods (especially alcohol), Neolin advocated resistance, both peaceful and armed. If all Indians west of the mountains united against the invaders, he declared, the Master of Life would once again look kindly upon his people. Ironically, Neolin's reference to a single Master of Life bore traces of his people's encounter with European Christianity.

Heeding Neolin's call in spring 1763, the Ottawa war chief Pontiac forged an unprecedented alliance among Hurons, Chippewas, Potawatomis, Delawares, Shawnees, and Mingoes (Pennsylvania Iroquois). Pontiac's forces besieged Fort Detroit while war parties attacked other British outposts in the Great Lakes. Detroit withstood the siege, but by late June the other forts west of Niagara and north of Fort Pitt (the renamed Fort Duquesne) had fallen to Pontiac's alliance. Indians raided the Virginia and Pennsylvania frontiers throughout the summer, killing at least two thousand settlers. Still, they could not take Niagara, Fort Pitt, or Detroit. In early August, colonial militiamen soundly defeated a combined Indian force at Bushy Run, Pennsylvania. Pontiac broke off the siege of Detroit in late October, and a treaty ending the war was finally negotiated three years later.

For nearly eighty years, European settlers and Indians who lived in "Penn's Woods" had avoided major conflicts. But the Indian attacks and the settlers' responses—especially the massacre of several families of defenseless Conestoga Indians in December 1763 by Scots-Irish vigilantes known as the Paxton Boys—revealed that violence in the region would become endemic.

Proclamation of 1763

London officials had no experience managing an area as vast as the territory Britain acquired from France, which included French settlers along the St. Lawrence, many Indian communities, and growing numbers of settlers and speculators. In October, George III's ministry issued the **Proclamation of 1763**, which designated the headwaters of rivers flowing into the Atlantic from the Appalachians as the western boundary for colonial settlement (see Map 5.1). Its promulgators expected the proclamation line to prevent clashes by forbidding colonists to move onto Indian lands. Instead, it infuriated land speculators and settlers who had already squatted west of the line.

After 1763, the speculators (who included George Washington, Thomas Jefferson, Patrick Henry, and Benjamin Franklin) lobbied vigorously to have their claims validated by colonial governments and London administrators. At a treaty conference in 1768 at Fort Stanwix, New York, they negotiated with Iroquois representatives to push the boundary line farther west and south. Still claiming to speak for the Delawares and the Shawnees, the Iroquois agreed to the deal, which brought them valuable trade goods and did not affect their own territories. Yet even though the Virginia land companies eventually gained the

Proclamation of 1763
England's attempt to end Indian problems by preventing westward movement by colonists.

support of the House of Burgesses, they never made any headway in London because administrators worried that western expansion would require funds they did not have.

George III

The British national debt doubled during the Seven Years' War, to £137 million. Financing Britain's war debt—and defending newly acquired territories—bedeviled King George III, who succeeded his grandfather, George II, in 1760. During the crucial years between 1763 and 1770, when the rift with the colonies widened, the king replaced cabinet ministers rapidly. Although determined to assert the power of the monarchy, George III stubbornly regarded adherence to the status quo as the hallmark of patriotism.

Selected as prime minister in 1763, George Grenville had to find new sources of funds, and the British people were already heavily taxed. Because the colonists had benefited greatly from wartime outlays, Grenville concluded, Anglo-Americans should shoulder a larger share of the empire's costs.

Theories of Representation

Americans believed they could be represented only by men who lived nearby and for whom they or their property-holding neighbors actually voted. Grenville and his English contemporaries, by contrast, believed that Parliament—king, lords, and commons acting together—represented all British subjects, wherever they resided and whether or not they could vote. In Parliament, the particular constituency that chose a member of the House of Commons had no special claim on that member's vote, nor did the member have to live near his constituents. According to this theory, called *virtual representation*, all Britons—including colonists—were represented in Parliament. Their consent to its laws could thus be presumed.

In the colonies, however, members of the lower houses of the assemblies were viewed as *actually* representing the regions that elected them. Voters cast their ballots for those they believed would advance the particular interests of a given district and province. Events of the 1760s revealed the incompatibility of these two understandings of representation.

Real Whigs

The colonists had grown accustomed to a faraway central government. They believed a good government was one that largely left them alone, a view in keeping with the theories of British writers known as the Real Whigs or Commonwealth thinkers. Drawing on a tradition of dissent that reached back to the English Civil War, the Real Whigs stressed the dangers inherent in a powerful government, particularly a monarchy. Some even favored republicanism, which proposed to eliminate monarchs and vest political power more directly in the people. Real Whig writers warned people to guard constantly against government's attempts to encroach on their liberty and seize their property.

As Britain tightened the reins in the 1760s and early 1770s, many Americans saw parallels in their circumstances and Real Whig ideology. Excessive and unjust taxation, they believed, could destroy their freedoms.

Sugar Act Act passed by British Parliament that sought to raise revenues by taxing colonial imports, notably the sugar trade.

Sugar and Currency Acts

In 1764, Parliament passed the **Sugar Act** and Currency Act. The Sugar Act (also known as the Revenue Act) revised existing customs regulations and laid new duties on some imports into the colonies. Influential Caribbean sugar planters lobbied for the act, which protected their commerce by preventing mainland rum distillers from smuggling molasses from the French islands. The act also established a vice-admiralty court at Halifax, Nova Scotia, to adjudicate violations of the law. Unlike the Navigation Acts, which the colonies considered legitimate, the Sugar Act was explicitly designed to raise revenue, not to channel American trade through Britain. The Currency Act outlawed most colonial paper money, because British merchants had complained that Americans paid their debts in inflated local currencies.

The Sugar Act and Currency Act were imposed on an already depressed economy. A business boom accompanied the Seven Years' War, but prosperity ended in 1760, when the fighting moved overseas. Urban merchants found fewer buyers for imported goods, and the loss of military demand for foodstuffs hurt American farmers. The bottom dropped out of the European tobacco market, threatening the livelihood of Chesapeake planters. Thus, the prospect of increased import duties and inadequate currency panicked merchants.

Without precedent for a campaign against acts of Parliament, eight colonial legislatures in 1764 sent separate petitions to Parliament requesting the Sugar Act's repeal. They argued that its commercial restrictions would hurt Britain as well as the colonies and that they had not consented to its passage. The protests had no effect.

The Stamp Act Crisis

How did James Otis and Patrick Henry offer different ways to address the Stamp Act crisis?

Stamp Act Obliged colonists to purchase and use special stamped (watermarked) paper for newspapers, customs documents, various licenses, college diplomas, and legal forms used for recovering debts, buying land, and making wills.

The **Stamp Act** (1765), Grenville's most important proposal, required tax stamps on most printed materials, placing the heaviest burden on members of the colonial elite, who used printed matter more intensively than did ordinary folk. Anyone who purchased a newspaper, made a will, transferred land, earned a diploma, bought dice or playing cards, applied for a license, accepted a government post, or took a loan would have to buy a stamp. It also required that scarce sterling coin be used to purchase tax stamps. The act broke with the colonial tradition of self-imposed taxation. Violators would be tried by vice-admiralty courts, in which judges alone rendered decisions, leading Americans to fear the loss of their right to trial by jury. And since the revenues would pay for British peacekeepers in North America, the tax also mobilized long-established fears of a standing army.

James Otis's *Rights of the British Colonies*

The most important colonial pamphlet protesting the Sugar Act and the proposed Stamp Act was *The Rights of the British Colonies Asserted and Proved*, by James Otis Jr., a brilliant young Massachusetts attorney. Otis exposed the dilemma that confounded the colonists for the next decade. How could they oppose certain acts of Parliament without questioning Parliament's authority over

them? Colonists, he asserted, were "entitled to all the natural, essential, inherent, and inseparable rights" of Britons, including the right not to be taxed without their consent. But Otis also accepted the prevailing theory of British government: Parliament was the supreme authority in the empire. Even its wrongheaded laws had to be obeyed until repealed. To resolve the dilemma, Otis proposed colonial representation in Parliament, an idea that was never taken seriously on either side of the Atlantic.

Like many Enlightenment thinkers, Otis reasoned from natural rights. But like very few writers at the time, he extended this natural rights logic to the enslaved. "The Colonists are by the law of nature free born, as indeed are all men, white or black," he wrote. It was common, in the 1760s, for colonists to protest that Britain's tyranny enslaved them. To receive the stamps "is Death—is worse than Death—it is slavery!" said Pennsylvania's John Dickinson. James Otis went further, warning "It is a clear truth, that those who every day barter away other mens liberty, will soon care little for their own." Slowly, the era's talk of liberty would begin to erode the intellectual foundations of human bondage.

Otis published his pamphlet before the Stamp Act was passed. When Americans first learned of the act's adoption in the spring of 1765, they reacted indecisively. Few colonists publicly favored the law, but colonial petitions had failed to prevent its adoption. Perhaps Otis was correct: Americans had to pay the tax, reluctantly but loyally.

Patrick Henry and the Virginia Stamp Act Resolves

Patrick Henry, a young Virginia attorney serving his first term in the House of Burgesses, was appalled by his fellow legislators' complacency. Near the end of the legislative session, when many burgesses had already departed, Henry introduced seven proposals against the Stamp Act. The few burgesses remaining adopted five of Henry's resolutions by a bare majority. But some colonial newspapers printed Henry's original resolutions as if the House had passed them all, even though one was rescinded and two others were never debated or voted on.

Link to Patrick Henry, Resolutions Against the Stamp Act (1765)

The four propositions adopted by the burgesses echoed Otis's arguments about taxation, asserting that colonists had never forfeited the rights of British subjects. The other three resolutions went much further. The repealed resolution claimed for the burgesses "the only exclusive right" to tax Virginians, and the two never considered asserted that Virginians need not obey tax laws passed by other legislative bodies—namely, Parliament.

Continuing Loyalty to Britain

Though willing to fight for their liberties as Britons within the empire, the colonists did not seek independence. Over the next decade, colonial leaders searched for a formula that would let them control their internal affairs, especially taxation, while remaining under British rule. But the British theory of government insisted that Parliament held absolute authority over all colonial possessions. In effect, the American rebels wanted British leaders to revise their fundamental understanding of how government worked. That was simply too much to expect.

The effectiveness of Americans' opposition to the Stamp Act rested on more than ideological arguments over parliamentary power. The battle was waged on the streets as well as on the page.

Anti–Stamp Act Demonstrations

In August, the Loyal Nine, a Boston artisans' social club, organized a protest against the Stamp Act. Hoping to show that people of all ranks opposed the act, they convinced rival labor associations, composed of workers and poor tradesmen, to lay aside their differences for the demonstration.

On August 14, the demonstrators hung an effigy of Andrew Oliver, the province's stamp distributor, from a tree on Boston Common. That night a large crowd led by a group of about fifty well-dressed tradesmen paraded the effigy around the city. Demonstrators then built a bonfire near Oliver's house and fed the effigy to the flames. They broke most of Oliver's windows and threw stones at officials. The Loyal Nine achieved success when Oliver publicly renounced the duties of his office. One Bostonian jubilantly wrote, "I believe people never was more Universally pleased."

Twelve days later, another crowd action—aimed this time at Oliver's brother-in-law, Lieutenant Governor Thomas Hutchinson—drew no praise from Boston's respectable citizens. On the night of August 26, a mob destroyed Hutchinson's elegant townhouse. The lieutenant governor reported that by the next morning, nothing was left of his mansion "but the bare walls and floors."

> Link to Thomas Hutchinson Recounts the Reaction to the Stamp Act in Boston (1765)

Americans' Divergent Interests

The differences between the two Boston mobs of August 1765 exposed divisions that would characterize subsequent protests. Skilled craftsmen as well as merchants, lawyers, and other educated elites preferred orderly demonstrations centered on political issues. For the city's laborers, economic grievances were paramount. Certainly, their "hellish Fury" as they wrecked Hutchinson's house suggests resentment of his ostentatious display of wealth.

The Stamp Act controversy for the first time drew ordinary folk into transatlantic politics. Matters that previously had been of concern only to an elite few were now discussed in every tavern and coffeehouse. Anti–Stamp Act demonstrations took place from Nova Scotia to the West Indies (see Map 5.3).

But though the act placed the heaviest tax burden on the Caribbean colonies—levying double or triple duty on large island land transfers, for example—protests there were notably tepid. On the largest, most populous, and richest islands—Jamaica and Barbados—planters complied with the tax. Since the wealthiest sugar barons were sojourners more than settlers, they had strong personal ties to Britain. They also depended on mercantilist legislation to favor their sugar exports. Finally, they relied upon British military might to protect them from their enslaved workforces. Over three-quarters of the revenues collected during the Stamp Act's brief life came from the West Indies.

On the mainland, street protests were so successful that by November 1, when the law was scheduled to take effect, not one stamp distributor on the mainland

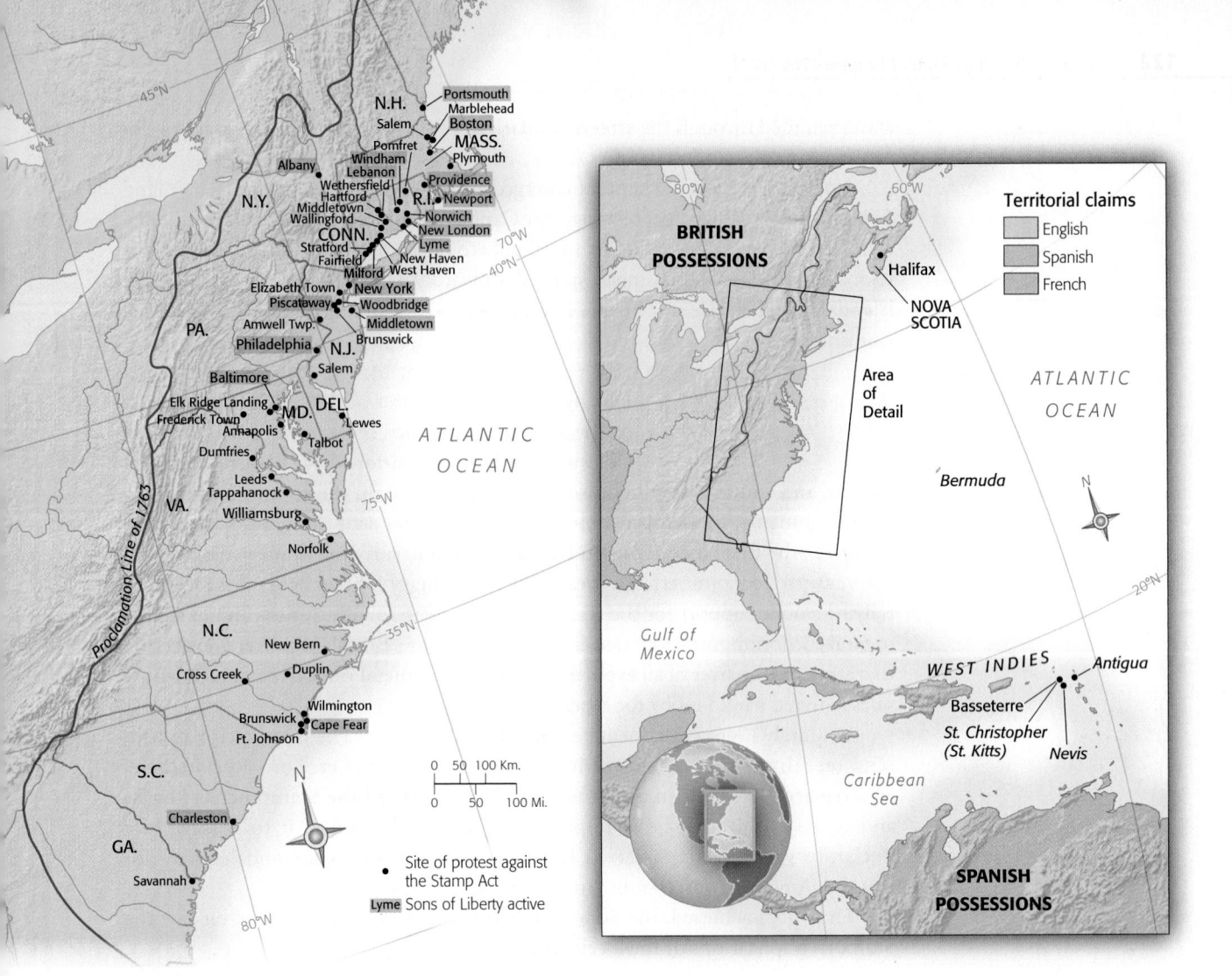

MAP 5.3

Colonial Resistance to the Stamp Act

All of the towns and islands labeled on this map witnessed crowd actions protesting the Stamp Act of 1765; British colonies outside the eventual United States joined in the nearly universal opposition to the hated measure. Source: Copyright © Cengage Learning 2015

was willing to enforce the act. Yet wealthy men recognized that mobs composed of the formerly powerless could endanger their dominance of society.

Sons of Liberty

Elites attempted to channel resistance into acceptable forms by creating an intercolonial association, the **Sons of Liberty**. Composed of merchants, lawyers, prosperous tradesmen, and tavern owners, the Sons of Liberty by early 1766 linked protest leaders from Charleston, South Carolina, to Portsmouth, New Hampshire.

The Sons of Liberty could influence events but not control them. In Charleston (formerly Charles Town) in October 1765, a crowd shouting, "Liberty Liberty and stamp'd paper" forced the resignation of the South Carolina stamp distributor. But the Charleston Sons of Liberty were horrified when in January 1766 local

Sons of Liberty Groups formed to resist the Stamp Act.

slaves paraded through the streets similarly crying, "Liberty!" The language of liberty could easily slip its channels.

No Sons of Liberty chapters emerged in the West Indies. Indeed, mainland Sons groups organized protests against Caribbean colonists as well as British officials. The *Boston Gazette* called on merchants to boycott "the SLAVISH Islands of Barbados and Antigua—Poor, mean spirited, Cowardly, Dastardly Creoles." The sugar islands should receive no "Fresh or Salt Provisions from any Son of liberty on the Continent."

Opposition and Repeal   During the fall and winter of 1765–1766, opponents of the Stamp Act pursued several different strategies. Colonial legislatures petitioned Parliament to repeal the law, and courts closed because they could not obtain the stamps required for legal documents. In October, nine mainland colonies sent delegates to a general congress—the first since 1754—in New York to draft a remonstrance stressing the law's adverse economic effects. Meanwhile, the Sons of Liberty held mass meetings, rallying public support for the resistance movement. Finally, American merchants organized nonimportation associations to pressure British exporters, expecting that since one-quarter of all exports went to the colonies, London merchants whose sales suffered would lobby for repeal.

In March 1766, Parliament repealed the Stamp Act. The main factor in winning repeal was the appointment of a new prime minister. Lord Rockingham, who replaced Grenville in the summer of 1765, opposed the Stamp Act as unwise and divisive. Although he championed repeal, he also linked it to passage of a **Declaratory Act**, which asserted Parliament's authority to tax and legislate for Britain's American possessions "in all cases whatsoever."

Declaratory Act Affirmed parliamentary power to legislate its colonies "in all cases whatsoever."

Their goal achieved, the Sons of Liberty dissolved. Few colonists yet saw the ominous implications of the Declaratory Act.

Resistance to the Townshend Acts

How did the American population become politicized in the late 1760s?

In summer 1766, another change in the ministry in London revealed how fragile the colonists' victory had been. The new prime minister, William Pitt, had fostered cooperation between the colonies and Britain during the Seven Years' War. But Pitt fell ill, and Charles Townshend became the dominant force in the ministry. An ally of Grenville, Townshend renewed efforts to obtain badly needed funds from Britain's American possessions (see Table 5.1).

The duties Townshend proposed in 1767 seemed to extend the Navigation Acts by focusing on trade goods like paper, glass, and tea. But they differed, first by applying to British imports, not to those from foreign countries. Second, the revenues would pay some colonial officials, thereby eliminating assemblies' ability to threaten to withhold salaries from uncooperative officials. Additionally, Townshend's scheme established an American Board of Customs Commissioners and created vice-admiralty courts at Boston, Philadelphia, and Charleston. Both moves angered merchants, whose profits would be threatened by more vigorous enforcement of the Navigation Acts. Significantly, Townshend exempted the West Indies

Links TO THE WORLD

Writing and Stationery Supplies

In the seventeenth century, colonists stressed the importance of teaching children to read the Bible; writing was not seen as nearly so necessary. Yet as the eighteenth century progressed, and especially during the era of the American Revolution, writing skills acquired new significance. Family members parted by the war needed to communicate with each other, and new opportunities arose for merchants who could deal with distant correspondents.

Writing drew on a wide range of items from around the world. Paper was either imported from Britain or manufactured at an increasing number of American paper mills. The quill pens (goose feathers) that Americans used as writing implements often originated in Germany or Holland. Penknives, needed to sharpen blunt quills, and inkpots (made of brass, glass, or pewter, among other materials), also largely came from Britain. But the Americans could not write readily without additional items obtained from international trade.

For example, to absorb ink properly, paper needed to be treated with pounce, a powder made from a combination of gum sandarac (a tree resin from North Africa) and pumice, a powdered volcanic glass. Lacking envelopes, eighteenth-century writers folded their sheets of paper, addressed them on the outside, and sealed them with wax made in Holland or Britain from a combination of lac (a resinous secretion of insects, still used today for shellac) from India and cinnabar, a red quartz-like crystal, from Spain. Ink was manufactured from oak galls from Aleppo (in Syria), gum arabic (sap from acacia trees) from Sudan, and alum and copperas (derived from different stones) from Britain. Most ink was shipped from Britain in powdered form; in America, another key ingredient, urine, would be added to cause the alum to blend properly with the other substances to create the liquid ink.

When colonial elites drafted petitions against the Stamp Act, the implements they employed connected them to a long commercial chain stretching to Great Britain, the European continent, North Africa, and the Middle East.

Desk and Bookcase, c.1762 (mahogany, white cedar, yellow poplar, yellow pine, silvered glass & gilded brass), American School, (18th century) / Philadelphia Museum of Art, Pennsylvania, PA, USA / Purchased with the Mr. and Mrs. Walter H. Annenberg Fund for Major Acquisitions, and with supporting funds from the Henry P. McIlhenny Fund in memory of Frances P. McIlhenny, funds contributed by H. Richard Dietrich, Jr., and other private donors / The Bridgeman Art Library

This writing desk, made in Pennsylvania in the mid-to-late eighteenth century, would have been owned by a well-to-do family from the mid-Atlantic states. The pigeonholes would hold incoming and outgoing letters; the many drawers could store paper, ink, seals and sealing wax, and other supplies. The new importance of writing thus produced a perceived need for novel types of furniture.

TABLE 5.1 British Ministries and Their American Policies

Head of Ministry	Major Acts
George Grenville	Sugar Act (1764)
	Currency Act (1764)
	Stamp Act (1765)
Lord Rockingham	Stamp Act repealed (1766)
	Declaratory Act (1766)
William Pitt/ Charles Townshend	Townshend Acts (1767)
Lord North	Townshend duties (except for the tea tax) repealed (1770)
	Tea Act (1773)
	Coercive Acts (1774)
	Quebec Act (1774)

from key provisions of the new duties, a divide-and-conquer tactic revealing that Parliament had learned from the Stamp Act protests.

John Dickinson's Letters

Passage of the Townshend Acts drew a quick response from the colonies. One series of widely published essays in particular, *Letters from a Farmer in Pennsylvania*, by the prominent lawyer John Dickinson, expressed a broad consensus. Dickinson contended that Parliament could regulate colonial trade but could not raise revenue. By distinguishing between regulation and taxation, Dickinson avoided the sticky issue of the colonies' relationship to Parliament.

The Massachusetts assembly responded to the Townshend Acts by drafting a letter to the other colonial legislatures, suggesting a joint protest petition. When Lord Hillsborough, recently named to the new post of secretary of state for America, learned of the Massachusetts circular letter, he ordered the colony's governor, Francis Bernard, to demand that the assembly recall it. He also directed other governors to prevent their assemblies from discussing it. Hillsborough's order motivated colonial assemblies to unite against this new threat to their prerogatives. In late 1768, the Massachusetts legislature resoundingly rejected Bernard's recall order. Bernard dissolved the assembly, and other governors similarly responded.

Rituals of Resistance

The number of votes cast against recalling the circular letter—92—assumed ritual significance in the resistance movement. The number 45 already had symbolic meaning because **John Wilkes**, a radical Londoner sympathetic to the American cause, had been jailed for publishing a pamphlet entitled *The North Briton*, No. 45. In Boston, the silversmith Paul Revere made a punchbowl weighing 45 ounces that held 45 gills (half-cups) and was engraved with the names of the "glorious 92" opposition legislators; James Otis, John Adams, and others publicly drank 45 toasts from it.

John Wilkes British opponent of King George III who became a hero to American colonists.

Such public rituals familiarized common people with the terms of the argument. For example, when the Charleston Sons of Liberty held their meetings in public, crowds gathered to watch and listen. Songs supporting the American cause also helped to spread the word. American leaders urged colonists of all ranks and both sexes to sign agreements not to purchase or consume British products. The consumer revolution that had previously linked colonists culturally and economically now supplied them with a ready method of displaying their allegiance.

Daughters of Liberty

As the primary purchasers of textiles and household goods, women played a central role in the nonconsumption movement. More than three hundred Boston matrons publicly promised not to buy or drink tea, "Sickness excepted." The women of Wilmington, North Carolina, burned their tea after walking through town in a solemn procession. Women exchanged recipes for tea substitutes or drank coffee instead. The best known of the protests, the so-called Edenton Ladies Tea Party, was actually a meeting of prominent North Carolina women who pledged to work for the public good and to support resistance to British measures.

In many towns, young women calling themselves Daughters of Liberty met to spin in public squares to encourage colonists to end the colonies' dependence on British cloth by wearing homespun. These patriotic displays served the same purpose as the male rituals involving the numbers 45 and 92. When young ladies from well-to-do families sat outdoors at spinning wheels all day, eating only American food, drinking local herbal tea, and listening to patriotic sermons, they served as political instructors.

Divided Opinion Over Boycotts

The Stamp Act boycotts had helped revive a depressed economy by creating a demand for local products and reducing merchants' inventories. But by 1768 and 1769, merchants were again enjoying boom times and had no incentive to support boycotts. In contrast, artisans, who recognized that the absence of British goods would increase demand for their own manufactures, formed the core of the crowds that picketed importers' stores, publicized offending merchants' names, and sometimes destroyed property.

Such tactics were effective: colonial imports from England dropped dramatically in 1769. But the tactics also aroused heated opposition. Even some Americans who supported resistance to British measures questioned the use of violence to enforce the boycott. The threat to private property inherent in the campaign frightened wealthier and more conservative men and women.

Colonists were relieved when news arrived in April 1770 that the Townshend duties had been repealed, except for the tea tax. A new prime minister, Lord North, persuaded Parliament that duties on trade within the empire were ill advised. The other Townshend Acts remained in force, but repealing the duties made the provisions for paying officials' salaries and tightening customs enforcement appear less objectionable.

Visualizing THE PAST

Phillis Wheatley, Enslaved Poet in the Cradle of Liberty

In July 1761, the *Phillis* docked at Boston's Long Wharf after a long voyage during which nearly a quarter of its human cargo died. The captain placed an advertisement in the papers hawking "prime young slaves, from the Windward Coast." One of the least valuable among them was a little girl still missing her two front teeth. A merchant named John Wheatley purchased her as a gift for his wife, naming the child after the boat that brought her from Africa.

Phillis Wheatley grew up in a genteel house on King Street. The Wheatleys, influenced by the ideas of the Great Awakening, recognized her talents and educated her beyond the station of nearly all slaves and, indeed, of most white girls and women. She began to write

poetry. In 1770, her elegy on the death of George Whitefield made her famous in evangelical circles on both sides of the Atlantic. In 1773, a volume of her poems was published in London.

Wheatley's *Poems on Various Subjects* included an "elegant engraved likeness of the Author." Printed in an era when books seldom featured portraits of female authors and almost never bore the likenesses of people of African descent, Wheatley's image—probably based on a painting by the black Boston artist Scipio Moorhead—is a striking exception. What attributes does the portrait give the poet? How do the title page and the frontispiece represent her race, age, gender, and genius?

Wheatley frontispiece

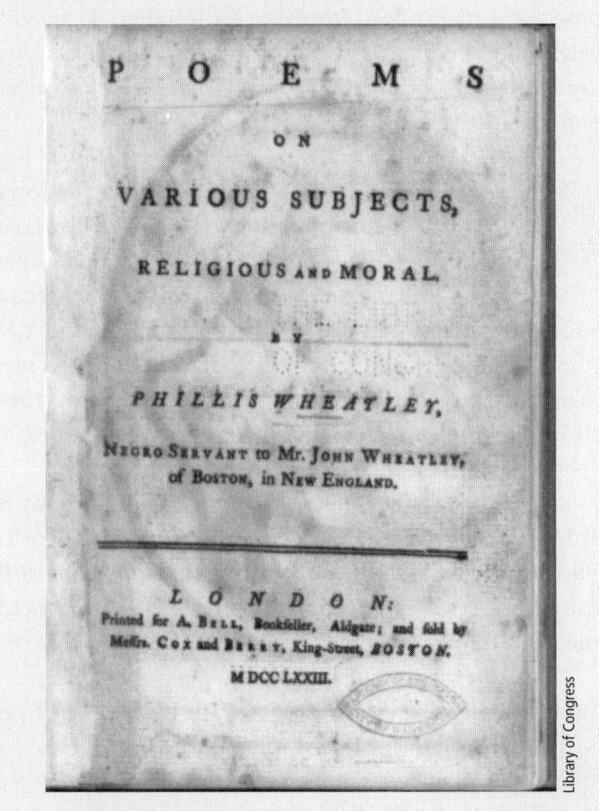

Wheatley title page

Library of Congress

Library of Congress

Confrontations in Boston

The decision to base the American Board of Customs Commissioners in Boston helped lead to the confrontation that patriots labeled the "**Boston Massacre**." Mobs targeted the customs officials from the day they arrived in November 1767. In June 1768, their seizure of the patriot leader John Hancock's sloop *Liberty* on suspicion of smuggling caused a riot. The ministry sent troops to maintain order. That October, two regiments of British regulars—about 700 men—marched up Long Wharf toward the Common. They served as constant visible reminders of the oppressive potential of British power. Patrols roamed the streets at all hours. Parents feared for the safety of their daughters, whom soldiers subjected to coarse sexual insults. Additionally, many redcoats sought employment in their off-duty hours, competing for unskilled jobs with the city's workingmen. The two groups brawled repeatedly in taverns and on the streets.

How did Samuel Adams's Committees of Correspondence mark a turning point in Americans' political thinking?

Boston Massacre Confrontation between colonists and British troops in which five colonists where shot and killed.

Boston Massacre

On the evening of March 5, 1770, a crowd of laborers threw hard-packed snowballs at troops guarding the Customs House. Against orders, the sentries fired on the crowd, killing four and wounding eight, one of whom died a few days later. Reportedly, the first to fall was Crispus Attucks, a sailor of mixed Nipmuck and African ancestry. Rebel leaders idealized Attucks and the other dead rioters as martyrs for liberty, holding a solemn funeral and later commemorating March 5 with patriotic orations.

Link to a description of the Boston Massacre from the *Boston Gazette* (March 12, 1770)

Despite the political benefits the patriots derived from the massacre, they probably did not approve of the crowd action that provoked it. Since the destruction of Hutchinson's house in August 1765, the Sons of Liberty had expressed distaste at uncontrolled riots. When the soldiers were tried for the killings, John Adams and Josiah Quincy Jr., both unwavering patriots, acted as their defense attorneys. Almost all the accused were acquitted, and the two men convicted were released after being branded on the thumb.

A British Plot?

The favorable outcome of the soldiers' trials persuaded London officials not to retaliate against Boston, and for more than two years after the massacre, the imperial crisis seemed to quiet. But the most outspoken newspapers, including the *Boston Gazette*, the *Pennsylvania Journal*, and the *South Carolina Gazette*, continued to publish essays pointing to the stationing of troops in Boston and the growing number of vice-admiralty courts as evidence of plans to enslave the colonists. Indeed, patriot writers played repeatedly on the word *enslavement*—though they rarely questioned the institution of slavery, as James Otis had in 1764. And none of them yet advocated American independence.

In fall 1772, the North ministry began to implement the Townshend Act that paid governors and judges from customs revenues. In early November, voters at a Boston town meeting established a **Committee of Correspondence** to publicize the decision by exchanging letters with other Massachusetts towns. Heading the committee was Samuel Adams.

Committee of Correspondence Local committees established throughout colonies to coordinate anti-British actions.

Shortly after the Boston Massacre, Paul Revere engraved this illustration of the confrontation near the Customs House on March 5, 1770. Offering visual support for the patriots' version of events, Revere depicted British soldiers firing on an unresisting crowd (instead of the aggressive mob described at the soldiers' trial) and—even worse—a gun firing from the building itself, which has been labeled "Butcher's Hall."

Samuel Adams and Committees of Correspondence

Aged fifty-one in 1772, Samuel Adams was about a decade older than other American resistance leaders, including his distant cousin John. He had been a Boston tax collector, a clerk of the Massachusetts assembly, and one of the Sons of Liberty. His Committee of Correspondence sought to create an informed consensus among the residents of Massachusetts. Such committees, which were eventually established throughout the colonies, broadened the protest movement beyond the seacoast and major cities and towns (see Map 5.3).

The statement prepared by the Boston Committee declared, "All persons born in the British American Colonies" had natural rights to life, liberty, and property. Grievances included taxation without representation, the increased presence of troops and customs officers on American soil, the expanded jurisdiction of vice-admiralty courts, and the nature of the instructions given to American governors by their superiors in London. No longer did resistance leaders—at least in Boston—mention the necessity of obedience to Parliament. They placed colonial rights first, loyalty to Britain a distant second.

Tea and Turmoil

How did the Tea Act push the colonies to the brink of revolution?

The tea tax was the only Townshend duty still in effect by 1773. After 1770, some Americans had continued to boycott English tea; others resumed drinking it. Tea figured prominently in the colonists' diet and their cultures, so the boycott meant forgoing a favorite beverage and altering everyday rituals.

Reactions to the Tea Act

In May 1773, Parliament passed the **Tea Act** to save the East India Company from bankruptcy. The company held a monopoly on British trade with the East Indies and was vital to the British economy. According to the Tea Act, only the East India Company's agents could sell tea in America. This enabled the company to avoid intermediaries and to price its tea competitively with that sold by smugglers. The net result would be cheaper tea for American consumers. Resistance leaders, however, interpreted the measure as designed to make them admit Parliament's right to tax them. Others saw the Tea Act as the first step in an East India Company monopoly on all colonial trade. Residents of the four cities designated to receive the first tea shipments prepared to respond to this perceived new threat to their freedom.

Tea Act England's attempt to bail out East India Company that heightened tensions between the British and the colonies.

A tea ship sent to New York City never arrived. In Philadelphia, Pennsylvania's governor persuaded the captain to return to Britain. Tea bound for Charleston was unloaded; some was destroyed, the rest sold in 1776 by the new state government.

The only confrontation occurred in Boston. The first of three tea ships, the *Dartmouth*, entered Boston harbor on November 28. Customs laws required cargo to be landed and duty paid within twenty days of a ship's arrival; otherwise, customs officers would seize the cargo. After several mass meetings, Bostonians voted to post guards on the wharf to prevent the tea from being unloaded. Governor Thomas Hutchinson refused to permit the three vessels to leave the harbor.

On December 16, one day before the cargo was to be confiscated, more than five thousand people crowded into Old South Church. The meeting, chaired by Samuel Adams, made a final attempt to convince Hutchinson to return the tea to England. But he refused. In the early evening Adams reportedly announced "that they had now done all they could for the Salvation of their Country." Cries rang out from the crowd: "Boston harbor a tea-pot tonight! The Mohawks are come!" Within a few minutes, about sixty men crudely disguised as Indians assembled at the wharf. They boarded the three ships and dumped their cargo into the harbor. By 9 PM, 342 chests of tea worth approximately £10,000 floated in splinters.

Coercive and Quebec Acts

The North administration reacted with outrage. In March 1774, Parliament adopted the first of four laws that colonists referred to as the **Coercive, or Intolerable, Acts**. It ordered the port of Boston closed until the tea was paid for, prohibiting all but coastal trade in food and firewood. Later that spring, Parliament passed three other punitive measures. The Massachusetts Government Act altered the province's charter, substituting an appointed council

Coercive, or Intolerable, Acts A series of restrictive laws comprised of the Boston Port Bill, the Massachusetts Government Act, the Justice Act, the Quartering Act, plus the unrelated Quebec Act. Intended by the British Parliament to primarily punish Massachusetts, the acts instead pushed most colonies to the brink of rebellion.

for the elected one, increasing the governor's powers, and forbidding most town meetings. The Justice Act allowed a person accused of committing murder while suppressing a riot or enforcing the laws to be tried outside the colony where the incident had occurred. Finally, the Quartering Act permitted military officers to commandeer privately owned buildings to house their troops.

Parliament then turned to reforming Quebec's government. The Quebec Act granted greater religious freedom to Catholics, alarming Protestant colonists who equated the Church of Rome with despotism. It also reinstated French civil law and established an appointed council (rather than an elected legislature). Finally, to protect northern Indians against Anglo-American settlement, the act annexed to Quebec the area west of the Appalachians, east of the Mississippi River, and north of the Ohio River—thereby removing the region from the jurisdiction of seacoast colonies. Wealthy speculators who hoped to develop the Ohio Country would now have to deal with officials in Quebec.

Resistance leaders saw the Coercive Acts and the Quebec Act as proof that Britain had embarked on a deliberate plan to oppress them. The Boston Committee of Correspondence urged all colonies to join an immediate boycott of British goods. But other provinces hesitated to take such a drastic step. In the British West Indies, even opponents of Parliament's evolving American policy thought the "Boston fire-brands" had gone too far and hoped the Coercive Acts might restore order. Rhode Island, Virginia, and Pennsylvania each suggested convening another intercolonial congress. Even the most ardent patriots remained loyal Britons and hoped for reconciliation. So the colonies agreed to send delegates to Philadelphia in September to attend a Continental Congress.

The Unsettled Backcountry

What internal struggles plagued the backcountry during the 1760s and 1770s?

In the same years that residents of British North America wrestled over deepening divisions between the colonies and the mother country, they contended over divisions *within* colonial society. Along the western edges of British settlement in the 1760s and 1770s, these internal struggles sometimes verged on civil war.

Land Riots in the North   By midcentury, with most fertile land east of the Appalachians purchased or occupied, conflicts over land escalated. The most serious land riots occurred along the Hudson River in 1765–1766. Late in the seventeenth century, the governor of New York had granted huge tracts in the lower Hudson Valley to prominent families. The proprietors in turn divided these estates into small farms, which they rented chiefly to poor Dutch and German migrants who regarded tenancy as a step toward independence. But in the eighteenth century, New Englanders and Europeans increasingly migrated to the region, resisting tenancy and often squatting. In the mid-1760s, the Philipse family sued farmers who had lived on Philipse land for two decades. The courts ordered squatters to make way for tenants with valid leases. Instead, farmers rebelled, terrorizing proprietors and tenants, and on one occasion battling a county sheriff and his posse. The rebellion lasted nearly a year, ending only when British troops captured its leaders.

"Regulators" in the South

The Regulator movements of the late 1760s (South Carolina) and early 1770s (North Carolina) pitted backcountry farmers against wealthy eastern planters who controlled the colonial governments. In South Carolina, Scots-Irish settlers protested their lack of an adequate voice in colonial political affairs. For months, they policed the countryside in vigilante bands known as Regulators, complaining of lax and biased law enforcement. North Carolina Regulators objected primarily to heavy taxation by the colonial legislature. In September 1770, they dragged a justice from the Rowan County Courthouse and then ransacked his house. The following May, several thousand Regulators fought and lost a battle with eastern militiamen at Alamance. A month later, six of the insurgents were hanged for treason.

Renewed Indian Warfare

In 1774, Virginia, headed by a new royally appointed governor, **Lord Dunmore**, asserted its title to the developing backcountry. Tensions mounted as Virginians surveyed land on the south side of the Ohio River—territory claimed by the Shawnees. In April, settlers attacked a Shawnee canoe carrying women and children as well as one man, murdering and scalping all nine. John Logan, a Mingo leader whose kin died in the attack, gathered warriors to retaliate against frontier settlements. When the governor dispatched some two thousand troops, these skirmishes escalated into a conflict known as **Lord Dunmore's War**. When the peace was finally settled in October, the Shawnee leader Cornstalk ceded the enormous territory that became the state of Kentucky to Dunmore's forces.

Lord Dunmore Royal governor of Virginia who promised freedom to slaves who fought to restore royal authority.

Lord Dunmore's War Confrontation between Virginians and the Shawnee Indians in 1774. During the peace conference that followed, Virginia gained uncontested rights to lands south of the Ohio country in exchange for its claims on the northern side.

Government by Congress and Committee

How did the First Continental Congress redefine America's relationship to England?

In the summer of 1774, while the Virginia backcountry bled and Boston suffered, fifty-six delegates from the mainland colonies readied for a "Grand **Continental Congress**" in Philadelphia. Because colonial governors had forbidden regular assemblies to conduct formal elections, most of the delegates had been chosen by extralegal conventions. The lawyer John Adams, one of four delegates from Massachusetts, anticipated that the Congress would serve as "a School of Political Prophets I Suppose—a Nursery of American Statesmen."

But what were American statesmen and what, indeed, was America? New England merchants and southern planters shared little common culture. So distinct were the interests of the British West Indies that those thirteen colonies sent no delegates at all—nor did Georgia. Even in the fall of 1774, as tavern talk throughout the colonies turned to the imminence of civil war, Great Britain remained the only nation the congressmen shared. They pledged their fealty to George III and pressed their claims not for American freedom but for "English liberty."

Continental Congress Group of representatives appointed by conventions in most of the North American colonies of Great Britain.

First Continental Congress

The colonies' leading political figures—mostly lawyers, merchants, and planters—attended the Philadelphia Congress. In addition to John Adams, the

Massachusetts delegation included his elder cousin Samuel Adams. Among others, New York sent John Jay, a talented young attorney. From Pennsylvania came the conservative Joseph Galloway and his longtime rival, John Dickinson. Virginia elected Richard Henry Lee, Patrick Henry, and George Washington.

The congressmen faced three tasks when they convened at Carpenters' Hall on September 5: defining American grievances, developing a resistance plan, and articulating their constitutional relationship with Great Britain. Radical congressmen, like Lee of Virginia, argued that colonists owed allegiance only to George III, not Parliament. The conservatives—Galloway and his allies—proposed a plan of union that would require Parliament and a new American legislature jointly to consent to laws governing the colonies. Delegates narrowly rejected Galloway's proposal, but they were not prepared to embrace the radicals' position either. Finally, they accepted wording proposed by John Adams. The crucial clauses in the Congress's Declaration of Rights and Grievances asserted that Americans would obey Parliament, but only voluntarily, and would resist all taxes in disguise.

Continental Association

The delegates agreed on the laws they wanted repealed (notably the Coercive Acts) and decided to implement an economic boycott while petitioning the king for relief. They adopted fourteen Articles of Association calling for nonimportation of British goods (effective December 1, 1774), nonconsumption of British products (effective March 1, 1775), and nonexportation of American goods to Britain and the British West Indies (effective September 10, 1775).

The Articles of Association (also known as the Continental Association) were designed to appeal to different groups and regions. The nonimportation agreement banned commerce in slaves as well as manufactures, which accorded with a long-standing desire of the Virginia gentry, whose members worried that slave importations discouraged skilled Europeans from immigrating. Delaying nonconsumption for three months after implementing nonimportation gave merchants time to sell items they acquired before December 1. In 1773, many Virginians had vowed to stop exporting tobacco in order to raise prices in a then-glutted market. So they welcomed an association that banned exportation while permitting them to profit from higher prices for their current crop. Postponing the nonexportation agreement also gave northern exporters of wood and foodstuffs to the Caribbean a final season of sales before the embargo.

West Indian grandees worried about the Articles of Association. Severing their supply lines from North America could bring famine, which could provoke widespread slave insurrection. The *Antigua Gazette* chided the mainland colonists for "their folly, madness, and ingratitude" in adopting the new resolutions.

Committees of Observation

To enforce the Continental Association, Congress recommended that every mainland locale elect committees of observation and inspection. By specifying that committee members be chosen by all men qualified to vote, Congress guaranteed the committees a broad popular base. The seven to eight thousand committeemen became local leaders of American resistance.

Legacy FOR A PEOPLE AND A NATION

Women's Political Activism

In the twenty-first century, female citizens of the United States participate at every level of American public life. Nancy Pelosi was elected Speaker of the House, third in line for the presidency, in January 2007; Hillary Rodham Clinton ran for president in 2008; Elena Kagan became the Supreme Court's third current female member in late 2010. The 2012 elections brought a record number of women to the 113th Congress: twenty sit in the Senate, and eighty-one in the House. Many women also serve as governors and in state offices. But before the 1760s, American women were seen as having no legitimate public role. A male essayist expressed the consensus in the mid-1730s: "Poli[ti]cks is what does not become them; the Governing Kingdoms and Ruling Provinces are Things too difficult and knotty for the fair Sex."

That changed when colonists resisted new British taxes and laws in the 1760s. Because women made household purchasing decisions, and because their labor in spinning and textile manufacture could replace imported clothing, it was vital for them to participate in the cause. For the first time in American history, women began to take formal political stands, deciding whether to boycott British goods. The groups they established to promote home manufactures—dubbed "Daughters of Liberty"—constituted the first American women's political organizations.

By the mid-nineteenth century, women's political involvement would begin to coalesce into a national "woman movement." In 1848, the leaders of a woman's rights convention at Seneca Falls, New York, drafted a Declaration of Sentiments, closely modeled on the language of the Declaration of Independence. The legacy of revolutionary-era women for the nation continues today in such groups as Emily's List and Concerned Women for America. Indeed, contemporary Americans would undoubtedly find it impossible to imagine their country without female activists of all affiliations.

Initially charged with overseeing implementation of the boycott, within six months these committees became de facto governments. They examined merchants' records, publicizing those who continued to import British goods. They promoted home manufactures and urged Americans to abandon expensive leisure-time activities, which were believed to reflect vice and corruption.

The committees gradually extended their authority. They attempted to identify opponents of American resistance, developed elaborate spy networks, circulated copies of the Continental Association for signature, and investigated reports of questionable activities. Suspected dissenters were urged to support the colonial cause publicly; if they refused, the committees had them watched, restricted their movements, or even tried to force them into exile.

Provincial Conventions While the committees of observation expanded their power during the winter and early spring of 1775, the regular colonial governments edged toward collapse. In most colonies, popularly elected provincial conventions took over the government, sometimes replacing the legislatures or holding concurrent sessions. In late 1774 and early 1775, these conventions approved the Continental Association, elected delegates to a Second Continental Congress (scheduled for May), organized militias, and gathered arms. Royal officials suffered repeated humiliation. Courts were prevented from meeting, and militiamen mustered only when committees ordered. During the six months preceding the battles at Lexington and Concord, ordinary Americans forged independence at the local level, even though the vast majority of them still proclaimed loyalty to Great Britain.

Summary

At the outbreak of the Seven Years' War in the Ohio Country, no one could have predicted such dramatic change in Britain's mainland colonies. Yet that conflict simultaneously removed France from North America and created a huge debt that Britain had to repay, developments with major implications for the imperial relationship.

After the war ended in 1763, the number of mainland colonists who considered themselves political actors increased substantially, and they began to develop an American identity. Their concept of the political process differed from that of the mother country, and they held a different definition of what constituted representation and consent to government actions. They also came to understand that their economic interests were sometimes distinct from those of Great Britain. Colonial political leaders reached such conclusions only after a long train of events, some of them violent. While many colonists questioned the imperial relationship with Britain, bloodshed in the backcountry revealed persistent divisions *within* American society, including battles between frontier settlers and displaced Indians.

In late 1774, Americans were committed to resistance but not to independence. During the next decades, they would forge a new American nationality.

Chapter Review

From the Ohio Country to Global War

What was at stake in the Seven Years' War?

The Seven Years' War was ultimately a contest over land between the British, French, Native Americans, and some settlers. All parties vied for control of large tracts of western land. France sought to hold and expand its possessions along the Ohio River, which it relied on for trade. After battling with Indians, France continued to push southward in its land grabbing, and Anglo-American colonists gathered in Albany, New York, to address the French threat. The colonists sought to forge a stronger alliance with the Iroquois and to coordinate plans for intercolonial defense, but they failed on both counts. England declared war in 1756 and, after winning the protracted battle, the issue of land between European nations was settled when France ceded most of its North American territories to Britain.

1763: A Turning Point

How did colonists' ideas about government differ from those of the British in the 1760s?

British authorities believed that Parliament—which included the king, lords, and commons—represented *all* British subjects regardless of where they lived. In this system of virtual representation, the people's consent to Parliament's actions was assumed. Americans, on the other hand, increasingly believed in direct representation, that they could only be represented by men who lived nearby and whom they elected. Moreover, they understood the lower houses as representing the regions that elected them. Living on the other side of the ocean, colonists were also accustomed to a central government with limited authority and embraced the Real Whig notion that good government was one that left them alone to manage their affairs. As England imposed taxes and greater control over the colonies beginning in 1763, many colonists believed their freedom was endangered and questioned whether authority should lie with the monarchy or the people.

The Stamp Act Crisis

 How did James Otis and Patrick Henry offer different ways to address the Stamp Act Crisis?

Angry about the heavy taxes and questioning Britain's right to impose them, colonists began to wonder how they might resist Parliament yet remain British subjects. At issue for essayists such as James Otis was how to oppose certain acts of Parliament while at the same time recognizing that Parliament was a supreme authority to which they must yield. He argued that Americans had to pay the tax, reluctantly but loyally. In contrast, Patrick Henry introduced seven proposals against the stamp act to the Virginia House of Burgesses. The four propositions adopted by the burgesses echoed Otis's arguments about taxation, but the other three argued that local governments rather than Parliament should have the right to raise taxes. Some colonial newspapers printed all seven resolutions as though they were passed, thus contributing to the spread of these ideas.

Resistance to the Townshend Acts

 How did the American population become politicized in the late 1760s?

Ordinary Americans were not accustomed to being involved in political affairs, which they understood as handled by elites. The Sons of Liberty made a conscious effort to draw people from all ranks into their anti-Townshend campaign, partly because they needed widespread participation for their boycott of British products designed in protest to the act. Although colonial leaders created rituals that would teach illiterate Americans about the reasons for resistance, including celebrations commemorating previous demonstrations and political songs, the people too were involved in the process. Women helped by spinning yarn outdoors in public, symbolically displaying their patriotism for all to see.

Confrontations in Boston

 How did Samuel Adams's Committees of Correspondence mark a turning point in Americans' political thinking?

An original member of the Sons of Liberty, Adams wanted to widen the movement's scope beyond its stronghold in New England cities and seacoast towns and create consensus among Massachusetts residents for the cause of liberty. The pamphlet he produced for the Boston Committee of Correspondence in 1772 was widely distributed. It stated the rights of colonists to life, liberty, and property, and it outlined complaints against England for taxation without representation, unnecessary troops and customs officers on American soil, the use of imperial revenues to pay colonial officials, and the expanded jurisdiction of vice-admiralty courts. Far more radical than earlier documents, this one did not seek to define the limits of parliamentary authority but instead declared colonists' allegiance to America first and England a distant second.

Tea and Turmoil

How did the Tea Act push the colonies to the brink of revolution?

When Parliament imposed the Tea Act on the colonies in May 1773, it was attempting to save the East India Company from bankruptcy, but colonists recognized it was designed in part to make them admit Parliament's right to tax them. Citizens in several cities wanted to prevent the tea from being unloaded from ships; in Boston, that led to a protest in which the tea was dumped in the harbor by men dressed as Indians. Parliament responded with punitive laws, known as the Coercive or Intolerable Acts, ordering the city to pay for the tea and closing the port until it did. Other acts reorganized the state's government, banned town meetings, and allowed officers to commandeer private buildings to house troops. Colonists saw such measures as proof that Britain would oppress them and sent delegates to a Continental Congress in Philadelphia in 1774 to decide how to respond.

The Unsettled Backcountry

What internal struggles plagued the backcountry during the 1760s and 1770s?

In the North, conflicts over land escalated. In 1765–1766, land riots erupted along the Hudson River, as New Englanders and Europeans who migrated to the region squatted on claimed land. When the court ordered the squatters to clear the land for valid tenants, they rebelled. In the South, Regulator movements formed in South Carolina in the late 1760s and in North Carolina in the early 1770s. Their protests often grew violent, such as in May 1771 when North Carolina Regulators fought and lost a battle with militiamen at Almanace. Additionally, Indian warfare escalated. Lord Dunmore's War resulted in the Shawnee leader Cornstalk ceding the territory that became Kentucky to Dunmore's forces.

Government by Congress and Committee

How did the First Continental Congress redefine America's relationship to England?

Congressmen meeting at the First Continental Congress in September 1774 were not ready for a complete break from England, but they did outline America's grievances, develop a resistance plan, and define America's relationship to Great Britain. Debate covered the spectrum of opinion from the radical call to obey only the king and not Parliament to the more conservative view that would have Parliament and a new American legislature jointly enacting colonial laws. In the end, the group compromised and agreed in the Declaration of Rights and Grievances to obey Parliament on a voluntary basis (rather than as subjects) and resist all taxes imposed by Parliament.

Suggestions for Further Reading

Fred Anderson, *The War That Made America: A Short History of the French and Indian War* (2005)

Bernard Bailyn, *The Ideological Origins of the American Revolution* (1967)

Christopher Leslie Brown, *Moral Capital: Foundations of British Abolitionism* (2006)

Colin G. Calloway, *The Scratch of a Pen: 1763 and the Transformation of North America* (2006)

Vincent Caretta, *Phillis Wheatley: Biography of a Genius in Bondage* (2011)

Benjamin H. Irvin, *Clothed in Robes of Sovereignty: The Continental Congress and the People out of Doors* (2011)

Marjoleine Kars, *Breaking Loose Together: The Regulator Rebellion in Pre-Revolutionary North Carolina* (2002)

Pauline R. Maier, *From Resistance to Revolution: Colonial Radicals and the Development of American Opposition to Britain, 1765–1776* (1972)

Gary B. Nash, *The Unknown American Revolution: The Unruly Birth of Democracy and the Struggle to Create America* (2005)

Andrew Jackson O'Shaughnessy, *An Empire Divided: The American Revolution and the British Caribbean* (2000)

American Revolutions

1775–1783

The Mohawks knew her as Konwatsitsiaenni, a leader in the Turtle clan. To the British, she was Molly Brant, common-law wife of the continent's most powerful Indian agent, Sir William Johnson. After the Seven Years' War, Molly Brant became the first lady of Mohawk country, one of the busiest trading regions in the Atlantic world. Her power and influence, wrote one British official, was "far superior to that of all their Chiefs put together."

In the 1760s, people of all nations journeyed to Johnson Hall, the English-style manor that Brant shared with Johnson and their growing biracial family. There visitors might smoke the calumet and drink tea served by African slaves, bury the hatchet and play billiards, view a collection of English silver and Algonquian wampum. Worlds met and mingled at Johnson Hall, and in Molly Brant. She wore Mohawk dress and refused to speak English; Johnson spoke Mohawk and sometimes painted his face in the manner of native warriors. Yet Brant and Johnson named four of their eight mixed-race children after British monarchs: Mary, Elizabeth, Anne, and George.

William Johnson died in 1774, on the eve of a war that would destroy the world he and Molly Brant had built at the western edge of Britain's empire. As Brant returned to her home village of Canajoharie, Mohawk country was transformed into a battleground. When the Americans took up arms against King George, Molly and her younger brother Joseph rallied the Mohawks behind the British. The Oneidas threw in with the patriots, who professed themselves "afraid" that Brant's "influence may give us some trouble."

Through the summer of 1777, Mohawk country burned and bled. Johnson Hall stood abandoned. Tipped off by Brant, pro-British militia and Mohawk warriors ambushed American forces and their native allies at the Oneida village of Oriskany (Oriske) that August. The daylong battle left two hundred patriots and fifty loyalists dead. Joseph Brant's Mohawks torched what remained of Oriskany; Oneida warriors and American troops razed Canajoharie. Soldiers plundered Molly Brant's house. Her people became refugees, hounded and sometimes horsewhipped by patriot forces as they marched north to seek shelter at Fort Niagara.

After the war, Molly Brant settled in the town of Kingston, in the new British colony of Upper Canada. In compensation for all she had done and for all she had lost, the British government awarded her an annual pension of £100. Her daughters married Canadian officials. Only her surviving son chose to live among the Iroquois, in the new Six Nations reserve on Grand River, north of the new national border dividing what had once been his mother's homeland.

The American Revolution created an enduring republic from thirteen separate colonies. But as Molly Brant's experience shows, it was also a bloody civil war. The fighting uprooted countless families and forced roughly sixty thousand loyalists—black, white, and native—into exile. The rupture of trading relationships between colonies and empire wreaked havoc upon the American economy.

The struggle for independence required revolutionary leaders to accomplish three closely related aims. The first was political and ideological: transforming a loyal resistance into a movement demanding separation from Britain. The colonies' elected officials worked to enlist all European Americans in the patriot cause, and to ensure the neutrality of Indians and slaves.

To win independence, patriot leaders also needed to secure international recognition and aid, particularly from France. They dispatched to Paris the most experienced American diplomat, Benjamin Franklin, who skillfully negotiated the Franco-American alliance of 1778, which proved crucial to the American war effort.

Only the third task directly involved the British. George Washington, named commander-in-chief of the American army in the summer of 1775, soon recognized that his primary goal should be not to win battles so much as to preserve his army to fight another day. Consequently, the story of the Revolutionary War often unfolds in British action and American reaction, British attacks and American defenses and withdrawals.

The challenges the rebellion presented to the British army aided the American war effort. King George's fighting forces—at least 100,000 men over the course of the war—had to cross 3,000 miles of ocean. Over such vast distances, men, materiel, and vital news traveled achingly slowly. The theater of war was itself immense as well. And the United Colonies had no single capital whose conquest would wipe out the rebellion. Against an enemy so various and dispersed, priorities were difficult to assign, especially after the entry of the French on the American side. Faced with such complexities, British military planners made grave errors. In the end, the Americans' improbable triumph owed as much to their geography, their endurance, and their enemy's missteps as to their military prowess.

American victories on the battlefield violently severed the political bonds tying thirteen of the former colonies to Great Britain. But military success does not alone make a nation; that task required profound changes in politics, culture, and society. The triumph of the Continental army only began the long work of creating the United States.

As you read this chapter, keep the following questions in mind:

- **What choices of allegiance confronted residents of North America after 1774? Why did people make the choices they did?**

- **What strategies did the British and American military forces adopt, and why?**

- **How did the United States win independence and forge the outlines of a new national government?**

Chronology

1775	Battles of Lexington and Concord; first shots of war fired
	Siege of Boston begins
	Second Continental Congress begins
	Washington named commander-in-chief of Continental army
	"Olive Branch" petition seeks reconciliation with Britain
	Dunmore's proclamation offers freedom to Virginia patriots' slaves who join British forces
1776	Thomas Paine advocates independence in *Common Sense*
	British evacuate Boston
	Second Continental Congress directs states to draft constitutions
	Declaration of Independence adopted
	New York City falls to British
1777	Articles of Confederation sent to states for ratification
	Philadelphia falls to British
	Burgoyne surrenders at Saratoga
1778	French alliance brings vital assistance to America
	British evacuate Philadelphia
1779	Sullivan expedition destroys Iroquois villages
1780	Charleston falls to British
1781	Articles of Confederation ratified
	Americans take Yorktown; Cornwallis surrenders
1782	British victory over French at Battle of the Saintes secures Jamaica
	Peace negotiations begin
1783	Treaty of Paris grants independence to the United States

Toward War

What were the problems with Great Britain's war strategy?

On January 27, 1775, Lord Dartmouth, Britain's secretary of state for America, wrote to General Thomas Gage in Boston, urging him to act. Opposition could not be "very formidable," Dartmouth wrote.

Battles of Lexington and Concord

Gage, the commander-in-chief of Britain's forces in America and, since the departure of Thomas Hutchinson, also the governor of Massachusetts, received Dartmouth's letter on April 14. He quickly dispatched an expedition to confiscate the stockpile of colonial military supplies at Concord. Boston sent two messengers, William Dawes and Paul Revere (later joined by Dr. Samuel Prescott), to rouse the countryside. When several hundred British regulars approached Lexington at dawn on April 19, they found just seventy militiamen mustered on the common. The Americans' commander ordered his men to withdraw, but as they dispersed, a shot rang out. British soldiers then fired. When they stopped, eight Americans lay dead, and another ten wounded. The British marched on to Concord, five miles away.

There the militia contingents were larger. At the North Bridge, three British soldiers were killed and nine wounded. Then thousands of militiamen hidden in houses and behind trees fired at the British forces as they retreated toward Boston. By day's end, the redcoats had suffered 272 casualties, including 70 deaths. The Americans suffered just 93 casualties.

The Siege of Boston

By April 20, some twenty thousand American militiamen had gathered around Boston. Many soon went home for spring planting, but those who remained were organized into formal units. Boston was thus besieged by patriot militia whose presence effectively contained Gage's forces within the beleaguered town. For nearly a year, the two armies stared at each other across the battlements. The redcoats attacked only once, on June 17, when they drove the Americans from trenches atop Breed's Hill in Charlestown. In that misnamed Battle of Bunker Hill, the British incurred their greatest wartime losses: over 800 wounded and 228 killed. The Americans lost less than half that number.

First Year of War

During the same eleven-month period, patriots captured the British Fort Ticonderoga on Lake Champlain, acquiring much-needed cannon. Trying to bring Canada into the war, they also mounted a northern campaign that ended in disaster at Quebec in early 1776. But the long lull in fighting between the main armies at Boston during the war's first year gave both sides a chance to organize and strategize.

Prime Minister Lord North and his new American secretary, Lord George Germain, made three central assumptions about the war. First, they forecast that patriot forces could not withstand the assaults of trained British regulars. Accordingly, they dispatched Great Britain's largest force ever: 370 transport ships carrying 32,000 troops and tons of supplies, accompanied by 73 naval vessels and 13,000 sailors. Among them were thousands of professional German soldiers (many from the state of Hesse) who had been hired out to Britain. Second, British officials and army officers believed that capturing major cities—a central aim in European warfare—would defeat the rebel army. Third, they assumed that military victory would regain the colonies' allegiance.

All three assumptions proved false. North and Germain vastly underestimated Americans' commitment to resistance. Officials also missed the significance of the American population's dispersal. Although Britain would control each of the largest mainland ports at some time during the war, less than 5 percent of the population lived in those cities. Furthermore, with a vast coastline, commerce was easily rerouted. Capturing cities did relatively little damage to the American cause.

Most of all, London officials did not initially understand that military triumph would not alone bring political victory. Securing the colonies would require Americans to resume their allegiance to the empire. After 1778, King George's ministry determined to achieve that goal by expanding the use of loyalist forces and restoring civilian authority in occupied areas. But the policy came too late. Britain's leaders never fully realized they were fighting an entirely new kind of conflict: not a conventional European war but the first modern war of national liberation.

Second Continental Congress

Britain had a bureaucracy to supervise the war; Americans had only the Second Continental Congress. The delegates who convened in Philadelphia on May 10, 1775, had to assume the mantle of intercolonial government. As spring edged into summer, Congress organized the United Colonies to prosecute the war. The delegates authorized the printing of money, established a committee to supervise foreign relations, strengthened the militia, and ordered ships built for a new Continental navy. In July, Pennsylvania's John Dickinson proclaimed, "We are reduced to the alternative of chusing an unconditional submission to the tyranny of irritated ministers, or resistance by force.—The latter is our choice."

Yet for many delegates, hesitation remained. That same month, Dickinson drafted a petition beseeching the king to halt the growing conflict. Approved by Congress on July 5, 1775, the address, now known as the Olive Branch petition, asserted that its 48 signatories remained "your Majesty's faithful subjects in the colonies."

Even while preparing the Olive Branch petition—which the king would ultimately reject—Congress pursued its most urgent task: creating the Continental army and appointing its leadership. Many delegates recognized the importance of naming a commander-in-chief who was not a New Englander. In mid-June, John Adams proposed the appointment of a fellow delegate to Congress, **George Washington** of Virginia. Congress unanimously concurred.

George Washington
American military leader and the first President of the United States (1789–1797).

George Washington

Devoted to the American cause, Washington was dignified, conservative, and respectable—a man of unimpeachable integrity. The early death of his older brother and his marriage to the wealthy widow Martha Custis had made him one of the wealthiest planters in Virginia. Though a slaveholding aristocrat, Washington was committed to representative government. After his mistakes early in the Seven Years' War, he had repaired his reputation by maintaining a calm demeanor under fire.

Washington took command of the army surrounding Boston in July 1775. In March 1776, the arrival of cannon captured at Ticonderoga finally enabled him to pressure the redcoats, yet an assault on Boston proved unnecessary. Sir William Howe, Britain's new commander, wanted to transfer his men to New York City, where he expected support from **loyalists**. On March 17, the British and more than a thousand of their supporters abandoned Boston forever.

loyalists Colonists who retained a profound reverence for the British crown and believed that if they failed to defend their king, they would sacrifice their personal honor.

Forging an Independent Republic

How did Thomas Paine's Common Sense *help reshape the war's purpose?*

Well before the British fleet (along with many loyalist exiles) sailed north to await reinforcements in Halifax, the colonies were moving inexorably toward independence. By the late summer of 1775, Congress had begun to mold the tenets of republican thought into the structures of republican governments and to fashion the rituals and symbols of a nation.

Varieties of Republicanism

Since its first meeting, in the autumn of 1774, Congress's actions had been strongly influenced by republican thought. Three different definitions of republicanism jockeyed for preeminence in the new United States. Despite their differences, all three strands contrasted the industrious virtue of America with the decadence of Britain and Europe. Most agreed that a virtuous country would be composed of hardworking citizens who would dress simply, live plainly, and elect wise leaders to public office.

Ancient history and political theory informed the first concept, embraced chiefly by members of the educated elite (such as the Adamses of Massachusetts). The histories of Greece and Rome suggested that republics fared best when they were small and homogeneous. Unless a republic's citizens were willing to sacrifice their private interests for the public good, government would collapse. A truly virtuous man, classical republican theory insisted, had the temperament—and the resources—to forgo personal profit and work for the best interests of the nation. Society would be governed by members of a "natural aristocracy," men whose talent elevated them to positions of power. Rank would be founded on merit rather than birth.

A second definition, advanced by other elites and some skilled craftsmen, followed the Scottish thinker Adam Smith, whose treatise entitled *An Inquiry into the Nature and Causes of the Wealth of Nations* was published just weeks before Congress declared American independence. Smith argued that republican virtue would be achieved through the pursuit of private interests, rather than through the subordination of personal profit to communal ideals.

The third notion of republicanism was more egalitarian. Men who advanced this version—including many with scant formal education—wanted government to respond directly to the needs of ordinary folk, and rejected the notion that the "lesser sort" should defer to their "betters." They were democrats in more or less the modern sense, in an era when "democracy" was a term of insult, roughly equivalent to mob rule. For them, the untutored wisdom of the people embodied republican virtue. The most prominent advocate of this concept of republicanism was a radical English printer named Thomas Paine, who sailed to Philadelphia in 1774 bearing letters of introduction from Benjamin Franklin. In 1776, he would be one of the best-known writers in the world.

Common Sense A pamphlet written by Thomas Paine that advocated freedom from British rule.

Common Sense

First printed in January 1776, Thomas Paine's **Common Sense** sold for two shillings—about $15 in today's money. Perhaps one hundred thousand Americans bought copies or read sections reprinted in newspapers. Thousands more heard it read aloud in taverns, coffeehouses, and public squares. An estimated one in five American adults became familiar with Paine's arguments.

Paine's best seller did not create American independence, but it transformed the terms of debate. He wrote with passion verging on rage, in straightforward prose that reflected the oral culture of ordinary folk. *Common Sense* took the Bible—the only book familiar to most Americans—as its primary source of authority. As its title suggested, *Common Sense* aimed to cut through a fog of received wisdom—to see clearly and speak plain.

Paine insisted that America's independence was inevitable. Just as all children one day grow up, the "authority of Great Britain over this continent, is a form of government, which sooner or later must have an end." He said monarchs were "ridiculous" tyrants, and aristocrats greedy and corrupt. And for the frequently heard assertion that an independent America would be weak and divided, he substituted unlimited confidence in its future: "The sun never shined on a cause of greater worth."

Link to *Common Sense*

It is unclear how many were converted to the cause by *Common Sense*. But by late spring, towns, grand juries, and provincial legislatures drafted at least ninety different statements demanding American independence. Then, on June 7, Congress confirmed the movement toward separation. Virginia's Richard Henry Lee introduced the crucial resolution: "that these United Colonies are, and of right ought to be, free and independent States...that all political connection between them and the State of Great Britain is, and ought to be, totally dissolved." Congress postponed a vote on Lee's resolution to allow time for consultation and public reaction. In the meantime, they directed a five-man committee—including Thomas Jefferson, John Adams, and Benjamin Franklin—to draft a declaration of independence. The committee assigned primary responsibility for writing the document to Jefferson, a thirty-four-year-old Virginia lawyer known for his eloquence.

Jefferson and the Declaration of Independence

A member of the House of Burgesses, Thomas Jefferson had been educated at the College of William and Mary and in the law offices of a prominent attorney. His broad knowledge of history and political theory was evident in the Declaration and his draft of the Virginia state constitution. An intensely private man, Jefferson loved his home and family deeply. Not until after his wife Martha's death in 1782, from complications following the birth of their sixth (but only third surviving) child, did Jefferson fully commit himself to public service. He would not marry again. In the late 1780s, he began a long-lasting relationship with one of his slaves, Sally Hemings. Hemings was Martha Jefferson's half-sister, born of another relationship between a slave owner and enslaved woman. Between 1790 and 1808, she bore seven children whose father was almost certainly Thomas Jefferson.

Jefferson's draft of the **Declaration of Independence** reached Congress on June 28, 1776. The delegates voted for independence four days later, then refined the wording of the Declaration for two more days, adopting it with some changes on July 4. The Declaration of Independence (see Appendix) concentrated on the actions of George III, accusing him of attempting to destroy representative government in the colonies and of oppressing Americans.

Declaration of Independence Proposed by the Second Continental Congress, this document proclaimed independence of the Thirteen Colonies from British rule.

The Declaration's chief long-term importance lay in the first lines of its second paragraph, ringing statements of principle that have served ever since as the ideal to which Americans aspire: "We hold these truths to be self-evident: That all men are created equal; that they are endowed by their Creator with certain unalienable rights; that among these are life, liberty and the pursuit of happiness; that, to secure these rights, governments are instituted among men, deriving their just powers from the consent of the governed; that whenever any form of government becomes destructive of these ends, it is the right of the people to alter or to abolish it, and to institute new government."

By adopting the Declaration, the congressmen committed treason, a capital offense. When they concluded with the assertion that they "mutually pledge[d] to each other our lives, our fortunes, and our sacred honor," they spoke the truth.

Colonies to States

Shortly before adopting the Declaration, Congress directed the individual provinces to replace their colonial charters with state constitutions. After several years of experimentation with different methods, states eventually decided to elect conventions for the sole purpose of drafting constitutions. In this fashion, states sought authorization directly from the people to establish new governments. Delegates then submitted the constitutions they had drafted to voters for ratification.

Under their colonial charters, Americans learned to fear the power of governors and to see their legislatures as defenders of the people. Accordingly, the first state constitutions typically provided for the governor to be elected annually, mandated term limits, and gave him little independent authority. Pennsylvania's constitution featured no governor or upper legislative house.

The constitutions expanded the legislature's powers. Each state except Pennsylvania and Vermont retained a two-house structure, with members of the upper house serving longer terms and required to own more property than their counterparts in the lower house. But they also redrew electoral districts to more accurately reflect population patterns. Finally, most states lowered property qualifications for voting. Thus, the revolutionary era witnessed the first deliberate attempt to broaden the base of American government.

Limiting State Governments

Seven constitutions contained formal bills of rights, and others had similar clauses. Most guaranteed citizens freedom of the press, fair trials, the right to consent to taxation, and protection against general search warrants; an independent judiciary would uphold such rights. Most states also guaranteed freedom of religion, but seven states required that all officeholders be Christians, and some continued to support churches with tax money.

In general, state constitution makers put greater emphasis on preventing tyranny than on wielding political power effectively. But establishing such weak political units, especially in wartime, all but ensured that the constitutions would need revision. Revised versions increased the powers of the governor and reduced the legislature's authority.

American politicians initially concentrated on drafting state constitutions and devoted little attention to their national government. Not until late 1777 did Congress send the **Articles of Confederation**—which outlined a national government—to the states for ratification.

Articles of Confederation
The first document that sought to create the terms of a national government. It reserved substantial powers for the states, granting to each state its "sovereignty, freedom and independence."

Articles of Confederation

Under the Articles, the chief organ of national government was a unicameral (one-house) legislature in which each state had one vote. Its powers included conducting foreign relations, mediating interstate disputes, controlling maritime affairs, regulating Indian trade, and valuing state and national money. Congress could request but not compel the payment of taxes. (See the Appendix for the text of the Articles of Confederation.)

The Articles required the unanimous consent of state legislatures for ratification or amendment, and a clause concerning western lands proved troublesome. The draft Congress accepted in 1777 allowed states to retain land claims from their original charters. But states with definite western boundaries (such as Maryland and New Jersey) wanted the others to cede to the national government their landholdings west of the Appalachian Mountains. Maryland refused to accept the Articles until 1781, when Virginia finally surrendered its western holdings to national jurisdiction (see Map 7.1).

Funding a Revolution
Finance posed the most persistent problem faced by both state and national governments. Congress borrowed what it could at home and abroad, but such mechanisms went only so far. With limited credit and even less power to tax, Congress turned to printing paper money.

Through 1775 and the first half of 1776, these paper dollars—dubbed "Continentals"—passed at face value. But in late 1776, as the American army suffered reverses, prices rose, confidence in the nation's credit fell, and the value of the Continental began to depreciate. State governments tried to prop up the ailing currency by requiring acceptance of paper money on an equal footing with specie (coins). States borrowed funds, established lotteries, and levied taxes. But they also printed their own competing currencies. State currencies—totaling roughly $209 million—funded nearly 40 percent of the cost of the war. But as the conflict dragged on, they too plummeted in value.

By the end of 1780, the Continental had declined so far that it took 100 paper dollars to purchase one Spanish silver dollar (see Figure 6.1). Congress responded

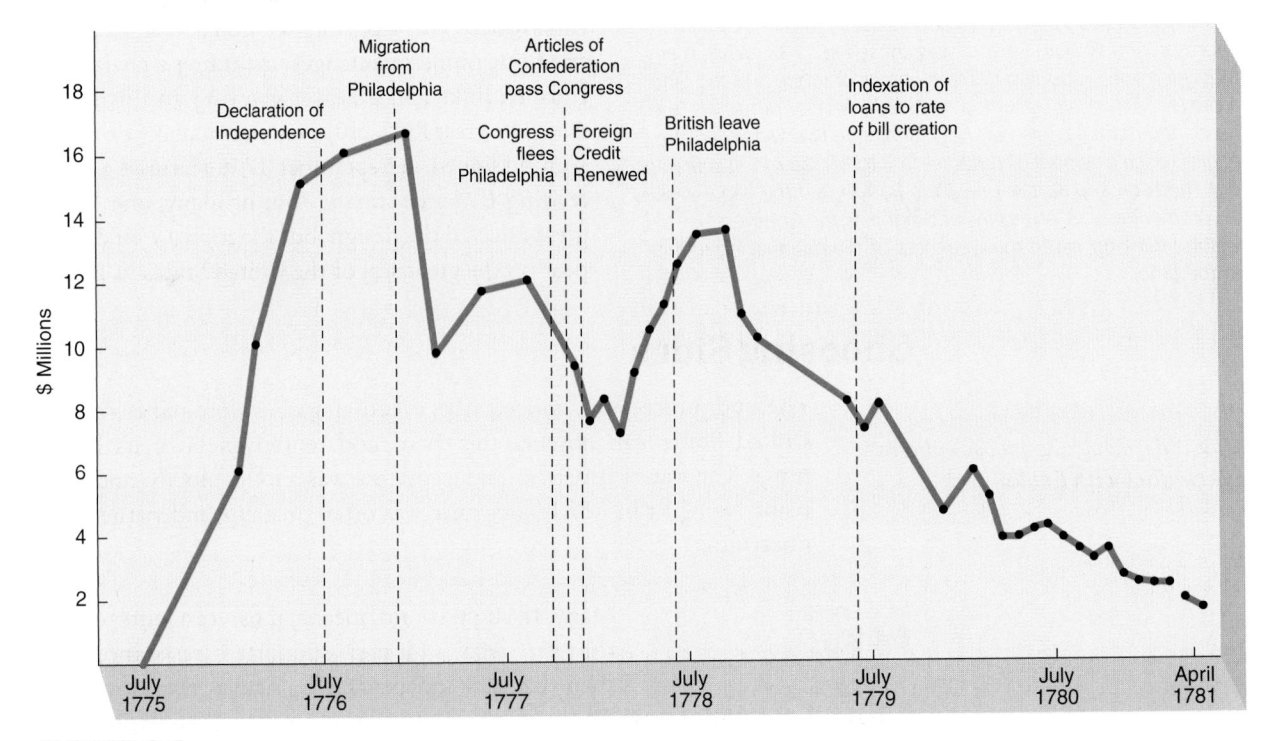

FIGURE 6.1
The Changing Value of the Continental Dollar, 1777–1781

This graph, illustrating the total value in silver coin of congressional bills of credit issued during the Revolution, shows that confidence in the new American currency was high at the beginning of the war. In 1777 and early 1778, the Continental's value sank with American defeats and rose with American victories. But after July 1778, the enormous number of bills in circulation caused their value to plummet. By the end of the war, they were virtually worthless.

(Source: Adapted from Charles W. Calormis, "Institutional Failure, Monetary Scarcity, and the Depreciation of the Continental," *Journal of Economic History*, Vol. 48, No. 1 (March 1988), p. 56.)

National Archives

Congress debated the design of a proper emblem for the new nation for six years before this national seal, drawn by Charles Thomson and William Barton, was chosen in 1782. While many of its elements, including thirteen stripes of white and red, and a cluster of thirteen stars, had surfaced in earlier proposals, the fierce and martial eagle was new. Benjamin Franklin called the eagle—once a symbol of Britain—"a Bird of bad moral character." But Thomson and Barton prevailed. Barton said the eagle evoked "supreme Power & Authority, and signifies the Congress"— wishful thinking, given the weakness of the national legislature at the time.

by devaluing its notes, accepting Continental dollars in payment of taxes at one-fortieth of their face value. This scheme succeeded in retiring much of the "old tenor" paper, at an enormous cost to people who had taken the notes. All told, Congress issued more than $200 million worth of Continental dollars—funding about 40 percent of the cost of the war—before stopping the presses.

Symbolizing a Nation

In addition to passing laws and mustering troops, Congress devised a wide array of symbols and ceremonies to promote a sense of "we" in the everyday interactions of ordinary citizens. The United States shared no common language or lineage. When they printed money, coined medals, invented seals, designed uniforms, and proclaimed festivals, members of Congress worked to create unity from the diversity of former British subjects who must now become Americans. The Continental dollar, for example, tried out numerous images, including a chain with thirteen links and a beaver gnawing an unyielding oak. The crest for a proposed national coat of arms commissioned in September 1776 featured a scroll reading *E Pluribus Unum*: "out of many, one." Congress rejected the design, but the motto would reappear on the great seal of the United States in 1782.

Choosing Sides

How did Americans choose sides in the conflict with England?

The endurance—and, indeed, the eventual global dominance—of the United States can obscure the chaos and tentativeness of its beginnings. The war of American independence was a long, bloody, and multisided conflict in which allegiance was often unstable and virtue often uncertain.

Patriots

Many though by no means most residents of the thirteen rebel colonies supported resistance and then backed independence. Active revolutionaries accounted for about two-fifths of the European American population and included small and middling farmers, members of dominant Protestant sects, Chesapeake gentry, merchants, urban artisans, elected officeholders, and people of English descent. Wives usually, but not always, fell in with their husbands about politics. Although such groups supported the Revolution, some patriots sought more sweeping political reform than others. Many fought for social and economic change instead or as well.

Link to John Dickinson, *Letters from a Farmer in Pennsylvania* (1768)

New Nations

The American Revolution created the United States and led to the formation of three other nations: Canada, Sierra Leone, and Australia.

In modern Canada before the Revolution, only Nova Scotia had many English-speaking settlers. Largely New Englanders, they were recruited after 1758 to repopulate the region forcibly taken from the exiled Acadians. During and after the Revolution, loyalist families moved to the region that is now Canada, which remained under British rule. In just a few years, the refugees transformed the former French colony, laying the foundation of the modern Canadian nation.

An early view of the settlement of black loyalists in West Africa, the foundation of the modern nation of Sierra Leone.

The New York Public Library/Art Resource, NY

Sierra Leone, too, was founded by colonial exiles— African Americans who fled to the British army during the war. Many of them ended up in London. Seeing the refugees' poverty, charitable merchants— calling themselves the Committee for Relief of the Black Poor—developed a plan to resettle the African Americans elsewhere. The refugees rejected the Bahamas, fearing reenslavement there. They accepted a return to their ancestors' homeland. In early 1787, vessels carrying about four hundred settlers reached Sierra Leone in West Africa, where representatives of the Black Poor committee had acquired land. The first years were difficult, and many of the newcomers died of disease and deprivation. But in 1792, several thousand loyalist African Americans left Nova Scotia to join the struggling colony. The influx ensured Sierra Leone's survival; it remained a part of the British empire until achieving independence in 1961.

At the Paris peace negotiations in 1782, American diplomats refused to allow the United States to continue to serve as a dumping ground for British convicts. Britain thus needed another destination for the felons its courts sentenced to transportation. It sent them to Australia, claimed for Britain in 1770. Britain continued this practice until 1868, but voluntary migrants also came. The modern nation was created on January 1, 1901.

Thus, the founding of the United States links the nation to the formation of its northern neighbor and to new nations in West Africa and the Pacific.

National Library of Australia

Thomas Rowlandson, an English artist, sketched the boatloads of male and female convicts as they were being ferried to the ships that would take them to their new lives in the prison colony of Australia. Note the gibbet on the shore with two hanging bodies— symbolizing the fate these people were escaping.

Loyalists

At least one-fifth of the European American population rejected independence. Their objections to violent protest, their desire to uphold legally constituted government, and their fears of anarchy combined to make them sensitive to its dangers. British-appointed government officials; Anglican clergy everywhere and lay Anglicans in the North; tenant farmers; members of persecuted religious sects; backcountry southerners who had rebelled against eastern rule in the late 1760s and early 1770s; and non-English ethnic minorities, especially Scots: all believed that the colonial assemblies had shown little concern for their welfare in the past. Joined by merchants whose trade depended on imperial connections, and by former British military men who had settled in America after 1763, they formed a loyalist core.

Whole regions of British America continued within the empire. Halifax, Quebec, and St. John (Prince Edward Island) in what became Canada; as well as East and West Florida, the Bahamas, Barbados, Dominica, Grenada, Jamaica, the Leeward Islands, and St. Vincent remained loyal to Britain, while Bermuda steered a precarious neutral course. The unfolding war cannot be understood without accounting for Britain's desire to protect its valuable Caribbean possessions, especially Jamaica.

After the war, roughly sixty thousand American loyalists scattered to different parts of the British empire. Their number included some eight to ten thousand escaped slaves. In addition, slave-owning loyalists carried an estimated fifteen thousand enslaved African Americans along the varied paths of their diaspora from the United States.

Neutrals

Between the patriots and the loyalists, there remained in the uneasy middle perhaps two-fifths of the European American population. Some, such as Quakers, were sincere pacifists. Others shifted their allegiance to whichever side appeared to be winning, or cared little about politics and deferred to those in power. Neutral colonists resisted British and Americans alike when taxes became too high or when calls for militia service came too often. Neutrals made up an especially large proportion of the population in the backcountry, where Scots-Irish settlers had little love for either the patriot gentry or British authorities.

To patriots, apathy or neutrality was as heinous as loyalism. In the winter of 1775–1776, the Second Continental Congress recommended that all "disaffected" persons be disarmed and arrested. State legislatures began to require voters (or, in some cases, all free adult men) to take oaths of allegiance; refusal usually meant banishment to England or extra taxes. The patriots' policies helped to prevent their opponents from banding together to threaten the revolutionary cause.

Native Americans

Their grievances against European American newcomers flooding the backcountry predisposed many Native Americans toward an alliance with Great Britain. Yet some chiefs urged caution: the British abandonment of Fort Pitt (and them) suggested that the Crown might not protect them in the future. Moreover,

British officials understood that neither the Indians' style of fighting nor their war aims necessarily coincided with British goals and methods. Accordingly, they at first sought from Indians only a promise of neutrality.

Patriots also courted Indians' neutrality. In 1775, the Second Continental Congress sent a message to Indian communities, describing the war as "a family quarrel between us and Old England" and requesting that native warriors "not join on either side." The Iroquois Confederacy responded with a pledge of neutrality that would prove short-lived.

The British victory over France in 1763 had destroyed the Indian nations' most effective means of maintaining their independence: playing European powers against one another. Only a few communities (among them the Stockbridge of New England and the Oneidas in New York) unwaveringly supported the American revolt; most native villages either remained neutral or sporadically aligned themselves with the British.

Warfare between settlers and Indians persisted in the backcountry long after fighting between patriot and redcoat armies had ceased. Indeed, the Revolutionary War constituted a brief chapter in the ongoing struggle for control of the region west of the Appalachians, which continued through the next century.

African Americans

So, too, the African Americans' Revolution formed but one battle in an epic freedom struggle that continues in the twenty-first century. African Americans did not need revolutionary ideology to tell them that slavery was wrong, but the pervasive talk of liberty added fuel to their struggle. Above all, the goal of bondspeople was *personal* independence—liberation from slavery.

In New England, where blacks comprised the smallest share of the population, many joined the patriot ranks. But most slaves in most colonies thought they stood a better chance with the British. Groups of bondsmen from Massachusetts to South Carolina offered to assist the British army in exchange for freedom. In April 1775, several Williamsburg, Virginia, slaves sent word to the royal governor, Lord Dunmore, that they were prepared to "take up arms" on his behalf. Dunmore began to formulate the policy he announced in November, with a proclamation offering to free any Virginia slaves and indentured servants who abandoned their patriot masters and joined the British. An estimated 2,500 enslaved Virginians—among them numerous women and children—did so. The surviving men (many perished in a smallpox epidemic) were organized into the British Ethiopian Regiment.

The best recent estimates suggest that some thirty to forty thousand, more than two-thirds of whom were women and children, escaped their bondage during the conflict. Those who survived till the war's end left with the redcoats, joining the global loyalist diaspora.

Patriots could never completely ignore the threats posed by loyalists and neutrals, or the particular aims of Indians and African Americans. But the difficulties of a large-scale slave revolt on the mainland, coupled with dissension in Indian communities and the patriots' successful campaign to neutralize loyalists, generally allowed the revolutionaries to remain in control of the countryside.

The Struggle in the North

What was France's role in the American Revolution?

In late June 1776, the first ships carrying Sir William Howe's troops from Halifax appeared off the coast of New York (see Map 6.1). Taking New York, home to numerous loyalists, would allow the British to consolidate their colonial allies, isolate New England, and, as Howe's successor put it, "gain the hearts & subdue the minds of America." On July 2, redcoats landed on Staten Island, but Howe waited for reinforcements from England before attacking. Washington therefore had time to march his army of seventeen thousand south from Boston to defend Manhattan.

MAP 6.1
The War in the North, 1775–1778

The early phase of the Revolutionary War was dominated by British troop movements in the Boston area, the redcoats' evacuation to Nova Scotia in the spring of 1776, and the subsequent British invasion of New York and New Jersey. Source: Copyright © Cengage Learning 2015

New York and New Jersey

By August, when British forces reached full strength, they comprised some twenty-four thousand men, including at least eight hundred fugitive slaves. Washington and his men, still inexperienced, made major mistakes, losing battles at Brooklyn Heights and on Manhattan Island. In September, New York City fell to the British, who captured nearly three thousand American soldiers.

As Washington and his men slowly retreated into Pennsylvania, British forces took control of most of New Jersey. But Washington determined to strike back. He crossed the Delaware River at night to attack a Hessian encampment at **Trenton** early on December 26. The patriots captured more than nine hundred Hessians and killed another thirty; only three Americans were wounded. Several days later, Washington defeated British forces at Princeton. Having gained command of the field, Washington set up winter quarters at Morristown, New Jersey.

Trenton New Jersey battle where Washington took almost a thousand Hessian prisoners on December 26. It significantly boosted the flailing morale of Washington's troops to fight on.

Campaign of 1777

British strategy for 1777 still aimed to isolate New England from the other colonies. General John Burgoyne would lead redcoat and Indian invaders down the Hudson River from Canada to rendezvous near Albany with a similar force moving east. The combined forces would then presumably link up with Howe's troops in New York City. But Howe was planning to capture Philadelphia. Thus in 1777 this independent operation of British armies in America ultimately resulted in disaster.

Howe delayed beginning the Philadelphia campaign for months, and then took precious weeks to transport his troops by sea. By the time British forces advanced, Washington had had time to prepare his defenses. The two armies clashed at Brandywine Creek in September, and then at Germantown a month later. Although the British won both engagements, the Americans acquitted themselves well. The redcoats captured Philadelphia in late September, forcing Congress to move inland. But the campaign season was nearly over, and the revolutionary army had gained skill and confidence.

Far to the north, Burgoyne was headed toward defeat. He and his men had set out from Montreal in mid-June. An easy British triumph at Fort Ticonderoga in July was followed by two setbacks in August—the redcoats and Mohawks halted their march east after the battle at Oriskany, New York; and in a clash near Bennington, Vermont, American militiamen nearly wiped out eight hundred of Burgoyne's German mercenaries.

Harvey A. Andruss Library Special Collections at Bloomsburg University

The Stockbridge Indians of western Massachusetts were among the only native groups to ally themselves firmly with the Continental army. Johann von Ewald, a Hessian captain whose unit battled the Stockbridge troops at White Plains, New York, drew this sketch of a Stockbridge warrior. Ewald noted that native soldiers marched in deerskin shoes and carried bows, arrows, and battle-axes along with their muskets. "Through the nose and in the ears they wore rings," Ewald wrote in his journal. Elements of traditional Stockbridge culture had survived many years among Christian missionaries.

Molly and Joseph Brant
Mohawk leaders who supported the British.

Iroquois Confederacy Splinters

The August 1777 battle at Oriskany revealed new divisions within the Six Nations of the Iroquois Confederacy, formally pledged to neutrality. The loyalist Mohawk bands led by **Molly and Joseph Brant** won over the Senecas and the Cayugas. The Oneidas—committed to the American side—brought in the Tuscaroras before fragmenting into pro-British, pro-patriot, and neutral factions. At Oriskany, some Oneidas and Tuscaroras fought with patriot militiamen against their Mohawk brethren, shattering a three-hundred-year-old league of friendship.

The collapse of Iroquois unity and the confederacy's abandonment of neutrality had devastating consequences. In 1778, British-allied warriors raided villages in western Pennsylvania and New York. The Americans the following summer dispatched an expedition to burn Iroquois crops and settlements. The devastation forced many bands to seek food and shelter north of the Great Lakes during the winter of 1779–1780. Many Iroquois followed Molly Brant's path into exile, settling permanently in Canada.

Saratoga A turning point in the American Revolution. The American victory in this battle convinced France that Americans could win the war, leading France to ally with the colonists.

Burgoyne's Surrender

After several skirmishes with American soldiers commanded by General Horatio Gates, Burgoyne was surrounded near **Saratoga**, New York. On October 17, 1777, he surrendered his entire force.

Burgoyne's defeat buoyed patriots and disheartened Britons. Most important, the American victory at Saratoga drew France formally into the conflict. The American Revolution gave the French an opportunity to avenge their defeat in the Seven Years' War. Even before Benjamin Franklin arrived in Paris in late 1776, France covertly supplied the revolutionaries with military necessities. Indeed, 90 percent of the gunpowder used by the Americans during the war's first two years came from France, transported via its Caribbean colony in Martinique.

Franco-American Alliance of 1778

Franklin worked tirelessly to strengthen ties between the two nations. Adopting a plain style of dress, he played on the French image of Americans as virtuous farmers. In February 1778, the countries signed two treaties. In the Treaty of Amity and Commerce, France recognized American independence and established trade ties. In the Treaty of Alliance, France and the United States pledged that neither would negotiate peace with the British without consulting the other. France also abandoned any future claim to Canada and to North American territory east of the Mississippi River.

The French alliance had two major benefits for the patriot cause. First, France began to aid the Americans openly, sending troops, warships, arms, ammunition, clothing, and blankets. Second, Britain now had to fight France in the Caribbean and elsewhere. Spain's entry into the war as an ally of France (but not of the United States) in 1779, followed by Holland's in 1780, turned what had been a colonial rebellion into a global war. The French aided the Americans throughout the conflict, but in its latter half that assistance proved vital.

Battlefield and Home Front

How was the Continental army staffed?

The shooting war remained in the northern and mid-Atlantic colonies through 1778. After France entered the conflict, Britain's attention shifted southward, and the colonies north of Pennsylvania saw little action. Yet the war also extended far beyond the battlefield, and it affected colonists across North America for eight long years. Roughly two hundred thousand men—nearly 40 percent of the free male population over the age of sixteen—served either in state militia units or in the Continental army over the course of the conflict. Their sacrifice and suffering changed their lives, and the lives of everyone in their households.

Militia Units

Only in the first months of the war was the revolutionaries' army manned primarily by the semi-mythical "citizen-soldier," the militiaman who swapped his plow for a musket. After a few months, early arrivals went home. They reenlisted only briefly when the contending armies neared their farms and towns. In such militia units, elected officers and the soldiers who chose them reflected local status hierarchies, yet these units retained a flexibility absent from the Continental army, composed of men in statewide units led by appointed officers.

Continental Army

As in Britain's military, the Continental army's officer corps was composed of gentlemen—men of property—who exercised strict control over soldiers. The soldiers were primarily young, single, or propertyless men. They enlisted for long periods or for the war's duration. Some were ardent patriots; others saw the army as a chance to earn monetary bonuses or land. To meet their quotas, towns and states recruited everyone they could, including recent immigrants. Nearly half of Pennsylvania soldiers were of Irish origin, and about 13 percent were German.

Dunmore's proclamation led Congress in January 1776 to modify an earlier policy prohibiting African Americans in the regular army. Recruiters in northern states turned increasingly to bondsmen, often promising them freedom after the war. Southern states initially resisted, but all except Georgia and South Carolina eventually enlisted black soldiers. Approximately five thousand African Americans served in the Continental army, commonly in racially integrated units. They were assigned tasks that others shunned, such as burying the dead and foraging for food. At any given time they composed about 10 percent of the regular army, but they seldom served in militia units.

American wives and widows of poor soldiers came to the army with their menfolk because they were too impoverished to survive alone. Such camp followers—roughly 3 percent of the total number of troops—worked as cooks, nurses, and launderers.

Officer Corps

Officers in the Continental army lived according to different rules of conduct and compensation than did enlisted men. A colonel earned seven times as much as a common soldier, and a junior officer was paid one and one-half times as much. Officers were discouraged from fraternizing with enlisted men, and sometimes punished for doing so.

Continental officers developed an intense sense of pride and commitment to the revolutionary cause. Officers' wives, too, prided themselves on their and their husbands' service. Unlike poor women, they did not travel with the army but instead made extended visits while the troops were in camp. Martha Washington and other officers' wives, for example, lived at Valley Forge in the winter of 1777–1778. They brought food, clothing, and household furnishings to make their stay more comfortable, and they entertained each other and their menfolk at teas, dinners, and dances. They created friendships later renewed when some of their husbands became the new nation's leaders.

Hardship and Disease

Ordinary soldiers endured great hardship. Wages were low, and often the army could not meet the payroll. Soldiers occasionally hired themselves out as laborers to nearby farmers to augment their meager earnings. Rations (a daily allotment of bread, meat, vegetables, milk, and beer) did not always appear, leaving men to forage for food. When conditions deteriorated, troops threatened mutiny (though only a few carried out that threat) or simply deserted. Punishments for desertion, theft, and assault were harsh; convicted soldiers were sentenced to hundreds of lashes, whereas officers were publicly humiliated, deprived of their commissions, and discharged in disgrace.

Disease—especially dysentery, various fevers, and, early in the war, smallpox—was a constant feature of camp life. Because most British soldiers had already survived smallpox (which was endemic in Europe), it did not pose as significant a threat to redcoat troops. In early 1777, Washington ordered that the entire regular army be inoculated. Inoculation, coupled with the increasing numbers of foreign-born (and mostly immune) men who enlisted, helped to protect Continental soldiers later in the war, contributing significantly to the eventual American victory.

American soldiers and sailors unfortunate enough to be captured by the British endured great suffering, especially those held in makeshift prisons or on prison ships (known as hulks) in or near Manhattan. Redcoat officers regarded the patriots as rebellious traitors rather than as prisoners of war. Fed meager rations and kept in crowded, unsanitary conditions, over half of these prisoners eventually fell victim to disease.

Home Front

Wartime disruptions affected the lives of all Americans. Both American and British soldiers plundered farms and houses. Moreover, troops carried disease wherever they went, including when they returned home. People suffered from shortages of salt, soap, flour, and other necessities. Severe inflation hampered spending (see Figure 6.1). With export markets curtailed, income fell dramatically.

Even such basic social patterns as gender roles were profoundly altered by the war. With men absent from their homes, wives who previously had handled only the "indoor affairs" of their households found themselves responsible for "outdoor affairs" as well. Most white women did not work in the fields themselves, but they supervised field hands and managed their families' finances. These new responsibilities added to the burdens of wives and mothers, but also gave some of them a sense of independence and a connection to the public life of the new nation.

Visualizing THE PAST

Frontier Refugees

In 1763, following its victory in the Seven Years' War, Great Britain took command of Fort Detroit. Shown here in an eighteenth-century watercolor, the fort was located on the narrow strait connecting Lake Huron to Lake Erie. The strategic site controlled water access to the three westernmost Great Lakes; such water travel was crucial in an era with few and poor frontier roads. Patriot forces tried twice to capture Detroit, from which Indian raiding parties attacked frontier settlements. Britain's native allies defeated the revolutionaries both times.

Throughout the war, Detroit served as a magnet for loyalist refugees. Among them was Marie-Therese Berthelet Lasselle, who fled with her family to the fort from their trading post at what is now Fort Wayne, Indiana. Depicted here is her self-portrait in watercolor on silk, with additional silk embroidery. What can we learn about frontier female refugees from such sources? What does this tell us about her aspirations, as well as her skills?

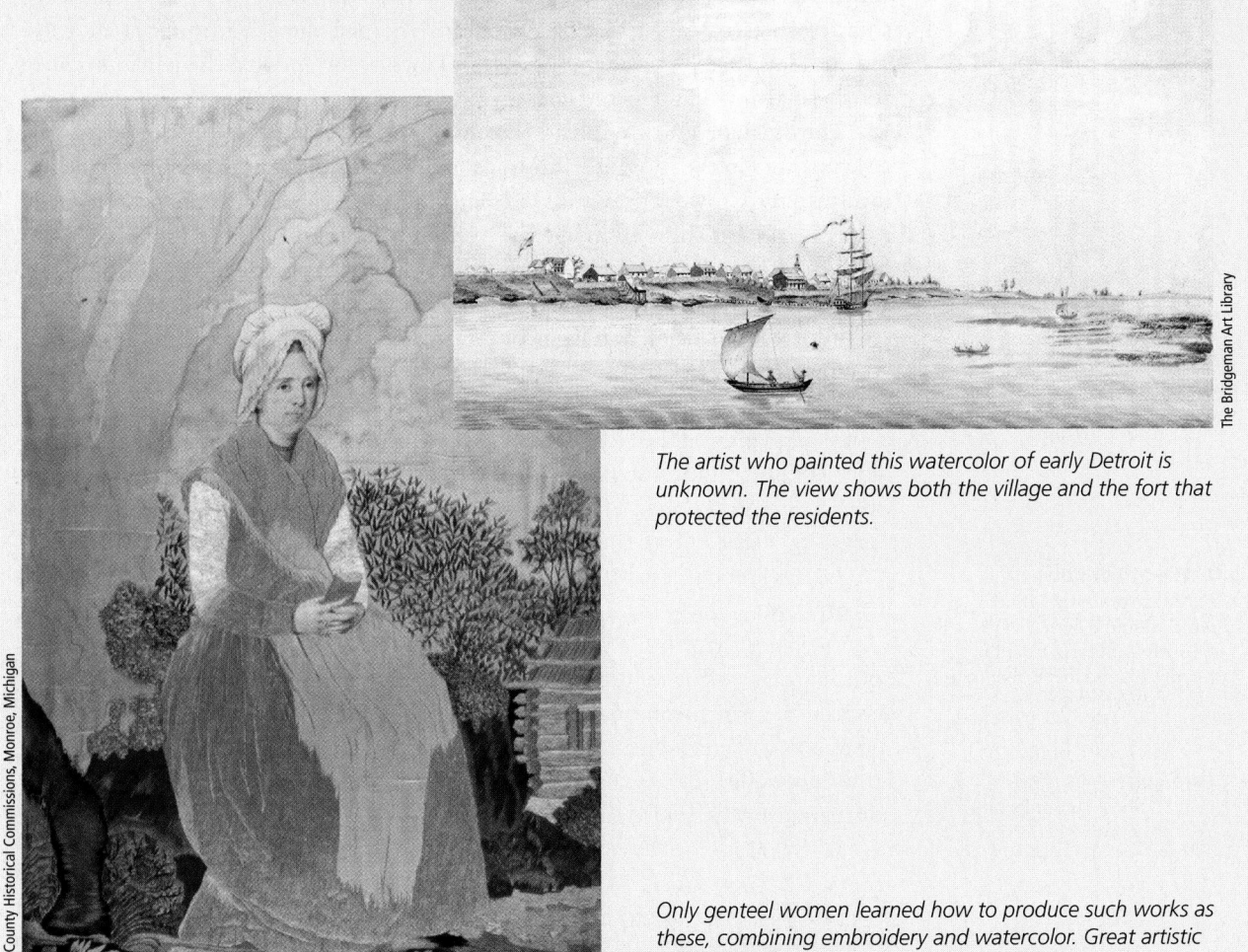

Monroe County Historical Commissions, Monroe, Michigan

The Bridgeman Art Library

The artist who painted this watercolor of early Detroit is unknown. The view shows both the village and the fort that protected the residents.

Only genteel women learned how to produce such works as these, combining embroidery and watercolor. Great artistic skills contribute to this remarkable self-portrait by Marie-Therese Berthelet Lasselle.

The War Moves South

What events led the British to cease offensive operations and begin peace negotiations in 1782?

In the wake of the Saratoga disaster, British military leaders reassessed their strategy. With France (and soon Spain) in the fight, the North American theater shrank in importance; defending the West Indies, and even England and Ireland, became priorities. Britain's attention shifted toward the southern colonies in large part to create a base of operations from which to sustain and protect its Caribbean dominions. After 1778, Britain continued the American war chiefly to serve the ends of empire in the West Indies and in Europe.

South Carolina and the Caribbean

In June 1778, Sir Henry Clinton, who replaced Howe as Britain's commander, ordered the evacuation of Philadelphia and sent a convoy that captured the French Caribbean island of St. Lucia, thereafter a key British base. Clinton also dispatched a small expedition to Georgia. When Savannah and then Augusta fell into British hands, he became convinced that a southern strategy could succeed. In late 1779, he sailed from New York to besiege Charleston (see Map 6.2). The Americans trapped there held out for months, but on May 12, 1780, General Benjamin Lincoln surrendered the patriots' entire southern army—5,500 men.

The redcoats quickly spread through South Carolina, establishing garrisons at key points in the interior. Hundreds of South Carolinians proclaimed renewed loyalty to the Crown. Thousands of escaped slaves streamed into Charleston, ready to assist the British in exchange for freedom. Clinton began the process of pacifying the south. Because there were three sides in this phase of the conflict—the British army, the Continental army, and over twenty thousand African Americans seeking freedom from bondage—one historian labels the southern campaign a "triagonal war."

The entry of France, Spain, and Holland made the southern campaign a naval as well as a land war. France's powerful navy picked off Britain's Caribbean islands one by one, including Grenada—second only to Jamaica in sugar production—and, in 1781, St. Christopher. The British capture of the Dutch island of St. Eustatius in early 1781 actually cost them dearly, for Admiral Sir George Rodney neglected to pursue the French fleet to Virginia, where it would play a major role in the **battle at Yorktown**.

On land, the fall of Charleston failed to dishearten the patriots; instead, it spurred them to greater exertions. Patriot women in four states formed the Ladies Association, which collected money to purchase shirts for needy soldiers. Recruiting efforts were revitalized. Nevertheless, at Camden in August 1780, forces under **Lord Cornwallis**, the new British commander in the South, defeated a reorganized southern army led by Horatio Gates.

Greene and the Southern Campaign

After the Camden defeat, Washington (who remained in the North to contain the British garrison at New York) appointed General Nathanael Greene to command the southern campaign.

battle at Yorktown The battle at Yorktown, Virginia, which resulted in the defeat of British military leader Lord Cornwallis and his surrender to George Washington.

Lord Cornwallis British general whose surrender at York town in 1781 effectively ended the Revolutionary War.

MAP 6.2

The War in the South

The southern war—after the British invasion of Georgia in late 1778—was characterized by a series of British thrusts into the interior, leading to battles with American defenders in both North and South Carolina. Finally, after promising beginnings, Cornwallis's foray into Virginia ended with disaster at Yorktown in October 1781. Source: Copyright © Cengage Learning 2015

Greene adopted a conciliatory policy toward the many Americans who had switched sides. He ordered his troops to treat captives fairly and not to loot loyalist property. He helped the shattered provincial congresses of Georgia and South Carolina reestablish civilian authority in the interior—a goal the British had failed to accomplish. Greene also pursued diplomacy with Indians. Although redcoat invaders initially won some native allies, by war's end, only the Creeks remained allied with Great Britain.

Even before Greene took command in December 1780, the tide had begun to turn. At King's Mountain, in western North Carolina, a backcountry force defeated redcoats and loyalists that October. Then in January 1781, Greene's aide Daniel Morgan routed the British regiment Tarleton's Legion at nearby Cowpens. Greene confronted British troops under Lord Cornwallis at Guilford Court House, North Carolina, in March. Although Cornwallis controlled the field at day's end, most of his army had been destroyed. Greene returned to South Carolina, where he forced the redcoats to retire to Charleston.

Surrender at Yorktown

Cornwallis headed north into Virginia, where he joined forces with redcoats commanded by the American traitor Benedict Arnold. He then withdrew to the peninsula between the York and James rivers, where he fortified Yorktown. Washington sent more than seven thousand French and American troops south from New York. When the French fleet arrived from the Caribbean just in time to defeat the Royal Navy vessels sent to relieve Cornwallis, the British general was trapped. On October 19, 1781, Cornwallis surrendered.

Link to diary entries of Anna Rawle, daughter of a loyalist, following the surrender of Cornwallis, 1781

The catastrophe at Yorktown, coupled with losses in West Florida, Minorca, and India, and compounded by Spanish and French ships then besieging Gibraltar and menacing the English Channel, forced Britain to give up its rebel colonies for lost. In January 1782, Parliament voted to cease offensive operations in America and begin peace negotiations.

Uncertain Victories

What risky—but ultimately wise— move did American diplomats make in negotiating peace with England after the American Revolution?

The Battle at Yorktown marked the last engagement between the British and Continental armies, not the end of the Revolutionary War. Not until more than a year after Cornwallis's surrender were preliminary peace terms agreed upon; ratifying the Treaty of Paris took another nine months.

Saving Jamaica

British officials turned their full attention to the most valuable of all their country's American possessions: Jamaica. Jamaica produced two-fifths of Britain's sugar and nine-tenths of its rum. Its human capital—over two hundred thousand slaves on the eve of revolution—likewise added to the balance sheet of empire. Through the autumn of 1781, Jamaica faced increased threat from France and Spain.

If the patriots' revolution ended in British defeat in Virginia in October 1781, Britain's American war ended in victory over the French at the Battle of the Saintes in April 1782. The win, led by redeemed General George Rodney, helped Britain obtain favorable peace terms from France in the negotiations under way in Paris.

DEA / G. NIMATALLAH/Getty Images

Admiral George Rodney's triumph over the French navy at the Battle of the Saintes in April 1782 preserved Britain's control of Jamaica, an economic cornerstone of the empire. The victory—a crucial success that stood out amidst the broader pattern of British losses in the American War— was celebrated with heroic sculptures and maritime paintings like this one, part of a series of images of the battle that Nicholas Pocock was commissioned to begin in 1782.

Treaty of Paris

Americans rejoiced when they learned of the signing of the preliminary peace **treaty of Paris** in November 1782. The American diplomats—Benjamin Franklin, John Jay, and John Adams—ignored Congress's instructions to let France take the lead and negotiated directly with Great Britain. Their instincts were sound: the French government was more an enemy to Britain than a friend to the United States. (In fact, French ministers worked secretly to try to prevent the establishment of a strong, unified government in America.) Spain's desire to claim the region between the Appalachian Mountains and the Mississippi River further complicated the negotiations. But the American delegates achieved their main goal: independence as a united nation.

Signed on September 3, 1783, the Treaty of Paris granted unconditional independence to the United States of America. Generous boundaries delineated the new nation: to the north, approximately the present-day boundary with Canada; to the south, the 31st parallel (about the northern border of modern Florida); to the west, the Mississippi River. Florida, acquired by Britain in 1763, reverted to Spain (see Map 7.1). In ceding so much land to the United States, Britain ignored the territorial rights of its Indian allies. British diplomats also poorly served loyalists and British merchants, who were disappointed in the outcome.

Some provisions of the treaty rankled in the United States as well. Article Four, which allowed British merchants to recover prewar debts that Americans owed them, and Article Five, which recommended that loyalists be allowed to recover their confiscated property, aroused considerable opposition in America.

treaty of Paris A treaty signed in 1783 when the British recognized American independence and agreed to withdraw all royal troops from the colonies.

Revolutionary Origins

Many historians today contend that the American Revolution was not truly "revolutionary," if *revolution* means overturning an earlier power structure. The nation won its independence and established a republic, both radical events in the eighteenth century. But with the exception of British officials, essentially the same men who had led the colonies also led the new country. In contrast, the nearly contemporary French Revolution witnessed the execution of the monarch and many aristocrats, and a significant redistribution of authority. So the legacy of the American Revolution appears at once radical and conservative.

Throughout the more than two hundred years since the "Revolution," varying groups have claimed to represent its true meaning. People protesting discriminatory policies against women and minorities (usually dubbed "liberals") invoke the "created equal" language of the Declaration of Independence. Left-wing organizations rail against concentrations of wealth and power. Those protesting higher taxes (usually called "conservatives") often adopt the symbolism of the Boston Tea Party, as in the "tea party" movement that arose in the spring of 2009 to oppose Obama administration policies. Right-wing militias arm themselves, preparing to defend their homes and families against a malevolent government, just as they believe the minutemen did in 1775. Indeed, vigilante groups styling themselves "minutemen" patrol the United States–Mexico border to defend it against illegal aliens. The message of the Revolution can be invoked to support extralegal demonstrations of any description, from invasions of military bases by antiwar protesters to demonstrations outside abortion clinics. But the Revolution can also be invoked to oppose such street protests because—some would argue—in a republic, change should come peacefully, via the ballot box.

Just as Americans in the eighteenth century disagreed over the meaning of their struggle, so the legacy of revolution remains contested in the twenty-first century.

Summary

The war finally over, victorious Americans could contemplate their achievement with satisfaction and even awe. Having forged a working coalition among the disparate mainland colonies, they declared their membership in the family of nations and entered a successful alliance with France. With an inexperienced army, they had defeated the world's greatest military power. They won only a few battles—most notably, at Trenton, Saratoga, and Yorktown—but their army always survived to fight again. Ultimately, the Americans wore down an enemy that had other parts of its empire to shore up.

In winning the war, the Americans reshaped the physical and mental landscapes in which they lived. They excluded from their new nation their loyalist neighbors. They established republican governments and created new national loyalties. They also laid claim to most of the territory east of the Mississippi River and south of the Great Lakes, thereby greatly expanding the land potentially open to their settlements and threatening native dominance of the interior. They had also begun, sometimes without recognizing it, the long national reckoning with slavery that would last nearly another century.

In the future, Americans would face a great new challenge: defining their nation and ensuring its survival in a world dominated by the bitter rivalries among Britain, France, and Spain and threatened by divisions within the American people as well.

Chapter Review

Toward War

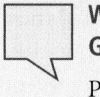

What were the problems with Great Britain's war strategy?

Prime Minister Lord North and American Secretary Lord George Germain believed that an unprecedented fighting force would overwhelm the colonists. They targeted major American cities, believing that this typical goal of European warfare would work in America as well. And they reasoned that once the colonists surrendered, they would return their allegiance to Great Britain. But American forces proved more resistant that the British had predicted, even in the face of such a powerful opposing army. The British captured the largest mainland port cities, but less than 5 percent of the colonists lived there. Finally, military victory could not alone restore the authority of the Crown in the colonies. Rather, a British political victory rested upon the Americans' resuming their allegiance to the empire, a step most were not willing to take.

Forging an Independent Republic

How did Thomas Paine's *Common Sense* help reshape the war's purpose?

While Americans had been at war with Great Britain for months, most leaders denied seeking a complete break from England and focused on achieving some autonomy and a redress for various grievances. In January 1776, Paine's widely popular pamphlet called for independence and the establishment of a republic (a government by the people with no king or nobility). He argued that once America broke from European control, it would become strong and prosperous. Within months of its publication, the Second Continental Congress passed a resolution that the colonies should be free and all ties to Great Britain dissolved and charged five men, among them Thomas Jefferson, to write a declaration of independence.

Choosing Sides

How did Americans choose sides in the conflict with England?

Only two-fifths of the European American population of the thirteen colonies were patriots seeking to separate from England—among them small and middling farmers, Chesapeake gentry, merchants, city artisans, elected officeholders—and even then, their specific goals varied. Loyalists who opposed the break with England represented one-fifth of the population and included Anglican clergy; parishioners in the North; tenant farmers; members of persecuted religious sects; backcountry southerners; ethnic minorities, especially Scots; and merchants who relied on British trade. Two-fifths of the population remained neutral, including pacifist groups such as the Quakers. Only a few Indian communities supported the American revolt; most native villages either remained neutral or sporadically aligned themselves with the British. Finally, free blacks in the North and in the middle colonies took the patriots' side, while southern bondspeople thought they'd have a better chance at personal freedom by allying with the British, who made such promises to runaway slaves.

The Struggle in the North

What was France's role in the American Revolution?

Initially, France secretly sent military supplies to the Americans and regarded the revolution as a chance to avenge its defeat to Britain in the Seven Years' War. Once Americans won the Battle of Saratoga, the French openly supported them, sending naval vessels, ammunition, and troops. France's assistance proved vital to American victory in the final years of the war. Americans and the French signed two treaties in 1778, the Treaty of Amity and Commerce, which recognized American independence and set up trade relations; and the Treaty of Alliance, which promised neither side would negotiate peace (in conflicts with Britain) without consulting the other. France also abandoned claims to Canada and to North American territory east of the Mississippi River.

Battlefield and Home Front

How was the Continental army staffed?

Only in the war's earliest months were battlefields filled by militiamen, who left their fields to fight. After that, American leaders organized an army comprising young, single, often propertyless men who enlisted for a period of time for money or land. Towns were required to send their quota of soldiers and did so by enlisting everyone, including recent immigrants. Initially, African Americans were banned from the army, but by 1776, that prohibition was lifted, as northern recruiters promised slaves their freedom after the war. About five thousand enlisted, comprising 10 percent of the army. African Americans were typically in integrated units but were often given tasks others rejected, such as burying the dead. Wives and widows of poor soldiers often followed the camps, too, working as cooks, nurses, and launderers for rations or low wages.

The War Moves South

What events led the British to cease offensive operations and begin peace negotiations in 1782?

The British conceded the war after suffering losses both on the mainland and around the world. Beginning in late 1780, American forces began a string of victories in the South. They defeated the British at King's Mountain and Cowpens, and they inflicted heavy losses on Cornwallis's men at Guilford Court House. With the help of the French navy, Americans surrounded Cornwallis at Yorktown, where he surrendered on October 19, 1781. In addition, the British suffered losses in West Florida, Minorca, and India, and they endured Spanish and French ships menacing the English Channel. These worldwide catastrophes led Parliament to cease offensive operations in America in January 1782.

Uncertain Victories

What risky—but ultimately wise—move did American diplomats make in negotiating peace with England after the American Revolution?

During the signing of a preliminary peace treaty in Paris in 1782 ending the American Revolution,

diplomats Benjamin Franklin, John Jay, and John Adams ignored Congress's instructions to let Paris lead the way. Congress wanted them to follow the terms of the 1778 Treaty of Alliance, in which Americans promised not to make peace with England without consulting France first (and vice versa). Instead, the diplomats trusted their instincts and negotiated on their own. Turns out they were right: French ministers had secretly tried to prevent a strong government from taking hold in America. War-weary Britain not only gave America its independence, but also ceded vast tracts of land and unlimited fishing rights off Newfoundland.

Suggestions for Further Reading

Edwin G. Burrows, *Forgotten Patriots: The Untold Story of American Prisoners during the Revolutionary War* (2008)

Colin Calloway, *The American Revolution in Indian Country* (1995)

Emma Christopher, *A Merciless Place: The Fate of Britain's Convicts after the American Revolution* (2011)

Stephen Conway, *The British Isles and the War of American Independence* (2000)

Caroline Cox, *A Proper Sense of Honor: Service and Sacrifice in George Washington's Army* (2004)

David Hackett Fischer, *Paul Revere's Ride* (1995)

Alan Gilbert, *Black Patriots and Loyalists: Fighting for Emancipation in the War for Independence* (2012)

Edward G. Gray and Jane Kamensky, eds., *The Oxford Handbook of the American Revolution* (2012)

Maya Jasanoff, *Liberty's Exiles: American Loyalists in the Revolutionary World* (2011)

Jill Lepore, *The Whites of Their Eyes: The Tea Party's Revolution and the Battle over American History* (2010)

Piers Mackesy, *The War for America, 1775–1783* (1964)

Pauline Maier, *American Scripture: Making the Declaration of Independence* (1997)

Mary Beth Norton, *Liberty's Daughters: The Revolutionary Experience of American Women, 1750–1800* (2nd ed., 1996)

Andrew Jackson O'Shaughnessy, *The Men Who Lost America: British Leadership, the American Revolution, and the Fate of the Empire* (2013)

Forging a Nation

1783–1800

7

The pullout began in March 1783, when news reached New York City that America and Britain had agreed upon preliminary terms of peace. Twenty thousand British troops had to be shipped to other corners of the empire, and thirty-five thousand loyalist civilians needed to find homes in a new world they had neither imagined nor embraced. Like their counterparts in Savannah and Charleston, most of New York's loyalists would rebuild their shattered lives in exile. In April, transport ships began to depart, bound for Nova Scotia, Quebec, London, and the Bahamas. The fate of thousands of African American loyalists was especially insecure. A British commission met weekly in a tavern on Pearl Street to arbitrate the claims of former bondspeople. Had they served the British cause and spent at least a year behind British lines, thus earning freedom by the terms of the treaty? Or would they be re-enslaved, recovered as lost property by their aggrieved owners?

Each Wednesday, the commissioners granted passage to the lucky ones whose names they recorded in a ledger called the "Book of Negroes." One of the first ships out, called *L'Abondance*, carried 132 free blacks to new lives in Nova Scotia. Among them was a man whom Lord Dunmore had recruited from the workforce of a Virginia patriot when the war began. Harry Washington escaped Mount Vernon and never looked back, not even when his former owner assumed command of the Continental army. His exodus would take him from the Chesapeake to New York to a small settlement south of Halifax and eventually to the African American colony in Sierra Leone, whose capital the former slaves and their patrons named Freetown.

On November 25, 1783, months after *L'Abondance* spirited Harry Washington to lasting freedom, his onetime master rode into New York City in triumph. General George Washington processed to the fort at the southern tip of Manhattan. At one o'clock, a cannon fired as the last British troops in the new United States climbed into longboats and rowed out to ships facing east, toward home.

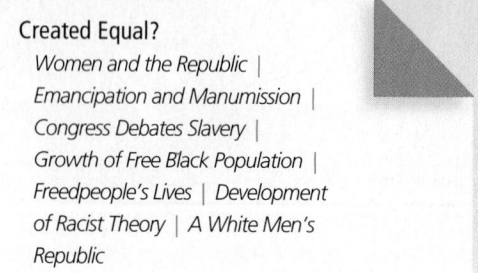

The evacuation of New York City marked one ending of the American Revolution. But Americans now confronted urgent questions about their future. How could they create and sustain a virtuous republic? How would that republic take its place "among the powers of the earth," as the Declaration of Independence had put it? And how could the country's leaders foster consensus among a populace so varied in a nation so vast?

Fighting the British dissolved at least some of the boundaries that had long divided American colonists, inspiring new loyalties to the new nation. But throughout the long civil war, Americans had remained a stunningly diverse people. *E Pluribus Unum*, the nation's new Great Seal proclaimed: "from many, one." Making one nation of many peoples—settling the Revolution—was the enormous task of the 1780s and 1790s, and remains unfinished still.

Nation making involved formal politics and diplomacy, as the leading men of the United States set out to fashion a unified government from diverse polities and divergent republican ideals. The country's first such government, under the Articles of Confederation, proved too weak and decentralized. Political leaders tried another approach when they drafted the Constitution in 1787.

Ratifying the Constitution provoked heated and sometimes violent contests in 1787 and 1788. Those battles between Federalists (supporters of the Constitution) and Antifederalists (its opponents) foreshadowed still wider divisions over major questions confronting the republic: the relationship between national power and states' rights, the formulation of foreign policy, the future of Indian nations encompassed within the borders of the United States, and the limits of dissent. Americans could not fully accept the division of the nation's citizens into competing factions known as Federalists and Republicans (or Democratic-Republicans). In republics, they believed, consensus should prevail; the rise of factions signified decay and corruption. Yet political leaders worked actively to galvanize supporters, thereby reworking the nation's political practice, if not its theory.

The hard work of settling the Revolution also took place in the less distinct but more populous realms of culture and ideas. In the early United States, novelists, painters, and educators at every level pursued explicitly moral goals. Women's education became newly important, for the mothers of the republic's "rising generation" were primarily responsible for ensuring the nation's future.

And then there were Thomas Jefferson's soaring words in the Declaration of Independence: "all men are created equal." Given that bold statement of principle, how could white republicans justify holding African Americans in perpetual bondage? During the war, thousands of bondsmen and bondswomen had answered that question by freeing themselves. Some white Americans, too, freed their slaves or voted for state laws that abolished slavery. Others redoubled their defense of the institution.

"We the People of the United States": in their name, and by their power, was the federal Constitution ratified. But who, precisely, were "the People," and how did various groups among them encounter the new nation? Some of the answers were clearer in 1800 than they had been in 1776. But as Thomas Jefferson assumed the presidency, the long work of settling the Revolution had barely begun.

As you read this chapter, keep the following questions in mind:

- **What challenges confronted the new nation's leaders at home and abroad during the 1780s and 1790s?**

- **What were the elements of the new national identity? How did poor farmers, women, Indians, and African Americans fit into that identity?**

- **What disputes divided the nation's citizens, and how did Americans react to those disputes?**

Trials of the Confederation

What was the significance of the Northwest Ordinance?

Under the Articles of Confederation, the unicameral legislature, called the Second Continental Congress until 1781 and the Confederation Congress thereafter, proved inefficient and unwieldy. It was simultaneously a legislative body and a collective executive; there was no judiciary. It had no independent income and no authority to compel the states to accept its rulings. In the 1780s, the limitations of the Articles would become glaring.

Foreign Affairs

Because the Articles denied Congress the power to establish a national commercial policy, foreign trade exposed the new government's weaknesses. After the war, Britain, France, and Spain restricted America's trade with their colonies. Congress watched helplessly as British goods flooded the United States while American produce could no longer be sold in the British West Indies.

The Spanish presence on the nation's southern and western borders caused Congress other difficulties. Spain in 1784 closed the Mississippi River to American navigation. The United States opened negotiations with Spain in 1785, but the talks collapsed when Congress divided. Southerners and westerners insisted on navigation rights, whereas northerners focused on winning commercial concessions in the West Indies.

The refusal of state and local governments to comply with provisions of the Treaty of Paris relating to the payment of prewar debts and the confiscated property of loyalists gave Britain an excuse to maintain military posts on the Great Lakes. Furthermore, Congress's inability to convince states to implement the treaty disclosed its lack of power.

Chronology

1777	Vermont becomes first jurisdiction to abolish slavery
1783	British expelled from New York City
1784	United States signs treaty with Iroquois at Fort Stanwix; Iroquois repudiate it two years later
1785	Land Ordinance of 1785 provides for surveying and sale of national lands in Northwest Territory
1785–86	United States negotiates treaties with Choctaws, Chickasaws, and Cherokees
1786	Annapolis Convention discusses reforming government
1786–87	Shays's Rebellion in western Massachusetts raises questions about future of the republic
1787	Constitutional Convention drafts new form of government
1788	Hamilton, Jay, and Madison urge ratification of the Constitution in *The Federalist*
	Constitution ratified
1789	Washington inaugurated as first president
	French Revolution begins
1790	Hamilton's *Report on Public Credit* proposes assumption of state debts
1791	First ten amendments (Bill of Rights) ratified
	First national bank chartered
	Haitian Revolution begins
1793	France declares war on Britain, Spain, and the Netherlands
	Washington proclaims American neutrality in Europe's war
	Democratic societies founded, the first grassroots political organizations
1794	Whiskey Rebellion in western Pennsylvania protests taxation
1795	Jay Treaty with Britain resolves issues remaining from the Revolution
	Pinckney's Treaty with Spain establishes southern boundary of the United States
	Treaty of Greenville with Miami Confederacy opens Ohio to settlement
1796	First contested presidential election: Adams elected president, Jefferson vice president
1798	XYZ Affair arouses American opinion against France
	Sedition Act penalizes dissent
1798–99	Quasi-War with France
	Fries's Rebellion in Pennsylvania protests taxation
1800	Gabriel's Rebellion threatens Virginia slave owners
1800–01	Jefferson elected president by the House of Representatives after stalemate in electoral college

Order and Disorder in the West

Beyond the Appalachians, individual states jockeyed over the vague western boundaries indicated by their colonial charters (see Map 7.1). The United States assumed the Treaty of Paris cleared its title to all land east of the Mississippi except the area still held by Spain. Still, recognizing that land cessions should be obtained from powerful tribes, Congress initiated negotiations with northern and southern Indians (see Map 7.2).

At Fort Stanwix, New York, in 1784, American diplomats negotiated a treaty with chiefs who claimed to represent the Iroquois; at Hopewell, South Carolina, in late 1785 and early 1786, they negotiated with emissaries from the Choctaw, Chickasaw, and Cherokee nations. In 1786, the Iroquois repudiated the Fort Stanwix treaty, denying that the negotiators were authorized to speak for the Six Nations. The confederacy threatened new attacks on frontier settlements, but the flawed treaty stood. By 1790, the once-dominant confederacy was confined to a few scattered reservations.

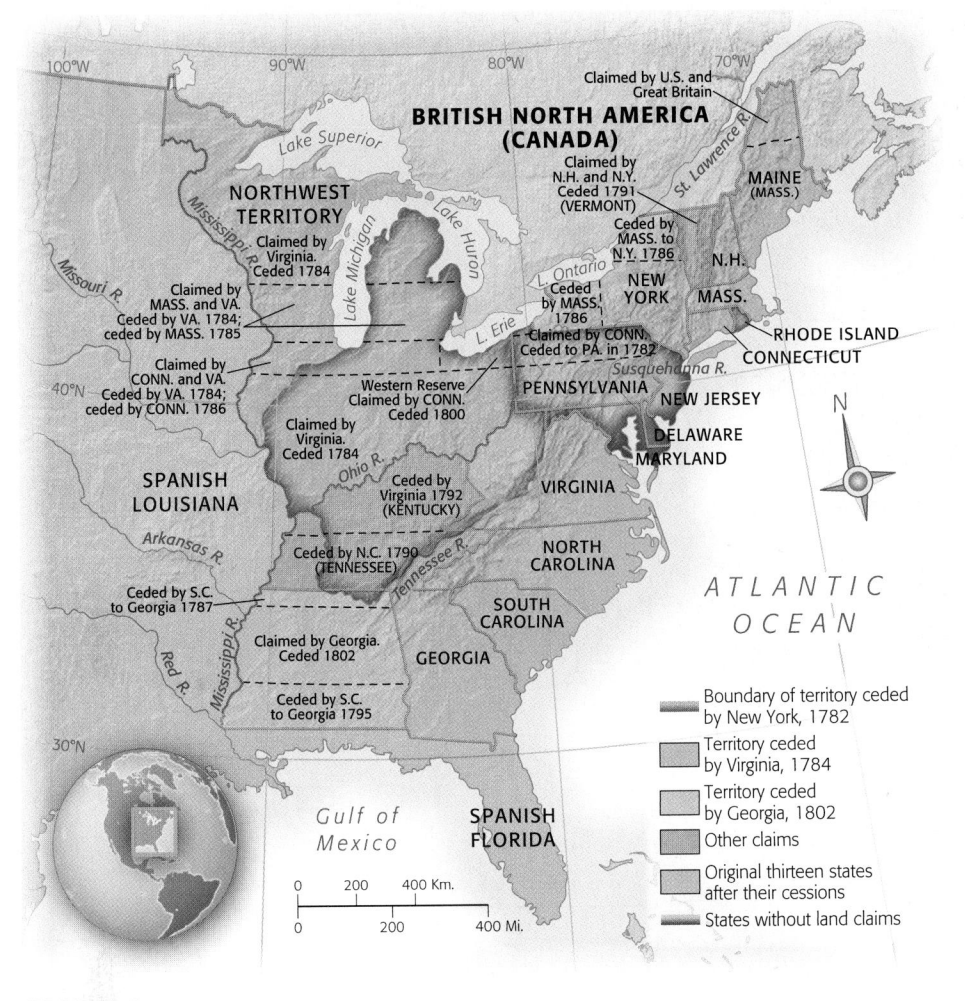

MAP 7.1

Western Land Claims and Cessions, 1782–1802

After the United States achieved independence, states competed with one another for control of valuable lands to which their original charters granted them possible and sometimes overlapping claims. That competition led to a series of compromises among the states or between individual states and the new nation, indicated on this map. Source: Copyright © Cengage Learning 2015

In the South, too, the United States took the treaties as confirmation of its sovereignty. European Americans poured over the southern Appalachians, provoking the Creeks to declare war. In 1790, they came to terms with the United States.

Ordinance of 1785

Western nations, such as the Shawnees, Chippewas, Ottawas, and Potawatomis, challenged Iroquois hegemony as early as the 1750s. After Iroquois power collapsed, they formed a confederacy and demanded negotiations with the United States. At first, the American government ignored the western confederacy. Shortly after state land cessions were completed, Congress organized the Northwest Territory, bounded by the Mississippi River, the Great Lakes, and the Ohio River

MAP 7.2

Cession of Tribal Lands to the United States, 1775–1790

The land claims of the United States meant little as long as Indian nations still controlled vast territories within the new country's formal boundaries. A series of treaties in the 1780s and 1790s spelled the end of native territorial sovereignty over some lands, which were opened to white settlement. Source: From Lester J. Cappon et al., eds., *Atlas of Early American History: The Revolutionary Era, 1760–1790* Copyright © 1976 by Princeton University Press.

(see Map 7.1). Ordinances passed in 1784, 1785, and 1787 outlined the process through which the land could be sold to settlers and formal governments created. The 1784 law created procedures for settlers to form governments and organize new states that would join the federal union "on an equal footing with the original states." Congress in 1785 directed that the Northwest Territory be surveyed into townships 6 miles square, each divided into thirty-six sections of 640 acres (one square mile). One dollar was the minimum price per acre; the minimum sale was one section. The resulting minimum outlay, $640, lay beyond the reach of small farmers, except veterans who received part of their army pay in land warrants. Proceeds from western land sales constituted the first independent revenues available to the national government.

Northwest Ordinance

The Northwest Ordinance of 1787 contained a bill of rights that guaranteed settlers freedom of religion and the right to jury trial, forbade cruel and unusual punishments, and nominally prohibited slavery. Eventually, that prohibition became an important symbol for antislavery northerners, but at the time it had little effect. Some residents already held slaves, and Congress would not deprive them of their property. The ordinance also allowed slave owners to "lawfully reclaim" runaways who took refuge in the territory—the first national fugitive slave law. Not until 1848 was enslavement abolished throughout the Old Northwest.

The ordinance of 1787 also specified the process by which territorial residents could organize state governments and seek admission to the Union "on an equal footing with the original States." Early in the nation's history, therefore, Congress assured residents of the territories the same rights held by citizens of the original states.

Although the Northwest Ordinance is often viewed as one of the few lasting accomplishments of the Confederation Congress, it remained largely theoretical in 1787. Miamis, Shawnees, and Delawares in the region refused to acknowledge American sovereignty. They opposed settlement violently, attacking pioneers who ventured too far north of the Ohio River. Not until after the Articles of Confederation were replaced with a new constitution could the United States muster sufficient force to implement the ordinance.

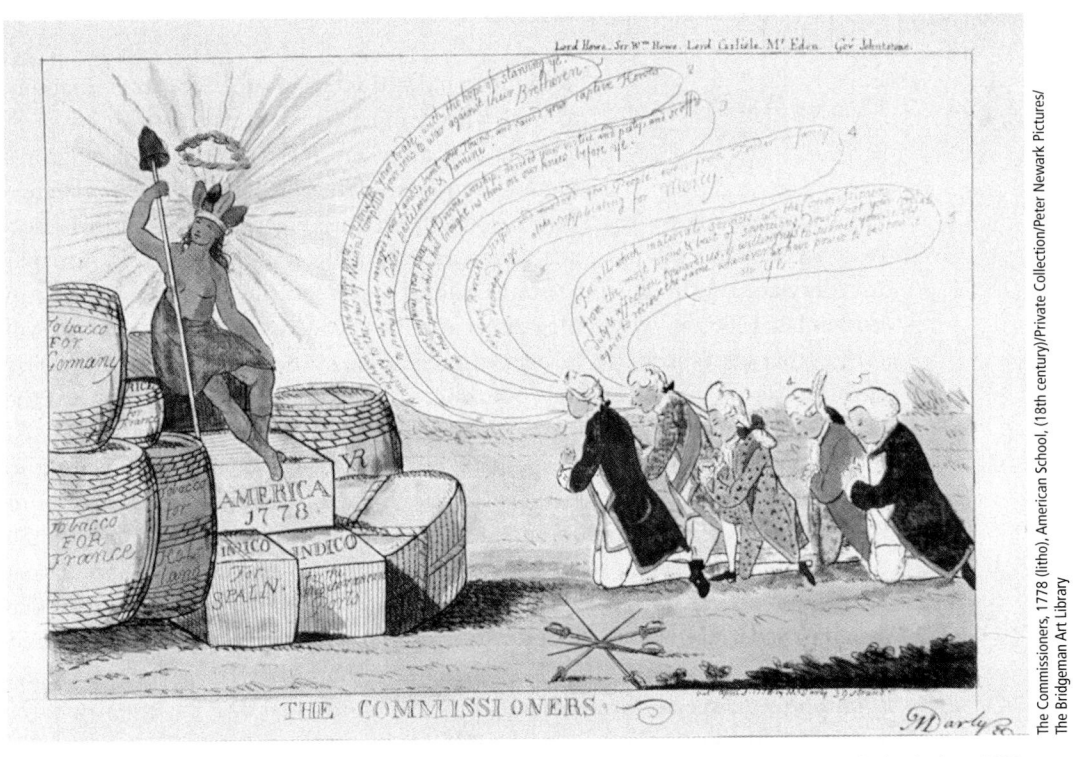

The Commissioners, 1778 (litho), American School, (18th century)/Private Collection/Peter Newark Pictures/ The Bridgeman Art Library

A British cartoon ironically reflected Americans' hopes for postwar trade, hopes that were dashed after 1783. The Indian woman symbolizing America sits on a pile of tobacco bales, with rice and indigo casks bound for Europe nearby. The artist was satirizing the failed 1778 British peace commission and Britons' willingness to make concessions to the rebellious colonies, but his image captured Americans' belief in the importance of their produce.

The First American Depression

The Articles were ill equipped to confront the transformation of the American economy. During the war, trade between Europe (especially Britain) and North America ceased almost entirely. As vital sources of income and goods dried up, the plummeting value of the Continental dollar diminished purchasing power. After the peace, exporters of staple crops and importers of manufactured goods suffered from restrictions that European powers imposed on American commerce.

Although recovery began by 1786, the war's effects proved hard to erase. By 1790, per capita income had dropped more than 40 percent from its prewar average, nearly equaling Americans' losses in the early years of the Great Depression.

The near-total cessation of foreign commerce during the war did stimulate domestic manufacturing. Moreover, America's export trade shifted from Europe and toward the West Indies. Foodstuffs shipped to the French and Dutch Caribbean colonies became America's largest single export, replacing tobacco (and thus accelerating the Chesapeake's conversion to grain).

From Crisis to the Constitution

How did the question of slavery become linked to the new U.S. Constitution?

By the mid-1780s, Americans involved in overseas trade, western land speculation, foreign affairs, and finance had become acutely aware of the inadequacies of the Articles of Confederation.

Annapolis Convention

Recognizing the Confederation Congress's inability to deal with commercial matters, representatives of Virginia and Maryland met at George Washington's Mount Vernon in March 1785 to negotiate an agreement about trade on the Potomac River. The meeting prompted an invitation to other states to discuss trade policy more broadly at a convention in Annapolis, Maryland. Although nine states named representatives to the gathering in September 1786, only five delegations attended. Consequently, they issued a call for another convention, to be held in Philadelphia nine months later, "to devise such further provisions as shall appear necessary to render the constitution of the federal government adequate to the exigencies of the Union."

At first, few other states responded. But the nation's economic problems also caused taxation woes. The states had run up huge war debts, issuing securities to pay soldiers, purchase supplies, and underwrite loans. During the hard times of the early 1780s, many veterans and other creditors sold those securities to speculators for pennies on the dollar. In 1785, Congress requisitioned still more taxes from the states to cover national war bonds. When states tried to comply, they succeeded primarily in arousing popular protests. In Massachusetts, which levied heavy taxes at full price in specie, farmers faced with selling their land to pay the new taxes responded furiously. The actions of men from the state's western counties, many of them veterans from leading families, proved that reform was needed.

Shays's Rebellion

Daniel Shays, a former Continental army officer, led the disgruntled westerners. On January 25, 1787, about fifteen hundred troops assaulted the Springfield federal armory. Terming Massachusetts "tyrannical" and styling themselves "Regulators" (like backcountry Carolinians in the 1760s), Shaysites linked their rebellion with the struggle for American independence. The militiamen defending the armory fired on their former comrades in arms, who suffered twenty-four casualties. Some (including Shays) fled the state; two were hanged; most paid fines and took oaths of allegiance to Massachusetts. The state legislature soon reduced the burden on landowners, easing tax collections and enacting new import duties instead.

Constitutional Convention

To political leaders, the rebellion confirmed the need for a stronger federal government. After most states appointed delegates, the Confederation Congress belatedly endorsed the Philadelphia convention, "for the sole and express purpose of revising the Articles of Confederation." In mid-May 1787, fifty-five men, representing all the states but Rhode Island, assembled in the Pennsylvania State House. George Washington was elected presiding officer.

Most delegates to the Constitutional Convention were substantial men of property. Their ranks included merchants, planters, physicians, generals, governors, and especially lawyers. More than half of them had attended college. Most wanted to give the national government new authority, yet they also sought to advance their states' divergent interests.

A dozen men did the bulk of the convention's work. Of those, **James Madison** of Virginia most fully deserves the title "Father of the Constitution." A Princeton graduate from western Virginia, he had served on the local Committee of Safety and was elected to the provincial convention, the state's lower and upper houses, and the Continental Congress (1780–1783).

To prepare for the Philadelphia meeting, Madison ordered more than two hundred books on history and government from Paris, analyzing their accounts of past confederacies and republics. Rejecting the common assertion that republics had to be small to survive, Madison asserted that a large, diverse republic was less likely to succumb to the influence of a particular faction. No one set of interests would be able to control it, and political stability would result from compromises among contending parties.

James Madison Known as the "Father of the Constitution" and was elected President of the United States in 1808.

Virginia and New Jersey Plans

The so-called **Virginia Plan**, introduced on May 29 by that state's governor, Edmund Randolph, embodied Madison's conception of national government. The plan provided for a two-house legislature with the lower house elected directly by the people and the upper house selected by the lower; representation in both houses proportional to property or population; an executive elected by Congress; a national judiciary; and congressional veto over state laws.

Many delegates believed the Virginia Plan went too far toward national consolidation. After two weeks of debate, disaffected delegates—particularly those from small states—united under William Paterson of New Jersey. The **New Jersey Plan**, presented June 15, proposed retaining a unicameral Congress in which each state had an equal vote, while giving Congress new powers of taxation and regulation.

Virginia Plan A proposal calling for the establishment of a strong central government rather than a confederation of states. It gave Congress virtually unrestricted rights of legislation and taxation, power to veto any state law, and authority to use military force against the states.

New Jersey Plan A proposal calling for a single-chamber congress in which each state had an equal vote, just as the Articles, but strengthened the taxing and commercial powers of Congress.

Although the convention initially rejected Paterson's position, he and his allies won several victories in subsequent months.

The delegates agreed that the new government should have a two-house (bicameral) legislature. Further, they concurred that "the people," however defined, should be directly represented in at least one house. But they differed on three key questions: Should representation in both houses of Congress be proportional to population? How was representation in either house to be apportioned among the states? And, finally, how would the members of the two houses be elected?

The last issue proved easiest to resolve. To quote John Dickinson, delegates deemed it "essential" that the lower branch of Congress be elected directly by the people and "expedient" that members of the upper house be chosen by state legislatures. The plan had the virtue of placing the election of one house of Congress a step removed from the "lesser sort," whose judgment the wealthy convention delegates did not trust.

The possibility of proportional representation in the Senate caused greater disagreement. Small states argued for equal representation, which would give them relatively more power at the national level. Large states supported a proportional plan, which would allot them more votes in the upper house. For weeks, the convention deadlocked. A committee appointed to work out a compromise recommended equal representation in the Senate, with a proviso that all appropriation bills originate in the lower house. Only the absence of several opponents of the compromise at the time of the vote averted a breakdown.

Slavery and the Constitution

The question of how to apportion representation in the lower house divided the nation along sectional lines. Delegates concurred that a census should be conducted every ten years to determine the nation's population, and they agreed that Indians, who paid no taxes, should be excluded for purposes of representation. Delegates from states with large slave populations wanted to count African and European inhabitants equally for the purposes of representation (though not for taxation); delegates from states with few slaves wanted to count only free people.

Delegates resolved the dispute by using a formula developed by the Confederation Congress in 1783 to allocate financial assessments among states: three-fifths of slaves would be included in population totals. (The formula reflected delegates' judgment that slaves were less efficient producers of wealth than free people, not that they were three-fifths human and two-fifths property.) What came to be known as the "three-fifths compromise" on representation won unanimous approval.

three-fifths clause Allowed three-fifths of all slaves to be counted for congressional representation and, thereby, in the electoral college that selected the president.

The **three-fifths clause** assured southern voters congressional representation out of proportion to their numbers and a disproportionate influence on the selection of the president. In return for southerners' agreement that Congress could pass commercial regulations by a simple majority vote, New Englanders agreed that Congress could not end the importation of slaves for twenty years. Further, the fugitive slave clause (Article IV, Section 2) required all states to return runaways to their masters. By guaranteeing national assistance to any states threatened with "domestic violence," the Constitution promised aid in putting down future slave revolts and incidents like Shays's Rebellion. Although the words *slave* and *slavery* do not appear in the Constitution (the framers used such euphemisms as "other persons"), eleven of its eighty-four clauses concerned slavery in some fashion. All but one of those protected the institution.

Congressional and Presidential Powers

The delegates concurred that the national government needed the authority to tax and to regulate foreign and interstate commerce. The convention implied but did not explicitly authorize a national judicial veto of state laws. Delegates also drafted a long list of actions forbidden to states, and they stipulated that religious tests could never be required of U.S. officeholders.

The convention placed primary responsibility for foreign affairs with a new official, the president, who was also designated commander-in-chief of the armed forces. With the Senate's consent, the president could appoint judges and other federal officers. To select the president, delegates established the electoral college, whose members would be chosen in each state by legislatures or voters. If a majority of electors failed to unite behind one candidate, the House of Representatives (voting as states, not as individuals) would choose the president, who would serve for four years but be eligible for reelection.

The key to the Constitution was the distribution of political authority (**separation of powers**) among executive, legislative, and judicial branches of the national government, and the division of powers between states and nation (called *federalism*). The president could veto congressional legislation, but that veto could be overridden by two-thirds majorities in both houses, and his treaties and major appointments required the Senate's consent. Congress could impeach the president and federal judges, but courts appeared to have the final say on interpreting the Constitution. Two-thirds of Congress and three-fourths of the states had to concur on amendments. These **checks and balances** would prevent the government from becoming tyrannical, but at times they prevented the government from acting decisively. And the line between state and national powers remained so blurry that the United States fought a civil war in the next century over that issue.

The convention held its last session on September 17, 1787. All but three of the 42 delegates still present then signed the Constitution. (See the appendix for the text of the Constitution.) Congress submitted the document to the states in late September. The ratification clause provided for the new system to take effect after approval by special conventions in at least nine states. Thus, the national Constitution, unlike the Articles of Confederation, would rest directly on popular authority.

Federalists and Antifederalists

Every newspaper in the country printed the full text of the Constitution, and most supported its adoption. Although most citizens concurred that the national government needed more power over taxation and commerce, some believed the proposed government held the potential for tyranny. The unprecedented debate frequently spilled into the streets.

Those supporting the Constitution called themselves **Federalists**. They drew upon classical republicanism, promoting a virtuous, self-sacrificing republic led by a manly aristocracy of talent. They argued that the separation of powers among legislative, executive, and judicial branches, and the division of powers between states and nation, would preclude tyranny.

separation of powers The establishment of three distinct branches of government each with varying political powers.

federalism System in which states and central governments have distinctive roles and powers.

checks and balances A separation of powers between the various branches of government, designed to prevent one branch from dominating the others.

Federalists The name supporters of new Constitution gave themselves during the ratification struggle.

Antifederalists So dubbed by the Federalists, the Antifederalists were opposed to the Constitution because they feared it gave too much power to the central government and it did not contain a bill of rights.

The Federalists termed those who opposed the Constitution **Antifederalists**, thus casting them in a negative light. Antifederalists recognized the need for a national source of revenue. But they saw the states as the chief protectors of individual rights and believed that weakening the states would promote the rise of arbitrary power. Heirs of the Real Whig ideology of the late 1760s and early 1770s, Antifederalists stressed the need for constant popular vigilance to avert oppression. Indeed, some of those who had originally promulgated such ideas—Samuel Adams, Patrick Henry, and Richard Henry Lee—led the opposition to the Constitution. Joining them were small farmers determined to safeguard their property from excessive taxation, backcountry Baptists and Presbyterians, and upwardly mobile men who would benefit from an economic and political system less tightly controlled than that the Constitution envisioned.

Bill of Rights The first ten amendments of the Constitution that guaranteed personal liberties.

Bill of Rights

The Constitution's lack of specific guarantees to protect the rights of the people against the tyranny of a powerful central government troubled Antifederalists, who wanted the document to incorporate a bill of rights, as did Britain's governing documents since the Glorious Revolution. Most state constitutions had done so as well. *Letters of a Federal Farmer*, perhaps the most widely read Antifederalist pamphlet, listed the rights that should be enshrined: freedom of the press and religion, trial by jury, and protection from unreasonable searches.

Ratification

In June 1788, when New Hampshire ratified, the Constitution's requirement of nine states was satisfied. But New York and Virginia had not yet voted, and the new framework could not succeed without those powerful states.

TABLE 7.1 Ratification of the Constitution by State Conventions

State	Date	Vote
Delaware	December 7, 1787	30–0
Pennsylvania	December 12, 1787	46–23
New Jersey	December 18, 1787	38–0
Georgia	January 2, 1788	26–0
Connecticut	January 9, 1788	128–40
Massachusetts	February 6, 1788	187–168
Maryland	April 28, 1788	63–11
South Carolina	May 23, 1788	149–73
New Hampshire	June 21, 1788	57–47
Virginia	June 25, 1788	89–79
New York	July 26, 1788	30–27
North Carolina	November 21, 1789	194–77
Rhode Island	May 29, 1790	34–32

Pro-Constitution forces won by ten votes in the Virginia convention, which, like Massachusetts, recommended that a list of specific rights be added. In New York, James Madison, John Jay, and Alexander Hamilton, writing under the pseudonym "Publius," published *The Federalist*, a series of eighty-five essays explaining the theory behind the Constitution and answering critics. Their arguments, coupled with Federalists' promise to add a bill of rights, helped win the battle there. On July 26, 1788, New York ratified the Constitution by just three votes. Although the last states—North Carolina and Rhode Island—did not join the Union for over a year, the new government was a reality.

Link to James Madison, *The Federalist Papers* (1787–88)

Promoting a Virtuous Citizenry

How were notions of republican virtue engendered in post-revolutionary America?

As citizens of the United States constructed their republic, they sought to embody republican principles of nationalism and virtue not only in their governments but also in their society and culture.

Virtue and the Arts

Republican writers and artists strove to counter the notion that the fine arts signaled luxury and corruption. William Hill Brown's *The Power of Sympathy* (1789), the first novel published in the United States, unfolded a story of seduction as a warning to "the Young Ladies of United Columbia," and promised to "Inspire the Female Mind with a Principle of Self Complacency." Mason Locke Weems published *Life of Washington* in 1800 shortly after George Washington's death. This moralizing biography—with its invented tale of the boy who chopped down the cherry tree and could not tell a lie—became the era's most popular secular work.

Painters, too, used their works to elevate republican taste. Prominent artists Gilbert Stuart and Charles Willson Peale painted portraits of upstanding republican citizens. Stuart's portraits of George Washington—three painted from life, from which the artist made scores of copies, which in turn spawned countless engravings—came to represent the face of the young republic around the world. Stuart's own motives were commercial as well as patriotic. When he returned to the United States in 1793 after nearly two decades in Britain, he told a friend, "I expect to make a fortune by Washington alone."

Bequest of Mrs. Benjamin Ogle Tayloe; Collection of The Corcoran Gallery of Art/Corbis

Gilbert Stuart completed this portrait of George Washington in 1800, after Washington's death renewed the frenzy of interest in the first president's likeness. For this version, Stuart copied his own famed "Athenaeum" portrait, which he had painted when Washington sat for him in 1796. Copies of Stuart's copies— painted as well as engraved—decorated homes throughout the early United States and surfaced as far away as Canton, China.

Educational Reform

Americans' concern for the future of the infant republic focused their attention on children. Education had previously been seen as the concern of families. But if young

Judith Sargent Stevens (later Murray), by John Singleton Copley, ca. 1769. The eventual author of essays advocating improvements in women's education sat for this portrait on the eve of her first marriage, some two decades before she began to publish her work. Her direct gaze and high forehead suggest both her intelligence and her seriousness of purpose.

people were to resist vice and become useful citizens, they would need education. In fact, the very survival of the nation depended on it. Some northern states began using tax money to support public elementary schools.

To instruct their children adequately, mothers would have to be properly educated. Massachusetts insisted that town elementary schools teach girls as well as boys. Throughout the United States, private academies were founded to give teenage girls from well-to-do families advanced schooling. Colleges remained closed to women, but a few fortunate girls could study history, geography, rhetoric, and mathematics along with fancy needlework—the only artistic endeavor considered appropriate for ladies.

Judith Sargent Murray Judith Sargent Murray of Gloucester, Massachusetts, became the chief theorist of women's education in the early republic. In powerful essays published in the 1780s and 1790s, Murray argued that women and men had equal intellects but unequal schooling. Boys and girls should be educated alike, Murray insisted, and girls should be taught to support themselves by their own efforts: "Independence should be placed within their grasp." Murray's writings were part of a general rethinking of women's position that occurred in a climate of political upheaval.

Building a Workable Government

How did the chartering of the Bank of the United States provoke an early constitutional debate?

Only a few Antifederalists ran for office in the congressional elections held late in 1788; even fewer were elected. The drafters of the Constitution had deliberately left many key issues undecided, so the nationalists' domination of the First U.S. Congress meant that their views prevailed.

First Congress Congress faced four immediate tasks when it convened in April 1789: raising revenue, responding to calls for a bill of rights, setting up executive departments, and organizing the federal judiciary. James Madison, representing Virginia in the House of Representatives, persuaded Congress to adopt the Revenue Act of 1789, imposing a 5 percent tariff on certain imports. The First Congress thus achieved an effective national tax law.

Madison also took the lead with respect to constitutional amendments. When introducing nineteen proposed amendments in June, he told his fellow representatives they needed to respond to the people's will, noting that North Carolina had vowed not to ratify the Constitution without a Bill of Rights. After heated debates, Congress approved twelve amendments. The states ratified ten, which became part of the Constitution on December 15, 1791.

The First Amendment prohibited Congress from restricting freedom of religion, speech, the press, peaceable assembly, or petition. The Second Amendment guaranteed the right "to keep and bear arms" because of the need for a "well regulated Militia." The Third Amendment limited the quartering of troops in private homes. The next five pertained to judicial procedures. The Fourth Amendment prohibited "unreasonable searches and seizures," the Fifth and Sixth established the rights of accused persons, the Seventh specified the conditions for jury trials in civil cases, and the Eighth forbade "cruel and unusual punishments." The Ninth and Tenth Amendments reserved to the people and the states other unspecified rights and powers.

Executive and Judiciary

Congress also considered the organization of the executive branch, preserving the three administrative departments established under the Articles of Confederation: War, Foreign Affairs (renamed State), and Treasury. Congress also instituted two lesser posts: the attorney general—the nation's official lawyer—and the postmaster general. Further, the House and Senate agreed that the president could dismiss officials whom he had appointed, making the heads of executive departments accountable solely to the president.

The most far-reaching law, the **Judiciary Act of 1789**, defined the jurisdiction of the federal judiciary and established a six-member Supreme Court, thirteen district courts, and three appellate courts. Its most important provision, Section 25, allowed appeals from state to federal courts when cases raised certain constitutional questions.

Judiciary Act of 1789
Outlined the federal judiciary's jurisdiction and established the Supreme Court, as well as district and appellate courts. How did the chartering of the Bank of the United States provoke an early constitutional debate?

Washington's First Steps

George Washington did not seek the presidency. In 1783, he resigned his army commission and retired to Mount Vernon. Yet after the adoption of the new government, only Washington was thought to have sufficient stature to serve as the first president, an office largely designed with him in mind. The unanimous vote of the electoral college merely formalized that consensus. Symbolically, Washington donned a suit of homespun for the inaugural ceremony in April 1789.

Washington acted cautiously during his first months in office, knowing he would set precedents. His first major task was to choose the heads of the executive departments. For the War Department, he selected an old comrade in arms, Henry Knox of Massachusetts. He chose for the State Department fellow Virginian Thomas Jefferson, who had been minister to France. For secretary of the treasury, the president chose the brilliant, ambitious **Alexander Hamilton**.

Alexander Hamilton Secretary of Treasury under President George Washington.

Alexander Hamilton

The illegitimate son of a Scottish aristocrat, Hamilton—no relation to Dr. Alexander Hamilton who toured the colonies in 1744 (see Chapter 4)—was born in the British West Indies in 1757. He spent his early years in poverty, but in 1773, financial support from friends allowed him to enroll at King's College (later Columbia University) in New York. Hamilton volunteered for service in the American army, where he came to Washington's attention. After the war, Hamilton practiced law in New York City and served as a delegate to the Annapolis Convention and the Constitutional Convention. His contributions to *The Federalist* in 1788 revealed him as one of the republic's chief political thinkers.

Caribbean-born, Hamilton had no natal ties to any state. His primary loyalty lay with the nation. He never feared the exercise of centralized executive authority, and he favored close ties with Britain. Believing people to be motivated primarily by economic self-interest, his notion of republicanism placed little weight on self-sacrifice for the common good. Those beliefs significantly influenced the way he tackled the new nation's tangled finances.

National and State Debts

Hamilton's first task was to deal with the public debt. Americans agreed that their new government could establish its credit only by repaying at full face value the obligations the nation had incurred while winning independence. But the state debts were another matter. Some states—notably, Virginia, Maryland, North Carolina, and Georgia—had largely paid off their war debts. They opposed taxing their citizens so the national government could assume other states' debts. Massachusetts, Connecticut, and South Carolina, by contrast, still had sizable unpaid debts and would welcome national assumption. The possible assumption of state debts also had political implications; such a move would concentrate economic and political power at the national level.

Report on Public Credit
Hamilton's plan to ensure that wealthy merchants, who held the public debt, would be linked to the government's financial survival.

Hamilton's Financial Plan

Hamilton's first **Report on Public Credit**, sent to Congress in January 1790, proposed that Congress assume outstanding state debts, combine them with national obligations, and issue securities covering both principal and accumulated unpaid interest. Hamilton hoped to ensure that holders of the public debt—many of them wealthy merchants and speculators—had a significant financial stake in the new government's survival. Opposition coalesced around James Madison, whose state of Virginia had mostly eliminated its debt, and who wanted to avoid rewarding wealthy speculators who purchased debt certificates at deep discounts from needy veterans and farmers.

The House initially rejected the assumption of state debts. But the Senate adopted Hamilton's plan largely intact. Compromises followed, linking the assumption bill to another controversial issue: the location of the permanent national capital. A southern site on the Potomac River was selected, and the first part of Hamilton's financial program became law in August 1790.

First Bank of the United States

Four months later, Hamilton submitted to Congress a second report on public credit, recommending the creation of a national bank modeled on the Bank of England. The Bank of the United States was to be chartered for twenty years with $10 million of paid-in capital—$2 million from public funds, and the balance from private investors. The bank would collect and disburse moneys for the treasury, and its notes would circulate as the nation's currency. But another issue loomed: did the Constitution give Congress the power to establish such a bank?

Madison thought not. The Constitutional Convention had rejected a clause authorizing Congress to issue corporate charters. Attorney General Edmund Randolph and Secretary of State Thomas Jefferson agreed with Madison. Washington asked Hamilton to reply to his critics. In his *Defense of the Constitutionality of the Bank*, Hamilton argued that Congress could choose any means not specifically prohibited by the Constitution to achieve a constitutional end. Washington concurred, and the bill became law.

The Bank of the United States proved successful, as did the debt program. The new nation's securities became desirable investments at home and abroad. The resulting influx of capital, coupled with the high prices that American grain now commanded in European markets, eased farmers' debt burdens and contributed to a new prosperity.

Hamilton's *Report on Manufactures* (1791) outlined an ambitious plan to promote the United States' industrial development through limited use of protective tariffs. But Congress rejected the report, believing that America's future lay in agriculture and the carrying (shipping) trade and that the mainstay of the republic was the yeoman farmer.

Also controversial was another feature of Hamilton's financial program enacted in 1791: an excise tax on whiskey to provide additional income to the national government. The tax affected a relatively small number of westerners—the farmers who grew corn and the distillers who turned it into whiskey—and might also reduce the consumption of whiskey. (Eighteenth-century Americans consumed about twice as much alcohol per capita as Americans do today.) Moreover, western farmers and distillers tended to support Jefferson, and Hamilton saw the benefits of taxing them rather than his own merchant supporters.

Whiskey Rebellion

News of the tax sparked protests in the West, where residents were upset that the same government that protected them inadequately from Indian attacks was now proposing to tax them disproportionately. For two years, large groups on the frontiers of Pennsylvania, Maryland, and Virginia drafted petitions protesting the tax, imitated crowd actions of the 1760s, and occasionally harassed tax collectors.

President Washington responded with restraint until July 1794, when western Pennsylvania farmers resisted two tax collectors. When about seven thousand rebels convened on August 1 to plot the destruction of Pittsburgh, Washington acted to prevent a repeat of Shays's Rebellion. On August 7, he told insurgents to disperse and summoned nearly thirteen thousand militiamen. Federal forces marched westward in October and November, led at times by Washington himself. The troops met no resistance and arrested only twenty suspects. Two men were convicted of treason; Washington pardoned both.

The suppression of the **Whiskey Rebellion** demonstrated that the national government would not allow violent resistance to its laws. In the republic, people dissatisfied with a given law should try to amend or repeal it.

Whiskey Rebellion Tax protest by western farmers that turned violent. Washington's response, sending in troops, demonstrated that only peaceful protests would be tolerated in a republic.

Building a Nation Among Nations

What was the underlying purpose of the Alien and Sedition Acts of 1798?

By 1794, some Americans were beginning to seek change through electoral politics. In a government of the people, sustained factional disagreement was taken as a sign of corruption, but that did little to check partisanship.

Republicans and Federalists

As early as 1792, Jefferson and Madison became convinced that Hamilton's policies of favoring wealthy commercial interests at the expense of agriculture threatened the United States. Characterizing themselves as the true heirs of the Revolution, they charged Hamilton with plotting to subvert republican principles. They and their followers began calling themselves Republicans. Hamilton likewise accused Jefferson and Madison of attempting to destroy the republic. To link themselves with the Constitution, Hamilton and his supporters called themselves Federalists. Newspapers aligned with each side fanned the flames of partisanship.

The growing controversy persuaded Washington to promote political unity by seeking office again in 1792. But after 1793, developments in Europe magnified the disagreements, as France (America's wartime ally) and Great Britain (America's most important trading partner) resumed hostilities.

French Revolution

In 1789, many Americans welcomed the news of revolution in France. The French people's success in overthrowing an oppressive monarchy enabled Americans to see themselves as the vanguard of a trend that would reshape the world.

But by 1793, the reports from France had grown alarming. Political leaders succeeded each other with bewildering rapidity. Executions mounted; the king was beheaded that January. Although many Americans, including Jefferson and Madison, retained sympathy for the revolution, others—Hamilton among them—began to cite France as a prime example of the perversion of republicanism.

Debates within the United States intensified when republican France declared war on Austria in 1792, and then on Britain, Spain, and Holland the following year. That confronted the Americans with a dilemma. The 1778 Treaty of Alliance with France bound them as allies "forever." Yet the United States remained connected to Great Britain through a shared history, language, and commerce.

Edmond Genêt French minister to the United States

The situation intensified in April 1793, when **Edmond Genêt**, a representative of the French government, landed in Charleston, South Carolina. Genêt's arrival raised troubling questions for President Washington. Should he receive Genêt, thus officially recognizing France's revolutionary government? Should he acknowledge an obligation to aid France under the terms of the 1778 treaty? Washington received Genêt but also issued a proclamation stating that the United States would adopt "conduct friendly and impartial toward the belligerent powers." Federalist newspapers defended the neutrality proclamation, while Republicans who favored assisting France only reluctantly accepted the popular policy.

Newspapers of the Early Republic

In the 1790s newspapers did not attempt to present news objectively, and indeed, none of their readers expected them to do so. Instead, newspapers were linked to the rapidly expanding political factions of the new nation—the partisan groupings (not yet political parties in the modern sense) terming themselves *Federalists* and *Republicans*. The "official" paper of the Federalists was *The Gazette of the United States* (colonial papers supported by individual governments too had been called *gazettes*—just as the *London Gazette* was tied to the English government). Among the Republicans' many allied newspapers was *The New-York Journal, and Patriotic Register*. A reader comparing the front pages of any two issues could see at a glance the differences between them. *The Gazette of the United States* filled its first page with sober news articles, whereas the face *The New-York Journal* presented to the world was consumed entirely with advertisements, some headed by intriguing design elements. Which would appeal more directly to America's artisans and forward-thinking yeomen, and why?

Democratic Societies

Genêt's faction fell from power in Paris, and he subsequently sought political asylum in the United States. But his disappearance from the diplomatic scene did not diminish the impact of the French Revolution in America. More than forty Democratic societies, formed by Americans sympathetic to the French Revolution, organized between 1793 and 1800. Members cast themselves in the mold of the 1760s resistance movement, as defenders of fragile liberty from corrupt and self-serving Federalist rulers.

The rapid spread of citizens' groups outspokenly critical of the administration disturbed Hamilton and Washington. Federalist writers charged that the societies' "real design" was "to involve the country in war, to assume the reins of government and tyrannize over the people." In the fall of 1794, Washington accused the clubs of fomenting the Whiskey Rebellion. As the first organized political dissenters in the United States, the Democratic societies alarmed officials who had not yet accepted the idea that one component of a free government was an organized loyal opposition.

Jay Treaty Debate

In 1794, George Washington dispatched Chief Justice John Jay to London to negotiate unresolved questions in Anglo-American relations. The United States wanted to establish freedom of the seas and to assert its right, as a neutral nation, to unfettered trade with both combatants. Further, Great Britain still held posts in the American Northwest, thus violating the 1783 peace treaty. Southern planters also wanted compensation for the slaves who left with the British army after the war.

Jay had little to offer the British, but Britain agreed to evacuate the western forts and reduce restrictions on American trade to England and the Caribbean. The **Jay Treaty** established two arbitration commissions—one to deal with prewar debts Americans owed to British creditors and the other to hear claims for captured American merchant ships—but Britain adamantly refused to compensate slave owners for their bondspeople. Most Americans, including the president, at first expressed dissatisfaction with the treaty, which was nevertheless ratified by the Senate in secret in late June 1795.

After the treaty was published, Republican newspapers organized rallies and urged Washington to reject it. Federalists countered with gatherings and essays of their own, contending that Jay's treaty was preferable to no treaty at all. Washington signed the pact in mid-August. Just one opportunity remained to prevent it from taking effect: Congress had to appropriate funds to carry out the treaty, and appropriation bills had to originate in the House of Representatives.

Hoping the opposition would dissipate, Washington delayed submitting the treaty to the House until March 1796. Pressure on the House to appropriate the funds to carry out the treaty built quickly. Federalists successfully linked the Jay Treaty with another, more popular pact that Thomas Pinckney of South Carolina had negotiated with Spain the previous year. **Pinckney's Treaty** gave the United States valuable navigation privileges on the Mississippi River and the right to land and store goods at New Orleans tax-free. The overwhelming support it received helped to overcome opposition to the Jay Treaty. In late April, a divided House appropriated the money by a three-vote margin.

Jay Treaty Pact that sought to resolve mounting tensions between Britain and the United States in the years after the Revolution. Britain agreed to relinquish control of its western U.S. posts, establish commissions to receive claims for ships damaged by British seizures, and broaden U.S. access to trade with the West and British.

Pinckney's Treaty Also called the Treaty of San Lorenzo, it won westerners the right of duty-free access to New Orleans and the use of the Mississippi River for commerce.

Ironically, the Federalists' campaign to sway public opinion violated their fundamental philosophy of government—that ordinary people should defer to the judgment of elected leaders. The Federalists won the battle, but in the long run they would lose the war, for Republicans ultimately proved more effective in appealing to the citizenry.

The terms used by Jefferson and Madison ("the people" versus "aristocrats") or by Hamilton and Washington ("true patriots" versus "subversive rabble") do not adequately describe the growing divisions in the electorate. Republicans, especially strong in the southern and middle states, tended to be confident and optimistic. Southern planters foresaw a prosperous future fueled by westward expansion. Republicans employed democratic rhetoric to win over small farmers in southern and mid-Atlantic states. Members of non-English ethnic groups found Republicans' message attractive, as did artisans. Republicans prized America's internal resources and remained sympathetic to France.

Federalists, concentrated among the commercial interests of New England, stressed the need for order, hierarchy, and obedience to authority. In their eyes, the nation's internal and external enemies made alliance with Great Britain essential. The Federalists' vision of international affairs may have been accurate, but it was also unappealing. Federalists offered voters little hope of a better future, and the Republicans prevailed in the end.

Washington's Farewell Address

After the treaty debate, wearied by the criticism, George Washington decided not to seek reelection. In September, Washington published his Farewell Address, most of which Hamilton wrote. The address outlined two principles that guided American foreign policy at least until the late 1940s: to maintain commercial but not political ties to other nations, and to reject permanent alliances. Washington also stressed America's uniqueness—its exceptionalism—and the need for independent action in foreign affairs, today called *unilateralism*.

Some interpret Washington's plea for an end to partisan strife as a call for politicians to consider the good of the whole nation. But in the context of the impending presidential election, the Farewell Address appears rather as an attack on the Republican opposition. Washington advocated unity behind the Federalist banner.

Election of 1796

The presidential **election of 1796** saw the first serious contest for the position. Federalists in Congress put forward Vice President John Adams, with the diplomat Thomas Pinckney as his running mate. Congressional Republicans chose Thomas Jefferson as their presidential candidate; the lawyer, Revolutionary War veteran, and politician Aaron Burr of New York ran for vice president. But the method of voting in the electoral college did not take into account the possibility of party slates. The Constitution's drafters had not foreseen the emergence of competing political organizations, so the document provided no way to express support for one candidate for president and another for vice president. The electors simply voted for two people. The man with the highest total became president; the second highest, vice president.

election of 1796 Federalist John Adams won by three votes and, as the second-highest vote-getter in the electoral college, Thomas Jefferson became vice president.

That procedure was the Federalists' undoing. Adams won the presidency with 71 votes. With 68 votes, the next highest total, Jefferson would become vice president. During the next four years, the new president and vice president, once allies, became bitter enemies.

XYZ Affair

As president, John Adams clung to an outdated notion that the president should remain above politics. Thus, Adams kept Washington's cabinet intact, despite its key members' allegiance to his chief Federalist rival, Alexander Hamilton. Adams was often passive, letting others (usually Hamilton) take the lead. But Adams's detachment did enable him to weather the greatest international crisis the republic had yet faced.

The Jay Treaty improved America's relationship with Great Britain, but it provoked France to retaliate by seizing American vessels carrying British goods. In response, Congress authorized building ships and stockpiling weapons and ammunition. President Adams also sent three commissioners to Paris to negotiate a settlement, but agents of Talleyrand, the French foreign minister, demanded a bribe of $250,000 before negotiations could begin. The Americans refused and reported the incident in dispatches the president received in March 1798. Adams informed Congress and recommended further increases in military spending.

Convinced that Adams had deliberately sabotaged negotiations, Republicans insisted that the dispatches be turned over to Congress. Adams complied, withholding only the names of the French agents, whom he labeled X, Y, and Z. The revelation that the Americans had been treated with contempt stimulated anti-French sentiment in the United States and became known as the **XYZ Affair**. Congress abrogated the Treaty of Alliance and authorized American ships to commandeer French vessels.

XYZ Affair French demand for bribes from American negotiators that triggered great anger.

Quasi-War with France

Thus began an undeclared war with France fought in Caribbean waters between warships of the U.S. Navy and French privateers. Although Americans initially suffered heavy losses, by early 1799 the U.S. Navy had established its superiority, easing the threat to America's vital Caribbean trade.

Republicans, who opposed war and sympathized with France, could not quell anti-French feelings. Because Agent Y had boasted of a "French party in America," Federalists accused Republicans of traitorous designs.

Alien and Sedition Acts

Federalists moved to codify their belief that Republicans were subversive foreign agents. In 1798, the Federalist-controlled Congress adopted four laws known as the **Alien and Sedition Acts**, intended to weaken the Republican faction. Three of the acts targeted recently arrived immigrants, whom Federalists accurately suspected of sympathizing with Republicans. The Naturalization Act lengthened the residency period required for citizenship and ordered resident aliens to register with the federal government. The two Alien Acts provided for the detention of enemy aliens during wartime and gave the president authority to deport any alien he deemed dangerous to national security.

Alien and Sedition Acts A series of laws passed in 1789 under the label of national security but that were intended to suppress dissent and block the rise of the Republican faction.

The fourth statute, the Sedition Act, outlawed conspiracies to prevent the enforcement of federal laws. Violations were punishable by five years in prison and a $5,000 fine. The act also made writing, printing, or uttering "false, scandalous and malicious" statements "with intent to defame" the government or the president a crime punishable by as much as two years' imprisonment and a fine of $2,000. Today, a law punishing political speech would be unconstitutional. But in the eighteenth century, when organized opposition was suspect, many Americans supported such restrictions.

The Sedition Act led to fifteen indictments and ten guilty verdicts. Republican newspaper editors nevertheless continued their criticisms of Federalists, energized rather than quashed by the persecution. Jefferson and Madison combated the acts in another way. Petitioning the Federalist-controlled Congress to repeal the laws would clearly fail, and Federalist judges refused to allow accused individuals to question the Sedition Act's constitutionality. Accordingly, Republican leaders turned to the state legislatures. Concealing their role to avoid being indicted for sedition, Jefferson and Madison drafted resolutions that were introduced into the Kentucky and Virginia legislatures, respectively, in the fall of 1798. Because a compact among the states had created the Constitution, the resolutions contended, people speaking through their states had a right to judge the constitutionality of federal actions. Both legislatures pronounced the Alien and Sedition Acts unconstitutional, thus advancing the doctrine later known as nullification.

Although no other state endorsed them, the **Virginia and Kentucky Resolutions** placed the opposition party squarely in the revolutionary tradition of resistance to tyrannical authority. Jefferson and Madison had identified a key constitutional issue: How far could states go in opposing the national government? This question would not be definitively answered until the Civil War.

Link to the Virginia Resolution

Virginia and Kentucky Resolutions Jefferson's and Madison's response to the Alien and Sedition Acts. The Resolution stressed states' rights and the power of nullification in response to Alien and Sedition Acts.

The Convention of 1800

Just as northern legislatures were rejecting the Virginia and Kentucky Resolutions, Federalists split over France. Hamilton and his supporters called for a declaration legitimizing the undeclared naval war. Adams, though, received private signals that the French government regretted its treatment of the American commissioners. In response, he dispatched William Vans Murray to Paris to negotiate with Napoleon Bonaparte, France's new leader. The United States sought compensation for ships France had seized since 1793 and abrogation of the treaty of 1778. The Convention of 1800, which ended the Quasi-War, conceded only the latter point. Still, it freed the United States to follow the independent course George Washington had urged in his Farewell Address.

The West in the New Nation

How did the new nation begin to expand its boundaries westward?

By 1800, the nation had added three states (Vermont, Kentucky, and Tennessee) and more than 1 million people to the nearly 4 million counted by the 1790 census. It claimed sovereignty east of the Mississippi River and north of Spanish Florida. But the United States had control of the Northwest Territory only after American troops battled a powerful confederacy of eight Indian nations led by the Miamis.

War in the Northwest Territory

In 1789, General Arthur St. Clair, first governor of the Northwest Territory, failed to open more land to settlement through treaty negotiations with the western confederacy. Subsequently, Little Turtle, the confederacy's able war chief, defeated forces led by General Josiah Harmar (1790) and by St. Clair (1791) in battles near the border between modern Indiana and Ohio. In the United States' worst defeat in frontier history, more than six hundred of St. Clair's men died, and scores more were wounded.

The Miami Confederacy declared that peace could be achieved only if the United States recognized the Ohio River as its northwestern boundary. But the national government refused. In August 1794, a newly invigorated army under the command of General Anthony Wayne, a Revolutionary War hero, defeated the confederacy at the Battle of Fallen Timbers, near present-day Toledo, Ohio (see Map 7.2). Eager to avoid a costly and prolonged frontier conflict, the general reached agreement with the confederacy in August 1795.

The resulting Treaty of Greenville gave the United States the right to settle much of what was to become Ohio. In turn, the United States formally accepted the principle of Indian sovereignty, by virtue of residence, over all lands the native peoples had not ceded. Never again would the United States government claim that it had acquired Indian territory solely through negotiation with a European or North American country.

"Civilizing" the Indians

Even Indian peoples who lived independent of federal authority came within the orbit of American influence. The nation's stated goal was to "civilize" them. To promote "a love for exclusive property" among Indian peoples, Henry Knox proposed that the government give livestock and agricultural training to individual natives. Four years later, the **Indian Trade and Intercourse Act of 1793** codified the secretary of war's proposals.

Indian Trade and Intercourse Act of 1793 Series of U.S. laws that attempted to "civilize" Indians according to European American standards.

The plan incorrectly posited that Indians' traditional commitment to communal landowning could easily be overcome, and it ignored their centuries-old agricultural practices. Policymakers focused on Indian men: because they hunted, male Indians were "savages" who should be "civilized" by learning to farm. That women traditionally farmed was irrelevant because, to officials, Indian women—like those of European descent—should confine themselves to child rearing, household chores, and home manufacturing.

Many Indian nations responded cautiously to the "civilizing" plan. The Iroquois Confederacy had been devastated by the war. Restricted to small reservations increasingly surrounded by Anglo-American farmlands, men could no longer hunt and often spent their days idle. Quaker missionaries started a demonstration farm among the Senecas to teach men to plow, but women showed greater interest.

Iroquois men became more receptive to the reformers after the spring of 1799, when a Seneca named Handsome Lake experienced remarkable visions. Like earlier prophets, Handsome Lake preached that Indian peoples should renounce alcohol, gambling, and other destructive European customs. He directed followers to reorient men's and women's work assignments as Quakers advocated, as he recognized

Greenville County Museum of Art, Gift of The Museum Association, Inc. with funds donated by Corporate Partners: Ernst and Young; Fluor Daniel; Director's Circle Members: Mr. and Mrs. Alester G. Furman III; Mr. and Mrs. M. Dexter Hagy; Thomas P. Hartness; Mr. and Mrs. E. Erwin Maddrey II; Mary M. Pearce; Mr. and Mrs. John D. Pellett, Jr.; Mr. W. Thomas Smith; Mr. and Mrs. Edward H. Stall; Eleanor and Irvine Welling; Museum Antiques Show, 1989, 1990, 1991, Elliott, Davis & Company, CPAs sponsor; Collectors Group 1990, 1991

In 1805, an unidentified artist painted Benjamin Hawkins, a trader and U.S. agent to the Indians of the Southeast, at the Creek agency near Macon, Georgia. Hawkins introduced European-style agriculture to the Creeks, who are shown here with vegetables from their fields. Throughout the eastern United States, Indian nations had to make similar adaptations of their traditional lifestyles in order to maintain their group identity.

that only by adopting the European sexual division of labor could the Iroquois retain their autonomy.

Created Equal?

The Constitution distinguished between "persons" and "citizens." All persons inhabiting the United States comprised, in some vague sense, *the people* who were sovereign in a republic. But only *citizens* voted and fully possessed the rights enumerated in the Constitution's first ten amendments. The language of Jefferson's Declaration of Independence, however, was far more sweeping: "all men are created equal." In eighteenth-century parlance, *all men* meant *all persons*. After independence, women, the enslaved, free persons of color, and radical thinkers wrestled anew with the contradictions between such capacious notions of liberty and the laws and customs of the young United States.

What contributed to the growing number of free blacks in America after the Revolution?

Women and the Republic

"I long to hear that you have declared an independancy," wrote **Abigail Adams** to her husband John in March 1776. And "by the way," she continued, "in the new Code of Laws which I suppose it will be necessary for you to make I desire you would Remember the Ladies, and be more generous and favourable to them than your ancestors." She hoped that Congress would "not

Abigail Adams Wife of Revolutionary figure John Adams (and second U.S. President). Influenced by the ideology of the Revolution, her letter to her husband is considered an early effort for greater rights for women.

DEA PICTURE LIBRARY/Getty Images

Mary Wollstonecraft (1759–1797) was one of the most famous thinkers of her day. In her youth she worked as a teacher, governess, and part-time author. In 1792, she published A Vindication of the Rights of Woman, *which argued that the radical equality envisioned by the revolutionaries in France should be extended to relations between the sexes.* Vindication *became an international best seller, with French, German, and American editions printed within the year. Engravings based on this portrait of Wollstonecraft by John Opie served as the frontispiece to later editions of her works, and circulated widely in the United States.*

put such unlimited power into the Hands of the Husbands," who traditionally held near-absolute authority over their wives' property and persons. "If perticuliar care and attention is not paid to the Laidies [sic] we are determined to foment a Rebelion, and will not hold ourselves bound by any Laws in which we have no voice, or Representation." Like many other disfranchised Americans in the age of revolution, Abigail Adams adapted patriot ideology to serve purposes revolutionary leaders had never intended.

Abigail Adams did not ask for woman suffrage, but others did, and some authors began to discuss and define the "rights of women" in general terms. Judith Sargent Murray, Thomas Paine, and James Otis all published essays on the topic, as did many transatlantic radicals. In 1792, Britain's Mary Wollstonecraft inflamed readers throughout the English-speaking world with her tract entitled *A Vindication of the Rights of Woman.*

Nor was the battle for women's rights confined to the page. The New Jersey state constitution in 1776 defined voters as "all free inhabitants"; subsequent state laws explicitly enfranchised female voters. For several decades, women who met the state's property qualifications—as well as free black landowners—voted in New Jersey's elections. That women chose to vote was evidence of their altered perception of their place in the country's political life.

As political contests grew more openly combative, women's role in the public sphere came to seem more threatening—both to the republic and to womanhood itself. Increasingly, thinkers emphasized the differences between men and women rather than their shared humanity. After an election marred by drunken violence, New Jersey's state legislature abolished female voting in 1807. Throughout the nation, as property qualifications for white male voters shrank, the presumed distinction between white men and everyone else grew.

Emancipation and Manumission

How did approximately seven hundred thousand enslaved and free blacks—persons but not citizens, who comprised 20 percent of the American population—fit into the developing nation? In the late 1770s and early 1780s, enslaved men and women in New Hampshire, Connecticut, and Massachusetts petitioned their courts and legislatures for freedom.

Such agitation catalyzed the gradual abolition of slavery in the North, a process now known as "the first emancipation." Vermont banned slavery in its 1777 constitution. Responding to lawsuits filed by enslaved men and women, Massachusetts courts ruled in 1783 that the state constitution prohibited slavery. Other states adopted gradual emancipation laws between 1780 (Pennsylvania) and 1804 (New Jersey). No southern state passed a general emancipation law, but the legislatures of Virginia (1782), Delaware (1787), and Maryland (1790 and 1796) altered statutes that restricted slave owners' ability to free their bondspeople.

Congress Debates Slavery

At the national level, too, the Revolution transformed slavery from an unspoken assumption to an open question. In 1790, three groups of Quakers submitted petitions to Congress calling for the abolition of slavery and the international slave trade. Southerners vigorously asserted that Congress should not even consider the petitions. They insisted that slavery was integral to the Union and that abolition would cause more problems than it solved. Congress accepted a committee report denying it the power to halt slave importations before 1808 or to emancipate slaves at any time, that authority "remaining with the several States alone." The precedent that Congress could not abolish slavery endured until the Civil War.

Revolutionary ideology thus had limited impact on the well-entrenched interests of large slaveholders. Even in the northern states—societies with slaves, not slave societies—lawmakers' concern for the *property* rights of owners led them to favor gradual over immediate emancipation. New York's law freed children born into slavery after July 4, 1799, but only after they reached their mid-twenties. And not until the late 1840s did Rhode Island and Connecticut abolish all vestiges of slavery.

Growth of Free Black Population

The number of free people of African descent grew dramatically after the Revolution. Wartime escapees from plantations, bondsmen who served in the Continental army, and others emancipated by their owners or by new state laws were now free. By 1790, nearly 60,000 free people of color lived in the United States; ten years later, they numbered more than 108,000, more than 10 percent of the African American population.

A sailor of African descent posed proudly for this portrait around 1790. Unfortunately, neither the name of the sailor nor the name of the artist is known today.

Private Collection/Picture Research Consultants & Archives

MAP 7.3
African American Population, 1790: Proportion of Total Population

The first national census clearly indicated that the African American population was heavily concentrated in the coastal South. Although there were growing numbers of blacks in the backcountry—presumably taken there by migrating slave owners—most parts of the North and East had few African American residents. But slavery shaped the economy of the entire U.S. in the early republic, and even in the mid-Atlantic and the North, its abolition took place gradually, sometimes over decades. Source: CAPPON, LESTER J.; ATLAS OF EARLY AMERICAN HISTORY, © 1976 Princeton University Press, 2004 renewed PUP. Reprinted by permission of Princeton University Press.

In the Chesapeake, manumissions were speeded by the shift from tobacco to grain production. Because grain cultivation was less labor intensive, planters complained about "excess" slaves, and occasionally freed some of their less productive or more favored laborers. The enslaved also negotiated agreements allowing them to live and work independently until they could save enough to purchase themselves. Virginia's free black population more than doubled in the two decades after 1790. By 1810, nearly one-quarter of Maryland's African American population lived outside of legal bondage.

Freedpeople's Lives   Freedpeople from rural areas often headed to port cities, especially Boston, Philadelphia, and the new boomtown of Baltimore. Women outnumbered men among the migrants, for they had better employment opportunities, especially in domestic service. Some freedmen also worked in domestic service, but larger numbers were unskilled laborers and sailors. A few women and a sizable proportion of men (nearly one-third of those in Philadelphia in 1795) were skilled workers or retailers. Many replaced the surnames of former masters with names like Newman or Brown and established independent two-parent families. They also began to occupy distinct neighborhoods, probably due to discrimination.

Even whites who recognized African Americans' right to freedom were unwilling to accept them as equals. Several states—including Delaware, Maryland, and South Carolina—adopted laws denying property-owning black men the vote. South Carolina forbade free blacks from testifying against whites in court. New Englanders used indenture contracts to control freed youths, who were often barred from public schools. Freedmen found it difficult to purchase property and find good jobs.

To survive and prosper, freedpeople came to rely on collective effort. In Charleston, mulattos formed the Brown Fellowship Society, which provided them insurance, financed a school, and helped to support orphans. In 1794, former slaves in Philadelphia and Baltimore, led by the African American clergyman

Richard Allen, founded societies that eventually became the **African Methodist Episcopal (AME) church**. AME congregations—along with African Baptist, African Episcopal, and African Presbyterian churches—became cultural centers of free black communities.

Development of Racist Theory

Their endeavors were especially important because the post-revolutionary years witnessed the development of racist theory in the United States. European Americans had long regarded their slaves as inferior, but the most influential thinkers reasoned that bondspeople's seemingly debased character derived from their enslavement, rather than enslavement's being the consequence of inherited inferiority. After the Revolution, slave owners skirted the contradiction between slaveholding practice and the egalitarian implications of revolutionary theory. They argued that people of African descent were less than fully human and thus the principles of republican equality applied only to European Americans.

Simultaneously, the concept of "race" began to be applied to groups defined by skin color. Egalitarian thinking among European Americans at once downplayed status distinctions within their own group, and distinguished all "whites" from all others. Notions of "whiteness," "redness," and "blackness" developed alongside beliefs in European Americans' superiority.

With this new racial thought came the assertion that, as Thomas Jefferson insisted in 1781, blacks were "inferior to the whites in the endowments both of body and mind." There followed the belief that those with black skin were inherently lazy, even though owners had often argued that slaves made "natural" workers. Another notion was that blacks were sexually promiscuous, and that African American men lusted after European American women. The more common sexual exploitation of enslaved women by their masters generally aroused little concern, though Federalist newspaper editors did not hesitate to use Jefferson's long-standing relationship with Sally Hemings to inflame public opinion against him.

African Americans challenged these racist notions. In 1791, Benjamin Banneker, a free black mathematical genius, sent Jefferson a copy of his latest almanac (which included his astronomical calculations) to show blacks' mental powers. Jefferson admitted Banneker's intelligence but regarded him as exceptional, and said he would need more evidence to change his mind about people of African descent.

A White Men's Republic

Though many men of African descent had served with honor in the Continental army, laws from the 1770s on linked male citizenship rights to "whiteness." Some historians argue that, just as excluding women from the political realm reserved all power for men, so identifying common racial antagonists helped to foster white solidarity across class lines. The division of American society between slave and free was transformed into a division between blacks—some of whom were free—and whites.

Haitian Refugees

Less than a decade after winning independence, the United States confronted its first immigration crisis. Among the approximately 600,000 residents of St. Domingue in the early 1790s were about 100,000 free people, almost all of them slave owners; half were whites, the rest of mixed race. After the French Revolution those free mulattos sought greater social and political equality. Slaves then seized the opportunity to revolt. By 1793, they had triumphed under the leadership of a former bondsman, Toussaint L'Ouverture. In 1804 they ousted the French, establishing the republic of Haiti. Thousands of whites and mulattos, accompanied by as many slaves as they could transport, sought asylum in the United States.

Southern plantation owners worried that refugee slaves so familiar with ideas of freedom and equality would mingle with their own bondspeople. Many were uncomfortable with the arrival of numerous free people of color. Most southern states adopted laws forbidding the entry of Haitian slaves and free mulattos, but the laws were difficult to enforce, as was a similar congressional act. More than fifteen thousand refugees—white, black, and mixed race—flooded into the United States and Spanish Louisiana. Many ended up in Virginia (which did not pass an exclusion law) or in the cities of Charleston, Savannah, and New Orleans.

In both New Orleans and Charleston, the influx of Haitians of mixed race aroused a heightened color consciousness that placed light-skinned people atop a hierarchy of people of color. After the United States purchased Louisiana in 1803, the number of free people of color there almost doubled in three years, largely because of a final surge of immigration from Haiti. And, in Virginia, the Haitian revolt inspired slaves in 1800 to plan the action now known as Gabriel's Rebellion.

The Haitian refugees thus linked European Americans and African Americans to events in the West Indies.

Courtesy of the Collections of the Louisiana State Museum

A free woman of color in Louisiana early in the nineteenth century, possibly one of the refugees from Haiti. Esteban Rodriguez Mir, named governor of Spanish Louisiana in 1782, ordered all slave and free black women to wear head wraps rather than hats—which were reserved for whites—but this woman and many others subverted his order by nominally complying, but nevertheless creating elaborate headdresses.

"Revolutions" at the End of the Century

What gave rise to new potential revolutions in America at the end of the eighteenth century?

Three events in the last two years of the eighteenth century can be deemed real or potential revolutions: Fries's Rebellion, Gabriel's Rebellion, and the election of Thomas Jefferson. Each mirrored the tensions and uncertainties of the young republic.

Fries's Rebellion

The tax resistance movement named for Revolutionary War veteran John Fries arose among German American farmers in Pennsylvania's Lehigh Valley in 1798–1799. To finance the Quasi-War, Congress taxed land, houses, and legal documents. German Americans, imbued with revolutionary ideals (nearly half were veterans), saw in the taxes a threat to their liberties and livelihoods. Asserting their right to resist unconstitutional laws, they raised liberty poles, petitioned Congress, and barred assessors from their homes.

When a federal judge ordered the arrest of twenty resisters, Fries led 120 militiamen to Bethlehem, where they surrounded a tavern temporarily housing the prisoners. President Adams described the militiamen's actions as acts of war. Fries and many of his neighbors were arrested and tried; he and two others were convicted of treason, thirty-two more of violating the Sedition Act. Although Fries and the other "traitors" were sentenced to hang, Adams pardoned them just two days before their scheduled execution. Despite clemency from a Federalist president, the region's residents became, and remained, Republican partisans.

Gabriel's Rebellion

Gabriel, an enslaved Virginia blacksmith who planned the second end-of-the-century revolution, drew on both Haitian and American revolutionary experiences. He first recruited other skilled African American artisans who lived, as he did, under minimal supervision. Next, he enlisted rural slaves. The rebels planned to attack Richmond on the night of August 30, 1800. They would set fire to the city, seize the capitol building, and capture the governor, James Monroe. At that point, Gabriel believed, other slaves and poor whites would join the movement.

Heavy rain forced a postponement. Several planters then learned of the plot. Gabriel avoided arrest for weeks, but militia troops apprehended and interrogated other rebel leaders. Twenty-six rebels, including Gabriel, were hanged. Southern state legislatures responded to the plot by passing increasingly severe laws regulating slavery, which became even more firmly entrenched as an economic institution and way of life in the region.

Election of 1800

The third end-of-the-century revolution was the election of Thomas Jefferson as president and a Congress dominated by Republicans. Leading up to November 1800, Federalists and Republicans openly campaigned for congressional seats and maneuvered to control the electoral college. Republicans again nominated Jefferson and Burr; Federalists named John Adams, with Charles Cotesworth Pinckney of South Carolina as vice president. When the votes were counted, Jefferson and Burr had tied with 73, while Adams garnered 64 and Pinckney 63. Under the Constitution, the existing House of Representatives would decide the election.

Voting in the House continued for six days; in the end, a deal was struck that gave Jefferson the presidency on the thirty-sixth ballot. The bitterly fought election prompted the adoption of the Twelfth Amendment, which provided that electors would thenceforth cast separate ballots for president and vice president.

In an 1820 letter to then-president James Monroe, Jefferson linked "the revolution of 1776" to "that of 1800." Historians debate whether the so-called Revolution

Dissent During Wartime

The Quasi-War with France in 1798–1799 spawned the nation's first attempt to suppress dissent. By criminalizing dissenting speech, the Sedition Act of 1798 tried to mute criticism of the war and President John Adams. Fifteen men were indicted and ten fined and jailed after being convicted under the statute.

Although Americans might assume that their right to free speech under the First Amendment, now more fully accepted than it was two centuries ago, protects dissenters during wartime, history suggests otherwise. Every conflict has stimulated efforts to suppress dissenters. During the Civil War, the Union jailed civilian Confederate sympathizers. During the First World War, the government deported immigrant aliens who criticized the war effort. World War II brought the silencing of those who had opposed American entry into the war. The consequences of antiwar protests in the Vietnam era still affect the nation today, for the American people remain divided over whether the proper course of action in the 1960s and 1970s was dissent from, or acquiescence to, government policy.

The USA PATRIOT Act, adopted after the terrorist attacks of September 11, 2001, removed long-standing restrictions on federal government surveillance of citizens, controversially granting access to library records. Criticism of the wars in Iraq and Afghanistan has raised questions: Do newspapers that publish classified information or pictures of abused prisoners overstep the First Amendment? Can political figures censure the conduct of the wars without being labeled unpatriotic?

Freedom of speech is never easy to maintain, and wartime conditions make it much more difficult. When the nation comes under attack, many argue that dissent should cease. Others contend that people must always have the right to speak freely. Events in the United States since the 9/11 attacks suggest that this legacy remains contentious for the American people.

of 1800 deserves the name Jefferson later gave it. Many of the Republicans' promised reforms failed to materialize. The defeated Federalists retained and indeed strengthened their hold on the federal judiciary. But at the very least, Jefferson's inauguration—which marked the first peaceful transfer of power from one faction to another in a modern republic—ushered in a new era in American political culture, one in which republican theory and partisan practice could coexist. "We are all Republicans, we are all Federalists," the new president proclaimed in his first inaugural address. The unifying sentiment was welcome, but hardly accurate.

Summary

During the 1780s, the republic's upheavals convinced many leaders that the United States needed a more powerful central government. Drafted in 1787, the Constitution created that stronger national framework. The document's supporters—called Federalists—contended that their design was just as "republican" as the flawed Articles of Confederation had been. Those labeled Antifederalists argued otherwise, but ultimately lost the fight.

Inhabitants of the early United States faced changed lives and changed politics. Indian peoples east of the Mississippi River found aspects of their traditional cultures under assault. Enslaved African Americans faced increasingly restrictive laws in the southern colonies. In the North, freedom suits, manumissions, and gradual eman- cipation laws fostered a growing free black community. At the same time, a newly systematic and defensive pro-slavery argument emphasized race (rather than slave or free status) as the determinant of African Americans' standing in the nation. Imag- ined chiefly as mothers of the next generation and selfless contributors to the nation's welfare, white women played a limited role in American public life. Writers and artists promoted such feminine self-sacrifice and other republican virtues.

The years between 1788 and 1800 established enduring precedents for Con- gress, the presidency, and the federal judiciary. The United States forged diplomatic independence. The French Revolution prompted debates over foreign and domestic policy. In the 1790s, the United States saw the emergence of organized factionalism and grassroots politicking involving both men and women. In 1801, after more than a decade of struggle, the Jeffersonian view of an agrarian, decentralized republic prevailed over Alexander Hamilton's vision of a centralized economy and a strong national government.

Chapter Review

Trials of the Confederation

What was the significance of the Northwest Ordinance?

The Northwest Ordinance of 1787 included a bill of rights guaranteeing freedom of religion and the right to a jury trial, and it forbade cruel and unusual pun- ishments and nominally prohibited slavery. But its ban on slavery was more symbolic than actual because it did not deny slaveholders living in the territory the right to their human property and included the first fugitive slave law. The Northwest Ordinance also specified the process by which residents of the territories could organize state governments and seek admission to the Union "on an equal footing with the original States." Congress there- fore assured territorial residents the same rights held by citizens of the original states.

From Crisis to the Constitution

How did the question of slavery become linked to the new U.S. Constitution?

Slavery came into play at the Constitutional Con- vention as states debated how their populations should be counted in determining the number of representa- tives each would get in the lower house of Congress. Slave states wanted their bondspeople fully counted, while those from states with few slaves wanted only free people counted. The dispute was resolved by a formula known as the three-fifths compromise, noting that three-fifths of slaves would be included in population totals used to determine congressional districts. While the words *slave* and *slavery* are not used in the Constitution, it nonethe- less included direct and indirect protections for slavery, among them assistance in putting down revolts, return- ing fugitive slaves to masters, and agreeing not to end the importation of bondspeople for twenty years.

Promoting a Virtuous Citizenry

How were notions of republican virtue engendered in post-revolutionary America?

Republican writers and artists produced works that reinforced republican notions. For example, Mason Locke Weems's *Life of Washington* offered a moralizing tale of honesty and integrity. Americans, especially in the North, began to focus on public education as a means to help children become useful citizens. Some argued that since child rearing was women's role, they, too, would need education to help raise virtuous future citizens. The essaying Judith Sargent Murray argued that women and men had equal intellects but unequal schooling and pro- posed that boys and girls be educated alike. Her writings were part of a general rethinking of women's position.

Building a Workable Government

How did the chartering of the Bank of the United States provoke an early constitutional debate?

Treasury Secretary Alexander Hamilton asked Congress to charter a national bank, modeled on England's, which would act as a collecting and disbursing agent for the treasury and the source for national currency. Some political leaders, like James Madison and Thomas Jefferson argued that the Constitution did not give Congress the power to establish the bank. Hamilton, by contrast, stated that Congress could use any means not prohibited by the Constitution to achieve a constitutional end. President Washington agreed, and the bill establishing the Bank of the United States became law.

Building a Nation Among Nations

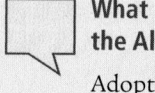

What was the underlying purpose of the Alien and Sedition Acts of 1798?

Adopted by the Federalist-controlled Congress, these acts were designed to suppress dissent—still seen as dangerous and subversive rather than a natural part of a republic—and weaken the competing Republican faction. Hence, the acts targeted recent immigrants, typically Republican supporters, by lengthening the residency requirement for citizenship, among other rules, as well as allowing the president to detain or deport any alien considered dangerous to national security. The Sedition Act outlawed antigovernment conspiracies and curbed free speech by making the writing or uttering of false, malicious, or scandalous statements against the government illegal. Although the Federalists expected the acts to weaken their critics, the laws only increased dissent.

The West in the New Nation

How did the new nation begin to expand its boundaries westward?

The United States nominally controlled the land east of the Mississippi and north of Spanish Florida, and later, through warfare and treaty, managed to extend its northernmost boundary to the Ohio River. Initially, leaders attempted to negotiate with Indians living there for the land; when that failed, war with eight Indian nations ensued, culminating in 1795 with the Treaty of Greenville. This agreement allowed the United States to settle most of what would become Ohio in exchange for acknowledging the principle of Indian sovereignty—by virtue of residence—over lands that had not been ceded.

Created Equal?

What contributed to the growing number of free blacks in America after the Revolution?

Slaves who escaped plantations during the war, those who served in the military, or those who had been freed by their owners or state laws accounted for many of the 60,000 free people of color in the United States by 1790 and 108,000 by 1800. Northern states, which were less reliant on slave labor, increasingly freed slaves and were more likely to adopt laws abolishing slavery. But even there, many states respected owners' "property rights" and preferred gradual manumission over outright abolition. In the courts, too, blacks challenged the contradictions between forced bondage and the ideology of the Revolution, and while often unsuccessful, their actions forced policymakers to grapple with this issue. Postwar economic changes also spurred manumissions, particularly in the Chesapeake, where the shift from tobacco to grain production meant far fewer slaves were required, doubling the free black population in Virginia between 1790 and 1810, for example.

"Revolutions" at the End of the Century

What gave rise to new potential revolutions in America at the end of the eighteenth century?

Three events revealed unresolved issues—and growing tensions—in the new republic. First, Fries's Rebellion questioned the power of the central government to tax, seeing it—much as early revolutionaries had—as a threat to personal liberties and livelihoods. Second, Gabriel's Rebellion of semifree blacks sought to challenge the slave system in the Chesapeake (but ended up inspiring stricter slave laws in the South). And finally, the hotly contested 1800 presidential election revealed a structural flaw in the Constitution, which required that presidential electors vote for two men without designating one as president and the other as vice president, thus creating the tie between Jefferson and Burr. It led to the Twelfth Amendment, which provided that electors cast separate ballots for presidential and vice presidential candidates.

Suggestions for Further Reading

Annette Gordon-Reed, *The Hemingses of Monticello: An American Family* (2008)

Eliga Gould, *Among the Powers of the Earth: The American Revolution and the Making of a New World Empire* (2012)

Woody Holton, *Unruly Americans and the Origins of the Constitution* (2007)

David Jaffe, *A New Nation of Goods: The Material Culture of Early America* (2010)

Catherine O'Donnell Kaplan, *Men of Letters in the Early Republic: Cultivating Forums of Citizenship* (2008)

Pauline Maier, *Ratification: The People Debate the Constitution, 1787–1788* (2010)

David Andrew Nichols, *Red Gentlemen & White Savages: Indians, Federalists, and the Search for Order on the American Frontier* (2008)

Jeffrey L. Pasley, *"The Tyranny of Printers": Newspaper Politics in the Early American Republic* (2001)

David Waldstreicher, *Slavery's Constitution: From Revolution to Ratification* (2009)

Rosemarie Zagarri, *Revolutionary Backlash: Women and Politics in the Early American Republic* (2007)

Defining the Nation

1801–1823

Eager to distinguish himself from the allegedly aristocratic ways of his Federalist predecessors, President Thomas Jefferson displayed impatience for ceremony. But on his first New Year's Day in office, he awaited the ceremonial presentation of a much-heralded tribute to his commitment, as one gift bearer put it, to "defend Republicanism and baffle all the arts of Aristocracy." Crafted in Massachusetts, the belated inaugural gift weighed more than twelve hundred pounds and measured four feet in diameter, bearing the inscription "THE GREATEST CHEESE IN AMERICA—FOR THE GREATEST MAN IN AMERICA."

The "mammoth cheese" was devised the previous July and made by the "Ladies" of Cheshire, a western Massachusetts farming community as Jeffersonian-Republican as it was Baptist. As a religious minority in largely Congregationalist New England, the Cheshire Baptists celebrated a president whose vision featured agrarianism and separation of church and state.

Federalist editors joked that the mammoth cheese's maggot-infested condition upon delivery symbolized the nation under Republican rule. Its size resulted from the excesses of democracy, in which even women and backwoods preachers could play leading roles.

The Federalists' derision of the mammoth cheese inspired further demonstrations of democratic pride. In subsequent months, a Philadelphia baker sold "Mammoth Bread," and two years later, in 1804, a "mammoth loaf" was served in the Capitol to a crowd of Federalist-disparaging Republicans, including President Jefferson.

People excluded from formal political participation—the vote—expressed ideal visions for the nation's future when they petitioned legislatures, marched in parades, debated in taverns—and sent the president a mammoth cheese. Behind such symbolism lay serious political ideologies. Jeffersonians believed virtue derived from agricultural endeavors and thus celebrated the acquisition of the Louisiana Territory. Their efforts to expand their agriculturally based "empire of liberty" westward were resisted by Native Americans and their European allies, and sometimes by Federalists. The War of 1812 largely removed such resistance, facilitating the United States' nearly unbridled expansion west. Although that war ended with few issues resolved, it secured the United States' sovereignty, opened much of the West to European Americans and their African American slaves, and helped spur revolutions in transportation and industry.

Contemporary observers hailed postwar nationalism as an "Era of Good Feelings," but when economic boom turned to bust, nationalistic optimism faded. No issue proved more divisive than slavery's future in the West, as Missouri's petition for statehood revealed.

As you read this chapter, keep the following questions in mind:

- **What characterized the two main competing visions for national development?**

- **How did America's relationship with Europe influence political and economic developments?**

- **In what ways did nonvoting Americans—most blacks, women, and Native Americans—take part in defining the new nation?**

Political Visions

Was Jefferson's election and political vision truly "the revolution of 1800"?

In his inaugural address, Jefferson appealed to opponents and supporters as citizens with common republican beliefs: "We are all republicans, we are all federalists.... A wise and frugal government, which shall restrain men from injuring one another, which shall leave them free to regulate their pursuits of industry and improvement, and shall not take from the mouth of labor the bread it had earned. This is the sum of good government."

Outgoing president John Adams missed Jefferson's call for unity, having left Washington before dawn. Former friends, he and Jefferson now disliked each other. Democratic-Republicans—as the Republicans of the 1790s now called themselves—and Federalists bitterly disagreed on how society and government should be organized. Federalists advocated a strong national government to promote economic development. Democratic-Republicans believed that limited government would foster republican virtue. Nearly two decades later, Jefferson would call his election "the revolution of 1800."

Separation of Church and State

On the day he received the overripe cheese, Jefferson reciprocated with a letter to the Baptist association in Danbury, Connecticut, proclaiming that the

Chronology

1801	Marshall becomes chief justice
	Jefferson inaugurated as president
1801–05	United States defeats Barbary pirates
1803	*Marbury v. Madison*
	Louisiana Purchases
1804	Jefferson reelected president
1804–06	Lewis and Clark Expedition
1805	Tenskwatawa emerges as Shawnee leader
1807	Chesapeake affair
	Embargo Act
1808	Congress bans slave importation
	Madison elected president
1808–13	Tenskwatawa and Tecumseh organize Indian resistance
1811	National Road begun
1812	Madison reelected president
1812–15	War of 1812
1813	Tecumseh's death
	Boston Manufacturing Company starts textile mill in Waltham, Massachusetts
1814	Treaty of Ghent
1814–15	Hartford Convention
1815	Battle of New Orleans
1817	Regular steamboat travel begins on Mississippi
1817–25	Erie Canal constructed
1819	*McCulloch v. Maryland*
	Adams-Onís Treaty
1819–early 1820s	First major depression
1820–21	Missouri Compromise
1822	Colonization of Liberia begins (formally established in 1824)
1823	Monroe Doctrine

Constitution's First Amendment supported a "wall of separation between church and state." New England Baptists hailed Jefferson as a hero, but New England Federalists believed their worst fears were confirmed. During the 1800 election, Federalists waged a venomous campaign, incorrectly labeling Jefferson an atheist. Their rhetoric proved so effective that, after Jefferson's election, some New England women hid their Bibles in their gardens to foil Democratic-Republicans allegedly bent on confiscating them.

Religious Revivals

Jefferson became president during a period of religious revivalism, particularly among Methodists and Baptists, whose democratic preaching—all humans, they said, were equal in God's eyes—encouraged a growing democratic political culture. The most famous revival was at Cane Ridge, Kentucky, in August 1801. According to one report, twenty-five thousand men and women, free and enslaved, attended. The call to personal repentance and conversion invigorated southern Protestantism, giving churches an evangelical base. All revivalists believed in individual self-improvement, but northern revivalists also emphasized communal improvement, becoming missionaries for individual salvation and social reform (see Chapter 10).

Emboldened by secular and religious ideologies about equality, society's non-elites articulated their own political visions and worked to reshape the debates. When the Cheshire Baptists sent their cheese to President Jefferson, for example, they pointedly informed the Virginia planter that it had been made "without a single slave to assist."

Political Mobilization

The revolution of 1800, which gave the Democratic-Republicans majorities in both houses of Congress along with the presidency, resulted from an electorate limited largely to property-holding men. Under the Constitution, states regulated voting. Nowhere but New Jersey could property-owning, single women vote; that right was granted inadvertently and revoked in 1807. In 1800, free black men meeting property qualifications could vote everywhere but Delaware, Georgia, South Carolina, and Virginia, though local custom often kept them from exercising that right. Nonetheless, partisan politics captured Americans' imaginations. Political mobilization took place locally, as candidates rallied popular support on militia training grounds, in taverns and churches, at court gatherings, and during holiday celebrations. Voters and nonvoters expressed their views through parades, petitions, songs, and debates. Most important, they devoured a growing print culture of pamphlets, broadsides (posters), almanacs, and newspapers.

The Partisan Press

Read aloud in taverns, artisans' workshops, and homes, newspapers gave national importance to local events. In 1800, the nation had 260 newspapers; by 1810, it had 396—virtually all unabashedly partisan.

Courtesy Winterthur Museum, Museum purchase, 1959.131

Although most places limited the vote to property-owning white men, elections, such as this one in Philadelphia, drew multiracial crowds of men, women, and children.

The parties adopted official organs. After his election, Jefferson persuaded the *National Intelligencer* to move from Philadelphia to Washington, where it became the Democratic-Republicans' voice. In 1801, Alexander Hamilton launched the *New York Evening Post* as the Federalist vehicle. Published six or seven times a week, party papers helped invigorate the growing obsession with partisan politics.

Limited Government

To bring into his administration men sharing his vision of individual liberty, an agrarian republic, and limited government, Jefferson rejected appointments that Adams made in his presidency's last days and dismissed Federalist customs collectors. He awarded treasury and judicial offices to Republicans. Jeffersonians worked to make the government leaner. If Alexander Hamilton had viewed the national debt as the engine of economic growth, Jefferson deemed it the source of government corruption. Secretary of the Treasury Albert Gallatin halved the army budget and reduced the 1802 navy budget by two-thirds. He moved to reduce the national debt from $83 million to $57 million, hoping to retire it by 1817. Jefferson closed two of the nation's five diplomatic missions abroad, at The Hague and in Berlin. And the Democratic-Republican–controlled Congress oversaw the repeal of all internal taxes, including the despised whiskey tax of 1791.

Ideas of liberty also distinguished Democratic-Republicans from Federalists. Opposition to the Alien and Sedition Acts of 1798 had united Republicans. Jefferson now declined to use the acts against his opponents, instead pardoning those convicted of violating them.

Congress let the Sedition Act expire in 1801 and the Alien Act in 1802, and repealed the Naturalization Act of 1798, which required fourteen years of residency for citizenship. The 1802 act that replaced it required only five years of residency, loyalty to the Constitution, and the forsaking of foreign allegiances and titles. It remained the basis of naturalized American citizenship into the twentieth century.

Judicial Politics

To many Democratic-Republicans, the judiciary represented a centralizing and undemocratic force, since judges were appointed, not elected, and served for life. At Jefferson's prompting, the House impeached (indicted) and the Senate convicted Federal District Judge John Pickering of New Hampshire, whose alleged alcoholism made him an easy target. The House impeached Supreme Court Justice Samuel Chase for judicial misconduct. A staunch Federalist, Chase had pushed for prosecutions under the Sedition Act, campaigned for Adams in 1800, and denounced Jefferson's administration. But Democratic-Republicans failed to muster the two-thirds Senate majority necessary for conviction. The failure to remove Chase preserved the Court's independence and established the precedent that criminal actions, not political disagreements, justified removal from office.

The Marshall Court

Although Jefferson appointed three new Supreme Court justices, the Court remained a Federalist stronghold under John Marshall. Even after the Democratic-Republicans achieved a majority of Court seats in 1811, Marshall remained influential as chief justice. Under the Marshall Court (1801–1835), the Supreme Court upheld federal supremacy over the states while protecting commercial interests.

Marshall made the Court an equal branch of government. He strengthened the Court by having it speak with a more unified voice; rather than issuing individual concurring judgments, justices now issued joint majority opinions. From 1801 through 1805, Marshall wrote twenty-four of the Court's twenty-six decisions; through 1810, he wrote 85 percent of the opinions.

Judicial Review

In his last hours as president, Adams named Federalist William Marbury a justice of the peace in the District of Columbia. Jefferson's secretary of state, James Madison, declined to certify the appointment, allowing the new president to appoint a Democratic-Republican. Marbury sued, requesting a writ of mandamus (a court order forcing the president to appoint him). If the Supreme Court ruled in Marbury's favor in **Marbury v. Madison**, the president probably would not comply, and the Court could not force him to do so. Yet by refusing to issue the writ, the Federalist-dominated bench would hand the Democratic-Republicans a victory.

Instead, Marshall recast the issue. He ruled that Marbury had a right to his appointment but that the Supreme Court could not compel Madison to honor it because the Constitution did not grant the Court power to issue a writ of mandamus. Without specific mention in the Constitution, Marshall wrote, the section of the Judiciary Act of 1789 authorizing the Court to issue writs was unconstitutional. Thus, the Supreme Court denied itself the power to issue writs of mandamus but established its far greater power to judge the constitutionality of laws. In doing so, Marshall fashioned the theory of judicial review. Because the Constitution was "the supreme law of the land," Marshall wrote, any federal or state act contrary to the Constitution must be null and void. This power of the Supreme Court to determine the constitutionality of legislation and presidential acts permanently enhanced the independence of the judiciary and breathed life into the Constitution.

Marbury v. Madison Case in which the Supreme Court's power to determine the constitutionality of laws was established.

Election of 1804

In the first election after the Twelfth Amendment's ratification, Jefferson dropped Aaron Burr as his running mate and, to establish a North–South balance, chose George Clinton of New York. They swamped their opponents—South Carolinian Charles Cotesworth Pinckney and New Yorker Rufus King—in the electoral college by 162 votes to 14, carrying fifteen of the seventeen states. The 1804 election escalated the animosity between Burr and Hamilton, who supported Burr's rival in the New York gubernatorial election. When Hamilton called Burr a liar, Burr challenged Hamilton to a duel. Because New York had outlawed dueling, the encounter occurred in New Jersey. Details of the duel remain hazy but Hamilton died after being shot by Burr. New York and New Jersey prosecutors indicted Burr for murder.

Burr fled to the West. While historians disagree about his motives, the "Burr Conspiracy" was understood at the time as a scheme with Brigadier General James Wilkinson to create a new empire by militarily taking what is now Texas and by persuading existing western territories to leave the United States. Tried for treason in 1807, Burr faced a prosecution aided by President Jefferson but overseen by Jefferson's rival Chief Justice Marshall. Prompted by Marshall to interpret treason narrowly, the jury acquitted Burr, who fled to Europe.

Nationalism and Culture

As statesmen bickered, other Americans conveyed their nationalist visions artistically. Painters continued to memorialize great birth scenes of American nationhood, such as the Declaration of Independence's signing, Revolutionary War battles, and the Constitutional Convention. Four of John Trumbull's revolutionary scenes, commissioned in 1817, still hang in the Capitol building rotunda in Washington.

Architecturally, Americans self-consciously constructed a new, independent nation. Designed by Major Pierre Charles L'Enfant, the city of Washington was meant to embody a "reciprocity of sight:" each of the government's three branches—legislative, judicial, and executive—should keep an eye on one another. Across America, wealthier citizens commissioned Federal-style homes, which imitated the simplicity of classical architecture and used indigenous building materials.

The era's best-selling book was Noah Webster's spelling book, which proposed making English more "republican." It sold nearly 100 million copies by the end of the nineteenth century. Webster supported a national language that, unlike "King's English," would not require elite training. Words should be spelled as they sound—for example, "honor" should replace "honour."

Continental Expansion and Indian Resistance

Why was the Louisiana Purchase among Jefferson's most popular decisions as president?

By 1800, hundreds of thousands of white Americans had settled in the rich Ohio River and Mississippi River valleys, intruding on Indian lands. In the Northwest they raised foodstuffs, primarily wheat; in the Southwest they cultivated cotton. During the American Revolution, cotton production was profitable only for the Sea Island planters in South Carolina and Georgia, who grew the long-staple variety. Short-staple cotton, which grew in the interior, was unmarketable because its sticky seeds required removal by hand. After New England inventor **Eli Whitney** designed a cotton gin in 1793, allowing one person to remove the same number of seeds that previously required fifty people, cultivation of short-staple cotton spread rapidly into Louisiana, Mississippi, Alabama, Arkansas, and Tennessee. The cotton gin greatly increased the demand for slaves who seeded, tended, and harvested cotton fields.

Eli Whitney Invented the cotton gin, which made cleaning of southern cotton faster and cheaper.

American settlers depended on free access to the Mississippi River and its Gulf port, New Orleans. Whoever controlled the port of New Orleans had a hand on the American economy's throat.

New Orleans

Spain, which acquired France's territory west of the Mississippi after the Seven Years' War (1763), secretly transferred it back to France in 1800 and 1801.

MAP 8.1

Louisiana Purchase

The Louisiana Purchase (1803) doubled the area of the United States and opened the trans-Mississippi West for American settlement. Source: Copyright © Cengage Learning 2015

American officials discovered this in 1802, when Napoleon seemed poised to rebuild a French empire in the New World. American concerns intensified when Spanish officials, on the eve of ceding control to the French, violated Pinckney's Treaty by barring Americans from storing their products at New Orleans prior to transshipment to foreign markets. Western farmers and eastern merchants thought Napoleon had closed the port; they talked war.

To relieve the pressure for war and win western farmers' support, Jefferson urged Congress to authorize the call-up of eighty thousand militiamen. He also sent Virginia's Governor James Monroe to join Robert Livingston in France to buy the port of New Orleans and as much of the Mississippi Valley as possible. Arriving in Paris in April 1803, Monroe learned that France had already offered to sell Louisiana to the United States for just $15 million. With St. Domingue torn from French control by revolution and slave revolt, Napoleon abandoned dreams of a New World empire, and instead now urgently needed money to wage war against Britain. On April 30, Monroe and Livingston signed a treaty to buy the 827,000-square-mile territory (see Map 8.1).

Louisiana Purchase

The **Louisiana Purchase** ensured that the United States would control the Mississippi's mouth, pleasing western settlers who relied on the river to market

Louisiana Purchase The U.S. purchase of the Louisiana Territory (the area from the Mississippi River to the Rocky Mountains) from France in 1803 for $15 million. The purchase virtually doubled the area of the United States.

Link to Thomas Jefferson: Constitutionality of the Louisiana Purchase (1803)

their goods. It also inspired those who imagined the United States as the nexus of international trade networks between Europe and Asia. Louisiana promised to fulfill easterners' dreams of cheap, fertile lands. Its vast expanse meant, too, that land could be reserved for Indians displaced by white settlers and their black slaves. But critics doubted its constitutionality (even Jefferson agonized over it); others worried that it belied the Democratic-Republicans' commitment to debt reduction. And some New England Federalists complained that it undermined their commercial interests and threatened the republic by spreading the population beyond where it could be controlled. Overall, though, the Louisiana Purchase was the most popular achievement of Jefferson's presidency.

When the United States acquired the territory, hundreds of thousands of people there became American subjects, including Native Americans as well as people of European and African descent. Around New Orleans, Louisiana's colonial heritage was reflected in its people: creoles of French and Spanish descent; slaves of African descent; free people of color; Acadians, or Cajuns (descendants of French settlers in eastern Canada); and some Germans, Irish, and English. The 1810 census reported that 97,000 non-Indians lived in the area. Although Jefferson imagined the West as an "empire of liberty," free people of color soon discovered their exclusion from the Louisiana Purchase treaty's provision that "the inhabitants of the ceded territory" would gain American citizenship. Denied the right to vote and serve on juries, New Orleans' people of color fought to retain their rights to form families and to bequeath property and belongings as they pleased, and some succeeded.

Lewis and Clark Expedition

Jefferson feared that, if Americans did not claim the trans-Mississippi West, the British, who still controlled present-day Canada and parts of the Pacific Northwest, would. He launched a military-style mission to chart the region's commercial possibilities—its water passages to the Pacific and trading opportunities with Indians—while cataloguing its geography, peoples, flora, and fauna.

The Corps of Discovery expedition, headed by Meriwether Lewis and William Clark, began in May 1804 and lasted for more than two years; it traveled up the Missouri River, across the Rockies, and down the Columbia to the Pacific Ocean—and back. The **Lewis and Clark Expedition** members "discovered" (as they saw it) dozens of previously unknown Indian tribes, many of whom had long before discovered Europeans. Although the expedition was prepared for possible conflict, its goal was peaceable: to foster trade relations, win political allies, and tap into Indians' knowledge of the landscape. Lewis and Clark brought twenty-one bags of gifts for Native American leaders to establish goodwill and to stimulate interest in trade. Most of the interactions were cordial, but when Indians were unimpressed by the gifts, tensions arose.

The Corps of Discovery proved democratic in seating enlisted men on courts-martial and allowing Clark's black slave York and the expedition's female guide **Sacagawea** to vote on where to locate winter quarters in 1805. But unlike the expedition's other members, neither York nor Sacagawea drew wages, and when York later demanded his freedom, Clark repaid him with "a severe trouncing."

Lewis and Clark Expedition Expedition led by Meriwether Lewis and William Clark to explore the Louisiana Territory.

Sacagawea Female Native American guide who aided Lewis and Clark in exploring the Louisiana Territory.

Lewis and Clark failed to discover a Northwest Passage to the Pacific, but their explorations contributed to nationalist visions of American expansion. Fossils and Native American artifacts they collected were displayed in Charles Willson Peale's museum at Independence Hall in Philadelphia, an institution emphasizing the uniqueness of America's geography and republican experiment.

Nationalists overlooked Indians' land claims. Although Jefferson had more sympathy for Indians than many of his contemporaries—he expressed interest in their cultures and believed Indians to be intellectually equal to whites—he nonetheless lobbied, unsuccessfully, for a constitutional amendment that would transport them west of the Mississippi into Louisiana Territory. He became involved in efforts to pressure the Chickasaws to sell their land, and if legal methods failed, he advocated trickery. Traders, he suggested, might run them into debt, which they would have to repay "by a cessation of lands."

Divisions Among Indian Peoples

Some Indian nations adopted white customs as a means of survival and often agreed to sell their lands and move west. These "accommodationists" (or "progressives") were opposed by "traditionalists," who urged adherence to native ways and refused to relinquish their lands. Distinctions between accommodationists and traditionalists were not always clear-cut, however.

In the early 1800s, two Shawnee brothers, Tenskwatawa (1775–1837) and **Tecumseh** (1768–1813), led a traditionalist revolt against American encroachment by fostering a pan-Indian federation centered in the Old Northwest and reaching into parts of the South. By the 1800s, the Shawnees lost most of their Ohio land, occupying scattered sites there and in the Michigan and Louisiana territories. Despondent, Lalawethika—Tenskwatawa's name as a youth—turned to a combination of European remedies (particularly whiskey) and Native American ones, becoming a shaman in 1804. But when European diseases ravaged his village, he despaired.

Tecumseh The Shawnee leader who sought to unite several tribes from Canada to Georgia against encroachment on their lands by American settlers; allied with the British in the War of 1812.

Tenskwatawa and Tecumseh

Lalawethika emerged from an illness in 1805 as a new man, renamed Tenskwatawa ("the Open Door") or—by whites—"the Prophet." Claiming to have died and been resurrected, he traveled in the Ohio River valley as a religious leader, attacking the decline of moral values among Native Americans, warning against whiskey, and condemning intertribal battles. He urged Indians to return to the old ways and to abandon white ways: to hunt with bows and arrows, not guns; to stop wearing hats; and to give up bread for corn and beans.

By 1808, Tenskwatawa and his older brother Tecumseh had turned their focus to resisting American aggression. They invited all Indians to settle in pan-Indian towns in Indiana, first at Greenville (1806–1808) and then at Prophetstown (1808–1812). This challenged the treaty-making process by denying the claims of Indians who were guaranteed the same land under the 1795 Treaty of Greenville. Younger Indians flocked to Tecumseh, the more political of the two brothers.

Convinced that only an Indian federation could stop white settlement, Tecumseh sought to unify northern and southern Indians from Canada to Georgia. Among southern Indians, only one Creek faction welcomed him, but his efforts alarmed

This Charles M. Russell painting of the Lewis and Clark Expedition depicts Sacagawea talking with Chinook Indians. A Shoshone, Sacagawea knew the land and the languages of the mountain Indians, and helped guide the Corps of Discovery.

Russell, Charles Marion (1865–1926)/Peter Newark American Pictures/Bridgeman Art Library

white settlers and government officials. In November 1811, while Tecumseh was in the South, Indiana governor William Henry Harrison moved against Tenskwatawa and his followers. During the battle of Tippecanoe, the army burned their town; as they fled, the Indians exacted revenge on white settlers. When Harrison vowed reprisals, Tecumseh allied with the British. This alliance in the West, combined with American issues over neutrality rights on the high seas, propelled the United States toward war with Britain.

The Nation in the Orbit of Europe

What led to the War of 1812?

The early republic's economy relied heavily on fishing and the carrying trade, with the American merchant marine transporting commodities between nations. Merchants in Boston, Salem, and Philadelphia traded with China, sending cloth and metal to swap for furs with Chinook Indians on the Oregon coast, and then sailing to China to trade for porcelain, tea, and silk. The slave trade lured American ships to Africa. Not long after Jefferson's first inaugural address, the United States was at war with Tripoli—a state along the Barbary Coast of North Africa—over a principle that would long be a cornerstone of American foreign policy: freedom of the seas. That is, outside national territorial waters, the high seas should be open for free transit.

First Barbary War

In 1801, the bashaw (pasha) of Tripoli declared war on the United States for its refusal to pay tribute for safe passage of its ships through the Mediterranean. Jefferson deployed a naval squadron to protect American ships. After two years of stalemate, Jefferson declared a blockade of Tripoli, but when the American frigate *Philadelphia* ran aground in the harbor, its three hundred officers and sailors were imprisoned. Jefferson refused to ransom them, and a small American force accompanied by Arab, Greek, and African mercenaries marched from Egypt to the "shores of Tripoli" to seize the port of Derne. A treaty ended the war in 1805, but the United States continued to pay tribute to the three other Barbary states—Algiers, Morocco, and Tunis—until 1815. In the intervening years, the United States became embroiled in European conflicts.

At first, Jefferson distanced the nation from European turmoil in the wake of the French Revolution. After the Senate ratified the Jay Treaty in 1795, the United States and Great Britain reconciled. Britain withdrew from its western forts on American soil and interfered less in American trade with France. Then, in May 1803, two weeks after Napoleon sold Louisiana to the United States, France was at war against Britain and, later, Britain's continental allies, Prussia, Austria, and Russia. Initially, the United States benefited, as American merchants gained control of most of the West Indian trade. After 1805, when Britain defeated the French and Spanish fleets at Trafalgar, Britain's Royal Navy tightened its control of the oceans. Two months later, Napoleon crushed the Russian and Austrian armies at Austerlitz. Stalemated, France and Britain launched a commercial war, blockading trade and costing the United States dearly.

Threats to American Sovereignty

To replenish their supply of sailors, British vessels stopped American ships and impressed (forcibly recruited) British deserters, British-born naturalized American seamen, and other sailors suspected of being British. Perhaps six to eight thousand Americans were impressed between 1803 and 1812. Alleged deserters—many of them American citizens—faced British courts-martial. Americans saw the principle of "once a British subject, always a British subject" as a mockery of U.S. citizenship and national sovereignty. Americans also resented the British interfering with their West Indian trade and seizing American vessels within U.S. territorial waters.

In April 1806, Congress responded with the Non-Importation Act, barring British manufactured goods from American ports. Because the act exempted most cloth and metal articles, it had little impact on British trade; instead, it warned the British what to expect if they continued to violate American neutral rights. In November, Jefferson suspended the act while Baltimore lawyer William Pinkney joined James Monroe in London to negotiate a settlement. The treaty they carried home did not mention impressments; hence the president never submitted it for ratification.

Difficult Anglo-American relations came to a head in June 1807 when the USS *Chesapeake*, sailing from Norfolk for the Mediterranean, was stopped by the British frigate *Leopard*, whose officers demanded to search the ship for British deserters. Refused, the *Leopard* opened fire, killing three Americans and wounding eighteen others. The British seized four deserters, three of whom held American citizenship; one was hanged. The incident outraged Americans while exposing American military weakness.

The Embargo of 1807

Jefferson responded with what he called "peaceable coercion." In July, the president closed American waters to British warships and increased military and naval expenditures. In December 1807, Jefferson put economic pressure on Great Britain by invoking the Non-Importation Act, then implementing the **Embargo Act of 1807**. The embargo, which forbade exports from the United States to any country, was a short-term measure to avoid war by pressuring Britain and France to respect American rights and by preventing confrontation between American merchant vessels and European warships.

Embargo Act of 1807 Act that forbade exports from the United States to any country.

The embargo's biggest economic impact, however, fell on the United States. Exports declined by 80 percent in 1808, squeezing New England shippers and workers. Manufacturers received a boost, as the domestic market became theirs exclusively. Merchants began to shift from shipping to manufacturing. In 1807, there were twenty cotton and woolen mills in New England; by 1813, there were more than two hundred.

International Slave Trade

With Jefferson's encouragement, Congress voted in 1807 to abolish the international slave trade as of January 1, 1808—the earliest date permissible under the Constitution. South Carolina still allowed the legal importation of slaves, but most of the state's planters favored a ban, nervous about adding to the black population of a state where whites were outnumbered. The final bill provided that smuggled slaves would be sold according to the laws of the state or territory in which they arrived, underscoring that even illegal slaves were property. Had the bill not done so, threatened one Georgia congressman, the result might have been "resistance to the authority of the Government," even civil war.

During the last four months of 1807, sixteen thousand African slaves arrived at Gadsden Wharf in Charleston, where they were detained by merchants eager to wait out the January 1 deadline. Although hundreds, if not thousands of these slaves died in the disease-ridden holding pens before they could be sold, merchants calculated that the increased value of those who survived would outweigh the losses. Even after January 1, 1808, a brisk and profitable illegal trade emerged. In 1819, Congress authorized the president to use force to intercept slave ships along the African coast, but the small American navy could not have halted the illicit trade.

Early Abolitionism and Colonization

From the nation's earliest days—in Philadelphia, New York, Albany, Boston, and Nantucket—free blacks formed societies to petition legislatures, seek judicial

redress, stage marches, and publish tracts chroni-
cling slavery's horrors. By 1830, the nation had fifty
African American abolitionist societies.

After the Revolution, white abolitionists also
formed antislavery organizations in places like
Boston and Philadelphia, with its large population
of Quakers, whose religious beliefs emphasized
human equality. These reformers pressed for gradual
abolition and an end to the international slave trade.
Although they aided African Americans seeking
freedom through judicial decisions, their assumptions about blacks' racial inferiority kept them from
advocating for equal rights. Early white abolitionists
were typically wealthy men whose societies excluded
women, African Americans, and nonelites.

Elites often supported the colonization movement, which crystallized in 1816 with the organization of the American Colonization Society.
Its members planned to purchase and relocate
American slaves and free blacks to Africa or the
Caribbean. Supporters included Thomas Jefferson,
James Madison, James Monroe, and Henry Clay. In
1824, the society founded Liberia, on Africa's west
coast, and began a settlement for African Americans
who were willing to go. The society had resettled
nearly twelve thousand by 1860. Some coloniza-
tionists aimed to strengthen slavery by ridding the South of troublesome slaves or
to purge the North of African Americans altogether. Others hoped colonization
would improve African Americans' conditions. Although some African Americans
supported the movement, black abolitionists generally denounced it.

*In an effort to win support for measures to end the international
slave trade and slavery itself, abolitionists published drawings
of the inhumanely cramped slave ships, where each person
was allotted a space roughly the size of a coffin. Disease spread
rapidly under such conditions, causing many slaves to die before
reaching American shores.*

Election of 1808

Once congressional discussion of the international
slave trade subsided, politicians focused on the
embargo, especially as the 1808 presidential elec-
tion neared. Democratic-Republicans suffered from factional dissent in seaboard
states hobbled by trade restrictions. Although nine state legislatures passed resolutions urging Jefferson to run again, the president declined and supported James
Madison, his secretary of state. Madison won the endorsement of the party's congressional caucus, but Virginia Democratic-Republicans put forth James Monroe,
who later withdrew. Madison and Vice President George Clinton headed the ticket.
Charles Cotesworth Pinckney and Rufus King again ran on the Federalist ticket.

The younger Federalists played up widespread disaffection with Democratic-
Republican policy, especially the embargo. Pinckney received 47 electoral votes
to Madison's 122, but he carried all of New England except Vermont, and won
Delaware. Federalists also gained seats in Congress and captured the New York
State legislature. Still, the transition from one Democratic-Republican administra-
tion to the next went smoothly.

Emigration to Liberia

Even as European immigrants sought republican freedoms in the United States, close to twelve thousand African Americans sought similar opportunities in Liberia—first a colony organized by the American Colonization Society (1822), then an independent nation (1847) along Africa's west coast.

Excluded from the American Revolution's promises of equality, some African Americans advocated resettlement in the Caribbean, Canada, and, especially, Africa. In 1816, Paul Cuffee, an abolitionist and shipping merchant of African American and Native American descent, resettled nine African American families in Sierra Leone, a British colony established for freed slaves. After his death the following year, the American Colonization Society (ACS) continued his work, with such members as President James Monroe and Senator Henry Clay. In 1824, the ACS formally established Liberia, to which it encouraged immigration of freeborn and recently freed African Americans. The ACS's members held wide-ranging views; some saw slavery as a threat to American principles or prosperity, while others aimed primarily to deport free blacks, widely seen as a threat to slavery. Because ACS leaders called blacks "useless and pernicious" (Henry Clay) and reasoned that colonization would secure American slavery, many African Americans denounced ACS-sponsored emigration.

But others saw Liberia as the best opportunity for freedom and as a chance to enlighten native Africans. Initially, American transplants succumbed in large numbers to malaria and struggled to wrestle land and power from indigenous populations. Within a generation, though, the Americo-Liberians had established themselves as elites, subjecting native populations to the second-class citizenship they themselves experienced in the United States.

The Republic of Liberia declared its independence from the ACS in 1847, and today only about 5 percent of its population descends from original settlers. But its constitution is modeled on the U.S. Constitution, its official language is English, its flag resembles the American stars-and-bars, and the American dollar is accepted alongside the Liberian dollar. For the past three decades, the nation has suffered from violent political turmoil over who should rule: the descendants of the nineteenth-century Americo-Liberians or leaders of indigenous ethnic groups. Begun in the 1820s, African American emigration to Liberia forged a link with both immediate and enduring consequences.

Eager to persuade readers of Liberia's success as a colony for former American slaves, colonizationists published images such as this one of the president's house in Monrovia, in which sparsely clad African natives are juxtaposed with genteel American transplants. Even as the image lauds the supposed superiority of African Americans to Africans, it implies that African Americans will themselves fare much better in Africa than they could in the United States.

CORBIS

Women and Politics

Wives of elected and appointed officials played crucial roles in facilitating the transition, fostering conversation and diplomatic negotiation, providing an ear or a voice for unofficial messages, and—in international affairs—standing as surrogates for their nation. Elite women hosted events that muted partisan rivalries. Political wives' interactions among themselves served political purposes, too: when First Lady Dolley Madison visited congressmen's wives, she cultivated goodwill for her husband while collecting recipes so she could serve regional cuisine at White House functions.

Jeffersonians appealed directly for women's support of their embargo. Sympathetic women responded by spurning imported fabric and making (or directing their slaves to make) homespun clothing. Federalists, however, encouraged women to "keep commerce alive," and sympathetic women bought smuggled goods.

Failed Policies

Facing domestic opposition, the embargo collapsed. Instead, the Non-Intercourse Act of 1809 reopened trade with all nations except Britain and France, and authorized the president to resume trade with those two nations once they respected American neutral rights. In June 1809, President Madison reopened trade with Britain after its minister to the United States promised that Britain would repeal restrictions on American trade. But His Majesty's government in London repudiated the minister's assurances, leading Madison to revert to nonintercourse.

When the Non-Intercourse Act expired in 1810, Congress substituted Macon's Bill Number 2, reopening trade with both Great Britain and France but providing that, when either nation stopped violating American commercial rights, the president would suspend American commerce with the other. When Napoleon accepted, Madison declared nonintercourse on Great Britain in 1811. Although the French continued to seize American ships, Britain became the main focus of American hostility because it dominated the seas.

In spring 1812, the British admiralty ordered its ships not to stop, search, or seize American warships, and in June Britain reopened the seas to American shipping. But before word of this policy change reached America, Congress declared war.

Mr. Madison's War

The House voted 79 to 49 for war; the Senate, 19 to 13. Democratic-Republicans favored war by 98 to 23; Federalists opposed it 39 to 0. Those who favored war, including President Madison, pointed to assaults on American sovereignty and honor: impressment, violation of neutral trading rights, and British alliances with western Indians. Others saw an opportunity to conquer and annex British Canada. Most militant were land-hungry southerners and westerners—the "**War Hawks**" —led by John C. Calhoun of South Carolina and first-term congressman and House Speaker Henry Clay of Kentucky. Most representatives from the coastal states, and especially the Northeast, feared trade disruption to commerce and opposed "Mr. Madison's War."

Initially, the Federalists benefited from antiwar sentiment. They joined renegade Democratic-Republicans in supporting New York City mayor DeWitt Clinton for president in 1812. Clinton lost to Madison by 128 to 89 electoral votes, but Federalists gained some congressional seats and carried many local elections. The pro-war South and West remained solidly Democratic-Republican.

Link to James Madison's "War Message" to the Senate and House of Representatives, June 1, 1812

War Hawks Militant Republicans of the early nineteenth century who demanded more aggressive policies and who wanted war with Britain.

MAP 8.2

Major Campaigns of the War of 1812

The land war centered on the U.S.–Canadian border, the Chesapeake Bay, and the Louisiana and Mississippi territories.

Source: Copyright © Cengage Learning 2015

The War of 1812

What were the consequences of the War of 1812?

Lasting from 1812 to 1815, the war unfolded in skirmishes (see Map 8.2) for which the U.S. armed forces were ill prepared. The U.S. Military Academy at West Point, founded in 1802, produced only eighty-nine regular officers, and campaigns were executed poorly. Although the U.S. Navy had a corps of experienced officers, it proved no match for the Royal Navy.

The government's efforts to lure recruits—with sign-up bonuses and promises of three months' pay and rights to purchase 160 acres of western land—had mixed success. At first, recruitment went well among westerners motivated by civic spirit, desire for land, anti-Indian sentiment, and fears of Tecumseh's pan-Indian organization. But with pay delays and inadequate supplies, recruitment dwindled. In New England, Federalists discouraged enlistments. Militias in New England and New York often refused to fight outside their states. Desperate for soldiers, New York offered freedom to slaves who enlisted and compensation to their owners, and the U.S. Army made the same offer to slaves in the Old Northwest and Canada. But in the Deep South, fear of arming slaves kept them out of the military except in New Orleans, where a free black militia dated back to Spanish control of Louisiana. The British recruited slaves by promising freedom in exchange for service. In the end, British forces outnumbered the Americans.

Invasion of Canada

Despite recruitment problems, Americans expected to take Canada easily. Canada's population was sparse, its army small, and the Great Lakes inaccessible to the Royal Navy in the Atlantic. Americans hoped, too, that French Canadians might welcome U.S. forces.

Americans aimed to split Canadian forces and isolate pro-British Indians, especially Tecumseh, whom the British had promised an Indian nation in the Great Lakes region. In July 1812, U.S. general William Hull, territorial governor of Michigan, marched his troops—who outnumbered those of the British—into Upper Canada (modern Ontario), hoping to conquer Montreal. But by abandoning Mackinac Island and Fort Dearborn, and by surrendering Fort Detroit, he left the Midwest exposed. Captain Zachary Taylor provided the only bright spot, giving the Americans a land victory with his September 1812 defense of Fort Harrison in Indiana Territory. By the winter of 1812–1813, the British controlled half of the Old Northwest.

Naval Battles

Despite victories on the Atlantic by the USS *Constitution* (nicknamed "Old Ironsides"), the USS *Wasp*, and the USS *United States*, the American navy—which began the war with just seventeen ships—could not match the powerful Royal Navy. By 1814, the Royal Navy blockaded nearly all American ports along the Atlantic and Gulf coasts. After 1811, American trade overseas declined by nearly 90 percent, and the lost customs duties threatened to bankrupt the federal government and prostrate New England.

The contest for control of the Great Lakes, the key to the war in the Northwest, evolved as a shipbuilding race. Under Master Commandant Oliver Hazard Perry and shipbuilder Noah Brown, the United States outbuilt the British on Lake Erie and defeated them at the bloody Battle of Put-in-Bay on September 10, 1813, gaining control of Lake Erie.

Burning Capitals

A ragged group of Kentucky militia volunteers, armed with swords and knives, marched 20 to 30 miles a day to join General William Henry Harrison's forces in Ohio. Now 4,500 strong, Harrison's troops took Detroit before crossing into Canada, where at the Battle of the Thames they defeated British, Shawnee, and Chippewa forces in October 1813. Among the dead was Tecumseh. The Americans then razed the Canadian capital of York (now Toronto).

Visualizing THE PAST

Selling War

The War of 1812 was not always a popular war, but afterward many Americans trumpeted the war's successes. To the left, we see a recruitment poster from 1812, in which General William Henry Harrison seeks additional cavalrymen. Hampered partly by transportation difficulties, Harrison is unable to offer much—soldiers are even requested to supply their own bacon and horses—but he promises that the expedition will be short, undoubtedly a concern to men eager to return to the fall harvest. To the right, we see a handkerchief made in 1815, after the Treaty of Ghent and the Battle of New Orleans; it features the United States' victories against the world's greatest naval power, Great Britain. Featuring a decorative border, the kerchief may have been for display. What similar values do we see promoted in the two images, and what factors—such as their intended audiences, their purposes, and when they were created—might account for any differences between them?

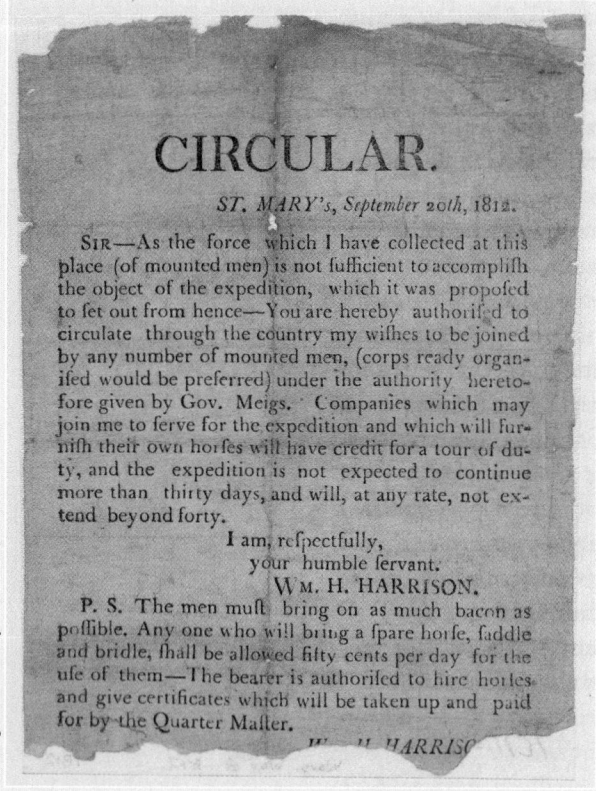

Recruitment Poster for the War of 1812 (litho), American School, (19th century)/© Chicago History Museum, USA/ The Bridgeman Art Library

With a tiny regular army, the United States often had to rely on short-term recruits to wage war on the British.

Kerchief commemorating the victories of the War of 1812, c.1815 (cotton), American School, (19th century)/© Collection of the New-York Historical Society, USA/ The Bridgeman Art Library

Made in 1815 from cotton textiles—whose domestic production soared during the War of 1812, with trade cut off from Britain—this handkerchief helps promote American "liberty and independence."

After defeating Napoleon in Europe in April 1814, the British launched a land counteroffensive against the United States, concentrating on the Chesapeake Bay. Royal troops occupied Washington, D.C., in August and set it ablaze. The presidential mansion and parts of the city burned all night. The president and cabinet fled. Dolley Madison stayed to oversee removal of cabinet documents and save a Gilbert Stuart portrait of George Washington.

The British intended the attack on Washington as a diversion. The major battle occurred in September 1814 at Baltimore, where the Americans held firm. Francis Scott Key, detained on a British ship, watched the bombardment of Fort McHenry and later wrote "The Star-Spangled Banner" (which became the national anthem in 1931). The British inflicted heavy damage but achieved little militarily; their offensive on Lake Champlain also failed. The war reached a stalemate.

War in the South

To the south, two wars were happening simultaneously. In the Patriot War, a private army of Americans secretly supported by the Madison administration tried to seize East Florida from Spain. What started as a settlers' rebellion along the Georgia-Florida border—to grab more land, strike at the Spaniards' Indian allies, and later to protest the Spaniards' arming of black soldiers—turned into a war. Federalists condemned the invasion of a neutral territory, and the Senate refused twice (in 1812 and 1813) to support military seizure of Florida. Embarrassed, Madison withdrew his support, and the movement collapsed in May 1814.

In the war with Britain, the southern theater proved more successful. The final campaign began with an American attack on the Red Stick Creeks along the Gulf of Mexico and the British around New Orleans, and it ended with Americans gaining new territory. Responding to Tecumseh's call to resist U.S. expansion, in 1813 the Red Sticks attacked Fort Mims, about forty miles from Mobile, killing hundreds of white men, women, and children. Seeking revenge, General Andrew Jackson of Tennessee rallied his militiamen and Indian opponents of the Red Sticks and crushed them at Horseshoe Bend (in present-day Alabama) in March 1814. This led to the Treaty of Fort Jackson, in which the Creeks ceded 23 million acres, or about half of their holdings, and withdrew to the southern and western Mississippi Territory.

Jackson became a major general and continued south toward the Gulf of Mexico. After seizing Pensacola (in Spanish Florida) and securing Mobile, Jackson's forces marched to New Orleans. Three weeks later, on January 8, 1815, Jackson's poorly trained army held its ground against two British frontal assaults. At day's end, more than two thousand British soldiers lay dead or wounded, while the Americans suffered only twenty-one casualties.

The Battle of New Orleans occurred two weeks after the war's conclusion: word had not yet reached America that British and United States diplomats had signed the **Treaty of Ghent** on December 24, 1814. Still, the Battle of New Orleans catapulted General Andrew Jackson to national political prominence.

Treaty of Ghent Treaty that ended the War of 1812, restoring the prewar status quo.

Treaty of Ghent

The Treaty of Ghent essentially restored the prewar status quo. It provided for an end to hostilities, release of prisoners, restoration of conquered territory, and arbitration of boundary disputes. But the United States received no satisfaction on impressment, blockades, or other maritime rights for neutrals, and the British demands for territorial cessions from Maine to Minnesota went unmet. The British dropped their promise of an independent Indian nation.

Napoleon's defeat allowed the United States to discard its prewar demands because peace in Europe made impressment and interference with American commerce moot issues. Similarly, war-weary Britain stopped pressing for military victory.

American Sovereignty Reasserted

The War of 1812 affirmed the independence of the American republic and ensured Canada's independence from the United States. Trade and territorial disputes with Great Britain continued, but they never again led to war. The return of peace allowed the United States to again focus on the Barbary Coast, where the dey (governor) of Algiers had declared war on the United States. In the Second Barbary War, U.S. forces held hundreds of Algerians while negotiating a treaty in the summer of 1815 that forever freed the United States from paying tributes for passage in the Mediterranean. The Second Barbary War reaffirmed America's commitment to freedom of the seas.

Domestic Consequences

The War of 1812 had profound domestic consequences. Federalists' hopes of returning to national prominence evaporated with the **Hartford Convention**. New England delegates—frustrated by the stalemated war and the shattered New England economy—met in Hartford, Connecticut, in the winter of 1814-1815 to discuss revising the national compact or pulling out of the republic. Although moderates prevented a secession resolution—withdrawal from the Union—delegates condemned the war and the embargo while endorsing constitutional changes that would weaken the South's power and make it harder to declare war. When news arrived of Jackson's victory in New Orleans and the Treaty of Ghent, the Hartford Convention made the Federalists look wrongheaded, even treasonous. By the 1820s, the party faded from the national scene.

Hartford Convention
Federalist meeting that was perceived as disloyalty during time of war and began the downfall of the party.

With Tecumseh's death, midwestern Indians lost their powerful leader; with the British withdrawal, they lost their strongest ally. Some accommodationists, such as the Cherokees, temporarily flourished, but the war effectively disarmed traditionalists bent on resisting American expansion. Although the Treaty of Ghent pledged the United States to end hostilities with Indians and to restore their prewar "possessions, rights, and privileges," Indians could not make the United States honor the agreement.

For American farmers, the war opened formerly Indian land for cultivating cotton in the Old Southwest and wheat in the Old Northwest. It also stimulated industry, as Americans could no longer rely on overseas imports. The War of 1812 thus fueled demand for raw cotton, and the newly acquired lands in the Southwest beckoned southerners, who migrated there with slaves or hopes of someday owning slaves. The war's conclusion accelerated three trends that would dominate U.S. history for decades: industrial takeoff, slavery's entrenchment, and westward expansion.

Early Industrialization

As a result of the embargo and the War of 1812, the North underwent an accelerated industrial development as the South became more dependent on cotton production (see Chapter 9). Although the two regions' economies followed different paths, they remained interconnected.

How did early industrialization bridge older farm/family production with newer systems of production for market?

Preindustrial Farms

Before the War of 1812, most American farmers practiced mixed agriculture, raising a variety of crops and livestock. When they produced more than they needed, they traded the surplus with neighbors or sold it to local storekeepers. Such transactions often transpired without money; farmers might trade eggs for shoes, or they might work their neighbor's fields in exchange for bales of hay.

Family members provided most farm labor, though some yeoman farmers, North and South, relied on slaves or indentured servants. Men and boys worked in the fields, herded livestock, chopped firewood, fished, and hunted. Women and girls tended gardens, milked cows, spun cloth, processed and preserved food, prepared meals, washed clothes, and tended infants and toddlers.

Farmers lent each other farm tools, harvested each other's fields, bartered goods, and raised their neighbors' barns and husked their corn. Little cash exchanged hands, mostly because money was scarce. Still, New England farmers often kept elaborate account books, whereas southern farmers made mental notes of debts. Years might pass without debts repaid. In the local economy—where farmers exchanged goods with people they knew—a system of "just price" prevailed, in which neighbors calculated value based on how much labor was involved. When farmers engaged in long-distance trade they set prices based on what the market would bear.

Preindustrial Artisans

Farmers who lived near towns often purchased crafted goods from local cobblers, saddlers, blacksmiths, gunsmiths, silversmiths, and tailors. Most artisans, though, lived in the nation's seaports, where master craftsmen (businessmen who owned shops and tools) employed apprentices and journeymen. Although the majority of craftsmen, North and South, were white, free blacks were well represented in some cities' trades, such as tailoring and carpentry in Charleston, South Carolina. Teenage apprentices lived with masters, who taught, lodged, and fed them in exchange for labor. The master's wife and daughters cooked, cleaned, and sewed for the workers. When their apprenticeship expired, apprentices became journeymen who earned wages, hoping to one day own shops. The workplace had little division of labor or specialization. A tailor measured, designed, and sewed an entire suit, for example.

Men, women, and children worked long days on farms and in workshops, but the pace was uneven and unregimented. When busy, they worked dawn to dusk;

work slowed after the harvest or when a large order was completed. Husking bees and barn raisings brought people together to shuck corn and build, and to eat, drink, and dance. Busy periods did not stop artisans from taking grog breaks, from reading the newspaper aloud, or even from attending a political meeting. Journeymen often staggered in late on Monday mornings, if they showed up at all, after carousing on their day off. In this way, workers exerted influence over the workplace.

Putting-Out and Early Factories

Early industry reorganized daily work routines and market relationships. In the late eighteenth and early nineteenth centuries a "putting-out" system developed, particularly in Massachusetts, New Jersey, and Pennsylvania. Women and children continued to produce goods, but now a merchant supplied raw materials, paid them a wage (usually a price for each piece produced), and sold their wares in distant markets, pocketing the profits himself. This "outwork" appealed to women eager for cash, whether to secure economic independence or to save money for land where their children might establish farms. Particularly in New England—where population density, small farms, and tired soil constricted farming opportunities—the putting-out system provided opportunities to earn money with which to buy more fertile western lands.

The earliest factories grew in tandem with the putting-out system. When Samuel Slater helped set up the first American water-powered spinning mill in Rhode Island in 1790—using children to card and spin raw cotton into thread—he sent the spun thread to nearby farm families who were paid to weave it into cloth. Although the work remained familiar, women now operated looms for wages and produced cloth primarily for the market.

Despite their separate identity, Americans relied on British technology to combine the many steps of textile manufacturing—carding (or disentangling) fibers, spinning yarn, and weaving cloth—under one factory roof. Slater, a British immigrant, had reconstructed from memory the complex machines he'd had in England. But Slater's mill only carded and spun yarn; hand-weaving it into cloth was often done by farm women. In 1810, Bostonian Francis Cabot Lowell visited the British textile center of Manchester, touring factories and later sketching from memory what he had seen. In 1813, he and his business associates founded the Boston Manufacturing Company, uniting all phases of textile manufacturing under one roof in Waltham, Massachusetts. A decade later, the Boston Manufacturing Company established its model industrial village—named for its now-deceased founder—along the Merrimack River. At Lowell, Massachusetts, there would be boardinghouses for workers, a healthy alternative to Manchester's tenements and slums.

Northern industrialization was linked to slavery. Much of the capital came from merchants who partly made their fortunes through the slave trade. Two of the most prominent industries—textiles and shoes—expanded alongside a growing southern cotton economy. Southern cotton fed northern textile mills, and northern shoe factories sold "Negro brogans" (work shoes) to southern planters.

Courtesy Gore Place Society, Waltham, Mass.

This contemporary painting shows the Boston Manufacturing Company's 1814 textile factory at Waltham, Massachusetts. All manufacturing processes were brought together under one roof, and the company built its first factories in rural New England to tap roaring rivers as a power source.

Sectionalism and Nationalism

How did the American System mark the triumph of Federalist economic policy?

Following the War of 1812, Madison and the Democratic-Republicans absorbed the Federalist idea that the national government should encourage growth. His agenda, which Henry Clay later called the American System, included a national bank, improved transportation, and a protective tariff—a tax on imported goods to protect American manufacturers from foreign competition. Yet true to his Jeffersonian roots, Madison argued that only a constitutional amendment could authorize the federal government to build local roads and canals. Instead, most internal improvements would fall to the states.

American System

Clay and congressional leaders such as Calhoun of South Carolina believed the American System would ease sectional divides. The tariff would stimulate

New England industry, whose goods would find markets in the South and West. The South's and West's agricultural products—cotton and foodstuffs—would feed New England mills and workers. Manufactured and agricultural products would move along roads and canals that tariff revenues would fund. A national bank would handle the transactions.

In 1816, Congress chartered the Second Bank of the United States (the first bank's charter expired in 1811) to serve as a depository for federal funds and to issue currency, collect taxes, and pay government debts. The Second Bank of the United States would also oversee state and local banks, ensuring that their paper money had backing in specie (precious metals). Like its predecessor, the bank mixed public and private ownership; the government provided one-fifth of the bank's capital and appointed one-fifth of its directors.

Congress also passed the Tariff of 1816, which taxed imported woolens and cottons as well as iron, leather, hats, paper, and sugar. This tariff divided the nation. New England, western, and Middle Atlantic states would benefit from it and thus applauded it, whereas many southerners objected that it raised prices on consumer goods and could prompt Britain to retaliate with a tariff on cotton.

Southerners such as Calhoun promoted roads and canals to "bind the republic together." However, on March 3, 1817, the day before leaving office, President Madison, citing constitutional scruples, vetoed Calhoun's "Bonus Bill," which would have authorized federal funding for such public works.

Early Internal Improvements

Federalists and Democratic-Republicans agreed that improved transportation would promote national prosperity. For Federalists, roads and canals were necessary for commercial development; for Jeffersonians, they would spur western expansion and agrarian growth. In 1806, Congress passed (and Jefferson signed) a bill authorizing funding for the Cumberland Road (later, the National Road), running 130 miles between Cumberland, Maryland, and Wheeling, Virginia (now West Virginia). In 1820, Congress authorized a survey of the National Road to Columbus, Ohio, a project completed in 1833.

Erie Canal Major canal that linked the Great Lakes to the Atlantic seaboard, opening the upper Midwest to wider development.

Most transportation initiatives received funding from states and/or private investors. Between 1817 and 1825, New York constructed the **Erie Canal**, linking the Great Lakes to the Atlantic seaboard. Although southern states constructed modest canals, the South's trade used river-going steamboats after 1817, when steamboats began traveling regularly upriver on the Mississippi. With canals and steamboats, western agricultural products traveled faster and inexpensively, fueling westward expansion. Canals expanded commercial networks into regions without natural waterways and reoriented midwestern commerce through the North.

Panic of 1819

Immediately following the War of 1812, the international demand for (and price of) American commodities soared. Poor weather in Europe led to crop failures, increasing demand for northern foodstuffs and southern cotton, which, in turn, triggered western land speculation. Speculators raced to buy large tracts at modest, government-established prices and then to resell them at hefty profits to would-be settlers.

The young nation's dirt roads meant bumpy and dusty travel for goods as well as passengers, prompting calls for transportation innovations, such as canals and, later, railroads, to spur economic growth.

Prosperity proved short-lived. By the late 1810s Europeans could grow their own food, and Britain's new Corn Laws established high tariffs on imports. Cotton prices fell in England. Wars in Latin America interfered with mining and reduced the supply of precious metals, leading European nations to hoard specie. American banks furiously printed paper money and expanded credit further. Fearful of inflation, the Second Bank of the United States demanded in 1819 that state banks repay loans in specie. State banks then called in the loans and mortgages they had made. Falling commodities prices meant that farmers could not pay their mortgages, and plummeting land values—50 to 75 percent declines in portions of the West—meant they could not meet debts even by selling their farms. The nation's banking system collapsed, triggering a financial panic.

Foreclosures soared and unemployment skyrocketed, reaching 75 percent in Philadelphia. Workers and their families could not make it through the winter without charitable donations of food, clothing, and firewood. Americans everywhere contemplated the virtues and hazards of rapid market expansion, disagreeing on whom to blame for its shortcomings. Even as the nation's economy rebounded in the early 1820s amid a flurry of internal improvements, no one could predict in what region or sector the nation's fortunes would lie.

Missouri Compromise	America also faced a political crisis in 1819 about slavery's westward expansion. Residents of the Missouri Territory petitioned Congress for admission to

the Union with a constitution permitting slavery. Missouri's admission would give slaveholding states a two-vote majority in the Senate and set a precedent for new western states created from the Louisiana Purchase.

Following the Louisiana Purchase and after the War of 1812, the American population surged westward, leading five new states to join the Union: Louisiana (1812), Indiana (1816), Mississippi (1817), Illinois (1818), and Alabama (1819). Of these, Louisiana, Mississippi, and Alabama permitted slavery. Because Missouri was on the same latitude as free Illinois, Indiana, and Ohio, its admission as a slave state would push slavery farther westward and northward.

For two and a half years the issue dominated Congress. When Representative James Tallmadge Jr. of New York proposed gradual emancipation in Missouri, some southerners accused the North of threatening to destroy the Union. The House, which had a northern majority, passed the Tallmadge Amendment, but the Senate rejected it.

House Speaker Henry Clay—himself a western slaveholder—offered a compromise in 1820. Maine, carved out of Massachusetts, would enter as a free state, followed by Missouri as a slave state, maintaining the balance between slave and free states. In the rest of the Louisiana Territory north of Missouri's southern border of 36°30′, slavery would be prohibited (see Map 8.3).

The compromise carried but almost unraveled when Missouri submitted a constitution barring free blacks from the state. Opponents contended that it violated the federal constitutional provision that citizens of each state were "entitled to all privileges and immunities of citizens in the several States." Proponents countered that many states already barred free blacks. In 1821, Clay proposed a second compromise: Missouri would guarantee that its laws would not discriminate against citizens of other states. (Once admitted to the Union, Missouri twice adopted laws barring free blacks.) For more than three decades, the **Missouri Compromise** governed congressional policy toward admitting new slave states. But it masked rather than suppressed the simmering political conflict over slavery's westward expansion.

The Era of Good Feelings	So, too, did the so-called "**Era of Good Feelings**," as a Boston newspaper dubbed the presidency of James Monroe, which was marked by a lack of partisan political discord. Madison's successor, Monroe was the

third Virginian elected president since 1801. A former senator and twice governor of Virginia, he served under Madison as secretary of state and of war and used his association with Jefferson and Madison to attain the presidency. In 1816, he and his running mate, Daniel Tompkins, trounced the last Federalist presidential nominee, Rufus King, garnering all the electoral votes except those of the Federalist strongholds of Massachusetts, Connecticut, and Delaware.

Led by Federalist chief justice John Marshall, the Supreme Court became the bulwark of the nationalist agenda. In **McCulloch v. Maryland** (1819), the Court struck down a Maryland law taxing banks that were not chartered by its legislature—a law aimed at hindering the Baltimore branch of the Second Bank

Missouri Compromise
Attempt to end the debate over the number of slave and free states admitted to the Union by admitting Missouri as a slave state and Maine as a free state and banning slavery in the Louisiana Territory north of the 36°30′ latitude line.

Era of Good Feelings
Period of one-party politics during administration of James Monroe.

McCulloch v. Maryland
Supreme Court decision that restated national supremacy over the states.

MAP 8.3

Missouri Compromise and the State of the Union, 1820

The compromise worked out by House Speaker Henry Clay established a formula that avoided debate over whether new states would allow or prohibit slavery. In the process, it divided the United States into northern and southern regions. Source: Copyright © Cengage Learning 2015

of the United States. The bank refused to pay the tax and sued. At issue was state versus federal jurisdiction. Writing for a unanimous Court, Marshall asserted the supremacy of the federal government over the states. The Court ruled, too, that Congress had the power to charter banks. The Marshall Court thus supported the Federalist view that the federal government could promote interstate commerce.

Government Promotion of Market Expansion

Later Supreme Court cases validated government promotion of economic development and encouraged business enterprise. In *Gibbons v. Ogden* (1824), the Supreme Court overturned the New York law granting Robert Fulton and Robert Livingston (and their successor, Aaron Ogden) a monopoly on the New York–New Jersey steamboat trade. Chief Justice Marshall ruled that the federal power to license new enterprises took precedence over New York's grant of monopoly rights and declared that Congress's power under the commerce clause of the Constitution extended to "every species of commercial intercourse." Within two years, the number of steamboats in New York increased from six to forty-three. A later ruling in *Charles River Bridge v. Warren Bridge* (1837), encouraged new enterprises and technologies by favoring competition over monopoly, and the public interest over implied privileges in old contracts.

Federal and state courts, in conjunction with state legislatures, encouraged the proliferation of corporations—organizations holding property and transacting business as if they were individuals. Corporation owners, called shareholders, were granted limited liability, or freedom from personal responsibility for the company's debts beyond their original investment. The federal government assisted commercial development, too, by expanding the number of U.S. post offices from three thousand in 1815 to fourteen thousand in 1845 and by protecting inventions through patent laws and domestic industries through tariffs on foreign imports.

Boundary Settlements

Monroe's secretary of state, John Quincy Adams, son of John and Abigail Adams, managed the nation's foreign policy from 1817 to 1825. He pushed for expansion of American fishing rights in Atlantic waters, political distance from Europe, and peace. Under Adams's leadership, in 1817 the United States and Great Britain signed the Rush-Bagot Treaty limiting them to one ship each on Lake Champlain and Lake Ontario and to two ships each on the remaining Great Lakes. This first modern disarmament treaty demilitarized the U.S.-Canadian border. Adams pushed for the Convention of 1818, which fixed the U.S.-Canadian boundary from Lake of the Woods in Minnesota westward to the Rockies along the 49th parallel. The delegates disagreed on the boundary west of the Rockies, so Britain and the United States settled on joint occupation of Oregon for ten years (renewed indefinitely in 1827).

Adams's negotiations also resulted in the Adams-Onís Treaty, in which the United States gained Florida. Although the Louisiana Purchase omitted reference to Spanish-ruled West Florida, the United States claimed the territory as far east as the Perdido River (the present-day Florida-Alabama border). During the War of 1812, the United States seized Mobile and the remainder of West Florida; after the war Adams claimed East Florida. In 1819, Don Luís de Onís, the Spanish minister to the United States, agreed to cede Florida to the United States without payment if the United States renounced its dubious claims to northern Mexico (Texas) and assumed $5 million of claims by American citizens against Spain. The treaty also defined the southwestern boundary of the Louisiana Purchase and divided Spanish Mexico and Oregon Country at the 42nd parallel.

Monroe Doctrine

Adams's desire to insulate the United States and the Western Hemisphere from European conflict inspired his greatest achievement: the **Monroe Doctrine**. Between 1808 and 1822, the United Provinces of Río de la Plata (present-day northern Argentina, Paraguay, and Uruguay), Chile, Peru, Colombia, and Mexico all broke from Spain (see Map 8.4). In 1822, the United States became the first nation outside Latin America to recognize the new states. But with reactionary regimes ascending in Europe and France now occupying Spain, the United States feared that continental powers would attempt to return the new Latin American states to colonial rule.

Monroe's message to Congress in December 1823 became known as the Monroe Doctrine. He announced that the American continents "are henceforth not to be considered subjects for future colonization by any European power." This

Monroe Doctrine Foreign policy statement that proclaimed that the American continents were not to be subjected to European colonization and demanded nonintervention by Europe in New World nations.

OREGON
COUNTRY
(Joint U.S.-British
occupation)

BRITISH NORTH AMERICA
(CANADA)
(Gr. Br.)

Mississippi R.

Colorado R.

New York

• Philadelphia
Washington, D.C.

UNITED STATES

• Charleston

N

ATLANTIC
OCEAN

MEXICO
1821

Rio Grande

San
Antonio

New Orleans

Gulf of Mexico

BAHAMA IS.
(Gr. Br.)

40°W

40°N

Mexico City •

• Veracruz

Havana
CUBA
(Spain)

HAITI 1804

PUERTO RICO (Spain)

20°N

BRITISH
HONDURAS (Gr. Br.)
GUATEMALA
• Guatemala City

JAMAICA
(Gr. Br.)

Caribbean Sea

TRINIDAD (Gr. Br.)

UNITED PROVINCES OF
CENTRAL AMERICA
1823–1839

Panama

Magdalena R.

Caracas

VENEZUELA
• Socorro
Bogotá

Orinoco R.

BR. GUIANA (Gr. Br.)

DUTCH GUIANA (Neth.)

FRENCH GUIANA (France)

Galápagos
Islands

GRAN COLOMBIA
1819–1830

Quito •
ECUADOR

Amazon R.

Equator   0°

PACIFIC

OCEAN

Lima •

PERU
1824

EMPIRE OF BRAZIL
1822

• Salvador

BOLIVIA
1825
• La Paz

• Sucre

20°S

PARAGUAY
1811

Paraná R.

• Río de Janeiro

São Paulo •

CHILE
1817

UNITED
PROVINCES OF
THE RIO DE
LA PLATA
1816

URUGUAY
1828

Valparaíso •
Santiago •

ARGENTINA

Buenos Aires
Bahía
Blanca •

Montevideo

PATAGONIA
(Disputed between
Argentina and Chile)

Islas Malvinas
(Falkland Islands)

80°W   60°W

0   500   1000 Km.

0   500   1000 Mi.

1811 Year independence gained

Colony

MAP 8.4

Latin American Independence, 1840

With Central and South American colonies triumphing in their wars of independence against European colonial powers,
President Monroe sought to enhance the United States' security by warning European nations against meddling in the region.

Source: Copyright © Cengage Learning 2015

States' Rights and Nullification

Under the Constitution, the exact nature of the relationship between the states and the federal government was ambiguous because Constitutional Convention delegates disagreed on whether states or the nation should prevail in an irreconcilable conflict. The Tenth Amendment offered a slight clarification: powers not delegated to the central government, it said, were reserved to the states or to the people.

When New England Federalists met in Hartford in late 1814 to prepare a list of grievances against "Mr. Madison's War," they drew on the doctrine of nullification, first announced sixteen years earlier in the Kentucky and Virginia Resolutions, written by Thomas Jefferson and James Madison, respectively. Opposing the Alien and Sedition Acts, these founding fathers asserted that, if the national government assumed powers not delegated to it by the Constitution, states could nullify federal actions—that is, declare them inoperative within state borders. Some New England Federalists discussed taking nullification further by seceding. Their formulation of states' rights to nullify federal authority left a legacy for dissent that has recurred in crises up to the present.

In the following decade, South Carolina nullified federal tariffs, and in 1861 southern states threatened by Abraham Lincoln's election as president claimed the right of secession. Although the Civil War supposedly settled the issue—states could neither nullify federal law nor secede—southern states opposing the Supreme Court's 1954 ruling in favor of school integration again claimed the right to nullify "unauthorized" federal policy within their borders. In the early twenty-first century, as the U.S. Congress failed to muster a two-thirds majority to propose a constitutional amendment banning gay marriage, dozens of states ratified their own such constitutional amendments. Symbolically, the threat of secession remains potent. Decrying the 2009 federal stimulus package to jump-start the ailing national economy, Texas governor Rick Perry declared that his state might secede rather than face unwanted spending, taxation, and debt. In 2012, after the Supreme Court affirmed the constitutionality of the Patient Protection and Affordable Care Act ("Obamacare"), opponents renewed grassroots calls for their states' secession. The Hartford Convention's legacy for a people and a nation provides Americans who dissent from national policy with a model for using state governments, and threats of secession, as protest vehicles.

addressed American anxiety about Latin America and Russian expansion beyond Alaska and its settlements in California. Monroe demanded nonintervention by Europe in the affairs of independent New World nations, and he pledged U.S. noninterference in European affairs including Europe's existing New World colonies. European nations stayed out of New World affairs because they feared the British Royal Navy, not the United States' proclamations.

Summary

The partisanship of the 1790s made the early republic a period of vigorous political engagement. With a vision of an agrarian nation that protected individual liberty, Jeffersonians promoted a limited national government—one that stayed out of religious affairs and spent little on military forces, diplomatic missions, and economic initiatives. The rival Federalists, who exerted their influence through the judiciary, declared federal supremacy over states even as the judiciary affirmed its supremacy over other government branches. Federalists hoped a strengthened federal government would promote commerce and industry.

Despite his belief in limited government, Jefferson considered the Louisiana Territory acquisition and the Corps of Discovery his greatest presidential accomplishments. Americans soon streamed into the Louisiana Territory, and more would have gone if not for Indians (and their British allies) and poorly developed transportation routes.

With its economy focused on international shipping, the greatest threats to the United States soon came from abroad. In its wars with the Barbary states, the United States sought to guard its commerce and ships on the high seas. Although the War of 1812 was a military stalemate, it inspired a new sense of nationalism and launched an era of American development.

The Treaty of Ghent reaffirmed American independence; thereafter, the nation settled disputes with Great Britain by negotiation. The war also seriously impaired Indian resistance in the Midwest and Southwest, while accelerating American industrial growth. Federalists' opposition to the war undermined their credibility, and their party faded from the national political scene by 1820. The absence of partisan conflict created what contemporaries called an Era of Good Feelings.

Still, competing visions of America's route to prosperity endured. Under Chief Justice John Marshall, the Supreme Court supported the Federalist agenda, issuing rulings that stimulated commerce and industry. Democratic-Republicans looked, instead, toward the Louisiana Territory. But most Americans agreed on the need for improved transportation, though most improvements took place in the North.

In 1819 the postwar economic boom ended, as congressmen debated whether to admit Missouri as a slave state. Henry Clay's compromise removed slavery's expansion from political center stage, but did not permanently settle the issue.

The United States also acquired Florida. Fearful of European intentions to reassert influence in the Americas and emboldened by the nation's expanding boundaries, President Monroe proclaimed that the United States would not tolerate European intervention in American affairs. But even as its expanding boundaries strengthened the United States' international presence, territorial expansion threatened political unity at home.

Chapter Review

Political Visions

Was Jefferson's election and political vision truly "the revolution of 1800"?

Jefferson considered his election in 1800 a revolution, since it also gave his Democratic-Republican Party a majority in both houses of Congress. That made it easier to enact his vision of limited government, individual liberty (which required the separation of church and state), and an agrarian (versus commercial) republic.

Since Democratic-Republicans viewed national debt as a sign of corruption, he authorized his treasury secretary to cut the federal budget and decrease the national debt (which Federalists saw as a tool to stimulate the economy). Jefferson also pardoned those convicted under the Alien and Sedition Acts, which he regarded as a violation of liberties, and attempted to remove a Supreme Court justice opposed to his brand of politics. (He was ultimately unsuccessful, which maintained the Court's independence.)

Continental Expansion and Indian Resistance

Why was the Louisiana Purchase among Jefferson's most popular decisions as president?

The purchase of 827,000 square miles of land west of the Mississippi from France doubled the size of the United States, secured American interests from potential European incursion at its inland borders, and opened more land for American settlement (even though Native Americans were already living there). Moreover, by purchasing the land on the other side of the river, the United States controlled access to the Mississippi, which appealed to western settlers who relied on it to get their goods to market. Finally, it fed dreams of cheap, fertile lands for would-be settlers.

The Nation in the Orbit of Europe

What led to the War of 1812?

Continuing disputes with Great Britain over the nature of American independence. Ongoing hostilities between European nations spilled over onto American ships, as Great Britain often stopped and seized U.S. ships and forced British deserters and British-born but naturalized American citizens into military service. As many as six to eight thousand Americans were impressed from 1803 to 1812. American trade vessels were also seized. Trade embargoes did little to stop the practice and ultimately hurt American merchants and the U.S. economy. In seeking Congressional support for war, Madison pointed to violation of neutral trading rights, British alliances with western Indians, and affronts to American independence as additional causes, while others saw war as an opportunity to annex British Canada. Although Britain reopened the seas and ordered its ships not to disturb American warships by June of 1812, news of the policy change did not reach America until long after Congress declared war.

The War of 1812

What were the consequences of the War of 1812?

The most important outcome of the war was that it affirmed American independence and autonomy as a nation and guaranteed no future battles with Britain over trade or territory. In other ways, the Treaty of Ghent that ended the fighting, simply restored the prewar status quo: the United States did not get the results it wanted on impressments, blockades, and maritime rights for neutral parties. On the home front, the war shattered the U.S. economy and led some New England Federalists to threaten secession, which contributed to the party's demise when the war soon ended. Indians who had supported the British lost a major ally. And while Indians had their land and rights restored by the Treaty of Ghent, they had no power to enforce it. With the end of war, three trends emerged that were pivotal for the nation's future: westward expansion, the entrenchment of slavery, and industrial development.

Early Industrialization

How did early industrialization bridge older farm/family production with newer systems of production for market?

The South continued as an agricultural region and expanded its slave system, while the North transformed quickly into a market economy. With the war cutting off European trade, northern entrepreneurs invested in domestic production and factories. Former artisans and farmers increasingly shifted from producers to wage workers. Early forms of market changes came from piecework or outwork, where manufacturers hired women and children in their homes to produce goods, often paying them for each piece produced. After the first mills were opened in the 1790s, women and children went to work there. People increasingly bought goods—clothes, shoes, and soap—that they once made for themselves. Commercial farming emerged in the North to meet the growing demand for foodstuffs that was created when people shifted from farming to factory jobs. Those farmers who remained in agriculture shifted increasingly to cash crops.

Sectionalism and Nationalism

How did the American System mark the triumph of Federalist economic policy?

Long opposed to big government, Democratic-Republicans amended this philosophy to adopt the Federalist notion that the central government should aid economic growth and encourage the development of commerce and industry. Their program was dubbed the American System, and included a national bank, development of transportation networks, and a protective tariff that would tax imported goods to protect American products from foreign competitors. Advocates of the American System, such as South Carolina leader

John C. Calhoun, believed it could bridge sectional divides and expand the nation. Both parties embraced internal improvements for different reasons: Federalists saw them as spurring commercial development, while Jeffersonians (Democratic-Republicans) thought they would lead to western and agrarian expansion.

Suggestions for Further Reading

Stephen Aron, *American Confluence: The Missouri Frontier from Borderland to Border State* (2006)

Claude A. Clegg III, *The Price of Liberty: African Americans and the Making of Liberia* (2004)

David Edmunds, *Tecumseh and the Quest for Indian Leadership* (2006)

Richard S. Newman, *The Transformation of American Abolitionism: Fighting Slavery in the Early Republic* (2002)

Kent Newmyer, *John Marshall and the Heroic Age of the Supreme Court* (2001)

Jeffrey Ostler, *The Plains Sioux and U.S. Colonialism from Lewis and Clark to Wounded Knee* (2004)

Jeffrey Pasley, Andrew Robertson, and David Waldstreicher, eds., *Beyond the Founders: New Approaches to the Political History of the Early American Republic* (2004)

Alan Taylor, *The Civil War of 1812: American Citizens, British Subjects, Irish Rebels, and Indian Allies* (2010)

Gordon S. Wood, *Empire of Liberty: A History of the Early Republic, 1789–1815* (2009)

The Rise of the South

1815–1860

Thomas Jefferson died, as he lived, in debt, on July 4, 1826, the same day his longtime rival John Adams died. At Jefferson's Virginia home, Monticello, anxiety filled his white and black "families."

On January 15, 1827, a five-day estate sale took place at Monticello. Among the paintings, furniture, and mementoes were "130 valuable negroes." Monticello's blacksmith, Joseph Fossett, watched his wife Edith and eight children sold to four different bidders.

Jefferson was reportedly a caring slaveholder, who tried to keep families together. After his wife, Martha (with whom he had two daughters), died in 1782, Jefferson had six children with his slave, Sally Hemings, four of whom lived beyond infancy. Sally was the half sister of Jefferson's wife, and part of an extended family of light-skinned Hemingses.

Joe Fossett, as Jefferson promised, became free one year after his master's death. Jefferson had earlier freed his four children with Hemings: William Beverly Hemings, Harriet Hemings II, James Madison Hemings, and Thomas Eston Hemings. Jefferson never freed Sally; Virginia law would have required him to attain, publicly, a dispensation from the state legislature to free her without removing her from the state, and Jefferson wanted no more salacious publicity about his house servant and mistress. Sally died a slave, in Charlottesville, Virginia, in 1835 at age sixty-two. Monticello itself was sold in 1831. But across the South in the 1820s, the "business" of slavery expansion and cotton production was hardly over.

In 1815, the southern states and territories, with fertile soil and a growing slave labor force, were poised for growth and prosperity. New lands were settled, new states were peopled, and the South emerged as the world's most extensive commercial agricultural economy. The Old South's wealth came from export crops, land, and slaves, and its population was almost wholly rural. Racial slavery affected values, customs, laws, class structure, and the region's relationship to the nation and the world. As slaves were increasingly defined as chattel, they struggled to survive and resist, sometimes overtly, but often simply in daily life and culture. By 1860, white southerners asserted the moral and economic benefits of slavery and sought to advance their political power over the national government.

As you read this chapter, keep the following questions in mind:

- **How and why was the Old South a "slave society," with slavery permeating every class and group within it, free or unfree?**

- **How and why did white southerners come to see cotton as "king" of a global economy, and how did the cotton trade's international reach shape southern society from 1815 to 1860?**

- **How did African American slaves build and sustain a meaningful life and a sense of community amid the potential chaos and destruction of their circumstances?**

- **How would you weigh the comparative significance of the following central themes in the history of the Old South: class, race, migration, power, liberty, wealth?**

VISUALIZING THE PAST *Imaging Nat Turner's Rebellion*

LEGACY FOR A PEOPLE AND A NATION *Reparations for Slavery*

SUMMARY

The "Distinctive" South

What made the antebellum South different from the North?

In the first half of the 1800s, slaveholding states from the Chesapeake and Virginia to Missouri, and from Florida across to Texas, came to be designated as the South. Today, many consider it America's most distinctive region. Historians have long examined how the Old South was like and unlike the rest of the nation. Because of its unique history, has the South, in the words of poet Allen Tate, always been "Uncle Sam's other province"? Analyzing why the South seems more religious, conservative, or tragic than other regions has been an enduring practice.

Certain American values, such as materialism, individualism, and faith in progress, have been associated with the North and values such as tradition, honor, and family loyalty, with the South. Stereotype has also labeled the South as static, even "backward," and the North as dynamic in the pre–Civil War decades. In truth, there were many Souths: low-country rice and cotton regions with dense slave populations; mountainous regions of small farmers; semitropical wetlands in the Southeast; **plantation** culture in the cotton belt and Mississippi Valley; Texas grasslands; tobacco- and wheat-growing regions in Virginia and North Carolina; bustling port cities; wilderness areas with rare hillfolk homesteads.

plantation Large landholding devoted to a cash crop such as cotton or tobacco.

Chronology

1810–20	An estimated 137,000 slaves are forced to move from the Upper South to Alabama, Mississippi, and other western regions
1822	Vesey's insurrection plot is discovered in South Carolina
1830s	Vast majority of African American slaves in America are native born
1830s–40s	Cotton trade grows into largest source of commercial wealth and America's leading export
1831	Turner leads a violent slave rebellion in Virginia
1832	Virginia holds the last debate in the South about the future of slavery; gradual abolition is voted down
	Publication of Dew's proslavery tract *Abolition of Negro Slavery*
1836	Arkansas gains admission to the Union as a slave state
1839	Mississippi's Married Women's Property Act gives married women some property rights
1845	Florida and Texas gain admission to the Union as slave states
	Publication of Douglass's *Narrative of the Life of Frederick Douglass, an American Slave, Written by Himself*
1850	Planters' share of agricultural wealth in the South is 90 to 95 percent
1850–60	Of some 300,000 slaves who migrate from the Upper to the Lower South, 60 to 70 percent go by outright sale
1857	Publication of Hinton R. Helper's *The Impending Crisis*, denouncing the slave system
	Publication of George Fitzhugh's *Southern Thought*, an aggressive defense of slavery
1860	There are 405,751 mulattos in the United States, accounting for 12.5 percent of the African American population
	Three-quarters of all southern white families own no slaves
	South produces largest cotton crop ever

South-North Similarity

The South shared much in common with the rest of the nation. The geographic sizes of the South and the North were roughly the same. In 1815, white southerners and fellow northerners shared heroes and ideology from the American Revolution and War of 1812. They worshipped the same Protestant God as northerners, lived under the same Constitution, and similarly combined nationalism and localism in their attitudes toward government. But as slavery and the plantation economy expanded (see Map 9.1), the South did not become a land of individual opportunity in the same manner as the North.

Research has shown that, despite enormous cruelties, slavery was a profitable labor system for planters. Southerners and northerners shared an expanding capitalist economy. As it grew, the slave-based economy reflected planters' rational choices. More land and more slaves generally converted into more wealth.

By the eve of the Civil War in 1860, the distribution of wealth and property in the two sections was almost identical: 50 percent of free adult males owned only 1 percent of real and personal property, and the richest 1 percent owned 27 percent of the wealth. North and South had ruling classes. Entrepreneurs in both sections sought their fortunes in an expanding market economy. The southern "master class" was more likely than propertied northerners to move west to make a profit.

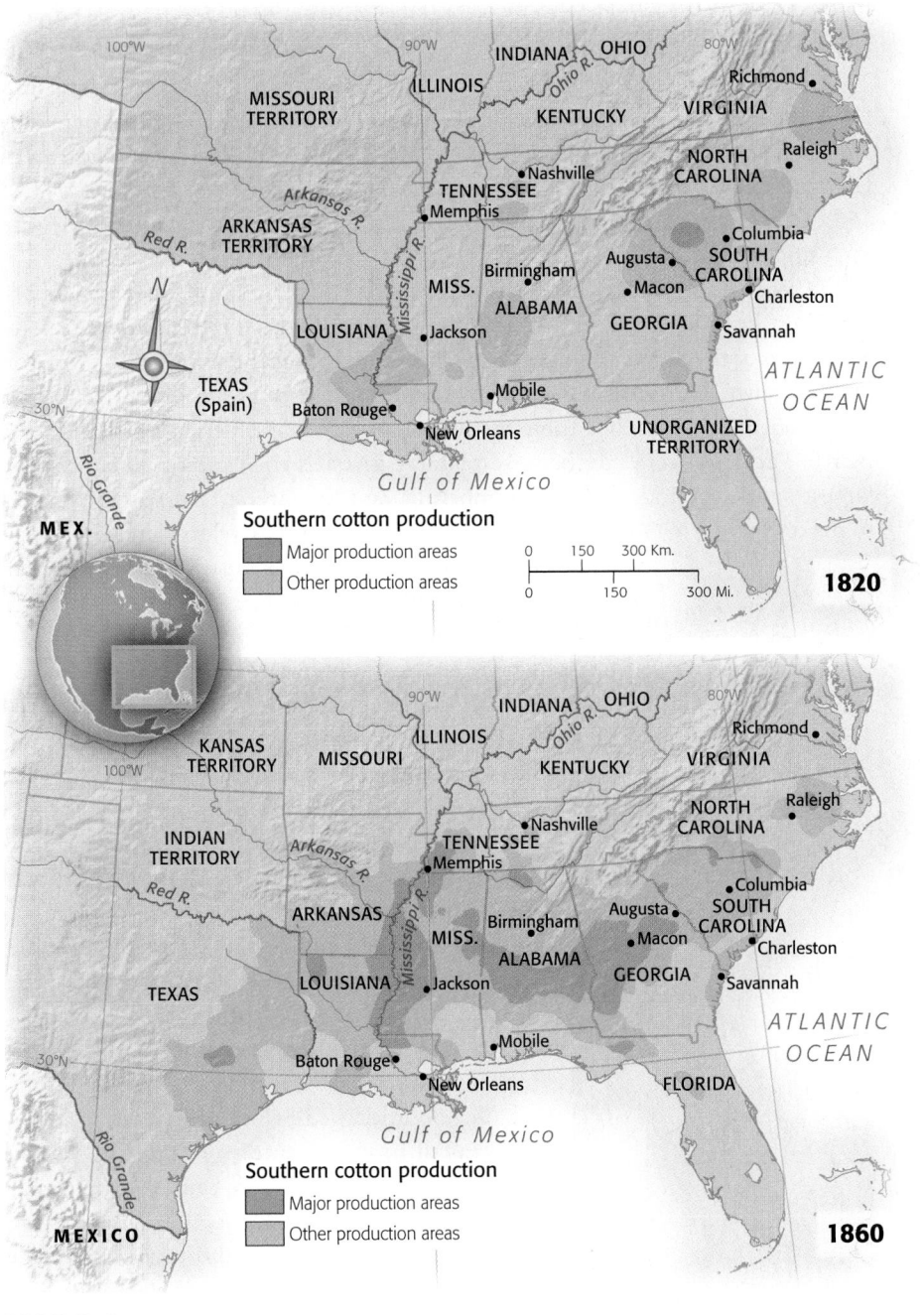

MAP 9.1

Cotton Production in the South

These two maps reveal the rapid westward expansion of cotton production and its importance to the antebellum South. Source: Copyright © Cengage Learning 2015

South-North Dissimilarity

In terms of differences, the South's climate and longer growing season gave it a rural and agricultural destiny. Many great rivers provided rich soil and transportation routes. The South developed as a biracial society of brutal inequality, where the liberty of one race depended on the enslavement of another.

Cotton growers spread over large areas to maximize production and income. Consequently, population density in the South was low; by 1860, there were only 2.3 people per square mile in largely unsettled Texas, 15.6 in Louisiana, and 18.0 in Georgia. The Northeast averaged 65.4 people per square mile—Massachusetts had 153.1 people per square mile, and New York City compressed 86,400 people into each square mile.

Where people were scarce, it was difficult to finance and operate schools, churches, libraries, inns, and restaurants. Similarly, the South's rural character and vision of the plantation as self-sufficient meant that the section spent little on public health. Southerners were strongly committed to their churches, and some embraced universities, but these institutions were far less developed than in the North. Factories were rare because planters invested their capital in slaves. The largest southern "industry" was lumbering, and the largest factories used slaves to make cigars. The South was slower than the North to develop a unified market economy and a regional transportation network and had only 35 percent of the nation's railroad mileage in 1860.

The Old South never developed its own banking and shipping capacity to any degree and relied on the North for both. Most southern bank deposits were in the North, and as early as 1822, one-sixth of all southern cotton cleared for Liverpool or Le Havre from the port of New York. With cotton constituting two-fifths of New York's exports, merchants and bankers there became interested in the fate of slavery and cotton prices. In economic conventions from 1837 to 1839, southern delegates debated foreign trade, dependence on northern importers and financiers, and other alleged threats to their commercial independence.

The South lagged behind the North in industrial growth. Its urban centers were mostly ports like New Orleans and Charleston, which became crossroads of commerce and small-scale manufacturing. In the interior were small market towns dependent on agricultural trade. Lacking manufacturing jobs, the South did not attract immigrants as readily as the North. By 1860, only 13 percent of the nation's foreign-born population lived in slave states.

Like most northerners, antebellum southerners embraced evangelical Christianity. Americans everywhere believed in a personal God and in conversion and piety as the means to salvation. But southern evangelical Baptists and Methodists concentrated on personal rather than social

Library of Congress

America, 1841, lithograph and watercolor by Edward Williams Clay. An idealized portrayal of loyal and contented slaves, likely distributed by northern apologists for slavery. All is well on the plantation as well-dressed slaves dance and express their gratitude to their master and his perfect family. The text includes the old slave saying: "God bless you master! You feed and clothe us. When we are sick you nurse us, and when too old to work, you provide for us!" The master replies piously: "These poor creatures are a sacred legacy from my ancestors and while a dollar is left me, nothing shall be spared to increase their comfort and happiness."

improvement. By the 1830s in the North, evangelicalism was a wellspring of reform movements (see Chapter 10); but in states where blacks were numerous and unfree, religion, as one scholar has written, preached "a hands-off policy concerning slavery." Moreover, distance and sparse population prevented reform-minded women from developing associations with each other. The only reform movements that grew in the emerging southern Bible Belt, such as temperance, focused exclusively on personal behavior.

A Southern Worldview and the Proslavery Argument

In the wake of the American Revolution, Enlightenment ideas of natural rights and equality stimulated antislavery sentiment in the Upper South, produced a brief flurry of manumissions, and inspired hope for gradual emancipation. But that confidence waned in the new nation. As slavery spread, southerners vigorously defended it.

By the 1820s, white southerners justified slavery as a "**positive good**," not merely a "necessary evil." They used the antiquity of slavery, as well as the Bible's many references to slaveholding, to foster a historical argument for bondage. But at the heart of the proslavery rationale was a deep and abiding racism. Whites were the more intellectual race, they claimed, and blacks more inherently physical and therefore destined for labor. In an 1851 proslavery tract, John Campbell declared that "there is as much difference between the lowest tribe of negroes and the white Frenchman, Englishman, or American, as there is between the monkey and the negro."

Some southerners defended slavery in practical terms: their bondsmen were economic necessities. In 1845, James Henry Hammond of South Carolina argued that slaveholding was a matter of property rights protected by the Constitution. The deepest root of the proslavery argument was a hierarchical view of the social order with slavery prescribed by God. Southerners cherished tradition, believing social change should come slowly, in increments, if at all. As Nat Turner's slave rebellion compelled the Virginia legislature to debate the gradual abolition of slavery in 1831–1832, Thomas R. Dew, a slaveholder and professor at the College of William and Mary, contended that "that which is the growth of *ages* may require ages to remove." Dew's widely read *Abolition of Negro Slavery* (1832) ushered in an outpouring of proslavery writing that would intensify over the next thirty years. As slavery expanded westward and fueled national prosperity, Dew cautioned that gradual abolition threatened the South's "irremediable ruin." Dew declared black slavery the "order of nature" and the basis of the "well-ordered, well-established liberty" of white Americans. Dew's well-ordered society also included the proper division of men and women into separate spheres and functions.

Proslavery advocates invoked natural-law doctrine, arguing that the natural state of humankind was inequality of ability and condition, not equality. Proslavery writers believed that people were born to certain stations in life; they stressed dependence over autonomy and duty over rights as the human condition. As Virginia writer George Fitzhugh put it in 1854, "Men are not born entitled to equal rights. It would be far nearer the truth to say, that some were born with saddles on their backs, and others booted and spurred to ride them." Given the persistence

positive good Southern justification for slavery as beneficial to the larger society, both to white owners and their black slaves.

of modern racism throughout the U.S., it is especially important to comprehend antebellum southerner's rationalizations for slavery.

Many slaveholders saw themselves in a paternal role, as guardians of a familial relationship between masters and slaves. Although contradicted by countless examples of slave resistance and escape, and by slave sales, planters needed to believe in and exerted great energy in constructing the idea of the contented slave.

A Slave Society

Slavery and race affected everything in the South. There, whites and blacks were socialized, married, reared children, worked, conceived of property, and honed their habits of behavior under the influence of slavery. This was true of slaveholding and nonslaveholding whites and of enslaved and free blacks. Slavery shaped the South's social structure, fueled its economy, and dominated its politics.

Still, the South was interdependent with the North, West, and Europe in a growing capitalist market system. For its cotton trade, southerners relied on northern banks, steamship companies, and merchants. But there were elements of this system that southerners increasingly disliked, especially urbanism, wage labor, a broadening right to vote, and threats to their racial and class order. Distinctive or national, the South's story begins in what we have come to call the Old South, a term only conceivable after the eviction of native peoples from the region.

Southern Expansion, Indian Resistance, and Removal

How did Native Americans living in western territories respond to increasing migration by southern whites?

When the trans-Appalachian frontier opened in the wake of the War of 1812, 5 to 10 percent of the population moved annually, usually westward. In the first two decades of the century, they poured into the Ohio Valley; by the 1820s, they were migrating into the Mississippi River valley and beyond. By 1850, two-thirds of Americans lived west of the Appalachians.

A Southern Westward Movement

After 1820, the heart of cotton cultivation and the slave-based plantation system shifted from the coastal states to Alabama and the newly settled Mississippi Valley—Tennessee, Louisiana, Arkansas, and Mississippi. Southern slaveholders took slaves with them to the newer areas of the South, and **yeoman** farmers followed, hoping for new wealth through cheap land and slaves.

yeoman Independent small farmer, usually nonslaveholding.

A wave of migration was evident everywhere in the Southeast. As early as 1817, a Charleston, South Carolina, newspaper reported that migration out of that state had reached "unprecedented proportions." Almost half of the white people born in South Carolina after 1800 left the state, most for the Southwest.

The way to wealth for southern seaboard planters was to go west to grow cotton for the booming world markets, by purchasing more land and slaves. Mississippi's population soared from 73,000 in 1820 to 607,000 in 1850, with African American slaves in the majority. Across the Mississippi River, Arkansas' population went from

14,000 in 1820 to 210,000 in 1850. By 1835, the American immigrant population in Texas reached 35,000, including 3,000 slaves, outnumbering Mexicans two to one. American settlers declared Texas's independence from Mexico in 1836, spurring further American immigration into the region. By 1845, "Texas fever" boosted the Anglo population to 125,000. Statehood that year opened the floodgates to more immigrants and to a confrontation with Mexico that would lead to war.

As the **cotton kingdom** grew to what southern political leaders dreamed would be national and world dominion, this westward migration, fueled initially by optimistic nationalism, ultimately made migrant planters more sectional and southern. By the 1840s, these capitalist planters, fearful that their slave-based economy was under attack, sought to protect and expand their system. Increasingly, they saw themselves, as one historian has written, less as "landowners who happened to own slaves" than as "slaveholders who happened to own land."

cotton kingdom A broad swath of territory where cotton was a mainstay that stretched from South Carolina, Georgia, and northern Florida in the east through Alabama, Mississippi, central and western Tennessee, and Louisiana, and from there on to Arkansas and Texas.

For most white Americans, the Indians were in the way of their growing empire. Before 1830, large swaths of upper Georgia belonged to the Cherokees, and huge regions of Alabama and Mississippi were Creek, Choctaw, or Chickasaw land. Indians were also on the move, but in forced migrations. Taking Indian land, so the reasoning went, merely reflected the natural course of progress: the "civilizers" had to displace the "children of the forest." National leaders provided the rhetoric and justification needed. As president in 1830, Andrew Jackson explained why the Indians must go. "What good man would prefer a country," he asked, "covered with forests and ranged by a few thousand savages to our extensive Republic, studded with cities, towns, and prosperous farms?"

Indian Treaty Making

In theory, under the U.S. Constitution, the federal government recognized Indian sovereignty and treated Indian peoples as foreign nations. Agreements between Indian nations and the United States were signed and ratified like other international treaties. In practice, however, fraud dominated the government's approach to treaty making and Indian sovereignty. As the country expanded, new treaties would shrink Indian landholdings.

Although Indian resistance persisted against such pressure after the War of 1812, it only slowed the process. In the 1820s, native peoples in the middle West, Ohio Valley, Mississippi Valley, and other parts of the cotton South ceded 200 million acres for a pittance.

Indian Accommodation

Increasingly, Indian nations east of the Mississippi sought to survive through accommodation. In the first three decades of the century, the Choctaw, Creek, and Chickasaw peoples in the lower Mississippi became suppliers and traders. Under treaty provisions, Indian commerce took place through trading posts and stores that provided Indians with supplies, and purchased or bartered Indian-produced goods. The trading posts extended credit to chiefs, who increasingly fell into debt that they could pay off to the federal government only by selling their land.

By 1822, the Choctaw nation had sold 13 million acres but still carried a $13,000 debt. The Indians struggled, increasing agricultural production and hunting, working as farmhands and craftsmen, and selling produce at market stalls in

The Amistad Case

In April 1839, a Spanish slave ship, *Tecora*, sailed from Lomboko, the West African region that became Sierra Leone. On board were Mende people, sold by their African enemies. In June, they arrived in Havana, Cuba, a Spanish colony. Two Spaniards purchased fifty-three of the Mende and sailed aboard *La Amistad* for their plantations elsewhere in Cuba. After three days at sea, the Africans revolted. Led by a man the Spaniards called Joseph Cinque, they killed the captain and took control. They ordered the two Spaniards to return them to Africa, but the slaveholders tried to reach the American South. Far off course, *La Amistad* was seized by the USS *Washington* in Long Island Sound and brought ashore in Connecticut.

The "Amistad Africans" soon became a cause for abolitionists and slaveholders, as well as an issue in U.S.–Spanish relations. The Africans were imprisoned in New Haven, and a dispute ensued: Were they slaves and murderers, and the property of Cuban owners, or were they free people exercising their natural rights? Were they Spanish property, seized on the high seas in violation of a 1795 treaty? If a northern state could "free" captive Africans, what did it mean for enslaved African Americans in the South? Connecticut abolitionists went to court, where a U.S. circuit court judge dismissed the mutiny and murder charges but refused to release the Africans because their Spanish owners claimed them as property.

Meanwhile, a Yale professor of ancient languages, Josiah Gibbs, visited the captives and learned their words for numbers. In New York, he walked along the docks repeating the Mende words until an African seaman, James Covey, responded. Covey journeyed to New Haven, conversed with the jubilant Africans, and soon their tale garnered sympathy throughout New England.

In a new trial, the judge ruled that the Africans were illegally enslaved and ordered them returned to their homeland. Slave trade between Africa and the Americas had been outlawed in a treaty between Spain and Great Britain. Spain's lawyers demanded the return of their "merchandise." Needing southern votes to win reelection, President Martin Van Buren supported Spanish claims.

The administration appealed to the Supreme Court in February 1841. Arguing the abolitionists' case, former president John Quincy Adams pointed to a copy of the Declaration of Independence on the court wall, invoked the natural rights to life and liberty, and chastised Van Buren. In a 7-to-1 decision, the Court ruled that the Africans were "free-born."

On November 27, 1841, thirty-five survivors and five American missionaries embarked for Africa, arriving in Sierra Leone on January 15, 1842. The Amistad case showed how intertwined slavery was with freedom, and the United States with the world. It poisoned diplomatic relations between America and Spain for a generation, and stimulated Christian mission work in Africa.

Joseph Cinque, by Nathaniel Jocelyn, 1840. Cinque led the rebellion aboard La Amistad, *a Spanish ship carrying captive Africans along the coast of Cuba in 1839. They commandeered the ship and sailed it north toward New England, where they were rescued off the coast of Connecticut. Cinque, celebrated as a great leader, sat for the painting while he and his people awaited trial. They were freed by a decision of the U.S. Supreme Court in 1841 and returned to their homeland in Sierra Leone in West Africa.*

AP Photo/New Haven Colony Historical Society

Natchez and New Orleans. As the United States expanded westward, white Americans promoted their assimilation through education and conversion to Christianity. In 1819, in response to missionary lobbying, Congress appropriated $10,000 annually for "civilization of the tribes adjoining the frontier settlements."

Within five years, thirty-two boarding schools run by Protestant missionaries enrolled Indian students. They substituted English for American Indian languages and taught agriculture alongside the Christian gospel. But settlers still eyed Indian land. Wherever native peoples lived, illegal settlers disrupted their lives. The federal government halfheartedly enforced treaties, as legitimate Indian land rights gave way to the advance of white civilization.

With loss of land came dependency. The Choctaws relied on white Americans for manufactured goods and even food. Disease further facilitated removal of American Indian peoples to western lands. While other groups increased rapidly, the Indian population fell, some nations declining by 50 percent in three decades. As many as one hundred thousand eastern and southern Indian peoples were removed between 1820 and 1850; about thirty thousand died in the process.

Removal had a profound impact on Shawnees, the people of the Prophet and Tecumseh (see pages 207–208). After giving up 17 million acres in Ohio in a 1795 treaty, the Shawnees scattered to Indiana and eastern Missouri. Others moved to the Kansas Territory in 1825. By 1854, Kansas was open to white settlement, and the Shawnees had ceded seven-eighths of their land, or 1.4 million acres. Men lost their traditional role as providers; their skills hunting woodland animals were useless on the Kansas prairies. As grain became the tribe's dietary staple, Shawnee women played a greater role as providers, supplemented by government aid under treaty provisions. Remarkably, the Shawnees preserved their language and culture despite these devastating dislocations.

Indian Removal as Federal Policy

Cherokees, Creeks, Choctaws, Chickasaws, and Seminoles aggressively resisted white encroachment after the War of 1812. In his last annual message to Congress in late 1824, President James Monroe proposed that all Indians be moved beyond the Mississippi River. Monroe considered this an "honorable" proposal that would protect Indians from invasion and provide them with independence for "improvement and civilization." He believed force would be unnecessary. But all five tribes unanimously rejected Monroe's proposition. Between 1789 and 1825, the five nations negotiated thirty treaties with the United States, and they reached their limit. Most wished to remain on what little was left of their ancestral land.

Pressure from Georgia prompted Monroe's policy. In the 1820s, the state accused the federal government of not fulfilling its 1802 promise to remove the Cherokees and Creeks from northwestern Georgia in return for the state's renunciation of its claim to western lands. In 1826, under federal pressure, the Creek nation ceded all but a small strip of its Georgia acreage, but for Georgians only their complete removal would resolve the conflict. In an unsuccessful attempt to retain the remainder of their traditional lands in Alabama, the Creeks radically altered their political structure. In 1829, they centralized tribal authority and forbade any chief from ceding land.

Indian Removal Act
Legislation authorizing Andrew Jackson to exchange public lands in the West for Indian territories in the East and appropriated federal funds to cover the expenses of removal.

Link to President Jackson Reports on Indian Removal, 1830

In 1830, after a narrow vote, Congress passed the **Indian Removal Act** authorizing the president to negotiate removal treaties with all tribes living east of the Mississippi. The bill, which provided federal funds for such relocations, would likely not have passed the House without the additional representation afforded slave states due to the Constitution's three-fifths clause.

Cherokees

No people met the challenge of assimilating to American standards more than the Cherokees, whose traditional home centered on eastern Tennessee and northern Alabama and Georgia. Between 1819 and 1829, the tribe became economically self-sufficient and politically self-governing; during this Cherokee renaissance the nearly fifteen thousand adult Cherokees regarded themselves as a nation, not a collection of villages. In 1821 and 1822, Sequoyah, a self-educated Cherokee, devised an eighty-six-character phonetic alphabet that made possible a Cherokee-language Bible and a bilingual tribal newspaper, *Cherokee Phoenix* (1828). Between 1820 and 1823, the Cherokees created a formal government with a bicameral legislature, a court system, and in 1827 they adopted a written constitution modeled after that of the United States. They transformed their economy from hunting, gathering, and subsistence agriculture to commodity trade based on barter, cash, and credit. The Cherokee nation, however, collectively owned all tribal land and forbade land sales to outsiders. Nonetheless, many became individual farmers and slaveholders; by 1833, they held fifteen hundred black slaves, and over time Cherokee racial identity became very complex.

But Cherokee transformations failed to win respect or acceptance from white southerners. In the 1820s, Georgia pressed them to sell the 7,200 square miles they held in the state. Congress appropriated $30,000 in 1822 to buy the Georgia land, but the Cherokees resisted. Impatient, Georgia annulled the Cherokees' constitution, extended the state's sovereignty over them, prohibited the Cherokee National Council from meeting except to cede land, and ordered their lands seized. The discovery of gold on Cherokee land in 1829 further whetted Georgia's appetite for Cherokee territory.

Cherokee Nation v. Georgia

The Cherokees under Chief John Ross turned to the federal courts to defend their treaty with the United States. In *Cherokee Nation v. Georgia* (1831), Chief Justice John Marshall ruled that under the Constitution an Indian tribe was neither a foreign nation nor a state and therefore had no standing in federal courts. Indians were deemed "domestic, dependent nations." Legally, they were in but not of the United States. Nonetheless, said Marshall, the Indians had a right to their lands; they could lose title only by voluntarily giving it up.

A year later, in *Worcester v. Georgia*, Marshall declared that the Cherokee nation was a distinct political community in which "the laws of Georgia can have no force" and into which Georgians could not enter without permission or treaty. The Cherokees celebrated. Jackson, however, whose reputation was built as an Indian fighter, tried to usurp the Court's action. Newspapers reported that Jackson had said, "John Marshall has made his decision: now let him enforce it." To open up new lands for settlement, Jackson favored expelling the Cherokees.

Georgians, too, refused to comply; they would not tolerate a sovereign Cherokee nation within their borders. A Cherokee census indicated that they owned thirty-three grist mills, thirteen sawmills, one powder mill, sixty-nine blacksmith shops, two tanneries, 762 looms, 2,486 spinning wheels, 172 wagons, 2,923 plows, 7,683 horses, 22,531 cattle, 46,732 pigs, and 2,566 sheep. "You asked us to…form a republican government," declared the Cherokee leader John Ridge in 1832. "We did so—adopting your own as a model. You asked us to cultivate the earth, and learn the mechanic arts: We did so. You asked us to learn to read: We did so. You asked us to cast away our idols, and worship your God: We did so." But neither the plow nor the Bible earned the Cherokees respect in the face of the economic, imperial, and racial quests of fellow southerners (see Map 9.2).

MAP 9.2
Removal of Native Americans from the South, 1820–1840

Over a twenty-year period, the federal government and southern states forced Native Americans to exchange their traditional homes for western land. Some tribal groups remained in the South, but most settled in the alien western environment.

Source: Copyright © Cengage Learning 2015

Trail of Tears

The Choctaws made the forced journey from Mississippi and Alabama to the West in the winter of 1831 and 1832. Alexis de Tocqueville was visiting Memphis when they passed through: "The wounded, the sick, newborn babies, and the old men on the point of death.... the sight will never fade from my memory," he wrote. The Creeks in Alabama resisted removal until 1836, when the army pushed them westward. A year later, the Chickasaws followed.

Some Cherokees believed that further resistance was hopeless and accepted removal, agreeing in 1835 to exchange their southern home for western land, in the Treaty of New Echota. Most wanted to stand firm. John Ross, with petitions signed by fifteen thousand Cherokees, lobbied the Senate against ratification of the treaty. He lost. But when the time for evacuation came in 1838, most Cherokees refused to move. President Martin Van Buren sent federal troops; about twenty thousand Cherokees were evicted, held in detention camps, and marched under military escort to Indian Territory in present-day Oklahoma. Nearly one-quarter died of disease and exhaustion on what came to be known as the **Trail of Tears**.

When the forced march ended, the Indians had traded about 100 million acres east of the Mississippi for 32 million acres west of the river plus $68 million. Forced removal had a disastrous impact on the Cherokees and other displaced Indian nations. In the West, they encountered an alien environment. Unable to live off the land, many became dependent on government payments. In 1839, followers of John Ross assassinated leaders of the protreaty faction. Violence continued sporadically until a new treaty in 1846 imposed a temporary truce. In time, the Cherokees reestablished their political institutions and a governing body in Tahlequah, in northeastern Oklahoma.

Trail of Tears Forced migration in 1838 of Cherokee Indians from their homelands in the southeast to what is now Oklahoma.

GILCREASE MUSEUM, TULSA OK

The Trail of Tears, *by twentieth-century Pawnee artist Brummet Echohawk. About twenty thousand Cherokees were evicted in 1838–1839, and about one-quarter of them died on the forced march to present-day Oklahoma.*

Seminole Wars

In Florida, some Seminole leaders agreed in the 1832 Treaty of Payne's Landing to relocate to the West within three years, but others opposed the treaty. A minority under Osceola, a charismatic leader, fought the protreaty group. When federal troops were sent to impose removal in 1835, Osceola waged a guerrilla war against them.

Florida Indians were a varied group that included many Creeks and mixed Indian–African Americans (ex-slaves or descendants of runaway slaves). The U.S. Army, however, considered them all Seminoles. General Thomas Jesup believed that the runaway slave population was the key to the war. "And if it be not speedily put down," he wrote a friend in 1836, "the South will feel the effects of it on their slave population before the end of the next season."

Osceola was captured and died in an army prison in 1838, but the Seminoles fought on under Chief Coacoochee (Wild Cat). In 1842, the United States abandoned removal. Most of Osceola's followers agreed to move west to Indian Territory after another war in 1858, but some remained in the Florida Everglades.

Social Pyramid in the Old South

What class tensions emerged in the antebellum South?

A large majority of white southern families (three-quarters in 1860) were yeoman farmers who owned land but no slaves. The social distance between poorer whites and the planter class could be great; still greater was the distance between whites and free blacks. White yeomen, landless whites, and free blacks occupied the broad base of the social pyramid in the Old South.

Yeoman Farmers

After the War of 1812, white farmers moved in waves down the southern Appalachians into the Gulf lands or through the Cumberland Gap into Kentucky and Tennessee. In large sections of the South, especially inland from the coast and away from large rivers, small, self-sufficient farms were the norm. Lured by stories of good land, many men repeatedly uprooted their wives and children.

Their status as a numerical majority did not mean they set the political or economic direction of the larger society. Self-reliant and often isolated, they operated both apart from and within the slave-based staple-crop economy.

On the southern frontier, men cleared fields, built log cabins, and established farms while their wives labored in the household economy and patiently re-created the social ties—to relatives, neighbors, fellow churchgoers—that enriched everyone's experience. Women dreaded the isolation and loneliness of the frontier.

Some yeomen acquired large tracts of land, purchased slaves, and became planters. They forged part of the new wealth of the cotton boom states of Mississippi and Louisiana, where mobility into the slave-owning class was possible. Others clung to familiar mountainous areas or sought self-sufficiency. As one historian has written, though they owned no slaves, yeomen were jealous of their independence, and "the household grounded their own claims to masterhood."

Yeoman Folk Culture

Yeomen enjoyed a folk culture based on family, church, and local region. Their speech patterns recalled their

Scots-Irish and Irish backgrounds. They flocked to religious revivals called camp meetings, and in between got together for house-raisings, logrollings, quilting bees, corn-shuckings, and hunting. Such occasions combined work with fun and fellowship, offering food and liquor in abundance.

Demanding work and family responsibilities shaped women's lives in the home. They worked in the fields but food preparation consumed much of women's time. Household tasks continued during frequent pregnancies and child care. Nursing and medical care also fell to mothers, who relied on folk wisdom. Women, too, wanted to be masters of their household, although with such heavy workloads, it often came at the price of their health.

Yeomen's Livelihoods   Probably typical of southern yeomen, Ferdinand L. Steel moved as a young man from North Carolina to Tennessee to work as a river boatman but eventually took up farming in Mississippi. Steel and his family raised corn and wheat, though cotton was their cash product: they sold five or six bales a year to obtain money for sugar, coffee, salt, calico, gunpowder, and other store-bought goods.

Thus, Steel entered the market economy as a small farmer, but with mixed results. He picked his own cotton and complained that it was brutal work and unprofitable. He felt like a serf in cotton's kingdom. When cotton prices fell, a small farmer like Steel could be driven into debt or lose his farm.

Steel's family in Mississippi in the 1840s retained much of the flavor of the frontier, and he survived on a household economy. He made all the family's shoes; his wife and sister sewed dresses, shirts, and "pantaloons." The Steel women rendered their own soap and spun and wove cotton into cloth; the men hunted game. Steel doctored his illnesses with boneset tea and herbs. As the nation fell deeper into crisis over slave labor and the planter class strove more aggressively to preserve its slave society, this independent farmer never came close to owning a slave.

The focus of Steel's life was family and religion. Family members prayed together daily, and he studied Scripture for an hour after lunch. "My Faith increases, & I enjoy much of that peace which the world cannot give," he wrote in 1841. Seeking to prepare himself for Judgment Day, Steel borrowed histories, Latin and Greek grammars, and religious books from his church. Eventually, he became a traveling Methodist minister. "My life is one of toil," he reflected, "but blessed be God that it is as well with me as it is."

Landless Whites   Roughly 25 to 40 percent of white southerners were hired hands who owned no land and worked for others. Their property consisted of a few household items and some animals—usually pigs. The landless included some immigrants, especially Irish, who did heavy and dangerous work, such as building railroads and digging ditches.

In the countryside, white farm laborers struggled to purchase land in the face of low wages or, if they rented, unpredictable market prices for their crops. Scrimping, some climbed yeoman ranks. When James and Nancy Bennitt of North Carolina succeeded in their ten-year struggle to buy land, they avoided the unstable cotton market and raised extra corn and wheat for cash. People like the Bennitts were both participants in and victims of an economy dominated by cotton producers who relied on slave labor.

Herdsmen with pigs and other livestock faced a desperate struggle. By 1860, as the South anticipated war to preserve its society, between 300,000 and 400,000 white people in Virginia, North and South Carolina, and Georgia—approximately one-fifth of the total white population—lived in poverty. Land and slaves determined wealth in the Old South, and many whites possessed neither.

Yeomen's Demands and White Class Relations

Class tensions emerged in the western, nonslaveholding parts of the seaboard states by the 1830s. There, yeoman farmers resented their underrepresentation in state legislatures and the corruption in local government. Voters in the more recently settled states of the Old Southwest adopted white manhood suffrage and other electoral reforms, including popular election of governors, legislative apportionment based on white population only, and locally chosen county government. Slave owners with new wealth, however, were determined to hold the reins of power.

Historians have offered several explanations why tensions between slaveholders and nonslaveholders did not fuel greater conflict. One of the most important factors was race. The South's racial ideology stressed the superiority of all whites to blacks. Thus, slavery became the basis of equality among whites, and white privilege inflated the status of poor whites, giving them a common interest with the rich. The dream of upward mobility blunted some class conflict.

Most important, before the Civil War yeomen worked their farms and avoided debt, largely unhindered by slaveholding planters. Likewise, slaveholders pursued their goals independently of yeomen. Suppression of dissent also played an increasing role. After 1830, white southerners who criticized the slave system were intimidated, attacked, or rendered politically powerless in a society held together partly by white racial solidarity.

Still, there were signs of class conflict. As cotton lands filled up, nonslaveholders faced narrower economic prospects; meanwhile, wealthy planters enjoyed expanding profits. The risks of entering cotton production were becoming too great and the cost of slaves too high for many yeomen to rise in society. From 1830 to 1860, the percentage of white southern families holding slaves declined steadily, from 36 to 25 percent. Although slave owners were a minority in the white population, planters' share of the South's agricultural wealth remained between 90 and 95 percent.

Anticipating possible secession, slave owners stood secure. In the 1850s, they occupied from 50 to 85 percent of the seats in state legislatures and a similarly high percentage of the South's congressional seats. And planters' interests controlled all other major social institutions, such as churches and colleges.

Free Blacks

The nearly quarter-million free blacks in the South in 1860 often fared little better than slaves. Upper South free blacks were usually descendants of people manumitted by their owners in the 1780s and 1790s. A remarkable number of slaveholders in Virginia and the Chesapeake had freed their slaves because of religious principles and revolutionary ideals in the wake of American independence (see Chapter 7). Many free blacks also became free as runaways, especially by the 1830s. A small number purchased their own freedom.

Some free blacks worked in towns or cities, but most lived in rural areas and struggled to survive. They usually did not own land and labored in someone else's fields, often alongside slaves. By law, free blacks could not own a gun, buy liquor, violate curfew, assemble except in church, testify in court, or (throughout the South after 1835) vote. Despite these obstacles, a minority bought land, and others found jobs as skilled craftsmen, especially in cities.

A few free blacks prospered and bought slaves. In 1830, there were 3,775 free black slaveholders in the South; 80 percent lived in Louisiana, South Carolina, Virginia, and Maryland, and half of the total lived in New Orleans and Charleston. Most purchased their own wives and children, whom they could not free because laws required newly emancipated blacks to leave their state. To free family members they had purchased, hundreds of black slaveholders petitioned for exemption from anti-manumission laws. At the same time, a few mulattos in New Orleans were active slave traders. Although rare in the United States, the greed and the tragic quest for power that lay at the root of slavery could cross racial or ethnic barriers.

Free Black Communities

In the cotton belt and Gulf regions, a large proportion of free blacks were mulattos, the privileged offspring of wealthy white planters. Not all planters freed their mixed-race offspring, but those who did often gave their children a good education and financial backing. In cities like New Orleans, Charleston, and Mobile, extensive interracial sex, as well as migrations from the Caribbean, produced a mulatto population that was recognized as a distinct class.

In many southern cities by the 1840s, free black communities formed, especially around churches. By the late 1850s, Baltimore had fifteen such churches, Louisville nine, and Nashville and St. Louis four each—most of them African Methodist Episcopal. In 1840, Baltimore contained 17,967 free blacks and 3,199 slaves out of a total population of 102,313. These free people of color worked in menial jobs, from domestic servants to dockworkers and draymen, and they also suffered under a strict Black Code, denying civil or political rights and restricting their movements.

The Planters' World

How did cotton shape the lives of planters and their families?

At the top of the southern social pyramid were slaveholding planters. Most lived in comfortable farmhouses, not in the opulence that legend suggests. The grand plantation mansions with outlying slave quarters are an enduring symbol of the Old South. But in 1850, 50 percent of southern slaveholders had fewer than five slaves; 72 percent had fewer than ten; 88 percent had fewer than twenty. Thus, the average slaveholder was not a wealthy aristocrat but an aspiring farmer.

The Newly Rich

In the 1840s, newly rich Louisiana cotton planter Bennet Barrow was preoccupied with moneymaking. He worried about his cotton crop, and to overcome his worries, he hunted and had a passion for racing horses and raising hounds. He could report the loss of a slave without feeling, but became emotional when illness afflicted his sporting animals. His strongest feelings surfaced when his horse Jos Bell "broke down running a mile … ruined for Ever." The same day, Barrow gave his human property a "general Whipping."

The richest planters used their wealth to model genteel sophistication. Extended visits, parties, and balls to which women wore the latest fashions provided opportunities for friendship, courtship, and display. These entertainments were important diversions for plantation women, who relished social events to break the monotony of their domestic lives. Yet socializing also sustained a rigidly gendered society.

Most of the planters in the cotton-boom states of Alabama and Mississippi were newly rich by the 1840s. As one historian put it, "a number of men mounted from log cabin to plantation mansion on a stairway of cotton bales, accumulating slaves as they climbed." And many did not live like rich men. They put their new wealth into cotton acreage and slaves even as they sought refinement and high social status.

The cotton boom in the Mississippi Valley created one-generation aristocrats. A case in point is Greenwood Leflore, a Chocktaw chieftain who owned a plantation in Mississippi with four hundred slaves. After selling his cotton on the world market, he spent $10,000 in France to furnish a single room of his mansion with handwoven carpets, furniture upholstered with gold leaf, tables and cabinets ornamented with tortoiseshell inlay, a variety of mirrors and paintings, and a clock and candelabra of brass and ebony.

Social Status and Planters' Values

Slave ownership was the main determinant of wealth in the South. Slaves were a commodity and an investment, much like gold; people bought them on speculation, hoping for a rise in their market value. Many slaveholders mortgaged their slaves and used them as collateral. People who could not pay cash for slaves would ask the sellers to purchase the mortgage, just as banks give mortgages on houses today. The slaveholder would repay the loan in installments with interest.

The availability of slave labor tended to devalue free labor: where strenuous work under supervision was reserved for an enslaved race, few free people relished it. When Alexis de Tocqueville crossed from Ohio into Kentucky in his 1831 travels, he observed "On the right bank of the Ohio [River] everything is activity, industry; labor is honoured; there are no slaves. Pass to the left bank and the scene changes so suddenly… the enterprising spirit is gone. There, work is not only painful; it is shameful."

Aristocratic values—lineage, privilege, pride, honor, and refinement of person and manner—commanded respect throughout the South. Many of those qualities were in short supply, however, in the recently settled portions of the cotton kingdom, where frontier values of courage and self-reliance ruled during the 1820s and 1830s. By the 1850s, a settled aristocratic group of planters did rule, however, much of the Mississippi Valley.

Aristocratic planters expected to wield power and receive deference from poorer whites. But the independent yeoman class resented infringements of its rights, and many yeomen belonged to evangelical faiths that exalted simplicity and condemned the planters' wealth. Much of the planters' power and claims to leadership were, after all, built on their assumption of a monopoly on world cotton and a foundation of black slave labor.

King Cotton in a Global Economy

The American South so dominated the world's supply of cotton that southern planters gained enormous confidence that the cotton boom was permanent and that the industrializing nations of England and France would always bow to **King Cotton**.

King Cotton Term expressing the southern belief that the U.S. and British economies depended on cotton, making it "king."

American cotton production doubled in yield each decade after 1800 and provided three-fourths of the world's supply by the 1840s. Southern staple crops were three-fifths of American exports by 1850, and one of seven workers in England depended on American cotton for a job. Cotton production made slaves the most valuable financial asset in the United States—greater than banks, railroads, and manufacturing combined. In 1860 dollars, the slaves' total value as property equaled an estimated $3.5 billion (roughly $75 billion in early twenty-first-century dollars).

"Cotton is King," the *Southern Cultivator* declared in 1859. Until 1840, cotton furnished much of the export capital to finance northern economic growth. After that, the northern economy expanded without dependence on cotton profits. Nevertheless, southerners boasted of King Cotton's supremacy. "No power on earth dares…to make war on cotton," James Hammond lectured the U.S. Senate in 1858. Although the South produced 4.5 million bales in 1861, its greatest cotton crop ever, such world dominance was about to collapse.

Paternalism

Slaveholding men often embraced a paternalistic ideology that justified their dominance over black slaves and white women. They stressed their obligations, viewing themselves as custodians of society and of the black families they owned. The paternalistic planter saw himself not as an oppressor but as the benevolent guardian of an inferior race.

Paul Carrington Cameron, North Carolina's largest slaveholder, exemplifies this mentality. After a period of sickness among his one thousand North Carolina slaves (he had hundreds more in Alabama and Mississippi), Cameron wrote, "I fear the Negroes have suffered much from the want of proper attention and kindness under this late distemper no love of lucre shall ever induce me to be cruel." He later described to his sister his sense of responsibility: "Do you remember a cold & frosty morning, during [our mother's] illness, when she said to me Paul my son the people ought to be shod' this is ever in my ears, whenever I see any ones shoes in bad order; and in my ears it will be, so long as I am master."

This comforting self-image let rich planters obscure the harsh dimensions of slave treatment. And slaves—accommodating to the realities of power—encouraged masters to think that their benevolence was appreciated. Paternalism also served as a defense against abolitionist criticism. In reality, paternalism grew as a give-and-take relationship between masters and slaves—owners took labor from the bondsmen, while slaves sought to obligate masters to provide them a measure of autonomy and living space.

But Cameron's benevolence vanished with changed circumstances. After the Civil War, he bristled at African Americans' efforts to be free and made sweeping economic decisions without regard for their welfare. Writing on Christmas Day 1865, Cameron showed little Christian charity (but a healthy profit motive) when he declared, "I am convinced that the people who gets rid of the free negro first will be the first to advance in improved agriculture. Have made no effort to retain any of mine." He turned off his land nearly a thousand black people, rented his fields to several white farmers, and invested in industry.

Virginia Luxuries, *folk painting, artist unknown. Abby Aldrich Rockefeller Folk Art Museum, the Colonial Williamsburg Foundation.*

Relations between men and women in the planter class were similarly defined by paternalism. The upper-class southern woman was raised to be a wife, mother, and subordinate companion to men. South Carolina's Mary Boykin Chesnut wrote of her husband, "He is master of the house....All the comfort of my life depends upon his being in a good humor." Women found it difficult to challenge society's rules on sexual or racial relations.

Planters' daughters usually attended one of the South's rapidly multiplying boarding schools. Typically, the young woman could entertain suitors whom her parents approved. But she quickly had to choose a husband and commit herself to a man whom she generally had known only briefly. Young women had to follow the wishes of their family, especially their father.

Upon marriage, a planter-class woman ceded to her husband most of her legal rights, becoming part of his family. She was isolated on a large plantation, where she supervised the cooking and preserving of food, managed the house, watched children, and attended sick slaves. These realities were more confining on the frontier, where isolation was greater. Men on plantations could occasionally escape into the public realm—to town, business, or politics. Women could retreat from rural plantation culture only into kinship and associations with other women.

Marriage and Family Among Planters

A perceptive young white woman approached marriage with anxiety. Lucy Breckinridge, a wealthy Virginia girl of twenty, lamented the autonomy she surrendered at the altar. In her diary, she recorded: "A woman's life after she is married, unless there is an immense amount of love, is nothing but suffering and hard work."

Childbearing often involved grief, poor health, and death. In 1840, the birth rate for white southern women was almost 30 percent higher than the national average. The average southern white woman would bear eight children in 1800; by 1860, the figure had decreased to only six. Childbirth complications were a major cause of death, occurring twice as often in the hot South as in the Northeast.

Sexual relations between planters and slaves were another problem that white women endured but were not supposed to notice. "Violations of the moral law … made mulattos as common as blackberries," protested a woman in Georgia, but wives had to play "the ostrich game." Such habits produced a large mixed race population by the 1850s.

In the 1840s and 1850s, as abolitionist attacks on slavery increased, southern men published several articles stressing that women should restrict their concerns to the home. The *Southern Quarterly Review* declared, "The proper place for a woman is at home. One of her highest privileges is to be politically merged in the existence of her husband."

But a study of women in Petersburg, Virginia, a large tobacco-manufacturing town, revealed behavior that valued financial autonomy. Over several decades before 1860, the proportion of women who never married, or did not remarry after a spouse's death, grew to exceed 33 percent. Likewise, the number of women who worked for wages, controlled their own property, and ran dressmaking businesses increased.

Slave Life and Labor

What was the true nature of the master-slave relationship?

Slaves knew a life of poverty, coercion, toil, and resentment. They provided the strength and know-how to build an agricultural empire. But they embodied a fundamental contradiction: in the world's model republic, slaves were on the wrong side of a brutally unequal power relationship.

Slaves' Everyday Conditions

Southern slaves enjoyed few material comforts. Although they generally had enough to eat, their diet was monotonous and nonnutritious. Clothing was coarse and inexpensive. Few slaves received more than two changes of clothing for hot and cold seasons and one blanket each winter. Children of both sexes ran naked in hot weather and wore long cotton shirts in winter. Many slaves went without shoes until December. Conditions were better in cities, where slaves frequently lived in the same dwelling as their owners and were regularly hired out, enabling them to accumulate their own money.

On plantations, the average slave lived in a crude, one-room cabin. Each dwelling housed one or two families. Crowding and lack of sanitation spread infection and such contagious diseases as typhoid fever, malaria, and dysentery. White plantation doctors were hired to care for sick slaves, and some "slave doctors" attained a degree of power in the quarters and with masters by healing through herbalism and spiritualism.

Slave Work Routines

Long hours and large work gangs characterized Gulf Coast cotton districts. Overseers rang the morning bell before dawn, and black people, tools in hand, walked toward the fields. Slaves who cultivated tobacco in the Upper South worked long hours picking the sticky, sometimes noxious, leaves under harsh discipline. As one woman recalled when interviewed in the 1930s, "it was way after sundown fore they could stop that field work. Then they had to hustle to finish their night work [such as watering livestock or cleaning cotton] in time for supper, or go to bed without it."

Working "from sun to sun" became a norm in much of the South. Profit took precedence over paternalism. Slave women did heavy fieldwork, even during pregnancy. Old people cared for young children, doing light chores, or carding, ginning, and spinning cotton.

South Carolina and Georgia low country planters used a **task system** whereby slaves were assigned measured amounts of work to be performed in a given time period. So much cotton per day was to be picked from a designated field, so many rows hoed or plowed in a specified section. Upon completion, slaves' time was their own for working garden plots, tending hogs, even hiring out their own labor. From this experience, many slaves developed a sense of property ownership.

Of the 1860 population of 4 million slaves, fully half were under the age of sixteen. "A child raised every two years," wrote Thomas Jefferson, "is of more profit than the crop of the best laboring man." In 1858, a slave owner writing in an agricultural magazine calculated that a slave girl purchased in 1827 for $400 had borne three sons now worth $3,000 as field hands. Slave children gathered kindling, carried water to the fields, swept the yard, lifted cut sugar-cane stalks into carts, stacked wheat, chased birds away from sprouting rice plants, and labored in cotton and tobacco production.

As slave children matured, they faced psychological traumas including powerlessness and an awareness that their parents could not protect them. They had to fight to keep from internalizing what whites labeled their inferiority. Many former slaves resented their denial of education. And for girls reaching maturity, the potential trauma of sexual abuse loomed.

task system Labor system in which each slave had a daily or weekly quota of tasks to complete.

Link to *Twelve Years a Slave* by Solomon Northup, 1853

Violence and Intimidation Against Slaves

Whites throughout the South believed that slaves "can't be governed except with the whip." One South Carolinian explained to a northern journalist that he whipped his slaves regularly, because "the fear of the lash kept them in good order." Evidence suggests that whippings were less frequent on small farms than on large plantations. But beatings symbolized authority to the master and tyranny to the slaves, who used them to evaluate a master. Former slaves said a good owner was one who did not "whip too much," whereas a bad owner "whipped till he's bloodied you and blistered you."

The master wielded absolute authority on his plantation. Slaveholders rarely had to answer to the law or to the state. Yet physical cruelty may have been less prevalent in the United States than in other slaveholding parts of the New World. Especially in some of the Caribbean sugar islands, death rates from violence were so high that the heavily male slave population shrank. In the United States, the slave population experienced a steady natural increase, as births exceeded deaths.

The worst evil of American slavery was the nature of slavery itself: coercion, belonging to another person, and having virtually no hope for change. Recalling their time in bondage, some former slaves emphasized the physical abuse, memories focused on the tyranny of whipping as much as the pain. Delia Garlic made the point: "It's bad to belong to folks that own you soul an' body…you couldn't guess the awfulness of it." To be a slave was to be the object of another person's will and material gain, as the saying went, "from the cradle to the grave."

Most American slaves retained their mental independence and self-respect despite their bondage. They had to be subservient and speak honeyed words to their masters, but they talked and behaved differently among themselves. In *Narrative of the Life of Frederick Douglass, an American Slave, Written by Himself* (1845), **Frederick Douglass** wrote that most slaves, when asked about "their condition and the character of their masters, almost universally say they are contented, and that their masters are kind." Slaves did this, said Douglass, because they were governed by the maxim that "a still tongue makes a wise head."

Frederick Douglass
A former slave who was the leading black abolitionist during the antebellum period.

Slave-Master Relationships

Some former slaves remembered warm feelings between masters and slaves, but the prevailing attitudes were distrust and antagonism. One woman said her mistress was "a mighty good somebody to belong to" but only "'cause she was raisin' us to work for her."

Slaves were alert to the daily signs of their degraded status. One man recalled the general rule that slaves ate cornbread and owners ate biscuits. If blacks did get biscuits, "the flour that we made the biscuits out of was the third-grade sorts." If the owner took his slaves' garden produce to town to sell for them, slaves often suspected him of pocketing part of the profits.

Suspicion often grew into hatred. When a yellow fever epidemic struck in 1852, many slaves saw it as God's retribution. An elderly ex-slave named Minnie Fulkes cherished the conviction that God was going to punish white people for their cruelty to blacks. On the plantation, of course, slaves had to keep such thoughts to themselves and created many ways to survive and to sustain their humanity in this world of repression.

Slave Culture and Resistance

How did slaves adapt Christianity to make it their own?

The resource that enabled slaves to maintain defiance was their culture: beliefs, values, and practices born of their past and maintained in the present. As best they could, they built a community knitted together by stories, music, a religious worldview, leadership, the smells of their cooking, the sounds of their voices, and the tapping of their feet. "The values expressed in folklore," wrote African American poet Sterling Brown, provided a "wellspring to which slaves … could return in times of doubt to be refreshed."

African Cultural Survival

Slave culture changed significantly after 1808, when Congress banned further importation of slaves and the generations born in Africa died out. South Carolina illegally reopened the international slave trade, but by the 1830s, the majority of slaves in the South were native-born Americans.

Yet African influences remained strong. Some slave men plaited their hair into rows and designs; slave women often wore their hair tied in small bunches secured by a string or piece of cloth. A few men and many women wrapped their heads in kerchiefs of the styles and colors of West Africa.

Music, religion, and folktales were part of daily life for slaves. Borrowing from their African background and forging new American folkways, they developed what scholars have called a sacred worldview, which affected work, leisure, and self-understanding. Slaves made musical instruments with carved motifs that resembled African stringed instruments. One visitor to Georgia in the 1860s described an African ritual dance called the ring shout: "A ring of singers is formed.... They then utter a kind of melodious chant, which gradually increases in strength, and in noise, until it fairly shakes the house, and it can be heard for a long distance."

Many slaves continued to believe in spirit possession. While whites believed in ghosts and charms, slaves' belief resembled the African concept of the living dead—deceased relatives visiting the earth for years until the process of dying is complete. Slaves also practiced conjuration and quasi-magical root medicine. By the 1850s, noted conjurers and root doctors were reputed to live in South Carolina, Georgia, Louisiana, and other isolated coastal areas with high slave populations.

As they became African Americans, slaves increasingly developed a racial identity. In the colonial period, Africans arrived in America from many states and kingdoms, represented in distinctive languages and traditions. Africans landed in the New World with virtually no concept of "race;" by the antebellum era, their descendants had learned through bitter experience that race was the defining feature of their lives.

Slaves' Religion and Music

Over time, more and more slaves adopted Christianity, fashioning it into an instrument of support and resistance. Theirs was a religion of justice and deliverance, quite unlike their masters' religious propaganda. "You ought to have heard that preachin,'" said one man. "'Obey your master and mistress, don't steal chickens and eggs and meat,' but nary a word about havin' a soul to save." In slaves' interpretations of biblical stories, as one historian has said, they were "willing themselves reborn."

Devout slaves worshipped every day. Some slaves held secret prayer meetings that lasted into the night. Many nurtured the belief that God would end their bondage. This faith—and the emotional release that accompanied worship—sustained them.

Slaves also adapted Christianity to African practices. In West African belief, devotees are possessed by a god so thoroughly that the god's personality replaces the human personality. In the late antebellum era, Christian slaves experienced possession by the Protestant "Holy Spirit." The combination of shouting, singing, and dancing that seemed to overtake black worshippers formed the heart of their religious faith. "The old meeting house caught fire," recalled an ex-slave preacher. "The spirit was there.... God saw our need and came to us." In brush arbors or meetinghouses, slaves thrust their arms to heaven, made music with their feet, and sang away their woes.

Rhythm and physical movement were crucial to slaves' religious experience. In black preachers' chanted sermons, an American tradition was born. The chanted sermon was a scriptural message and patterned form that required audience response punctuated by "yes sirs!" and "amens!" But through song the slaves left their most sublime gift to American culture.

Through the spirituals, slaves tried to impose order on the chaos of their lives. Often referred to later as the "sorrow songs," lyrics covered many themes, including imminent rebirth. Sadness could give way to joy: "Oh, Oh, Freedom/Oh, Oh, Freedom over me—/But before I'll be a slave,/I'll be buried in my grave,/And go home to my Lord,/And Be Free!"

Many songs also express intimacy and closeness with God. Some display rebelliousness, such as the enduring "He said, and if I had my way/If I had my way, if I had my way,/I'd tear this building down!" And some spirituals reached for a collective sense of hope in the black community.

> O, gracious Lord! When shall it be,
> That we poor souls shall all be free;
> Lord, break them slavery powers—
> Will you go along with me?
> Lord break them slavery powers,
> Go sound the jubilee!

In many ways, American slaves converted the Christian God to themselves. They sought an alternative world—a home other than the earthly one fate had given them. With variations on the Br'er Rabbit folktales—in which the weak survive by wit and power is reversed—and in songs, they fashioned survival from their own cultural imagination.

The Black Family in Slavery

Although American law did not recognize slave families, slave owners *expected* slaves to form families and have children. As a result, there was a normal ratio of men to women, young to old. On some of the largest South Carolina cotton plantations, when masters allowed their slaves increased autonomy through the task system, the property accumulation in livestock, tools, and garden produce led to more stable and healthier families.

Following African kinship traditions, African Americans avoided marriage between cousins (commonplace among aristocratic slave owners). By naming their children after relatives of past generations, African Americans emphasized family histories. Kinship networks and extended families held life together in many slave communities.

For slave women, sexual abuse and rape by white masters were ever-present threats. By 1860, there were 405,751 mulattos in the United States, comprising 12.5 percent of the African American population. White planters were sometimes open with their behavior toward slave women, but not in the way they talked about it. Buying slaves for sex was common at the New Orleans slave market. In what was called the "fancy trade" (a "fancy" was a young, attractive slave girl), females were sold for prices as much as 300 percent higher than average. At such auctions, slaveholders exhibited some of the ugliest values of the slave system by paying $3,000 to $5,000 for female "companions."

Slave women like Harriet Jacobs spent years dodging their owners' sexual pursuit. In recollecting her desperate effort to protect her children, Jacobs asked a haunting question: "Why does the slave ever love? Why allow the tendrils of the heart to twine around objects which may at any moment be wrenched away by the hand of violence?"

The Domestic Slave Trade

Slave families most feared and hated separation by violence from those they loved, sexual appropriation, and sale. Many struggled to keep their children together and, after emancipation, to reestablish contact with loved ones lost by forced migration and sale. Between 1820 and 1860, roughly 2 million slaves were moved into the region from western Georgia to eastern Texas. When the Union army registered thousands of black marriages in Mississippi and Louisiana in 1864 and 1865, 25 percent of the men over age forty reported that they had been forcibly separated from a previous wife. Thousands of black families were disrupted annually to serve the expanding cotton economy.

Many antebellum white southerners made their living from the slave trade. In South Carolina by the 1850s, there were more than one hundred slave-trading firms selling approximately 6,500 slaves annually to southwestern states. One 1858 estimate indicated that slave sales in Richmond, Virginia, that year netted $4 million. A market guide to 1858 Richmond slave sales listed average prices for "likely ploughboys," ages twelve to fourteen, at $850 to $1,050; "extra number 1 fieldgirls" at $1,300 to $1,350; and "extra number 1 men" at $1,500.

At slave "pens" in cities like New Orleans, traders promoted "a large and commodious showroom … prepared to accommodate over 200 Negroes for sale." Traders made slaves appear young, healthy, and happy, cutting gray whiskers off men; using paddles as discipline to avoid scarring their merchandise; and forcing people to dance and sing as buyers arrived. When transported to the southwestern markets, slaves were often chained together, making journeys of 500 miles or more on foot.

The complacent mixture of racism and business among traders is evident in their own language. "I refused a girl 20 year[s] old at 700 yesterday," one trader wrote in 1853. "She is very badly whipped but good teeth." Some sales were transacted at owners' requests, often for tragically inhumane reasons. "Bought a cook yesterday that was to go out of state," wrote a trader; "she just made the people mad that was all."

Strategies of Resistance

Slaves brought to their resistance the same common sense and determination that characterized their struggle to secure family lives. The scales weighed against overt revolution, but they seized opportunities to alter work conditions. They sometimes slacked off when they were not watched. Daily discontent and desperation were also manifest in equipment sabotage; carelessness about work; theft of food, livestock, or crops; or getting drunk on stolen liquor. A woman named Ellen, hired as a cook in Tennessee in 1856, put mercury poison into a roasted apple for her unsuspecting mistress. And some slave women

Missouri Historical Museum

A bill of sale documents that this slave woman, Louisa, was owned by the young child whom she holds on her lap. In the future, Louisa's life would be subject to the child's wishes and decisions.

resisted by trying to control their own pregnancy, either by avoiding it or by seeking to improve their conditions.

Male, and some female, slaves sometimes violently attacked overseers or owners. Southern court records and newspapers contain accounts of these resistant slaves who contradicted the image of the docile bondsman. Rebels were customarily flogged, sold, or hanged. Many slaves attempted to run away to the North, and some received assistance from the loose network known as the Underground Railroad (see page 348). But it was more common for slaves to run off temporarily to hide in the woods. Approximately 80 percent of runaways were male; children prevented women from fleeing. Fear, disgruntlement over treatment, or family separation might motivate slaves to flee. Only a minority made it to freedom in the North, but these fugitives made slavery an insecure institution by the 1850s.

American slavery also produced fearless revolutionaries. Gabriel's Rebellion involved about a thousand slaves when it was discovered in 1800, before it would have exploded in Richmond, Virginia (see page 193). According to controversial court testimony, a similar conspiracy existed in Charleston in 1822, led by Denmark Vesey, a free black. Born a slave in the Caribbean, Vesey won a lottery of $1,500 in 1799, bought his freedom, and became a religious leader. According to one long-argued interpretation, Vesey was a heroic revolutionary determined to free his people. But in a recent challenge, historian Michael Johnson notes that the court testimony is the only reliable source on the alleged insurrection. Might the testimony reveal less of reality than of white South Carolina's fears of slave rebellion? The court, says Johnson, built its case on rumors and intimidated witnesses, and "conjured into being" an insurrection that was not truly about to occur. Nonetheless, thirty-seven "conspirators" were executed, and more than three dozen others were banished from the state.

Nat Turner A slave who led a bloody rebellion in Southampton County, Virginia, in 1831.

Nat Turner's Insurrection

The most famous rebel, **Nat Turner**, struck for freedom in Southampton County, Virginia, in 1831. The son of a woman who passionately hated her enslavement and a father who escaped to freedom, Turner learned to read as a child and was encouraged by his first owner to study the Bible. He enjoyed certain privileges but also endured hard work and changes of masters.

Young Nat became a preacher known for eloquence and mysticism. After planning for years, Turner led rebels from farm to farm in the predawn darkness of August 22, 1831. The group severed limbs and crushed skulls with axes or shot victims. Before planters stopped them, Nat Turner and his followers had in forty-eight hours slaughtered sixty whites. In retaliation whites randomly killed slaves across the region, and Turner was caught and hanged. As many as two hundred African Americans lost their lives as a result of the rebellion.

Nat Turner remains a haunting symbol in America's unresolved history of racial slavery and discrimination. While in jail, Turner was interviewed by Virginia lawyer and slaveholder, Thomas R. Gray. Their intriguing creation, *The Confessions of Nat Turner*, became a best seller within a month of Turner's hanging. Gray called the rebel a "gloomy fanatic," but in a manner that made him fascinating and produced one of the most remarkable documents of American slavery. After Turner's insurrection, many states passed stiffened legal codes against black education and religious practice.

Imaging Nat Turner's Rebellion

Below is the title page from *The Confessions of Nat Turner,* by Thomas R. Gray, 1831. This nearly twenty-page document was published by the lawyer who recorded and likely refashioned Turner's lengthy statement during an interview in his jail cell before his execution. *The Confessions* became a widely sold and sensational documentation of Turner's identity and his motivations and methods during the rebellion. It portrayed Turner as a religious mystic and fanatic and allowed the public to imagine the mind of a religiously motivated slave rebel. Below and to the right is "Horrid Massacre in Virginia," 1831, woodcut. This composite of scenes depicts the slaughter of innocent women and children, as well as white men as victims and resistants. The fear, confusion, and retribution that dominated the aftermath of the Turner rebellion are on display here. Why was Nat Turner's insurrection such a shock to the nation as well as to the South? What kind of impact did Nat Turner's rebellion have on the South's evolving defense of slavery in the coming decades?

THE
CONFESSIONS
OF
NAT TURNER,
THE LEADER
OF
THE LATE INSURRECTION
IN SOUTHAMPTON, VA.

AS FULLY AND VOLUNTARILY MADE TO

THOMAS R. GRAY,

In the prison where he was confined, and acknowledged by him to be such,
when read before the Court of Southampton; with the
certificate, under seal of the Court convened at
Jerusalem, Nov. 5, 1831, for his trial.

ALSO,

AN AUTHENTIC ACCOUNT
OF THE
WHOLE INSURRECTION,
WITH
Lists of the Whites who were Murdered,
AND OF THE
*Negroes brought before the Court of Southampton,
and there sentenced, &c.*

RICHMOND:
PUBLISHED BY THOMAS R. GRAY.
T. W. WHITE, PRINTER.
1832.

Everett Collection

Library of Congress

259

Reparations for Slavery

How should the United States come to terms with 250 years of racial slavery? Is this period best forgotten as a terrible passage, or does the nation owe a long-overdue debt to black people for their oppression? After emancipation in 1865, and rooted in vague federal promises, many former slaves believed they were entitled to "forty acres and a mule," but these never materialized.

In 1897, Callie House, a poor mother of four born in 1865 in a contraband camp for ex-slaves, organized the National Ex-Slave Pension and Bounty Association, modeled after soldiers' pension systems. House traveled throughout the South, recruiting 250,000 members at 10-cent dues. Her lobbying of the federal government for slave pensions failed; she was accused of mail fraud and imprisoned for one year in 1916.

More recently, widespread debate over "reparations" for slavery has emerged. In the rewriting of slavery's history since the 1960s, Americans have learned how slave labor created American wealth: how insurance companies insured slaves, how complicit the U.S. government was in slavery's expansion, and how slaves built the U.S. Capitol while their owners received $5 a month for their labor.

The debate is fueled by analogies: reparations paid to Japanese Americans interned during World War II; reparations paid to Native American tribes for stolen land; the reparations paid to Holocaust survivors; and a suit settled in 1999 that will pay an estimated $2 billion to some twenty thousand black farmers for discrimination by the Agriculture Department in the early twentieth century.

Some argue that, because there are no living former slaves or slaveholders, reparations can never take the form of money. But in 2002, a lawsuit was filed against three major corporations that allegedly profited from slavery, and the National Reparations Coordinating Committee promises a suit against the U.S. government. Some city councils have passed resolutions forcing companies in their jurisdictions to investigate possible past complicity with slave trading or ownership, prompting some firms to establish scholarship programs for African Americans.

Critics argue that resources would be better spent "making sure black kids have a credible education" and rebuilding inner cities. Advocates contend that, when "government participates in a crime against humanity," it is "obliged to make the victims whole." The movement for reparations has sparked broad public debate. The legacy of slavery for a people and a nation promises to become America's most traumatic test of how to reconcile its history with justice.

Most important, in 1832 a shocked Virginia held a legislative and public debate over gradual emancipation to rid itself of slavery and of blacks. The plan would not have freed any slaves until 1858 and provided that eventually all blacks would be colonized outside Virginia. When the House of Delegates voted, gradual abolition lost, 73 to 58. Virginia merely reinforced its defense of slavery. It was the last time white southerners would debate emancipation until war forced their hand.

Summary

During the four decades before the Civil War, the South grew in land, wealth, and power along with the rest of the country. Although southern states were enmeshed in the nation's heritage and political economy, they also developed as a distinctive region, ideologically and economically, because of slavery. More than the North, the antebellum South was a biracial society; whites grew up influenced by black folkways and culture; and blacks, the vast majority of whom were slaves, became cobuilders of a rural, agricultural society.

With the cotton boom and state and federal policies of Indian removal, the South became a huge slave society. The coercive influence of slavery affected southern life and politics and increasingly produced a leadership determined to preserve a hierarchical social and racial order. Despite their shared white supremacy, yeomen's democratic values often clashed with aristocratic planters' profit motives. Slaveholders' benevolent self-image and paternalistic ideology was tested by slaves' own judgments. African American slaves responded by fashioning a rich folk culture and a religion of deliverance. Their experiences could differ regionally and by labor type. Some blacks were crushed by bondage; others transcended it through survival and resistance.

By 1850, through their wits and on the backs of African labor, white southerners had aggressively built one of the last profitable, expanding slave societies on earth. North of them and deeply intertwined with them in the same nation, economy, constitutional system, and history, a different kind of society had grown even faster—driven by industrialism and free labor. The clash of these two deeply connected—yet mutually divided societies—would soon explode in political storms over the nation's future.

Chapter Review

The "Distinctive" South

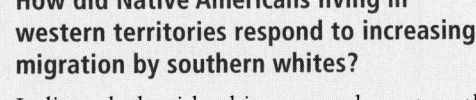

What made the antebellum South different from the North?

Both regions were capitalist and Christian (largely Protestant) and embraced the heroes and causes of the American Revolution. They were also roughly the same physical size. But they differed in their economic development: because of its climate and longer growing season, the South's development was agricultural and rural, whereas the North became increasingly urban and industrial. With a comparatively low population density and people spread out from each other, the South had little income for developing its commercial, educational, and health-related institutions. The South was also slower to develop a regional transportation network and relied on slaves for labor and the North for banking and shipping of its products. The South had fewer urban areas, and those that existed were primarily port cities, such as Charleston, that provided a link for commerce and small manufacturing. With few labor opportunities, the South also did not attract as many immigrants as the North.

Southern Expansion, Indian Resistance, and Removal

How did Native Americans living in western territories respond to increasing migration by southern whites?

Indians dealt with white encroachment on their land in several ways. Some embraced accommodation, establishing trading posts to exchange supplies with settlers, often ultimately falling into heavy debt that could only be repaid by selling their land. Others resisted, rejecting removal/relocation plans that whites offered, and holding fast to their land. The Creeks and Cherokees assimilated to American standards—even changed their political structure to more closely resemble that of whites—in an effort to keep their land. When Congress narrowly passed the Indian Removal Act in 1830, which provided funds to relocate Indians to territory farther west, the Cherokees refused to leave and sued the state of Georgia in federal court. While the courts found them entitled to their land, President Andrew Jackson ignored the ruling and sent in troops to evacuate thousands of Cherokees and march them from Georgia to present-day

Oklahoma. Many refused to go and were imprisoned; others died of disease and exhaustion on the trek known as the Trail of Tears.

Social Pyramid in the Old South

What class tensions emerged in the antebellum South?

Although they were fewer in number, the slave-holding planter class occupied the highest rungs of southern society and dominated its political life (controlling up to 85 percent of legislative posts) as well as churches and colleges. Before the 1830s, the vast socioeconomic differences between rich planters and small, independent, nonslaveholding yeomen farmers were mediated by their shared racial status as white. However, tensions emerged as yeomen began to resent their underrepresentation in state government and the corruption of local governments. They sought universal manhood suffrage and other reforms, including popular election of governors and legislative apportionment based solely on the white population—all of which planters resisted. Moreover, as cotton farming made land less and less available, nonslaveholders faced fewer opportunities to improve their station, while planters enjoyed greater and greater profits.

The Planters' World

How did cotton shape the lives of planters and their families?

Cotton production touched every aspect of slave society; during the boom years, it made many families rich. Most, however, lived in farmhouses and not the mansions of legend. Wealth in the cotton south was measured in terms of slave ownership; planters typically put their profits back into slaves and land. Along with a racial hierarchy, the society was also organized in terms of class and gender. White elites expected deference from poorer whites (though many yeomen resisted). Elite women were to be wives, mothers and subordinate to men, who were masters of the entire household. When a woman married, her legal and property rights were ceded to her husband. Women often felt isolated, their relationships restricted to family and other women, while men could engage in the broader world of business and politics. Slaveholding men justified their dominance over black slaves and wives and children via an ideology of paternalism, viewing themselves as custodians of their families, which

included slaves. The truth of their treatment of slaves and wives often made a lie of such paternalism, however.

Slave Life and Labor

What was the true nature of the master-slave relationship?

Generally speaking, slaves' lives belied the paternalism white masters claimed. They enjoyed few material comforts, occupying one-room cabins, often with other families. They were worked long, arduous days into the night, and while they typically had enough to eat, their diet was not nutritious. Slaves in the task system could be hired out once they completed assigned chores and were sometimes allowed to keep a portion of what they earned. But instead of being truly treated as family members, most slaves were recognized as property upon which wealth for whites could be built. Profit was the primary definer of master-slave relationships. There was also much cruelty and brutality—rather than paternalism—on the part of many owners, including whippings and the rape of slave women. Slave families were often separated, as one or more members were sold away to other plantations. For slaves, the vulnerability and frustration of being owned and at the mercy of another human being, along with being used for harsh physical labor, sparked resentment, resistance, and sometimes outright rebellion.

Slave Culture and Resistance

How did slaves adapt Christianity to make it their own?

While many slaves maintained and adapted aspects of the African heritage to their new circumstances, they also embraced and remade Christianity as a form of resistance. In secret prayer meetings, slaves focused on justice and deliverance, believing God would liberate them from their servitude and exact retribution from those who unjustly enslaved or abused them. They also merged their Christianity with African practices, adding shouting, singing, dancing, and other rituals to their religious meetings, along with chanted sermons, which were regarded as vital for the conversion experience. Their religious rituals not only attempted to restore order and meaning to their lives but also to establish closeness with God and hope for the future. Finally, while prayer meetings were often held in secret, they helped forge relationships and community in slave quarters.

Suggestions for Further Reading

Ira Berlin, *Generations of Captivity: A History of African American Slaves* (2003)

David Brion Davis, *Inhuman Bondage: The Rise and Fall of Slavery in the New World* (2006)

Erskine Clarke, *Dwelling Place: A Plantation Epic* (2005)

Steven Deyle, *Carry Me Back: The Domestic Slave Trade in American Life* (2005)

Annette Gordon-Reed, *The Hemingses of Monticello: An American Family* (2008)

Walter Johnson, *Soul by Soul: Life Inside the Antebellum Slave Market* (1999)

Charles Joyner, *Down by the Riverside: A South Carolina Slave Community* (1984)

James D. Miller, *South by Southwest: Planter Emigration and Identity in the Slave South* (2002)

James Oakes, *Slavery and Freedom: An Interpretation of the Old South* (1991)

Michael O'Brien, *Conjectures of Order: Intellectual Life and the American South, 1810–1860*, 2 vols. (2004)

Seth Rockman, *Scraping By: Wage Labor, Slavery, and Survival in Early Baltimore* (2009)

Daniel H. Usner Jr., *American Indians in the Lower Mississippi Valley* (1998)

The Restless North

1815–1860

After 25 stormy days at sea, Mary Ann and James Archbald and their four children finally arrived in New York on April 17, 1807. The couple left their ancestral homeland in Scotland, envisioning a bright future in which their children would be beholden to no one—neither landlord nor employer. They were pursuing the Jeffersonian dream of republican independence.

The Archbalds bought a farm in central New York, along a Hudson River tributary, where they raised sheep, grew hay and vegetables, skinned rabbits for meat and fur—and then sold whatever they did not need. From the wool shorn by her husband and sons, Mary Ann and her daughters spun thread and wove cloth for their own use and for sale. They used the cash to pay their mortgage. Twenty-one years after leaving Scotland, Mary Ann, in anticipation of making their last payment, declared: "being out of debt is, in my estimation, being rich." By then, her sons were young adults with visions of wealth that centered on water, not land.

On April 17, 1817—a decade after the Archbalds reached American shores—the New York State legislature authorized construction of a canal connecting Lake Erie to the Hudson River, and surveyors mapped a route through the Archbalds' farm. The sons helped dig the canal, while Mary Ann and her daughters cooked and cleaned for the twenty Irish laborers whom the sons hired. The Archbald sons soon tried commercial speculation, borrowing money to buy wheat and lumber in western New York to resell it at substantial profits to merchants in Albany and New York City. As early as 1808, Mary Ann had reached an unpleasant conclusion about her new home: "We are a nation of traders in spite of all Mr. Jefferson can say or do."

After the War of 1812, the market economy took off in unanticipated ways. In the North, steamboats, canals, and then railroads remapped the young republic's geography and economy, setting off booms in westward migration, industry, commerce, and urban growth.

Chapter Outline

Still, even after the War of 1812, the United States' financial connections to Europe, particularly Britain, remained profound. When Europeans suffered hard times, so did American merchants, manufacturers, farmers, and workers. For wage-earning Americans, economic downturns meant unemployment and destitution.

The economy's rapid expansion following the War of 1812 inspired fears that, if not properly controlled, market growth would threaten the nation's moral fiber. It upset traditional family patterns and relied on unskilled workers—often immigrants and free African Americans—who seemed unfit for republican citizenship. Commercially minded Americans saw cities as exemplars of civilization and breeding grounds of depravity. Anxious about the era's rapid changes, many Americans turned to evangelical religion, which in turn inspired reform movements.

Only through faith in improvement, progress, and upward mobility could Americans remain hopeful that the nation's greatness lay with commercial expansion. They did so partly by articulating a free-labor ideology that rationalized the negative aspects of market expansion while promoting the northern labor system as superior to the South's.

As you read this chapter, keep the following questions in mind:

- **What factors contributed to the commercialization of northern society, and why did they have less of an influence on the South?**

- **How did the daily lives—work, family, leisure—of northerners (rural and urban) change between 1815 and 1860?**

- **In what ways did reformers try to preserve existing American ideals and in what ways did they try to change them?**

Or Was the North Distinctive?

What happened to the North and South economically after the War of 1812?

Historian James McPherson has proposed a new twist to the old question of southern distinctiveness: perhaps it was the *North*—New England, the Middle Atlantic, and the Old Northwest—that diverged from the norm. At the republic's birth, the two regions had much in common: slavery, ethnic homogeneity, a majority of the population engaged in agriculture, a small urban population. But that started to change with economic development after the War of 1812. State and local governments and private entrepreneurs engaged in

Chronology

1790s–1840s	Second Great Awakening
1820s	Model penitentiaries established
1820s–1840s	Utopian communities founded
1824	*Gibbons v. Ogden* prohibits steamboat monopolies
1825	Erie Canal completed
1826	American Society for Promotion of Temperance founded
1827	Construction begins on Baltimore and Ohio (B&O) Railroad
1830	First locomotive runs on B&O Railroad
	Joseph Smith organizes Mormon Church
1830s	Penny press emerges
1830s–50s	Urban riots commonplace
1833	American Antislavery Society founded
1834	Women workers strike at Lowell
1837–42	Croton Aqueduct constructed
1839–43	Hard times spread unemployment and deflation
1840	Split in abolitionist movement; Liberty Party founded
1840s	Female mill workers' publications appear
1844	Federal government sponsors first telegraph line
	Lowell Female Reform Association formed
1845	Massive Irish immigration begins
1846	Smithsonian Institute founded
1848	American Association for the Advancement of Science established
1850s	Free-labor ideology spreads

development, which happened faster and more extensively in the North. As the North embraced economic progress, it—rather than the South—diverged from the norm. The North, writes McPherson, "hurtled forward toward a future that many Southerners found distasteful if not frightening." With its continual quest for improvement, the North—much more so than the South—embodied what Frenchman Alexis de Tocqueville, who toured the United States in 1831–1832, called the nation's "restless spirit."

While the South expanded as a slave society, the North transformed, as one historian has put it, from a society with markets to a market society. In the colonial era, settlers lived in a society in which they engaged in long-distance trade—selling their surpluses to merchants, who in turn sent raw materials to Europe, using the proceeds to purchase finished goods for resale—but in which most settlers remained self-sufficient. During and after the War of 1812, the North became a market society in which participation in long-distance commerce altered individuals' aspirations and activities. With European trade largely halted during the war, entrepreneurs invested in domestic factories. More men, women, and children began working for others rather than on family farms, increasing domestic demand for foodstuffs. Farming became commercialized, with farmers abandoning self-sufficiency and specializing in crops that would yield cash on the market. Farmers then used the cash to buy goods they once made for themselves, such as cloth and soap along with some luxuries. Unlike the typical southern yeoman, they were not self-reliant, and isolation was rare. In the North, market expansion altered much of life. Some historians see these rapid changes as a market revolution.

The Transportation Revolution

How did the transportation revolution help lay the groundwork for a market economy?

To market goods far from where they were produced, Americans needed internal improvements. Before the War of 1812, natural waterways provided the most readily available and cheapest transportation routes for people and goods, but with limitations. Boatmen poled bateaux (cargo boats) down shallow rivers or floated flatboats down deep ones. Cargo generally moved downstream only, and most boats were destroyed for lumber at their destination. Upstream commerce was limited.

Roads

Overland transport was limited, too. Roads constructed during the colonial and revolutionary eras often became obstructed by fallen trees, soaked by mud, or clouded in dust. To reduce mud and dust, turnpike companies built "corduroy" roads, whose tightly lined-up logs resembled the ribbed cotton fabric. But the continual jolts caused nausea among passengers and discouraged merchants from shipping fragile wares. Land transportation was slow and expensive. In 1800, it cost as much to ship a ton of goods thirty miles into the interior as to ship it from New York to England. The lack of cheap, quick transportation impeded westward expansion and industrial growth.

Aside from the National Road (see Chapter 8), financing fell to states and private investors, and enthusiasm for building turnpikes greatly outpaced the money and manpower expended. Turnpike companies sometimes adopted improvements, such as laying hard surfaces made of crushed stone and gravel, but many of the newly built roads suffered from old problems.

Steamboats

In 1807, Robert Fulton's *Clermont* traveled between New York and Albany on the Hudson River in thirty-two hours, demonstrating the feasibility of using steam engines to power boats. After the Supreme Court's ruling against steamboat monopolies in *Gibbons v. Ogden* (1824), steamboat companies flourished on eastern rivers and, to a lesser extent, on the Great Lakes. They transported settlers to the Midwest, where they would grow grain and raise pigs that fed northeastern factory workers. Along western rivers like the Mississippi and the Ohio, steamboats carried midwestern timber and grain and southern cotton to New Orleans, where they were transferred to oceangoing vessels destined for northern and international ports. To travel between Ohio and New Orleans by flatboat in 1815 took several months; in 1840, the same trip by steamboat took just ten days. In the 1850s, steamboats became subject to federal regulations after deadly accidents in which boilers exploded, fires ignited, and boats collided.

Canals

In the late eighteenth and early nineteenth centuries, private companies (sometimes with state subsidies) built small canals to transport goods to and from interior locations. These projects rarely reaped substantial profits, discouraging future investment. In 1815, only three canals measured more than 2 miles long;

the longest was 27 miles. After Madison's veto of the Bonus Bill (see Chapter 8) dashed commercially minded New Yorkers' hopes for a canal connecting Lake Erie to the port of New York, Governor DeWitt Clinton pushed successfully for a state-sponsored initiative. What later became the **Erie Canal** was to run 363 miles between Buffalo and Albany, and was to be four feet deep.

Erie Canal Major canal that linked the Great Lakes to New York City, opening the upper Midwest to wider development.

Construction began on July 4, 1817. The canal, its promoters emphasized, would help demonstrate how American ingenuity and hard work could overcome obstacles, including the combined ascent and descent of 680 feet between Buffalo and Albany. By so doing, it would help unify the nation and secure its commercial independence from Europe.

Over the next eight years, nine thousand laborers felled forests, shoveled dirt, blasted rock, hauled boulders, rechanneled streams, and molded the canal bed. Stonemasons and carpenters built aqueducts and locks. The work was dangerous, sometimes fatal, with workers succumbing to malaria, rattlesnake bites, gunpowder explosions, and asphyxiation from collapsed canal beds.

The canal's promoters celebrated the waterway as the work of "republican free men," but few canal workers would have perceived their construction jobs as fulfilling Jefferson's notion of republican freedom. Once completed, the Erie Canal relied on child labor: Boys led the horses who pulled the canal boats between the canal's eighty-three locks, while girls cooked and cleaned on the boats. When the canal froze shut in winter, many workers lost their jobs.

Once completed in 1825, the Erie Canal proved immediately successful. Horse-drawn boats, stacked with bushels of wheat, barrels of oats, and piles of logs, streamed eastward from Lake Erie and western New York. Forty thousand passengers in 1825 alone traveled the new waterway. The canal shortened the journey between Buffalo and New York City from twenty to six days and reduced freight charges by nearly 95 percent—thus securing New York City's position as the nation's preeminent port. None of the other new canals enjoyed the Erie's financial success. As the cost of construction combined with an economic contraction, investment slumped in the 1830s. Several midwestern states could not repay their canal loans, leading them to bankruptcy or near-bankruptcy. By midcentury, the canal era had ended, though the Erie Canal (by then twice enlarged and rerouted) continued to prosper, still operates today (as the New York State Barge Canal), though primarily for leisure travel.

Railroads

The future belonged to railroads. Trains moved faster than canal boats and operated year-round. Railroads could connect remote locations to national and international markets. By 1860, the United States had 60,000 miles of track, mostly in the North. Railroads dramatically reduced the cost and the time involved in shipping goods.

The U.S. railroad era began in 1830 when Peter Cooper's locomotive, Tom Thumb, steamed along 13 miles of Baltimore and Ohio Railroad track. Not until the 1850s did railroads offer long-distance service at reasonable rates. Even then, lack of a common standard for track width thwarted development of a national system. A journey from Philadelphia to Charleston involved eight different gauges, requiring passengers and freight to change trains seven times. Only at Bowling Green, Kentucky, did northern and southern railroads connect. Despite the race to construct internal improvements, the nation's canals and railroads did little to unite the regions and promote nationalism, as proponents of government-sponsored internal improvements had hoped.

Northern governments and investors spent more on internal improvements than did southerners. Pennsylvania and New York together accounted for half of all state monies invested. Southern states invested in railroads, but—with smaller free populations—they collected fewer taxes and had less to spend.

The North and South laid roughly the same amount of railroad track per person before the Civil War, but when measured in mileage, the more populous North had tracks that stretched farther, forming an integrated system of local lines branching off major trunk lines. In the South, railroads remained local. Neither people nor goods moved easily across the South, unless they traveled via steamboat or flatboat along the Mississippi River system—and even then, flooded banks often disrupted passage.

Regional Connections The North's frenzy of canal and railroad building expanded transportation networks far into the hinterlands. In 1815, nearly all produce from the Old Northwest floated down the Mississippi to New Orleans, tying that region's fortunes to the South. By the 1850s, though, canals and railroads strengthened the economic, cultural, and political links between the Old Northwest—particularly the more densely populated northern regions—and the Northeast. (See Map 10.1.)

Internal improvements hastened westward migration, making western settlement more appealing by providing easy access to eastern markets. News, visitors, and luxuries now traveled regularly to previously remote areas of the Northeast and Midwest. Delighted that the Erie Canal brought fresh seafood to central New York, Mary Archbald explained that "distance . . . is reduced to nothing here."

Samuel F. B. Morse's invention of the telegraph in 1844 allowed news to travel almost instantaneously along telegraph wires. By 1852, more than 23,000 miles of lines were strung nationwide. The telegraph enabled the birth of modern business practices involving the coordination of market conditions, production, and supply across great distances.

Ambivalence Toward Progress Many northerners hailed internal improvements as symbols of progress. They proclaimed that, by building canals and railroads, they had completed God's design for the North American continent. Practically speaking, canals and railroads allowed them to seek opportunities in the West.

But even people who welcomed such opportunities could find much to lament. Mary Ann Archbald savored fresh seafood dinners but regretted that her sons turned to speculation. Others decried the Irish canal diggers and railroad track layers, whom they deemed depraved and racially inferior. Still others worried that, by promoting urban growth, transportation innovations fostered social ills.

MAP 10.1

Major Roads, Canals, and Railroads, 1850

A transportation network linked the seaboard to the interior. Settlers followed those routes westward, and they sent back grain, grain products, and cotton to the port cities. Source: Copyright © Cengage Learning 2015

The degradation of the natural world proved worrisome, too. When streams were rerouted, swamps drained, and forests felled, natural habitats were disturbed, even destroyed. Deprived of waterpower, mills no longer ran. Without forests, wild animals—on which many rural people had relied for protein—sought homes elsewhere. Fishermen, too, found their sources of protein (and cash) dried up when natural waterways were dammed or rerouted to feed canals.

Factories and Industrialization

How was factory work different from the work life people previously knew?

By lowering transportation costs, internal improvements facilitated the Northeast's rapid manufacturing and commercial expansion. Western farmers supplied raw materials and foodstuffs for northeastern factories and workers. They also expanded the domestic market for northeastern manufactured goods. Focused on cultivating their lands, western settlers preferred to buy rather than make cloth, shoes, and other goods.

Factory Work

Much early industrialization involved processing raw materials—milling flour, turning hogs into packaged meat, sawing lumber. The pork-packing industry illustrates how specialization turned skilled craftsmen into laborers. Traditionally, each butcher carved an entire pig. Under the new industrial organization, each worker performed a particular task—such as cutting off the right front leg—as the pig traveled down a "disassembly line."

Factory work, with its impersonal and regimented nature, contrasted with more informal artisan shops and farm households. In large factories, laborers never saw owners, working instead under paid supervisors, nor did they see the final product. Factory workers lost their sense of autonomy, as the bell or steam whistle governed their day. Competition from cheaper, less-skilled workers—particularly after European immigration soared in the 1840s—created job insecurity and few opportunities for advancement.

Initially Americans imported or copied British machines that made mass production possible. Soon they built their own. The **American System of manufacturing** used machinery to produce interchangeable parts. Eli Whitney, the cotton gin's inventor, promoted interchangeable parts in 1798, when he contracted with the federal government to make ten thousand rifles in twenty-eight months. The American System quickly produced the machine-tool industry—the manufacture of machines for the purpose of mass production. The new system permitted large-scale production of inexpensive but high-quality household items.

American System of manufacturing System of manufacturing that used interchangeable parts.

Textile Mills

Mechanization was most dramatic in textiles, with production centered in New England, near water sources to power spinning machines and looms. After 1815, New England's rudimentary cotton mills developed into modern factories with mass-produced goods. Cotton cloth production rose from 4 million yards in 1817 to 323 million in 1840. In the mid-1840s, cotton mills employed approximately eighty thousand "operatives"; more than half were women.

With labor scarce near the mills, managers recruited New England farm daughters, whom they housed in dormitories in what became known as the **Waltham** or **Lowell** plan of industrialization. People who farmed were often suspicious of those who did not—particularly in the United States, where an agrarian lifestyle was associated with virtue. To ease such concerns, mill managers offered paternalistic oversight of mill girls; they enforced curfews and required church attendance.

Despite restrictions, the Waltham system offered farm girls opportunities to socialize and earn wages to help their families, save for their dowries or education, or spend on such items as clothing. Workers wrote literary pieces for the owner-subsidized *Lowell Offering* and attended educational lectures in the evenings. Working conditions in textile mills—the deafening roar of the power looms, the long hours, and regimentation—made young women cling to notions that their jobs were temporary. The average girl arrived at sixteen and stayed five years, usually leaving to get married.

Although the Waltham plan drew international attention, more common was the Rhode Island (or Fall River) plan employed by **Samuel Slater**, among others. Mills hired entire families, lodging them in boardinghouses. Men worked farm

Waltham, Lowell Sites of early textile mills in New England, which were precursors to modern factories. Nearly 80 percent of the workers in Waltham, Lowell, and similar mills were young, unmarried women who had been lured from farms by the promise of wages.

Link to "A Week in the Mill" *Lowell Offering,* October 1845

Samuel Slater British mechanic who carried plans for textile mills to the United States.

Links TO THE WORLD

Internal Improvements

On July 4, 1827, ninety-one-year-old Charles Carroll, the only surviving signer of the Declaration of Independence, shoveled the first spadeful of earth on the Baltimore and Ohio Railroad, the nation's first westward railroad. Internal improvements, he and others believed, would cement the United States' economic independence by supplying the nation's growing industrial centers with food and raw materials, while transporting manufactured goods back to its rural population.

Although boosters championed canals and railroads as the triumph of American republicanism, such projects depended on technology, funding, and labor from abroad. American engineers scrutinized canals and railroads in France, the Low Countries, and England. Railroad companies purchased locomotives from English manufacturers. Foreign investors financed significant portions of projects. Thousands of immigrants, mostly from Ireland, worked blasting boulders, draining malaria-filled swamps, picking at roots and rocks, and heaving dirt. After the Civil War, Chinese immigrants helped build the transcontinental railroad.

Internal improvements allowed people, raw materials, and goods to move inexpensively and quickly across the continent, spurring the nation's growth—but also strengthening ties to Europe. Cotton and grain moved eastward, with much of it sold overseas. Cotton fed European textile mills; grain fed their workers. Thus, whenever economic conditions constricted in Europe, reverberations were felt on cotton and wheat farmss across America.

Canals and railroads, hailed as symbols of American independence, linked American farmers to an increasingly complex and volatile international economy.

Erie Canal, NY, 1831 (graphite, w/c and gouache on paper), Hill, John William (1812–79)/ © Collection of the New-York Historical Society, USA/The Bridgeman Art Library

Workers repair a section of the Erie Canal, near Little Falls, in 1831. While hailed as a great achievement of human progress, the canal required frequent repairs, frustrating travelers, merchants, boat workers, and people living along its banks.

plots nearby while wives and children worked in the mills, though as the system developed, men worked in the factories supervising wives and children in family-based work units.

Labor Protests

Mill life grew more difficult, especially during the depression of 1837 to 1843, when demand for cloth declined and mills ran part time. To increase productivity, managers sped up machines and required each worker to operate more machines. To boost profits, owners lengthened hours, cut wages, and packed the boardinghouses.

Workers organized, and in 1834 (and again in 1836), reacting to a 25 percent wage cut, they unsuccessfully "turned out" (struck) against the Lowell mills. In 1844, Massachusetts mill women formed the Lowell Female Reform Association and joined other workers in pressing, unsuccessfully, for state legislation mandating a ten- instead of fourteen-hour day.

Women aired their complaints in worker-run newspapers: in 1842, the *Factory Girl* appeared in New Hampshire, the *Wampanoag and Operatives' Journal* in Massachusetts. Two years later, mill workers founded the *Factory Girl's Garland* and the *Voice of Industry*, nicknamed "the factory girl's voice." Even the owner-sponsored *Lowell Offering* faced controversy when workers charged its editors with suppressing articles criticizing working conditions.

Few militant native-born mill workers stayed to fight the managers and owners, and gradually, fewer New England daughters entered the mills. In the 1850s, Irish immigrant women replaced them. Technological improvements made the work less skilled, enabling mills to hire lower-paid laborers. Male workers, too, protested changes wrought by the **market economy**. As voters, they formed labor political parties first in Pennsylvania, New York, and Massachusetts in the 1820s, and then elsewhere. They advocated free public education and an end to imprisonment for debt, and opposed banks and monopolies. Aspiring to own land, some advocated for free homesteads.

market economy Newly developing commercial economy that depended on goods and crops produced for sale rather than for personal consumption.

Labor Unions

The courts provided organized labor's greatest victory: protection from conspiracy laws. When journeyman shoemakers organized during the early 1800s, employers accused them of criminal conspiracy. The cordwainers' (shoemakers') cases between 1806 and 1815 left labor organizations in an uncertain position. Although the courts acknowledged the journeymen's right to organize, judges viewed strikes as illegal until a Massachusetts case, ***Commonwealth v. Hunt*** (1842), ruled that Boston journeyman bootmakers could strike "to subserve their own interests."

The first unions represented journeymen in printing, woodworking, shoemaking, and tailoring. Locally organized, they sought protection against competition from inferior workmen by regulating apprenticeships and establishing minimum wages. Umbrella organizations of individual craft unions, like the National Trade Union (1834), arose in several cities in the 1820s and 1830s. But the movement disintegrated amid wage reductions and unemployment in the depression of 1839–1843.

Commonwealth v. Hunt A court case in 1842 where the Massachusetts Supreme Judicial Court ruled that labor unions were not illegal monopolies that restrained trade.

Permanent labor organizations were difficult to sustain. Skilled craftsmen disdained less skilled workers. Moreover, workers divided along ethnic, religious, racial, and gender lines.

Consumption and Commercialization

How did farm women's work change as the commercial economy expanded?

By producing inexpensive cloth, New England mills spawned the ready-made clothing industry. Before the 1820s, women sewed most clothing at home. Tailors and seamstresses made wealthy men's and women's clothing to order. By the 1820s and 1830s, much clothing was mass-produced for sale in clothing stores. A division of labor took hold: one worker cut patterns all day, another sewed hems, another affixed buttons. The sewing machine, invented in 1846 and widely available in the 1850s, accelerated the process. Many farm families still made their own clothing yet bought clothes when they could afford to, freeing time for raising both crops and children.

The Garment Industry

Market expansion created demand for mass-produced clothing. Girls working in factories no longer had time to sew clothes. Young immigrant men—separated from mothers and sisters—bought the crudely made, loose-fitting clothing. But the biggest market for ready-made clothes was in the cotton South. Planters bought ready-made shoes and clothes for slaves, in whose hands they would rather place a hoe than a needle and thread.

Retailers often bought goods wholesale, though many manufactured shirts and trousers in their own factories. Lewis and Hanford of New York City boasted of cutting more than 100,000 garments in winter 1848–1849. The New York firm did business mostly in the South and owned a retail outlet in New Orleans. While southerners and westerners engaged in the clothing trade, its center remained in New York.

The garment industry often took the form of what some historians call metropolitan industrialization, which relied on reorganization of labor, similar to the earlier putting-out system. Much production of ready-made clothing, for example, occurred in tenements throughout New York City, where thousands of women spent long hours sewing buttons onto a piece of ready-made clothing, while others sewed hem after hem.

Specialization of Commerce

Commercial specialization transformed some urban traders into merchant princes. After the Erie Canal opened, New York City became a stop on every major trade route from Europe, southern ports, and the West. Traders sometimes invested in factories, further stimulating urban manufacturing. Some cities specialized: Rochester became a milling center ("The Flour City"), and Cincinnati ("Porkopolis") became the first meatpacking center.

Merchants who engaged in complex commercial transactions required large, mostly male, office staffs. At the bottom were messenger boys, often preteens, who delivered documents. Above them were copyists, who hand-copied documents. Clerks processed documents and did translations. Above them were the bookkeeper and confidential chief clerk. Those seeking employment in such countinghouses took a course from a writing master. All hoped to rise to partner, although their chances grew increasingly slim.

Specialization lagged in small towns, where merchants continued to exchange goods with local farm women and craftsmen continued to sell finished goods, such as shoes and clothing. In some rural areas, peddlers were general merchants. But as transportation improved and towns grew, small-town merchants increasingly specialized.

Commercial Farming

Even amid commercial booms, agriculture remained the northern economy's backbone. But the **transportation revolution** and market expansion transformed semi-subsistence farms into commercial enterprises. Many families abandoned mixed agriculture for specialization in cash crops. By the 1820s, eastern farmers had cultivated nearly all available land, and their small farms, often with uneven terrains, were ill suited for the labor-saving farm implements introduced in the 1830s, such as mechanical sowers, reapers, and threshers. Many northern farmers thus either moved west or quit farming for jobs in merchants' houses and factories.

transportation revolution Rapid expansion of canals, steamships, and railroads.

In 1820, about one-third of northern produce was intended for the market, but by 1850 that amount surpassed 50 percent. As farmers shifted toward market-oriented production, they invested in additional land, new equipment, and new labor sources (hired hands). Many New England and Middle Atlantic farm families faced competition from midwestern farmers after the Erie Canal opened. They abandoned wheat and corn production, shifting to livestock and vegetable and fruit production. Much of what they produced fed the North's rapidly growing urban and manufacturing populations.

Farmers financed innovations through land sales and debts. Indeed, increasing land values promised the greatest profit. Farm families who owned land flourished, but it became harder to become a farmer. The number of tenant farmers and hired hands increased, and farmers who had previously employed unpaid family members and enslaved workers now leased portions of their farms or hired paid labor.

Farm Women's Changing Labor

As the commercial economy expanded, rural women assumed additional responsibilities. Some did outwork (see Chapter 8). Many increased production of eggs, dairy products, and garden produce for sale; others raised bees or silkworms.

With the New England textile mills producing more finished cloth, farm women and children often abandoned time-consuming spinning and weaving, bought factory-produced cloth, and produced more marketable products, such as butter and cheese. Some mixed-agriculture farms converted entirely to dairy production, with men taking over formerly female tasks. Canals and railroads carried cheese to eastern ports, where wholesalers sold it worldwide.

Rural Communities

Despite pressure to manage farms like time-efficient businesses, some farmers clung to old practices such as barn raisings and husking bees. But by the 1830s with young women working in textile mills and young men laboring as clerks or factory hands, there were fewer people at such events. While farmers continued to swap labor and socialize with neighbors, they increasingly reckoned debts in dollars and watched national and international markets more closely. When financial panics hit, cash shortages almost halted business activity, casting many farmers further into debt, sometimes bankruptcy. Faced with potentially losing their land, farmers called in neighbors' debts, sometimes rupturing long-established relationships.

Cycles of Boom and Bust

With market expansion came booms and busts that often hit the Northeast hardest. Prosperity stimulated demand for finished goods, such as clothing and furniture, which led to higher prices and still higher production and to land speculation. Investment money was plentiful as Americans saved and foreign, mostly British, investors bought U.S. bonds and securities. Then production surpassed demand. Prices and wages fell; land and stock values collapsed, and investment money left the United States.

Although the 1820s and 1830s were boom times, financial panic triggered a bust cycle in 1837, the year after the Second Bank of the United States closed. Economic contraction remained severe through 1843. Many banks could not repay depositors, and states, facing deficits, defaulted on their bonds. Because of the **Panic of 1837**, European, especially British, investors became suspicious of U.S. loans and withdrew money from the United States.

Panic of 1837 A severe depression that struck the United States beginning in May 1837.

Hard times had come. "The streets seemed deserted," Sidney George Fisher observed of Philadelphia in 1842. "The largest [merchant] houses are shut up and to rent, there is no business … no money, no confidence." The hungry formed lines at soup societies, and beggars crowded the sidewalks. Laborers demanding their deposits gathered at closed banks. Sheriffs sold seized property at one-quarter of former prices. Congress passed the Federal Bankruptcy Law of 1841; by the time the law was repealed two years later, 41,000 bankrupts had sought protection under its provisions.

Families in Flux

Anxieties about economic fluctuations reverberated into northern homes. Sweeping changes in the household economy led to new family ideals. In the preindustrial era, families were the primary economic units; now they became a moral and cultural institution, though in reality few families could live up to this ideal.

How were men's and women's roles within the family redefined in the new industrial era?

The "Ideal" Family

In the North, the market economy increasingly separated the home from the workplace, leading to a new middle-class ideal in which men functioned in the public sphere while women oversaw the private or domestic sphere. The home became, in theory, an emotional retreat from the competitive, selfish business world. Men provided and protected, while women nurtured and guarded the family's morality. Childhood expanded: children were to remain at home until their late teens or early twenties. This ideal became known as separate-spheres ideology, the cult of domesticity, or the cult of true womanhood. Although it rigidly separated the male and female spheres, this ideology elevated domestic responsibilities. In her widely read *Treatise on Domestic Economy* (1841), Catharine Beecher approached housekeeping as a science while trumpeting mothers' role as their family's moral guardian. Beecher maintained that women's natural superiority as moral, nurturing caregivers made them especially suited for teaching (when single) and parenting (once married).

Shrinking Families

These new domestic ideals depended on smaller families enabling parents, particularly mothers, to offer children greater attention, education, and financial help. With the market economy, parents could afford to have fewer children because children no longer played a vital economic role. Urban families produced fewer household goods, and commercial farmers, unlike self-sufficient ones, relied on hired laborers. Although smaller families resulted partly from first marriages' occurring at a later age, they also resulted from planning, made easier when cheap rubber condoms became available in the 1850s. Some women chose, too, to end accidental pregnancies with abortion.

In 1800, American women bore seven or eight children; by 1860, five or six. This decline occurred even though immigrants with large-family traditions were settling in the United States; thus, the birth rate among native-born women declined more sharply. Although rural families remained larger than urban ones, birth rates among both groups declined comparably.

Still, few northern women could fulfill the middle-class ideal of **separate spheres**. Most wage-earning women provided essential income for their families and could not stay home. They often saw domestic ideals as oppressive, as middle-class reformers mistook poverty for immorality, condemning working mothers for letting their children work or scavenge rather than attend school. Although most middle-class women stayed home, new standards of cleanliness proved time-consuming. Although their household contributions were generally assessed in moral terms, their economic contributions were significant. They provided, without remuneration, the labor for which wealthier women paid when they hired domestic servants to perform chores. Without servants, women could not devote themselves primarily to their children, making the ideals of the cult of domesticity impossible for many middle-class families.

> **separate spheres** Middle-class ideology that emerged with the market revolution and divided men's and women's roles into distinct and separate categories based on their perceived gender differences, abilities, and social functions. Men were assigned the public realm of business and politics, while women were assigned to the private world of home and family.

Women's Paid Labor

In working-class families, girls left home as early as age twelve, earning wages most of their lives, with short respites for bearing and rearing children. Unmarried girls and women worked primarily as domestic servants or in factories; married and widowed women worked as laundresses, seamstresses, and cooks. Some hawked food and wares on city streets; others did piecework; and some became prostitutes. Few could support themselves or a family comfortably.

Middle-class Americans sought to keep daughters closer to home, except for brief stints as mill girls or teachers. In the 1830s, Catharine Beecher successfully campaigned for teacher-training schools for women. She argued both for women's moral superiority and their economic value; because these women would be single, she contended, they need not earn as much as their male counterparts, whom she presumed to be married (not all were). Unmarried women earned about half the salary of male teachers. By 1850, schoolteaching had become a woman's profession.

The proportion of single women in the population increased significantly in the nineteenth century. As more young men headed west, some eastern communities were disproportionately female. Other women chose to remain independent, seeking opportunities opened by the market economy and urban expansion. Because women's work generally paid poorly, those who forswore marriage faced serious challenges, leaving many single women dependent on charitable or family assistance.

The Growth of Cities

How could cities be seen at once as symbols of progress and of moral decay?

No period in American history saw more rapid urbanization than between 1820 and 1860. The percentage of people living in urban areas (defined by a population of 2,500 or more) grew from 7 percent in 1820 to nearly 20 percent in 1860. The greatest growth occurred in the Northeast and the Midwest. Although most northerners continued to live on farms or in small villages, cities boomed. Many urban residents were temporary, and many were immigrants.

Urban Boom

In 1820, the United States had thirteen places with a population greater than ten thousand; in 1860, it had ninety-three (see Map 10.2). New York City, already the nation's largest city in 1820, saw its population grow from 123,709 in that year to 813,669 in 1860. Philadelphia, the nation's second-largest city, saw its population multiply ninefold during that forty-year period. In 1815, Rochester, New York, had just 300 residents. By 1830, the Erie Canal turned the sleepy agricultural town into the nation's twenty-fifth-largest city, with a population of over 9,000.

Cities experienced geographic expansion too. In 1825, Fourteenth Street was New York City's northern boundary. By 1860, Forty-second Street was its northern limit. Public transit made city expansion possible. By the 1850s, all big cities had horse-drawn streetcars, allowing wealthier residents who could afford the fare to settle on the cities' outskirts.

Market-Related Development

The period between 1820 and 1860 saw the creation of many inland cities in the North—usually places that emerged with the creation of transportation lines or manufacturing establishments. The Boston Manufacturing Company, for example, selected the site for Lowell, Massachusetts, because of its proximity to the Merrimack River, which could power its textile mill. Incorporated in 1826, by the 1850s Lowell was the second-largest city in New England.

Northern cities developed elaborate municipal services but lacked taxing power to provide services for all. New services and basic sanitation depended on residents' ability to pay. Another solution was to charter private companies to sell basic services. Baltimore first chartered a private gas company in 1816. By midcentury, every major city had done so. Private firms lacked capital to build adequate water systems, and they laid pipe only in commercial and well-to-do residential areas. Supplying water ultimately fell to city governments.

Extremes of Wealth

Wealth was concentrating among a relatively small number of people. By 1860, the top 5 percent of

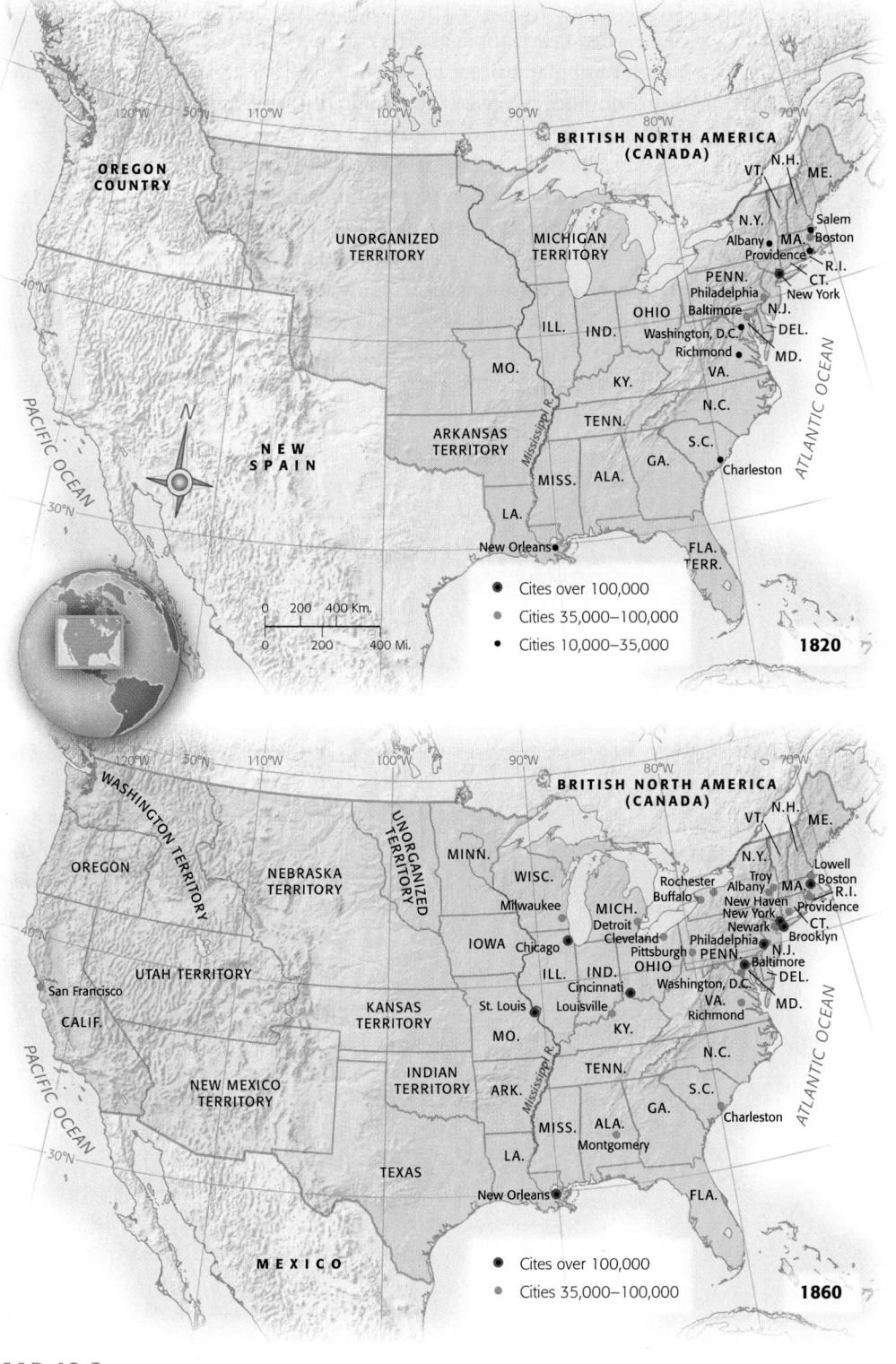

MAP 10.2

Major American Cities in 1820 and 1860

The number of Americans who lived in cities increased rapidly between 1820 and 1860, and the number of large cities grew as well. In 1820, only New York City had a population exceeding 100,000; forty years later, eight more cities had surpassed that level. Source: Copyright © Cengage Learning 2015

American families owned more than half of the nation's wealth, and the top 10 percent owned nearly three-quarters. In the South, income extremes were most apparent on rural plantations, but in the North, cities revealed economic inequities.

A number of factors contributed to widespread poverty in America's industrial cities: poor wages, lack of full-time employment, and the increasingly widespread employment of women and children, which drove down wages for everyone. Women and children, employers rationalized, did not need a living wage because they were dependent, meaning they relied on men to support them. In reality, though, not all women or children had men to support them, nor were men's wages always adequate to support a family comfortably.

New York provides an example of the extremes of wealth accompanying industrialization. Houses built for two families often held four. Some families took in lodgers to pay the rent; such crowding encouraged poorer New Yorkers to head

Visible signs of urban poverty in the 1850s were the homeless and orphaned children, most of them immigrants, who wandered the streets of New York City. The Home for the Friendless Orphanage, at Twenty-ninth Street and Madison Avenue, provided shelter for some of the orphan girls.

outdoors. But poor neighborhoods were filthy. Excess sewage from outhouses drained into ditches, carrying urine and fecal matter into the streets. People piled garbage into gutters, backyards, or alleys. Pigs, geese, dogs, and vultures scavenged the streets, while rats roamed under wooden sidewalks and through large buildings. Typhoid, dysentery, malaria, and tuberculosis thrived in such conditions, and cholera epidemics struck in 1831, 1849, and 1866.

Just beyond poverty-stricken neighborhoods were lavish mansions, whose residents escaped to country estates during the summer's heat or epidemics. Much of this wealth was inherited. Rich New Yorkers increased their fortunes by investing in commerce and manufacturing.

The middle class was larger than the wealthy elite but smaller than the working classes. They were businessmen, traders, and professionals, and the rapid turn toward industrialization and commercial specialization made them a larger presence in northern cities than in southern ones. Middle-class families enjoyed new consumer items: wool carpeting, fine wallpaper, and rooms full of furniture. Houses were large, from four to six rooms. By the 1840s and 1850s, middle-class families used indoor toilets that were mechanical, though not yet flushing. These families formed the backbone of urban clubs and societies, filled the family pews in church, and sent their sons to college.

Immigration

Many of the urban poor were immigrants. The 5 million immigrants to the United States between 1830 and 1860 outnumbered the country's entire population in 1790 (see Figure 10.1). During the peak period of pre–Civil War immigration (1847–1857), 3.3 million immigrants entered the United States, including 1.3 million Irish and 1.1 million Germans. By 1860, 15 percent of the white population was foreign born, with 90 percent of immigrants living in northern states.

Various factors "pushed" Europeans from their homes and "pulled" them to the northern United States. In Ireland, the potato famine (1845–1850)—a period of widespread starvation caused by a diseased potato crop—drove millions from their homeland. Although economic conditions pushed most Germans, some were political refugees—liberals, freethinkers, socialists, communists, and anarchists—who fled after the abortive revolutions of 1848. Employers, states, and shipping companies promoted opportunities in America with this message: work and prosper in America or starve in Europe. Once in the United States, immigrants soon saw the fallacy of promoters' promises of riches, and hundreds of thousands returned home.

Many early immigrants lived or worked in rural areas. Like the Archbalds, a few settled on farms and bought land. Others worked as hired farmhands, canal diggers, or railroad track layers—often hoping to buy land later. By the 1840s and 1850s—when immigration soared—the prospects of buying land became increasingly remote.

By 1860, most immigrants settled in cities, often near where they arrived. The most destitute could not afford the fare farther inland. Some had resources but fell victim to swindlers. Others liked the cities' ethnic flair. In 1855, 52 percent of New York's 623,000 inhabitants were immigrants, 28 percent from Ireland and 16 percent from the German states. Throughout the 1850s, about 35 percent of Boston was foreign born; more than two-thirds were Irish.

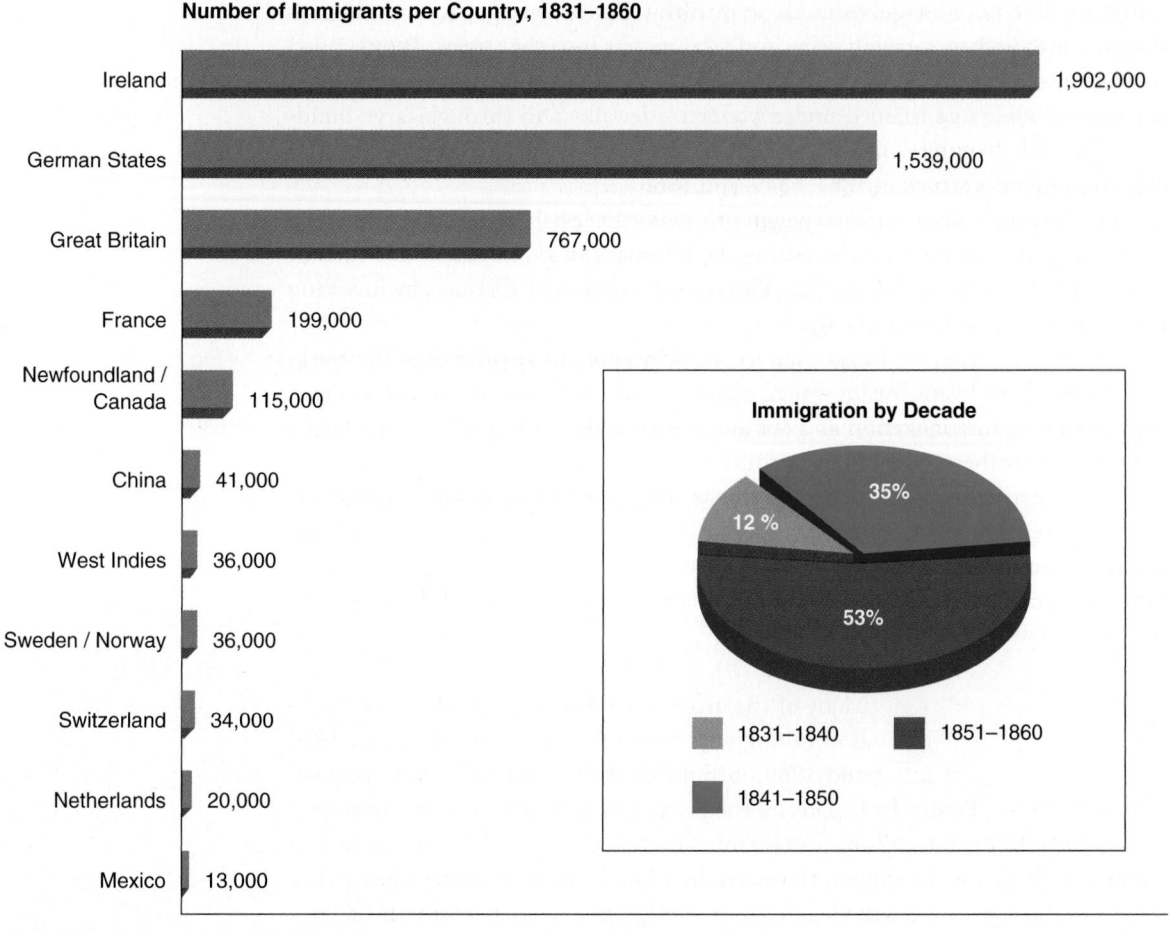

FIGURE 10.1

Major Sources of Immigration to the United States, 1831–1860

Most immigrants came from two areas: Great Britain, of which Ireland was a part, and the German states. These two areas sent more immigrants between 1830 and 1860 than the inhabitants of the United States enumerated at the first census in 1790. By 1860, 15 percent of the white population was of foreign birth.

(Source: Data from Stephan Thernstrom, ed., *Harvard Encyclopedia of American Ethnic Groups* [Cambridge, Mass., and London: Harvard University Press, 1980], 1047.)

Most of the new Irish immigrants were young, poor, rural, and Roman Catholic. Women worked as domestic servants or mill hands, while men labored in construction or transportation. Most Germans came with enough resources to head to states such as Ohio, Illinois, Wisconsin, and Missouri. Although some southern cities like Charleston and Savannah had Irish immigrants, most European immigrants disliked slavery and semitropical heat and preferred the Northeast or Midwest.

Ethnic Tensions

Tension—often about the era's economic changes—characterized the relationship between native-born Americans and immigrants, particularly Irish Catholics. Native-born workers blamed immigrants for scarce job opportunities and low wages. Middle-class whites blamed them for poverty and crime. They believed immigrants' moral depravity—not poor wages—led to poverty.

White northerners often portrayed Irish immigrants as nonwhite, as African in appearance. But Irish and African Americans did not develop a sense of solidarity. Instead, some of the era's most virulent riots erupted between Irish immigrants and African Americans.

Anti-Catholicism became strident in the 1830s. In Boston, anti-Catholic riots occurred frequently. Nearby Charlestown, Massachusetts, saw a mob burn a convent in 1834. In Philadelphia, a crowd attacked priests and nuns and vandalized churches in 1844. Urban riots usually attracted more newspaper attention, fueling fears that cities were violent, depraved places.

Protestant German immigrants fared better than the Irish. Because Germans generally arrived with resources and skills, Americans stereotyped them as hardworking. But non-Protestant Germans—Catholics and Jews (whom white Americans considered a separate race) frequently encountered racial and religious prejudice.

Immigrants often lived in ethnic enclaves, setting up social clubs and mutual aid societies. Irish Catholics had their own neighborhoods, where they established Catholic churches and schools. In larger cities, immigrants from the same German states clustered together.

A Female Employment Office (oil on canvas), Burr, William Henry (1819–1908)/© Collection of the New-York Historical Society, USA/ The Bridgeman Art Library

Domestic servants await their fate at a hiring office. Because servants resided with their employers, concerns about honesty often topped an employer's list of priorities for a suitable servant.

People of Color

African Methodist Episcopal churches First American denomination established by and for African Americans.

African Americans also forged their own communities and culture. By 1860 nearly 250,000 (many of them refugees from southern slavery) lived in the urban North. **African Methodist Episcopal churches** and preachers helped forge communities. Ministers were political leaders; churches hosted political forums and protest meetings.

White racism impinged on northern African Americans' lives. Streetcars, hotels, restaurants, and theaters could turn away African Americans without legal penalty. City laws barred African Americans from public buildings. Even where laws were liberal, whites' attitudes constrained African Americans' opportunities. In Massachusetts, for example, African Americans enjoyed more legal rights than anywhere else. Still, whites often refused to shop at black businesses. African Americans were excluded from factory and clerical jobs. Women worked as house servants, cooks, washerwomen, and child nurses. Most African American men worked as construction workers, porters, longshoremen, or day laborers—all jobs subject to frequent unemployment. Others took lower-paying but stable jobs as servants, waiters, cooks, barbers, and janitors. Many African American men became sailors and merchant seamen, jobs offering regular employment and advancement, though not protection from racial taunts.

In cities, African Americans turned service occupations into businesses, opening restaurants, taverns, hotels, barbershops, and employment agencies for domestic servants. Some sold used clothing or were junk dealers. A few became wealthy, invested in real estate, and loaned money. With professionals—ministers, teachers, physicians, dentists, lawyers, and newspaper editors—they formed a small but growing African American middle class.

Still, African Americans became targets of urban violence. White rioters clubbed and stoned African Americans, destroying their houses, churches, and businesses—and sent many fleeing for their lives. Philadelphia experienced five major riots in the 1830s and 1840s. By 1860, hundreds of African Americans had died in urban riots.

Urban Culture

Living in cramped, squalid conditions, working-class families spent little time indoors. In the 1840s, a working-class youth culture developed on the Bowery, one of New York's entertainment strips. Lined with theaters, dance halls, and cafés, it became an urban midway. The Bowery boys' greased hair, distinctive clothing, and swaggering gait frightened many middle-class New Yorkers, as did Bowery girls' colorful costumes. Equally scandalous were the middle-class clerks who succumbed to urban temptations, notably prostitution.

Gangs of garishly dressed young men and women flaunting their sexuality and drinking excessively drove respectable citizenry to establish private clubs. Some men joined the Masonic order, which offered members an elaborate code of deference between ranks, while women organized literary clubs and benevolent societies.

Increasingly, urban recreation and sports became commodities. Horse racing, walking races, and, in the 1850s, baseball attracted urban men. Wall Street office workers formed the Knickerbocker Club in 1842 and in 1845 drew up rules for playing baseball. Large cities boasted two or more theaters catering to different

On May 10, 1849, a working-class protest at the elitist Astor Place Theater led to a clash with state militia, resulting in at least twenty-two deaths and over one hundred and fifty injuries.

classes. Some plays cut across class lines—Shakespeare was so widely performed that even illiterate theatergoers knew his plays.

In the 1840s, singing groups, theater troupes, and circuses traveled from city to city. Minstrel shows were popular, featuring white men (often Irish) in makeup imitating African Americans in song, dance, and patter. In the early 1830s, Thomas D. Rice of New York became famous for portraying Jim Crow, an old southern slave. In patched clothing and torn shoes, the blackface Rice danced and sang. Minstrel performers told jokes mocking economic and political elites, and evoked nostalgia for preindustrial work habits and morality. But blackface actors encouraged a racist stereotyping of African Americans as sensual and lazy.

The Penny Press

Accounts of urban culture peppered the penny press, which emerged in the 1830s, soon sweeping northern cities. Made possible by technological advances—the advent of the steam-powered press, improved methods for producing paper, and transportation innovations—the penny press (each newspaper cost one cent) differed from traditional (six-cent) newspapers. The older papers covered mostly commercial news and identified strongly with a political party; the penny press proclaimed political independence and hired reporters to cover local, national, and international stories. Where six-cent newspapers relied on subscriptions and political contributions, penny newspapers were sold by newsboys on the street. They earned money from advertising, and drew an economically diverse readership. Working-class people could now regularly afford newspapers.

Penny newspapers focused on daily life, giving one social class the opportunity to peer into the lives of other classes, ethnicities, and races. The penny press often sensationalized the news, thereby influencing urban dwellers' views of one another and of cities.

Cities as Symbols of Progress

To many northerners, cities symbolized progress and decay. Cities nurtured churches, schools, civil governments, and museums—signs of civilization and culture. As canals and railroads opened the West for mass settlement, many white northerners applauded the appearance of church steeples and public buildings in areas that had been "savage wilderness," or territory controlled by Native Americans.

Yet some middle-class Americans deplored the nation's largest cities, which they saw as havens of disease, poverty, crime, and vice—emblems of moral decline. They considered epidemics to be divine scourges, striking the filthy, intemperate, and immoral. Theft and prostitution provided evidence of moral vice, and wealthy observers perceived these crimes not as by-products of poverty but as proof of individual failing. They pushed city officials to establish the first police forces. Boston hired daytime policemen in 1838, and New York formed its police force in 1845.

Middle-class reformers focused on purifying cities of disease and vice. If disease was divine punishment, then Americans would have to become more godly. Reformers sought to convince the urban working classes that life would improve if they gave up alcohol, worked harder, and prayed frequently. This belief became central to northerners' ideas about progress.

Revivals and Reform

How did religious revival movements lead to social reform?

Second Great Awakening
Religious revival that swept the country and helped inspire reform movements.

Religious revivals in the late eighteenth and early nineteenth centuries—sometimes called the **Second Great Awakening** for their resemblance to the eighteenth-century Great Awakening—raised people's hopes for the Second Coming of the Christian messiah and the establishment of God's kingdom on earth. Revivalists created communities of believers resolved to speed the millennium, or the thousand years of peace that would accompany Christ's Second Coming, by combating sin. Some believed the United States had a special mission in God's design. If evil could be eliminated, individuals and society could be perfected, readying the earth for Christ's return.

Revivalists strove for large-scale conversions. Rural women, men, and children traveled long distances to camp meetings, where they heard fiery sermons preached day and night from hastily constructed platforms and tents in forests or fields. In cities, women in particular attended daily services and prayer meetings. Converts vowed to live sanctified lives and help others see the light.

Revivals

Northern revivalists emphasized social reform. The most prominent preachers were Lyman Beecher, who began in New England before moving to Cincinnati, and **Charles G. Finney**, who traveled the canals and roads linking the Northeast to the Midwest. Revivalist preachers argued that evil was avoidable, that Christians were not doomed by original sin, and that anyone could achieve salvation. Revivalism thrived among Methodists and Baptists, whose denominational structures maximized democratic participation and drew ministers from ordinary folk.

Finney achieved his greatest successes in sections of western New York experiencing rapid changes in transportation and industrialization—in what he called the "Burned-Over District" because of the region's intense evangelical fires. Rapid change raised fears of social disorder—family dissolution, drinking, swearing, and prostitution. Many individuals worried, too, about their economic fate during the era's booms and busts.

When northern revivalist preachers emphasized good works—good deeds— they helped ignite social reform movements, first in the Burned-Over District and then in New England, the Middle Atlantic, and the upper Midwest. Evangelically inspired reform associations constituted what historians call the "benevolent empire." They shared a commitment to human perfectibility and often turned to the same wealthy men for financial resources and advice.

Charles G. Finney A lawyer-turned-Presbyterian minister who conducted revivals in towns like Utica along the Erie Canal and who stressed individual responsibility.

Moral Reform

Those resources enabled reformers to use the era's new technologies—steam presses and railroads. By mass-producing pamphlets and newspapers for distribution into the country's interior, reformers spread their message widely. With canals and railroads making travel easier, reformers could attend conventions and host speakers from distant places. Most reform organizations sponsored weekly newspapers, creating a community of reformers.

While industrialists and merchants provided financial resources for evangelical reform, their wives and daughters solicited new members and circulated petitions. Reforms expanded the cult of domesticity's role for women—beyond moral guardians for the family—to the public realm. Women established reformatories for wayward youth or asylums for orphans. Participation in reform movements allowed women to exercise moral authority outside the household, giving them new influence.

Many female reformers had attended a female academy or seminary—which embraced women as men's intellectual equals—where the curriculum included arts of "refinement"—music, dance, penmanship—but focused on science and literature. By 1820, approximately equal numbers of men and women attended institutions of higher education. Women prepared themselves to influence public opinion even as many maintained substantial domestic responsibilities. A few women became prominent editors and writers, but most influenced society as educators and reformers.

The aftermath of an 1830 exposé of prostitution in New York City illustrates reformers' public influence and belief in moral uplift. Female reformers there organized a shelter and tried to secure respectable employment for prostitutes. They also publicized brothel clients' names to shame these men. Organizing as the Female Moral Reform Society, by 1840 this group had 555 affiliated chapters nationwide. It soon lobbied successfully for criminal sanctions in New York State against men who seduced women into prostitution.

Penitentiaries and Asylums

A similar belief in perfectibility led reformers to establish penitentiaries aimed to transform criminals into productive members of society through disciplined regimens. Other reformers sought to improve treatment of the mentally ill, who were often imprisoned alongside criminals, and put in cages or dark dungeons. **Dorothea Dix**, the movement's leader, exemplifies the reformer who started with a religious belief in human perfectibility and moved into social action. Investigating asylums, petitioning the Massachusetts legislature, and lobbying other states and Congress, Dix had encouraged twenty-eight states to build institutions for the mentally ill by 1860.

Dorothea Dix Leader of movement to improve conditions for the insane.

Temperance

Temperance reformers, who advocated partial or full abstinence from alcoholic beverages, likewise crossed into the political sphere. Drinking was widespread in the early nineteenth century, when men gathered in public houses and inns to drink, talk, and play cards. Contracts were sealed and celebrations commemorated with liquor.

temperance Abstinence from alcohol; name of the movement against alcohol.

Evangelicals considered drinking sinful, and forsaking alcohol was often part of conversion. Preachers condemned Sunday drinkers of alcohol for violating the Sabbath—workers' one day off. Factory owners claimed alcohol made workers unreliable. Civic leaders connected alcohol with crime. Middle-class reformers, often women, condemned it for diverting men from family responsibilities and fostering abusive behavior. In the early 1840s, thousands of women formed Martha Washington societies to reform alcoholics, raise children as teetotalers, and spread the temperance message.

Link to Reverend M'Ilvaine Denounces Intemperance, 1839

As the temperance movement grew, its goal shifted from moderation to abstinence to prohibition. By the mid-1830s, five thousand state and local temperance societies touted teetotalism, and more than a million people had pledged abstinence. Per capita consumption of alcohol fell from five gallons per year in 1800 to below two gallons in the 1840s. The American Society for the Promotion of Temperance, organized in 1826, pushed for legislation ending alcohol manufacture and sale. In 1851, Maine became the first state to ban alcohol except for medicinal purposes; by 1855, similar laws were passed throughout New England and in New York, Pennsylvania, and the Midwest.

The temperance campaign had an anti-immigrant and anti-Catholic strain to it. Along the nation's canals, reformers lamented taverns catering to Irish workers, and in the cities, they expressed outrage at the Sunday tradition of German families' gathering at beer gardens. Some Catholics heeded the message, pledging abstinence and forming organizations such as the St. Mary's Mutual Benevolence Total Abstinence Society in Boston.

But many workers—Protestants and Catholics—rejected reformers' imposition of their middle-class values. Workers agreed that poverty and crime were problems but blamed poor wages, not drinking habits. Even some who resisted alcohol opposed prohibition, believing that nondrinking should be about self-control, not state coercion.

Public Schools

Public education usually included religious education, but when teachers taught Protestant beliefs and used the King James Bible, Catholics established their own

Visualizing THE PAST

Engaging Children

Hundreds of thousands of children joined the temperance movement, often by enlisting in the so-called Cold Water Army. Like adult temperance societies, the Cold Water Army advocated for complete abstinence from alcoholic beverages. On holidays such as George Washington's birthday and the Fourth of July, they marched at public gatherings, singing temperance songs and carrying banners and fans such as the one pictured below. Reverend Thomas P. Hunt, a Presbyterian minister, founded the Cold Water Army because he believed that by recruiting children, he stood a greater chance of eradicating alcohol consumption than if he aimed his temperance efforts directly at adults. What might have been his logic? Why might children have wanted to join a Cold Water Army? Do the images on the certificate and fan offer any clues? What were the benefits of participating in the movement? What were the implied consequences of failing to do so? Why might Hunt have chosen the term *army*, and what about that choice might have proved appealing to his young recruits?

Children who participated in a Cold Water Army often received a certificate that acknowledged their commitment to the cause while reiterating the pledge they had taken.

Children in Cold Water Army parades sometimes carried decorative fans, which they may have displayed in their homes as well, as reminders to themselves and their parents of temperance's virtues.

schools. Some Protestants feared that Catholics would never assimilate into American culture and charged Catholics with plotting to impose papal control. Still, public education touched more Americans than did any other reform movement. **Horace Mann**, a Massachusetts lawyer and reformer from humble beginnings advocated free, tax-supported education to replace church schools and private schools. Universal education, Mann proposed, would "prepare children to become good citizens," end crime and help Americanize immigrants.

During Mann's tenure as secretary of the Massachusetts Board of Education from 1837 to 1848, Massachusetts led the "common school" movement, establishing teacher training, lengthening the school year, and raising salaries to make teaching more attractive. Adhering to notions that women had special claims to morality and could be paid less as men's dependents, Mann envisioned a system in which women educated future clerks, farmers, and workers with a practical curriculum that emphasized geography, arithmetic, and science. Due partly to expanding public education in the North, by 1850 most native-born white Americans were literate.

Horace Mann First secretary of the newly created Massachusetts Board of Education who presided over sweeping reforms to transform schools into institutions that occupied most of a child's time and energy.

Engineering and Science

Public education's emphasis on science reflected a broader belief that engineering and science could help remedy the nation's problems. Scientists and doctors blamed not immorality but unclean, stagnant water for causing epidemics. After the devastating 1832 cholera epidemic, New York City planned a massive waterworks, and between 1837 and 1842 built the forty-one-mile Croton Aqueduct that brought water from upstate New York to Manhattan.

Several scientific institutions were also founded in this era. After James Smithson, a wealthy British scientist, left his estate to the United States government, Congress established the Smithsonian Institution (1846), which promoted scientific knowledge. Joseph Henry, the Smithsonian's director, was a renowned scientist; his experiments in electromagnetism helped make possible the telegraph and, later, the telephone. Like Henry, many nineteenth-century Americans considered religion and science compatible. They saw scientific discoveries as signs of progress, symbolizing that the millennium was approaching. God created the natural world, they believed, and it was their Christian duty to perfect it in preparation for God's return.

Utopian Experiments

What were the goals of utopian communities?

Some idealists dreamed of a new social order. They established dozens of utopian communities based on religious principles, a resistance to the market economy's excessive individualism, or both. Some groups, like the **Mormons**, arose during the Second Great Awakening. Utopian communities attempted to recapture what they perceived as the past's more communal nature, even while offering radical departures from marriage and child rearing.

Mormons Members of the Church of Jesus Christ of Latter-day Saints, the first major denomination founded in the United States; members were persecuted for many years.

Mormons

No utopian experiment was more enduring than the Church of Jesus Christ of Latter-day Saints, whose members were known as Mormons. During the 1820s religious ferment in western New York, **Joseph Smith**, a young farmer, reported that an angel called Moroni gave him divinely engraved gold plates. Smith published his revelations as the *Book of Mormon* and organized a church in 1830. The next year,

Joseph Smith Founder of the Mormon Church.

the community moved to Ohio to build a "New Jerusalem" and await the Second Coming of Jesus.

After angry mobs drove the Mormons from Ohio, they settled in Missouri. Anti-Mormons charged that Mormonism was a scam created by Joseph Smith, and feared Mormon economic and political power. In 1838, Missouri's governor charged Smith with fomenting insurrection and worked to indict him and other leaders for treason.

Smith and his followers left for Nauvoo, Illinois. The state legislature gave them a city charter making them self-governing. But again the Mormons met antagonism, especially after Smith introduced polygamy in 1841, allowing men to have several wives at once. In 1844, after Smith and his brother were charged with treason and jailed, then murdered, the Mormons left Illinois to seek security in the western wilderness. Under Brigham Young's leadership, they established a cooperative community in the Great Salt Lake Valley.

Shakers

The **Shakers**, the largest communal utopian experiment, reached their peak between 1820 and 1860, with six thousand members in twenty settlements in eight states. Shaker communities emphasized agriculture and handcrafts, contrasting with the new factory regime. Founded in England in 1772 by Mother Ann Lee, their name derived from their worship service, which included shaking their entire bodies. Ann Lee's children died in infancy, and she saw their deaths as retribution for her sin of intercourse; thus, she advocated celibacy. After imprisonment in England in 1773–1774, she settled in America.

Shakers lived communally, with men and women in separate quarters; individual families were abolished. Men and women shared leadership equally. Many Shaker settlements became temporary refuges for orphans, widows, runaways, abused wives, and laid-off workers. Their settlements depended on new recruits, partly because celibacy meant no reproduction and because some members left, unsuited to communal living or the Shakers' spiritual message.

Shakers Utopian sect that stressed celibacy and emphasized agriculture and handcrafts; became known for furniture designs long after the community itself ceased to exist.

Oneidans, Owenites, and Fourierists

Other utopian communities joined in resisting social change. John Humphrey Noyes, a lawyer converted by Finney's revivals, established two perfectionist communities: in Putney, Vermont, in 1835, and—after being indicted for adultery—in Oneida, New York, in 1848. Noyes advocated communal property, communal child rearing, and "complex marriage," in which all the community's men were married to all its women, but a woman could reject a sexual proposition. Couples applied to Noyes for permission to have a child, or Noyes assigned two people to reproduce. Robert Dale Owen's community in **New Harmony**, Indiana (1825–1828), also abolished private property and advocated communal child rearing. The Fourierists, named after French philosopher Charles Fourier, established more than two dozen communities in the Northeast and Midwest that resisted individualism and promoted gender equality.

The most famous Fourier community was Brook Farm, in West Roxbury, Massachusetts. Inspired by **transcendentalism**—the belief that the physical world is secondary to the spiritual realm, which human beings can reach only by intuition—Brook Farm's rural communalism combined spirituality, manual labor, intellectual life, and

New Harmony An important and well-known utopian community, founded in Indiana by Robert Owen.

transcendentalism The belief that the physical world is secondary to the spiritual realm, which humans can reach only by intuition.

play. Founded in 1841 by Unitarian minister George Ripley, Brook Farm attracted farmers, craftsmen, and writers, including novelist Nathaniel Hawthorne. In 1845, Brook Farm's one hundred members organized themselves into phalanxes (working-living units), following Fourier's model. As regimentation replaced individualism, membership dropped. A year after a disastrous fire in 1846, the experiment collapsed.

| American Renaissance |

Ralph Waldo Emerson, a pillar of transcendentalism, was the prime inspiration for a literary outpouring now known as the American Renaissance. After quitting his Boston Unitarian ministry in 1831, he spent two years in Europe before returning to lecture and write, preaching self-reliance. Widely admired, he influenced Hawthorne, *Dial* editor Margaret Fuller, Herman Melville, and Henry David Thoreau. The American Renaissance was distinctively American and an outgrowth of the European romantic movement. It addressed universal themes using American settings and characters. Hawthorne, for instance, used Puritan New England as a backdrop.

Thoreau championed individualism. In his 1849 essay on "Resistance to Civil Government" (known after his death as "Civil Disobedience"), Thoreau advocated resistance to a government engaged in immoral acts. During the War with Mexico (see Chapter 13), Thoreau refused to pay his taxes, believing they would aid an immoral war to expand slavery, and was briefly jailed. Later, defying federal law, Thoreau helped escaped slaves on their way to freedom.

Abolitionism

How did evangelicalism transform the antislavery movement?

Thoreau joined evangelical abolitionists trying to eradicate slavery, which they deemed a sin. Their efforts built on an earlier generation of antislavery activism among blacks and whites.

William Lloyd Garrison
Founder of *The Liberator* and a controversial white advocate of abolition, he demanded an immediate end to slavery and embraced civil rights for blacks on par with those of whites.

| Evangelical Abolitionism |

In the early 1830s, a new group of radical white abolitionists—most prominently, **William Lloyd Garrison**—rejected earlier gradualism and colonization (see Chapter 8) and demanded immediate and uncompensated emancipation. Garrison began publishing his abolitionist newspaper *The Liberator* in 1831; in 1833, he founded the American Antislavery Society, the era's largest abolitionist organization.

Immediatists believed slavery was a sin needing eradication. They were influenced by African American abolitionist societies and evangelicals' notion that humans, not God, determined their spiritual fate by choosing good or evil. When all humans had chosen good, the millennium would come. Slavery, however, denied enslaved men and women the ability to act as what Finney called "moral free agents."

Garrison advocated "moral suasion," hoping to bring emancipation by winning over slave owners and others who supported or tolerated slavery. Evangelical abolitionism depended, then, on large numbers of ministers and laypeople spreading the word nationwide.

| The American Antislavery Society |

By 1838, at its peak, the society had two thousand local affiliates and over 300,000 members. Unlike earlier white abolitionists, the immediatists welcomed men and women of all races and classes. Lydia Maria Child, Maria Chapman, and Lucretia Mott served on its executive committee; Child edited its official paper, the *National Anti-Slavery Standard*, from 1841 to 1843, and the society sponsored black and female speakers.

With the "great postal campaign" in 1835, the society flooded the mails with antislavery tracts. Women went door to door collecting signatures on antislavery petitions; by 1838, more than 400,000 petitions were sent to Congress. Abolitionist-minded women met in "sewing circles," making clothes for escaped slaves while organizing activities, such as antislavery fairs at which they sold goods—often hand-made—donating the proceeds to antislavery causes.

African American Abolitionists

At the same time, African Americans continued independent efforts to end slavery and improve free African Americans' status. Former slaves—famously, Frederick Douglass, Henry Bibb, Harriet Tubman, and Sojourner Truth—fought slavery through speeches, publications, and participation in a secret network known as the Underground Railroad, which spirited enslaved men, women, and children to freedom. By the thousands, African Americans established churches, moral reform societies, newspapers, and schools and orphanages.

Opposition to Abolitionism

But abolitionists' visibility inspired virulent opposition among southerners and northerners who recognized cotton's vital economic role and feared that emancipation would prompt an influx of freed slaves into the North. They questioned the institution's morality but believed blacks to be inherently inferior and incapable of the virtue and diligence required of freedom and citizenship.

Opposition to abolitionism could become violent. In Boston, David Walker, a southern-born free black, died under mysterious circumstances in 1830, one year after advocating the violent overthrow of slavery in his *Appeal ... to the Colored Citizens*. Among northerners who despised abolitionists, most were elites with economic connections to the southern cotton economy and political connections to leading southerners. Northern gentlemen incited anti-abolitionist riots. Mob violence peaked in 1835, with more than fifty riots aimed at abolitionists or African Americans. In 1837, in Alton, Illinois, a mob murdered white abolitionist editor Elijah P. Lovejoy, and rioters sacked his printing office.

Moral Suasion Versus Political Action

Violence made some immediatists question moral suasion as a tactic. James G. Birney, the son of a Kentucky slave owner, believed abolition could be effected only through politics. Involving women violated the natural order and detracted from the ultimate goal: freedom for slaves. Thus, when William Lloyd Garrison, an ardent women's rights supporter, endorsed Abby Kelley's appointment to the American Antislavery Society's business committee in 1840, he provoked an irreparable split in the abolitionist movement. Arthur Tappan and Theodore Weld led a dissident group that established the American and Foreign Anti-Slavery Society. That society formed a new political party: the Liberty Party, which nominated Birney for president in 1840 and 1844.

The Burning of Pennsylvania Hall, 1838 (colour litho), American School, (19th century)/Library Company of Philadelphia, PA, USA/The Bridgeman Art Library

Destruction by Fire of Pennsylvania Hall,
On the night of the 17th May, **1838**

Three days after its dedication in 1838, Pennsylvania Hall—an abolitionist center in Philadelphia—was burned to the ground by anti-abolitionist rioters.

Although committed to immediate abolition, the Liberty Party thought only states had the jurisdiction to determine slavery's legality. They believed the federal government could act only in western territories; the party demanded that new territories prohibit slavery. Prominent black abolitionists, including Frederick Douglass, endorsed the party, whose leaders also emphasized combating northern prejudice.

Free-Labor Ideology   Secular and religious belief in progress—and upward mobility—coalesced into the notion of free labor (that, in a competitive marketplace, those who worked hard and lived virtuous lives could improve their status). Many laborers initially rejected free-labor ideology, seeing it as a veiled attempt to rationalize poor wages, denigrate Catholicism, and quell worker protest. But by the 1850s, with slavery's expansion into the West, more northerners embraced free-labor ideology and saw slavery as antithetical to it. This way of thinking especially made the North distinctive.

P. T. Barnum's Publicity Stunts

Usually remembered for the Ringling Brothers and Barnum & Bailey Circus, P. T. Barnum (1810–1891) left another legacy: the publicity stunt. Using hoaxes and spectacles, Barnum's American Museum in New York City drew tens of millions of visitors between 1841 and 1868, making Barnum the era's second wealthiest American.

Barnum first gained widespread publicity in 1835 with his traveling exhibition of Joice Heth, whom he claimed was George Washington's 161-year-old former slave. When interest waned, Barnum planted a rumor that she was a machine made of leather and bones. The penny press reveled in the ensuing controversy, swelling admissions and earning Barnum enough to purchase the American Museum, whose "500,000 natural and artificial curiosities" he promoted through similar stunts. Barnum also hosted the nation's first beauty pageant in 1854. Offensive to middle-class sensibilities, it flopped, but Barnum persevered with pageants featuring dogs, babies, and chickens. The baby show alone attracted 61,000 visitors. Selling more than a million copies, Barnum's autobiography inspired generations of entrepreneurs.

Many cultural icons began as promotional gimmicks, including the Miss America Pageant (1921), the Macy's Thanksgiving Day parade (1924), and the Goodyear blimp (1925). Since 1916, Nathan's has hosted a Fourth of July hot dog–eating contest, now attracting forty thousand spectators and a television audience. The *Guinness Book of World Records*, begun as an Irish beer company's promotional brochure, inspires thousands each year to attempt to break records. Even failed attempts generate publicity.

By staging stunts for media exposure, today's entrepreneurs reveal the enduring legacy of P. T. Barnum, the self-proclaimed greatest showman on earth.

P. T. Barnum's first great success came in 1835 when he charged admission to see Joice Heth, whom he claimed was the 161-year-old former slave of George Washington.

Collections, Somers Historical Society, Somers, NY

Summary

During the first half of the nineteenth century, the North became enmeshed in commercial culture. Northern states and capitalists invested heavily in internal improvements, which lay the groundwork for market expansion. Most northerners shifted toward commercial farming or, in smaller numbers, toward industrial wage labor. Farmers specialized in cash crops, while their children worked in factories or countinghouses.

To many northerners, the market economy symbolized progress, bringing easier access to cheap western lands, employment for surplus farm laborers, and commercial availability of goods that had been time-consuming to produce. But the market economy also led to increased specialization, a depersonalized workplace, and a sharper divide between work and leisure. The market economy tied northerners to fluctuating national and international markets, and during economic downturns, many northern families experienced destitution.

With less need for children's labor, northerners began producing smaller families. Even as working-class children worked, middle-class families created a model of childhood that had parents shielding children from the world's dangers. Mothers, in theory, became moral guardians, keeping the home safe from the new economy's competitiveness. Few women, though, could devote themselves entirely to nurturing their families.

Immigrants and free African Americans performed the lowest-paying work, and many native-born whites blamed them for problems spurred by rapid economic change. Anti-immigrant (especially anti-Catholic) and antiblack riots became commonplace. Immigrants and African Americans responded by forming their own communities.

Cities came to symbolize the possibilities and limits of market expansion. Urban areas were marked by extremes of wealth, vibrant working-class cultures, as well as poverty, crime, and mob violence. To reconcile the seeming contradictions, middle-class northerners articulated free-labor ideology, touting the possibility for upward mobility in a competitive marketplace. This ideology would become increasingly central to northern regional identity.

Chapter Review

Or Was the North Distinctive?

What happened to the North and South economically after the War of 1812?

The South continued as an agricultural region and expanded its slave system, while the North transformed quickly into a market economy. With the war cutting off European trade, northern entrepreneurs invested in domestic production and factories. Commercial farming emerged in the North, with farmers shifting from producing just what they needed—with small amounts for trade—to specializing in crops that would generate cash, which they could use to buy goods they formerly made at home, such as soap and cloth.

The Transportation Revolution

> **How did the transportation revolution help lay the groundwork for a market economy?**

The lack of inexpensive, quick, and convenient transportation impeded westward expansion and industrial growth until the early nineteenth century. Beginning in the 1800s, however, several innovations—steamboats, canals, and railroads—dramatically reduced the cost and time to transport raw materials, goods, and people. Canals connected regions and shortened travel times, and steamboats reduced trips that previously took months to just days. Faster and less costly to build, railroads soon replaced canals, with transportation costs overall cut by as much as 95 percent. Goods that were previously unavailable in the nation's interior now could be had easily and cheaply. Westward migration expanded, creating new markets and cultural links between previously distant regions, as news, products, and people of various backgrounds fanned out from the Northeast to the Northwest.

Factories and Industrialization

> **How was factory work different from the work life people previously knew?**

The artisan shops and family farms that predated factories had fewer formal rules and less structure than the factories that arose in the late eighteenth and early nineteenth centuries. Artisans traditionally saw themselves as producers, in charge of their labor and its outcome and working side by side with hired helpers. In factories, workers infrequently saw owners and worked for wages under the watchful eye of supervisors with strict rules and a clock governing their day. Instead of learning how to make something from start to finish, workers now specialized in only one part of the process and never saw the finished item. There was no job security, and employers often cut wages or eliminated jobs during economic downturns. Workers resisted by organizing strikes—as the mill girls did—or forming unions.

Consumption and Commercialization

> **How did farm women's work change as the commercial economy expanded?**

Along with their regular farm and household duties, rural women took on new responsibilities to help pay for some of the items they now bought (such as textiles) instead of bartering for or making on their own. Some took in outwork; others increased production of eggs, milk, butter, and produce and other items for sale in the market. Daughters often went to work in textile mills, sending part of their wages home to aid their families.

Families in Flux

> **How were men's and women's roles within the family redefined in the new industrial era?**

Before the rise of the market economy, families were the center of production and economic activity. As industrialization took hold, however, new ideals transformed families into moral and cultural institutions. Men, particularly middle-class men, occupied the public sphere, providing for and protecting their families. In this new "separate spheres" ideology, women's roles were confined to the home, and they were charged with making it a retreat for husbands and children from the harshness of economic life. This ideology, which elevated women's domestic roles, was later dubbed *the cult of domesticity* or *the cult of true womanhood*. However, this ideology was rarely realized in practice.

The Growth of Cities

> **How could cities be seen at once as symbols of progress and of moral decay?**

America experienced rapid urbanization between 1820 and 1860, particularly in the Northeast and Midwest, as some previously agricultural regions—such as Rochester near the Erie Canal—became cities and existing cities grew dramatically in population and size. People flocked to cities, seeking opportunities. On the one hand, cities served as transportation and industrial hubs and nurtured schools, churches, civil governments, and museums—all signs of progress. On the other hand, some middle-class Americans regarded them as centers of disease, poverty, crowding, crime, and vice—symbols of moral decline. Prostitution, vagrancy, and theft led reformers to seek to purify cities. They targeted the working class, who many saw as contributing to urban decay, with the promise of upward mobility and free-labor ideology—that those who worked hard, lived virtuous lives, and gave up alcohol would become successful. Workers initially rejected such notions as an imposition on their lives, but with slavery's potential expansion westward in the 1850s, many embraced free-labor ideology.

From Revival to Reform

How did religious revival movements lead to social reform?

Ministers and preachers in the Second Great Awakening raised hope for their audiences that the second coming of Jesus Christ was at hand—as long as listeners were able to renounce sin and purge society of sinful behaviors such as drinking, swearing, and even slavery. Revivalists stressed human perfectibility and promoted self-improvement. They preached that there was a direct link between how people lived and whether they would enter God's Kingdom, and in so doing, inspired social and moral reform. Women were often a major force in reform movements, expanding their domestic roles in the home into efforts to counteract the evils of the market economy. Reform goals included reformatories for wayward youth, orphan asylums, rehabilitation for criminals, temperance, and improvements in education.

Utopian Experiments

What were the goals of utopian communities?

Often inspired by religious revivalism, the utopian movement sought to hold the line on the rapid social change that members found disturbing, in particular, the rising market economy's excessive individualism. Some dreamed of creating a new social order; others wanted to recapture the supposed communal nature of the past and at the same time reshape marriage, child rearing, and other social arrangements. The Shakers, for example, built a profitable community around agriculture and handcrafts, but also abolished individual families in favor of men and women living in separate quarters and sharing leadership. The Oneida community centered on communal property ownership, communal child rearing, and "complex marriage" in which all men were married to all women. The Fourierists included writers and intellectuals who inspired an American renaissance in literature and the arts, with Brook Farm in West Roxbury, Massachusetts, their most famous community. During its brief existence, the community

embraced transcendentalism, the notion that the physical world is secondary to the spiritual realm.

Abolitionism

How did evangelicalism transform the antislavery movement?

Abolitionism dates back to the nation's earliest days, when efforts to end slavery were initiated by both free blacks and elite whites. After 1830, however, evangelical abolitionists seeking to eradicate America's sins focused on slavery with renewed vigor. The activist and newspaper editor William Lloyd Garrison led a new, more radical strain of abolitionism known as "immediatism," which called for the immediate and complete end of slavery without compensating slave owners. Immediatists shared the evangelical belief that people determined their spiritual fate through good or evil acts and that by ending slavery, they could bring about the millennium, or Christ's return to earth. These abolitionists welcomed women and African Americans to the movement, inviting former slaves to serve as speakers and encouraging women to not only join but serve on executive committees, a controversial move that ultimately led to the split of the abolitionist movement in 1840.

Suggestions for Further Reading

Jeanne Boydston, *Home and Work: Housework, Wages, and the Ideology of Labor in the Early Republic* (1990)

Nancy Cott, *The Bonds of Womanhood: "Women's Sphere" in New England, 1780–1835* (1977)

Daniel Walker Howe, *What Hath God Wrought: The Transformation of America, 1815–1848* (2007)

Mary Kelley, *Learning to Stand and Speak: Women, Education, and Public Life in America's Republic* (2006)

Bruce Laurie, *Artisans into Workers: Labor in Nineteenth-Century America* (1989)

Steven Mintz, *Moralists and Modernizers: America's Pre–Civil War Reformers* (1995)

Carol Sheriff, *The Artificial River: The Erie Canal and the Paradox of Progress, 1817–1862* (1996)

Christine Stansell, *City of Women: Sex and Class in New York, 1789–1860* (1986)

Melvyn Stokes and Stephen Conway, eds., *The Market Revolution in America: Social, Political, and Religious Expressions, 1800–1880* (1996)

George Rogers Taylor, *The Transportation Revolution, 1815–1860* (1951)

The Contested West

1815–1860

To eight-year-old Henry Clay Bruce, moving west was an adventure. In April 1844, the Virginia boy began a 1,500-mile, two-month trip to his new home in Missouri. Henry marveled at the beautiful terrain, impressive towns, and steamboat ride from Louisville to St. Louis. Once in Missouri, Henry noticed how much the West differed from the East. Farms were farther apart, and the countryside abounded with wild fruits, game, and fish. Still, rattlesnakes, wolves, and vicious hogs kept Henry and his playmates close to home.

A slave, Henry made the trip with his mother and siblings after his owner, Pettis Perkinson, decided to seek a fresh start in the West. Perkinson and three other white Virginians crammed their families, slaves, and whatever belongings they could fit into three wagons. In Missouri, Pettis resided with his brother, who—according to Henry—readily yelled at and whipped his own slaves. Henry's first year in Missouri was as carefree as a slave child's life could be. The boy fished, hunted (with dogs, not guns), and gathered prairie chickens' eggs. But by age nine, Henry was hired out, first to a brickmaker, then to a tobacco factory. He worked sunup to sundown, and when he failed to satisfy his bosses, he was whipped.

Meanwhile, Pettis Perkinson, unenamored with Missouri, returned to Virginia, later summoning some of his slaves, including Henry. Slaves' work was less rigorous in Virginia, but that did not compensate for leaving loved ones behind in Missouri. Soon Pettis Perkinson again grew weary of Virginia and renewed his quest for opportunity in the West, this time in Mississippi, where his sister lived. But cotton plantation life suited neither Henry nor his master, who now decided—to his slaves' joy—to give Missouri another chance.

Two years later, Perkinson headed for Texas. Henry, now in his late teens, and his brothers refused to go. Although livid, Pettis Perkinson abandoned his plans rather than contend with recalcitrant slaves. Henry became the foreman on Perkinson's Missouri farm, where he remained until escaping during the Civil War to the free state of Kansas. Finally, Henry Clay Bruce found the opportunity and freedom that had led so many westward.

In 1820, about 20 percent of the nation's population lived west of the Appalachian Mountains. By 1860, nearly 50 percent did. Most whites and free blacks moved west seeking better opportunities. Easterners envisioned in the West enormous tracts of fertile, uncultivated land, or, beginning in the late 1840s, gold or silver mines. Some saw opportunities for lumbering or ranching or for selling goods or services to farmers, miners, lumbermen, and cattlemen.

For some white Americans, mostly southerners, the ability to own slaves in the West signaled the epitome of their own freedom. For other northerners and southerners, slavery's westward expansion frustrated dreams for a new beginning in a region free from what they saw as slavery's degrading influence on white labor. Northerners often set their sights on the Oregon Territory, where they hoped to find agricultural prosperity in a land free from blacks, enslaved and free.

Men often decided to go west without consulting their wives and children, and slaves' wishes received less consideration. Nor did western settlers consider the impact of their migration on Indian peoples living there on lands they had occupied for generations, or since being relocated by the U.S. government.

Beyond removing Indians, the federal government made laws regulating settlement and the establishment of territorial governments, surveyed and fixed prices on public lands, sold those lands, invested in transportation routes, and established a military presence.

In the 1820s, the Mexican government, too, encouraged Anglo-American settlement in the West along its northern borderlands, which it would later regret. U.S. settlers vied with the region's other inhabitants—Indians, Hispanics, and people of mixed heritage—for land and natural resources. A decade later, Mexico's northern province of Texas declared its independence and sought annexation by the United States. Thus began heightened tensions between the United States and Mexico, and within the United States as Texas's future became entangled with slavery.

Human interactions in the West involved cooperation and conflict. But with each passing decade, conflict—between expectations and reality, between people with different aspirations and worldviews—would increasingly define daily life.

As you read this chapter, keep the following questions in mind:

- **How did conditions and tensions in the East influence western migration and settlement?**

- **How did public, private, and individual initiatives converge to shape the West's development?**

- **What motivated cooperation in the West, and what spurred conflict?**

The West in the American Imagination

What were the myths that helped shape white Americans' perceptions of the West?

For historian Frederick Jackson Turner, writing in the late nineteenth century, the western frontier, with its abundance of free land, was the "meeting point between savagery and civilization." It bred American democracy, shaped the American character, and made the United States exceptional. Modern historians generally eschew the notion of

Chronology

1812	General Land Office established	1834	McCormick reaper patented
1820	Price lowered on public lands	1836	Lone Star Republic founded
1821	Santa Fe Trail charted		U.S. Army Corps of Topographical Engineers established
	Mexico's independence	1840–60	250,000 to 500,000 migrants travel overland
1823	Mexico allows Stephen Austin to settle U.S. citizens	1841	Log Cabin Bill
1824	Congressional General Survey Act		Texas annexed (See Chapter 12)
	Jedediah Smith's South Pass publicized	1846–48	War with Mexico (Chapter 12)
	Indian Office established	1847	Mormons settle Great Salt Lake valley
1825–32	*Empresario* contracts signed	1848	California gold discovered
1826	Fredonia rebellion fails	1849–50s	Migrants stream into Great Plains and Far West
1830	Indian Removal Act (see Chapter 9)	1857–58	Mormons and U.S. Army in armed conflict
1830–46	Comanche, Navajo, and Apache raiders devastate northern Mexican states	1862	Homestead Act
1832	Black Hawk War		

American exceptionalism, stressing instead the deep and complex connections between the United States and the rest of the world. Although today's scholars reject the racialist assumptions of Turner's definition of *frontier*, some see continued value in the term to signify a meeting place of different cultures. Others see the West as a place, not a process, though they disagree over what delineates it.

Defining the West
For early-nineteenth-century Americans of European descent, the West included anything west of the Appalachian Mountains. It represented the future—a place offering economic and social betterment, typically through landownership. The West's seeming abundance of land meant that anyone could hope to own a farm and achieve independence. Men who already owned land, like Pettis Perkinson, looked westward for cheaper, bigger, and more fertile landholdings. With the discovery of gold in California in 1848, the West became a place to strike it rich. Others went west by force, including slaves and Indians removed from their eastern homelands by the U.S. military under the Indian Removal Act of 1830.

To others, the notion of the West would have been baffling. Emigrants from Mexico and Central or South America traveled north to get to what European Americans called the West. Chinese nationals traveled eastward to California. Many Indians simply considered the West home. Other Indians and French Canadians journeyed southward to the West. All arrived in the western portion of the North American continent because of a combination of factors pushing and pulling them.

Frontier Literature

For European Americans, Daniel Boone became the archetypical frontiersman, whose daring individualism opened the Eden-like West for hardworking freedom lovers. Through biographies, Boone became a familiar figure in American and European households. The mythical Boone lived in the wilderness and shrank from society. He overpowered bears and Indians and became the pathfinder for civilization. As a friend wrote, Boone "has been the instrument of opening the road to millions of the human family … to a Land flowing with milk and honey." By borrowing biblical language—the land of milk and honey denoting the Promised Land—Boone's friend suggested that Boone was Moses-like, leading his people to a land of abundance.

With the invention of the steam press in the early 1830s, western adventure stories became cheap and widely read. Davy Crockett, another real-life figure turned into mythical hero, was featured in many of them. Crockett first fought the Creeks under Andrew Jackson but later championed Indian rights. Still, after his death

MAP 11.1
Westward Expansion, 1800–1860

Through exploration, purchase, war, and treaty, the United States became a continental nation, stretching from the Atlantic to the Pacific. Source: Copyright © Cengage Learning 2015 defending the Alamo mission during Texas's fight for independence (1836), Crockett nonetheless appeared in stories portraying the West as violent, a place where one escaped civilized society and fought Indians and Mexicans. But even in this myth, the American West symbolized what white Americans saw as their nation's core value: freedom.

Western Art

Artists' images often revealed more about white Americans' ideals than about the West itself. In these portrayals, the West was sometimes an untamed wilderness inhabited by savages (noble or otherwise), and sometimes a cultivated garden, a land of milk and honey where the Jeffersonian agrarian dream was realized.

The first Anglo-American artists to travel west were Samuel Seymour and Titian Ramsay Peale, whom the federal government hired to accompany explorer Stephen H. Long to the Rocky Mountains in 1830. They pioneered an influential art genre: facsimiles in government reports. Between 1840 and 1860, Congress published nearly sixty works on western exploration, featuring hundreds of lithographs and engravings of plants, animals, and people. Some reports became best sellers. The government distributed more than 53,000 copies of its popular twelve-volume Pacific Railway Survey (1855–1860), which helped easterners visualize the continent's western reaches.

Sometimes government reports made telling alterations to the paintings they included. When Richard Kern accompanied explorer James H. Simpson in 1849 to the Southwest, he painted a Navajo man in a submissive pose. The reproduction transformed the man's pose into a rebellious one. In other cases, the government reports changed artists' depictions of Indian-occupied landscapes into empty terrain free for the taking.

Artists' cultural assumptions colored their portrayals of the West, too, and commercial artists produced what they thought the public craved. When **George Catlin** traveled west immediately following the Indian Removal Act of 1830, he painted the region with a moral in mind. Indians came in two varieties—those who preserved their original, almost noble qualities of freedom and moderation, and those who, after coming in contact with whites, had become "dissolute." Indians, he implied, benefited from removal from white Americans' corrupting influence.

In one of his most famous portraits, George Catlin painted Wi-Jun-Jon, an Assiniboine Indian, both before and after he had mingled with white men. In the "before" stance, the Indian is a dignified, peace-pipe-bearing warrior; in the "after" portrait, the "corrupted" Indian has abandoned dignity for vanity and his peace pipe for a cigar.

George Catlin American painter who traveled throughout the West and produced numerous portraits of Native Americans that reflected his fascination with and beliefs about them.

Countering the Myths

But western realities often clashed with promoters' promises, and disappointed settlers sometimes tried to clarify matters for future migrants. Rebecca Burlend and her son were lured to Illinois by a fellow Englishman's letters extolling "a land flowing with milk and honey." Later, Burlend and her son wrote *A True Picture of Emigration* (1831), which described Illinois' hardships—intemperate weather, difficult working conditions, and swindlers. Her account sought not to discourage emigration, but to substitute a realistic for a rosy description.

Expansion and Resistance in the Trans-Appalachian West

What made the Midwest especially appealing to white settlers?

In the 1820s and 1830s, settlers streamed into the Old Northwest and the Old Southwest by foot, horseback, wagon, canal boat, steamboat, or a combination of means. Many people, like Pettis Perkinson and his slaves, moved several times, and when opportunities failed to materialize, some returned home.

Both the Old Northwest and the Old Southwest saw population explosions during the early nineteenth century. While the Old Southwest grew by 50 percent each decade, the Northwest's population grew exponentially. In 1790, the Northwest region's white population numbered just a few hundred. By 1860, nearly 7 million people called it home. Between 1810 and 1830, Ohio's population more than quadrupled, while Indiana and Illinois grew fourteenfold and thirteenfold, respectively. Michigan's population multiplied fiftyfold between 1820 and 1850. Migration accounted for most of this growth. Once in the Old Northwest, people did not stay put. By the 1840s, more people left Ohio than moved into it. Geographic mobility, the search for better opportunities, and connections to the market economy defined the region that became known as the Midwest.

Deciding Where to Move

Moving west meant leaving behind worn-out soil and settled areas with little land available for purchase. The journey was arduous; the labor of clearing new lands, backbreaking. The West was a land of opportunity but also of uncertainty. What if the soil proved less fertile than anticipated? What if neighbors proved unfriendly, or worse? Like Pettis Perkinson, people often relocated where they had relatives or friends and traveled with acquaintances. They chose areas with familiar climates. Migrants also settled in ethnic communities or with people of similar religious affiliations. As a result, the Midwest was—in the words of two historians—"more like an ethnic and cultural checkerboard than the proverbial melting pot."

The legal status of slavery influenced where people settled. Some white southerners, tired of the planter elite's power, sought areas free from slavery—or at least where there were few plantations. Many others went west to improve their chances of owning slaves, or of purchasing additional slaves. White northerners hoped to distance themselves from slavery as well as from free blacks. In the 1850s, many midwestern states passed "black laws" prohibiting African Americans, free or enslaved, from living within their boundaries. Ironically, free blacks migrated west to free themselves from eastern prejudice. Enslaved people moved west in enormous numbers after 1815. Some traveled with their owners; others with slave traders. When white parents gave their westward-bound children slaves, they tore those slaves from their own spouses, children, or parents. For those traveling with slave traders, their first destination in the West was the slave pen, often in New Orleans, where they were auctioned to the highest bidder, who became their new owner and took them farther west. Nonetheless, some slaves took advantage of frontier conditions—vast forests, inconsistent law enforcement, and the proximity of Native American communities willing to harbor runaway slaves—to seize their freedom.

Between 1815 and 1860, few western migrants settled on the Great Plains, a region reserved for Indians until the 1850s, and few easterners risked the overland journey to California and Oregon before the transcontinental railroad's

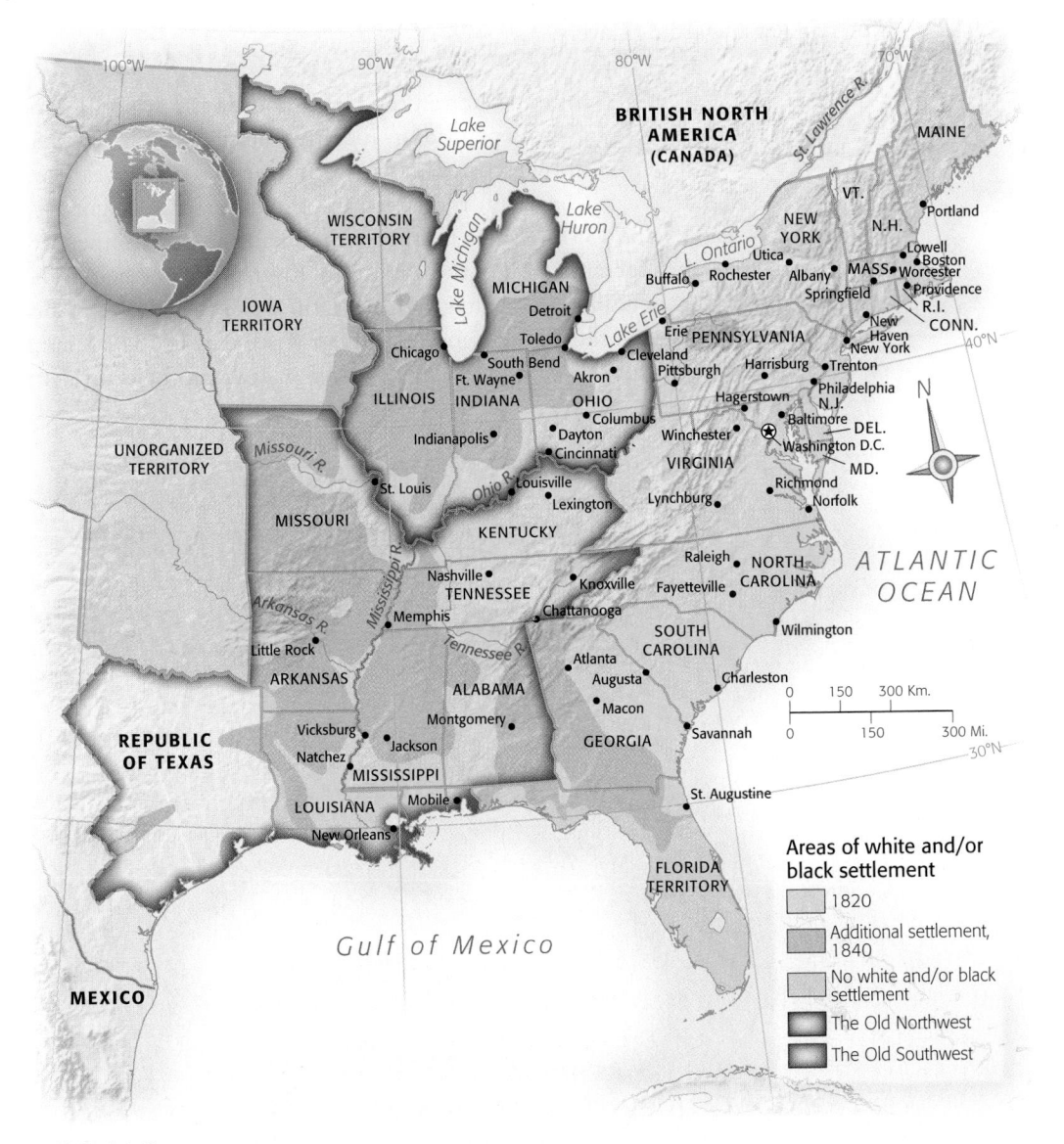

MAP 11.2

Settlement in the Old Southwest and Old Northwest, 1820 and 1840

Removal of Indians and a growing transportation network opened up land to white and black settlers in the regions known as the Old Southwest and the Old Northwest, as the U.S. population grew from 9.6 million in 1820 to 17.1 million in 1840. Source: Copyright © Cengage Learning 2015 completion in 1869. At first the Southwest appealed most to settlers. But beginning in the 1820s, the Midwest drew more settlers with its better-developed transportation routes, democratic access to economic markets, smaller African American population, cheaper average landholding, and climatic similarity to New England and northern Europe. The Old Northwest's thriving transportation hubs also made good first stops for western migrants lacking cash to purchase land. They found work unloading canal boats, planting and harvesting wheat, grinding wheat into flour, sawing trees into lumber—or, more often, cobbling together a combination of seasonal jobs. With the Old Northwest's population growing quickly, white southerners worried increasingly about congressional representation and laws regarding slavery.

Indian Removal and Resistance

In the Midwest and the Southwest, white settlement depended on Indian removal. Even as the U.S. Army escorted Indians from the Old Southwest (see Chapter 9), the federal government arranged eighty-six treaties between 1829 and 1851 in which northeastern Indian nations relinquished land titles in exchange for lands west of the Mississippi River. Some northern Indians evaded removal, including the Miamis in Indiana, the Ottawas and Chippewas in the upper Midwest, and the Winnebagos in southern Wisconsin. In 1840, Miami chiefs acceded to pressure to exchange 500,000 acres in Indiana for equivalent

In 1834, Karl Bodmer painted a farm on the Illinois prairie, depicting the more permanent, if still modest, structures that farmers built after the initial urgency to clear fields for cultivation had subsided.

Joslyn Art Museum, Omaha, Nebraska

acreage in Indian Country. Under the treaty, their people had five years to move or be escorted out by federal troops. But about half of the Miami nation dodged the soldiers—and many of those who trekked to Indian Country later returned. In Wisconsin, some Winnebagos eluded removal or returned to Wisconsin after being escorted west by soldiers.

Black Hawk War

In a series of treaties between 1804 and 1830, Sauks (or "Sacs") and Fox leaders exchanged lands in northwestern Illinois and southwestern Wisconsin for lands across the Mississippi River in Iowa Territory. Black Hawk, a Sauk warrior, disputed the treaties' validity and in 1832 led Sauk and Fox families to Illinois, panicking white settlers. The state's governor activated the militia, who were joined by militia from surrounding states and territories and U.S. Army regular soldiers. Over several months, hundreds of Indians and dozens of whites died under often gruesome circumstances in the Black Hawk War. As the Sauks and Fox tried to flee across the Mississippi River, American soldiers fired indiscriminately. Those who survived the river crossing met gunfire from Lakota (Sioux), now allied with the Americans.

Black Hawk surrendered, and U.S. officials impressed upon him and other leaders the futility of resistance. After being imprisoned, then sent to Washington, D.C., along a route meant to underscore the United States' immense size and population, and imprisoned again, the Indians were returned home. The Black Hawk War ended militant Indian uprisings in the Old Northwest.

Selling the West

Land speculators, developers of "paper towns" (ones existing on paper only), steamboat companies, and manufacturers of farming implements promoted the Midwest as a tranquil place of unbounded opportunity. Land proprietors emphasized the region's connections to eastern customs and markets. They knew that, when families moved west, they did not seek to escape civilization.

Western settlement generally followed connections to national and international markets. Eastern farmers, looking to shed tired soil or tenancy, sought fertile lands for commercial crops. Labor-saving devices, such as Cyrus McCormick's reaper (1834) and John Deere's steel plow (1837), made the West more alluring. McCormick, a Virginia inventor, patented a horse-drawn reaper that allowed two men to harvest the same number of acres of wheat that previously required between four and sixteen men. The reaper's efficiency achieved its greatest payoffs on the large, flat prairie lands, so McCormick relocated his factory to Chicago in 1847. Without John Deere's steel plow, which could break through tough grass and roots without constant cleaning, "breaking the plains" might not have been possible.

Clearing the Land

After locating a suitable land claim, settlers constructed a rudimentary cabin if none already existed. Time did not permit elaborate structures; settlers first had to clear the land. At the rate of five to ten acres a year, depending on a family's size, the average family needed ten years to fully clear a farm. Prairie land took less time.

Whereas farming attracted families, lumbering and, later, mining appealed to single young men (although employers regarded married men as the most stable workforce, they only wanted "good Families without children," whose wives would work as cooks or laundresses). By the 1840s, as eastern forests became depleted, northeastern lumber companies and laborers migrated to Wisconsin, Michigan, and Minnesota. Recently arrived Scandinavians and French Canadians also worked in the lumber industry. As the Great Lakes forests thinned, lumbermen moved again—some to the Gulf States' pine forests, some to Canada, and some to the Far West, where Mexicans in California and British in Canada had already established flourishing lumber industries. With the rapid growth of California's cities following the **Gold Rush** of 1849, timber's demand soared, drawing midwestern lumbermen farther west.

Gold Rush After an American carpenter discovered gold in the foothills of California's Sierra Nevada range in 1848, Americans and people from around the world moved to California to look for gold.

Midwestern cities nurtured the surrounding countryside's settlement. Steamboats turned river settlements like Louisville and Cincinnati into commercial centers, while Chicago, Detroit, and Cleveland grew up on the Great Lakes' banks. By the mid-nineteenth century, Chicago, with its railroads, stockyards, and grain elevators, dominated the region's economy; western farmers transported livestock and grain by rail to that city, where pigs became packed meat and grain became flour before being shipped east. The promise of future flour and pigs gave rise to commodities markets. Some of the world's most sophisticated and speculative economic practices took place in Chicago.

The Federal Government and Westward Expansion

How did the federal government sponsor and speed up westward expansion?

Few white Americans considered settling in the West before the region had been explored, surveyed, secured, and "civilized," which meant Indian removal and the establishment of churches, businesses, and American legal structures. Wide-scale settlement depended on the federal government's sponsorship.

The Fur Trade

Fur trappers were among the first white Americans in the trans-Appalachian West, but their lives bore faint resemblance to their mythical representation as mountain men who dared to go where whites never trod. Fur trappers lived among Indians, became multilingual, and often married Indian women. Indian women transformed animal carcasses into finished pelts, and they smoothed trade relations between husbands and their native communities. The offspring of such marriages—métis or mestizos (people of mixed Indian and European heritage)—added to the West's cultural complexity.

The fur trade was an international business, with pelts from America reaching Europe and Asia. Until the 1820s, British companies dominated the trade, but American ventures prospered in the 1820s and 1830s. The American Fur Company made John Jacob Astor—who managed his business from New York City—the nation's wealthiest man. Beginning in the 1820s, trappers and traders met annually for a "rendezvous"—a multiday gathering where they traded fur for guns, tobacco,

Explorers' routes

→ Pike, 1805
-→ Pike, 1806–1807
→ Long, 1819–1820

Fremont

→ 1842
-→ 1843
→ 1845
-→ 1848
→ 1854

UTE Major Indian tribe, 1850
—— U.S. boundaries, by 1854

MAP 11.3

Western Indians and Routes of Exploration

Although western explorers believed they were discovering new routes and places, Indians had long lived in most of the areas through which explorers traveled. Source: Robert Utley, *The Indian Frontier of the American West, 1846–1890*, University of New Mexico Press, 1984, p. 5. Reprinted by permission of the University of New Mexico Press. © Cengage Learning 2015

and beads that they could exchange with Indians. Modeled on Indian gatherings, the rendezvous united Americans, Indians, Mexicans, and people of mixed heritage to trade, gamble, and socialize.

By 1840, the American fur trade was fading. Beavers had been overhunted and fashions had shifted, with silk supplanting beaver fur for hats. The traders' legacy includes resource extraction and depletion, introducing native peoples to devastating diseases, and developing trails across the trans-Mississippi West.

Santa Fe Trail Trading route from St. Louis, Missouri, to Santa Fe, New Mexico, that enabled commerce to expand its reach farther west.

Transcontinental Exploration

A desire for quicker and safer routes for transporting goods to trading posts drove much early exploration. In 1821, merchant William Becknell helped chart the **Santa Fe Trail** running between Missouri and Santa Fe, New Mexico, where it connected to the Chihuahua Trail running into Mexico, allowing American and Mexican merchants to develop a vibrant trade. In 1824, fur trader Jedediah Smith rediscovered the South Pass, a twenty-mile break in the Rocky Mountains in present-day Wyoming previously known only to Native Americans and some Pacific Fur Company trappers. The South Pass became the route followed by most overland travelers to California and Oregon.

Lewis and Clark's Corps of Discovery was the first of many federally sponsored expeditions to chart the trans-Mississippi West. These expeditions sought to establish cordial relations with Indian groups with whom Americans might trade or enter military alliances. Some were scientific, exploring the region's native inhabitants, flora, and fauna. But they were always commercial. Like Lewis and Clark, later explorers hoped to locate land, water, and rail routes that would allow American businessmen and farmers to trade nationally and internationally.

In 1805, the U.S. Army dispatched Zebulon Pike to find the Mississippi River's source and a navigable route west. He was instructed to research natural resources and native peoples and foster diplomatic relationships with Indian leaders. Before the Supreme Court ruled in *Johnson v. M'Intosh* (1823) that Indians did not own land but merely had a "right of occupancy," government officials instructed Pike and other explorers to purchase lands for military garrisons.

Although Pike failed to identify the Mississippi's source and had limited success in purchasing land, he gathered important information. When Pike and his men wandered into Spanish territory to the south, military officials held Pike captive for several months in Mexico, inadvertently showing him areas that he might not have otherwise explored. After his release, Pike wrote about a potential market in furs and precious metals in southwestern cities. The province of Tejas (Texas), with its fertile soil, enchanted him. But Pike dismissed other northern provinces of Mexico, whose boundaries stretched to present-day northern Nevada and Utah, as unsuitable for human habitation. Although nomadic Indians might sustain themselves there, he explained, the region was unfit for civilized people.

John C. Frémont Explorer who played a role in a California rebellion against Mexico; later a senator and presidential candidate and force in national politics.

Link to Frémont, The Exploring Expedition to the Rocky Mountains, Oregon, and California

In 1820, army explorer Stephen Long similarly deemed modern-day Oklahoma, Kansas, and Nebraska as "the Great American Desert," incapable of cultivation. Until the 1850s, when a transcontinental railroad was planned, this "desert" was reserved for Indian settlement. In 1838, Congress established the U.S. Army Corps of Topographical Engineers to systematically explore the West. As second lieutenant in that corps, **John C. Frémont** undertook three expeditions to the region between the upper Mississippi and Missouri rivers, the Rockies, the Great Basin, Oregon, and California. He helped survey the Oregon Trail. Aided by his wife, Jessie Benton Frémont, he published best-selling accounts of his explorations. The Corps of Topographical Engineers' most significant contributions came in the 1850s with its surveying of possible routes for a transcontinental railroad.

A Military Presence The army also helped ready the West for settlement. With the General Survey Act of 1824, Congress empowered the military to chart transportation improvements vital to military protection or commercial growth. Army engineers helped design state- and privately sponsored roads, canals, and railroads, and army soldiers cleared forests and laid roadbeds. A related bill, also in 1824, authorized the army to improve the Ohio and Mississippi rivers; a later amendment did the same for the Missouri.

By the 1850s, 90 percent of the U.S. military was stationed west of the Mississippi River. When Indians refused to relinquish their lands, the army escorted them westward; when they harmed whites, the army waged war. The army sometimes destroyed crops and buildings of white squatters refusing to vacate lands settled illegally. But, primarily, the army assisted overland migration. Army forts intimidated Indians, defended settlers from Indian attacks, and supplied information and provisions. In theory, the army was also supposed to protect Indians by driving settlers off Indian lands and enforcing laws prohibiting alcohol sales to Indians. Yet the army's small size relative to the territory made it virtually impossible to do so.

The Office of Indian Affairs handled the government's other Indian interactions, including treaty negotiations, school management, and trade oversight. Created in 1824 as part of the War Department, the Indian Office cooperated with the military in removing Indians from lands necessary for American expansion and in protecting citizens who relocated in the West. In 1849 the Indian Office became part of the newly established Department of the Interior, and soon shifted from removal to civilization, through a reservation system. Whereas some Indians accepted reservations as protection from white incursion, others rejected them, sometimes sparking deadly intratribal disagreements.

Public Lands The federal government controlled vast tracts of land, procured either from the states' cessions of their western claims after the Revolution or through treaties with foreign powers, including Indian nations. The General Land Office, established in 1812 as part of the Treasury Department, handled those lands' distribution. Its earliest policies divided western lands into 640-acre tracts to be auctioned at a minimum of $2 an acre. These policies favored speculators—who bought up millions of acres—over individual, cash-poor farmers. Many settlers became squatters, prompting Congress in 1820 to lower land prices to $1.25 per acre and to sell tracts as small as 80 acres. Twelve years later, it sold 40-acre tracts. Yet it demanded that the land be bought outright; few would-be western settlers (particularly after the Panic of 1819) had enough cash to purchase government land. Because speculators sold land on credit, many small-time farmers bought from them at inflated prices.

Farmers pressed for a federal policy of preemption—that is, the right to settle on land without obtaining title, to improve it, and buy it later at the legal minimum price ($1.25 an acre). Some states offered lands through preemption, and Congress sometimes authorized preemption of federal lands in the 1820s and 1830s. But the first general preemption law, the so-called Log Cabin Bill, came in 1841, and it applied only to surveyed land. Preemption extended to unsurveyed

Gold in California

When James Marshall discovered gold in Sutter's Mill, California, in January 1848, word spread quickly worldwide. Within a year, tens of thousands of adventurers from other countries rushed to California, making it the most cosmopolitan place in North America.

In an era before the telegraph crossed the oceans, the news traveled surprisingly fast. Mexicans heard first. Next, word spread to Chile, Peru, and throughout South America; then across the Pacific to Hawai'i, China, and Australia; and then to Europe—Ireland, France, and the German states. Overland travelers brought the news south to Baja California and Sonora in Mexico. By spring 1849, some six thousand Mexicans were panning for gold. Many of the Mexicans came seasonally, spreading news of California on every trip home.

The newspaper *Honolulu Polynesian* announced California gold in the kingdom on June 24, 1848.

Regular steamship service between Hawai'i and California transported gold seekers as early as 1853.

A ship brought news of California gold discoveries to Valparaiso, Chile, in August 1848. People in Chile's cities talked feverishly about gold, and newspapers reported rumors of California's overnight riches. Before year's end, two thousand Chileans had left for California.

Word of gold and California reached Australia in December 1848, and by 1850 every ship in Sydney Harbour was California-bound. News reached China in mid-1848. Widespread poverty and gold's allure prompted many Chinese to migrate. By the mid-1850s, one in five gold miners was Chinese.

In 1850, the new state of California had nearly 40 percent foreign-born inhabitants, the majority non-European. Through word of mouth, rumor, letters home, and newspaper reports, the 1848 discovery of gold linked California to millions of ordinary people around the globe.

The Art Archive at Art Resource, NY

This 1855 Frank Marryat drawing of a San Francisco saloon dramatizes the international nature of the California gold rush. Like theater performers, the patrons of the saloon dress their parts as Yankees, Mexicans, Asians, and South Americans.

lands with the **Homestead Act** of 1862, which provided that land would be provided free to any U.S. citizen (or foreigner who declared the intention of becoming a citizen), after residing on it for five years and improving it. Alternatively, settlers could buy land outright at $1.25 an acre after six months of residency, which allowed them to use the land as collateral for loans for additional land, farming supplies, or machinery.

Homestead Act Passed in 1862, it embodied the Republican Party's ideal of "free soil, free labor, free men" by granting 160 acres of public land to settlers who resided on it for five years and improved it.

The Southwestern Borderlands

What factors led white Americans to settle in Texas?

Along the Louisiana Territory's southwestern border lay vast provinces controlled mostly by the Comanches and other Indians but claimed first by Spain and then—after 1821—by the newly independent nation of Mexico. **New Mexico**, with commercial centers in Albuquerque and Santa Fe, remained under Mexican control until the United States conquered the territory during its War with Mexico. Texas became an autonomous state in 1824, giving it greater independence from federal authorities than New Mexico enjoyed. This situation fostered Texas's struggle for national independence and then annexation to the United States, which returned slavery to the forefront of American political debate (see Chapter 12).

New Mexico Former Spanish colony in the upper Rio Grande Valley that became part of Mexico after 1821.

Southwestern Slavery

Slavery in the Southwest was centuries old. Yet as practiced by indigenous peoples—Comanches, Apaches, Kiowas, Navajos, Utes, and Pueblos—and by Spaniards, slavery centered on capturing women and children, who were then assimilated into their captors' communities, where they provided labor and status while fostering economic and diplomatic exchanges with their former communities.

This system was built on racial mixing—a practice anathema to most white Americans. As white slaveholders from the Southeast pushed into Mexican territory during the 1820s and 1830s, they often justified their conquest in racial terms. The region's Hispanic settlers, they reasoned, had been rendered lazy and barbarous by racial intermixing and were thus destined to be supplanted.

The New Mexican Frontier

When Mexico gained independence from Spain in 1821, New Mexico's Hispanic population outnumbered the indigenous Pueblo peoples by three to one. There were 28,000 Hispanics, including people born in Spain and *criollos*, people born in New Spain to parents of Spanish descent. Most New Mexicans engaged in irrigated agriculture, but to the south, larger farms and ranches predominated. Rancheros became wealthy selling wool and corn in distant markets, and from using unpaid laborers, often relatives, bound by debt. Threatened by the province's raiding Indian tribes—Apaches, Utes, Navajos, and Comanches—Hispanics, Pueblos, and mestizos sometimes united in defense. But their numerical superiority allowed Hispanics to seize many Pueblo villages and lands in the rich northern river valleys.

The Santa Fe Trail caused a commercial explosion in New Mexico, doubling the value of imports in two years. Whereas the Spanish tried to keep foreigners out, the Mexican government offered enormous land grants to Anglo-American and French entrepreneurs, hoping they would develop the region's industry and agriculture and strengthen commercial ties with the United States.

Although commercial relationships grew, few Americans settled in New Mexico during the 1820s and 1830s. The best lands were occupied by Indians and Hispanics. And Americans seeking cheap, fertile land could find it in Texas.

The Texas Frontier

In 1821, indigenous Indians remained the dominant group in Texas, though there were also Hispanics, Anglos, mestizos, and immigrant Indians. Of the thirty thousand indigenous people, most were Comanches. Texas was part of what one historian has called the Comanche Empire, an enormous territory from northern Mexico to Louisiana that the Comanches dominated through kinship, trade, diplomacy, and violence. People of European heritage were a small presence in Texas in 1821. Hispanic peoples had been there since the 1500s, establishing missions and presidios, but by 1820, they numbered only five thousand.

MAP 11.4
Mexico's Far North
What is now considered the American Southwest was made up of the northern provinces of Mexico until the United States conquered the territory during the Mexican War (1846–1848). Source: Copyright © Cengage Learning 2015

Most raised livestock on ranches, while others traded with Indians. They formed a distinctive identity as **Tejanos** (or Texans) rather than as Spaniards. Many intermarried with Indians.

After the War of 1812, Anglo-Americans started entering Texas, where they sought furs, silver, or adventure. They traded manufactured goods—guns, ammunition, and kettles—for animal hides, horses, and mules, quickly supplanting the Tejanos as the Indians' trading partners. Although some Anglos settled in Texas, most traveled the Santa Fe and Chihuahua trails without settling.

Tejanos A native Texan of Mexican descent.

The Comanche Empire

As Indians competed for resources, the southwestern borderlands experienced intermittent but brutal violence. Mounted on horses, the Comanches hunted bison, took captives, and stole horses, livestock, and crops from their enemies. Smaller Indian groups, such as the Wichitas and Caddos, grew corn, beans, squash, and pumpkin. When crops failed, farmers turned to bison hunting, sometimes causing conflict with the Comanches.

Tensions increased around the time of Mexican independence, when another ten thousand Indians migrated into the region. From the Old Northwest came Shawnees and Kickapoos—former members of Tecumseh's confederacy. From the Old Southwest came Cherokees, Creeks, Choctaws, Chickasaws, and Seminoles, some with African American slaves. Indian newcomers vied for land and animals, often clashing with established groups. Some immigrant Indians, having adopted Anglo clothing and racial ideologies, dismissed as "savage" the indigenous Indians who hunted buffalo, wore skins, and did not regard land as a commodity.

Smithsonian American Art Museum, Washington, DC/Art Resource, NY

The Comanche controlled a vast empire along the Louisiana Territory's southwestern border with Mexico. Here, in a George Catlin painting from 1834, Comanche women dress robes and dry meat.

Paintings and Cultural Impressions

Although few people of Spanish descent settled in Texas, those who did developed a distinctive and proud cultural identity. Calling themselves Tejanos, they adapted their inherited culture—music, dances, and cuisine—to their new surroundings. In the painting below of an 1844 celebration in San Antonio, French-born painter Theodore Gentilz captures the mixture of cultural carryovers and frontier adaptations. Which elements of the scene seem reminiscent of life in Spain or in the colonial capital of Mexico City? Which elements seem to be adaptations to life along a cultural frontier and political borderland? Which elements of the painting seem to celebrate Tejano culture, and which, if any, seem critical of it? If you were using this painting as a source of information about Tejano culture and its influence on contemporary music and dance, what else would you want to know about the artist and the scene he has captured?

Although the musician in Gentilz's painting is playing the fiddle, other artistic depictions record the widespread use of the guitar, which helped give rise to the corrido, a folk ballad whose legacy is still apparent in today's country and western music.

bpk, Berlin/Art Resource, NY

Daughters of the Republic of Texas Library

Theodore Gentilz arrived in Texas in the 1840s and soon began portraying the region's culture with his paintbrush. Here, Tejano settlers perform the fandango, a Spanish dance.

Because violence threatened Indian removal and disrupted trade, the U.S. government brokered a treaty in 1835: the Comanches would allow immigrants onto their lands in exchange for trade opportunities. Trade soon boomed. Immigrant Indians swapped agricultural products and manufactured goods, such as rifles and ammunition, for the Comanches' meats, robes, and horses. That same year, the Comanches ended their longstanding war with the Osages. With peace came American traders. Meanwhile, the U.S. government's Indian removal continued, fueling Americans' commitment to cotton cultivation and expansionism.

American *Empresarios* A decade earlier, before Mexican independence, the Spanish worried about the security of Texas, which they considered a buffer between hostile Indians and the United States. Their solution was to populate the region. Thus when Missouri miner and trader Moses Austin approached Spanish authorities in January 1821 about settling Americans in Texas, they agreed as long as Austin brought Americans willing to assimilate into Texas society. In exchange for promising to bring three hundred Catholic families—and no slaves—Austin would receive two hundred thousand acres along the Brazos River. Before Austin could act, though, he died, and Mexico won its independence from Spain in September 1821.

Austin's son, Stephen, pursued his father's scheme, pressing the new Mexican government to honor the grant, which it did in 1823, provided that Austin renounce his American citizenship and become a Mexican national. By 1825, Stephen Austin had settled two thousand white people and four hundred "contract laborers" of African descent. With ninety-year contracts, these African Americans were essentially slaves. Austin later brought nine hundred additional families in exchange for more land.

Satisfied with the Austin experiment, in 1824 Mexico passed a Colonization Law providing land and tax incentives to future foreign settlers. The state of Coahuila y Texas specified that the head of a family could obtain up to 4,428 acres of grazing land or 177 acres of farming land. The land was cheap and could be paid for in installments over six years, with nothing due until the fourth year. Foreigners had to be upstanding Christians and permanent residents. To encourage settlers to assimilate into Mexican society, the Coahuila y Texas government provided additional land to those who married Mexican women.

Most U.S. citizens who settled in Mexico did so under an *empresario,* or immigration agent, who selected "moral" colonists, distributed lands, and enforced regulations. In exchange, he received nearly 25,000 acres of grazing land and 1,000 acres of farming land for every hundred families he settled. Between 1825 and 1832, approximately twenty-four empresario contracts (seventeen of which went to Anglo-Americans) were signed for eight thousand families. The land grants covered almost all of present-day Texas.

During the 1820s, some Anglo-Americans who emigrated to Texas felt pushed by the Panic of 1819 and pulled by cheap land and generous credit terms. Despite Mexican efforts to encourage assimilation, these Americans tended to settle in separate communities. Anglo-Americans outnumbered Tejanos two to one. Authorities worried that the transplanted Americans would try to make Texas part of the United States.

Texas Politics

In 1826, an empresario named Haden Edwards called for an independent Texas, the "Fredonia Republic." Other empresarios, seeing advantages in peaceful relations with the Mexican government, resisted Edwards's secessionist movement. Although the Fredonia revolt failed, Mexican authorities dreaded what it might foreshadow.

Consequently, in 1830 Mexican authorities terminated legal immigration from the United States while encouraging immigration from Europe and other parts of Mexico. They prohibited American slaves from entering Texas, which brought Texas in line with the rest of Mexico—where slavery had been outlawed the previous year. Yet these laws did not discourage Americans and their slaves from coming; soon they controlled most of the Texas coastline and its U.S. border. Mexican authorities repealed the anti-immigration law in 1833, reasoning that it discouraged upstanding settlers without deterring undesirables. By 1835, the non-Indian population of Texas was nearly thirty thousand, with Americans outnumbering Tejanos seven to one.

Among white Texans, some, like Stephen Austin, favored staying in Mexico but demanded more autonomy, the legalization of slavery, and free trade with the United States. Others pushed for Texas secession from Mexico and wanted annexation to the United States. In 1835, the secessionists overtook a Mexican military installation charged with collecting taxes at Galveston Bay. Austin advocated a peaceful resolution, but, suspicious, Mexican authorities jailed him for eighteen months, which converted him to the independence cause.

The Lone Star Republic

General Santa Anna Mexican president and dictator whose actions led Texans to revolt.

With discontent over Texas increasing throughout Mexico, Mexican president **General Santa Anna** declared himself dictator and marched his army toward Texas. Fearing Santa Anna would free their slaves, Texans rebelled. After initial defeats at the Alamo mission in San Antonio and at Goliad in March 1836, the Texans easily triumphed by year's end. They declared themselves the Lone Star Republic and elected **Sam Houston** as president. Their constitution legalized slavery and banned free blacks.

Sam Houston Military and political leader of Texas during and after the Texas Revolution.

Texas then faced the challenge of nation building, which to its leaders involved Indian removal. When the Indians refused to leave, Mirabeau Lamar, the nation's second president, mobilized the Texas Rangers—mounted nonuniformed militia—to drive them out through terror. The Rangers raided Indian villages, where they robbed, raped, and murdered. This "ethnic cleansing," as one historian has labeled it, ultimately cleared the land of native settlers to make room for white Americans and their African American slaves.

"War of a Thousand Deserts"

Since the early 1830s, Mexico's ten northern states had been wracked by raiding warfare perpetrated by Plains Indians—Comanches, Navajos, and Apaches. When Mexicans resisted by killing Comanches or their Kiowa allies, the Comanches escalated their violence ravishing the countryside and its inhabitants in what one historian has deemed vengeance killings. When additional Comanches fell in the course of avenging a killing, then another round of

Plains Indians, including the Apaches portrayed here, frequently and brutally raided the northern provinces of Mexico beginning in the 1830s, leading to a cycle of vengeance killings that devastated the region and made it more vulnerable to invasion by the United States Army during the War with Mexico in the mid-1840s.

revenge killing ensued. The raiders devastated Mexican settlements, where once-thriving farms became man-made "deserts."

With the Mexican government's concerns focused on U.S. and French threats, individual Mexican states responded to the raids themselves, and often turned against one another, with Mexicans killing other Mexicans. The resulting carnage fed U.S. proponents of **manifest destiny**—those who believed that racially superior (white) Americans were destined to spread their culture westward to regions inhabited by inferior races (Indians and Mexicans). The United States would use manifest destiny to justify its war with Mexico from 1846 to 1848 (see Chapter 12). When American soldiers marched to Mexico's capital with seeming ease, they did so because they traversed huge swaths of Mexican territory that had been devastated or deserted by fifteen years of Indian raiding.

manifest destiny Coined by editor John L. O'Sullivan, it was the belief that the United States was endowed by God with a mission to spread its republican government and brand of freedom and Christianity to less fortunate and uncivilized peoples; it also justified U.S. territorial expansion.

Wartime Losses and Profits

After annexing Texas in 1845, the United States, seeking further territorial expansion, waged war against Mexico. In the borderlands, as in Mexico, civilians—Indians, Tejanos, Californios, and Mexicans—lost their lives, and many suffered wartime depredations. If they aided the Mexicans, the U.S. Army destroyed their homes; if they refused aid to the Mexicans, the Mexicans destroyed their homes. An 1847 U.S. Army report acknowledged that its "wild volunteers … committed … all sorts of atrocities on the persons and property of Mexicans." After the war ended in the borderlands, violence continued, with Texas Rangers slaughtering Indians from 1847 to 1848.

Some civilians profited from the war. Farmers sold provisions and mules to the armies, peddlers sold alcohol and food to soldiers, and others set up gambling and prostitution businesses near army camps.

Cultural Frontiers in the Far West

How did the gold rush influence the development of the Far West?

Even before the United States seized expansive territory during the War with Mexico, some Americans moved to the Far West, often to California, Utah, and other places Mexico controlled. Some sought religious freedom or to convert others to Christianity, but most wanted fertile farmland.

Western Missionaries

Catholic missionaries maintained a strong presence in the Far West. In Spanish missions, priests introduced Indians to Catholic sacraments; enforced rigid rules about prayer, sexual conduct, and work; and treated them as legal minors. Indians who did not measure up were subject to corporal punishment. When they ran away, they were forcibly returned. With few options, Indians often responded to abusive practices with armed uprisings, ultimately weakening the mission system.

A Mexican law secularized the California missions in 1833, using them to organize Indian labor. Some Indians stayed at the missions; others left to farm their own land or to find employment elsewhere, but for almost all, secularization brought enhanced personal freedom despite limited legal rights.

Still, Catholic missionaries—Americans, Europeans, and converted Indians—continued ministering to immigrants, working to convert Indians. Missionaries founded schools and colleges, introduced medical services, and aided in railroad explorations.

In the Pacific Northwest, Catholics vied directly with Protestants for Indian souls. Under the auspices of the American Board of Commissioners for Foreign Missions, two missionary couples—credited as being the first white migrants along the Oregon Trail—traveled to the Pacific Northwest in 1836. Narcissa and Marcus Whitman built a meetinghouse for Cayuse Indians in Waiilatpu, near present-day Walla Walla, Washington, while Eliza and Henry Spalding worked to convert the Nez Percé at Lapwai, in what is now Idaho. The Whitmans did little to endear themselves to the Cayuses, whom Narcissa deemed "insolent"; their dark skin, fitting of their "heathenism." The Cayuse, in turn, saw the Whitmans as "severe and hard," and none converted. The Whitmans turned their attention to white migrants flowing into Oregon in the 1840s.

These migrants' arrival escalated tensions with the Cayuses, and when a devastating measles epidemic struck in 1847, the Cayuses saw it as a calculated assault. They retaliated by murdering the Whitmans and twelve other missionaries. The Spaldings abandoned their successful mission, blamed Catholics for inciting the massacre, and became farmers in Oregon.

Mormons

Persecuted in Missouri and Illinois, the Mormons in 1847 followed Brigham Young to their "Promised Land" in the Great Salt Lake valley, still under Mexican control but soon to become part of the U.S. territory of Utah. As non-Mormons settled in Utah, Young diluted their influence by attracting new Mormon settlers to what he called the state of Deseret.

The Mormons' arrival in the Great Basin complicated relations among Indians. The Utes, for example, had long traded in stolen goods and captured people, particularly Paiutes. After Mormons tried to curtail the slave trade, Ute slavers tortured Paiute captives, particularly children, calculating that Mormons would buy them. The purchased children often worked as servants in Mormon homes. Although the Mormons tried to convert the Paiutes, their condescending treatment caused friction, even violence. Sharing the Utes as a common enemy, the Mormons and Paiutes formed an uneasy alliance in the early 1850s.

With their slave trade threatened and their economy in shambles, the Utes attacked Mormon and Paiute settlements. War erupted in 1853, and although an uneasy truce was reached in 1854, tensions continued between the Mormons and Indians.

And between Mormons and their white neighbors. Although Mormons prospered from providing services and supplies to California-bound settlers, Young discouraged "gentiles" (his term for non-Mormons) from settling in Deseret and advocated boycotts of gentile businesses. When in 1852 the Mormons openly sanctioned polygamy, anti-Mormon sentiment increased nationwide. In June 1857, President James Buchanan dispatched 2,500 federal troops to suppress an alleged Mormon rebellion. Anxious over their safety, some Mormons joined some Paiutes in attacking a passing wagon train of non-Mormon migrants. Approximately 120 men, women, and children died in the so-called Mountain Meadows Massacre in August 1857. In the next two years, the U.S. Army and the Mormons engaged in armed conflict, with property destruction but no fatalities.

| **Oregon and California Trails** | From 1840 until 1860, between 250,000 and 500,000 people, including many children, walked across much of the continent, usually over seven months. Although they traveled armed, most of their encounters with Indians were peaceful, if tense. |

The overland journeys began at one of the so-called jumping-off points—towns such as Independence, St. Joseph, and Westport Landing—along the Missouri River, where migrants bought supplies for the 2,000-mile trip. While miners frequently traveled alone or with fortune-seeking young men, farmers traveled with relatives, neighbors, church members, and other acquaintances.

They timed their departures to be late enough to find forage grass for their oxen and livestock, but not so late that they would encounter the treacherous snows of the Rockies and the Sierra Nevada. Not all were successful. From 1846 to 1847, the Donner Party took a wrong turn, got caught in a blizzard, and resorted to cannibalism. More fortunate overland migrants trudged alongside their wagons, averaging fifteen miles a day, in weather from freezing cold to blistering heat. Men generally tended livestock, while women set up camp, prepared meals, and tended small children. Indians were usually peaceful, if cautious. During the trails' early days, Indians provided food and information or ferried migrants across rivers. In exchange, migrants offered wool blankets, knives, metal pots, tobacco, ornamental beads, and other items. When exchanges went wrong—due to misunderstandings or conscious attempts to swindle—tensions escalated.

Indian Treaties

Still, the U.S. Indian Office negotiated treaties to keep Indians—and their intertribal conflicts—from interfering with western migration and commerce.

Fort Laramie Treaty A treaty between the United States and eight northern Plains tribes in which the Indians agreed to maintain intertribal peace, accepted the U.S.-defined territorial regions for each tribe, and allowed the United States to construct roads. In exchange, they received annual payouts of provisions and agricultural necessities.

The **Fort Laramie Treaty** of 1851 (or the Horse Creek Council Treaty) was signed by the United States and eight northern Plains tribes—the Lakotas, Cheyennes, Arapahos, Crows, Assiniboines, Gros-Ventres, Mandans, and Arrickaras—who occupied the Platte River valley through which the three great overland routes westward—the Oregon, California, and Mormon trails—all passed. Two years later, in 1853, the United States signed a treaty with three southwestern nations, the Comanches, Kiowas, and Apaches, who lived near the Sante Fe Trail. Under both treaties, the Indians agreed to maintain peace, recognize government-delineated tribal boundaries, allow the United States to construct roads and forts within those boundaries, refrain from depredations against western migrants, and issue restitution for any depredations nonetheless committed. In return, they would receive annual allotments from the U.S. government for ten years, paid with provisions, domestic animals, and agricultural implements.

Contrary to U.S. expectations, Indian chiefs did not see such treaties as perpetually binding. Government officials, meanwhile, promised allotments but did little to ensure their timely arrival, often leaving Indians starving. Treaties did not end intertribal warfare, nor did they secure overlanders' safety. But they represented the U.S. government's efforts to promote expansion and protect westward-bound citizens.

Ecological Consequences of Cultural Contact

Armed conflict took relatively few lives compared to cholera, smallpox, and other maladies. The trails' jumping-off points bred disease, which migrants inadvertently carried to their Indian trading partners. Fearful of infection, Indians and migrants increasingly shied away from trading.

The disappearance of the buffalo (American bison) from the region further inflamed tensions. The buffalo provided protein to Plains Indians and held spiritual significance. Many Native Americans blamed the migrants for the buffalo's disappearance, even though most overlanders never saw a buffalo. By the time the overland migration peaked in the late 1840s and the 1850s, the herds were long overhunted, partly by Native Americans eager to trade their hides. The surviving buffalo scattered to where the grass was safe from the overlanders' livestock. On rare occasions when wagon trains stumbled upon bison herds, men rushed to fulfill their frontier fantasies and shot the animals. For sport, overlanders also hunted antelopes, wolves, bears, and birds—animals that held spiritual significance for many Native Americans.

Gold Rush

Migrants especially intruded on Indian life near the California gold strikes. In January 1848, John Wilson Marshall discovered gold on John Sutter's property along a shallow tributary to the American River near present-day Sacramento, California. During the next year, tens of thousands of "forty-niners" rushed to California, where they practiced placer mining, panning and dredging for gold, seeking instant riches.

Some did indeed make fortunes. Peter Brown, a black man from Ste. Genevieve, Missouri, wrote his wife in 1851 that "California is the best country in the world to make money. It is also the best place for black folks on the globe." Most forty-niners, however, never found enough gold to pay their expenses. With their dreams dashed, many forty-niners took wage-paying jobs with large mining companies that used dangerous machinery to cut deep into the earth's surface.

As a remote Mexican province, California had small settlements surrounded by military forts (presidios) and missions. It was inhabited mostly by Indians, along with some Mexican rancheros, who raised cattle and sheep on enormous landholdings worked by coerced Indian laborers. With gold strikes, new migrants—from South America, Asia, Australia, and Europe—rushed to California. Although a California Supreme Court ruling—*People v. Hall* (1854)—made it impossible to prevent violence against Chinese immigrants, Chinese citizens continued to seek their fortune in California; by 1859, approximately 35,000 of them worked in the goldfields.

With hungry gold miners to feed, California experienced an agricultural boom. Wheat became the preferred crop: it required minimal investment, was easily planted, and had a short growing season. California's large-scale wheat farming depended on bonded Indian laborers.

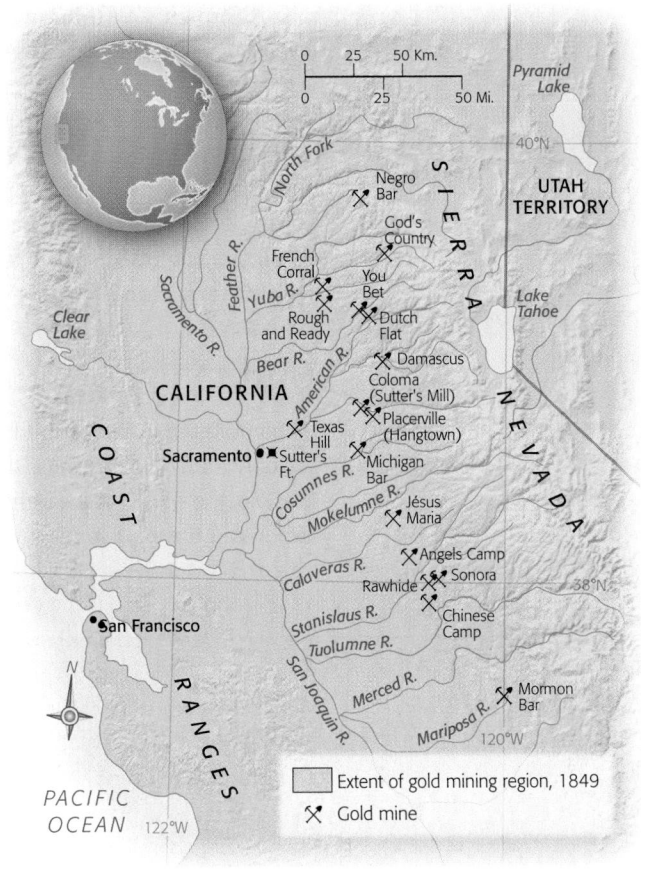

MAP 11.5
The California Gold Rush
Gold was discovered at Sutter's Mill in 1848, sparking the California gold rush that took place mostly along the western foothills of the Sierra Nevada Mountains. Source: Copyright © Cengage Learning 2015

Mining Settlements

Mining brought a commercial and industrial boom, too, as enterprising merchants rushed to supply new settlers. Among them was Levi Strauss, a German Jewish immigrant, whose tough mining pants found a ready market among prospectors. Because men greatly outnumbered women, women's skills (and company) were in demand. As men set up all-male households and performed traditionally female tasks, women received high fees for cooking, laundering, and sewing. Women also ran boardinghouses, hotels, and brothels.

Cities sprang up. In 1848, San Francisco was a small mission settlement of about 1,000 Mexicans, Anglos, soldiers, friars, and Indians. With the gold rush, it became a city, ballooning to 35,000 people in 1850. It was the West Coast gateway to the interior, and ships bringing people and supplies jammed the harbor.

Although California was admitted into the Union as a free state in 1850, its legislature soon passed "An Act for the Government and Protection of Indians" that legalized Indians' enslavement. Using enslaved Indians in the mines between 1849 and 1851 ended when newly arrived miners brutally attacked the Indian workers, believing they degraded white labor and gave an unfair advantage to established miners. Those slaves who survived the violence became field workers and house servants. Between 1821 and 1860, the Indian population of California fell from 200,000 to 30,000, as Indians died from disease, starvation, and violence. Because masters separated male and female workers, Indians failed to reproduce in large numbers.

Summary

Encouraged by literary and artistic images of the frontier as a place of natural abundance and opportunity, millions poured into the Old Southwest and Old Northwest in the early nineteenth century. The federal government promoted westward expansion through support for transportation improvements, surveying, cheap land,

Legacy FOR A PEOPLE AND A NATION

Descendants of Early Latino Settlers

Today, American news media frequently report on Latinos in the United States, for current census figures identify them as the nation's largest racial or ethnic minority. Stories focus on the growing number of documented and undocumented Latino immigrants, their increasing social impact, and their occasionally difficult relationships with African Americans. Yet all the attention to recent arrivals overlooks the sizable number of Latinos who are descended from people whose residency in North America predated the existence of the United States.

When the region stretching from eastern Texas to California was acquired by the United States in the 1840s, its population included indigenous Indian nations and thousands of people with at least partial European ancestry, primarily Spanish or Portuguese. Their descendants have included such U.S. congress-people as Manuel Luján (1969–1988) and such senators as Kenneth Salazar (who served from 2004 to

2009, when he resigned to become secretary of the interior). Their families have resided in what is now U.S. territory for twelve or fourteen generations.

Persuasive evidence suggests that many of the early Iberian settlers in New Mexico were *conversos*, or of New Christian descent—that is, people whose Jewish ancestors converted to Catholicism in the fifteenth century to avoid religious persecution. After Jews were expelled from Spain and Portugal in 1492, many fled to the Spanish empire's far corners. Some participated in Juan de Oñate's 1598 expedition to New Mexico. There, some secretly maintained such Jewish customs as Sabbath observances and food restrictions. Today, some Latino residents of New Mexico have acknowledged their converso roots and reclaimed a Jewish identity.

These long-standing Latino citizens of the United States, not just those of converso descent, have given the nation and its people an important multicultural legacy.

and protection from Indians. Still, western migrants did not always find what they were seeking. Some returned home, some moved elsewhere, and some stayed in the West, abandoning their dreams of economic independence.

Large numbers of African American slaves were moved westward by owners or slave traders between 1820 and 1860. Native Americans saw their lands and livelihoods constrict, and their environments drastically altered, threatening their economic and spiritual lives. Some Indians responded to white incursion through accommodation and peaceful overtures; others resisted. For Indians in Texas and California, white incursions brought devastation, yet not before the Comanches and their allies ravaged farming settlements along the Mexico-U.S. border, paving the way for the U.S. Army to invade its southern neighbor from 1846 to 1848.

White beliefs about Native Americans' supposed inferiority allowed many to rationalize the Indians' fate; white attitudes toward black people and slavery drove where they settled in the West. Those who believed that slavery degraded white labor headed along a northern trajectory, whereas those who dreamed of slave ownership headed southward, where they clashed with yet another group they deemed racially inferior: Mexicans. When American settlers in Texas achieved independence from Mexico and legalized slavery, they triggered events that would bring the divisive issue of slavery's westward expansion forward in American politics.

Chapter Review

The West in the American Imagination

What were the myths that helped shape white Americans' perceptions of the West?

In novels, artists' paintings, and materials recruiting settlers, the West was depicted as a place of cheap or free, abundant, and unoccupied land where anyone could seek to better himself or herself. They often neglected the reality that many of these lands were home to native peoples. Artists often depicted Indians as savages (sometimes noble savages) or as docile and easily conquered. Frontiersmen like Daniel Boone were portrayed as having the courage and independent spirit needed to tame the so-called uncivilized wilderness and open the West to freedom-loving white settlers. The West effectively symbolized core American values of freedom, independence, and opportunity.

Expansion and Resistance in the Trans-Appalachian West

What made the Midwest especially appealing to white settlers?

Migrants who headed west in search of a better life often chose the Midwest because they wanted a region with a climate, features, and conveniences similar to those where they previously lived. The Midwest, compared to the Old Southwest, had better-developed transportation routes, easier access to markets, a smaller African American population, cheaper landholdings, and a climate similar to New England's. The region proved a good first stop for those who did not yet have enough cash to purchase land; in the Midwest, they could obtain jobs unloading canal boats or working in farms or mills, before moving on.

The Federal Government and Westward Expansion

How did the federal government sponsor and speed up westward expansion?

U.S. federal policies regarding Indians and land, particularly Indian removal from desirable lands, did much to encourage white movement into the West. Many whites, in fact, awaited government efforts to clear lands before moving there. The federal government funded expeditions to chart the trans-Mississippi West, including efforts to find the best location for a transcontinental railroad. Army engineers helped design roads, canals, and railroads, while soldiers cleared forests and did other work. The military also established forts that intimidated Indians, removed Indians from lands that whites desired, defended settlers from Indian attacks, or pushed squatters from land they did not own. Sales of government-controlled land also encouraged settlement.

The Southwestern Borderlands

What factors led white Americans to settle in Texas?

First, the Panic of 1819 pushed some Anglo-Americans to seek cheap land and a fresh start in the Texas territory controlled by Mexico. Beginning in 1824, officials in Mexico also encouraged settlement by offering tax incentives and land grants to foreigners. American Stephen Austin initially settled over two thousand whites, who, contrary to their agreement, brought four hundred slaves. He later brought another nine hundred families. Mexico required settlers be Christians willing to establish permanent residences and to assimilate. But early on, Mexican officials rightly feared that the transplanted Americans would seek to annex Texas to the United States. Beginning in 1826, there were calls for an independent Texas under the name "Fredonia Republic"; as the proportion of Americans to Tejanos reached seven to one in 1835, demand for secession heightened, culminating in battles and the eventual declaration of Texas as the Lone Star Republic in 1836.

Cultural Frontiers in the Far West

How did the gold rush influence the development of the Far West?

As miners flooded into California seeking gold, an agricultural boom emerged, with wheat becoming the main crop, often farmed by Indian slaves. Wherever mining areas sprung up, a commercial and industrial boom usually followed, as merchants provided necessities and other goods to new settlers. Cities also grew up fast; San Francisco went from one thousand people in 1848 to thirty-five thousand two years later. While California was admitted as a free state that year, it quickly legalized the enslavement of Indians, using them to work in the mines and later in fields or homes.

Suggestions for Further Reading

Gary Clayton Anderson, *The Conquest of Texas: Ethnic Cleansing in the Promised Land, 1820–1875* (2005)

Stuart Banner, *How the Indians Lost Their Land: Law and Power on the Frontier* (2005)

Ned Blackhawk, *Violence over the Land: Indians and Empires in the Early American West* (2006)

Andrew R. L. Cayton and Peter S. Onuf, *The Midwest and the Nation: Rethinking the History of an American Region* (1990)

William Cronon, *Nature's Metropolis: Chicago and the Great West* (1991)

Brian DeLay, *War of a Thousand Deserts: Indian Raids and the U.S.-Mexican War* (2008)

Pekka Hämäläinen, *The Comanche Empire* (2008)

Robert V. Hine and John Mack Faragher, *The American West: A New Interpretive History* (2000)

Albert L. Hurtado, *Indian Survival on the California Frontier* (1998)

Anne F. Hyde, *Empires, Nations & Families: A History of the North American West, 1800–1860* (2011)

Susan L. Johnson, *Roaring Camp: The Social World of the California Gold Rush* (2000)

Andrés Reséndez, *Changing National Identities at the Frontier: Texas and New Mexico, 1800–1850* (2005)

Michael L. Tate, *Indians and Emigrants: Encounters on the Overland Trails* (2006)

Politics and the Fate of the Union

12

1824–1859

Never has a work of popular literature so caught the tide of politics as Harriet Beecher Stowe's **Uncle Tom's Cabin** (1852). While Stowe created many enduring scenes, especially powerful was that of the young slave Eliza, child in arms, escaping across the Ohio River, after her owner sold the infant to a slave trader. "Nerved with strength such as God gives only to the desperate," continued Stowe, "with one wild cry and flying leap, she [Eliza] vaulted clear over the turbid current … on to the raft of ice beyond…. she … felt nothing, till dimly, as in a dream, she saw the Ohio side, and a man helping her up the bank."

The daughter and sister of prominent preachers and theologians, Stowe saw her story first serialized in a Washington, D.C., newspaper in 1851, and published as a book in 1852. The novel captured the agonies of slave families broken apart and sold. Stowe spread the blame widely in her indictment of slavery. For example, the most evil slaveholder (Simon Legree) is a transplanted New Englander. The story's humane slaveholder, St. Clair, is southern bred, but almost too good for this corrupt world, and dies before he can reform it. In Eliza, Little Eva, Topsy, and Uncle Tom himself, a Christ-like figure whom the story ushers toward unforgettable martyrdom, the nation and the world vicariously experienced not only slavery's inhumanity, but its destruction of the human soul, as it also threatened the life of the republic.

By mid-1853, the book had sold over 1 million copies and was soon translated into numerous foreign languages. Its popularity alarmed white southerners, inspiring nearly twenty anti-Uncle Tom novels in the 1850s. Southern writers justified slavery as more humane than northern wage labor, and attacked Stowe for breaking gender conventions by engaging in a public critique of the South. In stories such as J. W. Page's *Uncle Robin in his Cabin and Tom Without One in Boston*, fiendish abolitionists induced slaves to run away, only to starve in northern cities. In these novels, masters are benevolent and slaves loyal as they perform roles dictated by nature and God. Many novels let slaves philosophize on slavery's behalf. In *Aunt Phillis's Cabin*, Phillis visits the North

327

Uncle Tom's Cabin Harriet
Beecher Stowe's best-selling
1852 novel that aroused
widespread northern sympathy
for slaves (especially fugitives)
and widespread southern anger.

with her owners, where abolitionists encourage her to escape. "I want none of your help," she declares; she refuses to "steal" herself, longing instead for her southern "home."

In *Uncle Tom's Cabin*, Stowe cast a feminist, abolitionist thunderbolt into the slavery debate. That debate had been largely submerged in the political system dominated, beginning in the 1830s, by the Jacksonian Democrats and Whigs.

Yet Democrats and Whigs varied on other issues. Democrats typically emphasized small government, whereas Whigs advocated an activist federal government to promote economic development. Democrats championed agricultural expansion into the West, while Whigs urged commercial growth in the East, via their "American System" of high protective tariffs, centralized banking, and federally funded internal improvements. Together, Whigs and Democrats forged the second party system.

Sectional conflict resurfaced after Texas's annexation in 1845. From 1846 to 1848, the United States went to war against Mexico, escalating the problem of slavery's expansion. The Compromise of 1850's fugitive slave law sent thousands of enslaved blacks fleeing into Canada, and prompted Stowe to write her novel. In Kansas Territory by 1855, open warfare exploded between proslavery and antislavery settlers. The following year, the Supreme Court issued a dramatic decision about slavery's constitutionality and the status of African American citizenship. And by 1858, abolitionist John Brown was planning a raid into Virginia to start a slave rebellion.

As the 1850s advanced, slavery divided Americans, North and South. The old nationwide political parties fractured, replaced by virulent sectionalism. People everywhere believed America's future was at stake. In 1855, the famous black leader Frederick Douglass spoke for the enslaved when he wrote that "the thought of only being a creature of the past and present, troubled me, and I longed to have a future – a future with hope in it."

As you read this chapter, keep the following questions in mind:

- **What were the main issues dividing Democrats and Whigs?**

- **After 1845, how and why did westward expansion become so intertwined with the future of slavery and freedom?**

- **During the 1850s, why did Americans (white males, virtually all of whom could vote, and blacks, few of whom had the franchise) care so deeply about electoral politics?**

Jacksonianism and Party Politics

Throughout the 1820s and 1830s, politicians sought to appeal to an increasingly broad-based electorate. Hotly contested elections helped make politics the great nineteenth-century American pastime among voters and nonvoters alike. But they also fueled bitter rivalries.

How did changes in voting laws influence the outcome of the 1824 presidential election and the future of political parties?

Expanding Political Participation

Property restrictions for voters remained in just seven of twenty-six states by 1840. Some even allowed foreign nationals who officially declared their intention of becoming American citizens to vote. Between 1824 and 1828 the number of votes cast in presidential elections tripled, from 360,000 to over 1.1 million. The proportion of eligible voters who cast ballots also grew, from about 27 percent in 1824 to more than 80 percent in 1840.

The selection of presidential electors also became more democratic. Previously, a caucus of party leaders typically picked them, but by 1824 eighteen out of twenty-four states chose electors by popular vote. Consequently, politicians augmented their appeals to voters, and the 1824 election saw the end of the congressional caucus, when House and Senate members of the same political party selected their candidate.

Election of 1824

As a result, five Democratic-Republican candidates entered the presidential campaign of 1824. The Republican caucus chose William H. Crawford of

Eliza Crossing the Ice Flows of the Ohio River, *depicting one of the most famous scenes in American literature, illustration from* Uncle Tom's Cabin, *engraved by Charles Bour.*

Eliza crossing the ice floes of the Ohio river to freedom, illustration from 'Uncle Tom's Cabin' by Harriet Beecher Stowe, engraved by Charles Bour (1814–81) (litho) (see also 90903), Bayot, Adolphe Jean-Baptiste (1810–66) (after)/Private Collection/The Bridgeman Art Library

Chronology

1824	No electoral college majority in presidential election
1825	House of Representatives elects Adams president
1828	Tariff of Abominations
	Jackson elected president
1830s–40s	Democratic-Whig competition gels in second party system
1831	Antimasons hold first national political convention
1832	Jackson vetoes rechartering Second Bank of the United States
	Jackson reelected president
1832–33	Nullification Crisis
1836	Specie Circular
	Van Buren elected president
1837	Financial panic ends boom of the 1830s
1839–43	Hard times spread unemployment and deflation
1840	Whigs win presidency under Harrison
1841	Tyler assumes presidency after Harrison's death
1845	Texas annexed
	"Manifest destiny" term coined
1846	War with Mexico begins
	Oregon Treaty negotiated
	Wilmot Proviso inflames sectional divisions
1847	Cass proposes idea of popular sovereignty
1848	Treaty of Guadalupe Hidalgo gives United States new territory in the Southwest
	Free-Soil Party formed
	Taylor elected president
	Gold discovered in California, which later applies for admission to Union as free state
	Seneca Falls Woman's Rights Convention
1850	Compromise of 1850 passes, containing controversial Fugitive Slave Act
1852	Stowe publishes *Uncle Tom's Cabin*
	Pierce elected president
1854	"Appeal of the Independent Democrats" published
	Kansas-Nebraska Act approved, igniting controversy
	Republican Party formed
	Fugitive Burns returned to slavery in Virginia
1856	Bleeding Kansas troubles nation
	Brooks attacks Sumner in Senate chamber
	Buchanan elected president, but Republican Frémont wins most northern states
1857	*Dred Scott v. Sanford* endorses white southern views on black citizenship and slavery in territories
	Economic panic and widespread unemployment begin
1858	Kansas voters reject Lecompton Constitution
	Lincoln-Douglas debates
	Douglas contends popular sovereignty prevails over *Dred Scott* decision in territories
1859	Brown raids Harpers Ferry

Georgia, secretary of the treasury. Instead of Congress, state legislatures now nominated candidates, offering the expanded electorate a slate of sectional candidates. John Quincy Adams drew support from New England, while westerners backed House Speaker Henry Clay of Kentucky. Some southerners initially supported Secretary of War John C. Calhoun, who later ran for the vice presidency instead. The Tennessee legislature nominated military hero Andrew Jackson.

Jackson led in electoral and popular votes, but no candidate received an electoral college majority. Adams finished second. Under the Constitution, the House of Representatives, voting by state delegation, one vote to a state, would select the next president from among the three electoral vote leaders. Clay, with the fewest votes, was dropped. Crawford, disabled from a stroke, never received consideration. Clay backed Adams, who won with thirteen of the twenty-four state delegations and became president (see Map 12.1). Adams named Clay secretary of state, the traditional stepping-stone to the presidency.

Angry Jacksonians denounced the election's outcome as a "corrupt bargain," claiming Adams had stolen the election by promising Clay a cabinet position for his votes. The Republican Party split. The Adams wing emerged as the National Republicans, and the Jacksonians became the **Democrats**.

As president, Adams proposed a strong nationalist policy incorporating Clay's American System of protective tariffs, a national bank, and internal improvements. Adams believed the federal government's active role should extend to education, science, and the arts. He proposed a national university in Washington, D.C. Brilliant as a diplomat and secretary of state, Adams fared less well as chief executive.

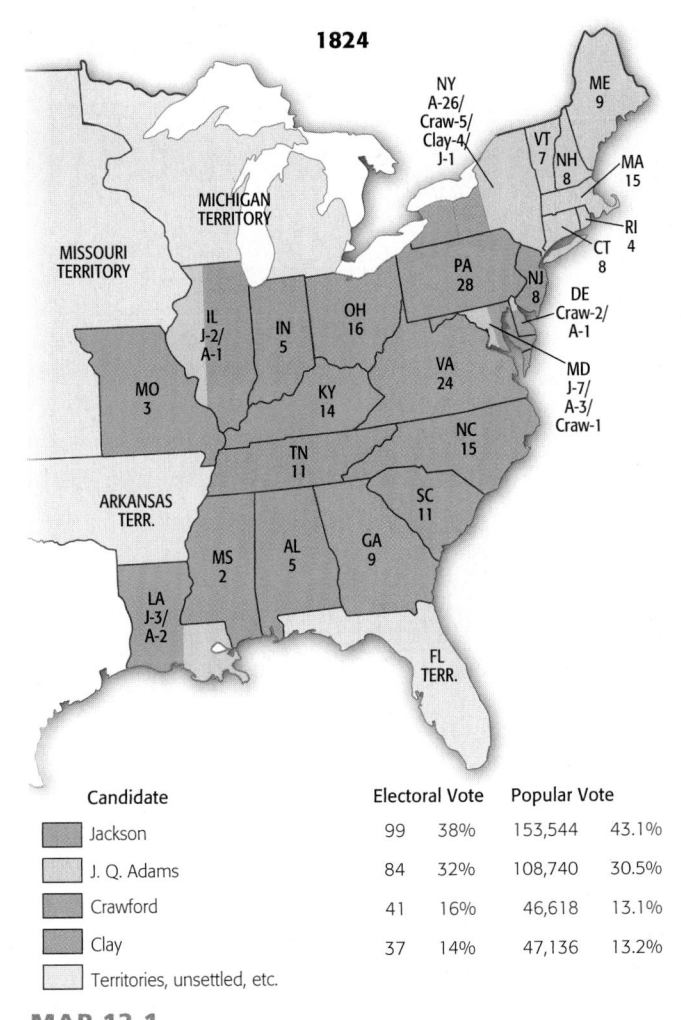

Candidate	Electoral Vote		Popular Vote	
Jackson	99	38%	153,544	43.1%
J. Q. Adams	84	32%	108,740	30.5%
Crawford	41	16%	46,618	13.1%
Clay	37	14%	47,136	13.2%
Territories, unsettled, etc.				

MAP 12.1
Presidential Election, 1824
Andrew Jackson led in both electoral and popular votes but failed to win a majority of electoral college votes. The House elected John Quincy Adams president. Source: Copyright © Cengage Learning 2015

Election of 1828	The 1828 election pitted Adams against Jackson. Nicknamed

"Old Hickory," Jackson was a tough, ambitious man. Born in South Carolina in 1767, he rose from humble beginnings to become a wealthy Tennessee planter and slaveholder. After leading the Tennessee militia to remove Creeks from the Alabama and Georgia frontier, Jackson garnered national acclaim in 1815 as the hero of the Battle of New Orleans; in 1818, his fame increased in an expedition against Seminoles in Spanish Florida. Jackson served as a congressman and senator from Tennessee and as the first territorial governor of Florida (1821).

Jackson's supporters accused Adams of stealing the 1824 election and, when he was envoy to Russia, of securing prostitutes for the czar. Adams supporters countered with reports that Jackson's wife, Rachel, married Jackson before divorcing her first husband. In 1806 while attempting to defend Rachel's integrity, Jackson killed a man during a duel, and the cry of "murderer!" reappeared in the election.

Democrats Members of the party that emerged from Jefferson's Republican Party as one of the two dominant parties in the second party system.

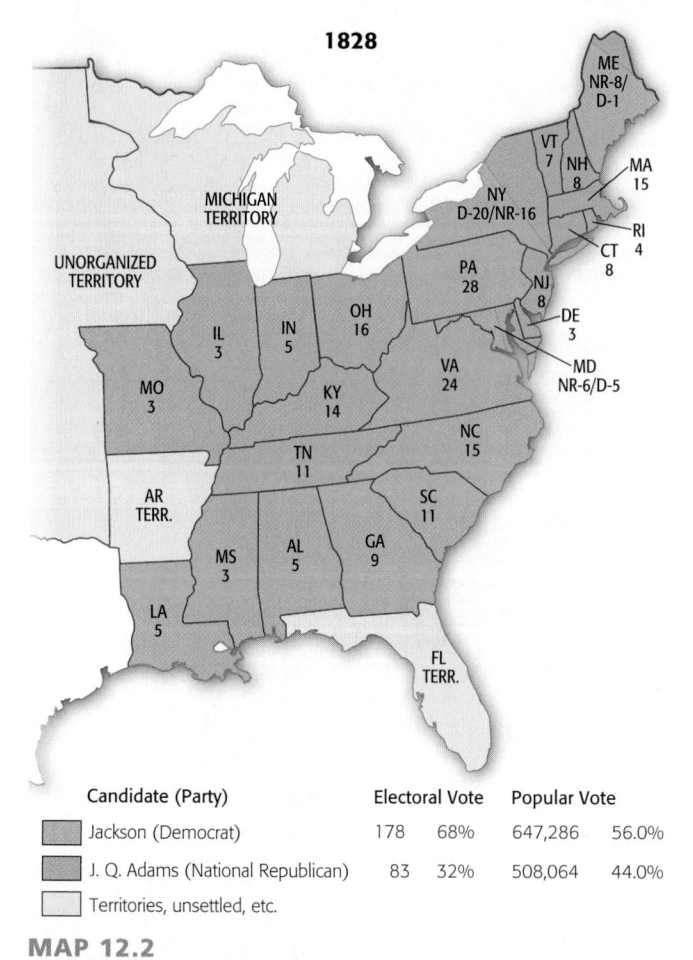

1828

ME
NR-8/
D-1

VT
7
NH
8
MA
15

NY
D-20/NR-16

RI
4

CT
8

PA
28

NJ
8

DE
3

MD
NR-6/D-5

MICHIGAN
TERRITORY

UNORGANIZED
TERRITORY

IL
3

IN
5

OH
16

VA
24

MO
3

KY
14

NC
15

TN
11

AR
TERR.

SC
11

MS
3

AL
5

GA
9

LA
5

FL
TERR.

Candidate (Party)	Electoral Vote		Popular Vote	
Jackson (Democrat)	178	68%	647,286	56.0%
J. Q. Adams (National Republican)	83	32%	508,064	44.0%
Territories, unsettled, etc.				

MAP 12.2
Presidential Election, 1828
Andrew Jackson avenged his 1824 loss of the presidency, sweeping the election in 1828. Source: Copyright © Cengage Learning 2015

Although Adams kept the states he won in 1824, Jackson swamped him, polling 56 percent of the popular vote and winning in the electoral college by 178 to 83 votes (Map 12.2). Through a coalition of state parties, political leaders, and newspaper editors, a popular movement had elected the president. The Democrats became the first well-organized national party.

Democrats

Democrats shared a commitment to the Jeffersonian concept of an agrarian society. They viewed a strong central government as antithetical to individual liberty, and they condemned government intervention in the economy as favoring the rich. Jacksonians called for federal intervention in westward expansion, however, with Jackson initiating Indian removal despite northeastern reformers' protests.

Like Jefferson, Jackson strengthened the government's executive branch while advocating limited government. He centralized power in the White House and relied on political friends, his "Kitchen Cabinet," for advice, rarely consulting his official cabinet. He appointed loyal Democrats to offices, a practice his critics called the **spoils system**, in which the victor gives the spoils of victory to supporters. The spoils system, opponents charged, corrupted the government because it based appointments on loyalty, not competency.

spoils system Practice of rewarding political supporters with public office.

King Andrew

Opponents mocked Jackson as "King Andrew I," charging him with abuse of power by ignoring the Supreme Court's ruling on Cherokee rights, sidestepping his cabinet, and replacing officeholders with his cronies. Jackson's critics especially disliked his frequent use of the veto to promote limited government. In 1830, he vetoed the Maysville Road bill, which would have funded construction of a sixty-mile turnpike from Maysville to Lexington, Kentucky. Constitutionally, he insisted, states bore responsibility for funding internal improvements within a single state. The veto undermined Clay's American System and underscored differences between the two parties.

The first six presidents vetoed nine bills; Jackson alone vetoed twelve. Previous presidents believed vetoes were justified only on constitutional grounds, but Jackson considered policy disagreements legitimate grounds. He made the veto an effective weapon for controlling Congress, which had to weigh the possibility of a veto as it deliberated.

Federalism at Issue: The Nullification and Bank Controversies

What was at issue in the Nullification Crisis?

The slave South feared federal power—especially South Carolina, where the planter class was strongest and slavery most concentrated. Southerners resented protectionist tariffs, which in 1824 and 1828 bolstered manufactures by imposing import duties on foreign cloth and iron. In protecting northern factories, the tariff raised the costs of manufactured goods to southerners, who labeled the high 1828 tariff the **Tariff of Abominations**.

Tariff of Abominations
Protective tariff of 1828 that infuriated southerners and spawned the Nullification Crisis.

Nullification

South Carolina's political leaders rejected the 1828 tariff, invoking the doctrine of nullification, maintaining that a state had the right to overrule, or nullify, federal legislation. Nullification borrowed from the 1798 Virginia and Kentucky Resolutions—that the states, representing the people, have a right to judge the constitutionality of federal actions. Jackson's vice president, John C. Calhoun of South Carolina, argued in his unsigned *Exposition and Protest* that, in disagreements between federal and state governments, a special state convention should decide the conflict by either nullifying or affirming the federal law.

As Jackson's running mate in 1828, Calhoun avoided endorsing nullification and embarrassing the Democratic ticket; he also sought Jackson's support as the Democratic presidential heir apparent. Thus, in early 1830, Calhoun presided silently over the Senate when Massachusetts Senator Daniel Webster and South Carolina Senator Robert Y. Hayne debated states' rights. The debate over the tariff soon focused on the nature of the Union, with nullification a subtext. Hayne charged the North with threatening to bring disunity. Webster defended New England and the republic.

Though sympathetic to states' rights and distrustful of the federal government, Jackson rejected state sovereignty and embraced the Union. The president articulated his position at a Jefferson Day dinner with the toast "Our Federal Union, it must and shall be preserved." Vice President Calhoun toasted "The Federal Union—next to our liberty the most dear," revealing his adherence to states' rights. Calhoun and Jackson grew apart, and Jackson eyed Secretary of State Martin Van Buren as his successor.

Tension resumed in 1832 when Congress passed a new tariff, reducing some duties but retaining high taxes on imported iron, cottons, and woolens. Although a majority of southern representatives supported the new tariff, South Carolinians did not. They feared the act could set a precedent for congressional legislation on slavery. In November 1832, a South Carolina state convention nullified the 1828 and 1832 tariffs, declaring it unlawful for federal officials to collect duties in the state.

The Force Bill

Jackson soon issued a proclamation opposing nullification. He moved troops to federal forts in South Carolina and prepared U.S. marshals to collect the duties. At Jackson's request, Congress passed the Force Bill, authorizing the president to call up troops but offering a way to avoid force by collecting duties before foreign ships reached Charleston's harbor. Jackson also extended an olive branch by recommending tariff reductions.

Calhoun resigned as vice president and won election to the U.S. Senate, where he worked with Henry Clay on the compromise Tariff of 1833. Quickly passed by Congress and signed by the president, the new tariff lengthened the list of duty-free items and reduced duties over nine years. Satisfied, South Carolina's convention repealed its nullification law.

Nullification became a debate on the principles of the republic. Each side believed it was upholding the Constitution. South Carolina opposed the tyranny of the federal government and manufacturing interests. Jackson fought the tyranny of South Carolina, whose actions threatened the republic. It took another crisis, over a central bank, to define the powers of the federal government more clearly.

Second Bank of the United States

At stake was the Second Bank of the United States, whose twenty-year charter would expire in 1836. The bank served as a depository for federal funds and provided business credit. Its bank notes circulated as currency nationwide and could be exchanged for gold. Through its twenty-five branch offices, the Second Bank acted as a clearinghouse for state banks, refusing notes lacking sufficient gold reserves. Most state banks saw the central bank's police role as potentially ruinous. Moreover, state banks could not compete with the Second Bank, which had more money in reserve.

Many states regarded the national bank as unresponsive to local needs. Western settlers and urban workers bitterly remembered the bank's conservative credit policies during the Panic of 1819. As a private, profit-making institution, its policies reflected its owners' interests, especially those of its president, Nicholas Biddle. An eastern patrician, Biddle symbolized what westerners resented about the bank, and what eastern workers disliked about the commercial elite.

Political Violence

Controversy over the Second Bank inflamed longstanding political animosities, igniting street violence. Elections often involved fraud, and with no secret ballot, political parties employed operatives to intimidate voters. New York City was home to the most powerful political machine, the Democrats' Tammany Hall, and thus in the midst of the Bank controversy, New York's mayoral election of 1834 sparked mayhem.

Whigs Formerly called the National Republicans; a major political party in the 1830s.

Three days of rioting began when Democratic operatives stormed Whig headquarters. After beating some **Whigs** unconscious, the Democrats attacked police; eight of them suffered severe wounds, and the mayor was also injured. Vowing revenge, more than five hundred Whigs stole weapons from the armory, but the state militia restored order.

Months later, an election-day riot in Philadelphia left two dead and five buildings burned to the ground. These two riots stood out for their intensity, but voter intimidation and fraud characterized the second party system.

Antimasonry

Violence was a catalyst for the formation of the Antimason Party, which started in upstate New York in the mid-1820s as a grassroots movement against Freemasonry, a secret male fraternity of prominent middle- and upper-class men. Antimasons claimed Masons colluded to bestow business and political favors on each other, and—in the incident that sparked the organized Antimasonry movement—Masons had obstructed justice in the investigation of the 1826 disappearance and presumed murder of a disgruntled former member who had written an exposé of the society. Evangelicals denounced Masonry, claiming its members neglected their families for alcohol and ribald entertainment. In the 1828 presidential election, the Antimasons opposed Jackson, a Mason. The Antimasons held the first national political convention in Baltimore in 1831, nominating William Wirt of Maryland for president and Amos Ellmaker of Pennsylvania for vice president.

Election of 1832

Democrats and National Republicans held conventions. Democrats reaffirmed Jackson for president and nominated Martin Van Buren of New York for vice president. The National Republican convention selected Clay and John Sergeant of Pennsylvania. The Independent Democrats ran John Floyd and Henry Lee of Virginia.

The Bank of the United States became the election's main issue. Jacksonians denounced it as a vehicle for special privilege, while the Republicans supported it. The bank's charter was valid until 1836, but Clay persuaded Biddle to ask Congress for an early rechartering. If Jackson signed the rechartering bill, then Clay could attack the president's inconsistency. If he vetoed it, Clay hoped voters would favor him. The plan backfired. The president vetoed the bill with a message appealing to voters who feared that rapid economic development spread advantages undemocratically. Jackson stood against special interests seeking to use the government to their own advantage and won 54 percent of the popular vote to Clay's 37 percent. He captured 76 percent of the electoral college. The Antimasons won only Vermont but galvanized anti-Jackson opposition.

Jackson's Second Term

Jackson began in 1833 dismantling the Second Bank and depositing federal funds in state-chartered banks. When its federal charter expired in 1836, it became just another Pennsylvania-chartered private bank, closing five years later. Congress passed the Deposit Act of 1836, authorizing the secretary of the treasury to designate one bank per state and territory to provide services formerly performed by the Bank of the United States. The act also provided that federal surplus exceeding $5 million—income derived from the sale of public lands to speculators, who gobbled it up to resell at a profit—be distributed to the states as interest-free loans beginning in 1837. Eager to use the money for state-funded internal improvements, Democrats joined Whigs in supporting the measure. Fearing that the act would

Whigs, who named themselves after the loyal opposition in Britain, delighted in portraying Andrew Jackson as a power-hungry leader eager to turn a republic into a monarchy.

fuel speculation, promote inflation, and thus undermine farmers' interests, Jackson opposed it. Because support was strong enough to override a veto, Jackson signed the bill but first insisted on a provision prohibiting state banks from issuing or accepting small-denomination paper money. Jackson hoped that by encouraging the use of coins, the provision would prevent unscrupulous businessmen from paying workers in devalued paper bills.

Specie Circular

The president then ordered treasury secretary Levi Woodbury to issue the Specie Circular, which provided that, after August 1836, only settlers could use paper money to buy land; speculators had to use specie (gold or silver). The policy proved disastrous, significantly reducing public land sales, which in turn reduced the federal government's surplus and its loans to the states. A banking crisis emerged. Fearful that bank notes would lose value, people redeemed them for specie, creating a shortage that forced the banks to suspend payment. In the waning days of Jackson's administration, Congress repealed the circular, but the president pocket-vetoed the bill by holding it unsigned until Congress adjourned. In May 1838, after Jackson had left office, a joint resolution of Congress overturned the circular.

The Second Party System

How did Whigs and Democrats differ ideologically?

In the 1830s, opponents of the Democrats, including remnants of the National Republican and Antimason parties, united as the Whig Party. From 1834 through the 1840s, Whigs and the Democrats competed on nearly equal footing, and each drew supporters from all regions. The era's political competition—the second party system— thrived on ideological rivalry.

Democrats and Whigs

The two parties differed about the route to national prosperity. Democrats embraced westward expansion's opportunities for independent landownership. Whigs were suspicious of rapid westward expansion, and instead pushed for commercial development within the nation's current boundaries.

The Whigs' economic vision demanded an activist government, while Democrats promoted limited government. Whigs supported corporate charters, a national bank, and paper currency; Democrats opposed all three. Whigs believed in progress and perfectibility, and they favored social reforms, including public schools, prison and asylum reform, and temperance. Jacksonians criticized reformers for undermining the people's will. Nor did Whigs object to helping special interests if it promoted the general welfare. The chartering of corporations, they argued, expanded opportunity for everyone. Whigs stressed a "harmony of interests" among all classes while Democrats saw society as divided into the "haves" and the "have nots." Whigs preferred to see society ruled from the top down; they believed in free-labor ideology and thought that society's wealthy had risen by merit. Democrats alleged that the wealthy had benefited from special favors.

Political Coalitions

Religion and ethnicity, as much as class, influenced party affiliation. The Whigs' support for moral reform appealed to evangelical Protestants along with free black voters. In many locales, membership rolls of reform societies overlapped those of the party. Whigs' rallies resembled camp meetings; their speeches employed pulpit rhetoric; their programs embodied reformers' perfectionist beliefs.

By appealing to evangelicals, Whigs alienated other faiths. The evangelicals' ideal Christian state had no room for nonevangelical Protestants, Catholics, Mormons, or religious freethinkers. Consequently, more than 95 percent of Irish Catholics, 90 percent of Reformed Dutch, and 80 percent of German Catholics voted Democratic.

The parties' platforms thus attracted seemingly odd coalitions of voters. Democrats' promises to open additional lands for settlement attracted yeoman farmers, wage earners, frontier slave owners, and immigrants. The Whigs' preference for slower, controlled settlement of western lands attracted groups as diverse as black New Englanders and slave owners in the Upper South; the former hoped to undercut slavery itself, and the latter wanted to protect their investments from cheap western competition. With broad voter coalitions, room existed within each party for a spectrum of beliefs, particularly regarding slavery.

Some politicians went to extremes to keep the potentially divisive issue of slavery out of national political debate. Responding to the American Antislavery Society's petitioning campaign, the House of Representatives in 1836 adopted what abolitionists labeled the "gag rule," which automatically tabled abolitionist petitions. Former president John Quincy Adams, now a representative from Massachusetts, defended the right to petition and spoke against the gag rule, which was repealed in 1844.

Election of 1836

Vice President Martin Van Buren headed the Democratic ticket in the 1836 presidential election. A career politician, Van Buren built a political machine—the Albany Regency—in New York and joined Jackson's cabinet in 1829, first as secretary of state and then as American minister to Great Britain.

Not yet a national party in 1836, Whigs entered three sectional candidates: Daniel Webster (New England), Hugh White (the South), and William Henry Harrison (the West). Van Buren captured the electoral college even though he had only a 25,000-vote lead. No vice presidential candidate received a majority of electoral votes, and for the only time in American history, the Senate decided a vice presidential race, selecting Democratic candidate Richard M. Johnson of Kentucky.

Van Buren and Hard Times

Weeks after Van Buren took office, the American credit system collapsed. With banks refusing to redeem paper currency with gold in response to the Specie Circular, a downward economic spiral curtailed bank loans. After a brief recovery, hard times persisted from 1839 until 1843.

Van Buren followed Jackson's hard-money, antibank policies, proposing the Independent Treasury Bill, which became law in 1840 but was repealed in 1841. The independent treasury created regional treasury branches that accepted and dispersed only gold and silver coin; they did not accept paper currency or checks drawn on state banks, and thus accelerated deflation. Whigs favored new banks, more paper currency, and readily available corporate and bank charters. As the party of hard money, Democrats favored eliminating paper currency; by the mid-1840s, most favored eliminating bank corporations.

William Henry Harrison and the Election of 1840

With the nation facing hard times, Whigs confidently approached the election of 1840 with a simple strategy: maintain loyal supporters and court independents by blaming hardship on Democrats. Whigs rallied behind military hero General William Henry Harrison, conqueror of the Shawnees at Tippecanoe Creek in 1811. The Democrats renominated President Van Buren, and the newly formed Liberty Party ran James Birney.

Harrison and his running mate, John Tyler of Virginia, ran a people's crusade against the aristocratic president in "the Palace." Although descended from a Virginia plantation family, Harrison presented himself as an ordinary farmer. Whigs wooed voters with rallies, parades, songs, posters, campaign mementos, and a party newspaper, *The Log Cabin*. They appealed to voters as well as nonvoters, including women, who attended rallies and actively promoted the Whig cause. Roughly 80 percent of eligible voters cast ballots. Narrowly winning the popular vote, Harrison swept the electoral college, 234 to 60.

Women's Rights

What inspired the rise of the women's movement in the mid-nineteenth century?

Although women participated in electoral campaigns, states denied them the right to vote, along with other rights afforded male citizens. The movement for women's rights gained steam with the 1830s religious revivalism and reform movements (see Chapter 10). While revivals emphasized human equality, reform movements brought middle-class women into the public sphere.

By the 1840s, female abolitionists took the lead in demanding women's legal and political rights. Committed to notions of human equality, they were frustrated by their subordinated status within the abolitionist movement. Dismayed that female abolitionists were denied seats in the main hall at the first World Anti-Slavery Convention in London in 1840, Lucretia Mott and Elizabeth Cady

Stanton united eight years later to organize the first American women's rights convention. **Angelina and Sarah Grimké**, sisters who were born into a South Carolina slaveholding family, became abolitionists in the North, where critics attacked them for speaking to audiences that included men. Some thought the next step was obvious: full citizenship rights for women.

Angelina and Sarah Grimké Southern-born sisters who were powerful antislavery speakers; later leaders of the women's rights movement.

Legal Rights

After independence, American states carried over traditional English marriage law, giving husbands control over the family. Husbands owned their wives' property and whatever they or their children produced or earned. Fathers were their children's legal guardians and could deny their daughters' choice of husband, though by 1800 few did.

Married women made modest gains in property and spousal rights after 1830. Arkansas in 1835 passed the first married women's property law, and by 1860 sixteen states allowed women to own and convey property and write wills. When a wife inherited property, it was hers, though money earned still belonged to her husband. Such laws were popular among wealthy Americans, hoping to protect family fortunes during economic downturns; property in a woman's name was safe from her husband's creditors. In the 1830s, states also added cruelty and desertion as grounds for divorce, but divorce remained rare.

Political Rights

The movement to secure women's political rights was launched in July 1848, with the first Woman's Rights Convention at **Seneca Falls**, New York. The three hundred women and men in attendance demanded women's social and economic equality. Their Declaration of Sentiments, modeled on the Declaration of Independence, broadcast the injustices suffered by women and proclaimed "all men and women are created equal." The similarities between abolitionism and women's rights led reformers, including former slaves like Sojourner Truth, to work for both movements in the 1850s. Abolitionists William Lloyd Garrison and Frederick Douglass supported women's right to vote, but most men opposed it. The Seneca Falls suffrage resolution passed only after Douglass passionately endorsed it. In 1851, **Elizabeth Cady Stanton** joined with temperance advocate **Susan B. Anthony** to become the most vocal suffrage activists. They won relatively few converts and many critics, however.

Seneca Falls The location of a women's rights convention in 1848.

Elizabeth Cady Stanton, Susan B. Anthony Vocal advocates of women's suffrage.

The Politics of Territorial Expansion

How did territorial expansion expose political fissures?

After taking office in 1841, President Harrison convened Congress in special session to pass the Whig program: repeal of the independent treasury system, a new national bank, and a higher protective tariff. But the sixty-eight-year-old Harrison caught pneumonia and died within a month of his inauguration. John Tyler, who left the Democratic Party to protest Jackson's nullification proclamation, became the first vice president to succeed to the presidency. Tyler assumed executive powers, setting a precedent that would not be codified in the Constitution until 1967 with the Twenty-fifth Amendment's ratification.

President Tyler

In office, Tyler became more Democrat than Whig. He vetoed Clay's protective tariffs, internal improvements, and bills to revive the Bank of the United States. After Tyler's second veto of a bank bill, the entire cabinet ultimately resigned. Tyler became a president without a party. Tyler's expansionist vision contained Whig elements, though: he eyed commercial markets in Hawai'i and China. During his presidency, the United States negotiated its first treaties with China, and Tyler expanded the Monroe Doctrine to include Hawai'i (or the Sandwich Islands). But Tyler fixed mostly on Texas and westward expansion.

Texas and "Manifest Destiny"

Soon after establishing the Lone Star Republic in 1836, Sam Houston approached American authorities to propose annexation as a state. But a new slave state would upset the balance of slave and free states in the Senate. Neither Whigs nor Democrats, wary of causing sectional divisions, wanted to address it. In the 1830s, Democratic presidents Andrew Jackson and Martin Van Buren—one a strong proponent of slavery, the other a mild opponent—sidestepped the issue. But by the mid-1840s—with cotton cultivation expanding rapidly—some Democratic politicians equated Texas's annexation with manifest destiny.

The belief that American expansion westward and southward was inevitable, just, and divinely ordained dated to the nation's founding but was first labeled "manifest destiny" in 1845 by John L. O'Sullivan, editor of the *United States Magazine and Democratic Review*. O'Sullivan claimed that Texas annexation would be "the fulfillment of our manifest destiny to overspread the continent allotted by Providence for the free development of our yearly multiplying millions." Manifest destiny implied that Americans had a God-given right, even obligation, to expand their republican and Christian institutions to less fortunate and less civilized peoples. Implicit in the idea of manifest destiny was the belief that American Indians and Hispanics, like people of African descent, were inferior peoples best controlled or conquered. Manifest destiny provided a political rationale for territorial expansion.

Link to John L. O'Sullivan, Annnexation (1845)

Fifty-Four Forty or Fight

To the north, Britain and the United States had jointly occupied the disputed Oregon Territory since 1818. Beginning with John Quincy Adams's administration, the United States tried to fix the boundary at the 49th parallel, but Britain wanted access to Puget Sound and the Columbia River. In the early 1840s, expansionists demanded the entire Oregon Country for the United States, up to its northernmost border at latitude 54°40′. Soon "fifty-four forty or fight" became their rallying cry.

President Tyler wanted Oregon and Texas, but was obsessed with Texas specifically. He argued that slavery's expansion would spread the nation's black population more thinly, causing the institution's gradual demise. But when word leaked out that Secretary of State John Calhoun had written to the British minister in Washington justifying Texas annexation to protect slavery, the Senate rejected annexation in 1844 by 35 to 16.

Polk and the Election of 1844

Worried southern Democrats persuaded their party's 1844 convention to require that the presidential nominee receive two-thirds of the convention votes, effectively allowing them to block the nomination of Martin Van Buren, who opposed annexation. Instead, the party ran House Speaker **James K. Polk**, an expansionist and slaveholding Tennessee cotton planter. The Democratic platform called for occupation of the entire Oregon Territory and annexation of Texas. The Whigs, who ran Henry Clay, argued that the Democrats' belligerent nationalism would trigger war with Great Britain or Mexico or both. Clay favored expansion through negotiation, whereas many northern Whigs opposed annexation altogether, fearful it would add slave states and strain relations with trading partners. Polk won the election by 170 electoral votes to 105, though with a margin of just 38,000 out of 2.7 million ballots cast.

James K. Polk President from 1845 to 1849; supporter of immediate annexation of Texas who wanted to gain California and Oregon for the United States as well.

Annexation of Texas

Interpreting Polk's victory as a mandate for annexation, President Tyler proposed that Texas be admitted by joint resolution of Congress. The usual method of annexation, by treaty negotiation, required a two-thirds majority in the Senate—which annexationists did not have. Joint resolution required a simple majority. On March 1, 1845, the resolution passed the House by 120 to 98 and the Senate by 27 to 25. Three days before leaving office, Tyler signed the measure. Mexico, which never recognized Texas independence, broke relations with the United States. In October, Texas citizens ratified annexation, and Texas joined the Union, with a constitution permitting slavery. The nation was on the brink of war with Mexico. That conflict would lay bare the inextricable relationships among westward expansion, slavery, and sectional discord.

The War with Mexico and Its Consequences

How did Polk's decisions push the United States toward war with Mexico?

The annexation of Texas did not make war with Mexico inevitable, but several of Polk's decisions did. During the annexation process, Polk urged Texans to seize all land to the Rio Grande and claim the river as their southern and western border. Mexico held that the Nueces River was the border; hence, the stage was set for conflict. Polk wanted Mexico's territory all the way to the Pacific, and all of Oregon Country as well. He and his expansionist cabinet achieved their goals, unaware of expansionism's impact on domestic harmony.

Oregon

During the 1844 campaign, Polk's supporters threatened war with Great Britain to gain Oregon. Polk, not wanting to fight Mexico and Great Britain simultaneously, sought diplomacy in the Northwest. In 1846, the Oregon Treaty gave the United States all of present-day Oregon, Washington, and Idaho, and parts of Wyoming and Montana (see Map 12.3). Thus, a new era of land acquisition and conquest had begun.

MAP 12.3
American Expansion in Oregon

The slogan of Polk's supporters had been "fifty-four forty or fight," but negotiation of a boundary at the forty-ninth parallel avoided the danger of war with Great Britain. Source: Copyright © Cengage Learning 2015

"Mr. Polk's War"

Toward Mexico, Polk was aggressive. In early 1846, he ordered American troops under General Zachary Taylor to defend the contested border of the Rio Grande. Polk saw California as the prize, and he attempted to buy from Mexico a huge tract extending to the Pacific. Failing that, Polk waited for war. After a three-week standoff, on April 24, 1846, Mexican cavalry ambushed a U.S. cavalry unit on the north side of the river; eleven Americans were killed, and sixty-three were captured. On April 26, Taylor sent a dispatch to Washington, D.C., announcing, "Hostilities may now be considered as commenced."

Polk then drafted a message to Congress: Mexico had "passed the boundary of the United States, had invaded our territory and shed American blood on American soil." Polk deceptively declared that "war exists by the act of Mexico itself." Two days later, on May 13, the House recognized a state of war with Mexico by a vote of 174 to 14, and the Senate, by 40 to 2. Because Polk withheld key facts, the full reality of what had happened on the distant Rio Grande was unknown.

Foreign War and the Popular Imagination

The idea of war unleashed public celebrations in southern and northern cities. After news came of General Taylor's first victories at Palo Alto and Resaca de la Palma, volunteers swarmed recruiting stations. In New York, writer Herman Melville remarked that "Nothing is talked of but the Halls of the Montezumas." Publishers rushed books about Mexican geography into print. New daily newspapers boosted sales by giving the war a romantic appeal.

Here was an adventurous war of conquest, the fulfillment of an Anglo-Saxon–Christian destiny to possess the North American continent and civilize the "semi-Indian" Mexicans. Racism fueled the expansionist spirit. In 1846, an Illinois newspaper justified the war by calling Mexicans "reptiles in the path of progressive democracy." War correspondents reported on battles, and ships from Vera Cruz on the Gulf Coast of Mexico carried news dispatches to New Orleans. Near war's end, news traveled by telegraph in only three days from New Orleans to Washington, D.C.

The war spawned poetry, song, drama, travel, literature, and lithographs that glorified the conflict. But not everyone cheered. Abolitionist James Russell Lowell considered the war a "national crime committed in behoof of slavery, our common sin." Even proslavery spokesman John C. Calhoun saw the perils of expansionism.

MAP 12.4

The War with Mexico

This map shows the territory disputed between the United States and Mexico. After U.S. gains in northeastern Mexico, in New Mexico, and in California, General Winfield Scott captured Mexico City in the decisive campaign of the war. Source: Copyright © Cengage Learning 2015

Conquest

Early in the war, U.S. forces made significant gains. In May 1846, Polk ordered Colonel Stephen Kearny to invade the remote provinces of New Mexico and California. General Zachary Taylor's forces attacked Monterrey, which surrendered in September, securing northeastern Mexico (see Map 12.4).

New Mexico proved more difficult to subdue, however. In January 1847, in Taos, northwest of Santa Fe, Hispanics and Indians led by Pablo Montoya and Tomas Romero rebelled against the Americans. In the Taos Revolt, some 500 Mexican and Indian insurgents laid siege to a mill in Arroyo Hondo, outside Taos. The U.S. command suppressed the revolt, and the insurgents retreated to a thick-walled church in Taos Pueblo. With cannon, the U.S. Army killed 150 and captured 400 rebels. Approximately 28 insurgent leaders were hanged in the Taos plaza, ending bloody resistance to U.S. occupation. Before the end of 1846, American forces also established dominion over California. General Winfield Scott then led fourteen thousand men toward Mexico City in what proved the war's decisive campaign. Outnumbered and threatened by yellow fever, Scott's men repeatedly discovered flanking routes around their foes. U.S. troops captured the Mexican capital.

Treaty of Guadalupe Hidalgo
Agreement that ended the U.S. War with Mexico, in which Mexico ceded vast amounts of its territory and was forced to recognize the Rio Grande as Texas's southern boundary.

Treaty of Guadalupe Hidalgo

Representatives of both countries signed the **Treaty of Guadalupe Hidalgo** in February 1848. The United States gained California and New Mexico (including present-day Nevada, Utah, and Arizona, and parts of Colorado and Wyoming), and recognition of the Rio Grande as Texas's southern boundary. The American government agreed to settle the $3.2 million in its citizens' claims against Mexico and to pay Mexico a mere $15 million.

The war's costs included the lives of thirteen thousand Americans (mostly from disease) and fifty thousand Mexicans. Enmity between Mexico and the United States endured into the twentieth century. Domestically, southwesterners and southern planters were enthusiastic about the war; New Englanders opposed it. Whigs in Congress charged that Polk, a Democrat, had "provoked" an unnecessary war and "usurped the power of Congress." Abolitionists and some antislavery Whigs charged that the war was a plot to extend slavery.

"Slave Power Conspiracy"

These charges fed northern fear of the "Slave Power." Abolitionists long warned of a slaveholding oligarchy that would dominate federal power. Slaveholders gained control of the South by suppressing dissent. They forced the gag rule on Congress in 1836. To many white northerners, this battle over free speech made the idea of a Slave Power credible. The War with Mexico deepened such fears.

Initially, some southern Whigs attacked the Democratic president for causing the war, and few southern congressmen saw slavery as the paramount issue. Many whites, North and South, feared that large land seizures would bring nonwhite Mexicans into the United States and upset the racial order. An Indiana politician did not want "any mixed races in our Union, nor men of any color except white, unless they be slaves." Despite their racism and exaggerations, many statesmen soon saw other potential outcomes of a war of conquest in the Southwest.

Wilmot Proviso

In August 1846, Pennsylvania Democrat David Wilmot proposed an amendment, or proviso, to a military appropriations bill: that "neither slavery nor involuntary servitude shall ever exist" in territories gained from Mexico. Although the proviso never passed, it transformed the debate over slavery's expansion. Southerners intensified efforts to protect slavery's future. Alexander H. Stephens declared that slavery was based on the Bible, and John C. Calhoun insisted that slaveholders had a constitutional right to take their slaves (as property) anywhere.

Visualizing THE PAST

The Mexican War in Popular Imagination

The War with Mexico was the first American foreign conflict to be covered by the press with actual correspondents and the first to stimulate the creation of widespread promotional popular art and commemorative objects. General Zachary Taylor, the American commander in Mexico, became the hero of the war, and in its wake was elected president in 1848 in a campaign that featured countless forms of this art. Why was the War with Mexico the first American foreign war to be covered by journalists and so widely depicted in political and military art? Do you think the artistic depictions of the War with Mexico increased or decreased the popularity of the war?

Presentation pitcher: ca. 1848–1850 (porcelain), French School (nineteenth century), Portrait of Zachary Taylor (1784–1850) on one side, twelfth president of the United States (1849–1850); landscape with battle on the other side, hero of the Mexican war (1846–1848), commemorates Taylor's triumph in the 1847 battle of Buena Vista.

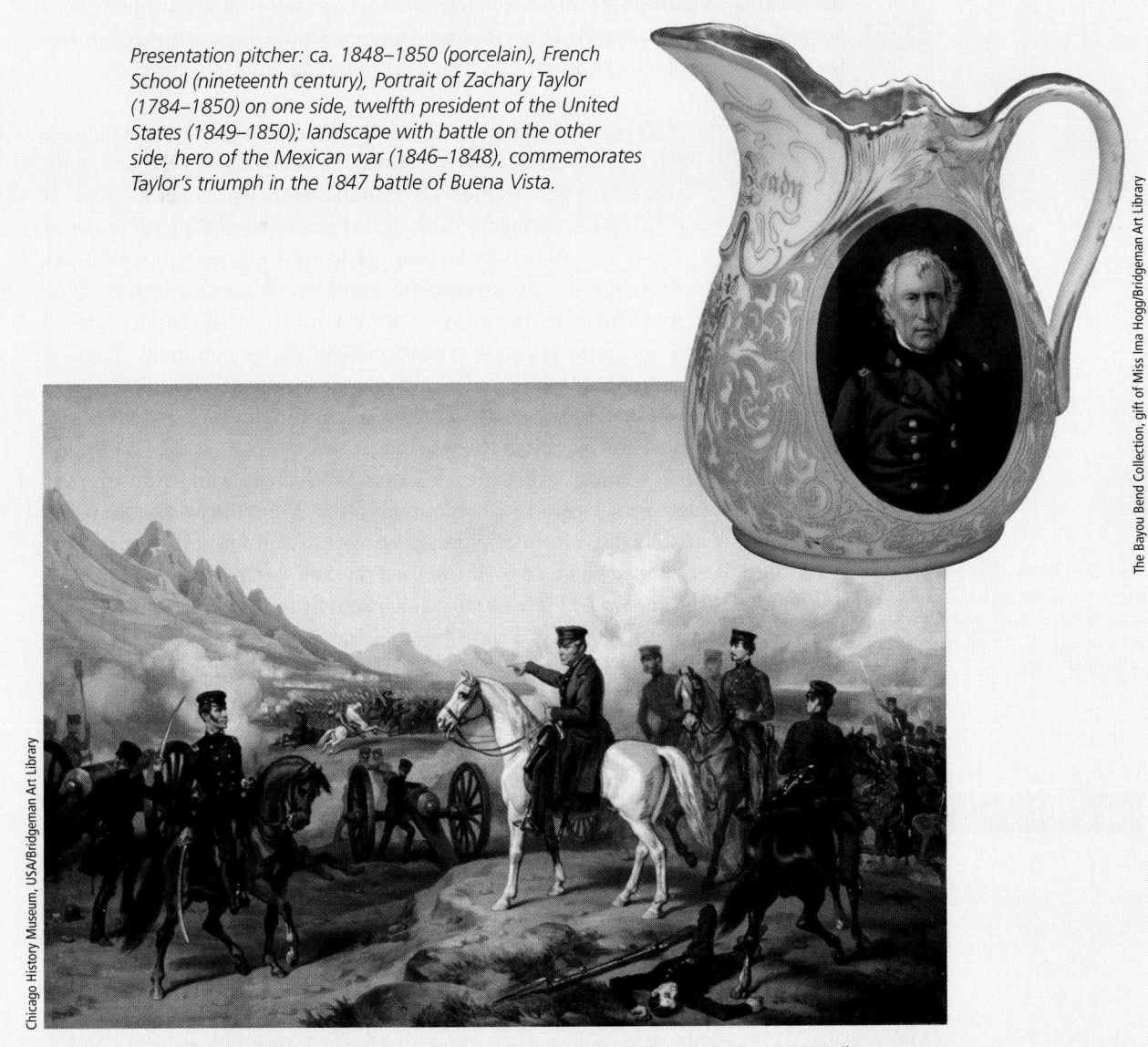

The Bayou Bend Collection, gift of Miss Ima Hogg/Bridgeman Art Library

Chicago History Museum, USA/Bridgeman Art Library

Painting, General Zachary Taylor in command at the Battle of Buena Vista, in Mexico, 1847, oil on canvas, by William Henry Powell (1823–1879).

This position, often called "state sovereignty," was a radical reversal of history. In 1787, the Confederation Congress discouraged slavery in the Northwest Territory; Article IV of the U.S. Constitution authorized Congress to make "all needful rules and regulations" for the territories; and the Missouri Compromise barred slavery from most of the Louisiana Purchase. Now southern leaders demanded guarantees for slavery.

Wilmot Proviso A proposed amendment that would have prohibited slavery in territories acquired from Mexico; though it never passed, it transformed the national debate over slavery.

The **Wilmot Proviso** became a rallying cry for abolitionists. While fourteen northern states endorsed it, not all supporters were abolitionists. Wilmot was neither an abolitionist nor an antislavery Whig. Instead, his goal was to obtain California "for free white labor."

The majority of white northerners were not active abolitionists, and their desire to keep the West slavery free was often matched by their desire to keep blacks out. At stake was the free individual's access to social mobility by acquiring western land. Slave labor, thousands of northerners believed, would degrade the toil of free men and render them unemployable. The West must therefore ban slavery.

The Election of 1848 and Popular Sovereignty

The divisive slavery question infested national politics. After Polk renounced a second term as president, the Democrats nominated Senator Lewis Cass of Michigan for president and General William Butler of Kentucky for vice president. Cass devised in 1847 the idea of "popular sovereignty"—letting residents in the western territories decide the slavery question for themselves. His party's platform declared that Congress lacked the power to interfere with slavery's expansion. The Whigs nominated General Zachary Taylor, a southern slaveholder and war hero; New York Congressman Millard Fillmore was his running mate. The Whig convention similarly denied that Congress had power over slavery in the territories.

Free-Soil Party A political party that sprang from and represented the movement to prevent slavery in the western territories.

Many southern Democrats distrusted Cass and voted for Taylor because he was a slaveholder. New York Democrats committed to the Wilmot Proviso nominated former president Martin Van Buren. Antislavery Whigs and former supporters of the Liberty Party joined them to organize the **Free-Soil Party**, with Van Buren as its candidate (see Table 12.1). This party, which sought to restrict slavery's expansion in the West and whose slogan was "Free Soil, Free Speech, Free Labor, and Free Men," won almost 300,000 northern votes. Taylor polled 1.4 million votes to Cass's 1.2 million and won the White House, but the results were ominous.

TABLE 12.1 New Political Parties

Party	Period of Influence	Area of Influence	Outcome
Liberty Party	1839–1848	North	Merged with other antislavery groups to form Free-Soil Party
Free-Soil Party	1848–1854	North	Merged with Republican Party
Know-Nothings (American Party)	1853–1856	Nationwide	Disappeared, freeing most to join Republican Party
Republican Party	1854–present	North (later nationwide)	Became rival of Democratic Party and won presidency in 1860

Sectionalism and religion, too, severed into northern and southern wings. As the 1850s dawned, the legacies of the War with Mexico threatened the nature of the Union.

1850: Compromise or Armistice?

What were the two troubling issues inherent in the Compromise of 1850?

More than eighty thousand Americans flooded into California during the 1849 gold rush. With Congress unable to agree on how to govern the territories, President Taylor urged settlers to apply for admission to the Union. They did, proposing a state constitution that banned slavery. Because California's admission as a free state would upset the Senate's sectional balance of power (the ratio of slave to free states was fifteen to fifteen), southern politicians wanted to postpone admission and make California a slave territory, or extend the Missouri Compromise to the Pacific.

Debate over Slavery in the Territories

Twice before—in 1820 and 1833—Henry Clay, the Whig leader and "Great Pacificator," had shaped sectional compromise; now he struggled one last time to preserve the nation. In the winter of 1850, Clay and Senator Stephen A. Douglas of Illinois steered their compromise package through debate and amendment.

The problems were numerous. Would California become a free state? How should the territory acquired from Mexico be organized? Texas, which allowed slavery, claimed large portions as far west as Santa Fe. Southerners complained that fugitive slaves were not returned as the Constitution required, and northerners objected to slave auctions in the nation's capital. Most troublesome, however, was the status of slavery in the territories.

Clay and Douglas found in the idea of popular sovereignty what one historian called a "charm of ambiguity." Ultimately, Congress would have to approve statehood for a territory, but "in the meantime," said Lewis Cass, it should allow the people living there "to regulate their own concerns in their own way." To avoid dissension within their party, northern and southern Democrats explained Cass's statement to their constituents in two incompatible ways. Southerners claimed that neither Congress nor a territorial legislature could bar slavery. Northerners, however, insisted that Americans living in a territory were entitled to local self-government and thus could outlaw slavery.

The cause of compromise gained a powerful supporter when Senator Daniel Webster committed his prestige to Clay's bill. Webster urged northerners not to "taunt or reproach" the South with antislavery measures. He warned that disunion inevitably would cause violence and destruction. Many of Webster's former abolitionist friends in New England accused him of going over to the "Devil."

Three days earlier, Calhoun was carried from his sickbed to speak against the compromise. When Calhoun was unable to speak, Senator James Mason of Virginia read his address, which predicted disunion if southern demands went unanswered, frightening some into support of compromise.

With Clay sick, Douglas reintroduced the compromise measures one at a time. Douglas realized that because southerners favored some bills and northerners the rest, a small majority for compromise could be achieved on each distinct issue. The strategy worked, and the Compromise of 1850 became law.

Compromise of 1850

The compromise had five essential measures:

1. California became a free state.
2. The Texas boundary was set at its present limits (see Map 12.5), and the United States paid Texas $10 million in compensation for the loss of New Mexico Territory.
3. The territories of New Mexico and Utah were organized on a basis of popular sovereignty.
4. The fugitive slave law was strengthened.
5. The slave trade was abolished in the District of Columbia.

At best, the Compromise of 1850 was an artful evasion. Douglas found a way to pass the five proposals without convincing northerners and southerners to agree on fundamentals. The compromise bought time, but it did not resolve territorial questions.

Furthermore, the compromise had two flaws. The first concerned the ambiguity of popular sovereignty. Southerners insisted on no prohibition of slavery during the territorial stage, and northerners declared that settlers could bar slavery whenever they wished. The compromise allowed for the appeal of a territorial legislature's action to the Supreme Court.

Fugitive Slave Act Part of the Compromise of 1850, this controversial measure gave additional powers to slave owners to recapture slaves and angered northerners by requiring them to hunt so-called fugitive slaves.

Fugitive Slave Act

The second flaw lay in the **Fugitive Slave Act**, which gave new—and controversial—protection to slavery. The law empowered slave owners to legally claim that a slave had escaped. That claim would then serve as proof of a person's slave status, even in free states and territories. Specially appointed federal commissioners adjudicated the identity of alleged fugitives, and those commissioners were paid fees that favored slaveholders: $10 if the alleged fugitive was returned, and $5 if not. Abolitionist newspapers attacked the Fugitive Slave Act as a violation of American rights. Why would northerners be arrested if they harbored runaways? The "free" states, moreover, were no longer a safe haven for black folk. An estimated twenty thousand fled to Canada in the wake of the Fugitive Slave Act.

Between 1850 and 1854, protests and violent resistance to slave catchers occurred in northern towns. Many abolitionists became convinced that violence was a legitimate means of opposing slavery. In an 1854 column, Frederick Douglass said that the only way to make the fugitive slave law "dead letter" was to make a "few dead slave catchers."

Underground Railroad A loosely organized route by which fugitive slaves, often of their own volition, escaped to freedom in the northern United States and Canada.

The Underground Railroad

By the 1850s, slaveholders were especially disturbed by the **Underground Railroad**, a loose, illegal network, spiriting runaways to freedom. Thousands of slaves escaped by these often disorganized routes, but largely through their own wits and courage with assistance from blacks in northern cities. Lewis Hayden in Boston, David Ruggles in New York, William Still in Philadelphia, and Jacob Gibbs in Washington, D.C., were among the many black abolitionists who managed fugitive slave escapes.

Harriet Tubman, herself an escapee in 1848, returned to her native Maryland and to Virginia at least a dozen times and secretly helped as many as three hundred slaves— some her family members—to freedom. Outraged Maryland planters offered a $40,000 reward for her capture.

In Ohio, white abolitionists, often Quakers, joined with blacks to help slaves cross the river to freedom. The Underground Railroad also had numerous maritime routes, as coastal slaves escaped aboard ships from Virginia, the Carolinas, or New Orleans, and ended up in northern port cities, the Caribbean, or England. Many fugitive slaves from the Lower South and Texas escaped to Mexico, which abolished slavery in 1829. Some joined Seminole communities in Florida, where they joined forces against the U.S. Army in the Seminole Wars of 1835–1842 and 1855–1858.

Slave escapes were a testament to human courage and the will for freedom. They never reached the scale believed by angry slaveholders or claimed by northern towns and local historical societies today. Nonetheless, the Underground Railroad applied pressure to the institution of slavery and gave slaves hope.

Election of 1852 and the Collapse of Compromise

The 1852 election had southern leaders optimistic that slavery would be secure under a new president. Franklin Pierce, a New Hampshire Democrat, won over Whig General Winfield Scott. Pierce supported the Compromise of 1850, where Scott's views on the compromise were unknown.

By 1852 sectionalism had essentially killed the Whig Party. President Pierce's enforcement of the Fugitive Slave Act provoked northern fear of the Slave Power, especially in the case of the fugitive slave Anthony Burns, who fled Virginia in 1852. In Boston, thinking he was safe, Burns began a new life. But in 1854, federal marshals placed him under guard in Boston's courthouse. An interracial crowd of abolitionists attacked the courthouse, killing a jailer while attempting to free Burns.

Pierce sent troops to Boston. Soldiers marched Burns to Boston harbor while his supporters, draped in black, hung American flags at half-mast. At a cost of $100,000, a single black man was returned to slavery.

This demonstration of federal support for slavery radicalized opinion, even among conservatives. Juries refused to convict the abolitionists who stormed the Boston courthouse. New England states passed personal liberty laws that blocked federal enforcement and absolved local judges from enforcing the Fugitive Slave Act, effectively nullifying federal authority. What northerners now saw as evidence of a dominating Slave Power, slaveholders saw as defense of their rights. Pierce constantly faced sectional conflict. His proposal for a transcontinental railroad derailed when congressmen disputed its location, through the North or South. An annexation treaty with Hawai'i failed because southern senators would not vote for another free state, and efforts to acquire slaveholding Cuba angered northerners.

Slavery Expansion and Collapse of the Party System

How did the Kansas-Nebraska Act lead to the collapse of existing political parties?

A greater controversy began in a surprising way. Stephen A. Douglas introduced a bill to establish the Kansas and Nebraska Territories. Ambitious for the presidency, Douglas did not view slavery as a fundamental problem, and was willing to risk controversy to economically aid his home state of Illinois. A transcontinental railroad would encourage Great Plains settlement and stimulate the Illinois economy. Thus, with these goals, Douglas further inflamed sectional passions.

Kansas-Nebraska Act
Effectively repealed the Missouri Compromise and inflamed sectional disputes around the expansion of slavery in the territories. The act left the decision of whether to allow slavery in the new territories of Kansas and Nebraska up to the people residing there (popular sovereignty).

The Kansas-Nebraska Act

The **Kansas-Nebraska Act** exposed conflicting interpretations of popular sovereignty. Douglas's bill left "all questions pertaining to slavery in the Territories … to the people residing therein." Northerners and southerners, however, disagreed over what territorial settlers could constitutionally do. Moreover, the Kansas and Nebraska Territories lay within the Louisiana Purchase, and the Missouri Compromise prohibited slavery there from latitude 36°30′ north to the Canadian border. If popular sovereignty were applied in Kansas and Nebraska, it would mean that the Missouri Compromise was no longer in effect.

Southern congressmen, anxious to establish slaveholders' right to take slaves into any territory, pressed Douglas for a repeal of the 36°30′ limitation in exchange for their support. During a carriage ride with Kentucky senator Archibald Dixon, Douglas conceded: "I will incorporate it in my bill, though I know it will raise a hell of a storm."

Douglas believed that climate and soil conditions would keep slavery out of Kansas and Nebraska. Nevertheless, his bill allowed slavery on land from which it had been prohibited for thirty-four years. Many Free-Soilers and antislavery forces considered this a betrayal of trust. The bill became law in May 1854 by a vote that demonstrated the dangerous sectionalization of American politics (see Map 12.5 and Table 12.2).

Meanwhile, opposition to the Fugitive Slave Act grew dramatically; between 1855 and 1859, Connecticut, Rhode Island, Massachusetts, Michigan, Maine, Ohio, and Wisconsin passed personal-liberty laws. These laws enraged southerners by providing counsel for alleged fugitives and requiring trial by jury. The Kansas-Nebraska Act devastated political parties. The weakened Whig Party broke into northern and southern wings. Democrats survived, but their northern support plummeted in the 1854 elections. Northern Democrats lost sixty-six of their ninety-one congressional seats and lost control of all but two free-state legislatures.

Birth of the Republican Party

The beneficiary of northern voters' wrath was a new political party. During debate on the Kansas-Nebraska Act, six congressmen—most prominently, Joshua Giddings, Salmon Chase, and Charles Sumner—published

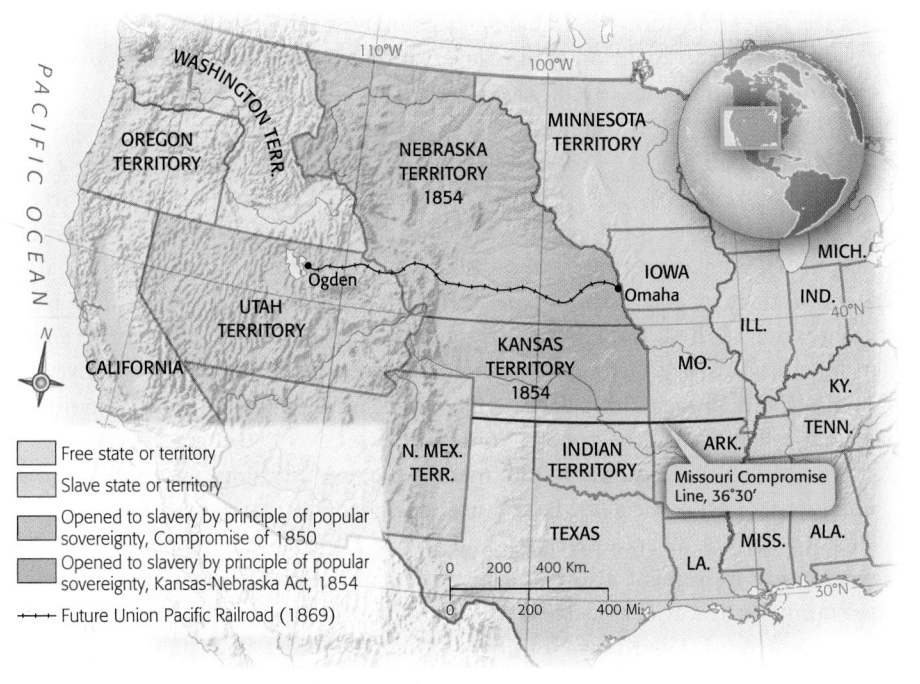

MAP 12.5

The Kansas-Nebraska Act and Slavery Expansion, 1854

The vote on the Kansas-Nebraska Act in the House of Representatives (see also Table 12.2) demonstrates the sectionalization of American politics due to the slavery question.

Source: Copyright © Cengage Learning 2015

an "Appeal of the Independent Democrats." In it they attacked Douglas's legislation as a "gross violation of a sacred pledge" (the Missouri Compromise) and a "criminal betrayal of precious rights" that would make free territory a "dreary region of despotism." Their appeal tapped a reservoir of northern concern, cogently expressed by Abraham Lincoln of Illinois.

Although Lincoln did not condemn southerners, he exposed the meaning of the Kansas-Nebraska Act. Lincoln argued that the founders, from love of liberty, banned slavery from the Northwest Territory, kept the word *slavery* out of the Constitution, and treated it as a "cancer" on the republic. The Kansas-Nebraska Act promised to extend slavery. America's future, Lincoln warned, was being mortgaged to slavery.

Thousands of white northerners agreed. During summer and fall 1854, antislavery Whigs and Democrats, Free-Soilers, and reformers throughout the Old Northwest formed the new Republican Party, dedicated to keeping slavery from the territories. Republicans' influence rapidly spread to the East. They won a stunning victory in the 1854 elections, capturing a majority of northern House seats and inspiring roughly a quarter of northern Democrats to desert their party.

TABLE 12.2 The Vote on the Kansas-Nebraska Act

The vote was 113 to 100 in favor.

	Aye	Nay
Northern Democrats	44	42
Southern Democrats	57	2
Northern Whigs	0	45
Southern Whigs	12	7
Northern Free-Soilers	0	4

For the first time, too, a sectional party gained significant power. The emergence of the Republican coalition of antislavery interests is the most rapid transformation in party allegiance in American history.

Know-Nothings

Know-Nothings Anti-Catholic and anti-immigrant party that enjoyed a brief surge of popularity in the early 1850s.

Republicans also drew into their coalition a fast-growing nativist movement, the American Party or **Know-Nothings** (because its first members kept their purposes secret, answering, "I know nothing" to questions). This group exploited fear of foreigners and Catholics. Between 1848 and 1860, nearly 3.5 million immigrants entered the United States—proportionally the heaviest inflow of foreigners in American history. Democrats courted these new citizens, but many native-born Anglo-Saxon Protestants believed that Irish and German Catholics would owe primary allegiance to the pope in Rome.

In 1854, anti-immigrant fears made the Know-Nothings successful in some northern states, especially Massachusetts, electing 11 congressmen, a governor, all state officers, all state senators, and all but 2 of 378 state representatives. The temperance movement also gained ground early in the 1850s with its promises to stamp out the evils associated with liquor and immigrants (a particularly anti-Irish campaign). The Know-Nothings strove to reinforce Protestant morality and to restrict voting and office holding to the native born. As the Whig Party disappeared, the Know-Nothings filled the void. But like the Whigs, the Know-Nothings could not keep their northern and southern wings together regarding slavery's expansion, and they dissolved after 1856. The growing Republican coalition wooed the nativists with temperance ordinances and laws postponing suffrage for naturalized citizens (see Table 12.1).

Party Realignment and the Republicans' Appeal

The Whig Party's demise ensured a major realignment of the political system. Immigration, temperance, homestead bills, the tariff, and internal improvements were crucial issues for voters during the 1850s. Commercial agriculture was booming in the Ohio–Mississippi–Great Lakes area, but residents desired more canals, roads, and river and harbor improvements. Because credit was scarce, a homestead program—the idea that western land should be free to individuals who would farm and make a home on it—attracted voters. Republicans appealed to those interested in the economic development of the West.

Partisan ideological appeals characterized the realigned political system. As Republicans preached, "Free Soil, Free Labor, Free Men," they captured many northerners' self-image. These phrases resonated with traditional ideals of equality, liberty, and opportunity under self-government—the heritage of republicanism. Invoking that heritage also undercut charges that the Republican Party was radical and abolitionist.

The northern economy was booming, and thousands of migrants moved west to establish farms and communities. Midwesterners multiplied their yields using new machines, such as mechanical reapers. Railroads were carrying their crops to urban markets. And industry was making available goods that recently had been unaffordable for most people.

Republican Ideology
Many people thought the key to progress was free labor—the dignity of work. Traditional republicanism hailed the virtuous common man as the nation's backbone. In Abraham Lincoln, a man of humble origins who became a successful lawyer and political leader, Republicans had a symbol of that tradition. They portrayed their party as the guardian of economic opportunity, giving individuals a chance to work, acquire land, and attain success. Republicans argued that the South, with little industry and slave labor, remained backward.

At stake in the crises of the 1850s were thus two competing definitions of "liberty:" southern planters' claims to protection of their liberty in the possession and transport of their slaves anywhere, and northern workers' and farmers' claims to protection of their liberty to seek a new start on free land, unimpeded by a system that defined labor as slave and black.

Opposition to slavery's extension helped create the Republican Party, but members broadened their appeal by adopting other causes. Their coalition ideology consisted of many elements: resentment of southern political power, devotion to unionism, antislavery sentiments based on free-labor arguments, moral revulsion to slavery, and racial prejudice. As *New York Tribune* editor Horace Greeley wrote in 1860, "an Anti-Slavery man per se cannot be elected." But, "a Tariff, River-and-Harbor, Pacific Railroad, Free Homestead man, may succeed although he is Anti-Slavery."

Southern Democrats
The disintegration of the Whig Party left many southerners at loose ends politically, including wealthy planters, smaller slaveholders, and urban businessmen. In the tense atmosphere of sectional crisis, these people were susceptible to states' rights positions and the defense of slavery. Hence, most formerly Whig slaveholders became Democratic.

Since Andrew Jackson's day, however, nonslaveholding yeomen had been the heart of the Democratic Party. Democratic politicians, though often slave owners, lauded the common man and claimed to advance his interests. According to the southern version of republicanism, white citizens in a slave society enjoyed liberty and equality because black people were enslaved. As Jefferson Davis explained in 1851, in the South, slavery elevated every white person to "stand upon the broad level of equality with the rich man." To retain support from ordinary whites, southern Democrats appealed to racism, asking, "Shall negroes govern white men, or white men govern negroes?"

Racial fears and traditional political loyalties kept the alliance between yeoman farmers and planters intact through the 1850s. Across class lines, white southerners united against what they perceived as the Republican Party's capacity to cause slave unrest. In the South, no viable party emerged to replace the Whigs, and political realignment sharpened sectional identities.

Political leaders of both sections used race in their arguments about opportunity. The *Montgomery* (Alabama) *Mail* warned southern whites in 1860 that the Republicans intended "to free the negroes and force amalgamation between them and the children of the poor men of the South." Republicans warned northern

William Walker and Filibustering

Between 1848 and 1861, the United States was at peace with foreign nations. But that did not stop private citizens, sometimes supported by politicians and businessmen, from launching adventurous attempts to take over foreign lands, especially in Mexico, Central America, and the Caribbean. The 1850s was the heyday of "filibustering," defined then as private military expeditions designed to destabilize or conquer foreign lands in the name of manifest destiny, commerce, the spread of slavery and white supremacy, or masculine daring.

At least a dozen filibustering schemes emerged in this era of expansion and sectional crises, all violations of the Neutrality Act of 1818. Such laws did not stop some senators, railroad and shipping entrepreneurs, or the self-styled soldier of fortune, William Walker, from seeking the "Southern dream" of a Latin American empire. They also did not stop several American presidents from attempting to annex Cuba.

Born in Tennessee, Walker studied in Europe in 1848 before returning to New Orleans for a stint editing a newspaper. He moved to California, practiced law, and courted conflict by fighting duels. After an ill-fated attempt in 1853 to forcibly create an American "colony" in Sonora and the Baja peninsula in Mexico, Walker turned to Nicaragua, whose isthmus was the fastest route to the California gold fields.

With a small army of mercenaries, Walker invaded Nicaragua in 1856, seized its government, declared himself president, and reintroduced slavery, which Nicaragua had banned. Defeated by a coalition of Nicaraguans and British in 1857, Walker returned to the United States and launched a fund-raising and speaking campaign on which he was often treated as a romantic hero. On his return to Nicaragua, he was arrested by a U.S. Navy squadron, brought to America, tried, and acquitted.

In 1860, Walker published an account of his exploits, *War in Nicaragua*. Famous for his swashbuckling character, Walker was regarded by some as a pirate serving the "Slave Power Conspiracy," and by others as the "grey-eyed man of destiny" advancing slavery and American hegemony. On Walker's third return to Central America in 1860, he was arrested and Honduran authorities executed him by firing squad. These filibustering adventures fired the imagination of manifest destiny and were small precursors of a larger United States exploitation and conquest of Latin America in the century to follow. Walker's legend, heroic and notorious, lives on today in Central America and in two American movies, *Burn* (1969), starring Marlon Brando, and *Walker* (1987), starring Ed Harris. Filibusters were links to the world that gave the United States a difficult legacy to overcome with its neighbors from Cuba to Hawai'i.

Library of Congress Prints and Photographs Division [LC-USZC4-10802]

Portrait of William Walker, Tennessee-born filibusterer, a self-styled soldier of fortune who attempted to create his own empire in Nicaragua, where he reinstituted slavery. To some, especially southerners, he was a romantic hero, but to others—especially northerners and the U.S. government—he was a notorious villain and arch proponent of the worst aspects of manifest destiny.

workers that, if slavery entered the territories, the great reservoir of opportunity for ordinary citizens would be poisoned.

Bleeding Kansas	The Kansas-Nebraska Act spawned violence as land-hungry partisans clashed in Kansas Territory.

Abolitionists and religious groups sent armed Free-Soil settlers; southerners sent reinforcements to establish slavery and prevent "northern hordes" from stealing Kansas. Conflicts led to bloodshed, and soon the nation was talking about "Bleeding Kansas."

Politics in the territory resembled war more than democracy. During 1855 elections for a territorial legislature, thousands of proslavery Missourians—known as Border Ruffians—invaded the polls and ran up a fraudulent majority for proslavery candidates. They murdered and intimidated free state settlers. The resulting legislature legalized slavery. Free-Soilers responded with an unauthorized convention at which they created their own government and constitution.

In May, a proslavery posse sent to arrest the Free-Soil leaders sacked the town of Lawrence, Kansas, killing several people and destroying a hotel. In revenge, radical abolitionist John Brown and his followers murdered five proslavery settlers along Pottawatomie Creek. The victims' heads and limbs were hacked by heavy broadswords. Brown did not wield a sword, but he fired a fatal shot into the head of one foe. Soon, armed bands of guerrillas battled over land claims as well as slavery.

Violence reached the U.S. Senate in May 1856, when Charles Sumner of Massachusetts denounced "the Crime against Kansas." Radically opposed to slavery, Sumner assailed the president, the South, and Senator Andrew P. Butler of South Carolina. Butler's cousin, Representative Preston Brooks, approached Sumner, raised his cane in defense of his kin's honor, and beat Sumner on the head. The senator collapsed.

Shocked northerners recoiled from another seeming case of wanton southern violence and assault on free speech. William Cullen Bryant, editor of the *New York Evening Post,* asked, "Has it come to this, that we must speak with bated breath in the presence of our southern masters?" Popular opinion in Massachusetts supported Sumner; South Carolina voters reelected Brooks.

Election of 1856	The election of 1856 showed extreme polarization. Democrats chose James Buchanan of Pennsylvania, who, as ambassador to Britain for four years, was unin-

volved in territorial controversies. Superior party organization helped Buchanan win 1.8 million votes and the election, but he owed his victory to southern support. Hence, he was labeled "a northern man with southern principles."

Eleven of sixteen free states voted against Buchanan, and Democrats did not regain those states for decades. The Republican candidate, John C. Frémont, won those eleven free states and 1.3 million votes; Republicans became the dominant party in the North after only two years of existence. The coming battle would pit a sectional Republican Party against an increasingly divided Democratic Party, with voter turnouts as high as 75 to 80 percent in many states.

Slavery and the Nation's Future

How did the issue of slavery—and the Dred Scott *decision—further divide the nation?*

For years, the issue of slavery in the territories convulsed Congress, and Congress tried to settle the issue. In 1857, the Supreme Court took up this emotionally charged issue and attempted to silence controversy with a definitive verdict.

Dred Scott Case

A Missouri slave named Dred Scott and his wife, Harriet Robinson Scott, sued for their freedom. Scott argued that his former owner, an army surgeon, had taken him for several years into Illinois, a free state, and to Fort Snelling in the Minnesota Territory, from which slavery was barred by the Missouri Compromise. Scott first won and then lost his case as it moved on appeal through the state courts, into the federal system, and after eleven years, to the Supreme Court.

The impetus for the lawsuit likely came as much from Harriet as from Dred Scott. They were legally married at Fort Snelling (free territory) in 1836 when Dred was forty and Harriet seventeen. She lived as a slave on free soil for about five years and had four children, also born on free soil: two sons who died in infancy and two daughters, Eliza and Lizzie, who lived. The quest for "freedom papers" through a lawsuit—begun in 1846 as two separate cases, one in his name and one in hers—possibly came as much from Harriet's desire to protect her teenage daughters from potential sale and sexual abuse. Her case for freedom may have been stronger than Dred's, but lawyers subsumed her case into his during the long appeal process.

After hesitation, the Supreme Court agreed to hear *Dred Scott v. Sanford* and decided to rule on the Missouri Compromise after all. The precedent before the court was this: Was a black person like Dred Scott a citizen of the United States and thus eligible to sue in federal court? Had residence in a free state or territory made him free? Did Congress have the power to prohibit or promote slavery in a territory? Two northern justices indicated they would dissent from the assigned opinion and argue for Scott's freedom and the constitutionality of the Missouri Compromise. This emboldened southerners on the Court, who were growing eager to declare the 1820 geographical restriction on slavery unconstitutional. In March 1857, Chief Justice Roger B. Taney of Maryland delivered the majority opinion of a divided Court (the vote was 7 to 2). Taney declared that Scott

Frank Leslie's Illustrated Newspaper, *June 27, 1857. Dred Scott and his wife, Harriet, below, and their two children, Eliza and Lizzie, above. Such dignified pictures and informative articles provided Americans broadly with images of the otherwise mysterious Dred Scott and his family in the landmark Supreme Court case.*

Library of Congress Prints and Photographs Division [LC-US262-79305]

was not a citizen of the United States or Missouri, that residence in free territory did not make Scott free, and that Congress had no power to bar slavery from any territory. The decision not only overturned a thirty-seven-year-old compromise, it also invalidated the Wilmot Proviso and popular sovereignty.

The Slave Power seemed to have won a major constitutional victory. African Americans were dismayed, for Taney's decision asserted that the founders had never intended for blacks to be citizens. At the nation's founding, the chief justice wrote, blacks had been regarded "as beings of an inferior order" with "no rights which the white man was bound to respect." Taney was mistaken, however. African Americans had been citizens in several original states and had voted.

Nevertheless, the ruling seemed to shut the door permanently on black hopes for justice. In northern black communities, rage and despair prevailed. Many fugitive slaves sought refuge in Canada; others considered the Caribbean or Africa. One black abolitionist said that the **Dred Scott** decision made slavery "the supreme law of the land." In this state of social dislocation and fear, blacks contemplated whether they had any future in the United States.

Northern whites who rejected the decision were suspicious of the circumstances that produced it. Five of the nine justices were southerners; three northern justices dissented or refused to concur in parts of the decision. The only northerner who supported Taney's opinion, Justice Robert Grier of Pennsylvania, was close to President Buchanan.

Link to The Dred Scott Decision, 1857

***Dred Scott* decision**
Controversial 1857 Supreme Court decision that stated that slaves were not U.S. citizens. It also deemed the Missouri Compromise unconstitutional because Congress lacked the authority to ban slavery in the territories.

Abraham Lincoln and the Slave Power

Republican politicians used these fears to strengthen their antislavery coalition. Abraham Lincoln declared as early as 1854 that the nation wanted the territories reserved as "homes of free white people. This they cannot be, to any considerable extent, if slavery shall be planted within them."

More important, Lincoln warned of slavery's increasing control over the nation. While the founders recognized slavery's existence, Lincoln argued in the "House Divided" speech of 1858, by which he launched his campaign against Stephen Douglas for the U.S. Senate from Illinois, the public believed that slavery would die naturally or by legislation. The next step in the unfolding Slave Power conspiracy, Lincoln alleged, would be a Supreme Court decision "declaring that the Constitution does not permit a State to exclude slavery from its limits." Indeed, lawsuits challenged state laws that freed slaves brought within their borders.

In the epic Lincoln-Douglas debates, staged before massive crowds in September-October, 1858, these two candidates squared off over the issues dividing the country: the westward expansion of slavery, abolitionism, federal power over property in slaves, whether the Declaration of Independence signaled racial equality, and ultimately, the American republic's future. Perhaps never before or since have Americans demonstrated such an appetite for democratic engagement.

As Lincoln showed in these debates, politically, Republicans were now locked in conflict with the *Dred Scott* decision. By endorsing the South's doctrine of state sovereignty, the Court had effectively declared that the Republican Party's central position—no extension of slavery—was unconstitutional. Republicans could only repudiate the decision, appealing to a "higher law," or hope to change the personnel of the Court.

The Lecompton Constitution and Disharmony Among Democrats

Northern voters were alarmed by the prospect that the territories would be opened to slavery. To retain their support, northern Democrats like Stephen Douglas had to reassure these voters. Yet, given his presidential ambitions, Douglas could not alienate southern Democrats.

Douglas chose to stand by popular sovereignty, even if the result angered southerners. In 1857, Kansans voted on a proslavery constitution drafted at Lecompton. It was defeated by more than ten thousand votes in a referendum boycotted by proslavery voters. Kansans overwhelmingly opposed slavery, yet President Buchanan tried to force the Lecompton Constitution through Congress to hastily organize the territory.

Never had the Slave Power's influence over the government seemed more blatant; the Buchanan administration and southerners demanded a proslavery outcome, contrary to majority will in Kansas. Douglas threw his weight against the Lecompton Constitution, infuriating southern Democrats like Senator Albert G. Brown of Mississippi. Increasingly, many southerners believed that their sectional rights and slavery would be safe only in a separate nation. And northern Democrats, led by Douglas, found it harder to support the territorial protection for slavery that southern Democrats insisted was a constitutional right.

John Brown's Raid on Harpers Ferry

Soon, the nation would be drawn to a new dimension of antislavery activism—armed rebellion. Born in Connecticut in 1800, John Brown was raised by religious antislavery parents. Between 1820 and 1855, he engaged in some twenty business ventures, nearly all failures. In his abolitionism, Brown relied on an Old Testament conception of justice—"an eye for an eye"—and he believed that slavery was an "unjustifiable" state of war. He also believed that violence in a righteous cause was a holy act. To Brown, the destruction of slavery in America required revolutionary acts.

On October 16, 1859, Brown led eighteen whites and blacks in an attack on the federal arsenal at Harpers Ferry, Virginia. Hoping to trigger a slave rebellion, Brown failed and was captured. In a celebrated trial in November and widely publicized execution in December, in Charles Town, Virginia, Brown became an enduring martyr, and villain, of American history.

White southerners were outraged when they learned that Brown received financial backing from prominent abolitionists and that such northern intellectuals as Ralph Waldo Emerson

The Metropolitan Museum of Art/Art Resource, NY

The Last Moments of John Brown, *depicting Brown's mythical kissing of the black child while leaving the jail for his journey to the gallows, by Thomas Hovenden, oil on canvas, 1882. Metropolitan Museum of Art, New York, Art Resource New York.*

Legacy FOR A PEOPLE AND A NATION

Coalition Politics

In a democracy, constituencies with diverse interests often form coalition parties to win elections. In the 1830s and 1840s Democrats and Whigs held varied beliefs, particularly regarding slavery. From the Mexican War into the 1850s, when third parties (the Free-Soilers and nativists) threatened the two-party system, and with the triumph of the Republicans in forging a new antislavery alliance that destroyed the second party system, the antebellum era provided a model of coalition politics.

The most rapidly successful third-party movement in American history was the Republican Party, founded in 1854. Never before or since has a coalition of politicians and voters from long-standing parties coalesced so clearly around a single goal—stopping slavery's spread.

Northern Democrats bolted to the Republicans; by the 1856 election, they formed 25 percent of the new party's vote. Northern Whigs also joined the Republicans. Radical abolitionists of the old Liberty or Free-Soil parties now found leadership positions among the exclusively northern Republicans.

This antislavery coalition forged divergent outlooks into a new worldview: resentment of southern society and political power; an aggressive antislavery, pro- free-labor argument; fear of disunion; moral revulsion to slavery as inhumane; a racist urge to keep free blacks from the West; and finally, commitment to the northern social order as the model of progress. Such a multi-part ideology coalesced against the common foe of the "Slave Power Conspiracy," an alleged concentration of southern power determined to control the nation's future.

Whether in the rural and urban reformers who formed the Populist and Progressive movements of the late nineteenth and early twentieth centuries; the mixture of urban working classes, rural southern whites, African Americans, and intellectuals of the New Deal coalition from the Great Depression to the 1970s; or the modern conservative counterrevolution, with its antigovernment determination to dismantle the New Deal's social contract, all coalitions have drawn upon this enduring legacy of pre–Civil War American politics.

and Henry David Thoreau praised Brown as a holy warrior. The South interpreted Brown's attack at Harpers Ferry as an act of terrorism and the fulfillment of their dread of "abolition emissaries" who would infiltrate the region to incite slave rebellion.

When Brown went to the gallows, he handed a note to his jailer with the famous prediction "I John Brown am now quite certain that the crimes of this guilty land will never be purged away, but with blood."

Summary

During the 1820s, politicians broadened their appeal to an expanding electorate of white men, helping give birth to the second party system with its rivalry between the Democrats and Whigs. Both parties favored economic development but Whigs advocated centralized government, whereas Democrats advocated limited government and agricultural expansion. Controversies over the Second Bank of the United States and nullification exposed different interpretations of the nation's founding principles. Although women participated in political campaigns and sought equality, activists won few supporters. Instead, the nation was focused on economic development and westward expansion.

The War with Mexico fostered massive land acquisition, which forced an open debate about slavery in the West. The Compromise of 1850 attempted to settle the dispute but only exacerbated sectional tensions, leading to the fateful Kansas-Nebraska Act of 1854, which tore asunder the political party system and gave birth to an antislavery coalition. With Bleeding Kansas and the *Dred Scott* decision by 1857, Americans faced clear and dangerous choices about the future of labor and the meaning of liberty in an expanding society. Finally, by 1859, when radical abolitionist John Brown attacked Harpers Ferry to foment a slave insurrection, southerners and northerners regarded each other in conspiratorial terms. Meanwhile, African Americans, slave and free, feared slave catchers and expected violent resolutions to their dreams of freedom in America.

During the 1850s, every southern victory in territorial expansion increased fear of the Slave Power, and each new expression of Free-Soil sentiment prompted slaveholders to harden their demands. In the profoundest sense, slavery was the root of the war. As a people and a nation, Americans reached the most fateful turning point in their history. Resolution would now come from the battlefield.

Chapter Review

Jacksonianism and Party Politics

How did changes in voting laws influence the outcome of the 1824 presidential election and the future of political parties?

As suffrage laws changed to eliminate property requirements and allow immigrants to vote, the number of eligible voters tripled from 1824 to 1828. Politicians broadened their outreach to these new voters and successfully urged states to shift from appointing presidential electors to electing them by popular vote. That, combined with the end of candidate selection by congressional caucus, meant that five Democratic-Republican candidates ran for president in 1824. Although Andrew Jackson led in both electoral and popular vote, no one had a clear majority, leaving the House of Representatives to choose the president. Its members chose second-place John Quincy Adams, which led to charges of election-stealing and divided the party into the National Republicans (behind Adams) and the Democrats (behind Jackson). With two parties and only two candidates in the 1828 election, Jackson handily won the presidency, and the Democratic Party became the first well-organized national political party in the United States.

Federalism at Issue: The Nullification and Bank Controversies

What was at issue in the Nullification Crisis?

At the core of the Nullification Crisis were differing interpretations of the Constitution regarding federal power and states' rights. The doctrine of nullification—that states could overrule federal legislation—was based on the Virginia and Kentucky Resolutions of 1798, which argued that states could judge whether federal actions were constitutional, and ultimately nullify federal laws that did not pass the test. President Jackson rejected state sovereignty and saw nullification as leading to disunion. When South Carolina nullified a federal tariff, Jackson threatened force to collect the duties. As a compromise, the tariff was reduced and South Carolina withdrew its nullification. But the debate on the nature of the republic and of federal power continued.

The Second Party System

How did Whigs and Democrats differ ideologically?

Unlike the Democrats, Whigs advocated for economic growth via an activist federal government. They were for corporate charters, a national bank, and paper currency and promoted public schools and prison reform. Nor did Whigs worry about government aiding special interests; to them, as long as the public benefited, they saw no problem in it. Democrats believed in the Jefferson model of limited government and embraced unrestricted westward expansion. Democrats saw the world divided into "haves" and "have nots" and saw in the West an opportunity for greater equality and social mobility for hardworking, independent farmers. Whigs worried about rapid westward expansion, thought government should be ruled from the top down, and believed that the wealthy obtained their status through their hard work, not political favors.

Women's Rights

What inspired the rise of the women's movement in the mid-nineteenth century?

The religious revivals of the Second Great Awakening provided the first impetus for a later women's movement by encouraging women to see themselves as equal spiritually to men and encouraging them to help reform society. Women's growing participation in the antislavery movement—and their subordinated status within it—lay the groundwork for the women's rights movement. After 1830, married women made small gains in property and spousal rights. Traditional marriage law, borrowed from the English, gave husbands control over the family, including wives' property and earnings, but new married women's property acts—beginning with Arkansas in 1835—enabled them to own and control inherited property. Eight years after being denied a seat at the World Anti-Slavery Convention because of their sex, Elizabeth Cady Stanton and Lucretia Mott joined others in holding the first Woman's Rights Convention in 1848 at Seneca Falls, New York. There, three hundred participants outlined their demands for political and social equality, including the right to vote, in their Declaration of Sentiments, a document that paralleled the Declaration of Independence.

The Politics of Territorial Expansion

How did territorial expansion expose political fissures?

Efforts to expand the territorial holdings of the United States ultimately magnified sharp regional and political divisions and ended the second party system's cross-sectional alliances. While Democrats embraced westward expansion as part of their vision of a society of independent white farmers, Whigs preferred to focus on commercial development within the nation's existing boundaries. Initially, both parties were able to reach compromises with factions in the North and South, until the divisive issue of slavery's role in westward expansion became unavoidable. Those who embraced widening America's territory to the Pacific as its manifest destiny sought to annex Texas—formerly Mexico's holding—and Oregon, which the United States jointly occupied with Great Britain. Whigs feared annexation of Texas would widen slavery's reach, tip the balance of free and slave states, lead to war with Mexico, and strain trade relations. Southern Democrats, including President James Polk, wanted to extend slavery as part of westward expansion, and took the first step by annexing Texas in 1845 as a slave state. The move made regional divisions unavoidable and moved the nation toward a war with Mexico and its own sectional crisis.

The War with Mexico and Its Consequences

How did Polk's decisions push the United States toward war with Mexico?

President Polk wanted to expand America's borders to the Pacific during the 1840s and was not going to take no for an answer. He supported annexation of Texas—which angered the Mexican government—and contested the U.S. border with Mexico, urging Texans to claim territory to the Rio Grande despite Mexico's strong objections that the boundary lay at the Nueces River. While unsuccessfully attempting to buy California from Mexico, Polk also sent troops to defend the Rio Grande dividing line. There, they were met by Mexican cavalry. After a three-week standoff, the Mexican cavalry ambushed a U.S. unit, killing eleven Americans and taking sixty-three captive. Polk informed Congress that Mexico had crossed what he considered the U.S. boundary (the disputed area), and thereby deceptively claimed that Mexico had incited the conflict that would become the War with Mexico.

1850: Compromise or Armistice?

What were the two troubling issues inherent in the Compromise of 1850?

The Compromise of 1850 attempted to resolve the debate between the North and South over slavery in the territories. In the end, it only furthered the controversy. First, it left the definition of popular sovereignty unclear so that southerners could interpret it to mean that a region could not ban slavery during the territorial stage, whereas northerners believed it was up to the people to decide at any point. Second, the Fugitive Slave Act enabled slave owners to present evidence in state courts that a slave had escaped, which would then serve as proof of slave status even in free states and territories—and without investigation into its truth. Moreover, the fees paid to commissioners were twice as much if a person were deemed to be a slave. Northerners could be arrested if they hid escaped slaves in their homes, which further angered northerners who saw this as a violation of their rights, thereby aggravating regional tensions.

Slavery Expansion and Collapse of the Party System

How did the Kansas-Nebraska Act lead to the collapse of existing political parties?

The Kansas-Nebraska Act, which ultimately eroded the 1850 Compromise, prompted sectional divisions within the political parties that led to each party's breakdown. The act established the Kansas and Nebraska Territories, but it applied popular sovereignty to let the territories decide what to do about slavery. Northerners argued that since the territories were within the Louisiana Purchase, they were subject to the Missouri Compromise (which prohibited slavery from latitude 36°30′ north to the Canadian border). When the act was passed in 1854, sectional divisions intensified. The weakened Whig Party split into northern and southern wings. Democrats' support in the North plummeted, costing them most of their congressional seats and control of all but two state legislatures. In late 1854, antislavery Whigs and Democrats, Free-Soilers, and reformers throughout the Old Northwest formed the new Republican Party to keep slavery from the territories.

Slavery and the Nation's Future

How did the issue of slavery—and the *Dred Scott* decision—further divide the nation?

The *Dred Scott* decision validated northern fears of a southern Slave Power, and inspired new fears about the territories being open to slavery. The Supreme Court was ultimately stacked in favor of the southern position on slavery and its extension into the new territories. Five of the nine justices were southerners, which had northerners fearing conspiracy. The court's decision in the *Dred Scott* case—that Scott was a slave despite the fact that he had lived in the free state of Illinois and the free territory of Missouri and that Congress could not make any laws that barred slavery from the territories—invalidated the Missouri Compromise. African Americans were devastated by the court's opinion that the nation's founders had never intended them to be citizens, while white northerners saw the decision as proof of the Slave Power's growing reach.

Suggestions for Further Reading

Edward L. Ayers and Carolyn R. Martin, eds., *America on the Eve of the Civil War* (2010)

Donald B. Cole, *Vindicating Andrew Jackson: The 1828 Election and the Rise of the Two-Party System* (2009)

Marc Egnal, *Clash of Extremes: The Economic Origins of the Civil War* (2009)

Nicole Etcheson, *Bleeding Kansas: Contested Liberty in the Civil War Era* (2004)

Don E. Fehrenbacher, *The Slaveholding Republic: An Account of the United States Government's Relations to Slavery* (2001)

Joan D. Hedrick, *Harriet Beecher Stowe: A Life* (1994)

Daniel Walker Howe, *What Hath God Wrought: The Transformation of America, 1815–1848* (2007)

Robert W. Johannsen, *To the Halls of the Montezumas: The Mexican War and the American Imagination* (1985)

Bruce Levine, *Half Slave and Half Free: The Roots of the Civil War* (2005)

Lynn Hudson Parsons, *The Birth of Modern Politics: Andrew Jackson, John Quincy Adams, and the Election of 1828* (2009)

Elizabeth R. Varon, *Disunion! The Coming of the American Civil War, 1789–1859* (2008)

Harry L. Watson, *Liberty and Power: The Politics of Jacksonian America* (2006)

Susan Zaeske, *Signatures of Citizenship: Petitioning, Antislavery, and Women's Political Identity* (2003)

Transforming Fire:
The Civil War,

13

1860–1865

Slave pens were the ugly crossroads of American history. Wallace Turnage, a seventeen-year-old slave from a cotton plantation in Pickens County, Alabama, entered wartime Mobile in December 1862 through the slave traders' yard; he would leave Mobile from that same yard twenty months later.

Turnage was born in 1846 on a tobacco farm near Snow Hill, North Carolina. In mid-1860, as the nation teetered toward disunion, he was sold to a Richmond, Virginia, slave trader named Hector Davis. Turnage worked in Davis's three-story slave jail, organizing auctions until he was sold for $1,000 in early 1861 to a cotton planter from Pickens County, Alabama. Frequently whipped, the desperate teenager tried four times over the next two years to escape to the Union army in Mississippi. He was captured each time and returned to his owner.

Frustrated, his owner sold Turnage for $2,000 at the Mobile slave traders' yard to a wealthy merchant in the port city. During 1864, as Mobile came under siege, its slaves were enlisted to build trenchworks. Turnage did many urban tasks for his new owner's family, including driving their carriage on errands.

In early August, Turnage crashed the carriage on a Mobile street. Furious, his owner took him to the slave pen, hiring the jailer to administer thirty lashes in the "whipping house." Stripped naked, his hands tied, Turnage was hoisted up on a hook. When it was over, his owner instructed Wallace to walk home. Instead, Turnage "took courage," as he wrote in his postwar narrative, and walked southwest through the Confederate encampment. The soldiers mistook the bloodied and tattered black teenager for one among hundreds of slaves who did camp labor.

For three weeks, Turnage crawled and waded twenty-five miles through the snake-infested swamps of the Foul River estuary, down the west edge of Mobile Bay. Nearly starved and narrowly escaping Confederate patrols, Turnage reached Cedar Point, where he could see Dauphin Island, now occupied by Union forces. Alligators swam nearby, as Turnage hid from

Confederates. He remembered: "It was death to go back and it was death to stay there and freedom was before me."

Then, Turnage noticed an old rowboat. He began to row out into the bay. Suddenly, he "heard the crash of oars and behold there was eight Yankees in a boat." Turnage jumped into the Union gunboat. For a few moments, the oarsmen in blue "were struck with silence" by the frail young black man crouched before them. Turnage looked back at Confederate soldiers on the shore and took his first breaths of freedom.

The Civil War brought astonishing changes to daily life, North and South. Millions of men were swept into training camps and regiments. Armies numbering in the hundreds of thousands marched over the South, devastating the countryside. Families struggled to survive without men; businesses coped with fewer workers. Women took on extra responsibilities and moved into new workforce jobs, including nurses and hospital workers.

But southerners also experienced defeat. For most, wealth changed to poverty as farms were ruined. Late in the war, many southerners yearned only for an end to inflation, shortages, slave escapes, and the death that visited most families. Southern slaves did not always encounter sympathetic liberators like those who aided Turnage, fed and clothed him, and took him before a Union general, where the freedman could either join a black regiment or become a white officer's camp servant. Until war's end, Turnage cooked for a Maryland captain.

In the North, farm boys and mechanics would be asked for heretofore unimagined sacrifices. The conflict ensured vast government expenditures and lucrative federal contracts. Businessmen found war profitable. "The battle of Bull Run," predicted an eminent financier in *Harper's Monthly,* "makes the fortune of every man in Wall Street who is not a natural idiot."

Change was most drastic in the South, where secessionists launched a conservative revolution for their section's independence. Born of states' rights doctrine, the Confederacy had to be transformed into a centralized nation to fight the war. Southern whites feared that a peacetime government of Republicans would interfere with slavery and ruin plantation life. Instead, their actions led to a war that turned southern society upside down and imperiled slavery's existence.

The war created social strains in North and South. Disaffection was strongest, though, in the Confederacy, where poverty and class resentment threatened the South from within. In the North, dissent also flourished, and antiwar sentiment occasionally erupted into violence.

The Civil War forced a social and political revolution regarding race. It compelled leaders and citizens to finally face the question of slavery. And blacks embraced the most fundamental turning point in their experience as Americans.

As you read this chapter, keep the following questions in mind:

- **How and why did the Civil War bring social transformations to both South and North?**

- **How did the war to preserve the Union or for southern independence become the war to free the slaves?**

- **By 1865, when Americans on all sides searched for the *meaning* of the war they had just fought, what might some of their answers have been?**

Election of 1860 and Secession Crisis

What were the issues leading to secession and the dissolution of the Union?

Many Americans believed the election of 1860 would decide the Union's fate. The Democratic Party was the only party that was truly national in scope. But at its 1860 convention in Charleston, South Carolina, the Democratic Party split.

Stephen Douglas wanted his party's presidential nomination, but he feared alienating northern voters by accepting the southern position on the territories. Southern Democrats, however, insisted on recognition of their rights—as defined by the *Dred Scott* decision. When Douglas obtained a majority for his version of the platform, delegates from the Deep South walked out. The Democrats presented two nominees: Douglas for the northern wing, and Vice President John C. Breckinridge of Kentucky for the southern.

Republicans nominated Abraham Lincoln, a reflection of the Midwest's growing power. Lincoln was perceived as more moderate on slavery than the early front-runner, Senator William H. Seward of New York. A Constitutional Union Party nominated John Bell of Tennessee.

Bell's only issue in the ensuing campaign was preserving the Union. Douglas sought to unite his northern and southern supporters, while Breckinridge backed away from the appearance of extremism, and his supporters in several states stressed his unionism. Although Lincoln and the Republicans denied any intent to interfere with slavery where it existed, they rejected its extension into the territories.

The 1860 election was sectional, and the only one in American history in which the losers refused to accept the result. Lincoln won, but Douglas, Breckinridge, and Bell together received a majority of the votes. Douglas had broad-based support but won few states. Breckinridge carried nine states in the Deep South. Bell won pluralities in Virginia, Kentucky, and Tennessee. Lincoln prevailed in the North, but in the four slave states that remained loyal to the Union (Missouri, Kentucky, Maryland, and Delaware—the border states) he gained only a plurality (see Table 13.1). Lincoln's victory was won in the electoral college. He polled only 40 percent of the total vote and was not on the ballot in ten slave states.

Chronology

1860	Election of Lincoln
	Secession of South Carolina
1861	Firing on Fort Sumter
	Battle of Bull Run
	McClellan organizes Union army
	Union blockade begins
	U.S. Congress passes first confiscation act
	Trent affair
1862	Union captures Fort Henry and Fort Donelson
	U.S. Navy captures New Orleans
	Battle of Shiloh shows the war's destructiveness
	Confederacy enacts conscription
	McClellan's peninsula campaign fails to take Richmond
	U.S. Congress passes second confiscation act, initiating emancipation
	Battle of Antietam ends Lee's drive into Maryland in September
	British intervention in the war on Confederate side is averted
1863	Emancipation Proclamation takes effect
	U.S. Congress passes National Banking Act
	Union enacts conscription

	African American soldiers join Union army
	Food riots occur in southern cities
	Battle of Chancellorsville ends in Confederate victory but Jackson's death
	Union wins key victories at Vicksburg and Gettysburg
	Draft riots take place in New York City
1864	Battles of the Wilderness and Spotsylvania produce heavy casualties on both sides
	Battle of Cold Harbor continues carnage in Virginia
	Sherman captures Atlanta
	Confederacy begins to collapse on home front
	Lincoln wins reelection, eliminating any Confederate hopes for negotiated end to war
	Jefferson Davis proposes arming slaves
	Sherman marches through Georgia to the sea
1865	Sherman marches through Carolinas
	U.S. Congress approves Thirteenth Amendment
	Lee surrenders at Appomattox Court House
	Lincoln assassinated
	Death toll in war reaches more than 700,000

Opposition to slavery's extension was the core issue for Lincoln and the Republican Party. Meanwhile, in the South, proslavery advocates and secessionists whipped up public opinion and demanded that state conventions assemble to consider secession.

Lincoln did not soften his party's position on the territories. Although many conservative Republicans—eastern businessmen and former Whigs who did not feel

TABLE 13.1   Presidential Vote in 1860

Lincoln (Republican)*	Carried all northern states and all electoral votes except 3 in New Jersey
Breckinridge (Southern Democrat)	Carried all slave states except Virginia, Kentucky, Tennessee, Missouri
Bell (Constitutional Union)	Carried Virginia, Kentucky, Tennessee
Douglas (Northern Democrat)	Carried only Missouri

*Lincoln received only 26,000 votes in the entire South and was not even on the ballot in ten slave states. Breckinridge was not on the ballot in three northern states.

strongly about slavery—hoped for a compromise, the original and most committed Republicans—old Free-Soilers and antislavery Whigs—held firm on slavery expansion.

In winter of 1860–1861, numerous compromise proposals were floated in Washington, including resurrecting the Missouri Compromise line, 36°30', and initiating a "plural presidency," with one president from each section. When Lincoln rejected concessions on the territorial issue, these peacemaking efforts collapsed.

Secession and the Confederate States of America

Meanwhile, on December 20, 1860, South Carolina passed an ordinance of secession. The Union was broken. Secessionists urged other states to follow South Carolina, believing that those favoring compromise could make a better deal outside the Union than in it.

Southern extremists called separate state conventions and passed secession ordinances in Mississippi, Florida, Alabama, Georgia, Louisiana, and Texas. By February 1861, these states joined South Carolina to form a new government in Montgomery, Alabama: the Confederate States of America. The delegates at Montgomery chose Jefferson Davis of Mississippi as their president.

Many southerners—perhaps even 40 percent in the Deep South—opposed immediate secession. In some state conventions, the secession vote was close and decided by overrepresentation of plantation districts. Four states in the Upper South—Virginia, North Carolina, Tennessee, and Arkansas—rejected secession and did not join the Confederacy until after fighting commenced. In border states, popular sentiment was divided; minorities in Kentucky and Missouri tried to secede, but these slave states ultimately came under Union control, along with Maryland and Delaware (see Map 13.1).

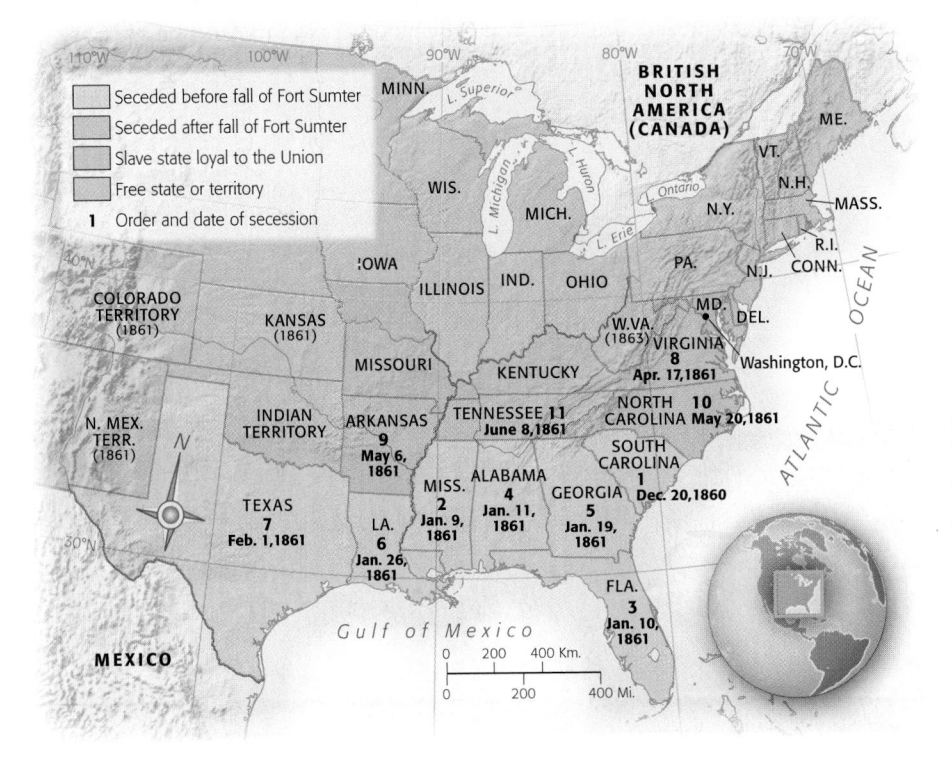

MAP 13.1

The Divided Nation—Slave and Free Areas, 1861

After fighting began, the Upper South joined the Deep South in the Confederacy. How does the nation's pattern of division correspond to the distribution of slavery and the percentage of blacks in the population? Source:

Copyright © Cengage Learning 2015

Secession posed new challenges for southerners. Analysis of election returns from 1860 and 1861 indicates that slaveholders and nonslaveholders were beginning to part company politically. Slaveholding counties strongly supported secession. But nonslaveholding areas proved less willing to support secession. With war looming, yeomen were beginning to consider their class interests and how far they would go to support slavery and slave owners.

As for why the Deep South bolted, the speeches and writings of the secession advocates prove revealing. Repeatedly, they stressed independence as the only way to preserve white racial security and the slave system. Only secession, said Alabama commissioner Stephen Hale to the Kentucky legislature, could sustain the "heaven-ordained superiority of the white over the black race."

Fort Sumter and Outbreak of War

President Lincoln's dilemma on Inauguration Day in March 1861 was how to maintain the authority of the federal government without provoking war. By holding onto forts in the states that had left the Union, he could assert federal sovereignty while awaiting restoration. But Jefferson Davis could not claim to lead a sovereign nation if the Confederate ports were under foreign (that is, U.S.) control.

The two sides collided early on April 12, 1861, at **Fort Sumter** in Charleston harbor. A federal garrison there ran low on food, and Lincoln notified the South Carolinians that he was sending a supply ship. For the Montgomery government, the alternatives were to attack the fort or acquiesce to Lincoln's authority. The Confederate secretary of war ordered local commanders to obtain a surrender or attack the fort. After two days of heavy bombardment, the federal garrison surrendered. Confederates permitted U.S. troops to sail away on unarmed vessels while Charlestonians celebrated. The Civil War—the bloodiest war in America's history—had begun.

Fort Sumter   Federal fort in Charleston harbor, South Carolina where the first shots of the Civil War were fired when the Union attempted to resupply troops.

Photograph of interior of Fort Sumter, in Charleston harbor, April 14, 1861, the day Major Robert Anderson and his troops surrendered and the Civil War began.

National Archives

Causation

Historians have debated the causes of the Civil War. Some have interpreted it as a clash of two civilizations on divergent historical trajectories. But the issues dividing Americans in 1861 were fundamental to the republic's future. Republican ideology tended toward abolishing slavery, even though Republicans denied such intention. Southern ideology led to establishing slavery everywhere, though southern leaders, too, denied such motives.

Lincoln put these facts succinctly. In a postelection letter to his old congressional colleague, Alexander Stephens of Georgia, soon to be vice president of the Confederacy, Lincoln stated, "You think slavery is right and ought to be expanded; while we think it is wrong and ought to be restricted. That I suppose is the rub."

Without slavery, there would have been no war. But the significance of states' rights, then as now, is always in the cause in which it is employed. If secession was an exercise in states' rights—then, to what end?

America goes to War, 1861–1862

What was the impact of the North's naval victories along the southern coast?

The onset of hostilities sparked patriotic sentiments, speeches, and ceremonies in both North and South. Northern communities raised companies of volunteers eager to save the Union. Southern recruits boasted of whipping the Yankees and returning home before Christmas. Southern women sewed dashing uniforms for men who would soon be lucky to wear drab gray or butternut homespun. Americans went to war in 1861 with romantic notions.

First Battle of Bull Run

Through the spring of 1861, both sides scrambled to organize and train their undisciplined armies. On July 21, 1861, the first battle took place outside Manassas Junction, Virginia, near a stream called **Bull Run**. General Irvin McDowell and thirty thousand Union troops attacked General P. G. T. Beauregard's twenty-two thousand southerners (see Map 13.2). Federal forces gained ground until they ran into a line of Virginia troops under General Thomas "Stonewall" Jackson. Jackson's line held, and the arrival of nine thousand Confederate reinforcements won the day for the South. Union troops fled to Washington.

Bull Run The location of the first major land battle in the Civil War.

The unexpected rout at Bull Run proved that although the United States enjoyed an advantage in resources, victory would not be easy. Pro-Union feeling was growing in western Virginia, and loyalties were divided in the four border slave states—Missouri, Kentucky, Maryland, and Delaware. But the rest of the Upper South—North Carolina, Virginia, Tennessee, and Arkansas—joined the Confederacy after Fort Sumter. Half a million southerners volunteered to fight—so many that the Confederate government could hardly arm them all. The United States therefore undertook a massive mobilization of troops around Washington, D.C.

Lincoln gave command of the army to General **George B. McClellan**, who proved better at organization and training than fighting. McClellan devoted fall and winter of 1861 to readying a force of a quarter-million men to take Richmond, the Confederate capital.

George B. McClellan Union general very popular with troops who proved better at organization and training than at fighting.

MAP 13.2
McClellan's Campaign

This map shows the water route chosen by McClellan to threaten Richmond during the peninsular campaign.

Source: Copyright © Cengage Learning 2015

Grand Strategy

While McClellan prepared, the Union began to implement other parts of its strategy, which called for a blockade of southern ports and capture of the Mississippi River. Like a constricting snake, this **"Anaconda plan"** would strangle the Confederacy. The Union navy had too few ships to patrol 3,550 miles of the southern coastline. Gradually, the navy increased the blockade's effectiveness, though it never stopped southern commerce completely.

"Anaconda plan" Called for the Union to blockade southern ports, capture the Mississippi River, and, like a snake, strangle the Confederacy.

The Confederate strategy was essentially defensive, given the South's claim of independence and the North's advantage in resources (see Figure 13.1). But Jefferson Davis called the southern strategy an "offensive defensive," maximizing opportunities to attack and using its transportation interior lines to concentrate troops at crucial points. The Confederacy did not need to conquer the North; the Union effort, however, required conquest of the South.

Both sides slighted the importance of the West, the expanse between Virginia and the Mississippi River and beyond. Guerrilla warfare broke out in 1861 in politically divided Missouri, and key locations along the Mississippi and other western rivers would prove crucial prizes in the North's victory. Beyond the Mississippi, the Confederacy hoped to gain an advantage by negotiating treaties with the Creeks, Choctaws, Chickasaws, Cherokees, Seminoles, and smaller groups of Plains Indians. Meanwhile, the Republican U.S. Congress carved the West into territories

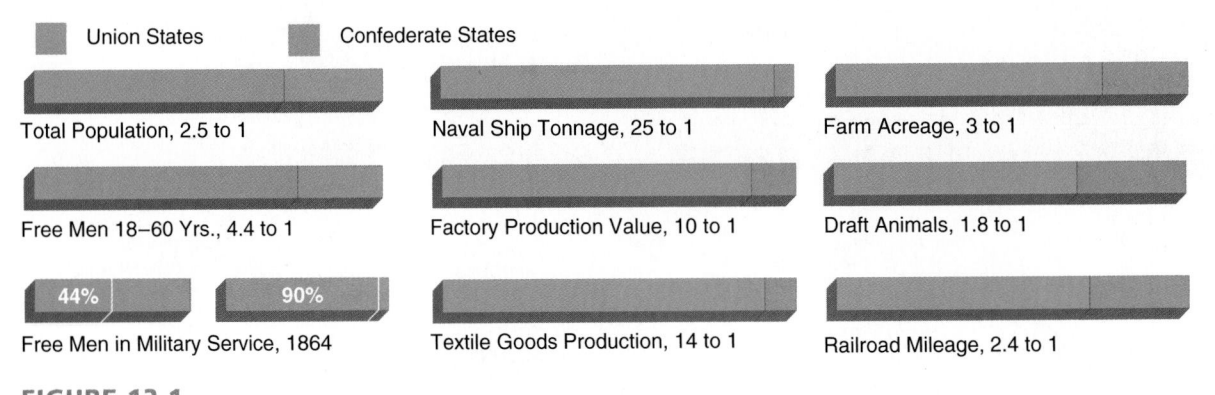

FIGURE 13.1
Comparative Resources, Union and Confederate States, 1861
The North had vastly superior resources. Although the North's advantages in manpower and industrial capacity proved very important, the South still had to be conquered, its society and its will crushed.

in anticipation of state making. For most Indians west of the Mississippi, the Civil War was nearly three decades of an enveloping strategy of conquest, relocation, and slaughter.

Union Naval Campaign The last half of 1861 brought no major land battles, but in late summer, Union naval forces captured Cape Hatteras and Hilton Head, one of the Sea Islands off Port Royal, South Carolina. A few months later, federal naval operations established significant beachheads along the Confederate coastline, including vital points in North Carolina, as well as Fort Pulaski, which defended Savannah (see Map 13.3).

The coastal victories off South Carolina foreshadowed a revolution in slave society. As federal gunboats approached, planters abandoned their land and fled. The Confederate cavalry tried to round up slaves and move them to the interior. But thousands of slaves greeted what they hoped to be freedom with rejoicing and broke the hated cotton gins. Some entered their masters' homes and took clothing and furniture. Many runaways poured into Union lines. Unwilling at first to wage a war against slavery, the federal government did not acknowledge the slaves' freedom—though it used their labor. These emancipated slaves, defined by Union officers as war "contraband" (confiscated enemy property), forced first a bitter debate within the Union army and government over how to treat the freedmen, and then an attempt to harness their labor and military power.

Spring 1862 brought stronger evidence of the war's gravity. In March, two ironclad ships—the *Monitor* (a Union warship) and the *Merrimack* (a Union ship that had been seized by the Confederacy)—fought off the coast of Virginia. Their battle, though indecisive, ushered in a new era in naval design. In April, Union ships commanded by Admiral David Farragut smashed through log booms blocking the Mississippi River and moved upstream to capture New Orleans. The South's greatest seaport and slave-trading center was now in federal hands.

MAP 13.3
The War in the West

Here is an overview of the Union's successful campaigns in the West and its seizure of the key points on the Mississippi River, as well as along the Atlantic coast in 1862 and 1863. These actions were decisive in paving the way for ultimate northern victory.

Source: Copyright © Cengage Learning 2015

War in the Far West

Farther west, three Confederate regiments were organized, mostly of Cherokees, but a Union victory at Elkhorn Tavern, Arkansas, shattered southern control of the region. Thereafter, Confederate operations in Indian Territory amounted to guerrilla raids.

In the westernmost campaign of the war, from February to May 1862, some three thousand Confederate and four thousand Union forces fought for control of New Mexico Territory. The Confederate invasion had aimed to access the trade riches of the Santa Fe Trail and seize gold mines in Colorado and California. But Colorado and New Mexico Unionists fought back, and in a series of battles at Glorieta Pass, twenty miles east of Santa Fe, on March 26 through 28, they blocked the Confederates. By May 1, Confederate forces straggled down the Rio Grande River into Texas, ending efforts to take New Mexico.

Grant's Tennessee Campaign and the Battle of Shiloh

Meanwhile, in February 1862, forces in northern Tennessee won significant Union victories. Union commander **Ulysses S Grant** saw the strategic importance of Fort Henry and Fort Donelson, the Confederate

Ulysses S Grant Commander of the Union army.

outposts guarding the Tennessee and Cumberland rivers. Over ten days, he seized the forts—cutting off the Confederates and demanding "unconditional surrender" of Fort Donelson. A path into Tennessee, Alabama, and Mississippi now lay open before the Union army.

Grant moved on into southern Tennessee and the first of the war's shockingly bloody encounters, the **Battle of Shiloh** (see Map 13.3). On April 6, Confederate general Albert Sidney Johnston caught federal troops with their backs to the Tennessee River, awaiting reinforcements. The Confederates attacked and inflicted heavy damage. Close to victory, General Johnston was killed. Union reinforcements arrived that night. The next day, the battle turned and, after ten hours of combat, the Confederates withdrew.

Neither side won a decisive victory at Shiloh, yet losses were staggering, and Confederates were forced to retreat into northern Mississippi. Northern troops lost thirteen thousand men (killed, wounded, or captured) out of sixty-three thousand; southerners sacrificed eleven thousand out of forty thousand. Total casualties in this single battle exceeded those in all three of America's previous wars combined. Before Shiloh, Grant hoped that southerners would soon tire of the conflict. After Shiloh, he recalled, "I gave up all idea of saving the Union except by complete conquest." Memories of the Shiloh battlefield would haunt surviving soldiers for the rest of their lives.

Battle of Shiloh The bloodiest battle in American history to that date (April 6–7, 1862).

McClellan and the Peninsula Campaign

On the Virginia front, President Lincoln had problems with General McClellan. Only thirty-six, McClellan had achieved success as an army officer and railroad president. Habitually overestimating the size of enemy forces, he called for reinforcements and ignored Lincoln's directions to advance. McClellan advocated a war of limited aims to ensure a quick reunion. He intended neither disruption of slavery nor war on noncombatants. McClellan finally sailed his troops down the Chesapeake, landing on the peninsula between the York and James rivers, and advanced on Richmond (see Map 13.2).

After a bloody battle at Fair Oaks on May 31 through June 1, the federal armies moved to within seven miles of the Confederate capital. The Confederate commanding general, Joseph E. Johnston, was wounded at Fair Oaks, and President **Jefferson Davis** placed his chief military adviser, **Robert E. Lee**, in command. The fifty-five-year-old Lee was an aristocratic Virginian, a lifelong military officer, and a veteran of the War with Mexico. Although he initially opposed secession, Lee gave his allegiance to his state and became a staunch Confederate. He soon foiled McClellan's legions.

Jefferson Davis President of the Confederacy.

Robert E. Lee Commander of the Confederate army.

First, Lee sent Stonewall Jackson's corps of seventeen thousand northwest into the Shenandoah Valley behind Union forces, where they threatened Washington, D.C., and drew some troops from Richmond to protect their own capital. Further, in mid-June, in an extraordinary four-day ride around the entire Union army, Confederate cavalry under J. E. B. Stuart confirmed the exposed position of McClellan's army north of the Chickahominy River. Then, in the Seven Days Battles, from June 26 through July 1, Lee struck at McClellan's army. Lee's daring move of taking the majority of his army northeast and attacking the Union right flank, while leaving only a small force to defend Richmond, forced McClellan to retreat toward the James River.

During the sustained fighting of the Seven Days, the Union forces suffered 20,614 casualties and the Confederates, 15,849. By August 3, McClellan withdrew his army to the environs of Washington. Richmond remained safe for almost two more years.

Confederate Offensive in Maryland and Kentucky

Buoyed by these results, Jefferson Davis conceived an ambitious plan to gain military advantage and recognition of the Confederacy by European nations. He ordered a general offensive, sending Lee north into Maryland and Generals Kirby Smith and Braxton Bragg into Kentucky. Calling on residents of Maryland and Kentucky, still slave states, to make peace with his government, Davis also invited northwestern states like Indiana, which sent much of their trade down the Mississippi to New Orleans, to leave the Union. This was an effort to take the war to the North and force a military and political turning point.

The plan was promising, but the offensive ultimately failed. Lee's forces achieved a striking success at the battle of Second Bull Run, August 29 through 30. The entire Union army retreated to the federal capital. Thousands of wounded occupied schools and churches, and two thousand suffered on cots in the U.S. Capitol rotunda.

Battle of Antietam First major battle on northern soil.

But in the bloodiest day of the war, September 17, 1862, McClellan turned Lee back from Sharpsburg, Maryland. In the **Battle of Antietam**, five thousand men died, and another eighteen thousand were wounded. McClellan intercepted a battle order, wrapped around cigars for each Confederate corps commander and lost by a courier. But McClellan moved slowly, failed to use his larger forces in simultaneous attacks, and allowed Lee's stricken army to retreat to across the Potomac. Lincoln removed McClellan from command.

In Kentucky, Generals Smith and Bragg secured Lexington and Frankfort, but their effort to force the Yankees back to the Ohio River was stopped at the Battle of Perryville on October 8. Bragg's army retreated back into Tennessee, where from December 31, 1862, to January 2, 1863, it fought an indecisive but bloody battle at Murfreesboro. Casualties exceeded even those of Shiloh.

Outnumbered and disadvantaged in resources, the South could not continue the offensive. Davis admitted to Confederate representatives that southerners were entering "the darkest and most dangerous period we have yet had."

But 1862 also brought painful lessons to the North. On December 13, Union general Ambrose Burnside, now in command of the Army of the Potomac, unwisely ordered his soldiers to attack Lee's army, which held fortified positions at

Library of Congress

Photograph of "Sunken Road," Antietam battlefield, taken shortly after the battle, September 1862, often called "The Harvest of Battle."

Fredericksburg, Virginia. Lee's men performed so efficiently in killing northerners that Lee was moved to say, "It is well that war is so terrible. We should grow too fond of it." Burnside's repeated assaults up Marye's Heights shocked his opponents, with thirteen hundred dead and ninety-six hundred wounded Union soldiers. The scale of carnage now challenged people on both sides to question the meaning of such a war.

War Transforms the South

What happened to the South's embrace of state sovereignty during the war?

War disrupted civilian life. One of the first traditions to fall was the southern preference for local and limited government. States' rights had been a formative ideology for the Confederacy, but state governments were weak. To withstand the North's massive power, the South needed to centralize; like the colonial revolutionaries, southerners could unite or die separately.

The Confederacy and Centralization

Jefferson Davis brought arms, supplies, and troops under centralized control. But by early 1862, the scope and duration of the conflict required more recruits. Tens of thousands of Confederate soldiers volunteered for one year, planning to return home in the spring to plant crops. Faced with a critical troop shortage, in April 1862 the Confederate government enacted the first national conscription (draft) law in American history.

Davis adopted a firm leadership role toward the Confederate Congress, which raised taxes and later passed a tax-in-kind—paid in farm products. Nearly forty-five hundred agents dispersed to collect the tax. Where opposition arose, the government suspended the writ of habeas corpus (which prevented individuals from being held without trial) and imposed martial law. Still, this tax system proved inadequate for the South's war effort.

To replace the food that men in uniform would have grown, Davis exhorted state governments to require farmers to switch from cash crops to food crops. But shortages continued. The War Department impressed slaves to work on fortifications, and after 1861 officers raided farms and carted away grain, meat, wagons, and draft animals to feed the troops. Such raids caused increased hardship and resentment for women managing farms without husbands and sons.

Soon, the Confederate administration gained control over the southern economy. The Confederate Congress also gave the central government almost complete control of the railroads. A large bureaucracy of over seventy thousand civilians administered Confederate operations. By the war's end, the southern bureaucracy was larger in proportion to population than its northern counterpart.

Confederate Nationalism

Historians have long argued over whether the Confederacy itself was a "rebellion," a "revolution," or the creation of a genuine "nation." Whatever label, Confederates created a culture and ideology of nationalism. In flags, songs, language, seals, school readers, and other national characteristics, Confederates crafted their own story.

Southerners believed the Confederacy was the true legacy of the American Revolution—a bulwark against centralized power that was in keeping with the war. To southerners, theirs was a continuing revolution against the excesses of Yankee democracy, and George Washington (a Virginian) on horseback formed the center of the Confederacy's official seal.

Also central to Confederate nationalism was a refurbished defense of slavery as a benign, protective institution, complete with the image of the "faithful slave." In wartime schoolbooks, children were instructed in the divinely inspired, paternalistic character of slavery. A poem popular among whites captured an old slave's rejection of the Emancipation Proclamation:

> Now, Massa, dis is berry fine, dese words
> You've spoke to me,
> No doubt you mean it kindly, but ole Dinah
> Won't be free …
> Ole Massa's berry good to me—and though I am
> His slave,
> He treats me like I'se kin to him—and I would
> Rather have
> A home in Massa's cabin, and eat his black
> Bread too,
> Dan leave ole Massa's children and go and
> Lib wid you.

Southern Cities and Industry

Clerks and subordinate officials crowded the cities where Confederate departments established offices. The sudden urban migration overwhelmed the housing supply and stimulated new construction. Richmond's population increased 250 percent. Mobile's population jumped from 29,000 to 41,000, and 10,000 people poured into war-related industries in little Selma, Alabama.

As the Union blockade disrupted imports, the traditionally agricultural South forged new industries. Many planters shared Davis's hope that industrialization would bring "deliverance … from all commercial dependence" on the North or the world. Indeed, the Confederacy achieved tremendous industrial development. Chief of Ordnance Josiah Gorgas increased the capacity of Richmond's Tredegar Iron Works and other factories so that by 1865 his Ordnance Bureau was supplying all Confederate small arms and ammunition. The government constructed new railroad lines and ironworks, using slaves relocated from farms and plantations.

Changing Roles of Women

White women, restricted to narrow roles in antebellum society, gained new responsibilities in wartime. The wives and mothers of soldiers now headed households and performed men's work, including raising crops and tending animals. Women in nonslaveholding families cultivated fields, while wealthier women acted as overseers. In the cities, white women—who had been largely excluded from the labor force—found respectable paying jobs, often in the Confederate bureaucracy. Female schoolteachers appeared in the South for the first time.

Patriotic sacrifice appealed to some women; others resented their new burdens. A Texas woman who had struggled to discipline slaves pronounced herself "sick of trying to do a man's business." Others grew angry over shortages, scornful of the war, and demanded that their men return to provide for their families.

Human Suffering, Hoarding, and Inflation

For millions of southerners, the war brought privation and suffering. Mass poverty descended on a large minority of the white population. Many yeoman families lost their breadwinners to the army. Women sought help from relatives, neighbors, friends, anyone. Sometimes they pleaded with the Confederate government to discharge their husbands.

The South was in many places so sparsely populated that the conscription of one craftsman could wreak hardship on an entire county. Often people begged together for the exemption or discharge of the local miller, neighborhood tanner, or wheelwright. Most serious, however, was the loss of a blacksmith, who could repair farming tools.

The blockade of Confederate shipping created shortages of important supplies—salt, sugar, coffee, nails—and speculation and hoarding made shortages worse. Greedy businessmen cornered the supply of some commodities; prosperous citizens stocked up on food. Inflation skyrocketed, fueled by the Confederate government's heavy borrowing and inadequate taxes, until prices increased almost 7,000 percent. Inflation particularly imperiled urban dwellers without their own food sources. As early as 1862, officials predicted that "women and children are bound to come to suffering if not starvation." A rudimentary relief program organized by the Confederacy failed to meet the need.

Inequities of the Confederate Draft

The Confederate government's policies decidedly favored the upper class. Until the war's last year, for example, prosperous southerners could avoid military service by hiring substitutes. Well over fifty thousand upper-class southerners purchased such substitutes, despite skyrocketing prices that reached $5,000 or $6,000 per man. Mary Boykin Chesnut knew of one aristocrat who "spent a fortune in substitutes.... He is at the end of his row now, for all able-bodied men are ordered to the front."

Anger at such discrimination exploded in October 1862, when the Confederate Congress exempted from military duty anyone who was supervising at least twenty slaves. Protests poured in from across the Confederacy, and North Carolina's legislators condemned the law. Its defenders argued, however, that exemption preserved order and aided food production, and the statute remained on the books.

This "twenty Negro" law is indicative of the racial fears many Confederates felt as the war threatened to overturn southern society. But it also fueled desertion and stimulated Unionism in nonslaveholding regions of the South. In Jones County, Mississippi, a wooded area with few slaves or plantations, Newt Knight, a Confederate soldier, led renegades who took over the county, declared their allegiance to the Union, and called their district the "Free State of Jones." They held out for the remainder of the war as an enclave of Union sympathizers.

The bitterness of letters to Confederate officials suggests the depth of the dissension and class anger. "If I and my little children suffer [and] die while there Father is in service," threatened one woman, "I invoke God Almighty that our blood rest upon the South." War magnified social tensions in the Confederacy.

Wartime Northern Economy and Society

How did the war affect workers in the North?

War dramatically altered northern society as well. Factories and citizens' associations geared up to support the war, and the federal government and its executive branch gained new powers. Idealism and greed flourished together, and the northern economy proved its awesome productivity.

Northern Business, Industry, and Agriculture

At first, the war was a shock to business. Northern firms lost their southern markets, and southern debts became uncollectible, jeopardizing northern merchants and western banks. Farm families struggled with a labor shortage caused by army enlistments. Cotton mills lacked cotton; construction declined; shoe manufacturers sold few of the cheap shoes that planters bought for slaves.

Certain entrepreneurs, such as wool producers, benefited from shortages of competing products, and soaring demand for war-related goods swept some businesses to new success. The U.S. Treasury issued $3.2 billion in bonds and paper money called "greenbacks," and the War Department spent over $360 million in revenues from new taxes, including the nation's first income tax.

War-related spending and government contracts revived business in many northern states. The northern economy also grew because of a complementary relationship between agriculture and industry. Mechanization of agriculture began before the war. Wartime recruitment and conscription gave western farmers an added incentive to purchase laborsaving machinery. Cyrus and William McCormick built an industrial empire in Chicago from the sale of their reapers. Between 1862 and 1864, the manufacture of mowers and reapers doubled to 70,000 yearly; by war's end, 375,000 reapers were in use, triple the number in 1861. Thus northern farm families whose breadwinners went to war did not suffer as much as did their counterparts in the South.

The Quartermaster and Military-Government Mobilization

This government-business marriage emerged from a greatly empowered Quartermaster Department, which became the single largest employer in the United States, issuing thousands of manufacturing contracts to hundreds of firms. Secretary of War Edwin M. Stanton's list of the weapons supplies needed by the Ordnance Department indicates the scope of the demand for government and business cooperation: "7,892 cannon, 11,787 artillery carriages, 4,022,130 small-arms, … 1,022,176,474 cartridges for small-arms, 1,220,555,435 percussion caps, … 26,440,054 pounds of gunpowder, … and 90,416,295 pounds of lead." The government also purchased huge quantities of uniforms, boots, food, camp equipment, saddles, horses, ships, and other necessities. By 1865, the government had purchased some 640,000 horses and 300,000 mules at a cost exceeding $100 million.

Two-thirds of U.S. war spending went to supply troops, and President Lincoln appointed West Point–trained engineer Montgomery Meigs to command that process. Meigs spent $1.8 billion to wage the war, more than all previous U.S. government expenditures since independence combined. His efforts, argued one historian, made the Union army "the best fed, most lavishly supplied army that had ever existed." The success of such military mobilization left an indelible mark on American political-economic history and provided perhaps the oldest root of the modern American "military-industrial state."

The story of Jay Cooke, a wealthy New York financier, best illustrates the wartime partnership between business and government. Cooke earned hefty commissions marketing government bonds to finance the war. But the financier's profit served the Union cause, as the interests of capitalism and government merged in American history's first era of "big government."

Northern Workers' Militancy

Northern industrial and urban workers did not fare as well. After the initial slump, jobs became plentiful, but inflation ate up much of a worker's paycheck. The price of coffee tripled; rice and sugar doubled; and between 1860 and 1864, consumer prices rose at least 76 percent, while daily wages rose only 42 percent. Workers' families consequently suffered a substantial decline in their standard of living.

Industrial workers also lost job security. To increase production, some employers replaced workers with laborsaving machines. Others urged the government to promote immigration to secure cheap labor. Workers responded by forming unions and sometimes by striking. Indeed, thirteen occupational groups—including tailors, coal miners, and railway engineers—formed national unions during the Civil War, and the number of strikes climbed.

Manufacturers viewed labor activism as a threat and formed statewide or craft-based associations to pool information. They shared blacklists of union members and required new workers to sign "yellow dog" contracts (promises not to join a union). To put down strikes, they hired strikebreakers, and sometimes used federal troops.

Labor militancy, however, did not keep employers from profiting or profiteering on government contracts. With immense demand for army supplies, unscrupulous businessmen sold clothing and blankets made of "shoddy"—wool fibers reclaimed from rags or worn cloth. Shoddy goods often came apart in the rain. Contractors sold inferior guns for double the usual price and passed off tainted meat as good. Rampant corruption led to a yearlong investigation by the House of Representatives.

Economic Nationalism and Government-Business Partnership

Legitimate enterprises also made healthy profits. The output of woolen mills increased so dramatically that industry dividends nearly tripled. Some cotton mills made record profits, even while reducing output. Brokerage houses earned unheard-of commissions. Railroads increased their business so much that railroad stocks skyrocketed.

Railroads were also a leading beneficiary of government largesse. With southern representatives absent from Congress, the northern route of the transcontinental railroad prevailed. In 1862 and 1864, Congress chartered two corporations—the Union Pacific Railroad and the Central Pacific Railroad—and assisted them financially in connecting Omaha, Nebraska, with Sacramento, California. For each mile of track laid, the railroads received a loan of $16,000 to $48,000 in government bonds plus 20 square miles of land along a free 400-foot-wide right of way. Overall, the two corporations gained approximately 20 million acres of land and nearly $60 million in loans.

Morrill Land Grant Act
Law in which Congress granted land to states to establish colleges focusing on agriculture, engineering, and military science.

Other businessmen benefited handsomely from the **Morrill Land Grant Act** (1862). To promote public education in agriculture, engineering, and military science, Congress granted each state thirty thousand acres of federal land for each of its congressional districts. The law eventually fostered sixty-nine colleges and universities as it also enriched a few prominent speculators. Similarly, the Homestead Act of 1862 offered cheap, and sometimes free, land to people who would settle the West and improve their property.

Before the war, banks operating under state charters issued seven thousand different kinds of currency notes. During the war, Congress and the Treasury Department established a national banking system to issue national bank notes, and by 1865 most state banks were forced by a prohibitive tax to join the national system. This created sounder currency but also inflexibility in the money supply and an eastern-oriented financial structure.

In the excitement of wartime moneymaking, an eagerness to display one's wealth flourished in the largest cities. The *New York Herald* noted: "This war has entirely changed the American character.... The individual who makes the most money—no matter how—and spends the most—no matter for what—is considered the greatest man."

The Union Cause

In the first two years of the war, northern morale remained high for a cause that today may seem abstract—the Union—but at the time meant the preservation of a social and political order that people cherished.

Secular and church leaders supported the cause, and even ministers who preferred to separate politics and pulpit denounced "the iniquity of causeless rebellion." Abolitionists campaigned to turn the war into a crusade against slavery. Free black communities and churches, both black and white, sent clothing, ministers, and teachers to aid the freedpeople. Indeed, thousands of northern blacks volunteered to join the war effort in spite of the initial rejection they received from the Lincoln administration. Thus, in wartime northern society, materialism and greed flourished alongside idealism, religious conviction, and self-sacrifice.

Northern Women on Home Front and Battlefront

U.S. Sanitary Commission
Civilian organization in the North staffed by large numbers of women that was a major source of medical and nutritional aid for soldiers.

Northern women, like their southern counterparts, took on new roles. They organized over ten thousand soldiers' aid societies, rolled bandages, and raised $3 million to aid injured troops. Women pressed for the first trained ambulance corps in the Union army, and they formed the backbone of the **U.S. Sanitary Commission**, a civilian agency recognized by the War Department in 1861, which provided nutritional and medical aid to soldiers. Although most of its officers were men, the volunteers who ran its seven thousand auxiliaries were primarily women. Women organized elaborate "Sanitary Fairs" to raise money and awareness for soldiers' health and hygiene.

Approximately thirty-two hundred women also served as nurses in frontline hospitals. Yet women had to fight to serve; the professionalization of medicine since the Revolution created a medical system dominated by men who resisted women's assistance. Even **Clara Barton**, famous for working in the worst hospitals at the front, was ousted from her post in 1863. But women such as Dorothea Dix, who sought to reform asylums for the insane, and Illinois widow Mary Ann Bickerdyke, who served in Sherman's army in the West, established a heroic tradition for Civil

Nurse Anne Bell tending to wounded soldiers in a federal hospital, Nashville, Tennessee, ca. 1863. The distant gaze of the man on the left and the grateful gaze of the one on the right realistically represent the agonies of military hospitals.

War nurses. They also advanced the professionalization of nursing, as several schools of nursing were established in northern cities during or after the war.

Clara Barton Nurse who worked for the Sanitary Commission and later founded the Red Cross.

Women also wrote sentimental war poetry, short stories, novels, and songs that reached thousands of readers in illustrated weeklies, monthly periodicals, and special "story papers." In many stories, female characters seek recognition for their loyalty and Union service, while others probe the suffering and death of loved ones. Louisa May Alcott arrived at her job as a nurse in Washington, D.C., after the horrific Union defeat at Fredericksburg, in December 1862. She later immortalized her experience in *Hospital Sketches* (1863), providing northern readers a view of the hospitals where loved ones agonized and perished. By 1863, many women found slaves' liberation an inspiring subject, as Julia Ward Howe did in her "Battle Hymn of the Republic":

> As He died to make men holy
> Let us die to make men free.

Walt Whitman's War

The poet **Walt Whitman** recorded his experiences as a volunteer nurse in Washington, D.C. As he dressed wounds and comforted suffering men, Whitman found "the marrow of the tragedy concentrated in those Army Hospitals." But he also found inspiration and a deepening faith in American democracy. In "The Wound Dresser," Whitman meditated unforgettably on the deaths he witnessed:

Walt Whitman Well-known poet and author of *Leaves of Grass*; Whitman wrote about his experiences as a nurse and his renewed faith in democracy.

> The crush'd head I dress, (poor crazed hand tear not the bandage away,)
> The neck of the cavalry-man with the bullet through and through I examine,
> Hard the breathing rattles, quite glazed already the eye, yet life struggles hard, (Come
> sweet death! be persuaded O beautiful death! In mercy come quickly.)

Indeed, the scale of death in this war shocked many Americans into believing that the conflict had to be for purposes larger than themselves.

The Advent of Emancipation

Why did Lincoln and Davis both avoid addressing the slavery issue in the early days of the war?

Despite the loyalty of soldiers and civilians, the governments of the United States and the Confederacy lacked clarity about the war's purpose. Throughout the war's early months, Davis and Lincoln avoided references to slavery. Davis realized that emphasis on the issue could increase class conflict in the South. Instead, he told southerners that they were fighting for constitutional liberty: northerners betrayed the founders' legacy, and southerners seceded to preserve it.

Lincoln had his reasons for avoiding slavery. It was crucial at first not to antagonize the Union's border slave states, whose loyalty was tenuous. Lincoln also hoped that a pro-Union majority would assert itself in the South and help coax the South back into the Union. And there were powerful political considerations. Some Republicans burned with moral outrage over slavery; others were frankly racist, dedicated to protecting free whites from the Slave Power and the competition of cheap slave labor. No Republican or northern consensus on slavery existed early in the war.

Lincoln and Emancipation

Lincoln's compassion, humility, and moral anguish during the war were evident in his speeches and writings. But as a politician, Lincoln distinguished between his convictions and his official acts. The latter were calculated for maximum advantage.

Many blacks attacked Lincoln during the first year of the war for his refusal to convert the struggle into an "abolition war." When Lincoln countermanded General John C. Frémont's order of liberation for slaves owned by disloyal masters in Missouri in September 1861, the *Anglo-African* declared that the president, by his actions, "hurls back into the hell of slavery thousands … rightfully set free." As late as July 1862, Frederick Douglass characterized administration policy as reconstruction of "the old union on the old and corrupting basis of compromise, by which slavery shall retain all the power that it ever had." Douglass wanted the old Union destroyed and the Constitution rewritten in the name of human equality. Within a year, just such a profound result began to take place.

Lincoln first substantively broached the subject of slavery in March 1862, when he proposed that states consider emancipation. He asked Congress to promise aid to any state that emancipated, appealing especially to border state representatives. What Lincoln proposed was gradual emancipation, with compensation for slaveholders and colonization of the freed slaves outside the United States.

Until well into 1864, Lincoln's administration promoted an impractical scheme to colonize 4.2 million freed slaves in Central America or the Caribbean. He was as yet unconvinced that America could become a biracial society, and he feared that white northerners might not support a war for black freedom. Black abolitionists vehemently opposed the Lincoln administration's machinations.

Radical Republicans A group of Republicans who assailed the U.S. president early in the war for failing to make emancipation a war goal and, later, for making it too easy for defeated rebel states to return to the Union.

A group of congressional Republicans, known as the **Radical Republicans** and led by George Julian, Charles Sumner, and Thaddeus Stevens, dedicated themselves to a war for emancipation. They were instrumental in creating a special House-Senate committee on the conduct of the war, which investigated Union reverses, sought to improve military efficiency, and prodded the president to take stronger measures against slavery.

A group of "contrabands" (liberated slaves), photographed at Cumberland Landing, Virginia, May 14, 1862, at a sensitive point in the war when their legal status was still not fully determined. The faces and generations of the women, men, and children represent the human drama of emancipation.

Confiscation Acts

In August 1861, at the Radicals' instigation, Congress passed its first confiscation act. Designed to punish the Confederates, the law confiscated all property used for "insurrectionary purposes." A second confiscation act (July 1862) confiscated the property of anyone who supported the rebellion, even those who resided in the South and paid Confederate taxes. Their slaves were declared "forever free of their servitude."

In summer 1862, Lincoln stood by his proposal of voluntary gradual emancipation. In protest, Horace Greeley, editor of the powerful *New York Tribune,* published an open letter to the president entitled "The Prayer of Twenty Millions." Greeley declared, "Mr. President, there is not one … intelligent champion of the Union cause who does not feel that all attempts to put down the Rebellion and at the same time uphold its inciting cause are preposterous and futile." Lincoln offered a calculated reply. He disagreed with those who would make slavery the paramount issue of the war and said, "If I could save the Union without freeing any slave I would do it, and if I could save it by freeing all the slaves I would do it; and if I could save it by freeing some and leaving others alone I would also do that. What I do about slavery, and the colored race, I do because I believe it helps to save the Union."

But Lincoln had already decided to boldly issue a presidential **Emancipation Proclamation**. He was waiting for a Union victory so that it would not appear an act of desperation. Yet the letter to Greeley represents Lincoln's concern with conditioning public opinion for the coming social revolution.

Emancipation Proclamation Lincoln's decree freeing all slaves in Confederate-held territories. It exempted border slave states that remained within the Union.

Emancipation Proclamations

On September 22, 1862, shortly after Union success at the Battle of Antietam, Lincoln issued the first of his two-part proclamation. Invoking his powers as commander-in-chief, he announced that on January 1, 1863, he would emancipate the slaves in the states "in rebellion" (those lacking legitimate representatives in the U.S. Congress by January). Thus, his September 1862 proclamation was less a declaration of the right of slaves to be free than a threat to southerners: unless they put down their arms and returned to Congress, they would lose their slaves. Lincoln had little expectation that southerners would give up, but he wanted a response.

Link to the Emancipation Proclamation, 1863

In the fateful January 1, 1863, proclamation, Lincoln declared that "all persons held as slaves" in areas in rebellion "shall be then, thenceforward, and forever free." But he excepted every Confederate county or city that had fallen under Union control. Those areas, he declared, "are, for the present, left precisely as if this proclamation were not issued." Nor did Lincoln liberate slaves in the border slave states that remained in the Union. "The President has … proclaimed emancipation only where he has notoriously no power to execute it," charged the anti-administration *New York World.*

But Lincoln was worried about the constitutionality of his acts, and he anticipated that after the war southerners might sue for restoration of their "property." Making the liberation of the slaves "a fit and necessary war measure" raised a variety of legal questions: Would it expire with the suppression of a rebellion? The proclamation did little to clarify the status or citizenship of the freed slaves, although it did open the possibility of military service for blacks. How, indeed, would this change the character and purpose of the war?

If the Emancipation Proclamation was legally ambiguous, as a moral and political document it had great meaning. Because the proclamation defined the war as a war against slavery, congressional Radicals could applaud it. Yet it also protected Lincoln's position with conservatives, enabling him to retreat and forcing no immediate changes on the border slave states. Most important, though, thousands of slaves had already reached Union lines across the South. They had "voted with their feet" for emancipation well before the proclamation. And now, every advance of federal forces into slave society was a liberating step.

Across the North and in Union-occupied sections of the South, blacks and their white allies celebrated the Emancipation Proclamation. At a large "contraband camp" in Washington, D.C., some six hundred black men, women, and children gathered at the superintendent's headquarters on New Year's Eve and sang through the night. In chorus after chorus of "Go Down, Moses" they announced the magnitude of their painful but beautiful exodus.

African American Recruits

The need for men soon convinced the administration to recruit northern and southern blacks for the Union army. By spring 1863, African American troops were answering the call of a dozen or more black recruiters in northern cities and towns. Lincoln came to see black soldiers as "the great available and yet unavailed of force for restoring the Union."

African American leaders hoped that military service would secure equal rights for their people. Once the black soldier had fought for the Union, wrote Frederick Douglass, "there is no power on earth which can deny that he has earned the right of citizenship in the United States."

In June 1864, with thousands of black former slaves in blue uniforms, Lincoln gave his support to a constitutional ban on slavery. On the eve of the Republican national convention, Lincoln called on the party to "put into the platform as the keystone, the amendment of the Constitution abolishing and prohibiting slavery forever." The party promptly called for the **Thirteenth Amendment**, which passed in early 1865 and was sent to the states for ratification. The war to save the Union had become the war to free the slaves.

Thirteenth Amendment
Ended slavery in all U.S. territory.

Who Freed the Slaves? It has long been debated whether Abraham Lincoln deserved the label (one he never claimed for himself) of "Great Emancipator." Was Lincoln ultimately a reluctant emancipator, following rather than leading Congress and public opinion? Or did Lincoln provide essential presidential leadership by going slow but, once moving, never backpedaling on black freedom? Once he focused on the unconditional surrender of the Confederates, Lincoln made slavery's destruction central to the war's purpose.

Others have argued, however, that the slaves were central in achieving their own freedom. When they were in proximity to war zones, slaves fled by the thousands. Some worked as camp laborers for the Union armies, and eventually more than 180,000 black men served in the Union army and navy. Some found freedom as individuals in 1861, and some not until 1865, as refugees trekking to contraband camps.

Nevertheless, emancipation was a historical confluence of a policy directed by and dependent on the military authority of the president and the will and courage of African Americans for self-emancipation. Wallace Turnage's escape in Mobile Bay in 1864 demonstrates that emancipation could result from both a slave's own heroism and Union forces. Most blacks comprehended their freedom as given and taken, but also as their human right. "I could now speak my opinion," Turnage concluded, "to men of all grades and colors."

A Confederate Plan of Emancipation Before the war was over, the Confederacy, too, addressed emancipation. Late in the war, Jefferson Davis was willing to sacrifice slavery to achieve independence. He proposed that the Confederate government purchase forty thousand slaves to work as army laborers, with a promise of freedom at the end of their service. He then called for the recruitment and arming of slaves as soldiers, who likewise would gain their freedom at war's end, as would their wives and children.

Bitter debate over Davis's plan resounded throughout the Confederacy. When the Confederate Congress finally approved slave enlistments in March 1865, owners had to comply only on a voluntary basis. With manpower shortages, General Lee supported the idea of slave soldiers, while most Confederate slaveholders vehemently opposed the enlistment plan. Supporters hoped to fight to a stalemate, achieve independence, and control the postwar racial order through their limited wartime emancipation schemes, but it was too late. By contrast, Lincoln's Emancipation Proclamation stimulated a vital infusion of forces into the Union armies: 134,000 former slaves (and 52,000 free blacks) fought for freedom and the Union. Their participation was pivotal in northern victory.

The Soldiers' War

What led previously reluctant white military leaders to accept black soldiers?

Military service completely altered soldiers' lives. Enlistment submerged young men in large organizations whose military discipline ignored their individuality. Army life meant tedium, physical hardship, and separation from loved ones. Yet it also had powerful attractions.

Ordinary Soldiers and Ideology

The old idea that Civil War soldiers fought largely because of unit cohesion and the devotion of fellow recruits is no longer an adequate explanation of why so many endured hardship for so long. Comradeship, duty, and honor were powerful motivators, as were "union," "home," "the government," "freedom," "flag," "liberty," and "states' rights." But according to recent studies, men on both sides were committed to the ideological purposes of the war. Literate soldiers left testimony in letters and regional newspapers of how they saw slavery at the heart of the matter. Members of Morgan's Confederate Brigade from Virginia declared: "any man who pretends to believe that this is not a war for the emancipation of the blacks ... is either a fool or a liar."

Hospitals and Camp Life

The soldiers' lot was often misery. They benefited from new products, such as canned condensed milk, but blankets, clothing, and arms were often poor quality. Hospitals were badly managed at first. Rules of hygiene in large camps were scarcely enforced. Water supplies were unsafe and typhoid epidemics common. About 57,000 men died from dysentery and diarrhea; 224,000 Union troops died from disease or accidents, double the 110,100 who died from battle. Confederate troops were less well supplied. Still, an extensive network of hospitals, aided by white female volunteers and black female slaves, sprang up.

On both sides, troops quickly learned that soldiering was far from glorious. Fighting, wrote a North Carolina volunteer in 1862, taught him "the realities of a soldier's life.... Without time to wash our clothes or our persons ... the whole army became lousy more or less with body lice." Union troops "skirmished" against lice by boiling their clothes, but to little avail.

War soon exposed them to the blasted bodies of friends and comrades. "It is a sad sight to see the dead and if possible more sad to see the wounded—shot in every possible way you can imagine," wrote one Confederate.

Still, as campaigns dragged on, soldiers who did not desert grew determined to see the struggle through. "We now, like true Soldiers go determined not to yield one inch," wrote a New York corporal. When the war was over, "it seemed like breaking up a family to separate," one man observed.

The Rifled Musket

Advances in technology made the Civil War particularly deadly. The most important were the rifle and the "minie ball." Bullets fired from a smoothbore musket were not accurate at distances over eighty yards. Cutting spiraled grooves inside the barrel gave the projectile greater accuracy, but rifles remained difficult to load and use until the Frenchman Claude Minie and the American James Burton developed a new kind of bullet that expanded on firing and flew accurately. With these bullets, rifles were deadly at four hundred yards.

This meant that soldiers assaulting a position defended by riflemen were in greater peril. While artillery now fired from a safe distance, there was no substitute for the infantry assault or the popular turning movements aimed at an enemy's flank. Thus, advancing soldiers exposed themselves repeatedly to accurate rifle fire. Because medical knowledge was rudimentary, even minor wounds often led to amputation and death through infection. Never before in Europe or America had such massive forces pummeled each other with weapons of such destructive power.

The Black Soldier's Fight for Manhood

At the outset of the war, racism in the Union army was strong. Most white soldiers wanted nothing to do with black people and regarded them as inferior. For many, acceptance of black troops grew only because they could do heavy labor and "stop Bullets as well as white people." A popular song celebrated "Sambo's Right to Be Kilt" as the only justification for black enlistments.

But white officers who volunteered to lead segregated black units to gain promotion found that experience altered their opinions. After one month with black troops, a white captain informed his wife, "I have a more elevated opinion of their abilities than I ever had before. I know that many of them are vastly the superiors of those … who would condemn them all to a life of brutal degradation."

Black troops had a mission to destroy slavery and demonstrate their equality. "When Rebellion is crushed," wrote a black volunteer from Connecticut, "who will be more proud than I to say, I was one of the first of the despised race to leave the free North with a rifle on my shoulder.…" Corporal James Henry Gooding of Massachusetts's black Fifty-fourth Regiment explained that his unit intended "to live down all prejudice against its color, by a determination to do well in any position it is put."

Indeed, blacks and whites of the Fifty-fourth Massachusetts forged deep bonds. Just before the regiment launched its costly assault on Fort Wagner in Charleston harbor, in July 1863, a black soldier called out to abolitionist Colonel Robert Gould Shaw, who would perish that day, "Colonel, I will stay by you till I die." "And he kept his word," noted a survivor of the attack. "He has never been seen since." The Fort Wagner assault was celebrated for demonstrating the valor of black men, but this bloody chapter in the history of American racism also proved that black men had to die in battle to be acknowledged as men.

Such valor emerged despite persistent discrimination. The Union government paid white privates $13 per month plus a clothing allowance of $3.50, whereas black privates earned only $10 per month less $3 for clothing. Outraged, several regiments refused to accept any pay, and Congress eventually remedied the inequity.

1863: The Tide of Battle Turns

What turned the tide of war toward Union victory?

The fighting in spring and summer 1863 did not settle the war, but it suggested the outcome. The campaigns began in a deceptively positive way for Confederates, as Lee's army performed brilliantly in battles in central Virginia.

Battle of Chancellorsville

On May 2 and 3, west of Fredericksburg, Virginia, some 130,000 members of the Union Army of the Potomac bore down on fewer than 60,000 Confederates. Boldly, Lee and Stonewall Jackson divided their forces, ordering 30,000 men under Jackson on a daylong march westward to prepare a flank attack.

Arriving at their position in late afternoon, Jackson's seasoned "foot cavalry" found unprepared Union troops laughing, smoking, and playing cards. The Confederate attack drove the entire right side of the Union army back. Eager to

Black Soldiers in the Civil War

The image below is of the storming of Fort Wagner in July 1863 by the Fifty-fourth Massachusetts Regiment in Charleston, South Carolina, by Chicago printmakers Kurtz and Allison. Kurtz and Allison issued vivid and colorful chromolithographs in the 1880s, celebrating the military valor of African Americans. This scene depicts the most famous combat action of black troops in the Civil War; the Fifty-fourth was the first northern-recruited black unit, and their bravery and sacrifice served as a measure of African American devotion to the Union cause. At right is a medal for valor won by a member of the Fifty-fourth Massachusetts Regiment. Why was this regiment such a symbolic test case for the military ability and political meaning of black soldiers in the Civil War? Why did black men have to die on battlefields for many Americans in the Civil War era to consider them fully men and citizens?

STORMING FORT WAGNER.

Library of Congress

Picture Research Consultants & Archives

press his advantage, Jackson rode forward with a few officers to study the ground. As Jackson and his team returned at twilight, southern troops mistook them for federals and fired, fatally wounding their commander. The next day, Union forces left in defeat. Southern forces won at Chancellorsville, but it cost them Stonewall Jackson, who would remain a legend in Confederate memory.

Siege of Vicksburg

July brought crushing defeats for the Confederacy in two critical battles—**Vicksburg** and **Gettysburg**—that damaged Confederate hopes for independence. Vicksburg was the last major fortification on the Mississippi River in southern hands (see Map 13.3). General Ulysses S. Grant laid siege to Vicksburg in May, bottling up the defending army of General John Pemberton. If Vicksburg fell, Union forces would control the river, cutting the Confederacy in two and gaining an open path into its interior. To stave off such results, Jefferson Davis put General Joseph E. Johnston in charge and beseeched him to aid Pemberton. Meanwhile, General Robert E. Lee proposed a Confederate invasion of the North, which, though it would not relieve Vicksburg directly, could stun the North and possibly lead to peace. By invading the North a second time, Lee hoped to move away from war-weary Virginia, garner civilian support in Maryland, win a major victory on northern soil, threaten major cities, and thereby force a Union capitulation.

As Lee's emboldened army advanced through western Maryland and into Pennsylvania, Confederate prospects along the Mississippi darkened. Davis repeatedly wired General Johnston, urging him to attack Grant's army. Johnston, however, considered "saving Vicksburg hopeless." Grant's men, meanwhile, were supplying themselves from the abundant crops of the Mississippi River valley and could continue their siege indefinitely.

Battle of Gettysburg

On July 4, 1863, Vicksburg's commander surrendered. The same day, a battle that had been raging for three days concluded at Gettysburg, Pennsylvania (see Map 13.4). On July 1, Confederate forces hunting for a supply of shoes collided with the Union army. Heavy fighting on the second day left federal forces in possession of high ground along Cemetery Ridge, where they were shielded by a stone wall and had a clear view of their foe across almost a mile of open field.

Undaunted, Lee believed his reinforced troops could break the Union line, and on July 3 he ordered an assault. Virginians under General George E. Pickett and North Carolinians under General James Pettigrew marched up the slope in a doomed assault known as Pickett's Charge.

Vicksburg Union victory that gave the North complete control of the Mississippi River.

Gettysburg Union victory that halted the Confederate invasion of Pennsylvania; turning point in the war in the East.

MAP 13.4
Battle of Gettysburg

In the war's greatest battle, fought around a small market town in southern Pennsylvania, Lee's invasion of the North was repulsed. Union forces had the advantage of the high ground, shorter lines, and superior numbers. The casualties for the two armies—dead, wounded, and missing—exceeded 50,000 men.

Source: Copyright © Cengage Learning 2015

They breached the enemy's line, but most fell in heavy slaughter. On July 4, Lee had to withdraw, having suffered almost four thousand dead and about twenty-four thousand missing and wounded. The Confederate general blamed himself and offered to resign, but President Davis refused. The Confederacy had reached what many consider its high-water mark at Gettysburg. Southern troops displayed unforgettable courage and dedication at Gettysburg, and under General George G. Meade, the Union army, which suffered 23,000 casualties (nearly one-quarter of the force), exhibited the same bravery in stopping the Confederate invasion.

After Gettysburg and Vicksburg, the Confederacy was split; west of the Mississippi, General E. Kirby Smith had to operate on his own, virtually independent of Richmond. Moreover, the heartland of Louisiana, Tennessee, and Mississippi lay exposed to invasion. Lee's northern defeat spelled the end of major southern offensive actions. By wearing down northern morale, the South might yet win, but its prospects were darker than before.

Disunity: South, North, and West

What were the causes of wartime dissent in the South?

Northern and southern governments waged the final two years of the war with increasing opposition at home. The gigantic costs of a civil war fed the unrest. But protest also arose from stresses in the region's social structures.

Union Occupation Zones

Wherever Union forces invaded, they imposed a military occupation consisting of three zones: garrisoned towns, with many troops controlling civilian and economic life; the Confederate frontier, areas still under southern control but with some federal military penetration; and "no man's land," regions between the two armies, beyond Confederate authority and under frequent Union patrols.

Roughly one hundred southern towns were garrisoned, causing severe social disruption. Large parts of Tennessee, Virginia, Louisiana, Mississippi, and Georgia were occupied and suffered food shortages, crop and property destruction, disease, roadway banditry, guerrilla warfare, summary executions, and the random flow of escaped slaves. After two years of occupation, a southern white woman wrote to a kinsman about their native Clarksville, Tennessee: "it is nothing but a dirty hole filled … with niggers and Yankees."

Disintegration of Confederate Unity

Vastly disadvantaged in industrial capacity, natural resources, and labor, southerners felt the cost of war more painfully than northerners. And internally, the southern class system threatened the Confederate cause.

Planters were increasingly opposed to their own government. Along with new taxation, Confederate military authorities impressed slaves to build fortifications. And when Union forces advanced, Confederate commanders burned cotton stores that lay in the enemy's path, enraging planters about such interference with their agricultural production and finances.

Years of opposition to the federal government within the Union had frozen southerners in a defensive posture. Now they erected the barrier of states' rights as a defense against change. Nor were the centralizing policies of the Davis administration popular. The Confederate constitution granted substantial powers to the central government, especially in wartime. But many planters took the position articulated by R. B. Rhett, editor of the *Charleston Mercury*, that the Confederate constitution "leaves the States untouched in their Sovereignty, and commits to the Confederate Government only a few simple objects, and a few simple powers to enforce them."

Confused and embittered planters struck out at Jefferson Davis. Conscription, thundered Governor Brown, was "subversive of [Georgia's] sovereignty, and at war with all the principles for the support of which Georgia entered into this revolution." To frustrate the law, Brown ordered local enrollment officials not to cooperate with the Confederacy.

Food Riots in Southern Cities

Widespread hunger and suffering sparked food riots in spring 1863 in Atlanta, Macon, Columbus, and Augusta, Georgia, and in Salisbury and High Point, North Carolina. On April 2, a crowd assembled in Richmond to demand relief. Responding to a passerby's questions about the group, a young girl replied, "We are starving. We are going to the bakeries and each of us will take a loaf of bread." That action fueled a riot that Davis ordered quelled at gunpoint.

Throughout the rural South, ordinary people resisted more quietly—by refusing to cooperate with conscription, tax collection, and impressments of food. Farmers who did provide food for the army refused to accept payment in certificates of credit or government bonds, as required by law. Conscription officers increasingly found no one to draft. In some areas, tax agents were killed.

Austere and private, Jefferson Davis was ill equipped to deal with such discontent. His class perspective also distanced him from common people's suffering. While his social circle in Richmond dined on duck and oysters, ordinary southerners went hungry.

Desertions from the Confederate Army

Such discontent affected the Confederate armies. Worried about their loved ones and resentful of what they saw as a rich man's war, large numbers of men abandoned the army, supported by friends and neighbors. Mary Chesnut observed a man being dragged back to the army as his wife looked on. "Desert agin, Jake!" she cried.

Desertion did not become a serious problem for the Confederacy until mid-1862, and stiffer policing solved the problem that year. But from 1863 on, the number of men on duty fell rapidly. By mid-1863, John A. Campbell, the South's assistant secretary of war, estimated that 40,000 to 50,000 troops were absent without leave and that 100,000 were evading duty. By November 1863, one-third of the army could not be accounted for.

The defeats at Gettysburg and Vicksburg dealt a heavy blow to Confederate morale. Desperate, President Davis and several state governors resorted to racial scare tactics to drive southern whites to further sacrifice. Defeat, Davis warned, would mean "extermination of yourselves, your wives, and children." Mississippi Governor Charles Clark predicted "elevation of the black race to a position of equality—aye, of superiority, that will make them your masters and rulers."

Internal disintegration of the Confederacy quickened. Confederate leaders realized they were losing the people's support. It is remarkable how long and effectively the Confederacy sustained a military effort while facing internal division.

Antiwar Sentiment, South and North

In North Carolina, William W. Holden, a popular Democratic politician and editor, led a growing peace movement. Over one hundred public meetings supporting peace negotiations took place during summer 1863. In Georgia early in 1864, Governor Brown and Alexander H. Stephens, vice president of the Confederacy, led a similar effort. Ultimately, the lack of a two-party system made questionable the legitimacy of any government criticism.

In the 1863 congressional elections, secessionists and supporters of the administration lost seats to men not identified with the government. In the war's last years, Davis's support in the Confederate Congress dwindled. Some newspaper editors and soldiers, especially in Lee's Army of Northern Virginia, kept the Confederacy alive despite disintegrating popular support.

By 1864, southerners were giving up the struggle. Deserters dominated some whole towns and counties. Active dissent was particularly common in upland and mountain regions, where Union support always held fast. Opposition to the war, though less severe, also existed in the North. Alarm intensified over the growing centralization of government. The draft sparked protest, especially among poor citizens, and the Union army struggled with a troubling desertion rate. But with greater human resources, the Union government's effectiveness was never threatened.

Moreover, unlike Davis, Lincoln knew how to stay in touch with the ordinary citizen. Through public letters to newspapers and private ones to soldiers' families, he reached the common people. The battlefield carnage, political problems, and criticism weighed on him, but his administration never lost control of the war effort.

Peace Democrats

Much of the wartime protest in the North was political. The Democratic Party fought to regain power by blaming Lincoln for the war's death toll, the expansion of federal powers, inflation and the high tariff, and the emancipation of blacks. Its leaders called for an end to the war and reunion on the basis of "the Constitution as it is and the Union as it was." Democrats denounced conscription and martial law and defended states' rights. They charged that Republican policies were designed to flood the North with blacks, threatening white men's privileges. In the 1862 congressional elections, Democrats made a strong comeback, with peace Democrats wielding influence in New York State and majorities in the legislatures of Illinois and Indiana.

Led by outspoken men like Representative Clement L. Vallandigham of Ohio, the peace Democrats became highly visible. Vallandigham criticized Lincoln as a "dictator" who suspended the writ of habeas corpus without congressional authority, arrested thousands of innocent citizens, and shut down opposition newspapers (charges that were true). He urged voters to depose "King Abraham." Vallandigham's attacks seemed so damaging that military authorities arrested him for treason. Lincoln wisely decided against punishment—and martyr's status—for the Ohioan and exiled him to the Confederacy. (Eventually, Vallandigham returned to the North through Canada.)

Some antiwar Democrats did encourage draft resistance, sabotage communications, and plot to aid the Confederacy. Republicans sometimes branded them—and by extension the peace Democrats—as **"Copperheads"**, after the poisonous snake. Although some Confederate agents were active in the North and Canada, they never genuinely threatened the Union war effort.

"Copperheads" Poisonous snakes; also the Republican nickname for antiwar northern Democrats. Some were pacifists, while others were activists who encouraged draft resistance, sabotage, and efforts to aid the Confederacy.

New York City Draft Riots

More violent opposition to the government arose from citizens facing the draft, which became law in 1863. Although many soldiers risked their lives willingly, others openly sought to avoid service.

Urban poor and immigrants in strongly Democratic areas were especially hostile to conscription. The North's poor viewed the system as discriminatory, and many immigrants suspected (wrongly, on the whole) that they were disproportionately called. (Approximately 200,000 men born in Germany and 150,000 born in Ireland served in the Union army.)

As a result, enrolling officers received rough treatment in many northern areas, and riots occurred in New Jersey, Ohio, Indiana, Pennsylvania, Illinois, and Wisconsin. The most serious violence occurred in New York City in July 1863. The war was unpopular there, and racial, ethnic, and class tensions ran high. Shippers had recently broken a longshoremen's strike by hiring black strikebreakers. Working-class New Yorkers feared an inflow of black labor from the South and regarded blacks as the cause of the war. Poor Irish workers resented being forced to serve in the place of others who could afford to avoid the draft.

Military police officers were attacked first, and then mobs crying, "Down with the rich" looted wealthy homes and stores. But blacks became the special target. Mobs rampaged through African American neighborhoods, beating and murdering people in the streets, and burning an orphan asylum. At least seventy-four people died during three days of violence. Army units directly from Gettysburg ended this tragic episode.

War Against Indians in the Far West

A civil war of another kind raged on the Great Plains and in the Southwest. By 1864, U.S. troops commanded by Colonel John Chivington waged full-scale war against the Sioux, Arapahos, and Cheyennes to eradicate Indian title to eastern Colorado. Indian chiefs sought peace, but American commanders had orders to "burn villages and kill Cheyennes." A Cheyenne chief, Lean Bear, was shot from his horse as he rode toward U.S. troops, holding papers given him by President Lincoln during a visit to Washington, D.C. Another chief, Black Kettle, was told by the U.S. command that his people would find a safe haven in Sand Creek, Colorado. Instead, on November 29, 1864, 700 cavalrymen, many drunk, attacked the Cheyenne village. With most men away hunting, the slaughter at the Sand Creek Massacre included 105 Cheyenne women and children and 28 men. American soldiers scalped and mutilated their victims, carrying women's body parts on their saddles or hats back to Denver.

In New Mexico and Arizona Territories, an authoritarian and brutal commander, General James Carleton, waged

THE RIOTS IN NEW YORK: DESTRUCTION OF THE COLORED ORPHAN ASYLUM.

A contemporary wood engraving of the destruction of the Colored Orphan Asylum during the New York City draft riots, July 13–16, 1863.

war on the Apaches and the Navajos. For generations both tribes raided the Pueblo and Hispanic peoples of the region to maintain their security and economy. During the Civil War years, Anglo-American farms also became Indian targets. In 1863, the New Mexico Volunteers, commanded by former mountain man Kit Carson, defeated the Mescalero Apaches and forced them onto a reservation at Bosque Redondo in the Pecos River valley.

But the Navajos resisted. Carson destroyed their livestock, orchards, and crops, causing the starving Navajos to surrender for food in January 1864. Three-quarters of the 12,000 Navajos were forced to march 400 miles (the "Long Walk") to the Bosque Redondo Reservation, suffering malnutrition and death en route. Permitted to return to a fraction of their homelands later that year, the Navajos never forgot the federal government's ruthless policies of removal and eradication of Indian peoples.

Election of 1864

Back east, war weariness reached a peak in summer of 1864, when the Democratic Party nominated popular general George B. McClellan for president and inserted a peace plank into its platform. Written by Vallandigham, it called for an armistice and spoke vaguely about preserving the Union. Democrats made racist appeals to white insecurity, calling Lincoln "Abe the nigger-lover." No incumbent president had been reelected since 1832, and some Republicans worked to dump Lincoln from their ticket for Salmon P. Chase or John C. Frémont, although little came of either effort.

With the fall of Atlanta and Union victories in the Shenandoah Valley by early September, Lincoln's prospects rose. A decisive factor: eighteen states allowed troops to vote at the front. Lincoln won 78 percent of the soldier vote. With 55 percent of the popular vote, Lincoln's reelection—a referendum on the war and emancipation—devastated southern morale. Without this political outcome, a Union military victory and a redefined nation might never have happened.

1864–1865: The Final Test of Wills

Why was it so crucial to northern military strategy that Europe remain neutral during the Civil War?

The Confederates could still have won their version of victory in the war's last year if military stalemate and northern antiwar sentiment had forced a negotiated settlement. But northern determination prevailed.

Northern Diplomatic Strategy

From the outset, the North had pursued one paramount goal: to prevent recognition of the Confederacy by European nations. Foreign recognition would belie Lincoln's claim that the United States was fighting an illegal rebellion and might lead to the financial and military aid that could ensure Confederate independence. Both England and France stood to benefit from a divided and weakened America. Thus, Lincoln and Secretary of State Seward needed to avoid serious military defeats and controversies with European powers.

Since the textile industry employed one-fifth of the British population, southerners banked on British recognition of the Confederacy. But at the war's start, British mills had a 50 percent surplus of cotton, and they later found new supplies in India, Egypt, and Brazil. The British government flirted with recognition of the Confederacy but awaited southern battlefield successes. France was unwilling to act without Britain. Confederate agents purchased arms and supplies in Europe and obtained loans from European financiers, but they never achieved a diplomatic breakthrough.

An acute crisis occurred in 1861 when the overzealous commander of an American frigate stopped the British steamer *Trent* and removed two Confederate ambassadors, James Mason and John Slidell, to a Boston prison. The British interpreted the capture as a violation of freedom of the seas and demanded the prisoners' release. Lincoln and Seward waited until northern public opinion cooled before releasing them. The incident strained U.S.-British relations.

Then the sale to the Confederacy of warships constructed in England sparked protest from U.S. ambassador Charles Francis Adams. Over twenty-two months, the English-built ship, the *Alabama,* destroyed or captured more than sixty U.S. ships.

Battlefield Stalemate and a Union Strategy for Victory	On the battlefield, northern victory was far from won in 1864. General Nathaniel Banks's Red River campaign to capture more of Louisiana and Texas fell apart, and the capture of Mobile Bay in August did not cause the fall of Mobile. Union general William

Tecumseh Sherman soon brought total war to the southern heartland. On the eastern front during winter 1863–1864, the two armies in Virginia settled into a stalemate, awaiting another northern spring offensive.

Military authorities have historically agreed that deep invasion is risky: the farther an army penetrates enemy territory, the more vulnerable its communications and supply lines become. Moreover, observed the Prussian expert Karl von Clausewitz, if the invader encounters a "truly national" resistance, his troops will be "everywhere exposed to attacks by an insurgent population."

General Grant, by now in command of the entire federal army, tested southern will with massive raids. Grant proposed to use armies to destroy Confederate railroads, thus ruining the enemy's transportation and economy. Union troops would live off the land while destroying resources useful to the Confederate military and to the civilian population. After General George H. Thomas's troops won the Battle of Chattanooga in November 1863, Georgia's heartland lay open. Grant entrusted General Sherman with 100,000 men for an invasion toward Atlanta's rail center.

Fall of Atlanta	Jefferson Davis positioned General Joseph E. Johnston's army in Sherman's path. Davis hoped for Lincoln's political defeat and the election of a presi-

dent who would bring peace. When General Johnston fell silent and continued to retreat, Davis replaced him with the one-legged General John Hood, who knew his job was to fight and preserve Atlanta.

Hood attacked but was beaten, and Sherman's army occupied Atlanta on September 2, 1864. The victory buoyed northern spirits and ensured Lincoln's reelection. Davis exhorted southerners to fight on. Hood's army marched north to cut Sherman's supply lines and force him to withdraw, but Sherman marched sixty thousand of his marauding men to the sea, destroying Confederate resources as he went (see Map 13.5).

Links TO THE WORLD

The Civil War in Britain

Because of the direct reliance of the British textile industry on southern cotton (cut off by the war), the American war was significant in Britain's economy and domestic politics. The British aristocracy and most cotton mill owners were pro-Confederate and proslavery, whereas clergymen, shopkeepers, artisans, and radical politicians worked for the Union and emancipation. Most British workers saw their future at stake in a war for slave emancipation. "Freedom" to the huge British working class (who could not vote) meant basic political and civil rights as well as jobs in an industrializing economy.

English aristocrats and conservatives believed in the superiority of the British system of government and looked askance at America's leveling tendencies. And some aristocratic British Liberals sympathized with the Confederacy's demand for independence. English racism also intensified, exemplified by the popularity of minstrelsy and the employment of science in racial theory.

The British propaganda war over the American conflict was widespread: public meetings organized by both sides were huge affairs, with competing banners, carts and floats, orators and resolutions. In a press war, the British argued over when rebellion is justified, whether secession was right or legal, whether slavery was at the heart of the conflict, and especially over the democratic image of America. This bitter debate became a test of reform in Britain: those eager for a broadened franchise and increased democracy were pro-Union, and those who preferred Britain's class-ridden political system favored the Confederacy.

The nature of the internal British debate was symbolized by the dozens of African Americans who served as pro-Union agents in England. The most popular was William Andrew Jackson, Confederate president Jefferson Davis's former coachman, who escaped from Richmond in September 1862. At British public meetings, Jackson countered pro-Confederate arguments that the war was not about slavery.

In the end, the British government did not recognize the Confederacy and, by 1864, English cotton lords found new sources in Egypt and India. But in this link between America and its English roots at its time of greatest travail, we can see the Civil War's international significance.

The Granger Collection, NYC

Some southern leaders pronounced that cotton was king and would bring Britain to their cause. This British cartoon shows King Cotton brought down in chains by the American eagle, anticipating the cotton famine to follow and the intense debate in Great Britain over the nature and meaning of the American Civil War.

Sherman's March to the Sea

Sherman's army was formidable, composed almost entirely of battle-tested veterans and officers who rose through the ranks from the midwestern states. Before the march, army doctors weeded out men who were weak or sick. Although many harbored racist attitudes, most now supported emancipation because, as one said, "Slavery stands in the way of putting down the rebellion."

As Sherman's men moved across Georgia, they cut a path 50 to 60 miles wide and more than 200 miles long. The massive destruction they caused later prompted historians to deem this the first modern "total war." A Georgia woman described the "Burnt Country" this way: "The fields were trampled down and the road was lined with carcasses of horses, hogs, and cattle that the invaders, unable either to consume or to carry with them, had wantonly shot down to starve our people."

After reaching Savannah in December, Sherman marched his armies into the Carolinas. To his soldiers, South Carolina was "the root of secession." They burned and destroyed as they marched, encountering little resistance. The opposing army of General Johnston was small, but Sherman's men should have faced guerrilla raids and attacks by local defense units. The absence of both led South Carolina's James Chesnut Jr. (a politician and Mary Chesnut's husband) to write that his state "was shamefully and unnecessarily lost." Southerners lost the will to continue.

In Georgia alone, nearly twenty thousand slaves followed the marauding Union troops. Others remained on plantations to await war's end because of either wariness of whites or negative experiences with federal soldiers. The destruction of food harmed slaves and white rebels, and many blacks lost livestock, crops, and other valuables to their liberators.

MAP 13.5
Sherman's March to the Sea

The Deep South proved a decisive theater at the end of the war. From Chattanooga, Union forces drove into Georgia, capturing Atlanta. Following the fall of Atlanta, General Sherman embarked on his march of destruction through Georgia to the coast and then northward through the Carolinas. Source: Copyright © Cengage Learning 2015

MAP 13.6
The War in Virginia

At great cost, Grant hammered away at Lee's army until the weakened southern forces finally surrendered at Appomattox Court House.

Source: Copyright © Cengage Learning 2015

Virginia's Bloody Soil

Intent on capturing Richmond, throughout spring and summer 1864, Grant hurled his troops at Lee's army and suffered appalling losses: almost eighteen thousand casualties in the Battle of the Wilderness; more than eight thousand at Spotsylvania; and twelve thousand in just hours at Cold Harbor (see Map 13.6).

Before the assault at Cold Harbor, Union troops pinned scraps of paper bearing their names to their backs, certain they would be mowed down as they rushed Lee's trenches. In four weeks in May and June, Grant lost as many men as were enrolled in Lee's entire army. From early May until July, when Union forces fought from forests west of Fredericksburg to Petersburg, south of Richmond, the two armies engaged each other nearly every day. Wagon trains carrying thousands of Union wounded crawled back toward Washington.

Undaunted, Grant kept up the pressure. Although costly, these battles enabled eventual victory: Lee's army shrank until offensive action was no longer possible, while Grant's army kept replenishing itself with new recruits. The siege of Petersburg, with the armies facing each other in miles of trenches, lasted throughout winter 1864–1865.

Surrender at Appomattox

With the numerical superiority of Grant's army now greater than two to one, Confederate defeat was inevitable. On April 2, Lee abandoned Richmond and Petersburg. On April 9, he surrendered at **Appomattox Court House**. Grant treated his rival respectfully and

Appomattox Court House
Site of Lee's surrender to Grant, marking the end of the Civil War.

paroled the defeated troops, allowing cavalrymen to keep their horses. Within weeks, Johnston surrendered to Sherman in North Carolina, and Davis, who fled Richmond, was captured in Georgia. The war was over. The North rejoiced, and most southerners fell into despair.

Lincoln lived to see but a few days of the war's aftermath. On the evening of April 14, he accompanied his wife to Ford's Theatre in Washington. There John Wilkes Booth, an embittered southern sympathizer, shot the president in the head at point-blank range. Lincoln died the next day. Twelve days later, troops tracked and killed Booth. Relief at the war's end mingled with a renewed sense of loss and anxiety about the future.

Financial Tally

Property damage and financial costs were enormous, though difficult to tally. U.S. loans and taxes during the conflict totaled almost $3 billion, and interest on the war debt was $2.8 billion. The Confederacy borrowed over $2 billion but lost far more in the destruction of homes, crops, livestock, and other property. Union troops looted factories and put two-thirds of the South's railroad system out of service.

Estimates of the war's total cost exceed $20 billion—five times the total expenditures of the federal government from its creation until 1861. By 1865, the federal government's spending soared to twenty times the prewar level and accounted for over 26 percent of the gross national product. Many changes were more or less permanent, as wartime measures left the government more deeply involved in manufacturing, banking, and transportation.

Death Toll and Its Impact

More men died in the Civil War than in all other American wars combined until Vietnam. The total number of casualties exceeded 1 million—frightfully high for a nation of 31 million people. Using microdata samples from the 1850, 1860, 1870, and 1880 censuses, a recent study has raised the official count of 620,000 dead in the Civil War to approximately 750,000. Scholarship also shows that we have never been able to carefully account for civilian casualties in the war, nor for the possibly one in four freed people who died in the process of achieving their own freedom. Not all died on the battlefield: 30,218 northerners died in southern prisons, and 25,976 Confederates died in Union prisons.

The scale and the anonymous nature of death overwhelmed American culture and led to the establishment of national cemeteries, where the large majority of the fallen were buried without identification. The desperate urge to memorialize individual soldiers in this war, writes historian Drew Faust, stemmed from "the anguish of wives, parents, siblings, and children who found undocumented, unconfirmed, and unrecognizable loss intolerable."

Summary

The Civil War altered American society forever. Although precise figures on enlistments are unavailable, it appears that 700,000 to 800,000 men served in the Confederate armies. Possibly 2.3 million served in the Union armies. All were taken from home, family; their lives, if they survived, were permanently altered. During the war, northern and southern women took on new roles to manage the hardships of the home front and support the war.

Abraham Lincoln's Second Inaugural Address

Historian Don Fehrenbacher wrote that "some of Lincoln's words have acquired transcendent meaning as contributions to the permanent literary treasure of the nation." How is this so with the short oration Lincoln delivered at the Capitol on March 4, 1865?

In a 701-word prose poem at his second inauguration, Lincoln probed the tragedy of the Civil War and interpreted its ultimate meanings. The first paragraph acknowledges the "progress of our arms" over four years of war. In the second paragraph, Lincoln entwines North and South in a mutual fate, but suggests responsibility for which side "would make war," and which side "would accept war," and leaves it to posterity: "And the war came."

Then, Lincoln offers a theological-historical explanation of the war that still resonates today in how Americans interpret this historical turning point. Lincoln declares that "all knew ... somehow" slavery was the "cause" of the conflict. Both sides appealed to the "same God." But Lincoln imagined slavery as an "offence" that came "in the providence of God," and brought "this mighty scourge of war" as its awful price.

Suddenly, in rhetoric unusual for presidential inaugurals, Lincoln assumed the prophet's mantle: "Yet if God wills that it [the war] continue, until all the wealth piled by the bond-man's two hundred and fifty years of unrequited toil shall be sunk, and until every drop of blood drawn by the lash, shall be paid by another drawn with the sword, as was said three thousand years ago, so still it must be said the judgments of the Lord are true and righteous altogether."

Famously, Lincoln ended by declaring "malice toward none ... charity for all" the healing balm for the "nation's wounds." Whether Lincoln was the nation's healer or its war maker who would demand any sacrifice to restore the Union and destroy slavery has animated the study of his personal story. The legacy of the Civil War, and Lincoln's place in it, are forever enmeshed in interpretations of this oratorical masterpiece.

Link to the text of Abraham Lincoln's Second Inaugural Address

Industrialization and economic enterprises grew exponentially with the war. Ordinary citizens' futures were increasingly tied to huge organizations. Under Republican leadership, the federal government expanded its power to preserve the Union and extend freedom. A social revolution and government authority emancipated the slaves. It was unclear at war's end how or whether the nation would use its power to protect former slaves' rights. The war left many unanswered questions: How would white southerners, embittered and impoverished, respond to efforts to reconstruct the nation? How would the country care for the maimed, the orphans, the widows? What would be the place of black men and women in American life?

In the West, a second civil war resulted in conquest of southwestern Indians by U.S. troops and land-hungry settlers. On the diplomatic front, the Union government managed to keep Great Britain and other foreign powers out of the war. Dissent played a crucial role in the Confederacy's collapse.

In the Civil War, Americans experienced a dramatic transformation. White southerners experienced a defeat that few other Americans ever faced. Blacks were moving proudly but anxiously from slavery to freedom. White northerners were self-conscious victors in a massive war for the nation's existence and for new definitions of freedom. The war would leave a compelling memory in American hearts and minds for generations.

Chapter Review

Election of 1860 and Secession Crisis

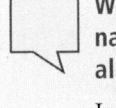

What were the issues leading to secession and the dissolution of the Union?

Abraham Lincoln's contested election in 1860, in which voters divided along regional lines, along with the inability to reach a compromise on the extension of slavery in the territories, ultimately fueled the movement to secede. Lincoln, the Republican candidate, won by carrying the North and winning in the electoral college, but for the first time in American history, the losing side (with its large southern base) refused to accept an election result. When President Lincoln rejected a compromise that would divide the territories into slave and free at the Missouri Compromise line (36°30′), hopes for preventing secession collapsed. South Carolina passed the first secession ordinance in December 1860; Mississippi, Florida, Alabama, Georgia, Louisiana, and Texas followed. A month after Lincoln's inauguration, these states established their own national capitol in Montgomery, Alabama, dubbing themselves the Confederate States of America.

America Goes to War, 1861–1862

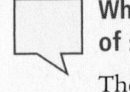

What was the impact of the North's naval victories for enslaved peoples along the southern coast?

In essence, they triggered a revolution in slave society. As federal gunboats drew near the South Carolina coast, planters fled their land. Confederate soldiers tried to round up slaves, who saw the arrival of the Union navy as a possible door to their freedom. Thousands of slaves celebrating by rebelling against the symbols of slavery: they broke cotton gins and stole clothing and furniture from masters' homes. Many ran away to join the Union army. While the Union initially did not acknowledge the slaves as free—and instead labeled them war "contraband"—it did put them to work for the Union army.

War Transforms the South

What happened to the South's embrace of state sovereignty during the war?

The state power that had been so sacred to the South before the war was forced—by the need to mobilize—to yield to a central authority. To maintain the war effort, the Confederacy centralized its operations, troops, and supplies, seeing the efforts of individual states as likely to fragment the greater cause. President Jefferson Davis took a firm leadership role toward the Confederate Congress and urged state governments to require farmers to switch from cash crops to food production. The central government assumed control of the southern economy and nearly complete control of the railroads. Much to the dismay of many secessionists, the southern bureaucracy ironically became larger than its northern counterpart and provided new employment opportunities for women.

Wartime Northern Economy and Society

How did the war affect workers in the North?

Northern urban and industrial workers did not fare as well as business owners and merchants during the war. While they enjoyed more job opportunities and higher wages as the wartime economy grew, inflation devoured much of their earnings. Consumer prices rose at nearly twice the rate of workers' salary increases, and workers' families saw their standard of living decline. They also lost job security as employers replaced workers with new laborsaving machines or cheap immigrant workers. Workers in several industries responded by starting unions or going out on strike, but manufacturers fought back with blacklists or by requiring workers to sign "yellow dog" contracts promising not to join a union.

The Advent of Emancipation

Why did Lincoln and Davis both avoid addressing the slavery issue in the early days of the war?

Davis feared the issue would increase class conflict between slaveless yeoman farmers and slave-owning plantation owners in the South. Instead, he preferred to say that southerners were fighting to preserve their constitutional liberties against northerners and for their independence. Lincoln avoided the topic of slavery to keep from antagonizing the Union's border states, whose loyalty he sought to preserve. He also hoped to inspire a pro-Union majority in the South that might push the region back to the national fold. Avoiding the topic was also politically expedient, since no consensus on slavery existed among Republicans or northerners early in the war—some were strident abolitionists, while others were racists who wanted to protect whites from both the southern Slave Power and the competition of slave labor.

The Soldiers' War

What led previously reluctant white military leaders to accept black soldiers?

At the beginning of the war, the Union army was racist, and many soldiers did not want to fight with blacks, whom they considered inferior. They tolerated them only as black recruits who would do the jobs white soldiers disliked. White officers' opinions changed when they witnessed the bravery and determination of the segregated black units they led. Black soldiers, too, felt they were fighting prejudice through their military successes, thereby proving their manhood and legitimate claim to freedom. Black soldiers' willingness to die in battle also earned the respect of white men. Many black soldiers who fought for white officers did forge deep ties, especially members of the ill-fated Fifty-fourth Massachusetts Regiment.

1863: The Tide of Battle Turns

What turned the tide of war toward Union victory?

Battles at Vicksburg and Gettysburg changed the course of war from a possible Confederate victory to assured victory for the Union. Vicksburg was the last major fortification on the Mississippi River in southern hands, while Gettysburg marked Lee's attempts to break the Union line and invade the North. Both battles produced heavy losses but also left the Confederate army divided, so that west of the Mississippi General E. Kirby Smith operated alone, while Louisiana, Tennessee, and Mississippi were vulnerable to invasions. After Gettysburg, there were no more Confederate offensive moves; severely weakened, the Confederate army could only act defensively.

Disunity: South, North, and West

What were the causes of wartime dissent in the South?

People across class lines increasingly disliked the actions taken by their government. Planters opposed new taxation and the impressments of their slaves to build fortifications. They also resented that Confederate commanders burned planters' cotton stores as Union soldiers

advanced. People universally rejected the increasing size and power of the central government in Richmond and conscription for military service. Many people faced food shortages and refused to comply with conscription, taxation, or the demand to provide food for soldiers. The ability of wealthy people to buy their way out of military service by hiring substitutes fueled resentment among soldiers, some of whom abandoned the army.

1864–1865: The Final Test of Wills

Why was it so crucial to northern military strategy that Europe remain neutral during the Civil War?

Lincoln believed that if foreign countries recognized the Confederacy, that action would legitimize what Lincoln considered an illegal rebellion. He also feared that foreign recognition could lead to military and financial aid that would facilitate a Confederate victory and ultimate independence. The president knew that both England and France would gain by a divided America, but France would not act without Britain, and Britain was not making a move until there were major southern battlefield successes. While England's relationship with southern textile mills made the Confederacy hopeful for an alliance, Britain's large cotton surplus and new supplies in India, Egypt, and Brazil kept it from doing more than selling arms and supplies or offering loans.

Suggestions for Further Reading

Stephen V. Ash, *When the Yankees Came: Conflict and Chaos in the Occupied South* (1995)

Edward L. Ayers, *In the Presence of Mine Enemies: War in the Heart of America, 1859–1863* (2002)

Ira Berlin et al., eds., *Freedom: A Documentary History of Emancipation, 1861–1867,* 3 vols. (1979–1982)

David W. Blight, *Frederick Douglass' Civil War: Keeping Faith in Jubilee* (1989)

Alice Fahs, *The Imagined Civil War: Popular Literature of the North and South* (2001)

Drew G. Faust, *This Republic of Suffering: Death and the American Civil War* (2008)

Gary W. Gallagher, *The Confederate War* (1997)

J. David Hacker, "A Census-Based Count of the Civil War Dead," *Civil War History,* (Dec. 2011).

Chandra Manning, *What This Cruel War Was Over: Soldiers, Slavery, and the Civil War* (2007)

James M. McPherson, *Battle Cry of Freedom: The Civil War Era* (1987)

Philip S. Paludan, *"A People's Contest": The Union and the Civil War* (1989)

Mark R. Wilson, *The Business of Civil War: Military Mobilization and the State, 1861–1865* (2006)

14

Reconstruction: An Unfinished Revolution

1865–1877

The lower half of secession's seedbed, Charleston, South Carolina, lay in ruin when most of the white population evacuated on February 18, 1865. A bombardment by Union forces around Charleston harbor destroyed many lovely, low-country planters' homes. Fires broke out everywhere. To many observers, the flames were the funeral pyres of a dying civilization.

Among the first Union troops to enter Charleston, the Twenty-first U.S. Colored Regiment received the city's surrender from its mayor. For black Charlestonians, who were mostly former slaves, this was a time to celebrate their freedom. Charleston's freedpeople converted Confederate ruin into a vision of Reconstruction based on Union victory and black liberation.

During the war's final year, Confederates transformed the planters' Race Course, a horse-racing track, and its famed Washington Jockey Club, into a prison. Kept outdoors in the interior of the track, 257 Union soldiers died of exposure and disease and were buried in a mass grave behind the grandstand. After the city fell, more than twenty black workmen reinterred the dead in marked graves. On the archway over the cemetery's entrance they painted the inscription "Martyrs of the Race Course."

On the morning of May 1, 1865, ten thousand people marched around the planters' Race Course, led by three thousand children carrying roses and singing "John Brown's Body." Black women with flowers and wreaths came next, followed by black men. The parade concluded with black and white Union regiments and white missionaries and teachers. At the gravesite, five black ministers read from scripture, and a black children's choir sang "America," "The Star-Spangled Banner," and Negro spirituals. After the ceremony, the crowd retired to the Race Course for speeches, picnics, and military festivities.

African Americans founded this "Decoration Day"—now Memorial Day—to remember those lost in battle. In their vision, they were creating the Independence Day of a Second American Revolution.

Chapter Outline

Wartime Reconstruction
Lincoln's 10 Percent Plan | Congress and the Wade-Davis Bill | Thirteenth Amendment | Freedmen's Bureau | Ruins and Enmity

The Meanings of Freedom
The Feel of Freedom | Reunion of African American Families | Blacks' Search for Independence | Freedpeople's Desire for Land | Black Embrace of Education | Growth of Black Churches | Rise of the Sharecropping System

VISUALIZING THE PAST *Sharecropping: Enslaved to Debt*

Johnson's Reconstruction Plan
Andrew Johnson of Tennessee | Johnson's Racial Views | Johnson's Pardon Policy | Presidential Reconstruction | Black Codes

The Congressional Reconstruction Plan
The Radicals | Congress Versus Johnson | Fourteenth Amendment | The South's and Johnson's Defiance | Reconstruction Acts of 1867–1868 | Failure of Land Redistribution | Constitutional Crisis | Impeachment of President Johnson | Election of 1868 | Fifteenth Amendment

Politics and Reconstruction in the South
White Resistance | Black Voters and the Southern Republican Party | Triumph of Republican Governments | Industrialization and Mill Towns | Republicans and Racial Equality | Myth of "Negro Rule" |

The Civil War and its aftermath wrought unprecedented changes in American society, law, and politics, but economic power, racism, and judicial conservatism limited Reconstruction's revolutionary potential. The nation had to determine the nature of federal-state relations, whether confiscated land could be redistributed, and how to bring justice to freedpeople and aggrieved white southerners. Americans also had to heal psychologically from a bloody fratricidal war. How they would negotiate the relationship between healing and justice would determine the fate of Reconstruction.

The turmoil of Reconstruction was most evident in national politics. Lincoln's successor, Andrew Johnson, fought with Congress over Reconstruction policies. Although a southerner, Johnson disliked the South's wealthy planters, and his first acts suggested that he would be tough on "traitors." Before late 1865, however, Johnson became the protector of white southern interests.

Johnson imagined a lenient and rapid "restoration" of the South to the Union rather than the fundamental "reconstruction" that Republican congressmen favored. Between 1866 and 1868, the president and Republican congressional leadership disagreed. Before it ended, Congress impeached the president, enfranchised freedmen, and gave them a role in reconstructing the South. The nation also adopted the Fourteenth and Fifteenth Amendments, ensuring equal protection of the law, citizenship, and universal manhood suffrage. But the cause of equal rights for African Americans fell almost as fast as it had risen.

By 1869, the Ku Klux Klan employed violence to thwart Reconstruction and undermine black freedom. As white Democrats in the South took over state governments, they encountered little opposition. Moreover, the wartime industrial boom created new opportunities and priorities. The West drew American resources like never before. Political corruption became a nationwide scandal, and bribery part of business.

The white South's desire to reclaim control of its states and of race relations overwhelmed the national interest in stopping it. Thus, Reconstruction became a revolution eclipsed, leaving legacies with which the nation has struggled ever since.

As you read this chapter, keep the following questions in mind:

- **Should the Reconstruction era be considered the Second American Revolution? By what criteria should we make such a judgment?**

- **What were the origins and meanings of the Fourteenth Amendment in the 1860s? What is its significance today?**

- **Reconstruction is judged to have "ended" in 1877. Over the course of the 1870s, what caused its end?**

Chronology

1865	Johnson begins rapid and lenient Reconstruction
	White southern governments pass restrictive black codes
	Congress refuses to seat southern representatives
	Thirteenth Amendment ratified, abolishing slavery
1866	Congress passes Civil Rights Act and renewal of Freedmen's Bureau over Johnson's veto
	Congress approves Fourteenth Amendment
	In *Ex parte Milligan*, the Supreme Court reasserts its influence
1867	Congress passes First Reconstruction Act and Tenure of Office Act
	Constitutional conventions called in southern states
1868	House impeaches and Senate acquits Johnson
	Most southern states readmitted to Union under Radical plan
	Fourteenth Amendment ratified
	Grant elected president

1869	Congress approves Fifteenth Amendment (ratified in 1870)
	Sharecropping takes hold across a cash-poor southern economy
1871	Congress passes second Enforcement Act and Ku Klux Klan Act
	Treaty with England settles *Alabama* claims
1872	Amnesty Act frees almost all remaining Confederates from restrictions on holding office
	Grant reelected
1873	*Slaughter-House* cases limit power of Fourteenth Amendment
	Panic of 1873 leads to widespread unemployment and labor strife
1874	Democrats win majority in House of Representatives
1875	Several Grant appointees indicted for corruption
	Congress passes weak Civil Rights Act
	Democratic Party increases control of southern states with white supremacy campaigns
1876	*U.S. v. Cruikshank* further weakens Fourteenth Amendment
	Presidential election disputed
1877	Congress elects Hayes president

Wartime Reconstruction

Which two political acts recognized the centrality of slavery to the war?

How best to reconstruct the Union was an issue as early as 1863, well before the war ended. Four vexing problems compelled early thinking and would haunt the Reconstruction era. One, who would rule in the South once it was defeated? Two, who would rule in the federal government—Congress or the president? Three, what were the dimensions of black freedom, and what rights under law would freedmen enjoy? And four, would Reconstruction be a preservation of the old republic or a second Revolution, reinventing a new republic?

Lincoln's 10 Percent Plan

Abraham Lincoln had never been anti-southern. His fear was that the war would collapse into guerrilla warfare by surviving Confederates. Lincoln insisted on leniency for southern soldiers once they surrendered. In his Second Inaugural Address, delivered a month before his assassination, Lincoln promised "malice toward none; with charity for all."

Lincoln planned early for a swift and moderate Reconstruction process. In his December 1863 "Proclamation of Amnesty and Reconstruction," he proposed replacing majority rule with "loyal rule" to reconstruct southern state governments.

He suggested pardons for ex-Confederates except the highest-ranking military and civilian officers. Once 10 percent of a given state's voting population in the 1860 general election had taken an oath to the United States and established a government, the new state would be recognized. Lincoln did not consult Congress in these plans, and "loyal" assemblies were created in Louisiana, Tennessee, and Arkansas in 1864, states largely occupied by Union troops on which they depended for survival.

Congress and the Wade-Davis Bill

Congress was hostile toward Lincoln's moves to readmit southern states prematurely. Radical Republicans, proponents of emancipation and of aggressively defeating the South, regarded the 10 percent plan a "mere mockery" of democracy. Led by Pennsylvania congressman Thaddeus Stevens and Massachusetts senator Charles Sumner, congressional Republicans proposed a harsher approach. Stevens advocated a "conquered provinces" theory, arguing that southerners organized as a foreign nation to war on the United States and, by secession, destroyed their statehood status. They therefore must be treated as "conquered foreign lands" and returned to the status of "unorganized territories" before applying for readmission.

In July 1864, the Wade-Davis bill, sponsored by Ohio senator Benjamin Wade and Maryland congressman Henry W. Davis, emerged from Congress with three specific conditions for southern readmission.

1. It demanded a "majority" of white male citizens participate in the creation of a new government.
2. To vote or be a delegate to constitutional conventions, men had to take an "ironclad" oath (declaring that they had never aided the Confederate war effort).
3. All officers above the rank of lieutenant and all civil officials in the Confederacy would be disfranchised and deemed "not a citizen of the United States."

Lincoln pocket-vetoed the bill and issued a conciliatory proclamation that he would not commit to any "one plan" of Reconstruction.

This exchange occurred when the outcome of the war and Lincoln's reelection were still in doubt. On August 5, Radical Republicans issued the "Wade-Davis Manifesto" to newspapers. It accused Lincoln of usurpation of presidential powers and disgraceful leniency toward an eventually conquered South. Lincoln saw Reconstruction as a means of weakening the Confederacy and winning the war; the Radicals saw it as a transformation of the nation's political and racial order.

Thirteenth Amendment

In early 1865, Congress and Lincoln joined in two important measures that recognized slavery's centrality to the war. On January 31, Congress passed the **Thirteenth Amendment**, which abolished involuntary servitude and declared that Congress shall have the power to enforce this outcome by "appropriate legislation." When the measure passed by 119 to 56, just 2 votes more than the necessary two-thirds, supporters in Congress rejoiced.

The Thirteenth Amendment emerged from a congressional debate and considerable petitioning and public advocacy. One of the first and most remarkable petitions for a constitutional amendment abolishing slavery was submitted in 1864

Thirteenth Amendment The constitutional amendment that abolished slavery; passed by Congress in 1865.

by Elizabeth Cady Stanton, Susan B. Anthony, and the Women's Loyal National League. Women throughout the Union accumulated thousands of signatures, even venturing into staunchly pro-Confederate regions of Kentucky and Missouri to secure supporters. It was a long road from the Emancipation Proclamation to the Thirteenth Amendment—through treacherous constitutional theory about individual "property rights," beliefs that the sacred document ought never to be altered, and partisan politics. But the logic of winning the war by crushing slavery, and securing a new beginning for the nation, prevailed. This story again gained attention in the 2012 movie, *Lincoln,* directed by Steven Spielberg.

Freedmen's Bureau

On March 3, 1865, Congress created the Bureau of Refugees, Freedmen, and Abandoned Lands—the **Freedmen's Bureau**, an unprecedented agency of social uplift. With thousands of refugees in the South, the government continued what private freedmen's aid societies started in 1862. In its four-year existence, the Freedmen's Bureau supplied food and medical services, built several thousand schools and some colleges, negotiated several hundred thousand employment contracts between freedmen and former masters, and managed confiscated land.

Freedmen's Bureau Created by Congress in March 1865, this agency had responsibility for the relief, education, and employment of former slaves as well as white refugees.

Link to the congressional act establishing the Freedmen's Bureau

The bureau was a controversial aspect of Reconstruction. Southern whites hated it, and politicians divided over its constitutionality. Some bureau agents were devoted to freedmen's rights; others exploited the chaos of the postwar South. The war prompted an eternal question of republics: what are the social welfare obligations of the state toward its people, and what do people owe their governments in return? Apart from conquest and displacement of the eastern Indians, Americans were inexperienced at the Freedmen's Bureau's task—social reform through military occupation.

Ruins and Enmity

In 1865, America was a land with ruins from the war. Some cities lay in rubble, large stretches of the southern countryside were depopulated and defoliated, and thousands of people, white and black, were refugees. Of the approximately 18,300,000 rations distributed across the South in the Freedmen's Bureau's first three years, 5,230,000 went to destitute whites.

In October 1865, after a five-month imprisonment in Boston, former Confederate vice president Alexander H. Stephens rode a train southward. When he reached northern Georgia, his native state, he expressed shock: "War has left a terrible impression.... Fences gone, fields all a-waste, houses burnt." Every northern traveler encountered hatred among white southerners. A North Carolina innkeeper told a journalist that Yankees had killed his sons, burned his house, and stolen his slaves, and left him "one inestimable privilege ... to hate 'em."

The Meanings of Freedom

How did blacks exert their newfound freedom?

Black southerners entered life after slavery with hope and circumspection. A Texas man recalled his father's words, "Our forever was going to be spent living among the Southerners, after they got licked." Often the changes people valued most were personal—alterations in employer or living arrangements.

The Feel of Freedom

For former slaves, Reconstruction meant a chance to explore freedom. Former slaves remembered singing into the night after federal troops, who confirmed rumors of their emancipation, reached their plantations. One angry grandmother dropped her hoe and confronted her mistress. "I'm free!" she yelled. "Yes, I'm free! Ain't got to work for you no more!" Another man recalled that he and others "started on the move," either to search for family members or just to move on.

As slaves, they learned to expect hostility from white people; they did not presume it would instantly disappear. Many freedpeople evaluated potential employers cautiously. After searching for better circumstances, a majority of blacks eventually settled as agricultural workers back on their former farms or plantations. But they relocated their houses and tried to control the conditions of their labor.

Reunion of African American Families

Throughout the South, former slaves focused on reuniting their families, separated during slavery by sale or hardship, and during the war by dislocation. By relying on the black community for help and by placing ads in black newspapers into the 1880s, some succeeded, while others searched in vain.

Husbands and wives who belonged to different masters established homes together to raise their own children. When her old master claimed a right to whip her children, a mother replied, "he warn't goin' to brush none of her chilluns no more."

Blacks' Search for Independence

Many black people wanted to minimize contact with whites because, as Reverend Garrison Frazier told General Sherman in January 1865, "There is a prejudice against us…that will take years to get over." Blacks abandoned slave quarters and fanned out to distant corners of the land they worked. Some described moving "across the creek." Other rural dwellers established small, all-black settlements that still exist along the South's back roads.

Freedpeople's Desire for Land

In addition to a fair employer, freedpeople most wanted to own land, which represented self-sufficiency and compensation for generations of bondage. General Sherman's special Field Order Number 15, issued in February 1865, set aside 400,000 acres of land in the Sea Islands for settlement of freedpeople. Hope swelled among ex-slaves as forty-acre plots and mules were promised to them. But President Johnson ordered them removed in October and the land returned to its original owners under army enforcement. Most members of both political parties opposed land redistribution to the freedmen. Even northern reformers who administered the Sea Islands during the war showed little sympathy for black aspirations. The former Sea Island slaves wanted small, self-sufficient farms. Northern soldiers, officials, and missionaries brought education and aid to the freedmen but insisted that they grow cotton for the competitive market. The U.S. government eventually sold thousands of acres in the Sea Islands, 90 percent of which went to wealthy investors from the North.

Black Embrace of Education

Blacks hungered for education that previously belonged only to whites. With freedom, they started schools and filled dirt-floor classrooms day and night. Children brought infants to school with them, and adults attended at night or after "the crops were laid by." Despite their poverty, many blacks paid tuition, typically $1 or $1.50 a month, which constituted major portions of a person's agricultural wages and totaled more than $1 million by 1870.

In its brief life, the Freedmen's Bureau founded over four thousand schools, and northern reformers established others funded by private philanthropy. The Yankee schoolmarm—dedicated, selfless, and religious—became an agent of progress in many southern communities. More than 600,000 African Americans were enrolled in elementary school by 1877.

Blacks and their white allies also established colleges and universities. The American Missionary Association founded seven colleges, including Fisk University and Atlanta University, between 1866 and 1869. The Freedmen's Bureau helped establish Howard University in Washington, D.C., and northern religious groups, such as the Methodists, Baptists, and Congregationalists, supported seminaries and teachers' colleges.

During Reconstruction, African American leaders often were highly educated members of the prewar elite of free people of color. Francis Cardozo, who held various offices in South Carolina, attended universities in Scotland and England. P. B. S. Pinchback, who became lieutenant governor of Louisiana, was the son of a planter who sent him to school in Cincinnati.

Growth of Black Churches

Freed from slavery's restrictions, blacks could build their own institutions. Slavery's secret churches became visible; in communities throughout the South, ex-slaves "started a brush arbor," which was "a sort of…shelter with leaves for a roof," where freed men and women worshipped.

Within a few years, branches of the Methodist and Baptist denominations attracted most southern black Christians. By 1877, in South Carolina, the African Methodist Episcopal (A.M.E.) Church had a thousand ministers, forty-four thousand members, and a school of theology, while the A.M.E. Zion Church had forty-five thousand members. In these churches, some of which became the wealthiest

Churches became a center of African American life, both social and political, during and after Reconstruction. Churches large and small, like this one, Faith Memorial Church in Hagley Landing, South Carolina, became the first black-owned institutions for the postfreedom generation.

Private Collection/Picture Research Consultants & Archives

and most autonomous institutions in black life, the freedpeople created enduring communities.

Rise of the Sharecropping System

Since former slaves lacked money to buy land, they preferred the next best thing: renting it. But the South had few sources of credit, and few whites would rent to blacks. Black farmers and white landowners therefore turned to **sharecropping**, a system in which the landlord or a merchant "furnished" food and supplies, such as draft animals and seed to farmers, and received as payment a portion of the crop. White landowners and black farmers bargained with one another. As the system matured during the 1870s and 1880s, most sharecroppers worked "on halves"—half for the owner and half for themselves.

> **sharecropping** A system where landowners and former slaves managed a new arrangement, with tenants paying landowners a portion of their crops for the use of the land on which they farmed, thereby usually ending up in permanent debt.

Sharecropping, which materialized by 1868, originated as a compromise between former slaves and landowners. It eased landowners' problems with cash and credit, and provided a permanent, dependent labor force; blacks accepted it because it freed them from supervision. But sharecropping proved disastrous. Owners and merchants developed a monopoly of control over the agricultural economy, as sharecroppers faced ever-increasing debt.

The fundamental problem was that southern farmers still concentrated on cotton. At the same time, freed black women valued making independent choices about gender roles and family and preferred domestic chores over picking cotton. Even as the South recovered its prewar share of British cotton purchases, cotton prices began a long decline, as world demand declined.

Thus, southern agriculture slipped into depression. Black sharecroppers struggled under growing debt that bound them to landowners and merchants almost as oppressively as slavery. Many white farmers gradually lost their land and became sharecroppers. By Reconstruction's end, over one-third of southern farms were worked by sharecropping tenants, white and black.

Johnson's Reconstruction Plan

What was Johnson's vision for Reconstruction?

Many people expected Reconstruction under President Andrew Johnson to be harsh. Throughout his career in Tennessee, he criticized wealthy planters and championed the small farmers. When an assassin's bullet thrust Johnson into the presidency, former slave owners feared Johnson would deal sternly with the South. When northern Radicals suggested the exile or execution of ten or twelve leading rebels, Johnson replied, "How are you going to pick out so small a number?"

Andrew Johnson of Tennessee

Like Lincoln, Johnson moved from obscurity to power. With no education, he became a tailor's apprentice. But from 1829, while in his early twenties, he held nearly every office in Tennessee politics: alderman, state representative, congressman, two terms as governor, and U.S. senator by 1857. Although elected as a Democrat, Johnson was the only senator from a seceded state who refused to leave the Union. Lincoln appointed him war governor of Tennessee in 1862; hence his symbolic place on the ticket in the president's 1864 bid for reelection.

Sharecropping: Enslaved to Debt

Sharecropping became an oppressive system in the postwar South. A new labor structure that began as a compromise between freedmen who wanted independence and landowners who wanted a stable workforce evolved into a method of working on "halves," where tenants owed endless debts to the furnishing merchants, who owned plantation stores like this one, photographed in Mississippi in 1868. Merchants recorded in ledger books, like the one at right, the debts that few sharecroppers were able to repay. Why did both former slaves and former slave owners initially find sharecropping an agreeable, if difficult, new labor arrangement? What were the short- and long-term consequences of the sharecropping system for the freedpeople and for the southern economy?

Amistad Center for Art & Culture, Hartford, CT. Simpson Collection/ Art Resource, New York

This Mississippi plantation store, shown in 1868, is a typical example of the new institution of the furnishing merchant and its power over postslavery agriculture in the South.

Division of Culture & the Arts, National Museum of American History, Behring Center, Smithsonian Institution.

Furnishing merchants kept ledger books such as this for decades; they became the record of how sharecroppers fell deeper in debt from year to year, and "owed their soul" to the country store.

Although a Unionist, Johnson's political beliefs made him an old Jacksonian Democrat. Before the war, he supported tax-funded public schools and homestead legislation, fashioning himself as a champion of the common man. Johnson advocated limited government. His philosophy toward Reconstruction? "The Constitution as it is, and the Union as it was."

Through 1865, Johnson alone controlled Reconstruction policy, for Congress recessed shortly before he became president and did not reconvene until December. Johnson formed new state governments in the South by using his power to grant pardons and offered terms to former Confederates.

Johnson's Racial Views

Johnson had owned house slaves, although he was never a planter. He accepted emancipation, but believed that black suffrage could never be imposed on southern states by the federal government. This set him on a collision course with the Radicals. On race, Johnson was a white supremacist. He declared in his 1867 annual message that blacks possessed less "capacity for government than any other race of people … wherever they have been left to their own devices they have shown a constant tendency to relapse into barbarism."

Such racial views influenced Johnson's policies. Where whites were concerned, however, Johnson proposed rules that would keep the wealthy planter class at least temporarily out of power.

Johnson's Pardon Policy

To gain amnesty or pardon, white southerners were required to swear an oath of loyalty, but Johnson refused this option to former federal officials, high-ranking Confederate officers, and political leaders or graduates of West Point or Annapolis who joined the Confederacy. He also barred ex-Confederates whose taxable property was worth more than $20,000. These individuals had to apply personally to the president for pardon. The president, it seemed, wanted revenge on the old planter elite and to promote a new yeoman leadership.

Johnson appointed provisional governors, who began Reconstruction by calling state constitutional conventions. The delegates had to draft new constitutions that eliminated slavery and invalidated secession. After ratification, new governments could be elected, and the states restored to the Union. But only southerners who had taken the oath of amnesty and were eligible voters when the state seceded could participate. Thus, unpardoned whites and former slaves were ineligible.

Presidential Reconstruction

The old white leadership proved resilient; prominent Confederates won elections and secured appointive offices. Then Johnson started pardoning planters and leading rebels. By September 1865, hundreds were issued in a single day. These pardons, plus the return of planters' abandoned lands, restored the old elite to power and made Johnson seem the South's champion.

Why did Johnson allow the planters to regain power? He may have enjoyed turning proud planters into pardon seekers. He also sought rapid Reconstruction to deny the Radicals any opportunity for thorough racial and political changes in the South. Johnson needed southern support in the 1866 elections; hence, he declared Reconstruction complete only eight months after Appomattox. In December 1865, many Confederate congressmen claimed seats in the U.S. Congress, including former Confederate vice president Alexander Stephens, who was now Georgia's senator-elect.

Black Codes

To define the status of freed men and women and control their labor, some legislatures revised the slave codes by substituting the word *freedmen* for *slaves.* The new black codes compelled former slaves to carry passes, observe a curfew, and live in housing provided by a landowner. Stiff vagrancy laws and restrictive labor contracts bound freedpeople to plantations, and "anti-enticement" laws punished anyone luring these workers to other employment. State-supported schools and orphanages excluded blacks.

Link to Louisiana Black Code

It seemed to northerners that the South was intent on returning African Americans to servility and that Johnson's Reconstruction policy held no one responsible for the war. Thus, the Republican majority in Congress halted Johnson's plan. The House and Senate refused to admit newly elected southern representatives. Instead, they bluntly challenged the president's authority and established a joint committee to study a new direction for Reconstruction.

The Congressional Reconstruction Plan

What made Radical Reconstruction different from Johnson's plan?

The Constitution mentioned neither secession nor reunion, but it gave Congress the primary role in admitting states. Moreover, the Constitution declared that the United States shall guarantee to each state a "republican form of government." This provision, legislators believed, gave them the authority to devise Reconstruction policies.

The key question: What had rebellion done to the relationship between southern states and the Union? Congressmen who favored vigorous Reconstruction measures argued that the war had broken the Union and that the South was subject to the victor's will. Moderate congressmen held that the states forfeited their rights through rebellion and thus came under congressional supervision.

The Radicals

Northern Democrats, weakened by their opposition to the war in its final year, denounced racial equality and supported Johnson's policies. Conservative Republicans, despite their party loyalty, favored a limited federal role in Reconstruction. Although a minority, Radical Republicans, led by Thaddeus Stevens, Charles Sumner, and George Julian, wanted to democratize the South, establish public education, and ensure freedpeople's rights. They favored black suffrage, supported some land confiscation and redistribution, and were willing to exclude the South from the Union for years to achieve their goals.

The Radicals brought a new civic vision; they wanted to create an activist federal government and the beginnings of racial equality. Many moderate Republicans,

Library of Congress

Photograph of Thaddeus Stevens, Republican congressman and staunch abolitionist from Pennsylvania, and leader of the "Radicals" during the creation of Reconstruction policies, from 1866 to 1868.

led by Lyman Trumbull, opposed Johnson's leniency but wanted to restrain the Radicals. They were, however, committed to federalizing the enforcement of civil, if not political, rights for freedmen.

With the 1866 elections looming, Johnson and the Democrats sabotaged the possibility of a conservative coalition by refusing to cooperate with conservative or moderate Republicans. They insisted that Reconstruction was over, that the new state governments were legitimate, and that southern representatives should be admitted to Congress. The Radicals' influence grew in proportion to Johnson's intransigence.

Congress Versus Johnson

Republicans believed they reached a compromise with Johnson in spring 1866. Under its terms, Johnson would modify his program by extending the Freedmen's Bureau for another year and passing a civil rights bill to counteract the black codes. This would force southern courts to practice equality under the scrutiny of the federal judiciary. Its provisions applied to public, not private, acts of discrimination. The Civil Rights Bill of 1866 was the first statutory definition of the rights of American citizens.

Johnson, however, destroyed the compromise by vetoing both bills (they became law when Congress overrode his veto). Because the civil rights bill defined U.S. citizens as native-born persons who were taxed, Johnson claimed it operated "in favor of the colored and against the white race."

Hope of presidential-congressional cooperation was dead. In 1866, newspapers reported daily violations of blacks' rights in the South and carried alarming accounts of antiblack violence. In Memphis, forty blacks were killed and twelve schools burned by white mobs, and in New Orleans, the toll was thirty-four African Americans dead and two hundred wounded. Violence convinced Republicans, and the northern public, that more needed to be done. A new Republican plan focused on the **Fourteenth Amendment** to the Constitution.

Fourteenth Amendment
Defined U.S. citizens as anyone born or naturalized in the United States, barred states from interfering with citizens' constitutional rights, and stated for the first time that voters must be male.

Fourteenth Amendment

Of the five sections of the Fourteenth Amendment, the first would have the greatest legal significance. It conferred citizenship on "all persons born or naturalized in the United States" and prohibited states from abridging their constitutional "privileges and immunities" (see the Appendix for the Constitution and all amendments). It also barred states from taking a person's life, liberty, or property "without due process of law" and from denying any person "equal protection of the laws." These phrases have become powerful guarantees of African Americans' civil rights—indeed, of the rights of all citizens, except for Indians, who were not granted citizenship rights until 1924.

Republicans almost universally agreed on the amendment's second and third sections. The fourth declared the Confederate debt null and void, and guaranteed the United States' war debt. Northerners rejected paying taxes to reimburse those who financed a rebellion, and business groups agreed on the necessity of upholding the U.S. government's credit, an element of the Fourteenth Amendment invoked in debates between congressional Republicans and the Obama administration over raising the federal "debt ceiling" in 2011 and 2013. The second and third sections barred Confederate leaders from holding state and federal office. Only Congress, by a two-thirds vote of each house, could remove the penalty. The amendment thus guaranteed some punishment for Confederate leaders.

The second section of the amendment also dealt with representation and embodied the compromises that produced the Constitution. Northerners disagreed about whether blacks should have the right to vote. Public will, North and South, lagged behind the egalitarianism of enactments that became new constitutional cornerstones. Many northern states still maintained black disfranchisement laws during Reconstruction.

Emancipation ended the three-fifths clause for the purpose of counting blacks, which would increase southern representation. Thus, the postwar South stood to gain power in Congress, and if white southerners did not allow blacks to vote, former secessionists would derive the political benefit from emancipation. So Republicans determined that, if a southern state did not grant black men the vote, their representation would be reduced proportionally and vice versa.

The Fourteenth Amendment specified for the first time that voters were "male." As such, it frustrated the women's rights movement. Advocates of women's equality worked with abolitionists for decades, often subordinating their cause to the slaves'. During the drafting of the Fourteenth Amendment, however, female activists such as Elizabeth Cady Stanton and Susan B. Anthony ended their alliance with abolitionists and fought for women, infusing new life into the women's rights movement. Other female activists, however, argued that it was "the Negro's hour." Many male former abolitionists were willing to delay woman suffrage to secure freedmen the vote in the South.

The South's and Johnson's Defiance

Johnson tried to block the Fourteenth Amendment. The president urged state legislatures in the South to vote against ratification, and all but Tennessee rejected the amendment by a wide margin.

To present his case to northerners, Johnson organized a National Union Convention. He boarded a special train for a "swing around the circle" that carried his message into the Northeast, Midwest, and back to Washington. Increasingly, audiences rejected his views, jeering at him. Johnson handed out American flags with thirty-six rather than twenty-five stars, declaring the Union restored. And, he labeled the Radicals "traitors" for attempting to take over Reconstruction.

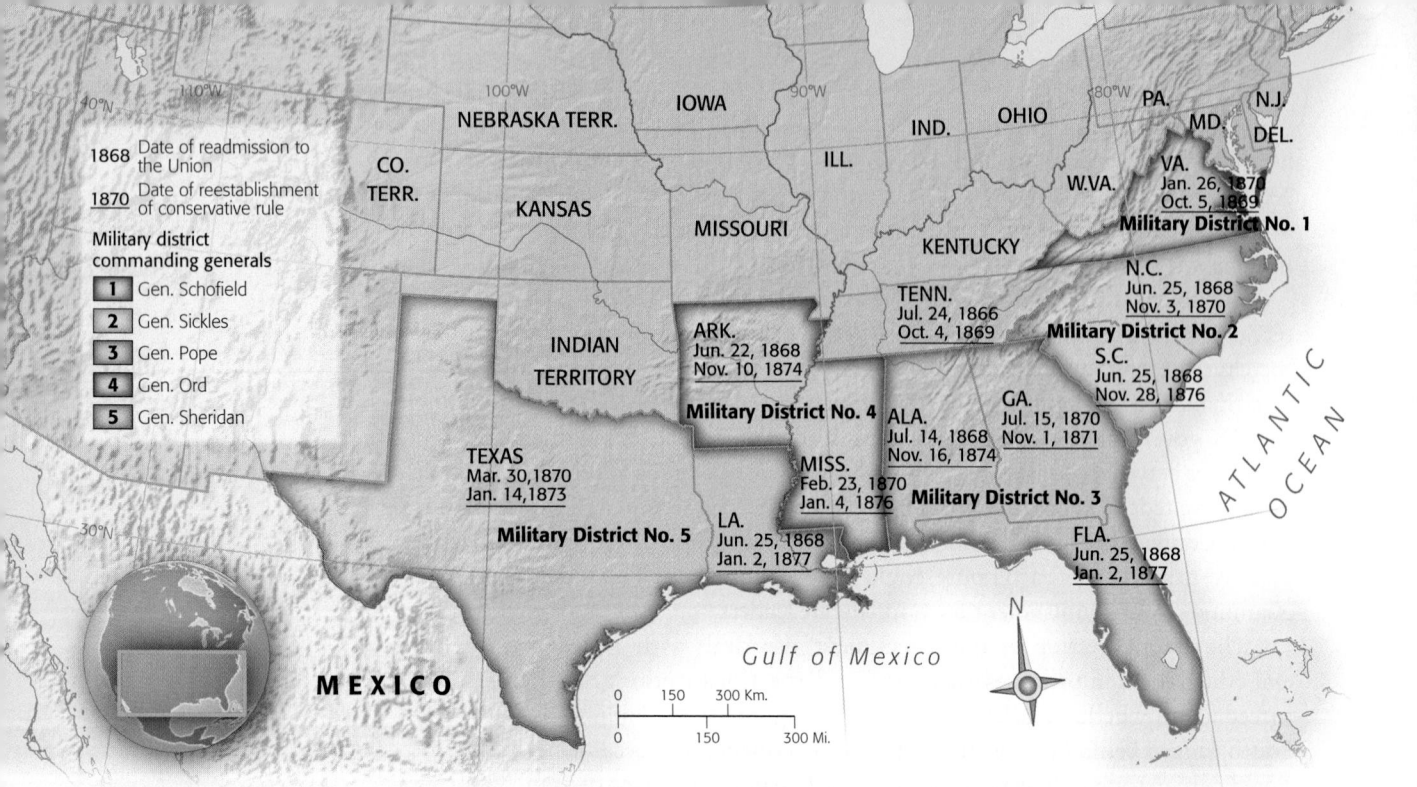

MAP 14.1

The Reconstruction Act of 1867

This map shows the five military districts established when Congress passed the Reconstruction Act of 1867. As the dates within each state indicate, conservative Democratic forces quickly regained control of government in four southern states. So-called Radical Reconstruction was curtailed in most of the others as factions within the weakened Republican Party began to cooperate with conservative Democrats. Source: Copyright © Cengage Learning 2015

In the 1866 elections, Radicals and moderates whom Johnson denounced won reelection by large margins, and the Republican majority grew to two-thirds of both congressional houses. The North was clear: Johnson's policies of states' rights and white supremacy were giving the advantage to rebels and traitors. Thus Republican congressional leaders won a mandate to pursue their Reconstruction plan.

But nothing could be accomplished as long as the "Johnson governments" existed and the southern electorate remained exclusively white. Republicans resolved to form new state governments in the South and enfranchise the freedmen.

Reconstruction Acts of 1867–1868

After debate, the First Reconstruction Act passed in March 1867. This plan, under which the southern states were readmitted to the Union, incorporated part of the Radical program. Union generals, commanding small garrisons and charged with supervising elections, assumed control in five military districts in the South (see Map 14.1). Confederate leaders designated in the Fourteenth Amendment were barred from voting until new state constitutions were ratified. The act guaranteed freedmen the right to vote and serve in state constitutional conventions. In addition, each southern state was required to ratify the Fourteenth Amendment and its new constitution by majority vote, then submit it to Congress for approval (see Table 14.1).

TABLE 14.1   Plans for Reconstruction Compared

	Johnson's Plan	Radicals' Plan	Fourteenth Amendment	Reconstruction Act of 1867
Voting	Whites only; high-ranking Confederate leaders must seek pardons	Give vote to black males	Southern whites may decide but can lose representation if they deny black suffrage	Black men gain vote; whites barred from office by Fourteenth Amendment cannot vote while new state governments are being formed
Office holding	Many prominent Confederates regain power	Only loyal white and black males eligible	Confederate leaders barred until Congress votes amnesty	Fourteenth Amendment in effect
Time out of Union	Brief	Several years; until South is thoroughly democratized	Brief	3–5 years after war
Other change in southern society	Little; gain of power by yeomen not realized; emancipation grudgingly accepted, but no black civil or political rights	Expand education; confiscate land and provide farms for freedmen; expansion of activist federal government	Probably slight, depending on enforcement	Considerable, depending on action of new state governments

The Second, Third, and Fourth Reconstruction Acts, passed between March 1867 and March 1868, provided the details for voter registration boards, the adoption of constitutions, and the administration of "good faith" oaths by white southerners.

Failure of Land Redistribution

The Radicals blocked Johnson, but they had hoped Congress could do much more. Thaddeus Stevens, for example, argued that economic opportunity was essential to the freedmen. He drew up a plan for extensive confiscation and redistribution of land, but it was never realized.

Racial fears and an American obsession with the sanctity of private property made land redistribution unpopular. Thus, black farmers had to seek work in a hostile environment in which landowners opposed their acquisition of land.

Constitutional Crisis

To restrict Johnson's influence and safeguard its plan, Congress passed several controversial laws. First, it limited Johnson's power over the army by requiring the president to issue military orders through the general of the army, Ulysses S Grant. Then Congress passed the Tenure of Office Act, which gave the Senate power to approve changes in the president's cabinet. Designed to protect Secretary of War Stanton, a Radical sympathizer, this law violated the tradition of presidents controlling cabinet appointments. These measures, along with the Reconstruction Acts, were passed by a two-thirds override of presidential vetoes.

In response, Johnson limited the military's power in the South, increasing the powers of the civil governments he created in 1865. Then he removed military officers who were enforcing Congress's new law, preferring commanders who allowed disqualified Confederates to vote. Finally, he tried to remove Secretary of War Stanton, pushing the confrontation to its climax.

Impeachment Process to remove a president from office; attempted but failed in case of Andrew Johnson.

Impeachment of President Johnson

Impeachment is a political procedure provided for in the Constitution as a remedy for crimes or serious abuses of power by presidents, federal judges, and other high government officials. Those impeached (politically indicted) in the House are then tried in the Senate. Historically, this power was not used to investigate and judge the private lives of presidents, although more recently it was used this way against President Bill Clinton.

Twice in 1867, the House Judiciary Committee considered impeachment of Johnson, first rejecting it and then recommending it by a 5-to-4 vote, which was defeated by the House. After Johnson tried to remove Stanton, however, a third attempt to impeach him carried in early 1868. The indictment concentrated on his violation of the Tenure of Office Act, though modern scholars regard his efforts to obstruct enforcement of the Reconstruction Act of 1867 as a more serious offense.

Johnson's trial in the Senate lasted more than three months. The prosecution, led by Radicals, attempted to prove that Johnson was guilty of "high crimes and misdemeanors." But they also argued that the trial was a means to judge Johnson's performance. The Senate rejected such reasoning, which could have made removal from office a political weapon against any chief executive who disagreed with Congress. The prosecution fell one vote short of the necessary two-thirds majority. Johnson remained in office, politically weakened.

Election of 1868

In the 1868 presidential election, Ulysses S. Grant, running as a Republican, defeated Horatio Seymour, a New York Democrat. Grant was not a Radical, but his

congressional Reconstruction The process by which the Republican-controlled Congress sought to make the Reconstruction of the ex-Confederate states longer, harsher, and under greater congressional control.

platform supported **congressional Reconstruction** and endorsed black suffrage in the South. (Significantly, Republicans stopped short of endorsing black suffrage in the North.) Democrats, meanwhile, denounced Reconstruction and preached white supremacy, conducting the most openly racist campaign to that point in American history. Both sides waved the "bloody shirt," blaming each other for the war's sacrifices. By associating with rebellion and Johnson's repudiated program, Democrats were defeated in all but eight states, though the popular vote was close. Blacks voted en masse for General Grant.

In office, Grant vacillated in dealings with the southern states, sometimes defending Republican regimes and sometimes currying favor with Democrats. On occasion, Grant called out federal troops to stop violence or enforce acts of Congress. But he never imposed a military occupation on the South. Rapid demobilization reduced a federal army of more than 1 million to 57,000 within a year of the Appomattox surrender. Thereafter, the number of troops in the South declined, until in 1874 there were only 4,000 in the southern states outside Texas. The legend of "military rule," so important to southern claims of victimization during Reconstruction, was steeped in myth.

Fifteenth Amendment

In 1869, the Radicals pushed through the **Fifteenth Amendment**, the final major measure in Reconstruction's constitutional revolution. It forbade states to deny the vote "on account of race, color, or previous condition of servitude." Such wording did not guarantee the right to vote. It left states free to restrict suffrage on other grounds so that northern states could continue to deny suffrage to women and certain men—Chinese immigrants, illiterates, and those too poor to pay poll taxes.

Fifteenth Amendment
Prohibited states from denying the vote to any citizen on account of "race, color, or previous condition of servitude."

The Fifteenth Amendment became law in 1870. Although African Americans rejoiced, it left open the possibility for states to create countless qualification tests to obstruct voting.

Politics and Reconstruction in the South

How did black voters in the early days of Reconstruction transform the South?

From the start, white southerners resisted Reconstruction and opposed emancipation, as evident in the black codes. The former planter class proved especially unbending because of its tremendous financial loss in slaves. For many poor whites who never owned slaves and yet sacrificed during the war, destitution, plummeting agricultural prices, disease, and the uncertainties of a growing urban industrialization drove them off land, toward cities, and into hatred of black equality.

White Resistance

Some planters attempted to postpone freeing slaves by denying or misrepresenting events. Former slaves reported that their owners "didn't tell them it was freedom" or "wouldn't let [them] go." To retain workers, some landowners claimed control over black children and used guardianship and apprentice laws to bind black families to the plantation.

Adamant resistance by whites soon manifested itself in other ways, including violence. A local North Carolina magistrate clubbed a black man on a public street, and in several states bands of "Regulators" terrorized blacks who displayed independence. And after President Johnson encouraged the South to resist congressional Reconstruction, many white conservatives captured the new state governments, while others boycotted the polls to defeat Congress's plans.

Black Voters and the Southern Republican Party

Enthusiastically, blacks went to the polls, voting Republican, as one man said, to "stick to the end with the party that freed me." Illiteracy did not prohibit blacks (or uneducated whites) from making intelligent choices. Mississippi's William Henry could read only "a little," but he said, "We saw D. Sledge vote; he owned half the county. We knowed he voted Democratic so we voted the other ticket so it would be Republican." Women, who could not vote, encouraged their husbands and sons, and preachers exhorted their congregations to use the franchise.

Thanks to a large black turnout and the restrictions on prominent Confederates, a new southern Republican Party came to power in the 1868–1870 constitutional conventions. Republican delegates consisted of a sizable black contingent

(265 out of the total of just over 1,000 delegates throughout the South), northerners who had moved to the South, and native southern whites seeking change. The new constitutions they drafted were more democratic than anything previously adopted in the South. They eliminated property qualifications for voting and holding office, turned many appointed offices into elective posts, and provided for public schools and institutions to care for the mentally ill, the blind, the deaf, the destitute, and the orphaned.

The conventions broadened women's rights in property holding and divorce. Usually the goal was not gender equality but providing relief to thousands of suffering debtors. Since husbands typically contracted the debts, giving women legal control over their own property provided some protection for families.

Triumph of Republican Governments

Under these new constitutions, southern states elected Republican-controlled governments. For the first time, state legislators in 1868 included black southerners. Contrary to what white southerners later claimed, Republican state governments did not disfranchise ex-Confederates as a group. James Lynch, a leading black politician from Mississippi, saw disfranchising whites as foolish. Landless former slaves "must be in friendly relations with the great body of the whites in the state," he explained. "Otherwise…peace can be maintained only by a standing army." Despised and lacking power, southern Republicans strove for safe ways to gain a foothold in a depressed economy.

Far from vindictive toward the race that enslaved them, most southern blacks appealed to white southerners to embrace fairness. Hence, the South's Republican Party condemned itself to defeat if white voters would not cooperate. Within a few years, most fledgling Republican parties in southern states would be struggling for survival against violent white hostility.

Industrialization and Mill Towns

Reconstruction governments promoted industry via loans, subsidies, and short-term exemptions from taxation. The southern railroad system was rebuilt and expanded, and coal and iron mining made possible Birmingham's steel plants. Between 1860 and 1880, the number of manufacturing establishments in the South nearly doubled.

This emphasis on big business, however, produced higher state debts and taxes, drew money

The Queen of Industry, Or, The New South.

The Queen of Industry, or the New South, *cartoon by Thomas Nast, 1882, contrasting the pre–Civil War plantation economy with the more industrialized economy of the 1880s.*

The Granger Collection, NYC

from schools and other programs, and multiplied possibilities for corruption. The alliance between business and government often operated at the expense of farmers and laborers. This conservative strategy also doomed Republicans' chances with poorer whites.

Poverty remained the lot of many southern whites. The war caused a massive onetime loss of income-producing wealth, such as livestock, and a steep decline in land values. In many regions, the old planter class still ruled the best land and access to credit or markets.

As poor whites and blacks found farming less tenable, they moved to cities and mill towns. Industrialization did not sweep the South as it did the North, but it laid deep roots. Attracting textile mills to southern towns became a competitive crusade. In 1860, the South counted some 10,000 mill workers; by 1880, the number grew to 16,741 and by century's end to 97,559. Many poor southerners moved from farmer to mill worker and other low-income wage work.

Republicans and Racial Equality

Whites who controlled the southern Republican Party were reluctant to allow blacks a share of offices proportionate to their electoral strength. Aware of their weakness, black leaders did not push hard for revolutionary change. Instead, they led efforts to establish public schools, although without pressing for integrated facilities. In 1870, South Carolina passed the first comprehensive school law in the South. By 1875, 50 percent of black school-age children were enrolled in school there, and approximately one-third of the three thousand teachers were black.

African American politicians who did fight for civil rights and integration were typically from cities such as New Orleans or Mobile, where large populations of light-skinned free blacks existed before the war. Their experience made them sensitive to status issues. Laws requiring equal accommodations won passage but often went unenforced.

Economic progress, particularly landownership, was a major concern for most freedpeople. Land reform failed because in most states whites were the majority, and former slave owners controlled the best land and financial resources. Much land did fall into state hands for nonpayment of taxes. Such land was sold in small lots. But most freedmen had too little cash to bid against investors or speculators. Any widespread land redistribution had to arise from Congress, which never supported such action.

Myth of "Negro Rule"

Within a few years, white hostility to congressional Reconstruction increasingly dominated. Conservatives, who had always wanted to fight Reconstruction through pressure and racist propaganda, began to do so. Charging that the South had been turned over to ignorant blacks, conservatives used "black domination" as a rallying cry for a return to white supremacy.

Such attacks were inflammatory propaganda and part of the growing myth of "Negro rule," which would become a central theme in battles over the memory of Reconstruction. African Americans participated in politics but hardly dominated. They were a majority in only two out of ten state constitutional conventions.

In state legislatures, only in South Carolina's lower house did blacks constitute a majority. Sixteen blacks won seats in Congress before Reconstruction was over. Only eighteen served in a high state office, such as lieutenant governor, treasurer, superintendent of education, or secretary of state.

Some four hundred blacks served in political office during Reconstruction, an enormous achievement. Elected officials, such as Robert Smalls in South Carolina, labored for cheaper land prices, better health care, access to schools, and the enforcement of civil rights. For too long, the black politicians of Reconstruction were forgotten heroes of this seedtime of America's long civil rights movement.

Carpetbaggers and Scalawags

"carpetbaggers" Derogatory nickname southerners gave to northerners who moved south after the Civil War, perceiving them as greedy opportunists who hoped to cash in on the South's plight.

Conservatives also assailed the allies of black Republicans. Their propaganda denounced northern whites as **"carpetbaggers,"** greedy crooks planning to pour stolen tax revenues into their luggage made of carpet material. In fact, most northerners who settled in the South had come seeking business opportunities, as schoolteachers, or to find a warmer climate; most never entered politics. Those who entered politics generally wanted to democratize the South and to introduce northern ways, such as industry and public education.

Carpetbaggers' real actions never matched the sensational stereotypes, although by the mid-1870s even some northerners who soured on Reconstruction endorsed the images. Thomas Wentworth Higginson, a Union officer and commander of an African American regiment during the Civil War, suggested that any Yankee politician still in the South by 1874 was a "mean man," a "scoundrel."

"scalawag" Term used by conservative southerners to describe other white southerners who were perceived as aiding or benefiting from Reconstruction.

Conservatives also invented the term **"scalawag"** to discredit white southerners cooperating with Republicans, as many wealthy men did. Most scalawags were yeoman farmers from mountain areas and nonslaveholding districts who were Unionists under the Confederacy. They hoped to benefit from the education and opportunities Republicans promoted. Sometimes banding with freedmen, they pursued common class interests to make headway against long-dominant planters. Ove time, however, most black-white coalitions floundered due to racism.

Tax Policy and Corruption as Political Wedges

Republicans wanted to repair the war's destruction, stimulate industry, and support such new ventures as public schools. But the Civil War damaged the South's tax base. One category of valuable property—slaves—had disappeared. Hundreds of thousands of citizens lost much of their property—money, livestock, fences, and buildings—to the war. Tax increases (sales, excise, and property) were necessary even to maintain traditional services. Inevitably, Republican tax policies aroused strong opposition, especially among yeomen.

Corruption charges also plagued Republicans. Many carpetbaggers and black politicians engaged in fraudulent schemes or sold their votes, participating in what scholars recognize was a nationwide surge of corruption in an age ruled by "spoilsmen" (see pages xxx). Corruption crossed party lines, but Democrats successfully blamed unqualified blacks and greedy carpetbaggers among southern Republicans.

Ku Klux Klan

Republican leaders also allowed factionalism along racial and class lines to undermine party unity. But in many southern states, the deathblow came through violence. The **Ku Klux Klan**, a secret veterans' club that began in Tennessee in 1866, spread through the South, rapidly becoming a terrorist organization. Klansmen sought to frustrate Reconstruction and keep the freedmen in subjection with nighttime harassment, whippings, beatings, rapes, and murders.

Although the Klan tormented blacks, its main purpose was political. Lawless night riders targeted Republicans, killing leading whites and blacks in several states. After freedmen who worked for a South Carolina scalawag started voting, terrorists visited the plantation and, as one victim noted, "whipped every … [black] man they could lay their hands on." Klansmen also attacked Union League clubs—Republican organizations that mobilized the black vote—and schoolteachers who aided freedmen.

Specific social forces shaped and directed Klan violence, with Alamance and Caswell Counties in North Carolina receiving the worst Klan violence. Slim Republican majorities there rested on cooperation between black voters and white yeomen. Together, these black and white Republicans ousted long-entrenched officials. The wealthy and powerful men who lost their accustomed political control were the Klan's county officers and local chieftains. By intimidation and murder, the Klan weakened the Republican coalition and restored a Democratic majority.

Klan violence ultimately destroyed Republicans across the South. One of every ten black delegates to the 1867–1868 state constitutional conventions was attacked, seven fatally. In one North Carolina judicial district, the Ku Klux Klan was responsible for twelve murders, over seven hundred beatings, rape, and arson. A single attack on Alabama Republicans in Eutaw left four blacks dead and fifty-four wounded. According to historian Eric Foner, the Klan "made it virtually impossible for Republicans to campaign or vote in large parts of Georgia."

Thus, Republican mistakes, racial hostility, and terror brought down the Republican regimes. In most southern states, Radical Reconstruction lasted only a few years (see Map 14.1). Its most enduring failure, however, was its inability to alter the South's social structure or its distribution of wealth and power.

Ku Klux Klan A terrorist organization established by six Confederate war veterans that sought to reestablish white supremacy in the South, suppress black voting, and topple Reconstruction governments.

Two members of the Ku Klux Klan, photographed in regalia, circa 1870. Dallas Historical Society,

Dallas Historical Society, Texas, USA/The Bridgeman Art Library

Retreat from Reconstruction

What led the North to lose interest in reconstructing the South?

During the 1870s, northerners lost the will to sustain Reconstruction, as they faced economic and social transformations in their region and the West. Radical Republicans like Albion Tourgée, a former Union soldier who moved to North Carolina and was elected a judge, condemned Congress's timidity. He, and many African Americans, believed that during Reconstruction, the North "threw all the Negroes on the world without any way of getting along." As the North lost interest in the South, Reconstruction collapsed.

Political Implications of Klan Terrorism

Whites in the old Confederacy referred to this decline of Reconstruction as "southern redemption." During the 1870s, "redeemer" Democrats claimed to be the South's saviors from alleged "black domination" and "carpetbag rule." Violence and terror emerged as tactics in politics.

Enforcement Acts Laws that sought to protect black voters, made violations of civil and political rights a federal offense, and sought to end Ku Klux Klan violence.

In 1870 and 1871, the Ku Klux Klan's violent campaigns forced Congress to pass two **Enforcement Acts** and an anti-Klan law. These laws made actions by individuals against the civil and political rights of others a federal criminal offense. They also provided for election supervisors and permitted martial law and suspension of the writ of habeas corpus to combat murders, beatings, and Klan threats. In 1872 and 1873, Mississippi and the Carolinas saw many prosecutions; but in other states, the laws were ignored. Southern juries sometimes refused to convict Klansmen; less than half of the 3,310 cases ended in convictions. Although many Klansmen fled their state to avoid prosecution, and the Klan officially disbanded, paramilitary organizations known as Rifle Clubs and Red Shirts often took the Klan's place.

Still, there were ominous signs that the North's commitment to racial justice was fading, as some influential Republicans opposed the anti-Klan laws. Rejecting other Republicans' arguments that the Thirteenth, Fourteenth, and Fifteenth Amendments made the federal government the protector of citizens' rights, dissenters charged that Congress was infringing on states' rights. This foreshadowed a general revolt within Republican ranks in 1872.

Industrial Expansion and Reconstruction in the North

Immigration and industrialization surged in the North. Between 1865 and 1873, 3 million immigrants entered the country, most settling in the industrial cities of the North and West. Within only eight years, industrial production increased by 75 percent. For the first time, nonagricultural workers outnumbered farmers, and wage earners outnumbered independent craftsmen. Government policies encouraged this rapid growth. Low taxes on investment and high tariffs on manufactured goods helped create a new class of powerful industrialists, especially railroad entrepreneurs.

From 1865 to 1873, thirty-five thousand miles of new track were laid, which fueled the banking industry and made Wall Street the center of American capitalism. Eastern railroad magnates, such as Thomas Scott of the Pennsylvania Railroad, created economic empires with the assistance of huge government subsidies of cash and land. Railroad corporations also bought up mining operations, granaries, and lumber companies. Big business now employed lobbyists to curry favor with government. Corruption ran rampant; some congressmen and legislators were paid annual retainers by major companies. The railroads brought modernity to the United States like almost nothing else; but they also taught the nation sordid lessons about the perils of monopoly and corruption, and by the late nineteenth century railroad entrepreneurs were the most hated men in the West.

As captains of industry amassed unprecedented fortunes in an age with no income tax, gross economic inequality polarized American society. The workforce, worried a prominent Massachusetts business leader, was in a "transition state…living in boarding houses" and becoming a "permanent factory population." In New York or Philadelphia, workers increasingly lived in unhealthy tenement housing. Thousands would list themselves on the census as "common laborer." In 1868, Republicans passed an eight-hour workday bill for federal workers. The "labor question" (see Chapter 16) now preoccupied northerners far more than the "southern" or the "freedmen" question.

Then the Panic of 1873 ushered in more than five years of economic contraction. Three million people lost their jobs, especially in large cities. Debtors and the unemployed sought easy-money policies to spur expansion (workers and farmers desperately needed cash). Businessmen, disturbed by the strikes and industrial violence that accompanied the panic, defended property rights and demanded "sound money" policies. The chasm between farmers and workers and wealthy industrialists widened.

Liberal Republican Revolt

Disenchanted with Reconstruction, a largely northern group calling itself the Liberal Republicans bolted the party in 1872 and nominated Horace Greeley, editor of the *New York Tribune,* for president. A varied group, Liberal Republicans included foes of corruption and advocates of a lower tariff. Two popular attitudes united them: distaste for federal intervention in the South and an elitist desire to let market forces and the "best men" determine policy.

Democrats also nominated Greeley in 1872, but it was not enough to stop Grant's reelection. Greeley's campaign for North-South reunion was a harbinger of the future in American politics. Organized Blue-Gray fraternalism (gatherings of Union and Confederate veterans) began in 1874. Grant continued to use military force sparingly and in 1875 refused a desperate request from Mississippi's governor for troops to quell racial and political terrorism there.

Grant made a series of poor appointments that fueled public dissatisfaction. His secretary of war, his private secretary, and officials in the treasury department and navy were involved in bribery or tax-cheating scandals. Instead of exposing the corruption, Grant defended the culprits. In 1874, Democrats recaptured the House of Representatives, signaling the end of the Radical Republican vision of Reconstruction.

General Amnesty

Democratic gains in Congress weakened legislative resolve on southern issues. Congress had already lifted the political disabilities of the Fourteenth Amendment from many former Confederates. In 1872, it adopted an Amnesty Act, which pardoned most of the remaining rebels. In 1875, Congress passed a **Civil Rights Act**,

Civil Rights Act An act designed to desegregate public places that lacked enforcement provisions.

partly in tribute to the recently deceased Charles Sumner, purporting to guarantee black people equal accommodations in public places, such as inns and theaters, but the bill was watered down and contained no enforcement provisions. (The Supreme Court later struck down this law; see page xxx.)

Democrats regained control of four state governments before 1872 and eight by late January 1876 (see Map 14.1). In the North, Democrats successfully stressed the failure and scandals of Reconstruction governments. Sectional reconciliation now seemed crucial for commerce. The nation was expanding westward, and the South was a new frontier for investment.

The West, Race, and Reconstruction

As the Fourteenth Amendment and other enactments granted blacks the beginnings of citizenship, other nonwhite peoples faced continued persecution. Across the West, the federal government pursued a containment policy against Native Americans. In California, where white farmers and ranchers often forced Indians into captive labor, some civilians practiced "Indian hunting." By 1880, thirty years of violence left an estimated forty-five hundred California Indians dead at the hands of white settlers.

In Texas and the Southwest, expansionists still deemed Mexicans and other mixed-race Hispanics to be "lazy," and incapable of self-government. In California and the Far West, initially few whites objected to Chinese immigrants who did the dangerous work of building railroads through the Rocky Mountains. But when the Chinese competed for urban, industrial jobs, conflict emerged. Anti-coolie clubs appeared in California in the 1870s, seeking laws against Chinese labor, fanning the racism flames, and organizing vigilante attacks on Chinese workers and the factories that employed them. Western politicians sought white votes by pandering to prejudice, and in 1879 the new California constitution denied Chinese the vote.

Viewing America from coast to coast, the Civil War and Reconstruction years dismantled racial slavery and fostered a volatile new racial complexity, especially in the West. Some African Americans asserted that they were more like whites than "uncivilized" Indians, while others, like the Creek freedmen of Indian Territory, sought an Indian identity. In Texas, whites, Indians, blacks, and Hispanics had mixed for decades, and by the 1870s forced reconsideration in law and custom of exactly who was "white."

America was undergoing what one historian has called a reconstruction of the concept of *race* itself. The turbulence of the expanding West reinforced the new nationalism and the reconciliation of North and South based on a resurgent white supremacy.

Foreign Expansion

In 1867, new expansion pressures led Secretary of State William H. Seward to purchase Alaska from Russia (see Chapter 19). Opponents ridiculed Seward's $7.2 million venture, but Seward convinced congressmen of Alaska's economic potential, and other lawmakers favored potential friendship with Russia.

Also in 1867, the United States took control of the Midway Islands, a thousand miles northwest of Hawai'i. Through diplomacy, Seward and his successor

The "Back to Africa" Movement

In the wake of the Civil War, and especially after the despairing end of Reconstruction, some African Americans sought to leave the South for the American West or North, but also to relocate to Africa. Liberia had been founded in the 1820s by the white-led American Colonization Society (ACS), an organization dedicated to relocating blacks "back" to Africa. Some eleven thousand African Americans had emigrated voluntarily to Liberia by 1860, with largely disastrous results. Many died of disease, and others felt disoriented in the strange new land and ultimately returned to the United States.

Reconstruction reinvigorated the emigration impulse, especially in cotton-growing districts where blacks had achieved political power before 1870 but were crushed by violence and intimidation in the following decade. When blacks felt confident in their future, the idea of leaving America fell quiet; but when threatened or under assault, whole black communities dreamed of a place where they could become an independent "race," a "people," or a "nation" as their appeals often announced. Often that dream, more imagined than realized, lay in West Africa.

Before the Civil War, most blacks denounced the ACS for its racism and hostility to their sense of American birthright. But letters of inquiry flooded the organization's headquarters after 1875. Wherever blacks felt the reversal of the promise of emancipation the keenest, they formed local groups such as the Liberia Exodus Association of Pinesville, Florida; or the Liberian Exodus Arkansas Colony; and many others.

At emigration conventions, and especially in churches, blacks penned letters to the ACS asking for maps or information about a new African homeland. Some local organizers would announce eighty or a hundred recruits "widawake for Liberia," although

such enthusiasm rarely converted into an Atlantic voyage. The impulse was genuine, however. "We wants to be a People," wrote the leader of a Mississippi emigration committee; "we can't be it heare and find that we ar compel to leve this Cuntry." Henry Adams, a former Louisiana slave, Union soldier, and itinerant emigration organizer, advocated Liberia, but also supported "Kansas fever" with both biblical and natural rights arguments. "God...has a place and a land for all his people," he wrote in 1879. "It...is the idea that pervades our breast 'that at last we will be free,' free from oppression, free from tyranny, free from bulldozing, murderous southern whites."

By the 1890s, Henry McNeal Turner, a freeborn former Georgia Reconstruction politician, and now bishop of the African Methodist Episcopal Church, made three trips to Africa and campaigned through press and pulpit for blacks to "Christianize" and "civilize" Africa. Two shiploads of African Americans sailed to Liberia, although most returned disillusioned or ill. Turner's plan of "Africa for the Africans" was as much a religious vision as an emigration system, but like all such efforts then and since, it reflected the despair of racial conditions in America more than realities in Africa. The numbers do not demonstrate the depth of the impulse in this link to the world: in 1879–1880, approximately twenty-five thousand southern blacks moved to Kansas, whereas from 1865 to 1900, just under four thousand emigrated to West Africa.

Departure of African American emigrants to Liberia aboard the Laurada, *Savannah, Georgia, March 1896. The large crowd bidding farewell to the much smaller group aboard the ship may indicate both the fascination with and the ambivalence about this issue among blacks in the South.*

Illustrated American/Historical/Corbis

Hamilton Fish arranged a financial settlement of claims on Britain for damage done by the *Alabama* and other cruisers built in England and sold to the Confederacy. Sectional reconciliation in Reconstruction America would serve new ambitions for world commerce and expansion.

Judicial Retreat from Reconstruction

Meanwhile, the Supreme Court played its part in the northern retreat from Reconstruction. During the Civil War, the Court was cautious and inactive. Reaction to the *Dred Scott* decision (1857) was so vehement, and the Union's wartime emergency so great, that the Court had avoided interference with government actions. But that changed in 1866 when *Ex parte Milligan* reached the Court.

Lambdin P. Milligan of Indiana had plotted to free Confederate prisoners of war and overthrow state governments. Consequently, a military court sentenced Milligan, a civilian, to death. Milligan challenged the military tribunal's authority, claiming he was entitled to a civil trial. The Supreme Court declared that military trials were illegal when civil courts were functioning.

In the 1870s, the Court successfully renewed its challenge to Congress's actions when it narrowed the meaning of the Fourteenth Amendment. The *Slaughter-House* cases (1873) began in 1869, when the Louisiana legislature granted one company a monopoly on livestock slaughtering in New Orleans. Rival butchers sued. Their attorney, former Supreme Court justice John A. Campbell, argued that Louisiana had violated the rights of some citizens in favor of others. The Fourteenth Amendment, Campbell contended, had brought individual rights under federal protection.

But in the *Slaughter-House* decision, the Supreme Court dealt a blow to the scope of the Fourteenth Amendment. It declared state citizenship and national citizenship separate. National citizenship involved only matters such as the right to travel freely from state to state, and only such narrow rights, held the Court, were protected by the Fourteenth Amendment.

Shrinking from a role as "perpetual censor" for civil rights, the Court's majority declared that the framers of recent amendments had not intended to "destroy" the federal system, in which the states exercised "powers for domestic and local government, including the regulation of civil rights." Thus, the justices severely limited the amendment's potential for protecting the rights of black citizens—its original intent.

The next day, the Court decided *Bradwell v. Illinois*, a case in which Myra Bradwell, a female attorney, was denied the right to practice law in Illinois because she was a married woman, and hence not a free agent. Using the Fourteenth Amendment, Bradwell's attorneys contended that the state had unconstitutionally abridged her "privileges and immunities" as a citizen. The Supreme Court disagreed, declaring a woman's "paramount destiny…to fulfill the noble and benign offices of wife and mother."

In 1876, the Court further weakened the Reconstruction era amendments. In *U.S. v. Cruikshank,* the Court overruled the conviction under the 1870 Enforcement Act of Louisiana whites who had attacked a meeting of blacks and conspired to deprive them of their rights. The justices ruled that the Fourteenth Amendment did not give the federal government power to act against these whites. The duty of protecting citizens' equal rights, the Court said, "rests alone with the States."

Such judicial conservatism blunted the revolutionary potential of the Civil War amendments.

Disputed Election of 1876 and Compromise of 1877

As the 1876 presidential election approached, the nation was focused on economic issues, and the North lost interest in Reconstruction. Samuel J. Tilden, the Democratic governor of New York, ran strongly in the South and needed one electoral vote to beat Rutherford B. Hayes, the Republican nominee. Nineteen electoral votes from Louisiana, South Carolina, and Florida (the only southern states not yet under Democratic rule) were disputed; both Democrats and Republicans claimed to have won those states despite fraud committed by their opponents (see Map 14.2).

To resolve this unprecedented situation, Congress established a fifteen-member electoral commission, balanced between Democrats and Republicans. Because Republicans held the majority in Congress, they prevailed, 8 to 7, on every attempt to count the returns, with commission members voting along party lines. Hayes would become president if Congress accepted the commission's findings.

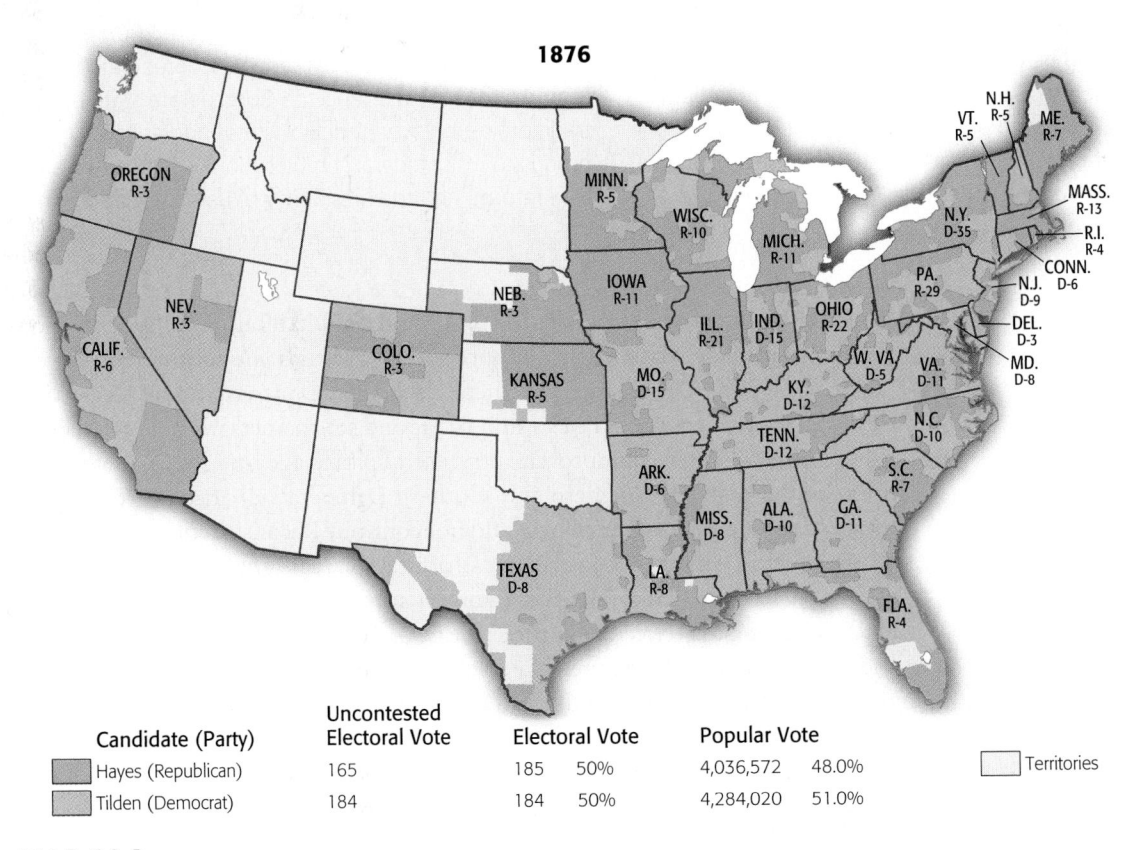

1876

Candidate (Party)	Uncontested Electoral Vote	Electoral Vote		Popular Vote	
Hayes (Republican)	165	185	50%	4,036,572	48.0%
Tilden (Democrat)	184	184	50%	4,284,020	51.0%

Territories

MAP 14.2
Presidential Election of 1876 and the Compromise of 1877

In 1876, a combination of solid southern support and Democratic gains in the North gave Samuel Tilden the majority of popular votes, but Rutherford B. Hayes won the disputed election in the electoral college, after a deal satisfied Democratic wishes for an end to Reconstruction. Source: Copyright © Cengage Learning 2015

Legacy FOR A PEOPLE AND A NATION

The Lost Cause

All major wars compel a struggle over their memory. After the Civil War, white southerners and their northern allies constructed a "Lost Cause" tradition, a racially exclusive version of the war and Reconstruction that persists today.

For ex-Confederates, the Lost Cause served as a psychological response to the trauma of defeat. Over time it also included reinterpretations of the war's causes; southern resistance to Reconstruction; doctrines of white supremacy; and a mythic popular culture enjoyed by northerners and southerners. Lost Cause advocates—from officers to soldiers to women leading memorial associations—argued that the war was never about slavery; that the Confederates lost due to Yankee numbers and resources; and that southern and northern sacrifice should be equally honored. In the industrial, urban, multiethnic America of the emerging twentieth century, an Old South of benevolent masters and faithful slaves, of Robert E. Lee as America's truest Christian soldier, provided a sentimentalized road to reunion.

By the 1890s, elite southern white women—among them the United Daughters of the Confederacy—built monuments, lobbied congressmen, delivered lectures, ran contests for schoolchildren, and strove to control the content of history textbooks, to exalt the South. Above all, Lost Causers advocated what one historian has called a "victory narrative" of the nation's triumph over Reconstruction's racial revolution and constitutional transformations. In his 1881 memoir, Jefferson Davis declared the Lost Cause not lost: "Well may we rejoice in the regained possession of self-government.... This is the great victory...a total noninterference by the Federal government in the domestic affairs of the States." These stories endure in Civil War memorabilia, such as the epic *Gone with the Wind,* the 2003 film *Gods and Generals*, and uses of the Confederate flag to oppose civil rights. And the Confederate state rights tradition is employed today by states and advocacy groups to resist federal stimulus money, national health care reform, and the presidency of Barack Obama.

But Democrats controlled the House and could filibuster to block action on the vote. Many citizens feared another civil war, as some southerners vowed, "Tilden or Fight!" The crisis ended when Democrats acquiesced in Hayes's election based on a "deal" between Hayes's supporters and southerners who wanted federal aid to railroads, internal improvements, federal patronage, and removal of troops from southern states. Northern and southern Democrats decided not to contest the election of a Republican who would not continue Reconstruction.

Southern Democrats rejoiced, but African Americans grieved over the betrayal of their hopes for equality. In a Fourth of July speech in Washington, D.C., in 1875, Frederick Douglass reflected on fifteen years of unparalleled change for his people and worried about white supremacy's hold on America's historical memory: "If war among the whites brought peace and liberty to the blacks, what will peace among the whites bring?"

Summary

Reconstruction left a contradictory record. It was an era of tragic aspirations and failures but also of unprecedented legal, political, and social change. The Union victory brought increased federal power, stronger nationalism, sweeping federal intervention in the southern states, and landmark constitutional amendments. It also sparked a revolution in how people would see the role of the state in their lives. But northern commitment to impose lasting change eroded, leaving the revolution unfinished. The promise for new lives and liberties among the freedpeople was tarnished, although not dead, by 1877.

The North embraced emancipation, black suffrage, and constitutional alterations strengthening the central government, primarily to defeat the rebellion. As wartime pressure declined, Americans, especially northerners, retreated from Reconstruction. The people and the courts maintained a preference for state authority and a distrust of federal power. Free-labor ideology stressed respect for property and individual self-reliance. Racism transformed into Klan terror and theories of black degeneration.

New challenges began to overwhelm the aims of Reconstruction. Industrialization promised prosperity but also wrought labor exploitation. Moreover, industry increased the nation's power and laid the foundation for an enlarged American role in international affairs.

In the wake of the Civil War, Americans faced two profound tasks—healing and dispensing justice. Making sectional reunion compatible with black freedom and equality overwhelmed American politics, and the nation still faced this ongoing dilemma more than a century later.

Chapter Review

Wartime Reconstruction

Which two political acts recognized the centrality of slavery to the war?

Passage of the Thirteenth Amendment and establishment of the Freedmen's Bureau in early 1865 sent a clear signal that slavery was a major cause for the Civil War. The Thirteenth Amendment first abolished slavery ("involuntary servitude") and, second, gave Congress the power to enforce it. Then, a few months later, Congress established the Bureau of Refugees, Freedmen and Abandoned Lands, known as the Freedmen's Bureau, to help former slaves. During its four years as a federal agency, it supplied food and medical services, built thousands of schools and colleges, negotiated job contracts between former slaves and masters, and managed confiscated lands.

The Meanings of Freedom

How did blacks exert their newfound freedom?

With emancipation, former slaves sought to reunite families broken apart through slave sales. Community also became important, as they built their own

churches that ultimately served to strengthen racial ties. Seeking greater control over their work lives, African Americans wanted fairer employers and hoped to own land; when that was not possible, they rented land from former masters under the sharecropping system, in which they paid for supplies and rent by giving owners half their crops on average. Former slaves also embraced the education that had been denied them under slavery and started schools, colleges, and universities throughout the South or attended those launched by the Freedmen's Bureau.

Johnson's Reconstruction Plan

What was Johnson's vision for Reconstruction?

Johnson's approach to Reconstruction could be summed up in a single quote: "The Constitution as it is, and the Union as it was." As president, he controlled Reconstruction policy through 1865, pardoning former Confederates and reestablishing state governments in the South. Despising the planter class, he initially insisted that ex-Confederates with property worth more than $20,000 apply directly to him for pardons. Gradually, Johnson pardoned planters, too, which restored the former elite to power, possibly because he wanted to block

Radical Republicans from implementing extensive racial and political changes in the South. Deeply racist, Johnson remained silent when southern states implemented black codes to restrict former slaves' freedom by requiring them to carry passes, obey curfew laws, and live in housing provided by a landowner. Nonetheless, after just eight months, Johnson declared Reconstruction was completed.

The Congressional Reconstruction Plan

What made Radical Reconstruction different from Johnson's plan?

Radical Republicans in Congress were upset at Johnson's moderate approach, which seemed to hold no one responsible for the war and reestablished racial hierarchies and the southern elite. Initially a minority, the Radicals' popularity grew as Johnson increasingly dug in his heels. Radicals wanted to democratize the South through black suffrage, civil rights, and land confiscation and redistribution. They secured passage of the Fourteenth Amendment, which conferred citizenship on "all persons born or naturalized in the United States." They also passed four strident Reconstruction acts with strict and detailed plans for readmitting southern states to the Union. They barred ex-Confederates from voting until freedmen could and outlined the rules for voter registration boards and the adoption of state constitutions. Unpopular, land redistribution never materialized, but in 1869, Radicals pushed through their final measure, the Fifteenth Amendment, which prohibited states from denying the vote based on "race, color, or previous condition of servitude."

Politics and Reconstruction in the South

How did black voters in the early days of Reconstruction transform the South?

With a large black voter turnout and prominent Confederates barred from the polls and political positions, a new southern variant on the Republican Party came to power during the 1868 to 1870 state constitutional conventions. These constitutions were highly democratic, eliminating property qualifications for voting and political office, shifting some appointed offices to elected ones, and establishing public schools. They also gave women greater rights in terms of property holding and divorce. Blacks became state legislators for the first time in 1868. Angry whites charged they were being ruled by Negroes, and some resorted to violent resistance. In truth, while blacks did play a greater role in government, they remained a minority.

Retreat from Reconstruction

What led the North to lose interest in reconstructing the South?

During the 1870s, northerners faced economic and social transformations at home and became increasingly disillusioned with Reconstruction. Some northerners thought federal expansion had cut too far into states' rights. Second, while immigration and industrialization made northern economies boom from 1865 to 1873, it also widened the gap between the richest and the poorest and created a powerful new class of industrialists. When the Panic of 1873 brought hard times and job losses, interest in Reconstruction faded beside regional economic concerns. The Supreme Court also played a role, challenging congressional Reconstruction in several decisions. The Court ultimately narrowed the meaning of the Fourteenth Amendment by declaring state and national citizenship as distinguishable and limited the amendment's ability to safeguard black citizens, as it was intended to do.

Suggestions for Further Reading

David W. Blight, *Race and Reunion: The Civil War in American Memory* (2001)

Gregory P. Downs, *Declarations of Dependence: The Long Reconstruction of Popular Politics in the South, 1861–1908* (2011)

W. E. B. Du Bois, *Black Reconstruction in America* (1935)

Eric Foner, *Reconstruction: America's Unfinished Revolution, 1863–1877* (1988)

William Gillette, *Retreat from Reconstruction, 1869–1879* (1980)

Gerald Jaynes, *Branches Without Roots: The Genesis of the Black Working Class in the American South, 1862–1882* (1986)

George Rable, *But There Was No Peace* (1984)

Heather Richardson, *West from Appomattox: The Reconstruction of America after the Civil War* (2007)

Elliot West, "Reconstructing Race," *Western Historical Quarterly* (Spring 2003)

Richard White, *Railroaded: The Transcontinentals and the Making of Modern America* (2011)

The Ecology of the West and South

15

1865–1900

Surrounded by eastern Arkansas lowlands that flooded annually, Nannie Stillwell Jackson kept a diary of her life as a late-nineteenth-century farmwife. Her tedious daily work routine and generosity represented the human ecology—the interaction between people and their environment—of her region and times.

A widow, Nannie married a widower ten years younger than herself who drank, stayed out late, and disliked her independence. One Saturday in 1890, for example, Nannie bought a pair of stockings on a trip to town, then later wrote in her diary, "…Mr. Jackson got mad because I bought what I did today but I can't help it if he did." She also participated in a supportive network of neighboring farm women, who visited each other and exchanged food, clothing, meals, and aid almost daily. Nature was Nannie's ally and enemy. She often sent her teenage daughter to bring "water from the bayou to wash with," but complained "no rain yet & we do need rain so bad." And waterborne typhoid fever killed several of her neighbors.

Nannie's experiences were shared across the American West and South, where people worked hard with—and sometimes against—the changing environment. Where Nannie Jackson lived, the nearby Missouri Pacific Railroad provided access to the outside world and its goods, such as the store-bought stockings she brought home. During her lifetime, a "New South" emerged, built upon railroads, factories, and cities. Farther west, the population grew rapidly as new migrants streamed in to develop the land and extract its wealth.

Historically, the region known as the "South" had a stable definition. It encompassed most of the states and territories beneath the thirty-ninth parallel westward to the Mississippi River and sometimes including Oklahoma and Texas, and its population rose from around 12.5 million in 1870 to 20 million in 1890. The meaning of the "West," however, changed. In the eighteenth century, the West encompassed everything beyond the Appalachian Mountains. With settlement of the Midwest after the Civil War, the West spanned the

Mississippi River to the Pacific Ocean, including the plains between the Mississippi and the Rocky Mountains, the Rockies, and the mountains and valleys of the Far West.

Before migrants arrived, the West was occupied by native inhabitants, whose human ecology of communities utilized natural resources differently from those who later occupied the region. On the Plains, for example, the Pawnees planted crops in springtime, left their fields in summer to hunt buffalo, then returned for harvesting. They sometimes battled with Cheyenne and Arapahoe over hunting grounds and crops. In what now is the American Southwest, natives shared the land and sometimes integrated with descendants of Spanish colonists. All these peoples survived by developing and using natural resources, with occasional access to outside markets. Between 1870 and 1890, the white population there swelled from 7 million to nearly 17 million, overwhelming native and Hispanic communities.

As newcomers built communities in the West and South, they exploited the environment for profit more extensively than did Indians. They excavated the earth for minerals, felled forests for homes, built railroads, dammed rivers, and plowed farmland with machines. Their goal included buying and selling in regional, national, and international markets. Nannie Jackson participated in such changes when she went to town to buy goods. The abundance of exploitable land and raw materials filled white Americans with faith that anyone persistent enough could succeed. This confidence also rested on a belief that white people were somehow superior, which asserted itself at the expense of minority people and the environment. As they transformed the landscape, their market economies transformed the nation. Both hope and hardship shaped the new human ecology.

As you read this chapter, keep the following questions in mind:

- **How did the interaction between people and the environment shape the physical landscapes of the West and South?**

- **Describe the societal and technological changes that revolutionized lives of farmers in the West and South.**

- **How did the U.S. government's relations with Native Americans change over time throughout the late nineteenth century?**

Chronology

1862	Homestead Act grants free land to citizens who live on and improve the land	1881–82	Chinese Exclusion Acts prohibit Chinese immigration to the United States
	Morrill Land Grant Act gives states public and to sell to finance agricultural and industrial colleges	1883	National time zones established
		1884	U.S. Supreme Court first defines Indians as wards under government protection
1864	Chivington's militia massacres Black Kettle's Cheyennes at Sand Creek	1887	Dawes Severalty Act ends communal ownership of Indian lands and grants land allotments to individual native families; "California Plan" advances irrigation
1869	First transcontinental railroad completed	1887–88	Devastating winter on Plains destroys countless livestock and forces farmers into economic hardship
1872	Yellowstone becomes first national park		
1876	Lakotas and Cheyennes ambush Custer's federal troops at Little Big Horn, Montana	1889	Asa Candler buys and develops Coca-Cola Company
1877	Nez Percé Indians under Young Joseph surrender to U.S. troops	1890	Final suppression of Plains Indians by U.S. Army at Wounded Knee
1878	Timber and Stone Act allows citizens to buy timberland cheaply but also enables large companies to acquire huge tracts of forestland		Census Bureau announces closing of the frontier
			Yosemite National Park established
1879	Carlisle School for Indians established in Pennsylvania	1892	Muir helps found Sierra Club
1880	Cigarette-making machine invented	1902	Newlands Reclamation Act passed

The Transformation of Native Cultures

What factors transformed Native Americans' subsistence economy and relationship to the land in the late nineteenth century?

Native Americans settled the West long before other Americans migrated there. Indians had shaped their environment for centuries. Nevertheless, several factors weakened native economic systems in the late nineteenth century.

Subsistence Cultures Western Indian ecologies varied. Some natives inhabited permanent settlements; others, temporary camps. Most Indians were participants and recipients in a flow of goods, culture, language, and disease carried by migrating bands. Indian economies were based in differing degrees on four activities: (1) crop growing; (2) livestock raising; (3) hunting, fishing, and gathering; and (4) trading and raiding. Corn was the most common crop; sheep and horses, acquired from Spanish colonizers and other Indians, were the livestock; and buffalo (American bison) and salmon were the primary prey of hunting and fishing. Indians raided one another for food, tools, and horses. When a buffalo hunt failed, they subsisted on crops. When crops failed, they hunted or stole food and horses, or traded livestock and furs for necessities.

For Indians on the Plains, life focused on buffalo. They cooked and preserved buffalo meat; fashioned hides into clothing, moccasins, and blankets; used sinew for thread and bowstrings; and carved tools from bones and horns. Buffalo were so valuable that Pawnees and Lakotas often fought over access to herds. **Plains Indians**

Plains Indians Diverse Native American societies inhabiting the region from the Dakotas to Texas.

Using buffalo hides to fashion garments, Indians often exhibited artistic skills in decorating their apparel. This Ute Indian hide dress shows symbolic as well as aesthetic representations.

altered the environment by periodically setting fire to tallgrass prairies, which burned away dead plants, facilitating growth of new grass so that horses could feed all summer.

In the Southwest, Indians led varying lifestyles, depending on the environment. For example, in southeastern Arizona and northwestern Mexico, some of the O'odham (in English, "The People") grew irrigated crops in the few river valleys, while those who inhabited the mountainous and desert regions followed a hunter–gatherer existence. The Navajo (or Dine', also meaning "The People") were herders, whose sheep, goats, and horses provided food, transportation, and status.

To Indians of the Northwest, salmon was important. Before the mid-nineteenth century, the Columbia River and its tributaries supported the densest population of native peoples in North America. To harvest fish, the Clatsops, Klamath, and S'Klallams developed technologies of stream diversion, platform construction, and special baskets to catch fish. They traded for horses, buffalo robes, beads, cloth, and knives.

Slaughter of Buffalo

On the Plains and in parts of the Southwest, native ecologies gradually dissolved after 1850, when whites competed with Indians for natural resources. Perceiving buffalo and Indians as hindrances, whites endeavored to eliminate both. The U.S. Army failed to enforce treaties that reserved hunting grounds for exclusive Indian use, so railroads sponsored buffalo hunts in which eastern sportsmen shot at buffalo from slow-moving trains, killing thousands.

Unbeknownst to Indians and whites, however, a combination of circumstances doomed the buffalo before the slaughter of the late 1800s. Natives contributed to the depletion of the herds by increasing their kills to trade hides with whites and other Indians. Also, in the dry years of the 1840s and 1850s, Indians relocated to river basins, pushing buffalo from grazing territory to face starvation. Whites, too, settled in river basins, further depriving buffalo of grasslands. And lethal animal diseases, such as anthrax and brucellosis, brought by white-owned livestock, decimated buffalo already weakened by malnutrition and drought. Increasing numbers of horses, oxen, and sheep, owned by white newcomers and some Indians, devoured vital grasses. The mass killing by railroads only struck the final blow. By the 1880s, only a few hundred of the 25 million buffalo estimated to exist on the Plains in 1820 remained.

Decline of Salmon

In the Northwest, salmon suffered a similar fate. White commercial fishermen and canneries moved into the Columbia and Willamette river valleys during the 1860s and 1870s, and by the 1880s they had greatly diminished salmon runs. By the early 1900s, construction of dams on the river and its tributaries further impeded salmon's reproduction. The U.S. government protected Indian fishing rights, and hatcheries restored some salmon supplies, but dams built to provide power, combined with overfishing and pollution, diminished salmon stocks.

| Influence of Young White Men |

Buffalo slaughter and salmon reduction undermined western Indian subsistence, but demographic changes also contributed. Throughout the nineteenth century, white migrants were overwhelmingly young, single males in their twenties and thirties, the age when they were most prone to violent behavior. In 1870 white men outnumbered white women by three to two in California, two to one in Colorado, and two to one in Dakota Territory. By 1900, preponderances of men remained throughout these places. Indians were likely to come into contact first with white traders, trappers, soldiers, prospectors, and cowboys—almost all of whom owned guns and would use them against animals and humans who got in their way.

Moreover, these men adopted prevailing attitudes that Indians were primitive, lazy, and devious. Such contempt made exploiting and killing natives easier, further justified by claims of threats to life and property. When Indians raided white settlements, they sometimes mutilated bodies, burned buildings, and kidnapped women, acts that were embellished in campfire stories and popular fiction to portray Indians as savages. In saloons and cabins, white men boasted about fighting Indians and showed off trophies of victims' scalps and other body parts.

Indian warriors, too, were young, armed, and prone to violence. Valuing bravery, they boasted of fighting white interlopers. But Indian communities contained excesses of women, the elderly, and children, making native bands less mobile and more vulnerable. They also were susceptible to bad habits of bachelor white society, copying their binges on cheap whiskey and prostitution. The syphilis and gonorrhea that Indian men contracted from Indian women infected by white men killed many and hindered reproduction, which their populations, already declining from smallpox and other white diseases, could not afford. Thus age and gender structures of the white frontier population, combined with racist contempt, further threatened western Indians' existence.

| Government Policy and Treaties |

U.S. government policy reinforced efforts to remove Indians. North American natives were organized not into tribes, as whites believed, but into bands, confederacies, and villages. Two hundred languages and dialects separated these groups, making it difficult for Indians to unite against white invaders. Although a language group could be defined as a tribe, separate bands and clans had different leaders, and seldom did a chief hold widespread power. Moreover, bands often spent more time battling among themselves than with white settlers.

Nevertheless, after 1795, American officials considered Indian tribes as nations with which they could make treaties ensuring peace and land boundaries. This was a faulty assumption because chiefs who agreed to a treaty did not always speak for the whole band and the group might not abide by it. Moreover, whites seldom accepted treaties as guarantees of Indians' land rights. On the Plains, whites settled wherever they wished, often commandeering choice farmland. In the Northwest, whites considered treaties protecting Indians' fishing rights on the Columbia River to be nuisances and ousted Indians from the best locations.

Reservation Policy

Prior to the 1880s, the federal government tried to force western Indians onto reservations, where they might be "civilized." Reservations usually consisted of areas in a group's previous territory that were least desirable to whites. The government promised protection from white encroachment, along with food, clothing, and other necessities.

Reservation policy helped make way for the market economy. In early years, trade benefited Indians and whites equally. Indians acquired clothing, guns, and horses in return for furs, hides, jewelry, and, sometimes, military assistance against other Indians. Over time, Indians became more dependent, and whites increasingly dictated trade. For example, white traders persuaded Navajo weavers in the Southwest to produce heavy rugs for eastern customers and to change designs and colors to boost sales. Meanwhile, Navajos raised fewer crops and were forced to buy food. Soon they were selling land and labor to whites, and their dependency made it easier to force them onto reservations.

Indians had no say over their affairs on reservations. Supreme Court decisions in 1884 and 1886 defined them as wards (like helpless children under government protection) and denied them U.S. citizenship. Thus they were unprotected by the Fourteenth and Fifteenth Amendments, which extended citizenship to African Americans. Second, pressure from white farmers, miners, and herders who sought Indian lands made it difficult for the government to preserve reservations intact. Third, the government ignored native history, even combining on one reservation enemy bands. Rather than serving as civilizing communities, reservations weakened Indian life.

Native Resistance

Not all Indians succumbed to market forces and reservation restrictions. Apaches in the Southwest battled whites even after being forced onto reservations. Pawnees in the Midwest resisted disadvantageous deals from white traders. In the Northwest, Nez Percé Indians escaped reservations by fleeing to Canada in 1877. They eluded U.S. troops until, 1,800 miles later in Montana, their leader, Young Joseph, recognized they could not succeed and ended the flight. Sent to a reservation, Joseph unsuccessfully petitioned the government to return his people's ancestral lands.

Whites responded to western Indian defiance militarily. In 1860, Navajos reacted by raiding Fort Defiance in Arizona Territory. The army then attacked and starved the Navajo into submission, and in 1863–1864 forced them on a "Long Walk" from their homelands to a reservation at Bosque Redondo in New Mexico. In the Sand Creek region of Colorado in 1864, a militia commanded by Methodist minister John Chivington attacked Cheyennes led by Black Kettle, killing almost every Indian. In 1879, four thousand U.S. soldiers forced surrender from Utes who were resisting further land concessions.

The most publicized battle occurred in June 1876, when 2,500 Lakotas and Cheyennes led by chiefs Rain-in-the-Face, Sitting Bull, and Crazy Horse annihilated 256 government troops led by Colonel George A. Custer near Little Big Horn River in southern Montana. Although Indians demonstrated military skill, supply shortages and relentless pursuit by U.S. soldiers, including African American units of Union army veterans called Buffalo Soldiers (so named by the Cheyennes and Comanches they fought), eventually overwhelmed armed Indian resistance. Native Americans were not so much conquered as they were harassed and starved into submission.

Reform of Indian Policy

In the 1870s and 1880s, reformers and government officials sought more purposely to "civilize" natives through landholding and education. This meant outlawing customs deemed to be "savage" and pressuring natives to adopt American values of ambition, thrift, and materialism. In this regard, the United States copied the imperialist policies of other nations, such as France, which banned native religious ceremonies in its Pacific island colonies. Others argued for sympathetic—and sometimes patronizing—treatment. Reform treatises, such as George Manypenny's *Our Indian Wards* (1880) and Helen Hunt Jackson's *A Century of Dishonor* (1881), aroused American humanitarianism.

In the United States, the most active Indian reform organizations were the Women's National Indian Association (WNIA) and Indian Rights Association (IRA). The WNIA sought to use women's domestic qualities of compassion to help needy people and urge gradual assimilation of Indians. The more influential IRA, which had few Native American members, advocated citizenship and landholding by individual Indians. Most white reformers believed Indians were culturally inferior and could succeed economically only by embracing middle-class values of diligence and education.

Reformers deplored Indians' sexual division of labor. Native women seemed to do all the work—tending crops, raising children, cooking, making tools and clothes—while being servile to men, who hunted but were otherwise idle. WNIA and IRA wanted Indian men to bear more responsibilities, treat Indian women more respectfully, and resemble male heads of white middle-class households. But when Indian men and women adopted this model of white society, Indian women lost the economic independence and power over daily life they once had.

Zitkala-Sa

Indians like Zitkala-Sa (Red Bird) used white-controlled education to their advantage. Born on South Dakota's Pine Ridge reservation in 1876, at age twelve this Yankton Sioux girl attended an Indiana boarding school and, later, Earlham College and the Boston Conservatory of Music. An accomplished orator and violinist, her major contribution was her writing on behalf of her people's needs and advocating of cultural preservation. In 1901, Zitkala-Sa published *Old Indian Legends,* translating Sioux oral tradition into stories. Zitkala-Sa married a mixed-race army captain who had taken the name Ray Bonnin and became known as Gertrude Bonnin. Subsequently, she served as editor of *American Indian Magazine,* all the while advocating for Indian rights.

Dawes Severalty Act U.S. law designed to "civilize" Indians by dividing up and distributing communal tribal lands to individuals.

Dawes Severalty Act

In 1887 Congress reversed its reservation policy and passed the **Dawes Severalty Act**. It authorized dissolution of community-owned Indian property and granted land to individual Indian families. The government held that land in trust for twenty-five years, so families could not sell their allotments. The law awarded citizenship to those accepting allotments (an act of Congress in 1906 delayed citizenship for those Indians who had not yet taken their allotment). It also entitled the government to sell unallocated land to whites.

Indian policy, under the Interior Department, now assumed two main features for assimilating Indians into white American culture. First, per the Dawes Act, the government distributed reservation land to families, arguing that property ownership would integrate Indians into the larger society as productive citizens. Second, officials believed that Indians would abandon their "barbaric" habits faster if their children were educated in boarding schools.

The Dawes Act represented a Euro-American and Christian worldview that a society of landholding families headed by men was ideal. Government agents and reformers were joined by educators who used schools to create a patriotic, industrious citizenry. Following Virginia's Hampton Institute, founded in 1869 to educate newly freed slaves, educators established the Carlisle School in Pennsylvania in 1879 as the flagship of the government's Indian school system. Boarding schools imposed white-defined sex roles: boys learned farming and carpentry, and girls learned sewing, cleaning, and cooking.

Ghost Dance Ritual where Sioux dancers moved in a circle, accelerating until they reached a trancelike state and experienced visions of the future where white society would vanish from Indian lands.

Ghost Dance

With resistance suppressed, Lakotas and others turned to the **Ghost Dance** as a spiritual means of preserving native culture. The Ghost Dance involved movement in a circle until dancers reached a trancelike state and envisioned dead ancestors who predicted buffalo would return and white civilization would be buried.

Ghost Dancers forswore violence, but as the religion spread, government agents worried about renewed Indian uprisings. Charging that the cult was anti-Christian, the army arrested Ghost Dancers. Late in 1890, the government sent the Seventh Cavalry, Custer's old regiment, to detain Lakotas moving toward Pine Ridge, South Dakota. Although the Indians were starving, the army assumed they were armed for revolt. Overtaking them at a creek called **Wounded Knee**, the troops massacred about three hundred men, women, and children.

Wounded Knee South Dakota site of a bloody clash between Sioux Indians and whites. Within minutes, white troops—mistakenly assuming the starving Indians were armed for revolt—slaughtered three hundred Indians, including seven infants.

The Losing of the West

Indian wars and the Dawes Act effectively reduced native control over land. Between 1887 and the 1930s, native landholdings dwindled from 138 million acres to 52 million. Land-grabbing whites were particularly cruel to the Ojibwas of the northern plains. In 1906, Minnesota Senator Moses E. Clapp attached to an Indian appropriations bill a rider declaring that mixed-blood adults on the White Earth reservation were "competent" (meaning educated in white ways) enough to sell their land without the Dawes Act's twenty-five-year waiting period. When the bill became law, speculators duped Ojibwas into signing away land for counterfeit money and worthless merchandise. The Ojibwas lost more than half their original holdings.

Visualizing THE PAST

Attempts to Make Indians Look and Act like "Americans"

Government officials believed that they could "civilize" Indian children in boarding schools by not only educating them to act like white people but also by making them look like white people. Thus the boys in the photograph on the left were given baseball uniforms and the girl on the right was made to wear a dress and carry a purse and umbrella, all of which were foreign to native people. These images convey information about how Indians were treated, but they also suggest attitudes of the photographer and the artist who made the images. What messages about "civilizing" natives did the person who photographed the baseball team and the artist who drew the picture of the girl reuniting with her people want the viewer to receive?

University of Washington Libraries, Special Collections NA4117

In an attempt to inculcate "American" customs into its native students, the Fort Spokane Indian School in Spokane, Washington, created a baseball team for the young men who boarded there.

Library of Congress

In an 1884 edition, Frank Leslie's Weekly, *one of the most popular illustrated news and fiction publications of the late nineteenth and early twentieth centuries, depicted an "Americanized" Indian girl dressed as a proper young lady returning from the Carlisle boarding school to visit her home at the Pine Ridge Agency in South Dakota.*

Government policy had other injurious effects on Indians' ways of life. Most schoolchildren returned to reservations from boarding schools demoralized by lessons that their inherited customs were inferior, rather than ready to assimilate into white society.

Ultimately, political and ecological crises overwhelmed western Indian groups. Buffalo extinction, enemy raids, and disease, along with U.S. military campaigns, hobbled subsistence culture until Native Americans could only yield their lands to market-oriented whites. Believing themselves superior, whites determined to transform Indians by teaching them about private property and American ideals and eradicating their "backward" languages, lifestyles, and religions. Indians tried to retain their culture, but by century's end, they lost control of their land and faced increasing pressure to shed their group identity.

The Extraction of Natural Resources

What sparked the rise of the conservation movement?

Unlike Indians, who used natural resources for subsistence and small-scale trading needs, white migrants to the West and Great Plains in the late nineteenth century saw the vast territory as untapped sources of wealth (see Map 15.1). Extracting its resources advanced settlement, created new markets at home and abroad, and fueled revolutions in transportation, agriculture, and industry across the United States. This ecological relationship between nature and humans led to wastefulness and fed racial and sexual oppression.

Mining

In the mid-1800s, the mining frontier drew thousands of people to Nevada, Idaho, Montana, Utah, and Colorado. California's gold rush helped populate a thriving state by 1850 and furnished many of the miners traveling to nearby states. Others followed traditional routes from the East to the West.

Prospectors climbed mountains and trekked across deserts seeking precious metals. They shot game for food and financed their explorations by convincing merchants to advance credit for equipment in return for a share of the as-yet-undiscovered lode. Unlucky prospectors whose credit ran out took jobs and saved up for another search.

Digging up and transporting minerals was expensive, so prospectors who made discoveries sold their claims to large mining syndicates, such as the Anaconda Copper Company. Financed by eastern capital, these companies brought in engineers, heavy machinery, railroad lines, and work crews, making western mining as corporate as eastern manufacturing. Mining operatives also settled cities and boosted populations in places such as El Paso and Tucson. Though discoveries of gold sparked national publicity, mining companies usually exploited more lucrative lead, zinc, tin, quartz, and copper.

Lumbering and Oil Drilling

Unlike mining, cutting trees for construction and heating materials required vast tracts of forestland to be profitable. Because tree supplies in the upper Midwest and South were depleted, lumber corporations

MAP 15.1

The Development and Natural Resources of the West

By 1890, mining, lumbering, and cattle ranching had penetrated many areas west of the Mississippi River, and railroad construction had linked together the western economy. These activities, along with the spread of mechanized agriculture, altered both the economy and the people who were involved in them. Source: Copyright © Cengage Learning 2015

moved into northwestern forests. The 1878 Timber and Stone Act sought to stimulate settlement in California, Nevada, Oregon, and Washington by allowing private citizens to buy inexpensive 160-acreplots. Lumber companies grabbed millions of acres by hiring seamen from waterfront boarding houses to register claims to timberland and then transfer them to the companies. By 1900, private citizens had bought over 3.5 million acres, but most of it belonged to corporations.

At the same time, oil companies began drilling wells in the Southwest. In 1900, petroleum came from the Appalachians and the Midwest, but rich oil reserves were discovered in southern California and eastern Texas, turning Los Angeles and Houston

The Australian Frontier

Australia, founded like the United States as a European colony, had a frontier society that resembled the American West in its mining development, folk society, and treatment of racial minorities. Australia experienced a gold rush in 1851, two years after the United States did, and large-scale mining companies moved into its western regions to extract mineral deposits.

The promise of mineral wealth lured thousands of mostly male immigrants—many from China—to Australia in the late nineteenth century. As in the United States, anti-Chinese riots erupted, and beginning in 1854, Australia passed laws restricting Chinese immigration. When the country became an independent British federation in 1901, it implemented a literacy test that terminated Chinese immigration for over fifty years.

As in the American West, the Australian frontier bred folk heroes who came to symbolize white masculinity as the epitome of self-reliance. But they also considered indigenous peoples, whom they called "Aborigines," as savages. Christian missionaries viewed Aborigines as pagan and tried to convert them. In 1869 the government of Victoria Province passed an Aborigine Protection Act that, like American policy toward Indians, encouraged removal of native children from their families to learn European customs in white schools. Aborigines adapted. They formed cricket teams, and those with light skin sometimes told census takers they were white. In the end, Australians resorted to reservations to "protect" Aborigines, just as Americans isolated native peoples on reserved land. Like the Americans, white Australians could not find a place for indigenous people in a land of opportunity.

Much like its American counterpart, the Australian frontier involved mining operations and was populated by indigenous people. Here, the Aborigines, as the natives were called, are using track to bring down ore extracted from a hill.

Alinari Archives/Getty Images

into boom cities. Although oil and kerosene were used mostly for lubrication and lighting, oil discovered in the Southwest later became a vital new fuel source.

Water and Irrigation

Glittering gold and gushing oil shaped popular images of the West, but finding a way to bring water to the arid soil was the key to its agricultural development. Western economic development is the story of how public and private interests used technology and organization to utilize the region's sometimes scarce water resources to make the land agriculturally productive.

For centuries, Indians irrigated southwestern fields for subsistence farming. When the Spanish arrived, they tapped the Rio Grande River to irrigate farms. Later they channeled water to San Diego and Los Angeles. The first Americans of European ancestry to practice extensive irrigation were the Mormons. After arriving in Utah in 1847, they diverted streams and rivers into canals, enabling them to farm the hard-baked soil. By 1890 Utah boasted over 263,000 irrigated acres supporting more than two hundred thousand people.

Rights to Water

Efforts at land reclamation through irrigation in Colorado and California sparked conflict over rights to the streams that flowed through the West. Americans inherited the English common-law principle of riparian rights, which held that the stream belonged to God; those who lived nearby could take water as needed but should not diminish the river. Intended to protect nature, this principle discouraged economic development by prohibiting property owners from damming or diverting water at the expense of others who lived downstream.

Western settlers rejected riparianism and embraced prior appropriation, which awarded a river's water to the first person claiming it. Westerners, taking cues from eastern Americans who diverted waterways to power mills, asserted that water existed to serve human needs. Anyone intending a "reasonable" (economically productive) use of river water should have the right to appropriation. The courts generally agreed.

Government Supervision of Water Rights

Under appropriation, those who dammed and diverted water often reduced its flow downstream. People disadvantaged by such action could sue or establish a public authority to regulate water usage. Thus in 1879, Colorado created several divisions to regulate water rights. In 1890, Wyoming added a constitutional provision declaring that the state's rivers were public property subject to supervision.

Destined to become the most productive agricultural state, California maintained a mixed legal system that upheld riparianism while allowing for some appropriation. This system disadvantaged irrigators, and they sought to change state law. In 1887, the legislature passed a bill permitting farmers to organize into districts that would construct and operate irrigation projects. An irrigation district could purchase water rights, seize private property for irrigation canals, and finance projects through taxation or by issuing bonds. Consequently, California had more than 1 million irrigated acres by 1890, making the state's fruit and vegetable agriculture the most profitable in the country.

Newlands Reclamation Act

Still, the federal government owned most western land in the 1890s. Prodded by land-hungry developers, states wanted the federal government to give them public domain lands, claiming they could make them profitable through reclamation (irrigation). Congress generally refused such transfers because of potential controversies. If, for example, California assumed control of the Truckee River, which flowed out of Lake Tahoe on the California-Nevada border, how would Nevadans ensure that California would allow them sufficient water? Only the federal government had the power to regulate interstate water development.

In 1902, after years of debates, Congress passed the **Newlands Reclamation Act**. Named for Nevada's Democratic congressman Francis Newlands, the law allowed the federal government to sell western public lands to individuals in parcels not to exceed 160 acres and to use proceeds to finance irrigation. The Newlands Act provided for control but not conservation of water, and instead fell within the tradition of development of nature for human profit. It represented a decision by the federal government to aid the agricultural and general economic development of the West.

Newlands Reclamation Act
Authorized the U.S. government to sell western public lands to finance dams and irrigation projects in the West.

Complex Communities

As the West developed, it became a multiracial society, including Native Americans, white migrants, Mexicans, African Americans, and Asians. A borderland from western Texas through New Mexico and Arizona to northern California (including Mexico) supported ranchers and sheepherders, descendants of early Spanish settlers. In New Mexico, Spaniards intermarried with Indians to form a *mestizo* population. Across the Southwest frontier, Mexican immigrants moved into American territory to find work. Some returned to Mexico seasonally. Although the Treaty of Guadalupe Hidalgo (1848) guaranteed property rights to Hispanics, "Anglo" (the Mexican name for a white American) miners, speculators, and railroads used fraud to claim Hispanic landholdings. Consequently, many Mexicanos moved to cities such as San Antonio and Tucson and became wage laborers.

Before the Chinese Exclusion Act of 1882 prohibited them from immigrating, some 200,000 Chinese—mostly young, single males—entered the United States, building communities in California, Oregon, and Washington. Many came with five-year labor contracts for railroad construction; others worked the fields. By the 1870s, Chinese composed half of California's agricultural workforce, often working in citrus groves. In cities such as San Francisco, they labored in textile and cigar factories.

Link to the Chinese Exclusion Act

Japanese and European immigrants, especially Irish, worked on railroads and in mining and agricultural communities. The region developed its own migrant economy, with workers relocating to take short-term jobs.

Many African Americans were **"exodusters,"** former slaves who fled the South and built all-black western towns. Nicodemus, Kansas, for example, was founded in 1877 by black migrants from Lexington, Kentucky. Despite early challenges, the town boasted newspapers, shops, churches, a hotel, and a bank. It declined when businesses left after the town failed to obtain railroad connections. Other black migrants, encouraged by editors and land speculators, went to Oklahoma Territory, where they founded thirty two all-black communities in the 1890s and early 1900s.

"exodusters" Freed people who migrated from the South to the North and Midwest for better opportunities.

Western Women

Although unmarried men dominated the frontier, many white women also headed west to find fortune. Most accompanied a husband or father and seldom prospected themselves. But many women earned money by cooking, laundering, and sometimes as sex workers in houses of prostitution. In the Northwest, they worked in canneries, cleaning and salting fish.

White women helped bolster family and community life as members of the home mission movement. They broke from traditional male-dominated Protestant missions. Using the slogan "Woman's work for women," they established missionary societies aiding women—unmarried mothers, Mormons, Indians, and Chinese—they believed had fallen prey to men or not yet adopted Christian virtue.

Significance of Race

To control labor and social relations within this human ecological complex, white settlers made race important. They classified people into five races: Caucasians (themselves), Indians, Mexicans (both Mexican Americans, who originally inhabited western lands, and Mexican immigrants), "Mongolians" (a term applied to Chinese), and "Negroes." With these categories, whites imposed racial distinctions on people who, with the possible exception of African Americans, had never before considered themselves a "race," and then judged them permanently inferior. In 1878, for example, a federal judge in California ruled that Chinese could not become U.S. citizens because they were not "white persons."

Racial and ethnic minorities occupied the bottom of a two-tiered labor system and experienced prejudice as whites tried to reserve for themselves the West's riches. Whites dominated the top tier of managerial and skilled labor positions, while Irish, Chinese, Mexican, and African American workers held unskilled positions. Anti-Chinese violence erupted during hard times. When the Union Pacific Railroad tried to replace white workers with lower-waged Chinese in Rock Springs, Wyoming, in 1885, unemployed whites burned down the Chinese part of town, killing twenty eight. Mexicans, many of whom were the original landowners in California and elsewhere, saw their property claims ignored or stolen by whites.

Because so many white male migrants were single, intermarriage or cohabitation with Mexican and Indian women was common. Such unions were acceptable for white men, but not for white women, especially with Asian immigrants. Most miscegenation laws passed by western legislatures sought to prevent Chinese and Japanese men from marrying white women.

Conservation Movement

Questions about natural resources caught Americans between desire for progress and fear of spoiling nature. After the Civil War, people eager to protect the natural landscape organized a conservation movement. Sports hunters, concerned about wildlife depletion, opposed commercial hunting and lobbied state legislatures to pass hunting regulations. Artists and tourists in 1864 persuaded Congress to preserve the Yosemite Valley by granting it to California, which reserved it for public use. In 1872, Congress designated the Yellowstone River region in Wyoming as the first national park. And in 1891 conservationists, led by naturalist John Muir, pressured Congress to authorize President Benjamin Harrison to create forest reserves—public lands protected from private timber cutters.

Link to Our Forests and National Parks, by John Muir, 1901

Despite Muir's activism and efforts by the Sierra Club (which Muir helped found in 1892) and corporations supporting rational resource development, opposition was loudest in the West, where people remained eager to exploit nature. By prohibiting trespass in areas such as Yosemite and Yellowstone, conservation policy deprived Indians and white settlers of wildlife, water, and firewood previously taken from federal lands.

Admission of New States

Development of mining and forest regions, along with farms and cities, brought western territories to the threshold of statehood (see Map 15.2). In 1889, Republicans seeking to solidify control of Congress passed an omnibus bill granting statehood to North Dakota, South Dakota, Washington, and Montana, where Republicans dominated. Wyoming and Idaho, which allowed women to vote, were admitted the following year. Congress denied statehood to Utah until 1896, wanting assurances from the Mormons, a majority of the territory's population, that they would prohibit polygamy.

Western states' varied communities spiced American folk culture and fostered a "go-getter" optimism that distinguished the American spirit. The lawlessness of places such as Deadwood, in Dakota Territory, and Tombstone, in Arizona

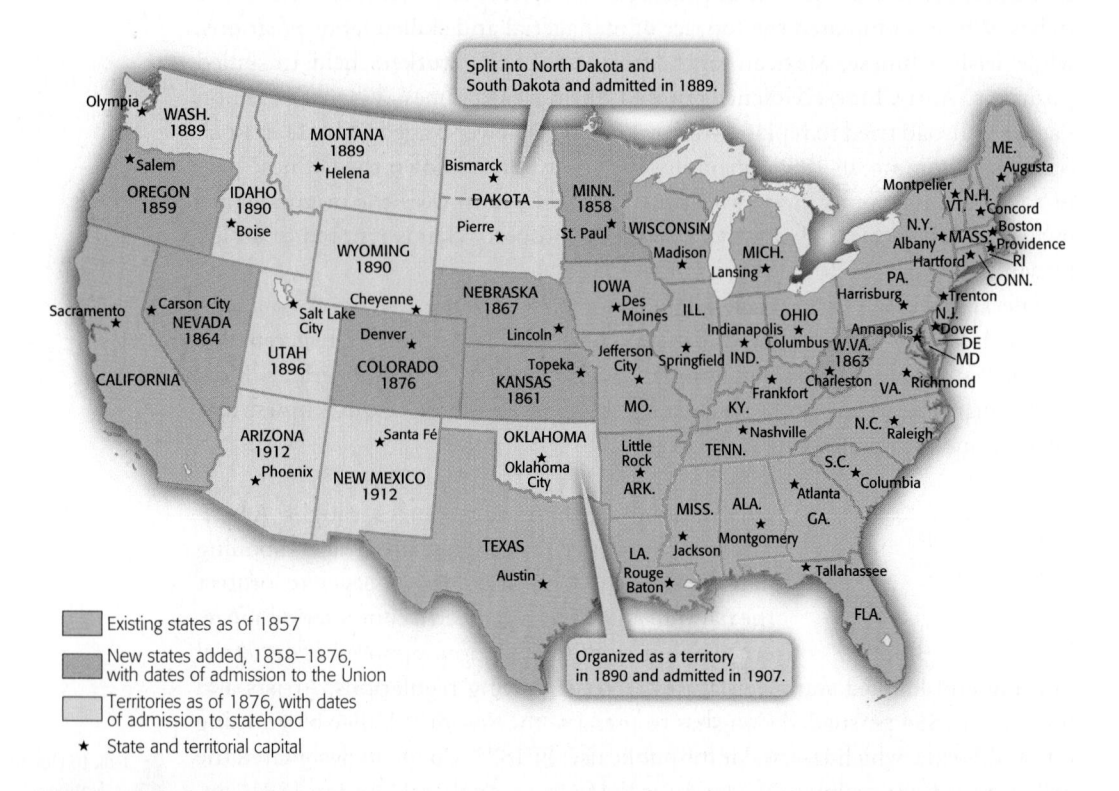

MAP 15.2
The United States, 1876–1912
A wave of admissions between 1889 and 1912 brought remaining territories to statehood and marked the final creation of new states until Alaska and Hawai'i were admitted in the 1950s. Source: Copyright © Cengage Learning 2015

Territory, gave their regions notoriety and romance. Legends arose about characters whose lives magnified the western experience, and promoters such as Buffalo Bill enhanced the western folklore's appeal.

Western Folk Heroes

Arizona's mining towns, with their free-flowing cash and loose law enforcement, attracted gamblers, thieves, and opportunists whose names came to symbolize the Wild West. Near Tombstone, the infamous Clanton family and their partner John Ringgold (Johnny Ringo) were smugglers and cattle rustlers. The Earp brothers—Wyatt, Jim, Morgan, Virgil, and Warren—and their friends William ("Bat") Masterson and John Henry ("Doc") Holliday operated on both sides of the law as gunmen, gamblers, and politicians. A feud between the Clantons and Earps climaxed on October 26, 1881, in a shootout at the OK Corral, where three Clantons were killed and Holliday and Morgan Earp were wounded.

Writers Mark Twain, Bret Harte, and others captured the flavor of western life, and characters such as Buffalo Bill, Annie Oakley, and Wild Bill Hickok became western folk heroes. But violence and eccentricity were uncommon. Most miners and lumbermen worked long hours, often for corporations, and had little time or money for gambling, carousing, or gunfights. Women worked as teachers, laundresses, storekeepers, and housewives. Only a few were sharpshooters or dance-hall queens. For most, western life was a struggle for survival.

The Age of Railroad Expansion

How did government policies aid the development of the West?

Between 1865 and 1890, railroad expansion boomed, as tracks grew from 35,000 to 200,000 miles, mostly west of the Mississippi River (see Map 15.1). By 1900, the United States contained one-third of all railroad track in the world. The Central Pacific employed thousands of Chinese; the Union Pacific used mainly Irish. Workers lived in shacks and tents that were dismantled, loaded on flatcars, and relocated each day.

After 1880, when steel rails replaced iron rails, railroads helped boost the nation's steel industry to international leadership. Railroads also spawned related industries, including coal production (for fuel), passenger and freight car manufacture, and depot construction. Railroads also fueled western urbanization. Transporting people and freight, railroads accelerated the growth of hubs such as Chicago, Omaha, Kansas City, Cheyenne, Los Angeles, Portland, and Seattle.

Railroad Subsidies

Railroads received some of the largest government subsidies in American history. Promoters argued that because railroads were a public benefit, the government should give them land from the public domain, which they could then sell to finance construction. During the Civil War, Congress, dominated by business-minded Republicans, granted railroad corporations over 180 million acres, mostly for interstate routes. Railroads funded construction by using the land as security for bonds or by selling it. State legislators, who often had financial interests in a railroad, granted some 50 million acres. Cities and towns also assisted, usually via loans or by purchasing railroad bonds or stocks.

Library of Congress

The rim of the horseshoe in this advertisement depicts reasons why railroad travel was better than other forms: one could avoid crowds of immigrants on steamships, move faster than a canal boat being towed by a mule, and be safe from bandits holding up a stagecoach. At the bottom of the poster are two depictions of luxurious dining and relaxed travel in a chair car that a railroad offered.

Government subsidies had mixed effects. Although capitalists often opposed government involvement in business, railroads accepted aid and pressured governments for assistance. The Southern Pacific, for example, threatened to bypass Los Angeles unless the city paid a bonus and built a depot. During the 1880s, the policy of generosity haunted communities whose zeal had prompted them to commit too much to railroads that were never built or that defaulted on loans. Some laborers and farmers fought subsidies, arguing that companies would become too powerful. Many communities boomed, however, as railroads attracted investment into the West and drew farmers into the market economy.

Standard Gauge, Standard Time

Railroad construction triggered important technological and organizational reforms. By the late 1880s, almost all lines had adopted standard-gauge rails so their tracks could connect. Air brakes, automatic car couplers, and other devices made rail transportation safer and more efficient. The need for gradings, tunnels, and bridges spurred the growth of the American engineering profession. Organizational advances included systems for coordinating passenger and freight schedules, and the adoption of uniform freight-classification systems. However, railroads also reinforced racism by segregating black and white passengers on cars and in stations.

Rail transportation altered conceptions of time and space. First, instead of expressing distance between places in miles, people referred to how long it took to travel from place to place. Second, railroad scheduling required nationwide standardization of time. Before railroads, local clocks struck noon when the sun was overhead, and people set clocks accordingly. But because the sun was not overhead at the same moment everywhere, time varied by place. Boston's clocks differed from New York's by almost twelve minutes. In 1883, without authority from Congress, the nation's railroads established four standard time zones for the country. Railroad time became national time.

Farming the Plains

What helped ease farmers' hardships as they settled the West?

While California led the nation agriculturally, the Great Plains developed rapidly. There, farming in the late 1800s exemplified two important achievements: the transformation of arid prairies into crop-producing land and the transformation of agriculture into big business via mechanization, long-distance transportation, and scientific cultivation.

Irrigation and mechanized agriculture enabled farmers to feed the nation's burgeoning population and turned the United States into the world's breadbasket.

Settlement of the Plains	During the 1870s and 1880s, more acres were put under cultivation in states such as Kansas, Nebraska, and Texas than in the entire nation during the previous 250 years.

The number of farms tripled between 1860 and 1910, as hundreds of thousands of hopeful migrants streamed into the Plains. The Homestead Act of 1862 and other measures to encourage western settlement offered cheap or free plots to people who would reside on and improve them. Land-rich railroads advertised cheap land, arranging credit and offering reduced fares. Railroad agents—often former immigrants—traveled to Denmark, Sweden, Germany, and other European nations to recruit settlers.

To most families, the West seemed to promise a better life. Railroad expansion enabled remote farmers to ship produce to market, and construction of grain elevators eased storage problems. Worldwide and national population growth sparked demand for farm products, and the prospects for commercial agriculture became increasingly favorable.

Hardship on the Plains	Farm life, however, was harder than advertisements and railroad agents insinuated. Migrants often encountered scarcities of essentials they had once

enjoyed. Barren prairies contained insufficient lumber so pioneer families built houses of sod and burned buffalo dung for heat. Water was sometimes scarce also. Machinery for drilling wells was expensive, as were windmills for drawing water to the surface.

Weather was even more formidable than the terrain. The climate between the Missouri River and the Rocky Mountains divides along a line running from Minnesota southwest through Oklahoma, then south, bisecting Texas. West of this line, annual rainfall averages less than twenty-eight inches, not enough for most crops (see Map 15.3).

Weather was unpredictable. Weeks of torrid summer heat and parching winds suddenly gave way to violent storms that washed away crops and property. Winter blizzards piled up snowdrifts that halted outdoor movement. Melting snow swelled streams, and floods threatened millions of acres. In fall, a rainless week turned dry grasslands into tinder, and the slightest spark could ignite a prairie fire. Severe drought in Texas between 1884 and 1886 drove many farmers off the land.

Nature could be cruel even under good conditions. Weather favorable for crops also bred insects. In the 1870s and 1880s, grasshopper swarms devoured everything: plants, tree bark, and clothing. One farmer lamented, the "hoppers left behind nothing but the mortgage."

Social Isolation	Settlers also faced social isolation. New England and European farmers lived in villages, traveling daily to and from nearby fields.

In the Plains, and in the Far West and South, peculiarities of land division compelled rural dwellers to live far apart. Because most farm plots were rectangular—usually encompassing

MAP 15.3

Agricultural Regions of the United States, 1890

In the Pacific Northwest and east of the twenty-eight-inch-rainfall line, farmers could grow a greater variety of crops. Territory west of the line was either too mountainous or too arid to support agriculture without irrigation. The grasslands that once fed buffalo herds could now feed beef cattle. Source: Copyright © Cengage Learning 2015

160 acres—at most four families could live nearby, but only if they built homes around their shared four-corner intersection. In practice, households lived back from boundary lines, with a half mile separating farmhouses. Women were especially isolated, confined by domestic chores to the household. Like Nannie Jackson, they visited and exchanged food and services with neighbors and occasionally went to town.

Letters that Ed Donnell, a young Nebraska homesteader, wrote to his family in Missouri reveal how circumstances could dull optimism. In the fall of 1885, Donnell rejoiced to his mother, "I like Nebr first rate…. Have got a good crop of corn, a floor in my house and got it ceiled overhead." But Donnell was lonely. "You wanted to know when I was going to get married. Just as quick as I can get money ahead to get a cow."

A year and a half later, Donnell's dreams were dissolving and, still a bachelor, he was considering relocating. By fall, Donnell lamented, "My health has been so poor this summer and the wind and the sun hurts my head…if I can sell I will…move to town for I can get $40 a month working in a grist mill." Thousands shared Donnell's hardships, and their cityward migration fueled late-nineteenth-century urban growth (see Chapter 16).

Mail-Order Companies and Rural Free Delivery

Farm families organized churches and clubs to ease isolation. By 1900, two developments brought rural settlers into closer contact with modern consumer society. First, mail-order companies, such as Montgomery Ward (founded 1872) and Sears Roebuck (founded 1893), made new products attainable. Ward and Sears received letters that reported family news and sought advice on needs from gifts to child care. A Washington man wrote, "As you advertise everything for sale that a person wants, I thought I would write you, as I am in need of a wife, and see what you could do for me."

Second, after farmers petitioned Congress for extension of the postal service, in 1896 the government made Rural Free Delivery (RFD) widely available. Farmers who previously picked up mail in town could now receive letters and catalogs in a roadside mailbox almost daily. In 1913, the postal service inaugurated parcel post, which made shipping costs much cheaper.

Mechanization of Agriculture

As with industrial production (see Chapter 16), machinery drove the late-nineteenth-century agricultural revolution. When the Civil War drew men from farms in the upper Mississippi River valley, women and older men left behind began using mechanical implements. After the war, demand encouraged farmers to utilize machines, and inventors developed new implements. Seeders, combines, binders, reapers, and rotary plows facilitated grain growing on the Plains and in California, while the centrifugal cream separator, patented in 1879, sped skimming cream from milk.

For centuries, farmers planted only what could be harvested by hand. Machines significantly increased productivity. Before mechanization, a farmer working alone could harvest about 7.5 acres of wheat. Using an automatic binder that cut and bundled the grain, he could harvest 135 acres. Machines dramatically reduced the time and cost of farming other crops as well.

Legislative and Scientific Aids

Meanwhile, Congress and scientists worked to improve existing crops and develop new ones. The 1862 Morrill Land Grant Act gave states federal lands to sell to finance agricultural research. Consequently, new public universities were established in Wisconsin, Illinois, Minnesota, California, and other states. A second Morrill Act in 1890 aided more schools, including several all-black colleges. The Hatch Act of 1887 provided for agricultural experiment stations in every state, further advancing agricultural science and technology.

Science also enabled farmers to use the soil more efficiently. Researchers developed dry farming, a plowing and harrowing technique that minimized evaporation. Botanists perfected varieties of "hard" wheat whose seeds could withstand northern winters. Agriculturists adapted new varieties of wheat from Russia and rice from Asia. George Washington Carver, son of black slaves who became a chemist and taught at Alabama's Tuskegee Institute, created hundreds of products from peanuts, soybeans, and sweet potatoes. Other scientists combatted plant and animal diseases. Technology helped American farmers expand productivity in the market economy (see Table 15.1).

TABLE 15.1   Summary: Government Land Policy

Railroad land grants (1850–1871)	Granted 181 million acres to railroads to encourage construction and development
Homestead Act (1862)	Gave 80 million acres to settlers to encourage settlement
Morrill Act (1862)	Granted 11 million acres to states to sell to fund public agricultural colleges
Other grants	Granted 129 million acres to states to sell for other educational and related purposes
Dawes Act (1887)	Allotted some reservation lands to individual Indians to promote private property and weaken tribal values among Indians and offered remaining reservation lands for sale to whites (by 1906, some 75 million acres had been acquired by whites)
Various laws	Permitted direct sales of 100 million acres by the Land Office

Source: Goldfield, David; Abbott, Carl; Anderson, Virginia Dejohn; Argersinger, Jo Ann; Argersinger, Peter H.; Barney, William L.; and Weir, Robert M., *The American Journey*, Volume II, 3 rd ed., © 2004. Reproduced by permission of Pearson Education, Inc., Upper Saddle River, New Jersey.

The Ranching Frontier

Western commercial farming ran headlong into one of the region's most romantic industries—ranching. Beginning in the sixteenth century, Spanish landholders raised cattle in Mexico and what would become the American Southwest. They employed Indian and Mexican cowboys, called *vaqueros,* who tended herds and rounded up cattle. Anglo ranchers moving into Texas and California in the early nineteenth century hired *vaqueros* to teach them roping, branding, horse training, and saddle making.

By the 1860s, cattle ranching became increasingly profitable, as population growth boosted demand for beef and railroads simplified transportation. By 1870 drovers were herding thousands of Texas cattle northward to Kansas, Missouri, and Wyoming (see Map 15.1). At the northern terminus, the cattle were sold or loaded onto trains bound for Chicago and St. Louis for slaughterhouses and international markets.

The long drive inspired images of bellowing cattle, buckskin-clad cowboys, and smoky campfires. Trekking a thousand miles or more for months made cattle sinewy and tough. Herds traveling through Indian Territory and farmers' fields were sometimes shot at. When cattlemen discovered that crossing Texas longhorns with heavier Hereford and Angus breeds made sturdier and more profitable animals, cattle raising expanded northward. Herds in Kansas, Nebraska, Colorado, Wyoming, Montana, and Dakota crowded out already declining buffalo populations.

The Open Range

Cattle raisers minimized expenses by purchasing a few acres bordering a stream and turning their herds loose on adjacent public domain that no one wanted because it lacked water access. By using open-range ranching, cattle raisers could utilize thousands of acres by owning a hundred. Neighboring ranchers often formed associations and allowed herds to graze together, burning an identifying brand into each animal's hide. But as ranchers flowed into the Plains, cattle overran the range, and other groups challenged ranchers over use of the land.

Sheepherders from California and New Mexico were also using the public domain, sparking territorial clashes. Ranchers complained that sheep ruined grassland by eating to the roots and that cattle refused to graze where sheep had been. Occasionally, ranchers and sheepherders resorted to violence rather than settle disagreements in court, where a judge might discover that both were using public land illegally.

More importantly, the farming frontier generated new land demands. Lacking sufficient timber and stone for fencing, western settlers could not easily define their property. Tensions flared when farmers accused cattlemen of allowing herds to trespass on cropland and when herders charged that farmers should fence their property.

Barbed Wire

The solution was barbed wire. Invented in 1873 by Joseph Glidden, a DeKalb, Illinois, farmer, this inexpensive and mass-produced fencing consisted of wires held in place by sharp spurs. It ended open-range ranching and made roundups unnecessary, as ranchers enclosed their herds on their property. Similarly, the development of the round silo for storing fodder enabled cattle raisers to feed herds without grazing.

Ranching as Big Business

By 1890, big businesses were taking over the cattle industry and applying scientific methods of breeding and feeding. Corporations also used technology to squeeze larger returns from meatpacking. Every part of a cow had uses: half was meat, but larger profits came from hides for leather, blood for fertilizer, hooves for glue, fat for candles and soap, and the rest for sausages. Cattle processing harmed the environment, as meatpackers and leather tanners dumped unsold goods into waterways. By the late nineteenth century, the Chicago River created a powerful stench that made nearby residents sick.

Open-range ranching made beef a staple of the American diet and created a few fortunes, but it could not survive the rush of history. Overgrazing destroyed Plains grass supplies, and the brutal winter of 1886–1887 destroyed 90 percent of some herds and drove small ranchers out of business. By 1890, large-scale ranchers owned or leased the land they used. Cowboys formed labor organizations and struck for higher pay. The myth of the cowboy's freedom and individualism lived on, but ranching became a corporate business.

The South After Reconstruction

In what ways was the South's economic development different from that of the West in the late nineteenth century?

The post–Civil War South developed its own human ecologies, involving resource exploitation, market economies, and land control. After the war, farmers concentrated on growing cotton, but high prices for seed and implements, declining crop prices, taxes, and debt trapped many white southerners in poverty. Conditions were worse for African Americans, who endured racism along with economic hardship.

Between 1860 and 1880, the total number of farms in southern states more than doubled, from 450,000 to 1.1 million. But a growing proportion of southern farmers rented, rather than owned, land. One-third of farmers counted in the 1880 federal census were sharecroppers and tenants; the proportion increased to two-thirds by 1920.

Sharecropping and Tenant Farming in the South

Unlike the Midwest, southern agriculture did not benefit much from mechanization. Tobacco and cotton, principal southern crops, required hoeing and weeding by hand. Tobacco leaves matured at different rates and stems were too fragile for machines. Also, mechanical devices were not precise enough to pick cotton. Thus, after the Civil War, southern agriculture remained labor intensive, and labor lords who utilized slaves became landlords who employed sharecroppers and tenant farmers.

Sharecropping and tenant farming—where farmers rented rather than owned land—entangled millions of black and white southerners in debt, weighed down by crop liens. Most farmers, too poor to have ready cash, borrowed to buy necessities, offering future crops as collateral. To get supplies, a farmer dealt with a "furnishing merchant," who would exchange provisions for a "lien," or legal claim, on the farmer's forthcoming crop. After the harvest was brought to market, the merchant claimed a portion to repay the loan. Often, however, the debt exceeded the crop's value. The farmer could pay off only part of the loan but borrowed more for the coming year, sinking deeper into debt.

Merchants frequently took advantage by inflating prices and charging excessive interest on the advances farmers received. If a farmer needed a 20-cent bag of seed, the furnishing merchant would sell it to him on credit, but for 28 cents. At year's end, that loan would have accumulated interest of 50 percent or more. The farmer, pledging more than his crop's worth against such debts, fell behind and never recovered, risking eviction.

In the southern backcountry—which in antebellum times was characterized by small, family-owned farms, few slaves, and diversified agriculture—economic changes compounded crop lien problems. Farmers increasingly shifted from subsistence agriculture to commercial farming, namely of cotton. This specialization came about for two reasons: constant debt forced farmers to grow crops that would net cash, and railroads enabled them to easily transport cotton to market. As backcountry yeomen devoted more acres to cotton, they produced less food and other supplies and were frequently at the mercy of merchants.

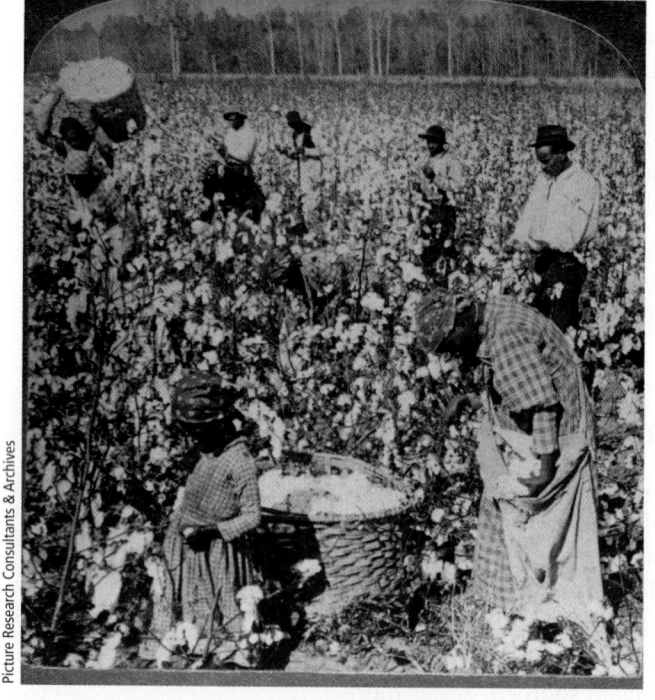

Picture Research Consultants & Archives

In a cotton field looking like it is snow covered, all members of this sharecropping African American family are engaged in picking cotton balls. The work was exacting, requiring constant stooping and lifting, and picking the cotton often left hands and fingers cut and calloused.

Closing the Southern Range

Before the 1870s, southern farmers, like western open-range ranchers, let their livestock roam on government-owned land in search of food and water. By custom, farmers built fences to protect their crops from foraging livestock. But as commercial agriculture reached the backcountry, large landowners and merchants induced county and state governments to require that animals be fenced in. Poor farmers with little land had to use more of their acreage for pasture. Such laws also forced people like Nannie Jackson to close themselves off from neighbors.

Poor whites in the rural South also feared that newly enfranchised blacks would challenge whatever political and social superiority (real and imagined) they enjoyed. Wealthy white landowners and merchants used racism to divide whites and blacks.

Leading Industries

Southern agriculture was closely tied to two leading industries: cotton and tobacco. In the 1870s, textile mills began to appear in the cotton belt, powered by the region's abundant rivers, manned by cheap labor, and aided by low taxes and northern investment. By 1900, the South had four hundred mills with a total of 4 million spindles, and was nearly eclipsing New England in textile-manufacturing supremacy. Proximity to raw materials and cheap labor also aided the tobacco industry, as did the invention in 1880 of a cigarette-making machine.

Cigarette factories, located in cities, employed black and white workers (in segregated sections). Textile mills, concentrated in small towns, employed women and children from poor white families and paid 50 cents a day for twelve or more hours of work—barely half what northern workers earned. Many companies built villages around their mills, where they controlled the housing, stores, schools, and churches. Company towns banned criticism of the management and squelched union organization.

Between 1890 and 1900, northern lumber syndicates moved into the Gulf States, boosting lumber production by 500 percent. During the 1880s, northern investors developed southern iron deposits into steel manufacturing, much of it in Birmingham, Alabama. What was to become the most famous southern product, Coca-Cola, was first formulated by Dr. John Pemberton, an Atlanta pharmacist, who in 1889 sold his formula to another Atlantan, Asa Candler, who made a fortune marketing the drink nationally. Coal mining and railroad construction also expanded rapidly, though, as with other southern industries, New York and London financiers dominated the boards of directors.

The New South

Local boosters heralded the emergence of a New South ready to compete with the West and North. Believing that the South should put its Civil War defeat behind it, businessmen advocated emulating northern industrialism. Henry Grady, editor of the *Atlanta Constitution* and a proponent of southern progress, proclaimed, "We have challenged your spinners in Massachusetts and your iron-makers in Pennsylvania.... We have fallen in love with work."

Yet the South in 1900 was as rural as in 1860. Staple-crop agriculture remained central to its ecology, and white supremacy permeated society. Furthermore, the South's low wages attracted few immigrants. A New South would not truly emerge until after a world war and a massive African American exodus had shaken up old habits.

National Parks

Embodying greatness in the majesty of national parks is a uniquely American contribution to world culture. Initially, however, Congress did not recognize this possibility: in 1872, it created Yellowstone National Park but appropriated no funds to protect it. In 1886, however, the secretary of the interior was granted cavalry soldiers to supervise the park; meant to be temporary, they stayed until 1922.

Slowly, Congress created other parks, including Yosemite and Sequoia in California in 1890 and sites in Oregon, Utah, Arizona, Montana, and Colorado between 1902 and 1915. But conflicts arose between those who, like naturalist John Muir and the Sierra Club, wished to preserve parks in pristine quality and those, such as Montana senator William A. Clark, who wanted to lease the land for logging, mining, railroads, and tourism. Congress in 1916 created the National Park Service (NPS) to conserve natural and historic territory for their enjoyment by future generations. Stephen Mather, head of the service, took preservation seriously but also allowed hotel construction in parks for visitors.

Initally, national parks were in the West, but after 1920 the Park Service established southern sites, beginning with the Great Smokies in Tennessee and North Carolina and Shenandoah in Virginia. In 1933, President Franklin Roosevelt transferred supervision of all national monuments and historic sites including the Statue of Liberty, Civil War battlefields, and Yosemite to the NPS. A few years later, the NPS added seashores, and from the 1960s onward urban sites such as Golden Gate National Recreation Area near San Francisco were included.

By 1950, 30 million people visited national parks annually. Roads fell into disrepair, campgrounds became dilapidated, and litter piled up. Moreover, those eager for the economic development of parklands lobbied for permission to expand roads and build hotels, gas stations, and restaurants. In 1964, Congress passed a bill providing funds for future parkland acquisition, but balancing preservation and public use remains controversial. Today, there are almost 400 national park units, encompassing more than 84 million acres. They stand as a legacy from the past that poses challenges for the future.

Summary

The complex interactions between people and their environments transformed the West, the South, and the nation. Indians, the West's original inhabitants, hunted, farmed, and depended on delicate resources, such as buffalo herds and salmon runs. When they came into contact with commerce-minded European Americans, their resistance to the market economy, diseases, and violence that whites brought into the West failed.

Mexicans, Chinese, African Americans, and Anglos discovered a reciprocal relationship between human activities and the environment. Miners, timber cutters, farmers, and builders extracted raw minerals for eastern factories, used irrigation and machines to yield agricultural abundance, filled pastures with cattle and sheep to expand food sources, and constructed railroads to tie the nation together. But the environment also exerted power through harsh climates, insects and parasites, and other hazards.

The West's settlers employed violence and greed that sustained discrimination within a multiracial society, left many farmers feeling cheated, provoked contests over water and pastures, and sacrificed environmental balance for market profits. The region's raw materials and agricultural products raised living standards and hastened industrial progress, but not without costs.

In the South, the end of slavery left African Americans tied to the land as tenant farmers and sharecroppers, while white yeoman farmers faced increasing disadvantages in expanding markets. To achieve sectional independence, southerners promoted industrialization, with some success, though by the 1900s many southern industries remained subsidiaries of northern firms. Moreover, southern planters, shippers, and manufacturers depended heavily on northern banks to finance their operations. Equally important, low wages discouraged potential immigrants who might have brought needed labor, skills, and capital. Thus although the South grew economically, it remained a dependent region in the national economy. Sectional differences continued to make the nation economically diverse.

Chapter Review

The Transformation of Native Cultures

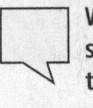

What factors transformed Native Americans' subsistence economy and relationship to the land in the late nineteenth century?

The Native American economic system was increasingly eroded after 1850 by a number of factors, some natural and some resulting from increasing interaction with, and encroachment by, whites. Southwestern and Plains Indian economies were devastated by the declining buffalo herd due to drought, diseases brought by white-owned livestock, excessive Native American hunting and trade, white settlement on Indian lands used for grazing, and whites' efforts to eliminate the buffalo to make way for railroads. Northwestern Indian economies, which relied on salmon fishing, similarly suffered when white commercial fisheries diminished salmon supplies and dammed up rivers and tributaries that were vital for fishing stocks. Finally, the U.S. government misunderstood differences between Indian groups, often negotiating faulty treaties or failing to guarantee land rights as promised in these agreements. Moreover, as Indians became increasingly dependent on trade with whites, they raised fewer crops and their need for cash to purchase goods forced them to sell their land, making it easier to force them onto reservations.

The Extraction of Natural Resources

What sparked the rise of the conservation movement?

Mining for precious metals, cutting trees for lumber, and drilling for oil drew thousands of people to the West seeking fortune and a better life. It also transformed the natural landscape, contributed to environmental wastefulness, and sparked a debate between the desire for progress and the need to preserve nature. This gave rise to a conservation movement after the Civil War. Recreational hunters and families that depended on wild game for meat lobbied legislatures; artists and tourists pressured Congress to protect Yosemite Valley by granting it to California for public use; and in 1862, the Yellowstone River region in Wyoming became the first national park. Congress also authorized President Benjamin Harrison to create forest reserves, at the urging of a group led by activist John Muir, who founded the environmental group the Sierra Club in 1892.

The Age of Railroad Expansion

How did government policies aid the development of the West?

First, during the Civil War era, government subsidies for railroad construction—among the largest in U.S. history—included massive land grants, which companies could use for interstate routes or sell to finance construction. Federal land grants topped 180 million acres, while states handed over another 50 million acres, and cities and towns helped by offering loans or buying railroad stocks. Second, through the Newlands Reclamation Act (1902), Congress supported the sale of western lands in parcels smaller than 160 acres to individuals, with the funds being used to finance irrigation projects in the region. That, in turn, facilitated agricultural and economic development and western urbanization. Cities and towns developed along railroad hubs, shipping farm products and manufactured goods nationwide.

Farming the Plains

What helped ease farmers' hardships as they settled the West?

Migrants hoped to find a better life in the West, but often experienced loneliness, isolation, the lack of essential products and services they previously knew, and even shortages of lumber needed to build homes. But the arrival of the railroad, the extension of the postal service into the West, and the advent of the mail-order business ended some of their problems by bringing consumer goods and people to the region. New technology and mechanization also made farming easier, and the creation of social clubs, churches, and other organizations helped ease social isolation.

The South After Reconstruction

In what ways was the South's economic development different from that of the West in the late nineteenth century?

In the South, the number of farms doubled between 1860 and 1880, yet more farmers rented rather than owned their land—the opposite of what occurred in the West. Southerners in the post–Civil War era relied increasingly on sharecropping or tenant farming, where land was rented and farmers borrowed money for supplies, using future crops as collateral. Ultimately, this simply pushed poor farmers further into debt, especially when merchants inflated prices and interest. Where the West benefited from technological advances in farm equipment, the South's reliance on staple crops of tobacco and cotton required human labor. While some southern industrial development (cigarette and textile factories, for example) was poised to compete with the North and West, the South would remain a largely agricultural and rural region based on staple crops until well into the twentieth century.

Suggestions for Further Reading

William Cronon, *Nature's* Metropolis: *Chicago and the Great West* (1991)

Karl Jacoby, *Crimes Against Nature: Squatters, Poachers, Thieves and the Hidden History of American Conservation* (2001)

Karl Jacoby, *Shadows at Dawn: A Borderlands Massacre and the Violence of History* (2009)

Patricia Nelson Limerick, *The Legacy of Conquest: The Unbroken Past of the American West* (1987)

Eugene P. Moehring, *Urbanism and Empire in the Far West, 1840–1890* (2004)

Robert M. Utley, *The Indian Frontier of the American West, 1846–1890* (1984)

Richard White, *"It's Your Misfortune and None of My Own": A New History of the American West* (1991)

Donald Worster, *A Passion for Nature: The Life of John Muir* (2008)

Building Factories, Building Cities

16

1877–1920

A s immigrants sailed into New York Harbor in the late nineteenth and early twentieth century, they saw Coney Island, a peninsula jutting out from Brooklyn. Its easy access from New York City by carriage road and ferry lines plus its beaches, parks, and attractions made Coney Island the world's largest entertainment resort. A 300-foot tower, with an elevator, was moved there after the 1876 Philadelphia World's Fair. Electric lamps lit the beaches for nighttime swimming. Racetracks and theaters attracted thousands of tourists. By 1904, the resort boasted three amusement parks—Steeplechase, Luna, and Dreamland. Rides, such as the world's first roller coaster, dazzled visitors. Before it burned down in 1896, there was even a hotel shaped like an elephant.

Coney Island blended the ingredients of modern America: new technology, materials, and products emerging from industrialization; and people and cultures emerging from urban growth. The industrialization that made Coney Island possible was a complex process featuring production of goods by machine. After two rounds of industrialization, by the late 1800s, the United States was the world's most productive industrial nation and the largest producer of raw materials and food (see Map 16.1). Four themes characterized American industrialization. First, manufacturers harnessed technology to serve production in new ways. Second, to increase production, factory owners divided work into repetitive tasks organized by the clock, turning workers who once saw themselves as producers into employees. Third, a new consumer society emerged as goods such as canned foods and machine-made clothing became common. Fourth, seeking growth and profits, corporation owners amassed power through new forms of corporate organization.

At the same time, urbanization—the process whereby cities and their areas expand more rapidly than surrounding environments—accelerated after the Civil War and by 1920, the census showed that, for the first time, a majority of Americans (51.4 percent) lived in cities. Urbanites propelled industrialization by furnishing

Chapter Outline

Technology and the Triumph of Industrialism
Birth of the Electrical Industry | Henry Ford and the Automobile Industry | Carnegie and Steel, du Pont and Chemicals | Technology and Southern Industry | Technology and Everyday Life

Big Business and its Critics
Trusts and Holding Companies | Social Darwinism | Dissenting Voices | Antitrust Legislation

Mechanization and the Changing Status of Labor
Frederick W. Taylor | Workers Become Employees | Women and Children in the Workforce | Freedom of Contract | Railroad Strikes of 1877 | Knights of Labor | American Federation of Labor | Homestead and Pullman Strikes | Labor Violence in the West | Women Unionists | The Nonunionized Workforce

VISUALIZING THE PAST *Impact of the 1911 Triangle Shirtwaist Fire*

Growth of the Modern American City
Mechanization of Mass Transportation | Population Growth | New Foreign Immigrants | Geographical and Social Mobility | Cultural Retention | Urban Borderlands | Racial Segregation and Violence | Mexican Barrios | Religious Diversity | Housing | Poverty and Crime | Water Purity and Waste Disposal | Political Machines | Civic and Social Reform

461

its workforces and benefited from its consumer goods, services, and entertainment, such as Coney Island. Migrants and immigrants to cities sought to free themselves from uncertainties of the past. But poverty and discrimination haunted many urban dwellers, combining the era's opportunities with persistent inequality. How people built cities and adjusted to the industrial environment shaped modern American society.

As you read this chapter, keep the following questions in mind:

- **How did mechanization affect the lives of average workers and the makeup of the labor force?**
- **What were the most important factors contributing to the urban growth of the period 1877–1920?**
- **How did immigrants adjust to and reshape their adopted homeland?**

Technology and the Triumph of Industrialism

How did technological innovations transform American industry?

Ingenuity drove the new industrialization. Between 1860 and 1930, the U.S. Patent Office granted 1.5 million patents for new inventions; it granted only 36,000 between 1790 and 1860. Inventions in electricity, internal combustion, and industrial chemistry often sprang from a marriage between technology and business organization.

Thomas Edison Inventor and founder of the first industrial research laboratory.

Birth of the Electrical Industry

Thomas Edison, who became America's most celebrated inventor, opened an "invention factory" in Menlo Park, New Jersey, in 1876. There, his application of electricity to light, sound, and images, plus his system of delivering electric power, laid the foundation for how Americans live today. His most notable invention was the incandescent light bulb. Additionally, his Edison Electric Light Company (founded in 1878) devised a system of power generation that provided electricity conveniently to manifold customers. Edison marketed his ideas with demonstrations of how electric lighting could transform night into day, brightening homes, offices, and places like Coney Island.

Other entrepreneurs further adapted electricity. Granville T. Woods, an Ohio engineer sometimes called "the black Edison," patented thirty-five devices vital to electronics and communications. Financiers Henry Villard and J. P. Morgan bought patents and merged equipment-manufacturing companies into the General Electric Company, including research laboratories.

Henry Ford: Founder of the Ford Motor Company and pioneer of modern assembly lines used in mass production.

Henry Ford and the Automobile Industry

Meanwhile, leading visionary manufacturer **Henry Ford** adapted the internal combustion engine—initially developed in Germany—to propel a vehicle.

Chronology

1869	Knights of Labor founded
1873–78	Economy declines
1876	National League of Professional Baseball Clubs founded
1877	Widespread railroad strikes protest wage cuts
1878	Edison Electric Light Company founded
1880s	"New" immigrants from eastern and southern Europe begin to arrive in large numbers
1882	Standard Oil Trust founded
1883	Pulitzer buys *New York World*, creating major publication for yellow journalism
1886	Haymarket riot in Chicago protests police brutality against labor demonstrations
	American Federation of Labor (AFL) founded
1890	Sherman Anti-Trust Act outlaws "combinations in restraint of trade"
1892	Homestead (Pennsylvania) steelworkers strike against Carnegie Steel Company
1893–97	Economic depression causes high unemployment and business failures
1895	*U.S. v. E. C. Knight Co.* limits Congress's power to regulate manufacturing
1896	*Holden v. Hardy* upholds law regulating miners' working hours
1900–10	Immigration reaches peak
1905	*Lochner v. New York* overturns law limiting bakery workers' working hours and limits labor protection law
	Intercollegiate Athletic Association, forerunner of National Intercollegiate Athletic Association (NCAA), is formed, restructuring rules of football
1908	*Muller v. Oregon* upholds law limiting women to ten-hour workday
	First Ford Model T built
1911	Triangle Shirtwaist Company fire in New York City leaves 146 workers dead
1913	Ford begins moving assembly-line production
1920	Majority (51.4 percent) of Americans live in cities

Through his organizational genius, Ford spawned a massive industry, predicting in 1909, "I am going to democratize the automobile. When I'm through, everybody will be able to afford one." Ford mass-produced identical cars on assembly lines that divided the manufacturing process into single tasks repeatedly performed by workers using specialized machines. By 1914, the Ford Motor Company outside of Detroit was producing 248,000 cars per year, and auto manufacturing spawned new industries in steel, oil, rubber, and glass. To enable his employees to afford a car, reduce labor turnover, and deter unionization, Ford began a Five-Dollar-Day pay plan that combined wages and profit sharing.

Link to Henry Ford Discusses Manufacturing and Marketing

Carnegie and Steel, du Pont and Chemicals

In America, Scottish immigrant **Andrew Carnegie** recognized the benefits of the British Bessemer process for producing steel, and in the 1870s he built steel-making plants near Pittsburgh that eventually furnished materials for rails, bridges, barbed wire, and household appliances. In 1892, Carnegie formed the Carnegie Steel Company and by 1900 controlled 60 percent of the country's steel business. In 1901, he sold his holdings to a group led by J. P. Morgan, who formed the huge U.S. Steel Corporation.

Industrial chemistry was pioneered by French immigrant E. I. du Pont, who manufactured gunpowder in Delaware in the early 1890s. In 1902, three du Pont

Andrew Carnegie Scottish immigrant who built an enormous steel company and became a renowned philanthropist.

Products manufactured in 20 largest cities

- 👕 Clothing
- 🗇 Flour milling
- 🗉 Food, beverage, and tobacco processing
- ◎ Foundry and machine shop products
- ⬡ Iron and steel
- ▯ Printing and publishing
- ◑ Slaughtering and meatpacking
- ◈ Textiles
- 🌐 Mixed or other

Natural resources

Ag	Silver	O	Oil (petroleum)
Au	Gold	Pb	Lead
C	Coal	Timber	Timber
Cu	Copper		
Fe	Iron ore		States with 25% or more of employees in manufacturing

MAP 16.1

Industrial Production, 1919

By the early twentieth century, each state could boast at least one kind of industrial production. Although the value of goods produced was still highest in the Northeast, states such as Minnesota and California had impressive dollar values of outputs.

Source: Data from U.S. Bureau of the Census, *Fourteenth Census of the United States, 1920*, Vol. IX, Manufacturing (Washington, D.C.: U.S. Government Printing Office, 1921)

cousins expanded the company into fertilizer, dyes, and other chemical products. In 1911, du Pont research labs adapted cellulose to produce such consumer goods as photographic film, textile fibers, and plastics.

Technology and Southern Industry

In the South, new industries developed around natural resources. The tobacco crop inspired North Carolinian James B. Duke to create a machine for making cigarettes. He began mass production in 1885 and attracted customers with advertising. By 1900, his American Tobacco Company was a global business. Also, electric-powered cotton looms and a cheap labor force enabled the southern textile industry to surpass water-powered New England mills. Many textile companies built villages around their mills and controlled housing, stores, schools, and churches. Northern capitalists invested in southern iron and steel, especially in

Birmingham, Alabama. And between 1890 and 1900, northern lumber syndicates moved into pine forests of the Gulf States, boosting wood production and prompting the relocation of furniture and paper production from North to South.

Technology and Everyday Life

Machines altered everyday life. Telephones and typewriters made face-to-face communications less important and facilitated correspondence. Electric sewing machines facilitated mass-produced clothing. Refrigeration enabled preservation and shipment of fresh meat, produce, and dairy products; canning preserved foods such as tomatoes, fish, and milk that otherwise would have spoiled easily. Dietary reformers William K. Kellogg and Charles W. Post mass-produced new breakfast foods such as cornflakes, and the discovery of vitamins heightened interest in food's health. Low-income families still consumed cheap dishes, but with increased availability of processed foods, American workers never suffered the severe malnutrition of other developing nations.

New technology even affected personal hygiene. Flush toilets, invented in England, reached American shores in the 1880s. Middle-class Americans began installing modern toilets in their urban houses, making bathrooms places of utmost privacy. Together, developments in communications, clothing, food, and plumbing contributed to a democratization of convenience via mass production.

Big Business and Its Critics

What led corporations to increasingly consolidate in the late nineteenth century?

Technological innovation required large capital investments. To expand, businesses borrowed from banks and sought higher profits to repay loans and reward stockholders. This spiraling process strangled small firms and caused uncertainty at the hint that a large debtor was about to fail. Economic downturns occurred regularly—in 1871, 1884, and 1893—as overproduction, underconsumption, and unregulated banking strained the system.

Corporations proved the best instruments for industrial expansion. These were companies that raised capital by selling shares to stockholders who shared profits without personal risk because laws limited their liability for company debts to the amount of their investments. Firms such as General Electric and the American Tobacco Corporation won judicial safeguards in 1888 when the Supreme Court declared that corporations, like individuals, are protected by laws preventing government from depriving them of property rights without due process of law. During the 1880s, corporations in the same industry made agreements, called *pools*, to share markets and profits.

Trusts and Holding Companies

Trusts came to dominate a few industries. These were large corporations formed to enable one company to control an industry by luring or forcing stockholders of smaller companies to yield their stock "in trust" to the larger company's board of trustees. This enabled companies such as **John D. Rockefeller**'s Standard Oil to achieve domination by combining with, or *vertically integrating*, other oil refineries. In 1898, New Jersey adopted laws allowing companies to own stock in other states, facilitating creation of holding companies, which

John D. Rockefeller
Creator of Standard Oil and master of the use of pools and trusts to monopolize an industry.

horizontal integration
Business strategy in which a holding company would seek to control all aspects of the industry in which it functioned, fusing related businesses together under one management.

merged several companies' assets (buildings, equipment, inventory, and cash) under single management. Using this **horizontal integration**, holding companies could dominate all aspects of an industry, including raw materials, manufacture, and distribution. For example, Gustavus Swift's Chicago meat-processing operation controlled livestock, slaughterhouses, refrigerator cars, and marketing.

Trusts and holding companies ensured orderly profits. Between 1889 and 1903, three hundred combinations formed, including American Sugar Refining Company and U.S. Rubber Company. A new species of businessman, the financier, aided the process by creating a holding company through stock sales and bank loans, then persuading firms to sell to him. This often put small companies out of business and made huge fortunes for shrewd bankers such as J. P. Morgan.

Corporate growth turned stock and bond exchanges into hubs of activity. In 1869, only 145 industrial corporations traded on the New York Stock Exchange; by 1914, 511 did. Foreign investors poured huge sums into American companies.

Social Darwinism Extended Charles Darwin's theory of "survival of the fittest" to the free-market system, arguing that competition would weed out weaker firms and allow stronger, fitter firms to thrive.

Social Darwinism

Business leaders justified their actions by invoking **Social Darwinism**. This philosophy loosely grafted Charles Darwin's theory of survival of the fittest onto laissez-faire, the doctrine that government should not interfere in private economic matters. Social Darwinists reasoned that in a free-market economy, wealth would naturally flow to those most capable of creating it.

Denouncing efforts to legislate maximum working hours or factory conditions as interference, corporate leaders nonetheless lobbied for public subsidies and tax relief to encourage business growth.

Dissenting Voices

Critics, however, charged that new forms of big business were unnatural because they stifled opportunity and fostered greed. Farmers, workers, and intellectuals feared that corporations were creating monopolies—domination of an economic activity by one powerful company—that crushed small businesses, fixed prices, and corrupted politicians.

By the mid-1880s, some intellectuals challenged Social Darwinism and laissez-faire. For example, sociologist Lester Ward, in his book *Dynamic Sociology* (1883), argued that a system that guaranteed survival only to the fittest was wasteful and brutal. Instead, cooperative activity fostered by government intervention was fairer.

Visionaries such as Henry George and Edward Bellamy questioned why the United States had so many poor people while a few became wealthy. George, a printer alarmed by the poverty of working people like himself, believed that inequality stemmed from the ability of property owners to profit from rising land values and the rents they charged. To prevent profiteering, George proposed replacing all taxes with a "single tax" on the rise in property values caused by increased market demand. George's scheme influenced subsequent reformers.

Novelist Edward Bellamy proposed that government own the means of production. In *Looking Backward* (1888), Bellamy depicted Boston in the year 2000 as a peaceful community where everyone had a job and a "principle of fraternal cooperation" replaced vicious competition. Bellamy's vision, called "Nationalism," sparked formation of Nationalist clubs nationwide and kindled efforts for political reform and government ownership of railroads and utilities.

Antitrust Legislation

Several states took steps to prohibit monopolies and regulate business. By 1900, twenty-seven states banned pools and fifteen outlawed trusts. Most were agricultural states in the South and West that were responding to antimonopolistic pressure from farmers (see Chapter 17). But states lacked the staff and judicial support to effectively attack big business, and corporations evaded restrictions.

In 1890 Congress passed the Sherman Anti-Trust Act that made illegal "every contract, combination in the form of trust or otherwise, or conspiracy in the restraint of trade." Those convicted of violating the law faced fines and jail terms, and victims could sue for triple damages. However, the law, under influence from pro-business eastern senators, did not clearly define "restraint of trade" and left interpretation of its provisions to the pro-business courts. When in 1895 the federal government prosecuted the Sugar Trust for owning 98 percent of the nation's sugar-refining capacity, eight of nine Supreme Court justices ruled in *U.S. v. E. C. Knight Co.* that control of sugar manufacturing did not necessarily mean control of trade. Between 1890 and 1900, the federal government prosecuted only eighteen cases under the Sherman Anti-Trust Act, mostly against railroads. Ironically, the act equipped the government to break up labor unions, which, when they went on strike, were deemed in restraint of trade.

A cartoon protesting John D. Rockefeller's power over the oil and railroad industries shows him wearing a golden crown and regal robe, and standing on an oil storage tank labeled "Standard Oil." The huge crown is topped with a dollar sign and made of oil tanks and railroad cars from four railroad companies owned by Rockefeller: Lehigh Valley Railroad, St. Paul Railroad, Jersey Central Railroad, and Reading Rail Road.

Library of Congress

Mechanization and the Changing Status of Labor

How did mechanization and new systems of management change the nature and status of work?

As mechanized assembly lines made large-scale production more economical, owners invested in machines and hired fewer workers. Profitability relied on efficiency in production. Where previously workers controlled the methods of production, by the 1890s, engineers and managers with expert knowledge used standardization to reduce the need for human skills.

Frederick W. Taylor

The most influential advocate of efficiency was Frederick W. Taylor. As engineer for a Pennsylvania steel company in the 1880s, Taylor concluded that companies could best reduce costs and increase profits by applying studies of "how quickly the various kinds of work … ought to be done." This meant producing more for lower cost per unit, usually by eliminating unnecessary workers. He later outlined this system in his book, *Principles of Scientific Management* (1911). In 1898, Taylor took his stopwatch to Bethlehem Steel Company to apply his system. After observing workers shoveling iron ore, he designed fifteen kinds of shovels and prescribed proper motions for each, thereby reducing a crew of 600 men to 140. Soon other companies began implementing Taylor's theories. Taylor had little respect for ordinary laborers, calling steelworkers "stupid."

Workers Become Employees

Workers increasingly feared that they were becoming another interchangeable part in an industrial machine. No longer producers, who like farmers and craftsmen were paid according to the quality of what they produced, industrial workers instead were becoming wage earners who worked when someone hired and paid them. In mass production, tasks were regulated by the clock and carefully supervised. As a Massachusetts factory hand testified in 1879, "during working hours the men are not allowed to speak to each other, though working close together, on pain of discharge." Industrial accidents occurred often, killing hundreds of thousands each year. For those with mangled limbs and chronic illnesses, there was no disability insurance to replace lost income, and families suffered.

Workers attempted to retain autonomy. Artisans such as glassworkers and printers fought to preserve traditional customs, such as appointing a fellow worker to read a newspaper aloud while they labored. Immigrant factory workers tried to persuade foremen to hire their relatives and friends. After hours, workers enjoyed drinking and holiday celebrations, ignoring employers' efforts to control their social lives.

Women and Children in the Workforce

Employers cut labor costs by hiring women and children and paying them low wages. Between 1880 and 1900, numbers of employed women soared from 2.6 million to 8.6 million (see Figure 16.1). Inventions such as the typewriter and cash register simplified clerical tasks, and employers replaced males with females. Consequently, the proportion of women in domestic service (maids, cooks, laundresses), the most common and lowest paid form of female employment, declined. By 1920, women filled nearly half of all clerical jobs; in 1880 only 4 percent were women. Women were attracted to sales and secretarial positions because of their respectability and pleasant surroundings. Still, unskilled or uneducated women usually held menial positions in textile mills and food-processing plants that typically paid just $1.56 a week for seventy hours of work. (Unskilled men received $7 to $10.)

Mechanization in textile and shoe production created light tasks such as running errands, which children could handle cheaply. In 1890, more than 18 percent of children ages ten to fifteen were employed. In the South, textile mill owners

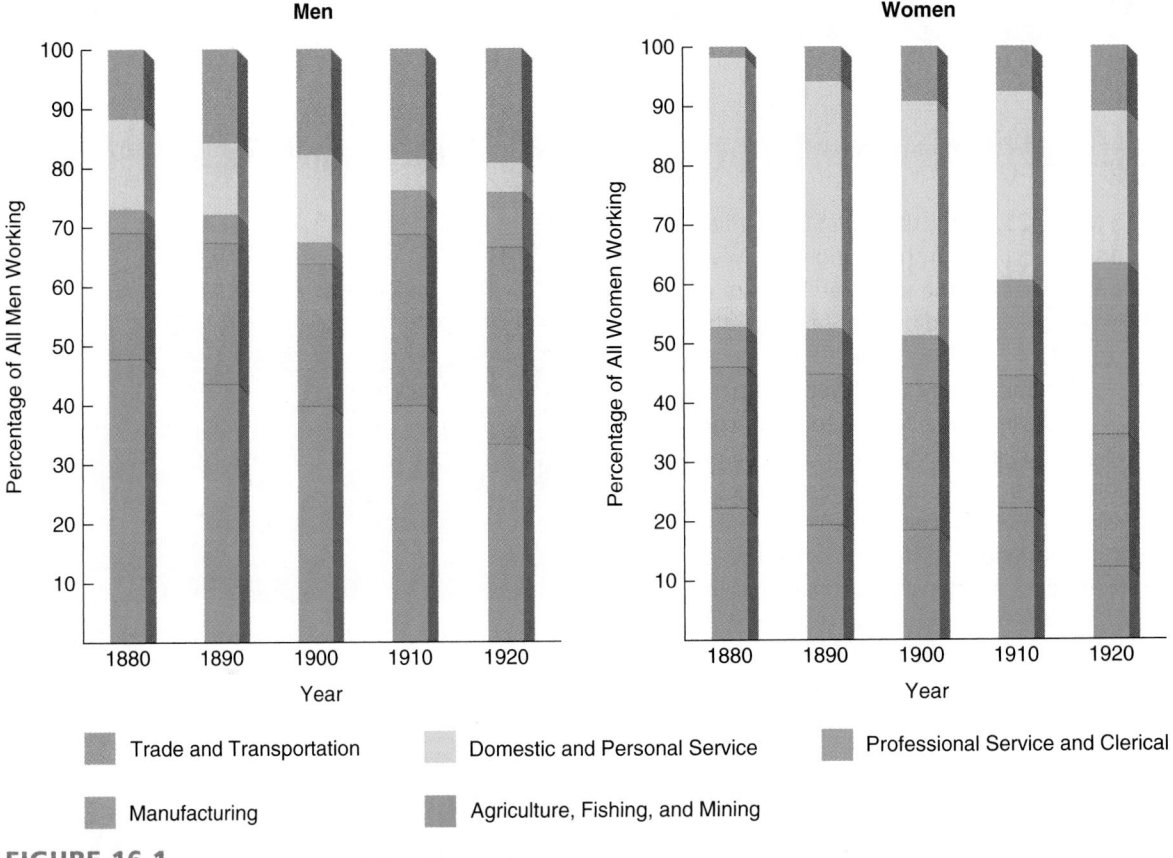

FIGURE 16.1

Distribution of Occupational Categories Among Employed Men and Women, 1880–1920

The changing lengths of the bar segments of each part of this graph represent trends in male and female employment. Over the forty years covered by this graph, the agriculture, fishing, and mining segment for men and the domestic service segment for women declined the most, whereas notable increases occurred in manufacturing for men and professional services (especially store clerks and teachers) for women.

Source: U.S. Bureau of the Census, *Census of the United States, 1880, 1890, 1900, 1910, 1920* (Washington, D.C.: U.S. Government Printing Office)

induced sharecroppers, desperate for extra income, to bind their children over to factories at miserably low wages. Several states, especially in the Northeast, passed laws limiting ages and hours of child laborers. But statutes regulated only firms operating within state borders, not those engaged in interstate commerce. Enforcing age requirements proved difficult because many parents, needing income, lied about their children's ages. Children also worked in street trades—peddling, shining shoes, and scavenging for discarded wood, coal, and furniture.

Freedom of Contract

To justify their treatment of workers, employers asserted the concept of "freedom of contract"—that since workers freely entered into a contract with bosses, workers could seek another job if they disliked the wages and hours. Actually, employers used supply and demand to set wages as low as laborers would accept. When some states tried to improve working conditions through legislation, business interests enlisted

Impact of the 1911 Triangle Shirtwaist Fire

On March 25, 1911, the worst factory fire in U.S. history occurred at the Triangle Shirtwaist Company, which occupied the top three floors of a building in New York City. Fed by piles of fabric, the fire spread quickly, killing 146 of the 500 young women, mostly Jewish immigrants, employed in the factory. Many of the victims were burned to death because they were locked inside workrooms by their employer; others plunged from windows. These images show three ways the public received news of the tragedy: through friends and relatives who came to identify and claim the bodies of victims, through a critical cartoon, and through the front page of a newspaper. Which of these images seems most powerful and likely to inspire reform? How do mass tragedies get communicated to the public today? What limitations in communications existed in 1911?

Bettmann/Corbis

Many of the victims of the Triangle Shirtwaist fire of 1911 were lined up in coffins, and their bodies were identified by relatives arriving at a makeshift morgue.

The Granger Collection, NYC

John French Sloan, an artist with radical leanings, drew this cartoon in the wake of the Triangle fire. Eager to assert that profit-minded capitalists were responsible for unnecessary deaths, Sloan used stark images to convey his message.

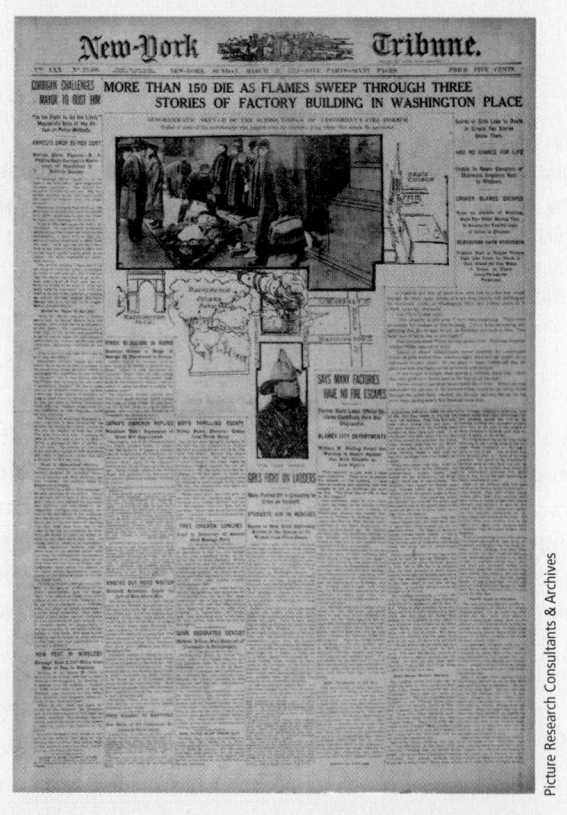

Picture Research Consultants & Archives

Using a large-print headline and grisly photograph, the New York Tribune, *one of New York City's and the nation's oldest and most respected newspapers, filled much of its front page with news of the event.*

courts, including the U.S. Supreme Court, to oppose such measures. *Holden v. Hardy* (1891) upheld a law restricting miners' working hours because overly long workdays increased potential injuries. But the court voided a law limiting bakery workers to a sixty-hour week and ten-hour day (*Lochner v. New York*, 1905), reasoning that baking was not dangerous enough to prevent workers from selling their labor freely.

In *Muller v. Oregon* (1908), the Supreme Court made an exception for women. It concluded that a law regulating hours of female laundry workers was constitutional because women's well-being as childbearers was "an object of public interest…" The case represented a victory for reformers seeking to safeguard women from exploitation. But because of the *Muller* decision, labor laws barred women from jobs such as printing and transportation, further confining women to low-paying, dead-end occupations.

Some workers tried to adjust to mechanization; others challenged the system by ignoring management's rules or quitting. Still others, disgruntled over low wages and anxious to restore independence, joined unions and went out on strikes.

Railroad Strikes of 1877

In 1877, a crisis in the railroad industry caused by four years of wage cuts, layoffs, and increased workloads climaxed with a series of strikes from Pennsylvania and West Virginia to Texas and California. State militia, organized and commanded by employers, broke up picket lines and fired upon strikers, and railroads hired strikebreakers. Pittsburgh saw the worst

TABLE 16.1   American Living Standards, 1890–1910

	1890	1910
Income and Earnings		
Annual income		
Clerical worker	$848	$1,156
Public schoolteacher	256	492
Industrial worker	486	630
Farm laborer	233	336
Hourly wage		
Soft-coal miner	0.18[a]	0.21
Ironworker	0.17[a]	0.23
Shoe worker	0.14[a]	0.19
Paper worker	0.12[a]	0.17
Labor Statistics		
Number of people in labor force	28.5 million	41.7 million[b]
Average workweek in manufacturing	60 hours	51 hours

[a] 1892

[b] 1920

violence; in July 1877, troopers attacked demonstrators, killing ten and wounding many more. A month later, President Rutherford B. Hayes sent in federal soldiers—the first significant use of the army to quell labor unrest.

Knights of Labor

About the same time, the Knights of Labor tried to organize a broad base of laborers. Aided by Terrence Powderly, a machinist and mayor of Scranton, Pennsylvania, who was elected grand master in 1879, the Knights built a membership of 730,000 by 1886. Unlike most craft unions, Knights welcomed unskilled and semiskilled workers, including women, African Americans, and immigrants (but not Chinese). The organization tried to bypass conflict between labor and management by establishing a cooperative society in which workers, not capitalists, owned factories, mines, and railroads. This ideal was unattainable because employers could outcompete laborers who might attempt to establish businesses. Powderly and other Knights leaders discouraged strikes, claiming they diverted attention from the long-term goal of a cooperative society and that workers lost more by striking. Some Knights, however, chose militant action. In 1886, they struck against southwestern railroads. When owner **Jay Gould** refused to negotiate, the strike spread. Ultimately, the Knights gave in. Thereafter Knights' membership dwindled, although its cooperative vision inspired the 1890s Populist movement (see Chapter 17).

Jay Gould Captain of industry and owner of the Union Pacific Railroad.

On May 1, 1886, in Chicago, one hundred thousand workers amassed for a huge demonstration, demanding an eight-hour workday. Two days later, fearing that anarchists were fomenting antigovernment violence, Chicago police mobilized and broke up a battle between unionists and strikebreakers, killing two and wounding others. On May 4, demonstrators protested police brutality at Haymarket Square near downtown Chicago. As police approached, a bomb exploded, killing seven and injuring sixty-seven. Authorities made arrests, and a court convicted eight anarchists of the bombing, despite questionable evidence. Four were executed, and one committed suicide in prison. Three received pardons in 1893 from Illinois governor John P. Altgeld.

The presence of foreign-born anarchists and socialists at Haymarket made civic leaders fearful that labor turmoil threatened social order. Consequently, governments strengthened police forces and employer associations circulated blacklists of union activists whom they would not employ.

American Federation of Labor (AFL) Skilled craft unions united under leadership of Samuel Gompers.

Samuel Gompers AFL leader who focused on practical goals like improved wages, hours, and working conditions.

Link to Samuel Gompers, Congressional Testimony Regarding AFL Unions (1914)

American Federation of Labor

The **American Federation of Labor (AFL)** emerged from the 1886 upheavals as the major workers' organization. Led by **Samuel Gompers**, former head of the Cigar Makers Union, the AFL pressed for higher wages, shorter hours, and the right to bargain collectively. The AFL accepted capitalism and worked to improve conditions within it.

The union avoided party politics, instead supporting labor's friends regardless of party. AFL membership grew to 1 million in 1901 and 2.5 million in 1917, when it consisted of 111 national unions.

Organized by craft rather than by workplace, the AFL rebuffed unskilled laborers and excluded women. Male unionists insisted that women would depress wages and should stay at home because, as one put it, "She is competing with the man who is her father or husband or is to become her husband." Most unions also excluded immigrants and African Americans, fearing job competition. Long-held prejudices were reinforced when blacks and immigrants, eager for work, served as strikebreakers.

Homestead and Pullman Strikes

The AFL and labor movement suffered setbacks in the early 1890s when violence again stirred public fears. In July 1892, the AFL-affiliated Amalgamated Association of Iron and Steelworkers struck Homestead Steel in Pennsylvania over pay cuts. Henry Frick, president of Carnegie Steel Company (Homestead's owner), responded to the **Homestead Strike** by hiring three hundred guards from the Pinkerton Detective Agency to protect the factory, but strikers attacked the guards. State troopers intervened and, after five months, the strikers gave up.

In 1894, employees at the Pullman Palace Car Company, maker of railroad passenger cars, walked out over exploitive policies at the company town near Chicago. The owner, George Pullman, controlled nearly everything in the town of twelve thousand: land, buildings, school, bank, and rents. When he cut wages without reducing rents, the American Railway Union, led by **Eugene V. Debs**, went on strike. Pullman closed the factory and the union refused to handle Pullman cars attached to any train. The railroad owners' association enlisted aid from the federal government and Debs was arrested for defying a court injunction against the strike. President Grover Cleveland ordered federal troops to Chicago. The union ended the strike and Debs received a six-month prison sentence.

Homestead Strike Worker walkout after wage cuts at a Carnegie Steel plant in 1892; officials responded to the strike by shutting down the plant.

Eugene V. Debs Indiana labor leader who organized workers in the Pullman Strike of 1893; would be the Socialist Party of America's presidential candidate five times between 1900 and 1920.

Labor Violence in the West

In the West, in 1894, fighting erupted in Cripple Creek, Colorado, when mine owners increased work hours without increasing pay. The governor called in state militia after two weeks, and owners agreed to restore the eight-hour workday. In Idaho, federal troops intervened three times in mining strikes. In 1905, former Idaho governor Frank Steuenberg was assassinated; speculation arose that the Western Federation of Miners (WFM) was exacting revenge for when Steuenberg imposed martial law during a strike in 1899. Authorities arrested WFM activist William "Big Bill" Haywood and tried him for murder in 1907. He was acquitted after his famous defense attorney, Clarence Darrow, proved that mine owners had paid a key witness.

In 1905, radical laborers formed the **Industrial Workers of the World (IWW)**. Like the Knights, the IWW (nicknamed the "Wobblies") tried to unite unskilled workers. Embracing violent tactics and socialism's rhetoric of class conflict, the "Wobblies" believed workers should seize and run the nation's industries. Their leaders—Haywood, coalfield organizer Mary "Mother" Jones, fiery orator Elizabeth Gurley Flynn, Italian radical Carlo Tresca, and songwriter Joe Hill—headed lumber, textile, and steel strikes. The union garnered publicity but collapsed during the First World War when federal prosecutors sent many of its leaders to prison and local police harassed IWW activities.

Industrial Workers of the World (IWW) Radical labor organization that sought to unionize all workers; nicknamed Wobblies, the IWW embraced socialism and led mass strikes of mine workers in Nevada and Minnesota and timber workers in Louisiana, Texas, and the Northwest.

Women Unionists

Despite exclusion from unions, some women organized and fought employers as strenuously as men. In 1909, male and female members of the International Ladies Garment Workers' Union staged a strike known as "Uprising of the 20,000" in New York City. Women also were prominent in the 1912 "Bread and Roses" strike against textile owners in Lawrence, Massachusetts, and their Telephone Operators' Department of the International Brotherhood of Electrical Workers sponsored a strike over wages that paralyzed the New England Bell telephone system in 1919. Without aid from male electrical workers, the telephone operators won higher wages and the right to bargain collectively.

The Women's Trade Union League (WTUL), founded in 1903, played a key role in representing laboring women. The WTUL sought legislation for shorter hours and better working conditions, supported strikes such as the "Uprising of the 20,000," sponsored educational activities, and campaigned for woman suffrage. Initially, sympathetic middle-class women held most WTUL offices, but after 1910 control shifted to working-class leaders, notably Agnes Nestor, a glove maker, and Rose Schneiderman, a capmaker. By inspiring working women to press for rights and training leaders, WTUL provided a vital link between labor and the women's movement into the 1920s.

The Nonunionized Workforce

The high-profile activities of organized labor obscure the fact that the vast majority of American wage workers in these years did not belong to unions. By 1920, union membership totalled 5 million—just 13 percent of all workers. For many, getting and keeping a job took priority over higher pay and shorter hours. Few companies employed workers year round; most hired during peak seasons and laid off employees during slack times. Moreover, union organizers excluded women, blacks, and immigrants.

The millions of men, women, and children who were not unionized tried to cope with industrial pressures. They joined societies such as the Polish Roman Catholic Union, African American Colored Brotherhood, and Jewish B'nai Brith, which for small fees provided life insurance, sickness benefits, and burial costs. Wages generally rose between 1877 and 1914, boosting purchasing power and consumerism; hourly pay averaged around 20 cents for skilled work and 10 cents for unskilled. But living costs rose faster, with the greatest effect felt in cities.

Growth of the Modern American City

What fueled urban growth in the late nineteenth century?

Initially trade centers, cities became arenas for industrial development in the late nineteenth century. As hubs for labor, transportation, communications, and consumption, cities supplied everything factories needed. Most cities housed various manufacturing enterprises, but product specialization was common. Mass-produced clothing concentrated in New York City, the shoe industry in Philadelphia, food processing in Minneapolis, meat processing in Chicago, fish canning in Seattle, steelmaking in Pittsburgh and Birmingham, and oil refining in Houston and Los Angeles. Such activities increased cities' attraction for people and capital.

Mechanization of Mass Transportation

As cities grew, settlement sprawled beyond original boundaries. Cities separated into distinct districts: working- and middle-class neighborhoods, commercial strips, downtown, and suburbs. Two forces created this new arrangement: first, mass transportation propelled people and enterprises outward. Second, economic change drew human and material resources inward.

By the 1870s, horse-drawn vehicles shared city streets with faster motor-driven conveyances. Commuter railroads and cable cars appeared, followed by electric-powered streetcars. In cities such as New York and Chicago, companies raised track onto trestles, enabling "elevated" trains to move above jammed streets. In Boston and New York, underground subways avoided traffic congestion.

Mass transit launched urban dwellers into outlying neighborhoods and created a commuting public. Working-class families, who needed every cent, found streetcars expensive. But the growing middle class who could afford the fare—usually five cents a ride—could escape to tree-lined neighborhoods on the outskirts and commute to the inner city for work, shopping, and entertainment. When consumers moved outward, shops, banks, and taverns followed. Meanwhile, the urban core became a work zone.

Population Growth

Between 1870 and 1920, the number of Americans living in cities increased from 10 million to 54 million, and the number of places with more than 100,000 people

Electric trolley cars and other forms of mass transit enabled middle-class people such as these women and men to reside on the urban outskirts and ride into the city center for work, shopping, and entertainment.

Picture Research Consultants & Archives

swelled from fifteen to sixty-four. Urban growth derived mainly from two sources. One was annexation of nearby territory. For example, New York City (Manhattan) merged with Brooklyn, Staten Island, and part of Queens in 1898, doubling from 1.5 million to 3 million people. Communities agreed to be annexed because they would gain access to cities' schools, water, and fire protection. More importantly, in-migration from the countryside and abroad contributed to urban population growth.

As debt and crop prices worsened, rural dwellers fled to cities such as Chicago and San Francisco, Indianapolis and Nashville. Young people were attracted by the independence of city life. Discrimination pushed many rural African Americans toward cities. By 1900, thirty-two cities, mostly in the South but in the North also, had more than ten thousand black residents. Because few factories would employ African Americans, most found service sector jobs—cleaning, cooking, and driving—usually at low wages.

"new immigrants" Wave of immigrants after 1880 coming from mainly southern and eastern Europe.

New Foreign Immigrants

More newcomers were foreign immigrants. Pushed by population pressures, land redistribution, religious persecution, and industrialization, they formed a global movement of people leaving Europe and Asia for Canada, Australia, Brazil, Argentina, and the United States. Before 1880, most immigrants came from northern and western Europe—England, Ireland, and Germany. But after 1880, many also came from eastern and southern Europe, Canada, Mexico, and Japan (see Map 16.2). Between 1900 and 1910, two-thirds of immigrants came from Italy, Austria-Hungary, and Russia. By 1910 arrivals from Mexico outnumbered those from Ireland. (See website for nationalities of immigrants.) Some wanted to make enough money to return home; most remained and helped to reshape American culture.

Many long-settled Americans feared these **"new immigrants,"** whose customs, Catholic and Jewish faiths, languages, and poverty made them seem particularly alien. Yet old and new immigrants relied on similar family-centered cultures to survive. New arrivals received aid from relatives who already immigrated, and family members pooled resources to help newcomers adapt.

Photo by Lewis W. Hine/George Eastman House/Getty Images

Male immigrants and an immigration official are looking through a wire fence at an Italian immigrant woman and her daughter who have recently arrived at the immigrant inspection station at Ellis Island, outside of New York City. The main port of entry for European immigrants after 1892, Ellis Island stands in the shadow of the Statue of Liberty.

Geographical and Social Mobility

Once in America, newcomers seldom stayed put. Via migration, people tried to escape poor housing and employment for better opportunities. Advances through work were available mostly to white males. Thousands of businesses were needed to serve burgeoning urban populations, and growing corporations hired new clerical personnel. Women also migrated within and between cities, but they usually went with husbands or fathers. Assigned to low-paying

MAP 16.2

Sources of European-Born Population, 1900 and 1920

In just a few decades, the proportion of European immigrants to the United States who came from northern and western Europe decreased (Ireland and Germany) or remained relatively stable (England and Scandinavia), while the proportion from eastern and southern Europe increased dramatically. Source: Data from U.S. Census Bureau, "Historical Census Statistics on the Foreign-Born Population of the United States: 1850–1990," February 1999, http://www.census.gov/population (accessed February 12, 2000).

occupations by prejudice, African Americans, American Indians, Mexican Americans, and Asian Americans made fewer gains.

Few individuals became rich by relocating, but many achieved moderate success. In fast-growing cities such as Atlanta and Los Angeles, approximately one in five white manual workers rose to white-collar or owner positions within ten years. Some men chose a steady job over the risk of starting a business. Many, particularly unskilled workers, could not maintain Old World occupations and had to accept low-paying jobs. Gaps between rich and poor widened, but urban economies created enough opportunities for those in between.

Cultural Retention

American cities were collections of subcommunities. Rather than completely assimilate, migrants and immigrants interacted with their environment to retain their identity while altering their outlook and urban society. Old World customs persisted in districts of Italians from the same province, Japanese from the same island, and Jews from the same Russian *shtetl*. Newcomers recreated aid organizations from their homelands, such as Chinese loan associations called *whey* that helped members start businesses. Southern Italians transferred the *padrone* system, whereby for a payoff a boss found jobs for immigrants. Newcomers practiced their religions and married within their group.

Urban Borderlands

In large cities, such as Chicago and Philadelphia, immigrants initially clustered in inner neighborhoods where jobs and cheap housing were available. These districts often were multi-ethnic "urban borderlands," where diverse people coexisted. Even in districts identified with a specific group, such as "Little Italy," rapid mobility undermined homogeneity as newcomers arrived and older inhabitants left. Businesses and institutions, such as bakeries, churches, and club headquarters—operated by and for one ethnic group—gave a neighborhood its identity.

For first- and second-generation immigrants, neighborhoods acted as havens until they were ready to leave the borderlands for other districts. European immigrants encountered prejudice, such as the exclusion of Jews from certain neighborhoods, professions, and clubs, but this discrimination was rarely systematic. For African Americans, Asians, and Mexicans, however, discrimination kept borderlands homogeneous.

Racial Segregation and Violence

By the late nineteenth century, racial bias forced African Americans into highly segregated ghettos. Within their neighborhoods, blacks nurtured institutions to cope with city life such as churches, newspapers, and clubs, and especially branches of Baptist and African Methodist Episcopal (AME) Protestantism. Religious associations dominated urban African American communities and fostered cooperation across class lines.

Often, the only way African Americans could relieve crowding in ghettos was to expand into surrounding, previously white neighborhoods, which resulted in attacks by white residents who feared blacks would reduce property values. Competition between blacks and whites for housing, jobs, and political influence sparked racial violence, in North and South. An influx of black strikebreakers into East St. Louis, Illinois, in 1917 heightened racial tensions, triggering a riot in which nine whites and thirty-nine blacks were killed and three hundred buildings were destroyed.

Though Chinese and Japanese immigrants usually preferred their own neighborhoods and business institutions in San Francisco, Seattle, Los Angeles, and New York, Anglos also tried to keep them separate. Using the slogan "The Chinese must go," Irish immigrant Denis Kearney and his followers intimidated employers into refusing to hire Chinese and drove hundreds of Asians from San Francisco. In 1880, the city banned Chinese laundries, which were social centers for immigrants, from white neighborhoods. In 1882, Congress passed the Chinese Exclusion Act suspending Chinese immigration, and in 1892 the Geary Act extended previous restrictions and required Chinese Americans to carry certificates of residence. Japanese, similarly, were prevented by law from becoming citizens.

Mexican Barrios

In southwestern cities such as Los Angeles, Tucson, Albuquerque, and San Antonio, Mexicans were the original inhabitants, Anglos the newcomers. But as Anglo arrivals increased, they pushed Mexicans into isolated districts called *barrios,* often away from multi-ethnic borderlands housing European immigrants. Such racial bias hindered the opportunities for African Americans, Asians, and Mexicans to remake their lives.

Virtually everywhere, immigrant culture mingled with existing realities. Although many foreigners identified themselves by their village or regional birthplace, native-born Americans categorized them by nationality. People from County Cork and County Limerick were merged into "Irish." Those from Calabria and Campobasso became "Italians." Moreover, the diversity of American cities prompted foreigners to modify habits. They learned the English language, used locally grown foods for traditional meals, fashioned mass-produced clothing into Old World styles, and went to American doctors while still practicing folk medicine.

Religious Diversity

The influx of multiple immigrants transformed the United States into a religiously diverse nation. Newcomers from Italy, Polish lands, and Slovakia joined Irish and Germans to increase Catholic populations in many cities, and New York City came to house one of the largest Jewish populations in the world. By 1920, Buddhism was well established among Japanese immigrants on the West Coast and in Hawai'i. Catholics and Jews tried to adjust their faiths to new environments by adopting English in services and altering traditional rituals. Still, Catholic immigrant parishes pressured bishops into appointing priests of the same ethnicity as parishioners, and Orthodox Jews retained Old World customs such as separating men and women in services. But when Catholics and Jews married co-religionists of different nationalities—an Italian marrying a Pole, for example—religious identity remained strong while ethnic identities blended.

The nation's broad diversity prevented domination by a single racial or ethnic majority and nurtured rich cultural variety: American folk literature, Italian and Mexican cuisine, Yiddish theater, African American music and dance, and much more. Newcomers changed their environment as much as it changed them.

Housing

Population growth outpaced housing supplies. With high rents and few options, those with low incomes shared space so that two or three families—and boarders—occupied single-family homes and apartments. The result was unprecedented crowding. In 1890, New York City's immigrant-packed Lower East Side averaged 702 people per acre. Cramped tenements and row houses in New York, Philadelphia, and New Orleans lacked light and fresh air. States such as New York passed regulations to establish ventilation and safety codes for new tenement buildings, but did not remedy existing buildings.

Improved furnaces, electric lighting, and indoor plumbing created more comfort for middle-class households and, later, for most others. Private enterprise made these technological advances possible, while major government-sponsored improvements were in street paving, modernized firefighting equipment, and electric street lighting.

Poverty and Crime

Poverty, however, continued to burden many urbanites. Employment, especially for unskilled workers, fluctuated with business cycles, triggering hardship for low-income families. Since colonial days, Americans believed that anyone could escape poverty through hard work and clean living; poverty, then, was due to moral weakness. Only those incapable of supporting themselves—orphans, people with disabilities, and widows—deserved relief. New York journalist Jacob Riis and other reformers concluded that people's environment contributed to poverty and therefore society bore responsibility to improve conditions. Riis's articles, combined into a book, *How the Other Half Lives* (1890), alerted readers to the deplorable conditions of slum housing. Some reformers advocated housing, education, and job initiatives to help the poor help themselves. Others, however, tolerated poor relief, but clung to the notion expressed by one charity worker that it "should be surrounded by circumstances that shall … repel everyone … from accepting it."

Crime and violence increased in American cities while falling in other industrializing nations. America's murder rate, for example, rose from 25 per million people in 1881 to 107 per million in 1898. Though police forces were increasingly professionalized, various urban groups disagreed about how best to enforce laws. Nativists were quick to blame immigrants for urban crime, and ethnic and racial minorities were more likely to be arrested. But lawbreakers included the native-born as well as foreigners.

Water Purity and Waste Disposal

Finding sources of pure water and ways to eliminate waste also challenged city dwellers. Old methods of sinking wells for water and dumping human and industrial waste in rivers no longer sufficed. By the 1880s, doctors increasingly embraced the theory that microorganisms caused disease, prompting concerns over where germs might breed. States gradually passed laws prohibiting disposal of raw sewage into rivers, and a few cities began to filter water and chemically treat sewage.

Trash, however, was a growing problem. Experts in 1900 estimated that every New Yorker annually generated 160 pounds of garbage (food), 1,200 pounds of ashes (from stoves and furnaces), and 105 pounds of rubbish. Factories created tons of solid waste (scrap metal, wood), and each of the 3.5 million horses in American cities daily dumped 20 pounds of manure and a gallon of urine on the streets. Women's groups convinced some cities to hire engineers to address the dilemma. One, George Waring, Jr., designed sewage disposal and street-cleaning systems for Memphis and New York. Cities became cleaner, but the trash problem continues to the present.

Political Machines

From the apparent confusion surrounding urban management arose **political machines**, organizations seeking to obtain and retain power. Machine politicians used fraud and bribery, but they also provided relief and service to their voters.

Big cities were typically run by political machines, with the most notable in New York, Philadelphia, and Chicago. Run by "**bosses**," these organizations built power bases among immigrant working classes. Bosses understood people's problems from firsthand experience. Bosses made politics their full-time profession. They attended weddings and wakes, sponsored picnics, and held open houses in saloons where neighborhood folk could speak to them. In return for jobs, food, clothing, and intervention when someone got arrested, people gave machine politicians the votes that kept them in power.

To finance their activities, bosses used political influence to control the awarding of public contracts. Recipients repaid the machine with a portion of their profits or salaries. Critics called this graft; bosses called it gratitude. Though waste and corruption were often involved, machine-led governments constructed much of the new urban infrastructure—public buildings, sewer systems, schools, and streetcar lines—and expanded services such as firefighting, police, and public health.

Bribes and kickbacks made machine projects costly. Bosses financed expansion with municipal bonds, and public debts soared. Also, payoffs from gambling and illegal liquor traffic were important sources of machine revenues. But bosses likely were no guiltier of greed and discrimination than businessmen who exploited workers, spoiled the environment, and manipulated government.

political machines
Organizations that emerged in urban, often working-class and immigrant neighborhoods. They solicited votes for particular candidates and promised jobs and other services to supporters; putting their candidates in office gave them power over local government.

bosses Headed political machines; often of similar background to constituents, these popular local figures exchanged votes for money, support, and other favors.

Civic and Social Reform

Middle- and upper-class civic reformers tried to replace machine politics with a government run efficiently, like a business. Structurally, they wanted tighter budget control, city manager and commission forms of government, and nonpartisan elections. A few reform mayors, such as Hazen Pingree of Detroit and Tom Johnson of Cleveland, went beyond governmental change to provide jobs and better housing for poor people. But civic reformers rarely held office for long.

Another group addressed social problems. Mostly middle class, this group pressed for building codes ensuring safer tenements, improved schools to prepare immigrants for citizenship, and medical care for the poor. Often led by women such as **Jane Addams** and **Florence Kelley**, social reformers also promoted safer food, public playgrounds, and school nurses. Environmental reformers, such as those in the City Beautiful movement, urged construction of civic centers, parks, and boulevards that would make cities economically efficient and attractive. Many plans, however, were only dreams. Neither government nor private businesses could finance large-scale projects, and planners disagreed over whether beautification would solve urban problems.

Urban reformers often failed to understand cities' diverse populations and people's varying visions of reform. To civic reformers, appointing government workers based on civil service exams rather than party loyalty meant progress, but to working-class men, civil service signified reduced job opportunities. Moral reformers believed

Jane Addams Social worker, pioneer of the settlement house movement, and founder of Chicago's Hull House, which provided education, training, and social activities for immigrants and the poor.

Florence Kelley Settlement house worker who became the chief factory inspector for Illinois in 1893.

that restricting alcoholic beverages would prevent husbands from squandering wages, but immigrants saw it as interference. Planners' visions of new boulevards and buildings often displaced the poor. Well-meaning humanitarians criticized how immigrant mothers shopped, cooked, and raised children without regard for their financial difficulties. Thus urban reform merged idealism with insensitivity.

Family Life and Individual Life

How did urbanization affect family life and structure?

Family cushioned urban dwellers from the world's uncertainties. But increasingly, new institutions—schools, political organizations, unions—competed with the family to provide education and security.

Until recently, when the number of single people living alone has risen markedly, most American households (75 percent or more) have consisted of nuclear families—a married couple with or without children. Because immigrants tended to be young, the population generally was young. In 1880, the median age was under twenty-one; by 1920, it was still only twenty-five. (Median age at present is thirty-seven.) Moreover, in 1900, death rates among people aged forty-five to sixty-four were double what they are today, and only 4 percent of the population was sixty-five and older versus 13 percent today. Thus in the late nineteenth century and early twentieth, fewer children than today had living grandparents, and three-generation households of children, parents, and grandparents were rare. Falling birth rates reduced family sizes. In 1880, there were 40 live births per 1,000 people; by 1900, births had dropped to 32; and by 1920, to 28. In part, this decline occurred because the United States was becoming an urban nation, and birth rates are historically lower in cities. Second, as nutrition and medical care improved, infant mortality fell and families did not have to bear many children to ensure that some would survive. Third, parents increasingly recognized that having three or four children instead of six meant improved quality of life for each child. Birth control technology—diaphragms and condoms—had existed for centuries, but in this era new materials made devices more convenient and dependable.

Family as a Resource

Many young adults who left home to work in cities became boarders in homes and lodging houses. Boarding was a transitional stage before setting up their own household. It also allowed families with spare space to obtain extra income.

At a time when welfare agencies were rare, people turned to their family when in need. Relatives often resided nearby and helped with child care, meals, advice, and consolation. As one family member recalled, "After two days my brother took me to the shop he was working in and his boss saw me and he gave me the job." But kinship obligations were not always welcome. Immigrant parents pressured daughters to stay home to help with housework, stifling opportunities for education and independence. Immigrant parents and American-born children often clashed over the abandonment of Old World ways or the amount of wages employed children should contribute.

The Unmarried

Although marriage rates were high, large numbers of city dwellers were unmarried. In 1890 almost 42 percent of adult men and 37 percent of women were single, almost twice as high as in 1960 (though lower than today). About half lived with parents, but others inhabited rented rooms. Mostly young, they developed a subculture that included dance halls, saloons, cafes, and the YMCA and YWCA.

Some unmarried people were part of homosexual populations that gathered in large cities such as New York, San Francisco, and Boston. Though difficult to estimate numerically, gay men patronized their own clubs, restaurants, coffeehouses, and theaters. A number of same-sex couples, especially women, formed lasting relationships, sometimes called "Boston marriages." People in this subculture were categorized more by how they acted—men acting like women, women acting like men—than by their sexual partners. The term "homosexual" was not used. Men who dressed and acted like women were called "fairies." Gay women remained hidden, and a visible lesbian subculture was rare until the 1920s.

Stages of Life

Before the late nineteenth century, stages of life were less distinct than today. Childhood was regarded as a period during which youngsters prepared for adulthood by gradually assuming responsibilities, such as caring for younger siblings. Subdivisions of youth—toddlers, schoolchildren, teenagers—were not recognized. Because married couples had more children over a longer time span, parenthood occupied most of adult life. Older people worked until they were physically incapable.

By the late nineteenth century, however, decreasing birth rates shortened the period of parenting, so more middle-aged couples experienced an "empty nest" when children grew up and left home. Longer life expectancy and a tendency by employers to force aged workers to retire separated the old from the young. As states passed compulsory school attendance laws in the 1870s and 1880s, childhood and adolescence became distinct stages, and peers rather than family influenced youngsters' behavior.

By 1900, new agencies assumed tasks formerly performed by families. Schools made education a community responsibility. Employment agencies, political machines, and labor unions became responsible for job recruitment and security. Yet kinship remained a dependable institution. Holiday celebrations—Thanksgiving, Christmas, and Easter—were times for family reunions. Birthdays, too, became increasingly festive, serving as milestones for measuring age-related life stages. In 1914, President Woodrow Wilson proclaimed the second Sunday in May as Mother's Day, capping a six-year campaign by schoolteacher Anna Jarvis, who believed children were neglecting their mothers. Ethnic, religious, and racial groups adapted celebrations to their cultures, preparing special foods and ceremonies.

New Leisure and Mass Culture

What fueled the rise of commercial leisure?

On December 2, 1889, as laborers paraded through Worcester, Massachusetts, seeking shorter working hours, carpenters hoisted a banner proclaiming, "Eight Hours for Work, Eight Hours for Rest, Eight Hours for What We Will." That last phrase claimed a new aspect of life: leisure.

Increase in Leisure Time

By the late 1800s, machines and assembly lines cut average workweeks from sixty-six hours in 1860 to sixty in 1890 and forty-seven in 1920, giving workers shorter workdays and freer weekends. White-collar employees worked eight to ten hours a day and often only half a day, if that, on weekends. Many Americans had time for recreation, and entrepreneurs profited from their new leisure time.

Amusement became a commercial activity. Production of games and toys expanded. By the 1890s, middle-class families were buying mass-produced pianos and sheet music that made singing a popular home entertainment. Organized sports, formerly a fashionable indulgence of elites, became a favorite pastime of all classes.

Baseball

Baseball was the most popular sport. Derived from older bat, ball, and base-circling games, baseball was formalized in 1845 by the Knickerbocker Club of New York City. By 1860 at least fifty baseball clubs existed, and youths played informal games on city lots and fields nationwide. The National League of Professional Baseball Clubs, founded in 1876, gave the sport a business structure, though as early as 1867, a "color line" excluded black players from major professional teams. In 1903 the National League and competing American League (formed in 1901) began a World Series between their championship teams. The Boston Americans (later, Red Sox) defeated the Pittsburgh Pirates.

Croquet and Cycling

Croquet and cycling were popular pastimes for men and women. Played on lawns, croquet encouraged socializing. Cycling was as popular as baseball, especially after 1885, when the cumbersome velocipede, with its huge front wheel and tall seat, gave way to safety bicycles with pneumatic tires and identical wheels. By 1900, Americans owned 10 million bicycles. Also, bicycles helped free women from constraints of Victorian fashion since safe riding required women to wear divided skirts and simple undergarments.

Football

American football, as an intercollegiate competition, attracted players and spectators wealthy enough to have access to higher education. By the late nineteenth century, however, the game appealed to a wider audience. While the Princeton-Yale game drew fifty thousand spectators, informal games were played throughout the country.

College football's violence and "tramp athletes"—nonstudents hired to help teams win—sparked a national scandal, climaxing in 1905 when eighteen players died from game-related injuries. President Theodore Roosevelt, an advocate of athletics, convened a White House conference to discuss the brutality. The gathering founded the Intercollegiate Athletic Association (renamed the National Collegiate Athletic Association, or NCAA, in 1910) to police college sports. In 1906, the association made the game less violent and tightened player eligibility.

Links TO THE WORLD

Japanese Baseball

Baseball, the "national pastime," was one new leisure-time pursuit that Americans took into different parts of the world. The Shanghai Base Ball Club was founded by Americans in China in 1863, but was denounced by the Imperial Court as spiritually corrupting. However, when Horace Wilson, an American teacher, taught baseball rules to his Japanese students around 1870, the game received an enthusiastic reception as a reinforcement of traditional virtues and became part of Japanese culture.

During the 1870s, Japanese high schools and colleges sponsored organized baseball, and in 1883 Hiroshi Hiraoka, a railroad engineer educated in Boston, founded the first official local team, the Shimbashi Athletic Club Athletics.

Before baseball, the Japanese had no team sports or recreational athletics. Once they learned about baseball, they found that the idea of a team sport fit their culture well. But for them, baseball was serious business, involving often brutal training. Practices at Ichiko, one of Japan's great high school baseball teams in the late

nineteenth century, were dubbed "Bloody Urine" because many players passed blood after a day's drilling. There was a spiritual quality, too, linked to Buddhist values. According to one Japanese coach, "Student baseball must be the baseball of self-discipline, or trying to attain the truth, just as in Zen Buddhism." This prompted the Japanese to consider baseball a new method for pursuing the spirit of Bushido, the way of the samurai.

When Americans played baseball in Japan, the Japanese admired their talent but found them lacking discipline and respect. Americans insulted the Japanese by refusing to remove their hats and bow when they stepped up to bat. An international dispute occurred in Tokyo in1891 when an American professor, late for a game, climbed over a sacred fence, for which fans attacked him. The American embassy lodged a complaint. Americans assumed their game would encourage Japanese to become like westerners, but the Japanese transformed baseball into a Japanese expression of team spirit, discipline, and nationalism that was uniquely Japanese.

Baseball Hall of Fame and Museum, Japan

Replete with bats, gloves, and uniforms, this Japanese baseball team of 1890 very much resembles its American counterpart of that era. The Japanese adopted baseball soon after Americans became involved in their country but also added their cultural qualities to the game.

As more women enrolled in college, they participated in sports such as rowing, track, swimming, archery, and baseball. Invented in 1891 as a winter sport for men, basketball—soon women's most popular sport—received women's rules (which limited dribbling and running, and encouraged passing) from Senda Berenson of Smith College.

Show Business

American show business, increasingly created by and for ordinary people, matured in these years. Theatrical performances offered audiences escape into adventure, melodrama, and comedy. Musical comedies entertained with songs, humor, and dance. **George M. Cohan**, a singer and dancer born into an Irish family, drew on patriotism and traditional values in songs such as "The Yankee Doodle Boy" and "You're a Grand Old Flag."

George M. Cohan Singer, dancer, and songwriter who drew on patriotic and traditional values in songs.

minstrel shows Early stage shows in which white men wore blackface makeup and played to the prejudices of white audiences by offering demeaning and caricatured portrayals of African Americans in songs, dances, and skits.

Probably the most popular mass entertainment by 1900, vaudeville offered something for everyone. Shows featured jugglers, magicians, acrobats, comedians, singers, dancers, and animal acts. Shrewd entrepreneurs made vaudeville big business. Famous producer Florenz Ziegfeld packaged stylish shows—the Ziegfeld Follies—and created the Ziegfeld Girl, whose graceful dancing and alluring costumes suggested a haunting sexuality.

Eva Tanguay was one of the most popular vaudeville performers of her era. A buxom singer who billed herself as "the girl who made vaudeville famous," Tanguay dressed in elaborate costumes and sang suggestive songs, many of which were written just for her and epitomized her carefree style.

Opportunities for Women and Minorities

Show business provided new opportunities for female, African American, and immigrant performers, but encouraged stereotyping and exploitation. Comic opera diva Lillian Russell, vaudeville comedienne-singer Fanny Brice, and burlesque queen Eva Tanguay attracted loyal fans and handsome fees. In contrast to the demure Victorian female, they conveyed pluck and creativity. Tanguay was both shocking and confident when she sang, "It's All Been Done Before But Not the Way I Do It." But lesser female performers were often exploited by male promoters and theater owners, who wanted to profit by titillating the public with scantily clad women.

Before the 1890s, **minstrel shows** were the chief commercial entertainment employing African Americans. Vaudeville provided new opportunities but reinforced demeaning stereotypes. Pandering to prejudices of white audiences, composers and white singers degraded blacks in songs such as "You May Be a Hawaiian on Old Broadway, But You're Just Another Nigger to Me." Bert Williams, an educated black comedian and dancer, achieved success by wearing blackface makeup and playing stereotypical roles of a smiling fool and dandy, but the humiliation tormented him.

Immigrants occupied the core of American popular entertainment. Performers reinforced ethnic stereotypes, but such distortions were more sympathetic than those involving blacks. A typical scene featuring Italians, for example, highlighted a character's uncertain grasp of English, which caused him to confuse *pallbearer* with *polar bear*. Such scenes allowed audiences to laugh with, rather than at, foibles of the human condition.

Movies

Shortly after 1900, live entertainment yielded to motion pictures. Perfected by Thomas Edison in the 1880s, movies began as slot-machine peep shows in arcades and billiard parlors. Eventually, images were projected onto a screen for large audiences. Producers, many of them from Jewish backgrounds, discovered that a film could tell an exciting story. Using themes of patriotism and working-class life, early filmmakers helped shift American culture away from straitlaced Victorian values to a more cosmopolitan outlook. Movies also presented social messages; *Birth of a Nation* (1915), directed by D. W. Griffith, was a stunning epic about the Civil War and Reconstruction that fanned racial prejudice by depicting African Americans as threats to white moral values. The National Association for the Advancement of Colored People (NAACP), formed in 1909, led protests against it. But the film's pioneering techniques—close-ups, fade-outs, and battle scenes—heightened its appeal.

Yellow Journalism

News also became a consumer product. Joseph Pulitzer, a Hungarian immigrant who bought the *New York World* in 1883, pioneered a new branch of journalism by filling *World* pages with stories of disasters, crimes, and scandals under screaming headlines in bold type. Pulitzer also popularized comics, and the yellow ink they were printed in brought about the term "yellow journalism" as a synonym for sensationalism. Soon other publishers, such as William Randolph Hearst, adopted Pulitzer's techniques. Pulitzer, Hearst, and their rivals boosted circulations by creating sports and women's sections. Also, magazines such as *Saturday Evening Post* and *Ladies Home Journal* became popular with human-interest stories, photographs, and eye-catching ads.

In 1891, there was less than 1 telephone for every 100 people in the United States; by 1901, the number doubled; and by 1921, it swelled to 12.6. In 1900, Americans used 4 billion postage stamps; in 1922, they bought 14.3 billion. More than ever, people in different parts of the country knew about and discussed the same news event. America was becoming a mass society where the same products, technology, and information dominated everyday life.

To some extent, new amusements allowed ethnic and social groups to share common experiences. Yet different groups used amusement parks such as at Coney Island, ball fields, vaudeville shows, movies, and feature sections of newspapers and magazines to suit their own needs. To the dismay of natives who hoped that public recreation and holidays would assimilate newcomers, immigrants converted picnics and Fourth of July celebrations into ethnic events and occasions for boisterous festivity. Young working-class men and women resisted parents' and moralizers' warnings and frequented dance halls, where they explored forms of courtship and sexual behavior. Thus, leisure—like work and politics—was shaped by the pluralistic forces that thrived in the new urban-industrial society.

Technology of Recorded Sound

Today's iPods and digital recorders derive from technology, chemistry, and human resourcefulness that came together in the late nineteenth century. In 1877, Thomas Edison devised a way to preserve and reproduce his voice by storing it on indentations made in tinfoil. Edison intended his "speaking machine" to help businesses store dictation. But in 1878, his rivalry with telephone inventor Alexander Graham Bell, who was working on a similar device, drew Edison to invent a phonograph for recorded music. By the 1890s, audiences paid to hear recorded sounds from these machines.

By 1901, companies such as the Columbia Phonograph Company produced machines that played music recorded on cylinders molded from a durable wax compound. Over the next ten years, inventors improved the phonograph so sound played from a stylus (needle) vibrating in the grooves of a shellac disc. Records' playing time increased from two minutes to four.

Phonograph records replaced sheet music as the most popular medium, but soon radio emerged and boosted record sales. Radio's popularity was only possible via another electronic technology: the microphone, a vast improvement over megaphones. As phonograph prices declined and sound quality advanced, more records became available.

The 1938 invention of the idler wheel, which enabled a phonograph turntable to spin a disc at speeds necessary for the stylus to pick up sound accurately, brought an important advance. Shortly thereafter, inventions in sound recording, such as the magnetic tape recorder, allowed for more manipulation of sound in the recording studio. In 1963 Philips, a Dutch electronics firm, introduced the compact audiocassette. Two decades later, Philips joined with the Japanese corporation Sony to adapt digital laser discs, invented by an American for video storage, to store music. The compact disc (CD) was born, and from there it was a short step for Apple Computers, Inc., to create the iPod, storing CD-quality music on an internal hard drive. Today, downloaded music has replaced records, tapes, and discs as a multibillion-dollar industry.

Summary

Industrialization, propelled by technology, and urbanization, enriched by waves of immigrants, dramatically altered the United States in the late nineteenth and early twentieth centuries. Industrial growth transformed the nation into a manufacturing, financial, and exporting power. Immigrant families outnumbered the native-born in many cities, and fueled the industrial economy as workers and consumers. And the era's new technologies made cities safer and life more comfortable.

But massive corporations transformed skilled producers into wage earners. Laborers fought to retain control of their work and organized unions. Finding adequate housing, jobs, and a safe environment posed challenges for newcomers. In cities, politics and reform took on new meanings, and family life reflected both change and continuity.

Wealth and power were unevenly distributed, however. Corporations consolidated to control resources. Though numerous, workers lacked influence, believing businesses profited at their expense. And the urban society that materialized when native inventiveness met the traditions of European, African, and Asian cultures seldom functioned smoothly, yet helped cities thrive. When the desire to retain one's culture met the need to fit in, it resulted in compound identifications: Irish American, Italian American, Polish American, and the like. By 1920, the foundation of the country's urban–industrial structure had been laid.

Chapter Review

Technology and the Triumph of Industrialism

How did technological innovations transform American industry?

New inventions and technological advances made production of goods and services faster and cheaper, which in turn fueled the rise of mass production and consumption. Big factories replaced small workshops as large-scale production became increasingly economical. Thomas Edison's system for inexpensively distributing electricity facilitated the emergence of countless other inventions in the late nineteenth and early twentieth centuries. Henry Ford built on a European invention for engines to create his assembly-line process that would mass-produce thousands of identical—ultimately affordable—cars in the early twentieth century. The du Pont family similarly revolutionized the chemical industry; electric looms advanced textile production and relocated it from North to South; while North Carolinian James B. Duke mass-produced cigarettes and remade the tobacco industry.

Big Business and Its Critics

What led corporations to increasingly consolidate in the late nineteenth century?

Big companies saw consolidation as a way to guarantee profits and control downward economic cycles. They believed the more they pooled resources to set prices and influence profits by determining how much to supply the market, the more they could manage a downturn. Until the 1880s, however, laws made it illegal for companies to own stock in another firm. Instead, businessmen such as John D. Rockefeller turned to trusts, luring stockholders of smaller companies to yield control of their stock "in trust" to the larger company's board of trustees. Once states allowed companies within their borders to own stock in corporations in other states, holding companies emerged, where one firm would own a partial or complete interest in another and merge their assets and resources. Holding companies also found it easier to dominate their markets by controlling all aspects of an industry, from raw materials to manufacturing to distribution. Business leaders also embraced a new theory—Social Darwinism—a survival of the fittest for the laissez-faire economy that justified their actions.

But critics questioned the concentration of wealth in a few hands and the growing poverty in a rich nation. Some wanted a more cooperative society and greater government involvement; others advocated government ownership of railroads and utilities. In the end, Congress passed antitrust legislation, though its potential was limited by vague language and pro-business courts.

Mechanization and the Changing Status of Labor

How did mechanization and new systems of management change the nature and status of work?

Innovation created new jobs, but laborsaving machines and assembly lines also meant that fewer workers could produce more in less time. This, along, with new ideas about efficiency (Frederick Taylor's "scientific management") replaced workers' skills with tasks regulated by supervisors and the clock. Instead of doing many different tasks, workers now did only one task repeatedly. As such, they were transformed from craftsmen and skilled producers into wage laborers. In the process, they lost control over their workdays and were regulated by the production mandates of bosses. The devaluing of skill and the urge to maximize profits led manufacturers to further cut labor costs by hiring women and children, whom they could pay much less. The advent of typewriters and other office machines opened clerical and white-collar jobs to educated women, though at a fraction of what men had earned. But in manufacturing, long days and often-hazardous working conditions led to an increasing number of accidents. Workers formed labor unions and participated in (sometimes violent) strikes, in the hope of regaining control over their work lives, with mixed results.

Growth of the Modern American City

What fueled urban growth in the late nineteenth century?

Cities grew two ways: first, by annexing areas that bordered them, as New York City did when it merged with Brooklyn, Staten Island, and parts of Queens, doubling its population to 3 million. Cities also expanded via in-migration from rural areas and, more importantly, immigration from abroad. New groups of immigrants from eastern and southern Europe joined earlier immigrants from northern and western European in seeking new opportunities in the United States between 1880 and 1920. Population pressures, land redistribution, industrialization, and religious persecution pushed many immigrants to leave Europe, Asia, Canada, and Latin America for the United States. Within the United States, low crop prices and heavy debts pushed some white farmers from the country in search of jobs in the city; in other cases, young men sought to escape economic hardship for the excitement of cities while young women left unhappy homes for greater independence. Similarly, African Americans headed to cities for better jobs and to escape crop liens and racial violence. As a result, cities became places of great cultural diversity.

Family Life and Individual Life

How did urbanization affect family life and structure?

In some ways, family life remained the same: it was still a central aspect of people's lives and provided resources and a safe haven from the harsh world beyond it. But in many ways the traditional family was transformed: institutions such as schools, unions, and political groups competed with the family in providing education and security, for example. With a rising population of young single immigrants and migrants, more people remained single—and for longer periods of time—than in the past, which meant more single people living alone or as boarders in other people's homes. Family size was reduced, too, with far fewer children born. This was due partly to lower infant mortality rates thanks to better nutrition and medical care, but also because birth rates tend to be lower in cities and because new and better materials for condoms and diaphragms made birth control devices more convenient and reliable. The notion of life stages emerged with lower birth rates and longer life expectancy, segmenting one's life into childhood, adolescence, and so on. With compulsory education, peer groups became more influential than families in shaping young people's behavior. Families continued to rely on each other as resources, especially immigrant families adjusting to life in America, but generations often clashed over Old World versus New World identities.

New Leisure and Mass Culture

What fueled the rise of commercial leisure?

Mechanization and new, more efficient means of production, along with labor activism, led to shorter workweeks and hours—which, in turn, gave workers more time to use as they saw fit. New mass entertainment rose to fill this need, including baseball and football leagues, bicycling, and other outdoor activities, as well as theater, vaudeville, and, later, film. Vaudeville was an early form of popular live entertainment, appealing to broad audiences with magic shows, comedians, singers and dancers, and providing work opportunities for blacks, immigrants and women (even while reinforcing negative stereotypes.) But by 1900, live entertainment was quickly replaced by the advent of movies, which began as slot machine peep shows in the 1880s, but evolved by the early twentieth century into a medium for story-telling. By focusing on a variety of themes, the medium of film helped shift American culture away from the straitlaced nature of Victorian society toward more cosmopolitan outlook.

Suggestions for Further Reading

John Bodnar, *The Transplanted: A History of Immigrants in Urban America* (1985)

Howard P. Chudacoff and Judith E. Smith, *The Evolution of American Urban Society*, 7th ed. (2010)

John D'Emilio and Estelle Freedman, *Intimate Matters: A History of Sexuality in America* (1988)

Steven J. Diner, *A Very Different Age: Americans of the Progressive Era* (1998)

Nancy Foner and George M. Frederickson, eds., *Not Just Black and White: Historical and Contemporary Perspectives on Immigration, Race, and Ethnicity in the United States* (2004)

Kenneth T. Jackson, *The Crabgrass Frontier: The Suburbanization of the United States* (1985)

Matthew Frye Jacobson, *Whiteness of a Different Color: European Immigrants and the Alchemy of Race* (1998)

John F. Kasson, *Civilizing the Machine: Technology and Republican Values in America, 1776–1900* (1976)

Alice Kessler-Harris, *Out to Work: A History of Wage-Earning Women in the United States* (2003)

T. J. Jackson Lears and Richard W. Fox, eds., *The Culture of Consumption: Critical Essays in American History, 1880–1980* (1983)

Robyn Muncy, *Creating a Female Dominion in American Reform, 1890–1935* (1991)

Kathy Peiss, *Cheap Amusements: Working Women and Leisure in Turn-of-the-Century New York* (1986)

Gilded Age Politics

1877–1900

W illiam Graham Sumner said of people who were lazy, immoral, or criminal that "it would have been better for society and would have involved no pain to them, if they had never been born." Born in New Jersey, Sumner was raised in Hartford, Connecticut, the son of a railroad employee and wife who had emigrated from England. In spite of his family's modest means, Sumner graduated from Yale College (later Yale University) in 1863. After studying in Germany and England, he was ordained an Episcopal priest in 1869. But society and economics were his real passions. So in 1872 he left the church and accepted a professorship in political and social science at Yale, where he remained until retiring in 1909.

Professor Sumner was a champion of laissez-faire, the ideology that government involvement in private affairs should be kept to a minimum. He was among those credited with adapting Charles Darwin's theory of the survival of the fittest to society and economics (see page 529). In an 1887 essay, Sumner expressed his laissez-faire views by asserting that the American people had "reached the point where individualism is possible," concluding that "whenever we try to get paternalized [meaning controlled by government] we only succeed in getting policed."

Sumner is an icon of the nation's rampant economic expansion. The traumatic Civil War and its aftermath plus the extraordinary rise of large corporations between 1877 and 1900 influenced politics and government and shaped everyday life. The era was characterized by greed, special interest, and political exclusion. The obsession with riches seemed so widespread that, when Mark Twain and his novelist friend Charles Dudley Warner satirized America as a nation of money-grubbers in their novel *The Gilded Age* (1874), the name stuck and is still used by historians to characterize the late nineteenth century.

At first glance, the Gilded Age may appear as the era in which laissez-faire triumphed. Corporations seemed to expand unfettered and government spending, especially on social programs, was kept to a minimum. The U.S. Congress was preoccupied with matters designed to aid business, and in several influential decisions, the Supreme Court limited the ability of government to control corporations.

Such a view, however, would miss the era's developments that expanded government power at federal, state, and local levels far more than people at the time realized. Though certain groups resisted government authority, others actively sought it. In spite of partisan and regional rivalries, Congress achieved legislative landmarks in railroad regulation, tariff and currency reform, the civil service, and other important issues. And in spite of Sumner's fear, state and local governments expanded their police power—the authority to protect the health, safety, and morals of citizens. Nevertheless, exclusion still prevented the majority of Americans—including women, southern blacks, Indians, uneducated whites, and unnaturalized immigrants—from voting and from the tools of democracy.

Until the 1890s, a stable party system and sectional balance maintained political equilibrium. Then, in the 1890s, rural discontent rumbled through the West and South, and a deep economic depression exposed the industrial system's flaws. The 1896 presidential campaign stirred Americans, as a new party system arose, old parties split, and sectional unity dissolved. The nation emerged from the turbulent 1890s with new economic and political configurations.

As you read this chapter, keep the following questions in mind:

- **What were the functions of government in the Gilded Age, and how did they change?**

- **How did policies of exclusion and discrimination make their mark on the political culture of the age?**

- **How did the economic climate give rise to the Populist movement?**

The Nature of Party Politics

How did factional disputes complicate party politics in the Gilded Age?

Public interest in elections reached an all-time high between 1870 and 1896. Around 80 percent of eligible voters (white and black males in the North and West, mostly white males in the South) consistently voted—a rate 20 to 30 percent higher than today's. Featuring parades, picnics, and speeches, politics served as recreation, with voting as its final step.

Chronology

1873	Congress ends coinage of silver dollars
1873–78	Economic hard times hit
1877	Georgia passes poll tax, disfranchising most African Americans
1878	Bland-Allison Act requires U.S. Treasury to buy between $2 million and $4 million in silver each month
1881	Garfield assassinated; Arthur assumes presidency
1883	Pendleton Civil Service Act introduces merit system
	Supreme Court strikes down 1883 Civil Rights Act
1886	*Wabash* case declares that only Congress can limit interstate commerce rates
1887	Farmers' Alliances form
	Interstate Commerce Commission begins regulating rates and practices of interstate shipping
1890	McKinley Tariff raises tariff rates
	Sherman Silver Purchase Act commits the U.S. Treasury to buying 4.5 million ounces of silver each month
	"Mississippi Plan" uses poll taxes and literacy tests to prevent African Americans from voting
	National American Woman Suffrage Association formed
1890s	Jim Crow laws, discriminating against African Americans in legal treatment and public accommodations, passed by southern states
1892	Populist convention in Omaha draws up reform platform
1893	Sherman Silver Purchase Act repealed
1893–97	Major economic depression hits United States
1894	Wilson-Gorman Tariff passes
	Coxey's Army marches on Washington, D.C.
1896	*Plessy v. Ferguson* establishes separate but equal doctrine
1898	Louisiana implements "grandfather clause" restricting voting by African Americans
1899	*Cumming v. County Board of Education* applies separate but equal doctrine to schools

Cultural-Political Alignments

In the Gilded Age, party loyalty was fierce. With some exceptions, people who opposed government interference in personal liberty identified with the Democratic Party; those who believed government could be an agent of reform identified with the Republicans. There was also a geographic dimension to these divisions. Northern Republicans capitalized on bitter memories of the Civil War by "waving the bloody shirt" at Democrats. Northern Democrats focused more on urban and economic issues, but southern Democratic candidates waved a different bloody shirt, calling Republicans traitors to white supremacy and states' rights.

Political allegiances were so evenly divided that no party gained dominance for long. Between 1877 and 1897, Republicans held the presidency for three terms, Democrats for two. Rarely did one party control the presidency and Congress simultaneously. From 1876 through 1892, presidential elections were close. The outcome often hinged on populous northern states—Connecticut, New York, New Jersey, Ohio, Indiana, and Illinois. Both parties tried to gain advantages by nominating presidential candidates from these states (and by committing vote fraud).

| Party Factions |

Internal quarrels split the Republican and Democratic parties. Among Republicans, New York's Senator Roscoe Conkling led one faction, known as "Stalwarts," and worked the spoils system to win government jobs for supporters. The Stalwarts' rivals were the "Half Breeds," led by Maine congressman James G. Blaine, who also blatantly pursued influence. On the sidelines stood more idealistic Republicans, or **"Mugwumps"** (supposedly an Indian term meaning "mug on one side of the fence, wump on the other"). Mugwumps, such as Missouri Republican senator Carl Schurz, believed that only righteous, educated men should govern. Republican allies of big business supported gold as the standard for currency, whereas those from western mining regions favored silver. Democrats subdivided into white supremacist southerners; working-class advocates; immigrant-stock supporters of urban political machines; business-oriented advocates of low tariffs and the gold standard; and debtor-oriented advocates of free silver.

In each state, one party usually dominated, and often the state "boss" was a senator who doled out jobs and parlayed his clout into national influence. (Until ratification of the Seventeenth Amendment to the Constitution in 1913, state legislatures elected U.S. senators.) These men exercised their power brazenly.

The Activism of Government

In what ways did the government become more activist—and expand its authority—in the late nineteenth century?

Still, government played a greater role in people's lives than previously. Along with laws, governments increasingly employed the constitutional provision of "police power," meaning the authority, within limits, to regulate and enforce order to ensure the health, safety, morals, and general welfare of the population.

| Uses of Police Power |

From the earliest days of the Republic, state and local governments intervened in people's lives to protect safety. By the Gilded Age, these laws and regulations greatly expanded. Laws banned mistreatment of animals and children; laws provided for the purity of foods and medicines; laws established minimum requirements for professionals such as doctors and teachers; and laws ensured the legitimacy of banks and insurance companies. Other laws required the licensing of, and sometimes prohibition of, liquor sales, prizefighting, and obscene literature; laws regulated rates and operations of streetcars and railroads; laws limited the working hours of women and children; and laws mandated racial segregation. Despite objections, state legislatures and city councils passed these laws with broad consent of the people they governed. Moreover, courts generally upheld them.

| Due Process |

Protesters who challenged police power asserted that governments were interfering with a person's or company's right to use of private property. This right was in the clause of the Fifth Amendment to the Constitution that stated that no person could "be deprived of life, liberty, or property, without due process of law; nor shall private property be taken for public use without just compensation." The restriction originally applied to actions by the federal government, but the Fourteenth Amendment (1868) extended it to state governments.

Railroad rates demonstrate how business interests tried to use due process as a protection against state and federal government regulation. In battling the competition for customers, railroads launched rate wars and angered shippers with inconsistent freight charges. On noncompetitive routes, railroads often boosted charges to compensate for unprofitably low rates on competitive routes. Railroads also played favorites, reducing rates to large shippers and offering free passes to preferred customers and politicians.

Railroad Regulation

Such favoritism stirred farmers, small merchants, and reform politicians to demand rate regulation. By 1880, fourteen states established commissions to limit freight and storage charges of state-chartered lines. Railroads fought back, arguing that the Fourteenth Amendment to the Constitution guaranteed them freedom to acquire and use property without government restraint. But in 1877, in *Munn v. Illinois,* the Supreme Court upheld state regulation, declaring that grain warehouses owned by railroads acted in the public interest and therefore must submit to regulation for "the common good."

Only the federal government could regulate interstate lines, as affirmed by the Supreme Court in the *Wabash* case of 1886. Reformers thereupon demanded federal action. Congress passed the **Interstate Commerce Act** in 1887, which prohibited rebates and rate discrimination and created the Interstate Commerce Commission (ICC), the nation's first regulatory agency, to investigate railroad rate-making and issue cease and desist orders against illegal practices. The legislation's weak enforcement provisions, however, left railroads room for evasion, and federal judges diminished state and ICC powers. In the *Maximum Freight Rate* case (1897), the Supreme Court evoked due process, ruling that regulation interfered with a railroad's right to a "fair return" from its property. Though weakened by a standoff between police power and due process, the principle of regulation remained in force.

Interstate Commerce Act
An 1887 law that established the Interstate Commerce Commission, the nation's first regulatory agency, to investigate railroad rate-making and discriminatory rate practices.

Veterans' Pensions

Issues of pensions, patronage abuses, tariffs, and currency also provoked debates and partisanship. From the end of the Civil War into the 1880s, Congress debated soldiers' pensions. The **Grand Army of the Republic**, an organization of Union army veterans, allied with the Republican Party and cajoled the government into providing pensions for former northern soldiers and their widows. Although the North spent $2 billion to fight the Civil War, veterans' pensions cost $8 billion, one of the largest welfare commitments the federal government has ever made. By 1900 soldiers' pensions accounted for roughly 40 percent of the federal budget. Confederate veterans, however, were excluded, though some southern states funded small pensions and built old-age homes for ex-soldiers.

Grand Army of the Republic (GAR) A social and political lobbying organization of northern Civil War veterans that convinced Congress to provide $8 billion in pensions for former Union soldiers and widows.

Civil Service Reform

Few politicians dared oppose pensions, but some attempted to dismantle the spoils system—the practice of awarding government jobs, or spoils—to political supporters regardless of their qualifications. During the Civil War, the federal government expanded considerably, and the spoils system flourished. As the postal service, diplomatic corps, and other government agencies grew, the number of federal jobs tripled, from 53,000 to 166,000. (There are about 1.9 million today.) Elected officials scrambled to control these to benefit their party. In return for short hours and high pay, appointees to federal positions pledged votes and part of their earnings to patrons.

Shocked by such corruption, especially after the Grant administration scandals, some reformers advocated appointments based on merit—civil service. Support for change accelerated in 1881 when a distraught job seeker assassinated President James Garfield. The **Pendleton Civil Service Act**, passed by Congress in 1882, created the Civil Service Commission to oversee competitive examinations for roughly 10 percent of federal jobs, but the president could expand the list. Because the Constitution barred Congress from interfering in state affairs, civil service at state and local levels developed more haphazardly.

Pendleton Civil Service Act
Attempt to end the spoils system; created the Civil Service Commission to oversee competitive exams for government jobs.

Tariff Policy

From 1789 onward, Congress created tariffs, which levied duties (taxes) on imported goods, to protect American products from foreign competition. But tariffs quickly became a tool special interests used to enhance profits. By the 1880s these interests succeeded in obtaining tariffs on more than four thousand items. A few economists and farmers argued for free trade, but most politicians insisted that tariffs were necessary to support industry and preserve jobs.

The Republican Party made protective tariffs its core agenda. Democrats complained that tariffs made prices artificially high by reducing less expensive imports, hurting farmers whose crops were not protected and consumers wanting to buy manufactured goods.

During the Gilded Age, revenues from tariffs and other levies created a federal budget surplus. Most Republicans liked that government was earning more than it spent and hoped to keep the surplus as a reserve or use it for projects that would aid commerce. Democrats acknowledged a need for protection of some manufactured goods and raw materials, but they favored lower tariff duties to encourage foreign trade and reduce the Treasury surplus.

Manufacturers and their congressional allies controlled tariff policy. The McKinley Tariff of 1890 boosted already-high rates by 4 percent. When House Democrats passed a bill to trim tariffs in 1894, Senate Republicans, aided by southern Democrats, added six hundred amendments restoring most cuts (the Wilson-Gorman Tariff). In 1897, the Dingley Tariff raised rates further. Attacks on duties, though unsuccessful, made tariffs a symbol of privileged business in the public mind.

Monetary Policy

When increased industrial and agricultural production caused prices to fall after the Civil War, debtors (have-nots) and creditors (haves) had opposing reactions. Farmers suffered because crop prices dropped and because demand for a limited supply of circulating money raised interest rates on loans, making it costly to borrow funds to pay mortgages and debts. They favored coinage of silver to increase the amount of currency in circulation, which in turn would reduce interest rates. Small businessmen, also in need of loans, agreed. Large businessmen and bankers favored a stable money supply backed only by gold, fearing currency fluctuations that would threaten investors' confidence in the U.S. economy. The money debate also reflected sectional cleavages: western silver-mining areas and agricultural regions of the South and West against the industrial Northeast.

Before the 1870s, the federal government bought gold and silver to back its paper money (dollars), setting a ratio that made a gold dollar worth sixteen times more than a silver dollar. Discovery and mining of gold in the West, however, increased gold supplies and lowered market prices relative to silver. Consequently, silver dollars disappeared from circulation as owners hoarded them. In 1873, Congress officially halted silver coinage. The United States unofficially adopted the gold standard.

Within a few years, new mines in the West began flooding the market with silver, and its price dropped. Gold now became relatively less plentiful, worth *more* than sixteen times that of silver, and it became worthwhile for people to spend rather than hoard silver dollars. Silver producers wanted the government to resume buying silver at the old sixteen-to-one ratio. Debtors, hurt by the economic hard times of 1873–1878, saw silver as a means of expanding the currency supply, so they pressed for resumption of silver coinage at the old sixteen-to-one ratio.

With parties split into silver and gold factions, Congress tried to compromise. The Bland-Allison Act (1878) authorized the Treasury to buy $2 million to $4 million worth of silver monthly, and the **Sherman Silver Purchase Act** (1890) increased the government's silver purchase by specifying weight (4.5 million ounces) rather than dollars. Neither measure satisfied various interest groups. Creditors wanted the government to stop buying silver, whereas for debtors, the legislation failed to expand the money supply satisfactorily. The issue would intensify during the 1896 presidential election (see pages 512–514).

Sherman Silver Purchase Act Law that instructed the treasury to buy, at current market prices, 4.5 million ounces of silver monthly.

Legislative Accomplishments

Congress addressed thorny issues under difficult conditions. Congressmen earned small salaries yet had to maintain two residences: in their home district and in Washington. Most congressmen had no private offices, worked long hours, wrote their own speeches, and paid for staff themselves. Yet, though corruption and greed tainted several, most politicians were principled and dedicated. They managed to pass significant legislation that increased the power of the federal government.

Presidential Initiative

What actions did American presidents between 1877 and 1900 take to restore authority to their office?

Operating under the cloud of Andrew Johnson's impeachment, Grant's scandals, and doubts about the legitimacy of the 1876 election (see Chapter 14), American presidents between 1877 and 1900 moved to restore authority to their office. Proper and honest, Presidents Rutherford Hayes (1877–1881), James Garfield (1881), Chester Arthur (1881–1885), Grover Cleveland (1885–1889 and 1893–1897), Benjamin Harrison (1889–1893), and William McKinley (1897–1901) tried to act as legislative and administrative leaders. Each president cautiously initiated legislation and used vetoes to guide national policy.

Hayes, Garfield, and Arthur

Rutherford B. Hayes had been a Union general and Ohio congressman and governor before his disputed election to the presidency, which prompted opponents to label him "Rutherfraud." Hayes served as conciliator, emphasizing national harmony over sectional rivalry and opposing racial violence. He tried to overhaul the spoils system by appointing civil service reformer Carl Schurz to his cabinet and by battling New York's patronage king, Senator Conkling.

When Hayes declined to run for reelection in 1880, Republicans nominated another Ohio congressman and Civil War hero, James A. Garfield, who won by 40,000 votes out of 9 million cast. By winning the pivotal states of New York and Indiana, Garfield carried the electoral college by 214 to 155. Garfield hoped to reduce the tariff and develop economic relations with Latin America, and he rebuffed Conkling's patronage demands. But in July 1881, Charles Guiteau shot him in a Washington railroad station. Garfield lingered for seventy-nine days before dying on September 19.

Garfield's successor was Vice President Chester A. Arthur, the New York Stalwart whom Hayes had fired. Arthur became a temperate executive. He signed the Pendleton Civil Service Act, urged Congress to modify outdated tariff rates, and supported federal railroad regulation. He wielded the veto aggressively, killing bills that excessively benefited railroads and corporations. Arthur wanted to run for president in 1884 but Republicans nominated James G. Blaine instead.

Democrats picked New York's governor, Grover Cleveland, a bachelor who admitted during the campaign that he had fathered an out-of-wedlock son. Cleveland beat Blaine by only 29,000 popular votes; his tiny margin of 1,149 votes in New York secured that state's 36 electoral votes, enough for a 219-to-182 victory in the electoral college. Cleveland may have won New York thanks to remarks of a Protestant minister, who equated Democrats with "rum, Romanism, and rebellion." Democrats publicized the slur among New York's large Irish-Catholic population, urging voters to support Cleveland.

Cleveland and Harrison

Cleveland, the first Democratic president since James Buchanan (1857–1861), expanded civil service, vetoed private pension bills, and urged Congress to cut tariff duties. When advisers worried about his chances for reelection, the president retorted, "What is the use of being elected or reelected, unless you stand for something?" Senate protectionists killed tariff reform, and when Democrats renominated Cleveland in 1888, businessmen convinced him to moderate his attacks on tariffs.

Republicans in 1888 nominated Benjamin Harrison, former Indiana senator and grandson of President William Henry Harrison (1841). Bribery and multiple voting helped him win Indiana by 2,300 votes and New York by 14,000. (Democrats also indulged in frauds, but Republicans proved more successful at them.) Although Cleveland outpolled Harrison by 90,000 popular votes, Harrison carried the electoral college by 233 to 168.

The first president since 1875 whose party had majorities in both congressional houses, Harrison influenced legislation by threats of vetoes, informal dinners,

The Spectacle of Gilded Age Politics

During the Gilded Age, political events, especially presidential elections, provided opportunity for elaborate spectacle, and politicians occupied the limelight as major celebrities. A presidential campaign functioned as a public festival at a time when mass entertainments such as movies and sports did not exist to offer people outlets for their emotions by attending parades, cheering, watching fireworks, and listening to marching bands. These two images, one an artist's rendering and the other a means for displaying one's preference for a particular candidate, present evidence of how people of the era might have expressed themselves politically. What similarities to modern-day campaign events and symbols do the images represent? In what ways are they different? Did politics and campaigning in the Gilded Age play a different role in the nation's culture than they do at present?

Collection of Janice L. and David J. Frent/ Corbis

Bettmann/CORBIS

The presidential campaign of Rutherford B. Hayes excited strong emotions. The inset image is that of a campaign brooch reminding voters of Hayes's Civil War record, and the drawing illustrates the gala of Hayes's inauguration in 1876.

and consultations with politicians. Partly in response, the Congress of 1889–1891 passed 517 bills, 200 more than the average passed by Congresses between 1875 and 1889. Harrison showed support for civil service by appointing reformer Theodore Roosevelt as civil service commissioner. But pressured by special interests, Harrison signed the Dependents' Pension Act, which provided pensions for Union veterans and widows and children, doubling the number of welfare recipients from 490,000 to 966,000.

The Pension Act and other appropriations pushed the 1890 federal budget past $1 billion for the first time. Democrats blamed the "Billion-Dollar Congress" on spendthrift Republicans. In 1890, voters reacted by unseating seventy-eight Republican congressmen. Capitalizing on voter unrest, Democrats nominated Grover Cleveland to run against Harrison in 1892. With large business contributions, Cleveland beat Harrison by 370,000 popular votes (3 percent of the total), easily winning the electoral vote.

In office again, Cleveland addressed currency, tariffs, and labor unrest, but his actions reflected political weakness. Cleveland promised sweeping tariff reform, but Senate protectionists undercut his efforts. And he bowed to requests from railroads, sending federal troops to put down the Pullman strike of 1894. In spite of Cleveland's efforts, major events—particularly economic downturn and agrarian ferment—pushed the country in another direction.

Discrimination and Disfranchisement

What legal means were used to discriminate against newly enfranchised African Americans in the decades following the Civil War?

Despite speeches about freedom and opportunity during the Gilded Age, policies of discrimination haunted more than half the nation's people. Racial issues long shaped politics in the South, home to the majority of African Americans. Southern white farmers and workers feared that newly enfranchised African American men would challenge their political and social superiority (real and imagined). Wealthy landowners and merchants fanned these fears, keeping blacks and whites from uniting to protest their own economic subjugation. Even some white feminists, such as Susan B. Anthony, opposed voting and other rights for blacks on grounds that white women deserved such rights before black men did.

In the North, custom more than law limited the opportunities of black people. Discrimination in housing, employment, and access to facilities such as parks, hotels, and department stores kept African Americans separate. Whether via low wages or lower crop returns, African Americans felt the sting of their imposed inferiority.

Violence Against African Americans

In 1880, 90 percent of southern blacks farmed or worked in personal and domestic service—just as they had as slaves. Between 1889 and 1909, more than seventeen hundred African Americans were lynched in the South. About a quarter of **lynching** victims were accused of assault—rarely proved—on a white woman. Most, however, had simply said or done something that made insecure whites feel disrespected, or they had succeeded in business or taken a job that made whites feel inferior.

lynching Vigilante hanging of those accused of crimes; used primarily against blacks.

Library of Congress Prints and Photographs Division, LC-US262-68958

Lynching could mean other than simple hanging. In 1893, a mob estimated at 10,000 gathered in Paris, Texas, to watch the torture and killing of a black man believed to have assaulted and murdered a four-year-old white girl. This photo was taken just as Henry Smith, the alleged assailant, was tortured fifty times by red-hot iron brands, then doused with kerosene and set on fire. After the gruesome event, the vengeful crowd burned down the scaffold.

Blacks did not suffer silently. Their most notable activist was **Ida B. Wells**, a Memphis schoolteacher, who was forcibly removed from a railroad car in 1884 when she refused to surrender her seat to a white man. In 1889, Wells became partner of a Memphis newspaper, the *Free Speech and Headlight*, in which she published attacks against white injustice, particularly the case of three black grocers lynched in 1892 after defending themselves against whites. She subsequently toured Europe, drumming up opposition to lynching and discrimination. Unable to return to hostile Memphis, she moved to Chicago and became a powerful advocate for racial justice.

Ida B. Wells African American journalist and activist who mounted a national anti-lynching campaign.

Disfranchisement

Southern white leaders instituted official measures of political discrimination. Despite threats and intimidation after Reconstruction, blacks still formed the backbone of the southern Republican Party and won numerous elective positions. In North Carolina, eleven African Americans served in the state senate and forty-three in the house between 1877 and 1890. This was unacceptable to racist whites, and beginning with Florida and Tennessee in 1889 (and eventually every southern state), governments levied taxes of $1 to $2 on all voters—prohibitive to most blacks, who were poor and in debt. Other schemes disfranchised or deprived the voting rights of blacks who could not read.

Furthering disfranchisement, the Supreme Court determined in *U.S. v. Reese* (1876) that Congress had no control over local and state elections other than upholding the Fifteenth Amendment, which prohibits states from denying the vote "on account of race, color, or previous condition of servitude." State legislators also found ways to exclude black voters. An 1890 state constitutional convention established the "Mississippi Plan," requiring voters to pay a poll tax eight months before each election, present the tax receipt at election time, and prove they could read and interpret the state constitution. Registration officials applied stiffer standards to blacks than to whites, even declaring black college graduates ineligible due to illiteracy. In 1898 Louisiana enacted the first "grandfather clause," which established literacy and property qualifications for voting but exempted sons and grandsons of those eligible to vote before 1867—a year in which no blacks could vote in Louisiana.

Such restrictions proved effective. In South Carolina, 70 percent of eligible blacks voted in the 1880 election; by 1896, the rate dropped to 11 percent. By the 1900s, African Americans effectively lost political rights in the South. More importantly, because voting is a right of citizenship, disfranchisement stripped African American men of their standing as U.S. citizens. Disfranchisement also affected poor whites, few of whom could meet poll tax, property, and literacy requirements. Consequently, the total number of eligible voters in Mississippi shrank from 257,000 in 1876 to 77,000 in 1892.

Legal Segregation

Existing customs of racial separation also expanded. During the 1870s, the Supreme Court opened the door to laws strengthening racial discrimination by ruling that the Fourteenth Amendment protected citizens' rights only against infringement by state governments, not by individuals, private businesses, or local governments. These rulings climaxed in 1883 when, in the *Civil Rights* cases, the Court struck down the 1875 Civil Rights Act, which prohibited segregation in facilities such as streetcars, theaters, and parks. Thus railroads, such as the Chesapeake & Ohio Railroad, could legally maintain discriminatory policies.

Plessy v. Ferguson Supreme Court ruling validating legal segregation; legalized separate facilities for blacks and whites as long as they were equal.

The Supreme Court also upheld legal segregation on a "separate but equal" basis in ***Plessy v. Ferguson*** (1896). This case began in 1892 when a New Orleans organization of African Americans chose Homer Plessy, a dark-skinned creole who was only one-eighth black (but considered black by Louisiana law), to sit in a whites-only railroad car. Plessy was arrested, and the appeal of his conviction reached the U.S. Supreme Court in 1896. The Court affirmed that a state law providing for separate facilities for the two races was reasonable because it preserved "public peace and good order." To the Court, a law separating the races did not necessarily "destroy the legal equality of the races." Although the ruling did not specify the phrase "separate but equal," it legalized separate facilities for black and white people as long as they were equal. In 1899, the Court legitimated school segregation in *Cumming v. County Board of Education*, until it was overturned by *Brown v. Board of Education* in 1954.

Link to "'Jim Crow' Street-Car Law Set to Catch Negroes," 1904

Segregation laws—known as Jim Crow laws—multiplied throughout the South, reminding African Americans of their inferior status. State and local statutes passed in the 1890s restricted blacks to the rear of streetcars, to separate public drinking fountains and toilets, and to separate sections of hospitals and cemeteries.

African American Activism

African American women and men challenged injustice. Some boycotted discriminatory businesses; others promoted "Negro enterprise." In 1898, Atlanta University professor John Hope urged blacks to become their own employers and support Negro Business Men's Leagues. Some blacks used higher education to elevate their status. In all-black teachers' colleges, men and women sought to expand opportunities for themselves and their race.

While disfranchisement pushed African American men from public life, African American women used domestic roles as mothers, educators, and moral guardians to uplift the race and seek improvements. Along with seeking the vote, they successfully lobbied southern governments for cleaner city streets, expanded charity services, and vocational education. While black women and white women sometimes united to achieve their goals, white women often sympathized with white men in supporting racial exclusion.

Woman Suffrage

Some women challenged male power structures by seeking the right to vote. An intensely religious woman, Frances Willard believed that (Christian) faith would empower women to uplift society. She urged women who joined the Woman's Christian Temperance Union to sign a pledge to abstain from alcohol to protect families from the evils of drink. But Willard also believed that the WCTU could best do the Lord's work if women could vote. Thus, at its 1884 convention, the WCTU passed a resolution deploring the "disenfranchisement of 12 million people who are citizens."

The more direct suffrage crusade was conducted by two organizations, the National Woman Suffrage Association (NWSA) and the American Woman Suffrage Association (AWSA). The NWSA, led by Elizabeth Cady Stanton and Susan B. Anthony, advocated women's rights in courts and workplaces as well as at the ballot box. The AWSA, led by former abolitionist Lucy Stone, focused narrowly on suffrage. The two groups merged in 1890 to form the National American Woman Suffrage Association with Stanton as president.

Anthony's argument for a constitutional amendment giving women the vote received little congressional support, with senators claiming suffrage would interfere with women's family obligations. Moreover, the women's suffrage campaign was tainted by racial intolerance. Many movement leaders espoused white superiority and accommodated racial prejudices to retain support from the AWSA's and NWSA's predominantly white, middle-class membership. Blacks who joined the WCTU had a separate Department of Colored Temperance. Also, leaders such as Anthony and Stanton felt resentment that the Fifteenth Amendment had enfranchised black men but not women. Many believed that "educated" white women should vote and that "illiterate" blacks should not.

Picture Research Consultants & Archives

Frances Willard became the second and best-known president of the national Woman's Christian Temperance Union (WCTU), founded in 1874. Beyond promoting abstinence from drinking alcohol, Willard and the WCTU also were involved in other reforms, including women's suffrage. In 1893, Willard took her crusade worldwide and became the first president of the International Council of Women. Here Willard's status is symbolized by her seat amid major American and British suffrage leaders, all officers of the World's WCTU.

Women did win partial victories. Between 1870 and 1910, eleven states (mostly in the West) legalized limited woman suffrage. By 1890, nineteen states allowed women to vote on school issues, and three granted suffrage on tax and bond issues. The right to vote in national elections awaited a later generation, but leaders such as Ida B. Wells, Susan B. Anthony, and Lucy Stone proved that women could be politically active even without the vote.

Agrarian Unrest and Populism

How did farmers' discontent crystallize in various movements in the late nineteenth century?

Economic inequity also sparked a mass movement. Despite rapid industrialization and urbanization in the Gilded Age, the United States remained an agrarian society with 64 percent of the population living in rural areas in 1890. The expression of farmers' discontent with economic hardship—a mixture of strident rhetoric, nostalgic dreams, and hardheaded egalitarianism—began in Grange organizations in the early 1870s. It accelerated when Farmers' Alliances formed in Texas in the late 1870s and spread across the South and Great Plains in the 1880s. The movement flourished where debt, bad weather, and insects demoralized struggling farmers and inspired visions of a cooperative, democratic society.

Hardship in the Midwest and West

In the Midwest, as growers cultivated more land, as mechanization boosted productivity, and as foreign competition increased, supplies of agricultural products exceeded national and worldwide demand. Prices for staple crops dropped steadily. A bushel of wheat that sold for $1.45 in 1866 brought only 80 cents in the mid-1880s and 49 cents by the mid-1890s. Meanwhile, transportation and storage fees remained high. To buy necessities and pay bills, farmers had to produce more. But the more they produced, the lower crop prices dropped (see Figure 17.1).

In Colorado, absentee capitalists seized control of transportation and water, and concentration of technology by large mining companies pushed out small firms. Charges of monopolistic behavior by railroads echoed among farmers, miners, and ranchers in Wyoming and Montana. In California, Washington, and Oregon, wheat and fruit growers found opportunities blocked by railroads' control of transportation and storage rates.

Grange Movement

With aid from Oliver H. Kelley, a U.S. Bureau of Agriculture employee, farmers organized in almost every state during the 1860s and 1870s, founding the Patrons of Husbandry—or the Grange—dedicated to improving economic and social conditions. By 1875 the Grange had twenty thousand branches and a million members. Strongest in the Midwest and South, Granges sponsored meetings and educational events to relieve the loneliness of rural life. Family oriented, Granges welcomed women's participation.

As membership flourished, Granges turned to economic and political action. Many members joined the **Greenback Labor Party**, formed in 1876 to advocate expanding the money supply by keeping "greenbacks"—paper money created by the

Greenback Labor Party
Advocated expanding the money supply through the government printing of money not backed by gold.

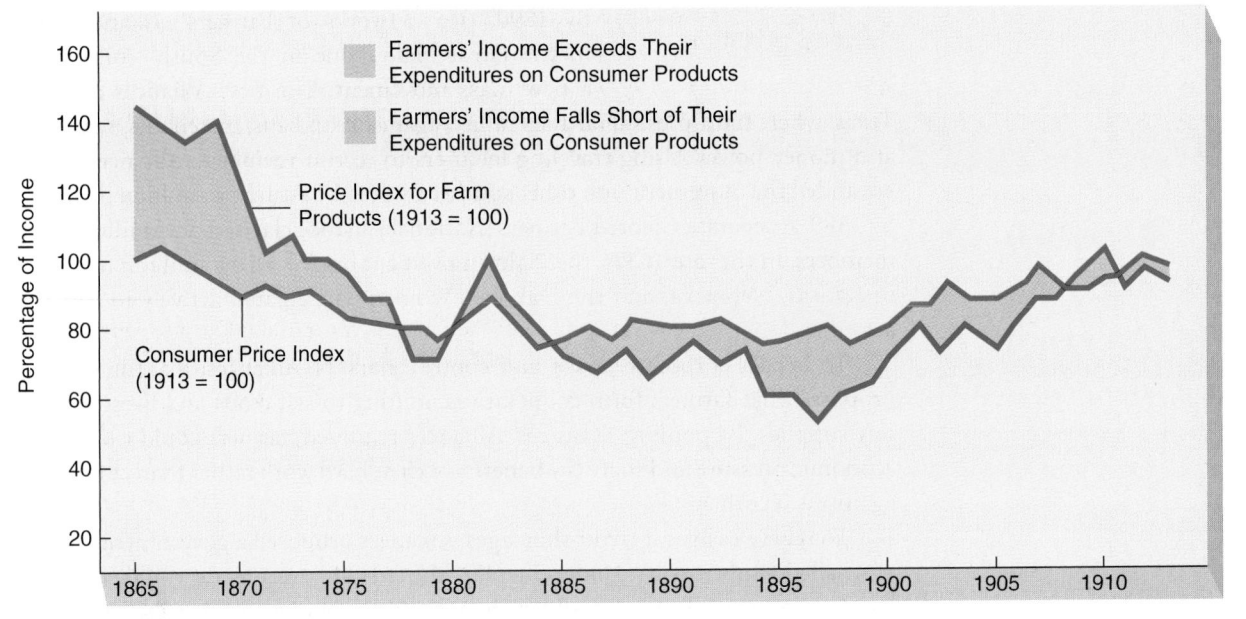

FIGURE 17.1
Consumer Prices and Farm Product Prices, 1865–1913
Until the late 1870s, in spite of falling farm prices, farmers were able to receive from their crops more income than they spent on consumer goods. But beginning in the mid-1880s, consumer prices leveled off and then rose, while prices for farm products continued to drop. As a result, farmers found it increasingly difficult to afford consumer goods, a problem that plagued them well into the twentieth century.

government during the Civil War—in circulation. Grange branches formed cooperative associations to buy supplies and market crops and livestock. A few Grangers ran farm implement factories and insurance companies. Most enterprises failed, however, because farmers lacked capital for large-scale buying and because large manufacturers and dealers undercut them.

In the late 1870s, Granges convinced states to establish agricultural colleges and pressed state legislatures for Granger laws to regulate transportation and storage rates. But in the 1886 *Wabash* case, the U.S. Supreme Court overturned Granger laws by denying states the power to regulate railroad rates. Disavowing party politics, Grangers did not challenge business interests within the two major parties. Their influence declined, and Granges became social organizations.

The White Hats

In the Southwest, migration of English-speaking ranchers onto pastureland used communally by Mecian farmers sparked sometimes violent resistance. In the late 1880s, a group calling itself Las Gorras Blancas, or White Hats, struggled to control formerly ancestral lands. In protest, they burned buildings, destroyed fences that Anglos had erected, and threatened the town of Las Vegas in New Mexico territory. However, they could not halt Anglos from legally buying and using public land. By 1900, many Hispanics had given up farming to work as agricultural laborers or migrate to cities.

Farmers' Alliances

By 1890, two networks of Farmers' Alliances—one in the Great Plains, one in the South—constituted a new mass movement. The first Alliances arose in Texas, where hard-pressed farmers rallied against crop liens, merchants, railroads, and money power. Using traveling lecturers to recruit members, Alliance leaders expanded the movement into other southern states, boasting two million members by 1889. A separate Colored Farmers' National Alliance claimed one million black members. In the late 1880s, the Plains movement organized two million members in Kansas, Nebraska, and the Dakotas. Women participated actively in Alliance activities.

To bypass corporate power and control markets, Alliances, like the Grange, proposed that farmers form cooperatives, uniting to sell crops and livestock and buy supplies. By pooling resources, Alliances reasoned, farmers could exert more economic pressure and share the benefits of their hard work rather than competing against each other.

To relieve cash and credit shortages, Alliances proposed a government aid system called a subtreasury. Under the plan, the federal government would construct warehouses where farmers could store nonperishable crops while awaiting higher market prices; the government would then loan farmers treasury notes amounting to 80 percent of the market price of stored crops. Farmers could use these notes to pay debts and make purchases. Once the crops were sold, farmers would repay the loans plus small interest and storage fees, thereby avoiding the exploitative crop lien system.

The subtreasury plan's second part would provide low-interest government loans to farmers to buy land. These loans, along with the treasury notes loaned to farmers who temporarily stored crops in government warehouses, would inject cash into the economy and encourage the kind of inflation that advocates hoped would raise crop prices without raising other prices.

Exhibited at the Chicago World's Fair of 1893, this cabin was the site of the first Farmers' Alliance meeting in Lampasas County, Texas. Using recruiters, rallies, and meetings replete with slogans like "We Are All Mortgaged But Our Votes," the organization voiced the grievances of rural America and laid the groundwork for formation of the Populist Party in the 1890s.

Private Collection/Picture Research Consultants & Archives

Problems in Achieving Alliance Unity

Had Farmers' Alliances been able to unite politically, they could have wielded formidable power; but racial voting restrictions weakened Alliance voter strength, and racism blocked acceptance of blacks by white Alliances. Some southern leaders, such as Georgia's Senator Tom Watson, tried to unite distressed black and white farmers, but poor whites held fast to prejudices. Many considered African Americans inferior and took comfort that there always would be people worse off than they were. Regional differences also prevented unity. Northern Alliances favored protective tariffs to keep out foreign grain, whereas white southerners wanted low tariffs to curb costs of imports. However, both favored railroad regulation, equitable taxation, currency reform, an end to alleged election frauds, and prohibition of landownership by foreign investors.

Rise of Populism

By 1890, farmers had elected several sympathetic officeholders, especially in the South, where Alliance allies won four governorships, eight state legislatures, forty-four seats in the House of Representatives, and three in the Senate. In the Midwest, Alliance candidates running on third-party tickets, such as the Greenback Party, won some victories in Kansas, Nebraska, and the Dakotas. Leaders crisscrossed the country to recruit support for a new party. In summer 1890, the Kansas Alliance held a "convention of the people" and nominated candidates who swept the state's fall elections. Formation of this People's Party, or **Populist Party**, gave a title to Alliance political activism. (Populism is the political doctrine that asserts the rights and powers of common people versus privileged elites.) By 1892, southern Alliance members joined northern counterparts in summoning a People's Party convention in Omaha, Nebraska, on July 4 to draft a platform and nominate a presidential candidate.

Populist Party "People's Party" that raised an agrarian-based, third-party challenge to the Republicans and Democrats and advocated for the rights of the common man.

Charging that inequality (between white classes) threatened to splinter society, the new party's platform declared, "The fruits of the toil of millions are boldly stolen to build up colossal fortunes for a few," and that "wealth belongs to him that creates it." It addressed three central sources of rural unrest: transportation, land, and money. Frustrated with weak regulation, Populists demanded government ownership of railroad and telegraph lines. The monetary plank called on the government to make more money available for farm loans and to restore unlimited coinage of silver. Other planks advocated a graduated income tax, direct election of U.S. senators, and a shorter workday. As its presidential candidate, the party nominated James B. Weaver of Iowa, a former Union general and supporter of an expanded money supply.

Populist Spokespeople

The Populist campaign featured dynamic personalities and rousing rhetoric. The Kansas plains rumbled with speeches by Mary Lease, who could allegedly "set a crowd hooting and harrahing at her will," and by "Sockless Jerry" Simpson, an unschooled but canny rural reformer who got his nickname after he ridiculed silk-stockinged wealthy people, causing a reporter to muse that Simpson probably never wore stockings. Minnesota's Ignatius Donnelly, pseudoscientist and writer of apocalyptic novels, became chief visionary of the northern plains, penning the

Russian Populism

Before American Populism, a different form of populism emerged in another largely rural country: Russia. Whereas American Populism came from the Alliance farm organizations, Russian populism was created by intellectuals seeking to educate peasants to agitate for social and economic freedom.

Russian society began to modernize in the mid-nineteenth century. Town governments were given control of local taxation, and education became more widespread. Perhaps most importantly, in 1861 Czar Alexander II signed an Edict of Emancipation, freeing Russian serfs (slaves attached to specific lands) and granting them compensation to buy land. Reforms progressed slowly, however, prompting some young, educated Russians called nihilists to press for radical reforms, including socialism. The reformers became known as *narodniki*, or populists, from *narod*, the Russian term for "peasant."

Narodniki envisioned a society of self-governing village communes, somewhat like the cooperatives proposed by American Farmers' Alliances. One leader, Peter Lavrov, believed intellectuals must get closer to the people and help them improve their lives. Russian populists believed only an uprising against the czar could realize their goals. When Alexander instituted repressive policies against the *narodniki* in the late 1870s, many turned to terrorism, culminating in Alexander II's assassination in 1881.

Russian peasants remained tied to tradition and could not abandon loyalty to the czar. Arrests and imprisonments after Alexander's assassination discouraged populists' efforts, and the movement declined. Nevertheless, populist ideas became the cornerstone of the Russian Revolution of 1917 and of subsequent Soviet social and political ideology.

Russian peasants, like American tenant farmers and owners of small landholdings, suffered from poverty and pressures of the expanded market economy. The plight of struggling Russian farm families stirred up empathy from young populist intellectuals, who adopted radical solutions that did not capture as much political fervor among farmers as American Populism did.

Bettmann/CORBIS

Omaha platform's thunderous language. The campaign also attracted opportunists, such as the one-eyed, sharp-tongued South Carolina senator "Pitchfork Ben" Tillman, who exploited agrarian resentments for their own political ends.

In the 1892 presidential election, Populist candidate James Weaver garnered 8 percent of the popular vote, majorities in four states, and twenty-two electoral votes. Not since 1856 had a third party done so well in its first national effort. Nevertheless, Populists were only successful in the West. The vote-rich Northeast ignored Weaver, and Alabama was the only southern state that gave Populists as much as one-third of its votes.

Still, Populism gave southern and western rural dwellers faith in a future of cooperation and democracy, as they looked toward the 1896 presidential election. Amid hardship and desperation, millions came to believe that a cooperative democracy in which government would ensure equal opportunity could overcome corporate power.

The Depression and Protests of the 1890s

Why did socialism fail to take hold in the United States amid the labor activism of the late nineteenth century?

In 1893, shortly before Grover Cleveland's second presidency began, the Philadelphia & Reading Railroad, once a thriving and profitable line, went bankrupt. Like other railroads, it had borrowed heavily to lay track and build stations and bridges. Overexpansion cut into profits, and the company was unable to pay its debts.

The same problem beset manufacturers. Output at McCormick farm machinery factories was nine times greater in 1893 than in 1879, but revenues had only tripled. The company bought more equipment and squeezed more work from fewer laborers, but it only increased debt and unemployment. Jobless workers could not pay their bills. Banks suffered when their customers defaulted. The failure of the National Cordage Company in May 1893 sparked a chain reaction of business and bank closings. By year's end, five hundred banks and sixteen hundred businesses had failed. Between 1893 and 1897, the nation suffered a staggering economic depression.

Nearly 20 percent of the labor force was jobless during the depression. Falling demand caused prices to drop between 1892 and 1895, but layoffs and wage cuts more than offset declining living costs. Many people could not afford basic necessities. The New York police estimated that twenty thousand homeless and jobless people roamed city streets.

Continuing Currency Problems

As the depression deepened, so did the currency dilemma. The Sherman Silver Purchase Act of 1890 committed the government to using treasury notes (silver certificates) to buy 4.5 million ounces of silver monthly. Recipients could redeem these certificates for gold, at the ratio of one ounce of gold for every sixteen ounces of silver. But a western mining boom increased silver supplies, causing its value to fall and prompting holders of silver certificates and greenback currency to exchange their notes for more valuable gold.

Consequently, the nation's gold reserves dwindled, falling below $100 million in early 1893.

Psychologically, if investors believed the country's gold reserves were disappearing, they would lose confidence in America's economic stability and refrain from investing. British capitalists, for example, owned $4 billion in American stocks and bonds and were likely to stop investing if dollars depreciated. The lower the gold reserve dropped, the more people rushed to redeem their money. Panic spread, causing more bankruptcies and unemployment.

To protect the gold reserve, President Cleveland called a special session of Congress to repeal the Sherman Silver Purchase Act. Repeal passed in late 1893, but the run on gold continued. In early 1895, reserves fell to $41 million, and, desperate, Cleveland accepted an offer of 3.5 million ounces of gold for $65 million worth of federal bonds from a banking syndicate led by financier J. P. Morgan. When the bankers resold the bonds, they made a $2 million profit. Cleveland claimed that he had saved the reserves, but discontented farmers, workers, silver miners, and some of Cleveland's Democratic allies saw only humiliation in the president's deal with big businessmen.

The deal between Cleveland and Morgan did not end the depression. After improving slightly in 1895, the economy plunged again. Farm income, declining since 1887, slid further; factories closed; banks restricted withdrawals. The tight money supply depressed housing construction, drying up jobs. Cities encouraged citizens to cultivate "potato patches" on vacant land to alleviate food shortages. Urban police stations filled up nightly with homeless people.

Consequences of Depression

In the late 1890s, gold discoveries in Alaska, good harvests, and industrial revival brought relief. But the downturn hastened the crumbling of the old economic system and emergence of a new one. The American economy expanded beyond sectional bases; when western farmers fell into debt, their depressed condition weakened railroads, farm-implement manufacturers, and banks in other regions. Moreover, the corporate consolidation that characterized the new business system tempted many companies to expand too rapidly. When the bubble burst in 1893, their reckless debts pulled other industries down with them.

A new global marketplace was emerging, forcing American farmers to contend with discriminatory transportation rates and falling crop prices at home, along with Canadian and Russian wheat growers, Argentine cattle ranchers, Indian and Egyptian cotton manufacturers, and Australian wool producers. Consequently, one country's economy affected that of other countries. With the glutted domestic market, American businessmen sought new markets abroad (see Chapter 19).

Depression-Era Protests

The depression exposed fundamental tensions in the industrial system. Technological and organizational changes had been widening the gap between employees and employers for half a century. Labor protest began with the railroad strikes of 1877. Their vehemence and support from working-class people raised fears that the United States would experience a popular uprising like the one in France in 1871, which briefly overturned the government and introduced communist principles. The 1886 Haymarket riot, prolonged 1892 strike at the Carnegie Homestead Steel plant, and labor violence among miners in the West heightened anxieties (see Chapter 16). In 1894, there were over thirteen hundred strikes and countless riots. Contrary to accusations of business leaders, few protesters were immigrant anarchists or communists. Rather, they were Americans who believed that in a democracy their voices should be heard.

Socialists

Small numbers of socialists participated in these confrontations. Some socialists believed that workers should control factories and businesses; others supported government ownership. All, however, opposed capitalism. Their ideas derived from Karl Marx (1818-1883), the German philosopher and father of communism, who contended that whoever controls the means of production determines how well people live. Marx wrote that industrial capitalism profits by paying workers less than the value of their labor and that mechanization and mass production alienate workers from their labor. According to Marx, only by abolishing the return on capital—profits—could labor receive its true value, possible only if workers owned the means of production. Marx predicted that workers worldwide would revolt and seize factories, farms, banks, and transportation lines. This revolution would establish a socialist order of justice and equality. Marx's vision appealed to some workers (even nonsocialists) because it promised independence and to some intellectuals because it promised to end class conflict and crass materialism.

In America, much of the movement was influenced by immigrants—first Germans, later Russian Jews, Italians, Hungarians, and Poles. It splintered into small groups, such as the Socialist Labor Party, which failed to attract the mass of laborers because it often focused on doctrine rather than workers' everyday needs. Nor could they rebut clergy and business leaders who celebrated opportunity, self-improvement, social mobility, and consumerism. Workers hoped that they or their children would benefit through education and acquisition of property or by becoming their own boss; they thus sought individual advancement rather than the betterment of all.

Eugene V. Debs

In 1894, a new and inspiring socialist leader emerged. The Indiana-born Eugene V. Debs headed the newly formed American Railway Union, which had carried out that year's strike against the Pullman Company. Jailed for defying the injunction against the strike, Debs read Karl Marx's works in prison. Once released, he became the leading spokesman for American socialism, combining visionary Marxism with Jeffersonian and Populist antimonopolism. Debs captivated audiences with attacks on the free-enterprise system. "Many of you think you are competing," he would lecture. "Against whom? Against Rockefeller? About as I would if I had a wheelbarrow and competed with the Santa Fe [railroad] from here to Kansas City." By 1900, the group—soon to be called the Socialist Party of America—was uniting around Debs.

Coxey's Army

In 1894, however, businessman Jacob Coxey from Massillon, Ohio, captured public attention. Coxey had believed that, to aid debtors, the government should issue $500 million of "legal tender" paper money and make low-interest loans to local governments, which would use the funds to pay unemployed men to build roads and other public works. He planned to publicize his scheme by leading a march from Massillon to Washington, D.C., gathering unemployed workers en route. "Coxey's Army" of about 200 left in March 1894. Hiking across Ohio into Pennsylvania, the marchers received food and housing in depressed industrial towns and rural villages and attracted additional recruits. A dozen similar processions from places such as Seattle, San Francisco, and Los Angeles also trekked eastward. Sore feet prompted some marchers to commandeer trains, but most marches were law-abiding.

Coxey's band of five hundred entered Washington, D.C., on April 30. The next day, the group, armed with "war clubs of peace," advanced to the Capitol. When Coxey and a few others vaulted a wall surrounding the grounds, mounted police routed the demonstrators. Police dragged Coxey away. As arrests and clubbings continued, Coxey's dream of a demonstration of four hundred thousand jobless workers dissolved. Like the strikes, the first people's march on Washington yielded to police muscle.

Unlike socialists, who wished to replace the capitalist system, Coxey's troops merely wanted more jobs and better living standards. Today, in an age of union contracts, regulation of business, and government-sponsored unemployment relief, their goals do not appear radical. The brutal reactions of officials, however, reveal how threatening dissenters like Coxey and Debs seemed to the existing social order.

Silver Crusade and the Election of 1896

How did Bryan's focus on free silver undermine his presidential campaign and the Populist Party?

Social protest and economic depression made the 1896 presidential election seem pivotal. Debates over money and power were climaxing as Democrats and Republicans battled to control Congress and the presidency. The key question, however, was whether voters would abandon old party loyalties for the Populist Party.

Free Silver

The Populist crusade against "money power" settled on the issue of silver, which many believed would solve the nation's complex ills. To them, coinage of silver symbolized an end to special privileges for the rich and return of government to the people by lifting struggling families out of debt, increasing the cash in circulation, and reducing interest rates.

As the 1896 election approached, Populists had to decide whether to join with sympathetic factions of the major parties, thus risking a loss of identity, or remain an independent third party. Except in mining areas of Rocky Mountain states, where free coinage of silver had strong support, Republicans were unlikely allies because their support for the gold standard and big business represented what Populists opposed.

Alliance with northern and western Democrats was more plausible since the party there retained vestiges of antimonopoly ideology and sympathy for a looser currency system, despite the influence of "gold Democrats," such as President Cleveland and Senator David Hill of New York. Linking with southern Democrats seemed less viable since candidates' failure to carry out their promises left southern farmers feeling betrayed. Whichever option they chose, Populists ensured that the 1896 election would be the most issue oriented since 1860.

Link to Populist Party Platform, 1896

Nomination of McKinley

Both major parties were divided. For a year, Ohio industrialist Marcus A. Hanna maneuvered to win the Republican nomination for Ohio's governor, William McKinley, and corralled enough delegates to succeed. The Republicans' only distress occurred when they adopted a platform supporting the gold standard, rejecting a prosilver stance proposed by Colorado senator Henry M. Teller. Teller, a party founder forty years earlier, left the convention in tears, taking a small group of silver Republicans with him.

During the Democratic convention, prosilver delegates wearing silver badges and waving silver banners paraded through the Chicago Amphitheatre. A *New York World* reporter remarked, "all the silverites need is a Moses." They found one in **William Jennings Bryan**.

William Jennings Bryan
Orator, anti-imperialist, champion of farm interests, and three-time Democratic presidential candidate.

William Jennings Bryan

Bryan arrived at the Democratic convention as a member of a contested Nebraska delegation. A former congressman whose support for coinage of silver annoyed President Cleveland, Bryan found the depression's impact on midwestern farmers distressing. Shortly after the convention seated Bryan, he joined the resolutions committee and helped write a platform calling for unlimited coinage of silver. Bryan's now-famous closing words ignited the delegates.

> Having behind us the producing masses of this nation and the world, supported by the commercial interests, the laboring interests, and the toilers everywhere, we will answer [the wealthy classes'] demand for a gold standard by saying to them: You shall not press down upon the brow of labor this crown of thorns, you shall not crucify mankind upon a cross of gold.

After that speech, it took five ballots to win Bryan the nomination, but the magnetic "Boy Orator" proved irresistible. In accepting the silverite goals of southerners and westerners and repudiating Cleveland's policies, the Democratic Party became more attractive to discontented farmers. But it alienated a minority gold wing, who withdrew and nominated their own candidate.

THE LOCKOUT IS ENDED; HE HOLDS THE KEY.

During the 1896 presidential campaign, Republicans depicted their candidate, William McKinley, as holding the key to prosperity for both the working man and the white-collar laborer, shown here raising their hats to the candidate. Republicans successfully made this economic theme— rather than the silver crusade of McKinley's unsuccessful opponent, William Jennings Bryan—the difference in the election's outcome.

Collection of Janice L. and David J. Frent/Corbis

Bryan's nomination presented the Populist Party convention with a dilemma. Should Populists join Democrats or nominate their own candidate? Some reasoned that supporting a separate candidate would split the anti-McKinley vote and guarantee a Republican victory. The convention compromised, first naming Tom Watson as its vice presidential nominee to preserve party identity (Democrats had nominated Maine shipping magnate Arthur Sewall) and then nominating Bryan for president.

The campaign, as Kansas journalist William Allen White observed, "took the form of religious frenzy." Bryan preached that "every great economic question is in reality a great moral question." Republicans countered Bryan's attacks on privilege by predicting chaos if he won. Hanna invited thousands of people to McKinley's home in Canton, Ohio, where the candidate plied them with homilies on moderation and prosperity, promising something for everyone. In an appeal to working-class voters, Republicans stressed the new jobs that a protective tariff would create.

Election Results

The election results revealed that the political standoff had ended. McKinley, symbol of urban and corporate ascendancy, beat Bryan by 600,000 popular votes and won in the electoral college by 271 to 176 (see Map 17.1). Bryan worked hard to rally the nation, but obsession with silver prevented Populists from building the urban-rural coalition that would have solidified their appeal. Urban workers, who might have benefited from Populist goals, feared that silver coinage would shrink the value of their wages. Labor leaders, such as the AFL's Samuel Gompers, would not commit fully because they viewed farmers as businessmen, not workers. And socialists denounced Populists as "retrograde" because they, unlike socialists, believed in free enterprise. Thus the Populist crusade collapsed. Although Populists and fusion candidates won a few state and congressional elections, the Bryan-Watson ticket of the Populist Party polled only 222,600 votes nationwide.

The McKinley Presidency

As president, McKinley reinforced his support of business by signing the Gold Standard Act (1900), requiring that all paper money be backed by gold. A seasoned politician, McKinley guided passage of record-high tariff rates as congressman in 1890. He accordingly supported the Dingley Tariff of 1897, which raised duties even higher. A believer in opening new markets abroad to sustain profits at home, McKinley encouraged imperialistic ventures in Latin America and the Pacific. Better times and victory in the Spanish-American War helped him beat Bryan again in 1900.

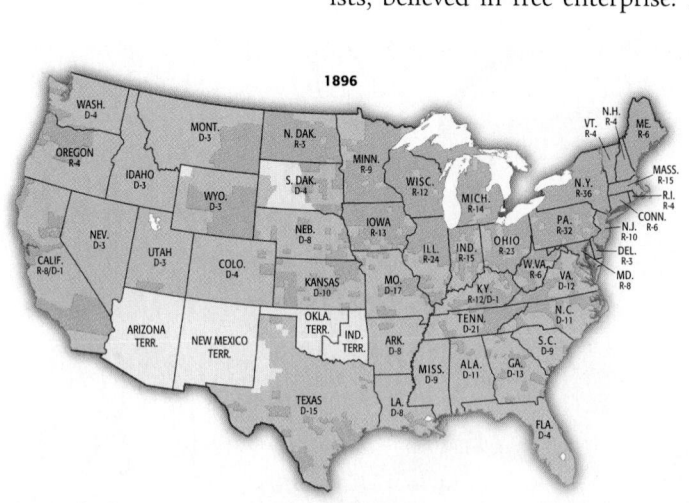

1896

Candidate (Party)	Electoral Vote		Popular Vote	
McKinley (Republican)	271	61%	7,102,246	51.1%
Bryan (Democrat)	176	39%	6,492,559	47.7%

Territories, Indian reservations, unsettled, etc.

MAP 17.1
Presidential Election, 1896

William Jennings Bryan had strong voter support in the South and West, but the numerically superior industrial states, plus California, created majorities for William McKinley. Source: Copyright © Cengage Learning 2015

Interpreting a Fairy Tale

The Wizard of Oz, released in 1939 and one of the all-time most popular movies, began as a work of juvenile literature penned by journalist L. Frank Baum in 1900. Originally titled *The Wonderful Wizard of Oz*, the story used memorable characters to create an adventurous quest.

Adults have long searched the story for hidden meanings. In 1964, scholar Henry M. Littlefield asserted that Baum intended to write a Populist parable illustrating the conditions of overburdened farmers and laborers. Dorothy, he theorized, symbolized the well-intentioned common person; the Scarecrow, the struggling farmer; the Tin Man, the industrial worker. Hoping for a better life, these friends, along with the Cowardly Lion (William Jennings Bryan), followed a yellow brick road (the gold standard) that led nowhere. The Emerald City was presided over by a wizard, who tried to be all things to all people, but Dorothy revealed him as a fraud. Dorothy was able to leave this muddled society and return to her simple Kansas farm family of Aunt Em and Uncle Henry by using her magical silver slippers (representing coinage of silver, though the movie made them red).

Subsequent theorists identified additional symbols, such as Oz being the abbreviation for ounces (oz.), the chief measurement of gold. The Wicked Witch of the East—who, Baum wrote, kept the little people (Munchkins) "in bondage,"—could represent industrial capitalism. But in 1983 historian William R. Leach asserted that Baum's tale actually was a celebration of urban consumer culture. Its language exalted the opulence of Emerald City, which to Leach resembled the "White City" of the Chicago World's Fair of 1893, and Dorothy's joviality symbolized the optimism of industrialization. Baum's career supported this new interpretation. Before writing, he designed display windows and was involved in theater—activities that gave him an appreciation of modern urban life.

The real legacy of *The Wonderful Wizard of Oz* has been its ability to provoke differing interpretations. Baum's fairy tale, the first truly American work of this sort, has bequeathed many fascinating images about the diversity and contradictions of American culture.

Summary

Though buffeted by special interests, Gilded Age politicians prepared the nation for the twentieth century. Laws encouraging economic growth with some principles of regulation, measures expanding government agencies while reducing crass patronage, and federal intervention in trade and currency issues evolved during the 1870s and 1880s, to the distress of Social Darwinists such as William Graham Sumner. Principles of police power clashed with those of due process, but many new laws set the stage for expanded government activism.

Nevertheless, the United States remained a nation of inconsistencies. Those who supported disfranchisement of African Americans and continued discrimination against women and racial minorities still dominated politics. People in power could not tolerate radical views like socialism or Populism, but many of these ideas continued to find supporters in the new century.

The 1896 election realigned national politics. The Republican Party, founded in the 1850s amid a crusade against slavery, became the majority party by emphasizing government aid to business, drawing the urban middle class, and playing down moralism. The Democratic Party miscalculated on the silver issue but held its support in the South and in urban political machines. At the national level, however, loyalties lacked their former potency. Suspicion of party politics increased, and voter participation declined. Populists tried to energize a third-party movement, but their success was fleeting.

Still, many Populist goals eventually were incorporated by the major parties, including regulation of railroads, banks, and utilities; shorter workdays; a variant of the sub-treasury plan; a graduated income tax; and direct election of senators. These reforms succeeded because various groups united behind them. Immigration, urbanization, and industrialization had transformed the United States into a pluralistic nation in which interest groups had to compromise. As the Gilded Age ended, business was still ascendant, and large segments of the population remained excluded from political and economic opportunity. But the winds of dissent and reform had begun to blow more strongly.

Chapter Review

The Nature of Party Politics

> How did factional disputes complicate party politics in the Gilded Age?

Most Democrats, who included immigrants and Catholics, sought to restrict government power, while most Republicans were native-born Protestants who believed government should play a bigger role in reforming society. Both parties were ultimately divided by factional rifts that kept them from simultaneously controlling the presidency and Congress or holding power in either for very long. Republican factions included Stalwarts and Half Breeds, who each sought to wield influence and award jobs to supporters, and Mugwumps, who thought only the most upstanding men should be allowed in government. Democrats split into white-supremacist southerners, immigrant and working-class advocates of urban political machines, businessmen who sought lower tariffs and the gold standard, and those who embraced free silver. Such divisions within parties made unity difficult.

The Activism of Government

> In what ways did the government become more activist—and expand its authority—in the late nineteenth century?

The government increasingly saw its role as ensuring public safety and setting standards for acceptable behavior throughout society. Laws more specifically banned certain behaviors—the mistreatment of children, for example—and regulated public safety, health, and morality, such as by setting maximum work hours

for women and children and prohibiting liquor sales and obscene literature. Efforts to regulate businesses, however, met with challenges under the due process provision of the Fifth Amendment to the Constitution, which, for example, railroads evoked to block efforts to regulate rates. The Supreme Court reaffirmed the federal government's authority to regulate interstate commerce, institutionalized when Congress passed the Interstate Commerce Act in 1887, complete with its own—and the nation's first—regulatory enforcement agency. The federal government also created the largest welfare commitment to that time via its pension program to Civil War veterans and their families, and broadened its powers over tariffs.

Presidential Initiative

> What actions did American presidents between 1877 and 1900 take to restore authority to their office?

After Andrew Johnson's impeachment and the scandals plaguing both the Grant administration and the 1876 election, the presidency was tarnished. Presidents Rutherford Hayes (1877–1881), James Garfield (1881), Chester Arthur (1881–1885), Grover Cleveland (1885–1889 and 1893–1897), Benjamin Harrison (1889–1893), and William McKinley (1897–1901) sought to bring integrity back to federal government through various legislative initiatives. They all supported civil service (and its expansion) as a means to end the corruption of the spoils system. With varying success, they addressed currency, tariffs, railroad regulation, and labor unrest.

Discrimination and Disfranchisement

 What legal means were used to discriminate against newly enfranchised African Americans in the decades following the Civil War?

To keep blacks from voting, southern leaders instituted measures such as poll taxes, which most blacks could not afford, and literacy tests. These measures were upheld in the Supreme Court, which noted that the Fifteenth Amendment could only prohibit states from denying the vote based on "race, color, or previous condition of servitude," but could not control the local election process. Similarly, Jim Crow, or segregation laws, confined African Americans to separate areas in public places such as streetcars, hospitals, and parks, thereby deliberately reminding them of their inferior status. These laws were upheld by the Supreme Court in *Plessy v. Ferguson*, which permitted statesto legally segregate on a "separate but equal" basis. Violence against African Americans—particularly lynching—provided a reminder of the extremes of white racism and hostility.

Agrarian Unrest and Populism

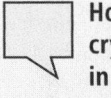 **How did farmers' discontent crystallize in various movements in the late nineteenth century?**

As farm prices dropped, farmers found it increasingly difficult to earn a living from their land. Those conditions were made worse by the fact that as smallholders, most could not compete with large firms, which could negotiate lower costs for transportation and supplies by virtue of their size. In response, farmers founded local organizations called Granges in the 1860s and 1870s, partly as social clubs and partly to enable them to join forces in cooperatives where they could get the same competitive advantage as larger firms. Granges declined in the late 1870s, replaced a decade later by Farmers' Alliances, which rallied against crop liens, merchants, railroads, and money power. Along with cooperatives, Alliances sought a government aid system called a subtreasury that they hoped would provide low-interest loans to farmers seeking to buy land and assist farmers in warehousing crops until market prices increased. By 1890, farmers allied politically, helping to form the Populist Party and elect candidates representing their interests.

The Depression and Protests of the 1890s

 Why did socialism fail to take hold in the United States amid the labor activism of the late nineteenth century?

The depression and thousands of strikes beginning with the 1877 railroad strike revealed general worker dissatisfaction that certainly created the conditions ripe for socialism to flourish, particularly once its charismatic leader Eugene V. Debs came to the fore in the 1890s. But American socialists could not agree on how best to implement Marxist strategies for worker control of the means of production and the end of capitalism's inequities. Socialism was also thwarted by that distinctly American celebration of social mobility and individual achievement. While workers found some aspects of socialism attractive, their ultimate aim was individual advancement, which they were unwilling to sacrifice for the greater good of all workers.

The Silver Crusade and the Election of 1896

 How did Bryan's focus on free silver undermine his presidential campaign and the Populist Party?

Populists embraced the issue of silver because they believed it would end special privileges for the rich by lifting mainstream Americans from debt, increasing the money in circulation, and lowering interest rates. Populists fused these ideas to the Democratic Party by joining forces with them behind William Jennings Bryan for president in 1896. Bryan was singularly focused on silver, but this cost him votes from urban workers, who feared silver coinage would cut their wages. Labor leaders equated farmers with businessmen, and as such, could not join forces with Populists on this issue. Bryan received only 222,600 votes nationwide, and while Populists continued to influence elections, the party itself collapsed.

Suggestions for Further Reading

Edward L. Ayers, *The Promise of the New South: Life After Reconstruction* (1992)

Jean Baker, *Sisters: The Lives of America's Suffragists* (2005)

Glenda Elizabeth Gilmore, *Gender and Jim Crow: Women and the Politics of White Supremacy in North Carolina, 1896–1920* (1996)

Steven Hahn, *A Nation Under Our Feet: Black Political Struggles in the Rural South, from Slavery to the Great Migration* (2003)

Michael Kazin, *The Populist Persuasion: An American History* (1995)

Jean V. Matthews, *The Rise of the New Woman: The Women's Movement in America, 1875–1930* (2003)

Nick Salvatore, *Eugene V. Debs: Citizen and Socialist* (1992)

The Progressive Era

18

1895-1920

What Ben Lindsey saw made him furious. As a young Colorado lawyer in the 1890s, a judge asked him to defend two boys, about twelve years old, accused of burglary. The boys had been imprisoned for sixty days without a trial and did not understand what the word *burglary* meant or how the justice system worked. Visiting them in jail, Lindsey found the youngsters playing poker with two older cellmates, a safecracker and a horse thief. Outraged that children were housed with hardened criminals, Lindsey later wrote, "Here were two boys, neither of them serious enemies of society, who were about to be convicted of burglary and have felony records.... I had made up my mind to smash the system that meant so much injustice to youth."

In 1901, Lindsey ran for county judge and began fighting for juvenile welfare. He spoke and wrote extensively about protecting children from criminal prosecution, abusive labor practices, and burdens of poverty. He and his wife, Henrietta, promoted a separate juvenile court system and aid to families with children at risk of becoming lawbreakers. They wrote reform laws adopted by many states and countries. The Lindseys' efforts to abolish injustice showed both compassion and middle-class bias, as a part of a broader movement seeking solutions to modern American social and economic problems.

During the 1890s, economic depression, labor violence, political upheaval, and foreign entanglements shook the nation. Numerous Americans continued to suffer from poverty and injustice. Some critics regarded industrialists as monsters who controlled markets and prices to maximize profits. Others believed government was corroded by bosses who abused power to enrich themselves. Tensions created by urbanization and industrialization fragmented society into conflicting interest groups.

By 1900, the previous decade's political tumult had calmed, and economic depression subsided. The nation emerged victorious from a war against Spain (see Chapter 19), and an era of new political leaders, including Theodore Roosevelt and Woodrow Wilson, was dawning. A sense of renewal both intensified anxiety

Chapter Outline

The Varied Progressive Impulse
National Associations and Foreign Influences | The New Middle Class and Muckrakers | Upper-Class Reformers | Settlement Houses | Working-Class Reformers | The Social Gospe | Socialists | Southern and Western Progressivism | Opponents of Progressivism

LINKS TO THE WORLD *Toynbee Hall, London*

Government and Legislative Reform
Restructuring Government | Labor Reform | Prohibition | Controlling Prostitution

New Ideas in Social Institutions
John Dewey and Progressive Education | Growth of Colleges and Universities | Progressive Legal Thought | Social Science | Eugenics

Challenges to Racial and Sexual Discrimination
Continued Discrimination for African Americans | Booker T. Washington and Self-Help | W. E. B. Du Bois and the "Talented Tenth" | Society of American Indians | "The Woman Movement" | Women's Clubs | Feminism | Margaret Sanger's Crusade | Woman Suffrage

VISUALIZING THE PAST *Heavyweight Boxing Champion Jack Johnson as Race Hero*

Theodore Roosevelt and Revival of the Presidency
Theodore Roosevelt | Regulation of Trusts | Pure Food and Drug Laws | Race Relations | Conservation | Gifford Pinchot |

over continuing problems and raised hopes that democracy could be reconciled with capitalism.

Between 1895 and 1920, a complex reform campaign emerged to renovate or restore American society, values, and institutions. By the 1910s, various reformers were calling themselves Progressives; in 1912, they formed their own political party. Historians have used the term *Progressivism* to refer to the era's spirit, while disagreeing over its meaning and over who actually was a Progressive.

The reform impulse had many sources. Industrial capitalism created awesome technology, unprecedented productivity, and abundant consumer goods. But it also brought harmful over-production, monopolies, labor strife, and destruction of natural resources. Burgeoning cities facilitated the distribution of goods and services, but also bred poverty, disease, and crime. Rising immigration and a new professional class reconfigured the social order. And the depression of the 1890s forced leading citizens to realize what working people already knew: America's central promise of equality of opportunity was elusive.

Middle-class reformers organized around three goals. First, they sought to end abuses of power by making trust-busting, consumers' rights, and good government compelling political issues. Second, Progressives like Ben Lindsey wished to supplant corrupt power with humane institutions, such as schools, courts, and medical clinics. They asserted that society had responsibility and power to improve individual lives and that government must protect the common good and elevate public interest above self-interest. They challenged entrenched views on women's roles, race relations, education, legal and scientific thought, and morality. Third, Progressives wanted to entrust experts who would end wasteful competition and promote social and economic order. Just as corporations applied scientific management to achieve economic efficiency, Progressives advocated expertise and planning to achieve social and political efficiency.

Progressives believed in humankind's ability to create a better world. Rising incomes, new educational opportunities, and increased availability of goods and services inspired confidence that social improvement would follow. Judge Lindsey expressed the Progressive creed when he wrote, "In the end the people are bound to do the right thing, no matter how much they fail at times."

As you read this chapter, keep the following questions in mind:

- **What were the major characteristics of Progressivism?**

- **In what ways did Progressive reform succeed, and in what ways did it fail?**

- **How did women and racial minorities challenge previous ways of thinking about American society?**

Chronology

1895	Booker T. Washington gives Atlanta Compromise speech
	National Association of Colored Women founded
1898	*Holden v. Hardy* upholds limits on miners' working hours
1901	McKinley assassinated; T. Roosevelt assumes presidency
1904	*Northern Securities* case dissolves railroad trust
1905	*Lochner v. New York* removes limits on bakers' working hours
1906	Hepburn Act tightens Interstate Commerce Commission (ICC) control over railroads
	Meat Inspection Act passed
	Pure Food and Drug Act passed
1908	*Muller v. Oregon* upholds limits on women's working hours
1909	National Association for the Advancement of Colored People (NAACP) founded

1910	Mann-Elkins Act reinforces ICC powers
	White Slave Traffic Act (Mann Act) prohibits transportation of women for "immoral purposes"
	Taft fires Pinchot
1911	Society of American Indians founded
1913	Sixteenth Amendment ratified, legalizing income tax
	Seventeenth Amendment ratified, providing for direct election of senators
	Underwood Tariff institutes income tax
	Federal Reserve Act establishes central banking system
1914	Federal Trade Commission created to investigate unfair trade practices
	Clayton Anti-Trust Act outlaws monopolistic business practices
1919	Eighteenth Amendment ratified, establishing prohibition of alcoholic beverages
1920	Nineteenth Amendment ratified, giving women the vote in federal elections

The Varied Progressive Impulse

How did Progressive reform cut across class lines?

Progressive reformers addressed decades-old issues in a new political climate. After the heated election of 1896, party loyalties eroded and voter turnout declined. In northern states, voter participation in presidential elections dropped from the 1880s level of 80 percent to under 60 percent by 1912. In southern states, where poll taxes and literacy tests prevented most African American and many poor white males from voting, it fell below 30 percent. New interest groups—championing their own causes—gained influence.

National Associations and Foreign Influences

Many formerly local organizations became national after 1890. These included professional associations, such as the American Bar Association; women's organizations, such as the National American Woman Suffrage Association; issue-oriented groups, such as the National Consumers League; civic-minded clubs, such as the National Municipal League; and minority-group associations, such as the National Negro Business League and the Society of American Indians. Such groups made politics more fragmented and issue focused than in earlier eras.

Some reform ideas were introduced by Americans who had encountered them while studying in England, France, and Germany; others, by foreigners visiting the United States. Americans borrowed from England the settlement house, in which reformers lived among and aided the urban poor, and workers' compensation for victims of industrial accidents. Other reforms, such as old-age insurance, subsidized workers' housing, and rural reconstruction, were also adopted in America.

The New Middle Class and Muckrakers

Progressive goals—ending abuse of power, protecting the welfare of all classes, reforming institutions, and promoting social efficiency—existed throughout society. But a new middle class in the professions of law, medicine, engineering, social service, religion, teaching, and business formed an important reform vanguard. Offended by corruption and immorality in business and government, they determined to apply the rational techniques of their professions to social problems. They also believed they could create a unified nation by "Americanizing" immigrants and Indians through education stressing middle-class customs.

Progressive views were voiced by journalists whom Theodore Roosevelt dubbed **muckrakers** (after a character in the Puritan allegory *Pilgrim's Progress,* who, rather than looking heavenward at beauty, looked downward and raked the muck). Muckrakers fed public tastes for scandal by exposing social, economic, and political wrongs. Investigative articles in popular magazines attacked adulterated foods, fraudulent insurance, prostitution, and political corruption. Lincoln Steffens hoped his exposés of bosses' misrule in *McClure's* would inspire reform. Other celebrated muckraking works included Upton Sinclair's *The Jungle* (1906), exposing outrages of the meatpacking industry, and Ida M. Tarbell's disparaging history of Standard Oil (first published in *McClure's,* 1902–1904).

muckrakers Journalists who wrote articles exposing urban political corruption and corporate wrongdoing.

Progressives advocated nonpartisan elections to prevent fraud and bribery bred by party loyalties. To make officeholders more responsible, they urged adoption of the initiative, which permitted voters to propose new laws; the referendum, which enabled voters to accept or reject a law; and the recall, which allowed voters to remove offending officials and judges from office.

Upper-Class Reformers

The Progressive spirit also stirred some businessmen and wealthy women. Executives like Alexander Cassatt of the Pennsylvania Railroad supported some government regulation and political restructuring to protect their interests from more radical reformers. Others, like E. A. Filene, founder of a Boston department store, were humanitarians who worked for social justice. Business-dominated organizations like the U.S. Chamber of Commerce thought that running schools, hospitals, and local government like efficient businesses would stabilize society. Elite women financed settlement houses and organizations like the Young Women's Christian Association (YWCA), which aided unmarried working women.

Settlement Houses

Young, educated, middle-class women and men worked to bridge the gap between social classes by living in inner-city settlement houses. Residents envisioned them as places where people could mitigate modern problems through education, art, and reform. Between 1886 and 1910, over 400 settlements were established, mostly in big cities, sponsoring activities such as English-language classes, kindergartens and nurseries, health clinics, vocational training, playgrounds, and art exhibits. The vanguard of Progressivism, settlement house workers backed housing and labor reform, offered meeting space to unions, and served as school nurses, juvenile probation officers, and teachers.

Though men helped initiate the settlement movement, the most influential participants were women. Jane Addams and Florence Kelley of Chicago's Hull House settlement, Lillian Wald of New York's Henry Street settlement, and Vida Scudder of Boston's Denison House broadened traditional female roles and used settlement work as a springboard to larger reform roles. Kelley's investigations into the exploitation of child labor prompted Illinois governor John Altgeld to appoint her state factory inspector; she later founded the National Consumers League. And Addams's efforts for world peace garnered her the Nobel Peace Prize in 1931.

Working-Class Reformers

Vital elements of what became modern American liberalism derived from working-class urban experiences. By 1900, many urban workers were pressing for bread-and-butter reforms such as safe factories, shorter workdays, workers' compensation, protection of child and women laborers, better housing, and a more equitable tax structure. Politicians who trained in machine politics tended to support political bosses, supposedly the enemies of reform. Yet bossism was not necessarily incompatible with humanitarianism. "Big Tim" Sullivan, an influential boss in New York's Tammany Hall machine, said he supported shorter workdays for women because "we ought to help these gals by giving 'em a law which will prevent 'em from being broken down while they're still young." As protectors of individual liberty, those representing the working-class opposed prohibition, Sunday closing laws, civil service, and nonpartisan elections, but often joined with other reformers to pass laws promoting social welfare.

The Social Gospel

Social Gospel Movement launched in the 1870s that stressed that true Christianity commits men and women to fight social injustice wherever it exists.

Much of Progressive reform rested on religious underpinnings. A movement known as the **Social Gospel**, led by Protestant ministers Walter Rauschenbusch, Washington Gladden, and Charles Sheldon, countered cutthroat capitalism by interjecting Christian churches into worldly matters, such as arbitrating industrial harmony and improving conditions of the poor. Believing that helping others provided the way to individual salvation and created God's kingdom on earth, Social Gospelers governed their lives by asking, "What would Jesus do?"

Others took secular pathways. Some tried to assimilate immigrants and Indians by expanding educational, economic, and cultural opportunities. But imposing their values on people of different cultures undermined their efforts. Working-class Catholic and Jewish immigrants, for example, sometimes rejected the Americanization efforts of Social Gospelers and resented middle-class reformers' interference in their child rearing.

Socialists

Disillusioned immigrant intellectuals, industrial workers, former Populists, and women's rights activists turned to socialism. They wanted the United States

Toynbee Hall, London

The settlement house movement, one of the Progressive Era's most idealized undertakings, owed much to Toynbee Hall in London, England. During the late nineteenth century, British middle-class university graduates began to feel uneasy about industrialization's failure to provide adequate living conditions for the urban working class. In 1884, Anglican clergyman Samuel Barnett and his wife Henrietta founded a residence in the London slums, where college students could live among working people and help them overcome poverty. The Barnetts named the settlement Toynbee Hall after their deceased friend, historian Arnold Toynbee. Toynbee Hall combined a religious mission to serve others with a scientific way of allaying class conflict through education and social welfare programs.

London and the nearby universities of Oxford and Cambridge at this time were destinations for young, idealistic Americans. Several took up temporary residence at Toynbee Hall, then returned to the United States to establish similar reform centers. Practically every Progressive Era U.S. settlement house founder was directly influenced by Toynbee Hall. Jane Addams, cofounder of Chicago's Hull House in 1889, visited Toynbee Hall in 1887 and called Hull House a "Toynbee Hall experiment." Vida Scudder, a Smith College graduate, undertook graduate studies at Oxford, and, influenced by Toynbee Hall, founded settlements in New York and Boston. In 1893, George Hodges opened Kingsley House in Pittsburgh after studying settlements in England.

More women participated in American settlements than in British, mainly because many were graduates of new women's colleges established in the United States between the 1870s and 1890s. Also, since funding came from outside donors, American settlements had more of a quality of professionalism than British settlements, where residents were normally unpaid volunteers. With the United States' growing ethnic and racial diversity, American settlements more explicitly adopted assimilation. Finally, British settlement workers accepted social distinctions, while Americans tried harder to improve the social status of the working class.

TOYNBEE·HALL·Commercial·Street·Whitechapel·London·E·   Mʳ E Hoole ·FRIBA·ARCHITECT·

Toynbee Hall, illustration from 'The Builder', February 14th, 1885 (litho), English School, (19th century)/Private Collection/The Bridgeman Art Library

Founded in 1884 and located in a working-class district in East London, the settlement of Toynbee Hall attracted graduates from Oxford and Cambridge universities who wished to live among impoverished industrial laborers, learn from them, and improve their conditions. The effort inspired young American social reformers to launch similar projects in American cities.

to follow the example of Germany, England, and France, where the government sponsored such socialist goals as low-cost housing, workers' compensation, old-age pensions, public ownership of municipal services, and labor reform. By 1912, the Socialist Party of America claimed 150,000 members and 700,000 subscribers to its newspaper *Appeal to Reason*.

Politically, socialists united behind Eugene V. Debs, the American Railway Union organizer who drew nearly 100,000 votes as Socialist Party presidential candidate in 1900. A spellbinding orator who appealed to urban immigrants and western farmers alike, Debs won 400,000 votes in 1904 and 900,000 in 1912, at the pinnacle of his and his party's career. Although Debs and other socialist leaders did not always agree on tactics, they made compelling overtures to reformers.

While some Progressives joined the Socialist Party, most reformers favored capitalism too much to want to overthrow it. Municipal ownership of public utilities represented their limit. Some AFL unions supported socialist goals and candidates, but many unions opposed reforms like unemployment insurance because it would increase taxes. Moreover, private real-estate interests opposed government intervention in housing, and manufacturers fought socialism by blacklisting militant laborers.

Southern and Western Progressivism

Progressive reform in the South included the same goals as in the North—railroad and utility regulation, factory safety, pure food and drug legislation, and moral reform. The South also pioneered some political reforms: the direct primary originated in North Carolina; the city commission plan arose in Galveston, Texas; and the city manager plan began in Staunton, Virginia.

In the West, several politicians championed regulation, putting the region at the forefront of campaigns to expand federal and state government functions. Nevada's Progressive senator Francis Newlands advocated national planning and federal control of water resources. California governor Hiram Johnson fought for direct primaries, regulation of child and women's labor, workers' compensation, a pure food and drug act, and educational reform.

In western states, women could vote on state and local matters but often women's reform efforts took place outside politics, in racially distinct projects. White women crusaded against child labor, founded social service organizations, and challenged unfair wages. African American women, as homemakers and religious leaders—which whites found more acceptable than political activism—advocated for cleaner streets, better education, and health reforms.

Opponents of Progressivism

It would be incorrect to assume that a Progressive spirit captivated all of American society between 1895 and 1920. Large numbers of people, heavily represented in Congress, disliked government interference in economic affairs and found no fault with existing power structures. They feared that government programs undermined the initiative and competition necessary to a free-market system. Further, tycoons like J. P. Morgan and John D. Rockefeller insisted that progress would result only from maintaining the profit incentive and an unfettered economy.

Moreover, Progressives were not always "progressive." Their attempts to Americanize immigrants reflected prejudice as well as naiveté. California governor Hiram Johnson promoted discrimination against Japanese Americans, and most southern governors—progressive or not—rested their power on appeals to white supremacy. In the South, the disfranchisement of blacks meant that electoral reforms affected only whites. Settlement houses in northern cities kept blacks and whites apart in separate programs and buildings.

Progressive reformers generally occupied the center of the ideological spectrum, believing on one hand that laissez-faire was obsolete and on the other that a radical departure from free enterprise was dangerous. Like Thomas Jefferson, they expressed faith in the will of the people; like Alexander Hamilton, they desired strong central government.

Government and Legislative Reform

According to Progressives, what was the government's role in improving society?

Mistrust of tyranny had traditionally prompted Americans to believe that democratic government should be small, interfere in private affairs only in unique circumstances, and withdraw when balance was restored. This viewpoint weakened in the late 1800s when economic problems seemed to overwhelm individual effort. Corporations pursued government aid and protection. Discontented farmers sought government regulation of railroads and other monopolistic businesses. City dwellers, accustomed to favors from political machines, expected government to act on their behalf. Before 1900, state governments were concerned largely with railroads and economic growth; the federal government focused primarily on tariffs and currency. After 1900, public opinion, roused by muckraking media, influenced change.

Restructuring Government

Middle-class Progressive reformers rejected the laissez-faire principle of government, reasoning that in a complex industrial age, public authority needed to counteract inefficiency and exploitation. But to tap this power, activists would have to reclaim government from politicians whose greed they believed soiled the democratic system.

Prior to the Progressive Era, reformers attacked city government corruption through such structural reforms as civil service, nonpartisan elections, and scrutiny of public expenditures. After 1900, campaigns promoting efficiency resulted in city-manager and commission forms of government, in which urban officials were chosen for professional expertise rather than for political connections.

At the state level, Progressives supported several skillful governors. Perhaps the most dynamic, Wisconsin's Robert M. La Follette, began as a small-town lawyer and rose through the state Republican Party to become governor in 1900. There, he initiated direct primaries, more equitable taxes, and railroad regulation. After three terms as governor, La Follette became a U.S. senator. "Battling Bob" displayed a rare ability to approach reform scientifically while proclaiming that his goal was "not to 'smash' corporations, but to drive them out of politics."

Crusades against corrupt politics made the system more democratic. Political reformers achieved a major goal in 1913 with adoption of the

Seventeenth Amendment to the Constitution, which provided for direct election of U.S. senators, replacing election by state legislatures. But party bosses were still able to control elections, and special-interest groups spent large sums to influence voting.

Labor Reform

Prodded by middle-class/working-class coalitions, many states enacted factory inspection laws, and by 1916 nearly two-thirds of states required compensation for victims of industrial accidents. Under pressure from the National Child Labor Committee, nearly every state set a minimum age for employment (varying from twelve to sixteen) and limited hours that children could work. Labor laws were imperfect, however. They seldom provided for the close inspection of factories that enforcement required. And families needing extra income falsified children's ages to employers.

Several groups also united to achieve restricted working hours for women and aided retirees. After the Supreme Court, in *Muller v. Oregon*, upheld Oregon's ten-hour workday limit in 1908, more states passed laws protecting female workers. In 1914, the American Association for Old Age Security secured old-age pensions in Arizona. Judges struck down the law, but demand for pensions continued, and in the 1920s many states enacted such laws.

Prohibition

Reformers did not always agree about whether laws should regulate behavior such as drinking and sexual conduct. For example, the **Anti-Saloon League**, formed in 1893, allied with the Woman's Christian Temperance Union (founded in 1874) to publicize alcoholism's role in health and family problems. The league successfully shifted attention from the immorality of drunkenness to breaking the alleged link between drinking and accidents, poverty, and poor productivity. The war on saloons prompted many states and localities to restrict liquor consumption. By 1900, one-fourth of the nation's population lived in "dry" communities prohibiting liquor sales.

Anti-Saloon League
Advocacy group founded in 1893 that sought to ban alcohol by publicizing its harmful effects on families and individuals and its link to accidents and health problems.

Still, alcohol consumption increased with the influx of immigrants whose cultures included social drinking, convincing prohibitionists that a nationwide ban was necessary. In 1918 Congress passed the **Eighteenth Amendment** (ratified in 1919 and implemented in 1920), outlawing the manufacture, sale, and transportation of intoxicating liquors. Not all prohibitionists were Progressive reformers, and vice versa. Nevertheless, the Eighteenth Amendment symbolized the Progressive goal to protect family and workplace through legislation.

Eighteenth Amendment
Amendment to the Constitution that established national prohibition of alcohol.

Controlling Prostitution

Moral outrage erupted when muckraking journalists charged that international gangs were kidnapping women and forcing them into prostitution, a practice called "white slavery." Accusations were exaggerated, but they alarmed moralists who falsely perceived a link between immigration and prostitution, and who feared that prostitutes were producing genetically inferior children. Reformers prodded governments to investigate and pass corrective legislation. The Chicago Vice Commission undertook a "scientific" survey of dance halls and illicit sex, and published its findings as *The Social Evil in Chicago* in 1911. The report concluded that poverty, gullibility, and desperation drove women into prostitution.

Reformers believed they could attack prostitution by punishing those who promoted and practiced it. In 1910, Congress passed the White Slave Traffic Act (Mann Act), prohibiting interstate and international transportation of a woman for immoral purposes. By 1915, nearly every state outlawed brothels and solicitation of sex. Such laws ostensibly protected young women from exploitation, but in reality they failed to address the more serious problem of sexual violence that women suffered at the hands of family members, presumed friends, and employers.

Like prohibition, the Mann Act reflected the sentiment that government could improve behavior by restricting it. Middle-class reformers believed the source of evil was not human nature but the social environment. Laws could help create a heaven on earth, although working classes resented such attempts to control them. Thus, when Chicagoans voted on a referendum to make their city dry before the Eighteenth Amendment was passed, three-fourths of the city's immigrant voters opposed it, and the measure was defeated.

New Ideas in Social Institutions

What was the impact of Progressive education reforms?

Progressive reformers' preoccupation with efficiency and scientific management infiltrated education, law, religion, and social science. Darwin's theory of evolution challenged beliefs in a God-created world, immigration created complex social diversity, and technology made old production habits obsolete. Professionals grappled with how to embrace newness yet preserve the best from the past.

John Dewey and Progressive Education

As late as 1870, when families needed children to do farmwork, Americans attended school only a few months a year for four years. By 1900, however, the urban-industrial economy and its expanding middle class advanced childhood as a special life stage, sheltering youngsters from society's dangers and promoting their physical and emotional growth. That meant ensuring that youngsters were exposed to age-appropriate educational materials and activities.

Educators argued that expanded schooling produced better citizens and workers. Consequently, in the 1870s and 1880s, state laws required children to attend school to age fourteen. The number of public high schools grew from five hundred in 1870 to ten thousand in 1910. By 1900, educational reformers, such as philosopher John Dewey, asserted that schools needed to prepare children for a modern world by making personal development the focus of curriculum.

Progressive education, based on Dewey's *The School and Society* (1899) and *Democracy and Education* (1916), stressed that learning should involve real-life problems and that children needed to learn from experience, not by rote memorization. Dewey and his wife, Alice, tested these ideas in their Laboratory School at the University of Chicago.

Growth of Colleges and Universities

A more practical curriculum also drove higher education reform. Previously, American colleges resembled their European counterparts in training a select few for careers in law, medicine, and religion. But in the late 1800s, institutions of higher learning multiplied via state and federal grants. Between 1870 and 1910, American colleges and universities grew from 563 to nearly 1,000. Curricula broadened to make learning more appealing and keep pace with technological and social changes. Harvard University, under President Charles W. Eliot, pioneered new teaching methods and substituted electives for required courses. Many schools considered athletics vital to a student's growth, and men's intercollegiate sports became a permanent feature.

Southern states created segregated colleges for blacks and whites. Aided by land grant funds, such schools as Alabama Agricultural and Mechanical University (A&M) opened their doors. "Separate" was a more accurate description of these institutions than "equal." Although African Americans continued to suffer from inferior educational opportunities, they found intellectual stimulation in all-black colleges and used education to help uplift their race.

Between 1890 and 1910, the number of women attending colleges and universities swelled from 56,000 to 140,000. Roughly 106,000 attended coeducational institutions (mostly state universities); the rest enrolled in women's colleges. By 1920, 283,000 women attended college, accounting for 47 percent of total enrollment. But discrimination lingered in admissions and curriculum policies. Women were encouraged (and usually sought) to take home economics and education courses, and most medical schools refused to admit women or imposed quotas. Separate women's medical schools trained female physicians, but most of these schools were absorbed or put out of business by larger, male-dominated institutions.

By 1920, 78 percent of children between ages five and seventeen were enrolled in public schools; another 8 percent attended private and parochial schools. There were 600,000 college and graduate students in 1920, compared with only 52,000 in 1870. Yet few people looked beyond the numbers to assess how well schools were doing their job.

Progressive Legal Thought

Harvard law professor Roscoe Pound and Oliver Wendell Holmes Jr., associate justice of the Supreme Court (1902–1932), led an attack on the traditional view of law as universal and unchanging. Their opinion that law should reflect society's needs challenged the practice of invoking inflexible legal precedents. Louis D. Brandeis, a lawyer who later joined Holmes on the Supreme Court, insisted that judges' opinions be based on scientifically gathered information about social realities. Brandeis collected extensive data on harmful effects of long working hours to convince the Supreme Court, in *Muller v. Oregon,* to uphold Oregon's ten-hour limit on women's workday.

Judges loyal to laissez-faire economics and strict interpretation of the Constitution overturned laws that Progressives thought necessary. Thus, despite Holmes's forceful dissent, in 1905 the Supreme Court, in *Lochner v. New York,* revoked a state law limiting bakers' working hours. The Court's majority argued that the Fourteenth Amendment protected an individual's right to make contracts without government interference. Several decisions, beginning with *Holden v. Hardy* (1898), in which the Supreme Court sustained a Utah law regulating miners' working hours, confirmed the use of state police power to protect health, safety, and morals. Judges also affirmed federal police power and Congress's authority over interstate commerce by upholding legislation, such as the Pure Food and Drug Act, the Meat Inspection Act, and the Mann Act.

But even if one agreed that laws should address society's needs, whose needs should prevail? In many localities, a native-born Protestant majority imposed Bible reading in public schools (offending Catholics and Jews), required businesses to close on Sundays, limited women's rights, restricted religious practices of Mormons and others, prohibited interracial marriage, and enforced racial segregation. Justice Holmes asserted that laws should be made for "people of fundamentally differing views," but how to accomplish that continues to spark debates today.

Social Science

Social science—the study of society and its institutions—also changed. Economics scholars used statistics to argue that laws governing economic relationships were not timeless but should reflect prevailing social conditions. A new breed of sociologists led by Lester Ward, Albion Small, and Edward A. Ross agreed, adding that citizens should work to cure social ills.

Meanwhile, historians Frederick Jackson Turner, Charles A. Beard, and Vernon L. Parrington examined the past to explain the present. Beard, like other Progressives, believed that the Constitution was a flexible document. His *Economic Interpretation of the Constitution* (1913) argued that a group of merchants and business-oriented lawyers created the Constitution to defend private property. If the Constitution served special interests in one age, he argued, it could be changed to serve broader interests in another.

In public health, organizations such as the National Consumers League (NCL), founded by Florence Kelley in 1899, joined physicians and social scientists to secure far-reaching Progressive reforms. NCL pursued protection of female and child laborers and elimination of potential health hazards. Local branches united with women's clubs to advance consumer protection measures, such as the licensing of food vendors and inspection of dairies. They urged city governments to fund neighborhood clinics providing medical care to the poor.

Eugenics

The Social Gospel served as a response to Social Darwinism, the application of natural selection and survival of the fittest to human interactions. Another movement, eugenics, embraced Darwinian principles and sought to apply them more intrusively. The brainchild of Francis Galton, an English statistician and cousin of Charles Darwin, eugenics rested on the belief that human character and habits could be inherited, including unwanted traits, such as criminality and mental illness. Eugenicists believed that society had an obligation to prevent the reproduction of the so-called mentally defective and criminally inclined by preventing them from marrying and, in extreme cases, sterilizing them. Such ideas targeted immigrants and people of color. Supported by such American notables as Alexander Graham Bell, Margaret Sanger, and W. E. B. Du Bois, eugenics was discredited, especially after it became a linchpin of Nazi racial policies.

Some reformers saw immigration restriction as a more acceptable way of controlling the composition of American society. Madison Grant's *The Passing of the Great Race* (1916) bolstered theories that immigrants from southern and eastern Europe threatened to weaken American society because they were inferior mentally and morally to earlier Nordic immigrants. Thus many people, including some Progressives, sought to curtail the influx of Poles, Italians, Jews, and other eastern and southern Europeans, and Asians. In the 1920s, restrictive legislation closed the door to "new" immigrants.

Challenges to Racial and Sexual Discrimination

What strategies did women use in their quest for equality in the early twentieth century?

White male reformers dealt primarily with politics and institutions and ignored issues affecting former slaves, nonwhite immigrants, Indians, and women. Yet these groups caught the Progressive spirit and made strides toward their own advancement. Their efforts, however, posed a dilemma. Should women and nonwhites aim to imitate white men's values? Or was there something unique about racial and sexual cultures worth preserving at the risk of sacrificing broader gains?

Continued Discrimination for African Americans

In 1900, nine-tenths of African Americans lived in the South, where repressive Jim Crow laws had multiplied in the 1880s and 1890s (see page 502). Denied legal and voting rights and socially segregated, southern blacks faced exclusion, intimidation, and violence—even lynching. In 1910, only 8,000 out of 970,000 high-school-age blacks were enrolled in southern high schools. Many African Americans responded by moving northward in the 1880s, accelerating their migration after 1900. Although conditions in places like Chicago, Cleveland, and Detroit represented improvement, job discrimination, inferior schools, and segregated housing prevailed there as well.

African American leaders differed over how—and whether—to assimilate. After emancipation, ex-slave Frederick Douglass urged "ultimate assimilation through self-assertion." Others supported emigration to Africa or the establishment of all-black communities in Oklahoma Territory and Kansas. Still others advocated militancy.

Booker T. Washington
Leading black activist of the late nineteenth century who advocated education and accommodation with white society as the best strategy for racial advancement.

Booker T. Washington and Self-Help

Most blacks could neither escape nor conquer white society. Self-help, a strategy articulated by educator **Booker T. Washington**, offered one popular alternative. Born into slavery in Virginia in 1856, Washington obtained an education and in 1881 founded Tuskegee Institute, an all-black vocational school, in Alabama. There he developed a philosophy that blacks' best hopes lay in at least temporarily accommodating whites. Rather than fighting for political rights, Washington counseled African Americans to work hard, acquire property, and prove they were worthy of respect. "Dignify and glorify common labor," he urged in an 1895 speech that became known as the Atlanta Compromise. Washington observed that "in all things that are purely social we can be as separate as the fingers, yet one as the hand in all matters essential to mutual progress."

Because he said what they wanted to hear, white businesspeople, reformers, and politicians regarded Washington as representing all African Americans. Although Washington endorsed a separate but equal policy, he never argued that blacks were inferior; rather, he asserted that they could enhance their dignity through self-improvement.

Some blacks, however, concluded that Washington endorsed second-class citizenship. In 1905, a group of "anti-Bookerites" convened near Niagara Falls and pledged militant pursuit of unrestricted voting rights, economic opportunity, integration, and equality before the law. Representing the Niagara movement was **W. E. B. Du Bois**, an outspoken critic of the Atlanta Compromise.

W. E. B. Du Bois and the "Talented Tenth"

A New Englander and the first African American to receive a PhD from Harvard, Du Bois was a Progressive and member of the black elite. While a faculty member at Atlanta University, Du Bois compiled sociological studies of black urban life and wrote in support of civil rights. He treated Washington politely but could not accept accommodation. Du Bois asserted that blacks must agitate for what was rightfully theirs, led by an intellectual vanguard of educated blacks dubbed the "Talented Tenth." In 1909, he joined white liberals also discontented with Washington's accommodationism to form the **National Association for the Advancement of Colored People (NAACP)** The organization aimed to end racial discrimination, eradicate lynching, and obtain voting rights through legal redress in the courts. By 1914, the NAACP had fifty branch offices and six thousand members.

African Americans struggled with questions about their place in white society. Du Bois voiced this dilemma, admitting that "one ever feels his twoness—an American, a Negro, two souls, two thoughts, two unreconciled strivings, two warring ideals in one dark body." As Du Bois wrote in 1903, a black "would not bleach his Negro soul in a flood of white Americanism, for he knows that Negro blood has a message for the world. He simply wishes to make it possible for a man to be both a Negro and an American." That simple wish would haunt the nation for decades to come.

W. E. B. Du Bois African American educator and activist who demanded full racial equality, including the same educational opportunities open to whites, and called on blacks to resist all forms of racism.

Link to W.E.B. Du Bois, Thoughts on Booker T. Washington (1903)

National Association for the Advancement of Colored People (NAACP) Organization that called for sustained activism, including legal challenges, to achieve political equality for blacks and full integration into American life.

Society of American Indians

Similarly, in 1911, middle-class Indians formed their own association, the Society of American Indians (SAI), to work for better education, civil rights, and health care. It also sponsored "American Indian Days" to cultivate pride and offset images of savage peoples promulgated in Wild West shows.

The SAI's emphasis on racial pride, however, was squeezed between pressures for assimilation and tribal allegiance. Its small membership did not fully represent the diverse and unconnected Indian nations. Individual hard work was not enough to overcome prejudice and condescension, and attempts to redress grievances through legal action faltered for lack of funds. Ultimately, the SAI had little

Heavyweight Boxing Champion Jack Johnson as Race Hero

It is probable that more African Americans in the 1910s paid attention to Jack Johnson than to Booker T. Washington or W. E. B. Du Bois. In 1908, Jackson became the first black heavyweight champion of the world by knocking out Tommy Burns. Immediately, white boxing fans began searching for a "Great White Hope" to recapture the title, and in 1910, former champion James J. Jeffries came out of retirement to fight Johnson, boasting that he would "demonstrate that a white man is king of them all." But after fifteen rounds of pummeling from Johnson, Jeffries gave up. African Americans around the nation celebrated their hero's victory, and in some places race riots erupted as angry whites attacked jubilant revelers. Racist reaction was particularly strong because Johnson refused to accept white standards for the way a black man should behave. He courted and married white women, flaunted his consumer tastes, and dealt with opponents and reporters with a pompous attitude. In 1915, Johnson, then thirty-seven years old, lost his title to Jess Willard in Cuba. The fight took place outside the country because in 1913 Johnson had been convicted of violating the Mann Act in transporting Belle Schreiber, a white prostitute, across state lines for "immoral purposes." Sentenced to a year in jail, Johnson fled the country, but he returned in 1920 to serve his sentence. How do these three images reveal racial attitudes, both black and white, toward Jack Johnson? What messages do they convey to the viewer?

The Italian poster artist Achille Beltrame depicted Jack Johnson's reception by jubilant African Americans in his hometown of Chicago after his triumph over James Jeffries in 1910. As a result of that victory, Johnson acquired an international as well as national reputation.

Jack Johnson's first wife was Etta Terry Duryea, a socialite and former wife of an automobile manufacturer. Their turbulent marriage ended in 1912 when Duryea committed suicide.

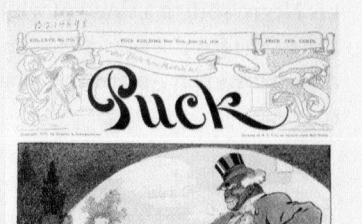

Puck, America's first successful humor magazine, caricatured how Uncle Tom's Cabin would have to be performed if Jack Johnson were to beat James Jeffries in 1910. The magazine cover shows Johnson as a large, wealthy man knocking down the slaveholder Simon Legree.

effect on poverty-stricken Indians, who seldom knew that the organization existed. Torn by internal disputes, the association folded in the early 1920s.

"The Woman Movement"

Women's groups faced similar struggles about their place in society and the tactics they should use to achieve rights. Should they try to achieve equality within a male-dominated society? Or assert female qualities to create new social roles for women?

The answers that women found involved a subtle but important shift in their politics. Before 1910, women's rights activists defined themselves as "the woman movement." Often middle-class, these women strove to move beyond the household into higher education and paid professions. They employed the theory that women's special, even superior, traits as guardians of family and morality would humanize society. Settlement house founder Jane Addams endorsed woman suffrage by asking, "If women have in any sense been responsible for the gentler side of life which softens and blurs some of its harsher conditions, may not they have a duty to perform in our American cities?"

Women's Clubs

Originating as literary and educational organizations, women's clubs began taking stands on public affairs in the late nineteenth century. They asserted traditional female responsibilities for home and family as the rationale for reforming society through an enterprise that historians have called "social housekeeping." These female reformers worked for factory inspection, regulation of children's and women's labor, improved housing, and consumer protection.

African American women had their own club movement, including the Colored Women's Federation, which sought to establish a training school for "colored girls." Founded in 1895, the National Association of Colored Women was the nation's first African American social service organization; it concentrated on establishing nurseries, kindergartens, and retirement homes. Black women also developed reform organizations within Black Baptist and African Methodist Episcopal churches.

Feminism

Around 1910, some people concerned with women's place in society began using the term *feminism*. Whereas the woman movement spoke of moral purity, feminists emphasized rights and self-development.

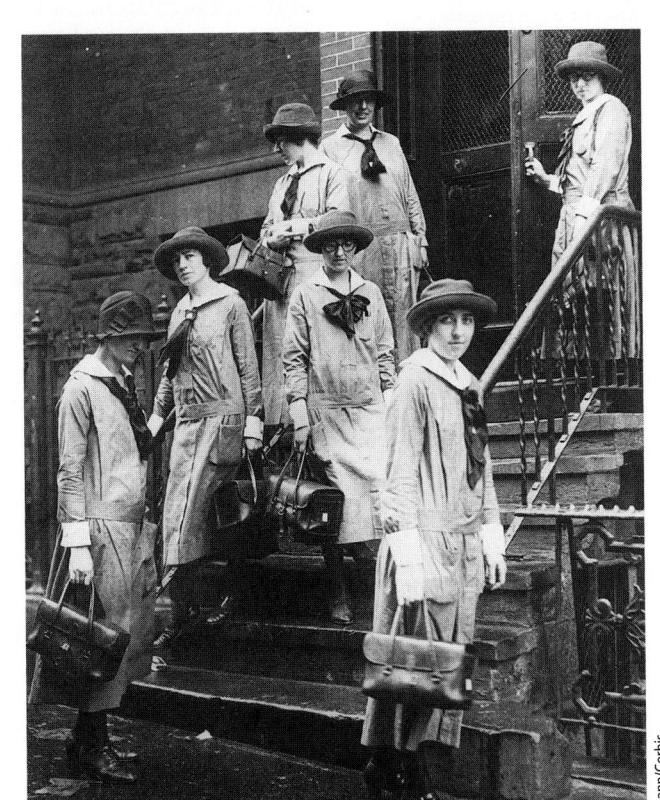

Bettmann/Corbis

The rise of the settlement house movement and of the Visiting Nurse Association provided young middle-class women with opportunities to aid inner-city working-class neighborhoods and formed the basis of the social work profession. Here a group of visiting nurses prepares to apply their medical training to the disadvantaged.

Charlotte Perkins Gilman, a major figure in the movement, declared in her book *Women and Economics* (1898) that domesticity and purity were obsolete and attacked men's monopoly on economic opportunity. Arguing that paid employees should handle domestic chores, such as cooking, cleaning, and child care, Gilman asserted that modern women must have access to jobs to be independent.

Margaret Sanger's Crusade

Several feminists joined the birth control movement led by Margaret Sanger. A former visiting nurse who believed in women's rights to sexual pleasure and to determine when to have a child, Sanger helped reverse state and federal laws banning distribution of information about sex and contraception. Opposition came from those who saw birth control as a threat to family and morality. Sanger also was a eugenicist who perceived birth control as a means of limiting the numbers of children born to "inferior" immigrant and non-white mothers. In 1921, she formed the American Birth Control League, enlisting physicians and social workers to convince judges to allow distribution of birth control information. Most states still prohibited the sale of contraceptives, but Sanger provoked public debate.

Carrie Chapman Catt
President of the National American Woman Suffrage Association in the early twentieth century.

Woman Suffrage

A new generation of Progressive feminists, represented by Harriot Stanton Blatch, daughter of nineteenth-century suffragist Elizabeth Cady Stanton, carried on women's battle for the vote. Blatch linked voting rights to the improvement of women's working conditions. She joined the Women's Trade Union League and founded the Equality League of Self Supporting Women in 1907. Declaring that every woman worked, for wages or unpaid housework, Blatch believed all women's efforts contributed to society's betterment. Thus, women should exercise the vote to promote and protect women's economic roles.

Nine states, all in the West, allowed women to vote in state and local elections by 1912 (see Map 18.1). As they pressed for national suffrage, advocates' tactics ranged from letter writing and publications of the National American Woman Suffrage Association, led by **Carrie Chapman Catt**, to meetings and militant marches of the National Woman's Party, led by Alice Paul and Harriot Stanton Blatch. More decisive, however, was women's service during the First World War as factory laborers, medical volunteers, and municipal workers. By convincing legislators that women could shoulder public responsibilities, women's wartime

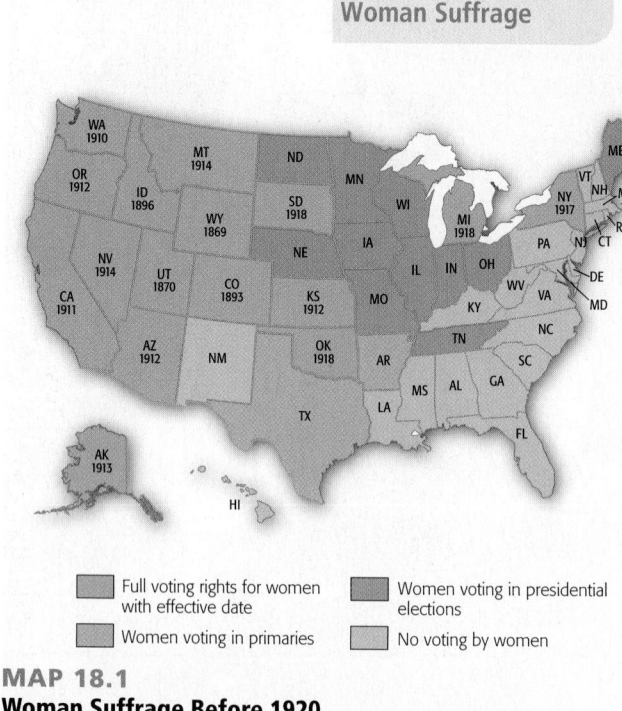

Full voting rights for women with effective date

Women voting in primaries

Women voting in presidential elections

No voting by women

MAP 18.1
Woman Suffrage Before 1920
Before Congress passed and the states ratified the Nineteenth Amendment, woman suffrage already existed, but mainly in the West. Several midwestern states allowed women to vote only in presidential elections, but legislatures in the South and the Northeast generally refused such rights until forced to do so by constitutional amendment.

Source: Copyright © Cengage Learning 2015

contributions facilitated passage of the national suffrage amendment (the Nineteenth Amendment) in 1920.

During the Progressive Era, the resolve and energy of leaders like Blatch, Paul, and Catt helped clarify issues that concerned women, but winning the vote was only a step. Discrimination in employment, education, and law continued to shadow women for decades.

Theodore Roosevelt and Revival of the Presidency

Theodore Roosevelt was known as a trustbuster, but was he?

The Progressive Era's reform focused on the federal government as the foremost agent of change. Although the federal government had notable accomplishments during the Gilded Age, its role was mainly to support rather than control economic expansion. Then, in September 1901, the assassination of President William McKinley by anarchist Leon Czolgosz vaulted **Theodore Roosevelt**, the young vice president (he was forty-two), into the White House. As governor of New York, Roosevelt angered state Republican bosses by showing sympathy for regulatory legislation. He would become the nation's most forceful president since Abraham Lincoln, one who bestowed the office with much of its twentieth-century character.

Theodore Roosevelt Youthful successor to slain president William McKinley in 1901; U.S. president, 1901–1909; promoted an agenda of progressive reform.

Theodore Roosevelt

Driven by a lifelong obsession to overcome his physical limitations of asthma and nearsightedness, Roosevelt exerted what he called "manliness"—a zest for action and display of courage. In his teens, he became a marksman and horseman, and later competed on Harvard's boxing and wrestling teams. In the 1880s, he lived on a Dakota ranch, roping cattle and brawling with cowboys. Descended from a Dutch aristocratic family, Roosevelt had wealth, but he also inherited a sense of civic responsibility that guided him into public service. He served three terms in the New York legislature, sat on the federal Civil Service Commission, served as New York City's police commissioner, was assistant secretary of the navy, and earned a reputation as a combative, crafty leader. In 1898, he thrust himself into the Spanish-American War by organizing a volunteer cavalry brigade, called the Rough Riders, to fight in Cuba. Although his dramatic act had little impact on the war's outcome, it made him a media hero.

Roosevelt carried his youthful exuberance into the White House. A Progressive, he concurred with his allies that a small, uninvolved government would not suffice in the industrial era. Instead, economic progress necessitated a government powerful enough to guide national affairs. In economic matters, Roosevelt wanted government to decide when big business was good and when it was bad.

Library of Congress

Looking eager for battle in his neatly pressed new uniform from the elite haberdasher Brooks Brothers, Theodore Roosevelt served as a colonel in the U.S. Volunteers and joined the U.S. Army's campaign to oust Spain from Cuba in 1898. His bravado helped propel his political ascendancy into the governorship of New York and vice presidency of the United States.

Regulation of Trusts

The federal regulation of business that characterized American history began with Roosevelt's presidency. Although labeled a trustbuster, Roosevelt actually considered business consolidation an efficient means to material progress, but he believed in distinguishing between good and bad trusts, and preventing bad ones from manipulating markets. Thus, he instructed the U.S. Justice Department to use antitrust laws to prosecute railroad, meatpacking, and oil trusts, which he believed exploited the public. Roosevelt's policy triumphed in 1904 when the Supreme Court ordered the breakup of Northern Securities Company, the huge railroad combination created by J. P. Morgan. Roosevelt did not attack other trusts, such as U.S. Steel, another of Morgan's creations.

When prosecution of Northern Securities began, Morgan reportedly asked Roosevelt, "If we have done anything wrong, send your man to my man and they can fix it up." The president refused but was more sympathetic to cooperation between business and government than might seem. He urged the Bureau of Corporations (part of the newly created Department of Labor and Commerce) to assist companies in merging and expanding. Through investigation and consultation, the administration cajoled businesses to regulate themselves.

Hepburn Act Legislation that strengthened regulatory powers of the Interstate Commerce Commission, particularly over railroads, and later other businesses and industries.

Roosevelt also supported regulatory legislation. After a year of wrangling, Roosevelt persuaded Congress to pass the **Hepburn Act** (1906), which gave the Interstate Commerce Commission (ICC) the authority to set railroad freight rates and rates for ferries, express companies, storage facilities, and oil pipelines. The Hepburn Act still allowed courts to overturn ICC decisions, but it now required shippers to prove they had not violated regulations, rather than making the government demonstrate violations.

Pure Food and Drug Laws

Roosevelt showed willingness to compromise to ensure pure food and drug legislation. For decades, reformers sought government regulation of processed meat and patent medicines. Public outrage at fraud flared in 1906 when Upton Sinclair published *The Jungle*, a fictionalized exposé of Chicago meatpacking plants. Sinclair, a socialist who wanted to improve working conditions, shocked public sensibilities with vivid descriptions, such as:

> There would be meat stored in great piles in rooms; and the water from the leaky roofs would drip over it, and thousands of rats would race about on it … a man could run his hand over these piles of meat and sweep off handfuls of dried dung of rats. These rats were a nuisance, and the packers would put poisoned bread out for them; they would die, and then rats, bread, and meat would go into the hoppers together.

Link to Upton Sinclair, "The Condemned-Meat Industry," 1906

Roosevelt ordered an investigation. Finding Sinclair's descriptions accurate, he supported the Meat Inspection Act (1906). But as part of a compromise with meatpackers and their congressional allies, the government had to finance inspections, and meatpackers could appeal adverse decisions. Nor were companies required to provide date-of-processing information on canned meats. Most large meatpackers welcomed the legislation because it restored foreign confidence in American meat products.

The Pure Food and Drug Act (1906) also addressed abuses in the patent medicine industry. Makers of tonics and pills had long made undue claims about their products' effects and used alcohol and narcotics as ingredients. The law required that labels list the ingredients—a goal consistent with Progressive confidence that with information, people would make wiser purchases.

Roosevelt's approach to labor resembled his compromises with business. When the United Mine Workers struck against Pennsylvania coal mine owners in 1902 over an eight-hour workday and higher pay, the president urged arbitration. Owners refused to recognize the union or to arbitrate grievances. As winter approached and nationwide fuel shortages loomed, Roosevelt threatened to use federal troops to reopen the mines, thus forcing management to negotiate. The arbitration commission supported higher wages and reduced hours and required management to deal with miners' grievance committees. But it did not mandate recognition of the union. The decision, according to Roosevelt, provided a "square deal" for all. The settlement embodied Roosevelt's belief that the president or his representatives should determine which labor demands were legitimate and which were not.

Race Relations

Although he angered southern congressmen by inviting Booker T. Washington to the White House to discuss racial matters, Roosevelt believed in white superiority and was neutral toward blacks only when it helped him politically. Case in point: in 1906 the army transferred African American soldiers from Nebraska to Brownsville, Texas. Anglo and Mexican residents resented their presence and banned them from parks and businesses. On August 14, a battle between blacks and whites broke out, and a white man was killed. Brownsville residents blamed soldiers, but the soldiers refused to help investigators identify participants. Consequently, Roosevelt discharged 167 black soldiers without a hearing and prevented them from receiving their pay and pensions despite lack of evidence. Black leaders were outraged. To preserve black support for Republican candidates in the 1906 elections, Roosevelt waited until after the elections to sign discharge papers.

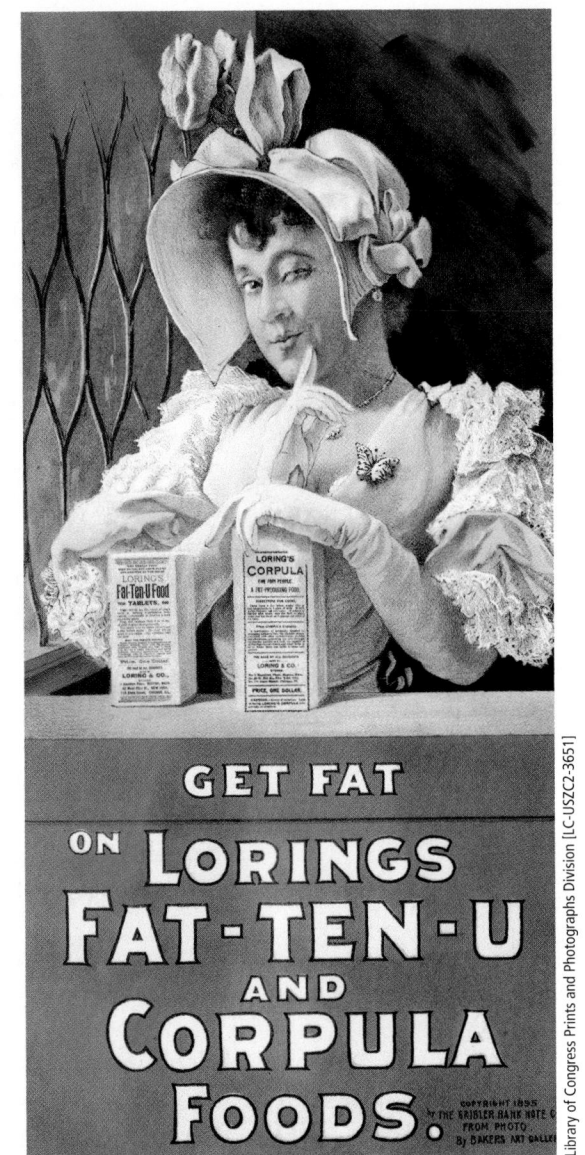

Library of Congress Prints and Photographs Division [LC-USZC2-3651]

Makers of unregulated patent medicines advertised their products' exorbitant abilities to cure almost any ailment and remedy any unwanted physical condition. Loring's Fat-Ten-U tablets and Loring's Corpula were two such products. The Pure Food and Drug Act of 1906 did not ban these items but tried to prevent manufacturers from making unsubstantiated claims.

Conservation

Roosevelt's Progressive impulse for efficiency and love for the outdoors inspired lasting contributions to resource conservation. Government establishment of national parks began in the late nineteenth century. Roosevelt advanced the movement by favoring *conservation* over *preservation*. Thus, he not only exercised presidential power to protect such natural wonders as the Grand Canyon in Arizona by declaring them national monuments, but also backed a policy of "wise use" of forests, waterways, and other resources. Previously, the government transferred ownership of natural resources on federal land to the states and private interests. Roosevelt, however, believed efficient resource conservation demanded federal management over lands in the public domain.

Roosevelt used federal authority over resources to create five national parks and fifty-one national bird reservations, protected waterpower sites from sale to private interests, and charged permit fees for users who wanted to produce hydroelectricity. He also supported the Newlands Reclamation Act of 1902, which controlled sale of irrigated federal land in the West (see page 445). Roosevelt tripled the number of national forests and backed conservationist Gifford Pinchot in creating the U.S. Forest Service.

Gifford Pinchot

As principal advocate of "wise use" policy, Pinchot promoted scientific management of the nation's woodlands. He obtained Roosevelt's support for transferring management of the national forests from the Interior Department to his bureau in the Agriculture Department. The Forest Service charged fees for grazing livestock within the national forests, supervised bidding for the cutting of timber, and hired university-trained foresters as federal employees.

Pinchot and Roosevelt did not seek to preserve resources permanently; rather, they wanted to conserve their efficient use and make companies profiting from using public lands pay the government. Many involved in natural resource development welcomed such a policy because it enabled them to manage their operations more effectively, such as when Roosevelt and Pinchot encouraged lumber companies to engage in reforestation.

Panic of 1907

In 1907, a financial panic caused by reckless speculation forced some New York banks to close to prevent frightened depositors from withdrawing money. J. P. Morgan helped stem the panic by persuading financiers to stop dumping stocks. In return for Morgan's aid, Roosevelt approved a deal allowing U.S. Steel to absorb the Tennessee Iron and Coal Company—a deal at odds with Roosevelt's trust-busting aims.

During his last year in office, Roosevelt retreated from the Republican Party's friendliness to big business. He supported stronger business regulation and heavier taxation of the rich. Promising that he would not seek reelection, Roosevelt backed Secretary of War **William Howard Taft** in 1908. Taft easily defeated three-time Democratic nominee William Jennings Bryan by 1.25 million popular votes and a 2-to-1 margin in the electoral college.

William Howard Taft
Roosevelt's handpicked successor for president (1909–1913); later served as chief justice of the U.S. Supreme Court.

Taft Administration

Taft faced political problems that Roosevelt had postponed, foremost: extremely high tariffs. Honoring Taft's pledge to cut tariffs, the House passed a bill providing numerous reductions. Protectionists in the Senate prepared to amend the bill and revise rates upward. But Senate Progressives led by La Follette attacked the tariff for benefiting special interests, trapping Taft between reformers who claimed to be preserving Roosevelt's antitrust campaign and protectionists who dominated the Republican Party. In the end, Rhode Island senator Nelson Aldrich restored most cuts, and Taft signed what became known as the Payne-Aldrich Tariff (1909). To Progressives, Taft failed to fill Roosevelt's shoes.

In reality, Taft was as sympathetic to reform as Roosevelt was. He prosecuted more trusts than Roosevelt; expanded national forest reserves; signed the Mann-Elkins Act (1910), which bolstered the ICC's regulatory powers; and supported such labor reforms as shorter work hours and mine safety legislation. The Sixteenth Amendment, which legalized the federal income tax, and the Seventeenth Amendment, which provided for direct election of U.S. senators, were initiated during Taft's presidency (and ratified in 1913). Like Roosevelt, Taft compromised with big business, but he was unable to manipulate the public with spirited rhetoric. Roosevelt had expanded presidential power. Taft, by contrast, believed in the strict restraint of law. He had been a successful lawyer and judge, and returned to the bench as chief justice of the United States between 1921 and 1930.

Candidates in 1912

In 1910, Roosevelt found his party torn and tormented. Reformers formed the National Progressive Republican League and rallied behind Robert La Follette for president in 1912, though many hoped Roosevelt would run. Another wing of the party remained loyal to Taft. Disappointed by Taft, Roosevelt spoke out for "the welfare of the people" and stronger business regulation. When La Follette became ill early in 1912, Roosevelt, proclaiming himself fit as a "bull moose," sought the Republican presidential nomination.

Taft's supporters controlled the Republican convention and nominated him for a second term. In protest, Roosevelt's supporters formed a third party—the Progressive, or Bull Moose, Party—and nominated the former president. Meanwhile, Democrats took forty-six ballots to select their candidate, New Jersey's Progressive governor **Woodrow Wilson** Socialists, by now a growing party, again nominated Eugene V. Debs.

Woodrow Wilson Democratic president whose election in 1912 ushered in a second wave of progressive reforms on the national level; served as president until 1921.

New Nationalism Versus New Freedom

Central to Theodore Roosevelt's campaign was a scheme called the "New Nationalism," which envisioned an era of national unity in which government would coordinate and regulate economic activity. Roosevelt asserted that he would establish regulatory commissions to protect citizens' interests and ensure wise use of economic power.

Wilson's proposal, the "New Freedom," was more idealistic. He argued that concentrated economic power threatened individual liberty and that monopolies should be broken to ensure a free marketplace. But he would not restore laissez-faire. Like Roosevelt, Wilson would enhance government authority to protect and regulate. "Without the watchful … resolute interference of the government, there can be no fair play between individuals and such powerful institutions as the trust," he declared. Wilson stopped short, however, of advocating the cooperation between business and government inherent in Roosevelt's New Nationalism.

Roosevelt and Wilson stood closer together than their rhetoric implied. Both believed in individual freedom. Both supported equality of opportunity (chiefly for white males), conservation of natural resources, fair wages, and social betterment. Neither would hesitate to expand government intervention through strong leadership and bureaucratic reform.

In the election, the popular vote was inconclusive. The victorious Wilson won just 42 percent, though he did capture 435 out of 531 electoral votes. Roosevelt received 27 percent of the popular vote. Taft polled 23 percent of the popular vote and only 8 electoral votes. Debs won 6 percent but no electoral votes. Three-quarters of the electorate supported alternatives to Taft's view of restrained government.

Woodrow Wilson and Extension of Progressive Reform

How did participation in World War I alter Wilson's position on business?

Woodrow Wilson

Born in Virginia in 1856 and raised in the South, Wilson was the son of a Presbyterian minister. He earned a BA degree at Princeton University, studied law at the University of Virginia, received a PhD from Johns Hopkins University, and became a professor of history, jurisprudence, and political economy at Princeton. Between 1885 and 1908, he published several respected books on American history and government.

Wilson was a superb orator who could inspire loyalty with religious imagery and eloquent expressions of American ideals. But he harbored disdain for African Americans, had no misgivings about Jim Crow laws, and opposed admitting blacks to Princeton. At Princeton, he battled against aristocratic elements and earned a reputation as a reformer so that in 1910 New Jersey's Democrats nominated Wilson for governor. Once elected, Wilson repudiated the party bosses and promoted Progressive legislation. A poor administrator, he often lost his temper and refused to compromise. His accomplishments nevertheless won him the 1912 Democratic presidential nomination.

Wilson's Policy on Business Regulation

As president, Wilson blended New Freedom competition with New Nationalism regulation, setting the direction of future federal economic policy. Corporate consolidation made restoration of open competition impossible. Wilson sought to prevent abuses by expanding government's regulatory powers. He supported congressional passage in 1914 of the Clayton Anti-Trust Act and a bill creating the **Federal Trade Commission (FTC)**. The Clayton Act corrected deficiencies of the Sherman Anti-Trust Act of 1890 by outlawing such practices as price discrimination (lowering prices in some regions but not in others) and interlocking directorates (management of two or more competing companies by the same executives). The act also aided labor by exempting unions from its anti-combination provision, thereby making peaceful strikes, boycotts, and picketing less vulnerable to government interference. The FTC could investigate companies and issue cease and desist orders against unfair practices.

Federal Trade Commission (FTC) Agency formed in 1914 to ensure fair trade practices.

Under Wilson, the Federal Reserve Act (1913) established the nation's first central banking system since 1836. To break the power that syndicates like that of J. P. Morgan held over the money supply, the act created twelve district banks to hold reserves of member banks nationwide. District banks, supervised by the Federal Reserve Board, would lend money to member banks at a low interest rate called the discount rate. By adjusting this rate (and thus the amount a bank could afford to borrow), district banks could increase or decrease the amount of money in circulation, enabling the Federal Reserve Board to loosen or tighten credit, thereby making interest rates fairer.

Tariff and Tax Reform

Wilson and Congress attempted to restore competition with the Underwood Tariff of 1913. By reducing or eliminating certain tariffs, the Underwood Tariff encouraged importation of cheaper foreign goods. To replace revenues lost because of tariff reductions, the act levied a graduated income tax on U.S. residents. Incomes under $4,000 were exempt; thus, almost all factory workers and farmers escaped taxation. Individuals and corporations earning between $4,000 and $20,000 had to pay a 1 percent tax; thereafter rates rose to a maximum of 6 percent on earnings over $500,000.

The outbreak of World War I (see Chapter 20) and approaching 1916 presidential election campaign prompted Wilson to support stronger reforms. He backed the Federal Farm Loan Act, which created twelve federally supported banks that could lend money at moderate interest to farmers who belonged to credit institutions—a diluted version of the Populists' subtreasury plan proposed a generation earlier (see page 506). To forestall railroad strikes, Wilson in 1916 pushed passage of the Adamson Act, which mandated eight-hour workdays and time-and-a-half overtime pay for railroad laborers. He pleased Progressives by appointing Brandeis, the "people's advocate," to the Supreme Court, though an anti-Semitic backlash almost blocked Senate approval of the Court's first Jewish justice. Wilson also backed laws regulating child labor and providing workers' compensation for federal employees who suffered work-related injuries or illness.

But Wilson never overcame his racism. He fired several black federal officials, and his administration preserved racial separation in restrooms, restaurants, and government office buildings. When the pathbreaking but inflammatory film about the Civil War and Reconstruction, *The Birth of a Nation,* was released in 1915, Wilson allowed a showing at the White House, though he prohibited it during World War I.

Election of 1916

Republicans snubbed Theodore Roosevelt as their candidate in 1916, choosing Charles Evans Hughes, Supreme Court justice and former reform governor of New York. Aware of public anxiety over the world war in Europe since 1914, Wilson ran on neutrality and Progressivism, using the slogan "He Kept Us Out of War." The election was close. Wilson received 9.1 million votes to Hughes's 8.5 million and barely won in the electoral college, 277 to 254. The Socialist Party candidate drew only 600,000 votes, largely because Wilson's reforms won over some socialists and because the ailing Eugene Debs was no longer the party's standard-bearer.

During Wilson's second term, U.S. involvement in World War I increased government regulation of the economy. Mobilization and war, he believed, required greater coordination of production and cooperation between the public and private sectors. The War Industries Board exemplified this: private businesses

Margaret Sanger, Planned Parenthood, and the Birth Control Controversy

Some Progressive Era reforms illustrate how earnest intentions can become tangled in divisive moral issues. Such is the legacy of birth control advocate Margaret Sanger. In 1912, Sanger produced a column on sex education in the *New York Call* entitled "What Every Girl Should Know." Moralists accused her of writing obscene literature because she publicly discussed venereal disease and contraception. The issue of limiting family size, however, became her passion. She began counseling poor women on New York's Lower East Side about how to avoid frequent childbirth, miscarriage, and bungled abortion. In 1914, Sanger launched *The Woman Rebel*, a monthly newspaper advocating a woman's right to practice birth control. Indicted for distributing obscenity through the mails, she fled to England, where she gave speeches on family planning and enjoying sexuality without fear of pregnancy.

Returning to the United States, Sanger opened the country's first birth control clinic in Brooklyn in 1916. She was arrested, but when a court exempted physicians from a law prohibiting dissemination of contraceptive information, she set up a doctor-run clinic in 1923. Staffed by female doctors and social workers, the Birth Control Clinical Research Bureau became a model for other clinics. Sanger organized the American Birth Control League (1921) and sought support from medical and social reformers, even from the eugenics movement, for legalized birth control. After falling out with some allies, she resigned from the American Birth Control League in 1928.

The movement continued, and in 1938 the American Birth Control League and the Birth Control Clinical Research Bureau merged to form the Birth Control Federation of America, renamed the Planned Parenthood Federation of America (PPFA) in 1942. The organization's mission was to strengthen the family and stabilize society with governmental support, rather than focus on the right to voluntary motherhood. Throughout the 1940s, the PPFA emphasized family planning through making contraceptives more accessible. In 1970, it began receiving federal funds.

In the 1960s, new feminist agitation for women's rights and rising concerns about overpopulation made birth control and abortion controversial. Although PPFA initially dissociated from abortion, the debate between a woman's "choice" and a fetus's "right to life" drew the organization into the fray, especially after 1973, when the Supreme Court validated women's right to an abortion in *Roe v. Wade*. PPFA fought legislative and court attempts to make abortions illegal, and in 1989 it helped organize a women's march on Washington. Some Latino and African American groups attacked the PPFA's stance, charging that abortion was a eugenics program meant to reduce births among nonwhites.

Several of PPFA's clinics have been targets of picketing and violence by those who believe abortion is immoral. Most recently, debates have raged in Congress, statehouses, and political campaigns over whether to end government funding for Planned Parenthood clinics because the money might end up funding abortions. PPFA now operates nearly nine hundred health centers providing medical services and education to more than 5 million, mostly poor, women. But birth control has left a legacy to a people and a nation of disagreement over whose rights and whose morality should prevail.

submitted to the board's control on condition that their profit motives would be satisfied. After the war, Wilson's administration dropped such measures, including farm price supports, guarantees of collective bargaining, and high taxes. This retreat from regulation, prompted partly by the election of a Republican Congress in 1918, stimulated a new era of business ascendancy in the 1920s.

Summary

By 1920, a quarter-century of reform had wrought momentous changes. Progressives established the principle of public intervention to end abuses of power, reform institutions, and ensure fairness, health, and safety. Concern over poverty and injustice reached new heights.

Multiple and sometimes contradictory goals characterized the era because there was no single Progressive movement. National programs ranged from Roosevelt's faith in big government as a coordinator of big business to Wilson's promise to dissolve economic concentrations and legislate open competition. At state and local levels, reformers pursued causes as varied as neighborhood improvement, government reorganization, public ownership of utilities, and better working conditions. Women and African Americans developed a new consciousness about identity, and although women made some inroads into public life, both groups still found themselves in confined social positions.

Successes aside, the failure of many Progressive initiatives indicates the strength of the opposition and weaknesses within the reform movements. As issues such as Americanization, eugenics, prohibition, education, and moral uplift illustrate, social reform often merged into social control—attempts to impose one group's values on all of society. Courts asserted constitutional and liberty-of-contract doctrines in striking down key Progressive legislation, notably the federal law prohibiting child labor. Federal regulatory agencies rarely had enough resources for thorough enforcement; they had to depend on information from the companies they policed. In 1920, as in 1900, government remained under the influence of business.

Yet Progressive Era reforms reshaped the national outlook. Trust-busting, however faulty, made industrialists more sensitive to public opinion. Progressive legislation equipped government with tools to protect consumers against price fixing and dangerous products. Social reformers relieved some ills of urban and industrial life. Although the questions they raised about American life remained unresolved, Progressives made the nation acutely aware of its principles and promises.

Chapter Review

The Varied Progressive Impulse

How did Progressive reform cut across class lines?

The impulse to improve society at the turn of the twentieth century had variants in the working, middle, and wealthier classes. An emerging class of educated male and female professionals stood at the vanguard of Progressivism and sought to apply the techniques of professions such as law, engineering, medicine, social service, and teaching to end the abuse of power and inefficiency in business and government, and to protect the welfare of all classes. They also believed they could unify society through education and Americanization programs for new immigrants and Native Americans. Muckraking journalists exposed corruption and social wrongs, including fraudulent insurance, prostitution, and political corruption, as well as industrial outrages. One example was Upton Sinclair's exposé of the meatpacking industry. Workers, too, pressed for reforms to improve safety and housing and to include workers' compensation for injuries on the job. There was even a religious component as Protestant ministers sought to counter the negative impact of competitive capitalism and industrialization with a message of Christian salvation known as the "Social Gospel."

Government and Legislative Reform

 According to Progressives, what was the government's role in improving society?

Unlike earlier generations of Americans who believed in a limited role for government, Progressives felt the government not only had an obligation to improve society but could protect people and families by restricting behavior. Progressives pushed officials to adopt regulations that would end labor abuses and provide for factory inspections, compensation for injured workers, minimum age and wage laws, child labor laws, and protective legislation regulating the hours women could work. Many also supported women's suffrage. Next, Progressives focused on ending vice, pushing for the passage of state laws and later a constitutional amendment (the Eighteenth Amendment, implemented in 1920) banning the manufacture and sale of alcohol—which they believed contributed to accidents, poverty, and poor productivity. Inspired by muckraking articles about gangs forcing white women into prostitution (dubbed "white slavery"), Progressives called for government investigations and new laws. Congress passed the Mann Act in 1910, prohibiting the interstate and international transportation of women for immoral purposes. By 1915 nearly every state outlawed brothels and solicitation of sex.

New Ideas in Social Institutions

 What was the impact of Progressive education reforms?

Increasing concerns about the social impact of industrialization, along with a penchant for scientific management and efficiency, drove Progressive approaches to education. Reformers such as John Dewey not only wanted to ensure that children were exposed to age-appropriate materials, but they also focused on preparing children for the modern world by teaching them to use their ingenuity to solve real-life problems. College curricula shifted from their previous nearly exclusive focus on preparing primarily white men for a few professions such as medicine, religion, and law, to a focus on learning that kept pace with technological and social changes. Regarded as vital to a student's growth, athletics became a permanent feature. The number of colleges expanded, including all-black land grant colleges and women's colleges.

Challenges to Racial and Sexual Discrimination

 What strategies did women use in their quest for equality in the early twentieth century?

Women's organizations had long struggled over whether to focus on their shared humanity with men or accentuate their unique female qualities in pursuit of equality and new social roles for women. Calling themselves "the woman movement" before 1910, they played up women's special, even superior, traits as guardians of the family and morality. After that date, activists adopted the term *feminism,* emphasizing women's right to citizenship and self-development. Activist styles ranged from moderate to radical, but all saw the vote as a first and vital step to influencing the laws affecting them, be it improving women's working conditions or safeguarding their economic roles. Women's participation in the war effort also showed their ability and willingness to serve their country and made it impossible for legislators to continue to justify denying them the vote (which women finally received in 1920).

Theodore Roosevelt and the Revival of the Presidency

 Theodore Roosevelt was known as a trustbuster, but was he?

Yes and no. As a Progressive, Roosevelt believed government should guide national affairs and economic development and determine when business was a positive or negative force. But he also thought there were times when business consolidation and mergers could aid economic progress and urged the Bureau of Consolidation to assist in these efforts. At the same time, he was willing to step in when business consolidation led to corruption and market manipulation, as he did when he had the Justice Department use antitrust laws to prosecute railroad, meatpacking, and oil trusts, which he believed exploited the public. Roosevelt similarly supported regulatory legislation over interstate commerce and the quality of food and drugs. While Roosevelt supported the breakup of J. P. Morgan's Northern Securities Company, he did not break up the huge U.S. Steel Corporation and actually allowed it to acquire additional companies during the economic panic of 1907.

Woodrow Wilson and Extension of Progressive Reform

> **How did participation in World War I alter Wilson's position on business?**

In his first term as president, Wilson was disheartened by the corporate merger movement that seemed to weaken the prospects of fair business competition. To restore competition, he increased government regulation of the business sector, supporting the Clayton Antitrust Act and the establishment of the Federal Trade Commission to ensure fair business practices and protect labor. He also established banking regulation with the Federal Reserve Act of 1913 and similarly supported tariff reform and farm loans. With war mobilization a priority in his second term, Wilson sought greater cooperation between the private and public sector. Businesses agreed to submit to the federal War Industry Board's directives in exchange for the promise of profits. After the war, Wilson retreated from the regulation that had been his prewar policy, dropping farm supports, collective bargaining guarantees for labor, and high taxes, thereby inaugurating a new era of big business in the 1920s.

Suggestions for Further Reading

Francis L. Broderick, *Progressivism at Risk: Electing a President in 1912* (1989)

Nancy F. Cott, *The Grounding of Modern Feminism* (1987)

Steven J. Diner, *A Very Different Age: Americans of the Progressive Era* (1998)

Glenda Gilmore, *Who Were the Progressives?* (2002)

Hugh D. Hindman, *Child Labor: An American History* (2002)

Alice Kessler-Harris, *Out to Work: A History of Wage-Earning Women in the United States*, 20th anniversary ed. (2003)

Michael McGerr, *A Fierce Discontent: The Rise and Fall of the Progressive Movement in America, 1870–1920* (2003)

Patricia A. Schecter, *Ida B. Wells and American Reform, 1880–1930* (2001)

David Tyack, *Seeking Common Ground: Public Schools in a Diverse Society* (2003)

19

The Quest for Empire

1865–1914

"Foreign devil!" they shouted at Lottie Moon. The Southern Baptist missionary, half a world away from home, braced herself against the cries of the Chinese "rabble" whom she sought to convert to Christianity in the 1880s. She walked through the hecklers, silently vowing to win their acceptance and their souls.

Born in 1840 in Virginia and educated at what is now Hollins College, Charlotte Diggs Moon volunteered in 1873 for "woman's work" in northern China. There she taught and proselytized, largely among women and children, until her death in 1912.

In the 1870s and 1880s, Lottie Moon (Mu Ladi, or 幕拉第) made sometimes dangerous evangelizing trips to isolated Chinese hamlets. Curious peasant women pinched her, pulled on her skirts, and purred, "How white her hand is!" They asked: "How old are you?" "Where do you get money to live on?" Speaking in Chinese, Lottie held a picture book about Jesus Christ, drawing the crowd's attention to the "foreign doctrine" that she hoped would displace Confucianism, Buddhism, and Taoism.

In the 1890s, a "storm of persecution" against foreigners swept China, and missionaries upending traditional ways became hated targets. One missionary conceded that, in "believing Jesus," girls and women alarmed men who feared "disobedient wives and daughters" would no longer "worship the idols when told." In the Shaling village in early 1890, Lottie Moon's Christian converts were beaten. Fearing for her life, Moon left China for several months in 1900 during the Boxer Rebellion.

Lottie Moon and thousands of other missionaries converted only a small minority of Chinese people to Christianity. Although she, like other missionaries, probably never shed the Western view that she represented a superior religion and culture, she felt affection for the Chinese. In letters and articles directed to a U.S. audience, she lobbied to recruit Christian women, to stir up "a mighty wave of enthusiasm for Woman's Work for Woman." To this day, the Lottie Moon Christmas Offering in Southern Baptist churches raises millions of dollars for missions abroad.

Like many Americans who went overseas in the late nineteenth and early twentieth centuries, Lottie Moon helped spread American culture and influence abroad. Other peoples sometimes adopted and sometimes rejected American ways. American participants in this cultural expansion were transformed. Lottie Moon, for example, strove to understand the Chinese people and learn their language. She assumed their dress and abandoned such derogatory phrases as "heathen Chinese." She reminded less sensitive missionaries that the Chinese rightfully took pride in their own ancient history.

Lottie Moon also changed—in her own words—from "a timid self-distrustful girl into a brave self-reliant woman." As she questioned Chinese confinement of women, most conspicuous in arranged marriages, foot binding, and sexual segregation, she advanced women's rights. She knew she could not convert Chinese women unless they had the freedom to listen to her appeals. She also challenged male domination of America's religious missions. When the Southern Baptist Foreign Mission Board denied female missionaries the right to vote in meetings, she resigned. The board soon reversed itself.

Decades later, critics labeled missionaries' activities as "cultural imperialism," accusing them of subverting indigenous traditions and sparking destructive cultural clashes. Defenders of missionary work have celebrated their efforts to break down cultural barriers. Nonetheless, Lottie Moon's story illustrates how Americans in the late nineteenth century interacted with the world, how the categories "domestic" and "foreign" intersected, and how Americans expanded abroad for land, trade, investments, and strategic bases, as well as to promote American culture.

Between the Civil War and the First World War, an expansionist United States joined the great world powers. Before the Civil War, Americans repeatedly extended the frontier: they bought Louisiana; annexed Florida, Oregon, and Texas; pushed Indians from the path of white migration westward; seized California and other western areas from Mexico; and acquired southern parts of present-day Arizona and New Mexico from Mexico (the Gadsden Purchase). Americans also developed a lucrative foreign trade and promoted American culture everywhere. They rekindled their expansionist course after the Civil War, building and protecting an overseas empire.

It was an age of empire. By the 1870s, most of Europe's powers were carving up Africa and large parts of Asia and Oceania for themselves. By 1900 they had conquered more than 10 million square miles and 150 million people. As the century turned, France, Russia, and Germany were spending heavily on modern steel navies, challenging an overextended Great Britain. In Asia, a rapidly modernizing Japan expanded at China and Russia's expense.

Engineering advances altered the world's political geography through the Suez Canal (1869), the British Trans-Indian railroad (1870), and the Russian Trans-Siberian Railway (1904), while steamships, machine guns, telegraphs, and malaria drugs facilitated the imperialists' task. Simultaneously, European leaders' optimism in the 1850s and 1860s gave way to a pessimistic sense of impending warfare informed by notions of racial conflict and survival of the fittest.

Observant Americans argued that the United States risked being "left behind" if it failed to join the scramble for territory and markets. Republican senator Henry Cabot Lodge of Massachusetts claimed that "civilization and the advancement of the [Anglo-Saxon] race" were at stake. Such thinking encouraged Americans to reach beyond the continental United States for more land, markets, cultural penetration, and power.

By 1900, the United States emerged as a great power with particular clout in Latin America, especially as Spain declined and Britain disengaged from the Western Hemisphere. In the Pacific, the new U.S. empire included Hawai'i, American Samoa, and the Philippines. Theodore Roosevelt would, as president, seek to consolidate this power.

Most Americans applauded expansionism—the outward movement of goods, ships, dollars, people, and ideas. But many became uneasy whenever expansionism gave way to imperialism—the imposition of control over other peoples, undermining their sovereignty. Abroad, native nationalists, commercial competitors, and other imperial nations tried to block the spread of U.S. influence.

As you read this chapter, keep the following questions in mind:

- **What accounts for the increased importance of foreign policy concerns in American politics in the closing years of the nineteenth century?**

- **What key arguments were made by American anti-imperialists?**

- **How did late-nineteenth-century imperialism transform the United States?**

Imperial Dreams

What drove U.S. expansion overseas in the late nineteenth century?

Foreign policy assumed a new importance for Americans at the end of the nineteenth century. During the Gilded Age, they were preoccupied by internal matters, such as industrialization, the construction of the railroads, and the settlement of the West. Over time, however, political and business leaders began to look outward, advocating an activist approach to world affairs, emphasizing the supposed benefits to the country's domestic health.

That proponents of overseas expansion stressed the benefits that would accrue at home is hardly surprising, for foreign policy has always sprung from a nation's domestic setting—its needs and moods, ideology and culture. The leaders who guided America's expansionist foreign relations also guided the economic development of the machine age, forged the transcontinental railroad, built America's bustling cities and giant corporations, and shaped mass culture. They believed that the United States was an exceptional nation, superior to others because of its Anglo-Saxon heritage and its God-favored and prosperous history.

Along with exceptionalism, America's march toward empire was influenced by nationalism, capitalism, Social Darwinism, and a paternalistic attitude toward foreigners. "They are children and we are men in these deep matters of government," future president Woodrow Wilson announced in 1898. His words reveal the gender and age bias of American attitudes. Where these attitudes intersected with foreign cultures, the result was a mix of adoption, imitation, and rejection.

Chronology

1861–69	Seward sets expansionist course
1867	United States acquires Alaska and Midway
1876	Pro-U.S. Díaz begins thirty-four-year rule in Mexico
1878	United States gains naval rights in Samoa
1885	Strong's *Our Country* celebrates Anglo-Saxon destiny of dominance
1887	United States gains naval rights to Pearl Harbor, Hawai'i
	McKinley Tariff hurts Hawaiian sugar exports
1893	Economic crisis leads to business failures and mass unemployment
	Pro-U.S. interests stage successful coup against Queen Lili'uokalani of Hawai'i
1895	Cuban revolution against Spain begins
	Japan defeats China in war, annexes Korea and Formosa (Taiwan)
1898	United States formally annexes Hawai'i
	U.S. battleship *Maine* blows up in Havana harbor
	United States defeats Spain in Spanish-American War
1899	Treaty of Paris enlarges U.S. empire
	United Fruit Company forms and becomes influential in Central America
	Philippine insurrection breaks out, led by Emilio Aguinaldo
1901	McKinley assassinated; Theodore Roosevelt becomes president
1903	Panama grants canal rights to United States
	Platt Amendment subjugates Cuba
1904	Roosevelt Corollary declares United States a hemispheric "police power"
1905	Portsmouth Conference ends Russo-Japanese War
1906	San Francisco School Board segregates Asian schoolchildren
	United States invades Cuba to quell revolt
1907	"Great White Fleet" makes world tour
1910	Mexican revolution threatens U.S. interests
1914	U.S. troops invade Mexico
	First World War begins
	Panama Canal opens

Foreign Policy Elite

It would take time for most Americans to grasp the changes under way. Foreign policy is usually dominated by what scholars have labeled the "foreign policy elite"—opinion leaders in politics, journalism, business, agriculture, religion, education, and the military. Better read and better traveled than most Americans, more cosmopolitan and politically active in the post–Civil War era, these leaders believed that U.S. prosperity and security depended on the nation's influence abroad. Increasingly in the late nineteenth century, the expansionist-minded elite urged both formal and informal imperialism. They talked about building a bigger navy and digging a canal across Panama, Central America, or Mexico; establishing colonies; and selling surpluses abroad. Among them were Theodore Roosevelt, appointed assistant secretary of the navy in 1897; Senator Henry Cabot Lodge, who joined the Foreign Relations Committee in 1896; and corporate lawyer Elihu Root, who later served as secretary of war and secretary of state.

One reason these leaders believed in the importance of buying, selling, and investing in foreign marketplaces was for profits from foreign sales. Another reason was the belief that foreign commerce might serve as a safety valve to relieve overproduction, unemployment, and economic depression since the nation's farms and factories produced more than Americans could consume, especially during the

Visualizing THE PAST

Messages in Advertising

The American march toward empire was also reflected in advertising. On the front and back covers of this 1901 promotional booklet, the Singer Sewing Machine Company is marketing not only its product but the idea that a sewing machine can unite nations. The image that emerges of the United States is that of peacemaker and unifier. In the 1892 Singer sewing machine advertisement Imperial Dreams card, the Zulu natives are sewing American-style clothes. What message is being sent here, do you think? How does it compare to the recent advertising campaigns by firms such as Starbucks, Nike, and Subaru that push the product in question only indirectly and instead show people around the world connecting despite their differences?

Sewing machines and therefore world peace?

Picture Research Consultants & Archives

Singer sewing machine advertisement card, showing six people from Zululand (South Africa) with a Singer sewing machine.

Library of Congress

1890s depression. Economic ties also helped spread the American way of life, especially capitalism, while expansionism symbolized national stature.

Foreign Trade Expansion

Foreign trade figured prominently in the United States' economic growth after the Civil War. Foreign commerce stimulated the building of a larger protective navy, the professionalization of the foreign service, calls for more colonies, and an interventionist foreign policy. In 1865, U.S. exports totaled $234 million; by 1900, they climbed to $1.5 billion. By 1914, exports hit $2.5 billion. In 1874, the United States reversed its historically unfavorable balance of trade (importing more than it exported) and began to enjoy a long-term favorable balance. Most of America's products went to Britain, continental Europe, and Canada, but increasing amounts flowed to new markets in Latin America and Asia. Meanwhile, American investments abroad reached $3.5 billion by 1914, placing the United States among the top four investor countries.

Agricultural goods accounted for about three-fourths of total exports in 1870 and about two-thirds in 1900, with grain, cotton, meat, and dairy products topping the list. Farmers' livelihoods became tied to world market conditions and foreign wars. Wisconsin cheesemakers shipped to Britain; the Swift and Armour meat companies exported refrigerated beef to Europe.

In 1913, manufactured goods led U.S. exports for the first time (see Figure 19.1). Substantial proportions of America's steel, copper, and petroleum were sold abroad, making many workers in those industries dependent on American exports.

Race Thinking and the Male Ethos

In expanding U.S. influence overseas, many officials championed a nationalism based on notions of American supremacy. Some justified expansionism via new racist theories. For decades, the Western

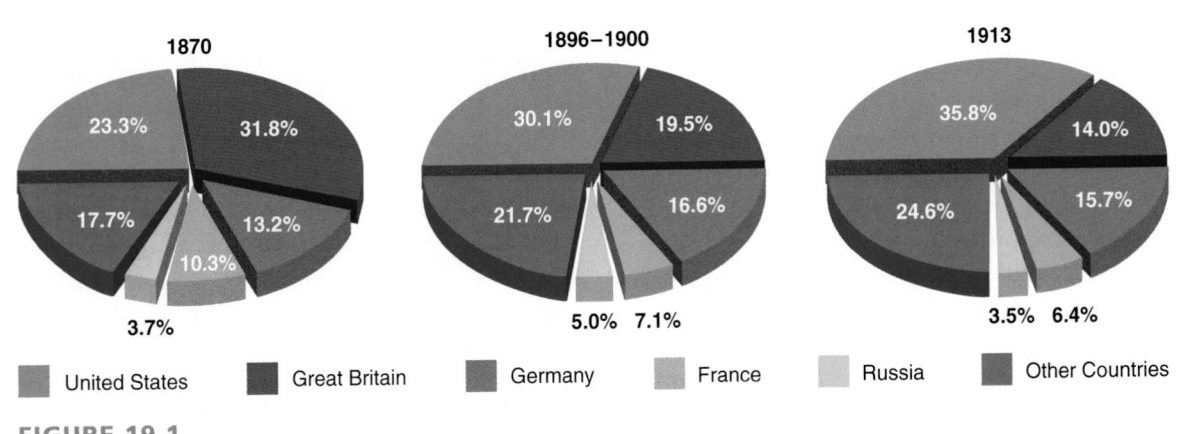

FIGURE 19.1
The Rise of U.S. Economic Power in the World
These pie charts showing percentage shares of world manufacturing production for the major nations of the world demonstrate that the United States came to surpass Great Britain in this significant economic measurement of power.

(Source: Friedberg, Aaron L.; *The Weary Titan.* © 1988 Princeton University Press, 1989 paperback edition. Reprinted by permission of Princeton University Press.)

National Geographic

In early 1888, thirty-three members of Washington, D.C.'s elite Cosmos Club considered "organizing a society for the increase and diffusion of geographical knowledge." The result was the National Geographic Society, the world's largest nonprofit scientific and educational institution.

At the heart of the enterprise was *National Geographic Magazine*, which debuted in October 1888. Early issues were brief and bland, and sales lagged. When Alexander Graham Bell became the society's president in 1898, he shifted emphasis from newsstand sales to society membership, reasoning correctly that belonging to a distinguished fellowship would draw members. He also appointed a talented editor, Gilbert H. Grosvenor, age twenty-three, who commissioned articles and filled eleven pages with photographs.

Early photos showed people posed in their native costumes, displayed as anthropological specimens. By 1908, pictures occupied half of the magazine. In 1910, the first color photographs appeared in a twenty-four-page spread on Korea and China—then the largest collection of color photographs published in a single issue of any magazine. *National Geographic*'s other photographic firsts included the first natural-color photos of Arctic life and the undersea world.

The society also sponsored expeditions, such as Robert Peary's and Matthew Henson's 1909 journey to the North Pole and, later, Jacques Cousteau's oceanic explorations and Jane Goodall's observations of wild chimpanzees. These adventures appeared in the magazine's pages. By the end of Grosvenor's tenure in 1954, circulation topped 2 million.

Less admirably, Grosvenor's editors pressured photographers for pictures of pretty girls. One photographer recalled, "Hundreds of bare-breasted women, all from poorer countries, were published at a time of booming subscription rates." Editors developed a well-earned reputation for presenting a rosy worldview. An article about Berlin published before the start of World War II, for example, contained no criticism of the Nazi regime and no mention of its persecution of Jews. Recently, the magazine has featured more newsworthy topics—AIDS, stem cell research, Hurricane Katrina, global warming—but in measured tones.

Throughout, the society expanded its reach, producing books, atlases, globes, and television documentaries. Targeting overseas readers, the society in 1995 launched a Japanese-language edition and subsequently added twenty-five other foreign editions. *National Geographic*, after a century of linking Americans to faraway places, now connected readers worldwide to the United States.

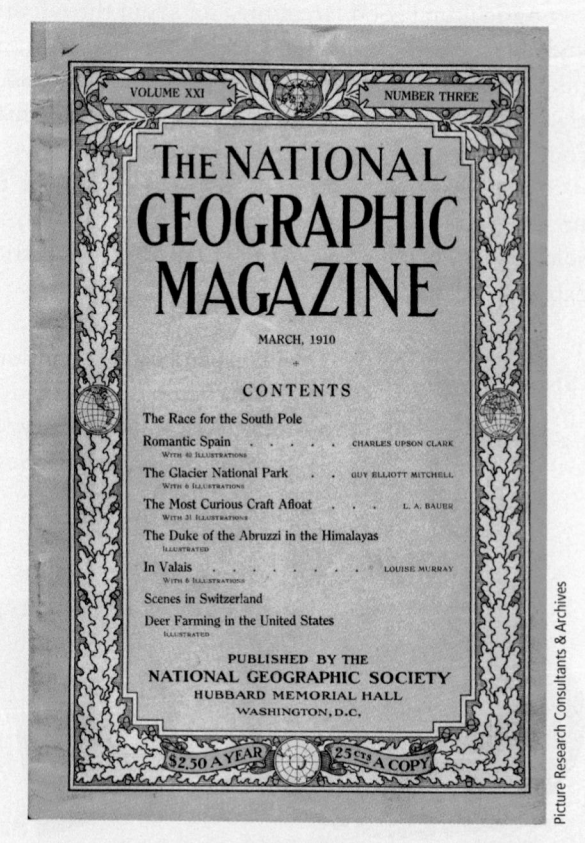

National Geographic had already gone through five different cover formats when Robert Weir Crouch, an English-born Canadian decorative artist, came up with a design that cemented the magazine's visual identity. Singular and immediately recognizable, the oak-and-laurel frame on the cover of the February 1910 issue would remain largely unchanged for nearly half a century, though the buff-colored border would be replaced with a golden one.

scientific establishment classified humankind by race, and students of physical anthropology drew on phrenology and physiognomy—the analysis of skull size and facial features—to produce a hierarchy of superior and inferior races. One French researcher claimed that blacks represented a female race and "like the woman, the black is deprived of political and scientific intelligence."

The language of U.S. leaders was also weighted with words like *manliness* and *weakling*. The warrior and president Theodore Roosevelt viewed people of color (or "darkeys," as he called them) as effeminate weaklings who were unable to govern themselves or cope with world politics. Americans debased Latin Americans as half-breeds needing supervision or distressed damsels begging for manly rescue. The gendered imagery in U.S. foreign relations joined race thinking to place women, people of color, and nations weaker than the United States low in the hierarchy of power and, hence, in a dependent status justifying U.S. dominance.

Reverend Josiah Strong's influential *Our Country* (1885) celebrated an Anglo-Saxon race destined to lead others. "As America goes, so goes the world," he declared. Social Darwinists saw Americans as a superior people certain to overcome competition.

Race thinking—popularized in magazine photos and cartoons, world's fairs, textbooks, museums, and political orations—reinforced notions of American greatness, influenced how U.S. leaders dealt with other peoples, and obviated the need to think about the subtle textures of other societies. *National Geographic*, which began publication in 1888, photographically chronicled America's new overseas involvements in Asia and the Pacific, featuring images of exotic, premodern peoples who had not become "Western." Fairs also put so-called uncivilized people of color on display in the "freak" section. Dog-eating Filipinos aroused comment at the 1904 St. Louis World's Fair. Such racism downgraded diplomacy and justified domination and war.

Similar thinking permeated attitudes toward immigrants, whose entry into the United States was first restricted in these years. Although the Burlingame Treaty (1868) provided for free immigration between the United States and China, anti-Chinese riots continuously erupted in the American West. An 1880 treaty permitted Congress to suspend Chinese immigration to the United States. Tensions continued: in 1885, white coal miners and railway workers in Rock Springs, Wyoming, massacred twenty-five Chinese.

In 1906, the San Francisco School Board ordered Chinese, Koreans, and Japanese segregated in special schools. Tokyo protested, and President Roosevelt quieted the crisis by striking a "gentleman's agreement" with Tokyo restricting Japanese immigration. San Francisco rescinded its segregation order. Relations with Tokyo worsened again in 1913 when the California legislature denied Japanese residents the right to own property.

Link to Josiah Strong, *Our Country* (1885)

The "Civilizing" Impulse

Expansionists believed that empire benefited Americans and those who came under their control. When the United States intervened in weaker states, Americans claimed that they were extending liberty and prosperity to less fortunate people. William Howard Taft, as civil governor of the Philippines (1901–1904), described the United States' mission in its new colony as

Cartoonists sometimes mocked the proselytizing efforts of U.S. and European missionaries. This illustration, from 1895, shows two missionaries, one British and one American, with bags of money and their respective militaries behind them, preaching to a Chinese man. The caption reads: "According to the ideas of our missionary maniacs, the Chinaman must be converted, even if it takes the whole military and naval forces of the two greatest nations of the world to do it." Note the labels on the guns.

Library of Congress

lifting Filipinos up "to a point of civilization" that will make them "call the name of the United States blessed." Later, Taft said about the Chinese that "the more civilized they become … the wealthier they become, and the better market they become for us."

Missionaries dispatched to Africa and Asia, like Lottie Moon, helped spur the transfer of American culture and power abroad—"the peaceful conquest of the world," as Reverend Frederick Gates put it. In 1915, ten thousand American missionaries worked overseas. In China by 1915, more than twenty-five hundred mostly female American Protestant missionaries taught, preached the gospel, and administered medical care.

Ambitions and Strategies

What happened to Seward's vision of an American empire?

The U.S. empire grew gradually, as American leaders defined guiding principles and built institutions to support overseas ambitions. William H. Seward, one of its chief architects, argued for extension of the American frontier as a senator from New York (1849–1861) and secretary of state (1861–1869). Seward envisioned a large U.S. empire encompassing Canada, the Caribbean, Cuba, Central America, Mexico, Hawai'i, Iceland, Greenland, and the Pacific islands. This empire would result from a natural process of gravitation toward the United States. Commerce would hurry the process, as would a canal across Central America, a transcontinental American railroad, and a telegraph system to speed communications.

Seward's Quest for Empire

Most of Seward's grandiose plans did not reach fruition in his lifetime. In 1867, his efforts for a treaty with Denmark to buy the Danish West Indies (Virgin

Islands) were scuttled by Senate foes and a hurricane that wrecked St. Thomas. The Virgin Islanders, who voted for annexation, would wait until 1917 for official U.S. status. Seward's scheme with unscrupulous Dominican Republic leaders to gain a Caribbean naval base at Samaná Bay also failed. The corruption surrounding this deal foiled President Ulysses S. Grant's initiative in 1870 to buy the island nation.

Anti-imperialism also blocked Seward. Opponents of empire such as Senator Carl Schurz argued that creating a showcase of democracy and prosperity on unsettled land at home would best persuade other peoples to adopt American principles. Some anti-imperialists, sharing the era's racism, opposed the annexation of territory populated by dark-skinned people.

Seward enjoyed some successes. In 1866, citing the Monroe Doctrine (see page 226), he sent troops to the Mexican border and demanded that France abandon its puppet regime there. Also facing angry Mexican nationalists, Napoleon III abandoned the Maximilian monarchy that he had forcibly installed three years earlier. In 1867, Seward paid Russia $7.2 million for the 591,000 square miles of Alaska—land twice the size of Texas. That same year, Seward claimed the Midway Islands (two small islands and a coral atoll northwest of Hawai'i).

International Communications

In 1866, through the efforts of financier Cyrus Field, an underwater transatlantic cable linked European and American telegraph networks. Backed by J. P. Morgan's capital, communications pioneer James A. Scrymser strung telegraph lines to Latin America, entering Chile in 1890. In 1903, a submarine cable spanned the Pacific to the Philippines; three years later, it reached Japan and China. Information about markets, crises, and war flowed steadily and quickly. Drawn closer to one another through improved communications and transportation, nations found that faraway events had greater impact on their prosperity and security.

Increasingly, American diplomats negotiated with Europeans as equals—signaling the United States' arrival on the international stage. Washington officials, for example, successfully confronted European powers over Samoa, South Pacific islands located four thousand miles from San Francisco on the trade route to Australia. In 1878, the United States gained exclusive rights to a coaling station at Samoa's coveted port of Pago Pago. Eyeing the same prize, Britain and Germany began to cultivate ties with Samoan leaders. Tensions grew, and war seemed possible. At the eleventh hour, however, Britain, Germany, and the United States met in Berlin in 1889 and, without consulting the Samoans, devised a three-part protectorate that limited Samoa's independence. Ten years later, the three powers partitioned Samoa: the United States received Pago Pago through annexation of part of the islands (now called American Samoa); Germany took what is today independent Western Samoa; and Britain obtained the Gilbert Islands and the Solomon Islands.

Alfred T. Mahan and Navalism

With eyes on all parts of the world, even on Africa, where U.S. interests were minimal, ardent expansionists embraced navalism—the campaign to build an imperial navy. Calling attention to the naval buildup

Captain Alfred Thayer Mahan Author of *The Influence of Sea Power upon History* (1890) and an advocate of a stronger navy and imperialism.

by European powers, notably Germany, they argued for a bigger, modernized navy, adding the "blue water" command of the seas to its traditional role of "brown water" coastline defense. **Captain Alfred Thayer Mahan**, a popularizer of this New Navy, argued that because foreign trade was essential, the nation required an efficient navy to protect its shipping; and a navy required colonies for bases. Mahan's ideas were published as *The Influence of Sea Power upon History* (1890). Theodore Roosevelt and Henry Cabot Lodge consulted Mahan, sharing his belief in the links between trade, navy, and colonies and his alarm over Germany's aggressive military spirit.

Moving toward naval modernization, Congress in 1883 authorized construction of the first steel-hulled warships. American factories produced steam engines, high-velocity shells, powerful guns, and precision instruments. The navy shifted from sail power to steam and from wood construction to steel. New Navy ships, such as the *Maine, Oregon,* and *Boston,* thrust the United States into naval prominence.

Crises in the 1890s: Hawai'i, Venezuela, and Cuba

What typically imperialist actions did the United States take in its dealings with Hawai'i and Venezuela?

In the depression-plagued 1890s, crises in Hawai'i and Cuba—and the belief that the frontier at home had closed—reinforced the expansionist argument. In 1893, historian Frederick Jackson Turner postulated that the ever-expanding continental frontier, which shaped the American character, was gone. He did not say a new frontier had to be found overseas, but he did claim that "American energy will continually demand a wider field for its exercise."

Hawai'i Island nation in the Pacific that became an American territory in 1898. It was significant from a military and economic standpoint.

Annexation of Hawai'i

Hawai'i, the Pacific Ocean archipelago of eight major islands two thousand miles from the U.S. west coast, emerged as America's new frontier. The Hawaiian Islands had long commanded American attention—commercial, missionary religious, naval, and diplomatic. By 1881, Secretary of State James Blaine already declared the Hawaiian Islands "essentially a part of the American system." By 1890, Americans owned about three-quarters of Hawai'i's wealth and subordinated its economy to that of the United States through sugar exports that entered the U.S. duty free.

In Hawai'i's multiracial society, Chinese and Japanese nationals far outnumbered Americans, who represented just 2.1 percent of the population. Prominent Americans on the islands organized secret clubs and military units to contest the royal government. In 1887, they forced the king to accept a constitution that granted foreigners the vote and shifted decision making from the monarchy to the legislature. The same year, Hawai'i granted the United States naval rights to Pearl Harbor. Many native Hawaiians (53 percent of the population in 1890) believed that the *haole* (foreigners)—especially Americans—were stealing their country.

The native government was further undermined when the 1890 McKinley Tariff eliminated the duty-free status of Hawaiian sugar exports in the United States. Suffering declining sugar prices and profits, the American island elite pressed for annexation by the United States, thereby classifying their sugar as domestic. When

Princess Lili'uokalani assumed the throne in 1891, she sought to roll back the political power of the *haole*. The next year, the white oligarchy formed the subversive Annexation Club.

Annexationists struck in January 1893 in collusion with John L. Stevens, America's chief diplomat in Hawai'i, who dispatched troops from the USS *Boston* to occupy Honolulu. The queen, arrested and confined, surrendered. Rather than yield to the new provisional regime, headed by Sanford B. Dole, son of missionaries and a prominent attorney, she relinquished authority to the U.S. government. President Benjamin Harrison hurriedly sent an annexation treaty to the Senate.

Sensing foul play, incoming president Grover Cleveland ordered an investigation, which confirmed a conspiracy that most Hawaiians opposed annexation. But when Hawai'i proved to be a strategic and commercial way station to Asia and the Philippines during the Spanish-American War, President William McKinley maneuvered annexation through Congress on July 7, 1898. Under the Organic Act of June 1900, the people of Hawai'i became U.S. citizens. Statehood came in 1959.

Queen Lili'uokalani (1838–1917), ousted from her throne in 1893 by wealthy revolutionaries, vigorously protested the U.S. annexation of Hawai'i in 1898. In her autobiography and diary, as well as in interviews, she defended Hawaiian nationalism and emphasized that American officials in 1893 had conspired with Sanford B. Dole and others to overthrow the native monarchy.

| Venezuelan Boundary Dispute |

The Venezuelan crisis of 1895 also saw the United States in an expansive mood. For decades Venezuela and Great Britain quarreled over the border between Venezuela and British Guiana, a territory containing rich gold deposits and a commercial gateway to northern South America via the Orinoco River. Venezuela sought U.S. help, and in July 1895, Secretary of State Richard Olney brashly lectured the British that the Monroe Doctrine prohibited European powers from denying self-government to nations in the Western Hemisphere. The British quietly retreated. With almost no Venezuelan input, in 1896 an Anglo-American arbitration board divided the disputed territory between Britain and Venezuela. Thus, the United States displayed a typical imperialist trait: disregard for the rights of small nations.

In 1895, Cuba was the site of another crisis. From 1868 to 1878, the Cubans battled Spain for their independence, winning only the end of slavery. While the Cuban economy suffered, repressive Spanish rule continued. Insurgents committed to *Cuba libre* waited for another chance, and José Martí, one of the heroes of Cuban history, collected money, arms, and men in the United States.

Revolution in Cuba

Culturally, Americans and Cubans intersected in many ways. Cubans of all classes had settled in Baltimore, New York, Boston, and Philadelphia. Prominent Cubans sent their children to U.S. schools. When Cuban expatriates returned home, many spoke English, had American names, played baseball, and jettisoned Catholicism for Protestant denominations.

The Cuban and U.S. economies were also intertwined. American investments of $50 million, mostly in sugar plantations, dominated the island. More than 90 percent of Cuba's sugar was exported to the United States, and most island imports came from the United States. Havana's famed cigar factories relocated to Key West and Tampa to evade U.S. tariffs. Martí, however, feared that "economic union means political union," for "the nation that buys, commands" and "the nation that sells, serves."

Martí's fears were prophetic. In 1894, the Wilson-Gorman Tariff imposed a duty on Cuban sugar. The Cuban economy, highly dependent on exports, plunged into crisis, hastening the island's revolution against Spain and its further incorporation into "the American system."

In 1895, from American soil, Martí launched a revolution against Spain. Rebels burned sugar-cane fields. U.S. investments were incinerated, and Cuban-American trade dwindled. To separate insurgents from their supporters, Spanish general Valeriano Weyler instituted a policy of "reconcentration." Some 300,000 Cubans were herded into fortified towns and camps, where starvation and disease caused tens of thousands of deaths. As reports of atrocities appeared in U.S. newspapers, Americans sympathized with the insurrectionists. In late 1897, a new government in Madrid modified reconcentration and promised some autonomy for Cuba, but the insurgents gained ground.

Sinking of the *Maine*

President William McKinley took office as an imperialist who advocated foreign bases for the New Navy, the export of surplus production, and U.S. supremacy in the Western Hemisphere. Vexed by Cuba's turmoil, he believed Spain should give up its colony and explored purchasing Cuba for $300 million. In January 1898, when antireform pro-Spanish loyalists and army troops rioted in Havana, Washington ordered the battleship *Maine* to Havana harbor to demonstrate U.S. concern and to protect American citizens.

On February 15, an explosion ripped the *Maine*, killing 266 of 354 American officers and crew. The naval board investigating the *Maine* disaster then reported that a mine had caused the explosion. Vengeful Americans blamed Spain. Congress complied unanimously with McKinley's request for $50 million for defense. (Later, official and unofficial studies attributed the sinking to an accidental internal explosion.)

McKinley's Ultimatum and War Decision

Though reluctant to go to war, McKinley sent Spain an ultimatum: accept an armistice, end reconcentration, and designate McKinley as arbiter. Madrid abolished reconcentration and rejected, then accepted, an armistice. The president would no longer tolerate chronic disorder ninety miles off the U.S. coast. On April 11, McKinley asked Congress for authorization to use force "to secure a full and final termination of hostilities between … Spain and … Cuba, and to secure in the island the establishment of a stable government, capable of maintaining order."

McKinley listed the reasons for war: the "cause of humanity"; the protection of American life and property; the "very serious injury to the commerce, trade, and business of our people"; and, referring to the destruction of the *Maine*, the "constant menace to our peace." On April 19, Congress declared Cuba free and independent and directed the president to use force to remove Spanish authority. The legislators also passed the Teller Amendment, which disclaimed U.S. intention to annex Cuba or control the island except to ensure its "pacification." McKinley blocked a congressional amendment to recognize the rebel government, arguing they were not ready for self-government.

The Spanish-American War and the Debate Over Empire

What were the anti-imperialist arguments against U.S. annexation of the Philippines after the Spanish-American War?

By the time the Spanish concessions were on the table, prospects for compromise appeared dim. Cuban insurgents wanted full independence, and no Spanish government could have given up and remained in office. Nor did the United States welcome a truly independent Cuban government that might attempt to reduce U.S. interests.

Motives for War   Mixed and complex motives drove Americans who favored war. McKinley's April message expressed a humanitarian impulse to stop the bloodletting and concern for commerce and property. Republicans wanted the Cuban question solved to secure their party's victory in upcoming congressional elections. Many businesspeople and farmers believed that ejecting Spain from Cuba would open new markets for surplus production.

Imperialists saw the war as an opportunity to fulfill expansionist dreams, while conservatives, alarmed by Populism and labor strikes, welcomed war as a national unifier. One senator commented that "internal discord" was disappearing in the "fervent heat of patriotism." Theodore Roosevelt and others too young to remember the bloody Civil War looked on war as adventure.

More than 263,000 regulars and volunteers served in the army and another 25,000 in the navy during the war. Most never left the United States. The typical volunteer was young (early twenties), white, unmarried, native born, and working class. Deaths numbered 5,462, mostly from diseases in Tennessee, Virginia and Florida. Only 379 died in combat. About 10,000 African American troops in segregated regiments found no relief from racism and Jim Crow, even though black troops were central to the victorious battle for Santiago de Cuba. For all, food, sanitary conditions, and medical care were bad. Still, Roosevelt could hardly contain himself. Although Roosevelt's Rough Riders, a motley unit of Ivy Leaguers and cowboys, proved undisciplined and ineffective, Roosevelt's self-serving publicity efforts ensured they received good press.

Dewey in the Philippines

The first war news came from Asia, from the Spanish colony of the Philippine Islands, where Filipinos were also seeking independence. On May 1, 1898, Commodore George Dewey's New Navy ship *Olympia* led an American squadron into Manila Bay and wrecked the Spanish fleet. Manila was a choice harbor, and the Philippines sat en route to China's potentially huge market.

Facing Americans and rebels in Cuba and the Philippines, Spanish resistance collapsed rapidly. U.S. ships blockaded Cuban ports and insurgents cut off supplies from the countryside, causing starvation and illness for Spanish soldiers. American troops landed near Santiago de Cuba on June 22 and laid siege to the city. On July 3, U.S. warships sank the Spanish Caribbean squadron in Santiago harbor. American forces assaulted the Spanish colony of Puerto Rico, gaining another Caribbean base for the navy and pushing Madrid to sue for peace.

Treaty of Paris

On August 12, Spain and the United States signed an armistice ending the war. In Paris, in December 1898, they agreed on the peace terms: independence for Cuba from Spain; cession of the Philippines, Puerto Rico, and the Pacific island of Guam to the United States for $20 million. The U.S. empire now stretched deep into Asia, and the annexation of Wake Island (1898), Hawai'i (1898), and Samoa (1899) gave American traders, missionaries, and naval promoters other stepping-stones to China.

During the war, the *Washington Post* detected "The taste of empire is in the mouth of the people." But anti-imperialists such as author Mark Twain, Nebraska politician William Jennings Bryan, reformer Jane Addams, and industrialist Andrew Carnegie argued against annexation of the Philippines. Their concern that a war to free Cuba had led to empire stimulated debate over American foreign policy.

Anti-Imperialist Arguments

Imperial control could be imposed formally (by military occupation, annexation, or colonialism) or informally (by economic domination, political manipulation, or the threat of intervention). Anti-imperialist ire focused mostly on formal imperial control. Some critics cited the Declaration of Independence and the Constitution: the conquest of people against their wills violated the right of self-determination.

Other anti-imperialists feared that the American character was being corrupted by imperialist zeal. Jane Addams, seeing children play war games on Chicago streets, noted that they were not freeing Cubans but rather slaying Spaniards. Hoping to build a foreign policy constituency from women's organizations, prominent women like Addams championed peace and an end to imperial conquest.

Some anti-imperialists protested that the United States was practicing a double standard—"offering liberty to the Cubans with one hand, cramming liberty down the throats of the Filipinos with the other, but with both feet planted upon the neck of the negro," as an African American politician from Massachusetts put it. Still others warned that annexing people of color would undermine Anglo-Saxon purity and supremacy at home.

For Samuel Gompers and other anti-imperialist labor leaders, the issue was jobs. Might not the new colonials be imported as cheap contract labor to drive down American wages? Would not exploitation of the weak abroad become contagious and lead to further exploitation of the weak at home? The anti-imperialists, however, never launched an effective campaign. Although they organized the Anti-Imperialist League in November 1898, they so differed on domestic issues that they were unable to speak with one voice on a foreign question. For example, Gompers favored the war but not the postwar annexations and Carnegie would accept colonies if they were not acquired by force.

Imperialist Arguments The imperialists answered their critics with appeals to patriotism, destiny, and commerce. They envisioned American merchant ships plying the waters to boundless Asian markets; naval vessels protecting America's Pacific interests; missionaries uplifting inferior peoples. It was America's duty, they insisted, quoting a then-popular Rudyard Kipling poem, to "take up the white man's burden." Furthermore, Filipino insurgents were beginning to resist U.S. rule, and it seemed cowardly to pull out under fire, especially with Germany and Japan ready to seize the islands.

In February 1899, by a 57-to-27 vote, the Senate passed the Treaty of Paris, ending the war with Spain. Most Republicans voted yes and most Democrats no. An amendment promising independence once the Filipinos formed a stable government lost by only the tie-breaking ballot of the vice president.

Asian Encounters: War in the Philippines, Diplomacy in China

Why was the Open Door policy such a key component of U.S. diplomacy?

The Philippine crisis was far from over. **Emilio Aguinaldo**, the Philippine nationalist leader who long battled the Spanish, believed that American officials promised independence for his country. But after the victory, U.S. officers ordered Aguinaldo out of Manila. In early 1899, he proclaimed an independent Philippine Republic and took up arms. U.S. officials stood against the rebellion.

Emilio Aguinaldo Nationalist leader of Filipino war against American occupation.

Philippine Insurrection and Pacification Both sides fought viciously; American soldiers burned villages and tortured captives, while Filipino forces staged brutal hit-and-run ambushes. U.S. troops introduced a variant of the Spanish reconcentration policy—in the province of Batangas, for instance, U.S. troops forced residents to live in designated zones to separate insurgents from supporters. Poor sanitation, starvation, and malaria and cholera killed thousands. Outside the secure areas, Americans destroyed food supplies to starve out rebels. At least one-quarter of the population of Batangas died or fled.

Before the Philippine insurrection was suppressed in 1902, 20,000 Filipinos died in combat, and 600,000 succumbed to starvation and disease. More than 4,000 Americans lay dead. Resistance to U.S. rule, however, continued. When the fiercely independent, often violent Muslim Filipinos of Moro Province refused to knuckle under, the U.S. military threatened extermination. In 1906, 600 Moros, including women and children, were slaughtered at the Battle of Bud Dajo.

U.S. officials soon tried to Americanize the Philippines, instituting a new educational system, with English as the main language. The architect Daniel Burnham,

MAP 19.1

Imperialism in Asia: Turn of the Century

China and the Pacific region had become imperialist hunting grounds by the turn of the century. The European powers and Japan controlled more areas than the United States, which nonetheless participated in the imperial race by annexing the Philippines, Wake, Guam, Hawai'i, and Samoa; announcing the Open Door policy; and expanding trade. As the spheres of influence in China demonstrate, that besieged nation succumbed to outsiders despite the Open Door policy. Source: Copyright © Cengage Learning 2015

leader of the City Beautiful movement, planned modern Manila. The Philippine economy grew as an American satellite, and a sedition act sent U.S. critics to prison. In 1916, the Jones Act vaguely promised independence once the Philippines established a "stable government." The United States finally ended its rule in 1946 during a post–World War II period of decolonization.

China and the Open Door Policy

In China, McKinley successfully focused on a policy emphasizing negotiation. Outsiders had pecked away at China since the 1840s. Taking advantage of the Qing (Manchu) dynasty's weakness, the major imperial powers carved out spheres of influence (regions over which they claimed political control and exclusive commercial privileges): Germany in Shandong, Russia in Manchuria, France in Yunnan and Hainan, and Britain in Kowloon and Hong Kong. Then, in 1895, Japan claimed victory over China in a short war and assumed control of Formosa and Korea and parts of China proper (see Map 19.1). American religious and business leaders petitioned Washington to halt the dismemberment of China before they were closed out.

Secretary of State John Hay knew that missionaries like Lottie Moon had become targets of Chinese nationalist anger and that American oil and textile companies had been disappointed with their investments there. Thus, in September 1899, Hay sent nations with spheres of influence in China a note seeking their respect for the principle of equal trade opportunity—an Open Door. The recipients sent evasive replies, privately complaining that the United States was seeking, for free, the trade rights in China that they had gained at considerable cost.

The next year, the Boxers, a Chinese secret society, sought to expel foreigners. They rioted, killing many outsiders and laying siege to the foreign legations in Beijing in what is known as the **Boxer Rebellion**. The United States joined the other imperial powers in sending troops. Hay also sent a second Open Door note instructing other nations to preserve China's territorial integrity and honor "equal and impartial trade." China continued for years to be fertile soil for foreign exploitation, especially by the Japanese.

Boxer Rebellion Chinese insurgency against Christians and foreigners, defeated by an international force.

The **Open Door policy** became a cornerstone of U.S. diplomacy. While the United States had long opposed barriers to international commerce, after 1900, when it emerged as the premier world trader, the Open Door policy became an instrument first to pry open markets and then to dominate them. The Open Door also developed as an ideology with several tenets: first, that America's domestic well-being required exports; second, that foreign trade would suffer interruption unless the United States intervened abroad; and third, that the closing of any area to American products, citizens, or ideas threatened the survival of the United States.

Open Door policy Foreign policy proposed by U.S. Secretary of State John Hay, in which he asked the major European powers to assure trading rights in China by opening the ports in their spheres of influence to all countries.

TR's World

What solidified U.S.-British ties heading into World War I?

Theodore Roosevelt played an important role in shaping U.S. foreign policy in the McKinley administration. As assistant secretary of the navy (1897–1898), as a Spanish-American War hero, and then as vice president in McKinley's second term, Roosevelt worked to make the United States a great power. Long fascinated by power, he also relished hunting and killing. Roosevelt justified the slaughtering of American Indians, if necessary, and took his Rough Riders to Cuba, desperate to get in on the fighting.

Like Americans of his day, Roosevelt assumed the superiority of Protestant Anglo-American culture and believed in using American power to shape world affairs (which he summarized by citing the West African proverb "Speak softly and carry a big stick, and you will go far"). In TR's world, there were "civilized" and "uncivilized" nations; the former, primarily white and Anglo-Saxon or Teutonic, had a right and a duty to intervene in the affairs of the latter (generally nonwhite, Latin, or Slavic, and therefore "backward") to preserve order and stability, even if that meant using violence.

Presidential Authority Roosevelt's love of the good fight caused many to rue his ascension to the presidency after McKinley's assassination in September 1901. But the cowboy was also an astute analyst of foreign policy. Roosevelt understood that American power, though growing, remained limited and that in many parts of the world the United States would have to rely on diplomacy to achieve satisfactory outcomes.

Roosevelt sought to centralize foreign policy in the White House. Congress was too large and unwieldy. This conviction that the executive branch should be supreme in foreign policy was to be shared by most presidents since TR, down to the present day.

Roosevelt's first efforts focused on Latin America, where U.S. economic and strategic interests towered (see Map 19.2). He also focused on Europe, where repeated disputes persuaded Americans to develop friendlier relations with Great Britain while avoiding the continent's troubles, which Americans blamed on Germany.

As U.S. economic interests expanded in Latin America, so did U.S. political influence. Exports to Latin America rose from $50 million in the 1870s to more than $120 million in 1901 and $300 million in 1914. Investments by U.S. citizens in Latin America climbed to $1.26 billion in 1914. In 1899, two large banana importers merged to form the United Fruit Company. United Fruit owned much of the land in Central America (more than a million acres in 1913) and the railroad and steamship lines. The company worked to eradicate yellow fever and malaria while bankrolling favored officeholders.

MAP 19.2
U.S. Hegemony in the Caribbean and Latin America

Through many interventions, territorial acquisitions, and robust economic expansion, the United States became the predominant power in Latin America in the early twentieth century. The United States often backed up the Roosevelt Corollary's declaration of a "police power" by dispatching troops to Caribbean nations, where they met nationalist opposition. Source: Copyright © Cengage Learning 2015

Cuba and the Platt Amendment

After the destructive war in Cuba, U.S. citizens and corporations dominated the island's economy, controlling the sugar, mining, tobacco, and utilities industries and most of the rural lands. Private U.S. investments grew from $50 million before the revolution to $220 million by 1913, and U.S. exports to the island rose from $26 million in 1900 to $196 million in 1917. The Teller Amendment outlawed the annexation of Cuba, but Washington officials used its call for "pacification" to justify U.S. control. American troops remained there until 1902.

U.S. authorities restricted voting rights to propertied Cuban males, excluding two-thirds of adult men and all women. American officials also forced Cubans to add the **Platt Amendment** to their constitution. This prohibited Cuba from making treaties that might impair its independence; in practice, this meant that all treaties required U.S. approval. Most important, the Platt Amendment granted the United States "the right to intervene" to preserve the island's independence and maintain domestic order. Finally, it required Cuba to lease a naval base to the United States (at Guantánamo Bay, still under U.S. jurisdiction today). Formalized in a 1903 treaty, the amendment governed Cuban-American relations until 1934.

Cubans protested the Platt Amendment, and a rebellion in 1906 prompted another U.S. invasion. The marines stayed until 1909, returning briefly in 1912 and again from 1917 to 1922. U.S. officials helped develop a transportation system, expand the public school system, found a national army, and increase sugar production. When Dr. Walter Reed's experiments, based on the theory of the Cuban physician Carlos Juan Finlay, proved that mosquitoes transmitted yellow fever, sanitary engineers eradicated the disease.

Puerto Rico, the Caribbean island taken as a spoil of war in the Treaty of Paris, also developed under U.S. tutelage. At first elites welcomed the United States as an improvement over Spain. But the U.S. military governor, General Guy V. Henry, regarded Puerto Ricans as children who needed "kindergarten instruction in controlling themselves without allowing them too much liberty." Some residents warned against the "Yankee peril"; others applauded the "Yankee model" and futilely anticipated statehood.

Platt Amendment Added to Cuba's constitution of 1903 under American pressure, it gave the United States the right to intervene if Cuban independence or internal order were threatened, and granted a naval base to the United States at Guantánamo Bay.

Link to the Platt Amendment

Panama Canal

Panama, meanwhile, became the site of a bold U.S. expansionist venture. In 1869, the world marveled when the newly completed Suez Canal facilitated travel between the Indian Ocean and Mediterranean Sea and enhanced the British empire's power. Surely that feat could be duplicated in the Western Hemisphere, possibly in Panama, a province of Colombia. Business interests joined politicians, diplomats, and navy officers in insisting that the United States control such an interoceanic canal.

But the Clayton-Bulwer Treaty with Britain (1850) provided for joint control of a canal. The British, recognizing their diminishing influence in the region and cultivating friendship with the United States as a counterweight to Germany, permitted a solely U.S.-run canal in the Hay-Pauncefote Treaty (1901). When Colombia resisted Washington's terms, Roosevelt encouraged Panamanian rebels to declare independence and ordered American warships to back them.

In a suit and hat, President Theodore Roosevelt occupies the controls of a ninety-five-ton power shovel at a Panama Canal work site. Roosevelt's November 1906 trip to inspect the massive project was the first time a sitting president left the United States.

Panama Canal Major waterway built by the United States for $352 million that traverses the Isthmus of Panama in Central America, connecting the Atlantic and Pacific oceans. Construction began in 1906 and was completed in 1914.

Link to the Roosevelt Corollary to the Monroe Doctrine

In 1903, the new Panama awarded the United States a canal zone and long-term rights to its control. The treaty also guaranteed Panama its independence. (In 1922, the United States paid Colombia $25 million in "conscience money" but did not apologize.) A technological achievement, the **Panama Canal** was completed in 1914.

Roosevelt Corollary

Elsewhere in the Caribbean, Roosevelt affirmed U.S. hegemony. Worried that Latin American nations' defaults on debts owed to European banks were provoking European intervention, the president in 1904 issued the Roosevelt Corollary to the Monroe Doctrine. He warned Latin Americans to stabilize their politics and finances or risk "intervention by some civilized nation." Roosevelt's declaration provided the rationale for frequent U.S. interventions in Latin America.

From 1900 to 1917, U.S. presidents ordered American troops to Cuba, Panama, Nicaragua, the Dominican Republic, Mexico, and Haiti to quell civil wars, thwart challenges to U.S. influence, gain ports and bases, and forestall European meddling (see Map 19.2). U.S. authorities ran elections, trained nationals, and shifted foreign debts to U.S. banks. They also controlled tariff revenues and government budgets (as in the Dominican Republic, from 1905 to 1941).

U.S.-Mexican Relations

U.S. officials paid attention to Mexico, where longtime dictator Porfirio Díaz (1876–1910) recruited foreign investors through tax incentives and land grants. American capitalists came to own Mexico's railroads and mines and invested heavily in petroleum and banking. By 1910, Americans controlled 43 percent of Mexican property and produced more than half of the country's oil. The Mexican revolutionaries who ousted Díaz in 1910 wanted to end their country's economic dependency on the United States.

The revolution descended into a bloody civil war with strong anti-Yankee overtones, and the Mexican government intended to nationalize American-owned properties. President Woodrow Wilson twice ordered troops onto Mexican soil: once in 1914, at Veracruz, to overthrow President Victoriano Huerta, and again in 1916, in northern Mexico, where General John J. "Black Jack" Pershing spent months pursuing Mexican rebel Pancho Villa for raiding an American border town. Failing to capture Villa and facing another nationalistic government, U.S. forces departed in January 1917.

As the United States reaffirmed the Monroe Doctrine, European nations reluctantly honored U.S. hegemony in Latin America. In turn, the United States continued to stand outside European embroilments. Theodore Roosevelt did help settle a Franco-German clash over Morocco by mediating a settlement at Algeciras, Spain (1906), but he drew American criticism for such involvement. Americans endorsed the Hague peace conferences (1899 and 1907) and negotiated arbitration treaties, but generally stayed outside the European arena, except for trade.

Peacemaking in East Asia

In East Asia, though, both Roosevelt and his successor, William Howard Taft, sought to preserve the Open Door and to contain Japan's rising power. Many race-minded Japanese interpreted the U.S. advance into the Pacific as an attempt by whites to gain ascendancy over Asians. The United States gradually had to make concessions to Japan to protect the Philippines and sustain the Open Door policy. Japan continued to plant interests in China and then smashed the Russians in the Russo-Japanese War (1904–1905). President Roosevelt mediated the negotiations at the Portsmouth Conference in New Hampshire and won the Nobel Peace Prize for helping to preserve a balance of power in Asia.

In 1905, in the Taft-Katsura Agreement, the United States conceded Japanese hegemony over Korea in return for Japan's respect for the U.S. position in the Philippines. Three years later, in the Root-Takahira Agreement, Washington recognized Japan's interests in Manchuria, whereas Japan again pledged the security of U.S. Pacific possessions and endorsed the Open Door in China. Roosevelt deterred the Japanese with reinforced naval power; in late 1907, he sent the navy's "Great White Fleet" on a world tour. Impressed, the Japanese expanded their navy.

Dollar Diplomacy

President Taft hoped to counter Japanese advances in Asia through dollar diplomacy—the use of private funds to serve American diplomatic goals and garner profits for American financiers—and bringing reform to less-developed countries. Taft induced American bankers to join an international consortium to build a railway in China. But it seemed only to embolden Japan to solidify its holdings in China.

In 1914, when World War I broke out in Europe, Japan seized Shandong and some Pacific islands from the Germans. In 1915, Japan issued its Twenty-One Demands, insisting on hegemony over China. The Chinese door was being slammed shut, but the United States lacked power in Asia to block Japan's imperialism. A new president, Woodrow Wilson, worried about how the "white race" could blunt the rise of "the yellow race."

Anglo-American Rapprochement

British officials shared this concern, though their attention was focused on rising tensions in Europe. Anglo-American cooperation blossomed during the Roosevelt-Taft years. The intense German-British rivalry and the rise of the United States to world power inspired London's quest for friendship with Washington. Already prepared by racial ideas of Anglo-Saxon kinship, the two nations shared a common language and respect for private property rights, and Americans appreciated British support in the 1898 war and the Hay-Pauncefote Treaty, London's virtual endorsement of the Roosevelt Corollary, and the withdrawal of British warships from the Caribbean.

British-American trade and U.S. investment in Britain also secured ties. By 1914, more than 140 American companies operated in Britain, including H. J. Heinz's processed foods and F. W. Woolworth's "penny markets." Many Britons decried an Americanization of British culture. The prickly character of the Anglo-American relationship, however, gave way to cooperation in world affairs, especially in 1917 when the United States entered World War I supporting the British against Germany.

Guantánamo Bay

Four hundred miles from Miami, near the south-eastern corner of Cuba, sits U.S. Naval Base Guantánamo Bay. The oldest American base outside the United States, it is the only one located in a country with which Washington does not have an open relationship. The United States has occupied Guantánamo since the aftermath of the Spanish-American War, leasing it from Cuba for $4,085 per year (originally, $2,000 in gold coins).

Cuban leaders were dissatisfied with the deal early on, and after Fidel Castro's communist takeover in 1959, Guantánamo fueled tensions between the two countries. Castro called it "a dagger pointed at Cuba's heart" and refused to cash the rent checks. That he cashed the very first check, however, enabled Washington to argue that Castro's government accepts the lease.

Since late 2001, "Gitmo" has contained a detainment camp for alleged combatants captured in Afghanistan and, later, Iraq and elsewhere. By late 2005, the number exceeded five hundred from forty countries. The George W. Bush administration called the detainees "unlawful enemy combatants" but promised to follow the Geneva accords governing prisoners of war. Soon there were allegations of abuse and complaints that holding detainees without trial, charges, or any prospect of release was unlawful. Some detainees committed suicide. For critics, the camp became an international symbol of American heavy-handedness that hurt America's image abroad.

In June 2006, the U.S. Supreme Court ruled that President Bush overstepped his power in establishing procedures for the Guantánamo detainees without congressional authority and that the procedures violated the Uniform Code of Military Justice and Geneva accords. In January 2009, President Barack Obama signed an executive order closing the detention center within one year, but strong opposition and complications concerning detainee trials and resettlements ensured the deadline would not be met. The question for a people and a nation remained: how would the United States balance security with due process and the rule of law?

Summary

From the Civil War to the First World War, expansionism and imperialism elevated the United States to world power status. By 1914, Americans held extensive economic, strategic, and political interests in a world made smaller by modern technology. The outward reach of U.S. foreign policy from Seward to Wilson sparked opposition from domestic critics, other imperialist nations, and foreign nationalists, but expansionists prevailed, and the trend toward empire endured.

Economic and strategic needs and ideology motivated and justified expansion. The belief that the United States needed foreign markets to absorb surplus production joined missionary zeal in reforming other societies through American products and culture. Notions of racial and male supremacy and appeals to national greatness also fed the appetite for foreign adventure. The greatly augmented navy became a primary means for satisfying America's expansionism.

Revealing the diversity of America's intersection with the world, missionaries like Moon in China, generals, companies, and politicians carried American ways, guns, and goods abroad to a mixed reception. A global power with far-flung interests to protect, the United States' self-proclaimed greatness and political isolation from Europe were tested when world war broke out in August 1914.

Chapter Review

Imperial Dreams

 What drove U.S. expansion overseas in the late nineteenth century?

American leaders increasingly believed in the decades after the Civil War that the nation's future prosperity and security depended on greater U.S. investment in and influence over other parts of the world. They believed foreign trade could prevent future U.S. economic downturns—an increasing concern after the depression of the 1890s—by shipping surplus products made here overseas. Economic ties also permitted political influence to be exerted abroad and helped spread the American way of life, especially capitalism, which fueled dramatic growth of U.S. exports. Leaders also embraced the notion of American "exceptionalism"—that the United States was unique and superior to other regions because of its heritage and God-favored prosperity. Nationalism, capitalism, Social Darwinism, and a paternalistic racism provided rationales for U.S. expansion and imperialism; hence, expansionists argued that when they intervened in and sometimes colonized these regions, they were helping to bring prosperity and liberty to weaker, less fortunate peoples.

Ambitions and Strategies

 What happened to Seward's vision of an American empire?

Secretary of State William Seward longed for a U.S. empire that would extend the frontier to include Canada, the Caribbean, Cuba, Central America, Mexico, Hawai'i, Iceland, Greenland, and the Pacific islands. He anticipated these areas would naturally gravitate to—and easily become enveloped by—the United States, and that foreign trade and certain infrastructure developments—such as a transcontinental U.S. railroad, a canal across Central America, and a telegraph system—would speed things along. Most of his vision never came to pass, blocked by anti-imperialists, political foes, and failed schemes. He had a few successes, however, including chasing the French puppet government from Mexico in 1866, purchasing Alaska from the Russians in 1867, and claiming the Midway Islands for the United States that year.

Crises in the 1890s: Hawai'i, Venezuela, and Cuba

 What typically imperialist actions did the United States take in its dealings with Hawai'i and Venezuela?

In both cases, the United States showed disregard for the rights of foreign peoples. Hawai'i was annexed despite the objections of its queen and most Hawaiians because it proved strategically and commercially important to the United States—particularly during the Spanish-American War, when it served as a way station to Asia and the Philippines. Venezuela, meanwhile, sought U.S. assistance in its border dispute with Great Britain over where its boundary with British Guiana should lie. The Anglo-American arbitration board divided up the territory, which was rich with gold and provided a commercial gateway to South America, between Britain and Venezuela, with almost no input from the latter.

The Spanish-American War and the Debate over Empire

What were the anti-imperialist arguments against U.S. annexation of the Philippines after the Spanish-American War?

Anti-imperialists expressed a wide range of concerns about the potential annexation of the Philippines. For many, it seemed hypocritical for Americans to fight a war for Cuban liberation, only to acquire another small nation in the process. Some argued that it violated the fundamental right of a people to self-determination that Americans themselves embraced in the Declaration of Independence and Constitution. Prominent women such as Jane Addams felt imperialist zeal corrupted the American character, and cited children's playing war games as evidence of this. Racists saw the annexation of a nonwhite nation as a potential threat to Anglo-Saxon purity and supremacy, while labor leaders feared the new colonists might become a cheap labor force to drive down American wages.

Asian Encounters: War in the Philippines, Diplomacy in China

 Why was the Open Door policy such a key component of U.S. diplomacy?

The Open Door policy originated in the late nineteenth century as a solution to U.S. trade difficulties in China. The concept called for nations with spheres of influence in turbulent China to respect the principle of equal trade opportunity in the region. After 1900, when the United States became the world's preeminent trader, the Open Door became the tool by which it could first pry open new markets and then dominate them. As it developed, the Open Door included the following tenets: that America's economy required exports to remain strong; that trade abroad could be interrupted unless the United States intervened; and that any effort to keep U.S. citizens, products, or ideas from other regions threatened U.S. survival.

TR's World

 What solidified U.S.-British ties heading into World War I?

Aside from their shared language and respect for private property rights, England and the United States were united by several other factors. To TR, the two countries' shared a superior white Anglo-Saxon heritage that justified their intervention into the affairs of "uncivilized" nations. Both were concerned about growing Japanese influence in Asia. U.S. investment in Britain, along with increased trade, further strengthened their bonds. British support for the Roosevelt Corollary to the Monroe Doctrine (granting the United States hegemony in the Western Hemisphere) and the withdrawal of British ships from the Caribbean made relations easier, as did England's respect for the United States' growing status as a world power. Increased tensions between Germany and England, along with British support for the 1898 war, increased cooperation between the two countries and ensured that many Americans would take England's side in the impending global conflict.

Suggestions for Further Reading

Gail Bederman, *Manliness and Cvilization: A Cultural History of Gender and Race in the United States, 1880–1917* (1995)

Kristin L. Hoganson, *Fighting for American Manhood: How Gender Politics Provoked the Spanish-American and Philippine-American Wars* (1998)

Michael H. Hunt, *Ideology and U.S. Foreign Policy* (1987)

Paul A. Kramer, *The Blood of Government: Race, Empire, the United States, and the Philippines* (2006)

Walter LaFeber, *The American Search for Opportunity, 1865–1913* (1993)

Brian M. Linn, *The Philippine War, 1899–1902* (2000)

Eric T. Love, *Race over Empire: Racism and U.S. Imperialism, 1865–1900* (2004)

Stuart Creighton Miller, *"Benevolent Assimilation": The American Conquest of the Philippines, 1899–1903* (1982)

John Offner, *An Unwanted War: The Diplomacy of the United States and Spain over Cuba, 1895–1898* (1992)

Louis A. Perez Jr., *The War of 1898: The United States and Cuba in History and Historiography* (1998)

Americans in the Great War

20

1914–1920

On May 7, 1915, Secretary of State William Jennings Bryan was lunching with cabinet members in Washington when he received a bulletin: the luxurious British ocean liner *Lusitania* had been sunk, apparently by a German submarine. He rushed to his office, and at 3:06 PM received confirmation from London: "THE LUSITANIA WAS TORPEDOED OFF THE IRISH COAST AND SANK IN HALF AN HOUR." The *Lusitania* sank in eighteen minutes; 1,198 people perished, including 128 Americans. With Europe at war, Bryan had feared such a calamity. Britain had imposed a naval blockade on Germany, and the Germans responded with submarine warfare against Allied shipping. As a passenger liner, the *Lusitania* should have been spared, but German officials warned Americans in newspapers that they traveled on British or Allied ships at their own risk; passenger liners suspected of carrying munitions or contraband were subject to attack. For weeks, Bryan urged President Woodrow Wilson to stop Americans from booking passage on British ships; Wilson refused.

The *Lusitania*, it soon emerged, *was* carrying munitions. Desperate to keep the United States out of the war, Bryan urged Wilson to condemn Germany and Britain's blockade and to ban Americans from traveling on belligerent ships. Others, including former president Theodore Roosevelt, called the sinking "an act of piracy" and pressed for war. Wilson did not want war, but he disagreed with Bryan about treating British and German violations the same. He sent a strong note to Berlin, insisting Germany end its submarine warfare.

As Bryan pressed his case, he became increasingly isolated within the administration. When in early June Wilson refused to ban Americans from travel on belligerent ships and sent a second protest note to Germany, Bryan resigned.

The division between the president and his secretary of state reflected divisions within the American populace over Europe's war. Eastern newspapers charged Bryan with betraying the country. But in the Midwest and South, he won praise from pacifists and German American groups for his "act of courage." Weeks

571

later, speaking to fifteen thousand people at Madison Square Garden, Bryan was applauded when he warned against "war with any of the belligerent nations." Although many Americans agreed with Wilson that honor ranked above peace, others shared Bryan's position that some sacrifice of neutral rights was reasonable to remain out of war.

Full-scale war seemed unthinkable. The new machine guns, howitzers, submarines, and dreadnoughts were awesome death engines; one social reformer lamented that using them would mean "civilization is all gone, and barbarism comes."

For almost three years, President Wilson kept America out of the war, while protecting U.S. trade interests and improving the nation's military posture. But American property, lives, and neutrality fell victim to British and German naval warfare. When, two years after the *Lusitania* went down, the president asked Congress for a declaration of war, he insisted America would not just win but "make the world safe for democracy."

A year and a half later, the Great War would be over. Some 10 million soldiers perished. Europeans experienced the destruction of ideals, confidence, and goodwill, along with immense economic damage. The Great War toppled four empires of the Old World—the German, Austro-Hungarian, Russian, and Ottoman Turkish—and left two others, the British and French, drastically weakened.

U.S. losses were comparatively small, yet Americans tipped the scales in favor of the Allies by contributing war materiel, troops, supplies, and loans. The war years also witnessed a massive international transfer of wealth from Europe across the Atlantic, as the United States went from being the world's largest debtor nation to its largest creditor. The conflict marked the United States as a world power.

At home, World War I intensified social divisions. Racial tensions accompanied the northward migration of southern blacks, and pacifists and German Americans were harassed. The federal government trampled on civil liberties to silence critics. After Russia's communist revolution, a Red Scare in America repressed radicals and tarnished America's democratic image. Although reformers continued to address issues like prohibition and woman suffrage, the war splintered the Progressive movement.

Abroad, Americans who marched to battle grew disillusioned with the peace process. They recoiled from victors squabbling over the spoils and chided Wilson for failing to deliver his promised "peace without victory." After negotiating the Treaty of Versailles at Paris following World War I, the president urged U.S. membership in the new League of Nations, which he believed would reform world politics. The Senate rejected his appeal (the League nonetheless organized without U.S. membership) because many Americans feared that the League might threaten U.S. interests and entangle Americans in Europe's problems.

As you read this chapter, keep the following questions in mind:

- **Why did the United States try to remain neutral and then enter the European war in 1917?**

- **How was American society changed by the war?**

- **What were the main elements of Woodrow Wilson's postwar vision, and why did he fail to realize them?**

Chronology

1914	First World War begins in Europe
1915	Germans sink *Lusitania* off coast of Ireland
1916	After torpedoing the *Sussex*, Germany pledges not to attack merchant ships without warning
	National Defense Act expands military
1917	Germany declares unrestricted submarine warfare
	Russian Revolution ousts the czar; Bolsheviks later take power
	United States enters First World War
	Selective Service Act creates draft
	Espionage Act limits First Amendment rights
	Race riot breaks out in East St. Louis, Illinois
1918	Wilson announces Fourteen Points for new world order
	Sedition Act further limits free speech
	U.S. troops at Château-Thierry help blunt German offensive
	U.S. troops intervene in Russia against Bolsheviks
	Spanish flu pandemic kills 25–40 million worldwide
	Armistice ends First World War
1919	Paris Peace Conference punishes Germany and launches League of Nations
	May Day bombings help instigate Red Scare
	American Legion organizes for veterans' benefits and antiradicalism
	Wilson suffers stroke after speaking tour
	Senate rejects Treaty of Versailles and U.S. membership in League of Nations
	Schenck v. U.S. upholds Espionage Act
1920	Palmer Raids round up suspected radicals

Precarious Neutrality

How viable was U.S. neutrality during World War I?

The war that erupted in August 1914 grew from years of European competition over trade, colonies, allies, and armaments. Two powerful alliance systems had formed: the Triple Alliance of Germany, Austria-Hungary, and Italy, and the Triple Entente of Britain, France, and Russia. All had imperial holdings and wanted more. As Germany challenged Great Britain for world leadership, many Americans saw Germany as an excessively militaristic nation that threatened U.S. interests in the Western Hemisphere.

Outbreak of the First World War

Crises in the Balkans triggered events that shattered Europe's delicate balance of power. Slavic nationalists sought to enlarge independent Serbia by annexing regions such as Bosnia, then a province of the Austro-Hungarian Empire. On June 28, 1914, Archduke Franz Ferdinand, heir to the Austro-Hungarian throne, was assassinated by a Serbian nationalist while visiting Sarajevo, the capital of Bosnia. Austria-Hungary consulted its Triple Alliance partner Germany, which urged toughness. When Serbia called on its Slavic friend Russia for help, Russia enlisted France and began mobilizing its armies.

Bound by alliances and stirred by turmoil in the Balkans, where Serbs repeatedly upended peace, the nations of Europe descended into war in the summer of 1914. Step by step, a Balkan crisis escalated into the "Great War."

Germany struck first, declaring war against Russia on August 1 and against France two days later. Britain hesitated, but when German forces slashed into neutral Belgium to get at France, London declared war against Germany on August 4. Eventually, Turkey (the Ottoman Empire) joined Germany and Austria-Hungary as the Central Powers, and Italy (switching sides) and Japan teamed up with Britain, France, and Russia as the Allies. Japan seized Shandong, Germany's area of influence in China.

President Wilson initially distanced America from the conflagration by proclaiming neutrality—the traditional U.S. policy toward European wars. He also asked Americans to refrain from taking sides, worrying that "otherwise our mixed populations would wage war on each other."

Link to President Wilson's Neutrality Policy

Taking Sides

Despite Wilson's appeal for unity at home, ethnic groups took opposing sides. Many German Americans and anti-British Irish Americans (Ireland was then trying to break free from British rule) cheered for the Central Powers. Americans with

MAP 20.1
Europe Goes to War, Summer 1914

Bound by alliances and stirred by turmoil in the Balkans, where Serbs repeatedly upended peace, the nations of Europe descended into war in the summer of 1914. Step by step, a Balkan crisis escalated into the "Great War." Source: Copyright © Cengage Learning 2015

1. **June 28**
   Assassination at Sarajevo

2. **July 28**
   Austria-Hungary declares war on Serbia

3. **July 30**
   Russia begins mobilization

4. **August 1**
   Germany declares war on Russia

5. **August 3**
   Germany declares war on France and invades Belgium

6. **August 4**
   Great Britain declares war on Germany

7. **August 6**
   Russia and Austria-Hungary at war

8. **August 12**
   Great Britain declares war on Austria-Hungary

Central Powers (Triple Alliance—except Italy—and allies)

The Allies (Triple Entente and allies)

Neutral nations

roots in Allied nations championed the Allied cause. Germany's attack on Belgium confirmed for many that Germany was the archetype of unbridled militarism.

The Wilson administration's pro-Allied sympathies also weakened the U.S. neutrality proclamation. Wilson shared the conviction with British leaders that a German victory would destroy free enterprise and government by law. If Germany won the war, he and his advisers agreed, "it would change the course of our civilization and make the United States a military nation."

U.S. economic links with the Allies also rendered neutrality difficult. England, a longtime customer, flooded America with new orders, especially for arms. Sales to the Allies helped end an American recession. Between 1914 and 1916, American exports to England and France grew 365 percent, from $753 million to $2.75 billion. Largely because of Britain's naval blockade, exports to Germany dropped by more than 90 percent, from $345 million to only $29 million. Loans to Britain and France from private American banks—totaling $2.3 billion during neutrality—financed much of U.S. trade with the Allies. Germany received only $27 million in the same period.

To Germans, the links between the American economy and the Allies meant that the United States had become the Allied arsenal and bank. Americans, however, worried that cutting economic ties with Britain would constitute a nonneutral act in favor of Germany. Under international law, Britain—which controlled the seas—could buy both contraband (war-related goods) and noncontraband from neutrals. It was Germany's responsibility, not America's, to stop such trade as international law prescribed by blockading the enemy's territory, seizing contraband from neutral (American) ships, or confiscating goods from belligerent (British) ships.

Wilsonianism

"Wilsonianism," the cluster of ideas that Wilson espoused, consisted of traditional American principles (such as democracy and the Open Door) and a conviction that the United States was a beacon of freedom. Only the United States could lead the convulsed world into a new, peaceful era of unobstructed commerce, free-market capitalism, democratic politics, and open diplomacy. "America had the infinite privilege of fulfilling her destiny and saving the world," Wilson claimed. Empires had to be dismantled to honor the principle of self-determination. Critics charged that Wilson often violated his own credos while forcing them on others—as his military interventions in Mexico in 1914, Haiti in 1915, and the Dominican Republic in 1916 testified. Nonetheless, his ideals served American commercial purposes.

To say that U.S. neutrality was never a possibility given ethnic loyalties, economic ties, and Wilsonian preferences is not to say that Wilson sought to enter the war. In early 1917, the president remarked that "we are the only one of the great white nations that is free from war today, and it would be a crime against civilization for us to go in." But go in the United States finally did. Why?

Violation of Neutral Rights

The short answer is that Americans got caught in the Allied–Central Power crossfire. British naval policy sought to cripple the German economy by severing trade. The British, "ruling the waves and waiving the rules," declared a blockade of water entrances to Germany and mined the North Sea. They seized cargoes and defined a broad list of contraband (including foodstuffs) that they prohibited neutrals from shipping to Germany. Furthermore, to counter German submarines, the British flouted international law by arming their merchant ships and flying neutral (sometimes American) flags. Wilson frequently protested British violations of neutral rights, but London deflected Washington's criticism by paying for confiscated cargoes, and German provocations made British behavior appear less offensive by comparison.

Germany looked for victory at sea by using submarines. In February 1915, Berlin declared a war zone around the British Isles, warned neutral vessels to stay out so as not to be mistakenly attacked, and advised passengers to stay off Allied ships. Wilson informed Germany that it would be held accountable for any losses of American life and property.

Wilson interpreted international law strictly and expected Germans to warn passenger or merchant ships before attacking, so that passengers and crew could disembark safely into lifeboats. The Germans thought that surfacing their slender and sluggish *Unterseebooten* (U-boats) would leave them vulnerable to attack. Berlin protested that Wilson was denying it the one weapon that could break the British economic stranglehold, disrupt the Allies' substantial connection with U.S. producers and bankers, and win the war. To British, Germans, and Americans, naval warfare became a matter of life and death.

The Decision for War

How did the Zimmermann telegram finally push Americans to abandon neutrality?

Ultimately, the war at sea doomed the prospects for U.S. neutrality. In early 1915, German U-boats sank ship after ship, notably the *Lusitania* on May 7. Germany's subsequent promise to refrain from attacking passenger liners ended in August when another British vessel, the *Arabic,* was sunk off Ireland. Three Americans died. Germany quickly pledged that an unarmed passenger ship would never again be attacked without warning. But the *Arabic* incident led critics to ask: why not require Americans to sail on American craft? From August 1914 to March 1917, after all, only 3 Americans died on an American ship (the tanker *Gulflight,* sunk by a German U-boat in May 1915), whereas about 190 were killed on belligerent ships.

Peace Advocates

In March 1916, a U-boat attack on the *Sussex*, a French vessel crossing the English Channel, injured four Americans and brought the United States closer to war. Stop the marauding submarines, Wilson lectured Berlin, or the United States will sever diplomatic relations. Again the Germans retreated. At the same time, U.S. relations with Britain soured after Britain's crushing of the Easter Rebellion in Ireland and further British restriction of U.S. trade with the Central Powers.

As the United States became more entangled in the Great War, many Americans urged Wilson to keep the nation out. In early 1915, Jane Addams, Carrie Chapman Catt, and other suffragists helped found the Woman's Peace Party, the U.S. section of the Women's International League for Peace and Freedom. Later that year, some pacifist Progressives organized an antiwar coalition, the American Union Against Militarism. Socialist Eugene Debs spoke for peace, while even businessmen such as Andrew Carnegie and Henry Ford financed peace groups.

Antiwar advocates emphasized that war drained a nation of its youth, resources, and reform impulse; that it fostered repression at home; that it violated Christian morality; and that wartime business barons reaped profits at the people's expense. Militarism and conscription, Addams pointed out, were what millions of immigrants left behind in Europe. Although the peace movement was splintered, it articulated several ideas that Wilson, who campaigned on a peace platform in the 1916 election, shared. Wilson futilely labored to bring the belligerents to the conference table, urging them in early 1917 to temper their acquisitive war aims and embrace "peace without victory."

Unrestricted Submarine Warfare

In Germany, Wilson's overture went unheeded. Since August 1916, German leaders had debated whether to resume the unrestricted U-boat campaign. Opponents feared a break with the United States, but proponents claimed that only through an all-out attack on Britain's supply shipping could Germany win the war. True, the United States might enter the war, but victory might be achieved before U.S. troops crossed the Atlantic. Consequently, in early February 1917, Germany launched unrestricted submarine warfare, attacking all warships and merchant vessels—belligerent or neutral—in the declared war zone. Wilson quickly broke diplomatic relations with Berlin.

In late February, British intelligence intercepted and passed to U.S. officials a telegram addressed to the German minister in Mexico from German foreign secretary Arthur Zimmermann. Its message: if Mexico joined a military alliance against the United States, Germany would help Mexico recover the territories it lost in 1848. Zimmermann hoped to "set new enemies on America's neck—enemies which give them plenty to take care of over there."

Link to the Zimmermann Telegram

Although Mexico City rejected Germany's offer, Wilson judged Zimmermann's telegram "a conspiracy against this country." The prospect of a German-Mexican collaboration turned the tide of opinion in the American Southwest, where antiwar sentiment had been strong.

Soon afterward, Wilson asked Congress for "armed neutrality" to defend American lives and commerce, seeking authority to arm American merchant ships, for example. During the debate, Wilson released Zimmermann's telegram to the press. Americans were outraged. Still, antiwar senators Robert M. La Follette and George Norris, among others, saw the armed-ship bill as a blank check for the president to move the country to war, and they filibustered it to death. Wilson armed America's commercial vessels anyway but acted too late to prevent the sinking of several American ships. War cries escalated.

War Message and War Declaration

On April 2, 1917, the president stepped before Congress and enumerated U.S. grievances: Germany's violation of freedom of the seas, disruption of commerce, interference with Mexico, and breach of human rights

Link to Wilson's war message to Congress, April 2, 1917

by killing innocent Americans. Congress declared war against Germany on April 6 by a vote of 373 to 50 in the House and 82 to 6 in the Senate. (This vote was for war against Germany only; a declaration of war against Austria-Hungary came months later, on December 7.) Montana's Jeannette Rankin, the first woman to sit in Congress, cast a ringing no vote.

Wilson took the United States into the Great War for principle, morality, honor, commerce, security, and reform. The submarine was certainly the culprit that drew a reluctant president and nation into the maelstrom. Critics blamed Wilson's rigid definition of international law and his contention that Americans should be entitled to travel anywhere, even on a belligerent ship loaded with contraband. Most Americans accepted Wilson's view that the Germans had to be checked to ensure an open, orderly world in which U.S. principles and interests would be safe.

America went to war to reform world politics, not to destroy Germany. By early 1917, the president concluded that America would not be able to claim a seat at the postwar peace conference unless it became a combatant. At the peace conference, Wilson intended to promote the principles he thought essential to a stable world order, to advance democracy and the Open Door, and to outlaw revolution and aggression. In designating the United States an "Associated" power rather than an Allied nation, Wilson tried to preserve part of his country's neutrality, but to no avail.

Winning the War

What was the impact of modern, trench warfare on soldiers?

Even before the U.S. declaration of war, the Wilson administration strengthened the military under the banner of "preparedness." The National Defense Act of 1916 provided for increases in the army and National Guard and for summer training camps modeled on the one in Plattsburgh, New York, where some of America's elite had trained in 1915 as "citizen-soldiers." The Navy Act of 1916 started the largest naval expansion in American history.

Selective Service Act Law that required all men between twenty-one and thirty (later expanded to eighteen through forty-five) to register with local draft boards.

The Draft and the Soldier

To raise an army, Congress in May 1917 passed the **Selective Service Act**, requiring males between age twenty-one and thirty (later changed to eighteen and forty-five) to register. National service, proponents believed, would prepare the nation for battle and instill patriotism and respect for order, democracy, and personal sacrifice. Critics feared it would lead to the militarization of American life.

On June 5, 1917, more than 9.5 million men signed up for the "great national lottery." By war's end, 4.8 million had served in the armed forces, 2 million of that number in France. Millions of laborers received deferments from military duty because they worked in war industries or had dependents.

The typical soldier was a draftee in his early to mid-twenties, white, single, American born, and poorly educated (most had not attended high school, and perhaps 30 percent could not read or write). Tens of thousands of women enlisted in the army Nurse Corps, served as "hello girls" (volunteer bilingual telephone operators) in the army Signal Corps, and became clerks in the navy and Marine Corps.

Some 400,000 African Americans also served in the military. Although many southern politicians feared arming blacks, the army drafted them into segregated units and assigned them to menial labor. They endured abuse and miserable conditions. Ultimately, more than 40,000 African Americans would see combat in Europe, and several black units served with distinction in the French army. The all-black 369th Infantry Regiment spent more time in the trenches—191 days—and received more medals than any other American outfit.

Although French officers were racially prejudiced and often treated the soldiers from their own African colonies poorly, black Americans serving with the French reported a degree of respect lacking in the American army. The irony was not lost on African American leaders, such as W. E. B. Du Bois, who endorsed the National Association for the Advancement of Colored People's (NAACP) support for the war and urged blacks to volunteer.

Nearly 65,000 draftees applied for conscientious-objector (CO) status (refusing to bear arms for religious or pacifist reasons), but some changed their minds or failed preinduction examinations. Quakers and Mennonites were numerous among the 4,000 inductees classified as COs. COs who refused noncombat service, such as in the medical corps, faced imprisonment. Approximately 3 million men evaded draft registration. Some were arrested, others fled to Mexico or Canada, but most stayed home and were never discovered. Another 338,000 men who registered never showed up for induction. According to arrest records, most "deserters" and "evaders" were lower-income agricultural and industrial laborers.

Trench Warfare

U.S. general **John J. Pershing,** head of the **American Expeditionary Forces (AEF)**, insisted that his "sturdy rookies" remain a separate army. He refused to turn over his "soldiers" to Allied commanders, who favored deadly trench warfare. Since fall 1914, zigzag trenches fronted by barbed wire and mines stretched across France. Between the muddy, stinking trenches lay "no man's land," denuded by artillery fire. When ordered out, soldiers would charge enemy trenches only to face machine gun fire and poison gas.

First used by the Germans in April 1915, chlorine gas stimulated overproduction of fluid in the lungs, leading to death by drowning. Gas in a variety of forms (mustard and phosgene, in addition to chlorine) would be used throughout the war, sometimes blistering, sometimes incapacitating, often killing.

The death toll in trench warfare was overwhelming. At the Battle of the Somme in 1916, the British and French suffered 600,000 dead or wounded to earn only 125 square miles; the Germans lost 400,000 men. At Verdun that year, 336,000 Germans perished, and at Passchendaele in 1917 more than 370,000 British men died to gain about 40 miles of mud and barbed wire.

Shell Shock

After arriving on the French front, U.S. units faced the horrors caused by advanced weaponry. Some suffered shell shock, a mental illness also known as war psychosis. Symptoms included a fixed, empty stare; violent tremors; paralyzed limbs; listlessness; jabbering; screaming; and haunting dreams. Even soldiers who appeared courageous cracked after days of incessant shelling and inescapable

John J. Pershing Commander of American Expeditionary Forces that fought in Europe.

American Expeditionary Forces U.S. soldiers who fought in Europe during World War I.

A U.S. soldier of Company K, 110th Infantry Regiment, receives aid during fighting at Verennes, France.

National Archives

human carnage. Red Cross canteens, staffed by women volunteers, provided relief and offered haircuts, food, and recreation.

In Paris, where forty large houses of prostitution thrived, venereal disease became such a problem that French prime minister Georges Clemenceau offered licensed, inspected prostitutes to the American army. By war's end, about 15 percent of America's soldiers had contracted venereal disease, costing the army $50 million and 7 million days of active duty. Periodic inspections, chemical prophylactic treatments, and the threat of court-martial for infected soldiers kept the problem from being greater.

American Units in France

Soldiers stationed in Europe filled their diaries and letters with descriptions of the local customs and "ancient" architecture, and noted how the grimy and war-torn French countryside bore little resemblance to the groomed landscapes in paintings. "Life in France for the American soldier meant marching in the dirt and mud, living in cellars in filth, being wet and cold and fighting," the chief of staff of the Fourth Division remarked.

With both sides exhausted, American participation tipped the balance toward the Allies. But not right away. Initially, the U.S. Navy battled submarines and escorted troop carriers, and pilots in the U.S. Air Service, flying mostly British and French aircraft, saw limited action. American "aces" like Eddie Rickenbacker defeated their German counterparts in aerial "dogfights" and became heroes in France and at home. But only ground troops could make a decisive difference, and American units did not engage in much combat until after the harsh winter of 1917–1918.

The Bolshevik Revolution

By then, the military and diplomatic situation changed dramatically as a result of the Bolshevik Revolution in Russia. In November 1917, the liberal-democratic government of Aleksander Kerensky, which led the country since the czar's abdication early in the year, was overthrown by V. I. Lenin's radical socialists. Lenin vowed to change world politics and end imperial rivalries on terms that challenged Wilson's. To Lenin, the war signaled the impending end of capitalism and the rise of a global revolution of workers. For Western leaders, the prospect of Bolshevik-style revolutions worldwide was too frightening to contemplate.

In the weeks following their takeover, the Bolsheviks attempted to embarrass the capitalist governments and incite world revolution. They published Allied secret agreements for dividing up the colonies and other territories of the Central Powers if the Allies were victorious. Wilson confided to Colonel House that he wanted to tell the Bolsheviks to "go to hell," but he accepted the colonel's argument that he would have to address Lenin's claims that there was little to distinguish the two warring sides and that socialism represented the future.

Fourteen Points

The result was the **Fourteen Points**, unveiled in January 1918, in which Wilson reaffirmed America's commitment to an international system governed by laws and renounced territorial gains as a legitimate war aim. The first five points called for diplomacy "in the public view," freedom of the seas, lower tariffs, armament reductions, and the decolonization of empires. The next eight points specified the evacuation of foreign troops from Russia, Belgium, and France, and appealed for self-determination for nationalities in Europe, such as the Poles. For Wilson, the fourteenth point was the mechanism for achieving the others: "a general association of nations" or League of Nations.

Lenin was unimpressed and called for an immediate end to the fighting, the eradication of colonialism, and self-determination for all peoples. Lenin also made a separate peace with Germany—the Treaty of Brest-Litovsk, signed on March 3, 1918. The deal erased centuries of Russian expansion, as Poland, Finland, and the Baltic states were taken from Russia and Ukraine was granted independence. One of Lenin's motives was to allow Russian troops loyal to the Bolsheviks to return home to fight anti-Bolshevik forces attempting to oust his government.

Lenin and Wilson's emerging feud contained the seeds of the superpower confrontation that would dominate the international system after 1945. Although each professed adherence to democratic principles, they defined democracy differently. For Lenin, it meant workers everywhere seizing control from the owners of capital and establishing worker-led governments. For Wilson, it meant independent governments operating within capitalist systems and according to republican political practices.

Americans in Battle

In March 1918, the Germans launched a major offensive. By May, they were within 50 miles of Paris. U.S. First Division troops helped blunt the German advance at Cantigny (see Map 20.2). In June the Third Division and French forces held positions along the Marne River at Château-Thierry, and the Second Division

Fourteen Points President Wilson's program for world peace; presented to Congress in a 1918 speech, in the midst of World War I.

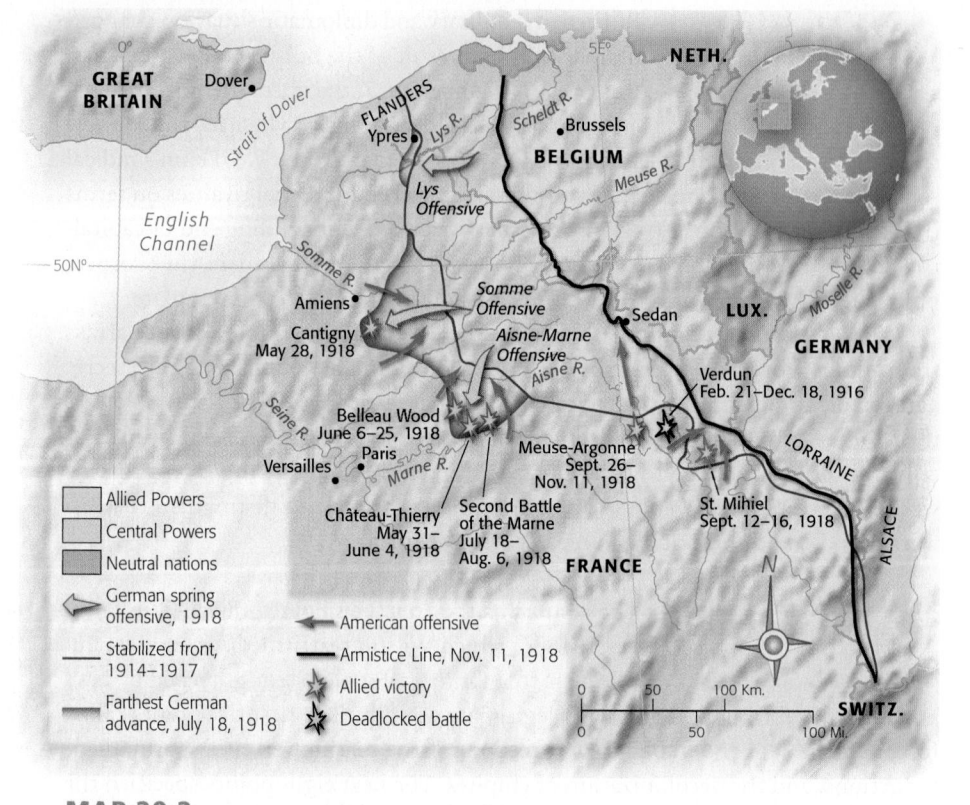

MAP 20.2
American Troops at the Western Front, 1918
America's 2 million troops in France met German forces head-on, ensuring the defeat of the Central Powers in 1918. Source: Copyright © Cengage Learning 2015

attacked the Germans in the Belleau Wood. American soldiers won the battle after three weeks of fighting, but thousands died or were wounded in sacrificial frontal assaults against German machine guns.

Allied victory in the Second Battle of the Marne in July 1918 stemmed German advances. In September, French and American forces took St. Mihiel in a ferocious battle. Then, in the Meuse-Argonne offensive, over 1 million Americans joined British and French troops in weeks of combat; some twenty-six thousand Americans died before the Allies claimed the Argonne Forest on October 10. For Germany—its ground and submarine war stymied, its troops and cities mutinous, its allies Turkey and Austria dropping out, its kaiser abdicating—peace became imperative. The Germans accepted a punishing armistice effective November 11, 1918.

Casualties

The cost of the war is impossible to compute: the belligerents counted 10 million soldiers and 6.6 million civilians dead and 21.3 million people wounded. Fifty-three thousand American soldiers died in battle, and another 62,000 died from disease, mainly a virulent strain of influenza that ravaged the world in late 1918. Economic damage was colossal and output dwindled, contributing to widespread starvation in Europe in the winter of 1918–1919.

The Influenza Pandemic of 1918

In summer and fall 1918, a terrible plague swept the earth. The massive outbreak of influenza claimed more than twice as many lives as the Great War—between 25 million and 40 million people. In the United States, 675,000 people died.

The first cases emerged in midwestern military camps in early March. At Fort Riley, Kansas, forty-eight men died. Soldiers shipped out to Europe in large numbers (eighty-four thousand in March), some unknowingly carrying the virus. The illness appeared on the western front in April. By June, an estimated 8 million Spaniards were infected, giving the disease its name, the Spanish flu.

In August, a second, deadlier form of influenza erupted simultaneously in three cities on three continents: Freetown, Sierra Leone, in Africa; Brest, France; and Boston, Massachusetts. In September, the disease swept down the East Coast, killing 12,000 Americans.

People could be healthy at the start of the weekend and dead by the end of it. Some experienced rapid accumulation of fluid in the lungs and literally drowned.

Others died slowly. Mortality rates were highest for twenty- to twenty-nine-year-olds—the same group dying in the war's trenches.

In October, the epidemic spread to Japan, India, Africa, and Latin America. In the United States, 200,000 perished. There was a nationwide shortage of caskets and gravediggers, and funerals were limited to fifteen minutes. Bodies were left in gutters or on front porches, to be picked up by trucks that drove the streets.

Suddenly, in November, for reasons still unclear, the epidemic eased, though the dying continued into 1919. In England and Wales, the final toll was 200,000, while in India the epidemic may have claimed 20 million. It was, in the historian Roy Porter's words, "the greatest single demographic shock mankind has ever experienced." World War I helped spread the disease, as did technological improvements that in the previous decade facilitated global travel. Americans, accustomed to thinking that two great oceans isolated them, were reminded that they were linked to the rest of humankind.

Health officials in gauze masks inspect street cleaners for Spanish influenza in Chicago in 1918.

Bettmann/CORBIS

War Industries Board Government agency established to coordinate military purchasing, ensure production efficiency, and provide weapons and supplies to the military.

The German, Austro-Hungarian, Ottoman, and Russian empires were gone. For a time, it appeared the Bolshevik Revolution might spread westward, as communist uprisings shook Germany and parts of central Europe. Before the armistice, revolutionaries temporarily took power in the German cities of Bremen, Hamburg, and Lübeck. In Moscow, the new Soviet state sought to consolidate its power.

Mobilizing the Home Front

How did wartime labor shortages create new opportunities for American workers?

Though the United States was belligerent for only nineteen months, the war had a tremendous impact on America. The federal government expanded its power over the economy to meet war needs and intervened in American life as never before. The enlarged Washington bureaucracy managed the economy, labor force, military, and public opinion. The government spent more than $760 million a month from April 1917 to August 1919. As tax revenues lagged, the administration resorted to deficit spending (see Figure 20.1). To Progressives of the New Nationalist persuasion, the wartime expansion and centralization of government power were welcome, but others worried about the dangers of concentrated federal power.

Business-Government Cooperation

The federal government and private business became partners during the war. But evidence of businesspeople cashing in on the national interest aroused public protest. The head of the aluminum advisory committee, for example, was also president of the largest aluminum company. Consequently, the committees disbanded in July 1917, replaced by a single manager, the **War Industries Board**. The government also suspended antitrust laws and signed cost-plus contracts, guaranteeing companies healthy profits and a means to pay higher wages to head off labor strikes. Competitive bidding was virtually abandoned, and big business grew bigger.

Hundreds of new government agencies, staffed primarily by businesspeople, used economic controls to shift the nation's resources to the Allies, the AEF, and war-related production. The Food Administration, led by engineer and investor Herbert Hoover, urged Americans to grow "victory gardens" and eat meatless and wheatless meals—but it also set prices and regulated distribution. The Railroad Administration took over the railway industry. The Fuel Administration controlled coal supplies and rationed gasoline. When strikes threatened the telephone and telegraph companies, the federal government seized and ran them.

FIGURE 20.1
The Federal Budget, 1914–1920
During the First World War, the federal government spent more money than it received from increased taxes. It borrowed from banks or sold bonds through Liberty Loan drives. To meet the mounting costs of the war, in other words, the federal government had to resort to deficit spending. Expenditures topped receipts by more than $13 billion in 1919. Given this wartime fiscal pattern, moreover, the U.S. federal debt rose from $1 billion in 1914 to $25 billion in 1919.
(Source: U.S. Department of Commerce, Historical Statistics of the United States: Colonial Times to 1957 [Washington, D.C.: Bureau of the Census, 1960], p. 711)

The largest of the superagencies was the War Industries Board (WIB), headed by the financier Bernard Baruch. This Wall Streeter told Henry Ford that he would dispatch the military to seize his plants unless the automaker accepted WIB limits on car production. Designed to coordinate the national economy, the WIB made purchases, allocated supplies, and fixed prices at levels that business requested. The WIB also ordered the standardization of goods to streamline production. The varieties of automobile tires, for example, were reduced from 287 to 3.

Economic Performance About one-quarter of American production was diverted to war needs. As farmers enjoyed boom years, they put more acreage into production and mechanized. Gross farm income from 1914 to 1919 increased more than 230 percent. Although manufacturing output leveled off in 1918, wartime demand fueled substantial growth for such industries as steel, which reached a peak production of 45 million tons in 1917, twice the prewar figure. Overall, the gross national product in 1920 stood 237 percent higher than in 1914.

Mistakes happened. Weapons deliveries fell short; the bloated bureaucracy of the War Shipping Board failed to build enough ships. In the severe winter of 1917–1918, coal companies reduced production to raise prices; railroads did not have enough coal cars; and harbors froze, closing out coal barges. People died from pneumonia and froze to death. To pay wartime bills, the government increased taxes. The Revenue Act in 1916 started by raising the surtax on high incomes and corporate profits, imposing a federal tax on large estates, and increasing the tax on munitions manufacturers. Still, taxation financed only one-third of the war. The other two-thirds came from loans, including Liberty bonds sold to the American people. The War Revenue Act of 1917 provided a steeply graduated personal income tax, a corporate income tax, an excess-profits tax, and increased excise taxes on alcoholic beverages, tobacco, and luxury items.

Although taxes curbed excessive corporate profiteering, there were loopholes. Sometimes companies inflated costs to conceal profits. Corporate net earnings for 1913 totaled $4 billion; in 1917 they reached $7 billion; and in 1918, after the tax bite and the war's end, they still stood at $4.5 billion. Profits and patriotism went hand in hand in America's war experience. The abrupt cancellation of billions of dollars' worth of contracts at war's end, however, caused a brief downturn, a short boom, and then an intense decline.

Labor Shortage For American workers, the full-employment wartime economy increased earnings. With the higher cost of living, however, workers saw minimal lifestyle improvement. Turnover rates escalated as workers switched jobs for higher pay and better conditions. Some employers sought to overcome labor shortages by expanding social programs and by expanding welfare and social programs.

To meet the labor crisis, the Department of Labor's U.S. Employment Service matched laborers with job vacancies, attracting workers from the South and Midwest to war industries in the East. The department also temporarily relaxed the literacy-test and head-tax provisions of immigration law to attract farm labor,

Eating to Win

The war effort mobilized Americans as never before and also demanded that they make sacrifices. Herbert Hoover's Food Administration used colorful posters to persuade Americans to change their eating habits. The poster below uses bold type and a man standing over a fallen German soldier to send a patriotic message to eat less and save food for the troops. The poster at right has a 1940s Uncle Sam as teacher with a book promoting City and Farm Gardens and asking folks to learn more. The poster below and to the right uses religion (and guilt) to motivate the public. Which poster do you find most effective, and why? How are Americans persuaded today to change their eating habits?

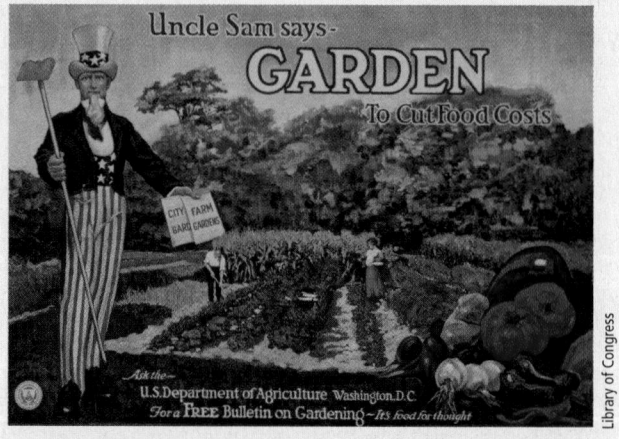

In this colorful 1917 poster, Uncle Sam, posing as a teacher, says, "Garden to cut food costs." The poster offers a free Department of Agriculture "bulletin on gardening—it's food for thought."

Hispanic artist Francis Luis Mora used strong graphics for his 1918 poster showing a man standing over a fallen German soldier.

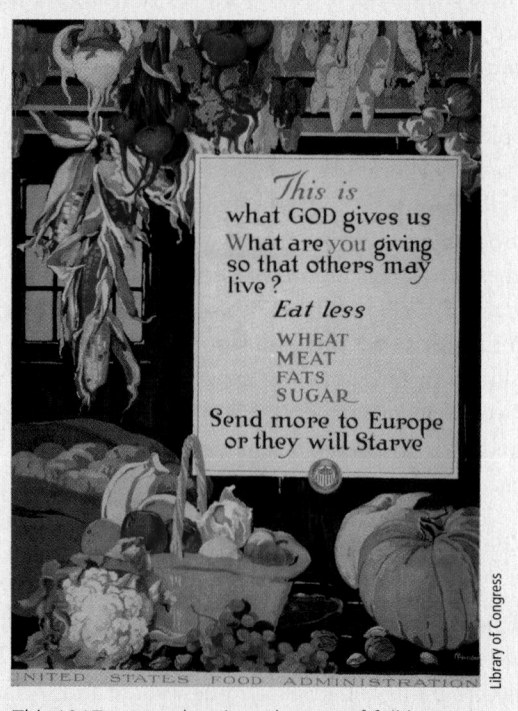

This 1917 poster showing a bounty of fall harvest fruits and vegetables—"This is what God gives us"—uses richly detailed illustration and colorful red type to get attention and ask the question, "What are you giving so that others may live?"

miners, and railroad workers from Mexico. As workers crammed into cities, the U.S. Housing Corporation and Emergency Fleet Corporation built row houses.

The tight wartime labor market meant new job opportunities for women. In Connecticut, a special motion picture, *Mr. and Mrs. Hines of Stamford Do Their Bit*, appealed to housewives' patriotism, urging them to take factory jobs. Although the number of women in the workforce increased slightly, the real story was that many women changed jobs, sometimes moving into formerly male jobs. Some white women left domestic service for factories, shifted from clerking in department stores to stenography and typing, or departed textile mills for employment in fire-arms plants. At least 20 percent of employees in the wartime electrical-machinery, airplane, and food industries were women. As white women took advantage of these new opportunities, black women took some of their places in domestic service and in textile factories. For the first time, department stores employed African American women as elevator operators and cafeteria waitresses. But most working women were single and remained in the sex-segregated occupations of typists, nurses, teachers, and domestic servants.

Women also served as volunteers, making clothing for refugees and soldiers, staffing Red Cross facilities, and teaching French to nurses assigned to the war zone. Many worked for the Women's Committee of the Council of National Defense, a network of state and local organizations publicizing government mobilization programs, encouraging home gardens, sponsoring drives to sell Liberty bonds, and promoting social welfare reforms. This patriotic work improved prospects for passing the Nineteenth Amendment granting woman suffrage. "We have made partners of women in this war," Wilson said as he endorsed woman suffrage in 1918. "Shall we admit them only to a partnership of suffering and sacrifice… and not to a partnership of privilege and right?"

War mobilization encouraged a great migration of southern African Americans to northern cities to work in railroad yards, packinghouses, steel mills, shipyards, and coal mines. Between 1910 and 1920, Cleveland's black population swelled by more than 300 percent, Detroit's by more than 600 percent, and Chicago's by 150 percent. All told, about a half-million African Americans moved to the North, with families pooling savings or selling household goods to fund the journey. Most migrants were unmarried and skilled or semiskilled males in their early twenties. Northern wartime

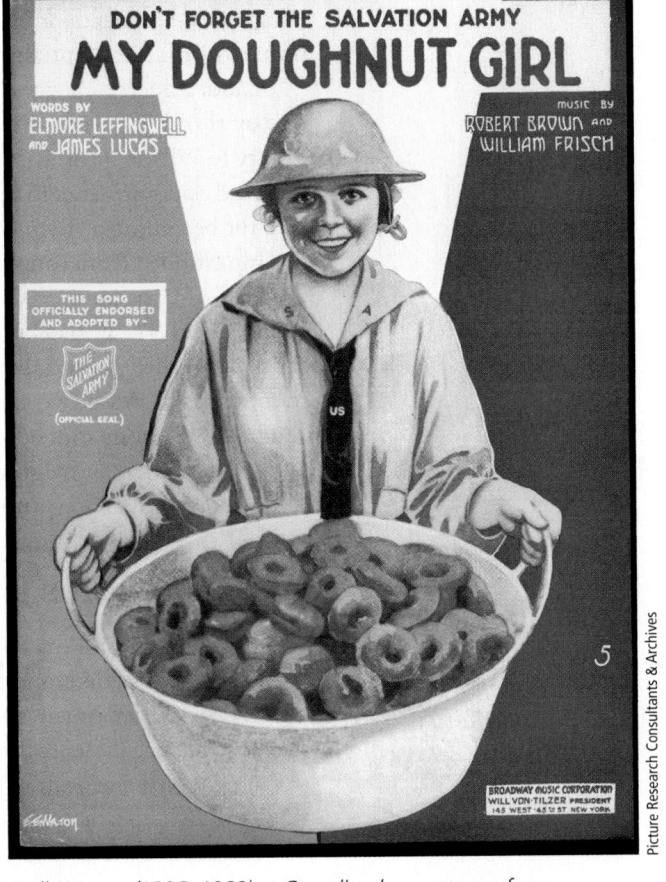

Picture Research Consultants & Archives

Stella Young (1896–1989), a Canadian-born woman from Chelsea, Massachusetts, became widely known as the "Doughnut Girl" because of her service during the First World War with the American branch of the Salvation Army, an international organization devoted to social work. She arrived in France in March 1918 and worked in emergency canteens near the battlefront, providing U.S. troops with coffee, cocoa, sandwiches, doughnuts, pie, and fruit. Stella Young became famous when this picture of her wearing a khaki uniform and a "doughboy" steel helmet was widely circulated as a postcard. A piece of sheet music was even written about her. She served again in World War II. Chelsea named a city square in her honor in 1968.

jobs provided an escape from low wages, sharecropping, tenancy, crop liens, debt peonage, lynchings, and political disfranchisement. One African American wrote to a friend in Mississippi, "I just begin to feel like a man.... I don't have to humble to no one... Will vote the next election."

National War Labor Board

To keep factories running smoothly, Wilson instituted the National War Labor Board (NWLB) in early 1918. The NWLB discouraged strikes and lockouts and urged management to negotiate with unions. In July, after the Western Union Company fired eight hundred union members for trying to organize the firm's workers, the president nationalized the telegraph lines and put the laborers back to work. But in September the NWLB ordered striking Bridgeport, Connecticut, machinists back to munitions factories, threatening to revoke the draft exemptions they received for working in an "essential" industry.

Labor leaders hoped the war would offer opportunities for recognition and better pay through partnership with government. Samuel Gompers threw the AFL's loyalty to Wilson, promising to deter strikes. He and other moderate labor leaders accepted appointments to federal agencies. The antiwar Socialist Party blasted the AFL for becoming a "fifth wheel on [the] capitalist war chariot," but union membership climbed from roughly 2.5 million in 1916 to more than 4 million in 1919.

The AFL, however, could not curb strikes by the radical Industrial Workers of the World (IWW, also known as "Wobblies") or rebellious AFL locals, especially those controlled by socialists. In the nineteen war months, more than six thousand strikes expressed workers' demands for a "living wage" and improved working conditions. Unions sought to create "industrial democracy," a more representative workplace with labor helping to determine job categories and content. Defying the AFL, labor parties had sprung up in twenty-three states by 1920.

Civil Liberties Under Challenge

How did free speech come under fire during World War I?

Wilson and his advisers enjoyed the support of most newspapers, religious leaders, and public officials. They were less certain, however, about ordinary Americans. An official and unofficial campaign soon began to silence dissenters who questioned Wilson's decision for war or who protested the draft. The Wilson administration compiled one of the worst civil liberties records in American history.

Targets of governmental and quasi-vigilante repression included hundreds of thousands of Americans and aliens: pacifists, conscientious objectors, socialists, radical labor groups, the debt-ridden Oklahoma tenant farmers who staged the Green Corn Rebellion against the draft, the Non-Partisan League, reformers like Robert La Follette and Jane Addams, and others. In the wartime debate over democratic free speech, the concept of "civil liberties" emerged for the first time as a major public policy issue (see "Legacy for a People and a Nation," page 597).

Committee on Public Information (CPI) Wartime propaganda agency, headed by journalist George Creel. While claiming merely to combat rumors with facts, the Creel committee in reality publicized the government's version of events and discredited all who questioned that version.

The Committee on Public Information

Spearheading the administration's war campaign was the **Committee on Public Information (CPI)**, formed in April 1917 and headed by Progressive journalist

George Creel. Employing talented writers and scholars, the CPI used propaganda to mobilize public opinion. Pamphlets and films demonized the Germans, and CPI "Four-Minute Men" spoke at movie theaters, schools, and churches to pump up patriotism. Encouraged by the CPI, film companies and the National Association of the Motion Picture Industry produced documentaries, newsreels, and anti-German movies, such as *The Kaiser, the Beast of Berlin* (1918).

The committee also urged the press to practice "self-censorship" and encouraged people to spy on neighbors. Ultrapatriotic groups, such as the Sedition Slammers and the American Defense Society, used vigilantism. In Hilger, Montana, citizens burned history texts mentioning Germany. By the end of the war, sixteen states had banned the teaching of the German language. To avoid trouble, the Kaiser-Kuhn grocery in St. Louis changed its name to Pioneer Grocery. The German shepherd became the Alsatian shepherd.

Nativist advocates of "100 percent Americanism" exploited the emotional atmosphere to exhort immigrants to shed their Old World cultures. Companies offered English language and naturalization classes and refused jobs and promotions to those who failed to learn English quickly. Labor's drive for compulsory health insurance, which gained support before the war, suffered a setback in the war atmosphere that had physicians and insurance companies denouncing health insurance as "Made in Germany."

Even institutions that had embraced tolerance became contaminated. Wellesley College economics professor Emily Greene Balch was fired for her pacifist views (she won the Nobel Peace Prize in 1946). Three Columbia University students were apprehended in mid-1917 for circulating an antiwar petition. Columbia fired Professor J. M. Cattell, a distinguished psychologist, for his antiwar stand. His colleague Charles Beard, a historian with a prowar perspective, resigned in protest. Local school boards also dismissed teachers who questioned the war.

Espionage and Sedition Acts

The Wilson administration guided through an obliging Congress the **Espionage Act** (1917) and the Sedition Act (1918), giving the government wide latitude to crack down on critics. The first statute forbade "false statements" designed to impede the draft or promote military insubordination, and it banned from the mails materials considered treasonous. The Sedition Act made it unlawful to obstruct the sale of war bonds and to use "disloyal, profane, scurrilous, or abusive" language to describe the government, the Constitution, the flag, or the military uniform. More than two thousand people were prosecuted under the acts, with many others intimidated into silence.

Espionage Act Law that set fines and prison sentences for a variety of loosely defined antiwar activities.

Progressives and conservatives alike used the war emergency to throttle the Industrial Workers of the World and the Socialist Party. Government agents raided IWW meetings, and the army put down IWW strikes. By war's end, most of the union's leaders were in jail. In summer 1918, Socialist Party leader Eugene V. Debs was arrested by federal agents for a speech extolling socialism and freedom of speech—including the freedom to criticize Wilson on the war. Given a ten-year sentence, Debs remained in prison until he was pardoned in late 1921.

The Supreme Court endorsed such convictions. In *Schenck v. U.S.* (1919), the Court upheld the conviction of a Socialist Party member who mailed pamphlets urging draft resistance. In wartime, Justice Oliver Wendell Holmes wrote, the First Amendment could be restricted when words "are of such a nature as to create a clear and present danger that they will bring about the substantial evils that Congress has a right to prevent."

Red Scare, Red Summer

What was the impact of the Red Scare in postwar America?

The line between wartime suppression of dissent and the postwar Red Scare is not easily drawn. Together, they stabbed at the Bill of Rights and wounded radicalism in America. While wartime fears focused on subversion, after the armistice it was revolution; and while in 1917 the target was often German Americans, in 1919 it was organized labor. Alarmed by the Russian Revolution and the communist uprisings in Europe, American fears grew in 1919 when the Soviet leadership formed the Communist International (or Comintern) to export revolution worldwide. Terrified conservatives sought out pro-Bolshevik sympathizers (or "Reds," from the communist red flag) in the United States, especially among immigrants and labor unions.

Labor Strikes

Labor union leaders emerged from the war determined to secure higher wages and retain wartime bargaining rights. Employers instead rescinded benefits they were forced to grant to labor during the war, including recognition of unions. The result was more than 3,300 strikes involving 4 million laborers in 1919. On May 1, a day of celebration for workers worldwide, bombs were sent to prominent Americans, though most were intercepted and dismantled. Police never captured the conspirators, but many blamed anarchists and others bent on destroying the American way of life. When the Boston police went on strike in September, some claimed a Bolshevik conspiracy, but others thought it ridiculous to label Boston's Irish American, Catholic cops "radicals."

Unrest in the steel industry in September stirred more ominous fears. Many steelworkers worked twelve hours a day, seven days a week, and lived in squalid housing, counting on the National Committee for Organizing Iron and Steel Workers to improve their lives. When postwar unemployment in the industry climbed and the U.S. Steel Corporation refused to meet with committee representatives, 350,000 workers walked off the job, demanding the right to collective bargaining, a shorter workday, and a living wage. The steel barons hired strikebreakers and sent agents to club strikers. The strike collapsed in early 1920.

Political and business leaders dismissed the steel strike as a foreign threat orchestrated by American radicals. There was no conspiracy, and the American left was splintered. Two defectors from the Socialist Party, John Reed and Benjamin Gitlow, founded the Communist Labor Party in 1919. The rival Communist Party of the United States of America, composed largely of aliens, was launched the same year. But their combined membership did not exceed 70,000—and in 1919 the harassed Socialist Party barely mustered 30,000 members.

American Legion

Although divisiveness signified radicals' weakness, Progressives and conservatives interpreted the advent of new parties as strengthening the radical menace.

Organized in May 1919 to lobby for veterans' benefits, the American Legion soon preached an antiradicalism that fueled the Red Scare. By 1920, 843,000 Legion members, mostly middle and upper class, embraced an impassioned Americanism demanding conformity.

Wilson's attorney general, A. Mitchell Palmer, also insisted that Americans think alike. A Progressive reformer, Quaker, and ambitious politician, Palmer appointed J. Edgar Hoover to head the Radical Division of the Department of Justice. Hoover compiled index cards naming allegedly radical individuals and organizations. During 1919, agents jailed IWW members, and Palmer made sure that 249 alien radicals, including the anarchist Emma Goldman, were deported to Russia.

States passed peacetime sedition acts and arrested hundreds of people. Vigilante groups and mobs flourished once again, their numbers swelled by returning veterans. In November 1919, in Centralia, Washington, American Legionnaires broke from a parade to storm the IWW hall. Several were wounded, others arrested, and one ex-soldier was taken from jail by a mob, then beaten, castrated, and shot. The New York State legislature expelled five elected Socialist Party members in early 1920.

Palmer Raids

The Red Scare peaked in January 1920 in the Palmer Raids. In raids that were planned and directed by J. Edgar Hoover, government agents in thirty-three cities broke into meeting halls and homes without search warrants, jailing four thousand people without counsel. In Boston, four hundred people were detained on bitterly cold Deer Island; two died of pneumonia, one leaped to his death, and another went insane. Because of court rulings and the courageous efforts of Assistant Secretary of Labor Louis Post, who deliberately held up paperwork, most of the arrestees were released, although in 1920–1921 nearly six hundred aliens were deported.

Palmer's disregard for elementary civil liberties drew criticism, with many charging that his tactics violated the Constitution. When Palmer called for a peacetime sedition act, he alarmed liberal and conservative leaders. His prediction that pro-Soviet radicals would incite violence on May Day 1920 proved mistaken—no disturbances occurred anywhere. Palmer, who called himself the "Fighting Quaker," was jeered as the "Quaking Fighter."

Racial Unrest

Palmer also blamed communists for the racial violence that gripped the nation, though the charge was baseless. African Americans realized well before war's end that their participation did little to change discriminatory white attitudes or segregation. The Ku Klux Klan was reviving, and D.W. Griffith's racist film *The Birth of a Nation* (1915) fed prejudice with its celebration of the Klan and demeaning depiction of blacks. Lynching statistics exposed the gap between wartime declarations of humanity and the American practice of inhumanity at home: between 1914 and 1920, 382 blacks were lynched, some in military uniform.

Northern whites who resented "the Negro invasion" rioted, as in East St. Louis, Illinois, in July 1917, and a month later in Houston. During the bloody "Red Summer" of 1919 (so named by black author James Weldon Johnson for the blood that was spilled), race riots rocked two dozen cities and towns. The worst violence occurred in Chicago, a favorite destination for migrating blacks. In the hot days of July 1919, a black youth swimming at a segregated white beach was hit by a thrown rock and drowned. Soon blacks and whites were battling each other. Stabbings, burnings, and shootings went on for days until state police restored some calm. Thirty-eight people died: twenty-three African Americans and fifteen whites.

A disillusioned W. E. B. Du Bois vowed a struggle. Or as poet Claude McKay put it after the Chicago riot in a poem he titled "If We Must Die,"

> Like men we'll face the murderous cowardly pack.
> Pressed to the wall, dying, but fighting back.

Black Militancy

Du Bois and McKay reflected a newfound militancy among black veterans and northern black communities. African American newspaper editorials harshly criticized white politicians while simultaneously imploring readers to embrace their own prowess and beauty. The NAACP stepped up its campaign for civil rights and equality, vowing in 1919 to publicize the terrors of lynching and to seek legislation against it. Other blacks, doubting the potential for equality, turned to a charismatic Jamaican immigrant named Marcus Garvey (see page 612), who called on African Americans to seek a separate black nation.

The crackdown on laborers and radicals, and the resurgence of racism in 1919, dashed wartime hopes. Although the passage of the **Nineteenth Amendment** in 1920, guaranteeing women the right to vote, showed that reform could happen, it was the exception. Unemployment, inflation, racial conflict, labor upheaval, and a campaign against free speech inspired disillusionment in the immediate postwar years.

Nineteenth Amendment
Amendment to the Constitution that granted women the right to vote.

An African American is confronted by state militia members during the race riots in Chicago in 1919. The troops were called in after Mayor Bill Thompson determined that the city police could not restore order.

The Granger Collection, NYC

The Defeat of Peace

President Wilson seemed more focused on confronting the threat of radicalism abroad than at home. Throughout the war's final months, he fretted about the Soviet takeover in Russia, and he revealed his anti-Bolshevism when he ordered five thousand American troops to northern Russia and ten thousand more to Siberia, joining other Allied contingents in fighting what was now a Russian civil war. Wilson did not consult Congress. He said the military expeditions would guard Allied supplies and Russian railroads from German seizure and would also rescue Czechs who wished to fight the Germans.

Wilson wanted to smash the infant Bolshevik government. Thus, he backed an economic blockade of Russia, sent arms to anti-Bolshevik forces, and refused to recognize Lenin's government. The United States also secretly passed military information to anti-Bolshevik forces and used food relief to shore up Soviet opponents in the Baltic region. Later, at the Paris Peace Conference, Soviets were denied a seat. U.S. troops did not leave Russia until spring 1920, after the Bolsheviks demonstrated their staying power.

Wilson faced a monumental task in securing a postwar settlement, though his political actions further complicated the process. During the 1918 congressional elections, Wilson misstepped in suggesting that patriotism required the election of a Democratic Congress; Republicans blasted the president for questioning their love of country. The GOP gained control of both houses, and Wilson aggravated his political problems by not naming a senator to his advisory American Peace Commission. He also refused to take any prominent Republicans to Paris or to consult with the Senate Foreign Relations Committee before the conference.

Wilson was greeted by adoring crowds in Paris, London, and Rome, but their leaders—Georges Clemenceau of France, David Lloyd George of Britain, and Vittorio Orlando of Italy (with Wilson, the Big Four)—became formidable adversaries. After four years of war, the Allies were not going to be cheated out of the fruits of victory. The late-arriving Americans had not suffered as France and Great Britain had. Germany would have to pay big for the calamity it caused.

Paris Peace Conference   At the Versailles peace conference, the Big Four tried to work out an agreement, mostly behind closed doors. The victors demanded that Germany (which had been excluded from the proceedings) pay a huge reparations bill. Wilson instead called for a small indemnity, fearing that an economically hobbled Germany might turn to Bolshevism. Unable to moderate the Allied position, the president reluctantly agreed to a clause blaming the war on Germany and to the creation of a commission to determine reparations (later set at $33 billion). Wilson acknowledged that the peace terms were "hard," but he also believed that "the German people must be made to hate war."

As for dismantling empires and the principle of self-determination, Wilson could only deliver some of his goals. The conferees created a League-administered "mandate" system that placed former German and Turkish colonies under the control of other imperial nations. Japan gained authority over Germany's Pacific colonies, while France obtained what became Lebanon and Syria, and the British received

MAP 20.3

Europe Transformed by War and Peace

After President Wilson and the other conferees at the Paris Peace Conference negotiated the Treaty of Versailles, empires were broken up. In eastern Europe in particular, new nations emerged. Source: Copyright © Cengage Learning 2015

the three former Ottoman provinces that became Iraq. Britain also secured Palestine, on the condition that it promote "the establishment in Palestine of a national home for the Jewish people" without prejudice to "the civil and religious rights of existing non-Jewish communities"—the so-called Balfour Declaration of 1917.

Elsewhere in Europe, Wilson's prescriptions fared better. Out of Austria-Hungary and Russia came the newly independent states of Austria, Hungary, Yugoslavia, Czechoslovakia, and Poland. Wilson and his colleagues also built a *cordon sanitaire* (buffer zone) of new westward-looking nations (Finland, Estonia, Latvia, and Lithuania) around Russia, to quarantine the Bolshevik contagion (see Map 20.3).

League of Nations and Article 10

Wilson worked hardest on the charter for the **League of Nations**, the centerpiece of his plans for the postwar world. He envisioned the League as having power over disputes among states; as such, it could transform international relations. Even so, the great powers would have preponderant say: the organization would have an influential council of five permanent members and elected delegates from smaller states, an assembly of all members, and a World Court.

League of Nations an international deliberative body, viewed as necessary to keep the peace; it was rejected by the U.S. Senate, and the United States never joined.

Wilson identified Article 10 as the "kingpin" of the League covenant: "The Members of the League undertake to respect and preserve as against external aggression the territorial integrity and existing political independence of all Members of the League." Wilson insisted that there could be no future peace with Germany without a league to oversee it.

German representatives initially refused to sign the punitive treaty but submitted in June 1919. They gave up 13 percent of Germany's territory, 10 percent of its population, all of its colonies, and a huge portion of its national wealth. Many wondered how the League could function in the poisoned atmosphere of humiliation and revenge. But Wilson waxed euphoric: "The stage is set, the destiny disclosed. It has come about by no plan of our conceiving, but by the hand of God."

Critics of the Treaty

Critics in the United States were not so sure. In March 1919, thirty-nine senators (enough to deny the treaty the necessary two-thirds vote) signed a petition stating that the League's structure did not adequately protect U.S. interests. Wilson denounced his critics as "pygmy" minds, but he persuaded the peace conference to exempt the Monroe Doctrine and domestic matters from League jurisdiction. Wilson would budge no more. Could his critics not see that membership in the League would give the United States "leadership in the world"?

By summer, criticism intensified: Wilson had bastardized his own principles. He conceded Shandong to Japan and killed a provision affirming the racial equality of all peoples. The treaty ignored freedom of the seas, and tariffs were not reduced. Reparations promised to be punishing on Germany. Critics on the left protested that the League would perpetuate empire. Conservative critics feared that the League would limit American freedom of action in world affairs, stymie U.S. expansion, and intrude on domestic questions. And Article 10 raised serious questions: Would the United States be obligated to use armed force to ensure collective security? And would the League feel compelled to crush colonial rebellions, such as in Ireland or India?

Henry Cabot Lodge of Massachusetts led the Senate opposition to the League. A Harvard-educated PhD and partisan Republican who disliked Wilson, Lodge packed the Foreign Relations Committee with critics and introduced several reservations to the treaty, most importantly that Congress had to approve any obligation under Article 10.

In September 1919, Wilson embarked on a speaking tour of the United States. Growing increasingly exhausted, he dismissed his antagonists as "contemptible quitters." While doubts about Article 10 multiplied, Wilson highlighted neglected features of the League charter—such as the arbitration of disputes and an international conference to abolish child labor. In Colorado, the president awoke to nausea and uncontrollable facial twitching. Days later, he suffered a massive stroke that paralyzed his left side. He became more stubborn, increasingly unable to conduct presidential business. More and more, his wife Edith had to select issues for his attention and delegate other matters to his cabinet heads. Advised to placate Lodge and other "Reservationist" senatorial critics so the Versailles treaty might receive congressional approval, Wilson rejected "dishonorable compromise."

Senate Rejection of the Treaty and League

Twice in November the Senate rejected the Treaty of Versailles and thus U.S. membership in the League. In March 1920, the Senate again voted; this time, a majority (49 for and 35 against) favored the treaty with reservations, but the tally fell short of the two-thirds needed. Had Wilson permitted Democrats to compromise—to accept reservations—he could have achieved his goal of membership in the League, which, despite the U.S. absence, came into being.

Within the debate lay a basic foreign policy issue: whether the United States would endorse collective security or continue the more solitary path articulated in George Washington's Farewell Address and the Monroe Doctrine. In a world dominated by imperialist states unwilling to subordinate their strategic ambitions to an international organization, Americans preferred their traditional nonalignment and freedom of choice over binding commitments to collective action. Wilson countered that the League promised something better than the status quo for the United States and the world: collective security in place of the frail protection of alliances and the instability of a balance of power.

An Unsafe World

Ultimately, World War I did not make the world safe for democracy, but it did make the United States a greater world power. By 1920, the United States was the world's leading economic power, producing 40 percent of its coal, 70 percent of its petroleum, and half of its pig iron. It also ranked first in world trade. American companies used the war to nudge Germans and British out of foreign markets, especially in Latin America. Meanwhile, the United States shifted from a debtor to a creditor nation, becoming the world's leading banker.

After the disappointment of Versailles, the peace movement revitalized, and the military became more professional. The Reserve Officers Training Corps (ROTC) became permanent; military colleges provided upper-echelon training; and the Army Industrial College, founded in 1924, pursued business-military cooperation in logistics and planning. The National Research Council, created in 1916 with government money and Carnegie and Rockefeller funds, continued a defense research alliance. Tanks, quick-firing guns, armor-piercing explosives, and oxygen masks for high-altitude-flying pilots were among the technological advances emerging from World War I.

The international system born in these years was unstable. Nationalist leaders active during World War I, such as Ho Chi Minh of Indochina and Mohandas K. Gandhi of India, vowed independence for their peoples. Communism became a disruptive force in world politics, and the Soviets bore a grudge against those who tried to thwart their revolution. The new states in central and eastern Europe proved weak. Germans bitterly resented the harsh peace settlement, and German war debts and reparations problems dogged international order for many years.

Legacy FOR A PEOPLE AND A NATION

Freedom of Speech and the ACLU

Before World War I, those with radical views often met with harsh treatment for exercising their constitutional right of freedom of speech. During the war, however, the Wilson administration's suppression of dissidents led some Americans to reformulate the traditional definition of allowable speech. Roger Baldwin, a conscientious objector, and woman suffrage activist Crystal Eastman were among the first to advance the idea that the content of political speech could be separated from the identity of the speaker and that patriotic Americans could—indeed should—defend the right of others to express political beliefs abhorrent to their own. After defending conscientious objectors, Baldwin and Eastman—joined by activists such as Jane Addams, Helen Keller, and Norman Thomas—formed the American Civil Liberties Union (ACLU).

Since 1920, the ACLU—which today has some three hundred thousand members nationwide—has aimed to protect the basic civil liberties of all Americans. It has been involved in almost every major civil liberties case in U.S. courts, among them the landmark *Brown v. Board of Education* case (1954), which ended federal tolerance of racial segregation. More recently, the ACLU was involved in the 1997 Supreme Court case ruling that the 1996 Communications Act banning "indecent speech" violated First Amendment rights.

Conservatives have long criticized the ACLU for its opposition to official prayers in public schools and its support of legal abortions, as well as its decisions on whose freedom of speech to defend. ACLU proponents counter that it has also defended those on the right, such as Oliver North, a key figure in the 1980s Iran-contra scandal.

Either way, the principle of free speech is today broadly accepted by Americans. ACLU membership skyrocketed after the September 11, 2001, terrorist attacks, due to concern about government policies eroding privacy and legal protections for Americans and for foreign detainees at Guantánamo Bay. Ironically, the Wilson administration's crackdown on dissent produced an expanded commitment to freedom of speech for a people and a nation.

Summary

The war years marked the emergence of the United States as a world power. But the war exposed deep divisions among Americans: white versus black, nativist versus immigrant, capital versus labor, men versus women, radical versus Progressive and conservative, pacifist versus interventionist, nationalist versus internationalist.

During the war, the federal government intervened in the economy and influenced people's everyday lives as never before. Although the Wilson administration shunned reconversion plans (war housing projects, for example, were sold to private investors) and quickly dismantled the many government agencies, the World War I experience of the activist state guided 1930s reformers battling the Great Depression (see Chapter 22). The government and business partnership in managing the wartime economy advanced the development of a mass society through the standardization of products and the promotion of efficiency. Wilsonian wartime policies also nourished the concentration of corporate ownership by suspending antitrust laws. Business power dominated the next decade. American labor entered lean years.

Although the disillusionment evident after Versailles did not cause the United States to adopt isolationism (see Chapter 22), skepticism about America's ability to right wrongs abroad marked the postwar American mood. People recoiled from photographs of shell-shocked faces and bodies dangling from barbed wire. American soldiers, tired of idealism, craved regular jobs. Many Progressives lost their enthusiasm for crusades.

By 1920, idealism faded. Americans were unsure of what their country's newfound status as a leading world power meant for the nation, or for their individual lives. With a mixed legacy from the Great War, the country entered the new era of the 1920s.

Chapter Review

Precarious Neutrality

How viable was U.S. neutrality during World War I?

President Woodrow Wilson, like most Americans, not only embraced neutrality, he took pride in America's being one of the few Western nations to be free from the war for its first three years. Still, U.S. economic links with Allied nations and Wilson's shared belief with the British that a German victory would spell the end of free enterprise and the rule of law made pure neutrality less believable to the outside world and less possible in the long run. The United States relied on sales to Allied nations to end its recession. It was also difficult to claim U.S. neutrality while American banks made extensive loans to Britain and France and sold arms to the Allies. Indirectly, or at least via commerce, the United States was engaged in the war even before officially entering the battlefields.

The Decision for War

How did the Zimmermann telegram finally push Americans to abandon neutrality?

For months in early 1917, Germany had launched a submarine attack on both warships and commercial vessels regardless of their stated neutrality. Americans were already outraged by this when British intelligence passed on to the United States an intercepted telegram in which the German minister in Mexico, Arthur Zimmermann, promised to help Mexico regain the territories it lost to the United States in 1848 if it united with Germany against the United States. The idea was to bring an enemy into America's backyard, but Mexico refused. Wilson released the telegram to the press, and anti-German sentiment skyrocketed. When several American ships were sunk shortly thereafter, war cries heightened, and Wilson asked Congress to declare war against Germany.

Winning the War

What was the impact of modern, trench warfare on soldiers?

Aside from an increased risk of casualty or fatality, trench warfare was mentally debilitating. Battles would be fought in zigzag, muddy, vile-smelling trenches across France fronted by barbed wire and mines. Soldiers would charge enemy trenches, often facing machine gun fire or poison gas. Many surviving soldiers suffered a mental illness dubbed "shell shock." Though not labeled as such at the time, its victims faced a kind of posttraumatic stress disorder, with symptoms including a fixed stare, violent tremors, paralyzed limbs, listlessness, jabbering, screaming, and nightmares. Trench warfare also produced extraordinarily high casualty rates.

Mobilizing the Home Front

How did wartime labor shortages create new opportunities for American workers?

A full-employment economy during the war not only meant that workers saw salaries increase (albeit sometimes only slightly ahead of inflation), but they also could easily leave jobs with low salaries or harsh conditions for something better. Worker shortages enabled women to move into higher-paying, formerly male jobs, trading domestic service for factories, shifting from clerking in department stores to stenography and typing, or leaving textile mills for firearms plants. Blacks made gains, too, as war mobilization pushed a half million African Americans to migrate to northern cities, leaving behind low-paid sharecropping and tenant farming for better wages in railroad yards, packinghouses, steel mills, shipyards, and coal mines.

Civil Liberties Under Challenge

> How did free speech come under fire during World War I?

Passage of the Espionage Act (1917) and the Sedition Act (1918) empowered the federal government to legally prosecute its critics (nearly twenty thousand were prosecuted), while others were intimidated into silence. Federal agents arrested Socialist Party leader Eugene V. Debs when he spoke out about socialism and freedom of speech, including the freedom to criticize Wilson's move to war. Professors who articulated pacifist views found themselves fired or forced to resign. Labor unions were similarly quashed. Outside government, ultrapatriotic groups employed vigilantism, burning textbooks that mentioned Germany or bullying people to buy war bonds.

Red Scare, Red Summer

> What was the impact of the Red Scare in postwar America?

Fears of a communist invasion began shortly after the Bolshevik Revolution and heightened when the Communist Party promised to spread its message worldwide. As membership in both the Socialist and Communist parties in the United States grew, nationwide crackdowns began against radicals, with labor a particular target. Political leaders – President Wilson included – worried about increased labor strikes and a possible link to Bolshevism in America. Attorney General A. Mitchell Palmer not only feared that the seeds of revolution were increasingly sown throughout society, but he appointed J. Edgar Hoover to head the Radical Division of the Justice Department and monitor allegedly radical people and organizations. The result: members of the labor union IWW were jailed; foreign activists such as Emma Goldman were among the 249 deported. Violations of the Bill of Rights and freedom of speech escalated, as did racism and racial violence. While Palmer blamed communists for racial violence, there was no truth to the charge. In truth, lynchings and violence against African Americans had more to do with resurgent racism in the postwar era and a revitalized Ku Klux Klan.

The Defeat of Peace

> What kept the United States out of the League of Nations?

While the League of Nations was Wilson's brainchild, the United States never joined. To Wilson, the League promised a more stable world based on collective security. But this notion of collectivity was problematic for a people used to operating independently in world affairs. Critics on the left feared that the League would perpetuate empire. Conservative critics worried that it might limit America's freedom to act as it saw fit in world affairs, block U.S. expansion, and intrude on domestic concerns. Worse, critics at home worried about being compelled to participate in collective action deemed necessary by the League.

Suggestions for Further Reading

John Milton Cooper Jr., *Breaking the Heart of the World: Woodrow Wilson and the Fight for the League of Nations* (2001)

Alan Dawley, *Changing the World: American Progressives in War and Revolution, 1914–1924* (2003)

David S. Foglesong, *America's Secret War Against Bolshevism* (1995)

James B. Grossman, *Land of Hope: Chicago, Black Southerners, and the Great Migration* (1989)

Michael Kazin, *A Godly Hero: The Life of William Jennings Bryan* (2006)

Jennifer D. Keene, *Doughboys, the Great War, and the Remaking of America* (2001)

David M. Kennedy, *Over Here: The Home Front in the First World War* (1980)

Thomas J. Knock, *To End All Wars: Woodrow Wilson and the Quest for a New World Order* (1992)

Margaret MacMillan, *Paris 1919: Six Months That Changed the World* (2002)

Robert H. Zieger, *America's Great War: World War I and the American Experience* (2000)

The New Era

21

1920–1929

Beth and Robert Gordon were incompatible marriage partners. Beth was frumpy and demanding; Robert liked to party. One evening at a nightclub, he met Sally Clark, who liked to party, too. When Robert came home smelling of perfume, the spouses argued, and shortly they divorced. Soon, Robert missed Beth's intellect. Meanwhile, Beth bought new clothes and makeup, turning herself into a glamorous beauty. Coincidentally, Beth and Robert visited the same summer resort and rekindled their romance. When Robert was injured in an accident, Beth nursed him back to health, much to Sally's disappointment. In the end, Beth and Robert remarried.

This story is the plot of the 1920 motion picture *Why Change Your Wife?*—one of dozens of films directed by Cecil B. DeMille. DeMille gave audiences what they fantasized about doing. Beth, Robert, and Sally dressed stylishly, went out dancing, listened to phonograph records, and visited resorts. Although DeMille's films and others of the 1920s usually ended by reinforcing marriage, ruling out premarital sex, and supporting the work ethic, they also exuded a new morality. Males and females shed old-style values for the pursuit of luxury, fun, and sexual freedom, just as actors such as Gloria Swanson and Thomas Meighan, the stars of *Why Change Your Wife?* did off-screen. In this way, *Why Change Your Wife?* was a harbinger of a new era.

During the 1920s, consumerism flourished. Although poverty beset small farmers, workers in declining industries, and nonwhites in inner cities, most other people enjoyed a high standard of living compared to previous generations. Spurred by advertising and installment buying, Americans acquired radios, automobiles, and stocks. Changes in work habits, family responsibilities, and health care fostered new uses of time and attitudes about behavior.

As in the Gilded Age, the federal government nurtured a favorable climate for business. But Progressive Era crusades for change at the national level cooled. Yet state and local governments undertook important reforms. The federal government and private organizations sought to secure world peace. Though many Americans embraced isolationism—meaning they wanted no part of Europe's political squabbles, military alliances, or the League of Nations—the nation remained active in global affairs in the 1920s to facilitate American prosperity and security.

An unseen storm lurked on the horizon, however. The glitter of consumer culture that dominated DeMille's films and everyday lives blinded Americans to rising debt and uneven prosperity. A devastating depression would bring the era to a brutal close.

As you read this chapter, keep the following questions in mind:

- **How did developments in technology stimulate social change and influence foreign policy during the 1920s?**

- **What were the benefits and costs of consumerism, and how did people deal with challenges to old-time values?**

- **What caused the stock market crash and the ensuing deep depression that signaled the end of the era?**

Economic Expansion

What helped turn the economy around in the 1920s?

The 1920s began with economic decline. After the First World War, industrial output dropped as wartime orders evaporated. In the West, railroads and the mining industry suffered. As demobilized soldiers flooded the workforce, unemployment, around 2 percent in 1919, passed 12 percent in 1921. Layoffs spread through New England as textile companies abandoned outdated factories for the South's convenient raw materials and cheap labor. Consumer spending dwindled, causing more contraction and joblessness.

Business Triumphant

Aided by electric energy, a recovery began in 1922 and continued unevenly until 1929. Electric motors enabled manufacturers to replace steam engines and produce goods more cheaply and efficiently. Most urban households now had electric service, enabling them to utilize new appliances such as refrigerators, toasters, and vacuum cleaners. The expanding economy gave Americans more spending money for products, and for restaurants, beauty salons, and movie theaters. Installment, or time-payment, plans drove the new consumerism. Of 3.5 million automobiles sold in 1923, 80 percent were bought on credit. By the late 1920s, the United States produced nearly half of the world's industrial goods and ranked first among exporters.

Economic expansion brought continued corporate consolidation. Although Progressive Era trust-busting achieved some business regulation, it had not eliminated oligopoly, the control of an industry by one or a few large firms. Now,

Chronology

1920	Volstead Act implements prohibition (Eighteenth Amendment)
	Nineteenth Amendment ratified, legalizing vote for women in federal elections
	Harding elected president
	KDKA transmits first commercial radio broadcast
1920–21	Postwar deflation and depression
1921	Federal Highway Act funds national highway system
	Emergency Quota Act establishes immigration quotas
	Sacco and Vanzetti convicted
	Sheppard-Towner Act allots funds to states to set up maternity and pediatric clinics
	Washington Conference limits naval arms
1922	Economic recovery raises standards of living
	Coronado Coal Company v. United Mine Workers rules that strikes may be illegal actions in restraint of trade
	Bailey v. Drexel Furniture Company voids restrictions on child labor

	Federal government ends strikes by railroad shop workers and miners
	Fordney-McCumber Tariff raises rates on imports
1923	Harding dies; Coolidge assumes presidency
	Adkins v. Children's Hospital overturns a minimum wage law affecting women
1923–24	Government scandals (Teapot Dome) exposed
1924	Snyder Act grants citizenship to all Indians not previously citizens
	National Origins Act revises immigration quotas
	Coolidge elected president
1925	Scopes trial highlights battle between religious fundamentalists and modernists
1927	Lindbergh pilots solo transatlantic flight
	The Jazz Singer, first movie with sound, released
1928	Stock market soars
	Kellogg-Briand Pact outlaws war
	Hoover elected president
1929	Stock market crashes; Great Depression begins

sprawling companies such as U.S. Steel and General Electric dominated basic industries, and oligopolies dominated marketing, distribution, and finance.

Languishing Agriculture

Agriculture, however, languished during the 1920s, as farmers faced international competition and went into debt when they tried to increase productivity by investing in machines, such as harvesters and tractors. Irrigation and mechanization made large-scale farming so efficient that fewer farmers could produce more crops. Consequently, crop prices plunged, big agribusinesses took over, and small landholders and tenants struggled as incomes plummeted and debts rose.

Economic Expansion Abroad

Business and government leaders attempted to use American prosperity to create stability and profits abroad. World War I left Europe in shambles. Between 1914 and 1924, Europe suffered tens of millions of casualties from world war, civil war, massacres, epidemics, and famine. Germany and France lost 10 percent of their workers. The American Relief Administration and private charities delivered food to needy people, including Russians wracked by famine in 1921 and 1922.

Because of World War I, the United States became a creditor nation and the financial capital of the world (see Figure 21.1). From 1914 to 1930, private

FIGURE 21.1

The United States in the World Economy

In the 1920s and 1930s, global depression and war scuttled the United States' hope for a stable economic order. This graph suggests, moreover, that high American tariffs meant lower exports, further impeding world trade. The Reciprocal Trade Agreements program initiated in the early 1930s was designed to ease tariff wars with other nations.

(Source: U.S. Bureau of the Census, *Historical Statistics of the United States, Colonial Times to 1970* (Washington, D.C., 1975).)

U.S. Dollars (in Billions)

Average Percentage

Underwood Tariff
Start of First World War

U.S. Enters War
Webb-Pomerene Act
Treaty of Paris / Edge Act

Fordney-McCumber Tariff

Dawes Plan

Start of Great Depression / Young Plan
Hawley-Smoot Tariff
Moratorium on War-Debts Payments
U.S. Withdraws from London Conference
Reciprocal Trade Agreements Act /
Export-Import Bank

Start of Second World War
Lend-Lease Act / U.S. Enters War

Bretton Woods Conference
End of Second World War

U.S. Exports (Merchandise) in Billions of Dollars

Average Tariff Duties Levied on Imports to U.S. (Percentage)

$2.4 billion
$8.1 billion
40.1%
38.1%
16.4%
$3.8 billion
40.1%
$5.2 billion
59.1%
$1.7 billion
37.8%
$3.3 billion
28.2%
$9.6 billion

1913 14 15 16 17 18 19 20 21 22 23 24 25 26 27 28 29 30 31 32 33 34 35 36 37 38 39 40 41 42 43 44 45 investment abroad grew fivefold, to more than $17 billion. U.S. firms began to challenge British control of oil in the Middle East. Also, American know-how became an export product. Germans marveled at Henry Ford's industrial techniques ("Fordismus"). The Phelps-Stokes Fund further advertised the American capitalist model, exporting to black Africa Booker T. Washington's Tuskegee philosophy of education, and the Rockefeller Foundation, battling diseases in Latin America and Africa, supporting colleges to train doctors in Lebanon and China, and funding medical research and nurses' training in Europe.

Investments in Latin America

American companies focused especially on Latin America, where they exploited Venezuela's petroleum resources, where the United Fruit Company became a huge landowner, and where Pan American Airways first developed air service. By 1929, American investment in the region totaled $3.5 billion and U.S. exports dominated trade. Countries there experienced repercussions from American economic and political decisions. For example, the price that Americans set for Chilean copper determined the health of Chile's economy. North American oil executives bribed Venezuelan politicians for tax breaks.

Latin American nationalists protested that their resources were being drained by U.S. companies. Distinguished Argentine writer Manuel Ugarte asserted that the United States had become a new Rome, annexing wealth rather than territory. Criticism mounted as years passed. In 1930, a Chilean newspaper warned that the American "Colossus" had "financial might" and that its aim was "Americas for the Americans—of the North."

Associations and "New Lobbying"

Business and professional organizations also expanded in the 1920s. Retailers and manufacturers formed trade associations to swap information; professional societies expanded. Farm bureaus promoted scientific agriculture and tried to stabilize markets. These groups participated in "new lobbying." With government playing an increasingly influential role, hundreds of organizations sought to convince, or lobby, legislators to support their interests.

Government policies helped business thrive, and legislators depended on lobbyists' expertise. Prodded by lobbyists, Congress cut taxes on corporations and wealthy individuals in 1921 and passed the Fordney-McCumber Tariff (1922) to raise tariffs. Presidents Warren G. Harding, Calvin Coolidge, and Herbert Hoover appointed cabinet officers who were favorable toward business. Regulatory agencies, such as the Federal Trade Commission and the Interstate Commerce Commission, cooperated with corporations more than they regulated them.

Key Supreme Court decisions sheltered business from government regulation and hindered organized labor. In *Coronado Coal Company v. United Mine Workers* (1922), chief justice and former president William Howard Taft ruled that a striking union, like a trust, could be prosecuted for illegal restraint of trade, yet in *Maple Floor Association v. U.S.* (1929), the Court decided that trade associations distributing anti-union information were not acting in restraint of trade. The Court also voided restrictions on child labor (*Bailey v. Drexel Furniture Company*, 1922) because they infringed on state power, and overturned a minimum wage

Pan American Airways

Air transportation and mail service between the United States and Latin America began in the 1920s, but anti-American hostility made establishing connections difficult. In 1926, the U.S. government, fearful that German aircraft might bomb the Panama Canal in future conflicts, signed a treaty with Panama giving American airplanes exclusive rights to Panamanian airports. Charles Lindbergh (see page 623) and former naval pilot Juan Trippe played key roles in expanding American air service throughout Latin America.

With help from his father-in-law, a banking partner of J. P. Morgan, Trippe established Pan American Airways (informally known as Pan Am) in 1927, and won a contract to carry mail between Florida and Cuba. In December of that year, Lindbergh persuaded the Mexicans to accept airline links to the United States. The next year, Lindbergh joined Pan Am and began flying company planes to Central and South America, helping Trippe initiate mail and passenger service to Panama, Mexico, and other Latin American countries in 1929.

Trippe advertised to wealthy Americans the opportunity to escape prohibition and enjoy Caribbean beaches via Pan Am.

Pan Am built airports that became essential connections between Latin America and the rest of the world. Trippe's employees created aerial maps that provided navigational aids. Pan Am linked Latin America more closely with the United States and helped connect parts of Latin America that had previously been divided by impenetrable mountain ranges. However, Pan Am cooperated with unsavory dictators, engaged in bribery, and violated human rights—in one case helping Bolivian police to corral local Indians behind barbed wire for days—to clear land for an airport.

Still, Pan Am enabled Americans to travel abroad and brought more foreigners to the United States. In 1942, its aircraft became the first to fly around the world. In the 1940s, the company began offering flights to Europe and Africa. Until its demise in 1991, Pan Am provided a leading link between the United States and the rest of the world.

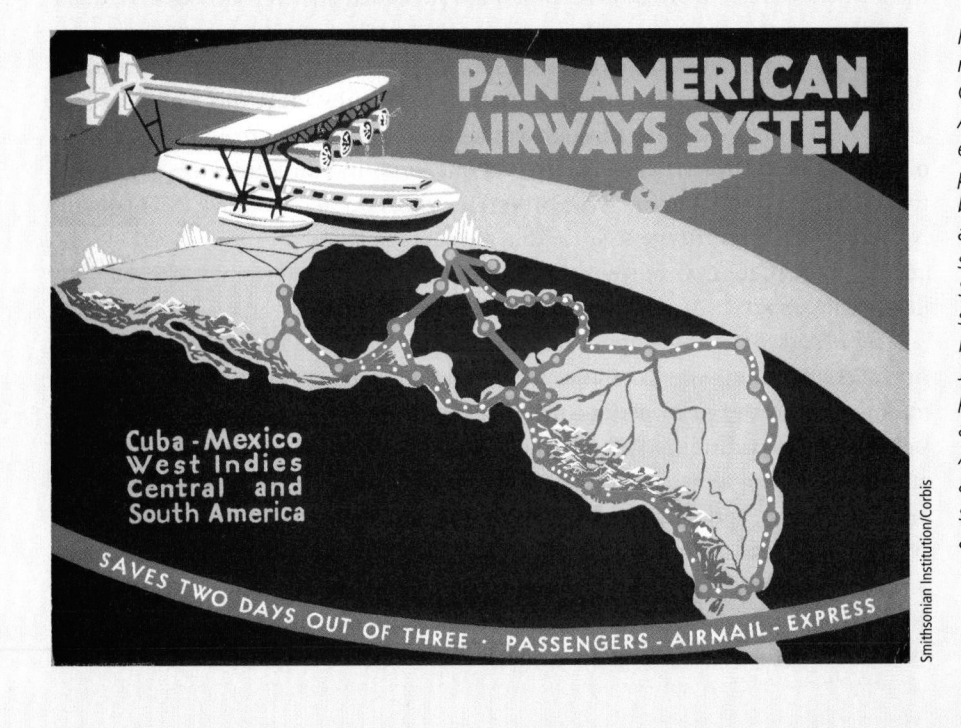

Providing air transport connections to the Caribbean, Central America, and South America, Pan American Airways established the first major passenger and cargo links between the United States and other nations. The aircraft shown in this illustration, the Sikorsky S-40 "Flying Clipper" seaplane, was added to the Pan Am fleet in October 1931. Juan Trippe, the company's president, called the seaplane a "flagship" and "the first American example of the great airliner of tomorrow that will speed trade and good will among nations."

Smithsonian Institution/Corbis

law affecting women because it infringed on liberty of contract (*Adkins v. Children's Hospital*, 1923).

| Setbacks for Organized Labor |

Public opinion turned against organized labor in the 1920s, linking it with communism brought to America by radical immigrants. Using Red Scare tactics, the Harding administration in 1922 obtained a court injunction to quash a strike by 400,000 railroad workers. State and federal courts issued injunctions to prevent other strikes and permitted businesses to sue unions for damages from labor actions.

Meanwhile, corporations imposed "yellow-dog contracts," which made refusal to join a union a condition of employment. Companies also countered the appeal of unions by offering pensions, profit sharing, and company-sponsored picnics—a policy known as "welfare capitalism." State legislators aided employers by prohibiting closed shops (workplaces where unions required all employees become union members) and permitting open shops (where employers could hire nonunion employees). Due to court action, welfare capitalism, and ineffective leadership, union membership fell from 5.1 million in 1920 to 3.6 million in 1929.

Government, Politics, and Reform

What happened to Progressive reform in the 1920s?

During the 1920s, politics shifted from Progressive Era activism, yet certain continuities remained and women, enfranchised nationally by the Nineteenth Amendment, influenced national and international affairs. Several Republican presidents reinforced Theodore Roosevelt's government-business cooperation, but they made government a compliant coordinator rather than the active manager Roosevelt advocated. Still, the government extended reform programs at home and embarked on new peace efforts abroad.

| Women and Politics |

Even with suffrage, women remained excluded from political power structures. Instead, they worked through voluntary organizations to lobby legislators on issues such as birth control, peace, education, Indian affairs, or opposition to lynching. The League of Women Voters, for example, reorganized out of the National Woman Suffrage Association, encouraged women to run for office, and actively lobbied for laws to improve conditions for employed women, the mentally ill, and the poor.

Sheppard-Towner Act
Sought to reduce infant mortality by providing matching funds to states to create prenatal and child health clinics. It was repealed in1929.

In 1921, women's groups persuaded Congress to pass the **Sheppard-Towner Act**, allotting funds to states to create maternity and pediatric clinics to reduce infant mortality. (The measure ended in 1929, when Congress, pressured by physicians, canceled funding.) The Cable Act of 1923 reversed the law under which an American woman who married a foreigner lost her U.S. citizenship and had to assume her husband's citizenship. At the state level, women achieved some rights, such as the ability to serve on juries.

As new voters, however, women pursued diverging goals. Women in the National Association of Colored Women, for example, fought for the rights of minorities. Other groups, such as the National Woman's Party, pressed for an equal rights amendment to ensure women's equality under the law. But such activity alienated the National Consumers League, the Women's Trade Union League, the League of Women Voters, and other organizations that supported protective legislation to limit hours and improve conditions for employed women.

Indian Affairs

Disturbed by the federal government's apathetic Indian policy, in the 1920s reform organizations such as the Indian Rights Association, the Indian Defense Association, and the General Federation of Women's Clubs worked to obtain justice and social services, including better education and return of tribal lands. Whites expected Indians to assimilate. But they overlooked important drawbacks. Severalty, the federal policy created by the Dawes Act of 1887 that allotted land to individuals rather than tribes, failed to make Indians self-supporting. Indian farmers suffered poor soil and unavailable irrigation, and attached to their land, they were disinclined to move to cities. Whites hoped to convert native peoples into "productive" citizens, typically ignoring indigenous cultures. Reformers were especially critical of Indian women, who rejected middle-class homemaking habits and balked at sending children to boarding schools.

Meanwhile, citizenship status remained unclear. The Dawes Act had conferred citizenship on Indians who accepted land allotments, but not those who remained on reservations. After several court challenges, Congress passed an Indian Citizenship Act (Snyder Act) in 1924, granting full citizenship to all Indians in hopes that Indians would help Indians to assimilate.

Presidency of Warren Harding

President **Warren G. Harding**, elected in 1920, was a symbol of government's goodwill toward business. He captured 16 million popular votes to 9 million for the Democratic nominee, Ohio governor James M. Cox and his running mate, New York governor Franklin D. Roosevelt (Teddy's cousin). (The total vote in the 1920 presidential election was 36 percent higher than in 1916, reflecting the first-time participation of women voters.)

Harding also benefited from voter disillusionment with the League of Nations and the collective world security system envisioned by Woodrow Wilson and the Democrats (see page 596). The League proved feeble because members failed to utilize it to settle disputes. Although the United States never joined, American officials participated discreetly in League meetings on public health, prostitution, drug and arms trafficking, counterfeiting, and other issues.

Warren G. Harding The twenty-ninth president of the United States, in office from 1921 to 1923.

Scandals of the Harding Administration

Harding appointed assistants who promoted business growth, notably Secretary of State Charles Evans Hughes, Secretary of Commerce Herbert Hoover, Secretary of the Treasury Andrew Mellon, and Secretary of Agriculture Henry C. Wallace. But Harding had personal weaknesses, notably his extramarital liaison with the wife of an Ohio merchant. In 1917, he began a relationship with Nan Britton, thirty-one years his junior, that resulted in a daughter born in 1919. Britton revealed the secret in a book, *The President's Daughter* (1927), although Harding never acknowledged his illegitimate offspring.

Of more consequence, Harding appointed cronies who used office holding for personal gain. Charles Forbes, head of the Veterans Bureau, went to federal prison, convicted of fraud and bribery in government contracts. Notoriously, a congressional inquiry in 1923 and 1924 revealed that Secretary of the Interior Albert Fall accepted bribes to lease government property to oil companies. Fall was fined $100,000 and spent a year in jail for his role in the so-called **Teapot Dome** scandal, named for the Wyoming oil reserve he handed to the Mammoth Oil Company.

Teapot Dome Scandal that rocked the Harding administration after Harding's secretary of the interior was found guilty of secretly leasing government oil reserves to two oilmen in exchange for a bribe.

By mid-1923, Harding had become disillusioned. On a speaking tour that summer, he became ill and died in San Francisco on August 2. Although his death preceded revelation of the Teapot Dome scandal, some speculated that, to avoid impeachment, Harding committed suicide or was poisoned by his wife. Most evidence, however, points to death from natural causes, probably heart disease.

Calvin Coolidge The thirtieth president of the United States; took office after the death of President Warren Harding in 1923.

Coolidge Prosperity

Vice President **Calvin Coolidge**, who became president, was less outgoing than Harding. As governor of Massachusetts, Coolidge attracted national attention in 1919 when he used the National Guard to end a policemen's strike, which won him business support and the 1920 vice presidential nomination. Respectful of private enterprise and aided by Treasury Secretary Andrew Mellon, Coolidge's administration reduced federal debt, lowered income tax rates (especially for the wealthy), and began construction of a national highway system.

With farm prices falling, Congress twice passed bills to establish government-backed price supports for staple crops (the McNary-Haugen bills of 1927 and 1928). Resembling the 1890s subtreasury scheme of the Farmers' Alliances, these bills proposed to establish a system whereby the government would buy surplus farm products and either hold them until prices rose or sell them abroad. Coolidge, however, vetoed the measures as improper government interference in the market economy.

"Coolidge prosperity" was the decisive issue in the 1924 presidential election. Both parties ran candidates who favored private initiative over government intervention. At their convention, Democrats voted 542 to 541 against condemning the revived Ku Klux Klan, and deadlocked for 103 ballots between southern prohibitionists, who supported former treasury secretary William G. McAdoo, and anti-prohibition easterners, who backed New York's governor, Alfred E. Smith. They finally compromised on New York corporate lawyer John W. Davis.

Remnants of the Progressive movement, along with farm, labor, and socialist groups, formed a new Progressive Party and nominated Robert M. La Follette, the aging Wisconsin reformer. The party stressed public ownership of railroads and power plants, conservation of natural resources, aid to farmers, rights for organized labor, and regulation of business. Coolidge beat Davis by 15.7 million to 8.4 million popular votes and 382 to 136 electoral votes. La Follette received 4.8 million popular votes and 13 electoral votes.

The urgency for political and economic reform that inspired the previous Progressive generation faded in the 1920s. Much reform, however, occurred at state and local levels. Following pre–World War I initiatives, thirty-four states instituted or expanded workers' compensation laws and public welfare programs in the 1920s. By 1926, every major city had planning and zoning commissions to harness physical growth to the common good. As a result of their efforts, a new generation of reformers who later influenced national affairs acquired valuable experience in statehouses, city halls, and universities.

The Search for Lasting Peace

The Progressive quest for humanity combined with a desire to prevent future world wars to energize a U.S. peace movement. Societies such as the National Council for Prevention of War kept alive Woodrow Wilson's dream for a world body to oversee peace. Women peace advocates, restricted by male leaders in these groups, formed their own organizations. Carrie Chapman Catt's moderate National Conference on the Cure and Cause of War formed in 1924, and the U.S. section of the Women's International League for Peace and Freedom (WILPF), organized in 1915 by Jane Addams and Emily Greene Balch, became the largest women's peace group. When Addams won the Nobel Peace Prize in 1921, she donated the money to the League of Nations.

Peace groups differed over strategies to ensure world order. Some urged cooperation with the League of Nations and the World Court. Others championed arbitration, disarmament and arms reduction, the outlawing of war, and neutrality during wars. The WILPF called for an end to U.S. economic imperialism, which it claimed compelled the United States to intervene militarily in Latin America to protect U.S. business interests. The Women's Peace Union (organized in 1921) lobbied for a constitutional amendment requiring a national referendum on a declaration of war. Quakers, YMCA officials, and Social Gospel clergy in 1917 created the American Friends Service Committee to identify pacifist alternatives to warmaking.

Washington Naval Conference and Kellogg-Briand Pact

Peace advocates influenced Warren G. Harding's administration to convene the **Washington Naval Conference** of November 1921–February 1922. Delegates from Britain, Japan, France, Italy, China, Portugal, Belgium, and the Netherlands joined a U.S. team led by Secretary of State Charles Evans Hughes to discuss limiting naval armaments. American leaders worried that an expansionist Japan, with the world's third largest navy, would overtake the United States, ranked second behind Britain.

Washington Naval Conference Multinational conference led by U.S. Secretary of State Hughes to address the problem of the United States, Great Britain, and Japan edging toward a dangerous (and costly) naval arms race.

Hughes opened the conference with the stunning proposal to scrap thirty major U.S. ships, totaling 846,000 tons. He urged the British and Japanese delegations to do away with smaller amounts. The final limit was 500,000 tons each for the Americans and the British, 300,000 tons for the Japanese, and 175,000 tons each for the French and the Italians. These limits were agreed to in the Five-Power Treaty, which also set a ten-year moratorium on building capital ships (battleships and aircraft carriers). The governments further pledged not to build new fortifications in their Pacific possessions (such as the Philippines).

Next, the Nine-Power Treaty reaffirmed the Open Door in China, recognizing Chinese sovereignty. Finally, in the Four-Power Treaty, the United States, Britain, Japan, and France agreed to respect one another's Pacific possessions. These treaties did not limit submarines, destroyers, or cruisers, nor did they provide enforcement powers for the Open Door. Still, Hughes achieved arms limitation and improved America's strategic position vis-à-vis Japan in the Pacific.

Peace advocates also applauded the Locarno Pact of 1925, agreements among European nations designed to reduce German-French tensions, and the Kellogg-Briand Pact of 1928. The latter document pledged sixty-two nations to "condemn recourse to war for the solution of international controversies, and renounce it as an instrument of national policy." The accord passed the U.S. Senate 85–1, but it lacked enforcement provisions. Nevertheless, the agreement reflected popular aversion to war and it stimulated further peace discussions.

A Consumer Society

How did the emergence of a consumer society change American life?

The consumerism depicted in *Why Change Your Wife?* reflected important economic changes. Between 1919 and 1929, the gross national product—the value of all goods and services produced in the United States—swelled by 40 percent. Wages and salaries also grew, while the cost of living remained stable. People had more purchasing power, and they spent as never before (see Table 21.1). New products and services were available, and not just to the rich. By 1929, two-thirds of all Americans lived in dwellings that had electricity, compared with one-sixth in 1912. In 1929, one-fourth of all families owned vacuum cleaners. Many could afford these goods plus radios, cosmetics, and movie tickets because several family members worked or because the breadwinner took a second job.

TABLE 21.1   Consumerism in the 1920s

1900	
2 bicycles	$ 70
Wringer and washboard	5
Brushes and brooms	5
Sewing machine (mechanical)	25
TOTAL	$ 105
1928	
Automobile	$ 700
Radio	75
Phonograph	50
Washing machine	150
Vacuum cleaner	50
Sewing machine (electric)	60
Other electrical equipment	25
Telephone (per year)	35
TOTAL	$ 1,145

Source: From an article in *Survey Magazine* in 1928 reprinted in *Another Part of the Twenties,* by Paul Carter. Copyright 1977 by Columbia University Press. Reprinted with permission of the publisher.

Effects of the Automobile

During the 1920s, automobile registrations soared from 8 million to 23 million, and by 1929 one in every five Americans had a car. Mass production and competition made cars affordable. A Ford Model T cost less than $300, and a Chevrolet sold for $700 by 1926—when factory workers earned about $1,300 a year and clerical workers about $2,300. At those prices, people could consider the car a necessity rather than a luxury.

Cars altered American life. Owners abandoned crowded trolleys; streets became cleaner as autos replaced horses. Female drivers achieved newfound independence, taking touring trips with friends. By 1927, most autos were enclosed (they previously had open tops), creating private space for youthful courtship and sex.

After World War I, motorists joined farmers and bicyclists in their decades-old campaign for improved roads. In 1921, Congress passed the Federal Highway Act, providing funds for state roads, and in 1923 the Bureau of Public Roads planned a national highway system. The oil-refining industry, which produced gasoline, became powerful. In 1920, the United States produced about 65 percent of the world's oil. Public officials paid more attention to traffic control, with General Electric Company producing the first timed stop-and-go traffic light in 1924.

Automobiles, such as the Ford Model T, gave middle-class women new mobility but did not necessarily lessen their domestic responsibilities, such as shopping for quality foods. The Ford Motor Company, however, tried to appeal to homemakers' sense of style and cost-consciousness by arguing that the new closed car was not only attention-getting but also a good economic value.

Picture Research Consultants & Archives

Advertising and Radio

By 1929, more money was spent on advertising than on formal education. Blending psychological theory with practical cynicism, advertising theorists asserted that any people's tastes could be manipulated. For example, cosmetics manufacturers like Max Factor, Helena Rubenstein, and African American entrepreneur Madame C. J. Walker used movie stars and beauty advice in magazines to entice female customers. Other advertisers hired baseball star Babe Ruth to endorse food and sporting goods.

Radio became an influential advertising medium. By 1929, over 10 million Americans owned radios, spending $850 million annually on radio equipment. In the early 1920s, Congress decided that broadcasting should be a private enterprise, not a tax-supported public service as in Great Britain. American programming focused on entertainment rather than educational content, because entertainment attracted larger audiences and higher advertising profits. Station KDKA in Pittsburgh, owned by Westinghouse Electric Company, pioneered commercial radio in 1920. In 1922, an AT&T-run station in New York City broadcast advertisements—commercials. By late 1922, there were 508 commercial stations.

Export of American Consumerism

America's economic prominence stimulated interest in American products abroad. Though some foreigners warned against Americanization, others accepted American products. Coca-Cola opened a bottling plant

612 The New Era, 1920–1929

in Essen, Germany. Ford built an automobile assembly factory in Cologne. German writer Hans Joachim claimed that cultural adoption might promote a peaceful, democratic world.

Products such as the automobile and radio helped create a new American people. Radio's mass marketing and standardized programming blurred ethnic boundaries and helped shape a homogeneous culture. And the automobile served as a social equalizer, prompting some to believe it might calm social unrest among ethnic groups. As one writer wrote in 1924, "It is hard to convince Steve Popovich, or Antonio Branca, or plain John Smith that he is being ground into the dust by Capital when at will he may drive the same highways… as the modern Midas."

Cities, Migrants, and Suburbs

What fueled the growth of cities in the 1920s?

The 1920 federal census revealed that, for the first time, a majority of Americans lived in urban areas (places with 2,500 or more people). Growth in manufacturing and services helped propel urbanization. Industries like steel, oil, and auto production energized Birmingham, Houston, and Detroit; services and retail trades boosted Seattle, Atlanta, and Minneapolis. During the 1920s, 6 million Americans left farms for the city. Young people, seeking excitement and openness, moved to regional centers like Kansas City or to the West. Between 1920 and 1930, California's population increased 67 percent, and California became a highly urbanized state while retaining its status as a leader in agricultural production.

African American Migration

African Americans, continuing their Great Migration that had begun in 1910, made up a sizable portion of people on the move during the 1920s. Pushed from cotton farming by a boll weevil plague and lured by industrial jobs, 1.5 million blacks moved, doubling the African American populations of New York, Chicago, Detroit, and Houston. They found menial jobs as janitors, longshoremen, and domestic servants.

Forced by low wages and discrimination to seek cheap housing, black newcomers squeezed into ghettos like Chicago's South Side or New York's Harlem. Blacks everywhere found better neighborhoods closed to them. They could either crowd into densely populated black neighborhoods or spill into nearby white neighborhoods. Fears of such "invasion" sparked violence and prompted neighborhood associations to adopt restrictive covenants, whereby white homeowners pledged not to sell or rent to blacks.

Marcus Garvey

In response to discrimination, threats, and violence, thousands of urban blacks joined movements that glorified racial independence. The most influential of these black nationalist groups was the Universal Negro Improvement Association (UNIA), led by **Marcus Garvey**, a Jamaican immigrant who believed blacks should separate from corrupt white society. Unlike the NAACP, formed by elite African American and white liberals, the UNIA was comprised exclusively of blacks, largely from the lower classes.

Marcus Garvey Charismatic black leader who promoted racial pride and independence and believed blacks should separate from white society.

Garvey furthered Booker T. Washington's ideas of economic independence by promoting black-owned businesses that would manufacture and sell products to black consumers. His newspaper, *Negro World*, preached black independence, and he founded the Black Star steamship line to transport manufactured goods to black businesses in North America, the Caribbean, and Africa.

The UNIA declined in the mid-1920s after mismanagement plagued Garvey's plans. In 1923, Garvey was imprisoned for mail fraud involving the bankrupt Black Star Line, and he was deported to Jamaica in 1927. His prosecution, however, was politically motivated. Middle-class black leaders, such as W. E. B. Du Bois, opposed the UNIA, fearing its extremism would undermine their efforts. In 1919, the U.S. Bureau of Investigation (BOI), forerunner to the FBI, began monitoring Garvey's radical activities and the BOI's deputy head, J. Edgar Hoover, proclaimed Garvey to be one of the most dangerous blacks in America. Nevertheless, for years the UNIA attracted a large following (contemporaries estimated 500,000; Garvey claimed 6 million), and Garvey's speeches instilled racial pride in many African Americans.

Newcomers from Mexico and Puerto Rico

The newest immigrants came from Mexico and Puerto Rico, where declining fortunes pushed people off the land. During the 1910s, Anglo farmers' associations encouraged Mexicans to provide cheap labor, and by the 1920s Mexican migrants constituted three-fourths of farm labor in the American West. Growers treated Mexican laborers as slaves, paying them extremely low wages. Although some achieved middle-class status, most crowded into urban low-rent districts plagued by poor sanitation, poor police protection, and poor schools. Mexicans moved back and forth across the border, creating a way of life that Mexicans called *sin fronteras*—without borders.

The 1920s also witnessed an influx of Puerto Ricans to the mainland, as the island's shift from sugar to coffee production created a labor surplus. Puerto Rico

Over half a million Mexicans immigrated to the United States during the 1920s. Many of them traveled in families and worked together in the fields and orchards of California and other western states. This family is shown pitting apricots in Los Angeles County in 1924.

Library of Congress

had been a U.S. possession since 1898, and Puerto Ricans were granted U.S. citizenship in 1916. Attracted by contracts from employers seeking cheap labor, they created *barrios* (communities) and found jobs in factories, hotels, restaurants, and domestic service. Like Mexicans, Puerto Ricans maintained customs and developed businesses—*bodegas* (grocery stores), cafés, boarding houses—and social organizations to help them adapt to American society. Educated elites—doctors, lawyers, and business owners—became community leaders.

| Suburbanization |

As urbanization peaked, suburban growth accelerated. Prosperity and automobile transportation in the 1920s made suburbs more accessible to those wishing to leave cities. Between 1920 and 1930, suburbs of Chicago (such as Oak Park and Evanston), Cleveland (Shaker Heights), and Los Angeles (Burbank and Inglewood) grew five to ten times faster than nearby central cities. Los Angeles builders erected 250,000 homes for auto-owning suburbanites. Most suburbs were middle- and upper-class bedroom communities; some, like Highland Park (near Detroit) were industrial satellites.

Increasingly, suburbs resisted annexation to core cities. Suburbanites wanted to escape big-city crime, grime, and taxes, and they fought to preserve control over police, schools, and water and gas services. Particularly in the Northeast and Midwest, the suburbs' independence prevented central cities from accessing the resources and tax bases of wealthier suburban residents. Population dispersal spread the environmental problems of city life—trash, pollution, noise—across the metropolitan area.

Most consumers who jammed shops, movie houses, and sporting arenas and who embraced fads like miniature golf lived in or around cities. They defied older morals by patronizing speakeasies (illegal saloons during prohibition), wearing outlandish clothes, and dancing to jazz, while others reminisced about the simplicity of a world gone by.

New Rhythms of Everyday Life

How did technological advances transform social life in America in the 1920s?

Amid expanding consumerism, Americans increasingly split their day into distinct time-based compartments: work, family, and leisure. For many, mechanization and resulting higher productivity enabled employers to shorten the workweek for industrial laborers from six days to five and a half. White-collar employees often worked a forty-hour week, enjoyed the weekend off, and received paid vacations.

Family time is harder to measure, but certain trends emerged. Family size decreased between 1920 and 1930 as birth control was increasingly practiced. Over half the women married in the 1870s and 1880s had five or more children; in the 1920s, only 20 percent did. Lower birth rates and longer life expectancy meant adults devoted less of their lives to child rearing. Meanwhile, divorce rates rose from 1 divorce for every 7.5 marriages in 1920 to 1 in 6 by 1929.

| Household Management |

Housewives still worked long hours cleaning, cooking, and raising children, but machines now lightened some tasks. Especially in middle-class households, electric irons and washing machines simplified chores.

Visualizing THE PAST

Expansion of Suburbs in the 1920s

An outburst of housing and highway construction made possible the rapid growth of suburbs in the 1920s. The Chicago suburb of Niles Center, ultimately called the Village of Skokie, was incorporated in 1888. Aided by the service of commuter railroads, the village began to grow in the early 1900s, and in 1913 the first permanently paved road in Cook County was built there. After 1920, a real estate boom began, and by the mid-1920s the village had its own water, sewer, and street lighting services, along with many more paved roads. Wealthy Chicagoans such as utilities and railroad investor Samuel Insull built lavish homes in Niles Center, and soon commercial and office buildings sprang up along its major thoroughfares. Population grew so rapidly that the community boasted that it was "The World's Largest Village." The Great Depression halted the boom in 1929, but significant growth resumed after the Second World War. How do you think daily life changed as a result of the growth of suburbs?

In some areas, real estate developers laid out streets and blocks in burgeoning suburbs, enticing offices, stores, and institutions before residences were even built. This photograph of Niles Center, Illinois, taken from an airplane around 1927, reveals how roads and automobiles had become essential to suburban expansion.

Provided by the Skokie Historical Society

Provided by the Skokie Historical Society

As the 1920s proceeded, suburban housing construction accelerated. These private homes, one still under construction, along Brown Street in Niles Center, Illinois, in 1926 reveal how an open prairie was converted into a residential community. Note the presence of autos, a flatbed truck, and electrical wires, all critical to suburban life.

Gas- and oil-powered central heating and hot water heaters eliminated the hauling of wood, coal, and water; maintaining a kitchen fire; and removing ashes.

But technology and economic change also created new demands on women's time. The pool of those who could help housewives with cleaning, cooking, and child care shrank because daughters stayed in school longer, and alternative forms of employment caused a shortage of domestic servants. Advertisers of washing machines, vacuum cleaners, and commercial soap tried to make women feel guilty for not doing enough housework. No longer a producer of food and clothing, a housewife became the family's shopper and chauffeur. One survey found that urban housewives spent seven and one-half hours per week driving to shop and transport children.

Health and Life Expectancy

With the discovery of vitamins between 1915 and 1930, nutritionists advocated certain foods to promote health. Producers of milk, canned fruits and vegetables, and other foods exploited the vitamin craze with claims about benefits that were hard to dispute because little was known about these invisible, tasteless ingredients. Welch's Grape Juice, for example, avoided mentioning the excess sugars when it advertised that it was "Rich in Health Values."

Better diets and improved hygiene made Americans healthier. Life expectancy at birth increased from fifty-four to sixty years between 1920 and 1930, and infant mortality decreased by two-thirds. Public sanitation and research in bacteriology reduced life-threatening diseases such as tuberculosis and diphtheria. But medical progress did not benefit everyone equally; infant mortality rates were 50 to 100 percent higher among nonwhites than among whites, and tuberculosis in inner-city slums remained alarmingly common. Nevertheless, the total population over age sixty-five grew 35 percent between 1920 and 1930.

Older Americans and Retirement

Industrialism put premiums on youth and agility, pushing older people into poverty from forced retirement and reduced income. Recognizing the needs of aging citizens, most European countries established state-supported pension systems in the early 1900s. Many Americans, however, believed that individuals should save for old age in their youth; pensions, they felt, smacked of socialism.

Most inmates in state poorhouses were older people, and almost one-third of Americans age sixty-five and older depended financially on someone else. Few employers, including the federal government, provided for retired employees. Resistance to pension plans broke at the state level in the 1920s. Led by the physician Isaac Max Rubinow and the journalist Abraham Epstein, reformers persuaded voluntary associations, labor unions, and legislators to endorse old-age assistance. By 1933, almost every state provided at least minimal support to needy elderly, opening the door to a national program of old-age insurance—Social Security.

Social Values

Social changes altered habits and values. Aided by new fabrics and chemical dyes, clothes became a means of self-expression as women and men wore more colorful styles than their parents' generation. The line between acceptable and inappropriate behavior blurred as smoking, drinking, and frankness about sex became fashionable.

Birth control gained a large following in respectable circles. Newspapers, magazines, motion pictures (such as *Why Change Your Wife?*), and popular songs (such as "I Don't Care") made certain that Americans did not suffer from "sex starvation."

Because restrictive child labor laws and compulsory attendance rules kept children in school longer, peer groups played a more influential role in socializing youngsters than parents. School classes, sports, and clubs constantly brought together children of the same age, separating them from the influence of adults.

Between 1890 and the mid-1920s, ritualized middle- and upper-class courtship, consisting of men formally "calling" on women and chaperoned social engagements, was replaced by unsupervised "dating." Unmarried young people, living away from family restraints, went on dates to new commercial amusements, such as movies and nightclubs. A woman's job seldom provided sufficient income for her entertainments, but she could enjoy them if a man "treated" her. Romance, and at times, sexual exploitation, accompanied the practice, especially when a woman was expected to trade sexual favors for being treated. Under the courtship system, a woman controlled who could "call" on her, bur reliance on a man's money for entertainment presented difficult moral choices.

Women in the Workforce

The practice of dating burgeoned after World War I, as women continued to stream into the labor force. By 1930, 10.8 million women held paying jobs, an increase of 2 million since war's end (see Figure 21.2). Sex segregation persisted; most women took jobs that men seldom sought. Thus, more than 1 million women were teachers and nurses; 2.2 million women were typists, bookkeepers, and filing clerks, a tenfold increase since 1920. Another 736,000 were store clerks, and growing numbers were waitresses and hairdressers. Women's wages seldom exceeded half of those paid to men. Although most married women did not hold paying jobs (only 12 percent were employed in 1930), married women as a proportion of the workforce rose by 30 percent during the 1920s, and the number of employed married women swelled from 1.9 million to 3.1 million.

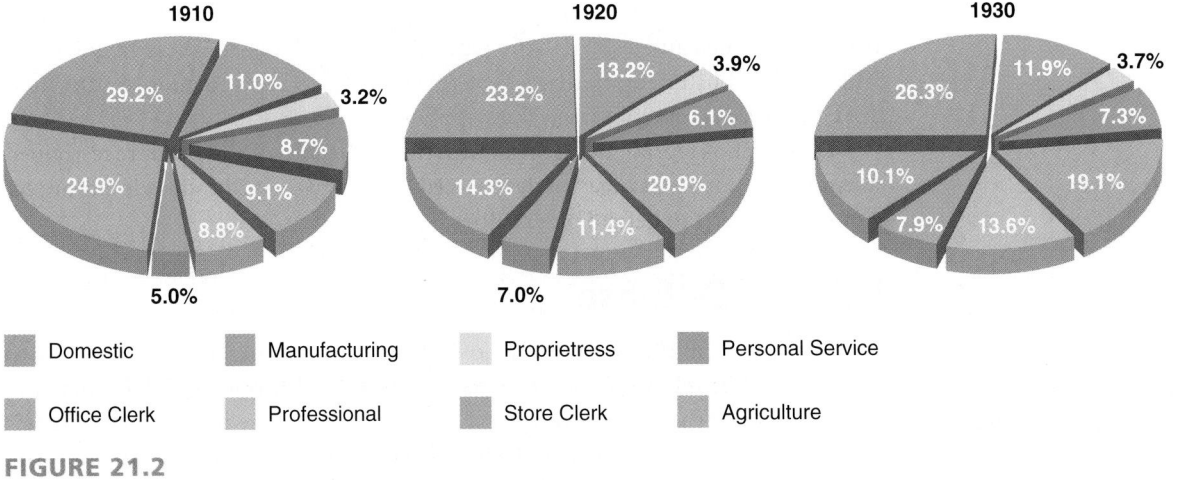

FIGURE 21.2

Changing Dimensions of Paid Female Labor, 1910–1930

These charts reveal the extraordinary growth in clerical and professional occupations among employed women and the accompanying decline in agricultural labor in the early twentieth century. Notice that manufacturing employment peaked in 1920 and that domestic service fluctuated as white immigrant women began to move out of these jobs and were replaced by women of color.

The proportion of racial and ethnic minority women in paid labor was double that of white women. Often they entered the workforce when husbands were unemployed or underemployed. The majority of employed African American women held domestic jobs. The few who had factory jobs performed the least desirable, lowest-paying tasks. Some opportunities opened for educated black women in social work, teaching, and nursing, but they faced discrimination and low incomes. More than white mothers, employed black mothers called on female relatives to help with child care. Mexican women in the Southwest worked as domestic servants, operatives in garment factories, and agricultural laborers. Next to black women, Japanese American women were the most likely to hold paying jobs, typically as field hands and domestics, facing racial bias and low pay.

Alternative Images of Femininity

Women remade the image of femininity, casting aside the heavy, floor-length dresses and long hair of previous generations. Instead, they embraced the short skirts and bobbed hair of the 1920s "flapper," which symbolized independence and sexual freedom. Although few women lived the flapper life, office workers, store clerks, and college students adopted the look. As Cecil B. DeMille's movies showed, new female icons included movie temptresses, such as Clara Bow, known as the "It Girl," and Gloria Swanson, notorious for torrid love affairs on and off the screen. Many women asserted new social equality with men. One observer described "the new woman" as intriguingly independent.

> She takes a man's point of view as her mother never could. … She will never make you a hatband or knit you a necktie, but she'll drive you from the station … in her own little sports car. She'll don knickers and go skiing with you, … she'll dive as well as you, perhaps better. …

Gay and Lesbian Culture

The era's sexual openness enabled the underground homosexual culture to surface somewhat. In nontraditional city neighborhoods, such as New York's Greenwich Village, cheap rents and a relative tolerance attracted gay men and lesbians, who patronized dance halls, speakeasies, and cafés. Still, gay establishments remained targets for police raids, demonstrating that there was little acceptance from the larger society.

These trends represented a break with the nineteenth century's more restrained culture. But social change rarely proceeds smoothly. As the decade advanced, groups mobilized to defend older values.

Lines of Defense

How did various groups seek to hold the line on social change in the 1920s?

Early in 1920, the leader of a newly formed organization hired two public relations experts, Edward Clarke and Elizabeth Tyler. They canvassed the South, Southwest, and Midwest, where they found countless people eager to pay a $10 membership fee and $6 for a white uniform. Clarke and Tyler pocketed $2.50 from each membership. Their success helped build the organization to 5 million members and four thousand chapters by 1923.

Ku Klux Klan

This was the Ku Klux Klan (KKK), a revived version of the hooded order that terrorized southern communities after the Civil War. Reconstituted in 1915 by William J. Simmons, an Atlanta, Georgia, evangelist and insurance salesman, the Klan adopted the hoods, intimidating tactics, and mystical terminology of its forerunner (its leader was the Imperial Wizard; its book of rituals, the Kloran). But the new Klan had broader objectives. It fanned outward from the Deep South, wielding political power in places as diverse as Oregon, where Portland's mayor was a Klan member, and Indiana, where Klansmen held the governorship and several legislative seats. Members included men from the urban middle class who feared losing social and economic gains and were nervous about a new youth culture that eluded family control. It included a women's adjunct with a half-million members.

One phrase summed up Klan goals: "Native, white, Protestant supremacy." *Native* meant no immigration, no "mongrelization" of American culture. According to Imperial Wizard Hiram Wesley Evans, "The world has been so made so that each race must fight for its life, must conquer, accept slavery, or die." Evans accused the Catholic Church of discouraging assimilation and enslaving people to priests and a foreign pope.

Using threatening assemblies, violence, and political and economic pressure, the Klan meted out vigilante justice to suspected bootleggers, wife beaters, and adulterers; forced schools to stop teaching evolution; campaigned against Catholic and Jewish political candidates; and fueled racial tensions against Mexicans in Texas border cities and against blacks everywhere. Klan women promoted native white Protestantism but also worked for moral reform and prohibition. Because the KKK vowed to protect women's virtue, housewives sometimes appealed to the Klan to punish abusive husbands. The Klan's method of justice was flogging.

By 1925, however, scandal undermined the Klan's moral base. Indiana grand dragon David Stephenson was convicted of second-degree murder after he kidnapped and raped a woman who later died. Eventually, the Klan's negative brand of patriotism and purity could not compete in a pluralistic society.

Intolerance pervaded American society in the 1920s. Nativists charged that Catholic and Jewish immigrants clogged city slums, flouted community norms, and stubbornly embraced alien religious and political beliefs. Fear of immigrant radicals also fueled a dramatic 1921 trial of two Italian anarchists, **Nicola Sacco and Bartolomeo Vanzetti**, convicted of murdering a paymaster and guard in Braintree, Massachusetts. Evidence for their guilt was flimsy.

Nicola Sacco and Bartolomeo Vanzetti Italian immigrants found guilty of a Massachusetts murder and sentenced to death. Sacco and Vanzetti were also anarchists and much of their murder trial focused on their radicalism.

Link to The United States Quota Act, 1921–1922

Immigration Quotas

Efforts to restrict immigration gathered support. Labor leaders warned that aliens would depress wages and raise unemployment. Business executives, who formerly desired cheap immigrant laborers, now realized that mechanization would keep wages low. Drawing support from such groups, Congress set yearly immigration allocations for each nationality in the Emergency Quota Act of 1921. By restricting annual immigration of a given nationality to 3 percent of immigrants from that nation already residing in the United States in 1910, the act favored Anglo-Saxon Protestant immigrants. It discriminated against Catholics and Jews from southern and eastern Europe, whose numbers were comparatively small in 1910.

National Origins Act of 1924
Restricted annual immigration from any foreign country to 2 percent of that nationality residing in the United States in 1890 (but barred Asians); also limited total annual immigration to 150,000.

In 1924, Congress replaced the Quota Act with the **National Origins Act**. This law limited annual immigration to 150,000 people and set quotas at 2 percent of each nationality residing in the United States in 1890, except for Asians, who were banned completely. The act further restricted southern and eastern Europeans since fewer of those groups lived in the United States in 1890 than in 1910, although it allowed foreign-born wives and children of U.S. citizens to enter as nonquota immigrants. In 1927, a revised National Origins Act apportioned redefined quotas to be distributed among European countries in proportion to the "national-origins" (country of birth or descent) of American inhabitants in 1920. People from the Western Hemisphere did not fall under the quotas (except for those whom the Labor Department defined as potential paupers), and soon they became the largest immigrant groups (see Figure 21.3).

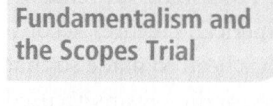

Whereas nativists tried to establish ethnic and racial purity, the pursuit of spiritual purity stirred religious fundamentalists. Millions of Americans sought

FIGURE 21.3
Sources of Immigration, 1907 and 1927
Immigration peaked in 1907 and 1908, when newcomers from southern and eastern Europe poured into the United States. After immigration restriction laws were passed in the 1920s, the greatest number of immigrants came from the Western Hemisphere (Canada and Mexico), which was exempted from the quotas, and the number coming from eastern and southern Europe shrank.

salvation by following Protestant evangelical denominations that interpreted the Bible literally. Believing that God's miracles created the world, they condemned the theory of evolution as heresy. Wherever fundamentalists constituted a majority of a community, they sought to determine what schools taught. Their enemies were "modernists," who used social sciences, such as psychology and anthropology, to interpret behavior. To modernists, God was important to the study of culture and history, but science advanced knowledge.

In 1925, Christian **fundamentalism** clashed with modernism in the **Scopes Trial** in Dayton, Tennessee. The state legislature banned public schools from teaching the theory that humans evolved from lower forms of life rather than descending from Adam and Eve. High school teacher John Thomas Scopes volunteered to serve as a test case and was arrested for violating the law. William Jennings Bryan, former secretary of state and three-time presidential candidate, argued for the prosecution, and civil liberties lawyers headed by Clarence Darrow represented Scopes. News correspondents crowded into town, and radio stations broadcast the trial.

Although Scopes was convicted—clearly he had broken the law—modernists claimed victory. The testimony, they believed, showed fundamentalism to be illogical. The trial's climax occurred when Bryan testified as an expert on the Bible. He asserted that Eve really had been created from Adam's rib, that the Tower of Babel was responsible for the diversity of languages, and that Jonah had been swallowed by a big fish. Spectators cheered Bryan, but the liberal press mocked him. Nevertheless, fundamentalism continued to expand and pressure schools to stop teaching evolution. These churches created an independent subculture, with their own schools, camps, radio ministries, and missionary societies.

fundamentalism Twentieth-century movement within Protestantism that taught literal interpretation of the Bible.

Scopes Trial Trial that took place after high school teacher John Scopes challenged a Tennessee law that banned teaching the theory of evolution in public schools.

Link to Scopes "Monkey" Trial transcripts (1925)

Religious Revivalism

Urban Pentecostal churches attracted African Americans and whites struggling with economic insecurity, nervous about modernism's attack on old-time religion, and swayed by their depiction of a personal Savior. Using modern advertising and staged radio broadcasts, magnetic preachers, such as Aimee Semple McPherson of Los Angeles, the former baseball player Billy Sunday, and Father Divine (an African American who amassed an interracial following) stirred revivalist fervor.

Clergy and teachers of all faiths condemned dancing, new dress styles, and sex in movies and parked cars. Many urban dwellers supported prohibition, believing it would end poverty, vice, and corruption. Yet most Americans sought balance as they tried to adjust to the modern order. Few refrained from the radio and movies like *Why Change Your Wife?*—activities that proved less corrupting than critics feared. Americans sought fellowship in civic organizations, such as Rotary, Elks, and women's clubs. Perhaps most important, people found release in leisure time.

The Age of Play

Why did movie and sports heroes become so important during the 1920s?

Americans embraced commercial entertainment, spending $2.5 billion on leisure in 1919; by 1929, spending topped $4.3 billion. Spectator amusements—movies, music, and sports—accounted for 21 percent of the 1929 total; the rest involved participatory recreation such as games, hobbies, and travel. Entrepreneurs fed an appetite for fads and spectacles. Early in the 1920s, mahjong, a Chinese tile game, was the craze. In the mid-1920s, devotees popularized crossword puzzles, printed in mass-circulation newspapers and magazines. By 1930, the nation boasted thirty thousand miniature golf courses. Dance crazes like the Charleston and recorded music on radio boosted the growing popularity of jazz.

| Movies and Sports |

Americans embraced movies and sports. In total capital investment, motion pictures became one of the nation's leading industries. In 1922, movies attracted 40 million viewers weekly; by 1929, nearly 100 million—at a time when the nation's population was 120 million and weekly church attendance was 60 million. Between 1922 and 1927, the Technicolor Corporation developed a means of producing movies in color. That, along with the introduction of sound in 1927's *The Jazz Singer*, made movies more exciting.

Although DeMille's romantic comedies like *Why Change Your Wife?* explored worldly themes, his most popular films—*The Ten Commandments* (1923) and *The King of Kings* (1927)—were biblical. Lurid dramas like *Souls for Sale* (1923) and *A Woman Who Sinned* (1924) drew big audiences, as did slapstick comedies starring Charlie Chaplin. In 1927, producers, bowing to pressure from legislators and religious leaders, instituted self-censorship, forbidding nudity, rough language, and plots that did not end with justice and morality triumphant. Movies also reproduced social prejudices—the few black actors were limited to playing maids and butlers.

Spectator sports drew millions every year. In an age when technology and mass production robbed experiences of their uniqueness, sports provided the unpredictability that people craved. Newspapers and radio magnified this tension, glorifying events with such dramatic narrative that promoters did not need advertising.

Excluded from playing in white-dominated professional baseball, African Americans organized their own teams and leagues. The Indianapolis ABCs, named after the American Brewing Company, was one of the more successful teams in the Negro National League during the 1920s and featured some of the best black baseball players of the era, including Oscar Charleston, Elwood "Bingo" DeMoss, and "Cannonball" Dick Redding.

National Baseball Hall of Fame, Cooperstown, N.Y.

Baseball's drawn-out suspense and potential for keeping statistics attracted a huge following. After the 1919 "Black Sox scandal"—when eight members of the Chicago White Sox were banned for allegedly throwing the World Series to the Cincinnati Reds (even though a jury acquitted them)—baseball transformed itself. A record three hundred thousand people attended the six-game 1921 World Series between the New York Giants and New York Yankees. Millions enjoyed games on the radio. Although African American ballplayers were prohibited from the major leagues, they formed their own teams, and in 1920 the first successful Negro League was founded.

Sports Heroes

As technology and mass society made the individual less significant, people clung to heroic personalities. Athletes like Bill Tilden in tennis, Gertrude Ederle in swimming (in 1926, she became the first woman to swim across the English Channel), and Bobby Jones in golf were famous. But boxing, football, and baseball produced the most popular sports heroes. Heavyweight champion Jack Dempsey, the "Manassa (Colorado) Mauler," attracted the first of several million-dollar gates in his fight with Frenchman Georges Carpentier in 1921.

Baseball's foremost hero was George Herman "Babe" Ruth, who began as a pitcher but broke records hitting home runs. Ruth hit twenty-nine homers in 1919, fifty-four in 1920 (the year the Boston Red Sox traded him to the New York Yankees), fifty-nine in 1921, and sixty in 1927—each year a record. His talent and boyish grin endeared him to millions. Known for overindulgence in food, drink, and sex, he charmed fans into forgiving his excesses by visiting hospitalized children.

Movie Stars and Public Heroes

Americans also fulfilled their yearning for romance and adventure through movie idols. One of the decade's most adored movie personalities was Italian-born Rudolph Valentino, whose looks made women swoon and men imitate him. When he died at thirty-one of complications from ulcers and appendicitis, the press turned his funeral into a public extravaganza.

The era's most celebrated hero, however, was **Charles A. Lindbergh**, an indomitable aviator who in May 1927 flew a plane solo from New York to Paris. The flight riveted America, as newspaper and telegraph reports followed Lindbergh's progress. After the pilot landed successfully, President Coolidge dispatched a warship to bring "Lucky Lindy" home, where he was greeted with a parade. Lindbergh received the Distinguished Flying Cross and the Congressional Medal of Honor. Promoters offered him millions of dollars to tour the world and $700,000 for a movie contract. His flight epitomized individual achievement and courage—old-fashioned values that attracted respect.

Charles A. Lindbergh
Popular aviator who flew solo across the Atlantic in his small single-engine plane, the *Spirit of St. Louis*, in May 1927.

Prohibition

The Eighteenth Amendment (1919), which prohibited the manufacture, sale, and transportation of alcoholic beverages, and the accompanying federal law (the Volstead Act of 1920) worked well initially. Per capita consumption of liquor dropped, as did arrests for drunkenness. But it was scarcely enforced. In 1922, Congress gave

Standing beside his plane, the Spirit of St. Louis, shortly before takeoff on his solo transatlantic flight, young Charles Lindbergh exhibits the self-reliance and determination that made him one of the most revered heroes of the 1920s. Lindbergh's feat signified a blend of new technology with old-fashioned individual effort.

the Prohibition Bureau less than $7 million for nationwide enforcement, and by 1927 most state budgets omitted funds to enforce prohibition.

After 1925, prohibition faltered as thousands made wine and gin illegally, and bootleg importers evaded the few patrols that existed. Moreover, drinking was a business with willing customers, and criminal organizations capitalized on public demand. The most notorious mob belonged to Al Capone, who seized control of illegal liquor and vice in Chicago, maintaining power over politicians and the vice business through intimidation, bribery, and violence. Americans wanted liquor, and until 1931, when a federal court convicted and imprisoned Capone for income tax evasion (the only charge for which authorities could obtain hard evidence), he supplied them.

Intellectuals were quick to expose the era's hypocrisies. Authors and artists felt at odds with society, and their rejection of materialism and conformity was biting and bitter. In protest, several writers from the so-called Lost Generation, including novelist Ernest Hemingway and poets Ezra Pound and T. S. Eliot, abandoned the United States for Europe. Others, like novelists William Faulkner, Sinclair Lewis, and Edith Wharton, remained in America but expressed disillusionment with the materialism that they witnessed.

Harlem Renaissance

Discontent inspired a new generation of African American artists. Middle-class, educated, and proud of their African heritage, black writers rejected white culture and exalted the militantly assertive "New Negro." In the "Negro Mecca" of New York's Harlem, black intellectuals and artists, aided by a few white patrons, celebrated black culture during what became known as the Harlem Renaissance.

The 1921 musical comedy *Shuffle Along* is often credited with launching the Harlem Renaissance. The show featured talented black artists, such as composer Eubie Blake and singer Josephine Baker. The Harlem Renaissance also fostered gifted writers, among them poets Langston Hughes, Countee Cullen, and Claude McKay; novelists Zora Neale Hurston and Jessie Fauset; and essayist Alain Locke. Though cherishing their African heritage and folk culture of the slave South, these artists and intellectuals realized that blacks had to come to terms with being free Americans. Langston Hughes wrote, "We younger Negro artists who create now intend to express our individual dark-skinned selves without fear or shame. If white people are pleased, we are glad. If they are not, it doesn't matter. We know we are beautiful."

Jazz

The Jazz Age, as the 1920s is sometimes called, evolved from African and African American folk music. Early jazz communicated exuberance, humor, and autonomy that African Americans seldom experienced in their public and political lives. Jazz's emotional rhythms and improvisation blurred the distinction between composer and performer. Urban dance halls and nightclubs, some of which included interracial audiences, featured performers like trumpeter Louis Armstrong and blues singer Bessie Smith. Music recorded by African American artists and aimed at African American consumers (sometimes called "race records") gave African Americans a place in commercial culture. More important, jazz endowed America with its own distinctive art form.

In many ways, the 1920s were the nation's most creative years. Painters such as Georgia O'Keeffe, Aaron Douglas, and John Marin forged a uniquely American style of visual art. Composer Henry Cowell pioneered electronic music, and Aaron Copland built orchestral works around native folk motifs. George Gershwin blended jazz rhythms, classical forms, and folk melodies in serious works (*Rhapsody in Blue,* 1924, and Piano Concerto in F, 1925, and hit tunes such as "The Man I Love"). In architecture, skyscrapers drew worldwide attention to American forms. The "emotional and aesthetic starvation" that essayist Harold Stearns lamented early in the decade was gone by 1929.

The Election of 1928 and End of the New Era

What were the early signs that the prosperity of the 1920s was coming to an end?

Intellectuals' uneasiness about materialism seldom altered the confident rhetoric of politics. Herbert Hoover voiced that confidence when he accepted the Republican nomination for president in 1928. "We in America today," Hoover boasted, "are nearer to the final triumph over poverty than ever before in the history of any land."

Herbert Hoover

Hoover was an apt Republican candidate (Coolidge chose not to seek reelection) because he fused the traditional value of individual hard work with modern emphasis on corporate action. A Quaker from Iowa, orphaned at age ten, Hoover put himself through Stanford University and became a wealthy mining engineer. During and after World War I, he distinguished himself as U.S. food administrator.

As secretary of commerce under Harding and Coolidge, Hoover promoted associationalism. Recognizing that nationwide associations dominated commerce and industry, Hoover sought business and government cooperation. He made the Commerce Department a center for the promotion of business, encouraging trade associations, holding conferences, and issuing reports, all aimed at improving productivity and profits.

Al Smith

As their candidate, Democrats in 1928 chose New York's governor Alfred E. Smith. Hoover had rural, native-born, Protestant, and business roots but had never run for office; Smith was an urbane politician of Irish stock with a career embedded in New York City's Tammany Hall political machine. He relished the give-and-take of city streets.

Smith was the first Roman Catholic to run for president on a major party ticket. His religion enhanced his appeal among urban ethnics, who increasingly voted, but intense anti-Catholic sentiments lost him southern and rural votes. Smith had a strong record on Progressive reform and civil rights, but his campaign stressed issues unlikely to unite these groups, particularly his opposition to prohibition.

Hoover, who emphasized national prosperity under Republican administrations, won the popular vote by 21 million to 15 million and the electoral vote by 444 to 87. Smith carried the nation's twelve largest cities, formerly Republican strongholds. For the next forty years, the Democratic Party solidified this urban base, which in conjunction with its traditional strength in the South made the party a formidable force in national elections.

Hoover's Administration

At his inaugural, Hoover proclaimed a New Day, "bright with hope." His cabinet featured mostly businessmen, including six millionaires. To lower ranking posts, Hoover appointed young professionals who agreed that a scientific approach could solve national problems. Like Hoover, Americans widely believed that individual effort led to success and that poverty suggested personal weakness. Prevailing opinion also held that fluctuations of the business cycle were natural and therefore not to be tampered with by government.

Stock Market Crash

This trust dissolved on October 24, 1929, known as Black Thursday, when stock market prices suddenly plunged, wiping out $10 billion in value (around $100 billion today). Panic set in. Prices of many stocks hit record lows; some sellers could find no buyers. At noon, leading bankers put up $20 million and ceremoniously began buying stocks. The mood brightened, and some stocks rallied.

But as news spread, frightened investors sold stocks to avoid further losses. On Black Tuesday, October 29, prices plummeted again. Hoover assured Americans that "the crisis will be over in sixty days." He shared the popular assumptions that the economy was strong enough to endure until the market righted itself. Instead, the crash ultimately unleashed a devastating worldwide depression.

In hindsight, the depression began long before the stock market crash. Prosperity in the 1920s was not as widespread as optimists believed. Agriculture had languished for decades, and many areas, especially in the South, were outside the new bounty of consumer society. Industries such as mining and textiles failed to sustain profits throughout the decade, and even the automotive and household goods industries had been stagnant since 1926. The fever of speculation included rash investment in California and Florida real estate, as well as in the stock market, and masked what was unhealthy in the national economy.

Declining Demand

The economic weakness that underlay the Great Depression had several interrelated causes. Since mid-1928, demand for new housing had faltered, reducing sales of building materials and unemployment. In growth industries, such as automobiles and electric appliances, demand leveled off, so factory owners cut production and workers. Retailers had amassed large inventories that were going unsold and started ordering less. Farm prices continued to sag, leaving farmers with less income for new machinery and goods. As wages and employment fell, families could not afford to buy consumer goods. Thus, by 1929, a sizable population of underconsumers was causing serious repercussions.

As the rich grew richer, middle- and lower-income Americans barely made modest gains. Although average per capita disposable income (income after taxes) rose about 9 percent between 1920 and 1929, income of the wealthiest 1 percent rose 75 percent. Much of this money went for stock market speculation, not consumer goods.

Corporate Debt and Stock Market Speculation

Furthermore, many businesses overloaded themselves with debt. To obtain loans, they misrepresented their assets in ways that hid their inability to repay. Such practices, overlooked by lending agencies, put the nation's banking system on a precarious footing.

Risky stock market speculation also precipitated the depression. Individuals and corporations bought millions of stocks on margin, meaning that they invested with a down payment of only a fraction of a stock's actual price and then used these partially paid-for stocks as collateral for more stock purchases. When stock prices stopped rising, investors tried to unload what they bought on margin. But with numerous investors selling simultaneously, prices plunged. Brokers demanded full payment for stocks bought on margin. The more obligations went unmet, the more the system tottered. Inevitably, banks and investment companies collapsed.

Economic Troubles Abroad; Federal Failure at Home

International economic conditions also contributed to the Great Depression. During and after World War I, Americans loaned billions to European nations. By the late 1920s, however, American investors instead kept their money in the lucrative U.S. stock market. Europeans, unable to borrow more or sell goods in the American market because of high tariffs, bought less from the United States. Moreover, the Allied nations depended on German war reparations to pay their debts to the United States, and the German government depended on American bank loans to pay those reparations. When the crash choked off American loans, the western economy ground to a halt.

Some Europeans branded the United States stingy for its handling of World War I debts and reparations. Twenty-eight nations became entangled in inter-Allied government debts totaling $26.5 billion ($9.6 billion of them owed to the U.S. government). Europeans owed private American creditors another $3 billion and urged Americans to erase government debts as a magnanimous contribution to the war effort. During the war, they angrily charged, Europe bled while America profited. American leaders insisted on repayment, some pointing out that the victorious European nations gained vast territory and resources as war spoils.

German Reparations

The debts question became linked to Germany's $33 billion reparations bill. Hobbled by inflation, Germany defaulted. To keep Germany afloat and forestall the radicalism that might thrive on economic troubles, American bankers loaned millions of dollars. A triangular relationship developed: U.S. investors' money flowed to Germany, Germany paid reparations to the Allies, and the Allies then paid some of their debts to the United States. The American-crafted 1924 Dawes Plan reduced Germany's annual payments, extended the repayment period, and provided more loans. The United States also gradually scaled down Allied obligations, cutting the debt by half during the 1920s.

But everything hinged on continued German borrowing in the United States, and in 1928 and 1929 American lending abroad dropped sharply in the face of more lucrative stock market opportunities. The U.S.-negotiated Young Plan of 1929, which reduced Germany's reparations, salvaged little as the world economy collapsed following the stock market crash. By 1931, the Allies had paid back only $2.6 billion. Staggered by the Great Depression—an international catastrophe—they defaulted on the rest. Annoyed, Congress in 1934 passed the Johnson Act, which forbade U.S. government loans to foreign governments in default to the United States.

Lack of Federal Regulation

Other federal policies also underlay the crisis. The government refrained from regulating speculation. In support of business expansion, the Federal Reserve Board pursued easy credit policies, charging low discount rates (interest on its loans to member banks) even though such loans were financing the speculative mania.

Neither experts nor people on the street realized what really happened in 1929. Conventional wisdom, based on previous depressions, held that economic downturns had to run their course. So in 1929, people waited for the tailspin to ease, never realizing that the "new era" had ended and that the economy, politics, and society would have to be rebuilt.

Intercollegiate Athletics

College sports spread widely in the late nineteenth century, but in 1924 brutality, academic fraud, and illegal payments to recruits prompted the Carnegie Foundation for the Advancement of Higher Education to undertake a five-year investigation of college sports. Its 1929 report recommended the abolition of varsity football, but had minimal effect. Football was immensely popular, and colleges built stadiums to attract spectators, bolster alumni allegiance, and enhance revenues.

From the 1920s to the present, intercollegiate sports has ranked as a major commercial entertainment. Still, American higher education has struggled to reconcile conflicts between the commercialism of athletic competition and the academic mission and ideal of amateurism. But the economic potential of competition has spawned expanding athletic departments and programs that compete with and sometimes overshadow an institution's academic mission.

Publicity about scandals and felonious behavior has sparked controversy in college sports since the 1920s. In 1952, after revelations of point-shaving (fixing the outcome) of basketball games at several colleges, the American Council on Education (ACE) undertook its own study. Its recommendations, including the elimination of football bowl games, went largely unheeded. In 1991, further abuses prompted the Knight Foundation Commission on Intercollegiate Athletics to urge college presidents to reform intercollegiate athletics. Few significant changes resulted, even after a follow-up study in 2001.

The most sweeping changes followed court rulings in the 1990s, mandating under Title IX of the Educational Amendments Act of 1972 that women's sports be treated equally with men's. Enforcement, however, provoked a backlash that aimed to prevent men's teams from being cut to satisfy Title IX. In 2012, the National Collegiate Athletic Association (NCAA) imposed severe penalties on Penn State University's football program for ignoring serial abuse of young boys by a former assistant coach. Recently also, the NCAA has attempted to regulate academic standards by monitoring athletes' academic progress, but reform's effectiveness depends on cooperation from member institutions. With millions of dollars involved, the system established in the 1920s has withstood most pressures for change.

Summary

Two critical events, the end of World War I and beginning of the Great Depression, marked the boundaries of the 1920s. After the war, traditional customs weakened as people sought new forms of self-expression and gratification. Modern science and technology touched the lives of rich and poor alike through mass media, movies, sports, automobiles, and electric appliances. Moreover, the decade's free-wheeling consumerism enabled ordinary Americans to emulate wealthier people by purchasing more and engaging in stock market speculation.

Beneath the "new era," prejudice and ethnic tensions tainted the American dream. Klansmen and immigration restrictionists encouraged discrimination against racial minorities and ethnic groups. Meanwhile, the distinguishing forces of twentieth-century life—technological change, bureaucratization, mass culture, and growth of the middle class—accelerated, making the decade truly "new."

Chapter Review

Economic Expansion

What helped turn the economy around in the 1920s?

Two factors helped transform the initial post–World War I recession into recovery: the advent of technologies such as electric energy in 1922 and new government pro-business initiatives. Electricity enabled goods to be produced more inexpensively, thereby driving consumer demand and stimulating the economy across the board. New installment or credit plans for purchasing big items such as cars also drove consumption. Business organizations successfully used new lobbying techniques to prompt government to implement pro-business policies that also stimulated growth. Congress cut taxes on corporations and wealthy individuals in 1921, and passed the Fordney-McCumber Tariff Act (1922). The Federal Trade Commission and the Interstate Commerce Commission tended to cooperate with corporations rather than regulate them. And several Supreme Court decisions sheltered business from government regulation and hindered organized labor. New investments abroad—especially in Latin America—further boosted U.S. corporate profits.

Government, Politics, and Reform

What happened to Progressive reform in the 1920s?

While Progressivism faded on a national level, its reform spirit continued to inspire local and state initiatives as well as those by women and ethnic groups. After the war, many states adopted or expanded workers' compensation laws and public welfare programs. Native American groups worked for better education and return of tribal lands, while white reformers held out hope of getting Indians to assimilate by adopting white middle-class standards of work, child rearing, and citizenship. Although women got the right to vote in 1920, they remained outside the national power structures. Instead, their voluntary organizations became the tools for lobbying for various issues including birth control, peace, education, opposition to lynching, and protective labor legislation. They also convinced Congress to pass legislation to reduce infant mortality and reverse the Cable Act, which cost a woman her U.S. citizenship if she married a man from another country. Remaining elements of the Progressive movement

formed a new political party, nominating Robert M. La Follette as their 1924 presidential candidate.

A Consumer Society

How did the emergence of a consumer society change American life?

In the 1920s, incomes increased, while new mass production methods kept the price of goods stable or made them more affordable. Consequently, greater numbers of Americans could afford products such as automobiles that once were the province of the wealthy. Car ownership led consumers to join with farmers in seeking improved roadways. At the same time, the emergence of advertising as a tool helped manipulate purchases and increasingly erased ethnic differences to create a more homogenous consumer society. And the growth of the radio, with its mass marketing and standardized programs, further blurred differences and heightened immigrants' assimilation into American culture and ways of life.

Cities, Migrants, and Suburbs

What fueled the growth of cities in the 1920s?

In 1920, for the first time in U.S. history, more people lived in urban areas than rural areas. In part, the shift was driven by young people, who left farms for the more exciting and varied life of cities. The demographic change was also driven by the migration of African Americans from poverty and a boll weevil plague on southern farms to seek better-paying factory jobs in the North. Once there, they faced discrimination in housing. Immigrants from Mexico and Puerto Rico similarly pushed off their land due to agricultural changes hoped to find better opportunities in America. Many Mexicans became underpaid and exploited farm laborers in the West, while Puerto Ricans found jobs in factories and restaurants or as domestic servants. Both maintained customs and developed local businesses or social clubs to help them adapt.

New Rhythms of Everyday Life

How did technological advances transform social life in America in the 1920s?

First, improved productivity and mechanization led to shorter workweeks, permitting the expansion of leisure activities and greater freedom, especially for young people. Industrialism privileged youth and agility over experience and forced older people to retire, which often meant economic hardship or poverty, as well as initiatives for old-age pensions (precursors to Social Security). Second, new appliances made housework less arduous and time-consuming and shifted women's roles from producer within the home to consumer for the family. But advertisers of new products also raised cleanliness standards and pressured women to do more to keep their homes clean. Third, advances in nutrition helped people live longer and healthier lives. Birth control also enabled families to separate sexuality from reproduction, and family size decreased. Finally, as products and services became more widely available, an increasing number of married women moved into the workforce to expand their families' purchasing power.

Lines of Defense

> How did various groups seek to hold the line on social change in the 1920s?

Troubled by the liberal social influences of the era, several groups emerged, seeking to restore what they considered to be traditional American values. The Ku Klux Klan was reconstituted in 1915 to reestablish native white American supremacy in the face of increasing immigration and black migration and to protect white women's virtue against so-called corrupting influences. The Klan was joined in its anti-immigration sentiment by other nativist groups, who pressed Congress to establish immigration quotas. Similarly, fundamentalist Christian groups sought to replace the modern emphasis on science with a renewed centrality of God's role in creation and daily life. Hence, the Tennessee legislature banned the teaching of the theory of evolution, resulting in the pivotal Scopes Trial in 1925. Religious revivalism likewise condemned the new social practices of dating, dancing, and fashion and the hint of sex in movies.

The Age of Play

> Why did movie and sports heroes become so important during the 1920s?

As mass consumption took hold, Americans felt robbed of a sense of individual distinctiveness. To recover that lost sensibility, Americans gravitated toward leisure activities that celebrated individual achievement or that inspired a sense of adventure or romance. Sports provided drama, unpredictability, and a chance to celebrate a particular player's talent. Motion pictures not only let viewers live vicariously through the exciting lives of characters, but also inspired the

hope for adventure in their own lives. Finally, national heroes such as aviator Charles Lindbergh made the possibility of greatness seem real and attainable, even if most Americans would never personally experience it for themselves. Middle-class, educated African Americans rejected white culture and celebrated their heritage in novels, poems, plays, and art, creating the literary and artistic movement known as the Harlem Renaissance. Black culture also produced the Jazz Age, creating a distinctly American musical form.

The Election of 1928 and the End of the New Era

> What were the early signs that the prosperity of the 1920s was coming to an end?

While the 1929 stock market crash put a definitive ending on the era's seeming prosperity, in truth, the seeds of recession were sown many years before. First, so-called prosperity had never reached farmers; agriculture had lagged for decades. Mining, textiles, and other industries did not remain profitable the entire decade, and even the automobile industry was stagnant after 1926. As demand faltered, factories cut back on production and workers, which in turn meant less disposable income to purchase consumer goods, triggering further cutbacks in retail orders and production. Housing demand dropped off after mid-1928, and at the same time, businesses were overloaded with debt. Together, this made for a perfect economic storm when the market crashed in 1929.

Suggestions for Further Reading

Patrick Cohrs, *The Unfinished Peace After World War I: America, Britain and the Stabilization of Europe, 1919–1932* (2006)

Lynn Dumenil, *The Modern Temper: American Culture and Society in the 1920s* (1995)

Colin Grant, *Negro with a Hat: The Rise and Fall of Marcus Garvey* (2008)

Maury Klein, *Rainbow's End: The Crash of 1929* (2003)

Roland Marchand, *Advertising the American Dream: Making Way for Modernity, 1920–1940* (1985)

Nathan Miller, *New World Coming: The 1920s and the Making of Modern America* (2004)

David Montgomery, *The Fall of the House of Labor: The Workplace, the State, and American Activism, 1865–1925* (1987)

Mae M. Ngai, *Impossible Subjects: Illegal Aliens and the Making of Modern America* (2004)

Thomas R. Pegram, *One Hundred Percent American: The Rebirth and Decline of the Ku Klux Klan in the 1920s* (2011)

George Sanchez, *Becoming Mexican American: Ethnicity, Culture and Identity in Chicano Los Angeles, 1900–1945* (1993)

Susan Thistle, *From Marriage to the Market: The Transformation of Women's Lives and Work* (2006)

The Great Depression and the New Deal

22

1929–1939

I n 1931, the rain stopped in the Great Plains. Montana and North Dakota became as arid as the Sonora Desert. Temperatures reached 115 degrees in Iowa. Farmers watched rich black dirt turn to gray dust. Then the winds began to blow. Farmers had stripped the Plains of native grasses in the 1920s, plowing up fifty thousand acres of new land daily. Now, with nothing to hold the earth, it began to blow away. The dust storms began in 1934—and worsened in 1935. Dust obscured the sun. Cattle, blinded by blowing grit, ran in circles until they died. Clouds of dust filled the skies of Kansas, Colorado, Oklahoma, Texas, and New Mexico—the Dust Bowl.

In late 1937, on a farm near Stigler, Oklahoma, Marvin Montgomery made a difficult decision. "The drought and such as that, it just got so hard," he told a congressional committee conducting hearings at a migratory labor camp in 1940. "I decided it would help me to change countries." So on December 29, 1937, Montgomery and his wife and four children loaded a secondhand Hudson automobile with their worldly goods—furniture, bedding, pots and pans—and headed for California.

The Montgomerys were not alone. At least a third of farms in the Dust Bowl were abandoned in the 1930s, and many families moved west, lured by advertisements promising work in California fields. Some three hundred thousand people migrated to California during the decade. Most of these were not displaced and poverty-stricken farm families like the Montgomerys; many were white-collar workers seeking better opportunities in California's cities. But the plight of families like the Montgomerys, captured in federal government–sponsored Farm Security Administration (FSA) photographs and immortalized in John Steinbeck's 1938 novel *The Grapes of Wrath*, came to represent the suffering of the Great Depression.

The Montgomerys ran out of money in Arizona and worked in the cotton fields there for five weeks before they moved on. In California, wages were low, and migrant families found little welcome. As they took over the agricultural labor formerly done by Mexicans and Mexican Americans, they learned that, by doing fieldwork, they had forfeited their "whiteness" in the eyes of many rural Californians. "Negroes and Okies' upstairs," read a sign in a San Joaquin Valley movie theater.

Most migrants to rural California lived in squalid camps, but the Montgomerys secured housing provided by the Farm Security Administration. For nine months the Montgomery family of six lived in a fourteen-by-sixteen-foot tent, which rented for 10 cents a day plus four hours of volunteer labor a month. Then they proudly moved into an FSA house, "with water, lights, and everything, yes sir; and a little garden spot furnished." Soon employment opportunities for the Montgomerys, as well as other newcomers, emerged in California's aircraft factories and shipyards mobilizing for the Second World War.

The Montgomerys' experience shows the human costs of the Great Depression that plunged the world into an economic crisis. Between 1929 and 1933, the U.S. gross national product was cut in half. Corporate profits fell from $10 billion to $1 billion; one hundred thousand businesses closed. Four million workers were unemployed in January 1930; by November, unemployment reached 6 million. When President Herbert Hoover left office in 1933, 13 million Americans—about one-fourth of the labor force—were idle. There was no national safety net: no welfare system, no unemployment compensation, no Social Security. And as banks failed by the thousands, with no federally guaranteed deposit insurance, families' savings disappeared.

Herbert Hoover, who had been elected president in the prosperous late 1920s, looked first to private enterprise for solutions. By the end of his term, he had extended the federal government's role in managing an economic crisis further than his predecessors. Nonetheless, the depression deepened and Americans became increasingly desperate. In the United States the economic catastrophe exacerbated existing racial and class tensions, while in Germany it propelled Adolf Hitler to power. By late 1932, many of America's leaders feared the depression was a crisis of capitalism, even of democracy itself.

In 1932, voters replaced Hoover with a man who promised a New Deal. Roosevelt's programs did not end the depression (only the massive mobilization for World War II did that), but they did alleviate suffering. For the first time, the federal government assumed responsibility for the nation's economy and its citizens' welfare.

Although some Americans saw the depression crisis as an opportunity for major economic change—even revolution—New Deal programs did not fundamentally alter the existing capitalist system or the distribution of wealth. Roosevelt did not directly challenge legal segregation in the South, either—in part because he relied on southern Democrats in Congress to pass New Deal legislation.

Despite its limits, the New Deal preserved America's democratic experiment through a time of uncertainty and crisis. By decade's end, a world war shifted America's focus from domestic to foreign policy. But the changes set in motion by the New Deal continued to transform the United States for decades to come.

As you read this chapter, keep the following questions in mind:

- **How did economic hard times during the 1930s affect Americans, and what differences were there in the experiences of specific groups and regions?**

- **How and why did the power of the federal government expand during the Great Depression?**

- **What were the successes and the failures of the New Deal?**

Hoover and Hard Times, 1929–1933

Why was Hoover reluctant to implement relief programs during the Great Depression?

By the early 1930s, tens of millions of Americans were desperately poor. In cities, the hungry lined up at soup kitchens; some scratched through garbage cans for food. In November 1932, *The Nation* told its readers that one-sixth of the American population risked starvation.

Families, unable to pay rent, were evicted. The new homeless poured into shantytowns, called "Hoovervilles" in ironic tribute to the formerly popular president. Over a million men took to the road or the rails in search of work. Couples delayed marriage. Married people put off having children, and in 1933 the birth rate sank below replacement rates.

Farmers and Industrial Workers

The agricultural sector, which employed almost one-quarter of American workers and missed the good times of the 1920s, was hit hard. As urbanites cut spending and foreign competitors dumped agricultural surpluses into the global market, farm prices hit bottom. Farmers tried to compensate by producing more, thus adding to the surplus and further depressing prices. By 1932, a bushel of wheat that cost North Dakota farmers 77 cents to produce brought only 33 cents. Throughout the nation, farmers could not pay their property taxes or mortgages. Banks foreclosed. In Mississippi, on a single day in April 1932 approximately one-fourth of the state's farmland was auctioned to meet debts. By the middle of the decade, the Dust Bowl would also drive thousands of farmers from their land.

America's industrial workers had seen their standard of living improve during the 1920s, and their consumer spending bolstered the nation's economic growth. But as incomes declined, sales of manufactured goods plummeted and factories closed—more than seventy thousand had gone out of business by 1933. As car sales dropped from 4.5 million in 1929 to 1 million in 1933, Ford laid off more than

Chronology

1929	Stock market crash (October); Great Depression begins
1930	Hawley-Smoot Tariff raises rates on imports
1931	"Scottsboro Boys" arrested in Alabama
1932	Banks fail throughout nation
	Bonus Army marches on Washington
	Hoover's Reconstruction Finance Corporation tries to stabilize banks, insurance companies, railroads
	Roosevelt elected president
1933	13 million Americans unemployed
	"First Hundred Days" of Roosevelt administration offer major legislation for economic recovery and poor relief
	Adolf Hitler becomes chancellor of Germany
	National bank holiday halts run on banks
	Agricultural Adjustment Act (AAA) encourages decreased farm production
	National Industrial Recovery Act (NIRA) attempts to spur industrial growth
	Tennessee Valley Authority (TVA) established
1934	Long starts Share Our Wealth Society
	Townsend proposes old-age pension plan
	Indian Reorganization Act restores lands to tribal ownership

1935	National Labor Relations (Wagner) Act guarantees workers' right to unionize
	Social Security Act establishes insurance for the aged, the unemployed, and needy children
	Works Progress Administration (WPA) creates jobs in public works projects
	Revenue (Wealth Tax) Act raises taxes on business and the wealthy
	Congress passes first Neutrality Act
1936	9 million Americans unemployed
	United Auto Workers win sit-down strike against General Motors
1937	Roosevelt's Court-packing plan fails
	Memorial Day massacre of striking steelworkers
	"Roosevelt recession" begins
	Sino-Japanese War breaks out
1938	10.4 million Americans unemployed
	80 million movie tickets sold each week
	Munich Conference grants part of Czechoslovakia to Germany
1939	Marian Anderson performs at Lincoln Memorial
	Germany invades Poland; Second World War begins

two-thirds of its Detroit workers. Almost one-quarter of industrial workers were unemployed, and those with jobs saw the average wage fall by almost one-third.

Marginal Workers　For workers on the lowest rungs of the employment ladder, the depression was crushing. In the South, where opportunities were already most limited for African Americans, jobs that many white men had considered below their dignity—bellhop, garbage collector—seemed suddenly desirable. In 1930, a short-lived fascist-style organization, the Black Shirts, recruited forty thousand members with the slogan "No Jobs for Niggers Until Every White Man Has a Job!" And as industry cut production in the North, African Americans were the first fired. By 1932, African American unemployment reached almost 50 percent.

Mexican Americans and Mexican nationals in the Southwest also felt the twin impacts of economic depression and racism. Their wages on California farms fell from a miserable 35 cents an hour in 1929 to a cruel 14 cents an hour by 1932. Throughout the Southwest, campaigns against "foreigners" hurt Mexican immigrants and American citizens of Hispanic descent whose families had lived in the Southwest for

This 1939 photograph, titled "Mother and Children on the Road," was taken in Tule Lake, California, by Farm Security Administration photographer Dorothea Lange. The FSA used photos like this one to build public support for New Deal programs to assist migrant workers and the rural poor.

Dorothea Lange/Library of Congress Prints and Photographs Division [LC-USF34-T01-020993-E]

centuries, long before the land belonged to the United States. In 1931, the Labor Department announced plans to deport illegal immigrants to free jobs for American citizens. This policy fell hardest on people of Mexican origin. Even those who had immigrated legally often lacked full documentation. The U.S. government deported 82,000 Mexicans between 1929 and 1935. Almost half a million people repatriated to Mexico during the 1930s. Some left voluntarily, but many were coerced or tricked into believing they had no choice.

Even before the economic crisis, women of all classes and races were barred from many jobs and were paid significantly less than men. Most Americans believed that men should be breadwinners and women homemakers. They worried that women who worked took jobs from men. In fact, men laid off from U.S. Steel would not likely have been hired as secretaries, "salesgirls," or maids. Nonetheless, when a 1936 Gallup poll asked whether wives should work if their husbands had jobs, 82 percent of respondents (including 75 percent of the women) answered no. Such beliefs translated into policy. Of fifteen hundred urban school systems surveyed in 1930 and 1931, 77 percent refused to hire married women as teachers, and 63 percent fired female teachers who married while employed.

The depression had a mixed impact on women workers. Women in low-wage manufacturing jobs were laid off before male employees, who were presumed to be supporting families. Almost one-quarter of women in domestic service—a high percentage of them African American—lost jobs as middle-class families economized. Despite discrimination and a poor economy, however, women's employment increased during the 1930s. "Women's jobs," such as teaching and clerical work, were not hit as hard as "men's jobs" in heavy industry, and women increasingly sought employment to keep their families afloat. Still, by 1940, only 15.2 percent of married women worked outside the home.

Middle-Class Workers and Families

Although unemployment climbed to 25 percent, most Americans did not lose homes or jobs during the depression. Professional and white-collar workers fared better than industrial workers and farmers. Even so, many middle-class families "made do" with less. Women cut back on household expenses by canning food or making their own clothes. Newspapers offered suggestions for using "extenders," cheap ingredients to make food go further ("Cracker-Stuffed Cabbage"). Although most families' incomes fell, the impact was cushioned by the falling cost of consumer goods.

Men who could no longer provide well for their families often deemed themselves "failures." But even for the relatively affluent, the psychological impact of the depression was inescapable. No one took economic security for granted anymore.

Hoover's Limited Solutions

Although **Herbert Hoover**, "the Great Engineer," had a reputation as a problem solver, no one, including Hoover, knew what to do about the crisis. Many business leaders believed that financial panics and depressions, though painful, were part of a natural "business cycle." Economic depressions, according to this theory, brought down inflated prices and cleared the way for real growth. Hoover disagreed. He put his faith in a voluntary system of "associationalism," in which the federal government coordinated efforts of business and professional organizations to solve the nation's economic problems by crafting programs that state and local governments, along with private industry, could voluntarily implement.

While many Americans thought that Hoover was doing nothing, in truth he stretched his beliefs about the role of government to their limit. He tried voluntarism, exhortation, and limited government intervention. First, he sought voluntary pledges from business groups to keep wages stable and renew investment. But when businesspeople looked at their own bottom lines, few could honor those promises.

As unemployment climbed, Hoover created the President's Organization on Unemployment Relief (POUR) to generate private contributions to aid the destitute. Although 1932 saw record charitable contributions, they were inadequate. By mid-1932, one-quarter of New York's private charities, funds exhausted, closed their doors. State and city officials found their treasuries drying up, too.

Hoover, however, held firm. He feared that government "relief" would destroy the spirit of self-reliance among the poor. Thus, he authorized federal funds to feed the drought-stricken livestock of Arkansas farmers but rejected a smaller grant to provide food for impoverished farm families. Many Americans became angry at Hoover's seeming insensitivity. Two years after his election, Hoover was the most hated man in America.

Hoover eventually endorsed limited federal action to combat the crisis, but it was too little. Federal public works projects, such as the Grand Coulee Dam in Washington, created some jobs. Hoover also signed into law the Hawley-Smoot Tariff (1930) to support American farmers and manufacturers by raising import duties to a staggering 40 percent. Instead, it hampered international trade as other nations created their own protective tariffs. And as other nations sold less to the United States, they had less money to repay their U.S. debts or buy American products. Fearing the collapse of the international monetary system, Hoover in 1931 announced a moratorium on the payment of First World War debts and reparations.

Picture Research Consultants & Archives

As the economic depression deepened, Americans had less money to spend, even on necessities, and manufacturers of consumer goods struggled to sell their products and stay in business. In this 1932 Ladies' Home Journal advertisement, Armour Foods tried to convince housewives who were making do with less that it was economical—"often as low as 10¢ a serving"—to purchase a whole ham instead of cheaper cuts of meat.

Herbert Hoover The thirty-first president of the United States, 1929–1933.

**Reconstruction Finance
Corporation (RFC)** Agency
set up under the Hoover
administration during the
Great Depression to make loans
to shore up banks and other
industries.

In January 1932, the administration took its most forceful action, creating the **Reconstruction Finance Corporation (RFC)** to provide federal loans to banks, insurance companies, and railroads, an action Hoover hoped would shore up those industries and halt the disinvestment in the American economy. Here, Hoover compromised his ideological principles. This was direct government intervention, not "voluntarism." If he would support direct assistance to private industries, why not direct relief to the millions of unemployed?

Protest and Social Unrest

More and more Americans asked that question. Social unrest grew as the depression deepened, and increasing violence raised the specter of popular revolt. Tens of thousands of farmers took the law into their own hands. Angry crowds forced auctioneers to accept just a few dollars for foreclosed property, and then returned it to the original owners. In August 1932, a new group, the Farmers' Holiday Association, encouraged farmers to take a "holiday"—to hold back agricultural products to limit supply and drive prices up. In the Midwest, farmers barricaded roads to stop other farmers' trucks, and then dumped the contents in roadside ditches.

In cities, the most militant actions came from Unemployed Councils, local groups for unemployed workers that were created and led by Communist Party members. Communist leaders believed the depression demonstrated capitalism's failure and offered an opportunity for revolution. Few of the quarter-million Americans who joined the local Unemployed Councils sought revolution, but they did demand action. Demonstrations often turned ugly. When three thousand members of Detroit Unemployment Councils marched on Ford's River Rouge plant in 1932, Ford security guards opened fire on the crowd, killing four men and wounding fifty.

As social unrest spread, so did racial violence. Vigilante committees offered bounties to force African American workers off the Illinois Central Railroad's payroll: $25 for maiming and $100 for killing black workers. Ten men were murdered and at least seven wounded. The Ku Klux Klan also gained strength. Thirty-eight black men were tortured, hanged, and mutilated by white mobs in the depression's early years. Racial violence was not restricted to the South; lynchings also took place in Pennsylvania, Minnesota, Colorado, and Ohio.

Bonus Army

The worst public confrontation shook the nation in the summer of 1932. More than fifteen thousand unemployed World War I veterans and their families converged on the nation's capital as Congress debated a bill authorizing immediate payment of cash "bonuses" that veterans were scheduled to receive in 1945. Calling themselves the Bonus Expeditionary Force, or Bonus Army, they set up a sprawling "Hooverville" shantytown across the river from the Capitol. Concerned about the impact on the federal budget, President Hoover opposed the bonus bill, and the Senate voted it down.

Most of the Bonus Marchers left Washington after this defeat, but several thousand stayed. The president called them "insurrectionists" and set a deadline for their departure. On July 28, Hoover sent in the U.S. Army, led by General

Douglas MacArthur. Four infantry companies, four troops of cavalry, a machine gun squadron, and six tanks converged on the veterans and their families. What followed shocked the nation. Men and women were chased down by horsemen; children were tear-gassed; shacks were set afire. Hoover was unrepentant, insisting in a campaign speech, "Thank God we still have a government that knows how to deal with a mob."

As the depression worsened, the appeal of a strong leader—someone who would take decisive action—grew. In February 1933, the U.S. Senate passed a resolution calling for newly elected president **Franklin D. Roosevelt** to assume "unlimited power." The rise to power of Hitler and his National Socialist Party in depression-ravaged Germany was an obvious parallel.

Franklin D. Roosevelt The thirty-second president of the United States, 1933–1945.

Franklin D. Roosevelt and the Launching of the New Deal

How did the federal government take on new roles during the period dubbed "The First Hundred Days"?

In the presidential campaign of 1932, Democratic challenger Franklin Delano Roosevelt insisted that the federal government had to play a greater role. He supported direct relief payments for the unemployed, declaring that such governmental aid was "a matter of social duty." He pledged "a new deal for the American people," though he was never very explicit about its outlines. His most concrete proposals were sometimes contradictory. But Roosevelt committed to use the power of the federal government to combat the paralyzing economic crisis. Voters chose Roosevelt over Hoover overwhelmingly: 22.8 million to 15.8 million in the popular vote (see Map 22.1).

Franklin Roosevelt, the twentieth-century president most beloved by America's "common people," was born into upper-class privilege. After graduating from Harvard College and Columbia Law School, he married **Eleanor Roosevelt**, Theodore Roosevelt's niece and his own fifth cousin, once removed. He served in the New York State legislature; was appointed assistant secretary of the navy by Woodrow Wilson; and at age thirty-eight, ran for vice president in 1920 on the Democratic Party's losing ticket.

Eleanor Roosevelt Widely popular and influential First Lady of the United States from 1933 to 1945.

Then, in 1921, Roosevelt was stricken with polio and bedridden for two years. He lost the use of his legs but gained, according to his wife Eleanor, a new strength of character. By 1928, Roosevelt was sufficiently recovered to run for—and win—the governorship of New York and then to accept the Democratic Party's presidential nomination in 1932.

Elected in November 1932, Roosevelt would not take office until March 4, 1933. (The Twentieth Amendment to the Constitution—the so-called Lame Duck Amendment, ratified in 1933—shifted future inaugurations to January 20.) In this long interregnum, the American banking system reached the verge of collapse.

Banking Crisis

The origins of the banking crisis lay in the flush years of World War I and the 1920s, when American banks made risky loans. After real estate and stock market bubbles burst in 1929 and agricultural prices collapsed, many of these loans went bad, leaving many banks without sufficient funds to cover customers' deposits. Afraid of losing their savings, depositors withdrew money from banks and put it

1932

Winner's percentage of
total popular vote

Under 50	50–80	Over 80	Candidate (Party)	Electoral Vote		Popular Vote			No returns
			Roosevelt (Democrat)	472	89%	22,821,857	57.3%		
			Hoover (Republican)	59	11%	15,761,841	39.6%		

MAP 22.1
Presidential Election, 1932

One factor above all decided the 1932 presidential election: the Great Depression. Roosevelt won 42 states and Hoover 6.

Source: Copyright © Cengage Learning 2015

Link to Franklin D. Roosevelt, First Inaugural Address (1933)

into gold or under mattresses. By Roosevelt's inauguration, every state had either suspended banking operations or restricted depositors' access to their money. The new president understood that the total collapse of the U.S. banking system would threaten the nation's survival.

The day after his inaugural address—in which he vowed to use federal power to face the crisis "frankly and boldly" and told Americans "that the only thing we have to fear is fear itself"—Roosevelt closed the nation's banks for a four-day "holiday" and summoned Congress to an emergency session. He introduced the Emergency Banking Relief Bill, which was passed sight unseen by unanimous House vote, approved 73 to 7 in the Senate, and signed into law the same day. This bill provided federal authority to reopen solvent banks and reorganize the rest, and authorized federal money to shore up private banks. Critics of the failed banking system had hoped Roosevelt planned to remove the banks from private hands. Instead, Roosevelt's banking policy was much like Hoover's—a fundamentally conservative approach that upheld the status quo.

The banking bill could save the U.S. banking system only if Americans were confident enough to deposit money in the reopened banks. In the first of his radio "Fireside Chats," Roosevelt asked Americans for support. The next morning, when

the banks opened, people lined up to deposit money. It was an enormous triumph for the new president. It also demonstrated that Roosevelt, though unafraid to take bold action, was not as radical as some wished or as others feared.

First Hundred Days

During the ninety-nine-day-long special session of Congress, dubbed by journalists "The First Hundred Days," the federal government took on dramatically new roles. Roosevelt, aided by a group of advisers—lawyers, university professors, and social workers collectively nicknamed "the Brain Trust"—and by the capable First Lady, set out to revive the American economy. These "New Dealers" had no single plan, and Roosevelt's policies fluctuated between balancing the budget and massive deficit spending (spending more than is taken in in taxes and borrowing the difference). But with a mandate for action and the support of a Democrat-controlled Congress, the new administration produced a flood of legislation. Two basic strategies emerged during the First Hundred Days: New Dealers experimented with national economic planning, and they created "relief" programs to help those in need.

National Industrial Recovery Act

At the heart of the New Deal experiment in planning were the **National Industrial Recovery Act (NIRA)** and the **Agricultural Adjustment Act (AAA)**. The NIRA was based on the belief that "destructive competition" had worsened industry's economic woes. Skirting antitrust regulation, the NIRA authorized competing businesses to cooperate in crafting industrywide codes that allowed manufacturers to establish industrywide prices and wages. With wages and prices stabilized, the theory went, consumer spending would increase, thus allowing industries to rehire workers. Significantly, Section 7(a) guaranteed industrial workers the right to "organize and bargain collectively"—in other words, to unionize. Individual businesses' participation in this program, administered by the **National Recovery Administration (NRA)**, was voluntary, so it was not very different from Hoover-era "associationalism."

From the beginning, the NRA faced serious problems. The majority of the 541 codes it approved reflected the interests of major corporations, not small-business owners, labor, or consumers. Most fundamentally, the NRA did not deliver economic recovery. In 1935, the Supreme Court ended the floundering system when it found that the NRA extended federal power past its constitutional bounds.

Agricultural Adjustment Act

The Agricultural Adjustment Act (AAA) had a more enduring effect. Establishing a national system of crop controls, it offered subsidies to farmers who agreed to limit production of specific crops. (Overproduction drove crop prices down.) In 1933, the nation's farmers agreed to destroy 8.5 million piglets and to plow under crops in the fields. Millions of hungry Americans found it difficult to understand this waste of food.

Government crop subsidies were a disaster for tenant farmers and sharecroppers, who were turned off their land as landlords cut production. In the South, the number of sharecropper farms dropped by almost one-third between 1930 and 1940

National Industrial Recovery Act (NIRA) Agency that brought together business leaders to draft codes of "fair competition" for their industries. These codes recognized workers' rights to establish unions, set production limits, prescribed wages and working conditions, and forbade price-cutting and unfair competitive practices.

Agricultural Adjustment Act (AAA) New Deal program that sought to curb the surplus farm production that depressed crop prices by offering payments for reducing production of seven farm products.

National Recovery Administration (NRA) Agency responsible for administering the National Industrial Recovery Act and establishing fair-trade codes for industries with the goal of stimulating the economy.

and dispossessed farmers—many of them African American—headed to cities and towns. But the subsidies did help many. In the Dakotas, for example, government payments accounted for almost three-quarters of the total farm income for 1934.

In 1936, the Supreme Court found that the AAA, like the NRA, was unconstitutional. But the legislation was rewritten to meet the Supreme Court's objections, and farm subsidies continue into the twenty-first century.

Relief Programs

Roosevelt moved quickly to implement poor relief: $3 billion in federal aid was allocated in 1935. New Dealers, however—like many other Americans—disapproved of direct relief payments. "Give a man a dole and you save his body and destroy his spirit; give him a job and pay him an assured wage and you save both the body and the spirit," wrote Harry Hopkins, Roosevelt's trusted adviser and head of the president's major relief agency, the Federal Emergency Relief Administration (FERA). Thus New Deal programs emphasized "work relief." By January 1934, the Civil Works Administration had hired 4 million people, most earning $15 a week. And the **Civilian Conservation Corps (CCC)** paid unmarried young men $1 a day to do hard outdoor labor: building dams and reservoirs, creating trails in national parks. The program was segregated by race but brought together young men from very different backgrounds. By 1942, the CCC had employed 2.5 million men, including 80,000 Native Americans working on western Indian reservations.

Civilian Conservation Corps (CCC) Relief program that employed jobless young men in such government projects as reforestation, park maintenance, and erosion control.

Work relief programs rarely addressed the needs of poor women. Mothers of young children were usually classified as "unemployable" and were offered relief instead of jobs. But in North Carolina, for example, the "mother's-aid" grant was one-sixth of the wage paid in a federal works program.

The **Public Works Administration (PWA)**, created by Title II of the National Industrial Recovery Act, used public funds to create jobs for men in the construction industry and building trades. In 1933, Congress appropriated $3.3 billion—or 165 percent of federal revenues for that year—to New Deal public works programs that would strengthen the nation's infrastructure. PWA workers built the Triborough Bridge in New York City, the Grand River Dam in Oklahoma, and school buildings in almost half of the nation's counties.

Public Works Administration (PWA) New Deal relief agency that appropriated $3.3 billion for large-scale public works projects to provide jobs and stimulate the economy.

The special session of Congress, convened by FDR in March, adjourned on June 16, 1933, having passed fifteen major pieces of legislation (see Table 22.1). In just over three months, the United States had rebounded from near collapse. As New Deal programs were implemented, unemployment fell steadily from 13 million in 1933 to 9 million in 1936, farm prices rose, along with wages and salaries, and business failures abated (see Figure 22.1).

Lowering Tariffs

Internationally, meanwhile, the Roosevelt administration worked to expand trade. Increased trade, Secretary of State Cordell Hull insisted, would not only help the United States pull itself out of the depression but also boost the chances for global peace. He successfully pressed Congress to pass the Reciprocal Trade Agreements Act in 1934, empowering the president to reduce U.S. tariffs by as much as 50 percent through special agreements with foreign countries. The act's central feature was the most-favored-nation principle, whereby the United States was entitled to the lowest tariff rate set by any nation with which it had an agreement.

TABLE 22.1 New Deal Achievements

Year	Labor	Agriculture and Environment	Business and Industrial Recovery	Relief	Reform
1933	Section 7(a) of NIRA	Agricultural Adjustment Act Farm Credit Act	Emergency Banking Relief Act Economy Act Beer-Wine Revenue Act Banking Act of 1933 (guaranteed deposits) National Industrial Recovery Act	Civilian Conservation Corps Federal Emergency Relief Act Home Owners Refinancing Act Public Works Administration Civil Works Administration	TVA Federal Securities Act
1934	National Labor Relations Board	Taylor Grazing Act			Securities Exchange Act Reciprocal Trade Agreements Act Export-Import Bank
1935	National Labor Relations (Wagner) Act	Resettlement Administration Rural Electrification Administration		Works Progress Administration National Youth Administration	Social Security Act Public Utility Holding Company Act Revenue Act (wealth tax)
1937		Farm Security Administration		National Housing Act	
1938	Fair Labor Standards Act	Agricultural Adjustment Act of 1938			

Source: Adapted from Charles Sellers, Henry May, and Neil R. McMillen, *A Synopsis of American History*, 6th ed. Copyright © 1985 by Houghton Mifflin Company. Reprinted by permission.

In 1934, Hull also helped create the Export-Import Bank, a government agency that provided loans to foreigners for the purchase of American goods. But in the short term, Hull's ambitious programs—examples of America's independent internationalism—brought only mixed results.

U.S. Recognition of the Soviet Union

Economic imperatives also motivated Roosevelt to extend diplomatic recognition to the Soviet Union. Throughout the 1920s, the Republicans had refused to open diplomatic relations with the Soviet government, which had failed to pay $600 million for confiscated American-owned property and had repudiated preexisting debts. Nonetheless, in the late 1920s U.S. businesses such as General Electric and International Harvester entered the Soviet marketplace, and by 1930 the Soviet Union was the largest buyer of American farm and industrial equipment.

Upon becoming president, Roosevelt speculated that closer Soviet-American relations might help the economy while deterring Japanese expansion. In 1933,

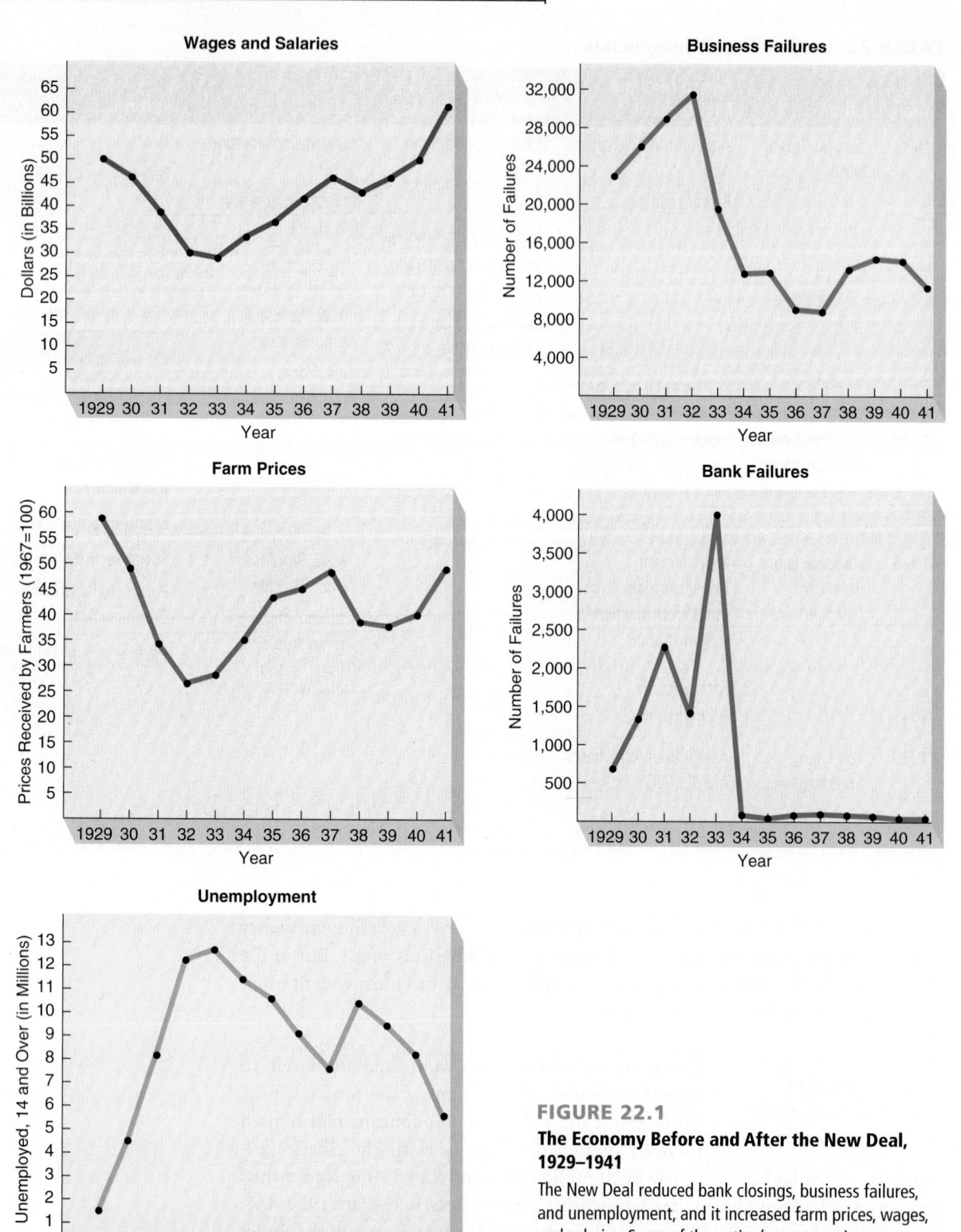

FIGURE 22.1

The Economy Before and After the New Deal, 1929–1941

The New Deal reduced bank closings, business failures, and unemployment, and it increased farm prices, wages, and salaries. Some of the nation's most persistent economic problems, however, did not disappear until the advent of the Second World War.

Roosevelt granted U.S. diplomatic recognition to the Soviet Union in return for Soviet agreement to discuss its debts and grant Americans in the Soviet Union religious freedom and legal rights.

Good Neighbor Policy
In Latin America, too, Roosevelt moved to reorient the direction of U.S. policy. He pledged the United States' participation in a **Good Neighbor policy**, by which he meant that Washington would be less blatant in its domination—less willing to defend exploitative business practices, less eager to launch military expeditions, and less reluctant to consult with Latin Americans. In reality, though, his administration continued to support and bolster dictators in the region, believing they would promote stability and preserve U.S. economic interests. When a revolution brought a radical government to power in Cuba in 1933, FDR instructed the American ambassador in Havana to work with conservative Cubans to replace the new government with a regime more friendly to U.S. interests. With Washington's support, army sergeant Fulgencio Batista took power in 1934.

> **Good Neighbor policy**
> Implemented by President Roosevelt, this Latin American policy stated that no nation had the right to intervene in the affairs of another; it replaced direct U.S. intervention with diplomacy and support for various leaders, businesses, and programs.

Political Pressure and the Second New Deal

> *What were the hallmarks of the Second New Deal?*

The unprecedented popular and congressional support for Roosevelt's New Deal did not last. Once the immediate crisis was averted, the struggle over solutions began in earnest. As some tried to stop the expansion of government power, others pushed for increased governmental action to combat continuing poverty and inequality.

Business Opposition
As the economy partially recovered, many wealthy business leaders criticized the New Deal. They condemned regulations and taxes, as well as budget-busting government spending for relief and jobs programs. In 1934, several corporate leaders joined former presidential candidate Al Smith and disaffected conservative Democrats to establish the American Liberty League to campaign against New Deal "radicalism." Hoping to turn southern whites against the New Deal, the Liberty League also secretly channeled funds to a racist group in the South that circulated pictures of the First Lady with African Americans.

Demagogues and Populists
Other Americans (sometimes called "populists") thought the government favored business over the people. Unemployment had decreased—but 9 million people were still jobless. In 1934, 1.5 million workers went on strike. In 1935, dust storms enveloped the southern plains, killing livestock and driving families like the Montgomerys from their land. As Americans' dissatisfaction mounted, so, too, did the appeal of various demagogues, who played to people's prejudices.

Father Charles Coughlin, a Roman Catholic priest whose weekly radio sermons reached 30 million listeners, spoke to those who felt they had lost control of their lives to distant elites and impersonal forces. Increasingly anti–New Deal, he was also anti-Semitic, telling his listeners that an international conspiracy of Jewish bankers caused their problems.

CANADA

Ottawa ✪

ATLANTIC OCEAN

UNITED STATES

• San Francisco

40°N

Washington, D.C. ✪

Roosevelt's Good Neighbor Policy, 1933

U.S. troops, 1917–1922
U.S. investors dominate sugar industry
Revolution of 1933
U.S. abrogates Platt Amendment, 1934
Batista era, 1934–1959

U.S. upholds right of intervention at
Pan American Conference, 1928

U.S. troops, 1915–1934
Financial supervision, 1916–1941

MEXICO

Gulf
of
Mexico

Miami •

THE
BAHAMAS
✪ Nassau

U.S. financial supervision, 1905–1941
U.S. troops withdrawn, 1924
Trujillo era, 1930–1961

Constitution of 1917 challenges U.S. interests
Nationalization of foreign oil companies, 1938
U.S.-Mexico agreement settles oil dispute, 1942

✪ Havana
CUBA
Guantánamo

DOMINICAN
REP.

San Juan
VIRGIN IS. (U.S./U.K.)

20°N

✪ Mexico
City

Belmopan ✪
BELIZE

JAMAICA
Kingston

HAITI
✪ ✪
Port-au-
Prince

Santo
Domingo

PUERTO
RICO (U.S.)

U.S. colony since 1917

GUATEMALA
Guatemala City ✪
San Salvador

HONDURAS
✪ Tegucigalpa
NICARAGUA
✪ Managua

Caribbean Sea

U.S. colony
Jones Act grants U.S. citizenship, 1917

EL SALVADOR
✪ San José

U.S. invasion, 1924
United Fruit Company active

COSTA
RICA
PANAMA

✪ Panama

✪ Caracas

GUYANA
Georgetown
✪

SURINAME
✪
• Cayenne
FRENCH GUIANA (Fr.)

VENEZUELA

U.S. financial supervision, 1911–1924
U.S. military occupation, 1912–1925
U.S. war against Sandino, 1926–1933
Somoza era, 1936–1979

✪ Bogotá

COLOMBIA

Paramaribo

SURINAME

Equator — 0°

U.S. control of Canal Zone
Declaration of Panama, 1939

✪ Quito
ECUADOR

U.S. oil investments

Amazon R.

BRAZIL

PERU

Lima •

BOLIVIA
✪ La Paz

✪ Brasília

PACIFIC
OCEAN

20°S

U.S. copper interests

PARAGUAY
✪ Asunción

Paraná R.

CHILE

N

Santiago ✪

URUGUAY

Buenos Aires ✪ ✪ Montevideo

ARGENTINA

U.S. votes for nonintervention pledge
at Pan-American Conference, 1936

40°S
40°W

0   500   1000 Km.
0   500   1000 Mi.

80°W   60°W

MAP 22.2
The United States and Latin America Between the Wars

The United States often intervened in other nations to maintain its hegemonic power in Latin America, where nationalists resented outside meddling in their sovereign affairs. The Good Neighbor policy decreased U.S. military interventions, but U.S. economic interests remained strong in the hemisphere. Source: Copyright © Cengage Learning 2015

Another challenge came from Dr. Francis E. Townsend, a public health officer in Long Beach, California, who was thrown out of work at age sixty-seven with only $100 in savings. Townsend proposed that Americans over the age of sixty should receive a government pension of $200 a month, financed by a new "transaction" (sales) tax. This plan was fiscally impossible (almost three-quarters of working Americans earned $200 a month or less) and profoundly regressive (because sales tax rates are the same for everyone, they take a larger share of income from those who earn the least). Nonetheless, 20 million Americans, or 1 in 5 adults, signed petitions supporting this plan.

Then there was Huey Long, the former governor of Louisiana and perhaps the most successful populist demagogue in American history. As a U.S. senator, Long initially supported the New Deal but soon decided that Roosevelt had fallen captive to big business. Long countered in 1934 with the Share Our Wealth Society. He proposed that the government take all income exceeding $1 million a year and wealth in excess of $5 million per family and use those funds to give each American family an annual income of $2,000 and a one-time homestead allowance of $5,000. (Long's plan was fiscally impossible but definitely not regressive.) By mid-1935, Long's movement claimed 7 million members, and few doubted that he aspired to the presidency. But Long was killed by a bodyguard's bullet during an assassination attempt in September 1935.

Left-Wing Critics

The political left also gained ground. Socialists and communists alike criticized the New Deal for trying to save capitalism instead of working to lessen the inequality of power and wealth in American society. In California, muckraker and socialist Upton Sinclair won the Democratic gubernatorial nomination in 1934 with the slogan "End Poverty in California." Disclaiming any intention of overthrowing the government, the U.S. Communist Party cooperated with left-wing labor unions, student groups, and writers' organizations in a **"Popular Front"** against fascism abroad and racism at home. It continued to fight racial discrimination through the League of Struggle for Negro Rights (founded in the late 1920s to fight lynching), and sent lawyers and funds to support the "Scottsboro Boys," who were falsely accused of raping two white women in Alabama (see page 658). In 1938, the party had fifty-five thousand members.

"Popular Front" Coalition of communist and politically left groups against fascism and racism.

Shaping the Second New Deal

It was not only external critics who pushed Roosevelt to focus on social justice. His administration—largely due to the tireless work and influence of Eleanor Roosevelt—included many progressive activists. **Frances Perkins**, America's first woman cabinet member, came from a social work background, as did Roosevelt's close adviser Harold Ickes. Women social reformers who coalesced around the First Lady played important roles. And by 1936, at least fifty black Americans held relatively important positions in New Deal agencies and cabinet-level departments. Journalists called these officials—who met on Friday evenings at the home of Mary McLeod Bethune, a distinguished educator and head of the Division of Negro Affairs for the National Youth Administration—the "black cabinet."

Frances Perkins Served as Secretary of Labor from 1933 to 1945, former Progressive reformer, and first woman cabinet member.

Mary McLeod Bethune, pictured here with her friend and supporter Eleanor Roosevelt, became the first African American woman to head a federal agency as director of the Division of Negro Affairs for the National Youth Administration.

Bettmann/CORBIS

As Roosevelt faced the election of 1936, he understood that he had to appeal to seemingly contradictory desires. Americans hit hard by the depression looked to the New Deal for help. Those with a tenuous hold on the middle class wanted security and stability. Still others wanted the New Deal to preserve American capitalism. With these lessons in mind, Roosevelt took the initiative again.

During the period historians call the Second New Deal, Roosevelt introduced progressive programs aimed at providing "greater security for the average man than he has ever known before in the history of America." The first triumph of the Second New Deal was the Emergency Relief Appropriation Act, which provided $4 billion in new deficit spending, primarily to create massive public works programs for the jobless. It also established the Resettlement Administration, which resettled destitute families and organized communities for low-income workers; the Rural Electrification Administration, which brought electricity to isolated rural areas; and the National Youth Administration, which sponsored work-relief programs for young adults.

Works Progress Administration (WPA)
Massive public works program that hired people to construct highways, roads, buildings; it also provided jobs for artists, actors, and writers in cultural programs.

Works Progress Administration

The largest and best-known program was the **Works Progress Administration (WPA)**, later renamed the Work Projects Administration. The WPA employed more than 8.5 million people who built 650,000 miles of highways and roads and 125,000 public buildings, as well as bridges, reservoirs, irrigation systems, sewage treatment plants, parks, playgrounds, and swimming pools.

The WPA also employed artists, musicians, writers, and actors, commissioning such tasks as decorating post office walls with murals depicting ordinary life in America and staffing government-sponsored orchestras. Through the Federal Writers' Project (FWP), authors created guidebooks for every state and wrote about the plain people of the United States, including a collection of "slave narratives" from more than two thousand elderly men and women who had been held in bondage before the Civil War. These cultural programs were also controversial, for many of the WPA artists, musicians, actors, and writers attempted to recover a tradition of American radicalism by celebrating the lives and labor of America's plain folk.

Social Security Act

Emergency Relief Recovery Act programs were part of a short-term "emergency" strategy. Roosevelt's long-term strategy centered around the **Social Security Act**. It created a federal pension system in which eligible workers paid mandatory Social Security taxes on their wages and their employers contributed an equivalent amount; these workers then received federal retirement benefits. The Social Security Act also created several welfare programs, including a cooperative federal-state system of unemployment compensation and Aid to Dependent Children (later renamed Aid to Families with Dependent Children, AFDC) for needy children in families without fathers present.

Social Security Act New Deal relief measure that launched a federal retirement benefits system as well as unemployment compensation, aid to needy children, and other welfare benefits.

Compared with the social security systems already in place in most western European nations, the U.S. system was fairly conservative. First, the government did not pay for old-age benefits; workers and their employers did. Second, the tax was regressive in that the more workers earned, the less they were taxed proportionally. Finally, the law did not cover agricultural labor, domestic service, and "casual labor not in the course of the employer's trade or business" (for example, janitorial work at a hospital). That meant that people of color, who disproportionately worked as farm laborers, as domestic servants, and in service jobs received no benefits. The act also excluded public-sector employees, so many teachers, nurses, librarians, and social workers (mostly women) went uncovered. Despite these limits, the federal government took some responsibility for the economic security of the aged, the temporarily unemployed, dependent children, and people with disabilities.

Roosevelt's Populist Strategies

As the election of 1936 approached, Roosevelt adopted the populist language of his critics. Denouncing "unjust concentration of wealth and power," he supported a new tax on business profits and increased taxes on inheritances, large gifts, and profits from the sale of property (see Figure 22.2).

In November 1936, Roosevelt won the presidency by a landslide, and the Democrats won huge majorities in the House and Senate. Roosevelt and the Democrats had forged a powerful "New Deal coalition" consisting of the urban working class (especially immigrants from southern and eastern Europe), organized labor, the eleven states of the former Confederacy (the "Solid South"), and northern blacks drawn away from the Republican Party, which they had long supported as the party of Lincoln. This New Deal coalition ensured that Democrats would occupy the White House for most of the next thirty years.

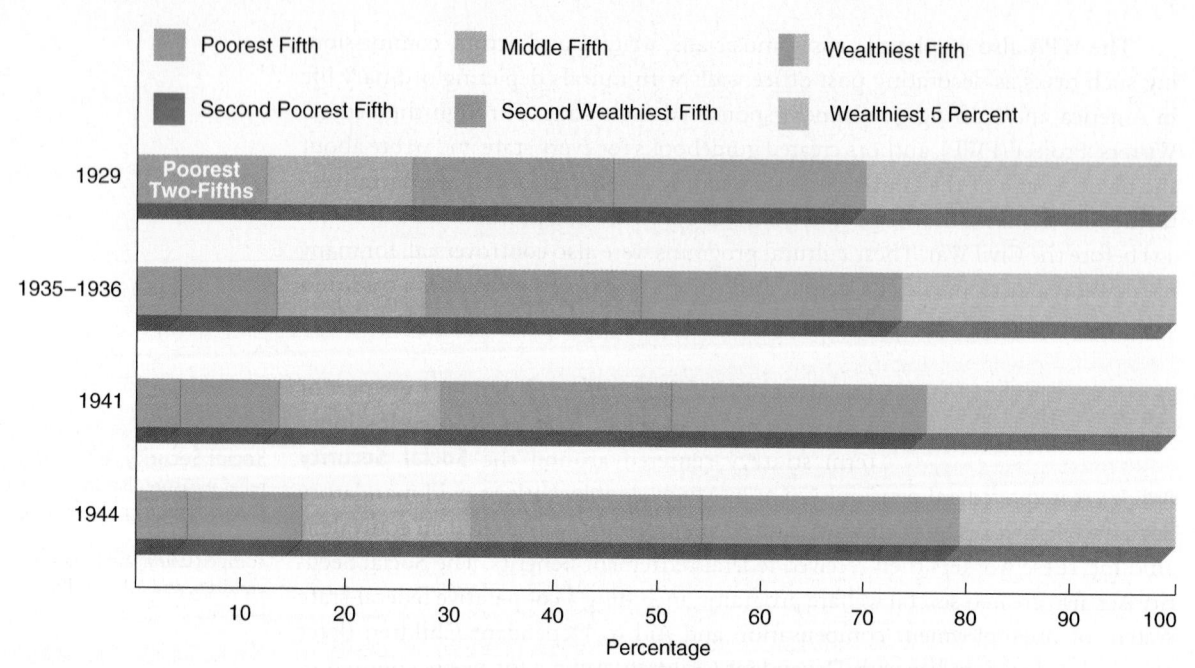

FIGURE 22.2

Distribution of Total Family Income Among the American People, 1929–1944 (percentage)

Although the New Deal provided economic relief to the American people, it did not, as its critics so often charged, significantly redistribute income downward from the rich to the poor.

(Source: Adapted from U.S. Bureau of the Census, *Historical Statistics of the United States, Colonial Times to 1970.* Bicentennial Edition, Washington, D.C.: U.S. Government Printing Office, 1975, page 301.)

Labor

How did Roosevelt provide support for labor?

During the depression's worst years, American workers struggled for the rights of labor. Management, however, fought back. Refusing to recognize unions, some even hired armed thugs to intimidate workers. One business publication declared that "a few hundred funerals will have a quieting influence." As employers refused to negotiate with union representatives, workers walked off the job. Local police or National Guard troops frequently intervened for management, smashing workers' picket lines. Violence erupted in the steel, automobile, and textile industries; among lumber workers in the Pacific Northwest; and among teamsters in the Midwest.

National Labor Relations (Wagner) Act Guaranteed workers the rights to organize and bargain collectively and outlawed unfair labor practices.

The Roosevelt administration supported labor with the 1935 **National Labor Relations (Wagner) Act**. This act guaranteed workers the right to organize unions and to bargain collectively. It outlawed "unfair labor practices," such as firing workers who joined unions; prohibited management from sponsoring company unions; and required employers to bargain with labor's elected union representatives on wages, hours, and working conditions. The Wagner Act also created an enforcement mechanism: the National Labor Relations Board (NLRB). With federal protection, union membership grew from 3.6 million in 1929 to 7 million in 1938. But the Wagner Act further alienated business leaders from the New Deal.

Rivalry between Craft and Industrial Unions

The growth and increasing militancy of the labor movement exacerbated an existing division between "craft" and "industrial" unions. Craft unions represented labor's elite: skilled workers in a particular trade, such as carpentry. Industrial unions represented all the workers, skilled and unskilled, in a given industry. In the 1930s, industrial unions grew dramatically.

Craft unions dominated the American Federation of Labor, the powerful umbrella organization for individual unions. Most AFL leaders offered little support for industrial organizing. Many looked down on industrial workers, disproportionately immigrants from southern and eastern Europe. Skilled workers had economic interests different from those of unskilled workers, and more conservative craft unionists were alarmed at what they saw as the radicalism of industrial unions.

In 1935, John L. Lewis, head of the United Mine Workers and the nation's most prominent labor leader, resigned as vice president of the AFL. He and other industrial unionists created the Committee for Industrial Organization (CIO); the AFL then suspended all CIO unions. By 1938, the slightly renamed **Congress of Industrial Organizations** had 3.7 million members, slightly more than the AFL's 3.4 million. Unlike the AFL, the CIO included women and people of color, giving these "marginal" workers greater employment security and the benefits of collective bargaining.

Congress of Industrial Organizations Association of 3.7 million members of industrial unions; included women and people of color.

Link to Cartoon about John L. Lewis, "Like Davey Crockett's Coon" 1937

Sit-Down Strikes

The most decisive labor conflict came when the United Auto Workers (UAW), an industrial union, demanded recognition from General Motors (GM), Chrysler, and Ford. When GM refused, UAW organizers and workers at the Fisher Body plant in Flint, Michigan, held a "sit-down strike" *inside* the factory on December 30, 1936. Refusing to leave, they immobilized GM production. GM tried to force the workers out by turning off the heat. When police attempted to take back the plant, strikers hurled steel bolts, coffee mugs, and bottles.

As the sit-down strike spread to adjacent plants, auto production plummeted. General Motors obtained a court order to evacuate the plant, but the strikers stood firm, risking imprisonment and fines. Michigan's governor refused to send in the National Guard to clear workers. After forty-four days, GM agreed to recognize the union, and Chrysler followed. Ford held out until 1941.

Memorial Day Massacre

On the heels of this triumph, however, came a reminder of the costs of labor's struggle. On Memorial Day 1937, picnicking workers and their families marched toward the Republic Steel plant in Chicago, intending to support strikers picketing there. Police ordered them to disperse. One marcher threw something at the police, and the police attacked. Ten men were killed, seven of them shot in the back. Thirty marchers were wounded, including a woman and three children. Many Americans, fed up with labor strife and violence, showed little sympathy for the workers.

At great cost, organized labor made great gains during the 1930s. Violence decreased as the NLRB effectively mediated disputes. And unionized workers—about

Visualizing THE PAST

The Women's Emergency Brigade and General Motors Sit-Down Strike

During the 1937 sit-down strike by automobile workers in Flint, Michigan, a women's "emergency brigade" of wives, daughters, sisters, and sweethearts demonstrated daily at the plant. When police tried to force the men out of Chevrolet Plant No. 9 by filling it with tear gas, the women used clubs to smash the plant's windows and let in fresh air. Sixteen people were injured that day in the riot between police and strikers. The following day the Women's Emergency Brigade marched again. Using this photograph as visual evidence: How did these women attempt to demonstrate the respectability and mainstream nature of their protest? How does that message fit with the clubs several still carry?

Gerenda Johnson, wife of a striker, leads a march past the GM Chevrolet small parts plant on the day following a violent conflict between police and strikers.

Bettmann/Corbis

652

23 percent of the nonagricultural workforce—saw their standard of living rise. By 1941, the average steelworker could afford to buy a pair of shoes for his children every other year.

Federal Power and the Nationalization of Culture

In what ways did the Depression inspire the emergence of a youth culture?

In the 1930s, national media, politics, and policies played an increasingly important role in the lives of Americans. Political power moved from the state and local level to the White House and Congress, and by the end of the decade almost 35 percent of the population had received some sort of federal government benefit. Americans in the 1930s began to expect the federal government to play a major and active role in the life of the nation.

New Deal in the West

The New Deal changed the American West more than any other region, as federally sponsored construction of dams and other public works projects reshaped the region's economy and environment. For example, the Boulder Dam (later renamed for Herbert Hoover) harnessed the Colorado River, providing water to southern California and using hydroelectric power to produce electricity for Los Angeles and southern Arizona. The water from this and other dams opened new areas to agriculture and allowed western cities to expand; the cheap electricity they produced attracted industry.

The federal government also brought millions of acres of western land under its control in the 1930s as it attempted to combat the environmental disaster of the Dust Bowl and to keep crop and livestock prices from falling further. In 1934, the Taylor Grazing Act imposed new restrictions on ranchers' use of public lands for grazing stock. Federal stock reduction programs probably saved the western cattle industry, but they destroyed the traditional economy of the Navajos by forcing them to reduce the size of sheep herds on their federally protected reservation lands.

New Deal for Native Americans

New federal activism also extended to the West's people. Previous federal policy toward Native Americans, especially those on reservations, was disastrous. The Bureau of Indian Affairs (BIA) was riddled with corruption; in its attempts to "assimilate" Native Americans, it had separated children from parents, suppressed native languages, and outlawed tribal religious practices. Division of tribal lands failed to promote individual landownership. In the early 1930s, Native Americans were the poorest group in the nation, plagued with an infant mortality rate twice that of white Americans.

In 1933, Roosevelt named one of the BIA's most vocal critics to head the agency. John Collier, founder of the American Indian Defense Agency, meant to completely reverse America's Indian policy. The **Indian Reorganization Act** (IRA, 1934) worked toward ending forced assimilation and restoring Indian lands to tribal ownership. Indian tribes regained their status as semi-sovereign nations, guaranteed "internal sovereignty" in matters not limited by acts of Congress.

Indian Reorganization Act
A 1934 measure that sought to restore Indian lands to tribal ownership and provided federal recognition of tribes as semi-sovereign nations.

Some Indians denounced the IRA as a "back-to-the-blanket" measure based on romantic notions of "authentic" Indian culture. The tribal government structure specified by the IRA was culturally alien to tribes such as the Papagos, whose language had no word for "representative." The Navajo nation refused to ratify the IRA. Eventually, however, 181 tribes organized under the IRA, which laid the groundwork for future economic development and limited political autonomy among native peoples.

New Deal in the South

New Dealers did not set out to transform the American West, but they did intend to transform the South. In 1929, the South's per capita income of $365 per year was less than half of the West's $921. More than half of southern farm families were tenants or sharecroppers. Roosevelt believed that as long as its people were too poor to participate in the nation's mass consumer economy, the South would be a drag on national economic recovery.

Tennessee Valley Authority (TVA) Ambitious plan of economic development that centered on creating an extensive hydroelectric power project in the poor Appalachian area.

The largest federal intervention in the South was the **Tennessee Valley Authority (TVA)**, authorized by Congress during Roosevelt's First Hundred Days. The TVA was created to develop a water and hydroelectric power project similar to the multipurpose dams of the West (see Map 22.3). However, confronted with the poverty and hopelessness of the Tennessee River Valley region (which included parts of Virginia, North Carolina, Tennessee, Georgia, Alabama, Mississippi, and Kentucky), the TVA expanded to promote economic development, bring electricity to rural areas, restore fields worn out from overuse, and fight malaria.

Although it benefited many poor southerners, the TVA was an environmental disaster. TVA strip mining caused soil erosion. Its coal-burning generators released sulfur oxides, which combined with water vapor to produce acid rain. Above all, the TVA degraded the water by dumping untreated sewage, toxic chemicals, and metal pollutants from strip mining into streams and rivers.

Southern senators benefited from the flow of federal dollars to their states, but they were also suspicious of federal intervention. Especially when federal action threatened the South's racial hierarchy, they resisted. As the nation's poorest and least educated region, the South would not easily be integrated into the national culture and economy. But New Deal programs began that process and improved the lives of at least some of the region's people.

Mass Media and Popular Culture

America's national mass media and popular culture helped break down regional boundaries and foster national connections. Radio filled the days and nights of the depression era. Manufacturers rushed to produce cheaper models, and by 1937 Americans were buying radios at the rate of twenty-eight a minute. By decade's end, 27.5 million households owned radios, and families listened on average five hours a day. Roosevelt went directly to the American people with radio "Fireside Chats" throughout his presidency.

In a time of uncertainty, radio gave citizens immediate access to political news. During hard times, radio offered escape: for children, the adventures of *Flash Gordon*; for housewives, new soap operas, such as *The Romance of Helen Trent*. Families gathered to listen to the comedy of ex-vaudevillians Jack Benny, George Burns,

MAP 22.3
The Tennessee Valley Authority

To control flooding and generate electricity, the Tennessee Valley Authority constructed dams along the Tennessee River and its tributaries from Paducah, Kentucky, to Knoxville, Tennessee. Source: Copyright © Cengage Learning 2015

and Gracie Allen. Listeners were carried to New York City for performances of the Metropolitan Opera on Saturday afternoons, and to major league baseball games (begun by the St. Louis Cardinals in 1935) in distant cities. Millions shared the horror of the kidnapping of aviator Charles Lindbergh's son in 1932; black Americans in the urban North and rural South experienced the triumphs of African American boxer Joe Louis ("the Brown Bomber"). Radio lessened isolation and helped create a more homogeneous mass culture across regional and class lines.

Hollywood movies also offered shared experiences. During the first years of the depression almost one-third of all movie theaters closed, but by the mid-1930s Americans were going to the movies again, and a nation of fewer than 130 million bought 80 million to 90 million movie tickets each week. Many Americans sought escape at the movies. Comedies were especially popular, from the slapstick of the Marx Brothers to the sophisticated banter of *My Man Godfrey*.

But some Americans were alarmed when *Little Caesar, Scarface,* and other gangster movies drew crowds in the early 1930s. Critics argued that the films glamorized crime. Faced with a boycott organized by the Roman Catholic Legion of Decency, in 1934 the film industry established a production code that would determine what American film audiences saw—and did not see—for decades.

Links TO THE WORLD

The 1936 Olympic Games

The 1936 Olympic Games, scheduled in Berlin under the Nazi regime, created a dilemma for the United States and other nations. Would participation in the Nazi-orchestrated spectacle lend credence to Hitler's regime? Or would victories won by other nations undermine Hitler's claims about the superiority of Germany's "Aryan race"?

Germany was excluded from the 1920 and 1924 Olympic Games following its World War I defeat, and the International Olympic Committee's choice (in 1931) of Berlin for the XI Olympiad was intended to welcome Germany back into the world community. However, with Hitler's rise to power in 1933, Germany determined to use the games as propaganda for the Nazi state. Campaigns to boycott the Berlin Olympics emerged in several nations, including the United States.

Americans were divided over the boycott. Some U.S. Jewish groups led campaigns against U.S. participation in Berlin, while others took no public position, concerned that their actions might lead to increased

Leonard de Selva/CORBIS

anti-Semitic violence within Germany. African Americans opposed the boycott and looked forward to demonstrating just how wrong Hitler's notions of Aryan superiority were. Some also pointed out the hypocrisy of American officials who criticized Germany while ignoring U.S. discrimination against black athletes.

The United States sent 312 athletes to Berlin; 18 were African Americans who won 14 medals, one-quarter of the U.S. total of 56. Track and field star Jesse Owens earned 4 gold medals. Jewish athletes won 13 medals; one of those athletes was American. But German athletes won 89, and despite the initial controversy, the XI Olympiad was a public relations triumph for Germany. The *New York Times*, impressed by the Germans' hospitality, proclaimed that the XI Olympiad put Germany "back in the fold of nations."

The idealistic vision of nations linked in peaceful athletic competition hit a low point at the 1936 Olympics. The 1940 Olympic Games, scheduled for Tokyo, were cancelled because of the escalating world war.

Bettmann/Corbis

The eleventh summer Olympic Games in Berlin were carefully crafted as propaganda for the Nazi state. And the spectacle of the 1936 games, as represented in the poster above, was impressive. But on the athletic fields, Nazi claims of Aryan superiority were challenged by athletes such as African American Jesse Owens, who is shown at left breaking the Olympic record in the 200-meter race.

Finally, in an unintended consequence, federal policies intended to channel jobs to male heads of households strengthened the power of national popular culture. During Roosevelt's first two years in office, 1.5 million youths lost jobs; many young people who would have gone to work at the age of fourteen in better times decided to stay in school. By decade's end, three-quarters of American youth went to high school—up from one-half in 1920—and graduation rates doubled. As more young people went to high school, more participated in national youth culture, increasingly listening to the same music and adopting similar clothing, dances, and speech. Paradoxically, the hard times of the depression caused youth culture to spread more widely among America's young.

The Limits of the New Deal

How did Roosevelt undermine his New Deal agenda?

Roosevelt began his second term with a strong mandate for reform. Almost immediately, however, the president's own actions undermined his New Deal agenda. Labor strife and racial issues divided America. As the world inched toward war, domestic initiatives lost ground to foreign affairs and defense. By late 1938, New Deal reform ground to a halt.

Court-Packing Plan

Following his landslide victory in 1936, Roosevelt sought to safeguard his progressive agenda. He saw the U.S. Supreme Court as its greatest threat. In ruling unconstitutional both the National Industrial Recovery Act (in 1935) and the Agricultural Adjustment Act (in 1936), the Court rejected not only specific legislative provisions but also the expansion of presidential and federal power such legislation entailed. Roosevelt was convinced the Court would invalidate most of the Second New Deal legislation. Citing the advanced age and heavy workload of the nine justices, he asked Congress for authority to appoint up to six new justices. But in an era that had seen the rise of Hitler, Mussolini, and Stalin, many Americans saw Roosevelt's plan as an attack on constitutional government. Congress rebelled, and Roosevelt experienced his first major congressional defeat.

Ironically, during the long public debate over Court packing, key swing-vote justices began to support liberal, pro–New Deal rulings. The Court upheld both the Wagner Act and the Social Security Act. Moreover, a new judicial pension program encouraged older judges to retire, and Roosevelt appointed seven new associate justices in the next four years. In the end, Roosevelt got what he wanted from the Supreme Court, but the Court-packing plan damaged his political credibility.

Roosevelt Recession

Another New Deal setback was the recession of 1937–1939, sometimes called the Roosevelt recession. In 1937, confident that the depression had reversed, Roosevelt began to cut government spending. The Federal Reserve Board, concerned about a 3.6 percent inflation rate, tightened credit. The two actions sent the economy into a tailspin: unemployment climbed from 7.7 million in 1937 to 10.4 million in 1938.

The New Deal was in trouble in 1937 and 1938. Roosevelt rejected calls for the resurrection of national economic planning as it had existed under the NRA, instead resuming deficit financing to stimulate consumer demand and create jobs. And in 1939, with conflict over the world war that had begun in Europe commanding more U.S. attention, the New Deal came to an end. Roosevelt sacrificed further domestic reforms in return for conservative support for his programs of military rearmament and preparedness.

Election of 1940

No president had ever served more than two terms, and Roosevelt seemed undecided until spring 1940, when Adolf Hitler's military advances in Europe apparently convinced him to stay on. Roosevelt promised Americans, "Your boys are not going to be sent into any foreign wars."

Roosevelt did not win this election in a landslide, but the New Deal coalition held. Roosevelt again won in the cities, supported by blue-collar workers, ethnic Americans, and African Americans. He also carried every southern state.

Race and the Limits of the New Deal

While the New Deal benefited many Americans, it fell short of equality for people of color. One problem was that national programs were implemented at the local level, and local custom often conflicted with national intent. In the South, African Americans received lower relief payments than whites and were paid less for WPA jobs. In Tucson, Arizona, Federal Emergency Relief Agency officials divided applicants into four groups—Anglos, Mexican Americans, Mexican immigrants, and Indians—and allocated relief payments in descending order.

The case of the Scottsboro Boys illustrates racism in conflicts between local and national power in 1930s America. One night in March 1931, young black and white "hobos" started fighting on a Southern Railroad freight train as it passed through Alabama. The black youths won and tossed the whites off the train. Afterward, a posse stopped the train and threw the black youths in the Scottsboro, Alabama, jail. Two white women "riding the rails" claimed that the men had raped them. Medical evidence later showed that the women were lying. But within two weeks, eight of the so-called Scottsboro Boys were convicted of rape by all-white juries and sentenced to death. The ninth, a boy of thirteen, was saved from the death penalty by one vote. The case—clearly a product of southern racism—became a cause célèbre, both in the nation and, through the efforts of the Communist Party, around the world.

The Supreme Court intervened, ruling that Alabama deprived black defendants of equal protection under the law by excluding African Americans from juries and denying defendants counsel. Alabama, however, staged new trials, convicting five of the young men (four would be paroled by 1950, and one escaped from prison). On issues of race, the South would not yield easily to federal power.

The gains made by people of color under the New Deal were limited by the political realities of southern resistance. In 1938, for example, southern Democrats blocked an antilynching bill with a six-week-long filibuster in the Senate. Roosevelt refused to use his political capital to break the filibuster and pass the bill. He knew that blacks would not desert the Democratic Party, but without southern senators, his legislative agenda was dead. Roosevelt wanted all Americans to enjoy the benefits of democracy, but he had no strong commitment to civil rights.

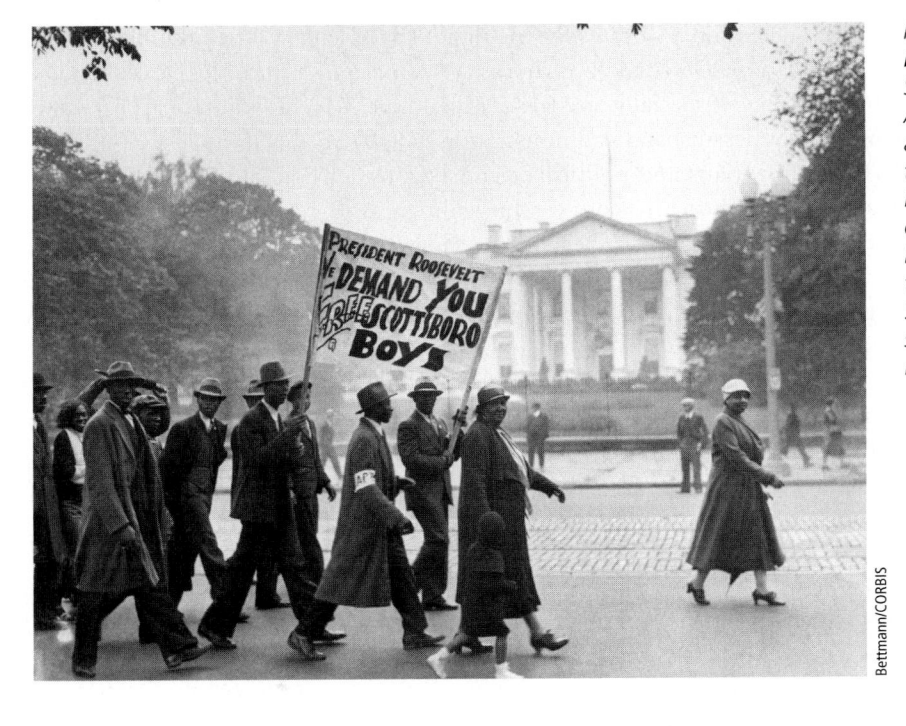

Marchers in Washington, D.C., demand freedom for the Scottsboro Boys, young African American men who were falsely accused and convicted of raping two white women in Alabama in 1931. This 1933 march was organized by the International Labor Defense, the legal arm of the Communist Party of the United States of America, which waged a strong campaign on behalf of the nine young men.

Bettmann/CORBIS

African American Support

Why, then, did African Americans support Roosevelt? Because despite discriminatory policies, the New Deal helped African Americans. By the end of the 1930s, almost one-third of African American households survived on income from a WPA job. African Americans held significant positions in the Roosevelt administration, and the First Lady publicly showed her commitment to racial equality. When the Daughters of the American Revolution refused to allow acclaimed black contralto Marian Anderson to perform in Washington's Constitution Hall, Eleanor Roosevelt arranged for Anderson to sing at the Lincoln Memorial on Easter Sunday 1939.

Nonetheless, given the limits of New Deal reform, some African Americans concluded that self-help and direct-action movements were a surer alternative. In 1934, black tenant farmers and sharecroppers joined with poor whites to form the Southern Tenant Farmers' Union. In the North, African American consumers boycotted white merchants who refused to hire blacks. Their slogan was "Don't Buy Where You Can't Work." And the Brotherhood of Sleeping Car Porters, led by A. Philip Randolph, fought for the rights of black workers.

An Assessment of the New Deal

Any analysis of the New Deal must begin with Roosevelt himself. Assessments of Roosevelt varied widely during his presidency: he was passionately hated and passionately loved. When he spoke to Americans in his Fireside Chats, hundreds of thousands wrote to him, asking for help and offering advice.

Eleanor Roosevelt played a crucial and unprecedented role in the Roosevelt administration. As First Lady, she worked for social justice, bringing reformers, trade unionists, and advocates for the rights of women and African Americans to the White House. Described by some as the conscience of the New Deal, she took public positions—especially on African American civil rights—far more progressive than those of her husband's administration.

Most historians and political scientists consider Franklin Roosevelt a truly great president, citing his courage, his willingness to experiment, and his capacity to inspire the nation. Some, who see the New Deal as a squandered opportunity for true change, charge that Roosevelt lacked vision. They judge Roosevelt by goals that were not his own: Roosevelt was a pragmatist whose goal was to preserve the system.

During his more than twelve years in office, Roosevelt strengthened not only the presidency but also the federal government. For the first time, the federal government took primary responsibility for safeguarding the economic security of the American people. New Deal programs saved millions of Americans from hunger and misery. However, as late as 1939, more than 10 million people remained jobless, and the nation's unemployment rate stood at 19 percent. It was not until 1941, as the nation mobilized for war, that unemployment declined to 10 percent. By 1944, only 1 percent of the labor force was jobless. World War II, not the New Deal, reinvigorated the American economy.

The Approach of War

How did President Roosevelt respond to the rising tensions in Europe between 1935 and the outbreak of war in 1939?

Roosevelt's effort to expand the federal government's power also had another source: the sharp rise in world tensions. The main threat came from a revitalized Germany. On March 5, 1933, one day after Roosevelt's inauguration, Germany's parliament granted dictatorial powers to the new chancellor, **Adolf Hitler**, leader of the **Nazi Party**. It was a stunning rise to power for Hitler, whose Nazis very likely would have remained a fringe party had the Great Depression not hit Germany with such force. Production plummeted 40 percent, and unemployment ballooned to 6 million, meaning that two workers out of five were jobless. A disintegrating banking system, which robbed millions of their savings, and widespread resentment among Germans over the Versailles peace settlement also fueled mass discontent.

Adolf Hitler German chancellor and Nazi dictator whose efforts to restore his nation's prominence included a brutal program to purify it of Jews and others he deemed "inferior races."

Nazi Party National Socialist German Workers' Party founded in Germany in 1919; it rose to prominence under the leadership of Adolf Hitler and stressed fascism and anti-Semitism.

Like Benito Mussolini, who had gained control of Italy in 1922, Hitler was a fascist. Fascism (called Nazism, or National Socialism, in Germany) celebrated supremacy of the state over the individual; dictatorship over democracy; authoritarianism over freedom of speech; a state-regulated economy over a free market; and militarism over peace. The Nazis vowed to revive Germany, cripple communism, and "purify" the German "race" by destroying Jews and other people, such as homosexuals and Gypsies, whom Hitler disparaged as inferiors. The Nuremberg Laws of 1935 stripped Jews of citizenship and outlawed intermarriage with non-Jews. Half of all German Jews were without work.

German Aggression Under Hitler

Determined to get out from under the Versailles treaty, Hitler withdrew Germany from the League of Nations, ended reparations payments, and began to rearm. While secretly laying plans to conquer neighboring states, he watched admiringly as Mussolini's troops invaded Ethiopia in 1935. The next year, Hitler ordered his own goose-stepping troopers into the Rhineland, an area demilitarized by the Versailles treaty.

In 1936, Italy and Germany formed an alliance called the Rome-Berlin Axis. Shortly thereafter, Germany and Japan united against the Soviet Union in the Anti-Comintern Pact. Britain and France responded with a policy of **appeasement**, hoping to curb Hitler's expansionism by permitting him a few territorial nibbles. Instead, the German leader continually raised his demands.

appeasement The process of making concessions to pacify, quiet, or satisfy the other party.

Early in 1938, Hitler again tested European tolerance when he sent soldiers to annex his birth nation, Austria. In September, he seized the largely German-speaking Sudeten region of Czechoslovakia. France and Britain, without consulting the Czechs, agreed at Munich to allow Hitler this territorial bite, in exchange for a pledge that he would not take more. British prime minister Neville Chamberlain returned home proclaiming "peace in our time." In March 1939, Hitler swallowed the rest of Czechoslovakia (see Map 22.4).

MAP 22.4
The German Advance

Hitler's drive to dominate Europe pushed German troops deep into France and the Soviet Union. Great Britain took a beating but held on with the help of American economic and military aid before the United States entered the Second World War in late 1941.

Source: Copyright © Cengage Learning 2015

Isolationist Views in the United States

Americans watched this buildup of tension in Europe with apprehension. A majority embraced isolationism, whose key elements were abhorrence of war and opposition to U.S. alliances with other nations. The vast majority of isolationists opposed fascism and condemned aggression, but they did not think the United States should do what Europeans themselves refused to do: block Hitler.

A 1937 Gallup poll found that nearly two-thirds of the respondents thought U.S. participation in World War I had been a mistake, and some isolationists charged that corporate "merchants of death" had promoted war and were assisting the aggressors. A congressional committee headed by Senator Gerald P. Nye held hearings from 1934 to 1936 on the role of business in the U.S. decision to enter the First World War. The Nye committee did not prove that American munitions makers had dragged the nation into that war, but it did uncover evidence that corporations had bribed foreign politicians to bolster arms sales in the 1920s and 1930s.

neutrality acts Laws passed in the mid-1930s to keep the United States out of any European wars.

Reflecting the popular desire for distance from Europe's disputes, Roosevelt signed a series of **neutrality acts**. The Neutrality Act of 1935 prohibited arms shipments to either side in a war, once the president declared the existence of belligerency. The Neutrality Act of 1936 forbade loans to belligerents. The Neutrality Act of 1937 introduced the cash-and-carry principle: warring nations wishing to trade with the United States would have to pay cash for their nonmilitary purchases and carry the goods from U.S. ports in their own ships. The act also forbade Americans from traveling on the ships of belligerent nations.

Roosevelt's Evolving Views

President Roosevelt shared the prevailing isolationist views in the early 1930s. Although prior to World War I he was an expansionist and interventionist, during the interwar period he talked more about the horrors of war. In an August 1936 speech at Chautauqua, New York, Roosevelt appealed to pacifist voters in advance of the presidential election. The United States, he promised, would remain unentangled in the European conflict. During the crisis over Czechoslovakia in 1938, Roosevelt endorsed appeasement.

Quietly, though, Roosevelt began readying the country for war. In early 1938, he successfully pressured the House of Representatives to defeat a constitutional amendment that would require a majority vote in a national referendum before a congressional declaration of war could go into effect (unless the United States were attacked). Later that year, in the wake of the Munich crisis, Roosevelt asked Congress for funds to build up the air force. In January 1939, the president secretly decided to sell bombers to France, saying privately that "our frontier is on the Rhine."

For Roosevelt and for other Western leaders, Hitler's swallowing of Czechoslovakia in March 1939 proved a turning point. Before then, they could explain away Hitler's actions by saying he was only trying to reunite German-speaking peoples. They now realized it would take force to stop him. When Hitler began eyeing Poland, London and Paris stood by the Poles. Undaunted, Berlin signed a nonaggression pact with Moscow in August 1939. The pact included a top-secret protocol that carved eastern Europe into German and Soviet zones and permitted the Soviets to grab the eastern half of Poland and the three Baltic states of Lithuania, Estonia, and Latvia, formerly part of the Russian Empire.

Poland and the Outbreak of World War II

Early on September 1, German tanks rolled into Poland. German fighting planes covered the advance, thereby launching a new type of warfare, the *blitzkrieg* (lightning war)—highly mobile land forces and armor combined with tactical aircraft. Within forty-eight hours, Britain and France declared war on Germany.

When Europe descended into war in September 1939, Roosevelt declared neutrality and pressed for repeal of the arms embargo. After much debate, Congress in November lifted the embargo on contraband and approved cash-and-carry exports of arms. Using "methods short of war," Roosevelt thus began to aid the Allies. Hitler sneered that a "half Judaized … half Negrified" United States was "incapable of conducting war."

German leader Adolf Hitler (1889–1945) is surrounded in this propagandistic painting by images that came to symbolize hate, genocide, and war: Nazi flags with emblems of the swastika, the iron cross on the dictator's pocket, Nazi troops in loyal salute. The anti-Semitic Hitler denounced the United States as a "Jewish rubbish heap" of "inferiority and decadence" that was "incapable of conducting war."

Asian Tensions

In Asia, meanwhile, Japan was on the march. The United States had interests at stake in the region: the Philippines and Pacific islands, religious missions, trade and investments, and the Open Door in China. In missionary fashion, Americans also believed that they were China's special friend and protector.

In the late 1920s, civil war broke out in China when Jiang Jieshi (Chiang Kai-shek) ousted Mao Zedong and his communist followers from the ruling Guomindang Party. Americans applauded this display of anti-Bolshevism and Jiang's conversion to Christianity in 1930. U.S. officials signed a treaty in 1928 restoring control of tariffs to the Chinese.

Japan continued to pressure the Chinese (see Map 22.5). In mid-1937, owing to Japanese provocation, the Sino-Japanese War erupted. Japanese forces seized Beijing and several coastal cities. To help China by permitting it to buy American arms, Roosevelt refused to declare the existence of war, thus avoiding activation of the Neutrality Acts.

MAP 22.5

Japanese Expansion Before Pearl Harbor

The Japanese quest for predominance began at the turn of the century and intensified in the 1930s. China suffered the most at the hands of Tokyo's military. Vulnerable U.S. possessions in Asia and the Pacific proved no obstacle to Japan's ambitions for a Greater East Asia Co-Prosperity Sphere. Source: Copyright © Cengage Learning 2015

Roosevelt's Quarantine Speech

On October 5, 1937, the president called for a "quarantine" to curb the "epidemic of world lawlessness." People who thought Washington had been too gentle with Japan cheered. Isolationists warned that Roosevelt was edging toward war. On December 12, Japanese aircraft sank the American gunboat *Panay*, an escort for Standard Oil Company tankers on the Yangtze River, killing two American sailors. Roosevelt was relieved when Tokyo apologized and offered to pay for damages.

Japan's declaration of a "New Order" in Asia, in the words of one American official, "banged, barred, and bolted" the Open Door. Alarmed, the Roosevelt administration during the late 1930s gave loans and sold military equipment to Jiang's Chinese government. In mid-1939, the United States abrogated its trade treaty with Tokyo, yet Americans continued to ship oil, cotton, and machinery to Japan. The administration hesitated to initiate economic sanctions because such pressure might spark a Japanese-American war at a time when Germany posed a more serious threat and the United States was unprepared for war.

Social Security

The New Deal's Social Security system expanded over subsequent decades, and now covers almost 99 percent of American workers. But today's Social Security system faces an uncertain future. Its troubles are due in part to decisions made during the 1930s. President Franklin Roosevelt did not want Social Security to be confused with poor relief. Instead, he created a system financed by payments from workers and their employers. This system, however, presented a short-term problem. If benefits came from their own contributions, workers who began receiving Social Security payments in 1940 would have received less than $1 a month. Therefore, Social Security payments from current workers paid the benefits of those already retired.

Over the years, this financing system has become increasingly unstable. In 1935, average life expectancy was lower than sixty-five years, the age one could collect benefits. Today, on average, American men live almost sixteen years past sixty-five, and women come close to twenty more years. In 1935, there were 16 current workers paying into the system for each person receiving retirement benefits. In 2010, there were 2.8 workers per retiree. Unless the system is reformed, many argue, the continuing retirement of the baby-boom cohort could even bankrupt the system.

While the stock market rose rapidly during the 1990s, some proposed that, because Social Security paid only a fraction of what individuals might have earned by investing their Social Security tax payments in stocks, Americans be allowed to do just that. Some opponents declared this proposal too risky; others asked if current workers kept their money to invest, where would benefits for current retirees come from? The stock market's huge drop in 2001 and then the long-lasting economic downturn that began in 2008 (and the losses sustained by private pension funds) slowed the push for privatization. Nonetheless, as baby boomers retire in growing numbers, questions about the future of Social Security remain an important part of the system's legacy.

Summary

In the 1930s, a major economic crisis and the approach of another world war threatened the future of the nation. By 1933, almost one-quarter of America's workers were unemployed. Millions were hungry or homeless. Herbert Hoover, elected president in 1928, believed that government should play a limited role in managing the economy and rejected both public jobs programs and aid to the poor. President Franklin Delano Roosevelt, elected in 1932, acted decisively to stabilize America's capitalist system and then worked to ameliorate its harshest impacts on the nation's people.

The New Deal expanded the role and power of the federal government. Because of New Deal reforms, banks, utilities, stock markets, farms, and most businesses operated under rules set by the federal government. Federal law guaranteed workers' right to join unions and required employers to negotiate with unions. New Deal programs offered public jobs to the unemployed and guaranteed many Americans the basic protection of a national welfare system.

The New Deal faced challenges from many directions, including populist demagogues and business leaders. As the federal government expanded its role, tensions between national and local authority sometimes flared up. Both the West and the

South were transformed by federal government action, but citizens there were suspicious of federal intervention, and white southerners resisted attempts to challenge systems of racial discrimination. The political realities of a fragile New Deal coalition and strong opposition shaped—and limited—New Deal programs of the 1930s and the social welfare systems with which Americans still live today.

New Deal programs helped many of America's people live better, more secure lives. But it took World War II and the economic boom it created to end the Great Depression. As the crises in Europe and Asia deepened in the last years of the 1930s, the Roosevelt administration sought to keep the United States out of the fray; even after Nazi forces invaded Poland in September 1939, thus sparking a new European struggle, the president declared American neutrality. As he did so, however, he sent aid to the Allies and began preparing the country for war.

Chapter Review

Hoover and Hard Times, 1929–1933

Why was Hoover reluctant to implement relief programs during the Great Depression?

Hoover believed in limited government and feared that government relief would promote entitlement and weaken self-reliance among the poor. When he made federal funds available to feed livestock, but not people, he was reviled by Americans. By the time he finally initiated federal jobs programs, it was too late to change public opinion. His public works projects, such as the Grand Coulee Dam, created some jobs, but nowhere near enough. Hoover's most direct government program—the Reconstruction Finance Corporation implemented in 1932—offered relief to businesses, but still provided no direct relief for the unemployed.

Franklin D. Roosevelt and the Launching of the New Deal

How did the federal government take on new roles during the period dubbed "The First Hundred Days"?

During this special session of Congress held after his election in 1932, Roosevelt sought to revive the economy through economic planning and relief programs. Both would expand federal power. The planning portion of this "New Deal" focused on the National Industrial Recovery Act (NIRA) and the Agricultural Adjustment Act (AAA). The NIRA encouraged industries to adopt wage and price standards that could erase competition and increase consumer spending and, therefore, demand for workers. The AAA established crop controls and offered farm subsidies. Roosevelt also spent $3 billion on work relief programs, such as the Civilian Conservation Corps, which hired young men to help build dams, reservoirs, and trails in national parks; and the Public Works Administration, whose workers built New York City's Triborough Bridge and hundreds of other public facilities. Fifteen laws were passed, and unemployment dropped from 13 million in 1933 to 9 million in 1936.

Political Pressure and the Second New Deal

What were the hallmarks of the Second New Deal?

Responding to political pressure, the Roosevelt administration increased direct economic support for Americans. The Emergency Relief Appropriation Act allocated $4 billion in deficit spending to provide public works jobs through the Works Progress Administration (WPA)—building roads, bridges, and parks and renovating schools and hospitals. It also employed artists, writers, and actors. The Resettlement Administration relocated poor families and organized communities for low-income workers, while the Rural Electrification Administration brought electricity to rural areas. The most important legislation was the Social Security Act, which created a federal pension system, unemployment benefits, and welfare for needy families.

Labor

How did Roosevelt provide support for labor?

Roosevelt bolstered labor's rights with the 1935 National Labor Relations (Wagner) Act, which guaranteed workers the right to organize unions and bargain collectively. The act made it illegal for businesses to fire workers who joined unions and banned management from sponsoring company unions. It also required firms to bargain with union representatives about wages, hours, and working conditions and created a National Labor Relations Board to mediate disputes. As the NLRB took hold, violence dissipated and workers' wages increased.

Federal Power and the Nationalization of Culture

In what ways did the Depression inspire the emergence of a youth culture?

Government policies focused on channeling jobs to the male heads of household. That meant that young boys who, at age fourteen, under normal economic conditions would have gone to work, could not find jobs. Hence, they stayed in school longer, and high school graduation rates doubled by the end of the decade. As young people spent more time in school, they developed a shared youth culture reflected in shared choices of music, clothing, and behavior.

The Limits of the New Deal

How did Roosevelt undermine his New Deal agenda?

Three of Roosevelt's decisions had negative consequences for the New Deal. Concerned that the Supreme Court would rule against future initiatives, Roosevelt in 1937 asked Congress to give him the authority to appoint six new justices, arguing that the present nine were getting old and were overworked. Congress refused and, although FDR was eventually able to name seven new associate justices, his political credibility was damaged. Second, Roosevelt reduced government spending in 1937, which, along with tightened credit, sent the economy into a tailspin. Third, in 1939, with war intensifying in Europe, Roosevelt traded further domestic reform for conservatives' support for military rearmament.

The Approach of War

How did President Roosevelt respond to the rising tensions in Europe between 1935 and the outbreak of war in 1939?

Roosevelt initially sought to keep the United States out of the war. Between 1935 and 1937, he signed three neutrality acts, which prohibited arms shipments, forbade loans to belligerents, and introduced the cash-and-carry principle. By 1938, however, he began quietly readying the country for war. Early that year, he successfully pressured the House of Representatives to defeat a constitutional amendment that would require a majority vote in a national referendum before a congressional declaration of war could take effect (unless the nation were attacked). After the Munich crisis, Roosevelt asked Congress for funds to build up the air force. In January 1939, he secretly decided to sell bombers to France. When Europe descended into war in September 1939, Roosevelt declared neutrality and pressed for repeal of the arms embargo. Congress in November lifted the embargo and approved cash-and-carry exports of arms. Using "methods short of war," Roosevelt thus began to aid the Allies.

Suggestions for Further Reading

Anthony J. Badger, *The New Deal: The Depression Years, 1933–1940* (1989)

Alan Brinkley, *The End of Reform: New Deal Liberalism in Recession and War* (1995)

Alan Brinkley, *Voices of Protest: Huey Long, Father Coughlin, and the Great Depression* (1982)

Lizabeth Cohen, *Making a New Deal: Industrial Workers in Chicago* (1990)

Blanche Wiesen Cook, *Eleanor Roosevelt*, Vols. 1 and 2 (1992, 1999)

Timothy Egan, *The Worst Hard Time* (2005)

Sidney Fine, *Sitdown: The General Motors Strike of 1936–37* (1969)

James E. Goodman, *Stories of Scottsboro* (1994)

David M. Kennedy, *Freedom from Fear: The American People in Depression and War* (1999)

Robert McElvaine, *The Great Depression: America, 1929–1941* (1984)

Eric Rauchway, *The Great Depression and the New Deal: A Very Short Introduction* (2008)

Jason Scott Smith, *Building New Deal Liberalism: The Political Economy of Public Works, 1933–1956* (2005)

Donald Worster, *Dust Bowl: The Southern Plains in the 1930s* (2004)

The Second World War at Home and Abroad

23

1939–1945

The first wave of planes launched before dawn from Japanese aircraft carriers less than three hundred miles north of O'ahu; a second wave followed soon thereafter. At the island's north shore, one group circled leeward toward the battleships anchored at Pearl Harbor; a second swept down the center of the island between the Ko'olau and the Waianae mountain ranges. Most of the people outside that Sunday morning paid them little mind, as war games were common in Hawai'i by that point. Watching planes diving on Pearl Harbor from the control tower at the adjacent army air base, Colonel William Farthing mused, "I wonder what the marines are doing to the navy so early on Sunday morning." Seconds later, a Japanese plane dived toward the air base and dropped a bomb.

On the battleship *West Virginia*, Ship's Cook Third Class Doris Miller was collecting laundry when the general quarters alarm sounded. Miller, a 6'3", three-hundred-pound African American man whom the navy restricted to mess service because of his race, reported to the bridge. Miller took over a .50-caliber Browning anti-aircraft gun—a weapon he'd never before fired—manning it until he ran out of ammunition and the order came to abandon the sinking ship. In Honolulu, seventeen-year-old Daniel Inouye—the son of a Japanese immigrant, who would win the Medal of Honor for heroism in the coming war and eventually serve as president pro tempore of the U.S. Senate—worked for twenty-four hours without rest at the Red Cross station at Lunalilo School. As casualties mounted, prostitutes turned the infamous brothels of Hotel Street into temporary hospital wards and nursed the badly wounded.

Japanese planes sank or severely damaged all eight of America's Pacific Fleet battleships. They destroyed or badly damaged 188 planes. More than 2,400 people died in the two-hour attack. That night the people of Hawai'i spent their first night under martial law, the islands completely dark against the threat of another attack.

By December 7, 1941, Europe and Asia were already in flames. Now the United States would join the world war.

For forty-five months, Americans fought abroad to subdue the German, Italian, and Japanese aggressors. The Second World War began badly for the United States, but by mid-1942 the Allies had halted the Axis powers' advance. In June 1944, American troops, together with Canadian, British, and Free French units, launched a massive invasion across the English Channel, landing at Normandy and pushing into Germany by the following spring. Battered by bombing raids, leaderless after Adolf Hitler's suicide, and pressed by a Soviet advance, the Nazis capitulated in May 1945. In the Pacific, Americans drove Japanese forces back. America's devastating conventional bombing of Japanese cities, followed by the atomic bombs that demolished Hiroshima and Nagasaki in August 1945 and the Soviet Union's declaration of war on Japan, led to surrender. At the end of the war, the nations that made up the "Grand Alliance"—Britain, the Soviet Union, and the United States—had very different visions of the postwar world.

The war was fought far from the United States, but it touched the lives of all Americans. This was a total war, in which the nation mobilized all sectors of its society and economy to defeat the Axis powers. The federal government, which had the monumental task of managing the war on all fronts, expanded its reach and power.

Committed to becoming the "arsenal of democracy," the United States built a massive war industry that demanded workers for seven-day-a-week, twenty-four-hour-a-day production. These factories created new opportunities for formerly marginal workers: women, African Americans, Latinos. After a decade of economic depression, Americans found new prosperity. The war strengthened unity and national purpose, but it also gave new shape to long-standing prejudices: the United States interned 112,000 Japanese nationals and Japanese Americans in remote "relocation camps" and fought the Axis with a racially segregated military. At war's end, although many Americans grieved for loved ones and worried about the stability of the emerging postwar order, the United States had unprecedented power and prosperity.

As you read this chapter, keep the following questions in mind:

- **What factors brought the United States into the war?**

- **What military, diplomatic, and social factors influenced decisions about how to fight the Second World War?**

- **How did World War II transform the United States?**

America's Entry into the Conflict

How did Roosevelt and Congress begin to aid the Allies after the German advances of early 1940?

When a new European war broke out in 1939, polls showed that Americans favored the Allies and that most supported aid to Britain and France, but the great majority emphatically wanted the United States to remain at peace. Troubled by this conflicting advice—oppose Hitler, aid the Allies, but stay out of the war—Roosevelt gradually moved the nation from neutrality to

Chronology

1939	Germany invades Poland; World War II begins
1940	France and the Low Countries fall to the Germans
1941	Lend-Lease Act passed by Congress
	Atlantic Charter issued by Roosevelt and Churchill
	Japan attacks Pearl Harbor
	United States enters World War II
1942	War Production Board created to oversee conversion to military production
	Allies losing war in Pacific to Japan; U.S. victory at Battle of Midway in June is turning point
	Office of Price Administration creates rationing system for food and consumer goods
	United States pursues "Europe First" war policy; Allies reject Stalin's demands for a second front and invade North Africa
	West Coast Japanese Americans relocated to internment camps
	Manhattan Project set up to create atomic bomb
	Congress of Racial Equality established
1943	Soviet army defeats German troops at Stalingrad

	Congress passes War Labor Disputes (Smith-Connally) Act following coal miners' strike
	"Zoot suit riots" in Los Angeles; race riots break out in Detroit and other cities
	Allies invade Italy
	Roosevelt, Churchill, and Stalin meet at Tehran Conference
1944	Allied troops land at Normandy on D-Day, June 6
	Roosevelt elected to fourth term as president
	United States retakes Philippines
1945	Roosevelt, Stalin, and Churchill meet at Yalta Conference
	British and U.S. forces firebomb Dresden, Germany
	Battles of Iwo Jima and Okinawa result in heavy Japanese and American losses
	Roosevelt dies; Truman becomes president
	Germany surrenders; Allied forces liberate Nazi death camps
	Potsdam Conference calls for Japan's "unconditional surrender"
	United States uses atomic bombs on Hiroshima and Nagasaki
	Japan surrenders

undeclared war against Germany and then, after the Japanese attack on Pearl Harbor, to full-scale war.

Because the stakes were so high, Americans vigorously debated the direction of their foreign policy from 1939 through 1941. Unprecedented numbers of Americans spoke out on foreign affairs and joined organizations that addressed the issues. Spine-chilling events and the widespread use of radio helped stimulate public interest. So did ethnic affiliations with the various belligerents and victims of aggression. The American Legion, the League of Women Voters, labor unions, and local chapters of the Committee to Defend America by Aiding the Allies and of the isolationist America First Committee (both organized in 1940) provided outlets for citizen participation in the national debate. African American churches organized anti-Italian boycotts to protest Mussolini's pummeling of Ethiopia.

In March 1940, the Soviet Union invaded Finland. In April, Germany conquered Denmark and Norway (see Map 22.4). On May 10, 1940, Germany attacked Belgium, the Netherlands, and France, ultimately pushing French and British forces back to the English Channel. At Dunkirk, France, between May 26 and June 6, more than three hundred thousand Allied soldiers frantically escaped to Britain on a flotilla of small boats. The Germans occupied Paris a week later. A new French government located in the town of Vichy collaborated with the Nazis and, on June 22, surrendered France to Berlin. With France out of the war, the German Luftwaffe (air force) launched massive bombing raids against Great Britain.

Alarmed by the swift defeat of one European nation after another, Americans gradually shed their isolationist sentiment. Assuring Americans that New Deal reforms would not be sacrificed for military preparedness, the president began to aid the Allies to prevent the fall of Britain. In May 1940, he ordered the sale of old surplus military equipment to Britain and France. In July, he cultivated bipartisan support by naming Republicans Henry L. Stimson and Frank Knox, backers of aid to the Allies, secretaries of war and the navy, respectively. In September, the president traded fifty overage American destroyers for leases to eight British military bases, including Newfoundland, Bermuda, and Jamaica.

First Peacetime Military Draft

Two weeks later, Roosevelt signed the hotly debated and narrowly passed **Selective Training and Service Act**, the first peacetime military draft in American history. The act called for the registration of all men between the ages of twenty-one and thirty-five; more than 16 million men signed up. Meanwhile, Roosevelt won reelection in November 1940 with promises of peace: "Your boys are not going to be sent into any foreign wars."

Roosevelt claimed that the United States could avoid war by enabling the British to win. In January 1941, Congress debated the president's **Lend-Lease bill**. Because Britain was broke, the president explained, the United States should lend rather than sell weapons. In March 1941, with pro-British sentiment running high, Congress passed the measure. The initial appropriation was $7 billion, but by the end of the war the amount had reached $50 billion, more than $31 billion of it for Britain.

To ensure delivery of Lend-Lease goods, Roosevelt ordered the U.S. Navy to patrol halfway across the Atlantic, and he sent American troops to Greenland and Iceland. He also sent Lend-Lease aid to the Soviet Union, which Hitler had attacked in June (thereby shattering the 1939 Nazi-Soviet nonaggression pact). If the Soviets could hold off two hundred German divisions in the east, Roosevelt calculated, Britain would gain some breathing room.

Atlantic Charter

In August 1941, **Winston Churchill** and Roosevelt met for four days on a British battleship off the coast of Newfoundland. The two leaders issued the **Atlantic Charter**, a set of war aims reminiscent of Wilsonianism: collective security, disarmament, self-determination, economic cooperation, and freedom of the seas. Churchill later recalled that the president told him in Newfoundland that he could not ask Congress for a declaration of war against Germany, but "he would wage war" and "become more and more provocative."

On September 4, a German submarine launched torpedoes at (but did not hit) the American destroyer *Greer*. Henceforth, Roosevelt said, the U.S. Navy would fire first when under threat. He also made good on a private promise to Churchill: American warships would convoy British merchant ships across the ocean. Thus, the

Selective Training and Service Act Law that required all men between twenty-one and thirty-five (later expanded to eighteen through forty-five) to register with local draft boards.

Lend-Lease bill Program proposed by Roosevelt to supply war material to cash-strapped Britain.

Winston Churchill British wartime prime minister; close friend of FDR and staunch ally of the United States; served 1940–1945 and 1951–1955.

Atlantic Charter Document that condemned international aggression, affirmed the right of national self-determination, and endorsed the principles of free trade, disarmament, and collective security.

Link to The Atlantic Charter (1941)

Men do conscription exercises as they become part of America's first peacetime military draft in 1940.

Photo by Ralph Morse/Pix Inc./Time Life Pictures/Getty Images

United States entered into an undeclared naval war with Germany. When in early October a German submarine torpedoed the U.S. destroyer *Kearny* off the coast of Iceland, the president announced that "history has recorded who fired the first shot." Later that month, when more than one hundred Americans died in the sinking of the destroyer *Reuben James*, Congress scrapped the cash-and-carry policy and revised the Neutrality Acts to permit transport of munitions to Britain on armed American merchant ships. The United States was edging close to being a belligerent.

U.S. Demands on Japan It seems ironic, therefore, that the Second World War came to the United States by way of Asia. Roosevelt wanted to avoid war with Japan in order to concentrate on Germany. In September 1940, after Germany, Italy, and Japan signed the Tripartite Pact (to form the Axis powers), Roosevelt slapped an embargo on shipments of aviation fuel and scrap metal to Japan. After Japanese troops occupied French Indochina in July 1941, Washington froze Japanese assets in the United States, virtually ending trade with Japan.

Tokyo recommended a summit meeting between Roosevelt and Prime Minister Prince Konoye, but American officials insisted that the Japanese first agree to respect China's sovereignty and honor the Open Door policy. Roosevelt supported Secretary Hull's hard-line policy against Japan's pursuit of the Greater East Asia Co-Prosperity Sphere—the name Tokyo gave to the vast Asian region it intended to dominate.

Roosevelt told his advisers to string out ongoing Japanese-American talks to gain time to fortify the Philippines and check the fascists in Europe. By breaking the Japanese diplomatic code, American officials learned that Tokyo's patience with diplomacy was dissipating. In late November, the Japanese rejected American demands to withdraw from Indochina. A message decoded on December 3 instructed the Japanese embassy in Washington to burn codes and destroy cipher machines, suggesting that war was coming.

Surprise Attack on Pearl Harbor In a daring raid on Pearl Harbor in Hawai'i, an armada of sixty Japanese ships, including six carriers bearing 360 airplanes, crossed three thousand miles of the Pacific Ocean. To avoid detection, they maintained radio silence. Early on December 7, some 230 miles northwest of Honolulu, the carriers unleashed their planes, dropping torpedoes and bombs on the unsuspecting American naval base and nearby airfields. A Japanese bomb that ignited explosives below the deck of the battleship USS *Arizona* killed more than 1,000 sailors. The USS *Nevada* was hit in a second aerial attack. A total of 2,403 died; 1,178 were wounded. The Pearl Harbor tragedy, from the perspective of the war's outcome, amounted to a military inconvenience more than a disaster.

Explaining Pearl Harbor How could the stunning attack on Pearl Harbor have happened? American cryptanalysts had broken the Japanese diplomatic code, but the intercepts never revealed naval or military plans and never mentioned Pearl Harbor specifically. Roosevelt did not, as some critics charged, conspire to leave the fleet vulnerable to attack so that the United States could enter the war through the "back door" of Asia. The base at Pearl Harbor was not on red alert because a message from Washington warning of the imminence of war had been too casually transmitted and had arrived too late. Base commanders believed Hawai'i too far from Japan to be a target. Like Roosevelt's advisers, they expected an assault on British Malaya, Thailand, or the Philippines (see Map 22.5). The Pearl Harbor calamity stemmed from mistakes and insufficient information, not from conspiracy.

On December 8, referring to the previous day as "a date which will live in infamy," Roosevelt asked Congress for a declaration of war against Japan. He noted that the Japanese had also attacked Malaya, Hong Kong, Guam, the Philippines, Wake, and Midway. A unanimous vote in the Senate and a 388-to-1 vote in the House thrust America into war. Representative Jeannette Rankin of Montana voted no, as she had for World War I. Britain declared war on Japan, but the Soviet Union did not. Three days later, Germany and Italy, honoring the Tripartite Pact they had signed with Japan in September 1940, declared war against the United States.

Link to President Roosevelt's Address to Congress, December 8th, 1941

A fundamental clash of systems explains why war came. Germany and Japan preferred a world divided into closed spheres of influence. The United States sought a liberal capitalist world order. American principles manifested respect for human rights; fascists in Europe and militarists in Asia trampled such rights. The United States prided itself on democracy; Germany and Japan embraced authoritarian regimes. When the United States protested against German and Japanese expansion, Berlin and Tokyo charged that Washington conveniently ignored its own sphere of influence in Latin America and its own history of military and economic aggrandizement. Such incompatible objectives and outlooks obstructed diplomacy and made war likely.

Avoidable War? War was likely, but perhaps not inevitable. Privately, American planners admitted they were largely powerless to affect Japan's moves in China; they further conceded among themselves that any Japanese withdrawal from China would take many months to carry out. So why not assent, grudgingly, to the Japanese presence in China and also reopen at least limited trade with the Tokyo government, in order to forestall further Japanese expansion in Southeast Asia? Such a policy would have delayed any showdown with Japan, allowed concentration on the European war, and given Washington more time to rearm. It was not to be, though, and the United States now prepared to wage war in two theaters half a world apart.

The United States at War

Was the United States prepared for war when it entered World War II?

Although the Japanese bombing of Hawai'i was a surprise, the United States had not stood idly as the rest of the world went to war. America's embargo of shipments to Japan and refusal to accept Japan's expansionist policies had brought the two nations to the brink of war, and the United States was deeply involved in an undeclared naval war with Germany well before Japan's attack on

Pearl Harbor. By December 1941, Roosevelt had long since instituted an unprecedented peacetime draft, created war mobilization agencies, and commissioned war plans for simultaneous struggle in Europe and the Pacific.

A Nation Unprepared

Nonetheless, the nation was not ready for war. Throughout the 1930s, military funding was a low priority. In September 1939 (when Hitler invaded Poland and began World War II), the U.S. Army ranked forty-fifth in size among the world's armies and could fully equip only one-third of its 227,000 men. The peacetime draft expanded the U.S. military to 2 million men, but Roosevelt's 1941 survey of war preparedness estimated that the United States could not be ready to fight before June 1943.

In December 1941, the Allies were losing the war (see Map 22.4). Hitler had claimed Austria, Czechoslovakia, Poland, the Netherlands, Denmark, and Norway. Romania was lost, then Greece and Bulgaria. France had fallen in June 1940. Britain fought on, but German planes rained bombs on London. More than 3 million German-led soldiers had penetrated deep into the Soviet Union and Africa. German U-boats controlled the Atlantic. Within months of America's entry into the war, German submarines sank 216 vessels—some so close to American shores that people could see the glow of burning ships.

War in the Pacific

In the Pacific, the war was largely America's to fight. The Soviets had not declared war on Japan, and there were too few British troops protecting Great Britain's Asian colonies to make much difference. By late spring 1942, Japan had captured most European colonial possessions in Southeast Asia. The Japanese attacked the Philippines hours after Pearl Harbor and destroyed U.S. air capability in the region. American and Filipino troops retreated to the Bataan Peninsula, hoping to hold the main island, Luzon, but Japanese forces were superior. In March 1942, General Douglas MacArthur, the commander of U.S. forces in the Far East, departed the Philippines for Australia, proclaiming, "I shall return."

Left behind were almost eighty thousand American and Filipino troops. Starving and sick, they held on for almost another month before surrendering. Japanese troops were not prepared to deal with a large number of prisoners, and most believed the prisoners had forfeited honorable treatment by surrendering. In what came to be known as the Bataan Death March, the Japanese force-marched their captives to prison camps 80 miles away, denying them food and water and bayoneting or beating to death those who fell behind. As many as ten thousand Filipinos and six hundred Americans died on the march. Tens of thousands of Filipino civilians also died under Japanese occupation.

The United States struck back. On April 18, sixteen American B-25s appeared over Japan. The Doolittle raid (named after the mission's leader) did little harm but pushed Japanese commander Yamamoto to bold action. Japan moved to lure the weakened United States into a "decisive battle." The target was Midway—two tiny islands about one thousand miles northwest of Honolulu. If Japan could take Midway, it would have a secure defensive perimeter far from the home islands (see Map 23.3). By using Guam, the Philippines, and perhaps even Australia as hostages, Japan believed, it could negotiate a favorable peace agreement with the United States.

General Yamamoto did not know that America's MAGIC code-breaking machines could decipher Japanese messages. When the Japanese fleet arrived, it found the U.S. Navy lying in wait. The Battle of Midway in June 1942 was a turning point in the Pacific war. Japan's hope to force the United States to withdraw, leaving Japan to control the Pacific, vanished. Now Japan was on the defensive.

"Europe First" Strategy

Despite the importance of these early Pacific battles, America's war strategy was "Europe First." American war planners believed that if Germany conquered the Soviet Union, it might directly threaten the United States. Roosevelt also feared that the Soviet Union, suffering almost unimaginable losses against Hitler, might pursue a separate peace with Germany and so undo the Allied coalition. Therefore, the United States would work with Britain and the USSR to defeat Germany, then deal with an isolated Japan.

British prime minister Winston Churchill and Soviet premier **Joseph Stalin** disagreed over strategy. By late 1941, before the Russian winter stalled their onslaught, German troops had nearly reached Moscow and Leningrad (present-day St. Petersburg) and had slashed into Ukraine, taking Kiev. Over a million Soviet soldiers had died. Stalin pressed for British and American troops to attack Germany from the west to draw German troops away from the Soviet front. Roosevelt agreed and promised to open a "second front" before the end of 1942. Churchill, however, blocked this plan. He had not forgotten Stalin's nonaggression pact with Hitler (see page 663), and British military commanders opposed launching a large-scale invasion of Europe. Churchill promoted air attacks on Germany. He wanted to win control of the North Atlantic shipping lanes and to launch a smaller attack on Axis positions in North Africa; halting the Germans there would protect British imperial possessions in the Mediterranean and the oil-rich Middle East.

Against his advisers' recommendation, Roosevelt accepted Churchill's plan. The U.S. military was not ready for a major campaign, and Roosevelt needed to show the American public some success in the European war. Thus, instead of rescuing the USSR, the British and Americans landed in North Africa in November 1942, winning quick victories in Algeria and Morocco. In Egypt, the British defeated General Erwin Rommel and his Afrika Korps in a struggle for control of the Suez Canal and the Middle East oil fields. Meanwhile, the Soviet Union lost 1.1 million men in the Battle of Stalingrad but defeated the German Sixth Army there in early 1943. Stalingrad, like Midway, was a major turning point in the war. By the spring of 1943, Germany, like Japan, was on the defensive. But relations among the Allies remained precarious, as the United States and Britain continued to resist Stalin's demand for a second front.

Joseph Stalin Soviet premier and dictator of the Soviet Union who came to power after the death of Vladimir Lenin in 1924 and ruled until his death in 1953.

The Production Front and American Workers

How did wartime production needs create a new relationship between government and business, and government and science?

Although the war would be fought on the battlefields of Europe and the Pacific, the nation's strategic advantage lay on the "production front" at home. Roosevelt pledged that America would serve as the world's "great arsenal of democracy"—making the machines that would win the war for the Allies—and would prevail through a "crushing superiority of equipment."

Goals for military production were staggering. In 1940, American factories built only 3,807 airplanes. Following Pearl Harbor, Roosevelt asked for 60,000 aircraft in 1942 and double that number in 1943. Plans called for building 16 million tons of shipping and 120,000 tanks. The military needed supplies for a force that would grow to almost 16 million men. Thus, for the duration of the war, military production took precedence. Automobile plants built tanks and airplanes instead of cars; dress factories sewed military uniforms. The **War Production Board**, established in early 1942, allocated resources and coordinated production among thousands of independent factories.

War Production Board
Government agency established during WWII that allocated resources, coordinated production among thousands of independent factories, and awarded government contracts for wartime production.

Businesses and the War Effort

During the war, American businesses, inspired by patriotism and generous financial incentives, overwhelmingly cooperated with government war-production plans. In 1940, as the United States produced armaments for the Allies, the American economy had begun to recover, and industrialists gained confidence as consumer spending rose. Automobile manufacturers, for example, expected to sell 25 percent more cars in 1941 than in 1939. Manufacturers understood that it would be enormously expensive to retool factories to produce planes or tanks instead of cars, and that such retooling would leave them dependent on a single client—the federal government.

The federal government, however, met business more than halfway. It paid for retooling and factory expansions; it guaranteed profits by allowing corporations to charge the government for production costs plus a fixed profit; it created generous tax write-offs and exemptions from antitrust laws. Consequently, corporations doubled their net profits between 1939 and 1943. Most military contracts went to America's largest corporations, which had the facilities and experience to guarantee rapid, efficient production. As a result, wartime government contracts further consolidated American manufacturing in the hands of a few giant corporations.

Manhattan Project

Wartime needs also created a new relationship between science and the U.S. military. Millions of dollars funded university research programs, which developed new technologies of warfare, such as vastly improved radar systems. The most important government-sponsored research program was the **Manhattan Project**, a $2 billion secret effort to build an atomic bomb. Roosevelt was convinced by scientists fleeing the Nazis in 1939 that Germany was developing an atomic weapon, and he resolved to beat them to it. The Manhattan Project achieved the world's first sustained nuclear chain reaction in 1942 at the University of Chicago, and in 1943 the federal government established a secret community at Los Alamos, New Mexico, where atomic scientists worked with Jewish refugees to develop the weapon that would change the world.

Manhattan Project Secret program to develop the atomic bomb.

New Opportunities for Workers

America's new defense factories required millions of workers. At first, workers were plentiful: 9 million Americans were still unemployed in 1940 when war mobilization began. But the armed forces took almost 16 million men, forcing industry to look elsewhere for workers. Women, African Americans, Mexican Americans, and poor whites from Appalachia and the Deep South streamed into defense jobs.

In some cases, federal action eased their path. As many industries refused to hire African Americans, **A. Philip Randolph**, head of the Brotherhood of Sleeping Car Porters, proposed a march on Washington, D.C., to demand equal access to defense industry jobs. Roosevelt, fearing race riots and that communists might infiltrate this March on Washington movement, offered a deal. In exchange for canceling the march, the president issued Executive Order No. 8802, which prohibited discrimination in the defense industry and established the Fair Employment Practices Committee (FEPC) to deal with violations. Although enforcement was uneven, hundreds of thousands of black Americans left the South, seeking work and new lives in the industrial cities of the North and West.

A. Philip Randolph Labor leader whose threatened march on Washington led to the creation of Executive Order No. 8802, which prohibited racial discrimination in war industries and government jobs.

Mexican workers also filled wartime jobs in the United States, through the **bracero program**. About 200,000 Mexican farmworkers, or *braceros*, were offered short-term contracts to fill agricultural jobs left vacant as Americans sought well-paid war work. Mexican and Mexican American workers faced discrimination and segregation, but they seized these new economic opportunities. In 1941, the Los Angeles shipyards employed not a single Mexican American; by 1944, 17,000 worked there.

bracero program Wartime "temporary worker" measure that brought in seasonal farm laborers from Mexico.

Early in the war production boom, employers insisted that women were not suited for industrial jobs. But labor shortages changed their position. The government's War Manpower Commission glorified the invented worker "**Rosie the Riveter**," who was featured on posters, in magazines, and in the recruiting jingle "Rosie's got a boyfriend, Charlie / Charlie, he's a marine / Rosie is protecting Charlie / Working overtime on the riveting machine."

Rosie the Riveter Symbol of the woman war worker; the bulging muscles represented her strength as she aided the nation's war effort by taking jobs vacated by men who fought in the war.

Rosie the Riveter was an inspiring, albeit inaccurate, image. Only 16 percent of female employees worked in defense plants, and women filled only 4.4 percent of "skilled" jobs (such as riveting). Nonetheless the number of women in the workforce grew by 57 percent, as more than 6 million women took wartime jobs, while

War production plans called for defense factories to build 120,000 new aircraft in 1943. Here, women workers take on "men's jobs" at Vultee Aircraft Corporation, using riveting guns and bucking bars to build the center section of wings for training planes.

Bettmann/Corbis

other women—including over 400,000 African American domestic workers—moved to higher-paying industrial jobs, often with union benefits.

Workers in defense plants were often expected to work ten days for every day off or to accept difficult night shifts. Businesses and the federal government offered new forms of support to keep workers on the job. The West Coast Kaiser shipyards offered high pay, child care, subsidized housing, and health care. The federal government also funded child care centers and before- and after-school programs.

Organized Labor During Wartime

Because America's war strategy relied on industrial production, the federal government tried to prevent strikes. Days after Pearl Harbor, a White House labor-management conference agreed to a no-strike/no-lockout pledge, and in 1942, Roosevelt created the National War Labor Board (NWLB) to settle disputes. The NWLB forged a temporary compromise between labor union demands for a "closed shop," in which only union members could work, and management's desire for "open" shops: workers could not be required to join a union, but unions could enroll as many members as possible. Between 1940 and 1945, union membership ballooned from 8.5 million to 14.75 million.

The government did restrict union power if it threatened war production. When coal miners in the United Mine Workers union went on strike in 1943 after the NWLB attempted to limit wage increases to a cost-of-living adjustment, railroads and steel mills shut down for lack of coal. Few Americans supported this strike. As anti-labor sentiment grew, Congress passed the War Labor Disputes (Smith-Connally) Act, which granted the president authority to seize and operate any strike-bound plant deemed necessary to the national security.

Success on the Production Front

For nearly four years, American factories operated twenty-four hours a day, seven days a week, turning out roughly 300,000 airplanes, 102,000 armored vehicles, 77,000 ships, 20 million small arms, 40 billion bullets, and 6 million tons of bombs. By war's end, the United States was producing 40 percent of the world's weaponry. This feat depended on transforming formerly skilled work into assembly-line mass production. Henry Ford, for example, created a massive bomber plant outside Detroit. The plant's assembly lines, almost a mile long, produced one B-24 Liberator bomber every hour.

But this increased production came at a cost. Workers did dirty, repetitive, and physically exhausting work day after day "for the duration." During the first two years of the war 102,000 men and women were killed doing war production work, and more than 350,000 were seriously injured.

Life on the Home Front

What was the impact of the war on family life?

Americans grieved the loss of loved ones abroad, but bombs did not fall on American cities; invading armies did not burn and rape and kill. Instead, war mobilization brought prosperity.

Supporting the War Effort

Still, the war was a constant presence for Americans on "the home front." Although Americans were never so unified as the widespread images of "the greatest generation" suggest, civilians supported the war effort in many ways, and "shared sacrifice" was a powerful ideal and significant reality. During the war, families planted 20 million "victory gardens" to replace food that went to America's fighting men. Housewives saved cooking fat, which yielded glycerin to make black powder used in shells or bullets.

Many consumer goods were rationed or unavailable. To save wool for military use, the War Production Board directed that men's suits would have narrow lapels, shorter jackets, and no vests or pant cuffs. Bathing suits, the WPB specified, must shrink by 10 percent. The Office of Price Administration (OPA), created by Congress in 1942, established a nationwide rationing system for sugar, coffee, gasoline, meat, and other consumer goods. By early 1943, the OPA had instituted a point system for rationing food. Each citizen—regardless of age—was allotted 48 blue points (canned fruits and vegetables) and 64 red points (meat, fish, and dairy) a month. In September 1944 a small bottle of ketchup "cost" 20 blue points and sirloin steak 13 red points a pound (in addition to their cost in dollars and cents. Rationed goods were available on the black market, but most Americans understood that sugar produced alcohol for weapons manufacture and meat fed "our boys" overseas.

Propaganda and Popular Culture

Although Americans strongly supported the war, government leaders worried that they would gradually become less willing to sacrifice. The Office of War Information (OWI), created in 1942, used Hollywood filmmakers and New York copywriters to sell the war at home. OWI posters exhorted Americans to sacrifice, and reminded them to watch what they said, for "loose lips sink ships."

Popular culture also reinforced wartime messages. Songs urged Americans to "Remember December 7th" or to "Accentuate the Positive." Others made fun of America's enemies ("You're a sap, Mr. Jap / Uncle Sam is gonna spanky").

Movies drew 90 million viewers a week in 1944—out of a total population of 132 million. During the war Hollywood tried to meet Eleanor Roosevelt's challenge to "Keep 'em laughing," though some films, such as *Bataan* or *Wake Island*, portrayed actual—if sanitized—war events. But even in comedies, the war was present. Theaters held "plasma premieres" with free admission to those who donated blood to the Red Cross. Before the film began, audiences sang "The Star Spangled Banner" and watched newsreels with carefully censored combat footage. In movie theaters, Americans saw the horror of Nazi death camps in May 1945. The Universal newsreel narrator ordered audiences, "Don't turn away. Look."

Wartime Prosperity

The war demanded sacrifice from Americans, but between 1939 and the end of the war, per capita income rose from $691 to $1,515. OPA-administered price controls kept inflation down so that wage increases did not disappear to higher costs. And with little to buy, people saved money.

Visualizing THE PAST

Portraying the Enemy

Racial stereotyping affected how both the Americans and the Japanese waged war. The Americans badly underestimated the Japanese, leaving themselves open for the surprise attack on Pearl Harbor and American forces in the Philippines. And the Japanese, believing Americans were barbarians who lacked a sense of honor, mistakenly expected that the United States would withdraw from East Asia once confronted with Japanese power and determination. This cover for *Collier's* magazine, appearing shortly after the first anniversary of Japan's attack on Pearl Harbor, shows some of the most extreme racial imagery of the war, but it was scarcely alone. How is Japan portrayed here? How might the fact that Japan had launched an immensely successful surprise attack on the United States have shaped this image, or Americans' reactions to it?

American propaganda caricatured all the Axis powers, but the Japanese were most likely to be portrayed as subhuman.

World War II cost the United States approximately $304 billion (more than $3 trillion in today's dollars). Instead of relying mainly on taxes to pay for the war, the government sold war bonds—thus borrowing money from those who bought them. The national debt skyrocketed from $49 billion in 1941 to $259 billion in 1945 (and was not paid off until 1970). However, wartime legislation increased the number of Americans paying personal income tax from 4 million to 42.6 million—at rates ranging from 6 to 94 percent—and introduced a new system in which employers "withheld" taxes from employee paychecks. For the first time, individual Americans paid more in taxes than corporations.

A Nation in Motion

Despite hardships and fears, the war offered home-front Americans new opportunities. More than 15 million civilians moved during the war (see Map 23.1), including seven hundred thousand black Americans who left the South.

The rapid influx of war workers to cities and towns strained community resources. Migrants crowded into substandard housing—even woodsheds, tents, or cellars. Disease spread: scabies and ringworm, polio, tuberculosis. Many long-term residents found the newcomers—especially the unmarried male war

Increase in population
- Over 20%
- 10–19%
- 5–9%
- 0–4%

Decrease in population
- 0–5%

National average
- 14.5 % increase

MAP 23.1
A Nation on the Move, 1940–1950
American migration during the 1940s was the largest on record to that time. The farm population dropped dramatically as men, women, and children moved to war-production areas and to army and navy bases, particularly on the West Coast. Well over 30 million Americans (civilian and military) migrated during the war. Many returned to their rural homes after the war, but 12 million migrants stayed in their new locations. Notice the population increases on the West Coast as well as in the Southwest and Florida. Source: Copyright © Cengage Learning 2015

workers—a rough bunch. In and around Detroit, where car factories now produced tanks and planes, established residents called war workers freshly arrived from southern Appalachia "hillbillies" and "white trash."

Racial Conflicts

As people from different backgrounds confronted one another under difficult conditions, tensions rose. In 1943, almost 250 racial conflicts exploded in forty-seven cities. In Detroit in June, white mobs, undeterred by police, roamed the city, attacking blacks. Blacks hurled rocks at police and dragged white passengers off streetcars. After thirty hours of rioting, twenty-five blacks and nine whites lay dead.

In Los Angeles, young Mexican American gang members, or *pachucos*, wore zoot suits: long jackets with wide padded shoulders, loose pants "pegged" below the knee, wide-brimmed hats, and dangling watch chains. With cloth rationed, wearing pants requiring five yards of fabric was a political statement, and although a high percentage of Mexican Americans served in the armed forces, many white servicemen believed otherwise. Rumors that *pachucos* had attacked white sailors led to violence. For four days, mobs of white men—mainly soldiers and sailors—roamed the streets, attacking and stripping zoot-suiters. Los Angeles outlawed zoot suits, but the "zoot suit riots" ended only when naval personnel were removed from the city.

Families in Wartime

The dislocations of war also had profound impacts on the nation's families. Despite policies exempting married men and fathers from the draft during most of the war, almost 3 million families were broken up. The divorce rate of 16 per 1,000 marriages in 1940 increased to 27 per 1,000 in 1944. At the same time, the number of marriages rose from 73 per 1,000 unmarried women in 1939 to 93 in 1942. Some couples scrambled to get married before the man was sent overseas; others sought military deferments. Births climbed from 2.4 million babies in 1939 to 3.1 million in 1943. Many were "goodbye babies," conceived with the idea that the father might not survive the war.

On college campuses, women complained, along with the song lyrics, "There is no available male." But other young women found plenty of male company, sparking concerns about wartime threats to sexual morality. *Newsweek*, for example, warned of "victory girls" or "cuddle bunnies" who were said to support the war effort by giving their all to men in uniform. Many young men and women behaved as they never would in peacetime. Often that meant hasty marriages to virtual strangers, especially if a baby was on the way. Despite changes in behavior, taboos against unwed motherhood remained strong, and only 1 percent of births during the war were to unmarried women. Wartime mobility also increased opportunities for same-sex relationships, and gay communities grew in such cities as San Francisco.

In many ways, the war reinforced traditional gender roles that had weakened during the depression, when many men lost the breadwinner role. Now men defended their nation while women "kept the home fires burning," sometimes filling jobs vacated by soldiers "for the duration." Women who worked were frequently blamed for neglecting their children and creating an "epidemic" of juvenile delinquency. Nonetheless, millions of women took on new responsibilities in wartime, whether on the factory floor or within their family.

The Limits of American Ideals

In what ways were American notions of civil liberties and basic freedoms tested during the war years?

In 1941, Roosevelt had pledged America to defend "four essential human freedoms"—freedom of speech, freedom of religion, freedom from want, and freedom from fear. Government-sponsored films contrasted American democracy and freedom with totalitarianism and fascism. Yet as America fought the totalitarian regimes of the Axis powers, the nation confronted questions: What limits on civil liberties were justified in the interest of national security? How freely could information flow without revealing military secrets and costing American lives? How could the United States protect itself against spies or saboteurs, especially from German, Italian, or Japanese citizens living in the United States? And what about America's ongoing domestic problems—particularly the problem of race? The answers revealed tensions between the nation's democratic claims and its wartime practices.

For the most part, America handled the issue of civil liberties well. American leaders embraced a "strategy of truth," declaring that citizens required a truthful accounting of the war's progress. However, the government closely controlled information about military matters, as even seemingly unimportant details might tip off enemies about troop movements. While government-created propaganda sometimes dehumanized the enemy, especially the Japanese, the government resorted to hatemongering much less frequently than during the First World War.

More complex was the question of how to handle dissent and guard against the possibility that enemy agents operated within the nation's borders. The 1940 Alien Registration (Smith) Act made it unlawful to advocate the overthrow of the U.S. government by force or violence, or to join any organization that did so. After Pearl Harbor, the government took thousands of Germans, Italians, and other Europeans into custody as suspected spies and potential traitors. During the war, the government interned 14,426 Europeans in Enemy Alien Camps and prohibited ten thousand Italian Americans from living or working in restricted zones along the California coast.

Internment of Japanese Americans

In March 1942, Roosevelt ordered that all 112,000 foreign-born Japanese and Japanese Americans living in California, Oregon, and the state of Washington (the vast majority of the mainland population) be removed from the West Coast to "relocation centers." Each of the Italian and German nationals interned by the U.S. government faced individual charges. Japanese nationals and Japanese Americans, however, were imprisoned as a group, under suspicion solely because they were of Japanese descent.

American anger at Japan's "sneak attack" on Pearl Harbor fueled calls for internment, as did fears that West Coast cities might be attacked. Long-standing racism was evident, and people in economic competition with Japanese Americans also supported internment. Although Japanese nationals could not become U.S. citizens or own property, American-born Nissei (second generation) and Sansei (third generation), all U.S. citizens, were increasingly successful in business and agriculture. The eviction order forced Japanese Americans to sell property valued at $500 million for a fraction of its worth.

Links TO THE WORLD

Radio News

In radio's early years, network executives believed their job was to entertain Americans and that current affairs should be left to newspapers. Yet radio could do something that no previous medium could do: report news as it happened.

Franklin Roosevelt was among the first to grasp radio's potential. As governor of New York, he occasionally went on the air, and after becoming president, he commenced his Fireside Chats, reassuring Americans during the depression that the government was working hard to help them. So successful were these broadcasts that, in the words of one journalist, "The President has only to look toward a radio to bring Congress to terms."

Across the Atlantic, Adolf Hitler also used the radio to carry speeches directly to the German people. His message: Germany had been wronged by enemies abroad and by Marxists and Jews at home. But the Nazis under Hitler's direction would lead the country back to greatness. As "Sieg Heil!" thundered over the airwaves, millions of Germans saw Hitler as their salvation.

In 1938, as events in Europe reached a crisis, American radio networks increased news coverage. When Hitler annexed Austria in March, NBC and CBS broke into scheduled programs to deliver bulletins. Then, on March 13, CBS broadcast the first international news roundup, a half-hour show featuring live reports. A new era in American radio was born.

When leaders from France and Britain met with Hitler in Munich later that year, millions of Americans listened intently to live radio updates. Correspondents became well known, none more so than Edward R. Murrow of CBS. During the Nazi air blitz of London in 1940–1941, Murrow's rich, understated, nicotine-scorched voice kept Americans spellbound as he tried, as he put it, to "report suffering to people [Americans] who have not suffered."

Murrow was pro-Allies, and his reports strengthened the interventionist voices in Washington by emphasizing Winston Churchill's greatness and England's bravery. More than that, though, radio reports from Europe made Americans feel more closely linked than before to people living an ocean away.

Library of Congress Prints and Photographs Division[LC-USZ62-119757]

Edward R. Murrow at his typewriter in wartime London.

The internees were sent to camps in Arkansas's Mississippi River floodplain; Wyoming's intermountain terrain; the western Arizona desert; and other desolate spots in the West. The camps were bleak. Behind barbed wire, families lived in a single room furnished only with cots, blankets, and a bare light bulb. Most had no running water. Toilets and dining and bathing facilities were communal. People nonetheless attempted to sustain community life, setting up consumer cooperatives, establishing sports leagues, and for many, maintaining Buddhist worship.

Betrayed by their government, many internees were ambivalent about their loyalty to the United States. Some sought legal remedy, but the Supreme Court upheld internment in *Korematsu v. U.S.* (1944). Almost 6,000 of the 120,000 internees renounced U.S. citizenship and demanded to be sent to Japan. Far more sought to demonstrate their loyalty. The all–Japanese American 442nd Regimental Combat Team, drawn heavily from young men in internment camps, was the most decorated unit of its size and received a Congressional Medal of Honor, 47 Distinguished Service Crosses, 350 Silver Stars, and more than 3,600 Purple Hearts. In 1988, Congress issued a public apology and largely symbolic payment of $20,000 to each of the 60,000 surviving Japanese American internees.

African Americans and "Double V"

African American leaders wanted the nation to confront the parallels between Nazi racist doctrines and Jim Crow segregation in the United States. Proclaiming a "Double V" campaign (victory at home and abroad), groups such as the National Association for the Advancement of Colored People (NAACP) hoped to "persuade, embarrass, compel and shame our government and our nation … into a more enlightened attitude toward a tenth of its people." The NAACP, 50,000 strong in 1940, had 450,000 members by 1946. And in 1942, civil rights activists, influenced by the philosophy of India's Mohandas Gandhi, founded the Congress of Racial Equality (CORE), which stressed "nonviolent direct action" and staged sit-ins to desegregate restaurants and movie theaters in Chicago and Washington, D.C.

Military service was a key issue for African Americans, who understood the link between the duty to defend one's country and the rights of citizenship. But the U.S. military remained segregated by race and resisted using black units as combat troops. As late as 1943, less than 6 percent of the armed forces were African American, compared with more than 10 percent of the population.

A Segregated Military

The federal government and War Department decided that the midst of world war was no time to integrate the military. The majority of Americans (approximately 89 percent of Americans were white) opposed integration. Racist beliefs were so entrenched that the Red Cross segregated blood plasma during the war. Integration of military installations, the majority of which were in the South, would have provoked a crisis as federal power contradicted state law. Government and military officials argued that wartime integration would incite even more racial violence, create disorder within the military, and hinder America's war effort. General George C. Marshall, Army Chief of Staff, proclaimed: "The army is not a sociological laboratory." Hopes for racial justice, so long deferred, were another casualty of the war.

Despite such discrimination, many African Americans stood up for their rights. Lieutenant Jackie Robinson refused to move to the back of the bus at the army's Camp Hood, Texas, in 1944—and faced court-martial, even though military regulations forbade racial discrimination on military vehicles. Black sailors disobeyed orders to return to work after an explosion that destroyed two ships and killed 320 men—an explosion caused by the navy practice of assigning untrained African

During World War II, for the first time, the War Department sanctioned the training and use of African American pilots. These members of the Ninety-ninth Pursuit Squadron—known as "Tuskegee Airmen" because they trained at Alabama's all-black Tuskegee Institute—joined combat over North Africa in June 1943. Like most African American units in the racially segregated armed forces, the men of the Ninety-ninth Pursuit Squadron were under the command of white officers.

National Archives and Records Administration

American men to load bombs onto Liberty ships. When they were court-martialed for mutiny, future Supreme Court justice and chief counsel for the NAACP Thurgood Marshall argued, "This is not fifty men on trial for mutiny. This is the Navy on trial for its whole vicious policy toward Negroes."

African American servicemen did eventually fight on the front lines, and fought well. The "Tuskegee Airmen," pilots trained at the Tuskegee Institute in Alabama, saw heroic service in all-black units, such as the Ninety-ninth Pursuit Squadron, which won eighty Distinguished Flying Crosses. After the war, African Americans—as some white Americans had feared—called on their wartime service to claim the full rights of citizenship. African Americans' wartime experiences were mixed, but the war was a turning point in the movement for equal rights.

America and the Holocaust

America's inaction in the face of what we now call the Holocaust is a tragic failure, though the consequences are clearer now than at the time. When, at the beginning of the war, the United States turned away refugees and refused to relax its immigration quotas to admit European Jews and others fleeing Hitler's Germany, almost no one foresaw that the future would bring death camps like Auschwitz. Americans knew they were turning away people fleeing dire persecution, and while anti-Semitism played a significant role in that decision, it was not unusual to refuse those seeking refuge, especially during a major economic crisis.

As early as 1942, American newspapers reported the "mass slaughter" of Jews and other "undesirables" (Gypsies, homosexuals, the physically and mentally handicapped) under Hitler. Many Americans, having been taken in by manufactured atrocity tales during World War I, wrongly discounted these stories. But Roosevelt knew about Nazi death camps capable of killing up to two thousand people an hour using the gas Zyklon-B.

In 1943, British and American representatives met in Bermuda to discuss the situation but took no action. Appalled, Secretary of the Treasury Henry Morgenthau Jr. charged that the State Department's foot dragging made the United States an accessory to murder. In 1944, stirred by Morgenthau's argument, Roosevelt created the War Refugee Board, which set up refugee camps in Europe and helped save 200,000 Jews. But it came too late. By war's end, the Nazis had systematically murdered almost 11 million people.

Millions of civilians were starved, gassed, machine gunned, or worked to death by their Nazi jailers during the war. Here, U.S. Army troops force Nazi Party members to exhume the bodies of two hundred Russian officers and others who were shot by the SS near Wuelfel, while the residents of Hannover watch. Allied troops often compelled local townspeople to watch exhumations of mass graves, attempting to make them confront the atrocities that many insisted they never knew were happening.

United States Holocaust Memorial Museum

Life in the Military

How did racial and gender norms play out in the military during World War II?

More than 15 million men and approximately 350,000 women served in the U.S. armed forces during World War II. Eighteen percent of American families had a father, son, or brother in the military. Some of these men (and all of the women) volunteered, but more than 10 million were draftees. The draft reached broadly and mostly equitably through the American population during World War II.

Selective Service   The Selective Service Act allowed deferments, but they did not disproportionately benefit the well-to-do: all four of Franklin and Eleanor Roosevelt's sons served. The small number of college deferments was balanced by deferments for many "critical occupations," including war industry workers and almost 2 million agricultural workers. Most exemptions were for men deemed physically or mentally unqualified to serve. Army physicians discovered the Great Depression's impact as draftees arrived with rotted teeth and deteriorated eyesight—signs of malnutrition. Military examiners also found evidence of the impact of racism and poverty. Half of African American draftees had no schooling beyond the sixth grade. Forty-six percent of African Americans and almost one-third of European Americans called for the draft were classified "4-F"—unfit for service.

Nonetheless, almost 12 percent of America's population served in the military. Regional differences were profound, and northerners and southerners often—literally—could not understand one another. Ethnic differences complicated things further. Although African Americans and Japanese Americans served in their own separate units, Hispanics, Native Americans, and Chinese Americans served in "white" units. The result was often tension, but many Americans became less prejudiced and less provincial as they served with men unlike themselves.

Fighting the War

Although military service was widespread, the burdens of combat were not equally shared. Women's roles in the U.S. military were much more restricted than in the British or Soviet militaries, where women served in combat-related positions. U.S. women served as nurses, in communications offices, and as typists or cooks. The recruiting slogan for the WACs (Women's Army Corps) was "Release a Man for Combat." However, most men in the armed forces never saw combat either; one-quarter never left the United States. One-third of U.S. military personnel served in clerical positions, filled mainly by well-educated men. African Americans, though assigned dirty and dangerous tasks, were largely kept from combat service. Lower-class, less-educated white men bore the brunt of the fighting.

Combat in World War II was horrible. Hollywood war films depicted men dying bravely, shot cleanly and comforted by their buddies in their last moments. In reality, less than 10 percent of casualties were caused by bullets. Most men were killed or wounded by mortars, bombs, or grenades. Seventy-five thousand American men remained missing in action at war's end, blown into fragments too small to identify. Combat meant sliding down a mud-slicked hill to land in a pile of putrid corpses and using flamethrowers that burned at 2,000 degrees Fahrenheit on other human beings. Service was "for the duration" of the war. Only death, serious injury, or victory offered release.

Close to three hundred thousand American servicemen died in combat. Almost 1 million American troops were wounded, half of them seriously. Medical advances, such as the development of penicillin and the use of blood plasma to prevent shock, helped wounded men survive—but many never fully recovered. Between 20 and 30 percent of combat casualties were psychoneurotic. The federal government strictly censored images of American combat deaths, consigning them to a secret file known as "the chamber of horrors." Americans at home rarely understood what combat had been like.

Winning the War

Why did Truman opt to use the atomic bomb to help end the war, rather than negotiate a peace with Japan?

Axis hopes for victory depended on a short war. German and Japanese leaders knew that, if the United States had time to fully mobilize its resources and men, the war was lost, but many believed that the United States would concede if it met with early, decisive defeats. By mid-1942, the Axis powers understood that they had underestimated American resolve and the willingness of other Allies to sacrifice their citizens to stop the Axis advance (see Map 23.2). The chance of an Axis victory grew slim as the months passed, but though the outcome was virtually certain after spring 1943, two years of fighting lay ahead.

Tensions among the Allies

The Allies' suspicions of one another undermined cooperation. The Soviets continued to press Britain and the United States to open a second front to draw

MAP 23.2

The Allies on the Offensive in Europe, 1942–1945

The United States pursued a "Europe First" policy: first defeat Germany, then focus on Japan. American military efforts began in North Africa in late 1942 and ended in Germany in 1945 on May 8 (V-E Day). Source: Copyright © Cengage Learning 2015

German troops away from the USSR, but the United States and Britain continued to delay. With the alliance badly strained, the three Allied leaders met in Tehran, Iran, in December 1943, where they agreed to launch **Operation Overlord**—the cross-channel invasion of France—in early 1944. And the Soviet Union promised to aid the Allies against Japan once Germany was defeated.

Operation Overlord Largest amphibious invasion in history, in which Allied troops stormed a sixty-mile stretch of the Normandy coast.

War in Europe

The second front opened in the dark morning hours of June 6, 1944: D-Day. In the largest amphibious landing in history, more than 140,000 Allied troops commanded by American general Dwight D. Eisenhower scrambled ashore at Normandy, France. Landing craft and soldiers immediately encountered the enemy; they triggered mines and were pinned down by fire from cliffside pillboxes. Although heavy bombardment and the clandestine work of saboteurs had softened the German defenses, the fighting was ferocious.

By late July, 1.4 million Allied troops spread across the countryside, liberating France and Belgium by the end of August, but leaving a path of devastation. Almost 37,000 Allied troops died in that struggle, and up to 20,000 French civilians were killed. German armored divisions counterattacked in Belgium's Ardennes Forest in December, hoping to push on to Antwerp to halt Allied supplies through that Belgian port. After weeks of heavy fighting in what has come to be called the **Battle of the Bulge**, the Allies gained control in late January 1945.

By that point, "strategic" bombing (though not nearly as precise as was publicly claimed) had destroyed Germany's war production and devastated its economy. In early 1945, the British and Americans began "morale" bombing, killing tens of thousands of civilians in aerial attacks on Berlin and then Dresden. Meanwhile, Soviet troops marched through Poland to Berlin. American forces crossed the Rhine River in March 1945 and captured the Ruhr Valley. Several units entered Austria and Czechoslovakia, where they met Soviet soldiers.

Battle of the Bulge Military offensive led by Germany. Named for the eighty-mile-long and fifty-mile-wide "bulge" that the German troops drove inside the American lines.

Yalta Conference

In early 1945, as the Battle of the Bulge raged, a very ill Franklin Roosevelt called for a summit meeting to discuss plans for the postwar world. The three Allied leaders met at Yalta, in the Russian Crimea, in February. Britain, its empire now vulnerable and shrinking, sought to protect its colonial possessions and to limit Soviet power. The Soviet Union, with 21 million dead, wanted German reparations for its massive rebuilding effort. The Soviets hoped to expand their sphere of influence throughout eastern Europe and to guarantee their national security; Germany, Stalin insisted, must be permanently weakened.

The United States also sought to expand its influence and to control the peace. Roosevelt lobbied for the United Nations Organization, approved in principle the

Allied ships unloading cargo during the first days of the Normandy invasion, June 1944. As this photograph shows, the scale of the operation was immense: Operation Overlord relied on 326,547 Allied troops, 11,590 aircraft, and 6,939 naval vessels.

Regional Council of Basse-Normandie/U.S. National Archives

previous year at Dumbarton Oaks in Washington, D.C., through which the United States hoped to exercise influence. The United States also wanted to avoid the debts-reparations fiasco that had plagued Europe after the First World War. U.S. goals included self-determination for liberated peoples; gradual decolonization; and management of world affairs by what Roosevelt called the Four Policemen: the Soviet Union, Great Britain, the United States, and China. (Roosevelt hoped China might help stabilize Asia after the war; the United States abolished the Chinese Exclusion Act in 1943 to consolidate ties between the two nations.) The United States was also determined to limit Soviet influence in the postwar world.

Military positions during the Yalta conference helped shape the negotiations. Soviet troops occupied eastern European nations, including Poland, where Moscow had installed a pro-Soviet regime despite a British-supported Polish government-in-exile in London. With Soviet troops in place, Britain and the United States had limited negotiating power over eastern Europe. The Big Three agreed that some eastern German territory would be transferred to Poland and the remainder divided into four zones—the fourth zone to be administered by France. Berlin, within the Soviet zone, would also be divided among the four victors. In exchange for U.S. promises to support Soviet claims on territory lost to Japan in the Russo-Japanese War of 1904–1905, Stalin agreed to a treaty of friendship with Jiang Jieshi (Chiang Kai-shek), America's ally in China, rather than with the communist Mao Zedong (Mao Tse-tung), and to declare war on Japan two or three months after Hitler's defeat.

Harry Truman

Franklin D. Roosevelt, reelected to an unprecedented fourth term in November 1944, died on April 12, 1945, and Vice President Harry S Truman became president. Truman, a senator from Missouri who had replaced former vice president Henry Wallace as Roosevelt's running mate in 1944, was inexperienced in foreign policy and was not informed about the top-secret atomic weapons project until after he became president. Eighteen days into Truman's presidency, Adolf Hitler killed himself in a bunker in bomb-ravaged Berlin. On May 8, Germany surrendered.

As the great powers jockeyed for influence after Germany's surrender, the Grand Alliance began to crumble. At the Potsdam Conference in mid-July, Truman was less patient with the Soviets than Roosevelt had been. And Truman learned during the conference that a test of the new atomic weapon had been successful. The United States no longer needed the Soviet Union's help in the Pacific war. The Allies did agree that Japan must surrender unconditionally. But with the defeat of Hitler and the end of the European war, wartime bonds among the Allies were strained.

The Pacific Campaign

In the Pacific, the war continued. Since the Battle of Midway in June 1942, American strategy had been to "island-hop" toward Japan, taking weaker islands in order to strand Japanese armies. By 1944, Allied troops—from the United States, Britain, Australia, and New Zealand—had secured the Solomon, Gilbert, Marshall, and Mariana Islands. General Douglas MacArthur landed at Leyte to retake the Philippines for the United States in October 1944 (see Map 23.3).

In February 1945, while the Big Three met at Yalta, U.S. and Japanese troops battled for Iwo Jima, a small island about seven hundred miles south of Tokyo. Twenty-one thousand Japanese defenders occupied the island's high ground.

MAP 23.3

The Pacific War

The strategy of the United States was to "island-hop"—from Hawai'i in 1942 to Iwo Jima and Okinawa in 1945. Naval battles were also decisive, notably the Battles of the Coral Sea and Midway in 1942. The war in the Pacific ended with Japan's surrender on August 15, 1945 (V-J Day). Source: Copyright © Cengage Learning 2015

Hidden in caves, trenches, and underground tunnels, they were protected from the aerial bombardment that U.S. forces used to clear the way for an amphibious landing. The island offered no cover, and marines were slaughtered as they came ashore. For twenty days, U.S. forces fought their way up Mount Suribachi, the island's highest and most heavily fortified point. The struggle for Iwo Jima cost the lives of 6,821 Americans and more than 20,000 Japanese. Only 200 Japanese survived.

A month later, American troops landed on Okinawa, an island in the Ryukyus chain at the southern tip of Japan, from which Allied forces planned to invade the main Japanese islands. Fighting raged for two months. The supporting fleet endured mass kamikaze (suicide) attacks, in which Japanese pilots intentionally crashed bomb-laden planes into American ships. On Okinawa, 7,374 American soldiers and marines died in battle. Almost the entire Japanese garrison of 100,000 was killed. More than one-quarter of Okinawa's people, or approximately 80,000 civilians, perished.

Bombing of Japan

Even with American forces just 350 miles from Japan's main islands, a powerful Japanese military faction was determined to preserve the emperor's sovereignty and avoid an unconditional surrender. On the night of March 9, 1945, 333 American B-29 Superfortresses dropped explosives on a four-by-three-mile area of Tokyo. They created a firestorm, a blaze so fierce that it sucked the oxygen from the air, producing hurricane-force winds and growing hot enough to melt concrete and steel. Almost 100,000 people were incinerated, suffocated, or boiled to death hiding in canals. Over the following five months, American bombers attacked sixty-six Japanese cities, leaving 8 million people homeless, killing almost 900,000.

Early in the summer of 1945, Japan put out peace feelers through the Soviets. Japan was not, however, willing to accept the "unconditional surrender" terms on which the Allied leaders had agreed at Potsdam, and Truman chose not to pursue a negotiated peace. U.S. troops were mobilizing to invade the Japanese home islands, but the Manhattan Project's success offered another option, and Truman took it. Using atomic bombs on Japan, Truman believed, would end the war quickly and save American lives. It would also demonstrate American power, keep the Soviet Union out of the final stages of the war, and give the United States control of the peace process.

Some historians argue that Japan was on the verge of unconditional surrender; others that the anti-surrender faction could have prevailed. No matter which is true, bombing (conventional or atomic) fit the U.S. strategy of using machines rather than men whenever possible. The decision to use the bomb did not seem as momentous to Truman as it does in retrospect. The moral line had already been crossed with wholesale bombing of civilian populations. The Japanese had bombed Shanghai in 1937. Germans had "terror-bombed" Warsaw, Rotterdam, and London. British and American bombers had purposely created firestorms in German cities, killing 225,000 people on a single night in Dresden. American conventional bombing of Japanese cities had already killed close to a million people. What distinguished the atomic bombs from conventional bombs was their power and their efficiency—not that they killed huge numbers of innocent civilians in unspeakably awful ways.

The shock waves and fires caused by the atomic bomb leveled great expanses of Hiroshima. Radiation released by the bomb caused lingering deaths for thousands who survived the explosion. The photo of the city shown here was taken eight months after the attack.

National Archives

On July 26, 1945, the Allies delivered an ultimatum to Japan: promising that the Japanese people would not be "enslaved," the **Potsdam Declaration** called for unconditional surrender or "prompt and utter destruction." Tokyo radio announced that the government would respond with *mokusatsu* (literally, "kill with silence," or ignore the ultimatum). On August 6, 1945, a B-29 bomber, the *Enola Gay*, dropped an atomic bomb above Hiroshima. A flash of dazzling light shot across the sky; then a huge, purplish mushroom cloud boiled forty thousand feet into the atmosphere. The bomb ignited a firestorm and killed 130,000 people. Tens of thousands more would suffer from radiation poisoning.

On August 8, the Soviet Union declared war on Japan. On August 9, the United States dropped a second atomic bomb on Nagasaki, killing at least 60,000 people. Five days later, on August 14, Japan surrendered. Recent histories argue that the Soviet declaration of war played a more significant role in Japan's decision to surrender than America's use of atomic weapons. In the end, the Allies promised that the Japanese emperor could remain as the nation's titular head. The Second World War was over.

Legacy FOR A PEOPLE AND A NATION

Nuclear Proliferation

Virtually from the moment of the Hiroshima and Nagasaki atomic bombings, American strategists grappled with the problem of keeping others, particularly the Soviet Union, from the "nuclear club." On September 23, 1949, President Truman informed shocked Americans that the Soviets had successfully tested an atomic device.

In the years thereafter, membership in the nuclear club grew, through a combination of huge national investments, espionage, and a black market of raw materials and technologies. There were successful detonations by Great Britain (1952), France (1960), China (1964), India (1974), and Pakistan (1998). Israel crossed the nuclear weapon threshold on the eve of the 1967 Six-Day War but to this day has refused to confirm that it has the bomb. Recently, creditable reports indicate that North Korea has a small nuclear arsenal and that Iran is working to get one.

Yet the number of nuclear states is fewer than experts predicted in the 1960s, when analysts warned that thirty nations might be so armed by the 1990s. It did not happen because the five existing nuclear powers committed themselves in the mid-1960s to promoting nonproliferation. Subsequently, 22 of 31 states that started down the nuclear path changed course and renounced the bomb. By late 2006, the Treaty on the Non-Proliferation of Nuclear Weapons (NPT), enacted on July 1, 1968, had 187 signatories and was hailed as one of the great international agreements of the post-1945 era.

Skeptics took a different view, noting that three states outside the NPT (Israel, India, and Pakistan) became nuclear powers. They charged the "original five" with preventing others from obtaining nuclear arms while keeping large stockpiles for themselves. With the world in 2013 awash in some 17,000 nuclear weapons (97 percent belonging to the United States and Russia), critics feared terrorist groups or other nonstate actors getting bombs. In that nightmare scenario, they warned, the de facto post-Nagasaki international moratorium on the use of nuclear weapons would be—literally—blown away.

Summary

World War II devastated much of the globe. One out of nine people in the Soviet Union had perished—at least 21 million military members and civilians. The Chinese lost 10 million; the Germans and Austrians, 6 million; the Japanese, 2.5 million. Up to 1 million died of famine in Japanese-controlled Indochina. Almost 11 million people were murdered in Nazi death camps. Across the globe, the Second World War killed at least 55 million people.

Waging war required the cooperation of Allied nations with very different goals. Tensions remained high as the United States and Britain resisted Stalin's demands for a second front. The United States, meanwhile, was fighting the Japanese in the Pacific. By the time Japan surrendered in August 1945, the strains between the Soviet Union and its English-speaking Allies made postwar stability unlikely.

American servicemen covered the globe, while on the home front, Americans worked around the clock to make the weapons that would win the war. Despite wartime sacrifices, many Americans found that the war had improved their lives. Mobilization ended the Great Depression. Americans moved to war-production centers. The influx of workers strained community resources and sometimes led to social friction and violence. But many Americans—African Americans, Mexican Americans, women, poor whites from the South— found new opportunities in well-paid war jobs. The federal government became a stronger presence, regulating business and employment; overseeing military conscription; and even controlling what people could buy to eat or to wear.

At war's end, only the United States had the economic resources to spur international recovery; only the United States was more prosperous than when war began. In the coming struggle to fashion a new world—the Cold War—the United States held a commanding position. For better or worse—and clearly there were elements of each—the Second World War was a turning point in the nation's history.

Chapter Review

America's Entry into the Conflict

> **How did Roosevelt and Congress aid the Allies following the German advances of early 1940?**

Alarmed by Germany's swift defeat of European nations, Americans gradually shed their isolationist sentiment, and the president began to aid the Allies to prevent the fall of Britain. In May 1940 he ordered the sale of surplus military equipment to Britain and France, and he urged Congress to let Britain borrow necessary arms. The president also signed the Selective Training and Service Act, the first peacetime military draft. In 1941, Congress passed Roosevelt's Lend-Lease Act. To ensure delivery of Lend-Lease goods, Roosevelt ordered the U.S. Navy to patrol halfway across the Atlantic. After German submarines attacked two U.S. destroyers, Congress scrapped the cash-and-carry policy and revised the Neutrality Acts to permit transport of munitions to Britain on armed American merchant ships.

The United States at War

> **Was the United States prepared for war when it entered World War II?**

Although the United States had been aiding the Allies, it was not prepared for war when it entered World War II following the bombing of Pearl Harbor in 1941.

Throughout the 1930s, military funding was a low priority. In September 1939 (when Hitler invaded Poland), the U.S. Army ranked forty-fifth among world armies, and there was only enough equipment for one-third of its troops. A peacetime draft instituted in 1940 expanded the U.S. military to 2 million men, but Roosevelt's 1941 survey of war preparedness estimated that the United States could not be ready to fight before June 1943.

The Production Front and American Workers

How did wartime production needs create a new relationship between government and business, and government and science?

Mobilizing for war required that factories shift from producing consumer goods to wartime necessities such as uniforms, arms, and tanks. The federal government enticed businesses to cooperate by offering generous tax write-offs and exemptions from antitrust laws. It also paid to retool or expand factories for war production and allowed corporations to charge production costs plus a fixed profit. Companies thus doubled their net profits from 1939 to 1944. The government ensured that labor strikes would not disrupt production by having the newly formed National War Labor Board settle disputes. The government spent millions on university research programs that would develop new war technologies, most importantly, the $2 billion secret Manhattan Project to build an atomic bomb.

Life on the Home Front

What was the impact of the war on family life?

Nearly 3 million families were broken up during the war years, despite government policies that exempted married men and fathers from the draft. Although divorce rates doubled, marriage rates also increased from 73 per 1,000 unmarried women in 1939 to 93 in 1942. Birth rates rose, too, from 2.4 million babies in 1939 to 3.1 million in 1943. Many were "goodbye babies," conceived with the idea that the father might not survive the war. Taboos against unwed motherhood remained strong, and only 1 percent of births during the war were to unmarried women. Wartime mobility also increased opportunities for same-sex relationships, and gay communities grew in such cities as San Francisco. Still, the

war reinforced traditional gender roles—men served as the nation's defenders while women were to "keep the home fires burning," sometimes filling jobs vacated by soldiers, albeit just "for the duration." Nonetheless, millions of women took on new responsibilities in wartime.

The Limits of American Ideals

In what ways were American notions of civil liberties and basic freedoms tested during the war years?

Tensions emerged between wartime practices and America's democratic ideals. Government propaganda films contrasted American democracy and freedom with totalitarianism and fascism. Although U.S. leaders embraced a "strategy of truth" that promised to honestly report the war's progress to the public, the government tightly controlled military information. Freedoms were curbed, as evident in passage of the 1940 Alien Registration (Smith Act), which made it illegal to advocate overthrowing the U.S. government. But the most grievous civil liberties violation was the treatment of ethnic Americans and resident aliens, notably the internment of the Japanese. In March 1942, Roosevelt ordered that all 112,000 foreign-born Japanese and Japanese Americans living in California, Oregon, and the state of Washington be removed from the West Coast to remote "relocation centers." There were no individual charges; they were imprisoned under suspicion solely because they were of Japanese descent.

Life in the Military

How did racial and gender norms play out in the military during World War II?

The discrimination that existed throughout American society was replicated in the armed services: African Americans and Japanese Americans served in units segregated from whites (although Hispanics, Native Americans, and Chinese Americans were part of "white" units). African Americans were given the dirtiest and most dangerous assignments, though they were largely kept from combat service. Less-educated, lower-class white men did most of the fighting. Women who volunteered for the Women's Army Corps and other female military organizations served as nurses, in communications offices, as typists, and as cooks—all military extensions of their traditional gender roles.

Winning the War

 Why did Truman opt to use the atomic bomb to help end the war, rather than negotiate a peace with Japan?

From a military standpoint, Truman would only agree to an unconditional surrender of the Japanese, something the Japanese were unlikely to accept. Truman believed that using the atomic bomb would end the war quickly and save U.S. soldiers' lives. He also believed the atomic bomb would demonstrate American power and prevent the Soviets from entering the Pacific war and controlling the peace process. Because extensive bombing of Japanese civilian areas had already occurred, Truman did not see the use of the bomb as crossing a moral line the way it would later come to be understood. What distinguished the atomic bombs from conventional bombs, as Truman saw it, was their power and efficiency—not that they killed huge numbers of civilians in unspeakably awful ways.

Suggestions for Further Reading

Michael C. C. Adams, *The Best War Ever: America and World War II* (1993)

Tsuyoshi Hasegawa, *Racing the Enemy: Stalin, Truman, and the Surrender of Japan* (2005)

William I. Hitchcock, *The Bitter Road to Freedom: A New History of the Liberation of Europe* (2008)

John Howard, *Concentration Camps on the Homefront: Japanese Americans in the House of Jim Crow* (2008)

David M. Kennedy, *Freedom from Fear: The American People in Depression and War, 1929–1945* (1999)

Warren F. Kimball, *Forged in War: Roosevelt, Churchill, and the Second World War* (1997)

Nelson Lichtenstein, *Labor's War at Home: The CIO in World War II* (1983)

Gerald F. Linderman, *The World Within War: America's Combat Experience in World War II* (1997)

Leisa Meyers, *Creating G.I. Jane: Sexuality and Power in the Women's Army Corps During World War II* (1996)

Williamson Murray and Allan Reed Millett, *A War to Be Won: Fighting the Second World War* (2009)

George Roeder, Jr., *The Censored War: American Visual Experience During World War II* (1993)

Barbara Dianne Savage, *Broadcasting Freedom: Radio, War, and the Politics of Race, 1938–1948* (1999)

Ronald Takaki, *Double Victory: A Multicultural History of America in World War II* (2000)

The Cold War and American Globalism

24

1945–1961

On July 16, 1945, the Deer Team leader parachuted into northern Vietnam, near Kimlung, a village in a valley of rice paddies. Colonel Allison Thomas and five other members of his Office of Strategic Services (OSS) unit could not know that the end of the Second World War was just weeks away. Their mission: to work with the Vietminh, a nationalist Vietnamese organization, to sabotage Japanese forces that in March had seized Vietnam from France. Ho Chi Minh, head of the Vietminh, offered the OSS team supper. The next day Ho denounced the French but remarked that "we welcome 10 million Americans." "Forget the Communist Bogy," Thomas radioed OSS headquarters in China.

A communist dedicated to winning his nation's independence from France, Ho joined the French Communist Party after World War I. For the next two decades, living in China, the Soviet Union, and elsewhere, he planned and fought to free his nation from French colonialism. During World War II, Ho's Vietminh warriors harassed French and Japanese forces and rescued downed American pilots. In March 1945, Ho met with U.S. officials in China. Receiving no aid from his ideological allies in the Soviet Union, Ho hoped that the United States would favor his nation's quest for liberation.

Other OSS personnel soon parachuted into Kimlung. Everywhere the Americans went, impoverished villagers thanked them with gifts of food and clothing, interpreting the foreigners' presence as a sign of U.S. anticolonial and anti-Japanese sentiments. In early August, the Deer Team began giving Vietminh soldiers weapons training. Ho hoped young Vietnamese could study in the United States and that American technicians could help build an independent Vietnam.

A second OSS unit, the Mercy Team, headed by Captain Archimedes Patti, arrived in the city of Hanoi on August 22. But unbeknownst to these OSS members, who believed that President Franklin D. Roosevelt's sympathy for eventual Vietnamese independence remained U.S. policy, the new Truman administration had decided to let France decide Vietnam's fate.

That policy change explains why Ho never received answers to the letters and telegrams he sent to Washington—the first dated August 30, 1945.

On September 2, 1945, with OSS personnel present, Ho Chi Minh read his declaration of independence for the Democratic Republic of Vietnam: "All men are created equal; they are endowed by their Creator with certain unalienable Rights; among these are Life, Liberty, and the pursuit of Happiness." Borrowing from the internationally renowned American document of 1776, Ho then itemized Vietnamese grievances against France.

In a last meeting with Captain Patti, Ho expressed sadness that the United States had armed the French to reestablish their colonial rule in Vietnam. Sure, Ho said, U.S. officials in Washington judged him a "Moscow puppet" because he was a communist. But Ho claimed that he drew inspiration from the American struggle for independence and that he was foremost "a free agent," a nationalist. Ho insisted the Vietnamese would go it alone. And they did—first against the French and eventually against more than half a million U.S. troops.

Because Ho Chi Minh and many of his nationalist followers had declared themselves communists, U.S. leaders rejected their appeal. Endorsing the containment doctrine against communism, American presidents from Truman to George H. W. Bush believed that a ruthless Soviet Union directed a worldwide communist conspiracy against peace, free-market capitalism, and democracy. Soviet leaders from Joseph Stalin to Mikhail Gorbachev protested that a militarized, economically aggressive United States sought world domination. This protracted contest between the United States and the Soviet Union acquired the name "the Cold War."

The Cold War was fundamentally a contest between the United States and the Soviet Union over spheres of influence. The competition between the capitalist "West" and the communist "East" dominated international relations for more than four decades and eventually took the lives of millions, cost trillions of dollars, spawned doomsday fears, and destabilized several nations. Occasionally, the two superpowers negotiated and signed agreements to temper their dangerous arms race; at other times they went to the brink of war and armed allies to fight vicious Third World conflicts. Sometimes these allies had their own ambitions and resisted pressure from one or both superpowers.

Vietnam was part of the Third World, a general term for nations that during the Cold War era wore neither the "West" (the "First World") nor the "East" (the "Second World") label. Sometimes called "developing countries," Third World nations were generally nonwhite, nonindustrialized, and located in the southern half of the globe—in Asia, Africa, the Middle East, and Latin

America. Many had been colonies of European nations or Japan. U.S. leaders often interpreted their anticolonialism as Soviet inspired rather than as expressions of indigenous nationalism. Vietnam became one among many sites where Cold War fears and Third World aspirations intersected, prompting American intervention and a globalist foreign policy that regarded the entire world as the appropriate sphere for America's influence.

Critics in the United States challenged Cold War exaggerations of threats from abroad, meddlesome interventions in the Third World, and militarization of foreign policy. But when leaders like Truman described the Cold War as a life-and-death struggle against a monstrous enemy, critics were drowned out by charges that dissenters were "soft on communism," if not un-American. U.S. leaders successfully cultivated a Cold War consensus that stifled debate and shaped the mindset of generations of Americans.

As you read this chapter, keep the following questions in mind:

- **Why did relations between the Soviet Union and the United States turn hostile soon after their victory in World War II?**

- **When and why did the Cold War expand from a struggle over the future of Europe and central Asia to one encompassing virtually the entire globe?**

- **By what means did the Truman and Eisenhower administrations seek to expand America's global influence in the late 1940s and the 1950s?**

From Allies to Adversaries

Was the Cold War inevitable?

World War II unsettled the international system. Germany was in ruins. Great Britain was overstrained; France was rent by internal division; and Italy was weakened. Japan was decimated and under occupation, and China was headed toward renewed civil war. Throughout Europe and Asia, factories, transportation, and communications links were reduced to rubble, and agricultural production plummeted. The United States and the Soviet Union offered different solutions to these problems. The collapse of Germany and Japan, moreover, had created power vacuums that drew the two major powers into collision as they sought influence. For example, in Greece and China, where civil wars raged between leftists and conservative regimes, the two powers supported different sides.

Decolonization

With empires disintegrating, a new Third World emerged. Financial constraints and nationalist rebellions forced the imperial states to set their colonies free. Britain exited India (and Pakistan) in 1947 and Burma and Sri Lanka (Ceylon) in 1948. The Philippines gained independence from the United States in 1946. The Dutch left Indonesia in 1949. In the Middle East, Lebanon (1943), Syria (1946), and Jordan (1946) gained independence, while in Palestine British officials faced

Chronology

1945	Roosevelt dies; Truman becomes president	1951	United States signs Mutual Security Treaty with Japan
	Atomic bombings of Japan	1953	Eisenhower becomes president
1946	Kennan's "long telegram" criticizes USSR		Stalin dies
	Vietnamese war against France erupts		United States helps restore shah to power in Iran
1947	Truman Doctrine seeks aid for Greece and Turkey		Korean War ends
	Marshall offers Europe economic assistance	1954	Geneva Accords partition Vietnam
	National Security Act reorganizes government		CIA-led coup overthrows Arbenz in Guatemala
1948	Communists take power in Czechoslovakia	1955	Soviets create Warsaw Pact
	Truman recognizes Israel	1956	Soviets crush uprising in Hungary
	United States organizes Berlin airlift		Suez crisis sparks war in Middle East
1949	NATO founded as anti-Soviet alliance	1957	Soviets fire first ICBM and launch *Sputnik*
	Soviet Union explodes atomic bomb	1958	U.S. troops land in Lebanon
	Mao's communists win power in China		Berlin crisis
1950	NSC-68 recommends major military buildup	1959	Castro ousts Batista in Cuba
	Korean War starts in June; China enters in fall	1960	Eighteen African colonies become independent
			Vietcong organized in South Vietnam

pressure from Zionists intent on creating a Jewish homeland and from Arab leaders opposed to the prospect. In Iraq, nationalist agitation increased against the British-installed government. Washington and Moscow saw these Third World states as potential allies that might provide military bases, resources, and markets. But some new nations, such as India, chose nonalignment in the Cold War.

Stalin's Aims

The United States and the Soviet Union assessed their most pressing tasks differently. The Soviets, though committed to victory over capitalist countries, were most concerned about preventing another invasion of their homeland. Its landmass was three times that of the United States, but it had only ten thousand miles of seacoast, much of which was under ice for a large part of the year. Russian leaders both before and after the revolution had made increased maritime access a chief foreign policy aim.

And the USSR's geographical frontiers were hard to defend. Siberia lay six thousand miles east of Moscow and was vulnerable to encroachment by Japan and China. In the west, the border with Poland had generated violent clashes since World War I, and more than 20 million Russians died after Hitler's invasion in 1941. Henceforth, Soviet leaders wanted no dangers along their western borders.

Overall, however, Soviet territorial objectives were limited. Although Americans compared Stalin to Hitler, Stalin's aims were more limited and resembled those of czars before him: he wanted to push the USSR's borders to include the Baltic states of Estonia, Latvia, and Lithuania, as well as the eastern part of prewar

Visualizing THE PAST

Stalin: Ally to Adversary

These two *Look* magazine portrayals of Soviet leader Stalin indicate how quickly the Grand Alliance of World War II disintegrated into the superpower confrontation of the Cold War. In the first piece, from mid-1944, correspondent Ralph Parker writes that Stalin spends half his time writing poetry and the other half reading it to the schoolchildren who clamor to sit on his knee. "Stalin," Parker adds, "is undoubtedly among the best-dressed of all world leaders making Churchill in his siren suit look positively shabby." Four years later, Louis Fischer paints a very different picture. "This small man with drooping shoulders tyrannizes one-fifth of the world," Fischer writes of the Soviet leader, adding that neither Hitler nor any Russian czar was as powerful or as menacing as the "Great Red Father." What do these two items suggest about American attitudes toward the outside world? What do they suggest about the role of the press in U.S. society?

"A Guy Named Joe" cover story of Look *magazine by Ralph Parker, June 27, 1944*

"Life Story of Stalin" by Louis Fischer in Look *magazine, June 8, 1948*

Poland. To the south, Stalin wanted a presence in northern Iran, and he pressed the Turks for naval bases and free access out of the Black Sea. The Soviets did not promote expanded world trade or the rapid rebuilding of the region's war-ravaged economies.

| U.S. Economic and Strategic Needs |

The United States, by contrast, came out of the war secure in its borders. American casualties were fewer than any of the other major combatants. With its fixed capital intact, its resources more plentiful than ever, and in lone possession of the atomic bomb, the United States was the strongest power in the world.

But government officials worried about complacency. Some other power—almost certainly the USSR—could eventually seize unstable areas of war-torn Europe and Asia. Therefore, Washington sought bases overseas to keep an airborne enemy at bay. To further enhance U.S. security, American planners sought the quick reconstruction of nations—including former enemies Germany and Japan—and a world economy based on free trade.

The Soviets, on the other hand, refused to join the new World Bank and International Monetary Fund (IMF), created at the July 1944 Bretton Woods Conference by forty-four nations to stabilize trade and finance. They held that the United States dominated both institutions and used them to promote private investment and open international commerce, which Moscow saw as capitalist tools. With the United States as its largest donor, the World Bank opened in 1945 and made loans to help members finance reconstruction projects; the IMF, also heavily U.S.-backed, helped members meet their balance-of-payments problems through currency loans.

| Stalin and Truman |

The personalities of the two countries' leaders also mattered. Stalin, though hostile to the Western powers and capable of ruthlessness against his own people (his periodic purges since the 1930s had taken the lives of millions), did not want war. He was aware of his country's weakness vis-à-vis the United States, and he appears to have initially believed he could achieve his aspirations through cooperation. Over the long term, though, he believed that Germany and Japan would threaten the USSR, and his suspicion of capitalist powers was boundless. Many have concluded that Stalin was clinically paranoid. As historian David Reynolds has noted, this paranoia, coupled with Stalin's xenophobia (fear of anything foreign) and his Marxist-Leninist ideology, created in the Soviet leader a mental map of "them" versus "us" that influenced his approach to world affairs.

Truman had none of Stalin's capacity for ruthlessness, but to a lesser degree he, too, was prone to a "them" versus "us" worldview. Truman preferred either/or answers over nuances, ambiguities, and counterevidence. He constantly exaggerated, as when he declared in his undelivered farewell address that he had "knocked the socks off the communists" in Korea. When Truman protested in a 1945 meeting at the White House that the Soviets were not fulfilling the Yalta agreement on Poland, the Soviet commissar of foreign affairs, V. M. Molotov, stormed out. Truman bragged after the encounter that "I gave it to him straight one-two to the jaw." The president self-consciously developed what he called his "tough method," which became a trademark of American Cold War diplomacy.

The Beginning of the Cold War

No precise start date for the Cold War's beginning can be given. It resulted from an ongoing process, one that arguably began in 1917 with the Bolshevik Revolution and the Western powers' hostile response, but in a more meaningful sense began in mid-1945, as World War II ended. By the spring of 1947, certainly, the struggle had begun.

One of the first Soviet-American clashes came in Poland in 1945, when the Soviets blocked the Polish government-in-exile in London from becoming part of the Moscow-sponsored communist government. The Soviets also extinguished civil liberties in Romania, arguing that the United States similarly manipulated Italy. Moscow initially allowed free elections in Hungary and Czechoslovakia, but as the Cold War accelerated and U.S. influence in Europe expanded, the Soviets encouraged communist coups in Hungary (1947) and Czechoslovakia (1948). Yugoslavia was unique: its independent communist government, led by Josip Broz Tito, broke with Stalin in 1948.

To defend their actions, Moscow officials noted that the United States was reviving Germany and meddling in Eastern Europe. They cited clandestine American meetings with anti-Soviet groups, repeated calls for elections likely to produce anti-Soviet regimes, and the use of loans to gain political influence (financial diplomacy). Moscow charged that the United States was pursuing a double standard—intervening in Eastern Europe but demanding that the Soviet Union stay out of Latin America and Asia. Americans called for free elections in the Soviet sphere, Moscow noted, but not in the U.S. sphere in Latin America.

Atomic Diplomacy

The Soviets believed that the United States was practicing "atomic diplomacy"—maintaining a nuclear monopoly to scare the Soviets into diplomatic concessions. Truman refused to turn over the weapon to an international control authority. In 1946, he backed the Baruch Plan, named after its author, financier Bernard Baruch, which provided for U.S. abandonment of its atomic monopoly only after the world's fissionable materials were controlled by an international agency. The Soviets retorted that this plan would require them to shut down their atomic bomb development project while the United States continued its own. Washington and Moscow soon became locked in a frightening nuclear arms race.

By the middle of 1946, Soviets and Americans clashed on every front. When the United States turned down a Soviet request for a reconstruction loan but gave one to Britain, Moscow upbraided Washington for using its dollars to manipulate foreign governments. The two Cold War powers also backed different groups in Iran, where the United States helped bring the pro-West shah to the throne. Unable to agree on the unification of Germany, the former allies built up their zones independently.

Warnings from Kennan and Churchill

After Stalin gave a speech in February 1946 that depicted the world as threatened by capitalist acquisitiveness, the American chargé d'affaires in Moscow,

George F. Kennan, sent a pessimistic "long telegram" to Washington. His widely circulated report fed a growing belief among American officials that only toughness would work with the fanatical Soviets. The following month, in Fulton, Missouri, former British prime minister Winston Churchill warned that a Soviet-erected "iron curtain" cut off Eastern European countries from the West. With an approving Truman nearby, Churchill called for an Anglo-American partnership to resist the new menace.

George F. Kennan American diplomat in Moscow, architect of the Cold War policy of containment.

Link to The Kennan Telegram, 1946

The growing Soviet-American tensions had major implications for the United Nations. The delegates who gathered in San Francisco in April 1945 to sign the UN charter agreed on an organization that included a General Assembly of all member states and a smaller Security Council that would take the lead on issues of peace and security. Five great powers were given permanent seats on the council—the United States, the Soviet Union, Great Britain, China, and France—and each could exercise a veto against any proposed action. Of the fifty-one founding states, twenty-two came from the Americas and another fifteen from Europe, which effectively gave the United States a large majority in the assembly. In retaliation, Moscow exercised its veto in the Security Council.

Some high-level U.S. officials were dismayed by the administration's harsh anti-Soviet posture. Secretary of Commerce Henry A. Wallace, who had been Roosevelt's vice president before Truman, charged that Truman's get-tough policy was substituting atomic and economic coercion for diplomacy. Wallace told a Madison Square Garden audience in September 1946, "The tougher we get, the tougher the Russians will get." Truman soon fired Wallace from the cabinet, blasting him privately as "a real Commie and a dangerous man."

Truman Doctrine

East-West tensions escalated further in early 1947, when Britain requested American help in Greece defending their conservative client-government (a government dependent on the economic or military support of a more powerful country) in a civil war against leftists. In his March 12, 1947, speech to Congress, Truman requested $400 million in aid to Greece and Turkey. But Republicans had won majorities in both houses of Congress in 1946, and they wanted less spending. Republican senator Arthur Vandenberg of Michigan, who backed Truman's request, told the president that he would have to "scare hell out of the American people" to gain congressional approval.

Link to the Truman Doctrine

Thus, the president delivered a speech laced with alarmist language. "If Greece should fall under the control of an armed minority," he concluded in an early version of the domino theory (see page 714), "the effect upon its neighbor, Turkey, would be immediate and serious. Confusion and disorder might well spread throughout the entire Middle East." He articulated what became known as the **Truman Doctrine**: "I believe that it must be the policy of the United States to support free peoples who are resisting attempted subjugation by armed minorities or by outside pressures."

Truman Doctrine U.S. policy designed to contain the spread of communism; began with President Truman's 1947 request to Congress for economic and military aid to the struggling countries of Greece and Turkey to prevent them from succumbing to Soviet pressure.

Critics correctly pointed out that the Soviet Union was little involved in the Greek civil war, that the communists in Greece were more pro-Tito than pro-Stalin, and that the resistance movement had noncommunist and communist members. Truman countered that, should communists gain control of Greece, they might open the door to Soviet power in the Mediterranean. The Senate approved Truman's request by 67 to 23 votes. Using U.S. dollars and military advisers, the Greek government defeated the insurgents in 1949, and Turkey became a U.S. ally on the Soviets' border.

Inevitable Cold War?

In the months after Truman's speech, the term *Cold War* slipped into the lexicon as a description of the Soviet-American relationship. Could the confrontation have been avoided? Not altogether, it seems clear. Even before World War II ended, observers anticipated that the two powerful but sharply different nations would seek to fill the power vacuum.

But it is far less clear that the conflict had to result in a Cold War. The "cold peace" that had prevailed from the revolution in 1917 through World War II could conceivably have been maintained into the postwar years as well. Neither side's leadership wanted war. Both hoped—at least initially—to maintain cooperation. The Cold War resulted from decisions by individual human beings who might have done more to maintain diplomatic dialogue and seek negotiated solutions to international problems.

Containment in Action

Was the U.S. containment policy successful?

To counter Soviet and communist expansion, the Truman team chose a policy of **containment**. Writing as "Mr. X" in the July 1947 issue of *Foreign Affairs* magazine, George Kennan, now at the State Department in Washington, advocated a "policy of firm containment, designed to confront the Russians with unalterable counterforce at every point where they show signs of encroaching upon the interests of a peaceful and stable world." Such counterforce, Kennan argued, would check Soviet expansion. Kennan's "X" article joined the Truman Doctrine as a key manifesto of Cold War policy.

containment U.S. policy uniting military, economic, and diplomatic strategies to prevent the spread of Soviet communism and to enhance America's security and influence abroad.

Lippmann's Critique

The veteran journalist Walter Lippmann opposed the containment doctrine in his powerful book *The Cold War* (1947), calling it a "strategic monstrosity" that failed to distinguish between areas vital and peripheral to U.S. security. Lippmann did not share Truman's conviction that the Soviet Union was plotting to take over the world. The president, he asserted, put too little emphasis on diplomacy. Ironically, Kennan agreed with much of Lippmann's critique, and he soon distanced himself from the doctrine he helped create.

Invoking the containment doctrine, the United States in 1947 and 1948 began to build an international economic and defensive network to protect American prosperity and security, and to advance U.S. hegemony. In Western Europe, the region of primary concern, American diplomats pursued economic reconstruction; the ouster of communists from governments, as occurred in 1947 in France and Italy; and blockage of "third force" or neutralist tendencies. Meanwhile, American culture—consumer goods, music, consumption ethic, and production techniques— permeated European societies. Some Europeans resisted Americanization, but transatlantic ties strengthened.

Marshall Plan

Americans, who had already spent billions of dollars on European relief and recovery by 1947, remembered well the troubles of the 1930s: global depression, political extremism, and war born of economic discontent. Such cataclysms could not be allowed to happen again; communism must not replace fascism. Hence, in June 1947, Secretary of State George C. Marshall announced that the United States would finance a massive European recovery program. Launched in 1948, the **Marshall Plan** sent $12.4 billion to Western Europe before the program ended in 1951 (see Map 24.1). To stimulate business at home, the legislation required that Europeans spend this aid on American-made products. The Marshall Plan proved a mixed success; it caused inflation, failed to solve a balance-of-payments problem, took only tentative steps toward economic integration, and further divided Europe between "East" and "West." But the program spurred Western European industrial production and investment, started the region toward self-sustaining economic growth, and—from the American perspective–helped contain communism.

Marshall Plan The Truman administration's proposal for massive U.S. economic aid to speed the recovery of war-torn Europe.

National Security Act

To streamline the administration of U.S. defense, Truman worked with Congress on the **National Security Act of July 1947**. The act created the Office of Secretary of Defense (which became the Department of Defense two years later) to oversee the armed services, the National Security Council (NSC) of high-level officials to advise the president, and the Central Intelligence Agency (CIA) to conduct spy operations and information gathering overseas. By the early 1950s, the CIA expanded its functions to include covert (secret) operations aimed at overthrowing unfriendly foreign leaders. The National Security Act gave the president increased powers regarding foreign policy.

National Security Act of July 1947 Act that unified the armed forces under a single agency, later called the Department of Defense. It also established the National Security Council to advise the president on matters of national security and created the Central Intelligence Agency (CIA).

In response, Stalin forbade communist satellite governments in Eastern Europe to accept Marshall Plan aid and ordered communist parties in Western Europe to work to thwart it. He tightened his grip on Eastern Europe—most notably, he engineered a coup in Czechoslovakia in February 1948 that ensured full Soviet control of the country—which heightened anxiety in the United States.

Berlin Blockade and Airlift

In June 1948, the Americans, French, and British agreed to fuse their German zones and integrate West Germany (the Federal Republic of Germany) into the Western European economy. Fearing a resurgent Germany tied to the American Cold War camp, the Soviets cut off western land access to the jointly occupied city of Berlin, located inside the Soviet zone. President Truman then ordered the **Berlin airlift**, a massive airlift of food, fuel, and other supplies to Berlin. The Soviets finally lifted the blockade in May 1949 and founded the German Democratic Republic, or East Germany.

Berlin airlift American program to deliver food and supplies to the people of the blockaded city of Berlin, Germany.

The successful airlift may have saved Harry Truman's political career: he narrowly defeated Republican Thomas E. Dewey in the November 1948 presidential election. Truman next formalized the military alliance among the United States, Canada, and Western Europe. In April 1949, twelve nations signed a mutual defense treaty, agreeing that an attack on any one of them would be considered an

MAP 24.1
Divided Europe

After the Second World War, Europe broke into two competing camps. When the United States launched the Marshall Plan in 1948, the Soviet Union countered with its own economic plan the following year. When the United States created NATO in 1949, the Soviet Union answered with the Warsaw Pact in 1955. On the whole, these two camps held firm until the late 1980s. Source: Copyright © Cengage Learning 2015

ICELAND
Reykjavík

Arctic Circle

20°W

ATLANTIC OCEAN

Joined Common Market, 1973

IRELAND $
Dublin

UNITED KINGDOM $
London

U.S. loan of $3.5 billion, 1946
Exploded first atomic bomb, 1952
Joined Common Market, 1973

Joined Common Market, 1986

PORTUGAL $
Lisbon

Joined NATO, 1982
Joined Common Market, 1986

SPAIN $
Madrid

Balearic Is.

Mediterranean Sea

Corsica

Sardinia

Sicily

Exploded first atomic bomb, 1960
Withdrew from NATO, 1966

FRANCE $
Paris

Brussels
BELGIUM $
LUX. $
NETHERLANDS $
Amsterdam

Joined Common Market, 1973

Bern
SWITZ.

Zones of occupation ended, 1955

Joined NATO, 1955

WEST GERMANY $
Bonn

DENMARK $
Copenhagen

North Sea

NORWAY $
Oslo

SWEDEN $
Stockholm

Baltic Sea

FINLAND
Helsinki

20°E

West Berlin
East Berlin

Berlin blockade, 1948–1949

EAST GERMANY

Prague
CZECHOSLOVAKIA

POLAND
Warsaw

Communist coup, 1948
U.S.S.R. invasion, 1968

ITALY $
Rome

Left COMECON, 1961
Withdrew from WP, 1968

Revolution, 1956

AUSTRIA $
Vienna

HUNGARY
Budapest

YUGOSLAVIA
Belgrade

Tito-Stalin schism, 1948

ALBANIA
Tiranë

GREECE
Athens

Truman Doctrine, 1947
Joined NATO, 1952
Joined Common Market, 1981

BULGARIA
Sofia

Danube R.

ROMANIA
Bucharest

Black Sea

Dnieper R.

UNION OF SOVIET SOCIALIST REPUBLICS

Moscow

Exploded first atomic bomb, 1949

40°E

60°N

Don R.

Volga R.

Caspian Sea

40°N

TURKEY
Ankara

CYPRUS Nicosia

Truman Doctrine, 1947
Joined NATO, 1952

N

0   200   400 Km.
0   200   400 Mi.

$ Participants in the Marshall Plan

Member of NATO,* formed in 1949

Member of COMECON ** formed in 1949; and the Warsaw Pact, organized in 1955

Member of the European Common Market, formed in 1958

Iron Curtain

* North Atlantic Treaty Organization
** Council for Mutual Economic Assistance

attack on all, and establishing the **North Atlantic Treaty Organization** (NATO; see Map 24.1), the first time since 1778 that the United States entered a formal European military alliance. Truman hoped that NATO would deter Soviet expansion and keep Western Europeans from embracing communism or even neutralism in the Cold War. The Senate ratified the treaty by 82 votes to 13, and the United States began to spend billions of dollars under the Mutual Defense Assistance Act.

By the summer of 1949, Truman and his advisers were basking in the successes of their foreign policy. Containment was working, West Germany was recovering, the Berlin blockade had been defeated, and NATO had been formed. True, there was trouble in China, where the communists under **Mao Zedong** were winning a civil war. But that struggle would likely wax and wane for years to come. Just possibly, some dared to think, Truman was on his way to winning the Cold War.

> **North Atlantic Treaty Organization** A mutual defense pact between the United States and eleven other nations promising to stand united in the face of military aggression, specifically by the Soviet Union.

> **Mao Zedong** Chinese military and political leader who established the communist People's Republic of China.

Twin Shocks

Then, suddenly, in late September, came the "twin shocks," two momentous developments that made Americans feel in even greater danger than ever before. First, an American reconnaissance aircraft detected unusually high radioactivity in the atmosphere: the Soviets had exploded an atomic device. With the American nuclear monopoly erased, Western Europe seemed more vulnerable. Second, the communists in China completed their conquest. Now the world's largest and most populous countries were ruled by communists, and one of them had the atomic bomb. The bipartisan foreign policy of 1945–1948 broke down, as Republicans, bitter over Truman's reelection, declared that traitors in America must have given Stalin the bomb and allowed China to be "lost."

Rejecting calls for high-level negotiations, Truman in early 1950 gave the go-ahead to begin production of a hydrogen bomb, the "Super." Kennan bemoaned the militarization of the Cold War and was replaced at the State Department by Paul Nitze. The National Security Council delivered to the president in April 1950 a significant top-secret document labeled **NSC-68**. Predicting continued tension with expansionistic communists, the report, whose primary author was Nitze, appealed for a much enlarged military budget and the mobilization of public support. The Cold War was about to become vastly more expensive and far-reaching.

> **NSC-68** Secret report by the National Security Council that would characterize U.S. Cold War strategy for decades; it saw the clash between the United States and the Soviet Union as a fight between good and evil and reversed the post–World War II military demobilization, focusing instead on a military buildup.

The Cold War in Asia

> *How did the Cold War turn "hot" in Asia?*

Though less important to both superpowers than Europe, Asia would be the continent where the Cold War most often turned hot and where the consequences of an expansive containment doctrine would exact their heaviest price on the United States.

From the start, Japan was crucial to U.S. strategy. The United States monopolized Japan's reconstruction through a military occupation directed by General Douglas MacArthur. Truman disliked "Mr. Prima Donna, Brass Hat," but MacArthur wrote a democratic constitution, gave women voting rights, revitalized the economy, and destroyed the nation's weapons. U.S. authorities also helped Americanize Japan by censoring films that criticized the United States (for the destruction of Hiroshima, for example) or depicted traditional Japanese customs, such as suicide, arranged marriages, and swordplay. In 1951, the United States and Japan signed a separate peace that restored Japan's sovereignty and ended the occupation. A Mutual Security Treaty that year provided for the stationing of U.S. forces in Japan, including a base on Okinawa.

Chinese Civil War

The administration had less success in China. The United States had long backed the Nationalists of Jiang Jieshi (Chiang Kai-shek) against Mao Zedong's communists. But after World War II, Generalissimo Jiang's government had become corrupt, inefficient, and out of touch with discontented peasants, whom the communists enlisted with promises of land reform. Jiang also subverted American efforts to negotiate a cease-fire and a coalition government.

American officials divided on the question of whether Mao was an Asian Tito—communist but independent—or, as most believed, part of an international communist movement that might give the Soviets a springboard into Asia. Thus, when Chinese communists made secret overtures to the United States for diplomatic talks in 1945 and again in 1949, American officials rebuffed them. Mao decided to "lean" to the Soviet side, but because of China's fierce independence, a Sino-Soviet schism soon opened.

Then came Mao's victory in September 1949. Jiang fled to the island of Formosa (Taiwan), and in Beijing (formerly Peking) Mao proclaimed the People's Republic of China (PRC). Truman hesitated to extend diplomatic recognition to the new government. U.S. officials became alarmed by the 1950 Sino-Soviet treaty of friendship and the harassment of Americans in China. Truman also chose nonrecognition because vocal Republican critics, the so-called China lobby, pinned Jiang's defeat on the administration. Not until 1979 did official Sino-American relations resume.

Vietnam's Quest for Independence

Mao's victory in China drew urgent American attention to Indochina, the southeast Asian peninsula held by France for the better part of a century. The Japanese

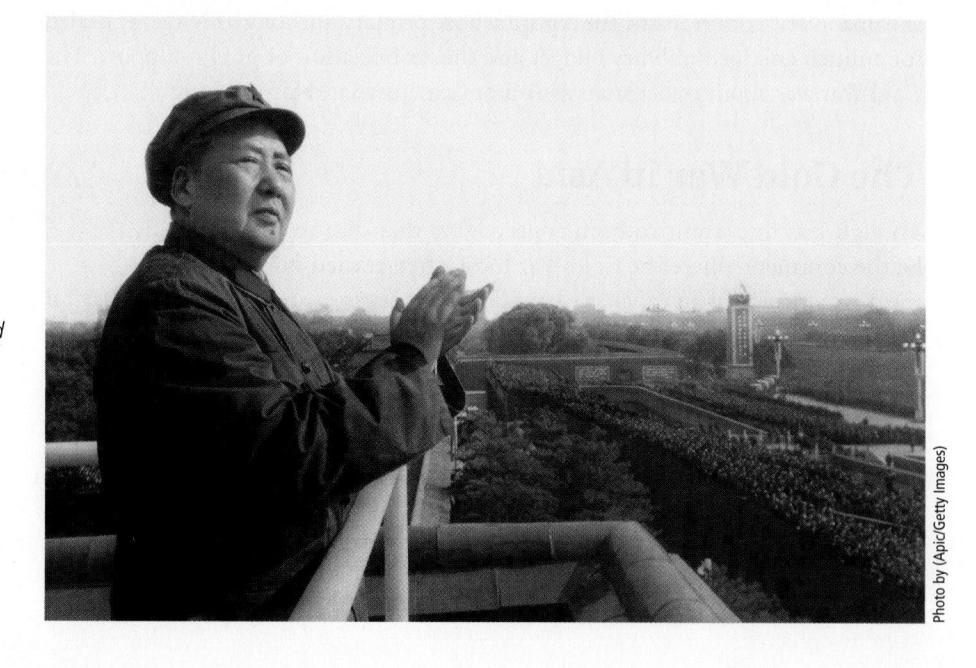

Mao Zedong was a military theoretician who also involved himself in day-to-day military decision making. He was responsible for, or at least approved, all of the major strategic moves the communists made on their way to power. This image shows him applauding soldiers and other supporters on Tiananmen Square in Beijing.

Photo by (Apic/Getty Images)

had wrested control over Indochina during World War II, but the Vietnamese nationalists had grown stronger. Their leader, Ho Chi Minh, hoped to use Japan's defeat to assert Vietnamese independence, and he sought U.S. support. American officials rejected Ho's appeals in favor of a restoration of French rule, mostly to ensure France's cooperation in the emerging Soviet-American confrontation. In addition, Ho, the State Department declared, was an "agent of international communism" who would assist Soviet and, after 1949, Chinese expansionism. Overlooking the native roots of the nationalist rebellion against French colonialism, Washington officials interpreted events in Indochina through a Cold War lens.

Even so, when war between the Vietminh and France broke out in 1946, the United States initially took a hands-off approach. But when Jiang's regime collapsed in China three years later, the Truman administration made two crucial decisions. First, in February 1950 it recognized the French puppet government of Bao Dai. To many Vietnamese, the United States thus became in essence a colonial power, an ally of the hated French. Second, in May, the administration agreed to send weapons and assistance to sustain the French in Indochina. From 1945 to 1954, the United States gave $2 billion of the $5 billion that France spent to keep Vietnam within its empire—to no avail (see Chapters 26 and 27). How Vietnam became the site of a major American war is one of the most remarkable and tragic stories of modern U.S. history.

The Korean War

Early on June 25, 1950, a large military force of the Democratic People's Republic of Korea (North Korea) moved across the thirty-eighth parallel into the Republic of Korea (South Korea). Colonized by Japan since 1910, Korea was divided in two after Japan's defeat in 1945. Although the Soviets had armed the North and the Americans had armed the South (U.S. aid had reached $100 million a year), the **Korean War** began as a civil war. Since its division, the two parts had been skirmishing while antigovernment (and anti-U.S.) guerrilla fighting flared in the South.

Both the North's communist leader, Kim Il Sung, and the South's president, Syngman Rhee, sought to reunify their nation. Kim's military gained strength when tens of thousands of Koreans returned home in 1949 after serving in Mao's army. Though President Truman claimed that the Soviets had masterminded the North Korean attack, Stalin only reluctantly approved it after Kim predicted an early victory and after Mao backed Kim. When the UN Security Council voted to defend South Korea, the Soviet representative was not present to veto because the Soviets were boycotting the United Nations for its refusal to admit the People's Republic of China. During the war, Moscow gave only limited aid to North Korea and China and reneged on promised Soviet airpower. Stalin did not want to be dragged into a costly war.

U.S. Forces Intervene Truman first ordered General Douglas MacArthur to send arms and troops to South Korea. Fearing lawmakers would initiate a lengthy debate, he did not seek congressional approval, thereby setting the precedent of waging war on executive authority alone. After the Security Council voted to assist South Korea, MacArthur

What were the consequences of the Korean War for the United States?

Korean War War between North Korea and South Korea with heavy U.S. and Soviet involvement (1950–1953), with each seeking to undermine the other via economic pressure and military raids.

MAP 24.2
The Korean War, 1950–1953
Beginning as a civil war between North and South, this war became international when the United States—under the auspices of the United Nations—and the People's Republic of China intervened with their military forces. Source: Copyright © Cengage Learning 2015

became commander of UN forces. Sixteen nations contributed troops, but 40 percent were South Korean and about 50 percent American. In the war's early weeks, North Korean tanks and superior firepower sent the South Korean army into retreat. The first American soldiers, taking heavy casualties, could not stop the North Korean advance. Within weeks, the South Koreans and Americans had been pushed into the tiny Pusan perimeter at South Korea's tip (see Map 24.2).

General MacArthur planned a daring amphibious landing at heavily fortified Inchon, several hundred miles behind North Korean lines. After U.S. bombs pounded Inchon, marines sprinted ashore on September 15, 1950. The operation soon liberated the South Korean capital of Seoul and pushed the North Koreans back to the thirty-eighth parallel. Even before Inchon, Truman had redefined the U.S. war goal from the containment of North Korea to the reunification of Korea by force. Communism would be rolled back.

Chinese Entry into the War

In September, UN forces drove deep into North Korea, and American aircraft began strikes against bridges on the Yalu River, the border between North Korea and China. Mao warned that China could not permit the bombing of its transportation links with Korea and would not accept annihilation of North Korea. MacArthur shrugged off the warnings, and Washington officials agreed, confident that the Soviets were not preparing for war.

MacArthur was right about the Soviets, but wrong about the Chinese. On October 25, Mao sent Chinese soldiers into the war near the Yalu. Perhaps to lure American forces into a trap or to signal willingness to negotiate, they pulled back after a successful offensive against South Korean troops. Then, after MacArthur sent the U.S. Eighth Army northward, tens of thousands of Chinese troops counterattacked on November 26, surprising American forces and driving them southward. One U.S. officer termed it "a sight that hasn't been seen for hundreds of years: the men of a whole United States Army fleeing from a battlefield, abandoning their wounded, running for their lives."

Truman's Firing of MacArthur

By 1951, the front had stabilized around the thirty-eighth parallel. Both Washington and Moscow welcomed negotiations, but MacArthur recklessly called for an attack on China and for Jiang's return. Denouncing the concept of limited war (war without nuclear weapons, confined to one place), MacArthur hinted that the president was practicing appeasement. In April, backed by the Joint Chiefs of Staff (the heads of the various armed services), Truman fired MacArthur, who returned home a hero. Truman's popularity sagged, but he weathered scattered demands for his impeachment.

Armistice talks began in July 1951, but the fighting continued for two more years. Defying the Geneva Prisoners of War Convention (1949), U.S. officials announced that only those North Korean and Chinese prisoners of war (POWs) who wished to go home would be returned. While Americans resisted forced repatriation, the North Koreans denounced forced retention. Both sides undertook "reeducation" or "brainwashing" of POWs.

Peace Agreement

Not until July 1953 was an armistice signed. Stalin's death in March and new leaders in both Moscow and Washington facilitated a settlement. The combatants agreed to hand over the POW question to a special panel of neutral nations, which later gave prisoners their choice of staying or leaving. Over half the North Korean and about a quarter of Chinese POWs returned home, whereas only a few Americans and South Koreans stayed in the north. The North Korean–South Korean borderline was set near the thirty-eighth parallel, the prewar boundary, and a demilitarized zone was created between the two Koreas.

American casualties totaled 54,246 dead and 103,284 wounded. Close to 5 million Asians died: 2 million North Korean civilians and 500,000 soldiers; 1 million South Korean civilians and 100,000 soldiers; and at least 1 million Chinese soldiers—ranking Korea as one of the costliest wars of the twentieth century.

Consequences of the War

The Korean War carried major domestic political consequences. The failure to achieve victory and the public's impatience with a stalemated war undoubtedly helped to elect Republican Dwight Eisenhower to the presidency in 1952, as the former general promised to "go to Korea" to end the war. The powers of the presidency grew as Congress repeatedly deferred to Truman. The president never asked Congress for a declaration of war, believing that, as commander-in-chief, he had the authority to send troops wherever he wished. He saw no need to consult Congress—except to get the $69.5 billion Korean War bill paid. In addition, the war, which occurred in the midst of the "who lost China?" debate, inflamed party politics in the United States. Republican lawmakers, including Wisconsin senator Joseph McCarthy, accused Truman and Secretary of State Dean Acheson of being "soft on communism"; this pushed the administration to take an uncompromising position in the negotiations.

The impact on foreign policy was even greater. The Sino-American hostility generated by the war made U.S. reconciliation with the Beijing government impossible and made South Korea and Formosa major recipients of American foreign aid. The alliance with Japan strengthened as its economy boomed after filling large U.S. procurement orders. Australia and New Zealand joined the United States in a mutual defense agreement, the ANZUS Treaty (1951). The U.S. Army sent four divisions to Europe and initiated plans to rearm West Germany. The Korean War also persuaded Truman to approve NSC-68. The military budget jumped from $14 billion in 1949 to $44 billion in 1953; it remained between $35 billion and $44 billion a year throughout the 1950s. The Soviet Union sought to match this military buildup, resulting in an arms race. Truman's legacy was a highly militarized U.S. foreign policy on a global scale.

Unrelenting Cold War

How did Dulles and Eisenhower raise the stakes in the Cold War?

President Eisenhower and Secretary of State **John Foster Dulles** largely sustained Truman's Cold War policies. As a general during the Second World War, Eisenhower had negotiated with world leaders. After the war, he had served as army chief of staff and NATO supreme commander. Dulles had been closely involved with U.S. diplomacy since the first decade of the century.

John Foster Dulles Secretary of state under Dwight D. Eisenhower. He spoke of a holy war against "atheistic communism" and rejected the policy of containment.

Eisenhower and Dulles accepted the Cold War consensus about the threat of communism and the need for global vigilance. Although Democrats promoted an image of Eisenhower as a bumbling, passive, aging hero, deferring most foreign policy matters to Dulles, the president in fact commanded the policymaking process and on occasion tamed the more hawkish proposals of Dulles and Vice President Richard Nixon. Even so, the secretary of state's influence was vast. He impressed people as averse to compromise, an essential ingredient in successful diplomacy. His assertion that neutrality was an "immoral and short-sighted conception" did not sit well with Third World leaders, who resented being told they had to choose between East and West.

"Massive Retaliation"

Considering containment too defensive, Dulles instead called for "liberation," freeing Eastern Europe from Soviet control. "Massive retaliation" was the administration's plan for the nuclear obliteration of the Soviet state or its assumed client, the People's Republic of China, if either one took aggressive actions. Officials believed massive retaliation would provide "deterrence," the prevention of hostile Soviet behavior.

In their "New Look" for the American military, Eisenhower and Dulles emphasized airpower and nuclear weaponry. The president's preference for heavy weapons stemmed in part from his desire to trim the federal budget ("more bang for the buck," as the saying went). Galvanized by the successful test of the world's first hydrogen bomb in November 1952, Eisenhower oversaw a massive stockpiling of nuclear weapons—from 1,200 at the start of his presidency to 22,229 at the end. With this huge military arsenal, the United States could practice "brinkmanship": not backing down in a crisis, even if it meant taking the nation to the brink of war. Eisenhower also popularized the **"domino theory"**: that small, weak neighboring nations would fall to communism like dominoes if they were not supported by the United States.

domino theory Eisenhower's prediction that if Vietnam went communist, then the smaller, neighboring communities of Thailand, Burma, Indonesia, and ultimately all of Asia would fall like dominoes.

CIA as Foreign Policy Instrument

Eisenhower increasingly utilized the Central Intelligence Agency as an instrument of foreign policy. The CIA put foreign leaders (such as King Hussein of Jordan) on its payroll; subsidized foreign labor unions, newspapers, and political parties; planted false stories in newspapers through its "disinformation" projects; and trained foreign military officers in counterrevolution. It hired American journalists and professors, secretly funded the National Student Association to spur contacts with foreign student leaders, and conducted experiments on unsuspecting Americans to determine the effects of "mind control" drugs. The CIA also launched covert operations (including assassination schemes) to subvert Third World governments, helping to overthrow the governments of Iran (1953) and Guatemala (1954) but failing to topple regimes in Indonesia (1958) and Cuba (1961).

The American intelligence community followed the principle of plausible deniability: covert operations should be conducted in such a way, and the decisions that launched them concealed so well, that the president could deny any knowledge of them. Thus, Eisenhower disavowed any U.S. role in Guatemala, even though he had ordered the operation. He and his successor, John F. Kennedy, also denied instructing the CIA to assassinate Cuba's Fidel Castro, whose regime after 1959 became stridently anti-American.

Nuclear Buildup

Leaders in Moscow soon became aware of Eisenhower's covert actions and stockpiling of nuclear weapons. They increased their own intelligence activity and tested their first H-bomb in 1953. Four years later, they fired the world's first intercontinental ballistic missile (ICBM) and propelled the satellite **Sputnik** into outer space. Americans felt more vulnerable to air attack, even though in 1957 the United States had 2,460 strategic weapons and a nuclear stockpile of 5,543, compared with the Soviet Union's 102 and 650. The administration deployed intermediate-range missiles in Europe, targeted against the Soviet Union. At the end of 1960, the United States added Polaris missile-bearing submarines to its navy. To foster future technological advancement, the National Aeronautics and Space Administration (NASA) was created in 1958.

Sputnik Soviet satellite that was the world's first successful launch in space in 1957; it dashed the American myth of unquestioned technological superiority.

Overall, though, Eisenhower sought to avoid military confrontation with the Soviet Union and China, content to follow Truman's *containment* of communism. Eisenhower refused to use nuclear weapons and proved more reluctant than many other Cold War presidents to send American soldiers into battle. He preferred to fight the Soviets at the level of propaganda, seeking to win the "hearts and minds" of people overseas. The "People-to-People" campaign, launched in 1956, used ordinary Americans and nongovernmental organizations to enhance the international image of the United States.

Sometimes, the propaganda war was waged on the Soviets' turf. In 1959, Vice President Richard Nixon traveled to Moscow to open an American products fair. In the display of a modern American kitchen, Nixon extolled capitalist consumerism, while Soviet premier Nikita Khrushchev, Stalin's successor, touted the merits of communism. The encounter became famous as the "kitchen debate."

The People-to-People Campaign

Just after the Cold War began, U.S. officials determined that the Soviet-American confrontation was as much psychological and ideological as military and economic. One result was the People-to-People campaign, a state-private venture initiated by the United States Information Agency (USIA) in 1956, which aimed to win the "hearts and minds" of people around the world. In this program, American propaganda experts used ordinary Americans, businesses, civic organizations, labor groups, and women's clubs to promote confidence abroad in American goodness. The People-to-People campaign, one USIA pamphlet said, made "every man an ambassador."

Campaign activities resembled the home-front mobilization efforts of World War II. Americans were told that $30 could send a ninety-nine-volume portable library of American books to schools and libraries overseas. Publishers donated magazines and books for free distribution to foreign countries. People-to-People committees organized sister-city affiliations, hosted exchange students, and organized traveling "People-to-People delegations." The travelers were urged to behave like goodwill ambassadors when abroad and to "help overcome any feeling that America is a land that thinks money can buy everything."

To extol everyday life in the United States, Camp Fire Girls in more than three thousand communities took photographs on the theme "This is our home. This is how we live. These are my People." The photographs were sent to girls in Latin America, Africa, Asia, and the Middle East. The Hobbies Committee, meanwhile, connected people with interests in radio, photography, coins, stamps, and horticulture.

The persistence to this day of the widespread impression that Americans are a provincial, materialistic people prompts skepticism about the People-to-People campaign's success. But alongside this negative image is a positive one that sees Americans as open, friendly, optimistic, and pragmatic. Whatever role the People-to-People campaign played in the larger Cold War struggle, it certainly linked ordinary Americans more closely to people in other parts of the world.

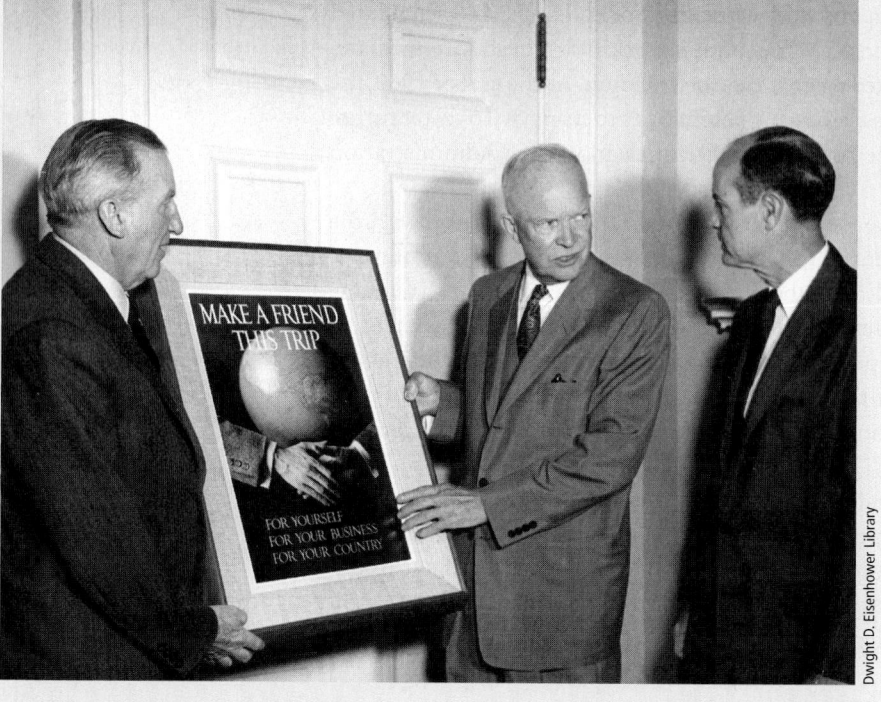

"Make a friend this trip," urges this framed People-to-People poster, delivered to President Eisenhower in May 1957, "for yourself, for your business, for your country." With the president are two of the campaign's leaders, John W. Hanes Jr. and Edward Lipscomb.

Dwight D. Eisenhower Library

Rebellion in Hungary

Eisenhower showed his restraint in 1956 when turmoil rocked parts of Eastern Europe. In February, Khrushchev called for "peaceful coexistence" between capitalists and communists, denounced Stalin, and suggested that Moscow would tolerate different brands of communism. Revolts against Soviet power promptly erupted in Poland and Hungary, testing Khrushchev's new permissiveness. After a new Hungarian government in 1956 withdrew from the Warsaw Pact (the Soviet military alliance formed in 1955 with communist countries of Eastern Europe), Soviet troops and tanks crushed the rebellion.

Although the Eisenhower administration's propaganda encouraged liberation efforts, U.S. officials could not aid the rebels without igniting a world war. Instead, they promised only to welcome more Hungarian immigrants than American quota laws allowed. The West could have reaped some propaganda advantage from this display of Soviet force had not British, French, and Israeli troops—U.S. allies—invaded Egypt during the Suez crisis just before the Soviets smashed the Hungarian uprising (see page 723).

The turmoil had hardly subsided when the divided city of Berlin again became a Cold War flash point. The Soviets railed against the placement in West Germany of American bombers capable of carrying nuclear warheads, and they complained that West Berlin had become an escape route for disaffected East Germans. In 1958, Khrushchev announced that the Soviet Union would recognize East German control of all of Berlin unless the United States and its allies began talks on German reunification and rearmament. The United States refused; Khrushchev backed down but promised to press the issue again.

U-2 Incident

On May 1, 1960, two weeks before a summit meeting in Paris, a U-2 spy plane carrying high-powered cameras crashed 1,200 miles inside the Soviet Union. Moscow claimed credit for shooting down the plane and displayed captured CIA pilot Francis Gary Powers and the pictures he had snapped of Soviet military sites. Khrushchev demanded an apology for the U.S. violation of Soviet airspace. When Washington refused, the Soviets left the Paris summit.

Meanwhile, both sides kept a wary eye on the People's Republic of China. Despite evidence of a widening Sino-Soviet split, most American officials treated communism as a monolithic movement. In 1954, in a dispute over miniscule islands off the Chinese coast—Mazu (Matsu) and the chain known as Jinmen (Quemoy)—the United States and the People's Republic of China lurched toward the brink. Taiwan's Jiang Jieshi held these islands and hoped to use them as a launching point to raid the mainland. Communist China's guns bombarded the islands in 1954. Thinking that U.S. credibility was at stake, Eisenhower defended the outposts and hinted that he might use nuclear weapons.

Formosa Resolution

In early 1955, Congress passed the Formosa Resolution, authorizing the president to deploy troops to defend Formosa and adjoining islands. In so doing, Congress formally surrendered to the president what it had informally given up in the 1950 Korea decision: the constitutional power to declare war. The crisis passed, but war loomed again in 1958 over Jinmen and Mazu. This time, as Jiang withdrew some troops, China relaxed its bombardments. But Eisenhower's nuclear threats persuaded the Chinese that they, too, needed nuclear arms. In 1964, China exploded its first nuclear bomb.

The Struggle for the Third World

How did racism in America interfere with U.S. leaders' ability to win Cold War allies among developing nations?

In much of the Third World, the process of decolonization that began during the First World War accelerated after World War II, when economically wracked imperial countries proved incapable of resisting their colonies' demands for freedom (see Map 24.3). From 1943 to 1994, a total of 125 countries became independent (including the former Soviet republics that departed the USSR in 1991). The emergence of new states shook the foundations of the international system. In the traditional U.S. sphere of influence, Latin America, nationalists once again challenged Washington's dominance.

Interests in the Third World

By the late 1940s, Soviet-American rivalry shifted increasingly to the Third World. The new nations could buy American goods, supply raw materials, and invite investments (more than one-third of America's private foreign investments were in Third World countries in 1959). Both great powers looked to these new states for votes in the United Nations and for military and intelligence bases. But often poor and unstable—and rife with tribal, ethnic, and class rivalries—many new nations sought to end the economic, military, and cultural hegemony of the West. They played the two superpowers against each other to garner more aid and arms. U.S. interventions—military and otherwise—in the Third World, American leaders believed, would impress Moscow with Washington's might.

To thwart nationalist, radical, and communist challenges, the United States directed more than 90 percent of U.S. foreign aid to developing nations by 1961. Washington also allied with undemocratic but anticommunist regimes, meddled in civil wars, and unleashed CIA covert operations. When some of the larger Third World states—notably India, Ghana, Egypt, and Indonesia—refused to take sides in the Cold War, Secretary of State Dulles declared that neutralism was a step toward communism. He and Eisenhower insisted that every nation should take a side.

American leaders argued that technologically "backward" Third World countries needed Western-induced capitalist development to enjoy economic growth and political moderation. Often these officials also ascribed stereotyped race-, age-, and gender-based characteristics to Third World peoples, seeing them as emotional and irrational, and therefore dependent on the fatherly tutelage of the United States.

Racism and Segregation as U.S. Handicaps

Race attitudes and segregation in the United States especially influenced U.S. relations with Third World countries. In 1955, G. L. Mehta, the Indian ambassador to the United States, was refused service in the whites-only section of a restaurant at Houston International Airport. Other Third World diplomats experienced similar indignities. Dulles, who apologized to Mehta, thought racial segregation spoiled American

MAP 24.3
The Rise of the Third World: Newly Independent Nations Since 1943

Accelerated by the Second World War, decolonization liberated many peoples from imperial rule. New nations emerged in the postwar international system dominated by the Cold War rivalry of the United States and the Soviet Union. Many newly independent states became targets of great-power intrigue but chose nonalignment in the Cold War. Source: Copyright © Cengage Learning 2015

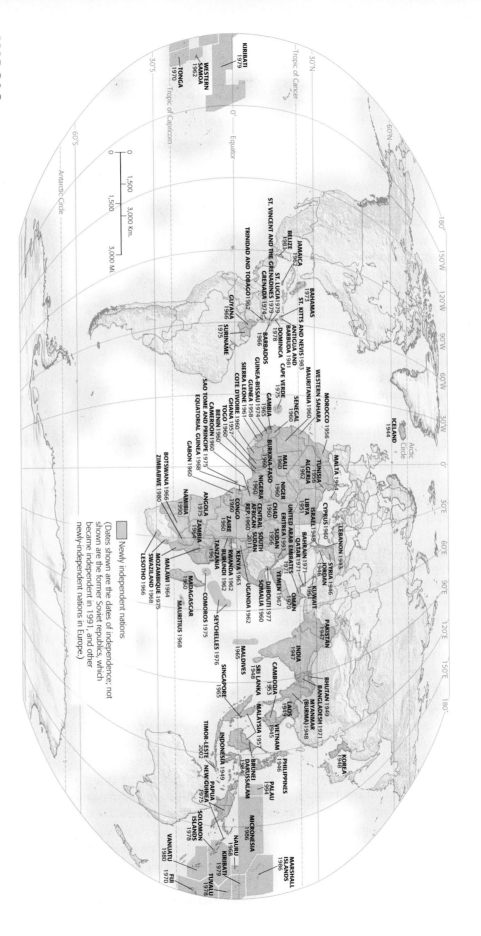

Newly independent nations

(Dates shown are the dates of independence; not shown are the former Soviet republics, which became independent in 1991, and other newly-independent nations in Europe.)

efforts to win friends in Third World countries and gave the Soviets a propaganda advantage.

Thus, when the U.S. attorney general appealed to the Supreme Court to strike down segregation in public schools, he underlined that the humiliation of dark-skinned diplomats "furnished grist for the Communist propaganda mills." When the Court announced its *Brown* decision in 1954 (see page 740), the government quickly broadcast news of the desegregation order around the world in thirty-five languages on its Voice of America overseas radio network. But the problem did not go away. For example, after the 1957 Little Rock crisis (see pages 742–743), Dulles remarked that racial bigotry was "ruining our foreign policy." Still, when a Department of State office countered Soviet propaganda by creating for the 1958 World's Fair in Brussels an exhibit titled "The Unfinished Work"—on U.S. strides toward desegregation—southern conservatives kicked up such a furor that the Eisenhower administration closed the display.

American hostility toward revolution also obstructed the quest for influence in the Third World. In the twentieth century, the United States opposed revolutions in Mexico, China, Russia, Cuba, Vietnam, Nicaragua, and Iran, among other nations. Preferring to maintain the status quo, the United States usually supported its European allies or the conservative, propertied classes in the Third World.

Development and Modernization

Yet idealism also inspired U.S. policy. Believing that Third World peoples craved modernization and the American economic model of private enterprise, American policymakers launched various "development" projects. Such projects promised economic growth, prosperity, and stability, which the benefactors hoped would undermine radicalism. In the 1950s, the Carnegie, Ford, and Rockefeller Foundations worked with the U.S. Agency for International Development (AID) to sponsor a Green Revolution promoting agricultural production. The Rockefeller Foundation supported foreign universities' efforts to train national leaders committed to nonradical development.

To persuade Third World peoples to abandon radical doctrines and neutralism, American leaders created propaganda campaigns. The United States Information Agency (USIA), founded in 1953, used films, radio broadcasts, the magazine *Free World*, exhibitions, exchange programs, and libraries (in 162 cities worldwide by 1961) to trumpet the theme of "People's Capitalism." Citing America's economic success—contrasted

In the 1950s, the United States Information Agency—known overseas as the United States Information Service or USIS—sought to generate favorable international perceptions of American ideas and culture, including in what the State Department called "isolated areas." Here, people crowd around a USIS mobile library on a road near Rangoon, Burma, in June 1953.

with "slave-labor" conditions in the Soviet Union—the message showcased well-paid American workers, political democracy, and religious freedom. To counter ugly pictures of segregation and racial violence, the USIA applauded success stories of individual African Americans, such as boxers Floyd Patterson and Sugar Ray Robinson. In 1960 alone, some 13.8 million people visited U.S. pavilions abroad.

Undoubtedly, the American way of life appealed to some Third World peoples. They, too, wanted to enjoy American consumer goods, rock music, economic status, and educational opportunities. But if foreigners often envied Americans, they also resented them for having and wasting so much and for allowing their corporations to extract high profits from overseas. Americans often received blame for the persistent poverty of the developing world, even though the leaders of those nations made decisions that hindered their own progress, such as pouring millions of dollars into their militaries while their people needed food. Nonetheless, anti-American resentments manifested in the late 1950s in attacks on USIA libraries in Calcutta, India; Beirut, Lebanon; and Bogotá, Colombia.

Intervention in Guatemala

When the more benign techniques of containment—aid, trade, cultural relations—proved insufficient to get Third World nations to line up on the American side in the Cold War, the Eisenhower administration often showed a willingness to press harder. In 1951, leftist Jacobo Arbenz Guzmán was elected president of Guatemala, a poor country whose largest landowner was the American-owned United Fruit Company, which owned 3 million acres of land throughout Latin America and operated railroads, ports, and telecommunications facilities. To fulfill his promise of land reform, Arbenz expropriated United Fruit's uncultivated land and offered compensation. The company dismissed the offer and charged that Arbenz posed a communist threat—a charge that CIA officials had already floated because Arbenz employed some communists in his government. The CIA began a secret plot to overthrow Arbenz. He turned to Moscow for military aid, thus reinforcing American suspicions. The CIA airlifted arms into Guatemala, dropping them at United Fruit facilities, and in mid-1954, CIA-supported Guatemalans struck from Honduras. U.S. planes bombed the capital city, and the invaders drove Arbenz from power. The new pro-American regime returned United Fruit's land, but an ensuing civil war staggered Guatemala for decades.

The Cuban Revolution and Fidel Castro

Eisenhower also worried as turmoil gripped Cuba in the late 1950s. In early 1959, Fidel Castro's rebels, or *barbudos* ("bearded ones"), driven by anti-American nationalism, ousted Fulgencio Batista, a longtime U.S. ally whose corrupt, dictatorial regime had turned Havana into a haven for gambling, prostitution, and organized crime. Cubans had resented U.S. domination since the early twentieth century, when the Platt Amendment had compromised their independence. Castro sought to roll back the influence of American business, which had invested some $1 billion on the island, and to break the U.S. grasp on Cuban trade.

In early 1960, after Cuba signed a trade treaty with the Soviet Union, Eisenhower ordered the CIA to organize Cuban exiles to overthrow the Castro government. The agency also plotted Castro's assassination. When Eisenhower drastically cut U.S. purchases of Cuban sugar, Castro seized North American–owned companies that had not yet been nationalized. Castro appealed to the Soviet Union, which offered loans and expanded trade. Before leaving office in early 1961, Eisenhower broke diplomatic relations with Cuba and advised president-elect John F. Kennedy to advance plans for the invasion, which came—and failed—in early 1961 (see page 764).

Arab-Israeli Conflict

In the Middle East, meanwhile, ongoing tensions between Arabs and Jews posed additional challenges (see Map 29.2). Before the end of World War II, only France and Britain among the great powers had been concerned with this region of the world. But the dissolution of empires and the rise of Cold War tensions drew in Washington, as did tensions in British-held Palestine. From 1945 to 1947, Britain tried to enlist U.S. officials to help resolve how to split Palestine between the Arabs and Jews. The Truman administration declined, and the British in 1947 turned the issue over to the United Nations, which voted to partition Palestine into separate Arab and Jewish states. Arab leaders opposed the decision, but in May 1948 Jewish leaders announced the creation of Israel.

The United States, which lobbied to secure the UN vote, immediately extended recognition to the new state. A moral conviction that Jews deserved a homeland after the Holocaust, and that Zionism would create a democratic Israel, influenced Truman's decision, as did the belief that Jewish votes might swing some states to the Democrats in the 1948 election. These beliefs trumped concerns that Arab oil producers might turn against the United States. The Soviet Union recognized Israel, but Israeli leaders kept Moscow at arm's length. Palestinian Arabs, displaced from land they considered theirs, joined with Israel's Arab neighbors to make immediate war on the new state. The Israelis fought for six months until a UN-backed truce was called.

In the years 1948–1950, hundreds of thousands of Jewish refugees arrived in the state of Israel. Legendary war photographer Robert Capa snapped this picture of refugees arriving on a boat in Haifa in 1949. A few years later, while on assignment for Life *magazine, Capa would be killed by a land mine in Indochina.*

Robert Capa/International Center of Photography/Magnum Photos

Thereafter, U.S. Middle East policy centered on ensuring Israel's survival and cementing ties with Arab oil producers. American companies produced about half of the region's petroleum in the 1950s. Eisenhower cultivated close relations with oil-rich Iran. Its ruling shah had granted American oil companies a 40 percent interest in a new petroleum consortium in return for CIA help in the successful overthrow, in 1953, of his rival, Mohammed Mossadegh.

American officials faced a more formidable foe in Egypt's Gamal Abdul Nasser, a towering figure in a pan-Arabic movement. Nasser vowed to expel the British from the Suez Canal and the Israelis from Palestine. The United States wished neither to anger the Arabs, for fear of losing valuable oil supplies, nor to alienate its ally Israel, supported at home by politically active American Jews. But when Nasser declared neutrality in the Cold War, Dulles lost patience.

Suez Crisis

In 1956, the United States reneged on its offer to help Egypt finance the Aswan Dam, which would provide inexpensive electricity and water for Nile valley farmland. Nasser responded by nationalizing the British-owned Suez Canal, intending to use its profits to build the dam. Fully 75 percent of Western Europe's oil came from the Middle East, most of it via the Suez Canal. Fearing an interruption, the British and French conspired with Israel to bring down Nasser. On October 29, 1956, the Israelis invaded Suez, joined two days later by British and French forces.

Eisenhower fumed, fearing the invasion would cause Nasser to seek help from the Soviets, inviting them into the Middle East. He sternly demanded that London, Paris, and Tel Aviv pull their troops out, and they did. Egypt took possession of the canal, the Soviets built the Aswan Dam, and Nasser became a hero to Third World peoples. The United States countered Nasser by supporting the notoriously corrupt conservative King Ibn Saud of Saudi Arabia, who renewed America's lease of an air base.

Eisenhower Doctrine

Washington officials worried that a "vacuum" existed in the Middle East—and that the Soviets might fill it. To protect American interests, the president proclaimed in the 1957 **Eisenhower Doctrine** that the United States would intervene in the Middle East if any government threatened by a communist takeover asked for help. In 1958, fourteen thousand American troops went to Lebanon to quell an internal political dispute that Washington feared might be exploited by pro-Nasser groups or communists. The restrained use of U.S. military power served to defuse the crisis.

Cold War concerns also drove Eisenhower's policy toward Vietnam. Despite substantial U.S. aid, the French lost steadily to the Vietminh. Finally, in early 1954, Ho's forces surrounded the French fortress at Dien Bien Phu in northwest Vietnam (see Map 26.1). Although some advisers advocated military intervention, Eisenhower moved cautiously. The United States had advised and bankrolled the French but had not committed troops to the war. If American airpower did not save the French, would ground troops be required next, and in hostile terrain? As one high-level doubter remarked, "One cannot go over Niagara Falls in a barrel only slightly."

At home, influential members of Congress—including Lyndon Baines Johnson of Texas, who as president would wage large-scale war in Vietnam—told Eisenhower

Eisenhower Doctrine The 1957 proclamation that the United States would send military aid and, if necessary, troops to any Middle Eastern nation threatened by "Communist aggression."

they wanted "no more Koreas" and warned him against any U.S. military commitment. The issue became moot on May 7, when the weary French defenders at Dien Bien Phu surrendered.

| Geneva Accords on Vietnam |

Peace talks, already under way in Geneva, brought together the United States, the Soviet Union, Britain, the People's Republic of China, Laos, Cambodia, and the competing Vietnamese regimes of Bao Dai and Ho Chi Minh. The 1954 Geneva Accords, signed by France and Ho's Democratic Republic of Vietnam, temporarily divided Vietnam at the seventeenth parallel; Ho's government was confined to the North, Bao Dai's to the South. The seventeenth parallel was meant as a truce line, not a national boundary; the country was scheduled to be reunified after national elections in 1956. Meanwhile, neither North nor South was to join a military alliance or permit foreign military bases on its soil.

Confident that the Geneva agreements ultimately would mean communist victory, the United States set about trying to undermine them. A CIA team undertook secret operations against North Vietnam, and in the South, the United States helped Ngo Dinh Diem push Bao Dai aside and inaugurate the Republic of Vietnam.

| National Liberation Front |

Diem proved a difficult ally. He abolished village elections and appointed supporters to public office. He threw dissenters in jail and shut down newspapers that criticized him. He ignored U.S. officials who urged him to implement land reform. Noncommunists and communists alike struck back at Diem's repressive government. In Hanoi, Ho's government in the late 1950s sent aid to southern insurgents, who assassinated hundreds of Diem's village officials. In late 1960, southern communists, acting at Hanoi's direction, organized the National Liberation Front (NLF), known as the Vietcong. The Vietcong attracted other anti-Diem groups in the South. And the Eisenhower administration, aware of Diem's shortcomings, continued to affirm its commitment to an independent, noncommunist South Vietnam. Diem remained depended on the United States, and he had little support in Vietnam.

Summary

The United States emerged from the Second World War as the preeminent world power, but officials worried that the unstable international system, an unfriendly Soviet Union, and the decolonizing Third World could upset American plans for the postwar peace. Locked with the Soviet Union in a "Cold War," U.S. leaders marshaled their nation's superior resources to influence and cajole other countries. Foreign economic aid, atomic diplomacy, military alliances, client states, covert operations, propaganda, and cultural infiltration became the instruments of the Cold War, which began as a conflict over the future of Europe but soon encompassed the globe.

America's claim to international leadership was welcomed by those who feared Soviet intentions. The reconstruction of former enemies Japan and (West) Germany helped those nations recover swiftly and become staunch members of the Western alliance. But U.S. policy also sparked resistance. Communist countries condemned

The National Security State

To build a cathedral, someone has observed, you first need a religion, and a religion needs inspiring texts that command authority. For decades, America's Cold War religion has been national security; its texts, the Truman Doctrine, the "X" article, and NSC-68; and its cathedral, the national security state. The word *state* in this case means "civil government." During the Cold War, the U.S. government essentially transformed itself into a huge military headquarters that interlocked with corporations and universities.

Overseen by the president and his National Security Council, the national security state's core is the Department of Defense. This department is a leading employer; its payroll by 2007 included 1.4 million people on active duty and almost 600,000 civilian personnel. Almost 700,000 of these troops and civilians served overseas, in 177 countries. Although national defense spending declined after the Cold War, it never fell below $290 billion. In the aftermath of the 9/11 terrorist attacks and the invasion of Iraq, the military budget rose again, reaching $439 billion in 2007. That figure equals the combined military spending of the twenty-five countries with the next-largest defense budgets. It does not include tens of billions of dollars in supplementary funds allocated by Congress to pay for operations in Afghanistan and Iraq.

Joining the Department of Defense as instruments of national security policy were the Joint Chiefs of Staff, the Central Intelligence Agency, and dozens more government bodies. These entities focused on finding the best means to combat real and potential threats from foreign governments. But what about threats from within? The terrorist attacks of September 2001 made starkly clear that enemies existed who, while perhaps beholden to a foreign entity—it need not be a government—launched their attacks from inside the nation's borders. Accordingly, in 2002 President George W. Bush created the Department of Homeland Security (DHS), with 170,000 employees encompassing all or part of twenty-two agencies, including the Coast Guard, the Customs Service, the Federal Emergency Management Administration (FEMA), and the Internal Revenue Service. It was the biggest overhaul of the federal bureaucracy since the Department of Defense was created, and it signified a more expansive notion of national security. By 2008, the number of DHS employees had risen to 208,000.

In 1961, President Eisenhower warned against a "military-industrial complex," while others feared a "warfare state." Despite the warnings, the national security state remained vigorous in the early twenty-first century, a lasting legacy of the early Cold War period for a people and a nation.

financial and atomic diplomacy, while Third World nations sought to undermine America's European allies and sometimes identified the United States as an imperial coconspirator. On occasion, even America's allies bristled at a United States that boldly proclaimed itself economic master and global policeman.

At home, critics protested that Presidents Truman and Eisenhower exaggerated the communist threat, wasting U.S. assets on immoral foreign ventures. Still, these presidents and their successors held firm to the mission of creating a nonradical, capitalist, free-trade international order. Determined to contain Soviet expansion, fearful of domestic charges of being "soft on communism," they enlarged the U.S. sphere of influence and held the line against the Soviet Union and the People's Republic of China and against revolution everywhere. One consequence was a dramatic increase in presidential power over foreign affairs—what the historian Arthur M. Schlesinger Jr. called "the Imperial Presidency."

The intensity of the Cold War obscured for Americans the indigenous roots of most Third World troubles, as the wars in Korea and Vietnam attested. Nor could the United States abide developing nations' drive for economic independence. Intertwined in the global economy as importer, exporter, and investor, the United States read challenges from this "periphery" as threats to the American standard of living. Overall, the rise of the Third World introduced new actors to the world stage, challenging the bipolarity of the international system. All the while, the threat of nuclear war unsettled Americans and foreigners alike.

Chapter Review

From Allies to Adversaries

Was the Cold War inevitable?

Aside from their alliance during World War II, the United States and Soviet Union had a tense relationship dating back to the 1917 Bolshevik Revolution. Since leaders of each country did not want war, their decades-old "cold peace" arguably could have continued. Some believe, however, that each nation's desire to fill the power vacuum left by the World War II defeat of Germany and Japan, along with their disparate goals and political ideologies, led individual leaders to make decisions that exacerbated tensions to the point of Cold War. Both countries backed different groups in Iran, could not agree on German reunification, and took many other opposing foreign policy positions. The U.S. nuclear monopoly only escalated strife, first because the Soviets believed the United States used its nuclear superiority to bully them into concessions, and later when the Soviets had their own nuclear bomb, by advancing an arms race.

Containment in Action

Was the U.S. containment policy successful?

In 1947, Truman and his aides adopted what they called the containment policy, which meant challenging the Soviets every time they attempted to spread communism beyond their borders. The policy was successful in building an international network by aiding European reconstruction and having communists removed from governments, as in Italy and France. The policy also led to the establishment of NATO (the North Atlantic Treaty Organization) in 1949. Truman hoped NATO would keep Europeans from turning communist and would deter Soviets from expansion. But containment failed when China became communist in 1949. Containment similarly could not keep the Soviet Union from becoming a nuclear power.

The Cold War in Asia

How did the Cold War turn "hot" in Asia?

U.S. foreign policy sought to keep communism from spreading to Asia. That often led to decisions that alienated potential allies. The United States refused diplomatic recognition to the People's Republic of China in 1949, fearing the nation was a likely Soviet ally. The United States also intervened militarily in Korea, to thwart what it saw as a Soviet-sponsored attack by the North against the South. After the Sino-Soviet treaty of friendship in 1950, U.S. policy focused on keeping Indochina from falling to the communists. Rather than recognizing tensions in Vietnam as a rebellion against French colonial rule, Truman and his aides blamed the Soviets for stirring up insurrection to expand communism. The United States lent military aid to the French, becoming increasingly engaged in what would develop into the Vietnam War.

The Korean War

What were the consequences of the Korean War for the United States?

Along with heavy casualties (54,246 Americans died and 103,284 were wounded), the conflict influenced politics in the United States. First, the powers of the U.S. president expanded, as Truman never sought congressional permission to declare war, believing that as commander-in-chief, he could dispatch troops at will. Consequently, he only turned to Congress for funding, and Congress also deferred to Truman rather than exercise its authority. As Republicans accused Truman of being soft on communism, he took an increasingly uncompromising position in negotiations for peace. But public frustration over U.S. failure in the war led to Eisenhower's election in 1952. Finally, the war generated increased hostilities between the United States and China, stoked the arms race with the Soviet Union, and strengthened the U.S. alliance with Japan.

Unrelenting Cold War

How did Dulles and Eisenhower raise the stakes in the Cold War?

While President Eisenhower and Secretary of State Dulles continued the containment policy, they also adopted more aggressive tactics. Militarily, Eisenhower increased the nuclear arsenal. Possessing the atomic bomb and the hydrogen bomb enabled the United States to practice brinkmanship, not backing down against the spread of communism, even to the brink of war. Eisenhower also popularized the domino theory—that neighboring countries would fall to communism like dominoes without U.S. assistance. At the same time, however, Eisenhower worked to avoid hot war. Instead, he utilized the Central Intelligence Agency to train foreign military officers in counterrevolution, subvert Third World governments, and attempt to influence international opinion with disinformation and pro-U.S. campaigns. Brinkmanship and espionage prompted a similar Soviet response, as the USSR tested its own H-bomb in 1953, fired the first intercontinental ballistic missile in 1957, and increased intelligence operations.

The Struggle for the Third World

How did racism in America interfere with U.S. leaders' ability to win Cold War allies among developing nations?

Racism harmed U.S. relations with Third World countries, whose leaders were often people of color. With segregation and discrimination rampant in the United States, it was difficult for U.S. leaders to claim a moral advantage over communism and win friends in new and developing nations. Matters were made worse when there were incidents of discrimination against visiting leaders. To counter this image, the U.S. government broadcast the positive news of the Supreme Court's school desegregation ruling.

Suggestions for Further Reading

Campbell Craig and Fredrik Logevall, *America's Cold War: The Politics of Insecurity* (2009)

Nick Cullather, *Secret History: The CIA's Classified Account of Its Operations in Guatemala, 1952–1954* (1999)

Bruce Cumings, *The Korean War: A History* (2010)

Mary L. Dudziak, *Cold War Civil Rights: Race and the Image of American Democracy* (2000)

John Lewis Gaddis, *Strategies of Containment*, 2nd ed. (2005)

Douglas Little, *American Orientalism: The United States and the Middle East Since 1945* (2002)

Fredrik Logevall, *Embers of War: The Fall of an Empire and the Making of America's Vietnam* (2012)

Geoffrey Roberts, *Stalin's Wars: From World War to Cold War, 1939–1953* (2007)

Marc Trachtenberg, *A Constructed Peace: The Making of the European Settlement, 1945–1963* (1999)

America at Midcentury

1945–1960

Isaac and Oleta Nelson wrapped themselves in blankets that morning in late January 1951 as they joined a hundred or so friends and neighbors from Cedar City, Utah, to watch the first atomic test on U.S. soil since the end of World War II. "We wanted to … show our patriotism," Isaac remembered. The red-orange flare of the bomb lit up the trees across the valley, more than ten miles away.

In the years immediately following World War II, the United States had tested atomic weapons on isolated islands in the south Pacific. U.S. officials knew the dangers of radioactivity. But as the USSR developed an atomic weapon and the hostilities in Korea escalated the Cold War, Atomic Energy Commission (AEC) members argued that testing outside U.S. borders might compromise national security. The danger to American public health and safety, they concluded (in a phrase from 1957 legal testimony), was offset by the threat of "total annihilation" by the Soviet enemy.

President Truman selected land in Nevada, already in use as a bombing and gunnery range, for nuclear testing. Advisers portrayed the land, which stretched across portions of Nevada, Arizona, and Utah and was downwind of Los Angeles and Las Vegas, as "virtually uninhabitable." Yet almost one hundred thousand people lived there, including descendants of Mormon settlers who had arrived in the 1840s and members of the Western Shoshone Nation, on whose land the test site lay. As radioactive clouds drifted over towns and farms, children played in the fallout as if it were snow.

After fallout from "Harry," a thirty-two-kiloton blast, saturated the region in 1953, forty-five hundred of the fourteen thousand sheep on local ranches died. The AEC blamed "unprecedented cold weather" and suppressed veterinary reports that documented lethal levels of radiation. In 1955, AEC medical staff told residents that radiation from nuclear tests amounted to only "about one-twentieth of that experienced in an X-ray." That same year, within hours of watching a fallout cloud, Oleta Nelson became nauseous, with violent diarrhea; her exposed skin turned bright red. A month later, her hair fell out. Oleta was diagnosed with a brain tumor in 1962. She died in 1965. By that time, the cancer rate for "downwinders" was one and a half times that of the rest of the U.S. population.

The Cold War did not affect most Americans so directly. Nonetheless, Cold War fears and policies shaped American life during the postwar era in ways both blatant and subtle. The United States emerged from World War II stronger and more prosperous. U.S. production capacity had increased during the war, and despite social tensions and inequalities, the fight against fascism gave Americans a unified purpose. But memories of sixteen years of depression and war would continue to shape the choices Americans made in their private lives, their domestic policies, and their relations with the world.

In the postwar era, the federal government's actions and individuals' choices reconfigured American society. Postwar social policies—often shaped by Cold War concerns—that sent millions of veterans to college on the GI Bill, linked the nation with high-speed interstate highways, fostered the growth of suburbs and the Sunbelt, and disrupted regional isolation helped to create a national middle-class culture that encompassed an unprecedented majority of citizens. Countless individual decisions—going to college, marrying young, having a family, moving to the suburbs, starting a business—were made possible by federal initiatives. Americans in the postwar era defined a new American Dream—one that centered on the family, greater material comfort and consumption, and a shared sense of a common culture. Elite cultural critics denounced this ideal of suburban comfort as "conformism," but many Americans found satisfaction in this new way of life.

Almost one-quarter of the American people did not share in the postwar prosperity—but they were ever less visible to the middle-class majority. Rural poverty continued, and inner cities became increasingly impoverished as more-affluent Americans moved to the suburbs and new migrants—poor black and white southerners, new immigrants from Mexico and Puerto Rico, and Native Americans resettled by the federal government from tribal lands—arrived.

As class and ethnicity became less important in suburbia, race continued to divide Americans. African Americans faced racism and discrimination nationwide, but the war marked a turning point in the struggle for equal rights. African Americans' initiatives led to important federal actions, including the Supreme Court's school desegregation decision in *Brown v. Board of Education*. Beginning in 1955, the yearlong Montgomery bus boycott launched the modern civil rights movement.

LINKS TO THE WORLD *Barbie*

The Limits of the Middle-Class Nation
Critics of Conformity |
Environmental Degradation |
Continuing Racism |
Poverty in an Age of Abundance

LEGACY FOR A PEOPLE AND A NATION
The Pledge of Allegiance

SUMMARY

The national politics of the postwar era were circumscribed. Truman pledged to expand the New Deal but was stymied by a conservative Congress. Eisenhower offered a solid Republican platform, seeking—though rarely attaining—a balanced budget, reduced taxes, and lower levels of government spending. Both men focused primarily on the foreign policy challenges of the Cold War. The most significant domestic political ferment, in fact, was a by-product of the Cold War: a ferocious anticommunism narrowed the boundaries of acceptable dissent.

The economic boom that began with the end of the war lasted twenty-five years. Although fears—of nuclear war, of returning hard times—lingered, prosperity bred complacency by the late 1950s. At decade's end, people sought satisfaction in their families and in consumer pleasures.

As you read this chapter, keep the following questions in mind:

- **How did the Cold War affect American society and politics?**

- **How did federal government actions following World War II change the nation?**

- **During the 1950s, many people began to think of their country as a middle-class nation. Were they correct?**

In this photograph, a scorched and disheveled male mannequin clad in a dark business suit stands in the desert with a female mannequin in the background, 7,000 feet from the forty-fourth nuclear test explosion. Taken a day after the blast, it indicated that humans could be burnt but still alive after such an explosion.

Photo by Loomis Dean/Time & Life Pictures/Getty Images

Chronology

1945	World War II ends
1946	Marriage and birth rates skyrocket
	2.2 million veterans seek higher education
	More than 5 million U.S. workers go on strike
1947	Taft-Hartley Act limits power of unions
	Truman orders loyalty investigation of 3 million government employees
	Mass-production techniques used to build Levittown houses
1948	Truman issues executive order desegregating armed forces and federal government
	Truman elected president
1949	Soviet Union explodes atomic bomb
1950	Korean War begins
	McCarthy alleges communists in government
	"Treaty of Detroit" creates model for new labor-management relations
1951	Race riots in Cicero, Illinois, as white residents oppose residential integration

1952	Eisenhower elected president
1953	Korean War ends
	Congress adopts termination policy for Native American tribes
	Rosenbergs executed as atomic spies
1954	*Brown v. Board of Education* decision reverses "separate but equal" doctrine
	Senate condemns McCarthy
1955	Montgomery bus boycott begins
1956	Highway Act launches interstate highway system
	Eisenhower reelected
	Elvis Presley appears on *The Ed Sullivan Show*
1957	King elected first president of Southern Christian Leadership Conference
	School desegregation crisis in Little Rock, Arkansas
	Congress passes Civil Rights Act
	Soviet Union launches *Sputnik*
1958	Congress passes National Defense Education Act
1959	Alaska and Hawai'i become forty-ninth and fiftieth states

Shaping Postwar America

> *What drove the mass migration of Americans to the suburbs after World War II?*

Americans faced many challenges at the end of World War II. The nation had to reintegrate war veterans into civilian society and transform a wartime economy to peacetime functions. It also had to contend with the domestic implications of the Cold War and the new global balance of power. Though unemployment rose and a wave of strikes rocked the nation, the economy soon flourished. This strong economy, along with new federal programs, transformed American society.

The Veterans Return

In 1945, as Germany and then Japan surrendered, the United States began to demobilize almost 15 million servicemen. Veterans' homecomings were often joyful but not always easy. Many veterans returned to wives whose lives had gone on without them, to children they barely knew. Some had serious physical injuries. Almost half a million veterans were diagnosed with neuropsychiatric disabilities, and the National Mental Health Act of 1946 passed largely because of awareness of the war's psychological toll on veterans.

Americans also worried about the economic impact of demobilization. As the end of the war approached, factories had begun to lay off workers. Ten days after the Allied victory over Japan,1.8 million people nationwide received pink slips, and 640,000 filed for unemployment compensation.

The GI Bill

The federal government had begun planning for demobilization during the war. In the spring of 1944, Congress unanimously passed the Servicemen's Readjustment Act, known as the **GI Bill** of Rights. The GI Bill showed the nation's gratitude to servicemen, but it also attempted to keep demobilized veterans from swamping the U.S. economy. Roughly half of all veterans received unemployment benefits, meant to stagger their entry into the job market. The GI Bill also provided low-interest home and business loans and stipends to cover the cost of college or technical school tuition and living expenses.

GI Bill Popular name for the Servicemen's Readjustment Act (1944), which sought to aid returning veterans—and maintain economic stability—by providing college tuition, job training, unemployment benefits, and low-interest home and farm loans.

The GI Bill, as written, covered all honorably discharged veterans, regardless of race or gender. But Congress assigned the Veteran's Administration to administer the GI Bill, even though it didn't have the capacity to manage the program. Thus decisions about implementation fell to state and local agencies, which allowed for discrimination. And because men and women charged with homosexuality were not honorably discharged, they were denied benefits.

Nonetheless, almost half of returning veterans used GI Bill education benefits. Sub-college programs drew 5.6 million veterans, while 2.2 attended college, graduate, or professional school. In 1947, about two-thirds of America's college students were veterans. While racial segregation persisted, Negro colleges grew. This flood of students and federal dollars created a golden age for higher education, and the resulting increase in well-educated or technically trained workers benefited the economy.

Education created social mobility: children of menial laborers became white-collar professionals. The GI Bill fostered a national middle-class culture, for as colleges exposed people to new ideas and to new experiences, students became less rooted in ethnic or regional cultures.

Economic Growth

American concerns that economic depression would return with war's end proved unfounded. After a difficult year of adjustment, the economy recovered quickly, fueled by consumer spending. Although Americans had brought home steady paychecks during the war, there was little to buy. Now Americans were ready to spend. Companies like General Motors, which expanded operations after the war, found millions of eager customers. And because most factories around the world were in ruins, U.S. corporations expanded their global dominance. Farming was also revolutionized. New machines, such as crop-dusting planes and mechanical cotton, tobacco, and grape pickers, along with increased use of fertilizers and pesticides, greatly increased the total value of farm output, as the productivity of farm labor tripled. The potential for profit drew large investors, and the average farm size increased from 195 to 306 acres.

Baby Boom

During the Great Depression, people had delayed marriage and America's birth rate had plummeted. But by 1946, the U.S. marriage rate was higher than that of any other recordkeeping nation (except Hungary) and a soaring birth rate reversed the downward trend of the past 150 years. "Take the 3,548,000 babies born in 1950," wrote Sylvia F. Porter in her syndicated newspaper column. "Bundle them into a batch, bounce them all over the bountiful land that is America. What do you get?" Porter's answer: "Boom. The biggest, boomiest boom ever known in history. Just imagine how much these extra people, these new markets, will absorb—in food, clothing, in gadgets, in housing, in services." Although the **baby boom** peaked in 1957, more than 4 million babies were born every year until 1965 (see Figure 25.1).

baby boom The soaring birth rate that occurred in the United States from 1946 through the early 1960s.

Suburbanization

Where would these baby boom families live? Scarcely any new housing had been built since the 1920s. Almost 2 million families were doubled up with relatives in 1948; 50,000 people lived in Quonset huts, and in Chicago housing was so tight that 250 used trolley cars were sold as homes.

A combination of market forces, government actions, and individual decisions solved the housing crisis and changed the way large numbers of Americans lived. In the postwar years, white Americans moved to the suburbs. Some moved to escape the crowds of the city. Rural people moved closer to city jobs. Some white families moved out of cities because African American families were moving in. Most who moved to the suburbs, however, simply wanted their own home—and suburban developments were affordable. Although suburban development predated World

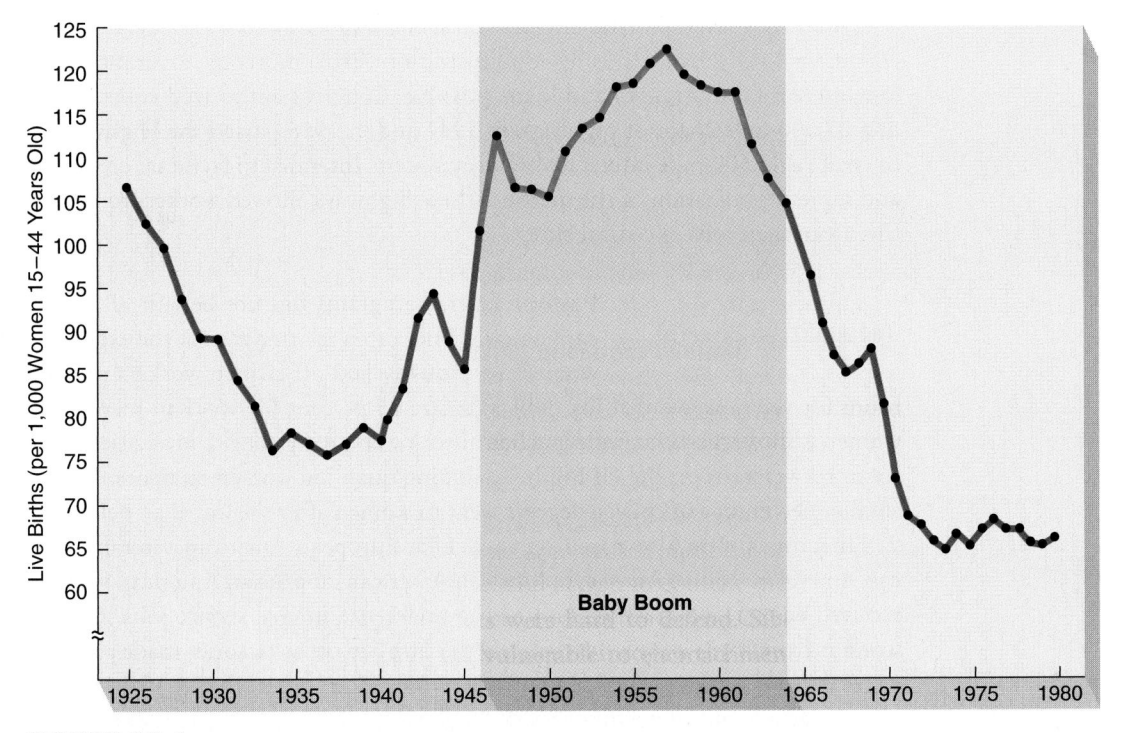

FIGURE 25.1

Birth Rate, 1945–1964

The birth rate began to rise in 1942 and 1943, but it skyrocketed during the postwar years beginning in 1946, reaching its peak in 1957. From 1954 to 1964, the United States recorded more than 4 million births every year.

(Source: Adapted from U.S. Bureau of the Census, *Historical Statistics of the United States, Colonial Times to 1970*, Bicentennial Edition (Washington, D.C.: U.S. Government Printing Office, 1975), p. 49.)

TABLE 25.1 **Geographic Distribution of the U.S. Population, 1930–1970 (in percentages)**

Year	Central Cities	Suburbs	Rural Areas and Small Towns
1930	31.8	18.0	50.2
1940	31.6	19.5	48.9
1950	32.3	23.8	43.9
1960	32.6	30.7	36.7
1970	31.4	37.6	31.0

Source: Adapted from U.S. Bureau of the Census, *Decennial Censuses, 1930–1970* (Washington, D.C.: U.S. Government Printing Office).

War II, the massive migration of 18 million Americans to the suburbs between 1950 and 1960 was on a wholly different scale (see Table 25.1).

In 1947, builder William Levitt adapted Henry Ford's assembly-line methods to revolutionize homebuilding. By 1949, instead of 4 or 5 custom homes per year, Levitt's company built 180 houses a week. They were very basic—four and a half rooms on a 60-by-100-foot lot, all with identical floor plans disguised by four different exteriors and seven different paint colors. In the Levittown on Long Island, the basic house sold for $7,990. Other homebuilders quickly adopted Levitt's techniques.

Suburban development happened on such a large scale because federal policies encouraged it. Federal Housing Administration (FHA) mortgage insurance made low-interest GI mortgages and loans possible. Congress authorized construction of a 37,000-mile chain of highways in 1947 and in 1956 passed the Highway Act to create a 42,500-mile interstate highway system. Intended to facilitate commerce and rapid mobilization of the military, these highways allowed workers to live farther from their jobs in central cities.

Inequality in Benefits

Postwar federal programs did not benefit all Americans equally. They often assisted men at the expense of women. As industry laid off civilian workers to make room for veterans, women lost jobs at a rate 75 percent higher than men. Many women still worked but were pushed into lower-paying jobs. Universities made room for veterans on the GI Bill by excluding qualified women students; a much smaller percentage of college degrees went to women after the war than before.

Inequities were also based on race. Like European American veterans, African American, Native American, Mexican American, and Asian American veterans received educational benefits and hiring preference in civil service jobs. But war workers from these groups were among the first laid off as factories made room for white, male veterans. Federal loan officers and bankers often labeled African American or racially mixed neighborhoods "high risk," denying mortgages to members of racial minorities regardless of individual creditworthiness. This practice, called "redlining" because such neighborhoods were outlined in red on lenders' maps, kept African Americans and many Hispanics from sharing the postwar economic explosion. White families who bought homes with federally guaranteed mortgages saw their small investments grow dramatically over the years.

Domestic Politics in the Cold War Era

What happened to New Deal–style liberalism after World War II?

During the postwar era, Democratic president Harry Truman attempted to build on the New Deal's liberal agenda, while Republican president Dwight D. Eisenhower sought balanced budgets and business-friendly policies. But both administrations focused on the challenges of the expanding Cold War, and neither came close to the activism of the 1930s New Deal.

Harry S Truman and Postwar Liberalism

Domestically, Truman oversaw reconversion from war to peace and attempted to keep a liberal agenda—the legacy of Roosevelt's New Deal—alive. In his 1944 State of the Union address, President Roosevelt had offered Americans a "Second Bill of Rights": the right to employment, health care, education, food, and housing. This declaration of government responsibility for citizens' welfare was the cornerstone of postwar liberalism. The Truman administration intended to preserve the federal government's active role in guaranteeing social welfare, promoting social justice, managing the economy, and regulating business. Truman proposed to increase the minimum wage; he supported the **Full Employment Act**, introduced by congressional Democrats in the winter of 1945, which guaranteed work to the able and willing, through public-sector employment if necessary.

To pay for his proposed social welfare programs, Truman gambled that full employment would generate sufficient tax revenue and that consumer spending would fuel economic growth. The gamble on economic growth paid off, but a conservative coalition of Republicans and southern Democrats in Congress refused to raise the minimum wage and gutted the Full Employment Act, which passed in 1946 without provisions regarding guaranteed work. But the act did reaffirm the federal government's responsibility for managing the economy and created a Council of Economic Advisers to help the president prevent economic downturns.

Full Employment Act Postwar liberal initiative that sought to stimulate economic growth by raising the minimum wage and guaranteeing jobs to those willing and able to work, through public-sector employment if necessary. The act passed without either of these provisions, which were blocked in Congress.

Postwar Strikes and the Taft-Hartley Act

The difficult conversion to a peacetime economy undermined Truman's domestic influence. As the end of wartime price controls sent inflation skyrocketing, more than 5 million workers went on strike in the year following Japan's surrender. Unions shut down the coal, automobile, steel, and electric industries, and halted railroad and maritime transportation. Americans began hoarding food and gasoline.

By the spring of 1946, Americans grew impatient with the strikes and partly blamed the Democratic administration. When unions threatened a national railway strike, President Truman announced that if strikers in an industry deemed vital to national security refused a presidential order to return to work, he would ask Congress to draft strikers into the armed forces. The Democratic Party would not offer unlimited support to organized labor.

The following year, pro-business Republicans and their conservative Democratic allies worked to restrict the power of labor unions. The 1947 **Taft-Hartley Act** allowed states to adopt right-to-work legislation that outlawed "closed shops," in which all workers were required to join the union if a majority favored a union

Taft-Hartley Act A 1947 law that amended some of the pro-labor provisions of the 1935 Wagner Act. It permitted states to outlaw the closed shop—workplaces where only union members could be hired—outlawed secondary boycotts, required union officials to sign loyalty oaths, and permitted the president to call a cooling-off period to delay any strike that might endanger national safety or health.

shop. The law also mandated an eighty-day cooling-off period before unions initiated strikes that imperiled national security. These restrictions limited unions' ability to expand their membership.

Truman did not support such limits on union power, but Congress passed the Taft-Hartley Act over his veto. As the president presided over the rocky transition to a peacetime economy, his approval rating plunged from 87 percent in late 1945 to 32 percent in 1946.

1948 Election

By 1948, it seemed that Republicans would win the White House in November. The party nominated Thomas Dewey, the man Roosevelt had defeated in 1944. Republicans hoped schisms in the Democratic Party would give them victory. Former New Dealer Henry A. Wallace was running on the **Progressive Party** ticket advocating friendly relations with the Soviet Union, racial desegregation, and nationalization of basic industries. And when the Democratic Party adopted a pro–civil rights plank in 1948, some white southerners created the States' Rights Democratic Party (the Dixiecrats), which nominated the fiercely segregationist governor of South Carolina, Strom Thurmond.

Truman refused to give up. He resorted to red-baiting, denouncing "Henry Wallace and his communists." He also sought support from African American voters in northern cities, becoming the first presidential candidate to campaign in Harlem. Truman prevailed; Roosevelt's New Deal coalition—African Americans, union members, northern urban voters, and most southern whites—had endured.

Progressive Party Party formed from a splintering within the Democratic Party in 1948 by those dissatisfied with Truman. It advocated friendly relations with the Soviet Union, racial desegregation, a ban on monopolies, and nationalization of basic industries.

Truman's Fair Deal

As he worked on his 1949 State of the Union message, Truman penciled in his intentions: "I expect to give every segment of our population a **fair deal**." Truman, unlike Roosevelt, pushed legislation supporting African American civil rights, including the anti-lynching bill. He proposed a national health insurance program and federal aid for education. But southern conservatives in Congress destroyed his civil rights legislation, the American Medical Association denounced his health insurance plan as "socialized medicine," and the Roman Catholic Church opposed aid to education because it would not include parochial schools.

fair deal Agenda proposed by President Truman that included civil rights, national health care legislation, and federal aid to education.

When Truman ordered troops to Korea in June 1950, many reservists and National Guardsmen resented being called to active duty. Americans, remembering the shortages of the last war, tried to stockpile food—thus causing inflation. In 1951, the president's approval rating was 23 percent.

Eisenhower's Dynamic Conservatism

In 1952 the Republicans insisted "It's Time for a Change," and voters agreed. Americans hoped that General **Dwight D. Eisenhower**, the popular World War II hero, could end the Korean War. And Eisenhower appealed to moderates in both parties; the Democrats also had tried to recruit him as their presidential candidate.

Dwight D. Eisenhower Republican president of the United States (1953–1961) known for his moderate politics, steering a middle course between Democratic liberalism and traditional Republican conservatism.

With a Republican in the White House for the first time in twenty years, conservatives hoped to roll back such New Deal liberal programs as Social Security. As a moderate, however, Eisenhower embraced what he called "dynamic conservatism": being "conservative when it comes to money and liberal when it comes to human beings." In 1954 Eisenhower signed legislation that raised Social Security benefits and added 7.5 million workers, mostly self-employed farmers, to its rolls. The Eisenhower administration, motivated by Cold War fears, also increased funding for education. In 1957, when the Soviet Union successfully launched *Sputnik*—the first earth-orbiting satellite—politicians and policymakers worried about America's scientific vulnerability. The resulting National Defense Education Act (NDEA) funded elementary and high school programs in mathematics, foreign languages, and the sciences and offered fellowships and loans to college students.

Growth of the Military-Industrial Complex

Overall, however, Eisenhower's administration was fiscally conservative and pro-business. Eisenhower tried to reduce federal spending and to balance the budget, but faced with three recessions (in 1953–1954, 1957–1958, and 1960–1961) and the cost of America's global activities, he turned to deficit spending. In 1959, federal spending climbed to $92 billion, about half of which went to support a standing military of 3.5 million men and to develop new weapons.

Eisenhower worried about this trajectory. In his farewell address in early 1961, he condemned this new "conjunction of an immense military establishment and a large arms industry" and warned that its "total influence—economic, political, even spiritual"—threatened the nation's democratic process. Eisenhower, the former five-star general and war hero, urged Americans to "guard against… the **military-industrial complex**."

military-industrial complex Term made famous by President Eisenhower's farewell speech in 1961; it refers to the U.S. military, arms industries, and related government and business interests, which together grew in power, size, and influence in the decades after World War II.

Link to Dwight Eisenhower, Farewell Address on the "Military-Industrial" Complex (1961)

Cold War Fears and Anticommunism

How did Cold War fears inspire a Red Scare in the United States?

International relations profoundly influenced America's domestic politics after World War II. Americans were frightened by the Cold War tensions between the United States and the Soviet Union, but reasonable fears spilled over into anticommunist demagoguery and witch hunts, which trampled civil liberties, suppressed dissent, and resulted in the persecution of thousands of innocent Americans.

Anticommunism was not new. A Red Scare had swept the nation following the Russian Revolution of 1917, and opponents of America's labor movement had used charges of communism to block unionization through the 1930s. Many saw the Soviet Union's virtual takeover of Eastern Europe in the late 1940s as an alarming parallel to Nazi Germany's takeover of neighboring states. People remembered the failure of "appeasement" at Munich and worried about being "too soft" toward the Soviet Union.

Espionage and Nuclear Fears

A top-secret U.S. government project, code-named "Venona," decrypted almost three thousand Soviet telegraphic cables that proved Soviet spies had infiltrated U.S. government agencies and nuclear programs. (The United States also had spies within the Soviet Union.) Intelligence officials withheld their evidence from the American public so that the Soviets would not realize their codes had been compromised. Thus even legitimate prosecution often appeared as persecution based on no evidence.

Fear of nuclear war also contributed to American anticommunism. After the Soviet Union exploded its own atomic device in 1949, President Truman initiated a national atomic civil defense program. Children practiced "duck-and-cover" in their classrooms, learning how to shield themselves "when the bomb falls." *Life* magazine featured backyard fallout shelters.

Politics of Anticommunism

American leaders did not always draw a sufficient line between attempts to prevent Soviet spies from infiltrating government agencies and anticommunist scaremongering. Republican politicians "red-baited" Democratic opponents, eventually targeting the Truman administration. In 1947, Truman ordered investigations into the loyalty of more than 3 million government employees. The government began discharging people deemed "security risks," among them alcoholics, homosexuals, and debtors thought susceptible to blackmail.

House Un-American Activities Committee (HUAC) Influential Congressional committee, originally created in 1938, which investigated communist influence in America and contributed to anticommunist hysteria in the postwar United States.

Leading the anticommunist crusade was the **House Un-American Activities Committee** (popularly known as HUAC). Created in 1938 to investigate "subversive and un-American propaganda," the anti–New Deal committee had quickly lost credibility by charging that film stars—including eight-year-old Shirley Temple—were Communist Party dupes. In 1947, HUAC attacked Hollywood again, using FBI files and the testimony of people like Screen Actors Guild president Ronald Reagan (who was a secret FBI informant). Ten screenwriters and directors, known as the "Hollywood Ten," were sent to prison for contempt of Congress when they refused to "name names" of suspected communists. Studios blacklisted hundreds of actors, screenwriters, directors, even makeup artists suspected of communist affiliations. With no evidence of wrongdoing, people's careers—and sometimes their lives—were ruined.

McCarthyism and the Growing "Witch Hunt"

University professors became targets of the growing "witch hunt" in 1949, when HUAC demanded lists of the textbooks used at eighty-one universities. When the board of regents at the University of California, Berkeley, instituted a loyalty oath for faculty, firing twenty-six who resisted on principle, nationwide protests forced the regents to back down. But many professors began to downplay controversial material in their courses. In the labor movement, the CIO expelled eleven unions, with more than nine hundred thousand members, for alleged communist domination.

Joseph R. McCarthy Wisconsin senator who launched a massive public campaign against communism and the Soviet spies and sympathizers he claimed were inside the federal government. He was later discredited.

The red panic reached its nadir in February 1950, when **Joseph R. McCarthy**, a relatively obscure Republican U.S. senator from Wisconsin, charged in a speech in Wheeling, West Virginia, that the U.S. State Department was "thoroughly infested with Communists." Not an especially credible source, McCarthy first claimed that there were 205 communists in the State Department, then 57, then 81. He had a severe drinking problem and a record of dishonesty as a lawyer and judge. But McCarthy crystallized Americans' anxieties, and anticommunist excesses came to be known as McCarthyism.

Anticommunism in Congress

In such a climate, most public figures found it risky to stand up against McCarthyist tactics. In 1950, Congress passed the Internal Security (McCarran) Act, which required members of "Communist-front" organizations to register with the government and prohibited them from holding government jobs or traveling abroad. In 1954, the Senate unanimously passed the Communist Control Act, which effectively made membership in the Communist Party illegal.

In 1948, Congressman Richard Nixon of California, a member of HUAC, was propelled onto the national stage when he accused former State Department official Alger Hiss of espionage. In 1950, Hiss was convicted of lying about his contacts with Soviet agents. That same year, **Ethel and Julius Rosenberg** were arrested for passing atomic secrets to the Soviets; they were found guilty of treason and executed in 1953. For decades, many historians believed that the Rosenbergs were victims of a witch hunt. In fact, there was strong evidence of Julius Rosenberg's guilt in cables decrypted at the time (as well as evidence that Ethel Rosenberg was less involved), but this evidence was not presented at their trial for national security reasons. The cables remained top secret until 1995, when a Clinton administration initiative opened the files.

Link to McCarran International Security Act (1950)

Ethel and Julius Rosenberg
Couple found guilty of conspiracy to commit espionage and executed in 1953.

Waning of the Red Scare

Some of the worst excesses of Cold War anticommunism waned when Senator McCarthy was discredited on national television in 1954. In previous years McCarthy had used the press masterfully. Knowing that newspapers buried corrections in their back pages, McCarthy made sensational accusations just before reporters' deadlines, leaving them no time to verify his claims. Journalists reported even his wildest charges in order to sell papers.

But McCarthy badly misunderstood the power of television. When McCarthy pushed the Senate to investigate his charge that the U.S. Army was protecting communists within its ranks, two networks broadcast gavel-to-gavel coverage of the resulting Army-McCarthy hearings. Apparently drunk, McCarthy ranted, slurred his words, and browbeat witnesses. Finally, after McCarthy maligned a young lawyer who was not even involved in the hearings, army counsel Joseph Welch intervened. "Have you no sense of decency, sir, at long last?" Welch asked, and the gallery erupted in applause. McCarthy's career as a witch-hunter was over. In December 1954, the Senate voted to "condemn" McCarthy for sullying the dignity of the Senate. He remained a senator, but exhaustion and alcohol took their toll and he died in 1957 at age forty-eight. Although the most virulent anticommunism had run its course, the use of fear tactics for political gain, and the narrowing of American freedoms and liberties, were chilling legacies of the Cold War.

The Struggle for Civil Rights

How did federal initiatives, Supreme Court decisions, and grassroots activism shape the struggle for civil rights after World War II?

The Cold War also shaped African American struggles for social justice and the nation's responses to them. Some African American leaders saw their struggle for equal rights in the United States as part of a larger, international movement. And American diplomats understood that if the United States continued to allow segregation, discrimination, disenfranchisement, and racial violence, it would struggle to pull the newly formed African and Asian nations into its sphere of influence. As the Soviet Union was quick to point out, the United States could hardly pose as the leader of the free world or condemn the Soviet Union's record on human rights while it practiced segregation at home. At the same time, many white Americans saw any criticism of their society as a Soviet-inspired attempt to weaken the United States in the ongoing Cold War. In this heated environment, African Americans struggled to seize the political initiative.

Black Political Power and Presidential Action African Americans who had helped win World War II were determined to enjoy better lives in postwar America, and politicians like Harry Truman were heeding black aspirations, especially as black voters in some urban-industrial states began to influence the political balance of power.

Truman had compelling political reasons for supporting African American civil rights, but he also genuinely believed that every American should enjoy the full rights of citizenship. He also was appalled by a resurgence of racial terrorism spearheaded by a revived Ku Klux Klan. Reports that police in Aiken, South Carolina, had gouged out the eyes of a black sergeant just three hours after he had been discharged from the army made Isaac Woodard a national symbol of injustice.

In December 1946, Truman signed an executive order establishing the President's Committee on Civil Rights. The committee's report, *To Secure These Rights*, would become the civil rights movement's agenda for the next twenty years. It called for laws to end lynching and segregation and to guarantee voting rights and equal employment opportunity.

In 1948 Truman issued two more executive orders. One proclaimed a policy of "fair employment" in federal jobs. The other, prompted in part by African American leaders who promised massive draft resistance if the military remained segregated, ordered the armed forces to end racial segregation. The military did not readily comply, but by the beginning of the Korean War it had begun to phase out segregated units.

Supreme Court Victories and School Desegregation African Americans successfully challenged racial discrimination in the courts and in state and local legislatures. Northern state legislatures, pressured by civil rights activists, passed measures prohibiting employment discrimination in the 1940s and 1950s. During the 1940s the NAACP's Legal Defense and Educational Fund, led by Thurgood Marshall, carried forward a plan to destroy the separate but equal doctrine established in *Plessy v. Ferguson* (1896). In higher education, the NAACP calculated, the cost of equality in racially separate schools would be prohibitive. "You can't build a cyclotron for one student," acknowledged one university president. NAACP lawsuits won African American students admission to professional and graduate schools at several formerly segregated state universities. The NAACP also won victories through the Supreme Court in *Smith v. Allwright* (1944), which outlawed the whites-only primaries held by the Democratic Party in some southern states; *Morgan v. Virginia* (1946), which struck down segregation in interstate bus transportation; and *Shelley v. Kraemer* (1948), which held that racially restrictive covenants (private agreements among white homeowners not to sell to blacks) could not legally be enforced.

Brown v. Board of Education of Topeka Landmark Supreme Court case (1954) that overturned *Plessy v. Ferguson* (1896); it desegregated public schools by arguing that racially separate schools are inherently unequal.

Even so, blacks continued to suffer segregation, disfranchisement, job discrimination, and violence. But in 1954, the NAACP won a historic Supreme Court victory: ***Brown v. Board of Education of Topeka***. Written by Chief Justice Earl Warren, the Court's unanimous decision concluded that "Separate educational facilities are inherently unequal." But the ruling that overturned *Plessy v. Ferguson* did not demand immediate compliance. A year later, the Court finally ordered school desegregation, but only "with all deliberate speed."

Montgomery Bus Boycott

By the mid-1950s, African Americans were engaged in a growing grassroots struggle for civil rights in both the North and the South, though southern struggles drew the most national attention. In 1955, Rosa Parks, a department store seamstress and NAACP activist, was arrested when she refused to give up her seat to a white man on a public bus in Montgomery, Alabama. Her arrest gave local black women's organizations and civil rights groups a cause around which to organize a boycott of the city's bus system. They selected as their leader a man who had just arrived in Montgomery: **Martin Luther King Jr.**, a twenty-six-year-old, recently ordained Baptist minister with a PhD from Boston University. King launched the boycott with a moving speech, declaring, "If we are wrong, the Constitution is wrong. If we are wrong, God Almighty is wrong … If we are wrong, justice is a lie." Committed to the transforming potential of Christian love and schooled in the teachings of India's leader Mohandas K. Gandhi, King believed in nonviolent civil disobedience as a vehicle to focus the nation's attention on the immorality of Jim Crow. King persisted in this struggle even as opponents bombed his house and he was jailed for "conspiring" to boycott.

During the yearlong Montgomery bus boycott, blacks rallied in their churches. They often walked miles a day. With the bus company near bankruptcy and downtown merchants suffering from declining sales, city officials adopted harassment tactics to end the boycott. But the black people of Montgomery persevered. Thirteen months after the boycott began, the Supreme Court declared Alabama's bus segregation laws unconstitutional.

Martin Luther King Jr. African American minister whose philosophy of civil disobedience fused the spirit of Christianity with the strategy of achieving racial justice by nonviolent resistance.

White Resistance

White reactions to the civil rights movement varied. Some communities in border states like Kansas and Maryland quietly implemented school desegregation, and many southern moderates advocated a gradual rollback of segregation. But others urged defiance. The Klan experienced another resurgence, and white violence against blacks increased. In August 1955, white men in Mississippi beat, mutilated, and murdered Emmett Till, a fourteen-year-old from Chicago, because they took offense at the way he spoke to a white woman; an all-white jury took only sixty-seven minutes to acquit those charged with the crime. Business and professional people created White Citizens' Councils (known familiarly as "uptown Ku Klux Klans") to resist school desegregation and use economic power against black civil rights activists. In keeping with the program of "massive resistance" proposed by Virginia's U.S. senator, Harry F. Byrd Sr., they pushed through state laws that provided private-school tuition for white children who left public schools to avoid integration and, in Virginia, refused state funding to integrated schools.

White resistance also mounted in northern cities. Chicago's African American population had increased from 275,000 in 1940 to 800,000 in 1960. Newcomers found good jobs in industry, and their numbers gave them political power. But they faced racism and segregation. In 1959 the U.S. Commission on Civil Rights

© Bettmann/Corbis

For leading the movement to gain equality for blacks riding city buses in Montgomery, Alabama, Martin Luther King Jr. (1929–1968) and other African Americans, including twenty-three other ministers, were indicted by an all-white jury for violating an old law banning boycotts. In late March 1956, King was convicted and fined $500. A crowd of well-wishers cheered a smiling King (here with his wife, Coretta) outside the courthouse, where King proudly declared, "The protest goes on!" King's arrest and conviction made the bus boycott front-page news across America.

described Chicago as "the most residentially segregated city in the nation." Detroit and other northern cities were not far behind. And because children attended neighborhood schools, education in the North was often segregated as well, though not by law, as it had been in the South.

Federal Authority and States' Rights

Although he disapproved of racial segregation, Eisenhower objected to "compulsory federal law," for he believed that race relations would improve "only if [desegregation] starts locally." He also feared that rapid desegregation would jeopardize Republican inroads in the South. Thus, Eisenhower did not state forthrightly that the federal government would enforce the *Brown* decision. He thereby tacitly encouraged white resistance. In 1956, 101 southern Democrats in Congress issued "The Southern Manifesto," condemning the *Brown* decision and commending states that sought to "resist forced integration by any lawful means."

Events in Little Rock, Arkansas, forced the president to act. In September 1957, Arkansas governor Orval E. Faubus defied a court-supported desegregation plan for Little Rock's Central High School, saying on television that "blood would run in the streets" if black students tried to enter. On the second day of school, eight black teenagers attempted to enter Central High, but they were turned away by Arkansas National Guard troops Faubus had deployed to block their entrance. The ninth student narrowly escaped a white mob with the help of a sympathetic white woman.

The "Little Rock Nine" first entered Central High more than two weeks later—and then only because a federal judge intervened. As an angry crowd surrounded the school and television broadcast the scene to the world, Eisenhower nationalized the Arkansas National Guard (placing it under federal, not state, control) and dispatched one thousand army paratroopers to guard the students for the rest of the year. Eisenhower had directly confronted the conflict between federal authority and states' rights. However, state power triumphed the following year, when Faubus closed all public high schools in Little Rock rather than desegregate them. Nonetheless, federal action continued.

In 1957, Congress passed the first Civil Rights Act since Reconstruction, creating the United States Commission on Civil Rights to investigate systemic discrimination, such as in voting. Although this measure, like a voting rights act passed three years later, was not fully effective, it lent federal recognition to civil rights.

Most important, however, was growing grassroots activism. In 1957, Martin Luther King Jr. became the first president of the Southern Christian Leadership Conference (SCLC), organized to coordinate civil rights activities. With the success in Montgomery and gains through the Supreme Court, African Americans were poised to launch a national civil rights movement.

Creating a Middle-Class Nation

What led to the emergence of a middle-class culture in the 1950s?

Despite massive resistance to civil rights during the 1950s, in other ways the United States was becoming more inclusive. National prosperity offered greater numbers of Americans material comfort and security through entrance into an economic middle class. Old European ethnic identities faded, as an ever smaller percentage of America's people was first- or second-generation immigrants.

In the new suburbs, people from different backgrounds created communities. Middle-class Americans increasingly looked to national media for advice on matters ranging from how to celebrate Thanksgiving to how to raise children. New opportunities for consumption also tied together Americans from different backgrounds. In the postwar years, a new middle-class way of life transformed the United States.

Prosperity for More Americans

During the 1950s, a growing economy gave more Americans than ever middle-class comforts and economic security. This economic boom was driven by consumer spending, as Americans bought goods unavailable during the war, and industries expanded production. As the Cold War deepened, government defense spending created jobs and stimulated the economy.

Cold War military and aerospace spending fueled the need for highly educated scientists, engineers, and other white-collar workers. The professional middle class thus grew. Universities received billions of dollars to fund research, expanding their roles in American life. Government-funded research also went beyond military weapons systems and the space race: the transistor, invented during the 1950s, was used in radios and sparked the computer revolution.

A new era of labor relations also helped bring economic prosperity to more Americans. The United Auto Workers (UAW) and General Motors led the way in providing workers with health insurance, pension plans, and guaranteed cost-of-living adjustments, or COLAs. The 1950 agreement that *Fortune* magazine called "The Treaty of Detroit" gave GM's workers a five-year contract, with regular wage increases tied to corporate productivity. With this agreement, labor cast its lot with management: workplace stability and efficiency, not strikes, would bring higher wages. During the 1950s, union families joined the economic middle class.

Sunbelt and Economic Growth

Sunbelt Southern and southwestern states whose rapid economic development brought many new residents during the postwar years.

During World War II, new defense industry plants and military training camps channeled federal money to the South, stimulating economic growth. In the postwar era, massive defense spending continued to shift economic development to the South and Southwest—the **Sunbelt** (see Map 25.1). Government actions—including tax breaks for oil companies, siting of military bases, and defense and aerospace contracts—were crucial to the region's new prosperity.

The Sunbelt's spectacular growth was also due to agribusiness, the oil industry, real estate development, and recreation. Sunbelt states successfully sought foreign investment and drew industry with low taxes, low heating bills, air conditioning, and right-to-work laws, which outlawed closed shops. Houston, Phoenix, Los Angeles, San Diego, Dallas, and Miami all boomed, and by 1963 California was the most populous state in the Union.

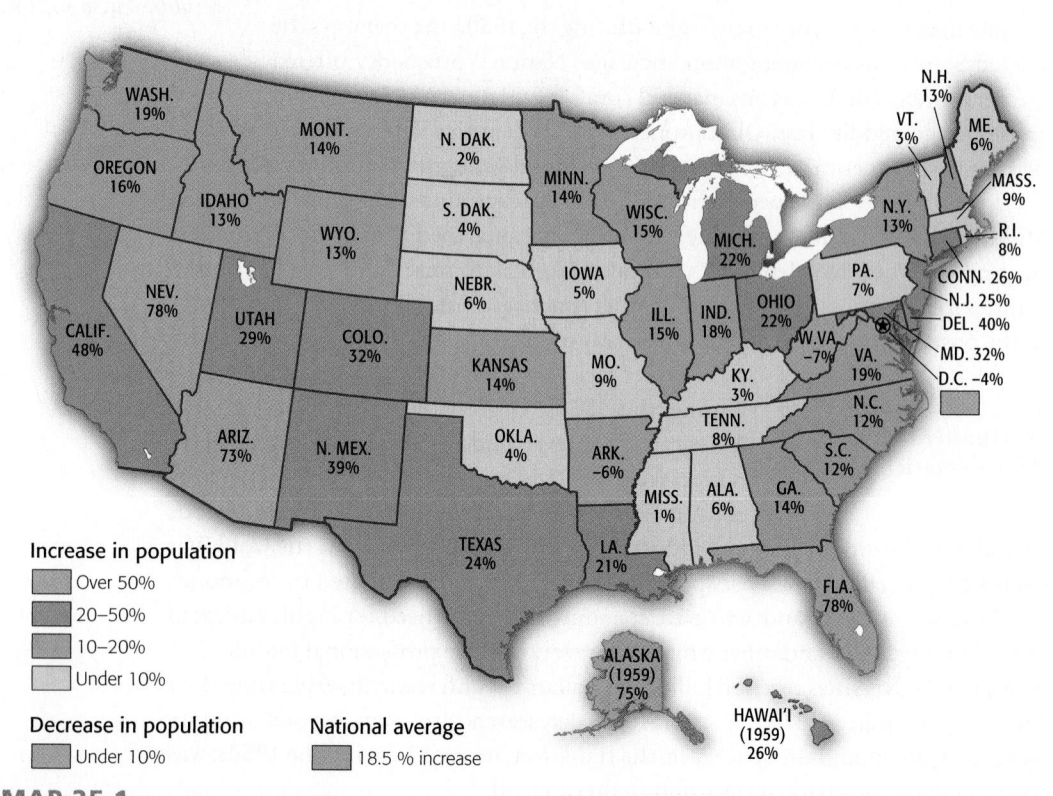

Increase in population
- Over 50%
- 20–50%
- 10–20%
- Under 10%

Decrease in population
- Under 10%

National average
- 18.5 % increase

MAP 25.1
Rise of the Sunbelt, 1950–1960

The years after the Second World War saw a continuation of the migration of Americans to the Sunbelt states of the Southwest and the West Coast. Source: Copyright © Cengage Learning 2015

Visualizing THE PAST

Moving to Levittown

Builder William Levitt's assembly-line methods created affordable homes for young families—although initially only "Caucasians" were allowed to buy homes in Levittown. This family, shown here on their moving day, would have received a copy of the Levittown *Homeowners Guide*, which contained a list of "do's" and "don'ts": for example, residents were not to hang laundry on Sundays, when their neighbors were "most likely to be relaxing on the rear lawn." What does this photograph reveal about the new Levittown family, and why might the community rule book promise to help residents "enjoy their new home"? From looking carefully at the map, including street names and public spaces, how did developers try to create neighborhood and community in a development of inexpensive and virtually identical homes?

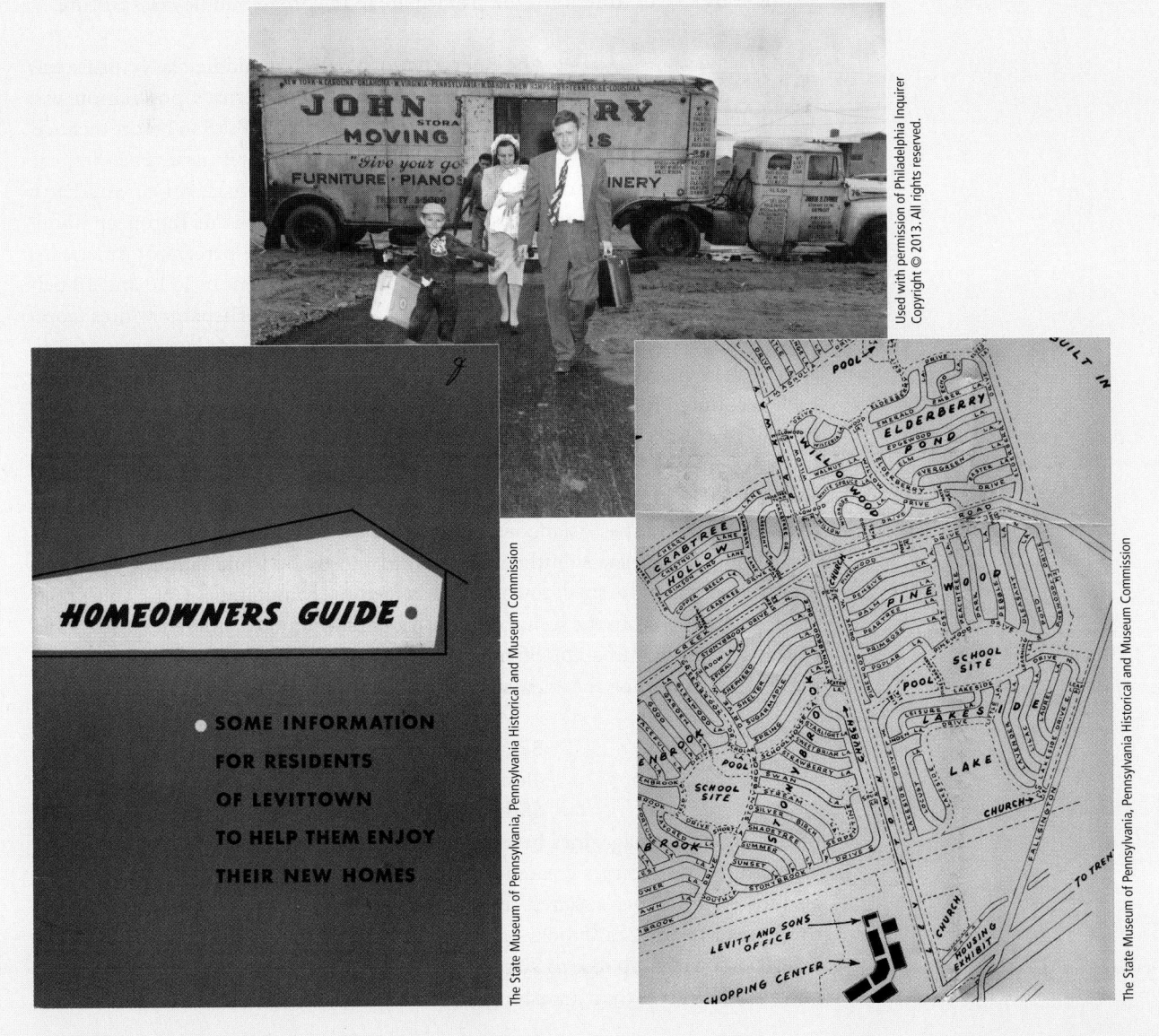

HOMEOWNERS GUIDE

- SOME INFORMATION
  FOR RESIDENTS
  OF LEVITTOWN
  TO HELP THEM ENJOY
  THEIR NEW HOMES

A New Middle-Class Culture

By the 1950s, unionized blue-collar workers had gained middle-class incomes, and veterans with GI Bill college educations had swelled the managerial and professional class. In 1956, for the first time, the United States had more white-collar than blue-collar workers, and 60 percent of families had incomes in the middle-class range (approximately $3,000 to $9,000 a year in the mid-1950s).

Paradoxically, the strength of unions in the postwar era contributed to a decline in working-class identity: as large numbers of blue-collar workers participated in suburban middle-class culture, the lines separating working class and middle class seemed less important. Increasingly, a family's standard of living mattered more than what sort of work made it possible. People of color did not share equally in America's postwar prosperity and were usually invisible in American representations of "the good life." However, many middle-income African Americans, Latinos, and Asian Americans did participate in the broad middle-class culture.

Whiteness and National Culture

The emergence of a national middle-class culture was possible in part because America's population was more homogeneous in the 1950s than before or since. In the nineteenth and early twentieth centuries, the United States restricted or prohibited immigration from Asia, Africa, and Latin America while accepting millions of Europeans. This large-scale European immigration was shut off in the 1920s, so that by 1960 only 5.7 percent of Americans were foreign born (compared with approximately 15 percent in 1910 and 13 percent in 2010). In 1950, 88 percent of Americans were non-Hispanic whites (compared with less than 64 percent in 2010), 10 percent of the population was African American, 2 percent was Hispanic, and Native Americans and Asian Americans each accounted for about one-fifth of 1 percent. But almost all European Americans were at least a generation removed from immigration. Instead of "Italians" or "Russians" or "Jews," they were increasingly likely to describe themselves as "white." In 1959, the addition of two new states, Alaska and Hawai'i, brought more people of native, Asian, or Pacific origin to the U.S. population.

Although the new suburbs were peopled mostly by white families, they were more diverse than the small towns and urban ethnic communities from which their residents had come. In the suburbs, many people encountered different customs and beliefs. But new suburbanites often traded the provincial homogeneity of specific ethnic or regional cultures for a new sort of homogeneity: a national middle-class culture.

Television

Because many white Americans were new to the middle class, they were uncertain about what was expected of them. They found instruction in the national mass media. Women's magazines helped housewives replace ethnic and regional dishes with "American" recipes created from national brand name products. Television also fostered America's shared culture. Although television sets cost about $300—the equivalent of $2,500 today—almost half of American homes had TVs by 1953. Television ownership rose to 90 percent by 1960, when more American households had a television set than a washing machine.

On television, suburban families like the Cleavers (*Leave It to Beaver*) ate dinner at a properly set dining room table. June Cleaver did housework in a carefully ironed dress. Every crisis was resolved through paternal wisdom. Popular family situation comedies reinforced the suburban middle-class ideal many American families sought.

The "middle-classness" of television programming was due in part to advertising. Corporations buying advertising did not want to offend potential consumers. Thus, although African American musician Nat King Cole drew millions of viewers to his NBC television show, it never found a sponsor. National corporations feared being linked to a black performer would hurt sales among whites—especially in the South. Because African Americans made up only about 10 percent of the population and many had little disposable income, they had little influence. The *Nat King Cole Show* was canceled within a year; it was a decade before the networks again anchored a show around a black performer.

With only network television available—ABC, CBS, and NBC (and, until 1956, DuMont)—at any one time 70 percent or more of all viewers might be watching the same program. (In the early twenty-first century, the most popular shows might attract 12 percent of the audience.) Television gave Americans shared experiences and helped create a more homogeneous, white-focused, middle-class culture.

Consumer Culture Americans also found common ground through consumer goods. After decades of scarcity, Americans embraced a dazzling array of choices with unmatched exuberance. People used consumer choices to express their personal identity and to claim status. Cars particularly embodied consumer fantasies. Expensive Cadillacs

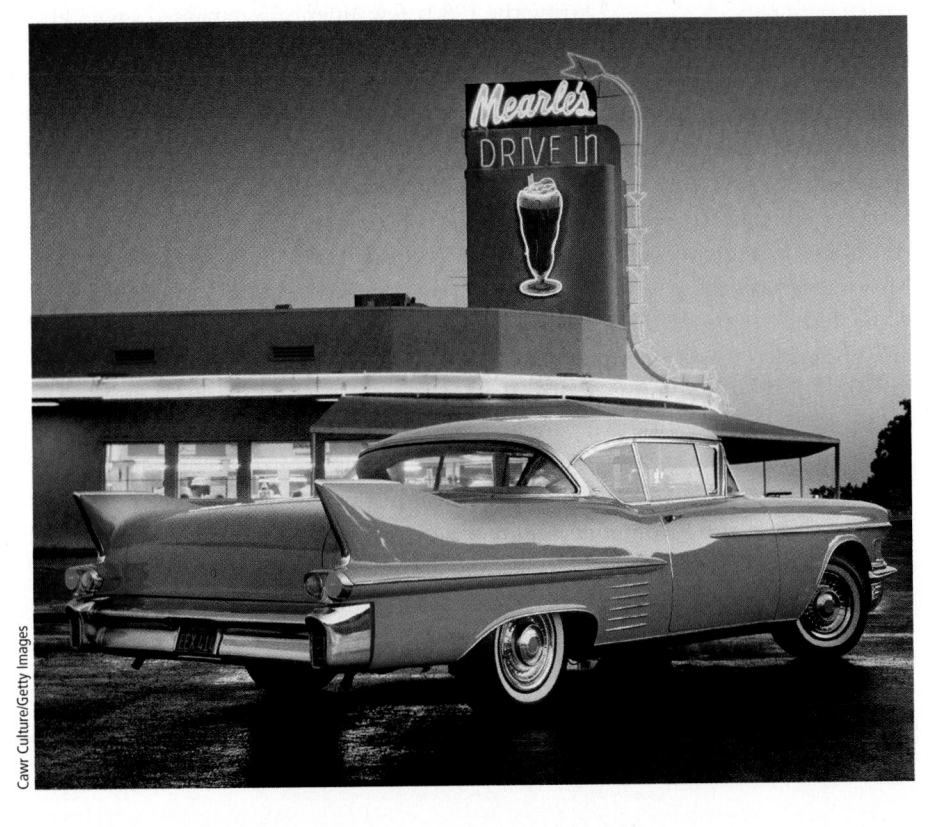

Consumer goods reflected a new exuberance during the 1950s, and none more than that decade's automobiles. This candy-pink 1958 Cadillac coupe, complete with swooping tail fins, stands in front of another 1950s institution: a California drive-in.

Cawr Culture/Getty Images

were the first to develop tail fins, soon added to midrange Chevys, Fords, and Plymouths. Americans spent $65 billion on automobiles in 1955—a figure equivalent to almost 20 percent of the gross national product. To pay for cars, suburban houses, and modern appliances, America's consumer debt rose from $5.7 billion in 1945 to $58 billion in 1961.

Religion

Church membership (primarily in mainline Christian churches) doubled between 1945 and the early 1960s. The destructive world war and the uncertainties of the nuclear age likely contributed to the resurgence of religion. The national mass media also played a role, as preachers like Billy Graham created national congregations from television audiences, preaching a message that combined the promise of salvation with Cold War patriotism. But local churches and synagogues also offered new suburbanites a sense of community, celebrating life's rituals and supporting those far from their extended families and old communities.

Men, Women, and Youth at Midcentury

How did the economic and social structure of the 1950s influence gender roles?

Having survived the Great Depression and a world war, many Americans sought fulfillment in private life; they saw their commitment to home and family as an expression of faith in the future. However, despite the satisfactions many found in family life, men and women found their life choices limited by social pressures to conform to narrowly defined gender roles.

Marriage and Families

During the 1950s, few Americans remained single, and most people married young. By 1959, almost half of American brides were under age nineteen; their husbands were usually only a year or so older. Early marriage was endorsed by experts and approved by most parents, in part to prevent premarital sex. Americans worried that premarital sex might leave the young woman pregnant, ruin her "reputation," or damage her psychologically.

Many young couples found freedom from parental authority by marrying. Most newlyweds quickly had babies—an average of three—completing their family while in their twenties. Birth control (condoms and diaphragms) was widely available and widely used, as couples planned family size. Two children were the American ideal in 1940; by 1960, most couples wanted four. About 88 percent of children under eighteen lived with two parents (in 2011, the figure was 69 percent). Fewer children were born outside marriage; only 3.9 percent of births were to unmarried women in 1950 (compared with 41 percent of births in 2011). Divorce rates were also lower, escalating from a new high of 9 divorces per 1,000 married couples in 1960 to a peak of 22 in the early 1980s, and down to approximately 16 divorces per 1,000 married couples today.

Gender Roles in 1950s Families

In 1950s families, men and women usually took distinct roles, with male breadwinners and female homemakers. This division of labor, contemporary commentators insisted, was based on essential differences between the sexes. In fact, the economic and social structure and cultural values of postwar America determined what choices were available to men and women.

During the 1950s, it was possible for many families to live in modest middle-class comfort on one (male) salary. There were incentives for women to stay at home, especially while children were young. Good child care was rarely available, and fewer families lived close to relatives. New child care experts, including **Dr. Spock**, whose 1946 *Baby and Child Care* sold millions of copies, insisted that a mother's full-time attention was necessary for her children's well-being. Because of hiring discrimination, women who could afford to stay home often did not find available jobs attractive enough to justify juggling paid employment with housework. Many women thus chose to devote their considerable energies to family life. America's schools and religious institutions also benefited immensely from their volunteer labor.

Dr. Spock Physician and author of *Baby and Child Care*, the best-selling child-rearing manual for parents of the baby boom generation.

Women and Work

Suburban domesticity left many women feeling isolated. The popular belief that one should find complete emotional satisfaction in private life put unrealistic pressures on marriages. And despite near-universal celebration of women's domestic roles, many women were managing both job and family responsibilities (see Figure 25.2). Twice as many women were employed in 1960 as in 1940, including 39 percent of women with children between the ages of six and seventeen. Most worked part time for some specific family goal: a new car, college tuition. They saw these jobs as service to the family, not independence from it.

Women faced discrimination in the world of work. Want ads were divided into "Help Wanted—Male" and "Help Wanted—Female" categories. Female full-time workers earned, on average, just 60 percent of what male full-time workers were paid and were restricted to lower-paid "female" fields, as maids, secretaries, teachers, and nurses. College psychology textbooks warned women not to "compete" with men; magazine articles described "career women" as a "third sex." Medical schools commonly limited the admission of women to 5 percent of each class. In 1960, less than 4 percent of lawyers and judges were female. When future Supreme Court Justice Ruth Bader Ginsburg graduated at the top of her Columbia Law School class in 1959, she could not find a job.

"Crisis of Masculinity"

While academics and mass media critics alike stressed the importance of "proper" female roles, they also devoted equal attention to the plight of the American male. American men faced a

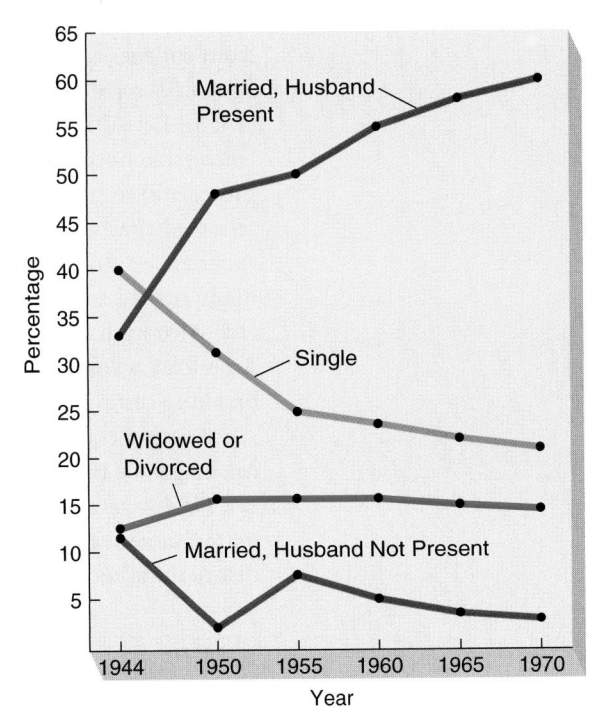

FIGURE 25.2
Marital Distribution of the Female Labor Force, 1944–1970

The composition of the female labor force changed dramatically from 1944 to 1970. In 1944, 41 percent of women in the labor force were single; in 1970, only 22 percent were single. During the same years, the percentage of the female labor force who had a husband in the home jumped from 34 to 59. The percentage who were widowed or divorced remained about the same from 1944 to 1970.

(Source: Adapted from U.S. Bureau of the Census, *Historical Statistics of the United States, Colonial Times to 1970*, Bicentennial Edition (Washington, D.C.: U.S. Government Printing Office, 1975), p. 133.)

"crisis of masculinity," proclaimed the nation's mass-circulation magazines. In a best-selling book, sociologist William H. Whyte explained that corporate employees had become "organization men," succeeding through cooperation and conformity, not initiative and risk. Experts claimed women's "natural" desire for security and comfort was stifling men's instinct for adventure. Some linked concerns about masculinity to the Cold War, arguing that, unless America's men recovered masculinity, the nation's future was at risk. At the same time, however, men who did not conform to standards of male responsibility—husband, father, breadwinner—were forcefully condemned and open to charges of "emotional immaturity" or "latent homosexuality."

Sexuality

Sexuality was complicated terrain in postwar America. Only heterosexual intercourse within marriage was deemed socially acceptable. Women who became pregnant outside marriage were often ostracized by friends and family and expelled from schools. Homosexuality was grounds for job dismissal, expulsion from college, even jail. At the same time, in his major works on human sexuality, *Sexual Behavior in the Human Male* (1948) and *Sexual Behavior in the Human Female* (1953), Dr. Alfred Kinsey, director of the Institute for Sex Research at Indiana University, noted that, while over 80 percent of his female sample disapproved of premarital sex on "moral grounds," half of them had had premarital sex. He also reported that at least 37 percent of American men had had "some homosexual experience." Americans made best sellers of Kinsey's dry, quantitative studies—as many rushed to condemn him. The *Chicago Tribune* called him a "menace to society." Although Kinsey's research did not provide a completely accurate picture of American sexual behavior, it told many Americans that they were not alone in breaking certain rules.

Another challenge to sexual rules came from Hugh Hefner, who launched *Playboy* magazine in 1953. Within three years, it had a circulation of 1 million. Hefner saw *Playboy* as an attack on America's "ferocious anti-sexuality" and his nude "playmates" as a means for men to combat what he considered the increasingly "blurred distinctions between the sexes" in family-centered suburban culture.

Youth Culture

As children grew up in relative stability and prosperity, a distinctive "youth culture" developed. Its customs and rituals were created within peer groups and shaped by national media—teen magazines, movies, radio, advertising, music.

The sheer numbers of "baby boom" youth made them a force in American society. America's corporations quickly learned the power of youth, as children's fads launched multimillion-dollar industries. Mr. Potato Head—probably the first toy advertised on television—had $4 million in sales in 1952. In the mid-1950s, when Walt Disney's television show *Disneyland* featured Davy Crockett, "King of the Wild Frontier," every child in America (and many adults) wanted a coonskin cap. As these baby boom children grew up, their buying power shaped American popular culture.

By 1960, America's 18 million teenagers were spending $10 billion a year. Seventy-two percent of movie tickets in the 1950s were sold to teenagers, and

Hollywood created teen films ranging from forgettable B movies to controversial and influential movies, such as James Dean's *Rebel Without a Cause*. Adults worried that teens would copy the delinquency romanticized in *Rebel Without a Cause*, and teenage boys did emulate Dean's rebellious look. The film, however, blamed parents for teenage confusion, drawing on popular psychological theories about sexuality and the "crisis of masculinity."

Nothing defined youth culture as much as music. Young Americans were electrified by the driving energy of Bill Haley and the Comets, Chuck Berry, Little Richard, and Buddy Holly. **Elvis Presley**'s 1956 appearance on TV's *Ed Sullivan Show* touched off a frenzy of teen adulation—and a flood of letters from parents scandalized by his "gyrations." Although few white musicians acknowledged the debt, the roots of rock 'n' roll lay in African American rhythm and blues. The raw energy and sometimes sexually suggestive lyrics of early rock music faded as the music industry sought white performers, like Pat Boone, to do blander, more acceptable "cover" versions of music by black artists.

Elvis Presley Popular rock 'n' roll musician who melded country, gospel, and rhythm and blues influences; his sexually charged style drew young fans and alarmed many adults.

Youth culture made many adults uneasy. Parents worried that "going steady" might encourage teens to "go too far" sexually. Crime rates for young people had risen dramatically after World War II, but much was "status" crime—curfew violations, sexual experimentation, underage drinking—activities that were only criminal because of the person's age. Congress held hearings on juvenile delinquency, with experts testifying to the corrupting power of youth-oriented popular culture, comic books in particular. Most youthful behavior, however, fit squarely into the consumer culture that youth shared with their parents. "Rebellious youth" rarely questioned the logic of postwar American culture.

Challenges to Middle-Class Culture

The growth of middle-class culture inspired pockets of cultural dissent. **Beat** (a word that suggested both "down and out" and "beatific") writers rejected middle-class social decorum and contemporary literary conventions. The Beat Generation embraced spontaneity in their art, sought freedom from the demands of everyday life, and enjoyed open sexuality and drug use. Perhaps the most significant beat work was Allen Ginsberg's angry, incantational poem "Howl" (1956), the subject of an obscenity trial whose verdict opened American publishing to a broader range of works. The mainstream press ridiculed the beats, dubbing them "beatniks" (after *Sputnik*, suggesting their un-Americanness). Their rebellion helped shape America's counterculture in the 1960s and 1970s.

Beat Nonconformist writers, such as Allen Ginsberg, who expressed scorn for the middle-class ideals of conformity, religion, family values, and materialism.

The Limits of the Middle-Class Nation

What were the limits of 1950s middle-class culture?

During the 1950s, influential critics condemned the new middle-class culture as a wasteland of conformity, homogeneity, and ugly consumerism.

Critics of Conformity

Americans, obsessed with self-criticism even as most participated wholeheartedly in the celebratory culture of their age, rushed to buy books like J. D. Salinger's *The Catcher in the Rye* and Norman Mailer's *The Naked and the Dead*, which

Barbie

Barbie, the "all-American doll," is—like many Americans—an immigrant. Although introduced in 1959 by the American toy company Mattel, Barbie's origins lie in Germany, where she was called Lilli.

The German Lilli doll was a novelty toy for adult men (as evidenced by her sexy outfits and her figure, equivalent to 39-21-31 in human proportions). She was based on a character that cartoonist Reinhard Beuthien drew for the German tabloid *Das Bild* in 1952. Lilli was so popular that she became a regular feature, later made three-dimensional as *Bild* Lilli, an eleven-and-a-half-inch-tall blonde doll—with the figure Barbie would make famous.

Lilli came to America with Ruth Handler, one of the founders and codirectors of the Mattel toy company. When she glimpsed Lilli while vacationing in Europe, Handler bought three—and gave one to her daughter Barbara, after whom Lilli would be renamed. Mattel bought the rights to Lilli and unveiled Barbie in March 1959. Despite mothers' hesitations about buying a doll that looked like Barbie, within the year Mattel had sold 351,000 Barbies at $3 each (or about $17 in 2000 dollars). The billionth Barbie was sold in 1997.

Within the United States, Barbie has been controversial—at least among adults. Some have worried that Barbie's wildly unrealistic figure fosters girls' dissatisfaction with their own body—a serious problem in a culture plagued with eating disorders. Others claim that, despite Barbie's 1980s "Girls Can Do Anything" makeover, Barbie represents empty-headed femininity, focused on endless consumption. And many have noted that blonde, blue-eyed Barbie failed to represent the diversity of America's people.

In 2002, international labor rights groups called for a boycott of Barbie. They cited studies showing that half of all Barbies were made by exploited young women workers in mainland China: of the $10 retail cost of an average Barbie, Chinese factories receive only 35 cents per doll to cover their costs, including labor. Saudi Arabia banned Barbie in 2003, arguing that her skimpy outfits and the values she represents are not suitable for a Muslim nation.

Even so, the doll remains popular worldwide, sold in more than 150 countries, with international sales rising as U.S. sales decline. For better or worse, Barbie continues to link the United States and the rest of the world.

Patrick Seeger/dpa/Corbis

Before Barbie became an American child's toy, she was Lilli, a German sex symbol. Mattel transformed the doll into a wholesome American teenager with a new wardrobe to match.

were profoundly critical of American society. Americans made best sellers of difficult academic works, such as David Riesman's *The Lonely Crowd* (1950) and William H. Whyte's *The Organization Man* (1955), both of which criticized conformity. Critiques also appeared in mass-circulation magazines like *Ladies' Home Journal* and *Reader's Digest*. Many Americans even understood *Invasion of the Body Snatchers*—a 1956 film in which zombielike aliens replace a town's human inhabitants—as criticism of suburban conformity and the homogeneity of postwar culture.

Most critics were attempting to understand significant changes in American society. Americans did lose some autonomy in work as large corporations replaced smaller businesses; they experienced the homogenizing force of mass production and a national consumer culture; they saw distinctions among ethnic groups and even among socioeconomic classes fade. Critics, however, were often elitist and antidemocratic, seeing only conformity and sterility and not understanding that inexpensive suburban housing gave healthier, perhaps happier, lives to millions raised in dark tenements or ramshackle farmhouses. In retrospect, however, other criticisms are obvious.

Environmental Degradation

The new consumer culture encouraged wasteful habits and harmed the environment. Americans replaced products because they were "out of date," not because they did not work, and automakers, encouraging the trend, revamped designs annually. By the 1960s, the United States, with only 5 percent of the world's population, consumed more than one-third of its goods and services.

Rapid economic growth exacted environmental costs. Steel mills, coal-powered generators, and internal-combustion car engines burning lead-based gasoline polluted the atmosphere and imperiled people's health. As suburbanites commuted greater distances to work, and neighborhoods were built without public transportation, Americans relied on private automobiles, consuming nonrenewable oil and gasoline and filling cities and suburbs with smog. Water was diverted from lakes and rivers to service Sunbelt cities, including the swimming pools and golf courses of parched Arizona and southern California.

Defense contractors and farmers were among the country's worst polluters. Refuse from nuclear weapons facilities at Hanford, Washington, and at Colorado's Rocky Flats arsenal poisoned soil and water resources. Agriculture employed pesticides and other chemicals. DDT, a chemical used on Pacific islands during the war to kill mosquitoes and lice, was used widely in the United States until after 1962, when wildlife biologist Rachel Carson indicted DDT for the deaths of mammals, birds, and fish in her best-selling book *Silent Spring*.

In the midst of prosperity, few understood the consequences of the economic transformation taking place. The nation was moving toward a postindustrial economy in which providing goods and services to consumers was more important than producing goods. Union membership grew slowly—because most new jobs were created in the union-resistant white-collar service trades. Technological advances increased productivity but also pushed people from relatively well-paid blue-collar jobs into the growing and lower-paid service sector.

1950

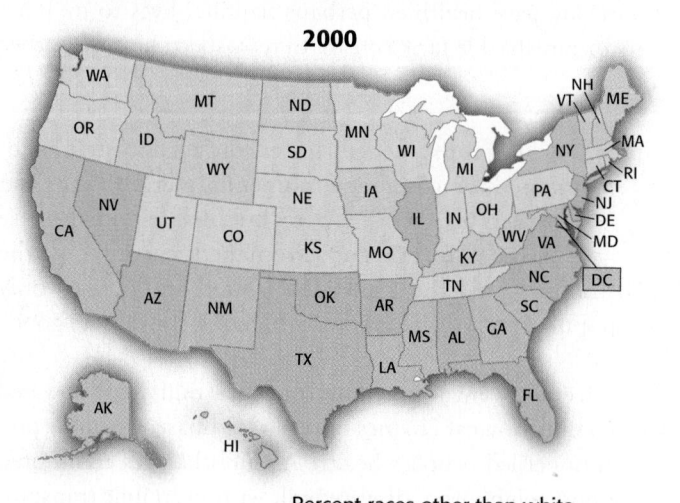

2000

Percent races other than white

■ Over 30%	■ Under 10%
■ 20–29%	▫ Not applicable
▫ 10–19%	

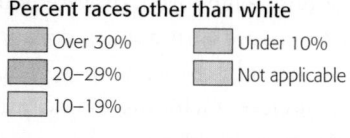

MAP 25.2

Racial Composition of the United States, 1950 and 2000

Compared with present-day America, most states were fairly racially homogeneous in 1950. The exception was the Deep South, where most African Americans still lived.

Source: Adapted from "Demographic Trends in the Twentieth Century," U.S. Census Bureau; www. census.gov/population/www/censusdata/hiscendata.html.

Continuing Racism

Racial discrimination stood unchallenged in most of 1950s America. Suburbs, North and South, were almost always racially segregated. Many white Americans had little or no contact with people of different races—not only because of residential segregation but also because the relatively small populations of nonwhite Americans were not dispersed equally throughout the nation. In 1960, there were 68 people of Chinese descent and 519 African Americans living in Vermont; 181 Native Americans lived in West Virginia; and Mississippi had just 178 Japanese American residents. Most white Americans in the 1950s did not think of the emerging middle-class culture as "white," but as "American," marginalizing people of color in image as in reality (see Map 25.2).

Poverty in an Age of Abundance

In an age of abundance, more than one in five Americans lived in poverty. One-fifth of the poor were people of color, including almost half of the nation's African Americans and more than half of all Native Americans. Two-thirds of the poor lived in households headed by a person with an eighth-grade education or less, one-fourth in households headed by a single woman. More than one-third of the poor were under age eighteen; one-fourth were over age sixty-five.

As millions of Americans (most of them white) settled in suburbs, the poor were concentrated in inner cities. African American migrants from the South were joined by poor whites from the southern Appalachians. Latin Americans arrived in growing numbers from Mexico, the Dominican Republic, Colombia, Ecuador, and Cuba.

Because of the strong economy, many newcomers gained a higher standard of living. But discrimination limited their advances, and they endured crowded and decrepit housing and poor schools. Federal programs that helped middle-class Americans sometimes made the lives of the poor worse. For example, the National Housing Act of 1949, passed to make available "a decent home … for every American family," provided for "urban redevelopment." Redevelopment meant slum clearance, replacing poor neighborhoods with luxury high-rise buildings, parking lots, and highways.

Legacy FOR A PEOPLE AND A NATION

The Pledge of Allegiance

The Pledge of Allegiance that Americans recite today was shaped by the Cold War. Congress added the phrase "under God" to the pledge in 1954 to emphasize the difference between the God-fearing United States and the "godless communists" of the Soviet Union.

The Pledge of Allegiance was not always an important part of American public life. The original version was written in 1892 by Francis Bellamy, editor of *The Youth's Companion*, to commemorate the four hundredth anniversary of Columbus's arrival in North America. In 1942, Congress officially adopted a revised version as an act of wartime patriotism. The Supreme Court ruled in 1943, however, that schoolchildren could not be forced to say the "Pledge to the Flag."

During the Cold War years, the pledge became an increasingly important symbol of U.S. loyalty. Cold War fears fueled a campaign by the Knights of Columbus, a Catholic men's service organization, to include "under God" in the pledge. Supporting the bill, President Eisenhower proclaimed that

in this way we shall constantly strengthen those spiritual weapons which forever will be our country's most powerful resource in peace and war. From this day forward, the millions of our schoolchildren will daily proclaim in every city and town, every village and every rural schoolhouse, the dedication of our nation and our people to the Almighty.

Some Americans, citing the doctrine of separation of church and state, have protested the inclusion of "under God." In June 2002, the Ninth District Court (covering California and eight other western states) sparked a major controversy by ruling that the 1954 version of the pledge was unconstitutional because it conveyed a "state endorsement" of a religious belief. Questions about the proper role of religion in American life remain controversial, a legacy for a people and a nation becoming even more diverse in the twenty-first century.

In rural areas, the growth of large agribusinesses pushed tenant farmers and owners of small farms off the land. From 1945 to 1961, the nation's farm population declined from 24.4 million to 14.8 million. When southern cotton harvesting was mechanized in the 1940s and 1950s, more than 4 million people were displaced. Southern tobacco growers dismissed tenant farmers, bought tractors, and hired migratory workers. In the West and Southwest, Mexican citizens continued to serve as cheap migrant labor under the *bracero* program. Almost 1 million Mexican workers came legally to the United States in 1959; many more were undocumented workers. Entire families labored, enduring conditions little better than in the Great Depression.

Native Americans were America's poorest people, with an average annual income barely half that of the poverty level. Conditions worsened under termination, a federal policy implemented during the Eisenhower administration. Termination reversed the Indian Reorganization Act of 1934, allowing Indians to terminate their tribal status and remove reservation lands from federal protection that prohibited their sale. Sixty-one tribes were terminated between 1954 and 1960. Termination could only occur with a tribe's agreement, but pressure was sometimes intense—especially when reservation land was rich in natural resources. Enticed by cash payments, almost four-fifths of the Klamaths of Oregon voted to sell their shares of forestland. With termination, their way of life collapsed. Many Indians left reservation land for the city. By the time termination was halted in the 1960s, observers compared the situation of Native Americans to the devastation their forebears had endured in the nineteenth century.

Overall, Americans who had lived through the Great Depression and World War II enjoyed the relative prosperity and economic security of the postwar era. But those who had made it to the comfortable middle class often ignored the plight of those left behind. It would be their children—the generation of the baby boom, many reared in suburban comfort—who would see racism, poverty, and the self-satisfaction of postwar suburban culture as a failure of American ideals.

Summary

In the years following World War II, Americans married and had children in record numbers. Millions of veterans used the GI Bill to attend college, buy homes, and start businesses. Consumer spending brought sustained growth, which lifted a majority of Americans into an expanding middle class.

The Cold War presidencies of Truman and Eisenhower focused on international relations rather than on domestic politics. Within the United States, Cold War fears provoked an extreme anticommunism that stifled political dissent and diminished Americans' civil liberties and freedoms.

The continuing African American struggle for civil rights drew national attention during the Montgomery bus boycott. African Americans won victories in the Supreme Court, including the landmark decision in *Brown v. Board of Education*. Truman and Eisenhower used federal power to guarantee the rights of black Americans, and a national civil rights movement began to coalesce.

Despite continued racial divisions, the United States became a more inclusive nation in the 1950s, as a majority of Americans participated in a national, consumer-oriented, middle-class culture. This culture largely ignored poverty in the nation's cities and rural areas, but for the growing number of middle-class Americans, the American dream seemed a reality.

Chapter Review

Shaping Postwar America

What drove the mass migration of Americans to the suburbs after World War II?

Demand for homes and federal policies facilitated massive migration to the suburbs. Few new houses or apartments were built during the Great Depression and World War II, and many young couples moved in with relatives or found creative solutions to the housing shortage. In the postwar years, developers applied assembly-line techniques to home construction, creating new suburbs on relatively inexpensive land outside cities. At the same time, the Federal Housing Authority offered low-interest mortgages and loans, and Congress authorized the construction of major roadways and interstate highways in the late 1940s and 1950s. These roads linked the new suburbs to jobs in the cities.

Domestic Politics in the Cold War Era

What happened to New Deal–style liberalism after World War II?

Truman embraced the New Deal idea of government responsibility for citizens' welfare. He sought an increase in the minimum wage, national health insurance, and federal aid for education. He additionally supported the Full Employment Act and civil rights legislation. But conservative Republicans and southern Democrats in Congress gutted the Full Employment Act and refused to raise the minimum wage, while southern conservatives destroyed civil rights legislation. Truman's medical insurance and educational funding proposals also met with resistance. A moderate Republican, Eisenhower signed amendments to the Social Security Act that increased benefits and made 7.5 million workers eligible. He also increased government funding for education. Still, neither Truman nor Eisenhower came close to the liberalism of the New Deal.

Cold War Fears and Anticommunism

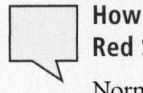

How did Cold War fears inspire a Red Scare in the United States?

Normal Cold War fears—of nuclear war or of a Soviet takeover—were replaced by irrational ones, inspiring a Red Scare. Mainstream Americans built bomb shelters; government employees could be deemed "security risks" (and fired) for such flimsy reasons as alcoholism, homosexuality, and high levels of debt. The House Un-American Activities Committee (HUAC) targeted Hollywood, university professors, and others. Consequently, studios blacklisted actors, screenwriters, and others suspected of communist affiliations, and university professors were threatened with firing for not taking loyalty oaths. Fears drove the CIO to purge itself of eleven unions—900,000 members—for alleged communist domination. The Red Scare waned after 1954 when Republican Senator Joseph McCarthy was discredited on national television for his claims about Communist Party members infiltrating the army.

The Struggle for Civil Rights

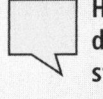

How did federal initiatives, Supreme Court decisions, and grassroots activism shape the struggle for civil rights after World War II?

African Americans who helped win World War II were determined to improve their status and end discrimination in the United States, and politicians like Truman were heeding black aspirations. Truman established the President's Commission on Civil Rights in 1946, which produced a report that became the civil rights movement's agenda for the next twenty years—calling for legislation to end lynching and segregation and guarantee voting rights and equality in employment. African Americans mounted successful challenges to racial discrimination in the courts, most notably the end of segregated schools in the 1954 landmark *Brown v. Board of Education of Topeka*. At the grassroots level, blacks fought discrimination, most visibly in the yearlong Montgomery bus boycott, which began in 1955 when Rosa Parks, a seamstress and NAACP activist, was arrested for refusing to give up her seat on a city bus to a white man.

Creating a Middle-Class Nation

What led to the emergence of a middle-class culture in the 1950s?

The unprecedented prosperity of the postwar era meant that there were more and better-paying jobs that enabled greater numbers of people to move into the ranks of the middle class. Even previously blue-collar manufacturing jobs now paid enough to make these families middle class, too. People of varying ethnic backgrounds came together via homeownership in the new suburbs, which, although still largely white, were more diverse than the communities where people previously resided. Newly affordable goods reached a wider segment of the population. And an emerging national mass media taught Americans how to behave and live like a single, unified, national middle class—with American foods replacing ethnic dishes, national brands replacing homemade products, and nationalized notions about how to raise children. Television shows also reinforced ideas about how middle-class people acted.

Men, Women, and Youth at Midcentury

How did the economic and social structure of the 1950s influence gender roles?

In the 1950s, middle-class families could survive on one income, typically the man's. Most Americans believed that men should be breadwinners and women homemakers—a role that left many women feeling isolated and unfulfilled. While many married women did work outside the home, it was often part time and for a specific goal, such as a new car. Child care was virtually nonexistent; popular child care experts such as Dr. Spock argued that children required a mother's full-time care; and hiring discrimination meant that there were few well-paying jobs open to women to make it worth juggling home and work responsibilities. Men who did not conform to standards of male responsibility—husband, father, breadwinner—were also socially condemned, and experts worried about the crisis in masculinity of a new generation of "organization men," corporate employees who succeeded through cooperation and conformity rather than initiative and risk.

The Limits of the Middle-Class Nation

What were the limits of 1950s middle-class culture?

Critics pointed out several negative consequences of 1950s middle-class culture. Instead of Americans replacing products when they wore out, now they replaced them when they seemed outdated. By the 1960s the United States, with only 5 percent of the world's population, consumed more than one-third of its goods and services. All of this consumption generated increased pollution and health concerns. Americans' dependence on the automobile led to increased reliance on gasoline, and water was shifted from lakes to swimming pools as the Sunbelt developed. Even in

the age of affluence, more than one-fifth of Americans were poor—often people of color (especially Native Americans and African Americans), many of whom were concentrated in inner cities. Racial discrimination continued, resulting in racially segregated suburbs. Programs that helped the middle class often hurt the poor, such as the National Housing Act of 1949, which replaced neighborhoods with luxury high-rise buildings, parking lots, and highways.

Suggestions for Further Reading

Glenn C. Altschuler and Stuart M. Blumin, *The GI Bill: A New Deal for Veterans* (2009)

Taylor Branch, *Parting the Waters: America in the King Years, 1954–1963* (1988)

Lizabeth Cohen, *A Consumer's Republic: The Politics of Mass Consumption in Postwar America* (2003)

Stephanie Coontz, *The Way We Never Were: American Families and the Nostalgia Trap* (1992)

Thomas Patrick Doherty, *Cold War, Cool Medium: Television, McCarthyism, and American Culture* (2003)

Mary Dudziak, *Cold War Civil Rights: Race and the Image of American Democracy* (2000)

James Gregory, *The Southern Diaspora: How the Great Migrations of Black and White Southerners Transformed the Nation* (2007)

Thomas Hine, *Populuxe* (1986)

Grace Palladino, *Teenagers* (1996)

Michael Sherry, *In the Shadow of War* (1995)

Thomas J. Sugrue, *Sweet Land of Liberty: The Forgotten Struggle for Civil Rights in the North* (2008)

The Tumultuous Sixties

1960–1968

It was late, and Ezell Blair had an exam the next day. But there he was with his friends in the dormitory, talking—as they often did—about injustice, about living in a nation that proclaimed equality for all but denied full citizenship to some because of the color of their skin. They were complaining about the do-nothing adults, condemning the black community of Greensboro, when Franklin McCain said, as if he meant it, "It's time to fish or cut bait." Joe McNeil and McCain's roommate, David Richmond, agreed. Blair, concerned about his exam, hesitated, but he was outvoted.

The next day, February 1, 1960, after their classes at North Carolina Agricultural and Technical College, the four freshmen walked into town. At the F. W. Woolworth's on South Elm Street, one of the most profitable stores in the national chain, each bought a few small things. Then, nervously, they sat down at the lunch counter and tried to order coffee. These seventeen- and eighteen-year-olds were prepared to be arrested, even attacked. But nothing happened. The counter help ignored them as long as possible; finally one worker reminded them, "We don't serve colored here." An elderly white woman told the boys how proud she was of them. The store closed; the manager turned out the lights. After forty-five minutes, the four men who had begun the sit-in movement left the store.

They returned the next day with twenty fellow students. By February 3, sixty-three of the sixty-five seats were taken. On February 4, students from other colleges arrived, and the sit-in spread to the S. H. Kress store across the street. By February 7, there were sit-ins in Winston-Salem; by February 8, in Charlotte; on February 9, in Raleigh. By the third week in February, students were picketing Woolworth's stores in the North. On July 26, 1960, they won. F. W. Woolworth's ended segregation in all of its stores.

When these four college freshmen sat down at the Woolworth's lunch counter in Greensboro, they signaled the beginning of a decade of public activism rarely matched in American history. During the 1960s, millions of Americans—many of them young—took to the streets. Passion over contemporary events revitalized democracy—and threatened to tear the nation apart.

John F. Kennedy, the nation's youngest president, told Americans as he took office in 1961, "The torch has been passed to a new generation." Despite his inspirational language, Kennedy had only modest success implementing his domestic agenda. In his third year as president, however, Kennedy responded to the bravery of civil rights activists and the intransigence of their white opponents by offering greater support for civil rights and proposing more ambitious domestic policies. But Kennedy was assassinated in November 1963. His death seemed, to many, the end of an era of hope.

Lyndon Johnson, Kennedy's successor, invoked the memory of the martyred president to launch an ambitious program of civil rights and liberal legislation. Johnson meant to use federal power to eliminate poverty and guarantee equal rights to all Americans. He called his vision the Great Society.

Despite liberal triumphs and civil rights gains, social tensions escalated during the mid-1960s. A revitalized conservative movement emerged, and Franklin Roosevelt's old New Deal coalition fractured as white southerners abandoned the Democratic Party. Many African Americans, especially in the North, were angry that poverty and racial discrimination persisted despite landmark civil rights laws, and their discontent exploded during the "long, hot summers" of the mid-1960s. White youth culture, which seemed intent on rejecting everything an older generation had worked for, created what Americans came to call "the generation gap."

Developments overseas also contributed to a growing national instability. After the 1962 Cuban missile crisis brought the Soviet Union and the United States close to nuclear disaster, President John F. Kennedy and Soviet leader Nikita Khrushchev moved to reduce bilateral tensions. Cold War pressures in Europe lessened. Everywhere else, however, the superpowers competed frantically. Throughout the 1960s, the United States tried a variety of approaches—including foreign aid, CIA covert actions, military assaults, cultural penetration, economic sanctions, and diplomacy—to win the Cold War. In Vietnam, Kennedy expanded U.S. involvement. Johnson "Americanized" the war, increasing U.S. troops to more than half a million in 1968.

By 1968, the Vietnam War had divided Americans and undermined Johnson's Great Society. With the assassinations of Martin Luther King Jr. and Robert Kennedy—two of America's brightest leaders—that spring, with cities in flames, and with tanks in the streets of Chicago in August, the fate of the nation seemed to hang in the balance.

As you read this chapter, keep the following questions in mind:

- **What were the successes and failures of American liberalism in the 1960s?**
- **Why did the United States expand its participation in the war in Vietnam and continue in the war so long?**
- **By 1968, many believed the fate of the nation hung in the balance. What did they think was at stake? What divided Americans, and how did they express their differences?**

Kennedy and the Cold War

How was the Cuban missile crisis a watershed in U.S.-Soviet relations?

Young, handsome, and intellectually curious, **John F. Kennedy** brought wit and sophistication to the White House. His Irish American grandfather had been mayor of Boston, and his millionaire father, Joseph P. Kennedy, had served as ambassador to Great Britain. In 1946, the young Kennedy returned from World War II a naval hero (the boat he commanded was sunk by a Japanese destroyer in 1943, and Kennedy saved his crew) and campaigned to represent Boston in the U.S. House of Representatives. He served three terms in the House, and in 1952 was elected to the Senate.

John F. Kennedy President from 1961 until his assassination in 1963.

John Fitzgerald Kennedy

As a Democrat, Kennedy inherited the New Deal commitment to America's social welfare system. But he avoided controversial issues, such as civil rights and the censure of Joseph McCarthy. Kennedy won a Pulitzer Prize for his *Profiles in Courage* (1956), a study of principled politicians, but he shaded the truth in claiming sole authorship of the book, which had been written largely by aide Theodore Sorensen (from more than one hundred pages of notes dictated by Kennedy). In foreign policy, Senator Kennedy endorsed containment. Despite an unimpressive legislative record, he enjoyed an enthusiastic following, especially after his landslide reelection to the Senate in 1958.

Kennedy and his handlers cultivated an image of him as a happy, healthy family man. But he was a chronic womanizer,

Many Americans were enchanted with the youthful and photogenic Kennedys. Here, the president and his family pose outside the Palm Beach, Florida, home of the president's father after a private Easter service, April 14, 1963.

AP Photo

Chronology

1960	Sit-ins begin in Greensboro
	Birth control pill approved
	John F. Kennedy elected president
	Young Americans for Freedom write Sharon Statement
1961	Freedom Rides protest segregation in transportation
1962	Students for a Democratic Society issues Port Huron Statement
	Cuban missile crisis courts nuclear war
1963	Civil rights March on Washington for Jobs and Freedom draws more than 250,000
	South Vietnamese leader Diem assassinated following U.S.-sanctioned coup d'état
	John F. Kennedy assassinated; Lyndon B. Johnson becomes president
1964	Civil Rights Act passed by Congress
	Race riots break out in first of the "long, hot summers"
	Gulf of Tonkin Resolution passed by Congress
	Free Speech Movement begins at University of California, Berkeley
	Lyndon B. Johnson elected president
1965	Lyndon Johnson launches Great Society programs
	United States commits ground troops to Vietnam and initiates bombing campaign
	Voting Rights Act outlaws practices preventing most African Americans from voting in southern states
	Immigration and Nationality Act lowers barriers to immigration from Asia and Latin America
	Malcolm X assassinated
1966	National Organization for Women founded
1967	"Summer of love" in San Francisco's Haight-Ashbury district
	Race riots erupt in Newark, Detroit, and other cities
1968	Tet Offensive deepens fear of losing war in Vietnam
	Martin Luther King Jr. assassinated
	Robert Kennedy assassinated
	Violence erupts at Democratic National Convention
	Richard Nixon elected president

even after his 1953 marriage to Jacqueline Bouvier. Nor was he the picture of physical vitality. As a child, he had almost died of scarlet fever. He later developed severe back problems, made worse by his experience in World War II. After the war, Kennedy was diagnosed with Addison's disease, an adrenaline deficiency that required daily cortisone injections and often left him in pain.

Election of 1960

Kennedy defeated Republican Richard Nixon in the 1960 presidential election by only 118,000 votes out of nearly 69 million cast. Kennedy achieved mixed success in the South but ran well in the Northeast and Midwest. His Roman Catholic faith hurt him in states where voters feared he would take direction from the pope, but helped in states with large Catholic populations. As the sitting vice president, Nixon had to answer for sagging economic figures and the Soviet downing of a U-2 spy plane. In televised debates against the telegenic Kennedy, Nixon looked nervous and surly, and the camera made him appear unshaven. Perhaps worse, when asked to list Nixon's significant decisions as vice president, Eisenhower replied, "If you give me a week, I might think of one."

The new president surrounded himself with young advisers whom writer David Halberstam called "the best and the brightest." Secretary of Defense Robert McNamara (age forty-four) had been an assistant professor at Harvard at twenty-four and later the whiz kid president of the Ford Motor Company. Kennedy's special assistant for national security affairs, McGeorge Bundy (age forty-one) had become a Harvard dean at thirty-four with only a bachelor's degree. Secretary of State Dean Rusk (fifty-two) had been a Rhodes Scholar in his youth. Kennedy was only forty-three, and his brother Robert, the attorney general, was thirty-five.

Kennedy gave top priority to waging the Cold War. In the campaign, he had criticized Eisenhower's foreign policy as unimaginative, accusing him of failing to reduce the threat of nuclear war with the Soviet Union and of weakening America's standing in the Third World. Kennedy's inaugural address suggested no halfway measures: "Let every nation know that we shall pay any price, bear any burden, meet any hardship, support any friend, oppose any foe to assure the survival and the success of liberty."

Nation Building in the Third World

In reality, Kennedy in office would not be prepared to pay any price or bear any burden in the struggle against communism. He came to understand, sooner than many of his advisers, that there were limits to American power abroad. He initiated dialog with the Soviets, sometimes using his brother Robert as a secret back channel to Moscow. Yet Kennedy also sought victory in the Cold War. After Soviet leader Nikita Khrushchev endorsed "wars of national liberation," such as the one in Vietnam, Kennedy called for "peaceful revolution" through nation building. The administration helped developing nations with aid aimed at improving agriculture, transportation, and communications. Kennedy thus oversaw the creation of the multibillion-dollar Alliance for Progress in 1961 to spur economic development in Latin America. In the same year, he also created the Peace Corps, dispatching American teachers, agricultural specialists, and health workers to assist authorities in developing nations. Cynics then and later dismissed the Alliance and the Peace Corps as Kennedy's Cold War tools for countering anti-Americanism and defeating communism in the developing world. The programs did have those aims, but both were also born of genuine humanitarianism.

Although Kennedy and his aides considered themselves supportive of social revolution in the Third World, they disapproved of communist involvement in such uprisings. The administration relied on counterinsurgency to defeat revolutionaries who challenged pro-American Third World governments. American military and technical advisers trained native troops and police to quell unrest.

Nation building and counterinsurgency encountered numerous problems. The Alliance for Progress was only partly successful; infant mortality rates improved, but Latin American economies registered unimpressive growth, and class divisions widened, exacerbating political unrest. Although many foreign peoples welcomed U.S. economic assistance and craved American material culture, they resented outside interference. And because aid was usually transmitted through a self-interested elite, it often never reached the poor.

Soviet-American Tensions

Kennedy also struggled in relations with the Soviet Union. A summit meeting with Soviet leader Nikita Khrushchev in Vienna in June 1961 went poorly, with the two leaders disagreeing over preconditions for peace and stability in the world. Consequently, the administration's first year witnessed little movement on controlling the nuclear arms race or getting a superpower ban on testing nuclear weapons in the atmosphere or underground. Instead, both superpowers accelerated arms production. In 1961, the U.S. military budget rose 15 percent; by mid-1964, U.S. nuclear weapons had increased by 150 percent. Government advice to citizens to build fallout shelters in their backyards intensified public fear of devastating war.

If war occurred, many believed Berlin would be the cause. In mid-1961, Khrushchev demanded an end to Western occupation of West Berlin and a reunification of East and West Germany. In August, the Soviets—at the urging of the East German regime—erected a concrete and barbed-wire barricade to halt the exodus of East Germans into the more prosperous and politically free West Berlin. The Berlin Wall inspired protests throughout the noncommunist world, but Kennedy privately sighed that "a wall is a hell of a lot better than a war." The ugly barrier shut off the flow of refugees, and the crisis passed.

Bay of Pigs Invasion

Yet Kennedy knew that Khrushchev would continue to press for advantage elsewhere. The president was particularly rankled by the growing Soviet assistance to Fidel Castro's Cuban government. The Eisenhower administration had bequeathed to the Kennedy administration a partially developed CIA plan to overthrow Castro: CIA-trained Cuban exiles would land and secure a beachhead; the Cuban people would rise up against Castro and welcome a new U.S.-backed government.

Kennedy approved the plan, and the attack took place on April 17, 1961, as twelve hundred exiles landed at the swampy Bay of Pigs in Cuba. Instead of meeting discontented Cubans, however, they were captured by Castro's troops. Kennedy had tried to keep U.S. participation in the operation hidden, but the CIA's role swiftly became public. Anti-American sentiment rose throughout Latin America. Castro, concluding that the United States might launch another invasion, looked even more toward the Soviet Union for a military and economic lifeline.

Embarrassed by the Bay of Pigs fiasco, Kennedy vowed to bring Castro down. The CIA hatched a project called Operation Mongoose to disrupt the island's trade, support raids on Cuba from Miami, and kill Castro. Assassination schemes included providing Castro with cigars laced with explosives and poison. The United States also tightened its economic blockade and undertook military maneuvers in the Caribbean. The Joint Chiefs of Staff sketched plans to spark a rebellion in Cuba that would be followed by an invasion of U.S. troops.

Cuban Missile Crisis

Both Castro and Khrushchev believed an invasion was coming, which partly explains the Soviet leader's risky decision in 1962 to secretly deploy nuclear missiles in Cuba as a deterrent. But Khrushchev also hoped the move would improve the Soviet position in the nuclear balance of power and force Kennedy to resolve the German problem. Khrushchev wanted the West out of Berlin, and he worried that Washington might provide West Germany with nuclear weapons. He thought he could prevent such a move by putting Soviet missiles just ninety miles off the coast of Florida. The world soon faced brinkmanship at its most frightening.

In mid-October 1962, a U-2 plane flying over Cuba photographed the missile sites. The president immediately organized a special Executive Committee (ExComm) to force the missiles and their nuclear warheads out of Cuba. Options considered ranged from invasion to limited bombing to quiet diplomacy. Kennedy settled on a naval quarantine of Cuba.

Kennedy addressed the nation on television on October 22 and demanded that the Soviets retreat. U.S. warships began crisscrossing the Caribbean, while B-52s with nuclear bombs took to the skies. Khrushchev agreed to withdraw the missiles if the United States pledged never to attack Cuba and remove Jupiter missiles aimed at the Soviet Union from Turkey. For days the world teetered on the brink of disaster. Then, on October 28, the United States agreed to Soviet demands in exchange for the withdrawal of Soviet offensive forces from Cuba. Khrushchev settled without consulting the Cubans. The missiles were removed from the island. At this most tense moment of the Cold War, Kennedy had proven equal to the task.

The **Cuban missile crisis** was a watershed in the Soviet-American relationship. In its aftermath, Kennedy and Khrushchev took steps toward improved relations. In August 1963, the adversaries signed a treaty banning nuclear tests in the atmosphere, the oceans, and outer space. They also installed a coded wire-telegraph "hot line" staffed around the clock to allow near-instant communication between the capitals. They refrained from further confrontation in Berlin.

By autumn 1963, Cold War tensions in Europe were subsiding as both sides accepted the status quo of a divided continent and a fortified border. Still, the arms race accelerated, and superpower competition in the Third World remained intense.

Cuban missile crisis
Confrontation between the Soviet Union and the United States in 1962 regarding the Soviet deployment of nuclear missiles in Cuba. It put the world on the brink of nuclear disaster until the two nations reached a compromise.

Marching for Freedom

What was Kennedy's reaction to growing civil rights activism?

Kennedy regarded the Cold War as the most important issue America faced. But in the early 1960s, young civil rights activists seized the national stage and demanded that the federal government mobilize behind them.

Students and the Movement

In 1960, six years after the *Brown* decision declared "separate but equal" unconstitutional, only 10 percent of southern public schools had begun desegregation. Fewer than one in four adult black Americans in the South could vote, and water fountains were still labeled "White Only" and "Colored Only." But one year after the young men had sat down at the all-white lunch counter in Greensboro, more than seventy thousand Americans—mostly college students—had participated in the sit-ins.

Student Nonviolent Coordinating Committee (SNCC) Civil rights organization founded by young people that played a key role in grassroots organizing in the South in the early 1960s.

The young people who created the **Student Nonviolent Coordinating Committee (SNCC)** in spring 1960 to help coordinate the sit-in movement were committed to nonviolence. In the years to come, such young people would risk their lives in the struggle for social justice.

Freedom Rides and Voter Registration

On May 4, 1961, thirteen members of the Congress of Racial Equality (CORE), a nonviolent civil rights organization formed during World War II, purchased bus tickets in Washington, D.C., for a 1,500-mile trip through the South to New Orleans. This racially integrated group, calling themselves Freedom Riders, meant to demonstrate that, despite Supreme Court rulings ordering the desegregation of interstate buses and bus stations, Jim Crow still ruled in the South. They knew they were risking their lives. One bus was firebombed outside Anniston, Alabama. Riders were badly beaten in Birmingham. In Montgomery, a thousand whites attacked riders with baseball bats and steel bars. Police stayed away; the commissioner called the freedom riders troublemakers.

News of the violent attacks made worldwide headlines. Soviet commentators pointed out the "savage nature of American freedom and democracy." In America, the violence forced many to confront racial discrimination and hatred in their nation. Middle- and upper-class white southerners had resisted integration following the *Brown* decision, but the Freedom Rides made some think differently. The *Atlanta Journal* editorialized: "[I]t is time for the decent people … to muzzle the jackals." The global outcry pushed a reluctant President Kennedy to send federal marshals to Alabama to safeguard the Freedom Riders. But bowing to white southern pressure, he allowed the Freedom Riders to be arrested in Mississippi.

While some activists pursued "direct action," others worked to build black political power in the South. Beginning in 1961, thousands of SNCC volunteers, many of them high school and college students, risked their lives encouraging African Americans in Mississippi and Georgia to register to vote. Some SNCC volunteers were white, and some were northerners, but many were black southerners, often from low-income families. They understood from experience the intersection of racism, powerlessness, and poverty.

Kennedy and Civil Rights

Kennedy was sympathetic—though not terribly committed—to the civil rights movement, and he realized that racial oppression hurt the United States in the Cold War struggle for international opinion. However, like Franklin D. Roosevelt, he feared alienating conservative southern Democrats in Congress. Thus, he appointed five die-hard segregationists to the federal bench in the Deep South and delayed fulfilling his campaign pledge to end segregation in federally subsidized housing until late 1962. Furthermore, he allowed FBI director J. Edgar Hoover to harass Martin Luther King and other civil rights leaders, using wiretaps and surveillance to gather personal information and circulating rumors of communist connections and personal improprieties to discredit their leadership.

But grassroots civil rights activism—and the violence of white mobs—forced Kennedy's hand. In September 1962, the president ordered 500 U.S. marshals to protect James Meredith, the first African American student to attend the University of Mississippi. Thousands of whites attacked the marshals with guns, gasoline bombs, bricks, and pipes. The violence killed two people and seriously wounded 160 federal marshals. The marshals did not back down, nor did Meredith. He broke the color line at "Ole Miss."

Birmingham and the Children's Crusade

Martin Luther King Jr. drew a lesson from the Freedom Rides and from Kennedy's reaction. While still committed to principles of nonviolence, King concluded that only by provoking a crisis that would attract national and international attention could the struggle for civil rights advance. He and his Southern Christian Leadership Conference (SCLC) planned a 1963 campaign in Birmingham, Alabama. Aware that their nonviolent protests would draw a violent response, they called their plan "Project C"—for "confrontation."

Throughout April 1963, nonviolent protests in Birmingham led to hundreds of arrests. Then, on May 2, in a controversial action, King and Birmingham parents put children, some as young as six, on the front lines. As about a thousand black children marched for civil rights, police commissioner Eugene "Bull" Connor ordered police to mow them down with monitor water guns—powerful enough to strip bark from a tree at 100 feet. Then police loosed attack dogs. The nation watched with horror on television, and President Kennedy demanded that Birmingham's white business and political elite negotiate a settlement; they agreed. The Birmingham movement won. Even more, activists had pushed civil rights to the fore of Kennedy's agenda.

"Segregation Forever!"

On June 11, defiant Alabama governor George C. Wallace fulfilled a promise to "bar the schoolhouse door" himself to prevent the desegregation of the University of Alabama. Hearing echoes of Wallace's January 1963 inaugural pledge "Segregation now, segregation tomorrow, segregation forever!" and facing a nation rocked by civil rights protests, Kennedy committed the federal government to guarantee racial justice—even over the opposition of individual states. On June 12, in a televised address, Kennedy said, "Now the time has come for this nation to fulfill its promise." A few hours later, thirty-seven-year-old civil rights leader Medgar Evers was murdered in his driveway in Jackson, Mississippi. The next week, the president asked Congress to pass a comprehensive civil rights bill ending legal racial discrimination.

March on Washington

On August 28, 1963, a quarter-million Americans gathered on the Washington Mall to show support for Kennedy's civil rights bill; many also wanted federal action to guarantee work opportunities. Behind the scenes, organizers from the major civil rights groups—SCLC, CORE, SNCC, the NAACP, the Urban League, and A. Philip Randolph's Brotherhood of Sleeping Car Porters—grappled with

Visualizing THE PAST

"Project C" and National Opinion

This photograph of a police dog attacking a seventeen-year-old demonstrator during a civil rights march in Birmingham, Alabama, appeared on the front page of the *New York Times* on May 4, 1963, just above a second photograph of a fireman spraying a group that included three teenage girls with a high-pressure fire hose. The following day, President Kennedy discussed this photo in a meeting in the White House. Some historians argue that photographs not only document history, they make it. Is that statement true in this case? How does this photograph fit into Martin Luther King's plans for "Project C" (see page 767)? What difference might it make that the *New York Times* editors chose to run this photograph rather than one of the many others taken that day?

Mass media coverage helped galvanize public opinion in support of civil rights protesters.

AP Photo/Bill Hudson

growing tensions within the movement. SNCC activists saw Kennedy's proposed legislation as too little, too late. King and other older leaders counseled moderation. The movement was splintering.

What most Americans saw, however, was a celebration of unity. Black and white celebrities joined hands; folksingers sang freedom songs. Television aired Martin Luther King Jr.'s prophecy of a day when "all God's children, black men and white men, Jews and Gentiles, Protestants and Catholics, will be able to join hands and sing in the words of the old Negro spiritual, Free at last! Free at last! Thank God Almighty, we are free at last!" The 1963 March on Washington for Jobs and Freedom was a triumph, but just days later, white supremacists bombed the Sixteenth Street Baptist Church in Birmingham, killing four black girls.

Freedom Summer In the face of violence, the struggle for racial justice continued. During the summer of 1964, more than one thousand white students joined the voter mobilization project in Mississippi. They formed Freedom Schools, teaching literacy and constitutional rights, and helped organize the Mississippi Freedom Democratic Party as an alternative to the white-only Democratic Party. SNCC organizers also believed that large numbers of white volunteers would focus national attention on Mississippi repression and violence. Not all went smoothly: local black activists were sometimes frustrated when well-educated white volunteers took decision-making roles, and tensions over interracial sexual relationships complicated an already difficult situation. Worse, project workers were arrested, shot at, bombed, and beaten. On June 21, local black activist James Cheney and two white volunteers, Michael Schwerner and Andrew Goodman, were murdered by a Klan mob. That summer, black and white activists risked their lives together, challenging the Deep South's racial caste system.

Liberalism and the Great Society

What made the War on Poverty controversial?

By 1963, with civil rights at the top of his domestic agenda, Kennedy seemed to be taking a new path. Campaigning in 1960, he had promised to lead Americans into a "New Frontier," with the federal government working to eradicate poverty, guarantee health care to the elderly, and provide decent schools for all children. But lacking a popular mandate in the 1960 election, fearful of alienating southern Democrats in Congress, and without a strong vision of domestic reform, Kennedy let his social policy agenda languish.

Instead, Kennedy focused on the economy, believing that continued prosperity would solve social problems. Kennedy's vision was perhaps best realized in America's space program. As the Soviets drew ahead in the space race, Kennedy vowed in 1961 to put a man on the moon before decade's end. With billions in new funding, the National Aeronautics and Space Administration (NASA) began the Apollo program. And in February 1962, astronaut John Glenn orbited the earth.

Kennedy Assassination The nation would not learn what sort of president John Kennedy might have become. On November 22, 1963, riding with his wife, Jackie, in an open-top limousine in Dallas, Texas, Kennedy was cheered by thousands along the motorcade's route. Suddenly, shots rang out. The president crumpled, shot in the head. Tears ran down the cheeks of CBS anchorman Walter Cronkite as he told the nation their president was dead.

That same day, police captured a suspect: Lee Harvey Oswald, a former U.S. Marine (dishonorably discharged) who had once attempted to gain Soviet citizenship. Two days later, Oswald was shot dead by nightclub owner Jack Ruby. Shocked Americans wondered if Ruby was silencing Oswald to prevent him from implicating others. (The seven-member Warren Commission, headed by U.S. Supreme Court Chief Justice Earl Warren, concluded the following year that Oswald had acted alone.)

Millions of Americans watched their president's funeral. In one awful moment in Dallas, the reality of the Kennedy presidency had been transformed into myth, the man into martyr. In the post-assassination atmosphere of grief and remorse, **Lyndon Johnson** invoked Kennedy's memory to push through the most ambitious program of legislation since the New Deal.

Lyndon Johnson The 36th president of the United States; champion of civil rights legislation and the war on poverty.

Johnson and the Great Society

While Kennedy came from wealth and was educated at Harvard, Johnson had grown up in modest circumstances in the Texas hill country and graduated from Southwest Texas State Teachers' College. He was as earthy as Kennedy was elegant, prone to curses and willing to use his physical size to his advantage. Johnson first came to Congress in 1937. As Senate majority leader from 1954 to 1960, he learned how to manipulate people and wield power. As president, he used these political skills in an attempt to unite the nation.

the Great Society President Johnson's vision for America; LBJ believed the federal government must act to alleviate poverty, end racial injustice, and improve the lives of all Americans.

Johnson, a liberal in the style of Franklin D. Roosevelt, believed that the federal government must work actively to improve Americans' lives. In a 1964 commencement address at the University of Michigan, he described his vision of a nation built on "abundance and liberty for all … demand[ing] an end to poverty and racial injustice … where men are more concerned with the quality of their goals than the quantity of their goods." Johnson called this vision "**the Great Society**."

Link to President Johnson's Great Society Speech

Civil Rights Act

Johnson made civil rights his top legislative priority, and in July he signed into law the **Civil Rights Act of 1964**. Originally crafted by the Kennedy administration, the bill ended *legal* discrimination on the basis of race, color, religion, or national origin in employment, federal programs, voting, and public accommodation. The original bill did not include sex discrimination; that was introduced by a southern congressman who hoped it would engender opposition to torpedo the bill. But a bipartisan group of women members of the House of Representatives ensured its passage with sex as a protected category. In the Senate a "southern bloc" had filibustered for 57 days, but growing public support for civil rights, pressure from the Johnson administration, savvy legislative maneuvering, and compromise brought the bill to a vote.

Civil Rights Act of 1964 The most significant civil rights law in U.S. history; ended legal discrimination and segregation in public accommodations.

The Civil Rights Act of 1964 also provided means to enforce its provisions: federal authority to withhold funds from public agencies or federal contractors that discriminated, and an Equal Employment Opportunity Commission (EEOC) to investigate job discrimination claims. However, in the first years after the bill was passed the EEOC did not take sex discrimination seriously, despite a flood of complaints from women. Frustrated by such responses, a group of about three hundred prominent women and men came together in 1966 to form the **National Organization for Women (NOW)**, an organization created to pressure the EEOC to enforce the law and to work for women's equality in American society.

Many white southerners resented federal intervention in what they considered local customs, and throughout the nation, millions of conservative Americans believed that the federal government had overstepped its constitutional boundaries. They wanted to reinforce local control and states' rights. In the 1964 election, this conservative vision was championed by the Republican candidate, Arizona senator Barry Goldwater.

National Organization for Women (NOW) Civil rights group for women that lobbied for equal opportunity, filed lawsuits against gender discrimination, and mobilized public opinion against sexism.

Election of 1964

Goldwater had voted against the 1964 Civil Rights Act and opposed Social Security. Like many conservatives, he believed that individual *liberty*, not equality, mattered most. Goldwater's calls for "law and order" drew cheers from voters. He also believed that the United States needed a more powerful national military to fight communism and suggested that the United States should use tactical nuclear weapons against its enemies. "Extremism in the defense of liberty is no vice," he told delegates at the 1964 Republican National Convention.

Johnson campaigned on an unemployment rate under 4 percent and economic growth at better than 6 percent. But he knew that his support of civil rights had broken the New Deal coalition, telling an aide, "I think we just delivered the south to the Republican Party for my lifetime and yours."

Tensions exploded at the 1964 Democratic National Convention. Two delegations from Mississippi demanded to be seated. The Democratic Party's official delegation was exclusively white; the Mississippi Freedom Democratic Party (MFDP) sent a racially mixed delegation to represent a state in which literacy tests and violence disenfranchised black citizens. White southern delegates threatened to walk out if the MFDP delegates were seated. MFDP delegate Fannie Lou Hamer offered powerful testimony to the convention's credentials committee, concluding, "[If] the Freedom Party is not seated now, I question America." Johnson sought a compromise, but the MFDP declined. "We didn't come all this way for no two seats," Hamer said, and the delegation walked out.

Johnson lost the MFDP, and he lost the Deep South—the first Democrat since the Civil War to do so. Yet he won the election by a landslide, and voters elected the most liberal Congress in American history. With the mandate provided by a record 61.1 percent of the popular vote, Johnson launched his Great Society. Congress passed the most sweeping reform legislation since 1935.

Civil rights remained a critical issue. In late 1964, the SCLC made voting rights its top priority. Martin Luther King Jr. and other leaders turned to Selma, Alabama, seeking another public confrontation that would mobilize national support and federal action. It came on March 6, 1965, when state troopers turned electric cattle prods, chains, and tear gas against peaceful marchers as they crossed the Edmund Pettus Bridge on the way to Montgomery. On March 15, the president offered full support for a second monumental civil rights bill, the

Voting Rights Act Law that outlawed practices that prevented blacks in the South from voting.

Immigration Act of 1965 Law that abolished the national-origins quotas of the 1920s and transformed America's racial and ethnic kaleidoscope.

War on Poverty Name of campaign launched by Lyndon B. Johnson to bring the poor into mainstream society by promoting greater opportunity through public works and training programs.

Medicare Program created by President Johnson to provide government health insurance for those sixty-five and older.

Medicaid Program created by President Johnson to provide health care for the poor.

Voting Rights Act. This act outlawed practices that prevented most blacks in the Deep South from voting and provided for federal election oversight in districts with evidence of past discrimination. Within two years, the percentage of African Americans registered to vote in Mississippi jumped from 7 percent to almost 60 percent. Black elected officials became increasingly common in southern states.

Improving American Life

Seeking to improve the quality of American life, the Johnson administration established new student loan and grant programs and created the National Endowment for the Arts and the National Endowment for the Humanities. The **Immigration Act of 1965** ended racially based quotas. And Johnson supported important consumer protection legislation, including the 1966 National Traffic and Motor Vehicle Safety Act, inspired by Ralph Nader's exposé of the automobile industry, *Unsafe at Any Speed* (1965). Johnson also signed "preservation" legislation to protect wilderness areas and supported laws to control environmental pollution.

War on Poverty

At the heart of Johnson's Great Society was the **War on Poverty**, which included major legislation beginning in 1964 (see Table 26.1). Johnson and other liberals believed that, in a time of affluence, the nation should use its resources to end "poverty, ignorance and hunger as intractable, permanent features of American society."

Johnson's goal was "to offer the forgotten fifth of our people opportunity, not doles." Local governments and school districts received billions of federal dollars to improve opportunities for the poor, from preschoolers (Head Start) to high schoolers (Upward Bound) to young adults (Job Corps). The Model Cities program targeted "blighted" urban neighborhoods with federal funds for employment, housing, education, and health. Community Action Programs channeled federal funds for antipoverty programs directly to neighborhood groups.

The Johnson administration also expanded the Food Stamp program and earmarked billions to construct public housing and subsidize rents. Two new federal programs guaranteed health care: **Medicare** for those sixty-five and older, and **Medicaid** for the poor. Finally, Aid to Families with Dependent Children (AFDC), the welfare program created during the New Deal, expanded both benefits and eligibility.

The War on Poverty was controversial. Leftists believed the government was doing too little to change structural inequality. Conserva-

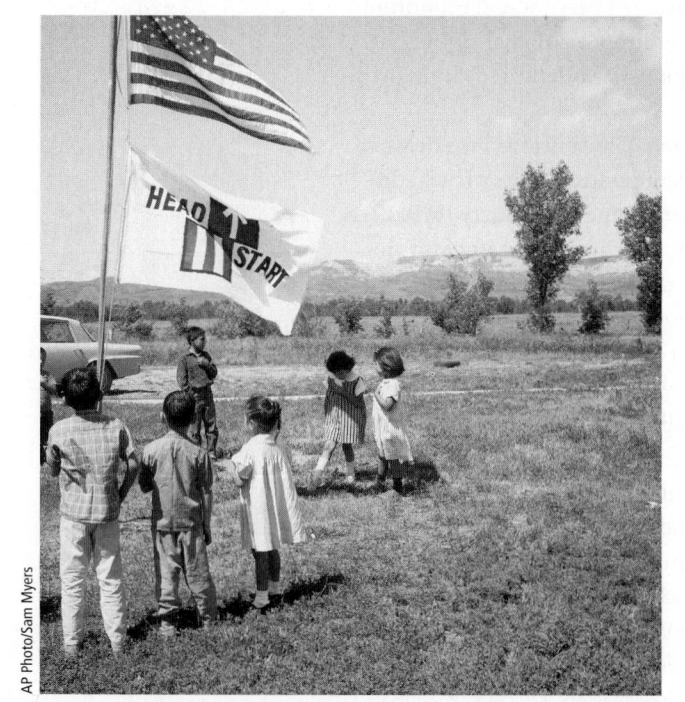

Sioux children pledge allegiance to the U.S. flag in a reservation-based Head Start program, Red Shirt, South Dakota, 1965. One of several programs established by the 1964 Economic Opportunity Act, Head Start prepared preschoolers from low-income families for grade school.

AP Photo/Sam Myers

TABLE 26.1   Great Society Achievements, 1964-1966

	1964	1965	1966
Civil Rights	Civil Rights Act Equal Employment Opportunity Commission Twenty-fourth Amendment	Voting Rights Act	
War on Poverty	Economic Opportunity Act Office of Economic Opportunity Job Corps Legal Services for the Poor VISTA		Model Cities
Education		Elementary and Secondary Education Act Head Start Upward Bound	
Environment		Water Quality Act Air Quality Act	Clean Water Restoration Act
New Government Agencies		Department of Housing and Urban Development National Endowments for the Arts and Humanities	Department of Transportation
Other		Medicare and Medicaid Immigration and Nationality Act	

Note: The Great Society of the mid-1960s saw the biggest burst of reform legislation since the New Deal of the 1930s.

tives argued that Great Society programs created dependency among America's poor. Policy analysts noted that specific programs were ill conceived and badly implemented. Decades later, most historians judge the War on Poverty a mixed success. Its programs improved the quality of housing, health care, and nutrition available to the poor. By 1975, for instance, the number of eligible Americans receiving food stamps had increased from 600,000 (in 1965) to 17 million. Poverty among the elderly fell from about 40 percent in 1960 to 16 percent in 1974, due largely to increased Social Security benefits and to Medicare (see Figure 26.1).

But War on Poverty programs less successfully addressed the root causes of poverty. Neither the Job Corps nor Community Action Programs showed significant results. Economic growth, not administration policies, was primarily responsible for the dramatic decrease in poverty rates during the 1960s—from 22.4 percent of Americans in 1959 to 11 percent in 1973. And one structural determinant of poverty remained unchanged: 11 million Americans in female-headed

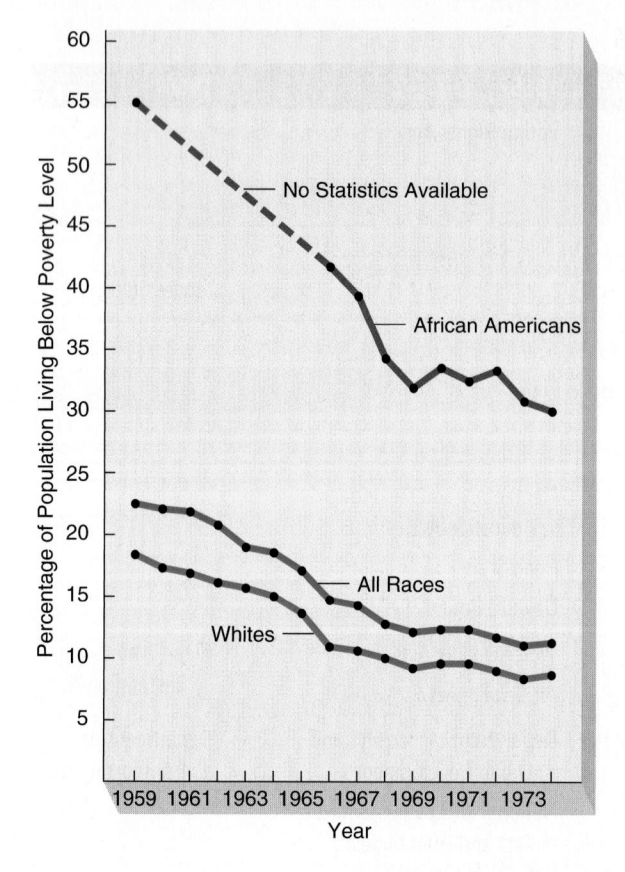

FIGURE 26.1

Poverty in America for Whites, African Americans, and All Races, 1959–1974

Because of rising levels of economic prosperity, combined with the impact of Great Society programs, the percentage of Americans living in poverty in 1974 was half as high as in 1959. African Americans still were far more likely than white Americans to be poor. In 1959, more than half of all blacks (55.1 percent) were poor; in 1974, the figure remained high (30.3 percent). The government did not record data on African American poverty for the years 1960 through 1965.

households remained poor at the end of the decade—the same number as in 1963.

Political compromises also created long-term problems. For example, Congress accommodated doctors and hospitals in its Medicare legislation by allowing federal reimbursements of hospitals' "reasonable costs" and doctors' "reasonable charges" in treating elderly patients. With no incentives for doctors or hospitals to hold prices down, national health care expenditures as a percentage of the gross national product rose by almost 44 percent from 1960 to 1971.

Johnson and Vietnam

How did the war in Vietnam become Americanized?

International affairs had never much interested Johnson, and he had little appreciation for foreign cultures. At the Taj Mahal in India, for example, Johnson tested the monument's echo with a Texas cowboy yell. "Foreigners," Johnson quipped early in his administration, only half-jokingly, "are not like the folks I am used to."

Kennedy's Legacy in Vietnam

Yet Johnson knew that foreign policy, especially regarding Vietnam, would demand his attention. Since the late 1950s, hostilities in Vietnam had increased, as Ho Chi Minh's North assisted the Vietcong guerrillas in the South to advance the reunification of the country under a communist government. Kennedy had increased aid to the Diem regime in Saigon, airdropped more raiding teams into North Vietnam, and launched crop destruction by herbicides to starve the Vietcong out of hiding. Kennedy also strengthened the U.S. military presence in South Vietnam; by 1963 more than sixteen thousand military advisers were there, some authorized to participate in combat alongside the U.S.-equipped Army of the Republic of Vietnam (ARVN).

Meanwhile, opposition to Diem's repressive regime increased. Peasants objected to being removed from their villages for their own safety, and Buddhist monks, protesting the Roman Catholic Diem's religious persecution, poured gasoline over their robes and ignited themselves in the streets of Saigon. Eventually, U.S. officials encouraged ambitious South Vietnamese generals to remove Diem. They murdered him on November 1, 1963, just a few weeks before Kennedy was killed.

The timing of Kennedy's murder ensured that Vietnam would be the most controversial aspect of his legacy. He expanded U.S. involvement and approved a coup against Diem, but despite the urgings of top advisers he refused to commit American ground forces. Over time, he became skeptical about South Vietnam's prospects and hinted that he would end the American commitment after winning reelection in 1964. What he would have done had he lived can never be known, but what seems clear is that Kennedy arrived in Dallas that fateful day still uncertain about how to solve the Vietnam problem.

Tonkin Gulf Incident and Resolution

Lyndon Johnson wanted to do nothing in Vietnam that could complicate his aim of winning the 1964 election. Yet he also sought victory in the struggle. As a result, throughout 1964 the administration secretly planned to expand the war to North Vietnam.

In early August 1964, U.S. destroyers reported coming under attack twice in three days from North Vietnamese patrol boats in the Gulf of Tonkin (see Map 26.1). Despite a lack of evidence that the second attack occurred, Johnson ordered retaliatory air strikes against North Vietnamese patrol boat bases and an oil depot. By a vote of 416 to 0 in the House and 88 to 2 in the Senate, Congress quickly passed the Gulf of Tonkin Resolution, which gave the president the authority to "take all necessary measures to repel any armed attack against the forces of the United States and to prevent further aggression." In so doing, Congress essentially surrendered its warmaking powers to the executive branch.

Decision for Escalation

President Johnson appreciated how the Gulf of Tonkin affair boosted his public approval ratings and removed Vietnam as a campaign issue for Barry Goldwater. On the ground in South Vietnam, however, the outlook remained grim, and officials planned to escalate American involvement.

In February 1965, in response to Vietcong attacks on American installations in South Vietnam that killed thirty-two Americans, Johnson ordered Operation Rolling Thunder, a bombing program which continued, more or less uninterrupted, until October 1968. Then, on March 8, the first U.S. combat battalions came ashore near Danang. The North Vietnamese responded by increasing infiltration into the South. In Saigon, meanwhile, coups and countercoups by self-serving military leaders undermined U.S. efforts.

In July 1965, Johnson convened a series of high-level discussions about U.S. policy. Although these deliberations had about them the character of a charade—Johnson wanted history to record that he agonized over a choice he had in fact already made—they did confirm that the American commitment would be more or less open ended. On July 28, Johnson publicly announced a significant troop increase, with others to follow. By the end of 1965, more than 180,000 U.S. ground troops were in South Vietnam. In 1966, the figure climbed to 385,000. In 1967

MAP 26.1

Southeast Asia and the Vietnam War

To prevent communists from coming to power in Vietnam, Cambodia, and Laos in the 1960s, the United States intervened massively in Southeast Asia. The interventions failed, and the remaining American troops made a hasty exit from Vietnam in 1975, when the victorious Vietcong and North Vietnamese took Saigon and renamed it Ho Chi Minh City. Source: Copyright © Cengage Learning 2015 alone, U.S. warplanes flew 108,000 sorties and dropped 226,000 tons of bombs on North Vietnam. In 1968, U.S. troop strength reached 536,100 (see Figure 26.2). Each American escalation brought a North Vietnamese escalation, as well as increased material assistance to Hanoi from the Soviet Union and China

Opposition to Americanization

Rolling Thunder and the U.S. troop commitment "Americanized" the war, transforming it from a civil war between North and South into an American war against the communist Hanoi government. Democratic leaders in the Senate, major newspapers such as the *New York Times* and the *Wall Street Journal*, and prominent columnists like Walter Lippmann warned against deepening involvement, as did Vice President Hubert H. Humphrey and Undersecretary of State George W. Ball. Virtually all of America's allies—including France, Britain, Canada, and Japan—cautioned against escalation and urged a political settlement. Remarkably, most top U.S. officials knew that the odds of success were small, but they hoped new measures would cause Hanoi to end the insurgency in the South.

Why, then, did America's leaders choose war? At stake was "credibility." They feared that, if the United States failed in Vietnam, other countries would find American power less credible. The Soviets and Chinese would challenge U.S. interests elsewhere, and allied governments might conclude that they could not depend on Washington. Johnson also worried that failure in Vietnam would harm his domestic agenda and cause personal humiliation. As for the stated objective of helping a South Vietnamese ally repulse external aggression, that, too, figured into the equation, but not as much as it would have had the Saigon government—racked with infighting and possessing little popular support—done more in its own defense.

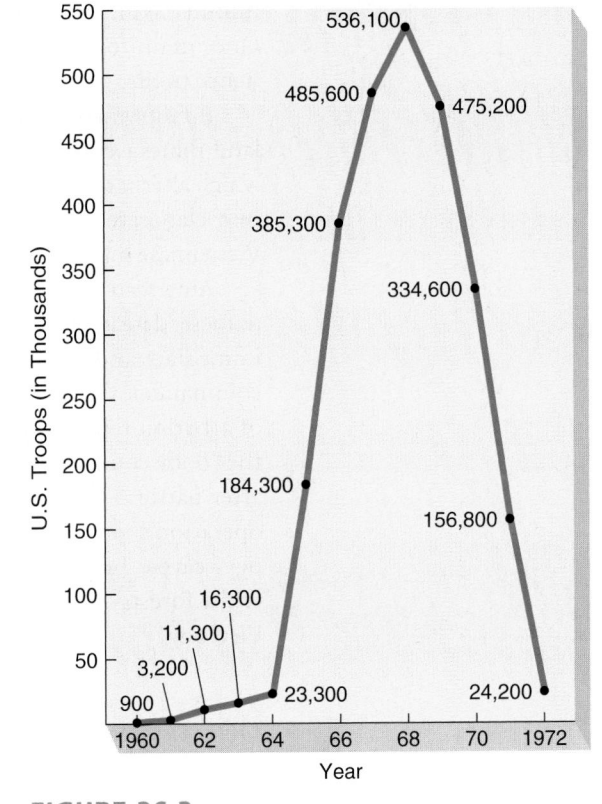

FIGURE 26.2

U.S. Troops in Vietnam, 1960–1972

These numbers show the Americanization of the Vietnam War under President Johnson, who ordered vast increases in troop levels. President Nixon reversed the escalation, so that by the time of the cease-fire in early 1973, fewer than 25,000 American troops remained in Vietnam. Data are for December 31 of each year.

(Source: U.S. Department of Defense)

American Soldiers in Vietnam

To minimize publicity about the war, Johnson refused to call up reserve forces. This decision forced the military to rely heavily on the draft, which made Vietnam a young man's war—the average age of soldiers was twenty-two, as compared with twenty-six in World War II. It also became a war of the poor and the working class. Through the years of heavy escalation (1965–1968), college students, teachers, and engineers could get deferments. (In 1969, the draft was changed so that some students were called up through a lottery system.) The armed services recruited hard in poor communities, many of them heavily African American and Latino, advertising the military as an avenue of training and advancement; very often, the pitch worked. Once in uniform, those with fewer skills were far more likely to see combat, and hence to die.

Infantrymen maneuvered into thick jungle growth, where booby traps and land mines were a constant threat. Boots and human skin rotted from the rains, which alternated with withering suns. The enemy was hard to find, often burrowed into elaborate underground tunnels or melded into the population, where any Vietnamese might be a Vietcong.

American forces fought well, and their entry helped stave off a South Vietnamese defeat at the time. In that sense, Americanization achieved its most immediate and basic objective. But the war soon became a stalemate. The U.S. commander, General William Westmoreland, mistakenly believed that a strategy of attrition represented the key to victory. Thus, the measure of success became the "body count"—the number of North Vietnamese and Vietcong corpses found after battle. The counts were manipulated by officers eager to demonstrate an operation's success. Worse, the American reliance on massive military technology—carpet bombing, napalm (jellied gasoline), crop defoliants that destroyed entire forests—alienated many South Vietnamese and brought new recruits to the Vietcong.

Divisions at Home

As television coverage brought the war into homes nightly, opposition grew. College professors and students organized debates and lectures on American policy. These public discussions became a form of protest, called "teach-ins" after the sit-ins of the civil rights movement. Pacifist groups, such as the American Friends Service Committee and the Women's International League for Peace and Freedom, organized early protests.

Wounded American soldiers after a battle in Vietnam.

Larry Burrows/Time Life Pictures/Getty Images

In early 1966, Senator William Fulbright held televised public hearings on whether the national interest was served by the war. George F. Kennan testified that his containment doctrine was meant for Europe, not volatile Southeast Asia. America's "preoccupation" with Vietnam, Kennan asserted, was undermining its global obligations. The Fulbright hearings provoked Americans to think about the conflict and the nation's role in it and revealed deep divisions on Vietnam among public officials.

Defense secretary Robert McNamara, who despite private misgivings championed the Americanization of the war in 1965, became increasingly troubled by the killing and bombing. Already in November 1965 he expressed skepticism that victory could ever be achieved. American credibility, far from being protected by the commitment, was suffering grievous damage, McNamara feared. But Johnson was determined to prevail in Vietnam. Although he occasionally halted the bombing to encourage Ho Chi Minh to negotiate (on America's terms) and to disarm critics, such pauses often were accompanied by increases in American troop strength. Ho rejected American terms, which amounted to abandonment of his lifelong dream of an independent, unified Vietnam.

A Nation Divided

As Johnson struggled in Vietnam, his Great Society faced challenges at home. American society was fracturing along many different lines: black and white, young and old, radical, liberal, and conservative.

What were the hallmarks of the youth movement in the 1960s?

Urban Unrest

In 1964, shortly after President Johnson signed the landmark Civil Rights Act, racial violence erupted in northern cities. Angry Harlem residents took to the streets after a white police officer shot a black teenager. The following summer, in the predominantly black Watts section of Los Angeles, crowds burned, looted, and battled police for five days and nights. The riot, which began when a white police officer attempted to arrest a black resident on suspicion of drunken driving, left thirty-four dead and over one thousand injured. In July 1967, twenty-six people were killed in street battles between African Americans and police and army troops in Newark, New Jersey. A week later, in Detroit, forty-three died as three square miles of the city burned. In 1967 alone, there were 167 violent outbreaks in 128 cities.

The "long, hot summers" of urban unrest in the 1960s differed from almost all previous race riots, which were typically started by whites. Here, black residents exploded in anger and frustration over the conditions of their lives. They looted and burned stores, most of them white owned, but in the process devastated their own neighborhoods.

In 1968, the National Advisory Commission on Civil Disorders, chaired by Governor Otto Kerner of Illinois, warned that America was "moving towards two societies, one white, one black—separate and unequal," and blamed white racism for the riots. Regarding the ghetto, the Kerner Commission concluded, "White institutions created it, white institutions maintain it, and white society condones it." Some white Americans disagreed, while others wondered why African

Americans were venting their frustration just when they were making real progress in civil rights.

The answer stemmed in part from regional differences. Although the *legal* disenfranchisement and discrimination in the South was a clear focal point for civil rights activism, most northern African Americans, increasingly concentrated in deteriorating inner-city ghettoes, lived in societies as segregated as any in the Deep South. They faced discrimination in housing, credit, and employment. The median income of northern blacks was little more than half that of northern whites, and their unemployment rate was twice as high. Many northern blacks had given up on the civil rights movement and Great Society liberalism.

Black Power

In this climate, a new voice urged blacks to seize freedom "by any means necessary." Malcolm X, a onetime pimp and street hustler who had converted while in prison to the Nation of Islam faith, offered African Americans new leadership. Members of the Nation of Islam, known as Black Muslims, espoused black pride and separatism from white society. Their faith, combining elements of traditional Islam with a belief that whites were subhuman "devils" whose race would soon be destroyed, also emphasized sobriety, thrift, and social responsibility. By the early 1960s, Malcolm X had become the Black Muslims' chief spokesperson. His advice was straightforward: "If someone puts a hand on you, send him to the cemetery." But Malcolm X was murdered in early 1965 by members of the Nation of Islam who felt betrayed when Malcolm X started his own, more racially tolerant organization. In death, Malcolm X became a powerful symbol of black defiance and self-respect.

A year after Malcolm X's death, Stokely Carmichael, SNCC chairman, denounced "the betrayal of black dreams by white America." To be truly free from white oppression, Carmichael proclaimed, blacks had to "stand up and take over"—to elect black candidates, to organize their own schools, to control their own institutions, to embrace "**Black Power**." That year, SNCC expelled its white members and repudiated nonviolence and integration. CORE followed suit in 1967.

Black Power Advocated in 1966 by SNCC president Stokely Carmichael, it promoted black nationalism, self-determination, and greater militance as a means of self-defense.

The best-known black radicals of the era were the Black Panthers, an organization formed in Oakland, California, in 1966. Blending black separatism and revolutionary communism, the Panthers dedicated themselves to destroying capitalism and "the military arm of our oppressors," the police. In contrast to earlier, nonviolent civil rights protesters, who had worn suits and ties or dresses to demonstrate respectability, male Panthers dressed in commando gear, carried weapons, and talked about killing "pigs"—and did kill eleven officers by 1970. Police responded in kind; most infamously, Chicago police murdered local Panther leader Fred Hampton in his bed. However, the Panthers also worked to improve life in their neighborhoods by creating free breakfast and health care programs for children, offering courses in African American history, and demanding jobs and housing.

Youth and Politics

By the mid-1960s, 41 percent of Americans were under the age of twenty. These young people spent more time in the world of peer culture than had any previous generation. Three-quarters of them graduated from high school (up from one-fifth in the 1920s) and almost half of them went to college (up from 16 percent in 1940). As this large baby boom generation came of age, many young people believed that they must provide democratic leadership for their nation. Inspired by the sit-in movement begun by black college students, white college students—from both political left and right—committed themselves to changing the system.

In fall 1960, a group of conservative college students met at William F. Buckley's family estate in Sharon, Connecticut, to create Young Americans for Freedom (YAF). Their manifesto, the "Sharon Statement," endorsed Cold War anticommunism and a vision of limited government opposed to New Deal liberalism. The YAF planned to capture the Republican Party and move it to the political right; Goldwater's 1964 presidential nomination demonstrated their early success.

At the other end of the political spectrum, an emerging "New Left" also rejected liberalism. Whereas conservatives believed liberalism's activist government encroached on individual liberty, the New Left believed that liberalism was not enough, that it could never offer equality to all Americans. At a meeting in Port Huron, Michigan, in 1962, founding members of Students for a Democratic Society (SDS) drafted their "Port Huron Statement," which condemned racism, poverty in the midst of plenty, and the Cold War. Calling for "participatory democracy," SDS sought to wrest power from the corporations, the military, and the politicians and return it to "the people."

Link to The Port Huron Statement of the Students for a Democratic Society (1962)

Free Speech Movement

The rise of activist white youth crystallized at the University of California, Berkeley. In the fall of 1964, the university administration banned political activity—including recruiting volunteers for civil rights work in Mississippi—from its traditional place along a university-owned sidewalk bordering the campus. When the administration called police to arrest a CORE worker who defied the order, four thousand students surrounded the police car.

Student political groups, left and right, united to create the **Free Speech Movement (FSM)**. The FSM won back the right to political speech, but not before state police had arrested almost eight hundred student protesters. Many saw the administration's actions as a failure of America's democratic promises, but the victory of the FSM also demonstrated to students their potential power. By decade's end, the activism born at Berkeley would spread to hundreds of colleges and universities.

Free Speech Movement (FSM) Coalition of student groups that insisted on the right to campus political activity; it began at the University of California, Berkeley.

Student Activism

Many student protesters sought greater control over their education, demanding more relevant class offerings, more freedom in course selection, and a greater voice in the running of universities. Students protested against the doctrine of in loco parentis, which until the late 1960s put universities legally "in the place of parents," allowing control over student behavior that went beyond the law. In loco parentis fell heaviest on women, who were subject to strict curfew regulations called parietals. Protesters demanded an end to sex discrimination, but rejected in loco parentis for other reasons as well. Protestors at the University of Kansas demanded that the administration explain how its statement that "college students are assumed to have maturity of judgment necessary for adult responsibility" squared with the minute regulation of students' nonacademic lives.

Youth and the War in Vietnam

It was the war in Vietnam, however, that mobilized a nationwide student movement. Believing it their civic duty to learn about and speak out on issues of national importance, university students and faculty held "teach-ins" about U.S. involvement in Vietnam as the war escalated in 1965. SDS sponsored the first major antiwar march that year, drawing twenty thousand protesters to Washington, D.C. On campuses everywhere, students adopted civil rights movement tactics, picketing ROTC buildings and protesting military research and recruiting done on their campuses. However, despite the visibility of antiwar protests, most students did not yet oppose the war: in 1967, only 30 percent of male students were "**doves**" on Vietnam, while 67 percent were "**hawks**." But as the war escalated, more of America's youth came to distrust the government, as well as the seemingly arbitrary authority of university administrations.

doves Term for opponents of American military involvement in Vietnam.

hawks Term for those who supported American goals in the Vietnam War.

Youth Culture and the Counterculture

The large baby boom generation changed the nation's culture more than its politics. Although many young people protested the war and marched for social justice, most did not. The sixties' "youth culture" was never homogeneous. Fraternity and sorority life stayed strong, even as radicalism flourished. And although there was some crossover, black, white, and Latino youth had different cultural styles, music, and clothes. Nonetheless, as potential consumers, young people exercised tremendous cultural authority and drove American popular culture in the late 1960s.

The most unifying element of youth culture was music. The Beatles had electrified American teenagers—73 million viewers watched their first television appearance on the *Ed Sullivan Show* in 1964. Bob Dylan promised revolutionary answers in "Blowin' in the Wind"; Janis Joplin brought the sexual power of the blues to white youth; James Brown and Aretha Franklin proclaimed black pride; the psychedelic rock of Jefferson Airplane and the Grateful Dead—along with hallucinogenic drugs—redefined reality. At the Woodstock Festival in upstate New York in 1969, more than four hundred thousand people reveled in the music and in a world of their own making, living in rain and mud for four days without shelter and without violence.

counterculture Youth movement that promoted drugs, free love, and an alternative way of life opposing the materialism and conformity of mainstream American society.

Some young people rejected what they saw as hypocritical middle-class values. They attempted to craft an alternative way of life, or **counterculture**, liberated from competitive materialism and celebrating pleasure. "Sex, drugs, and rock 'n' roll" became a mantra of sorts, offering these "hippies," or "freaks," a path to a new consciousness. Many did the hard work of creating communes and intentional communities, whether in cities or in hidden stretches of rural America. Although the New Left criticized the counterculture as apolitical, many freaks did envision revolutionary change through sex, drugs, or music.

The British Invasion

The British invasion began in earnest on February 7, 1964. Three thousand screaming American teenagers were waiting when Pan Am's *Yankee Clipper* touched down at New York's Kennedy Airport with four British "moptops" aboard. "I Want to Hold Your Hand" was at the top of the U.S. charts, and the largest television audience in history watched the Beatles on the *Ed Sullivan Show* the following Sunday night.

Although the Beatles led the invasion, they did not conquer America alone. The Rolling Stones' first U.S. hit single also came in 1964. The Dave Clark Five appeared on *Ed Sullivan* eighteen times. And there were many others, including Herman's Hermits, the Animals, the Yardbirds, the Hollies, the Kinks, and Petula Clark.

The British invasion was, at least in part, the triumphal return of American music, part of a transatlantic exchange that reinvigorated both nations. American rock 'n' roll had lost much of its early energy by the early 1960s, and in England, the London-centered popular music industry was pumping out a saccharine version of American pop. But other forms of American music had made their way across the Atlantic. By the late 1950s, young musicians in England's provincial cities were listening to the music of African American bluesmen Muddy Waters and Howlin' Wolf and the early rock 'n' roll of Buddy Holly and Chuck Berry. None of this music had a large popular audience in the United States, where the Singing Nun was at the top of the *Billboard* magazine charts just before the Beatles arrived.

Young British musicians, including John Lennon, Eric Clapton, and Mick Jagger, re-created American musical forms and reinvented rock 'n' roll. By the mid-1960s, the Beatles and the other British invasion bands were at the heart of a youth culture that transcended national boundaries. This music linked America's youth with young people throughout the world.

The Beatles perform on the Ed Sullivan Show *in February 1964. Although Britain's Queen Mother thought the Beatles "young, fresh, and vital," American parents were appalled when the "long" Beatles haircut swept the nation.*

AP Photo

The nascent counterculture had first burst on the national consciousness during the summer of 1967, when tens of thousands of young people poured into the Haight-Ashbury district of San Francisco, the heart of America's psychedelic culture, for the "summer of love." As an older generation of "straight" (or Establishment) Americans watched with horror, white youth adopted countercultural ways. Coats and ties disappeared, as did stockings—and bras. Young men grew long hair. Millions used marijuana or hallucinogenic drugs, read underground newspapers, and thought of themselves as alienated from "straight" culture even though they were attending high school or college and not completely "dropping out" of the Establishment.

Some of the most lasting cultural changes involved attitudes about sex. The mass media were fascinated with "free love," and some people embraced promiscuous sexuality. More important, however, premarital sex no longer destroyed a woman's "reputation." The birth control pill, widely available to single women by the late 1960s, greatly lessened the risk of unplanned pregnancy, and venereal diseases were easily cured by antibiotics. The number of unmarried couples living together increased 900 percent from 1960 to 1970. Still, 68 percent of American adults disapproved of premarital sex in 1969.

The adult generation that had grown up in the hard decades of depression and war, many of whom saw middle-class respectability as crucial to success and stability, did not understand. How could young people put such promising futures at risk by having sex without marriage, taking drugs, or protesting the war in Vietnam?

1968

What made 1968 distinctive?

By the beginning of 1968, it seemed that the nation was coming apart. Divided over the war in Vietnam, frustrated by the slow pace of social change, or angry over racial violence, Americans faced the most serious domestic crisis of the postwar era.

The Tet Offensive

On January 31, 1968, the first day of the Vietnamese New Year (Tet), Vietcong and North Vietnamese forces struck South Vietnam, capturing provincial capitals (see Map 26.1). The carefully planned offensive targeted the Saigon airport, the presidential palace, and the ARVN headquarters. U.S. and South Vietnamese units eventually regained control, inflicting heavy casualties and devastating villages.

Although the Tet Offensive was not the resounding battlefield victory Hanoi strategists sought, it called into question American military leaders' predictions that the war would soon be won. Had not the Vietcong and North Vietnamese demonstrated that they could strike when and where they wished? If America's airpower, dollars, and troops could not now defeat the Vietcong, could they ever do so? Had the American public been deceived? In February, the highly respected CBS television anchorman Walter Cronkite went to Vietnam to find out. The military brass in Saigon assured him that "we had the enemy just where we wanted him." The newsman recalled, "Tell that to the Marines, I thought—the Marines in the body bags on that helicopter."

Top presidential advisers sounded notes of despair. Clark Clifford, the new secretary of defense, told Johnson the war could not be won, even with the 206,000 additional soldiers Westmoreland requested. Aware that the nation was suffering a financial crisis prompted by rampant deficit spending, Johnson's advisers knew that taking the initiative in Vietnam would cost billions more, further derail the budget, panic foreign owners of dollars, and wreck the economy.

Johnson's Exit

Controversy over the war split the Democratic Party, just as a presidential election loomed in November. Senator Eugene McCarthy of Minnesota and Robert F. Kennedy (now a senator from New York), both strong opponents of Johnson's war policies, forcefully challenged the president in early primaries. During a March 31 television address, Johnson announced a halt to most of the bombing, asked Hanoi to negotiate, and stunned listeners by withdrawing from the presidential race. His presidency had become a casualty of the war. Peace talks began in May in Paris, but the war ground on.

Assassinations

Days after Johnson's shocking announcement, Martin Luther King Jr. was murdered in Memphis, where he had traveled to support striking sanitation workers. It remains unclear why James Earl Ray, a white forty-year-old drifter and petty criminal, shot King—or whether he acted alone. By 1968, King had become an outspoken critic of the Vietnam War and of American capitalism. Although some Americans hated what he stood for, most mourned his death, even as black rage and grief exploded in 130 cities. Once again, ghetto neighborhoods burned; thirty-four blacks and five whites died. The violence provoked a backlash from whites—primarily urban, working-class people who had no sympathy for black Americans' increasingly radical demands. In Chicago, Mayor Richard Daley ordered police to shoot rioters.

An already shaken nation watched in disbelief only two months later when Democratic presidential candidate Robert Kennedy was shot and killed after winning the California primary. His assassin, Sirhan Sirhan, an Arab nationalist, targeted Kennedy because he supported Israel.

Chicago Democratic National Convention

Violence erupted again in August at the Democratic National Convention in Chicago. Thousands of protesters converged on the city: students who'd gone

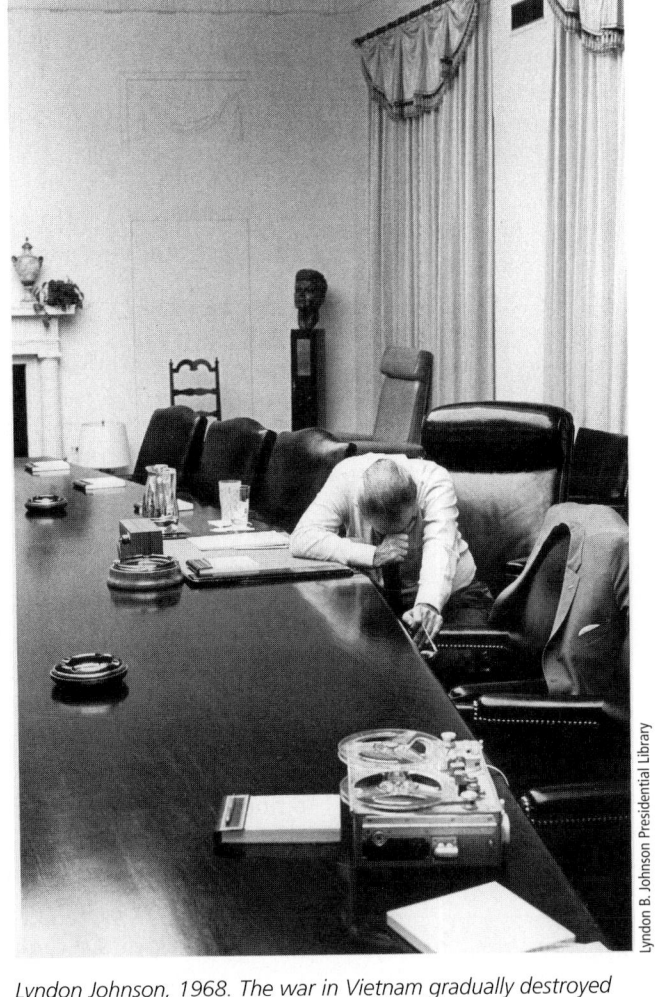

Lyndon Johnson, 1968. The war in Vietnam gradually destroyed his presidency and divided the nation.

Lyndon B. Johnson Presidential Library

"Clean for Gene," cutting long hair and donning "respectable" clothes to campaign for antiwar candidate Eugene McCarthy; members of America's counterculture drawn by a promise from the anarchist group, the Yippies, of a "Festival of Life" to counter the "Convention of Death"; and antiwar groups. Mayor Daley assigned twelve thousand police to twelve-hour shifts and had twelve thousand army troops with bazookas, rifles, and flamethrowers as backup. Police attacked peaceful anti-war protesters and journalists. "The whole world is watching," chanted the protesters, as police beat people.

Global Protest

Upheavals burst forth around the world that spring and summer. In France, university students protested academic policies and the Vietnam War. They received support from French workers, who occupied factories and paralyzed public transport; the turmoil contributed to the collapse of Charles de Gaulle's government the following year. In Italy, Germany, England, Ireland, Sweden, Canada, Mexico, Chile, Japan, and South Korea, students held similar protests. In Czechoslovakia, hundreds of thousands of demonstrators flooded Prague streets, demanding democracy and an end to Soviet repression. This so-called Prague Spring developed into a full-scale national rebellion before being crushed by Soviet tanks.

Why so many uprisings occurred simultaneously is not clear. The postwar baby boom experienced by many nations produced by the late 1960s a huge mass of young adults, many of whom grew up in relative prosperity, with high expectations for the future. Technological advances allowed the nearly instantaneous worldwide transmittal of televised images, so protests in one country could readily inspire similar actions in others. Demonstrations might have occurred in any case, but television news footage showing the wealthiest nation carpet-bombing a poor one surely helped fuel the agitation.

Nixon's Election

The presidential election of 1968 did little to heal the nation. Democratic nominee Hubert Humphrey, Johnson's vice president, seemed a continuation of old politics. Republican candidate Richard Nixon, like Goldwater in 1964, called for "law and order"—a phrase some understood as racist code words—to appeal to people tired of social unrest. He reached out to those he called "the great, quite forgotten majority—the nonshouters and the nondemonstrators." On Vietnam, Nixon vowed he would "end the war and win the peace." Governor George Wallace of Alabama, a segregationist who proposed using nuclear weapons on Vietnam, ran as a third-party candidate. Wallace carried five southern states, drawing almost 14 percent of the popular vote. Nixon won with the slimmest of margins. Divisions among Americans deepened.

Yet on Christmas Eve 1968—in a step toward fulfilling John Kennedy's pledge—*Apollo* 8 entered lunar orbit. Looking down on a troubled world, the astronauts broadcast photographs of a fragile blue orb floating in darkness and read aloud the opening passages of Genesis, "In the beginning, God created the heaven and the earth … and God saw that it was good." Many listeners found themselves in tears.

The Immigration Act of 1965

When President Johnson signed the 1965 Immigration Act in a ceremony at the Statue of Liberty, he believed its importance was that it "repair[ed] a very deep and painful flaw in the fabric of American justice" by ending national origins quotas. Nevertheless, the president and his advisers saw it as primarily symbolic. They were wrong. This relatively obscure act may have had greater long-term impact on Americans' lives than any other Great Society legislation.

The 1965 Immigration Act ended blatant discrimination against potential immigrants from Asia, Africa, and various Third World nations by substituting Eastern and Western Hemispheric "caps" for national quotas and allowing family reunification. The architects of the Immigration Act did not expect the scale or the sources of immigration to change, but world events decreed otherwise. Political instability, along with rapidly growing populations in many poorer nations, created a large pool of potential immigrants who were drawn by U.S. prosperity.

By the 1990s, immigration accounted for almost 60 percent of America's population growth. By 2000, more Americans were foreign born than at any time since the 1930s. The majority now came not from Europe but from Mexico, the Philippines, Vietnam, China, the Dominican Republic, Korea, India, the former USSR, Jamaica, and Iran.

More than two-thirds of the new immigrants settled in six states—New York, California, Florida, New Jersey, Illinois, and Texas—and later diversified other regions. By the late twentieth century, Spanish-language signs appeared in South Carolina, and Hmong farmers from the mountains of Southeast Asia offered produce at the farmers' market in Missoula, Montana. The legacy of the 1965 Immigration Act was unintended but profound: the people and the nation are today much more diverse than they otherwise would have been.

Summary

The 1960s began with high hopes for a more democratic America. Civil rights volunteers, often risking their lives, carried the quest for racial equality across the nation. The 1964 Civil Rights Act and the 1965 Voting Rights Act were major landmarks. America was shaken by the assassination of President John Kennedy in 1963, but under President Johnson, the liberal vision of government working to improve citizens' lives inspired legislation designed to create a Great Society.

The Cold War between the United States and the USSR intensified during the 1960s, and the 1962 Cuban missile crisis almost brought nuclear war. Determined not to let Vietnam "fall" to communists, the United States sent military forces to prevent the victory of communist Vietnamese nationalists led by Ho Chi Minh in that nation's civil war. By 1968, there were more than half a million American ground troops in Vietnam. The war divided Americans, undermined Great Society domestic programs, and destroyed Johnson's presidency.

Despite civil rights gains, many African Americans turned away from the civil rights movement, seeking more immediate change. Poor African American neighborhoods burned as violent unrest spread through the nation. Vocal young people—and some of their elders—questioned whether democracy truly existed in the United States.

Large numbers of the nation's white youth rebelled by embracing a "counterculture" that rejected white middle-class respectability. The year 1968 was one of crisis, of assassinations and violence in the streets. The decade that had started with such promise was ending in fierce political polarization.

Chapter Review

Kennedy and the Cold War

How was the Cuban missile crisis a watershed in U.S.-Soviet relations?

Tensions had long existed between the two superpowers, which both had nuclear weapons and disagreed over preconditions for peace and disarmament. In 1962, when the Soviets moved to place nuclear missiles in Cuba, ninety miles from the Florida coast, the United States and the Soviet Union were on the brink of a nuclear disaster. Stressful negotiations eventually led the Soviets to remove the missiles if the United States promised never to attack Cuba and to remove missiles aimed at the Soviet Union from Turkey. The Cuban missile crisis forced both leaders to take small steps toward improving their relationship. In August 1963, they signed a treaty banning nuclear tests in the atmosphere, oceans, and outer space.

Marching for Freedom

What was Kennedy's reaction to growing civil rights activism?

President Kennedy was sympathetic to civil rights and recognized that racism damaged America's international reputation, but he feared alienating southern white Democrats in Congress. He appointed segregationist judges to Deep South federal courts and delayed his campaign promise to end segregation in federally subsidized housing. He also permitted the FBI to harass civil rights leaders—Martin Luther King Jr. in particular. But continued African American activism and the often-violent responses of whites to actions such as the Freedom Rides and voter registration efforts—all covered by national and international media—pushed Kennedy to support the civil rights struggle. He ordered U.S. marshals to protect James Meredith, the first African American to attend the University of Mississippi, and in 1963, he asked Congress to pass a comprehensive civil rights bill.

Liberalism and the Great Society

What made the War on Poverty controversial?

As part of his Great Society programs, President Johnson believed he could use the nation's prosperity to end poverty. War on Poverty programs included public housing and subsidized rents, Medicare and Medicaid, Food Stamps, Head Start, Job Corps, and Community Action Programs. The War on Poverty triggered intense reactions. Those on the left felt the government failed to address the structural inequalities that caused poverty in the first place. Those on the right feared the programs would create dependency rather than inspire initiative among the poor. Analysts, too, thought many of the programs were poorly implemented.

Johnson and Vietnam

How did the war in Vietnam become Americanized?

In 1965, with the South Vietnamese government teetering on the brink of defeat, Lyndon Johnson dramatically expanded U.S. involvement in the conflict. He launched Operation Rolling Thunder, a sustained bombing program that would last until 1968, and he dispatched U.S. ground forces to the conflict; by the end of the year, 180,000 U.S. troops were on the ground, and the number would reach more than half a million by 1968. As the U.S. presence in South Vietnam grew, so did that of North Vietnam, as did the assistance to the North from the Soviet Union and China.

A Nation Divided

What were the hallmarks of the youth movement in the 1960s?

The baby boom generation of young Americans came of age determined to shape the future of the nation. Some were inspired by the civil rights movement. Many committed themselves to political change. Conservative college students formed Young Americans for Freedom in 1960, with a goal of limited government and opposition to New Deal–style liberalism. On the left, students who felt that liberalism had not gone far enough to bring equality to all Americans founded the Students for a Democratic Society (SDS) in 1962. Students protested a range of issues, from efforts to block free speech on campus to gender inequality and sexism to the Vietnam War. Other young Americans rejected what they saw as hypocritical middle-class values. They crafted an alternative way of life, or counterculture, liberated from competitive materialism and celebrating pleasure and personal freedom.

1968

What made 1968 distinctive?

1968 was a year of violent protest and political disillusionment. In the United States, people became increasingly frustrated with the war in Vietnam, as the Tet Offensive demonstrated that the war's end was nowhere in sight. Two national leaders—Martin Luther King and Robert Kennedy—were assassinated, dousing the hopes held by African Americans, political activists, and young voters for a different, more progressive America,

and sparking violent protests in 130 cities. Demonstrations at the Democratic National Convention in Chicago turned violent, as police and army troops attacked peaceful antiwar protesters and journalists. In France, students protested the war and rigid school policies, supported by workers who occupied factories and shut down public transportation. Within a year, similar student rebellions occurred in Italy, Germany, England, Ireland, Sweden, Canada, Mexico, Chile, Japan, and South Korea, while in Prague, Czechoslovakia, thousands of protesters demanded democracy and an end to Soviet repression, before their rebellion was crushed by Soviet tanks.

Suggestions for Further Reading

Beth Bailey, *Sex in the Heartland* (1999)

David Farber, *The Age of Great Dreams* (1994)

LawrenceFreedman, *Kennedy's Wars: Berlin, Cuba, Laos, and Vietnam* (2000)

George C. Herring, *LBJ and Vietnam: A Different Kind of War* (1994)

Peniel Joseph, *Waiting 'Til the Midnight Hour: A Narrative History of Black Power in America* (2006)

Michael Kazin and Maurice Isserman, *America Divided: The Civil War of the 1960s* (1999)

Fredrik Logevall, *Choosing War: The Lost Chance for Peace and the Escalation of War in Vietnam* (1999)

Lisa McGirr, *Suburban Warriors: The Origins of the New American Right* (2001)

Charles Payne, *I've Got the Light of Freedom: The Organizing Tradition and the Mississippi Freedom Struggle* (1995)

A Pivotal Era

1969–1980

I n 1969, Daniel Ellsberg was a thirty-eight-year-old former aide to Assistant Secretary of Defense John McNaughton. At the Pentagon, Ellsberg had worked on a top-secret study of U.S. decision making in Vietnam. When he left office following Richard Nixon's election, Ellsberg gained access to a copy of the study being stored at the Rand Corporation, where he intended to resume his pregovernment research career. He spent six months poring over the seven thousand pages that comprised what would come to be called the Pentagon Papers.

Initially supportive of U.S. military intervention in Vietnam, Ellsberg had grown disillusioned. A Harvard-trained PhD, former marine officer, and Cold Warrior, he spent from 1965 to 1967 in South Vietnam, assessing the war's progress for his superiors in Washington. He went on combat patrols and interviewed military officials, U.S. diplomats, and Vietnamese leaders. The war, he concluded, was in multiple respects—military, political, moral—a lost enterprise.

Loyal to the president, Ellsberg was initially reluctant to act. But when in 1969 it became clear that Nixon had no intention of ending the war, Ellsberg decided to risk imprisonment and make the Pentagon Papers public. The study, he believed, showed that presidents had escalated the American commitment in Vietnam despite uniformly pessimistic estimates from their advisers—and that they had repeatedly lied to the public about their actions and the results. Ellsberg hoped disclosing this information would generate sufficient uproar to force a policy change.

Aided by a Rand colleague, Ellsberg surreptitiously photocopied the study, then spent months pleading with antiwar senators and representatives to release it. When they refused, he went to the press. On June 13, 1971, the *New York Times* published a front-page article on the Pentagon Papers. Other newspapers soon printed excerpts as well.

Ellsberg's leak became intensely controversial. Nixon attempted to stop the papers' publication—among the first such efforts to muzzle the press since the American Revolution—and to discredit Ellsberg and deter other leakers through the illegal actions of petty operatives. Many Americans saw Ellsberg as a hero who acted to shorten an illegitimate war. To many others, he was a publicity-seeking traitor.

Most Americans experienced the 1970s as a series of jolts and crises, an era of continuing divisions, betrayed expectations, and new limits. Exposure of Richard Nixon's illegal acts in the political scandal known as "Watergate" shook the faith of Americans not already disillusioned by discovery that the administration had lied about its conduct of the Vietnam War. The movements for racial equality and social justice became more radical by the early 1970s, as some activists called for social revolution or embraced a form of "cultural nationalism" that emphasized the differences among America's peoples. An economic crisis sent the "misery index" (a combination of the unemployment rate and inflation) skyrocketing. Americans worried about social crisis as the rates of divorce and violent crime soared. Environmental crises also challenged the nation: in 1969, Ohio's sludge-filled Cuyahoga River caught fire; in 1979, a partial meltdown at Pennsylvania's Three Mile Island nuclear power plant became America's worst nuclear accident.

Overseas, Nixon and his national security adviser, Henry Kissinger, understood that the United States and the Soviet Union, weakened by the costs of competition and challenged by other nations, faced a world where power was diffused. Accordingly, even as they pressed for victory in Vietnam, Nixon and Kissinger sought improved relations with the People's Republic of China and the Soviet Union. They failed in Vietnam, but the great-power negotiations bore fruit, and diplomatic efforts continued under Nixon's successors, Gerald Ford and Jimmy Carter. But Carter's presidency was undermined by international events. In the Middle East—a region of growing importance in U.S. foreign policy—Carter helped broker a peace deal between Egypt and Israel but proved powerless to end a lengthy hostage crisis in Iran. An economic downturn caused by changes in the global economy worsened Carter's woes, and Cold War tensions revived following a Soviet invasion of Afghanistan in 1979.

Despite—and sometimes because of—these crises, the 1970s was a pivotal era. It was a time of triumph for many who sought a more egalitarian American society. It was also a time of major economic transformation. As international competition increased, the United States continued to lose well-paid industrial jobs. Well-educated Americans would benefit from new opportunities in technology, finance, and creative fields, while less educated Americans suffered as low-paid service jobs replaced often-unionized manufacturing jobs. The 1970s economic crisis compounded Americans' loss of confidence in their political leaders, and many Americans rejected the notion of an active federal government. The growth of a New Deal, Great Society model was challenged by a broad—though contested—turn toward the competitive marketplace as the means to address the nation's problems.

As you read this chapter, keep the following questions in mind:

- **How did American foreign policy change as a result of involvement in Vietnam?**

- **Why did Americans see this era as an age of limits?**

- **Some historians describe the period between 1968 and 1980 as a time when many Americans lost faith—in their government, in the possibility of joining together in a society that offered equality to all, in the possibility of consensus instead of conflict. Do you agree, or were the struggles and divisions of this era similar to those of previous decades?**

Rights, Liberation, and Nationalism

What were the successes of the women's movement during the 1970s?

By the end of the 1960s, as divisions among Americans deepened, movements for social justice and racial equality had become stronger, louder, and often more radical. The civil rights movement splintered as many young African Americans abandoned nonviolence, rejected integration in favor of separatism, and embraced a distinct African American culture. By the early 1970s Mexican Americans and Native Americans, inspired by African American claims, had created powerful "Brown Power" and "Red Power" movements that demanded recognition of their own cultures. As women claimed new rights, some feminists—along with gay men and lesbians—called for "liberation." All these claims were controversial; Americans disagreed on possible remedies and on the very definition of the problem.

African American Cultural Nationalism

By the late 1960s many black Americans, disillusioned by the racism that outlasted the end of legal segregation, believed that integration would leave them subordinated in a white-dominated society. Mainstream groups such as the NAACP continued to fight for equality through the nation's courts and ballot boxes, but other activists looked to culture rather than to narrow political action for social change. Rejecting European American standards of beauty, young people let their hair grow into "naturals" and "Afros," claiming the power of black "soul." Black students and young faculty members sought strength in their own histories and heritages, as colleges and universities met their demands for black studies programs. African traditions were reclaimed—or sometimes created. The new holiday Kwanzaa, invented in 1966 by Maulana Karenga, a professor of black studies at California State University, Long Beach, celebrated African heritage.

Chronology

1969	Stonewall Inn uprising begins gay liberation movement		*Roe v. Wade* legalizes abortion
			Agnew resigns; Ford named vice president
	Apollo 11 astronaut Neil Armstrong becomes first person to walk on moon's surface	1974	Nixon resigns under threat of impeachment; Ford becomes president
	National Chicano Liberation Youth Conference held in Denver	1975	In deepening economic recession, unemployment hits 8.5 percent
	Indians of All Tribes occupies Alcatraz Island		New York City saved from bankruptcy by federal loan guarantees
	Nixon administration begins affirmative action plan		Congress passes Indian Self-Determination and Education Assistance Act in response to Native American activists
1970	United States invades Cambodia	1976	Carter elected president
	Students at Kent State and Jackson State universities shot by National Guard troops	1978	*Regents of the University of California v. Bakke* outlaws quotas but upholds affirmative action
	First Earth Day celebrated		California voters approve Proposition 13
	Environmental Protection Agency created		
1971	Pentagon Papers published	1979	Three Mile Island nuclear accident raises fears
1972	Nixon visits China and Soviet Union		Camp David Accords signed by Israel and Egypt
	CREEP stages Watergate break-in		American hostages seized in Iran
	Congress approves Equal Rights Amendment		Soviet Union invades Afghanistan
1973	Peace agreement in Paris ends U.S. involvement in Vietnam		Consumer debt doubles from 1975 to hit $315 billion
	OPEC increases oil prices, creating U.S. energy crisis		

Mexican American Activism

In 1970, the nation's 9 million Mexican Americans (4.3 percent of the U.S. population) were concentrated in the Southwest and California. Although the federal census counted all Hispanics as white, they were often discriminated against in the job market, pay, housing, schools, and the courts. Almost half of Mexican Americans were functionally illiterate, and in 1974 only 21 percent of Mexican American males graduated high school. Almost one-quarter fell below the official poverty level.

The national Mexican American movement for social justice began with migrant farmworkers. Grape growers paid migrant workers as little as 10 cents an hour in 1965 (the minimum wage was $1.25), and frequently the housing they provided lacked running water and indoor toilets. Mexican American and Filipino grape workers launched a strike (*huelga*) against growers in California's San Joaquin Valley in 1965, and labor organizers **César Chávez** and Dolores Huerta offered leadership. It was, however, a national consumer boycott of table grapes led by Chávez and the AFL-CIO–affiliated United Farm Workers (UFW) that brought the growers to the bargaining table, and the UFW won better wages and working conditions in 1970. The UFW resembled nineteenth-century Mexican *mutualistas*, or cooperative associations. Its members founded cooperative groceries, a Spanish-language newspaper, and a theater group.

César Chávez Labor leader who founded the United Farm Workers and was the driving force in creating the Latino civil rights movement of the 1960s and 1970s; he fused nonviolence (using boycotts, strikes, and demonstrations) with the dignity of farmworkers and of Hispanic heritage.

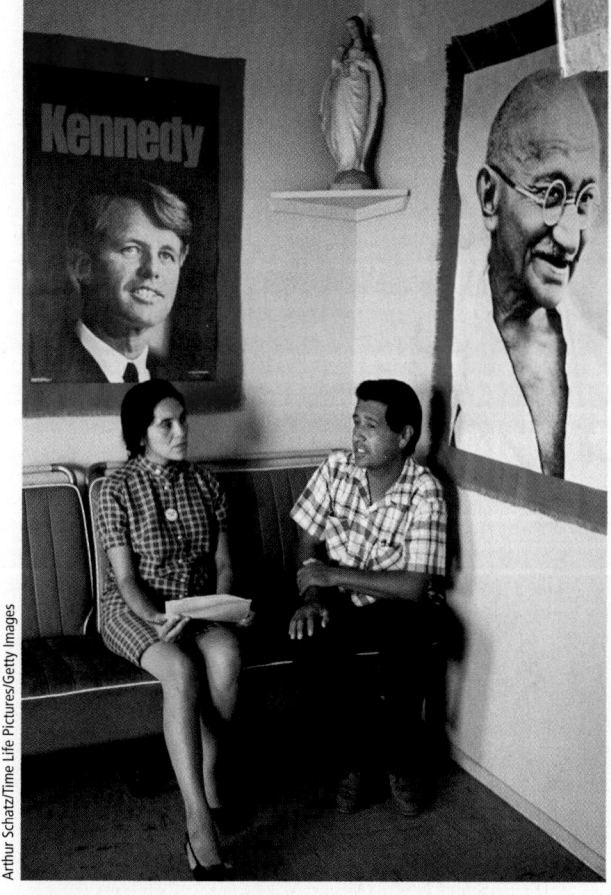

United Farm Workers leaders César Chávez and Dolores Huerta talk during the 1968 grape pickers' strike. The statue of the Virgin Mary, poster for presidential candidate Robert Kennedy, and photograph of Mahatma Gandhi suggest the guiding religious, political, and philosophical underpinnings of the movement.

Arthur Schatz/Time Life Pictures/Getty Images

Chicano Movement

During the same period, in northern New Mexico, Reies Tijerina created the Alianza Federal de Mercedes (Federal Alliance of Grants) to fight for the return of land it claimed belonged to local *hispano* villagers (whose ancestors had occupied the territory before it was claimed by the United States) under the 1848 Treaty of Guadalupe Hidalgo. In Denver, former boxer Rudolfo "Corky" Gonzáles drew Mexican American youth to the National Chicano Liberation Youth Conference in 1969. The conference adopted a manifesto, *El Plan Espiritual de Aztlan*, which condemned the "brutal 'Gringo' invasion of our territories."

These young activists did not seek equal rights through integration; instead, they wanted to liberate "La Raza" (from *La Raza de Bronze*, "the brown people") from oppressive American society and culture. They also rejected a hyphenated "Mexican-American" identity. The "Mexican American," they explained in *El Plan Espiritual de Aztlan*, "lacks respect for his culture." They called themselves "Chicanos" or "Chicanas"—barrio slang associated with *pachucos*, hip, rebellious, and definitely not respectable young men.

Many middle-class and older Mexican Americans never embraced the term *Chicano* or the separatist, cultural nationalist agenda of *el movimiento*. But younger activists succeeded in introducing Chicano studies into local high school and college curricula and in creating a unifying cultural identity for Mexican American youth. Some activists made political gains as well. La Raza Unida (RUP), a Southwest-based political party, registered tens of thousands of voters and won local elections.

Native American Activism

Young Native American activists also embraced cultural nationalism. Many, seeking a return to the "old ways," joined with older "traditionalists" to challenge tribal leaders who advocated assimilation.

In November 1969, a small group called "Indians of All Tribes" occupied Alcatraz Island in San Francisco Bay, demanding that the land be returned to native peoples. The protest lasted nineteen months and drew more than four hundred people from fifty different tribes. It marked the consolidation of a "pan-Indian" activism, which claimed a shared "Indian" identity that transcended tribal differences. Although the protesters did not reclaim Alcatraz Island, they attracted national attention to their struggle and inspired the growing "Red Power" movement. In 1972, the radical American Indian Movement occupied a Bureau of Indian Affairs office in Washington, D.C., and then in 1973 a trading post at Wounded Knee, South Dakota, where U.S. Army troops had massacred three hundred Sioux in 1890.

Meanwhile, more moderate activists, working through such pan-tribal organizations as the National Congress of American Indians and the Native American Rights Fund, lobbied Congress for greater rights and resources to govern themselves. In response, Congress and the federal courts returned millions of acres of land to tribal ownership, and in 1975 Congress passed the **Indian Self-Determination and Education Assistance Act**. Still, during the 1970s and 1980s American Indians had a higher rate of tuberculosis, alcoholism, and suicide than any other group. Nine of ten lived in substandard housing, and unemployment approached 40 percent.

Indian Self-Determination and Education Assistance Act The 1975 act that granted Native American tribes control of federal aid programs on the reservations and oversight of their own schools.

The Women's Movement

During the 1960s, a "second wave" of the American women's movement emerged, and by the 1970s activists waged a multifront battle for "women's liberation." Feminists did not always agree on methods or goals, but their struggles and successes made the 1970s a pivotal decade for American women.

In 1963, the surprise popularity of Betty Friedan's *The Feminine Mystique* signaled fuel for a revived women's movement. Writing as a housewife (though she had a long history of political activism as well), Friedan described "the problem with no name," the dissatisfaction of educated, middle-class wives and mothers like herself, who—looking at their homes and families—wondered guiltily if that was all there was to life. Instead of blaming women for failing to adapt to women's proper role, as 1950s magazines did, Friedan blamed the role itself and the society that created it.

The organized, liberal wing of the women's movement emerged in 1966, with the founding of the **National Organization for Women (NOW)**. NOW was initially a small group of educated, professional women. It served as a lobbying group; its goal was to pressure the EEOC to enforce the 1964 Civil Rights Act (see page 770). By 1970, NOW had one hundred chapters with more than three thousand members nationwide.

National Organization for Women (NOW) Women's rights organization founded in 1966 that lobbied for equal opportunity, filed lawsuits against gender discrimination, and mobilized public opinion against sexism.

Another strand of the women's movement developed from the nation's increasingly radical social justice movements. Many women working for civil rights or against the war in Vietnam were treated as second-class citizens—making coffee, not policy. As they analyzed inequality, these young women recognized their own oppression, and the oppression of all women. In 1968, a group of women protested the "degrading mindless-boob girlie symbol" represented by the Miss America Pageant in Atlantic City. Although nothing was burned, the pejorative 1970s term for feminists, "bra-burners," came from this event, in which women threw items of "enslavement" (girdles, high heels, curlers, and bras) into a "Freedom Trash Can."

Feminist Goals and Accomplishments

Feminism was never a single, coherent set of beliefs. Most radical feminists, however, practiced what they called "personal politics." They believed, as feminist author Charlotte Bunch explained, that "there is no private domain of a person's life that is not political, and there is no political issue that is not ultimately personal." In the early 1970s, women meeting in suburban

Roe v. Wade The 1973 Supreme Court ruling that privacy rights protected a woman's decision to end a pregnancy.

Link to *Roe v. Wade*, Justice Blackmun's Opinion of the Court

Equal Rights Amendment Proposed constitutional amendment guaranteeing equal rights for women; passed with strong support of both Democrats and Republicans in Congress but fell short of ratification by the states by the 1982 deadline.

kitchens, college dorm rooms, and churches or synagogues created "consciousness-raising" groups to talk about power and patriarchy, romance and marriage, sexuality, abortion, health care, work, and family.

Such conversations left many women convinced that it was crucial to gain the right to control their own bodies. The Boston Women's Health Collective published *Our Bodies, Ourselves* in 1971 (the original edition sold over 3 million copies), offering women new understanding of their sexual and reproductive health. Women who sought the right to safe and legal abortions won a major victory in 1973 when the Supreme Court, in a 7-to-2 decision on **Roe v. Wade**, ruled that privacy rights protected a woman's choice to end a pregnancy.

When the 1970s began, help-wanted ads specified "male" or "female." Unmarried women could be denied birth control; women were systematically excluded from juries; women frequently could not obtain credit in their own names. U.S. rape law mirrored the claim of a psychiatrist at the University of Kansas student health center: "A woman sometimes plays a big part in provoking her attacker by … her overall attitude and appearance"; courts allowed attorneys to use women's sexual histories to discredit them and did not recognize spousal rape. Only 4 percent of American attorneys were female; women made up only 1.3 percent of the military, and there was not a single female general. Less than 2 percent of college and university athletic budgets went to women's sports—and women received no athletic scholarships. No woman had ever been named a Rhodes Scholar, served as president of the *Harvard Law Review*, or been ordained as a pastor, rabbi, or (Episcopal) priest. All that would change by the end of the decade.

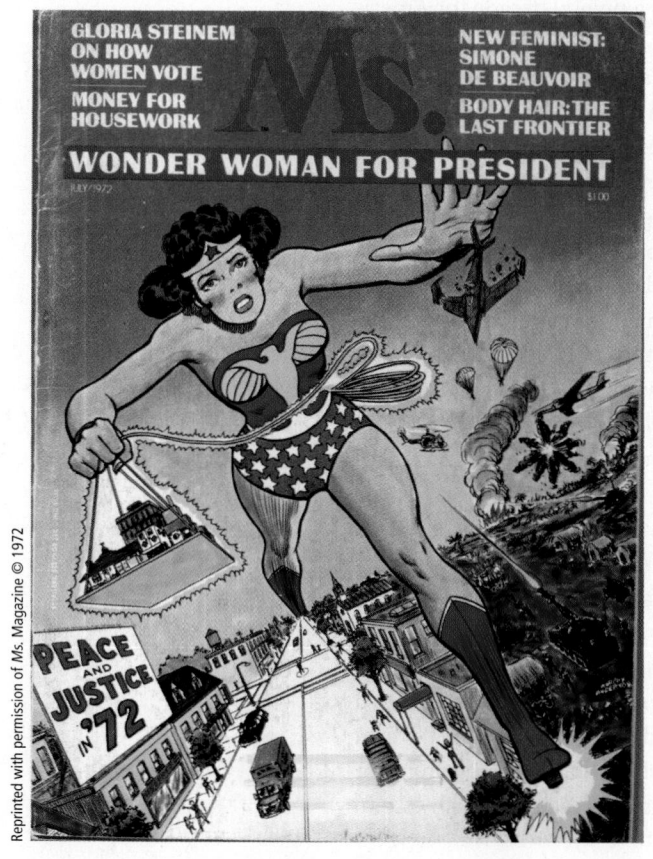

Reprinted with permission of *Ms.* Magazine © 1972

The 1940s comic book heroine Wonder Woman appeared on the cover of Ms. *magazine's first regular issue in July 1972. Wonder Woman represented the feminist belief in "womanpower," but the choice of Wonder Woman had a practical justification as well: the main financial investor in* Ms., *Warner Communications, was about to relaunch Wonder Woman comics.*

Opposition to the Women's Movement

Initially, the nation's elected representatives supported women's claims to equal rights. On March 22, 1972, Senate Republicans and Democrats approved the **Equal Rights Amendment**, first proposed by the National Woman's Party in the 1920s. By a vote of 82 to 8, senators confirmed that "equality of rights under the law shall not be denied or abridged by the United States or by any State on account of sex." By the end of the year, twenty-two states (of the thirty-eight necessary to amend the Constitution) had ratified the ERA.

But the women's movement also met powerful opposition—much of it from women. Many did not want to be "equal" if that meant giving up traditional gender roles in marriage or working at low-wage jobs. African American women and Latinas, many of whom had been active in movements for the liberation of their peoples and some of whom had helped create second-wave feminism, often regarded feminism as a "white" movement that ignored their cultural traditions and diverted attention from the fight for racial equality.

Organized opposition to feminism came primarily from conservative, often religiously motivated men and women. As one conservative Christian writer claimed, "The Bible clearly states that the wife is to submit to her husband's leadership." Such beliefs, along with fears about changing gender roles, fueled the STOP-ERA movement led by Phyllis Schlafly, a lawyer and conservative political activist. Schlafly attacked the women's movement as "a total assault on the role of the American woman as wife and mother." Schlafly's group argued that the ERA would decriminalize rape, force Americans to use unisex toilets, and make women subject to the military draft.

In fighting the ERA, tens of thousands of women became politically experienced; they fed a growing grassroots conservative movement that would blossom in the 1980s. By the mid-1970s, the STOP-ERA movement had stalled the Equal Rights Amendment. It fell three states short of ratification and expired in 1982.

Gay Liberation

In the early 1970s, gay men and lesbians faced widespread discrimination. Consensual sexual intercourse between people of the same sex was illegal in almost every state, and until 1973 the American Psychiatric Association labeled homosexuality a mental disorder. Homosexual couples did not receive partnership benefits, such as health insurance; they could not adopt children. The issue of gay and lesbian rights divided even progressive organizations: in 1970, the New York City chapter of NOW expelled its lesbian officers. Gay men and lesbians could conceal the identity that made them vulnerable to discrimination and harassment, but remaining "in the closet" made it difficult to organize politically.

There were small "homophile" organizations, such as the Mattachine Society and the Daughters of Bilitis, which had worked for gay rights since the 1950s. But the symbolic beginning of the gay liberation movement came on June 28, 1969, when New York City police raided the Stonewall Inn, a gay bar in Greenwich Village, for violating a city law that made it illegal for more than three homosexual patrons to occupy a bar at the same time. That night, patrons stood up to the police, and hundreds more joined them as word spread. The next morning, New Yorkers found a new slogan spray-painted on neighborhood walls: "Gay Power."

Inspired by the Stonewall riot, some men and women worked openly and militantly for gay rights. They focused on legal equality and the promotion of Gay Pride. Some rejected the notion of fitting into straight (heterosexual) culture and created distinctive gay communities. By 1973, there were about eight hundred gay organizations in the United States. Centered in big cities and on college campuses, most organizations created supportive environments for gay men and lesbians to come "out of the closet" and push for reform. By decade's end, gay men and lesbians were a political force in cities including New York, Miami, and San Francisco.

Affirmative Action

As activists made Americans increasingly aware of inequality, policymakers struggled to frame remedies. As early as 1965, President Johnson had acknowledged the limits of civil rights legislation, calling for "not just legal equality ... but equality as a fact and equality as a result." Johnson joined his belief that the federal government must help *individuals* attain competitive skills to a new concept: equality could be measured by *group* outcomes.

Practical issues helped shift emphasis to group outcomes. The 1964 Civil Rights Act outlawed discrimination but seemingly stipulated that action could be taken only when an employer "intentionally" discriminated against an individual. The tens of thousands of cases filed with the EEOC suggested that racial and sexual discrimination were widespread, but each alleged incident required proof that the employer intended to discriminate. Some argued that it was possible, instead, to prove discrimination by "results"—by the relative number of African Americans or women, for example, an employer hired or promoted.

In 1969, the Nixon administration implemented the first major government affirmative action program. The Philadelphia Plan (so called because it targeted government contracts in that city) required businesses contracting with the federal government to show (in Nixon's words) "affirmative action to meet the goals of increasing minority employment" and set specific numerical "goals," or quotas, for employers. Major government contracts soon required affirmative action for women and members of racial and ethnic minorities, and many corporations and universities began similar programs.

Supporters saw affirmative action as a remedy for the effects of past discrimination. Critics argued that creating proportional representation for women and minorities meant discrimination against others who had not created past discrimination, and that group-based remedies violated the principle of judging individuals on their own merits.

The End in Vietnam

What kept Nixon from ending the Vietnam War as quickly as he had hoped?

No issue divided Americans as pervasively as the Vietnam War. Nixon did not deliver on his vow "to stop that war. Fast." Like Johnson, he feared that a withdrawal would harm American credibility as well as his own domestic standing. Anxious to get American troops out of Vietnam, Nixon was equally committed to preserving an independent, noncommunist South Vietnam. He adopted a policy that at once contracted and expanded the war.

Invasion of Cambodia

Nixon's policy centered on "Vietnamization"—building up South Vietnamese forces to replace U.S. forces. Accordingly, the president decreased U.S. troops from 543,000 in the spring of 1969 to 156,800 by the end of 1971, and to 60,000 by the fall of 1972. Vietnamization helped limit domestic dissent, but it did not end the stalemate in the Paris peace talks under way since 1968. Even as he embarked on troop withdrawals, therefore, Nixon intensified the bombing of North Vietnam and enemy supply depots in neighboring Cambodia, hoping to pound Hanoi into concessions (see Map 26.1 on page 776).

The bombing of neutral Cambodia commenced in March 1969. For fourteen months, B-52 pilots flew 3,600 missions and dropped over one hundred thousand tons of bombs, initially in secret. When the North Vietnamese refused to buckle, Nixon turned up the heat: in April 1970, South Vietnamese and U.S. forces invaded Cambodia. The president announced publicly that he would not allow "the world's most powerful nation" to act "like a pitiful, helpless giant."

Protests and Counterdemonstrations

Instantly, the antiwar movement rose up, as students on about 450 college campuses went out on strike and hundreds of thousands of demonstrators protested the administration's policies. The crisis atmosphere intensified on May 4, when National Guardsmen in Ohio fired into a crowd of students at Kent State University, killing four and wounding eleven. Ten days later, police armed with automatic weapons blasted a women's dormitory at Jackson State, a historically black university in Mississippi, killing two students and wounding nine. Police claimed they had been shot at, but no such evidence could be found. In Congress, Nixon's widening of the war sparked outrage, and in June the Senate terminated the Tonkin Gulf Resolution of 1964. After two months, U.S. troops withdrew from Cambodia.

Although a majority of Americans told pollsters they thought the original U.S. troop commitment to Vietnam had been a mistake, 50 percent said they believed Nixon's claim that the Cambodia invasion would shorten the war. Angered by demonstrating college students, many voiced support for the war effort. In Washington, an "Honor America Day" program attracted more than two hundred thousand people who heard Billy Graham and Bob Hope laud administration policy. Nevertheless, the tumult over the invasion reduced Nixon's options on the war. Solid majorities would oppose any new missions for U.S. ground troops in Southeast Asia.

Nixon's troubles at home mounted in June 1971, when the *New York Times* began to publish the Pentagon Papers. Nixon secured an injunction to prevent publication, but the Supreme Court overturned the order. Americans learned from this study that political and military leaders frequently had lied to the public about their aims and strategies in Southeast Asia.

Equally troubling, morale and discipline among troops had been declining even before Nixon took office, and there were growing reports of drug addiction, desertion, racial discord, even the murder of unpopular officers by enlisted men (a practice called "fragging"). The court-martial and conviction in 1971 of Lieutenant William Calley, charged with overseeing the killing of more than three hundred unarmed South Vietnamese civilians in **My Lai** in 1968, got particular attention. An army photographer had captured the horror in graphic pictures.

Paris Peace Accords

The Nixon administration, meanwhile, stepped up efforts to pressure Hanoi into a settlement. When the North Vietnamese launched an offensive into South Vietnam in March 1972, Nixon responded with a massive aerial onslaught. That December, after an apparent peace agreement collapsed, the United States launched an air strike on the North—the so-called "Christmas bombing."

My Lai South Vietnamese village and site of an intended search-and-destroy mission by U.S. soldiers that evolved into a brutal massacre of more than 300 unarmed civilians, including women and children; some were lined up in ditches and shot, with their village then burned to the ground.

Visualizing THE PAST

The Image of War

The Vietnam War has been called the first "television war." More than ever before (or arguably since), news clips and photos brought Americans and others around the world face to face with the fighting and its victims. On June 8, 1972, as children and their families fled the village of Trang Bang, their bodies seared by napalm, Huynh Cong "Nick" Ut took this iconic photograph that became an antiwar rallying point and symbol of hope. The girl in the center, Phan Thi Kim Phuc, survived the attack but had to endure fourteen months of painful rehabilitation to treat the third-degree burns that covered more than half of her body. Kim later became a Canadian citizen and a Goodwill Ambassador for the United Nations Educational, Scientific and Cultural Organization (UNESCO). Some analysts have argued that a single image can become the voice of popular protest; others say that even indelible images such as this one cannot have that power. What do you think?

AP Photo/Nick Ut

But a diplomatic agreement was close. Most notably, Kissinger agreed that North Vietnamese troops could remain in the South after a settlement, while his North Vietnamese counterpart, Le Duc Tho, abandoned Hanoi's insistence that the Saigon government of Nguyen Van Thieu be removed. Nixon allowed concessions because he wanted to improve relations with the Soviet Union and China, win back the allegiance of America's allies, and restore stability at home. On January 27, 1973, Kissinger and Le Duc Tho signed a cease-fire agreement in Paris, and Nixon compelled a reluctant Thieu to accept it by threatening to cut off U.S. aid. The United States promised to withdraw its troops within sixty days. North Vietnamese troops could stay in South Vietnam, and a coalition government that included the Vietcong eventually would be formed in the South.

The United States pulled its troops out of Vietnam, leaving behind some military advisers. Soon, full-scale war erupted again. Just before the South Vietnamese surrendered, hundreds of Americans and Vietnamese who worked for them were hastily evacuated from Saigon. On April 29, 1975, the South Vietnamese government collapsed, and Vietnam was reunified under a communist government in Hanoi. Saigon was renamed Ho Chi Minh City for the persevering patriot who had died in 1969.

Costs of the Vietnam War

More than 58,000 Americans and 1.5 to 2 million Vietnamese had died in the war. Civilian deaths in Cambodia and Laos reached hundreds of thousands. The war cost the United States at least $170 billion, and billions more would be paid out in veterans' benefits. Money spent on the war was unavailable for domestic programs. The nation suffered inflation, political schism, and abuses of executive power. The war also delayed accommodation with the Soviet Union and the People's Republic of China, fueled friction with allies, and alienated Third World nations.

In 1975, communists formed repressive governments in Vietnam, Cambodia, and Laos, but beyond Indochina the domino effect once predicted by U.S. officials never occurred. Acute hunger afflicted the people of those devastated lands. Soon refugees—"boat people"—crowded aboard unsafe vessels to escape. Many emigrated to the United States, where they were received with mixed feelings by Americans reluctant to be reminded of defeat as well as their own responsibility for the plight of the Southeast Asian peoples.

Debate over the Lessons of Vietnam

Americans seemed angry and confused about the war. Hawkish observers claimed that failure in Vietnam undermined the nation's credibility. They pointed to a "Vietnam syndrome"—an American suspicion of foreign entanglements—which they feared would inhibit the future exercise of U.S. power. America lost in Vietnam, they asserted, because Americans lost their guts at home.

Dovish analysts blamed the war on an imperial presidency that permitted strong-willed men to act without restraint and on a weak Congress that conceded too much power to the executive branch. Make the president adhere to the checks-and-balances system—make him go to Congress for a declaration of war—these critics counseled.

This view found expression in the War Powers Act of 1973, which limited the president's war-making freedom and required congressional approval before committing U.S. forces to combat action lasting more than sixty days. That same year the draft came to an end.

Vietnam Veterans

Public discussion of the lessons of the Vietnam War was also stimulated by veterans' calls for help in dealing with posttraumatic stress disorder, which afflicted thousands of the 2.8 million Vietnam veterans. Doctors reported that the disorder, which caused nightmares and extreme nervousness, stemmed from soldiers' having seen so many children, women, and elderly people killed. Some GIs inadvertently killed these people; some killed them vengefully and later felt guilt. Other veterans publicized their deteriorating health from the effects of the defoliant Agent Orange and other herbicides they had handled or were accidentally sprayed with in Vietnam.

Nixon, Kissinger, and the World

How did the Vietnam War influence Nixon's approach to foreign policy?

The difficulties of the Vietnam War signified to Nixon and Kissinger that American power was limited and, in relative terms, in decline. This reality convinced them that the United States had to adapt to a new, multipolar international system no longer defined by the Soviet-American rivalry. Western Europe was becoming a major player, as was Japan. The Middle East loomed increasingly large, due in large part to America's growing dependence on oil. Above all, Americans had to come to grips with China by rethinking the policy of hostile isolation.

They were an unlikely duo—the reclusive, ambitious career politician from California, born of Quaker parents, and the sociable, dynamic Jewish intellectual who had fled Nazi Germany as a child. What the two men had in common was a tendency toward paranoia about rivals and a capacity to think in broad conceptual terms about America's place in the world.

Nixon Doctrine

In July 1969, Nixon and Kissinger acknowledged the limits of American power and resources when they announced the Nixon Doctrine. The United States, they said, would provide economic aid to allies, but these allies should not count on American troops. Washington could no longer afford to sustain its overseas commitments and would have to rely more on regional allies—including authoritarian regimes—to maintain an anticommunist world order. Nixon's doctrine amounted to a partial retreat from the 1947 Truman Doctrine's promise to support noncommunist governments facing threats.

détente Nixon's foreign policy initiative with the Soviet Union; it focused on mutual cooperation and sought to check expansion and reduce arms buildup through diplomacy and negotiation.

Détente

Another pillar of the new foreign policy was **détente**: measured cooperation with the Soviets through negotiations within a general environment of rivalry. Détente's primary purpose, like that of containment, was to check Soviet expansion and limit the Soviet arms buildup, though now that goal would be accomplished through diplomacy and mutual concessions. The second part of the strategy sought to curb revolution and radicalism in the Third World so as to quash threats to American interests. Specifically, expanded trade with friendlier Soviets and Chinese might reduce the huge U.S. balance-of-payments deficit. Improving relations with both communist giants, when Sino-Soviet tensions were increasing, might weaken communism.

The Soviet Union, too, found that the Cold War drained its resources. Improved ties with Washington would allow the USSR to focus on its increasingly fractious relations with China and might generate progress on outstanding European issues, including the status of Germany and Berlin. In May 1972, the United States and the USSR agreed in the ABM Treaty (officially the Treaty on the Limitation of Anti-Ballistic Missile Systems) to slow the arms race by limiting intercontinental ballistic missiles and antiballistic missile defenses.

Opening to China

Meanwhile, the United States took dramatic steps to end more than two decades of Sino-American hostility. The Chinese wanted to spur trade and hoped that friendlier Sino-American relations would make their onetime ally and now enemy, the Soviet Union, more cautious. In early 1972, Nixon made a historic trip to "Red China," where he and the venerable Chinese leaders Mao Zedong and Zhou Enlai agreed to disagree on a number of issues, except one: the Soviet Union should not be permitted to make gains in Asia. Sino-American relations improved slightly, and official diplomatic recognition came in 1979.

The opening to communist China and the policy of détente with the Soviet Union reflected Nixon's and Kissinger's belief in the importance of maintaining stability among the great powers. In the Third World, too, they sought stability, though there they hoped to get it not by change but by maintaining the status quo.

Wars in the Middle East

In the Middle East, the situation had grown more volatile after the Arab-Israeli Six-Day War in 1967. Israel had scored victories against Egypt and Syria, seizing the Sinai Peninsula and the Gaza Strip from Egypt, the West Bank and East Jerusalem from Jordan, and the Golan Heights from Syria (see Map 29.2). Israel gained 28,000 square miles and could henceforth defend itself against invading forces. But with Gaza and the West Bank as the ancestral home

"This was the week that changed the world," Richard Nixon said of his visit to China in February 1972. Many historians agree and consider the China opening Nixon's greatest achievement as president. When he and wife Pat visited the Great Wall, the president reportedly remarked: "This is a great wall."

National Archives and Records Administration

OPEC and the 1973 Oil Embargo

If one date can mark the relative decline of American power in the Cold War era and the arrival of Arab nations on the world stage, it would be October 20, 1973. That day, the Arab members of the Organization of Petroleum Exporting Countries (OPEC)—Saudi Arabia, Iraq, Kuwait, Libya, and Algeria—imposed an embargo on oil shipments to the United States and other Israeli allies. The move was in retaliation against U.S. support of Israel in the two-week-old Yom Kippur War. The embargo followed an OPEC price hike three days earlier from $3.01 to $5.12 per barrel. In December, the five Arab countries, joined by Iran, raised prices again, to $11.65 per barrel.

Gasoline prices surged across America, and some dealers ran low on supplies. Americans endured endless lines at the pumps and shivered in underheated homes. When the embargo was lifted in March 1974, oil prices stayed high, and the aftereffects of the embargo would linger through the decade. It confirmed the extent to which Americans no longer fully controlled their own economic destiny.

Just twenty years before, in the early 1950s, Americans had produced at home all the oil they needed. By the early 1960s, the picture had changed, as Americans depended on foreign sources for one out of every six barrels of oil they used. By 1972, the figure increased to about two out of six. As author Daniel Yergin has put it, "The shortfall struck at fundamental beliefs in the endless abundance of resources . . . that a large part of the public did not even know, up until October 1973, that the United States imported any oil at all."

When the embargo ended, Americans resumed their wastefulness, but in a changed world. The United States had become a dependent nation, its economic future linked to decisions by Arab leaders half a world away.

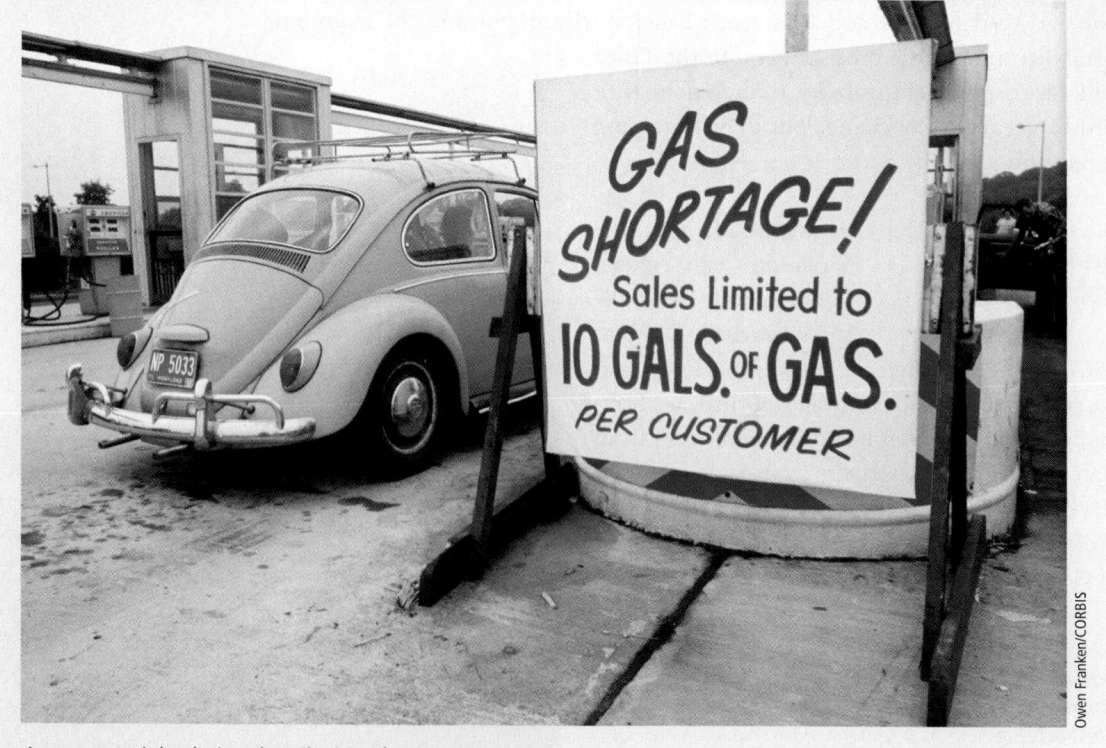

Owen Franken/CORBIS

A common sight during the oil crisis of 1973–74 was long lines and ominous signs at service stations in the United States. In this image, taken in early 1974, a station in Connecticut makes its point clearly.

of hundreds of thousands of Palestinians (see Chapter 24), Israel found itself governing people who wanted to see Israel destroyed. When the Israelis established Jewish settlements in their newly won areas, Arab resentment grew. Terrorists associated with the Palestinian Liberation Organization (PLO) made hit-and-run raids on Jewish settlements, hijacked jetliners, and murdered Israeli athletes at the 1972 Olympic Games in Munich, West Germany. The Israelis retaliated by assassinating PLO leaders.

In October 1973, on the Jewish High Holy Day of Yom Kippur, Egypt and Syria attacked Israel, primarily seeking revenge for the 1967 defeat. Surprised, Israel reeled before launching an effective counteroffensive against Soviet-armed Egyptian forces in the Sinai. To punish Americans for their pro-Israel stance, the Organization of Petroleum Exporting Countries (OPEC), a group of mostly Arab nations that had united to raise oil prices, embargoed oil shipments to the United States and other supporters of Israel. An energy crisis rocked the nation. Kissinger arranged a cease-fire in the war, but OPEC did not lift the oil embargo until March 1974. The next year, Kissinger persuaded Egypt and Israel to accept a UN peace-keeping force in the Sinai. But Arabs still vowed to destroy Israel, and Israelis built more Jewish settlements in occupied lands.

Antiradicalism in Latin America and Africa

In Latin America, the Nixon administration sought to thwart radical leftist challenges to authoritarian rule. In Chile, after voters in 1970 elected a Marxist president, Salvador Allende, the CIA secretly encouraged military officers to stage a coup. In 1973, a military junta ousted Allende and installed an authoritarian regime under General Augusto Pinochet. (Allende was subsequently murdered.) Washington publicly denied any role.

In Africa as well, Washington preferred the status quo, backing the white-minority regime in Rhodesia (now Zimbabwe) and activating the CIA in a failed effort to defeat a Soviet- and Cuban-backed faction in Angola's civil war. In South Africa, Nixon tolerated the white rulers who imposed segregationist apartheid on blacks and mixed-race "coloureds" (85 percent of the population), keeping them poor, disfranchised, and ghettoized in prisonlike townships. After the leftist government came to power in Angola, however, Washington took a keener interest in the rest of Africa, building economic ties and sending arms to friendly black nations, such as Kenya and the Congo, while distancing the United States from the white governments of Rhodesia and South Africa.

Presidential Politics and the Crisis of Leadership

How did Watergate bring down the Nixon administration?

Nixon's foreign policy accomplishments were overshadowed by his domestic failures. He betrayed the public trust and broke laws. His misconduct, combined with Americans' belief that their leaders had lied repeatedly about the war in Vietnam, shook Americans' faith in government. Suspicion of the government, exacerbated by Watergate, would limit what Gerald Ford and Jimmy Carter, Nixon's successors, could accomplish.

Nixon's Domestic Agenda

Richard Nixon was brilliant and politically cunning yet also crude, prejudiced against Jews and African Americans, happy to use dirty tricks and presidential power against his enemies, and driven by a resentment that bordered on paranoia. The son of a grocer from an agricultural region of southern California, Nixon loathed the liberal establishment, which loathed him back, and his presidency was driven by that hatred as much as by any strong philosophical commitment to conservative principles.

Much of Nixon's domestic agenda was liberal, expanding federal programs to improve society. His administration pioneered affirmative action. It doubled the budgets of the National Endowment for the Humanities (NEH) and National Endowment for the Arts (NEA). Nixon supported the ERA, signed major environmental legislation, created the Occupational Safety and Health Administration (OSHA), used deficit spending to manage the economy, and proposed a guaranteed minimum income for all Americans.

Yet Nixon also pursued a conservative agenda that involved "devolution," shifting federal government authority to states and localities. He promoted revenue-sharing programs that distributed federal funds back to the states, thus appealing to those who viewed high taxes as supporting liberal "giveaway" programs for poor and minority Americans. Nixon worked to equate the Republican Party with law and order and the Democrats with permissiveness, crime, drugs, radicalism, and the "hippie lifestyle." To capitalize on the backlash against the 1960s social movements and consolidate the support of those he called "the silent majority," Nixon fostered division, using his outspoken vice president, Spiro Agnew, to attack war protesters and critics as "naughty children." He appointed four conservative justices to the Supreme Court: Warren Burger, Harry Blackmun, Lewis Powell Jr., and William Rehnquist.

Determining whether Nixon was liberal, conservative, or simply pragmatic is complicated. For example, when the Nixon administration proposed a guaranteed minimum income for all Americans, his larger goal was to dismantle the federal welfare system. Nixon did not reject a powerful role for the federal government, but he was suspicious of federal bureaucrats, social change activists, and intellectual elites.

In addition, Nixon pursued a highly pragmatic "southern strategy" to attract white southerners to the Republican Party. He nominated two southerners to the Supreme Court—one of whom had a segregationist record—and when Congress declined to confirm either nominee, Nixon protested angrily. After the Supreme Court upheld a school desegregation plan requiring a highly segregated North Carolina school system to achieve racial integration by busing both black and white children throughout the county (*Swann v. Charlotte-Mecklenburg*, 1971), Nixon denounced busing. (Neither resistance to busing nor continuing segregation was purely southern, as Boston residents protested—sometimes violently—court-ordered busing to combat school segregation in 1974.)

George McGovern Liberal senator from South Dakota and Democratic candidate for president in 1972.

Enemies and Dirty Tricks

Nixon was almost sure of reelection in 1972. His Democratic opponent was **George McGovern**, a progressive senator from South Dakota and strong opponent of the Vietnam War who appealed to the left. Alabama governor George Wallace, running on a third-party ticket, withdrew after he was paralyzed in an assassination attempt. The Nixon campaign, however, took no chances. On June 17, five men tied to the Committee to Re-elect the President (CREEP) were caught breaking into the Democratic National Committee's offices at the Watergate complex in Washington, D.C. The break-in got little attention, and Nixon captured 60 percent of the popular vote in November. McGovern carried only Massachusetts and the District of Columbia. But even as Nixon triumphed, his downfall had begun.

Nixon obsessively believed he was surrounded by enemies. He made "enemies lists." On Nixon's order, his aide Charles Colson formed a secret group called the Plumbers. Their first job was to break into the office of the psychiatrist treating Daniel Ellsberg, the former Pentagon employee who made the **Pentagon Papers** public, looking for material to discredit him. The Plumbers expanded their "dirty tricks" operations during the 1972 presidential campaign, bugging phones, infiltrating campaign staffs, even writing anonymous letters falsely accusing Democratic candidates of sexual misconduct. They had already bugged the Democratic National Committee offices and were going back to plant more surveillance equipment when they were caught by the D.C. police at the Watergate complex.

Pentagon Papers A 47-volume U.S. government study from the end of WW II to the Vietnam War, tracing U.S. involvement in Southeast Asia. Released to the press by former Pentagon employee Daniel Ellsberg, the papers revealed military mistakes and a long history of White House lies to Congress, foreign leaders, and the American people.

Watergate Cover-up and Investigation

Nixon was not directly involved in the Watergate break-in. But instead of distancing himself and firing those responsible, he tried to cover it up, ordering the CIA to stop the FBI's investigation, claiming it imperiled national security. At this point, Nixon obstructed justice—a felony and an impeachable crime—but he also halted the investigation. However, two relatively unknown reporters for the *Washington Post*, Carl Bernstein and Bob Woodward, stayed on the story. Aided by an anonymous, highly placed government official whom they code-named Deep Throat (the title of a notorious 1972 X-rated film), they followed a money trail that led straight to the White House. (W. Mark Felt, second in command at the FBI in the early 1970s, identified himself as Watergate's Deep Throat in 2005.)

From May to August 1973, the Senate held televised public hearings on the Watergate affair. White House Counsel John Dean, fearful that he was being made the fall guy for the Watergate fiasco, gave damning testimony. On July 13, a White House aide told the Senate Committee that Nixon regularly recorded his conversations in the Oval Office. Nixon refused to turn the tapes over to Congress.

Impeachment and Resignation

Nixon faced scandals on other fronts. In October 1973, Vice President Spiro Agnew resigned, following charges that he had accepted bribes while governor of Maryland. Nixon appointed and Congress approved Michigan's **Gerald Ford**, the House minority leader, as Agnew's replacement. Meanwhile, Nixon's staff grew increasingly concerned about his excessive drinking and seeming mental instability. Then, on October 24, 1973, the House of Representatives began impeachment proceedings.

Under court order, Nixon released edited portions of the Oval Office tapes. Although the first tapes revealed nothing criminal, the public was shocked by

Gerald Ford Michigan congressman who took the place of Vice President Spiro Agnew when Agnew resigned following charges of corruption. Ford became the thirty-eighth president of the nation when Nixon resigned in 1974.

Nixon's obscenities and racist slurs. In July 1974, the Supreme Court ruled that Nixon must release all the tapes. Despite erasures on two key tapes, the House Judiciary Committee found evidence of three impeachable offenses: obstruction of justice, abuse of power, and contempt of Congress. On August 9, 1974, facing certain impeachment and conviction, Richard Nixon became the first president of the United States to resign.

The Watergate scandal shook Americans' confidence in their government. It also prompted Congress to pass several bills aimed at restricting presidential power, including the War Powers Act.

Ford's Presidency

Gerald Ford, the nation's first unelected president, faced a cynical nation. The presidency was discredited. The economy was in decline. The people were divided. When in one of his first official acts as president, Ford issued a full pardon to Nixon, his approval ratings plummeted from 71 to 41 percent.

While Ford was, overall, a decent and honorable man who tried to end what he called "the long national nightmare," he accomplished little during his two and a half years in office. The Democrats gained a large margin in the 1974 congressional elections and, after Watergate, Congress was willing to exercise its power. Ford almost routinely vetoed its bills—thirty-nine in one year—but Congress often overrode his veto. Ford was often portrayed as a buffoon and a klutz in political cartoons, comedy monologs, and on the new hit television show *Saturday Night Live*. After Nixon's actions, no longer would respect for the presidency prevent the media from reporting presidential stumbles, frailties, or misconduct.

Jimmy Carter The thirty-ninth president of the United States (1977–1981).

Carter as "Outsider" President

Jimmy Carter, who was elected in 1976 by a slim margin, initially benefited from Americans' suspicion of politicians. Carter was a one-term Georgia governor, one of the new southern leaders committed to racial equality. He had grown up on his family's peanut farm in rural Plains, Georgia, graduated from the Naval Academy, then served as an engineer in the navy's nuclear submarine program. Carter, a born-again Christian, promised Americans "I will never lie to you."

From his inauguration, when he broke with the convention of a motorcade and walked down Pennsylvania Avenue holding hands with his wife and close adviser, Rosalynn, and their daughter, Amy, Carter emphasized his populist, outsider appeal. But that status proved problematic as president, as he scorned the deal making necessary to get legislation through Congress.

More than any other post–World War II American leader, Carter was willing to tell Americans things they did not want to hear. As shortages of natural gas forced schools and businesses to close during the bitterly cold winter of 1977, Carter went on television—wearing a cardigan sweater—to call for "sacrifice" in a new era of limits. He also submitted a conservation-based energy plan to Congress. In the defining speech of his presidency Carter told Americans that the nation suffered from a crisis of the spirit. He talked about the false lures of "self-indulgence and consumption" and called for a "new commitment to the path of common purpose." But his words failed to inspire Americans to break free of what was then described as a national malaise.

Carter did score some domestic accomplishments. He eased burdensome government regulations without destroying consumer and worker safeguards, and created the Department of Energy and the Department of Education. He also established a $1.6 billion "superfund" to clean up abandoned chemical waste sites and placed more than 100 million acres of Alaskan land under federal government protection.

Economic Crisis

What were the long-term effects of the 1970s recession?

Since World War II, except for a few brief downturns, prosperity dominated American life. It had made possible the great liberal initiatives of the 1960s and improved the lives of America's poor and elderly citizens. But in the early 1970s, that long period of economic expansion ended. In 1974 alone, the gross national product dropped 2 percentage points. Industrial production fell 9 percent. Inflation skyrocketed, and unemployment grew.

Stagflation and Its Causes

Throughout most of the 1970s, the U.S. economy floundered in what economists dubbed "stagflation": a stagnant economy characterized by high unemployment combined with out-of-control inflation (see Figure 27.1). When the federal government increased spending to stimulate the economy and reduce unemployment, inflation grew. When it tried to control inflation by cutting government spending or tightening the money supply, the recession deepened and unemployment skyrocketed.

The causes of the economic crisis were complex. President Johnson had created inflationary pressure by waging an expensive war in Vietnam while expanding domestic spending in his Great Society programs. But America's changing role in the global economy also created problems. By the early 1970s, both of America's major wartime adversaries, Japan and Germany, had become major economic powers—and competitors in global trade. In 1971, for the first time since the end of the nineteenth century, the United States imported more than it exported, beginning an era of American trade deficits.

American corporations were also to blame. During the years of global dominance, few American compa-

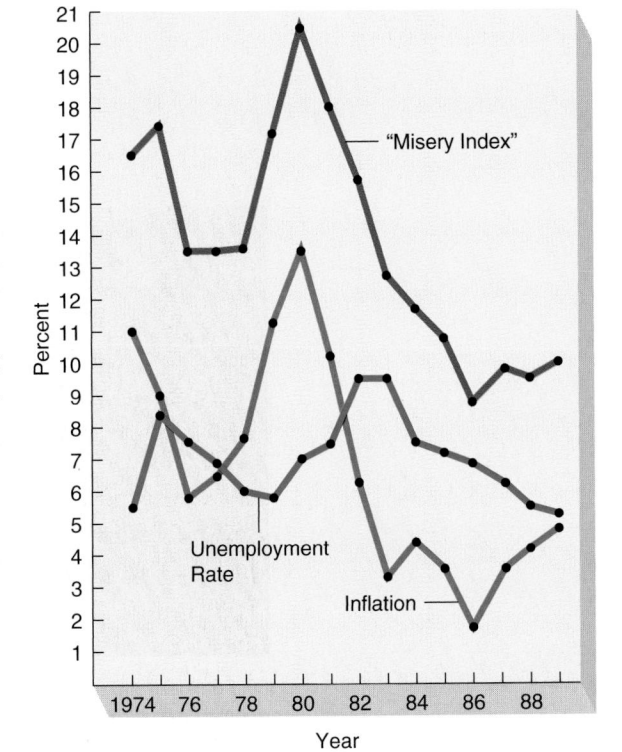

FIGURE 27.1

"Misery Index" (Unemployment Plus Inflation), 1974–1989

Americans' economic discomfort directly determined their political behavior. When the "misery index" was high in 1976 and 1980, Americans voted for a change in presidents. When economic discomfort declined in 1984 and 1988, Ronald Reagan and George Bush were the political beneficiaries.

(Source: Adapted from *Economic Report of the President, 1992* (Washington, D.C.: 1992), pp. 340, 365.)

nies improved production techniques or educated workers, and thus American productivity—the average output of goods per hour of labor—declined. But wages rarely did. High labor costs combined with falling productivity made American goods increasingly expensive. Worse, American companies had allowed the quality of their goods to decline. From 1966 to 1973, for example, American car and truck manufacturers recalled almost 30 million vehicles because of serious defects.

America's global economic vulnerability was driven home by the energy crisis that began in 1973. The country depended on imported oil for almost one-third of its energy. When OPEC cut off shipments to the United States, U.S. oil prices rose 350 percent and increased the costs of heating, shipping, manufacturing, goods, and services. Inflation jumped from 3 percent in early 1973 to 11 percent in 1974. Sales of gas-guzzling American cars plummeted as people switched to energy-efficient subcompacts from Japan and Europe. GM laid off 6 percent of its domestic workforce and put larger numbers on rolling unpaid leaves. As the ailing automobile industry quit buying steel, glass, and rubber, manufacturers of these goods laid off workers, too.

Attempts to Fix the Economy

American political leaders tried desperately to manage the economic crisis, but their actions often exacerbated it. As America's rising trade deficit undermined

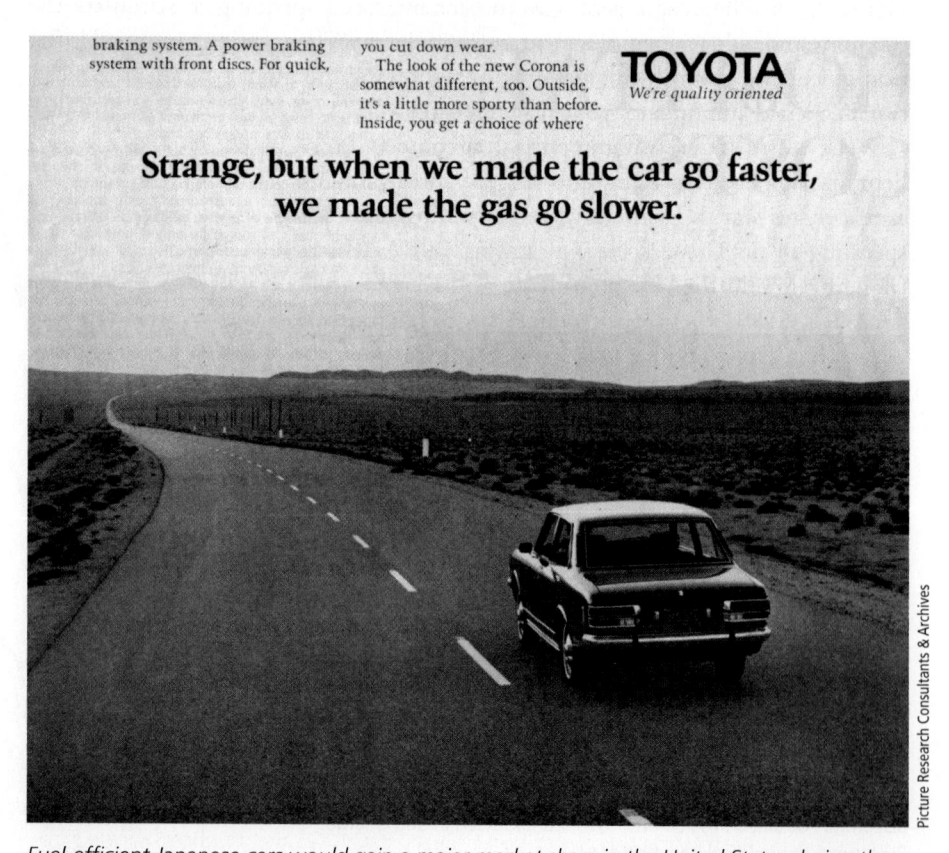

braking system. A power braking system with front discs. For quick, you cut down wear.

The look of the new Corona is somewhat different, too. Outside, it's a little more sporty than before. Inside, you get a choice of where

TOYOTA *We're quality oriented*

Strange, but when we made the car go faster, we made the gas go slower.

Picture Research Consultants & Archives

Fuel-efficient Japanese cars would gain a major market share in the United States during the energy crisis of the 1970s. This 1970 Toyota ad signals Japan's growing competitiveness in global trade.

international confidence in the dollar, the Nixon administration ended the dollar's link to the gold standard; free-floating exchange rates increased prices of foreign goods in the United States and stimulated inflation. Ford followed the tenets of monetary theory, which held that, with less money available to "chase" the supply of goods, price increases would gradually slow down, ending the inflationary spiral. He curbed federal spending and encouraged the Federal Reserve Board to tighten credit, which prompted the worst recession in forty years. In 1975, unemployment reached 8.5 percent. Carter, like Ford, pinned his hopes on market competition and led a bipartisan effort to deregulate airline, trucking, banking, and communications industries. But after a decade of decline, Americans were losing faith in the economy and in their leaders' ability to manage it.

Impacts of the Economic Crisis

The 1970s economic crisis accelerated the nation's transition from an industrial to a service economy. During the 1970s, the American economy "deindustrialized." Automobile companies laid off workers. Steel plant closings left communities devastated. Other manufacturing concerns moved overseas, seeking lower labor costs and fewer government regulations. New jobs were created—27 million of them—but they were overwhelmingly in the "service sector": retail sales, restaurants, warehouse and transportation work. These jobs were typically nonunion, paid lower wages, and lacked health care benefits. Formerly successful blue-collar workers saw their middle-class standard of living slipping away.

In addition, more people were chasing fewer jobs. Married homemakers looked for work because inflation ate away at their husbands' wages. The large numbers of baby boomers entering the labor market only added pressure.

As the old industrial regions of the North and Midwest declined, people fled the "snow belt" or the "rust belt," speeding up the Sunbelt boom already in progress (see Map 27.1). The federal government had invested heavily in the South and West during the postwar era, especially in military and defense industries. The Sunbelt was primed for the rapid growth of modern industries and services—aerospace, defense, electronics, transportation, research, banking and finance, and leisure. City and state governments competed for businesses and investment dollars, in part by preventing the growth of unions. Atlanta, Houston, and other southern cities marketed themselves as cosmopolitan and racially tolerant; they bought sports teams and built museums. This population shift south and west, combined with the flight of middle-class taxpayers to the suburbs, created disaster in northern and midwestern cities. Only federal loan guarantees saved New York City from bankruptcy in 1975, and Cleveland defaulted on its debts in 1978.

Tax Revolts

Even as stagflation and Sunbelt growth transformed American politics, a "tax revolt" movement emerged in the West. In California, inflation had driven property taxes up rapidly, hitting middle-class taxpayers hard. Instead of calling for wealthy citizens and major corporations to pay a larger share, voters, who now viewed government as the problem, rebelled against taxation itself. California's Proposition 13, passed by a landslide in 1978, rolled back property taxes and restricted future

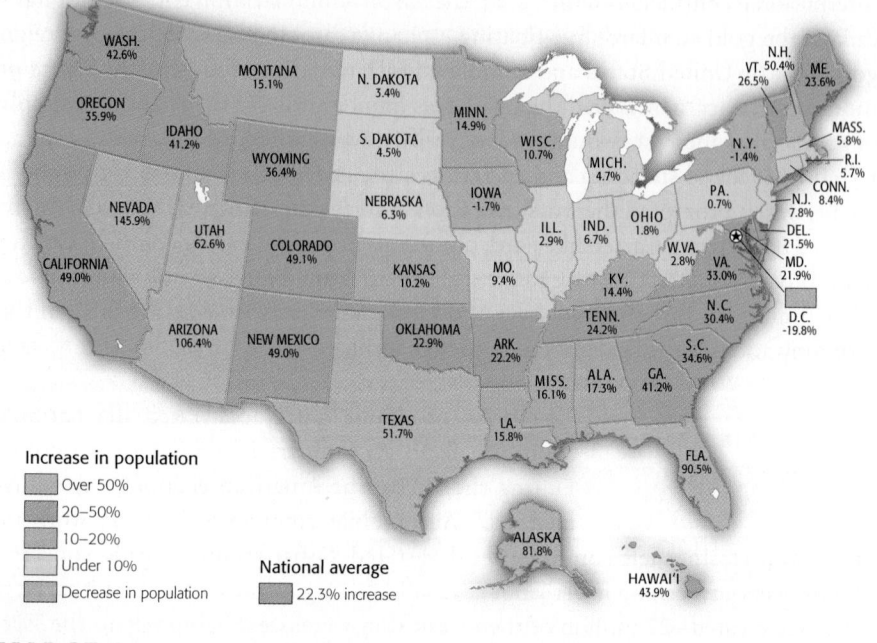

MAP 27.1

The Continued Shift to the Sunbelt in the 1970s and 1980s

Throughout the 1970s and 1980s, Americans continued to leave economically declining areas of the North and East in pursuit of opportunity in the Sunbelt. States in the Sunbelt and in the West had the largest population increases.

(Source: "Shift to the Sunbelt," *Newsweek*, September 10, 1990. Copyright © Cengage Learning 2015)

increases. Within months, thirty-seven states cut property taxes, and twenty-eight lowered state income tax rates.

The impact of Proposition 13 and similar initiatives was initially cushioned by state budget surpluses, but as those surpluses turned to deficits, states cut services—closing fire stations and public libraries, ending or limiting mental health services and programs for the disabled. Public schools were hit especially hard.

Credit and Investment

Before the runaway inflation of the 1970s, home mortgages and auto loans were the only major debt most Americans had. National credit cards had become common only in the late 1960s. In the 1970s, however, double-digit inflation rates made it economically smarter to buy goods before their prices went up—even if it meant borrowing the money. Because debt was paid off later with devalued dollars, the consumer came out ahead. In 1975, consumer debt hit a high of $167 billion; it almost doubled, to $315 billion, by 1979.

In the 1970s, Americans became investors rather than savers. Because banking regulations capped interest paid on individual savings accounts, a savings account bearing 5 percent interest actually *lost* more than 20 percent of its value from 1970 through 1980 because of inflation. That same money, invested at market rates, would have grown dramatically. Fidelity Investments, a mutual fund company, saw an opportunity: its money market accounts combined many smaller investments to purchase large-denomination Treasury bills and certificates of deposit, thus providing small investors the high interest rates normally available only to major investors. Money market investments grew from $1.7 billion in 1974 to $200 billion in 1982. Deregulation of the New York Stock Exchange spawned discount brokerage houses, whose low commission rates were affordable for middle-class investors.

An Era of Cultural Transformation

How did the new social mores of the 1970s impact family life?

As Americans struggled with economic recession, governmental betrayal, and social division, they also transformed American culture. The environmental movement, the growth of technology, the rise of born-again Christianity and a "therapeutic culture," contemporary forms of sexuality and the family, new roles for youth, and America's emphasis on diversity all have roots in the 1970s.

Environmentalism

A series of ecological crises drove home the fragility of the environment. In 1969, a major oil spill took place off the coast of Santa Barbara, California; that same year, the polluted Cuyahoga River, flowing through Cleveland, caught fire. In 1979, human error contributed to a nuclear accident at the Three Mile Island nuclear power plant near Harrisburg, Pennsylvania, and in 1980 President Carter declared a federal emergency at New York State's Love Canal, a dump site for a local chemical manufacturer, after it was discovered that 30 percent of local residents had suffered chromosome damage. Public activism produced major environmental initiatives, from the Environmental Protection Agency (EPA), created (under strong public pressure) in 1970 by the Nixon administration, to eighteen major environmental laws enacted by Congress during the decade.

When 20 million Americans—half of them schoolchildren—celebrated the first Earth Day on April 22, 1970, they signaled the triumph of a new understanding of environmentalism. Central to this movement was a recognition that the earth's resources were finite and must be both conserved and protected. Many also identified rapid global population growth as a problem, and state public health offices frequently dispensed contraceptives to stem this new "epidemic."

Technology

During these years, Americans became increasingly uneasy about the science and technology that had been one source of America's might. In a triumph of technology, American astronaut **Neil Armstrong** stepped onto the lunar surface on July 20, 1969. But technology could not cope with earthbound problems of poverty, crime, pollution, and urban decay; and the failure of technological warfare to deliver victory in Vietnam came at the same time antiwar protesters were questioning the morality of using such technology. Some Americans joined a movement for human-scale development, but the nation was profoundly dependent on complex technological systems. And it was during the 1970s that America's computer revolution began: the integrated circuit was created in 1970, and by 1975 the MITS Altair 8800—boasting 256 bytes of memory, and requiring about thirty hours to assemble—could be mail-ordered from Albuquerque, New Mexico.

Neil Armstrong First man to set foot on the moon.

Religion and the Therapeutic Culture

As Americans confronted material limits, they increasingly sought spiritual fulfillment. Although Methodist, Presbyterian, and Episcopalian churches lost members during this era, evangelical and fundamentalist Christian churches grew dramatically. Protestant evangelicals, describing themselves as "born again," emphasized the daily presence of God in their lives. Other Americans looked to the "New Age" movement, which drew from and often combined nonwestern spiritual and religious practices, including Zen Buddhism, yoga, and shamanism, along with insights from Western psychology and spiritually oriented environmentalism.

Also in the 1970s, America saw the emergence of a "therapeutic" culture. Although some were disgusted with the self-centeredness of the "Me Decade," best-selling books by therapists and self-help gurus insisted that individual feelings offered the ultimate measure of truth. Self-help books with titles like *I Ain't Much Baby—But I'm All I've Got* made up 15 percent of all best-selling books.

Sexuality and the Family

One such self-help book was *The Joy of Sex* (1972), which sold 3.8 million copies in two years. Sex became more visible in public culture during the 1970s, as television loosened its regulation of sexual content. In the early 1960s, married couples in television shows were required to occupy twin beds; in the 1970s, hit television shows included *Three's Company*, a comedy based on the then-scandalous premise that a single man shared an apartment with two beautiful female roommates—and got away with it by pretending he was gay. Donna Summers's 1975 disco hit "Love to Love You Baby" contained sixteen minutes of sexual moaning. Discos were sites of sexual display, both for gay men and for macho working-class cultures.

Sexual behaviors also changed. The seventies were the era of singles bars and gay bathhouses, but for most Americans, the "sexual revolution" meant broader public acceptance of premarital sex and a limited acceptance of homosexuality, especially among more educated Americans. More heterosexual young people lived together without marriage during the 1970s. When First Lady Betty Ford said on *60 Minutes* that she would not be surprised if her then-seventeen-year-old daughter Susan began a sexual relationship, it was clear that much had changed in the course of a decade.

Changes in sexual mores and in women's roles altered the American family as well. By the end of the 1970s, the birth rate had dropped almost 40 percent from its 1957 peak. Almost one-quarter of young single women in 1980 said they did not plan to have children. A rising percentage of babies was born to unmarried women, as the number of families headed by never-married women rose 400 percent. The divorce rate also rose, in part because states implemented "no fault" divorce. Americans also developed a greater acceptance of various family forms (like the blended family of television's *Brady Bunch*).

Youth

Young people gained new freedoms and responsibilities during the 1970s. In 1971, recognizing that the eighteen-year-old men who were eligible for the draft could not vote, Congress passed and the states quickly ratified the Twenty-sixth Amendment, which guaranteed the right of eighteen-year-olds to vote. Similarly, twenty-nine states lowered their minimum drinking age. Marijuana use skyrocketed, and several states moved toward decriminalization. In the early 1970s, some young people established communes and attempted to create countercultural worlds outside "the system." Later in the decade, others created the punk movement, which offered new physical and cultural spaces for youth through music and its do-it-yourself ethic.

Diversity

The racial justice and identity movements of the late 1960s and 1970s made Americans more aware of differences among the nation's peoples. The challenge was figuring out how to acknowledge the new importance of "difference" in public policy. The 1970s solution was the idea of "diversity." Difference was not a problem but a strength; the nation should not seek policies to diminish differences among its peoples but should instead seek to foster the "diversity" of its schools, workplaces, and public culture.

One major move in this direction came in the 1978 Supreme Court decision *Regents of the University of California v. Bakke.* Allan Bakke, a thirty-three-year-old white man with a strong academic record, had been denied admission to the medical school of the University of California at Davis. Bakke sued, charging that he had been denied "equal protection" of the law because the medical school's affirmative action program reserved 16 percent of its slots for racial minority candidates, who were held to lower standards. In 1978, the Supreme Court, in a split decision, decided in favor of Bakke. Four justices argued that any race-based decision violated the Civil Rights Act of 1964; four saw affirmative action programs as constitutionally acceptable. The deciding vote, though for Bakke, contained an important qualification. A "diverse student body," Justice Lewis Powell wrote, is "a constitutionally permissible goal for an institution of higher education." To achieve "diversity," educational institutions could consider race in admissions.

Renewed Cold War and Middle East Crisis

What was Carter's record regarding the Middle East?

When Jimmy Carter took office in 1977, he asked Americans to abandon their "inordinate fear of Communism." He vowed to reduce the U.S. military presence overseas, to cut back arms sales, and to slow the nuclear arms race. More than four hundred thousand American military personnel were stationed abroad, the United States had military links with ninety-two nations, and the CIA was active on every continent. Carter promised to avoid new Vietnams and to give more attention to environmental issues. He especially determined to improve human rights abroad—the freedom to vote, worship, travel, speak out, and get a fair trial. Like his predecessors, however, Carter identified revolutionary nationalism as a threat to America's global prominence.

Carter's Divided Administration

Carter spoke and acted inconsistently, partly because in the post-Vietnam years, no consensus existed in foreign policy and partly because his advisers squabbled among themselves. One source of the problem was

Zbigniew Brzezinski, a Polish-born political scientist who became Carter's national security adviser. An old-fashioned Cold Warrior, Brzezinski blamed foreign crises on Soviet expansionism. Carter gradually listened more to Brzezinski than to Secretary of State Cyrus Vance, an experienced public servant who advocated quiet diplomacy. Under Carter, détente deteriorated, and the Cold War deepened. Initially, Carter maintained fairly good relations with Moscow and scored some foreign policy successes around the world. The United States signed two treaties with Panama in 1977. One provided for the return of the Canal Zone to Panama in 2000, and the other guaranteed the United States the right to defend the canal after that time. The Senate narrowly endorsed both agreements in 1978. The majority agreed with Carter's argument that relinquishing the canal would improve U.S. relations with Latin America.

Camp David Accords

Agreements that were signed by Egypt's President Sadat and Israel's Prime Minister Begin following twelve days of secret negotiations—arranged by President Carter—at Camp David.

Camp David Accords

The crowning accomplishment of Carter's presidency was the **Camp David Accords**, the first mediated peace treaty between Israel and an Arab nation. In September 1978, at Camp David, Maryland, the president persuaded Israel and Egypt to agree to a peace treaty, gained Israel's promise to withdraw from the Sinai Peninsula, and forged a provisional agreement that provided for continued negotiations on the future status of the Palestinian people living in the occupied territories of Jordan's West Bank and Egypt's Gaza Strip (see Map 29.2). Other Arab states denounced the agreement for not requiring Israel to relinquish all occupied territories and for not guaranteeing a Palestinian homeland. But the accord, signed March 26, 1979, by Israeli prime minister Menachem Begin and Egyptian president Anwar al-Sadat, at least ended warfare along one frontier.

Soviet Invasion of Afghanistan

Carter's moment of diplomatic triumph did not last long. Relations with Moscow deteriorated, with U.S. and Soviet officials sparring over the Kremlin's reluctance to lift restrictions on Jewish emigration from the USSR, and over the Soviet decision to deploy new intermediate-range ballistic missiles aimed at Western Europe. Then, in December 1979, the Soviets invaded Afghanistan, a remote country whose strategic position made it a source of great-power conflict. Following World War II, Afghanistan struggled with ethnic and factional squabbling; in the 1970s, it spiraled into anarchy. In late 1979, the Red Army entered Afghanistan to shore up a faltering communist government under siege by Muslim rebels. Moscow officials calculated that they could be in and out of the country before anyone noticed.

Carter not only noticed but reacted forcefully. He suspended shipments of grain and high-technology equipment to the Soviet Union, withdrew a major new arms control treaty from Senate consideration, and initiated an international boycott of the 1980 Summer Olympics in Moscow. He also secretly authorized the CIA to distribute aid, including arms and military support, to the Mujahidin (Islamic guerillas) fighting the communist government and sanctioned military aid to their backer, Pakistan. Announcing the Carter Doctrine, the president asserted that the United States would intervene, unilaterally and militarily, should Soviet aggression threaten the petroleum-rich Persian Gulf. Carter warned aides that the Soviets, unless checked, would likely attack elsewhere in the Middle East, but declassified documents confirm what critics said: the Soviet invasion was limited and did not presage a push to the Persian Gulf.

Iranian Hostage Crisis   Carter simultaneously faced a tough foreign policy test in neighboring Iran. The shah, long the recipient of American favor, was dethroned by a broad coalition of Iranians, many of whom resented that their traditional ways had been dislocated by the shah's attempts at modernization. Riots led by anti-American Muslim clerics erupted in late 1978. The shah went into exile, and in April 1979 Islamic revolutionaries, led by the Ayatollah Khomeini, an elderly cleric who denounced the United States as the stronghold of capitalism and Western materialism, proclaimed a Shi'ite Islamic Republic. In November, with the exiled shah in the United States for medical treatment, mobs stormed the U.S. embassy in Tehran. They took American personnel as hostages, demanding the return of the shah to stand trial. The Iranians eventually released a few American prisoners, but fifty-two others suffered solitary confinement, beatings, and terrifying mock executions.

Unable to gain the hostages' freedom through diplomatic intermediaries, Carter took steps to isolate Iran economically, freezing Iranian assets in the United States. When the hostage takers paraded their blindfolded captives before television cameras, Americans felt taunted and humiliated. In April 1980, Carter broke diplomatic relations with Iran and ordered a daring rescue mission. But equipment failed and two aircraft collided, killing eight American soldiers. The hostages were not freed until January 1981, after Carter left office.

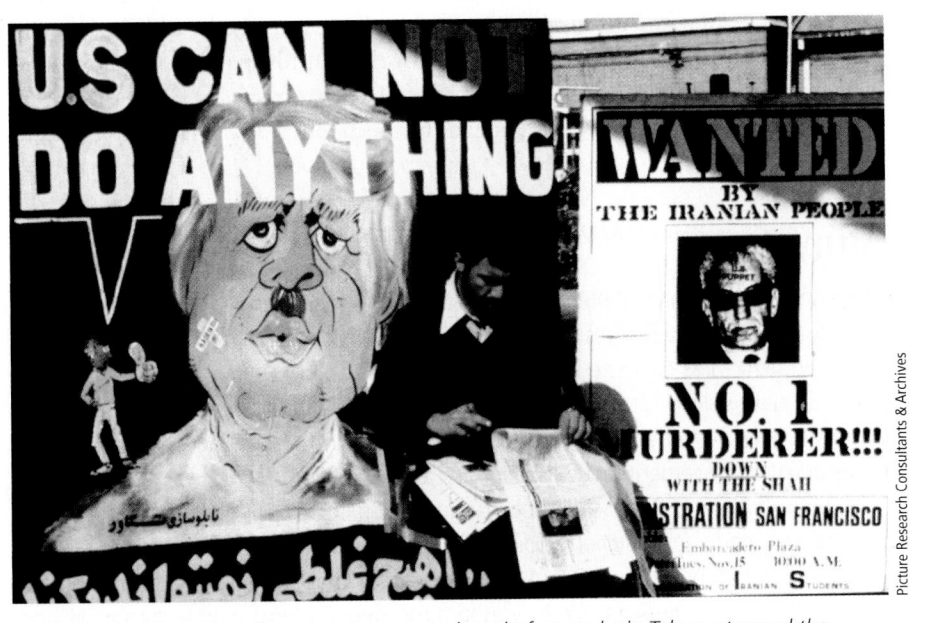

An Iranian is pictured reading a newspaper not long before mobs in Tehran stormed the American embassy and took more than fifty Americans hostage. Behind him are posters mocking U.S. president Carter and denouncing the shah.

Picture Research Consultants & Archives

The Iranian revolution, together with the rise of the Mujahidin in Afghanistan, signified the emergence of Islamic fundamentalism as a force in world affairs. Socialism and capitalism, the answers that the two superpowers offered to the problems of modernization, had failed to solve the problems in Central Asia and the Middle East. Nor had they assuaged feelings of humiliation generated by centuries of Western domination. As a result, Islamic orthodoxy found growing support for its calls to return to conservative Islamic values and Islamic law.

Rise of Saddam Hussein

U.S. officials took some consolation from Iran's troubles with the avowedly secular government in neighboring Iraq. Ruled by the quasi-socialist Ba'athist Party, Iraq had already won favor in Washington for its pursuit and execution of Iraqi communists. When a Ba'athist leader named Saddam Hussein took over as president of Iraq in 1979 and threatened the Tehran government, U.S. officials believed Saddam could offset the Iranian danger in the Persian Gulf. As border clashes between Iraqi and Iranian forces escalated into war in September 1980, Washington policymakers took an officially neutral position but soon tilted toward Iraq.

Carter earned some diplomatic successes in the Middle East, Africa, and Latin America, but the revived Cold War and the prolonged Iranian hostage crisis hurt the administration politically. Contrary to Carter's goals, more American military personnel were stationed overseas in 1980 than in 1976; the defense budget climbed and sales of arms grew to $15.3 billion in 1980. On human rights, the president practiced a double standard by applying the human rights test to some nations (the Soviet Union, Argentina, and Chile) but not to U.S. allies (South Korea, the shah's Iran, and the Philippines). Still, Carter's human rights policy saved the lives of some political prisoners, and he popularized and institutionalized concern for human rights around the world. But his inability to restore economic and military dominance dashed his reelection prospects. He lost the 1980 election to the hawkish Ronald Reagan, former Hollywood actor and governor of California.

Summary

From the crisis year of 1968 on, Americans were increasingly polarized—over the Vietnam War, over the best path to racial equality and equal rights, over the meaning of equality, and over the meaning of America itself. As many activists turned to "cultural nationalism," notions of American unity seemed a relic of the past. And though a new women's movement won victories against sex discrimination, a powerful opposition movement arose in response.

During this era, Americans became increasingly disillusioned with politics and presidential leadership. Richard Nixon's abuses of power in the Watergate scandal and cover–up, combined with growing awareness that the administration had lied repeatedly about America's role in Vietnam, produced a profound suspicion of government. A major economic crisis ended the post–World War II economic expansion,

The All-Volunteer Force

On June 30, 1973, the United States ended its military draft and turned to an all-volunteer force (AVF). The nation never had a peacetime draft before 1940, but as the country embraced global leadership after World War II, and as the dark shadow of the Cold War grew, the draft became an accepted part of American life. In 1973, more than 50 million American men had been inducted into the military since the end of World War II.

Richard Nixon had promised to end the draft during his 1968 presidential campaign, realizing that it was a focus for widespread protest against the Vietnam War. Ending the draft was not feasible during the war, but Nixon began planning for an all-volunteer force once in office. Many Americans supported the shift because they believed a president could not rely on a draft to compel people to fight a war they did not support.

The military, however, disliked Nixon's plan. The war in Vietnam had shattered morale and left the military—particularly the army— in disarray. Public opinion of the military was at an all-time low. How were they to attract volunteers?

The army, as the largest of the four services, required the most volunteers. To draw them, it ended make-work ("chickenshit") tasks and enhanced professionalism. It also turned to market research and advertising. Discovering that many men were afraid to lose their individuality in the army, the army's advertising agency launched a campaign telling potential volunteers, "Today's Army Wants to Join You."

The army needed about 225,000 recruits annually (compared to about 65,000 per year in 2009) and had difficulty attracting them. Within a decade, however, America's military boasted a higher rate of high school graduates than the comparable age population. During an era of relative peace, many young people found opportunities for education and training through military service. Military service was particularly attractive to capable but economically disadvantaged young people, a high percentage of whom were African American.

The proportion of women in the active military increased from 1.9 percent in 1972 to about 15 percent currently, and the roles they were allowed to fill widened. At the same time, the nation's understanding of military service changed. It was no longer an obligation of (male) citizenship. Instead, the military had to compete in the national labor market, often portraying service as "a good job." But in time of war, the legacy of the move to an AVF is highly charged. What does it mean when only a small number of volunteers bears the burden of warfare and most Americans never have to consider the possibility of going to war?

and Americans struggled with the psychological impact of a new age of limits and with the effects of stagflation.

Overseas, a string of setbacks—defeat in Vietnam, the oil embargo, and the Iranian hostage crisis—signified the waning of American power. Détente with the Soviet Union had flourished for a time; however, by 1980 Cold War tensions had again escalated. And the Middle East became an increasing focus of U.S. foreign policy.

Plagued by political, economic, and foreign policy crises, America ended the 1970s bruised, battered, and frustrated. The age of liberalism was long over; the turn toward marketplace solutions had begun, and the elements for a conservative resurgence were in place.

Chapter Review

Rights, Liberation, and Nationalism

What were the successes of the women's movement during the 1970s?

The women's movement made major gains in 1970s: the right of a married woman to obtain credit in her own name; the right of an unmarried woman to obtain birth control; women's right to serve on juries; and the end of sex-segregated help-wanted ads. Activists challenged definitions of rape that blamed the victim for the attack. Many worked for legalized abortion and won a major victory with the 1973 Supreme Court decision in *Roe v. Wade,* which ruled that privacy rights protected a woman's decision not to continue a pregnancy. By the end of the decade, more women worked as lawyers and served in the military, and women's athletics claimed a fairer share of university athletic budgets.

The End in Vietnam

What kept Nixon from ending the Vietnam War as quickly as he had hoped?

Nixon's policy in Vietnam was driven by a goal to end the war fast, partly so that it would not ruin his political career as it had Johnson's. But at the same time, he did not want to hurt American credibility as a world leader, and he still sought to prevent South Vietnam's defeat. Consequently, although he dramatically decreased the number of American troops from 543,000 in 1969 to 60,000 in 1970, he increased bombing of North Vietnam and neutral Cambodia, hoping to force the enemy into concessions. The North Vietnamese stood firm. A cease-fire was agreed to in 1973, and the communists claimed control of the entire country in 1975.

Nixon, Kissinger, and the World

How did the Vietnam War influence Nixon's approach to foreign policy?

The drawn-out struggle in Vietnam signified to Nixon that American power was limited. He adopted the Nixon Doctrine, which said the United States would provide economic aid but not troops to allies. In addition, he implemented détente, a policy aimed at creating improved Soviet-American relations and a reduced arms race within an environment of rivalry. With his historic trip to China in early 1972, he moved to end two decades of Sino-American hostility. Chinese leaders Mao Zedong and Zhou Enlai agreed with Nixon that the Soviet Union should be kept from making gains in Asia.

Presidential Politics and the Crisis of Leadership

How did Watergate bring down the Nixon administration?

Sometimes paranoid, Nixon directed aide Charles Colson to form a secret group called the Plumbers to dig up dirt on various groups, individuals, and political rivals. During Nixon's 1972 reelection campaign, some of the Plumbers were arrested while breaking into the Democratic National Committee headquarters in the Watergate complex. They had already bugged the Democratic National Committee offices and were going back to plant more surveillance equipment when they were caught by the D.C. police. While Nixon was not directly involved in this effort, he blocked FBI investigations into it—which constituted an obstruction of justice (an impeachable offense). He also initially refused to turn over his audiotapes of conversations in the Oval Office to congressional hearings. Eventually, he relinquished the tapes, although several contained significant gaps. Congress began impeachment hearings, and facing certain conviction and impeachment, on August 9, 1974, Nixon became the first U.S. president to resign.

Economic Crisis

What were the long-term effects of the 1970s recession?

The 1970s recession accelerated the nation's shift from an industrial to a service-based economy. As manufacturers in leading industries, such as automobiles and steel, laid off large numbers of workers or shifted to cheaper overseas production, new jobs opened in the lower-paid service sector, such as cashiers and waiters. Increasing numbers of married women went to work to keep their families afloat. Older industrial cities suffered decay, while the Sunbelt was well positioned to prosper with the growth of modern industries such as defense, aerospace, and finance. Double-digit inflation in the 1970s led people to buy goods before prices would rise, often on credit, fueling consumer indebtedness. Finally, with interest rates capped on savings accounts, people increasingly shifted to new forms of investment in mutual funds and the stock market.

An Era of Cultural Transformation

> How did the new social mores of the 1970s impact family life?

Increasing tolerance and openness about sex in the 1970s facilitated major changes in traditional notions of what constituted a family. There was a broader acceptance of premarital sex and limited acceptance of homosexuality. More heterosexual couples opted to live together without marrying. Though most did still marry, they married later and had fewer children. By decade's end, the birth rate dropped nearly 40 percent from its 1957 peak, and roughly 25 percent of single women said they did not intend to have children. Divorce rates rose as a result of new "no-fault" laws. Americans also developed a greater acceptance of a variety of family forms, including new blended families resulting from divorce and remarriage.

Renewed Cold War and Middle East Crisis

> What was Carter's record regarding the Middle East?

On the one hand, Carter achieved great success in mediating a peace treaty between Israel and Egypt in 1978. Although Arab states thought it fell short in not providing a Palestinian homeland and allowing Israel to maintain some of its occupied territories, it was a major first step toward a lasting settlement in the region. On the other hand, Carter angered Iranians when he provided protection for the exiled shah in the United States to seek medical treatment. Mobs stormed the U.S. embassy in Iran and took hostages to press for the shah to stand trial. Carter's inability to free the U.S. hostages contributed to his political downfall and defeat in his reelection bid in 1980.

Suggestions for Further Reading

Thomas Borstelman, *The 1970s: A New Global History from Civil Rights to Economic Inequality* (2012)

Jefferson R. Cowie, *Stayin' Alive: The 1970s and the Last Days of the Working Class* (2010)

Donald T. Critchlow, *Phyllis Schlafly and Grassroots Conservatism: A Woman's Crusade* (2005)

Daniel Ellsberg, *Secrets: A Memoir of Vietnam and the Pentagon Papers* (2002)

David Farber, *Taken Hostage: The Iran Hostage Crisis and America's First Encounter with Radical Islam* (2004)

Nancy MacLean, *Freedom Is Not Enough: The Opening of the American Workplace* (2006)

Lien-Hang Nguyen, *Hanoi's War: An International History of the War for Peace in Vietnam* (2012)

Rick Perlstein, *Nixonland: The Rise of a President and the Fracturing of America* (2008)

Ruth Rosen, *The World Split Open: How the Modern Women's Movement Changed America* (2000)

Hal Rothman, *The Greening of a Nation: Environmentalism in the U.S. Since 1945* (1997)

Odd Arne Westad, *The Global Cold War: Third World Interventions and the Making of Our Times* (2005)

28

Conservatism Revived

1980–1992

"It was hot and there was a lot of desert," Luisa Orellana remembered about crossing the Mexican border into the United States in the early 1980s. "All of us started running, each one with a child in our arms.... It rained so hard we couldn't see where we were going, but it helped because the Border Patrol couldn't see us either."

Three months earlier Luisa's father had been murdered. Tanis Stanislaus Orellana had worked in El Salvador with Archbishop Óscar Romero, the most powerful critic of the ruling military dictatorship whose death squads had murdered almost thirty thousand Salvadorans between 1979 and 1981. Romero was assassinated in 1980—shot as he consecrated the Eucharist during Mass. The civil war that followed lasted twelve years; an estimated 1 million Salvadorans fled to other nations, seeking refuge from the threat of torture, rape, and murder.

Luisa's family joined that exodus, fleeing after Tanis Orellana's murder. Taking a bus through Guatemala, they crossed illegally into Mexico and, sheltered by churches, made their way from Chiapas to Mexico City to Agua Prieta, on the U.S.-Mexico border.

Luisa and her family ran two miles through blinding rain. Cold, hungry, and scared, they were met by the Sanctuary movement, Americans who believed that the U.S. government's refugee policy offering asylum to those who fled violent repression and the threat of death or torture must include those who escaped the deadly civil wars ravaging Central America in the 1980s. The U.S. government had instead designated them "economic refugees" and denied them asylum.

The U.S. Sanctuary movement used church networks and human rights groups to verify Central American refugees' stories of rape, torture, and murder. Many members belonged to faith-based communities, although secular institutions, including several universities and the state of New Mexico, also participated. Some movement members went to prison, charged with transporting or harboring fugitives.

Luisa's family went from the sanctuary offered by Tucson churches, which were at the center of the movement, to live in the basement of a Spokane, Washington, Catholic church. In 1989, the U.S. government granted protection and work permits to Central American refugees. Luisa stayed in Washington, where she became a teacher of English as a second language.

The Orellana family was part of the "new immigration" that began in the early 1970s and grew throughout the 1980s, as record numbers of immigrants came to the United States from Asia, Mexico, Central and South America, and the Caribbean. Many from Central America, Vietnam, the Soviet Union, and Cuba were political refugees. The Orellanas found safety and peace in the United States, but not all immigrants—or all Americans—fared so well in the 1980s. Divisions between rich and poor increased. Social problems—drugs, violence, homelessness, the AIDS epidemic—made life even more difficult for the urban poor, while those on the other side of the economic divide enjoyed an era of luxury and ostentation.

Ronald Reagan's election in 1980 began a twelve-year period of Republican rule, as Reagan was succeeded by his vice president, George Bush, in 1988. Reagan was a popular president who seemed to embody the confidence shaken by the social, economic, and political crises of the 1970s. He drew support from a new conservative coalition: wealthy people who liked his pro-business policies; the religious New Right who sought the creation of "God's America"; and middle- and working-class whites attracted by Reagan's charisma and his embrace of "old-fashioned" values.

Reagan supported New Right social issues: he was anti-abortion, supported prayer in schools, ended Republican support for the Equal Rights Amendment, and appointed conservative Supreme Court and federal judges. Nonetheless, the Reagan administration focused primarily on political and economic conservative issues: reducing the size and power of the federal government and creating favorable conditions for business. The U.S. economy recovered from the stagflation of the 1970s and boomed through much of the 1980s. But corruption flourished in financial institutions freed from government oversight. By the end of the Reagan-Bush era, a combination of tax cuts and massive increases in defense spending had caused the budget deficit to increase fivefold.

Overseas, meanwhile, the Cold War intensified, then ended. The key figure in the intensification was Reagan, who promised to stand up to the Soviet Union. The key figure in ending the Cold War was Soviet leader Mikhail Gorbachev, who came to power in 1985. Gorbachev hoped to reform the Soviet system, not eradicate it, but he lost control of events as revolutions in Eastern Europe toppled communist regimes. In 1991, the Soviet Union disappeared. The Persian Gulf War of that same year demonstrated

LINKS TO THE WORLD *CNN*

LEGACY FOR A PEOPLE AND A NATION
The Americans with Disabilities Act

SUMMARY

America's unrivaled world power and the unprecedented importance of the Middle East in U.S. foreign policy.

As you read this chapter, keep the following questions in mind:

- **Ronald Reagan, campaigning for president in 1984, told voters, "It's morning again in America." How might Americans from different backgrounds judge the accuracy of his claim?**

- **What issues, beliefs, backgrounds, and economic realities divided Americans in the 1980s, and how do those divisions shape the culture and politics of contemporary America?**

- **Why did the Cold War intensify and then wane during the decade of the 1980s?**

A New Conservative Coalition

What factors contributed to the departure of working-class whites from the Democratic Party?

The 1970s were hard for Americans: defeat in Vietnam; the resignation of a disgraced president; the energy crisis; economic "stagflation," and the Iranian hostage crisis. Increasingly, Americans had lost faith in their government and in government-based solutions to the nation's problems. In 1980, when President Carter's approval rating stood at 21 percent, a diverse set of conservative groups forged a new coalition, coalescing around Republican candidate Ronald Reagan. The election of 1980 marked a sea change in American politics.

The End of the New Deal Coalition

The New Deal coalition—organized labor, urban ethnic and working-class whites, African Americans, and white southerners—had begun to splinter by the late 1960s, as large numbers of white southerners abandoned the Democratic Party. By 1980, the votes of urban working-class white Americans outside the South were also in play.

Changes in the economy had helped shift working-class politics. Labor unions had traditionally supported and been supported by the Democratic Party; as factories shut down or relocated to "right-to-work" states during the 1970s, union membership fell. Labor offered the Democratic Party smaller numbers, and loyalty to the Democratic Party had less pull on nonunionized workers.

As working-class whites faced new economic limits, government action often seemed incomprehensible or harmful. Affirmative action programs further reduced opportunities for working-class white men in a time of shrinking employment. White working-class parents often saw busing (sending children from racially segregated neighborhoods to other school districts to integrate schools) as threatening to their children. Some working-class whites felt outraged that they worked while others lived on taxpayer-funded welfare. While the majority of welfare recipients were white, opponents frequently portrayed welfare as a transfer of money from hardworking white families to indolent black ones.

Chronology

1980	Reagan elected president
1981	AIDS first observed in United States
	Economic problems continue; prime interest rate reaches 21.5 percent
	"Reaganomics" plan of budget and tax cuts approved by Congress
1982	Unemployment reaches 10.8 percent, highest rate since Great Depression
	ERA dies after STOP ERA campaign prevents ratification in key states
1983	Reagan introduces SDI
	Terrorists kill U.S. Marines in Lebanon
	U.S. invasion of Grenada
1984	Reagan aids contras despite congressional ban
	Economic recovery; unemployment rate drops and economy grows without inflation
	Reagan reelected
	Gorbachev promotes reforms in USSR
1986	Iran-contra scandal erupts
1987	Stock market drops 508 points in one day
	Palestinian *intifada* begins
1988	George H. W. Bush elected president
1989	Tiananmen Square massacre in China
	Berlin Wall torn down
	U.S. troops invade Panama
	Gulf between rich and poor at highest point since 1920s
1990	Americans with Disabilities Act passed
	Communist regimes in Eastern Europe collapse
	Iraq invades Kuwait
	South Africa begins to dismantle apartheid
1991	Persian Gulf War
	USSR dissolves into independent states
	United States enters recession
1992	Annual federal budget deficit reaches high of $300 billion at end of Bush presidency

Finally, many white working-class Americans were socially conservative. Catholics, for example, worried about government support for social change, including the Supreme Court's recognition of abortion rights in *Roe v. Wade*. Conservative questions about the proper limits of government gained a new hearing.

Growth of the Religious Right

By 1980, a newly powerful movement of social conservatives, based in fundamentalist Christian churches, was poised to influence American politics. Since the 1960s, America's mainline liberal Protestant churches—Episcopalian, Presbyterian, Methodist—had been losing members, while Southern Baptists and other denominations offering the experience of being "born again" through belief in Jesus Christ and the literal truth of the Bible (fundamentalism) had grown rapidly. Fundamentalist and evangelical preachers reached out through television: by the late 1970s, televangelist Oral Roberts was drawing 3.9 million viewers. Nearly 20 percent of Americans self-identified as fundamentalist Christians in 1980.

Most fundamentalist Christian churches stayed out of the social and political conflicts of the 1960s and early 1970s. But in the late 1970s, influential preachers began to mobilize for political struggle. In a 1980 "Washington for Jesus" rally, Pat Robertson told crowds, "We have enough votes to run the country." The Moral Majority, founded in 1979 by Jerry Falwell, sought to create a "Christian America," protecting the American family by fighting against the ERA and women's rights (he called NOW the "National Order of Witches"), gay rights, abortion, pornography, and the teaching of evolution and sex education in public schools.

Economic Conservatives

America's business community had also developed a strong political presence. The Business Roundtable, founded in 1972, brought together chief executive officers from *Fortune 500* corporations in order to leverage their financial power to shape politics. CEOs of corporations such as Sears, General Foods, and Westinghouse personally lobbied politicians, as the Roundtable pushed for deregulation and corporate tax breaks and investment credits.

Unlike the Business Roundtable, which emphasized the quiet influence of powerful CEOs, the U.S. Chamber of Commerce, which traced its origins to 1912, built a broadly based grassroots movement for capitalism that welcomed businesses of any size. By 1981, the chamber had 2,700 local Congressional Action Committees to lobby congressional representatives; they supported deregulation, lower taxes, and restricting the power of labor unions. And unlike the Business Roundtable, the chamber joined the religious right in its socially conservative agenda.

The Election of 1980

In 1980 inflation was in double digits. Mortgage rates approached 14 percent. Oil prices had skyrocketed. Unemployment lingered at the then-high rate of 7 percent. And fifty-two American hostages remained in captivity in Iran. Conservative leaders understood their opportunity to defeat Democratic incumbent Jimmy Carter.

Republican support quickly coalesced around **Ronald Reagan**, a former movie star and two-term governor of California. Reagan offered (in marked contrast to Carter) an optimistic vision of America's future. With his Hollywood charm and conservative credentials, he forged different sorts of American conservatives into a new political coalition.

Turnout was low on Election Day, but Reagan crushed Carter at the polls. And for the first time since 1952, the Senate majority went to the Republicans.

Ronald Reagan Former actor and California governor (1967–1975) who served as the fortieth president of the United States from 1981 to 1989.

Reagan's Conservative Agenda

Why did the emerging New Right support Ronald Reagan?

In the 1940s, as president of Hollywood's Screen Actors Guild, Reagan was a New Deal Democrat. But in the 1950s, as a corporate spokesman for General Electric, he became increasingly conservative. In 1964, Reagan's televised speech supporting Republican presidential candidate Barry Goldwater catapulted him to the forefront of conservative politics.

Elected governor of California two years later, Reagan became known for his right-wing rhetoric: America should "level Vietnam, pave it, paint stripes on it, and make a parking lot out of it." And in 1969, when student protesters occupied "People's Park" near the University of California in Berkeley, he threatened a "bloodbath," dispatching National Guard troops. Reagan was often pragmatic, however, about policy decisions. He denounced welfare but presided over reform of California's social welfare bureaucracy. And he signed one of the nation's most liberal abortion laws.

Reagan, at age sixty-nine the oldest American elected to the presidency, was not especially focused on the details of governing. When Carter briefed him on foreign and domestic policy, Reagan took no notes. Critics argued that his lack of knowledge could prove dangerous—as when he insisted that intercontinental ballistic missiles carrying nuclear warheads could be called back once launched.

But supporters insisted that Reagan focused on the big picture. While even supporters winced at his willingness to reduce complex policy issues to simple (and often misleading) stories, Reagan was to most Americans the "Great Communicator" who offered simple truths. He won admiration for his courage after he was seriously wounded in an assassination attempt just sixty-nine days into his presidency. Most important, Reagan had a clear vision for America's future. He and his advisers wanted to roll back fifty years of liberal policies that had made government increasingly responsible for the nation's economic health and for the social welfare of its citizens.

Attacks on Social Welfare Programs

Reagan, like traditional conservatives, believed that the federal government could not solve social problems. He also tapped into a backlash against Great Society programs. Many Americans who struggled to make ends meet resented paying taxes that, they believed, funded government "handouts." Lasting racial tensions also fueled public resentment: Reagan fed a stereotype of welfare recipients as unwed, black, teenage mothers who kept having babies to collect larger checks. In 1981, the administration cut welfare programs for the poor by $25 billion. But programs such as Aid to Families with Dependent Children and food stamps were small compared with Social Security and Medicare—social welfare programs that benefited Americans of all income levels. Major cuts for these popular programs proved impossible. The Reagan administration did shrink the *proportion* of the federal budget devoted to social welfare programs (including Social Security and Medicare) from 28 to 22 percent by the late 1980s—but only because it increased defense spending by $1.2 trillion.

Pro-Business Policies and the Environment

Reagan also attacked federal environmental, health, and safety regulations as reducing business profits and discouraging economic growth. Administration officials claimed that removing government regulation would restore the creativity of America's free-market system. However, they did not so much end government's role as deploy government power to aid corporate America.

Environmentalists were appalled when Reagan appointed James Watt, a well-known anti-environmentalist, as secretary of the interior. Watt was a leader in the "Sagebrush Rebellion," which sought to shift publicly owned lands in the West, such as national forests, from federal to state control. (The federal government controlled more than half of western lands.) But state control was not the sole issue; Watt's group wanted to open western public lands to private businesses for logging, mining, and ranching.

Telling Congress in 1981, "I don't know how many generations we can count on until the Lord returns," Watt dismissed concerns about protecting resources and public wilderness. He allowed private corporations to acquire oil, mineral, and timber rights to federal lands for minuscule payments. Watt was forced to resign in 1983 after he dismissively referred to a federal advisory panel as "a black … a woman, two Jews, and a cripple." But his appointment had already backfired, for his actions reenergized the environmental movement and provoked opposition from business leaders who understood that uncontrolled strip-mining and clear-cut logging could destroy lucrative tourism and recreation industries.

Attacks on Organized Labor

The pro-business Reagan administration undercut organized labor as well. In August 1981 Reagan intervened in a strike by the Professional Air Traffic Controllers Organization (PATCO). The air traffic controllers—federal employees, for whom striking was illegal—protested working conditions they believed compromised the safety of American air travel. Forty-eight hours into the strike, Reagan fired the 11,350 strikers, stipulating that they could never be rehired by the Federal Aviation Administration.

With the support of Reagan appointees to the National Labor Relations Board and an anti-union secretary of labor, businesses took an increasingly hard line with labor during the 1980s. Yet roughly 44 percent of union families had voted for Reagan in 1980, drawn to his espousal of old-fashioned values and vigorous anti-communist rhetoric.

The New Right

It is surprising that the religious New Right was drawn to Reagan, a divorced man without strong ties to religion or, seemingly, his own children. But Reagan endorsed the anti-abortion cause and prayer in public schools.

Reagan's judicial nominations also pleased the New Right. Though the Senate, in a bipartisan vote, refused to confirm Supreme Court nominee Robert Bork, Congress eventually confirmed Anthony M. Kennedy instead. Reagan also appointed Antonin Scalia, who would become a key conservative force, and Sandra Day O'Connor (the first female appointee) and elevated Nixon appointee William Rehnquist to chief justice. In 1986, the increasingly conservative Supreme Court upheld a Georgia law that punished consensual sex between men with up to twenty years in jail (*Bowers v. Hardwick*); in 1989, it ruled constitutional a Missouri law restricting the right to an abortion (*Webster v. Reproductive Health Services*), thus encouraging further challenges to *Roe v. Wade*. Overall, however, the Reagan administration did not push a conservative social agenda as strongly as some in the new Republican coalition had hoped.

Reaganomics

Why was the 1980s economic boom a mixed blessing?

The centerpiece of Reagan's domestic agenda was the economic program that took his name: Reaganomics. Traditional economic remedies failed to end stagflation: when the government increased spending to stimulate a stagnant economy, inflation skyrocketed; when it cut spending or tightened the money supply to reduce inflation, the economy plunged deeper into recession.

Reagan offered a simple answer. Instead of focusing on the complexities of global competition, deindustrialization, and OPEC's control of oil, Reagan argued that U.S. economic problems were caused by intrusive government regulation of business and industry, expensive social programs, high taxes, and deficit spending—in short, government itself. Reagan sought to "unshackle" the "free-enterprise" system from government regulation, slash social programs, cut taxes, and balance the budget by reducing the role of the federal government.

Supply-Side Economics

Reagan's economic policy was based largely on supply-side economics, the theory that tax cuts (rather than government spending) stimulate growth. According to a theory proposed by economist Arthur Laffer—his soon-to-be-famous Laffer curve—at some point rising tax rates discourage people from engaging in taxable activities (such as investing). As people invest less, the economy slows, and there is less tax revenue to collect. Cutting taxes reverses the cycle and increases tax revenues.

Although economists accepted the Laffer curve's broader principle, almost none believed that U.S. tax rates approached the point of disincentive. Even conservative economists were suspicious of supply-side principles. Reagan and his staff, however, sought a massive tax cut, arguing that corporations and individuals would invest funds freed up by lower tax rates, producing new plants, jobs, and products. And as prosperity returned, profits at the top would "trickle down" to the middle classes and even to the poor.

Reagan proposed to balance the federal budget through economic growth (created by tax cuts) and deep spending cuts, primarily in social programs. Congress cooperated with a three-year, $750 billion tax cut, at that point the largest in American history. Reagan's plan assumed $100 billion in cuts from programs including Social Security and Medicare, but Congress would not cut those benefits. Reagan, meanwhile, canceled out domestic spending cuts by dramatically increasing defense spending.

With major tax cuts, big increases in defense spending, and small cuts in social programs, the federal budget deficit exploded—from $59 billion in 1980 to more than $100 billion in 1982 to almost $300 billion by the end of George H. W. Bush's presidency in 1993. The Republican administrations borrowed money to make up the difference, transforming the United States from the world's largest creditor nation to its largest debtor (see Figure 28.1). The national debt grew to almost $3 trillion.

Harsh Medicine for Inflation

In 1981, the Federal Reserve Bank, an autonomous federal agency, raised interest rates for bank loans to an unprecedented 21.5 percent, battling inflation by tightening the money supply and slowing the economy. The nation plunged into recession. During the last three months of 1981, the gross national product (GNP) fell 5 percent and unemployment soared to 8 percent.

By late 1982, unemployment reached 10.8 percent, the highest rate since 1940. For African Americans, it was 20 percent. Reagan promised that consumers would lift the economy by spending their tax cuts. But as late as April 1983, unemployment remained at 10 percent, and people were angry. Jobless steelworkers paraded through McKeesport, Pennsylvania, carrying a coffin that bore the epitaph "American Dream." Agriculture, too, was faltering and near collapse. Farmers suffered from falling crop prices due to overproduction, as well as floods, droughts, and burdensome debts. Many lost their property to mortgage foreclosure; others filed for bankruptcy. Poverty rose to its highest level since 1965.

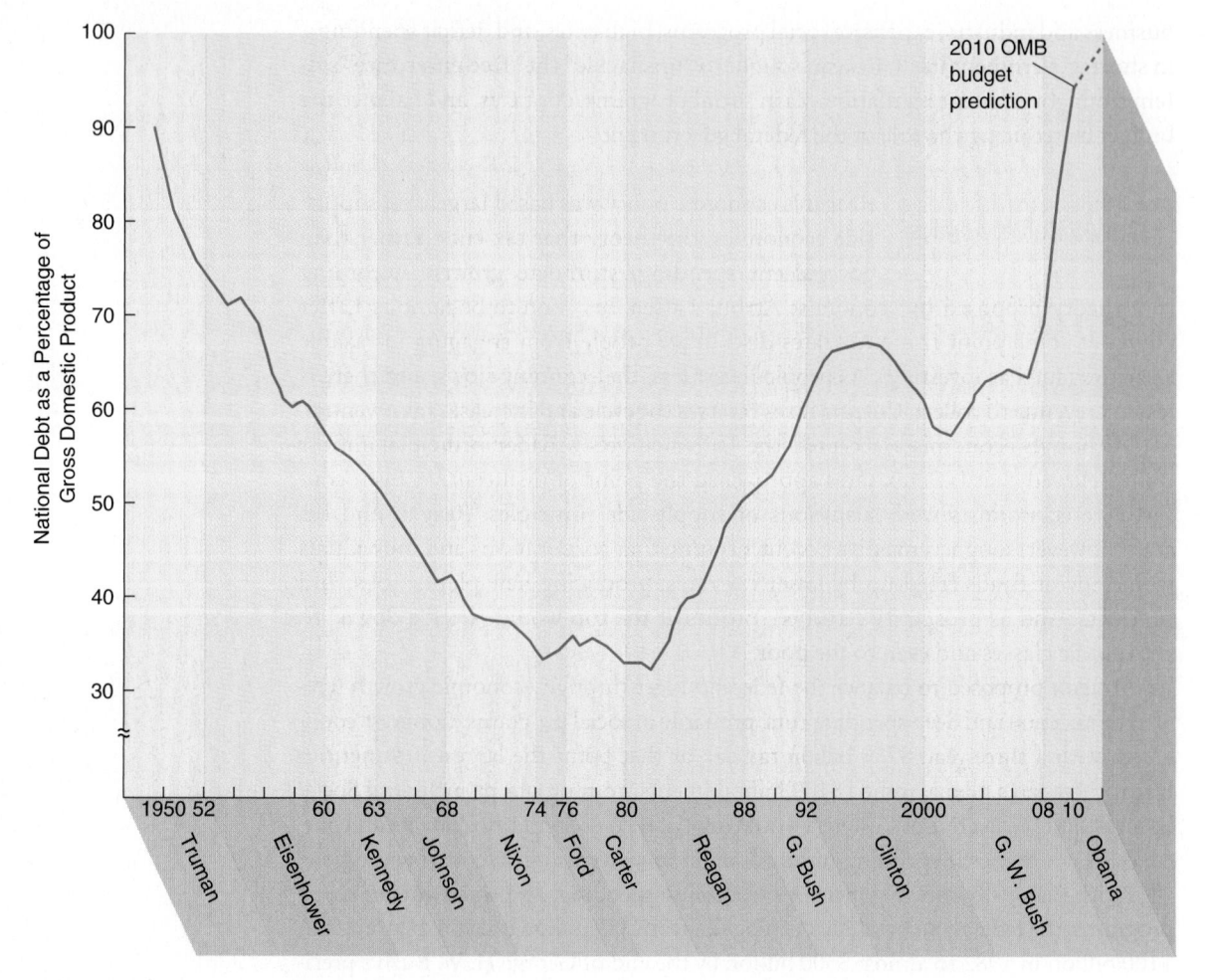

FIGURE 28.1

America's Rising National Debt, 1974–2010

America's national debt, which rose sporadically throughout the 1970s, soared to record heights during the 1980s. Under President Reagan, large defense expenditures and tax cuts caused the national debt to grow by $1.5 trillion.

(*Source:* Adapted from U.S. Bureau of the Census, *Statistical Abstract of the United States* (Washington, D.C.: 1992), p. 315.)

It was harsh medicine, but the Federal Reserve Bank's plan worked. High interest rates helped drop inflation from 12 percent in 1980 to less than 7 percent in 1982. The economy also benefited from OPEC's 1981 decision to increase oil production, thus lowering prices. In 1984, the GNP rose 7 percent, the sharpest increase since 1951, and midyear unemployment fell to a four-year low of 7 percent.

"Morning in America" Reagan got credit for the recovery, though it had little to do with his supply-side policies. In fact, the 1984 Democratic candidate, former vice president Walter Mondale, insisted that the growing budget deficit would have dire consequences for the American economy and said that he would raise taxes.

Mondale also emphasized fairness; not all Americans, he said, were prospering in Reagan's America. Reagan, in contrast, proclaimed, "It's morning again in America." Reagan won in a landslide, with 59 percent of the vote. Mondale, with running mate Geraldine Ferraro—U.S. congresswoman from New York and the first woman vice presidential candidate—carried only his home state of Minnesota.

Deregulation

Deregulation, begun under Carter and expanded under Reagan, created new opportunities for business. The 1978 deregulation of the airline industry lowered ticket prices; airline tickets cost almost 45 percent less in the early twenty-first century (in constant dollars) than in 1978. Deregulation of telecommunications industries created competition for the giant AT&T, and long-distance calling became inexpensive.

The Reagan administration loosened regulation of the banking and finance industries and cut the enforcement ability of the Securities and Exchange Commission (SEC), which oversees Wall Street. In the early 1980s, Congress deregulated the nation's savings and loan institutions (S&Ls), organizations previously required to invest depositors' savings in thirty-year, fixed-rate mortgages secured by property within a fifty-mile radius of the S&L's main office. By ending government oversight of investment practices, while covering losses from bad S&L investments, Congress left no penalties for failure. S&Ls increasingly put depositors' money into high-risk investments and engaged in shady—even criminal—deals.

Junk Bonds and Merger Mania

High-risk investments typified Wall Street as well, as Michael Milken, a reclusive bond trader, pioneered the "junk bond" industry and created lucrative investment possibilities. Milken offered financing to debt-ridden corporations unable to get traditional, low-interest bank loans, using bond issues that paid investors high interest rates because they were high-risk (thus "junk") bonds. Many of these corporations were attractive targets for takeover by other corporations or investors—who, in turn, could finance takeovers with junk bonds. Such "predators" could use the first corporation's existing debt as a tax write-off, sell off unprofitable units, and lay off employees to create a more profitable corporation.

By the mid-1980s, hundreds of major corporations—including giants Walt Disney and Conoco—fell prey to

President Ronald Reagan, who created a major budget deficit by pairing large tax cuts with large increases in defense spending, brandishes his "Tax Ax" at a Chamber of Commerce lunch in 1986.

Photo by Diana Walker/Time Life Pictures/Getty Images

merger mania and "hostile takeovers." Profits for investors were staggering: counting investment returns, Milken's income was about $1 billion a year by 1987.

The American economy boomed. Although the stock market plunged 508 points on a single day in October 1987—losing 22.6 percent of its value, or almost double the percentage loss in the crash of 1929—it rebounded quickly. But this high-risk boom also had significant costs. Heightened competition and corporate downsizing often increased efficiency, but it meant layoffs for white-collar employees. The wave of mergers and takeovers left American corporations increasingly burdened by debt. It also helped to consolidate sectors of the economy—such as the media—under the control of a few players.

| The Rich Get Richer |

The high-risk, deregulated boom of the 1980s was rotten with corruption. By the late 1980s, insider trading scandals—in which people used "inside" corporate information unavailable to the general public to make huge profits trading stocks—rocked financial markets and sent some of the most prominent Wall Street figures to jail. S&Ls lost billions in bad investments, sometimes turning to fraud to cover them up. The Reagan-Bush administration's bailout of the S&L industry had a total price tag of more than half a trillion dollars.

During the 1980s, the rich got richer, and the poor got poorer (see Figure 28.2). Ten times as many Americans reported an annual income of $500,000 in 1989 as in 1980. By 1989, CEOs received, on average, 71 times an average worker's pay, up from a 20 to 1 ratio in 1965 (the ratio was 231 to 1 in 2011, down from a 2000 high

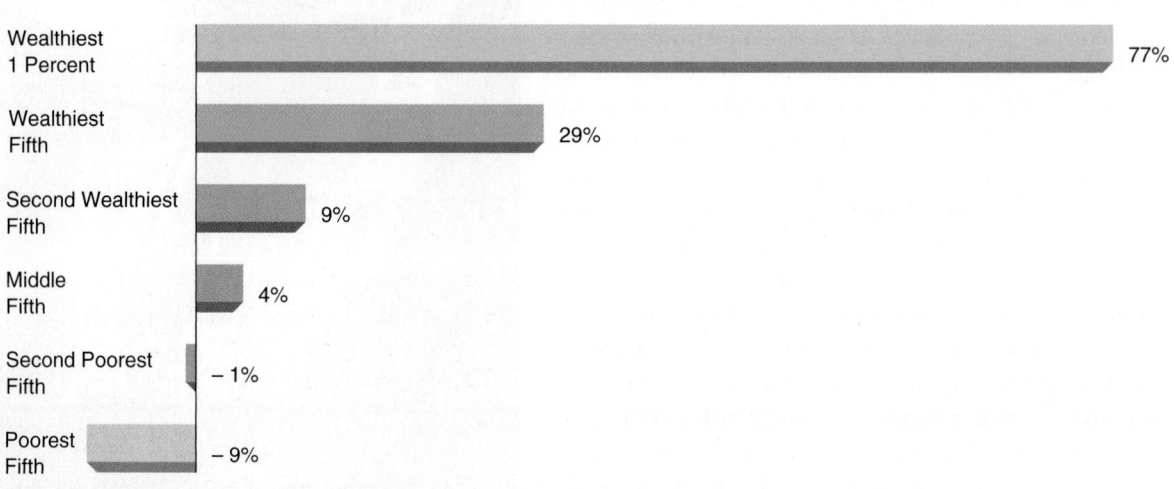

Percentage Increase in Pretax Income, 1977–1989

Wealthiest 1 Percent — 77%
Wealthiest Fifth — 29%
Second Wealthiest Fifth — 9%
Middle Fifth — 4%
Second Poorest Fifth — – 1%
Poorest Fifth — – 9%

FIGURE 28.2
While the Rich Got Richer in the 1980s, the Poor Got Poorer
Between 1977 and 1989, the richest 1 percent of American families reaped most of the gains from economic growth. In fact, the average pretax income of families in the top percentage rose 77 percent. At the same time, the typical family saw its income edge up only 4 percent. And the bottom 40 percent of families had actual declines in income.
(*Source:* Data from the *New York Times*, March 5, 1992.)

of 383 to 1). In 1987, the United States had forty-nine billionaires—up from one in 1978. But middle-class incomes were stagnant.

Most of the new inequality was due to Reagan's economic policies. His administration decreased the "total effective tax rates"—income taxes plus Social Security taxes—for the top 1 percent of American families by 14.4 percent. But it increased tax rates for the poorest 20 percent of families by 16 percent. By 1990, the richest 1 percent controlled 40 percent of the nation's wealth.

Reagan and the World

A key element in Reagan's winning strategy in the 1980 election was his call for the United States to assert itself in the world. Though lacking a firm grasp of international issues, history, and geography, Reagan adhered to a few core principles. One was a deep anticommunism; a second was an underlying optimism about the ability of American power and values to positively affect the world. Yet Reagan was also a political pragmatist, particularly as time went on and his administration became mired in scandal. Together, these elements help explain Reagan's aggressive anticommunist foreign policy and his positive response in his second term to Soviet leader Mikhail Gorbachev's call for "new thinking" in world affairs.

What characterized Reagan's approach to foreign policy?

Soviet-American Tension

Initially, Reagan and his advisers embraced the strident anticommunism of early Cold War U.S. foreign policy and rejected Nixon's détente and Carter's human rights focus. Where Nixon and Carter perceived an increasingly multipolar international system, the Reagan team reverted to a bipolar perspective defined by the Soviet-American relationship. Much of the intellectual ballast and moral fervor for this shift toward confrontation with Moscow came from **neoconservatives**, a small but influential group composed primarily of academics and intellectuals, many of them former Democrats who believed the party had lost its way after Vietnam. Key neoconservatives included Richard Perle and Paul Wolfowitz, who held mid-level positions in the administration.

When Poland's pro-Soviet leaders in 1981 cracked down on an independent labor organization, Solidarity, Washington restricted Soviet-American trade and hurled angry words at Moscow. In March 1983, Reagan told an audience of evangelical Christians in Florida that the Soviets were "an evil empire." That same year, Reagan restricted commercial flights to the Soviet Union after a Soviet fighter pilot mistakenly shot down a South Korean commercial jet that had strayed three hundred miles off course into Soviet airspace, killing 269 passengers.

Reagan believed that a substantial military buildup would thwart the Soviet threat. Accordingly, the administration launched the largest peacetime arms buildup in American history. In 1985, the military budget hit $294.7 billion (a doubling since 1980). Assigning low priority to arms control talks, Reagan announced in 1983 his desire for a space-based defense shield against incoming ballistic missiles: the **Strategic Defense Initiative (SDI)**. His critics tagged it "Star Wars" and

neoconservatives A small but influential group of intellectuals—typically former Democrats disillusioned with the party after Vietnam—who became part of Republican Ronald Reagan's conservative coalition.

Link to Ronald Reagan, "Evil Empire" Speech (1983)

Strategic Defense Initiative (SDI) Reagan's proposed program for developing a high-tech, space-based defense shield that would protect the United States against incoming ballistic missiles; nicknamed "Star Wars" by critics.

said perfecting such a system was scientifically impossible. Moreover, the critics warned, SDI would elevate the arms race to dangerous levels. SDI research and development consumed tens of billions of dollars.

Reagan Doctrine

Because he attributed Third World disorders to Soviet intrigue, the president declared the Reagan Doctrine: the United States would openly support anticommunist movements—"freedom fighters"—battling the Soviets or Soviet-backed governments. In Afghanistan, Reagan continued providing covert assistance, through Pakistan, to the Mujahidin rebels fighting Soviet occupation. When the Soviets stepped up the war in 1985, the Reagan administration sent high-tech weapons, including anti-aircraft Stinger missiles. Easily transportable and fired by a single soldier, the Stingers turned the tide in Afghanistan by making Soviet jets and helicopters vulnerable below twelve thousand feet.

The administration also applied the Reagan Doctrine aggressively in the Caribbean and Central America (see Map 28.1). In October 1983 Reagan sent U.S. troops into the tiny Caribbean island of Grenada to oust a pro-Marxist government. In El Salvador, he provided military and economic assistance to a military-dominated government struggling against left-wing revolutionaries. The regime used right-wing death squads, from which Luisa Orellana and her family fled. By decade's end, they had killed

MAP 28.1
The United States in the Caribbean and Central America

The United States has often intervened in the Caribbean and Central America. Geographical proximity, economic stakes, political disputes, security links, trade in illicit drugs, and Cuban leader Fidel Castro's longtime defiance of Washington have kept U.S. eyes fixed on events in the region. Source: Copyright © Cengage Learning 2015 forty thousand dissidents and citizens, as well as several American missionaries, and the United States had spent more than $6 billion there in a counterinsurgency war. In January 1992, the Salvadoran combatants finally negotiated a UN-sponsored peace.

Contra War in Nicaragua

The Reagan administration also meddled in the Nicaraguan civil war. In 1979, leftist insurgents overthrew Anastasio Somoza, a longtime U.S. ally. The revolutionaries called themselves Sandinistas in honor of Augusto César Sandino—who had headed the anti-imperialist Nicaraguan opposition against U.S. occupation in the 1930s and been assassinated by Somoza henchmen. When the Sandinistas aided rebels in El Salvador, bought Soviet weapons, and invited Cubans to help reorganize the Nicaraguan army, Reagan officials charged that Nicaragua was becoming a Soviet client. In 1981, the CIA began to train, arm, and direct more than ten thousand counterrevolutionaries, known as contras, to overthrow the Nicaraguan government.

Many Americans, including Democratic leaders in Congress, were skeptical about the communist threat and warned that Nicaragua could become another Vietnam. Congress in 1984 voted to stop U.S. military aid to the contras. Secretly, the Reagan administration lined up other countries, including Saudi Arabia, Panama, and South Korea, to funnel money and weapons to the contras, and in 1985 Reagan imposed an economic embargo against Nicaragua. In 1990, after Reagan had left office, Central American presidents brokered a settlement; in the national election that followed, the Sandinistas lost to a U.S.-funded party. After nearly a decade of civil war, thirty thousand Nicaraguans had died, and the ravaged economy was one of the poorest in the hemisphere.

Iran-Contra Scandal

Reagan's obsession with defeating the Sandinistas almost caused his political undoing. In November 1986, it became known that the president's national security adviser, John M. Poindexter, and an aide, marine lieutenant colonel **Oliver North**, in collusion with CIA director William J. Casey, had covertly sold weapons to Iran in an unsuccessful attempt to win the release of Americans held hostage by Islamic fundamentalist groups in the Middle East. Washington had condemned Iran as a terrorist nation and demanded that allies cease trade with the Islamic state. More damaging was the revelation that money from the Iran arms deal was illegally diverted to the contras. North later admitted he had lied to Congress to keep the operation clandestine: this after Congress had unambiguously rejected providing such aid.

Oliver North U.S. Marine colonel who became a central figure in the Iran-contra, arms-for-hostages scandal.

Although Reagan survived the **Iran-contra scandal**, his popularity declined, and Congress reasserted its authority over foreign affairs. In late 1992, outgoing president George Bush pardoned several former government officials convicted of lying to Congress. Critics smelled a cover-up, for Bush himself, as vice president, had participated in high-level meetings on Iran-contra deals. As for North, his conviction was overturned on a technicality.

Iran-contra scandal Scandal in which the Reagan administration illegally sold weapons to Iran to finance contras in Nicaragua.

U.S. Interests in the Middle East

The Iran-contra scandal also pointed to the increased importance in U.S. foreign policy of the Middle East and terrorism (see Map 29.1). The main U.S. goals in the Middle East remained preserving access to oil and supporting Israel, while checking Soviet influence. But in the 1980s American leaders faced new pressures from a deepened Israeli-Palestinian conflict and an anti-American and anti-Israeli Islamic fundamentalist movement that spread after the 1979 ouster of the shah of Iran.

The 1979 Camp David Accords between Israel and Egypt had raised hopes of a lasting settlement involving self-government for Palestinian Arabs living in the Israeli-occupied Gaza Strip and West Bank. Instead, Israel and the Palestinian Liberation Organization (PLO) remained at odds. In 1982, in retaliation for Palestinian shelling of Israel from Lebanon, Israeli troops invaded Lebanon. The beleaguered PLO and various Lebanese factions called on Syria to contain the Israelis. Thousands of civilians died. Soon after Reagan sent U.S. Marines to Lebanon to join a peacekeeping force, American troops became embroiled in a war between Christian and Muslim factions. In October 1983, terrorist bombs demolished a barracks in Lebanon's capital, Beirut, killing 241 American servicemen. Four months later, Reagan pulled the remaining marines out.

Terrorism

In the 1980s, numerous otherwise powerless groups, many of them associated with the Palestinian cause or with Islamic fundamentalism, relied on terrorism to further their aims. Often they targeted American citizens and property because of Washington's support of Israel and U.S. involvement in the Lebanese civil war. Of the 690 hijackings, kidnappings, bombings, and shootings around the world in 1985, 217 were against Americans, and most originated in Iran, Libya, Lebanon, and the Gaza Strip. Three years later, a Pan American passenger plane was destroyed over Scotland, probably by pro-Iranian terrorists.

Washington, allied with Israel, continued to propose plans for Israelis to give back occupied territories and for Arabs to stop attempting to push the Jews out of the Middle East. As the peace process stalled in 1987, Palestinians in the West Bank began an *intifada* (Arabic for "uprising") against Israeli forces. Israel refused to negotiate, but the United States talked with PLO chief Yasir Arafat after he renounced terrorism and accepted Israel's right to live in peace. For the PLO to recognize Israel and for the United States to recognize the PLO were major developments in the Arab-Israeli conflict.

In South Africa, too, American diplomacy became more aggressive. At first, the Reagan administration followed a policy of "constructive engagement"—asking the government to reform its white supremacist apartheid system. But many Americans demanded economic sanctions: cutting off imports from South Africa and pressuring 350 American companies to cease operations there. Some American cities and states passed divestment laws, withdrawing dollars from American companies active in South Africa. Public protest and congressional legislation forced the Reagan administration in 1986 to impose economic restrictions. Within two years, about half of the U.S. companies in South Africa left.

Enter Gorbachev

Many on the right disliked the South Africa sanctions policy—they believed the main black opposition group, the African National Congress (ANC), was dominated by communists, and they doubted the efficacy of sanctions. They also balked when Reagan, his popularity sagging, entered negotiations with the "evil empire." At a 1985 Geneva summit meeting, Reagan agreed in principle with new Soviet leader Mikhail S. Gorbachev's contention that strategic weapons should be substantially reduced, and at a 1986 Reykjavik, Iceland, meeting they came close to a major reduction agreement. SDI stood in the way: Gorbachev insisted it be shelved; Reagan refused. But Reagan and Gorbachev got along well, and Reagan toned down his anti-Soviet rhetoric.

Perestroika and *Glasnost*

The turnaround in Soviet-American relations stemmed more from changes abroad than from Reagan's decisions. Under Gorbachev, a younger generation of Soviet leaders came to power in 1985. They modernized the highly bureaucratized, decaying economy through a reform program known as *perestroika* ("restructuring") and liberalized the authoritarian political system through *glasnost* ("openness"). For these reforms to work, Soviet military expenditures had to be reduced.

In 1987, Gorbachev and Reagan signed the **Intermediate-Range Nuclear Forces (INF) Treaty** banning all land-based intermediate-range nuclear missiles in Europe. Gorbachev also reduced his nation's armed forces, helped settle regional conflicts, and began the withdrawal of Soviet troops from Afghanistan. The Cold War was coming to an end.

Intermediate-Range Nuclear Forces (INF) Treaty Treaty signed by U.S. president Reagan and Soviet leader Mikhail Gorbachev banning all land-based intermediate-range nuclear missiles in Europe, and resulting in the destruction of 2,800 missiles.

American Society in the 1980s

What divided Americans in the 1980s?

As the Cold War waned, so, too, did Americans' belief that the nation was united by shared, middle-class values. Indeed, many rejected that vision as undesirable. Though the 1980s were never as contentious as the 1960s and early 1970s, deep social and cultural divides split Americans. A newly powerful group of Christian conservatives challenged secular culture. A growing class of affluent Americans seemed a society apart from the urban poor. At the same time, immigration dramatically changed the composition of the population.

"Culture Wars"

Rejecting the "multiculturalist" belief that different cultures and lifestyle choices were equally valid, the New Right worked to make "God's law" the basis for American society. Concerned Women for America, founded by Beverly LaHaye in 1979, wanted elementary school readers containing "unacceptable" religious beliefs (including excerpts from *The Diary of Anne Frank* and *The Wizard of Oz*) removed from classrooms, and fundamentalist Christian groups again challenged teaching evolutionary theory in public schools. The Reagan administration frequently turned to James Dobson, founder of the conservative Focus on the Family organization, for policy advice.

Many other Americans vigorously opposed the New Right, which they saw as preaching intolerance and threatening basic freedoms—including freedom of religion. In 1982, prominent figures from the fields of business, religion, politics, and entertainment founded People for the American Way to support American civil

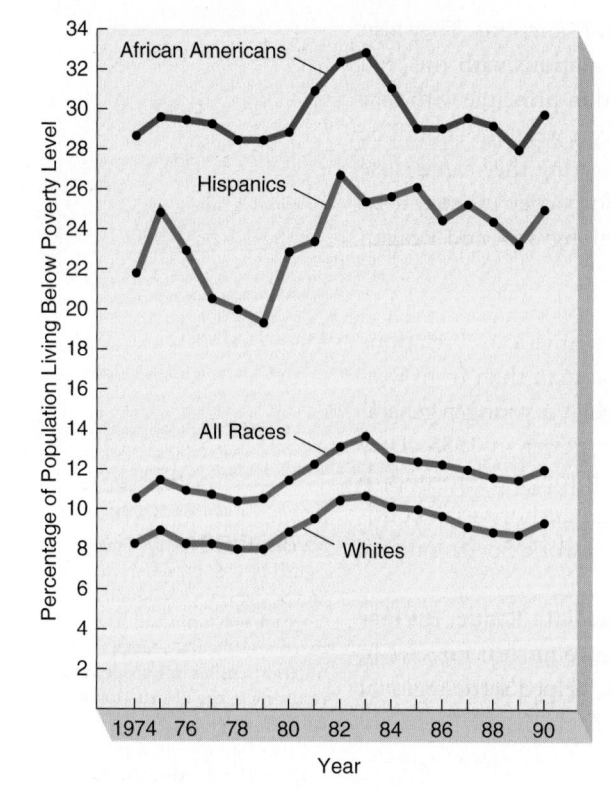

FIGURE 28.3

Poverty in America by Race, 1974–1990

Poverty in America rose in the early 1980s but subsided afterward. Many people of color, however, experienced little relief during the decade. Notice that the percentage of African Americans living below the poverty level was three times higher than that for whites. It was also much higher for Hispanics.

liberties, the separation of church and state, and tolerance and diversity. The struggle between the religious right and its opponents came to be known as the "culture wars."

Many New Right beliefs ran counter to the way most Americans lived—especially regarding women's roles. Legislation such as the Civil Rights Act of 1964 had opened both academic and athletic programs to girls and women. By 1985, more than half of married women with children under three worked outside the home—many from economic necessity. The religious right's insistence that women's place was in the home, subordinated to their husbands, contradicted the gains made toward sexual equality and the reality of many women's lives.

The New Inequality

As Americans fought the "culture wars" of the 1980s, another social divide threatened the nation. A 1988 national report on race relations looked back to the 1968 Kerner Commission report to claim, "America is again becoming two separate societies," white and black. The majority of America's poor were white, and the black middle class was expanding, but in 1980, 33 percent of blacks and 26 percent of Latinos lived in poverty, compared with 10 percent of whites (see Figure 28.3).

Reasons for poverty varied. For people of color, the legacies of racism played a role. The changing job structure was partly responsible, as well-paid jobs decreased, replaced by lower-paid service jobs. In addition, families headed by a single mother were more likely to be poor—five times more likely than families of the same race with two parents present. By 1990, a high rate of unwed pregnancy and a rising divorce rate meant that about one-quarter of all children lived in a single-parent household. Racial differences were significant: by 1992, 59 percent of African American children and 17 percent of white children lived in households headed by a single woman, and almost half of black children lived in poverty.

Social Crises in American Cities

In impoverished and often hopeless inner-city neighborhoods, violent crime—particularly homicides and gang warfare—grew alarmingly, as did school dropout rates, crime, and child abuse. Some people sought escape in hard drugs, especially crack, a derivative of cocaine, which first struck New York City's poorest neighborhoods in 1985. Gang shootouts over drugs were deadly: the toll in Los Angeles in 1987 was 387 deaths, more than half of them innocent bystanders. Many states instituted mandatory prison sentences for possessing small amounts of crack, making penalties for a gram of crack equivalent to those for 100 grams of cocaine, the drug of choice for more affluent, white Americans. This war on drugs, along with a crackdown on violent crime and a far more punitive criminal justice system, increased America's prison population almost four-fold. By 2000, young black men were more likely to have been arrested than to have graduated from a four-year college.

Homelessness also grew during the 1980s. Some of the homeless were impoverished families; many had drug or alcohol problems. About one-third were former psychiatric patients. By 1985, 80 percent of the total beds in state mental hospitals had been eliminated on the premise that small neighborhood programs would serve people better than large state hospitals. Such local programs never materialized. Consequently, many of America's mentally ill citizens wandered the streets.

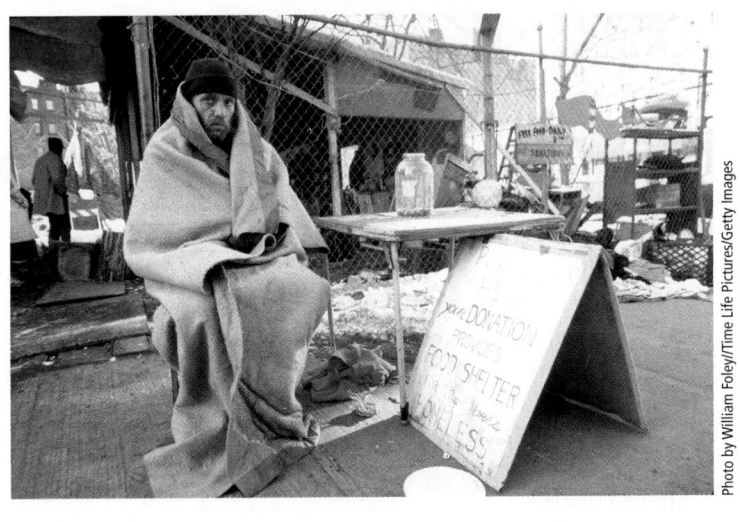

A homeless man collects donations for the Temple of Rainbow food kitchen in a vacant lot, 1988. Americans increasingly recognized homelessness as a major national problem during the 1980s.

The AIDS Epidemic

Another social crisis confronting Americans in the 1980s was the global spread of acquired immune deficiency syndrome, or **AIDS**. Caused by the human immunodeficiency virus (HIV), AIDS leaves its victims susceptible to deadly infections and cancers. HIV is spread through the exchange of blood or body fluids, often through sexual intercourse or needle sharing by intravenous drug users.

AIDS Acquired immune deficiency syndrome, first diagnosed in the United States in 1981; had a very high mortality rate in the 1980s.

AIDS was first diagnosed in the United States in 1981. During the 1980s it seemed an almost certain death sentence. Politicians were slow to devote resources to AIDS, in part because it was initially perceived as a "gay man's disease." A new group, ACT UP (the AIDS Coalition to Unleash Power), staged guerilla, agitprop demonstrations to confront "the system" that was so slow to address the threat of AIDS; for example, ACT UP wrapped the home of conservative senator Jesse Helms in a huge, custom-made condom. AIDS, and other sexually transmitted diseases such as genital herpes and chlamydia, ended an era defined by penicillin and "the Pill," in which sex was freed from the threat of serious disease or unwanted pregnancy.

New Immigrants from Asia

Social divisions were further complicated by the arrival of new immigrants. Between 1970 and 1990, the United States absorbed more than 13 million new arrivals, most from Latin America and Asia.

Before the immigration act reforms of 1965, less than 1 percent of Americans were of Asian ancestry; that percentage more than tripled by 1990. Before 1965, most Asian Americans were of Japanese ancestry; Chinese or Filipino Americans made up most of the rest. There were only 603 Vietnamese residents of the United States in 1964. By 1990, America had absorbed almost 800,000 refugees from Indochina, casualties of the Vietnam War. Immigrants flooded in from South Korea, Thailand, India, Pakistan, Bangladesh, Indonesia, Singapore, Laos, Cambodia, and Vietnam. Japanese Americans became only 15 percent of the Asian American population.

Immigrants from Asia were typically highly skilled or unskilled. Unsettled conditions in the Philippines created an exodus of well-educated Filipinos to the

Combating the Spread of AIDS

During the 1960s and 1970s, with penicillin offering a quick and painless cure for venereal diseases and with dependable, widely available contraceptives, such as the birth control pill, nonmonogamous sex had fewer physical risks than at any time in history. But new sexually transmitted diseases appeared during the 1980s. By far the most serious was HIV/AIDS (human immunodeficiency virus/acquired immune deficiency syndrome). Because AIDS initially was diagnosed in communities of gay men, many heterosexual Americans were slow to understand that they, too, might be at risk. Public health agencies and activist groups worked to raise awareness and promote safe sex. How is the couple in this ad portrayed? How does this image complicate widespread assumptions about who is at risk? And how does this public service advertisement make the case for "safe sex"?

Campaigns for "safe sex," such as this New York City subway ad, urged people to use condoms.

Sandro Tucci/Time Life Pictures/Getty Images

Applicants for visas wait in line at the U.S. embassy in New Delhi, India. In 1985, 140,000 people were on the waiting list for one of 20,000 annual immigrant visas. Many poorer nations, such as India, experienced a "brain drain" of highly educated people to the United States and Western Europe.

United States. India's abundance of physicians and health care workers increasingly emigrated, as did educated, skilled workers from Korea, Taiwan, and China. Other Chinese immigrants, however, had few job skills and spoke little or no English. Many crowded into neighborhoods like New York City's Chinatown, where women worked under terrible conditions in the city's nonunion garment industry. And even highly educated immigrants often found limited employment options.

The Growing Latino Population

Unprecedented immigration coupled with a high birth rate made Latinos the fastest-growing group of Americans. In 1970, Latinos comprised 4.5 percent of the nation's population; that jumped to 9 percent by 1990. Mexican Americans, concentrated in California and the Southwest, made up most of this population, but Puerto Ricans, Cubans, Dominicans, and other Caribbean immigrants also lived in the United States, clustered principally in East Coast cities.

During the 1980s, people from Guatemala and El Salvador, like the Orellana family, fled civil war and government violence. Many found their way to the United States even though the U.S. government commonly refused to grant them political asylum (about 113,000 Cubans received political refugee status during the 1980s, compared with fewer than 1,400 El Salvadorans) until 1989. Economic troubles in Mexico and throughout Central and South America also produced a flood of undocumented workers who crossed the poorly guarded two-thousand-mile border between the United States and Mexico, seeking economic opportunities. Some were sojourners who moved back and forth across the border. A majority meant to stay. These new Americans created a new hybrid culture that became an important part of the American mosaic.

Many Americans believed new arrivals threatened their jobs and economic security, and nativist violence and bigotry increased. In 1982, twenty-seven-year-old Vincent Chin was beaten to death in Detroit by an unemployed autoworker and his uncle. American auto plants were losing the competition with Japanese imports, and the two men seemingly mistook the Chinese American Chin for Japanese. In New

York, Philadelphia, and Los Angeles, inner-city African Americans boycotted Korean groceries. Riots broke out in Los Angeles schools between black students and newly arrived Mexicans. In Dade County, Florida, voters passed an antibilingual measure that removed Spanish-language signs on public transportation, while at the state and national level people debated declaring English the "official" U.S. language.

Concerned about illegal aliens, Congress passed the **Immigration Reform and Control (Simpson-Rodino) Act** in 1986. Its purpose was to discourage illegal immigration by imposing sanctions on employers who hired undocumented workers, but it also provided amnesty to millions who had immigrated illegally before 1982.

Immigration Reform and Control (Simpson-Rodino) Act A 1986 law that sought to discourage illegal immigration by fining employers who hired undocumented workers, but that also provided amnesty and a path to citizenship for millions who immigrated illegally before 1982.

New Ways of Life

Many Americans found their ways of life transformed during the 1980s due to new technologies and new models of distribution and consumption. American businesses made huge capital investments in technology as computers became central to the workplace. With new communications technology, large office parks could be located outside cities, where building costs were low, fostering "edge cities" or "technoburbs" filled with residents who lived, worked, and shopped outside the old city centers. New single-family homes grew larger; home prices rose from two and a half times the median household salary in 1980 to more than four times the median salary in 1988.

While the rich embraced ostentation (Donald Trump's $29 million yacht had gold-plated bathroom fixtures), people of more modest means also consumed more. Between 1980 and 1988, Wal-mart's sales jumped from $1.6 billion to $20.6 billion. The number of American shopping malls increased by two-thirds. Eating out became common. The percentage of overweight or obese Americans increased dramatically, even as people began to run marathons.

New technology went beyond the workplace. Almost half of American families owned a home computer by 1990. About half of all families subscribed to cable television by the middle of the decade. MTV (Music Television), launched in 1981, quickly became a national phenomenon. Early MTV stars included Michael Jackson, whose fourteen-minute "Thriller" video premiered there in 1983, and Madonna, whose creative manipulation of her own image, from "Boy Toy" sexuality to "Express Yourself" celebration of female empowerment, infuriated both sides in the culture wars. Movie attendance dropped as Americans bought newly affordable VCRs and rented movies.

The End of the Cold War and Global Disorder

What were the highs and lows of Bush's presidency?

The end of Ronald Reagan's presidency coincided with world events that brought the dawn of a new international system. Reagan's vice president, **George H. W. Bush**, would become president and oversee the transition. The scion of a Wall Street banker and former U.S. senator from Connecticut, Bush had attended an exclusive boarding school and then Yale. He had been a loyal vice president and possessed a formidable résumé—he had been ambassador to the United Nations, chairman of the Republican Party, special envoy to China, and director of the CIA. He had also been a war hero, flying fifty-eight combat missions in the Pacific in World War II and receiving the Distinguished Flying Cross.

George H. W. Bush The forty-first U.S. president (1989–1993).

George Herbert Walker Bush

In 1988, the Democratic Party nominated Massachusetts governor Michael Dukakis for president. On the Republican side, Bush built on Reagan's popularity, economic prosperity, and international stability. His camp also waged one of the most racially negative campaigns in American history, using a television commercial about a black convicted murderer from Massachusetts, Willie Horton, to charge that Dukakis was "soft on crime." Dukakis, while not personally attacking Bush, ran an uninspired campaign. Bush won by 8 percentage points in the popular vote, but the Democrats retained control of both houses of Congress.

From the start, Bush focused most of his attention on foreign policy, but domestic issues demanded his attention. Despite his oft-quoted campaign pledge, "Read my lips: no new taxes," when confronted with a rapidly growing federal deficit, Bush compromised with Congress and raised taxes. Bush believed that government could not solve the nation's social problems, yet he also believed government played an important role in the "kinder, gentler nation" he envisioned. In 1990, Bush signed the **Americans with Disabilities Act**, which banned job discrimination against those with disabilities who could, with reasonable accommodation, perform a job's essential tasks. It also required that "reasonable accommodations," such as wheelchair ramps, be made available. Much to the disappointment of conservatives, Bush signed the Clean Air Act, which sought to reduce acid rain by limiting factory and automobile emissions. And in 1991, Bush and Congress agreed on a civil rights bill that expanded the remedies victims of job discrimination could seek. However, Bush also nominated the highly conservative **Clarence Thomas** to the Supreme Court.

In world affairs, Bush was by nature cautious and reactive, much to the chagrin of neoconservatives. Gorbachev's reforms in the Soviet Union were now stimulating reforms in Eastern Europe that ultimately led to revolution. In 1989, thousands in East Germany, Poland, Hungary, Czechoslovakia, and Romania repudiated their communist governments and staged mass protests. In November 1989, Germans scaled the Berlin Wall and tore it down; the following October, the two Germanys reunited. By then, the other Eastern European communist governments had fallen or were near collapse.

Americans with Disabilities Act Law that barred discrimination against disabled persons in employment, transportation, public accommodation, communications, and governmental activities.

Clarence Thomas 1991 African American nominee for the Supreme Court appointed by Bush. As a justice, he has interpreted the Constitution narrowly, championing conservative social issues.

Pro-Democracy Movements

Challenges to communist rule in China met with less success. In June 1989, Chinese armed forces slaughtered hundreds—perhaps thousands—of unarmed students and citizens holding peaceful pro-democracy rallies in Beijing's Tiananmen Square. The Bush administration, anxious to preserve influence in Beijing, did no more than denounce the action, allowing the Chinese government to reject political liberalization.

Elsewhere, however, democratization efforts proved too powerful to resist. In South Africa, a new government under F. W. de Klerk began a cautious retreat from apartheid. In February 1990, de Klerk legalized all political parties in South Africa, including the ANC, and released Nelson Mandela, a hero to black South Africans, after a twenty-seven-year imprisonment. Then, the government repealed its apartheid laws over several years and allowed all citizens to vote. Mandela, who became South Africa's first black president in 1994, called the transformation "a small miracle."

| Collapse of Soviet Power | In 1990, the Soviet Union began to disintegrate. First the Baltic states of Lithuania, Latvia, and Estonia declared independence from Moscow. The following |

year, the Soviet Union ceased to exist, disintegrating into successor states—Russia, Ukraine, Tajikistan, and many others (see Map 28.2). Muscled aside by Russian reformers who thought he was moving too slowly toward democracy and free-market economics, Gorbachev lost power. The breakup of the Soviet empire, the dismantling of the Warsaw Pact (the Soviet military alliance formed in 1955 with communist countries of eastern Europe), the repudiation of communism by its leaders, German reunification, and a significantly reduced risk of nuclear war signaled the end of the Cold War.

The United States and its allies had won. The containment policy followed by nine presidents had many critics over the years, but it had succeeded on a most basic level: it had contained communism for four-plus decades without blowing up the world and without obliterating freedom at home. Two systems competed in this East-West confrontation, and that of the West had clearly triumphed.

Yet the Soviet empire might have survived longer had it not been for Gorbachev, one of the most influential figures of the twentieth century. Through a series of unexpected overtures and decisions, Gorbachev fundamentally transformed the superpower relationship in a way that could scarcely have been anticipated before. Reagan's role was less central but still vitally important because of his later willingness to negotiate and to treat Gorbachev more as a partner than as an adversary. Just as personalities mattered in starting the Cold War, so they mattered in ending it.

| Costs of Victory | The Cold War may never have become a hot war globally, but the period after 1945 nevertheless witnessed numerous Cold War–related conflicts claiming mil- |

lions of lives. In the Vietnam War alone, between 1.5 million and 2 million people died, more than 58,000 of them Americans. Military budgets ate up billions of dollars, shortchanging domestic programs. Some Americans wondered whether the communist threat was ever as grave as officials had claimed.

Bush proclaimed a "new world order" and signed important arms reduction treaties with the Soviet Union in 1991 and with the post-breakup Russia in 1993. But the United States sustained a large defense budget and continued to station large numbers of military forces overseas. Americans were therefore denied the "peace dividend" that they hoped would reduce taxes and free up funds to tackle domestic problems.

Link to George H. W. Bush, "New World Order" Speech (1991)

In Central America, the Bush administration cooled the zeal with which Reagan meddled, but Bush showed no reluctance to intervene to further U.S. aims. In December 1989, American troops invaded Panama to oust military leader Manuel Noriega. A longtime drug trafficker, Noriega had stayed in Washington's favor in the mid-1980s by providing logistical support for the Nicaraguan contras, but in the early 1990s, exposés of his sordid record changed Bush's mind. Noriega was captured and taken to Miami, where, in 1992, he was convicted of drug trafficking and imprisoned. Devastated Panama, meanwhile, became increasingly dependent on the United States, which offered little aid.

MAP 28.2

The End of the Cold War in Europe

When Mikhail Gorbachev came to power in the Soviet Union in 1985, he initiated reforms that ultimately undermined the communist regimes in Eastern Europe and East Germany and led to the breakup of the Soviet Union itself, ensuring an end to the Cold War.

Source: Copyright © Cengage Learning 2015

Saddam Hussein's Gamble

The strongest test of Bush's foreign policy came in the Middle East. The Iran-Iraq War ended inconclusively in August 1988, after eight years and almost four hundred thousand dead. The Reagan administration had assisted the Iraqis with weapons and intelligence, as had many NATO countries. In mid-1990, Iraqi president Saddam Hussein, facing massive war debts, invaded neighboring Kuwait, hoping to enhance his regional power, oil revenues, and domestic support. He hoped Washington would look the other way. Instead, Bush condemned the invasion and vowed to defend Kuwait, partly fearing that Iraq might threaten U.S. oil supplies in Kuwait and petroleum-rich Saudi Arabia.

Within weeks, Bush convinced virtually every important government, including most Arab and Islamic states, to agree to an economic boycott of Iraq. Then, in Operation Desert Shield, Bush dispatched more than 500,000 U.S. forces to the region, where they were joined by more than 200,000 from the allies. Likening Saddam to Hitler and declaring the moment the first post–Cold War "test of our mettle," Bush rallied a divided Congress to authorize "all necessary means" to oust Iraq from Kuwait (by a vote of 250 to 183 in the House and 52 to 47 in the Senate).

CNN

When Ted Turner launched CNN, his Cable News Network, on June 1, 1980, few people took it seriously. CNN, with a staff of three hundred—mostly young, mostly inexperienced—operated from the basement of a converted Atlanta country club. CNN was initially known for its on-air errors, as when a cleaning woman emptied anchor Bernard Shaw's trash during his live newscast. But by 1992, CNN was seen in more than 150 nations, and *Time* magazine named Ted Turner its "Man of the Year."

Throughout the 1980s, CNN built relations with local news outlets worldwide. When the Soviet Union wanted to denounce the 1989 U.S. invasion of Panama, officials called CNN's Moscow bureau instead of the U.S. embassy. Millions watched as CNN reporters broadcast live from Baghdad in the 1991 Gulf War. Saddam Hussein reportedly kept televisions in his bunker tuned to CNN, and in 1992, President George H. W. Bush noted, "I learn more from CNN than I do from the CIA."

Despite its global mission, CNN's American origins were often apparent. During the U.S. invasion of Panama, CNN cautioned correspondents not to refer to the American military forces as "our" troops. What CNN offered was a global experience: people throughout the world watching the major moments in contemporary history as they unfolded. CNN created new links among the world's people. But as *Time* magazine noted (while praising Turner as the "Prince of the Global Village"), such connections "did not produce instantaneous brotherhood, just a slowly dawning awareness of the implications of a world transfixed by a single TV image."

An employee at the CNN studios in Jerusalem dons a gas mask after an alarm sounds indicating an Iraqi missile attack on Israeli targets, January 19, 1991. CNN changed media history in the way its live coverage reported events as they unfolded.

Ricki Rosen/Corbis News/Corbis

Many Americans believed that economic sanctions should be given more time to work, but Bush would not wait. "This will not be another Vietnam," he said. Victory would come swiftly and cleanly.

Operation Desert Storm

Operation Desert Storm began on January 16, 1991, with the greatest air armada in history pummeling Iraqi targets. American missiles reinforced round-the-clock bombing raids on Baghdad, Iraq's capital. It was a television war, in which CNN reporters broadcast live from a Baghdad hotel as bombs fell. In late February, coalition forces under General Norman Schwarzkopf launched a ground war that quickly routed the Iraqis from Kuwait. When the war ended on March 1, at least 40,000 Iraqis had been killed, while allied forces lost 240 (148 of them Americans).

Bush rejected suggestions from advisers to take Baghdad and topple Hussein's regime. Coalition members would not have agreed to such a plan, and it was unclear who would replace Iraq's dictator. So Hussein remained, though with his authority curtailed. The UN maintained an arms and economic embargo, and the Security Council issued Resolution 687, demanding full disclosure of Iraq's program to develop weapons of mass destruction and ballistic missiles. In Resolution 688, the Security Council condemned the Iraqi regime's brutal crackdown against Kurds in northern Iraq and Shi'ite Muslims in the south and demanded access for humanitarian groups. The United States, Britain, and France seized on Resolution 688 to create a northern "no-fly zone" prohibiting Iraqi aircraft flights. A similar no-fly zone was set up in southern Iraq in 1992 and expanded in 1996.

Although some would later question Bush's decision to stop short of Baghdad, initially there were few objections. In the wake of Desert Storm, the president's popularity soared to 91 percent, beating the record 89 percent set by Harry Truman in June 1945 after Germany surrendered. Cocky advisers thought Bush could ride his popularity right through the 1992 election. But in the months following the Gulf War the nation entered a recession. Unemployment climbed to 8 percent. By late 1991, fewer than 40 percent of Americans felt comfortable with the nation's direction. By the time Bush and the Republicans entered the election year of 1992, the glow of military victory in the Gulf War had faded completely.

Legacy FOR A PEOPLE AND A NATION

The Americans with Disabilities Act

The Americans with Disabilities Act (ADA), passed by large bipartisan majorities in Congress and signed into law by President George Bush on July 26, 1990, built on the legacy of America's civil rights movement. Beyond prohibiting discrimination, it mandated that public and private entities—including schools, stores, restaurants and hotels, libraries and other government buildings, and public transportation authorities—provide "reasonable accommodations" to allow people with disabilities to participate fully in the life of their communities and their nation.

The equal-access provisions of the ADA have changed the landscape of America. Steep curbs and stairs once blocked access to wheelchair users; now ramps and lifts are common. Buses "kneel" for passengers with limited mobility; crosswalks and elevators use audible signals for the sight impaired. Colleges and universities offer qualified students (including those with learning disabilities) a wide range of assistance or accommodation. The National Park Service's "accessibility" program has enabled people with a whole spectrum of disabilities to travel into the Grand Canyon and on trails in many parks.

At the same time, ADA employment regulations have generated some difficult legal questions. Which conditions are covered by the ADA? (The Supreme Court has ruled that asymptomatic HIV infection is a covered disability and carpal tunnel syndrome is not.) Employers may not discriminate against qualified people who can, with "reasonable" accommodation, perform the "essential" tasks of a job—but what is "reasonable" and what is "essential"? The specific provisions of the ADA will likely continue to be contested and redefined in the courts. But as Attorney General Janet Reno noted, as she celebrated the tenth anniversary of the ADA, its true legacy is the determination "to find the best in everyone and to give everyone equal opportunity."

Summary

When Ronald Reagan left the White House in 1988, the *New York Times* wrote, "Ronald Reagan leaves no Vietnam War, no Watergate, no hostage crisis. But he leaves huge question marks—and much to do." George H. W. Bush met the foreign policy promises of the 1980s, as the Soviet Union collapsed and America won the Cold War. He also led the United States into war with Iraq, which ended swiftly but left Saddam Hussein in power.

During the 1980s, the United States moved from recession to prosperity. However, deep tax cuts and massive increases in defense spending increased the national debt from $994 billion to more than $2.9 trillion. Pro-business policies, such as deregulation, created opportunities for economic growth but also opened the door to corruption. Policies that benefited the wealthy at the expense of middle-class or poor Americans widened the gulf between the rich and everyone else. Drug addiction, crime, and violence grew, especially in the nation's most impoverished areas.

The 1980s also saw the coalescence of the "culture wars" between fundamentalist Christians who sought to "restore" America to God and opponents who championed separation of church and state and embraced liberal values. The nation shifted politically to the right, though the coalitions of economic and social conservatives that supported Reagan were fragile.

Finally, during the 1980s, American became more racially and ethnically diverse. The nation's Latino population grew in size and visibility. New immigrants from Asia arrived in large numbers. During the Reagan-Bush years, America had become both more divided and more diverse. In the years to come, Americans and their leaders would struggle with the legacies of the Reagan era.

Chapter Review

A New Conservative Coalition

> **What factors contributed to the departure of working-class whites from the Democratic Party?**

As factories relocated to "right-to-work" states or shut down during the 1970s, union membership fell. Labor offered the Democratic Party smaller numbers, and loyalty to the Democratic Party had less pull on nonunionized workers. At the same time, many working-class whites came to resent liberal government programs. They viewed affirmative action as reducing their opportunities in a time of shrinking employment. Parents viewed government busing programs as harmful to their children. White workers believed that their tax money went to support indolent blacks on welfare. Finally, many working-class families worried about federal government support for social change.

Reagan's Conservative Agenda

> **Why did the emerging New Right support Ronald Reagan?**

Reagan was a divorced man without strong ties to religion, but he supported New Right social issues. He endorsed the anti-abortion cause and prayer in public schools. His judicial nominations also pleased the religious New Right. He appointed Anthony Kennedy,

Antonin Scalia, and Sandra Day O'Connor and elevated William Rehnquist to chief justice. This increasingly conservative Court upheld a Georgia law that punished consensual sex between men with up to twenty years in jail and ruled that a Missouri law restricting the right to an abortion was constitutional. Overall, however, the Reagan administration did not push a conservative social agenda as strongly as some had hoped.

Reaganomics

Why was the 1980s economic boom a mixed blessing?

On the one hand, by 1984, the Federal Reserve's policy of increasing interest rates and tightening the money supply ended stagflation and reversed the economic downturn. And President Reagan's pro-business policies and deregulation helped create competition. On the other hand, deregulation allowed many businesses—particularly the financial services industry—to operate without accountability to governing authorities such as the SEC. Consequently, corruption was widespread, as some investors became rich via illegal insider trading. Shady deals in the savings and loan industry caused its collapse and required a federal bailout of half a trillion dollars. The high-risk investment climate fueled a stock market crash in 1987 and led to corporate downsizing and layoffs for white-collar workers. Finally, Reagan's tax cuts and other policies enabled the rich to get richer while the poor became poorer.

Reagan and the World

What characterized Reagan's approach to foreign policy?

In foreign policy, Reagan was both aggressive and flexible. In dealing with the Soviets, he initially adopted a strident anticommunist position, implementing the Reagan Doctrine to aid anticommunist "freedom fighters" around the world. He branded the Soviet Union as "an evil empire" and helped arm counterrevolutionaries to overthrow the Nicaraguan government he thought was becoming communist. Reagan launched the largest peacetime arms buildup in U.S. history, spending $294.7 billion in 1985 (twice as much as in 1980). But his optimism about the power of the United States to positively affect world events also led him in his second term to accept Soviet leader Mikhail Gorbachev's call for disarmament and new thinking in world affairs that led to the end of the Cold War.

American Society in the 1980s

What divided Americans in the 1980s?

Americans continued to feel the tug of unresolved racial and ethnic tensions, especially as the immigrant groups who arrived in the 1960s and 1970s (the majority from Asia and Latin America) changed the nation's demographic composition. The gulf—both economic and cultural—widened between well-off Americans and the urban poor. New lines were also being drawn between secular and religious forces, as a powerful new group of Christian conservatives sought to reverse what it regarded as society's increased permissiveness, to restore conservative family values, and to shape the nation's future around its Christian beliefs. The resulting battle, dubbed the "culture wars," pitted those who supported the separation of church and state and celebrated tolerance and diversity against this new religious right.

The End of the Cold War and Global Disorder

What were the highs and lows of Bush's presidency?

George H. W. Bush's popularity ratings soared to 91 percent after the United States' success in Operation Desert Storm. He scored kudos for passing the Americans with Disabilities Act, banning job discrimination against those with disabilities who can reasonably perform a job's task with minor accommodations. He also signed the Clean Air Act in 1990, which sought to reduce acid rain by restricting factory and auto emissions. But a recession emerged after the Gulf War, and unemployment climbed to 8 percent. By late 1991, less than 40 percent of Americans felt comfortable with the way the country was going.

Suggestions for Further Reading

Elijah Anderson, *Streetwise: Race, Class, and Change in an Urban Community* (1992)

Lou Cannon, *President Reagan: The Role of a Lifetime* (2000)

Robert M. Collins, *Transforming America: Politics and Culture During the Reagan Years* (2006)

Campbell Craig and Fredrik Logevall, *America's Cold War* (2009)

John Ehrman, *The Eighties: America in the Age of Reagan* (2005)

James A. Morone, *Hellfire Nation: The Politics of Sin in American History* (2003)

James Patterson, *The Restless Giant: The United States from Watergate to Bush v. Gore* (2005)

Kim Phillips-Fein, *Invisible Hands: The Making of the Conservative Movement from the New Deal to Reagan* (2009)

Mary Elise Sarotte, *1989: The Struggle to Create Post–Cold War Europe* (2009)

Into the Global Millennium

29

America Since 1992

A t 8:46 AM on that fateful Tuesday morning, Jan Demczur, a window washer, stepped into an elevator in the North Tower of the World Trade Center in New York City. The elevator started to climb, but before it reached its next landing, one of the six occupants recalled, "We felt a muted thud. The whole building shook. And the elevator swung from side to side like a pendulum." None of the occupants knew it, but American Airlines Flight 175 had just crashed into the building, at a speed of 440 miles per hour.

The elevator started plunging. Someone pushed the emergency stop button, and the descent stopped. Then a voice came over the intercom: there had been an explosion. As smoke seeped into the elevator, several men used the wooden handle of Demczur's squeegee to force open the doors. But they discovered they were on the fiftieth floor, where this elevator did not stop. In front of them was a wall.

Demczur, a Polish immigrant and former builder, saw that the wall was made of Sheetrock, a plasterboard he knew could be cut. Using the squeegee, the men took turns scraping and poking, and finally burst through to a men's bathroom. Startled firefighters guided them to a stairwell. They finally reached the street at 10:23 AM. Five minutes later, the tower collapsed.

It was September 11, 2001.

Later that day, Demczur learned that terrorists had hijacked four airliners and turned them into missiles. Two were flown into the World Trade Center; one slammed into the Pentagon in Washington, D.C.; and one crashed in a Pennsylvania field after passengers tried to retake the plane from the hijackers. Both World Trade Center towers collapsed, killing nearly three thousand people.

It was the deadliest attack the United States had ever suffered on its soil. The events sent shock waves around the globe, revealing just how interconnected the world had become at the dawn of the twenty-first century. At the World Trade Center alone, nearly five hundred foreigners from more than eighty countries perished. Many of the victims were, like Demczur, immigrants who had come to New York seeking a better life; others were on temporary work visas. But all helped to make the World Trade Center a kind of global city within a city, where some 50,000 people worked and another 140,000 visited daily.

A symbol of U.S. financial power, the World Trade Center towers also represented the globalization of trade that had marked the 1980s and 1990s. The towers housed the offices of more than four hundred businesses, including some of the world's leading financial institutions—Bank of America, Switzerland's Credit Suisse Group, Germany's Deutsche Bank, and Japan's Dai-Ichi Kangyo Bank.

Globalization was a 1990s buzzword and went beyond trade and investment to include connections in commerce, communications, and culture. While the terrorists, tied to a radical Islamic group called Al Qaeda, sought to bring down that globalization, their attack depended on the same international technological, economic, and travel infrastructure that fueled global integration. Cell phones, computers, intercontinental air travel—the plotters made full use of these instruments of globalization in carrying out their attack.

Americans struggled to comprehend the meaning of the attacks. For most of them, the 1990s offered good times. The stock market soared, unemployment dropped, and more Americans owned homes. But the 1990s were also marked by violence and cultural conflict—the first multiethnic uprising in Los Angeles, domestic terrorism in Oklahoma City, school shootings, and hate crimes.

These were also years of political volatility. From the first days of Bill Clinton's presidency, conservative Republicans blocked the Democrats' legislative programs, and the GOP routed Democrats in the 1994 midterm elections. But Republicans alienated voters by shutting down the federal government in a budget standoff during the winter of 1995–1996, and Clinton was reelected in 1996. However, scandal plagued the Clinton White House, compromising the president's ability to lead.

Clinton's successor, George W. Bush, successful in an extremely close and controversial election, responded to the 9/11 attacks by declaring a "war on terrorism." Bush ordered U.S. forces into large-scale military action, first in Afghanistan, where Al Qaeda was headquartered with the blessing of the ruling Taliban regime, then in Iraq to oust Saddam Hussein's government. Militarily, the Taliban and the Iraqi government were quickly beaten. Al Qaeda, however, remained a threat, and in Afghanistan fighting resumed. In Iraq, U.S. occupying forces battled a large-scale insurgency. Bush's high approval ratings dropped, and though he won reelection in 2004, his second term was undermined by

VISUALIZING THE PAST
American War Dead

LINKS TO THE WORLD
The "Swine Flu" Pandemic

LEGACY FOR A PEOPLE AND A NATION
Twitter Revolution

SUMMARY

continued bloodshed in Iraq and scandal at home. In 2008, Democratic candidate Barack Obama won the presidency on a platform of hope and change. The election of the nation's first African American president was a moment of great symbolic importance, but Obama, who inherited two wars and a major recession, struggled to create the domestic transformations he had promised. The economic crisis drastically limited the scope for policy initiatives, and Obama operated in a deeply polarized climate. Nevertheless, he ended American combat involvement in Iraq and got Congress to pass the Patient Protection and Affordable Care Act, the most significant overhaul of the U.S. health care system since 1965. In November 2012 he won reelection.

As you read this chapter, keep the following questions in mind:

- **What was "the new economy" of the 1990s, and how did it contribute to the globalization of business?**

- **Did the attacks of September 11, 2001, change America in fundamental ways? Explain.**

- **Why did the United States wage wars in Iraq and Afghanistan in the decade after 9/11, and why did it struggle to prevail in both despite massive technological superiority?**

Social Strains and New Political Directions

What political struggles complicated Bill Clinton's first presidency?

Although the 1990s would be remembered for relative peace and prosperity, the decade did not start that way. Drugs, homelessness, and crime plagued America's cities. Racial tensions worsened; the gulf between rich and poor widened. The economy tipped into recession. Public disillusionment with political leaders ran strong. As the 1992 presidential election year began, Americans wanted a change.

Turmoil in L.A.

Racial tensions that troubled the nation erupted in the South Central neighborhood of Los Angeles in 1992. The violence (which the Korean community called Sa-I-Gu, or 4/29, for the date it began) was a multiethnic uprising that left at least fifty-three people dead. There was an immediate cause. A jury with no African American members had acquitted four white police officers charged with beating a black man, Rodney King, who had fled a pursuing police car at speeds exceeding 110 miles per hour.

The roots of the violence went deeper. Almost one-third of South Central residents lived in poverty—a rate 75 percent higher than for the city as a whole—after well-paid jobs disappeared during the deindustrialization of the 1970s and 1980s. Tensions increased as new immigrants arrived—Latinos from Mexico and Central America who competed with African American residents for jobs, as well as Koreans who established grocery stores and small businesses. Outside the legitimate economy, the Rollin' 40s Crips (an African American gang) and the 18th Street

Chronology

1992	Violence erupts in Los Angeles over Rodney King verdict		2001	Supreme Court settles contested presidential election in favor of George W. Bush
	Major economic recession			Economy dips into recession; period of low growth and high unemployment begins
	Clinton elected president			Al Qaeda terrorists attack World Trade Center and Pentagon
1993	Congress approves North American Free Trade Agreement (NAFTA)			United States attacks Al Qaeda positions in Afghanistan, topples ruling Taliban regime
1994	Contract with America helps Republicans win majorities in House and Senate		2003	United States invades Iraq, ousts Saddam Hussein regime
	Genocide in Rwanda		2004	Bush reelected
1995	Domestic terrorist bombs Oklahoma City federal building		2005	Hurricane Katrina strikes Gulf Coast
	U.S. diplomats broker peace for Bosnia		2006	By end of year, U.S. deaths in the Iraq War reach three thousand
1996	Welfare reform bill places time limits on welfare payments		2007	Major economic recession begins in December
	Clinton reelected		2008	Barack Obama elected president
1999	NATO bombs Serbia over Kosovo crisis		2009	Obama announces increased U.S. military commitment to Afghanistan; U.S. continues troop drawdown in Iraq
	Anti-globalization demonstrators disrupt World Trade Organization (WTO) meeting in Seattle		2010	Congress passes Patient Protection and Affordable Care Act
2000	Nation records longest economic expansion in its history		2011	U.S. Navy SEALs kill Osama bin Laden
			2012	Obama reelected president

gang (Latino) struggled over territory as the crack epidemic further decimated the neighborhood and the homicide rate soared. Many African American and Latino residents saw high prices in Korean-owned shops as exploitation, while Korean shopkeepers complained of shoplifting, robberies, even beatings. And police tactics had alienated most neighborhood residents.

Other sources of the conflict affected the American people as a whole. During the Bush (senior) administration, the nation's economy had grown slowly or not at all. The state of California, left in an impossible position by 1978's Proposition 13—the first in a series of nationwide "tax revolts" that cut property taxes while the population boomed—faced bankruptcy in mid-1992. Thirty states were in financial trouble in the early 1990s. Factory employment plummeted, and corporate downsizing cost well-educated white-collar workers their jobs as well. In 1992, the number of poor people in America reached the highest level since 1964.

Clinton's Victory

As the American economy suffered, so did President George H. W. Bush's approval rating. Despite the credit Bush gained for ending the Cold War and the quick victory in the Gulf War, economic woes and a lack of what he called the "vision thing" left him vulnerable in the 1992 presidential election. On Election

Bill Clinton Forty-second U.S. president, serving from 1993 to 2001. Clinton served as the governor of Arkansas for twelve years prior to his election to the U.S. presidency.

Hillary Rodham Clinton Wife of President Bill Clinton, she was directly involved in policymaking during her husband's presidency. She later served as a New York senator (2001–2009), ran for president, and served as secretary of state.

Newt Gingrich Republican congressman who co-authored the 1994 "Contract with America" pledging tax cuts, congressional term limits, tougher crime laws, anti-pornography measures, a balanced-budget amendment, and other reforms.

Day, Democratic nominee **Bill Clinton** and his running mate, Tennessee senator Al Gore, swept New England, the West Coast, and much of the industrial Midwest, even making inroads into an almost solidly Republican South and drawing "Reagan Democrats" back into the fold.

Clinton and the "New Democrats"

Bill Clinton was a larger-than-life figure, a born politician from a small town called Hope who had wanted to be president most of his life. At Georgetown University in Washington, D.C., during the 1960s he had protested the Vietnam War and (like many of his generation) maneuvered to keep himself out of it. Clinton had won a Rhodes Scholarship to Oxford, earned his law degree from Yale, and returned to his home state of Arkansas, where he was elected governor in 1978 at age thirty-two. Bill Clinton's wife, **Hillary Rodham Clinton**, was the first First Lady to have a significant career of her own. They met when they were both law students at Yale, where Hillary Rodham had made Law Review (an honor not shared by her husband).

Politically, Bill Clinton was a "new Democrat," advocating a more centrist—though still socially progressive—position for the Democratic Party. Clinton and his colleagues emphasized private-sector economic development, focusing on job training and other policies they believed would promote opportunity, not dependency. They championed a global outlook in foreign policy and economic development and emphasized an ethic of "mutual responsibility" and "inclusiveness."

Clinton plunged into an ambitious program of reform and revitalization, beginning with appointing a cabinet that "looks like America" in its diversity. But Republicans, determined not to allow Clinton the traditional "honeymoon" period, maneuvered him into attempting to fulfill a campaign pledge to end the ban on gays in the military before he secured congressional or military support. Amid controversy, Clinton accepted a "don't ask, don't tell" compromise that alienated liberals, conservatives, the gay community, and the military.

Clinton's major goal was affordable health care. But special interests mobilized in opposition: the insurance industry worried about lost profits; the business community feared higher taxes; the medical community was concerned about more regulation, lower government reimbursement rates, and reduced health care quality. The health care task force, cochaired by Hillary Rodham Clinton, could not defeat these forces, and health care reform failed.

"Republican Revolution" and Political Compromise

New-style Republicans challenged the beleaguered Clinton. In September 1994, more than three hundred Republican candidates for the House of Representatives endorsed the "Contract with America." Developed under the leadership of Georgia congressman **Newt Gingrich**, the "Contract" promised "the end of [big] government … [and] the beginning of a Congress that respects the values and shares the faith of the American family." It called for a balanced-budget amendment to the Constitution, reduction of the capital gains tax, a two-year limit on welfare payments (while making unmarried mothers under eighteen ineligible), and increased defense spending.

In the midterm elections, the Republican Party mobilized socially conservative voters to take control of both houses of Congress for the first time since 1954. Many Republicans believed their attempts to weaken federal power and to dismantle the welfare state would succeed.

But while many Americans applauded the idea of cutting government spending, they opposed cuts to specific programs, including Medicare and Medicaid, education and college loans, highway construction, farm subsidies, veterans' benefits, and Social Security. Republicans made a bigger mistake when they issued President Clinton an ultimatum on the federal budget. Clinton refused to accept their terms, and the government was forced to suspend all nonessential action during the winter of 1995–1996. An angry public blamed the Republicans.

Such actions showed Clinton's resolve. But Clinton also compromised with those to his political right. He signed the 1996 Personal Responsibility and Work Opportunity Act, a welfare reform measure mandating that heads of families on welfare must find work within two years (though states could exempt 20 percent of recipients), limiting welfare benefits to five years over an individual's lifetime, and making many legal immigrants ineligible. He also signed the Telecommunications Act of 1996, which reduced diversity in media by permitting companies to own more television and radio stations.

Clinton and Gore were reelected in 1996 (defeating Republican Bob Dole and Reform Party candidate Ross Perot), in part because Clinton stole some of the conservatives' thunder. He declared that "the era of big government is over" and invoked family values, a centerpiece of the Republican campaign.

Clinton's legislative accomplishments were modest but included the Family and Medical Leave Act, which guaranteed 91 million workers the right to take time off to care for ailing relatives or newborn children. The Health Insurance Portability and Accountability Act ensured that, when Americans changed jobs, they would not lose health insurance because of preexisting medical conditions. Clinton created national parks that protected 3.2 million acres of American land and made progress cleaning up toxic waste dumps.

Political Partisanship and Scandal

Political battles were divisive and ugly as the political right attacked Clinton with vehemence. Hillary Clinton was a frequent target; when she told a hostile interviewer during her husband's first presidential campaign, "I suppose I could have stayed home and baked cookies and had teas. But what I decided to do was pursue my profession," the *New York Post* called her "a buffoon, an insult to most women." Rumors of scandal plagued the White House, and an independent counsel's office headed by conservative Republican and former judge Kenneth Starr would spend $72 million investigating allegations of wrongdoing by the Clintons.

Although Starr found no evidence that the Clintons had done anything wrong in the 1970 real estate deal (Whitewater) he was originally charged to investigate, he offered evidence that Clinton had committed perjury when he testified to a grand jury that he had not engaged in sexual relations with twenty-two-year-old White House intern Monica Lewinsky. In the wake of these charges, Clinton became the second president to be impeached by the House of Representatives. However, the Republican-controlled Senate, responding at least in part to popular opinion, acquitted Clinton.

Many Americans condemned Clinton's actions but did not believe they rose to the level of "high crimes and misdemeanors" required for impeachment. Clinton was not the first president to engage in illicit sex. But after the 1970s Watergate scandals, the media no longer turned a blind eye to presidential misconduct. Competitive twenty-four-hour news networks relied on scandal, spectacle, and crisis to lure viewers. Partisan political wars created a take-no-prisoners climate. Both Republican Speaker of the House Newt Gingrich and his successor, Robert Livingston, resigned when evidence of their own extramarital affairs surfaced. Finally, as former Clinton aide Sidney Blumenthal writes, the impeachment struggle was part of the "culture wars": "a monumental battle ... [about] cultural mores and the position of women in American society, and about the character of the American people."

Domestic Terrorism

Political extremism beyond Washington exploded on April 19, 1995, when 168 people were killed in a bomb blast that destroyed the nine-story Alfred P. Murrah Federal Building in Oklahoma City. At first, many blamed Middle Eastern terrorists. But a charred piece of truck axle two blocks away, with the vehicle identification number still legible, led investigators to Timothy McVeigh, a white American and Persian Gulf War veteran. McVeigh sought revenge for the deaths of members of the Branch Davidian religious sect, whom he believed the FBI had deliberately slaughtered in a standoff over firearms charges two years before in Waco, Texas.

In subsequent months, reporters and government investigators discovered militias, tax resisters, and white-supremacist groups nationwide. Many of these groups saw federal gun control laws, such as the Brady Bill, signed into law in 1993, as a dangerous usurpation of citizens' right to bear arms. Members of these groups believed that the federal government was controlled by "sinister forces," including Zionists, cultural elitists, and the United Nations.

Clinton's Diplomacy

Internationally, the Clinton team faced less tumult. The demise of the Soviet Union had created a one-superpower world, in which the United States stood far above others. Yet in his first term Clinton was more wary in traditional aspects of foreign policy—great-power diplomacy, arms control, regional disputes—than in facilitating American cultural and trade expansion. Recalling the public's impatience in the Vietnam debacle, he was deeply suspicious of foreign military involvements.

Clinton's mistrust of foreign interventions was cemented by the difficulties in Somalia. In 1992, Bush had sent U.S. Marines to the East African nation as part of a UN effort to ensure that humanitarian supplies reached starving Somalis. But in summer 1993, when Americans were attacked there, Clinton withdrew U.S. troops. And to his later regret he did not intervene in Rwanda, where in 1994 the majority Hutus butchered eight hundred thousand of the minority Tutsis in a brutal civil war.

Balkan Crisis

That Somalia and Rwanda were on the policy agenda at all testified to the growing importance of humanitarian concerns in post–Cold War U.S. policy. Many administration officials argued for using America's power to contain ethnic hatreds, support human rights, and promote democracy worldwide. The notion was tested in the Balkans, where Bosnian Muslims, Serbs, and Croats were killing one another. Clinton talked tough against Serbian aggression and atrocities in Bosnia-Herzegovina, especially the Serbs' "ethnic cleansing" of Muslims through massacres and rape camps. He occasionally ordered air strikes, but he primarily emphasized diplomacy. In late 1995, American diplomats brokered a fragile peace.

But Yugoslav president Slobodan Milosevic continued the anti-Muslim and anti-Croat fervor. When Serb forces moved to violently rid Serbia's southern province of Kosovo of its majority ethnic Albanians, reports of Serbian atrocities and a major refugee crisis stirred world opinion and convinced Clinton to respond. In 1999, U.S.-led NATO forces launched a massive aerial bombardment of Serbia. Milosevic withdrew from Kosovo, where U.S. troops joined a UN peacekeeping force. The International War Crimes Tribunal indicted Milosevic and his top aides for atrocities.

Agreements in the Middle East

In the Middle East, Clinton tried to help the Palestine Liberation Organization (PLO) and Israel settle their differences. In September 1993, the PLO's Yasir Arafat and Israel's prime minister, Yitzhak Rabin, signed an agreement at the White House for Palestinian self-rule in the Gaza Strip and the West Bank's Jericho. The following year Israel signed a peace accord with Jordan.

Villagers flee towards the town of Glogovac, in the Pristina district of central Kosovo, at the height of the Kosovo crisis in 1999.

David Brauchli/Sygma/Corbis

Radical anti-Arafat Palestinians, however, continued terrorist attacks on Israelis, while extremist Israelis killed Palestinians and, in November 1995, Rabin himself. Only after American-conducted negotiations and renewed violence in the West Bank did Israel agree in early 1997 to withdraw forces from the Palestinian city of Hebron. Thereafter, the peace process alternately sagged and spurted.

The same could be said of international environmentalism efforts, which gained momentum in the 1990s. The George H. W. Bush administration had opposed many provisions of the 1992 Rio de Janeiro Treaty protecting the diversity of plant and animal species, and resisted stricter rules to reduce **global warming**. Clinton, urged on by Vice President Al Gore, signed the 1997 Kyoto Protocol, which aimed to combat carbon dioxide and other emissions. But facing strong opposition, Clinton never submitted the protocol to the Republican-controlled Senate.

global warming Worldwide surge in average temperatures most scientists attribute to greenhouse gas emissions.

Bin Laden and Al Qaeda

Meanwhile, the threat to U.S. interests by Islamic fundamentalism loomed. Senior White House officials worried that **Al Qaeda** (Arabic for "the base"), an international terrorist network led by Osama bin Laden, wanted to purge Muslim countries of what it saw as the profane influence of the West.

Al Qaeda A radical Islamic group founded in the late 1980s and headed by Osama bin Laden; it relies on an international network of cells to carry out terrorist attacks against the West, particularly the United States and its allies, in the name of Islamic fundamentalism.

The son of a Yemen-born construction tycoon in Saudi Arabia, bin Laden had supported the Afghan Mujahidin in their struggle against Soviet occupation. He then founded Al Qaeda and financed terrorist projects with his inheritance. He eventually masterminded attacks on American targets. In 1995, a car bomb in Riyadh killed 7 people, 5 of them Americans. In 1998, bombings at the American embassies in Kenya and Tanzania killed 224 people, including 12 Americans. In Yemen in 2000, a boat laden with explosives hit the destroyer USS *Cole*, killing 17 American sailors. Although bin Laden masterminded and financed these attacks, he eluded U.S. attempts to apprehend him. In 1998, Clinton approved a plan to assassinate him, but it failed.

Globalization and Prosperity

What concerns did critics raise about globalization?

For most Americans, the late 1990s was a time of unprecedented peace and prosperity. Between 1991 and 1999, the Dow Jones Industrial Average climbed from 3,169 to a high of 11,497. The booming market benefited the middle class and the wealthy, as mutual funds, 401(k) plans, and other new investment vehicles drew a majority of Americans into the stock market. In 1952, 4 percent of American households owned stocks; by 2000, almost 60 percent did.

At the end of the 1990s, unemployment was 4.3 percent—the lowest peacetime rate since 1957. That made it easier to implement welfare reform, and welfare rolls declined 50 percent. Both the richest 5 percent and the least-well-off 20 percent of American households saw their incomes rise almost 25 percent. But that translated to an average gain of $50,000 for the top 5 percent and only $2,880 for the bottom 20 percent, further widening the gap between rich and poor. Still, by 1999, more than two-thirds of Americans were homeowners—the highest percentage in history.

Just how much credit Clinton deserved for the improved economy is debatable. The roots of the 1990s boom were in the 1970s, when American corporations began investing in new technologies, retooling plants, and cutting labor costs by moving operations to the union-weak South and West and to countries such as China and Mexico, with cheap labor and lax pollution controls.

Digital Revolution

The rapid development of "information technology"— computers, fax machines, cell phones, and the Internet— had a huge economic impact in the 1980s and 1990s. New companies and industries sprang up, many headquartered in California's "Silicon Valley." By the late 1990s, the *Forbes* list of the 400 richest Americans featured high-tech leaders such as Microsoft's Bill Gates, the wealthiest person in the world with worth approaching $100 billion.

The heart of this technological revolution was the microprocessor. Introduced in 1970 by Intel, the microprocessor miniaturized a computer's central processing unit, enabling small machines to perform calculations previously requiring large machines. Computing chores that took a week in the early 1970s took one minute by 2000; the cost of storing one megabyte of information fell from over $5,000 in 1975 to 17 cents in 1999.

Clinton and his advisers helped further spur economic growth by abandoning the middle-class tax cut and making deficit reduction a top priority. White House officials rightly concluded that, if the deficit—which topped $500 billion—could be brought under control, interest rates would drop and the economy would rebound. By 1997, the deficit had been erased, and the gross national product rose by an average of 3.5 to 4 percent annually.

Globalization of Business

Journalist Thomas L. Friedman asserted that the post–Cold War world was "the age of **globalization**," characterized by the integration of markets, finance, and technologies. U.S. officials lowered trade and investment barriers, completing the **North American Free Trade Agreement (NAFTA)** with Canada and Mexico in 1993, and in 1994 concluding the Uruguay Round of the General Agreement on Tariffs and Trade (GATT), which lowered tariffs for the seventy member nations that accounted for about 80 percent of world trade. The Clinton administration also endorsed the 1995 creation of the **World Trade Organization (WTO)** to administer and enforce agreements made at the Uruguay Round. Finally, the president formed the National Economic Council to promote worldwide trade missions.

Multinational corporations were the hallmark of this global economy. By 2000, there were 63,000 parent companies worldwide and 690,000 foreign affiliates. Some, such as Nike and Gap, Inc., subcontracted some production to developing countries with low labor costs. World exports, which totaled $5.4 trillion in 1998, had doubled in two decades. U.S. exports reached $680 billion in 1998, but imports rose to $907 billion (for a trade deficit of $227 billion). Sometimes the multinationals affected foreign policy, as when Clinton in 1995 extended full diplomatic recognition to Vietnam under pressure from

globalization The removal of barriers to the flow of capital, goods, and ideas across national borders.

North American Free Trade Agreement (NAFTA) Pact that admitted Mexico to the free-trade zone that the United States and Canada had created earlier.

Link to The North American Free Trade Agreement

World Trade Organization (WTO) International organization that regulates the global trading system and provides dispute resolution between member nations.

AP Photo/Beth A. Keiser

Protesting that the World Trade Organization (WTO) possessed the dangerous power to challenge any nation's environmental laws if the WTO deemed them barriers to trade, chanting demonstrators marched in the streets of Seattle on November 29, 1999. Critics of the WTO have claimed that sea turtles and dolphins had already been victimized by the organization. Demonstrators identified the WTO as an example of globalization gone wrong. The WTO meeting went on, but the results proved meager because nations could not agree on rules governing dumping, subsidies for farm goods, genetically altered foods, and lower tariffs on high-tech goods.

such corporations as Coca-Cola, Citigroup, General Motors, and United Airlines, which wanted to enter that emerging market.

The Debate over Globalization

While the administration promoted open markets, labor unions argued that free-trade agreements exacerbated the trade deficit and exported American jobs. Average real wages for American workers declined after 1973, from $320 per week to $260 by the mid-1990s. Other critics maintained that globalization widened the gap between rich and poor countries, creating a mass of "slave laborers" in poor countries. Environmentalists charged that globalization exported pollution to countries unprepared to deal with it. Still others warned about the power of multinational corporations over traditional cultures.

Anti-globalization activists staged mass demonstrations and also targeted corporations such as the Gap, Starbucks, Nike, and, especially, McDonald's, which by 1995 was serving 30 million customers daily in over one hundred countries. Critics assailed the company's slaughterhouse techniques, alleged exploitation of workers, its high-fat menu, and its role in creating an increasingly homogeneous world culture. For six years starting in 1996, McDonald's endured hundreds of often-violent protests, including bombings in Rome, Prague, London, Macao, Rio de Janeiro, and Jakarta.

Others decried the violence and the arguments of the anti-globalization campaigners. Some economists argued that if one included quality-of-life measurements, such as literacy and health, global inequality had declined. Some studies found that wage and job losses for U.S. workers were caused not primarily by globalization factors but by technological change that made production more efficient. Other researchers saw no evidence that globalization compromised governments' sovereignty or caused a "race to the bottom" in environmental standards.

As for creating a homogeneous global culture, McDonald's, others said, tailored its menu and operating practices to local tastes. And although American movies, TV programs, music, computer software, and other "intellectual property" often dominated world markets, foreign competition also arrived in America. American children, for example, were gripped by the Japanese Pokemon fad.

The Contested Election of 2000

The strong economy seemingly put Vice President **Al Gore** in position to prevail over Republican challenger **George W. Bush** (son of the forty-first president and two-time governor of Texas) in the 2000 presidential election. And on Election Day, Al Gore did narrowly win the popular vote. But he did not win the presidency. It all came down to Florida, where Bush's brother Jeb was governor, and its twenty-five electoral votes. In the initial tally, Bush edged Gore out in Florida, but the close margin legally required a recount. That recount was contentious. In several heavily African American counties, tens of thousands of votes went uncounted because voters failed to fully dislodge the "chads," small perforated squares, when punching the old-fashioned paper ballots. In Palm Beach County, it was discovered, many elderly Jewish residents had been confused by a poorly designed ballot and, thinking they were selecting Gore, had selected the allegedly anti-Semitic Pat Buchanan. After thirty-six days, with court cases at the state and federal levels, the Supreme Court voted 5 to 4 along narrowly partisan lines to end the recount process. Florida's electoral votes—and the presidency—went to Bush. Struggles over the election further polarized the nation.

With the close election, many believed Bush would govern from the center. Some also thought he had moved to the right only to ensure conservative evangelical Christian votes. But Bush governed from the right, arguably further to the right than any other modern administration.

Al Gore Longtime Democratic senator from Tennessee and vice president under Bill Clinton (1993–2001); unsuccessfully ran for president in the highly contested 2000 race; won a 2007 Nobel Peace Prize for his advocacy and expertise on environmental issues, particularly global warming.

George W. Bush Forty-third president of the United States, from 2001 to 2008; son of forty-first president George H. W. Bush.

9/11 and the War in Iraq

How did the events of September 11 change America's relationship to the world?

In international affairs, the administration charted a unilateralist course. Given America's preponderant power, senior officials reasoned, it did not need other countries' help. Accordingly, Bush withdrew the United States from the 1972 Anti-Ballistic Missile Treaty with Russia to develop a National Missile Defense system similar to Reagan's "Star Wars." The White House renounced the 1997 **Kyoto Protocol** on controlling global warming and opposed a protocol to strengthen the 1972 Biological and Toxin Weapons Convention. These decisions and the administration's hands-off policy toward the Israeli-Palestinian peace process caused consternation in Europe.

Kyoto Protocol A protocol setting strict emission targets for industrialized nations. President Bush refused to sign the agreement, making the United States one of only four nations that declined participation.

9/11

Then came September 11. Nineteen hijackers seized control of four commercial jets departing from East Coast airports. At 8:46 AM, one plane crashed into the 110-story North Tower of the World Trade Center in New York City. At 9:03 AM, a second flew into the South Tower. In less than two hours, both buildings collapsed, killing thousands of office workers, firefighters, and police officers. At 9:43, the third plane crashed into the Pentagon. The fourth plane was also headed toward Washington, but several passengers—learning of the World Trade Center attacks through cell phone conversations—stormed the cockpit; in the scuffle, the plane crashed in Somerset County, Pennsylvania, killing all aboard.

More than three thousand people died in the deadliest act of terrorism in history. The hijackers—fifteen Saudi Arabians, two Emiratis, one Lebanese, and an Egyptian—had ties to Al Qaeda.

Afghanistan War

President Bush responded with force. Al Qaeda operated out of Afghanistan with the blessing of the ruling Taliban, a repressive Islamic fundamentalist group. In early October, the United States launched a sustained bombing campaign against Taliban and Al Qaeda positions and sent special operations forces to help a resistance organization in northern Afghanistan. Within two months, the Taliban was driven from power, although bin Laden and top Taliban leaders eluded capture.

As administration officials acknowledged, military victory did not end the terrorist threat. Bush spoke of a long struggle against evil forces, in which the nations of the world were either with the United States or against it. Some questioned whether a "war on terrorism" could ever be won in a meaningful sense, given that the foe was a nonstate actor with little to lose. Stunned by September 11, most Americans experienced a renewed sense of national unity and pride. Bush's approval ratings skyrocketed.

USA PATRIOT Act
Controversial anti-terrorist law that extended the government's legal surveillance power to allow monitoring of telephone and Internet communications and library searches.

PATRIOT Act

But the new patriotism had a dark side. Congress passed the **USA PATRIOT Act** (Uniting and Strengthening America by Providing Appropriate Tools Required to Intercept and Obstruct Terrorism), making it easier for law enforcement to conduct searches, wiretap telephones, and obtain electronic records on individuals. Attorney General John Ashcroft approved giving FBI agents new powers to monitor the Internet, mosques, and rallies. Civil libertarians charged that the Justice Department overstepped, and some judges ruled against the tactics. Yet according to a June 2002 Gallup poll, 80 percent of Americans were willing to exchange some freedoms for security.

In Washington, Democrats and Republicans sparred over judicial appointments, energy policy, and the proposed new **Department of Homeland Security**, approved by Congress in November 2002 to coordinate intelligence and defense against terrorism.

Department of Homeland Security Cabinet-level department created by Congress to coordinate anti-terrorism efforts. Various agencies were placed under its jurisdiction, including the Coast Guard, the Customs Service, the Federal Emergency Management Agency (FEMA), and the Immigration and Naturalization Service.

Economic Uncertainty

Economically, the months before September 11 witnessed a collapse of some five hundred "dot-coms," Internet companies that were the darlings of Wall Street in the 1990s. Other economic warning signs included a meager 0.2 percent growth rate in goods and services for the second quarter of 2001 and falling corporate revenues.

Economic concerns deepened after 9/11 with a four-day closing of Wall Street and a sharp drop in stock prices. The Dow Jones Industrial Average plunged 14.26 percent. The markets eventually rebounded, but questions remained about the economy's health. Yet neither economic uncertainty nor the failure to capture **Osama bin Laden** dented Bush's popularity. In the 2002 midterm elections, Republicans retook the Senate and increased their majority in the House.

Osama bin Laden A wealthy Islamic fundamentalist militant expelled from his native Saudi Arabia in 1991; he took refuge in Sudan, where he financed large-scale construction and agricultural projects and amassed followers of his Al Qaeda terrorist organization. He masterminded several attacks, among them the September 11, 2001, attack on the United States.

International Responses

Overseas, the president's standing was not so high. Immediately after September 11, governments worldwide announced they would work with Washington against terrorism. Although Bush's good-versus-evil terminology put off many foreign observers, they initially swallowed their objections. But when the president hinted that America might unilaterally strike Saddam Hussein's Iraq or deal forcefully with North Korea or Iran—Bush's "axis of evil"—many allied governments objected.

Bush and other top officials argued that in an age of terrorism, the United States would not wait for a potential security threat to become real; it would strike first. Americans, Bush declared, had to be "ready for preemptive action when necessary to defend our liberty and to defend our lives." Critics, among them world leaders, called it reckless and contrary to international law.

But Bush was determined, particularly on Iraq. Several of his top advisers, including Secretary of Defense Donald Rumsfeld and Vice President Dick Cheney, had wanted to oust Saddam Hussein since the 1991 Gulf War. After 9/11, they folded Iraq into the war on terrorism—even though counterterrorism experts saw no link between Saddam and Al Qaeda. For a time, Secretary of State **Colin Powell**, the first African American in that post, kept the focus on Afghanistan, but gradually the White House shifted. By spring 2002, a secret consensus was reached: Saddam would be removed by force.

Colin Powell Four-star general who served as national security adviser (1987–1989), chairman of the Joint of Chiefs of Staff (1989–1993), and secretary of state (2001–2005).

Why Iraq?

In September 2002, Bush challenged the United Nations to enforce its resolutions against Iraq, or the United States would act on its own. He and his aides said Saddam was a major threat to the United States and its allies, a leader who possessed and would use banned biological and chemical "weapons of mass destruction" (WMDs) and who sought nuclear weapons. They claimed, contrary to their own intelligence, that he had ties to Al Qaeda and could be linked to the 9/11 attacks.

Beneath the surface lurked other motivations. Neoconservatives claimed that ousting Saddam would enhance Israel's security and start a chain reaction extending democracy throughout the region. White House political strategists believed a swift removal of a hated dictator would ensure Bush's reelection. Finally, Bush wanted to prevent an Iraq potentially armed with WMDs from destabilizing an oil-rich region.

Link to Secretary of State Colin Powell's speech to the UN advocating war with Iraq

Congressional Approval

Bush claimed he did not need congressional authorization for military action against Iraq, but he nevertheless sought it. In early October 2002, the House of Representatives voted 296 to 133 and the Senate 77 to 23 to authorize force. Many who voted in favor were unwilling to defy Bush so close to midterm elections, even though they opposed military action without UN sanction. Critics complained that the president had not presented evidence that Saddam Hussein constituted an imminent threat or was connected to the 9/11 attacks. Bush switched to a less hawkish stance, and in early November, the UN Security Council unanimously approved Resolution 1441, imposing rigorous arms inspections on Iraq.

But the Security Council was divided over the next move. In late January 2003, the weapons inspector's report castigated Iraq for failing to complete "the disarmament that was demanded of it" but also said it was too soon to tell whether inspections would succeed. Whereas U.S. and British officials said the time for diplomacy was up, France, Russia, and China called for more inspections. As the UN debate continued, and as antiwar demonstrations occurred worldwide, Bush sent about 250,000 soldiers to the region. Britain sent about 45,000 troops.

Fall of Baghdad

In late February, the United States floated a resolution to the UN that proposed issuing an ultimatum to Iraq, but only three of the fifteen Security Council members agreed. Bush abandoned the resolution and diplomatic efforts on March 17, when he ordered Saddam Hussein to leave Iraq within forty-eight hours or face attack. Saddam ignored the ultimatum, and on March 19 the United States and Britain launched an aerial bombardment. A ground invasion followed (see Map 29.1). On April 9, Baghdad fell.

When violence soon erupted, American planners seemed powerless to respond. The plight of ordinary Iraqis deteriorated as the occupation authority proved unable to maintain order. Decisions by the Coalition Provisional Authority (CPA), headed by Ambassador Paul Bremer, made matters worse—notably Bremer's move in May to disband the Iraqi army. An insurgency of Saddam loyalists, Iraqi nationalists, and foreign Islamic revolutionaries took shape; soon, U.S. occupying forces faced frequent ambushes. By October 2003, more troops had died from these attacks than had perished in the initial invasion.

The chaos in Iraq and the failure to find weapons of mass destruction had critics questioning the war. Even defenders of the invasion castigated the administration for failing to anticipate the occupation problems. In spring 2004, graphic photos showing Iraqi detainees being abused by American guards at Abu Ghraib prison were broadcast worldwide, generating international condemnation.

Election of 2004

President Bush, facing reelection, expressed disgust at the Abu Ghraib images and denied charges that he and top aides condoned the abuse. The White House also claimed the transfer of sovereignty to an interim Iraqi government in June would flatten the insurgency. Bush's Democratic opponent, Senator **John Kerry** of Massachusetts, a Vietnam veteran who had reluctantly voted for the Iraq resolution, never articulated a clear alternative strategy on the war. Bush won reelection with 51 percent of the popular vote to Kerry's 48 percent. The GOP also increased its majorities in the House and Senate.

John Kerry Senator from Massachusetts and Vietnam War veteran; Democratic nominee for president in 2004; served as secretary of state in the second Obama administration.

America Isolated

Internationally, Bush faced criticism on a number of fronts. The White House, critics said, rightly sought to prevent North Korea and Iran from joining the nuclear club but seemed incapable of making it happen. In Europe, Bush continued to be depicted as a gun-slinging cowboy whose aggressive policies threatened world peace.

Iraq, though, remained the chief problem. The bill for the Iraq War now exceeded $1 billion per week. In March 2005, American war dead reached 1,500; in December 2006, the figure reached 3,000. Iraqi civilian deaths, meanwhile,

MAP 29.1

The Middle East

The nations of the Middle East maintained precarious relations with the United States. To protect its interests, the United States extended large amounts of economic and military aid and sold huge quantities of weapons to the area. At times, Washington ordered U.S. troops to the region. The Arab-Israeli dispute particularly upended order, although the peace process moved forward intermittently. Source: Copyright © Cengage Learning 2015

The following labels and annotations appear on the map:

Soviet occupation, 1979–1989
U.S. aid to rebels, 1980s
International and Northern Alliance forces defeat Taliban, 2001

U.S. troops, 1958, 1983–1984

U.S. arms sales, 1955–1978: $20.8 billion
Shah overthrown, 1979
American hostages taken, 1979–1981

U.S. and allies launch First U.S.-Iraq War, 1991

U.S. arms sales, 1980s, during Iran-Iraq War
Iraq invades Kuwait, 1990
Second U.S.-Iraq War, 2003

Partner in U.S. efforts to eradicate al-Qaeda, 2001–

Oil embargo, 1973
Source of 17% of U.S. oil imports in 1975
Largest buyer of U.S. arms, 1978

U.S. troops assist in relief of famine, 1992–1993; U.S. troops withdrawn, 1994

Members of the Organization of Petroleum Exporting Countries (OPEC)

Oil field

ARAB-ISRAELI CONFLICT

Jewish state after UN partition of Palestine, 1947

Israel after War of 1948–1949

Area controlled by Israel after Six-Day War, 1967

Israeli-occupied area after Yom Kippur War, 1973

By Egyptian-Israeli agreements of 1975 and 1979, Israel withdrew from the Sinai in 1982. In 1981 Israel annexed the Golan Heights. Through negotiations between Israel and the PLO, Jericho and the Gaza Strip were placed under Palestinian self-rule, and Israeli troops were withdrawn in 1994. In 1994 Israel and Jordan signed an agreement opening their borders and normalizing their relations.

numbered in the tens of thousands. Iraqi casualties resulted from insurgent suicide attacks, U.S. bombing of suspected insurgent hideouts, and increasing sectarian violence between Sunnis and Shi'ites.

The Bush administration denied that Iraq had degenerated into civil war or that the struggle had become a Vietnam-like quagmire, but it seemed uncertain about how to end the fighting. In Congress and the press, calls for withdrawal from Iraq multiplied, but skeptics cautioned withdrawal could trigger sectarian bloodshed and a collapse of the Baghdad government. The power and regional influence of neighboring Iran would increase, and American credibility would be undermined throughout the Middle East. The 2007 "surge" contributed to a drastic reduction in violence, as commanders shifted to a counterinsurgency strategy emphasizing protection of the population. But the surge did little to promote political reconciliation among competing Iraqi factions.

Domestic Politics and Foreign Policy in Post–9/11 America

What was the decisive factor in the 2008 election?

The centerpiece of Bush's domestic agenda, achieved before the 9/11 attacks, was a $1.3 trillion tax cut—the largest in U.S. history. As Bush intended, it wiped out the $200 billion budget surplus he had inherited from the Clinton administration.

The Presidency of George W. Bush

Much of Bush's agenda fit with conservative principles. Religious conservatives liked the newly prominent role of religion in politics. The president spoke frequently of his faith; Attorney General John Ashcroft, a Pentecostal Christian, held morning prayer meetings in the Justice Department. And Bush appointed the medical director of a Christian pregnancy-counseling center whose website claimed that the "distribution of birth control is demeaning to women ... and adverse to human health and happiness" to head the federal family planning program.

Bush also advocated economic deregulation. His administration dismantled environmental restrictions on the oil, timber, and mining industries, and as Wall Street developed an array of risky financial instruments, he remained hands-off. While his plans to partially privatize Social Security and reform immigration failed, Bush did reshape the Supreme Court. Fifty-year-old conservative U.S. Circuit Court judge John Roberts was confirmed as chief justice after Chief Justice William Rehnquist died, and another strong conservative, fifty-five-year-old Samuel Alito, became junior associate justice when Sandra Day O'Connor resigned.

At the same time, Bush often turned to a form of "big government" conservatism. He dramatically increased the federal government's role in public education through his **"No Child Left Behind"** initiative. The legislation linked federal funding to state action: to receive federal education dollars, states had to set "high standards," evaluating students through a series of standardized tests that would hold failing schools accountable. And while conservatives traditionally argued against

"No Child Left Behind"
Label for Bush law mandating standardized testing in reading and math in grades four and eight.

federally subsidized medical care, the Bush administration created an expensive entitlement program covering prescription drugs for American seniors under Medicare.

Hurricane Katrina

Although Bush won reelection, perceptions of administrative incompetence began to undermine confidence in his administration. In late August 2005, **Hurricane Katrina** hit the U.S. Gulf Coast and New Orleans. It destroyed the levees that kept low-lying parts of New Orleans from being swamped by Lake Pontchartrain and surrounding canals. Floodwater covered 80 percent of New Orleans, and more than 1,800 people died.

Tens of thousands of people who lacked the resources to flee New Orleans sought shelter at the Superdome. Food and water quickly ran low, and toilets backed up; people wrapped the dead in blankets and waited for rescue. Those outside the Gulf region, watching the suffering crowd of mainly poor, black New Orleanians, discussed what Democratic Party leader Howard Dean called the "ugly truth": that poverty remains linked to race. The public also worried about local, state, and federal administrative mismanagement and the president's seeming indifference.

Economic Recession

But larger troubles were brewing: American home prices—a "housing bubble"—were about to collapse. After initial deregulation during the 1980s, financial institutions had begun experimenting with "subprime" mortgages for people who previously would not have qualified for credit. By 2006, one-fifth of all home loans were subprime. As demand for homes kept rising, so did prices. If a family defaulted on their mortgage and lost their house, the property could be sold for

Hurricane Katrina Worst natural disaster in U.S. history; resulting flooding destroyed much of New Orleans and the Gulf Coast in August 2005; poor handling of the crisis fueled cries of racism and tarnished the Bush administration.

New Orleans police officers and volunteers rescue residents from a flooded neighborhood during the devastation following Hurricane Katrina in August 2005. Katrina destroyed not only New Orleans, but much of the Gulf Coast from Louisiana into Alabama. The federal government designated 90,000 square miles as a disaster area. More than 1,800 people lost their lives in the storm.

AP Photo/Eric Gay

more than the mortgage was worth. Wall Street bought up mortgages, bundling them together, good and bad, into multibillion-dollar packages to sell to investors. These mortgage-backed securities—made possible by deregulation—were complex and risky.

This unstable structure began to fail in 2007, as more borrowers defaulted on mortgages. People tried to escape unaffordable mortgages by selling their houses, but housing prices plummeted. Increasingly, mortgages were larger than a home's value. And the financial institutions that had gambled on mortgage-backed securities did not have enough capital to sustain such losses. Worldwide, banks were on the verge of collapse.

The U.S. economy depends on the availability of credit—for business loans, car loans, home loans, credit cards. This crisis paralyzed the credit markets. Businesses could not get loans to buy raw materials or inventory; consumers couldn't get credit to buy large items, such as cars. And many Americans were already deeply in debt. In 2005, the average family spent more than it earned—and for those under thirty-five, the savings rate was minus 16 percent. People bought less, businesses laid off workers, and unemployment climbed. The Bush administration attempted to prevent the financial system's collapse by bailing out those banks and credit providers deemed "too big too fail." The Troubled Asset Relief Program (TARP) eventually provided $700 billion in loans to failing institutions, but many Americans on "Main Street" were angry that tax dollars rescued wealthy bankers on "Wall Street."

Barack Obama Forty-fourth president (first elected 2008) and the nation's first African American president, who took office in the midst of the worst economic crisis since the Great Depression.

Election of 2008

In the 2008 presidential election, the hard-fought Democratic primary pitted New York senator Hillary Clinton against Illinois senator **Barack Obama**, forcing Americans to confront the meaning of race and gender in American society. Obama won the nomination and ran against Arizona senator John McCain, a Vietnam veteran who survived five years in a P.O.W. camp. McCain never drew enthusiastic support from socially conservative Republicans. Obama mobilized the grassroots: young people, African Americans, people who had never voted before. He used social media to reach out to voters. People contributed millions of dollars through his website.

The economy was the deciding factor. McCain's claim, in the midst of Wall Street's September 2008 meltdown, that "the fundamentals of our economy are strong" backfired. Obama won in November.

Barack Obama

Barack Hussein Obama, the nation's forty-fourth president, was born in Hawai'i in 1961. His mother was a white woman from Kansas, his father a Kenyan graduate student at the University of Hawai'i. (The couple divorced when their child was two years old and each married again, giving Barack both African and Indonesian half-siblings.) Obama spent part of his childhood in Indonesia with his mother and attended high school in Hawai'i. After graduating from Harvard Law School, Obama worked as a community organizer in Chicago. There he met and married fellow Harvard Law graduate Michelle Robinson and worked as a civil rights lawyer and law professor at the University of Chicago before entering state politics in 1997. He gained national acclaim as a first-term senator for his keynote speech at the 2004 Democratic national convention.

More than seventy-five thousand people gathered in Chicago's Grant Park to celebrate Barack Obama's election on November 4, 2008.

Gary Hershorn/Reuters/Corbis Wire/Corbis

Obama was an inspirational speaker who offered messages of "hope" and "change." He began his presidency with ambitious goals. He vowed to pass a comprehensive health care reform bill within the year, but he also had to confront his inheritance: two wars, a massive federal deficit, and a major recession. In February 2009, Obama signed legislation creating a $787 billion economic stimulus package to jump-start the economy, and supported expanding TARP and bailing out failing auto giants GM and Chrysler. The economy began a slow recovery in 2009, but in 2010 the official unemployment rate remained close to 10 percent, and approximately 17 percent of those who wished to work were jobless or underemployed. One in eight Americans received food stamps from the government.

Partisan Impasse

Congress, during these years, was gridlocked by partisan conflict. Although Congress did finally pass a health care bill in March 2010—dubbed "Obamacare" by the plan's opponents—not a single Republican in the House of Representatives voted for it. Congress also approved legislation to end the "don't ask, don't tell" policy that prevented gay Americans from serving openly in the U.S. military.

Americans were frustrated that the Obama administration seemed incapable of solving the recession, and Republicans won a landslide victory in the 2010 midterm elections, gaining control of the House of Representatives. Spearheading this victory was a new grassroots movement: the tea party. The tea party mobilized Republican middle-class voters angry about big government and federal programs aimed at lower-income Americans, but wealthy conservatives provided financial and organizational support.

2012 Election

In 2012, Obama argued that his economic policies were working. GM and Chrysler were saved. America's major banks were stable. Unemployment, though still high, was dropping. Republican critics, including presidential candidate Mitt Romney, argued that recovery was too slow and that government spending was producing massive deficits.

Obama's victory in 2012 was narrower than his first, but his coalition held and he drew critical support from the growing Latino electorate. Treating his election as a mandate, Obama took firmer positions in negotiating with Republicans. But the nation continued to face struggles over debt, budget deficits, taxes, and government expenditures.

Obama and the World

In foreign affairs, Obama had more latitude. In Iraq, U.S. casualty figures continued to decline in 2009, and Obama stuck to a timeline for withdrawal to have combat forces out of the country by August 2010. Though some U.S. troops remained in Iraq as "advise and assist brigades" assigned to noncombat operations, in late 2011 these too were removed. On December 15, 2011, U.S. Defense Secretary Leon Panetta officially pronounced the Iraq War over. The last U.S. troops left Iraqi territory on December 18, 2011, but political stability in the country remained elusive.

As he drew down in Iraq, Obama ramped up U.S. involvement in Afghanistan, where the Taliban were regaining a foothold and appeared ready to threaten the existence of the government in Kabul, headed by Hamid Karzai. Obama ordered 17,000 more American combat troops to Afghanistan even before completion of the first review he had ordered.

Afghanistan "Surge"

On December 1, 2009, following another policy review, Obama announced a "surge" that would commit 33,000 additional U.S. troops to the struggle (for a total of 100,000), as well as 7,000 troops from NATO members and other allies. He rejected the advice of skeptics such as Vice President Joseph Biden, who questioned whether the surge would work and whether Karzai's government could take responsibility for its own security. To placate concerns of an open-ended war, Obama promised that "our troops will begin to come home" by summer 2011.

Progress was slow, however, and many analysts disagreed when Obama in June 2011 proclaimed the surge a success. The president pledged that the surge troops would be out of Afghanistan by summer 2012. The troops were duly withdrawn, leaving some 68,000 U.S. forces still in place. Although constant drone strikes and special operations raids took a toll on Al Qaeda, it was difficult for the administration to make the case that Afghanistan was stable or that Karzai's government could stand on its own. But as Obama's first term ended, the United States and its allies stuck to a plan to turn over all security responsibilities to the Afghans by the end of 2014.

Most voters in the 2012 presidential campaign gave Obama high marks on foreign policy for his drawdown in Iraq and his use of diplomacy and sanctions to try to compel Iran to halt its nuclear program. Critics faulted his cautious response when Syria headed toward chaos in 2012, but others thought him correct to encourage Saudi Arabia, Turkey, and other neighboring states to work together to undermine Bashar Assad's regime. On China, voters seemed comfortable with Obama's gradualist approach, which mixed strengthening economic ties while pressing Beijing on human rights issues and expanding military ties with smaller nations on China's periphery. And few Americans seemed inclined to penalize him for his scant success in furthering the Israeli-Palestinian peace process.

Death of Bin Laden

Obama's foreign policy trump card in the election was the violent death of the mastermind behind the 9/11 attacks, the man who had become the symbolic leader of global *jihad* against the West. In the very early hours of May 2, 2011, American Navy SEALs, in a daring operation later immortalized in the Hollywood film *Zero Dark Thirty*, shot and killed Osama bin Laden in Abbottabad, Pakistan, a garrison town north of Islamabad.

The operation took forty minutes, but the groundwork had been laid years before. With information acquired by interrogating detainees, CIA analysts identified one of the few Al Qaeda couriers bin Laden trusted. In August 2010 they tracked the courier to a compound in Abbottabad they speculated was bin Laden's location. On April 29, 2011, Obama gave the go-ahead for the operation. Three days later, U.S. commandos swooped down on the compound in stealth helicopters in the dead of night, moved through the buildings, and shot dead a total of five people including bin Laden.

Americans in the New Millennium

What demographic changes are Americans beginning to face in the twenty-first century?

In the second decade of the twenty-first century, the United States is a nation of extraordinary diversity. Immigration reform in the mid-1960s opened American borders to people from a wider variety of nations. New technologies—the Internet and cable and satellite television—replaced mass markets with niche markets. Everything from television shows to cosmetics to cars could be targeted toward specific groups defined by age, ethnicity, class, gender, or lifestyle choices. These changes helped to make Americans' understandings of identity more fluid and complex.

Race and Ethnicity in Today's America

In the 2000 U.S. government census, for the first time Americans could identify themselves as belonging to more than one race. The change acknowledged the growing number of Americans born to parents of different racial backgrounds. Critics worried that, because census data are used for allocating resources, the new "multiracial" option would reduce the clout of minority groups. Thus the federal government counted those who identified both as white and as members of a racial or ethnic minority as belonging to the minority group. Consequently, the official population of some groups, such as Native Americans, increased. Others rejected racial and ethnic categories altogether: 20 million people identified themselves simply as "American."

On October 17, 2006, the United States population passed 300 million. During the 1990s, the population of people of color grew twelve times as fast as the white population, fueled by immigration and birth rates. In 2003, Latinos passed African Americans to become the second largest ethnic or racial group (after non-Hispanic

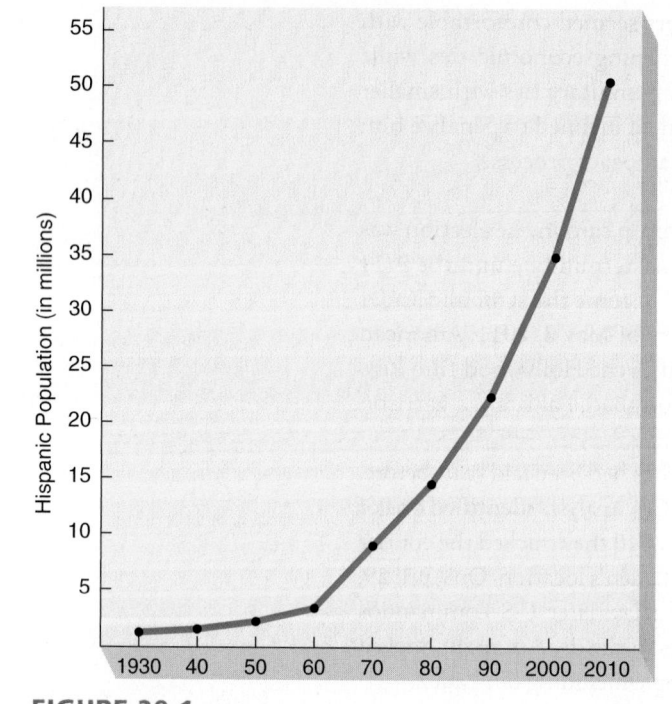

FIGURE 29.1

The Growth of the U.S. Hispanic Population

"Hispanic" combines people from a wide variety of national origins or ancestries—including all the nations of Central and South America, Mexico, Cuba, Puerto Rico, the Dominican Republic, Spain—as well as those who identify as Californio, Tejano, Nuevo Mexicano, and Mestizo.

(Source: Adapted from the U.S. Department of Commerce, Economics and Statistics Information, Bureau of the Census, 1993 report "We, the American…Hispanics"; also recent Census Bureau figures for the Hispanic population.)

whites), making the United States the fifth largest "Latino" country in the world (see Figure 29.1). Immigration from Asia also remained high, and in 2010, 5.6 percent of the U.S. population was Asian or Asian American. Most of this immigration is legal, but the number of people in the United States without official documentation peaked in 2007 at 12 million (up from 3 million in 1980), before falling to about 11 million during the economic recession.

These rapid demographic changes have altered the face of America. For example, in the small town of Ligonier, Indiana, the formerly empty Main Street now boasts three Mexican restaurants and a Mexican-owned Western-wear shop; Mexican immigrants drawn in the 1990s by plentiful industrial jobs cross paths with the newest immigrants, Yemenis, and with Amish families in horse-drawn buggies. Although many of America's schools and neighborhoods remain racially segregated and public debates about illegal immigration are heated, American popular culture has embraced the influences of this new multiethnic population. Economics were important: the buying power of the growing Latino population exceeded $798 billion in 2006 (and is projected to exceed $1.5 trillion by 2015), while average income for Asian American households tops that for all other groups. But American audiences also crossed racial and ethnic lines as, for example, African American rap and hip-hop attracted large followings of young white men.

The Changing American Family

Americans were divided over the meaning of other changes as well—especially the changing shape of American families (see Figure 29.2). Fewer and fewer American adults are married—barely half today, compared with almost three-quarters in 1960—and four out of ten Americans say they think marriage may be becoming obsolete. The median age at marriage continues to rise, reaching 28.7 for men and 26.5 for women in 2010. The number of people living together without marriage also continues to increase, and almost half of these cohabiting opposite-sex couples are over 35.

In the early twenty-first century, an antigay movement coexisted with rising support for the legal equality of gay, lesbian, transgendered, and bisexual Americans. Although the federal Defense of Marriage Act (DOMA), passed by Congress in 1996, defined marriage as a union between one man and one woman, many states and corporations extended domestic partner benefits to gay couples, and in 2002 the American Academy of Pediatrics endorsed adoption by gay couples. Between 2003 and 2013, same-sex marriage was legalized in twelve states, though DOMA

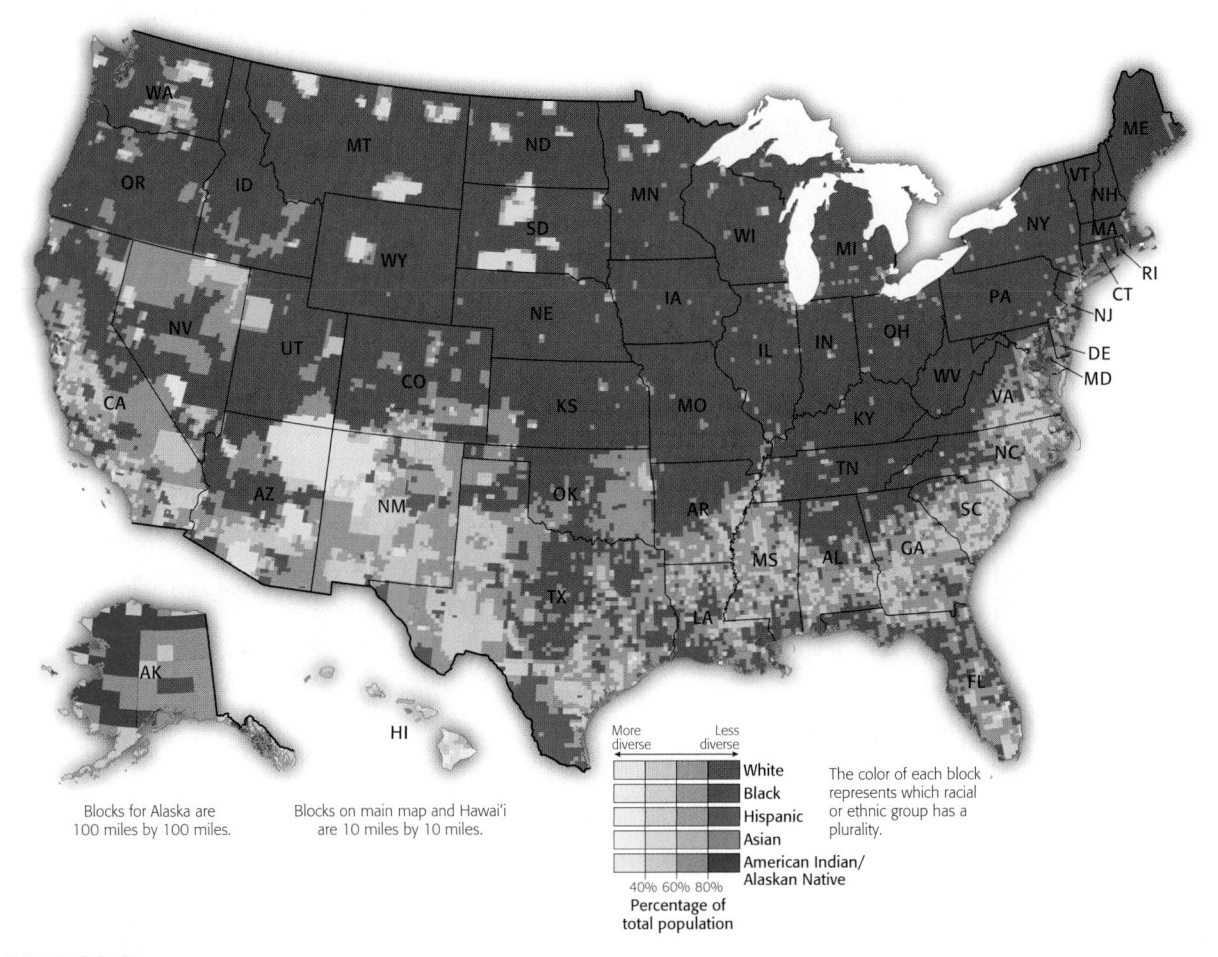

Blocks for Alaska are
100 miles by 100 miles.

Blocks on main map and Hawai'i
are 10 miles by 10 miles.

More diverse — Less diverse

White
Black
Hispanic
Asian
American Indian/
Alaskan Native

The color of each block
represents which racial
or ethnic group has a
plurality.

40% 60% 80%
Percentage of
total population

MAP 29.2
Mapping America's Diversity

Aggregate figures (more than 12 percent of the U.S. population was black and about 4 percent Asian in 2000, for example) convey America's ethnic and racial diversity. However, as this map shows, members of racial and ethnic groups are not distributed evenly throughout the nation.

prevented the federal government from recognizing same-sex couples as married. In June 2013 the Supreme Court, in a 5–4 decision, ruled DOMA unconstitutional, arguing that it "humiliates" children raised by same-sex couples and undermines state power to define marriage. Marriage equality made legally married same-sex couples eligible for military, health, and other federal benefits.

In the early-twenty-first-century United States, about 41 percent of babies were born to unmarried women, compared to 55 percent in Sweden and 2 percent in Japan. Although almost one-third of families with children had only one parent present—usually the mother—children also lived in blended families created by second marriages or moved back and forth between parents who had joint custody.

In 2006, the leading edge of the baby boom generation turned 60; the median age of the American population was 36.9 in 2012, up from 29.5 in 1967. As life expectancy

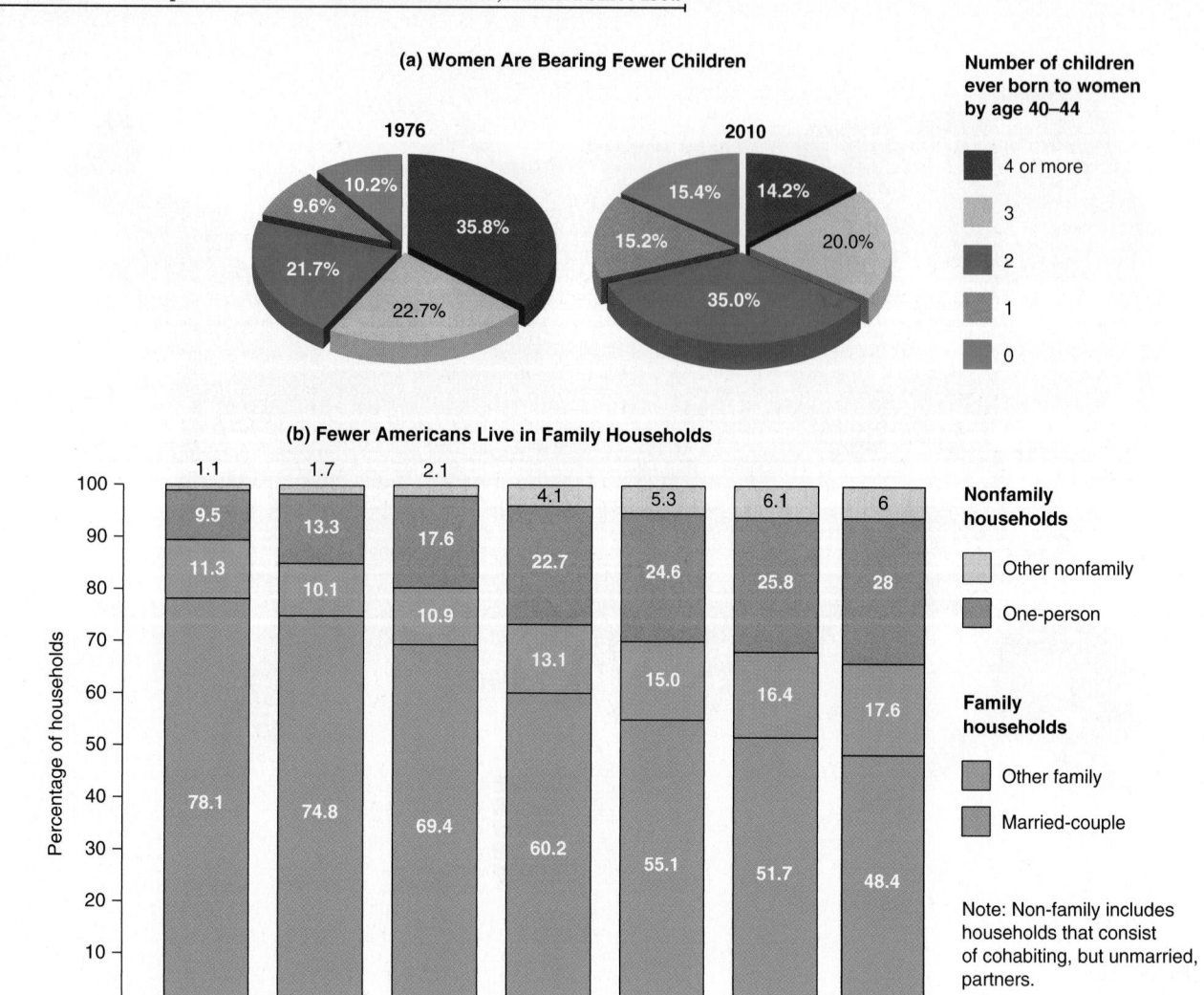

(a) Women Are Bearing Fewer Children

1976

2010

Number of children ever born to women by age 40–44

- 4 or more
- 3
- 2
- 1
- 0

1976: 35.8%, 22.7%, 21.7%, 9.6%, 10.2%

2010: 14.2%, 20.0%, 35.0%, 15.2%, 15.4%

(b) Fewer Americans Live in Family Households

Nonfamily households
- Other nonfamily
- One-person

Family households
- Other family
- Married-couple

Note: Non-family includes households that consist of cohabiting, but unmarried, partners.

FIGURE 29.2
The Changing American Family
American households became smaller in the latter part of the twentieth century, as more people lived alone and women had, on average, fewer children.
(Source: Adapted from U.S. Bureau of the Census, http://www.census.gov/prod/2002pubs/censr-4.pdf and http://www.census.gov/population/pop-profi le/2000/chap04.pdf.)

increases, the growing number of elderly Americans will put enormous pressure on the nation's health care system and family structure—who will care for people when they can no longer live independently?—and strain Social Security and Medicare.

Other health issues have become increasingly important. More than two-thirds of American adults are now overweight or obese—conditions linked to hypertension, cardiovascular disease, and diabetes. In 1995, no state had an adult obesity rate that hit 20 percent. By 2012, not a single state fell below 20 percent. Childhood obesity rates exceed 30 percent in twenty-nine states. On the other hand, cigarette smoking continues a slow decline. Slightly less than one-fifth of American adults smoked in 2010, down from about one-third in 1980.

Visualizing THE PAST

American War Dead

In 1991, as the United States prepared to go to war in the Persian Gulf, Defense Secretary Dick Cheney banned the media from photographing American war dead being returned to U.S. soil. The ban imposed by the George H. W. Bush administration may stem from a moment in the 1989 U.S. invasion of Panama, when ABC, CBS, and CNN ran coverage of caskets arriving at Dover Air Force Base and President Bush's White House news conference simultaneously on a split screen, making it appear that the president was not paying appropriate respect to those killed. During the twenty-first-century wars in Iraq and Afghanistan, the George W. Bush administration enforced a blanket ban on media photographs.

Critics argued that the Bush administration was hiding the tragic cost of America's wars, while supporters insisted that the policy protected the privacy of American military families. The ban was lifted by Robert M. Gates, President Obama's secretary of defense, in 2009, with the support of the U.S. Army. However, media access was granted only when the fallen soldier's family gave permission.

Is it possible that what Americans do not see is as important as what they do?

Coffins of U.S. military personnel arriving at Dover Air Force Base in Dover, Delaware. This undated photograph was released in response to a Freedom of Information Act request.

USAF/www.thememoryhole.org/Reuters/Corbis

Violence, Crime, and Incarceration

In the late twentieth and early twenty-first centuries, America was haunted by increasingly frequent and inexplicable mass murders (which the FBI defines as having four or more victims): sixty-two in the thirty years from 1982 to 2012. Americans were shocked in 1999 when two academically successful students at Columbine High School in Colorado murdered thirteen people (and injured twenty-three more) before committing suicide, but students also massacred classmates and teachers in Paducah, Kentucky; Springfield, Oregon; Jonesboro, Arkansas; and on the campuses of Virginia Tech and Okiah College in California. Armed men, most of them young, white, and mentally ill, committed mass murders at coffee shops and nursing homes, at workplaces, hotels, and places of worship, at a mall and a movie theater and an army post and an air force base. A gunman shot ten young girls in a one-room Amish schoolhouse in 2006. Twenty small children and six adults were murdered at Sandy Hook Elementary School in Newtown, Connecticut, in 2012.

Mass murders account for well below 1 percent of gun-related homicides. Shooting deaths and other homicides occur far more frequently in poor, inner-city neighborhoods. In Chicago, for example, 270 school-aged children were shot and killed between 2009 and 2012. At the same time, most Americans saw rapidly declining rates of violent crime after 1993.

The United States has the world's highest incarceration rate; as of 2008, approximately 1 of every 100 American adults was in prison or jail. The U.S. imprisonment rate of 751 per 100,000 compares to Russia's 577, Canada's 117, and Japan's 59. While the United States does have a higher rate of violent crime than most developed nations, high incarceration rates occur because the United States sentences more nonviolent criminals (including those convicted of drug crimes) to prison and, most importantly, the U.S. justice system imposes more mandatory and longer prison terms. According to the U.S. Justice Department, imprisonment of women has increased sevenfold since the 1970s, and in 2010 African American men were seven times more likely than white men and two and a half times more likely than Hispanic men to be incarcerated. Social costs are extraordinary, as men and women emerging from prison are too often unable to become productive members of society or to rejoin stable families and communities.

Medicine, Science, and Religion

As scientists and medical researchers struggle to find cures for devastating diseases, rapid advances in biogenetics offer new possibilities and raise ethical conundrums. During in vitro fertilizations—in which sperm and egg combine in a sterile dish and the fertilized egg or eggs are then transferred to the uterus—five- or six-cell blastocytes are formed. These blastocytes contain stem cells, unspecialized cells that can be induced to become cells with specialized functions. For example, stem cells might become insulin-producing cells of the pancreas, and thus a cure for diabetes. President Bush in 2001 called embryonic stem cell research "the leading edge of a series of moral hazards," because extracting stem cells destroys the blastocyte's "potential for life," and limited federally funded research to the existing seventy-eight stem cell lines, most of which turned out not to be viable. However, most Americans support stem cell research, believing that the moral good of curing diseases outweighs the moral good of preserving blastocytes. In 2009, President Obama signed an executive order ending the Bush restrictions.

Still, many Americans see a fundamental conflict between religious belief and scientific study. Fundamentalist Christians have struggled to prevent the teaching of evolution and to introduce parallel instruction of biblical "creationism" or "intelligent design," which holds that an intelligent creator lies behind the development of life on earth. The percentage of Americans who accept scientific evidence for evolution is lower than that in any other major nation except Turkey.

Century of Change

The twentieth century witnessed momentous changes, some bringing benefits, others threatening the existence of the human species. Research in the physical and biological sciences provided insight into the structure of matter and of the universe. And technology has made startling advances. Americans at the start of the twenty-first century were more connected to the rest of humankind than ever before. This was perhaps the most powerful product of globalization. A commodities trader in Chicago in February 2010 could send a text message to her fiancé in Tokyo while she spoke on the phone to a trader in Frankfurt and e-mailed another one in Bombay, all while watching NBC's live coverage of the Winter Olympics; within a minute, she could receive a reply from her fiancé saying that he missed her, too. If she felt sufficiently lovesick, she could board an airplane and be in Japan the following day.

Globalization and World Health

But there was a flip side to this growing connectivity. The rapid increase in international air travel was a potent force for the dissemination of global disease, as flying enabled people to reach the other side of the world in less time than the incubation period for many ailments. Environmental degradation also created global health threats. In 2003, the World Health Organization (WHO) estimated that nearly one-quarter of global disease and injury was related to environmental disruption. For example, 90 percent of diarrheal diseases (such as cholera), which were killing 3 million people a year, resulted from contaminated water. According to WHO, more than thirty infectious diseases were identified in humans for the first time from 1980 to 2000—including AIDS, Ebola virus, hantavirus, and hepatitis C and E. Environmentalists, meanwhile, insisted that the growing interaction of national economies harmed the ecosystem through climate change, ozone depletion, hazardous waste, and damage to fisheries.

Confronting Terrorism

The 9/11 attacks brought home what Americans had previously only dimly perceived: that globalization had shrunk the buffers that distance and two oceans provided the United States. Al Qaeda used the increasingly open, globalized world to expand its reach. It had shown that small terrorist cells could become transnational threats without any state sponsor or home base. According to American intelligence, Al Qaeda operated in more than ninety countries.

How would one go about vanquishing such a foe? Was decisive victory even possible? These remained open questions a dozen years after the World Trade

Links TO THE WORLD

The "Swine Flu" Pandemic

When United Flight 803 from Washington, D.C., landed at Tokyo's Narita airport on May 20, 2009, Japanese health officials boarded the plane. Wearing respirator masks, goggles, and disposable scrubs, they used thermal scanners to check passengers for elevated temperatures. If any symptoms were discovered, the plane might be quarantined. Japan had already closed its borders to travelers from Mexico, where the H1N1 "swine flu" virus had emerged about three weeks earlier. Mexico closed schools and businesses. Nevertheless the H1N1 virus had, by mid-May, already spread to more than twenty-two countries.

After several deaths in Mexico in late April, the World Health Organization raised its alert level to stage 5, expecting the virus to create the first major flu pandemic in more than forty years. Health analysts believed that the "right" pathogen emerging in the "right" place might spread worldwide in a day.

But global connections also offered new tools to combat pandemics. Global surveillance of disease might head off developing health threats. Individual nations and global organizations pool expertise as they develop vaccines and techniques to cope with pandemics. Some believe that a global culture where borders present little barrier may facilitate the growth of global immunities to infectious diseases.

People everywhere were relieved when the swine flu was ultimately no more deadly than a usual flu strain. Previously, SARS (severe, acute respiratory syndrome) and the H5N1 "bird flu" had also failed to become major worldwide heath threats. But the World Health Organization and the U.S. Centers for Disease Control cautioned that the emergence of a major pandemic

was simply a matter of time. In the era of globalization, diseases do not stop at borders or respect wealth and power, and the links between Americans and the rest of the world's peoples cannot be denied.

As the H1N1 virus—"swine flu"—spread rapidly in the spring of 2009, nations around the world attempted to prevent the spread of infection. Here, thermal cameras check the body temperatures of passengers arriving at Incheon International Airport in South Korea.

Center collapsed. Unchallenged militarily, the United States felt few constraints about intervening in Afghanistan and then Iraq. It continued to spend colossal sums on its military. (The Pentagon in 2011 spent more than $711 billion.) America had taken on military commitments all over the globe, from the Balkans and Iraq to Afghanistan and Korea (see Table 29.1). And although the huge infrastructure

TABLE 29.1   U.S. Military Personnel on Active Duty in Foreign Countries, 2012[1]

Region/Country[2]	Personnel	Region/Country[2]	Personnel
United States and Territories		Singapore	180
Continental U.S.	1,123,219	Thailand	114
Alaska	21,280	Bahrain	2,902
Hawai'i	49,242	Diego Garcia	516
Guam	5,646	Egypt	292
Puerto Rico	162	Israel	41
Europe		Oman	37
Belgium*	1,165	Pakistan	42
France*	70	Qatar	800
Germany*	45,596	Saudi Arabia	278
Greece*	361	United Arab Emirates	193
Greenland*	138	**Sub-Saharan Africa**	
Hungary	62	Djibouti	139
Italy*	10,916	Kenya	40
Netherlands*	374	South Africa	35
Norway*	90	**Western Hemisphere**	
Portugal*	713	Bahamas, The	50
Russia	67	Brazil	48
Spain*	1,600	Canada	146
Turkey*	1,491	Chile	38
United Kingdom*	9,310	Colombia	64
East Asia and Pacific		Cuba (Guantanamo)	988
Australia	183	Honduras	388
China, Communist	49	Peru	51
Japan	52,692	**Total Worldwide[2]**	1,372,522
Philippines	131	Undistributed[3]	39,157

*NATO countries

[1]Only countries with 30 or more U.S. military personnel are listed.

[2]Includes all regions/countries, not simply those listed.

[3]Undistributed includes Afghanistan, Iraq, Kuwait, Republic of Korea and any unknown/classified locations.

Source: *U.S. Department of Defense, Defense Manpower Data Center* (http://siadapp.dmdc.osd.mil/personnel/MILITARY/miltop.htm Accessed July 1, 2013)

and bureaucracy built up after 9/11 to prevent further terrorist attacks on U.S. soil succeeded in core respects, vulnerabilities remained: on April 15, 2013, two pressure-cooker bombs exploded near the finish line of the Boston Marathon, killing 3 and injuring 264.

Twitter Revolution

Twitter, a social networking and microblogging service founded in 2006 by Jack Dorsey and Biz Stone, has become one of the ten most visited websites on the planet, with more than 200 million monthly active users communicating via short bursts of information called tweets.

Along with Facebook, Flickr, and other social media sites, Twitter has spawned an important structural change in how information spreads. No longer is there a need to rely on the phone calls, faxes, and television shows prized by the Baby Boom generation. In addition to announcing personal opinions and achievements, the new sites have been used to organize protests—indeed, they have been credited with reinventing social activism. Thus the Arab Spring uprisings of 2010–11 and the Iranian election protests of 2009–10 were called "Twitter Revolutions" for the ways they upended the traditional relationship between political authority and popular will and enabled activists to collaborate and coordinate.

Social networks did not cause these upheavals. In Egypt, for example, sociopolitical tensions had long been acute, and Egyptian activists insisted that old-fashioned grassroots organizing, not social media, drove their revolution.

Yet if Twitter and other social media are not particularly effective at boosting popular *motivation* for a given cause, they can have an outsized impact on increasing *participation*. The Occupy Wall Street movement of 2011–12 began as a Twitter experiment in July 2011, when the Canadian anti-consumerism magazine *Adbusters* posted the idea of a march in Lower Manhattan. In subsequent months, protesters used Twitter, YouTube, and Facebook to coordinate efforts.

Twitter has also served as a de facto emergency communication system for breaking news. The Boston Police, for example, tweeted news of the arrest of a suspect in the 2013 Boston Marathon terrorist attack. Researchers are also studying using Twitter to track epidemics, and college professors are experimenting with using Twitter to promote student interaction.

For these and other dedicated tweeters, there could be no more fitting legacy of the twentieth century than the Internet and the social media it spawned.

Summary

The 1990s were, for most Americans, good times. A digitized revolution in communications and information generated prosperity and transformed life in America and worldwide. The longest economic expansion in American history—from 1991 to 2001—meant that most Americans who wanted jobs had them, that the stock market boomed, that the nation had a budget surplus, and that more Americans owned homes. The United States stood as the world's lone superpower.

Yet unsettling events troubled the nation. In 2000, the contested presidential election was decided by the Supreme Court in a partisan 5-to-4 vote; in 2001, the ten-year economic expansion came to an end. Then, on September 11 of that year, radical Islamic terrorists attacked the World Trade Center and the Pentagon, killing thousands. The new president, George W. Bush, declared a "war on terrorism." Bush won reelection in 2004, but his fortunes soon waned. Two costly wars and a severe economic crisis paved the way for Barack Obama's historic election in 2008. The new president secured passage of major health care reform legislation, but he struggled to combat the rise in unemployment and the lingering subprime mortgage crisis. Even so, in 2012 he won reelection.

The world that Americans found in the first years of the twenty-first century was much different from the one they had imagined on New Year's Eve 1999. The terror attacks of September 11, 2001, shook America to its core. Then came two lengthy and inconclusive wars, followed by the most severe economic downturn since the Great Depression. By the start of the new decade, Americans were deeply divided over how to respond to the nation's problems. As Obama's second term began, Americans continued to struggle over foreign and domestic priorities with the passion and commitment that keep democracy alive.

Chapter Review

Social Strains and New Political Directions

What political struggles complicated Bill Clinton's first term?

From the start, a new breed of conservative Republicans challenged many of Clinton's campaign goals, and ultimately took control of both houses of Congress after the midterm elections in 1994. Republicans successfully blocked Clinton's attempts at health care reform and forced him to change his position on gays in the military. Increasing partisan roadblocks led the beleaguered president to make compromises with the right—most notably, signing the 1996 Personal Responsibility and Work Opportunity Act (also known as "welfare reform"), which limited federal assistance for the needy to two years, and the Telecommunications Act, which allowed greater concentration of media ownership in fewer hands.

Globalization and Prosperity

What concerns did critics raise about globalization?

The so-called "age of globalization" that emerged in the late 1990s was characterized by greater worldwide integration of markets, finance, and technology. Labor unions feared losing jobs to less expensive overseas production, while critics argued that globalization widened the gap between rich and poor nations. Environmentalists charged that globalization resulted in greater pollution of developing countries, and others feared the power of multinational corporations over traditional cultures. Anti-global protests targeted McDonald's as symbolizing the creation of a homogeneous global culture.

9/11 and the War in Iraq

How did the events of September 11 change America's relationship to the world?

Immediately after the attacks, the world community united in support of the United States. But before long, as President Bush took a firm good-versus-evil stance that dictated countries were either with the United States or against it, he began to alienate allies and other friendly nations. Bush and his aides believed that the United States could not wait for threats to materialize; they had to strike first. And Bush differed with much of the UN Security Council over how to deal with Saddam Hussein's Iraq. The Security Council wanted to give arms inspections more time to succeed; the United States, backed by Britain, felt the time for diplomacy was over. The discord increased when Bush opted to launch an invasion. Bush also faced sharp international criticism for the military's abuse of war prisoners at Abu Ghraib.

Domestic Politics and Foreign Policy in Post–9/11 America

What was the decisive factor in the 2008 election?

While Americans were increasingly unhappy about the war in Iraq and disliked the Bush administration's handling of Hurricane Katrina, the biggest issue fueling voters' rejection of John McCain and the Republican Party was the deepening economic crisis. Years of deregulation led to risky investment practices in America's financial sector—particularly in housing and credit—that ultimately triggered a dangerous spiral of plummeting home values, foreclosures, and banking and credit problems. As credit tightened, businesses laid off workers and unemployment skyrocketed. The Bush administration provided $700 billion in loans to failing institutions, angering many Americans. When John McCain misspoke in the midst of the financial meltdown that "the fundamentals of our economy are strong," many questioned how in touch he was. The Democrat Barack Obama won the election.

Americans in the New Millennium

 What demographic changes are Americans beginning to face in the twenty-first century?

As the American population reached the 300 million mark in 2006, the country was more racially and ethnically diverse than ever. The population of people of color grew twelve times faster than that of whites, and Latinos became the second largest ethnic or racial group after non-Hispanic whites. Family structure has become increasingly varied. Fewer and fewer American adults are married—barely half today, compared with almost three-quarters in 1960. The country also faces an aging population, as the leading edge of the baby boom generation turned sixty in 2006. That, combined with greater life expectancy, presents new concerns of health care and additional family pressures. Meanwhile, debates about balancing science and religion—particularly over stem cell research and the teaching of evolution and creationism—continue to divide the nation.

Suggestions for Further Reading

Derek Chollet and James Goldgeier, *America Between the Wars: From 11/9 to 9/11* (2008)

Barbara Ehrenreich, *Nickled and Dimed: On (Not) Getting by in America* (2002)

David Halberstam, *War in a Time of Peace: Bush, Clinton, and the Generals* (2001)

John F. Harris, *The Survivor: Bill Clinton in the White House* (2005)

Jennifer L. Hochschild, *Facing Up to the American Dream: Race, Class, and the Soul of the Nation* (1995)

James Mann, *Rise of the Vulcans: The History of Bush's War Cabinet* (2004)

Alejandro Portes and Reuben G. Rumbaut, *Immigrant America: A Portrait*, 3rd ed. (2006)

Thomas E. Ricks, *The Gamble: General David Petraeus and the American Military Adventure in Iraq, 2006–2008* (2009)

Joseph E. Stiglitz, *Globalization and Its Discontents* (2002)

Appendix

Declaration of Independence in Congress, July 4, 1776

When, in the course of human events, it becomes necessary for one people to dissolve the political bonds which have connected them with another, and to assume, among the powers of the earth, the separate and equal station to which the laws of nature and of nature's God entitle them, a decent respect to the opinions of mankind requires that they should declare the causes which impel them to the separation.

We hold these truths to be self-evident: That all men are created equal; that they are endowed by their Creator with certain unalienable rights; that among these are life, liberty, and the pursuit of happiness; that, to secure these rights, governments are instituted among men, deriving their just powers from the consent of the governed; that whenever any form of government becomes destructive of these ends, it is the right of the people to alter or to abolish it, and to institute new government, laying its foundation on such principles, and organizing its powers in such form, as to them shall seem most likely to effect their safety and happiness. Prudence, indeed, will dictate that governments long established should not be changed for light and transient causes; and accordingly all experience hath shown that mankind are more disposed to suffer, while evils are sufferable, than to right themselves by abolishing the forms to which they are accustomed. But when a long train of abuses and usurpations, pursuing invariably the same object, evinces a design to reduce them under absolute despotism, it is their right, it is their duty, to throw off such government, and to provide new guards for their future security. Such has been the patient sufferance of these colonies; and such is now the necessity which constrains them to alter their former systems of government. The history of the present King of Great Britain is a history of repeated injuries and usurpations, all having in direct object the establishment of an absolute tyranny over these states. To prove this, let facts be submitted to a candid world.

He has refused his assent to laws, the most wholesome and necessary for the public good.

He has forbidden his governors to pass laws of immediate and pressing importance, unless suspended in their operation till his assent should be obtained; and, when so suspended, he has utterly neglected to attend to them.

He has refused to pass other laws for the accommodation of large districts of people, unless those people would relinquish the right of representation in the legislature, a right inestimable to them, and formidable to tyrants only.

He has called together legislative bodies at places unusual, uncomfortable, and distant from the depository of their public records, for the sole purpose of fatiguing them into compliance with his measures.

He has dissolved representative houses repeatedly, for opposing, with manly firmness, his invasions on the rights of the people.

He has refused for a long time, after such dissolutions, to cause others to be elected; whereby the legislative powers, incapable of annihilation, have returned to the people at large for their exercise; the state remaining, in the mean time, exposed to all the dangers of invasions from without and convulsions within.

He has endeavored to prevent the population of these states; for that purpose obstructing the laws for naturalization of foreigners; refusing to pass others to encourage their migration hither, and raising the conditions of new appropriations of lands.

He has obstructed the administration of justice, by refusing his assent to laws for establishing judiciary powers.

He has made judges dependent on his will alone, for the tenure of their offices, and the amount and payment of their salaries.

He has erected a multitude of new offices, and sent hither swarms of officers to harass our people and eat out their substance.

He has kept among us, in times of peace, standing armies, without the consent of our legislatures.

He has affected to render the military independent of, and superior to, the civil power.

He has combined with others to subject us to a jurisdiction foreign to our constitution, and unacknowledged by our laws, giving his assent to their acts of pretended legislation:

For quartering large bodies of armed troops among us;

For protecting them, by a mock trial, from punishment for any murders which they should commit on the inhabitants of these states;

For cutting off our trade with all parts of the world;

For imposing taxes on us without our consent;

For depriving us, in many cases, of the benefits of trial by jury;

For transporting us beyond seas, to be tried for pretended offenses;

For abolishing the free system of English laws in a neighboring province, establishing therein an arbitrary government, and enlarging its boundaries, so as to render it at once an example and fit instrument for introducing the same absolute rule into these colonies;

For taking away our charters, abolishing our most valuable laws, and altering fundamentally the forms of our governments;

For suspending our own legislatures, and declaring themselves invested with power to legislate for us in all cases whatsoever.

He has abdicated government here, by declaring us out of his protection and waging war against us.

He has plundered our seas, ravaged our coasts, burned our towns, and destroyed the lives of our people.

He is at this time transporting large armies of foreign mercenaries to complete the works of death, desolation, and tyranny already begun with circumstances of cruelty and perfidy scarcely paralleled in the most barbarous ages, and totally unworthy the head of a civilized nation.

He has constrained our fellow-citizens, taken captive on the high seas, to bear arms against their country, to become the executioners of their friends and brethren, or to fall themselves by their hands.

He has excited domestic insurrection among us, and has endeavored to bring on the inhabitants of our frontiers the merciless Indian savages, whose known rule of warfare is an undistinguished destruction of all ages, sexes, and conditions.

In every stage of these oppressions we have petitioned for redress in the most humble terms; our repeated petitions have been answered only by repeated injury. A prince, whose character is thus marked by every act which may define a tyrant, is unfit to be the ruler of a free people.

Nor have we been wanting in our attentions to our British brethren. We have warned them, from time to time, of attempts by their legislature to extend an unwarrantable jurisdiction over us. We have reminded them of the circumstances of our emigration and settlement here. We have appealed to their native justice and magnanimity; and we have conjured them, by the ties of our common kindred, to disavow these usurpations, which would inevitably interrupt our connections and correspondence. They, too, have been deaf to the voice of justice and of consanguinity. We must, therefore, acquiesce in the necessity which denounces our separation, and hold them, as we hold the rest of mankind, enemies in war, in peace friends.

We, therefore, the representatives of the United States of America, in General Congress assembled, appealing to the Supreme Judge of the world for the rectitude of our intentions, do, in the name and by the authority of the good people of these colonies, solemnly publish and declare, that these United Colonies are, and of right ought to be, FREE AND INDEPENDENT STATES; that they are absolved from all allegiance to the British crown, and that all political connection between them and the state of Great Britain is, and ought to be, totally dissolved; and that, as free and independent states, they have full power to levy war, conclude peace, contract alliances, establish commerce, and do all other acts and things which independent states may of right do. And for the support of this declaration, with a firm reliance on the protection of Divine Providence, we mutually pledge to each other our lives, our fortunes, and our sacred honor.

Articles of Confederation

Whereas the Delegates of the United States of America in Congress assembled did on the fifteenth day of November in the Year of our Lord One Thousand Seven Hundred and Seventy seven, and in the Second Year of the Independence of America agree to certain articles of Confederation and perpetual Union between the States of Newhampshire, Massachusetts Bay, Rhode Island and Providence Plantations, Connecticut, New York, New Jersey, Pennsylvania, Delaware, Maryland, Virginia, North Carolina, South Carolina and Georgia in the Words following, viz. "Articles of Confederation and perpetual Union between the states of Newhampshire, Massachusetts Bay, Rhode Island and Providence Plantations, Connecticut, New York, New Jersey, Pennsylvania, Delaware, Maryland, Virginia, North Carolina, South Carolina and Georgia.

Article I The Stile of this confederacy shall be "The United States of America."

Article II Each state retains its sovereignty, freedom and independence, and every Power, Jurisdiction and right, which is not by this confederation expressly delegated to the United States, in Congress assembled.

Article III The said states hereby severally enter into a firm league of friendship with each other, for their common defence, the security of their Liberties, and their mutual and general welfare, binding themselves to assist each other, against all force offered to, or attacks made upon them, or any of them, on account of religion, sovereignty, trade, or any other pretence whatever.

Article IV The better to secure and perpetuate mutual friendship and intercourse among the people of the different states in this union, the free inhabitants of each of these states, paupers, vagabonds and fugitives from Justice excepted, shall be entitled to all privileges and immunities of free citizens in the several states; and the people of each state shall have free ingress and regress to and from any other state, and shall enjoy therein all the privileges of trade and commerce, subject to the same duties, impositions and restrictions as the inhabitants thereof respectively, provided that such restriction shall not extend so far as to prevent the removal of property imported into any state, to any other state of which the Owner is an inhabitant; provided also that no imposition, duties or restriction shall be laid by any state, on the property of the united states, or either of them.

If any Person guilty of, or charged with treason, felony, or other high misdemeanor in any state, shall flee from Justice, and be found in any of the united states, he shall upon demand of the Governor or executive power, of the state from which he fled, be delivered up and removed to the state having jurisdiction of his offence.

Full faith and credit shall be given in each of these states to the records, acts and judicial proceedings of the courts and magistrates of every other state.

Article V For the more convenient management of the general interests of the united states, delegates shall be annually appointed in such manner as the legislature of each state shall direct, to meet in Congress on the first Monday in November, in every year, with a power reserved to each state, to recall its delegates, or any of them, at any time within the year, and to send others in their stead, for the remainder of the Year.

No state shall be represented in Congress by less than two, nor by more than seven Members; and no person shall be capable of being a delegate for more than three years in any term of six years; nor shall any person, being a delegate, be capable of holding any office under the united states, for which he, or another for his benefit receives any salary, fees or emolument of any kind.

Each state shall maintain its own delegates in a meeting of the states, and while they act as members of the committee of the states.

In determining questions in the united states, in Congress assembled, each state shall have one vote.

Freedom of speech and debate in Congress shall not be impeached or questioned in any Court, or place out of Congress, and the members of congress shall be protected in their persons from arrests and imprisonments, during the time of their going to and from, and attendance on congress, except for treason, felony, or breach of the peace.

Article VI No state without the Consent of the united states in congress assembled, shall send any embassy to, or receive any embassy from, or enter into any conference, agreement, or alliance or treaty with any King, prince or state; nor shall any person holding any office of profit or trust under the united states, or any of them, accept of any present, emolument, office or title of any kind whatever from any king, prince or foreign state; nor shall the united states in congress assembled, or any of them, grant any title of nobility.

No two or more states shall enter into any treaty, confederation or alliance whatever between them, without the consent of the united states in congress assembled, specifying accurately the purposes for which the same is to be entered into, and how long it shall continue.

No state shall lay any imposts or duties, which may interfere with any stipulations in treaties, entered into by the united states in congress assembled, with any king, prince or state, in pursuance of any treaties already proposed by congress, to the courts of France and Spain.

No vessels of war shall be kept up in time of peace by any state, except such number only, as shall be deemed necessary by the united states in congress assembled, for the defence of such state, or its trade; nor shall any body of forces be kept up by any state, in time of peace, except such number only, as in the judgment of the united states, in congress assembled, shall be deemed requisite to garrison the forts necessary for the defence of such state; but every state shall always keep up a well regulated and disciplined militia, sufficiently armed and accoutred, and shall provide and constantly have ready for use, in public stores, a due number of field pieces and tents, and a proper quantity of arms, ammunition and camp equipage.

No state shall engage in any war without the consent of the united states in congress assembled, unless such state be actually invaded by enemies, or shall have received certain advice of a resolution being formed by some nation of Indians to invade such state, and the danger is so imminent as not to admit of a delay, till the united states in congress assembled can be consulted: nor shall any state grant commissions to any ships or vessels of war, nor letters of marque or reprisal, except it be after a declaration of war by the united states in congress assembled, and then only against the kingdom or state and the subjects thereof, against which war has been so declared, and under such regulations as shall be established by the united states in congress assembled, unless such state be infested by pirates, in which case vessels of war may be fitted out for that occasion, and kept so long as the danger shall continue, or until the united states in congress assembled shall determine otherwise.

Article VII When land-forces are raised by any state for the common defence, all officers of or under the rank of colonel, shall be appointed by the legislature of each state respectively by whom such forces shall be raised, or in such manner as such state shall direct, and all vacancies shall be filled up by the state which first made the appointment.

Article VIII All charges of war, and all other expences that shall be incurred for the common defence or general welfare, and allowed by the united states in congress assembled, shall be defrayed out of a common treasury, which shall be supplied by the several states, in proportion to the value of all land within each state, granted to or surveyed for any Person, as such land and the buildings and improvements thereon shall be estimated according to such mode as the united states in congress assembled, shall from time to time direct and appoint. The taxes for paying that proportion shall be laid and levied by the authority and direction of the legislatures of the several states within the time agreed upon by the united states in congress assembled.

Article IX The united states in congress assembled, shall have the sole and exclusive right and power of determining on peace and war, except in the cases mentioned in the sixth article—of sending and receiving ambassadors—entering into treaties and alliances, provided that no treaty of commerce shall be made whereby the legislative power of the respective states shall be restrained from imposing such imposts and duties on foreigners, as their own people are subjected to, or from prohibiting the exportation or importation of any species of goods or commodities whatsoever—of establishing rules for deciding in all cases, what captures on land or water shall be legal, and in what manner prizes taken by land or naval forces in the service of the united states shall be divided or appropriated—of granting letters of marque and reprisal in times of peace—appointing courts for the trial of piracies and felonies committed on the high seas and establishing courts for receiving and determining final appeals in all cases of captures, provided that no member of congress shall be appointed a judge of any of the said courts.

The united states in congress assembled shall also be the last resort on appeal in all disputes and differences now subsisting or that hereafter may arise between two or more states concerning boundary, jurisdiction or any other cause whatever; which authority shall always be exercised in the manner following. Whenever the legislative or executive authority or lawful agent of any state in controversy with another shall present a petition to congress, stating the matter in question and praying for a hearing, notice thereof shall be given by order of congress to the legislative or executive authority of the other state in controversy, and a day assigned for the appearance of the parties by their lawful agents, who shall then be directed to appoint by joint consent, commissioners or judges to constitute a court for hearing and determining the matter in question: but if they cannot agree, congress shall name three persons out of each of the united states, and from the list of such persons each party shall alternately strike out one, the petitioners beginning, until the number shall be reduced to thirteen; and from that number not less than seven, nor more than nine names as congress shall direct, shall in the presence of congress be drawn out by lot, and the persons whose names shall be so drawn or any five of them, shall be commissioners or judges, to hear and finally determine the controversy, so always as a major part of the judges who shall hear the cause shall agree in the determination: and if either party shall neglect to attend at the day appointed, without showing reasons, which congress shall judge sufficient, or being present shall refuse to strike, the congress shall proceed to nominate three persons out of each state, and the secretary of congress shall strike in behalf of such party absent or refusing; and the judgment and sentence of the court to be appointed, in the manner before prescribed, shall be final and conclusive; and if any of the parties shall refuse to submit to the authority of such court, or to appear to defend their claim or cause, the court shall nevertheless proceed to pronounce sentence, or judgment, which shall in like manner be final and decisive, the judgment or sentence and other proceedings being in either case transmitted to congress, and lodged among the acts of congress for the security of the parties concerned: provided that every commissioner, before he sits in judgment, shall take an oath to be administered by one of the judges of the supreme or superior court of the state, where the cause shall be tried, "well and truly to hear and determine the matter in question, according to the best of his judgment, without favour, affection or hope of reward:" provided also that no state shall be deprived of territory for the benefit of the united states.

All controversies concerning the private right of soil claimed under different grants of two or more states, whose jurisdictions as they may respect such lands, and the states which passed such grants are adjusted, the said grants or either of them being at the same time claimed to have originated antecedent to such settlement of jurisdiction, shall on the petition of either party to the congress of the united states, be finally determined as near as may be in the same manner as is before prescribed for deciding disputes respecting territorial jurisdiction between different states.

The united states in congress assembled shall also have the sole and exclusive right and power of regulating the alloy and value of coin struck by their own authority, or by that of the respective states—fixing the standard of weights and measures throughout the united states—regulating the trade and managing all affairs with the Indians, not members of any of the states, provided that the legislative right of any state within its own limits be not infringed or violated—establishing and regulating post-offices from one state to another, throughout all the united states, and exacting such postage on the papers passing thro' the same as may be requisite to defray the expences of the said office—appointing all officers of the land forces, in the service of the united states, excepting regimental officers—appointing all the officers of the naval forces, and commissioning all officers whatever in the service of the united states—making rules for the government and regulation of the said land and naval forces, and directing their operations.

The united states in congress assembled shall have authority to appoint a committee, to sit in the recess of congress, to be denominated "A Committee of the States," and to consist of one delegate from each state; and to appoint such other committees and civil officers as may be necessary for managing the general affairs of the united states under their direction—to appoint one of their number to preside, provided that no person be allowed to serve in the office of president more than one year in any term of three years; to ascertain the necessary sums of Money to be raised for the service of the united states, and to appropriate and apply the same for defraying the public expences—to borrow money, or emit bills on the credit of the united states, transmitting every half year to the respective states an account of the sums of money so borrowed or emitted—to build and equip a navy—to agree upon the number of land forces, and to make requisitions from each state for its quota, in proportion to the number of white inhabitants in such state; which requisition shall be binding, and thereupon the legislature of each state shall appoint the regimental officers, raise the men and cloath, arm and equip them in a soldier like manner, at the expence of the united states, and the officers and men so cloathed, armed and equipped shall march to the place appointed, and within the time agreed on by the united states in congress assembled: But if the united states in congress assembled shall, on consideration of circumstances judge proper that any state should not raise men, or should raise a smaller number than its quota, and that any other state should raise a greater number of men than the quota thereof, such extra number shall be raised, officered, cloathed, armed and equipped in the same manner as the quota of such state, unless the legislature of such state shall judge that such extra number cannot be safely spared out of the same, in which case they shall raise, officer, cloath, arm and equip as many of such extra number as they judge can be safely spared. And the officers and men so cloathed, armed and equipped, shall march to the place appointed, and within the time agreed on by the united states in congress assembled.

The united states in congress assembled shall never engage in a war, nor grant letters of marque and reprisal in time of peace, nor enter into any treaties or alliances, nor coin money, nor regulate the value thereof, nor ascertain the sums and expences necessary for the defence and welfare of the united states, or any of them, nor emit bills, nor borrow money on the credit of the united states, nor appropriate money, nor agree upon the number of vessels of war, to be built or purchased, or the number of land or sea forces to be raised, nor appoint a commander in chief of the army or navy, unless nine states assent to the same: nor shall a question on any other point, except for adjourning from day to day be determined, unless by the votes of a majority of the united states in congress assembled.

The congress of the united states shall have power to adjourn to any time within the year, and to any place within the united states, so that no period of adjournment be for a longer duration than the space of six Months, and shall publish the Journal of their proceedings monthly, except such parts thereof relating to treaties, alliances or military operations as in their judgment require secrecy; and the yeas and nays of the delegates of each state on any question shall be entered on the Journal, when it is desired by any delegate; and the delegates of a state, or any of them, at his or their request shall be furnished with a transcript of the said Journal, except such parts as are above excepted, to lay before the legislatures of the several states.

Article X The committee of the states, or any nine of them, shall be authorised to execute, in the recess of congress, such of the powers of congress as the united states in congress assembled, by the consent of nine states, shall from time to time think expedient to vest them with; provided that no power be delegated to the said committee, for the exercise of which, by the articles of confederation, the voice of nine states in the congress of the united states assembled is requisite.

Article XI Canada acceding to this confederation, and joining in the measures of the united states, shall be admitted into, and entitled to all the advantages of this union: but no other colony shall be admitted into the same, unless such admission be agreed to by nine states.

Article XII All bills of credit emitted, monies borrowed and debts contracted by, or under the authority of congress, before the assembling of the united states, in pursuance of the present confederation, shall be deemed and considered as a charge against the united states, for payment and satisfaction whereof the said united states, and the public faith are hereby solemnly pledged.

Article XIII Every state shall abide by the determinations of the united states in congress assembled, on all questions which by this confederation are submitted to them. And the Articles of this confederation shall be inviolably observed by every state, and the union shall be perpetual; nor shall any alteration at any time hereafter be made in any of them; unless such alteration be agreed to in a congress of the united states, and be afterwards confirmed by the legislatures of every state.

AND WHEREAS it hath pleased the Great Governor of the World to incline the hearts of the legislatures we respectively represent in congress, to approve of, and to authorize us to ratify the said articles of confederation and perpetual union. Know Ye that we the under-signed delegates, by virtue of the power and authority to us given for that purpose, do by these presents, in the name and in behalf of our respective constituents, fully and entirely ratify and confirm each and every of the said articles of confederation and perpetual union, and all and singular the matters and things therein contained: And we do further solemnly plight and engage the faith of our respective constituents, that they shall abide by the determinations of the united states in congress assembled, on all questions, which by the said confederation are submitted to them. And that the articles thereof shall be inviolably observed by the states we respectively represent, and that the union shall be perpetual. In Witness whereof we have hereunto set our hands in Congress. Done at Philadelphia in the state of Pennsylvania the ninth Day of July in the Year of our Lord one Thousand seven Hundred and Seventy-eight, and in the third year of the independence of America.

Constitution of the United States of America and Amendments*

Preamble

We the people of the United States, in order to form a more perfect union, establish justice, insure domestic tranquillity, provide for the common defense, promote the general welfare, and secure the blessings of liberty to ourselves and our posterity, do ordain and establish this Constitution for the United States of America.

Article I

Section 1 All legislative powers herein granted shall be vested in a Congress of the United States, which shall consist of a Senate and a House of Representatives.

Section 2 The House of Representatives shall be composed of members chosen every second year by the people of the several States, and the electors in each State shall have the qualifications requisite for electors of the most numerous branch of the State Legislature.

No person shall be a Representative who shall not have attained to the age of twenty-five years, and been seven years a citizen of the United States, and who shall not, when elected, be an inhabitant of that State in which he shall be chosen.

Representatives and direct taxes shall be apportioned among the several States which may be included within this Union,

---

* Passages no longer in effect are printed in italic type.

according to their respective numbers, *which shall be determined by adding to the whole number of free persons, including those bound to service for a term of years and excluding Indians not taxed, three-fifths of all other persons.* The actual enumeration shall be made within three years after the first meeting of the Congress of the United States, and within every subsequent term of ten years, in such manner as they shall by law direct. The number of Representatives shall not exceed one for every thirty thousand, but each State shall have at least one Representative; *and until such enumeration shall be made, the State of New Hampshire shall be entitled to choose three, Massachusetts eight, Rhode Island and Providence Plantations one, Connecticut five, New York six, New Jersey four, Pennsylvania eight, Delaware one, Maryland six, Virginia ten, North Carolina five, South Carolina five, and Georgia three.*

When vacancies happen in the representation from any State, the Executive authority thereof shall issue writs of election to fill such vacancies.

The House of Representatives shall choose their Speaker and other officers; and shall have the sole power of impeachment.

Section 3 The Senate of the United States shall be composed of two Senators from each State, *chosen by the legislature thereof,* for six years; and each Senator shall have one vote.

Immediately after they shall be assembled in consequence of the first election, they shall be divided as equally as may be into three classes. The seats of the Senators of the first class shall be vacated at the expiration of the second year, of the second class at the expiration of the fourth year, and of the third class at the expiration of the sixth year, so that one-third may be chosen every second year; and if vacancies happen by resignation or otherwise, during the recess of the legislature of any State, the Executive thereof may make temporary appointments until the next meeting of the legislature, which shall then fill such vacancies.

No person shall be a Senator who shall not have attained to the age of thirty years, and been nine years a citizen of the United States, and who shall not, when elected, be an inhabitant of that State for which he shall be chosen.

The Vice-President of the United States shall be President of the Senate, but shall have no vote, unless they be equally divided.

The Senate shall choose their other officers, and also a President *pro tempore,* in the absence of the Vice-President, or when he shall exercise the office of President of the United States.

The Senate shall have the sole power to try all impeachments. When sitting for that purpose, they shall be on oath or affirmation. When the President of the United States is tried, the Chief Justice shall preside: and no person shall be convicted without the concurrence of two-thirds of the members present.

Judgment in cases of impeachment shall not extend further than to removal from the office, and disqualification to hold and enjoy any office of honor, trust or profit under the United States: but the party convicted shall nevertheless be liable and subject to indictment, trial, judgment and punishment, according to law.

Section 4 The times, places and manner of holding elections for Senators and Representatives shall be prescribed in each State by the legislature thereof; but the Congress may at any time by law make or alter such regulations, except as to the places of choosing Senators.

The Congress shall assemble at least once in every year, and such meeting *shall be on the first Monday in December, unless they shall by law appoint a different day.*

Section 5 Each house shall be the judge of the elections, returns and qualifications of its own members, and a majority of each shall constitute a quorum to do business; but a smaller number may adjourn from day to day, and may be authorized to compel the attendance of absent members, in such manner, and under such penalties, as each house may provide.

Each house may determine the rules of its proceedings, punish its members for disorderly behavior, and with the concurrence of two-thirds, expel a member.

Each house shall keep a journal of its proceedings, and from time to time publish the same, excepting such parts as may in their judgment require secrecy; and the yeas and nays of the members of either house on any question shall, at the desire of one-fifth of those present, be entered on the journal.

Neither house, during the session of Congress, shall, without the consent of the other, adjourn for more than three days, nor to any other place than that in which the two houses shall be sitting.

Section 6 The Senators and Representatives shall receive a compensation for their services, to be ascertained by law and paid out of the treasury of the United States. They shall in all cases except treason, felony and breach of the peace, be privileged from arrest during their attendance at the session of their respective houses, and in going to and returning from the same; and for any speech or debate in either house, they shall not be questioned in any other place.

No Senator or Representative shall, during the time for which he was elected, be appointed to any civil office under the authority of the United States, which shall have been created, or the emoluments whereof shall have been increased, during such time; and no person holding any office under the United States shall be a member of either house during his continuance in office.

Section 7 All bills for raising revenue shall originate in the House of Representatives; but the Senate may propose or concur with amendments as on other bills.

Every bill which shall have passed the House of Representatives and the Senate, shall, before it become a law, be presented to the President of the United States; if he approve he shall sign it, but if not he shall return it with objections to that house in which it originated, who shall enter the objections at large on their journal, and proceed to reconsider it. If after such reconsideration two-thirds of that house shall agree to pass the bill, it shall be sent, together with the objections, to the other house, by which it shall likewise be reconsidered, and, if approved by two-thirds of that house, it shall become a law. But in all such cases the votes of both houses shall be determined by yeas and nays, and the names of the persons voting for and against the bill shall be entered on the journal of each house respectively. If any bill shall not be returned by the President within ten days (Sundays excepted) after it shall have been presented to him, the same shall be a law, in like manner as if he had signed it, unless the Congress by their adjournment prevent its return, in which case it shall not be a law.

Every order, resolution, or vote to which the concurrence of the Senate and House of Representatives may be necessary (except on a question of adjournment) shall be presented to the President of the United States; and before the same shall take effect, shall be approved by him, or being disapproved by him, shall be repassed by two-thirds of the Senate and House of Representatives, according to the rules and limitations prescribed in the case of a bill.

Section 8 The Congress shall have power

To lay and collect taxes, duties, imposts, and excises, to pay the debts and provide for the common defense and general welfare of the United States; but all duties, imposts and excises shall be uniform throughout the United States;

To borrow money on the credit of the United States;

To regulate commerce with foreign nations, and among the several States, and with the Indian tribes;

To establish an uniform rule of naturalization, and uniform laws on the subject of bankruptcies throughout the United States;

To coin money, regulate the value thereof, and of foreign coin, and fix the standard of weights and measures;

To provide for the punishment of counterfeiting the securities and current coin of the United States;

To establish post offices and post roads;

To promote the progress of science and useful arts by securing for limited times to authors and inventors the exclusive right to their respective writings and discoveries;

To constitute tribunals inferior to the Supreme Court;

To define and punish piracies and felonies committed on the high seas and offenses against the law of nations;

To declare war, grant letters of marque and reprisal, and make rules concerning captures on land and water;

To raise and support armies, but no appropriation of money to that use shall be for a longer term than two years;

To provide and maintain a navy;

To make rules for the government and regulation of the land and naval forces;

To provide for calling forth the militia to execute the laws of the Union, suppress insurrections, and repel invasions;

To provide for organizing, arming, and disciplining the militia, and for governing such part of them as may be employed in the service of the United States, reserving to the States respectively the appointment of the officers, and the authority of training the militia according to the discipline prescribed by Congress;

To exercise exclusive legislation in all cases whatsoever, over such district (not exceeding ten miles square) as may, by cession of particular States, and the acceptance of Congress, become the seat of government of the United States, and to exercise like authority over all places purchased by the consent of the legislature of the State, in which the same shall be, for erection of forts, magazines, arsenals, dockyards, and other needful buildings; —and

To make all laws which shall be necessary and proper for carrying into execution the foregoing powers, and all other powers vested by this Constitution in the government of the United States, or in any department or officer thereof.

Section 9 *The migration or importation of such persons as any of the States now existing shall think proper to admit shall not be prohibited by the Congress prior to the year 1808; but a tax or duty may be imposed on such importation, not exceeding $10 for each person.*

The privilege of the writ of habeas corpus shall not be suspended, unless when in cases of rebellion or invasion the public safety may require it.

No bill of attainder or ex post facto law shall be passed.

No capitation, or other direct, tax shall be laid, unless in proportion to the census or enumeration herein before directed to be taken.

No tax or duty shall be laid on articles exported from any State.

No preference shall be given by any regulation of commerce or revenue to the ports of one State over those of another; nor shall vessels bound to, or from, one State, be obliged to enter, clear, or pay duties in another.

No money shall be drawn from the treasury, but in consequence of appropriations made by law; and a regular statement and account of the receipts and expenditures of all public money shall be published from time to time.

No title of nobility shall be granted by the United States: and no person holding any office of profit or trust under them, shall, without the consent of the Congress, accept of any present, emolument, office, or title, of any kind whatever, from any king, prince, or foreign state.

Section 10 No State shall enter into any treaty, alliance, or confederation; grant letters of marque and reprisal; coin money; emit bills of credit; make anything but gold and silver coin a tender in payment of debts; pass any bill of attainder, ex post facto law, or law impairing the obligation of contracts, or grant any title of nobility.

No State shall, without the consent of Congress, lay any imposts or duties on imports or exports, except what may be absolutely necessary for executing its inspection laws: and the net produce of all duties and imposts, laid by any State on imports or exports, shall be for the use of the treasury of the United States; and all such laws shall be subject to the revision and control of the Congress.

No State shall, without the consent of Congress, lay any duty of tonnage, keep troops or ships of war in time of peace, enter into any agreement or compact with another State, or with a foreign power, or engage in war, unless actually invaded, or in such imminent danger as will not admit of delay.

Article II

Section 1 The executive power shall be vested in a President of the United States of America. He shall hold his office during the term of four years, and, together with the Vice-President, chosen for the same term, be elected as follows:

Each State shall appoint, in such manner as the legislature thereof may direct, a number of electors, equal to the whole number of Senators and Representatives to which the State may be entitled in the Congress; but no Senator or Representative, or person holding an office of trust or profit under the United States, shall be appointed an elector.

The electors shall meet in their respective States, and vote by ballot for two persons, of

whom one at least shall not be an inhabitant of the same State with themselves. And they shall make a list of all the persons voted for, and of the number of votes for each; which list they shall sign and certify, and transmit sealed to the seat of government of the United States, directed to the President of the Senate. The President of the Senate shall, in the presence of the Senate and House of Representatives, open all the certificates, and the votes shall then be counted. The person having the greatest number of votes shall be the President, if such number be a majority of the whole number of electors appointed; and if there be more than one who have such majority, and have an equal number of votes, then the House of Representatives shall immediately choose by ballot one of them for President; and if no person have a majority, then from the five highest on the list said house shall in like manner choose the President. But in choosing the President the votes shall be taken by States, the representation from each State having one vote; a quorum for this purpose shall consist of a member or members from two-thirds of the States, and a majority of all the States shall be necessary to a choice. In every case, after the choice of the President, the person having the greatest number of votes of the electors shall be the Vice-President. But if there should remain two or more who have equal votes, the Senate shall choose from them by ballot the Vice-President.

The Congress may determine the time of choosing the electors and the day on which they shall give their votes; which day shall be the same throughout the United States.

No person except a natural-born citizen, *or a citizen of the United States at the time of the adoption of this Constitution,* shall be eligible to the office of President; neither shall any person be eligible to that office who shall not have attained to the age of thirty-five years, and been fourteen years a resident within the United States.

In cases of the removal of the President from office or of his death, resignation, or inability to discharge the powers and duties of the said office, the same shall devolve on the Vice-President, and the Congress may by law provide for the case of removal, death, resignation, or inability, both of the President and Vice-President, declaring what officer shall then act as President, and such officer shall act accordingly, until the disability be removed, or a President shall be elected.

The President shall, at stated times, receive for his services a compensation, which shall neither be increased nor diminished during the period for which he shall have been elected, and he shall not receive within that period any other emolument from the United States, or any of them.

Before he enter on the execution of his office, he shall take the following oath or affirmation:—"I do solemnly swear (or affirm) that I will faithfully execute the office of the President of the United States, and will to the best of my ability preserve, protect and defend the Constitution of the United States."

Section 2 The President shall be commander in chief of the army and navy of the United States, and of the militia of the several States, when called into the actual service of the United States; he may require the opinion, in writing, of the principal officer in each of the executive departments, upon any subject relating to the duties of their respective offices, and he shall have power to grant reprieves and pardons for offenses against the United States, except in cases of impeachment.

He shall have power, by and with the advice and consent of the Senate, to make treaties, provided two-thirds of the Senators present concur; and he shall nominate, and by and with the advice and consent of the Senate, shall appoint ambassadors, other public ministers and consuls, judges of the Supreme Court, and all other officers of the United States, whose appointments are not herein otherwise provided for, and which shall be established by law: but Congress may by law vest the appointment of such inferior officers, as they think proper, in the President alone, in the courts of law, or in the heads of departments.

The President shall have power to fill up all vacancies that may happen during the recess of the Senate, by granting commissions which shall expire at the end of their next session.

Section 3 He shall from time to time give to the Congress information of the state of the Union, and recommend to their consideration such measures as he shall judge necessary and expedient; he may, on extraordinary occasions, convene both houses, or either of them, and in case of disagreement between them, with respect to the time of adjournment, he may

adjourn them to such time as he shall think proper; he shall receive ambassadors and other public ministers; he shall take care that the laws be faithfully executed, and shall commission all the officers of the United States.

Section 4 The President, Vice-President and all civil officers of the United States shall be removed from office on impeachment for, and on conviction of, treason, bribery, or other high crimes and misdemeanors.

Article III

Section 1 The judicial power of the United States shall be vested in one Supreme Court, and in such inferior courts as the Congress may from time to time ordain and establish. The judges, both of the Supreme and inferior courts, shall hold their offices during good behavior, and shall, at stated times, receive for their services a compensation which shall not be diminished during their continuance in office.

Section 2 The judicial power shall extend to all cases, in law and equity, arising under this Constitution, the laws of the United States, and treaties made, or which shall be made, under their authority;—to all cases affecting ambassadors, other public ministers and consuls;—to all cases of admiralty and maritime jurisdiction;— to controversies to which the United States shall be a party;—to controversies between two or more States;— *between a State and citizens of another State;*—between citizens of different States;—between citizens of the same State claiming lands under grants of different States, and between a State, or the citizens thereof, and foreign states, citizens or subjects.

In all cases affecting ambassadors, other public ministers and consuls, and those in which a State shall be party, the Supreme Court shall have original jurisdiction. In all the other cases before mentioned, the Supreme Court shall have appellate jurisdiction, both as to law and fact, with such exceptions, and under such regulations, as the Congress shall make.

The trial of all crimes, except in cases of impeachment, shall be by jury; and such trial shall be held in the State where said crimes shall have been committed; but when not committed within any State, the trial shall be at such place or places as the Congress may by law have directed.

Section 3 Treason against the United States shall consist only in levying war against them, or in adhering to their enemies, giving them aid and comfort. No person shall be convicted of treason unless on the testimony of two witnesses to the same overt act, or on confession in open court.

The Congress shall have power to declare the punishment of treason, but no attainder of treason shall work corruption of blood, or forfeiture except during the life of the person attainted.

Article IV

Section 1 Full faith and credit shall be given in each State to the public acts, records, and judicial proceedings of every other State. And the Congress may by general laws prescribe the manner in which such acts, records, and proceedings shall be proved, and the effect thereof.

Section 2 The citizens of each State shall be entitled to all privileges and immunities of citizens in the several States.

A person charged in any State with treason, felony, or other crime, who shall flee from justice, and be found in another State, shall on demand of the executive authority of the State from which he fled, be delivered up, to be removed to the State having jurisdiction of the crime.

No person held to service or labor in one State, under the laws thereof, escaping into another, shall, in consequence of any law or regulation therein, be discharged from such service or labor, but shall be delivered up on claim of the party to whom such service or labor may be due.

Section 3 New States may be admitted by the Congress into this Union; but no new State shall be formed or erected within the jurisdiction of any other State; nor any State be formed by the junction of two or more States, or parts of States, without the consent of the legislatures of the States concerned as well as of the Congress.

The Congress shall have power to dispose of and make all needful rules and regulations respecting the territory or other property belonging to the United States; and nothing in this Constitution shall be so construed as to prejudice any claims of the United States, or of any particular State.

Section 4 The United States shall guarantee to every State in this Union a republican form of government, and shall protect each of them against invasion; and on application of the legislature, or of the executive (when the legislature cannot be convened), against domestic violence.

Article V

The Congress, whenever two-thirds of both houses shall deem it necessary, shall propose amendments to this Constitution, or, on the application of the legislatures of two-thirds of the several States, shall call a convention for proposing amendments, which, in either case, shall be valid to all intents and purposes, as part of this Constitution, when ratified by the legislatures of three-fourths of the several States, or by conventions in three-fourths thereof, as the one or the other mode of ratification may be proposed by the Congress; provided *that no amendments which may be made prior to the year one thousand eight hundred and eight shall in any manner affect the first and fourth clauses in the ninth section of the first article;* and that no State,

without its consent, shall be deprived of its equal suffrage in the Senate.

Article VI

All debts contracted and engagements entered into, before the adoption of this Constitution, shall be as valid against the United States under this Constitution, as under the Confederation.

This Constitution, and the laws of the United States which shall be made in pursuance thereof; and all treaties made, or which shall be made, under the authority of the United States, shall be the supreme law of the land; and the judges in every State shall be bound thereby, anything in the Constitution or laws of any State to the contrary notwithstanding.

The Senators and Representatives before mentioned, and the members of the several State legislatures, and all executive and judicial officers, both of the United States and of the several States, shall be bound by oath or affirmation to support this Constitution; but no religious test shall ever be required as a qualification to any office or public trust under the United States.

Article VII

The ratification of the conventions of nine States shall be sufficient for the establishment of this Constitution between the States so ratifying the same.

Done in Convention by the unanimous consent of the States present, the seventeenth day of September in the year of our Lord one thousand seven hundred and eighty-seven and of the Independence of the United States of America the twelfth. In witness whereof we have hereunto subscribed our names.

Amendments to the Constitution*

Amendment I

Congress shall make no law respecting an establishment of religion, or prohibiting the free exercise thereof; or abridging the freedom of speech, or of the press; or the right of the people peaceably to assemble, and to petition the government for a redress of grievances.

Amendment II

A well-regulated militia being necessary to the security of a free State, the right of the people to keep and bear arms shall not be infringed.

Amendment III

No soldier shall, in time of peace, be quartered in any house without the consent of the owner, nor in time of war, but in a manner to be prescribed by law.

Amendment IV

The right of the people to be secure in their persons, houses, papers, and effects, against unreasonable searches and seizures, shall not be violated, and no warrants shall issue but upon probable cause, supported by

*The first ten Amendments (the Bill of Rights) were adopted in 1791.

oath or affirmation, and particularly describing the place to be searched, and the persons or things to be seized.

Amendment V

No person shall be held to answer for a capital, or otherwise infamous crime, unless on a presentment or indictment of a grand jury, except in cases arising in the land or naval forces, or in the militia, when in actual service in time of war or public danger; nor shall any person be subject for the same offense to be twice put in jeopardy of life or limb; nor shall be compelled in any criminal case to be a witness against himself, nor be deprived of life, liberty, or property, without due process of law; nor shall private property be taken for public use without just compensation.

Amendment VI

In all criminal prosecutions, the accused shall enjoy the right to a speedy and public trial, by an impartial jury of the State and district wherein the crime shall have been committed, which district shall have been previously ascertained by law, and to be informed of the nature and cause of the accusation; to be confronted with the witnesses against him; to have compulsory process for obtaining witnesses in his favor, and to have the assistance of counsel for his defense.

Amendment VII

In suits at common law, where the value in controversy shall exceed twenty dollars, the right of trial by jury shall be preserved, and no fact tried by a jury shall be otherwise reexamined in any court of the United States, than according to the rules of the common law.

Amendment VIII

Excessive bail shall not be required, nor excessive fines imposed, nor cruel and unusual punishments inflicted.

Amendment IX

The enumeration in the Constitution, of certain rights, shall not be construed to deny or disparage others retained by the people.

Amendment X

The powers not delegated to the United States by the Constitution, nor prohibited by it to the States, are reserved to the States respectively, or to the people.

Amendment XI

[Adopted 1798]

The judicial power of the United States shall not be construed to extend to any suit in law or equity, commenced or prosecuted against one of the United States by citizens of another State, or by citizens or subjects of any foreign state.

Amendment XII

[Adopted 1804]

The electors shall meet in their respective States, and vote by ballot for President and Vice-President, one of whom, at least, shall not be an inhabitant of the same State with themselves; they shall name in their ballots the person voted for as President, and in distinct ballots the person voted for as Vice-President, and they shall make distinct lists of all persons voted for as President, and of all persons voted for as Vice-President, and of the number of votes for each, which lists they shall sign and certify, and transmit sealed to the seat of government of the United States, directed to the President of the Senate;— the President of the Senate shall, in the presence of the Senate and House of Representatives, open all the certificates and the votes shall then be counted;—the person having the greatest number of votes for President shall be the President, if such number be a majority of the whole number of electors appointed; and if no person have such majority, then from the persons having the highest numbers not exceeding three on the list of those voted for as President, the House of Representatives shall choose immediately, by ballot, the President. But in choosing the President, the votes shall be taken by States, the representation from each State having one vote; a quorum for this purpose shall consist of a member or members from two-thirds of the States, and a majority of all the States shall be necessary to a choice. And if the House of Representatives shall not choose a President whenever the right of choice shall devolve upon them, before *the fourth day of March* next following, then the Vice-President shall act as President, as in the case of the death or other constitutional disability of the President.

The person having the greatest number of votes as Vice-President shall be the Vice-President, if such number be a majority of the whole number of electors appointed; and if no person have a majority, then from the two highest numbers on the list the Senate shall choose the Vice-President; a quorum for the purpose shall consist of two-thirds of the whole number of Senators, and a majority of the whole number shall be necessary to a choice. But no person constitutionally ineligible to the office of President shall be eligible to that of Vice-President of the United States.

Amendment XIII

[Adopted 1865]

Section 1 Neither slavery nor involuntary servitude, except as a punishment for crime whereof the party shall have been duly convicted, shall exist within the United States, or any place subject to their jurisdiction.

Section 2 Congress shall have power to enforce this article by appropriate legislation.

Amendment XIV

[Adopted 1868]

Section 1 All persons born or naturalized in the United States, and subject to the jurisdiction thereof, are citizens of the United States and of the State wherein they reside. No State shall make or enforce any law which shall abridge the privileges or immunities of citizens of the United States; nor shall any State deprive any person of life, liberty, or property, without due process of law; nor deny to any person within its jurisdiction the equal protection of the laws.

Section 2 Representatives shall be apportioned among the several States according to their respective numbers, counting the whole number of persons in each State, excluding Indians not taxed. But when the right to vote at any election for the choice of Electors for President and Vice-President of the United States, Representatives in Congress, the executive and judicial officers of a State, or the members of the legislature thereof, is denied to any of the male inhabitants of such State, being twenty-one years of age and citizens of the United States, or in any way abridged, except for participation in rebellion, or other crime, the basis of representation therein shall be reduced in the proportion which the number of such male citizens shall bear to the whole number of male citizens twenty-one years of age in such State.

Section 3 No person shall be a Senator or Representative in Congress, or Elector of President and Vice-President, or hold any office, civil or military, under the United States, or under any State, who, having previously taken an oath, as a member of Congress, or as an officer of the United States, or as a member of any State legislature, or as an executive or judicial officer of any State, to support the Constitution of the United States, shall have engaged in insurrection or rebellion against the same, or given aid or comfort to the enemies thereof. Congress may, by a vote of two-thirds of each house, remove such disability.

Section 4 The validity of the public debt of the United States, authorized by law, including debts incurred for payment of pensions and bounties for services in suppressing insurrection or rebellion, shall not be questioned. But neither the United States nor any State shall assume or pay any debt or obligation incurred in aid of insurrection or rebellion against the United States, or any claim for the loss of emancipation of any slave; but all such debts, obligations, and claims shall be held illegal and void.

Section 5 The Congress shall have power to enforce, by appropriate legislation, the provisions of this article.

Amendment XV

[Adopted 1870]

Section 1 The right of citizens of the United States to vote shall not be denied or abridged by the United States or by any State on account of race, color, or previous condition of servitude.

Section 2 The Congress shall have power to enforce this article by appropriate legislation.

Amendment XVI

[Adopted 1913]

The Congress shall have power to lay and collect taxes on incomes, from whatever source derived, without apportionment among the several States, and without regard to any census or enumeration.

Amendment XVII

[Adopted 1913]

Section 1 The Senate of the United States shall be composed of two Senators from each State, elected by the people thereof, for six years; and each Senator shall have one vote. The electors in each State shall have the qualifications requisite for electors of [voters for] the most numerous branch of the State legislatures.

Section 2 When vacancies happen in the representation of any State in the Senate, the executive authority of such State shall issue writs of election to fill such vacancies: Provided, that the Legislature of any State may empower the executive thereof to make temporary appointments until the people fill the vacancies by election as the Legislature may direct.

Section 3 This amendment shall not be so construed as to affect the election or term of any Senator chosen before it becomes valid as part of the Constitution.

Amendment XVIII

[Adopted 1919; Repealed 1933]

Section 1 After one year from the ratification of this article the manufacture, sale, or transportation of intoxicating liquors within, the importation thereof into, or the exportation thereof from the United States and all territory subject to the jurisdiction thereof, for beverage purposes, is hereby prohibited.

Section 2 The Congress and the several States shall have concurrent power to enforce this article by appropriate legislation.

Section 3 This article shall be inoperative unless it shall have been ratified as an amendment to the Constitution by the legislatures of the several States, as provided by the Constitution, within seven years from the date of the submission thereof to the States by the Congress.

Amendment XIX

[Adopted 1920]

Section 1 The right of citizens of the United States to vote shall not be denied or abridged by the United States or by any State on account of sex.

Section 2 The Congress shall have power to enforce this article by appropriate legislation.

Amendment XX

[Adopted 1933]

Section 1 The terms of the President and Vice-President shall end at noon on the 20th day of January, and the terms of Senators and Representatives at noon on the 3rd day of January, of the years in which such terms would have ended if this article had not been ratified; and the terms of their successors shall then begin.

Section 2 The Congress shall assemble at least once in every year, and such meeting shall begin at noon on the 3rd day of January, unless they shall by law appoint a different day.

Section 3 If, at the time fixed for the beginning of the term of the President, the President-elect shall have died, the Vice-President-elect shall become President. If a President shall not have been chosen before the time fixed for the beginning of his term, or if the President-elect shall have failed to qualify, then the Vice-President-elect shall act as President until a President shall have qualified; and the Congress may by law provide for the case wherein neither a President-elect nor a Vice-President-elect shall have qualified, declaring who shall then act as President, or the manner in which one who is to act shall be selected, and such persons shall act accordingly until a President or Vice-President shall have qualified.

Section 4 The Congress may by law provide for the case of the death of any of the persons from whom the House of Representatives may choose a President whenever the right of choice shall have devolved upon them, and for the case of the death of any of the persons from whom the Senate may choose a Vice-President whenever the right of choice shall have devolved upon them.

Section 5 Sections 1 and 2 shall take effect on the 15th day of October following the ratification of this article.

Section 6 This article shall be inoperative unless it shall have been ratified as an amendment to the Constitution by the Legislatures of three-fourths of the several States within seven years from the date of its submission.

Amendment XXI

[Adopted 1933]

Section 1 The eighteenth article of amendment to the Constitution of the United States is hereby repealed.

Section 2 The transportation or importation into any State, Territory, or Possession of the United States for delivery or use therein of intoxicating liquors, in violation of the laws thereof, is hereby prohibited.

Section 3 This article shall be inoperative unless it shall have been ratified as an amendment to the Constitution by conventions in the several States, as provided in the Constitution, within seven years from the date of submission thereof to the States by the Congress.

Amendment XXII

[Adopted 1951]

Section 1 No person shall be elected to the office of President more than twice, and no person who has held the office of President, or acted as President, for more than two years of a term to which some other person was elected President shall be elected to the office of President more than once. But this article shall not apply to any person holding the office of President when this article was proposed by the Congress, and shall not prevent any person who may be holding the office of President, or acting as President, during the term within which this article becomes operative from holding the office of President or acting as President during the remainder of such term.

Section 2 This article shall be inoperative unless it shall have been ratified as an amendment to the Constitution by the legislatures of three-fourths of the several States within seven years from the date of its submission to the States by the Congress.

Amendment XXIII

[Adopted 1961]

Section 1 The District constituting the seat of Government of the United States shall appoint in such manner as the Congress may direct:

A number of electors of President and Vice-President equal to the whole number of Senators and Representatives in Congress to which the District would be entitled if it were a State, but in no event more than the least populous State; they shall be in addition to those appointed by the States, but they shall be considered for the purposes of the election of President and Vice-President, to be electors appointed by a State; and they shall meet in the District and perform such duties as provided by the twelfth article of amendment.

Section 2 The Congress shall have the power to enforce this article by appropriate legislation.

Amendment XXIV

[Adopted 1964]

Section 1 The right of citizens of the United States to vote in any primary or other election for President or Vice-President, for electors for President or Vice-President, or for Senator or Representative in Congress, shall not be denied or abridged by the United States or any State by reason of failure to pay any poll tax or other tax.

Section 2 The Congress shall have the power to enforce this article by appropriate legislation.

Amendment XXV

[Adopted 1967]

Section 1 In case of the removal of the President from office or of his death or resignation, the Vice-President shall become President.

Section 2 Whenever there is a vacancy in the office of the Vice-President, the President shall nominate a Vice-President who shall take office upon confirmation by a majority vote of both Houses of Congress.

Section 3 Whenever the President transmits to the President pro tempore of the Senate and the Speaker of the House of Representatives his written declaration that he is unable to discharge the powers and duties of his office, and until he transmits to them a written declaration to the contrary, such powers and duties shall be discharged by the Vice-President as Acting President.

Section 4 Whenever the Vice-President and a majority of either the principal officers of the executive departments or of such other body as Congress may by law provide, transmit to the President pro tempore of the Senate and the Speaker of the House of Representatives their written declaration that the President is unable to discharge the powers and duties of his office, the Vice-President shall immediately assume the powers and duties of the office as Acting President.

Thereafter, when the President transmits to the President pro tempore of the Senate and the Speaker of the House of Representatives his written declaration that no inability exists, he shall resume the powers and duties of his office unless the Vice-President and a majority of either the principal officers of the executive department[s] or of such other body as Congress may by law provide, transmit within four days to the President pro tempore of the Senate and the Speaker of the House of Representatives their written declaration that the President is unable to discharge the powers and duties of his office. Thereupon Congress shall decide the issue, assembling within forty-eight hours for that purpose if not in session. If the Congress, within twenty-one days after receipt of the latter written declaration, or, if Congress is not in session, within twenty-one days after Congress is required to assemble, determines by two-thirds vote of both Houses that the President is unable to discharge the powers and duties of his office, the Vice-President shall continue to discharge the same as Acting President; otherwise, the President shall resume the powers and duties of his office.

Amendment XXVI

[Adopted 1971]

Section 1 The right of citizens of the United States, who are eighteen years of age or older, to vote shall not be denied or abridged by the United States or by any State on account of age.

Section 2 The Congress shall have power to enforce this article by appropriate legislation.

Amendment XXVII

[Adopted 1992]

No law, varying the compensation for the services of the Senators and Representatives, shall take effect, until an election of Representatives shall have intervened.

Presidential Elections

Year	Number of States	Candidates	Parties	Popular Vote	% of Popular Vote	Electoral Vote	% Voter Participation[a]
1789	10	GEORGE WASHINGTON	No party designations			69	
		John Adams				34	
		Other candidates				35	
1792	15	GEORGE WASHINGTON	No party designations			132	
		John Adams				77	
		George Clinton				50	
		Other candidates				5	
1796	16	JOHN ADAMS	Federalist			71	
		Thomas Jefferson	Democratic-Republican			68	
		Thomas Pinckney	Federalist			59	
		Aaron Burr	Democratic-Republican			30	
		Other candidates				48	
1800	16	THOMAS JEFFERSON	Democratic-Republican			73	
		Aaron Burr	Democratic-Republican			73	
		John Adams	Federalist			65	
		Charles C. Pinckney	Federalist			64	
		John Jay	Federalist			1	
1804	17	THOMAS JEFFERSON	Democratic-Republican			162	
		Charles C. Pinckney	Federalist			14	
1808	17	JAMES MADISON	Democratic-Republican			122	
		Charles C. Pinckney	Federalist			47	
		George Clinton	Democratic-Republican			6	
1812	18	JAMES MADISON	Democratic-Republican			128	
		DeWitt Clinton	Federalist			89	
1816	19	JAMES MONROE	Democratic-Republican			183	
		Rufus King	Federalist			34	
1820	24	JAMES MONROE	Democratic-Republican			231	
		John Quincy Adams	Independent Republican			1	
1824	24	JOHN QUINCY ADAMS	Democratic-Republican	108,740	30.5	84	26.9
		Andrew Jackson	Democratic-Republican	153,544	43.1	99	
		Henry Clay	Democratic-Republican	47,136	13.2	37	
		William H. Crawford	Democratic-Republican	46,618	13.1	41	
1828	24	ANDREW JACKSON	Democratic	647,286	56.0	178	57.6
		John Quincy Adams	National Republican	508,064	44.0	83	
1832	24	ANDREW JACKSON	Democratic	701,780	54.2	219	55.4
		Henry Clay	National Republican	484,205	37.4	49	
		Other candidates		107,988	8.0	18	
1836	26	MARTIN VAN BUREN	Democratic	764,176	50.8	170	57.8
		William H. Harrison	Whig	550,816	36.6	73	
		Hugh L. White	Whig	146,107	9.7	26	
1840	26	WILLIAM H. HARRISON	Whig	1,274,624	53.1	234	80.2
		Martin Van Buren	Democratic	1,127,781	46.9	60	
1844	26	JAMES K. POLK	Democratic	1,338,464	49.6	170	78.9
		Henry Clay	Whig	1,300,097	48.1	105	
		James G. Birney	Liberty	62,300	2.3		

Presidential Elections (continued)

Year	Number of States	Candidates	Parties	Popular Vote	% of Popular Vote	Electoral Vote	% Voter Participation[a]
1848	30	ZACHARY TAYLOR	Whig	1,360,967	47.4	163	72.7
		Lewis Cass	Democratic	1,222,342	42.5	127	
		Martin Van Buren	Free Soil	291,263	10.1		
1852	31	FRANKLIN PIERCE	Democratic	1,601,117	50.9	254	69.6
		Winfield Scott	Whig	1,385,453	44.1	42	
		John P. Hale	Free Soil	155,825	5.0		
1856	31	JAMES BUCHANAN	Democratic	1,832,955	45.3	174	78.9
		John C. Frémont	Republican	1,339,932	33.1	114	
		Millard Fillmore	American	871,731	21.6		
1860	33	ABRAHAM LINCOLN	Republican	1,865,593	39.8	180	81.2
		Stephen A. Douglas	Democratic	1,382,713	29.5	12	
		John C. Breckinridge	Democratic	848,356	18.1	72	
		John Bell	Constitutional Union	592,906	12.6	39	
1864	36	ABRAHAM LINCOLN	Republican	2,206,938	55.0	212	73.8
		George B. McClellan	Democratic	1,803,787	45.0	21	
1868	37	ULYSSES S. GRANT	Republican	3,013,421	52.7	214	78.1
		Horatio Seymour	Democratic	2,706,829	47.3	80	
1872	37	ULYSSES S. GRANT	Republican	3,596,745	55.6	286	71.3
		Horace Greeley[b]	Democratic	2,843,446	43.9		
1876	38	RUTHERFORD B. HAYES	Republican	4,036,572	48.0	185	81.8
		Samuel J. Tilden	Democratic	4,284,020	51.0	184	
1880	38	JAMES A. GARFIELD	Republican	4,453,295	48.5	214	79.4
		Winfield S. Hancock	Democratic	4,414,082	48.1	155	
		James B. Weaver	Greenback-Labor	308,578	3.4		
1884	38	GROVER CLEVELAND	Democratic	4,879,507	48.5	219	77.5
		James G. Blaine	Republican	4,850,293	48.2	182	
		Benjamin F. Butler	Greenback-Labor	175,370	1.8		
		John P. St. John	Prohibition	150,369	1.5		
1888	38	BENJAMIN HARRISON	Republican	5,447,129	47.9	233	79.3
		Grover Cleveland	Democratic	5,537,857	48.6	168	
		Clinton B. Fisk	Prohibition	249,506	2.2		
		Anson J. Streeter	Union Labor	146,935	1.3		
1892	44	GROVER CLEVELAND	Democratic	5,555,426	46.1	277	74.7
		Benjamin Harrison	Republican	5,182,690	43.0	145	
		James B. Weaver	People's	1,029,846	8.5	22	
		John Bidwell	Prohibition	264,133	2.2		
1896	45	WILLIAM McKINLEY	Republican	7,102,246	51.1	271	79.3
		William J. Bryan	Democratic	6,492,559	47.7	176	
1900	45	WILLIAM McKINLEY	Republican	7,218,491	51.7	292	73.2
		William J. Bryan	Democratic; Populist	6,356,734	45.5	155	
		John C. Wooley	Prohibition	208,914	1.5		
1904	45	THEODORE ROOSEVELT	Republican	7,628,461	57.4	336	65.2
		Alton B. Parker	Democratic	5,084,223	37.6	140	
		Eugene V. Debs	Socialist	402,283	3.0		
		Silas C. Swallow	Prohibition	258,536	1.9		

Year	Number of States	Candidates	Parties	Popular Vote	% of Popular Vote	Electoral Vote	% Voter Participation[a]
1908	46	WILLIAM H. TAFT	Republican	7,675,320	51.6	321	65.4
		William J. Bryan	Democratic	6,412,294	43.1	162	
		Eugene V. Debs	Socialist	420,793	2.8		
		Eugene W. Chafin	Prohibition	253,840	1.7		
1912	48	WOODROW WILSON	Democratic	6,296,547	41.9	435	58.8
		Theodore Roosevelt	Progressive	4,118,571	27.4	88	
		William H. Taft	Republican	3,486,720	23.2	8	
		Eugene V. Debs	Socialist	900,672	6.0		
		Eugene W. Chafin	Prohibition	206,275	1.4		
1916	48	WOODROW WILSON	Democratic	9,127,695	49.4	277	61.6
		Charles E. Hughes	Republican	8,533,507	46.2	254	
		A. L. Benson	Socialist	585,113	3.2		
		J. Frank Hanly	Prohibition	220,506	1.2		
1920	48	WARREN G. HARDING	Republican	16,143,407	60.4	404	49.2
		James M. Cox	Democratic	9,130,328	34.2	127	
		Eugene V. Debs	Socialist	919,799	3.4		
		P. P. Christensen	Farmer-Labor	265,411	1.0		
1924	48	CALVIN COOLIDGE	Republican	15,718,211	54.0	382	48.9
		John W. Davis	Democratic	8,385,283	28.8	136	
		Robert M. La Follette	Progressive	4,831,289	16.6	13	
1928	48	HERBERT C. HOOVER	Republican	21,391,993	58.2	444	56.9
		Alfred E. Smith	Democratic	15,016,169	40.9	87	
1932	48	FRANKLIN D. ROOSEVELT	Democratic	22,821,857	57.4	472	56.9
		Herbert C. Hoover	Republican	15,761,841	39.7	59	
		Norman Thomas	Socialist	884,781	2.2		
1936	48	FRANKLIN D. ROOSEVELT	Democratic	27,752,869	60.8	523	61.0
		Alfred M. Landon	Republican	16,674,665	36.5	8	
		William Lemke	Union	882,479	1.9		
1940	48	FRANKLIN D. ROOSEVELT	Democratic	27,307,819	54.8	449	62.5
		Wendell L. Willkie	Republican	22,321,018	44.8	82	
1944	48	FRANKLIN D. ROOSEVELT	Democratic	25,606,585	53.5	432	55.9
		Thomas E. Dewey	Republican	22,014,745	46.0	99	
1948	48	HARRY S TRUMAN	Democratic	24,179,345	49.6	303	53.0
		Thomas E. Dewey	Republican	21,991,291	45.1	189	
		J. Strom Thurmond	States' Rights	1,176,125	2.4	39	
		Henry A. Wallace	Progressive	1,157,326	2.4		
1952	48	DWIGHT D. EISENHOWER	Republican	33,936,234	55.1	442	63.3
		Adlai E. Stevenson	Democratic	27,314,992	44.4	89	
1956	48	DWIGHT D. EISENHOWER	Republican	35,590,472	57.6	457	60.6
		Adlai E. Stevenson	Democratic	26,022,752	42.1	73	
1960	50	JOHN F. KENNEDY	Democratic	34,226,731	49.7	303	62.8
		Richard M. Nixon	Republican	34,108,157	49.5	219	
1964	50	LYNDON B. JOHNSON	Democratic	43,129,566	61.1	486	61.7
		Barry M. Goldwater	Republican	27,178,188	38.5	52	

Presidential Elections (continued)

Year	Number of States	Candidates	Parties	Popular Vote	% of Popular Vote	Electoral Vote	% Voter Participation[a]
1968	50	RICHARD M. NIXON	Republican	33,045,480	43.4	301	60.6
		Hubert H. Humphrey	Democratic	31,850,140	42.7	191	
		George C. Wallace	American Independent	171,422	13.5	46	
1972	50	RICHARD M. NIXON	Republican	47,169,911	60.7	520	55.2
		George S. McGovern	Democratic	29,170,383	37.5	17	
		John G. Schmitz	American	1,099,482	1.4		
1976	50	JAMES E. CARTER	Democratic	40,830,763	50.1	297	53.5
		Gerald R. Ford	Republican	39,147,793	48.0	240	
1980	50	RONALD W. REAGAN	Republican	43,904,153	50.7	489	52.6
		James E. Carter	Democratic	35,483,883	41.0	49	
		John B. Anderson	Independent	5,720,060	6.6		
		Ed Clark	Libertarian	921,299	1.1		
1984	50	RONALD W. REAGAN	Republican	54,455,075	58.8	525	53.3
		Walter F. Mondale	Democratic	37,577,185	40.6	13	
1988	50	GEORGE H. W. BUSH	Republican	48,886,097	53.4	426	50.1
		Michael S. Dukakis	Democratic	41,809,074	45.6	111[c]	
1992	50	WILLIAM J. CLINTON	Democratic	44,909,326	43.0	370	55.2
		George H. W. Bush	Republican	39,103,882	37.4	168	
		H. Ross Perot	Independent	19,741,048	18.9		
1996	50	WILLIAM J. CLINTON	Democratic	47,402,357	49.2	379	49.1
		Robert J. Dole	Republican	39,196,755	40.7	159	
		H. Ross Perot	Reform	8,085,402	8.4		
		Ralph Nader	Green	684,902	0.7		
2000	50	GEORGE W. BUSH	Republican	50,456,169	47.9	271	51.2
		Albert Gore	Democratic	50,996,116	48.4	266	
		Ralph Nader	Green	2,783,728	2.7		
2004	50	GEORGE W. BUSH	Republican	62,039,073	50.7	286	55.3
		John F. Kerry	Democratic	59,027,478	48.2	251	
		Ralph Nader	Independent	240,896	0.2		
2008	50	BARACK OBAMA	Democratic	69,498,459	53.0	365	61.7
		John McCain	Republican	59,948,283	46.0	173	
		Ralph Nader	Independent	739,165	0.55		
2012	50	BARACK OBAMA	Democratic	65,907,213	51.07	332	
		Mitt Romney	Republican	60,931,767	47.21	206	
		Gary Johnson	Independent	1,275,804	0.99		

Candidates receiving less than 1 percent of the popular vote have been omitted. Thus the percentage of popular vote given for any election year may not total 100 percent.

Before the passage of the Twelfth Amendment in 1804, the electoral college voted for two presidential candidates; the runner-up became vice president. Before 1824, most presidential electors were chosen by state legislatures, not by popular vote.

[a]Percent of voting-age population casting ballots.

[b]Greeley died shortly after the election; the electors supporting him then divided their votes among minor candidates.

[c]One elector from West Virginia cast her electoral college presidential ballot for Lloyd Bentsen, the Democratic Party's vice-presidential candidate.

Presidents and Vice Presidents

1. *President* George Washington 1789–1797
   Vice President John Adams 1789–1797

2. *President* John Adams 1797–1801
   Vice President Thomas Jefferson 1797–1801

3. *President* Thomas Jefferson 1801–1809
   Vice President Aaron Burr 1801–1805
   Vice President George Clinton 1805–1809

4. *President* James Madison 1809–1817
   Vice President George Clinton 1809–1813
   Vice President Elbridge Gerry 1813–1817

5. *President* James Monroe 1817–1825
   Vice Priesident Daniel Tompkins 1817–1825

6. *President* John Quincy Adams 1825–1829
   Vice President John C. Calhoun 1825–1829

7. *President* Andrew Jackson 1829–1837
   Vice President John C. Calhoun 1829–1833
   Vice President Martin Van Buren 1833–1837

8. *President* Martin Van Buren 1837–1841
   Vice President Richard M. Johnson 1837–1841

9. *President* William H. Harrison 1841
   Vice President John Tyler 1841

10. *President* John Tyler 1841–1845
    Vice President None

11. *President* James K. Polk 1845–1849
    Vice President George M. Dallas 1845–1849

12. *President* Zachary Taylor 1849–1850
    Vice President Millard Fillmore 1849–1850

13. *President* Millard Fillmore 1850–1853
    Vice President None

14. *President* Franklin Pierce 1853–1857
    Vice President William R. King 1853–1857

15. *President* James Buchanan 1857–1861
    Vice President John C. Breckinridge 1857–1861

16. *President* Abraham Lincoln 1861–1865
    Vice President Hannibal Hamlin 1861–1865
    Vice President Andrew Johnson 1865

17. *President* Andrew Johnson 1865–1869
    Vice President None

18. *President* Ulysses S. Grant 1869–1877
    Vice President Schuyler Colfax 1869–1873
    Vice President Henry Wilson 1873–1877

19. *President* Rutherford B. Hayes 1877–1881
    Vice President William A. Wheeler 1877–1881

20. *President* James A. Garfield 1881
    Vice President Chester A. Arthur 1881

21. *President* Chester A. Arthur 1881–1885
    Vice President None

22. *President* Grover Cleveland 1885–1889
    Vice President Thomas A. Hendricks 1885–1889

23. *President* Benjamin Harrison 1889–1893
    Vice President Levi P. Morton 1889–1893

24. *President* Grover Cleveland 1893–1897
    Vice President Adlai E. Stevenson 1893–1897

25. *President* William McKinley 1897–1901
    Vice President Garret A. Hobart 1897–1901
    Vice President Theodore Roosevelt 1901

26. *President* Theodore Roosevelt 1901–1909
    Vice President Charles Fairbanks 1905–1909

27. *President* William H. Taft 1909–1913
    Vice President James S. Sherman 1909–1913

28. *President* Woodrow Wilson 1913–1921
    Vice President Thomas R. Marshall 1913–1921

29. *President* Warren G. Harding 1921–1923
    Vice President Calvin Coolidge 1921–1923

30. *President* Calvin Coolidge 1923–1929
    Vice President Charles G. Dawes 1925–1929

31. *President* Herbert C. Hoover 1929–1933
    Vice President Charles Curtis 1929–1933

32. *President* Franklin D. Roosevelt 1933–1945
    Vice President John N. Garner 1933–1941
    Vice President Henry A. Wallace 1941–1945
    Vice President Harry S Truman 1945

33. *President* Harry S Truman 1945–1953
    Vice President Alben W. Barkley 1949–1953

34. *President* Dwight D. Eisenhower 1953–1961
    Vice President Richard M. Nixon 1953–1961

35. *President* John F. Kennedy 1961–1963
    Vice President Lyndon B. Johnson 1961–1963

36. *President* Lyndon B. Johnson 1963–1969
    Vice President Hubert H. Humphrey 1965–1969

37. *President* Richard M. Nixon 1969–1974
    Vice President Spiro T. Agnew 1969–1973
    Vice President Gerald R. Ford 1973–1974

38. *President* Gerald R. Ford 1974–1977
    Vice President Nelson A. Rockefeller 1974–1977

39. *President* James E. Carter 1977–1981
    Vice President Walter F. Mondale 1977–1981

40. *President* Ronald W. Reagan 1981–1989
    Vice President George H. W. Bush 1981–1989

41. *President* George H. W. Bush 1989–1993
    Vice President J. Danforth Quayle 1989–1993

42. *President* William J. Clinton 1993–2001
    Vice President Albert Gore 1993–2001

43. *President* George W. Bush 2001–2009
    Vice President Richard B. Cheney 2001–2009

44. *President* Barack H. Obama 2009–2017
    Vice President Joseph R. Biden 2009–2017

Justices of the Supreme Court

	Term of Service	Years of Service	Life Span		Term of Service	Years of Service	Life Span
John Jay	1789–1795	5	1745–1829	Noah H. Swayne	1862–1881	18	1804–1884
John Rutledge	1789–1791	1	1739–1800	Samuel F. Miller	1862–1890	28	1816–1890
William Cushing	1789–1810	20	1732–1810	David Davis	1862–1877	14	1815–1886
James Wilson	1789–1798	8	1742–1798	Stephen J. Field	1863–1897	34	1816–1899
John Blair	1789–1796	6	1732–1800	*Salmon P. Chase*	1864–1873	8	1808–1873
Robert H. Harrison	1789–1790	—	1745–1790	William Strong	1870–1880	10	1808–1895
James Iredell	1790–1799	9	1751–1799	Joseph P. Bradley	1870–1892	22	1813–1892
Thomas Johnson	1791–1793	1	1732–1819	Ward Hunt	1873–1882	9	1810–1886
William Paterson	1793–1806	13	1745–1806	*Morrison R. Waite*	1874–1888	14	1816–1888
*John Rutledge**	1795	—	1739–1800	John M. Harlan	1877–1911	34	1833–1911
Samuel Chase	1796–1811	15	1741–1811	William B. Woods	1880–1887	7	1824–1887
Oliver Ellsworth	1796–1800	4	1745–1807	Stanley Mathews	1881–1889	7	1824–1889
Bushrod Washington	1798–1829	31	1762–1829	Horace Gray	1882–1902	20	1828–1902
Alfred Moore	1799–1804	4	1755–1810	Samuel Blatchford	1882–1893	11	1820–1893
John Marshall	1801–1835	34	1755–1835	Lucius Q. C. Lamar	1888–1893	5	1825–1893
William Johnson	1804–1834	30	1771–1834	*Melville W. Fuller*	1888–1910	21	1833–1910
H. Brockholst Livingston	1806–1823	16	1757–1823	David J. Brewer	1890–1910	20	1837–1910
Thomas Todd	1807–1826	18	1765–1826	Henry B. Brown	1890–1906	16	1836–1913
Joseph Story	1811–1845	33	1779–1845	George Shiras Jr.	1892–1903	10	1832–1924
Gabriel Duval	1811–1835	24	1752–1844	Howell E. Jackson	1893–1895	2	1832–1895
Smith Thompson	1823–1843	20	1768–1843	Edward D. White	1894–1910	16	1845–1921
Robert Trimble	1826–1828	2	1777–1828	Rufus W. Peckham	1895–1909	14	1838–1909
John McLean	1829–1861	32	1785–1861	Joseph McKenna	1898–1925	26	1843–1926
Henry Baldwin	1830–1844	14	1780–1844	Oliver W. Holmes	1902–1932	30	1841–1935
James M. Wayne	1835–1867	32	1790–1867	William D. Day	1903–1922	19	1849–1923
Roger B. Taney	1836–1864	28	1777–1864	William H. Moody	1906–1910	3	1853–1917
Philip P. Barbour	1836–1841	4	1783–1841	Horace H. Lurton	1910–1914	4	1844–1914
John Catron	1837–1865	28	1786–1865	Charles E. Hughes	1910–1916	5	1862–1948
John McKinley	1837–1852	15	1780–1852	Willis Van Devanter	1911–1937	26	1859–1941
Peter V. Daniel	1841–1860	19	1784–1860	Joseph R. Lamar	1911–1916	5	1857–1916
Samuel Nelson	1845–1872	27	1792–1873	*Edward D. White*	1910–1921	11	1845–1921
Levi Woodbury	1845–1851	5	1789–1851	Mahlon Pitney	1912–1922	10	1858–1924
Robert C. Grier	1846–1870	23	1794–1870	James C. McReynolds	1914–1941	26	1862–1946
Benjamin R. Curtis	1851–1857	6	1809–1874	Louis D. Brandeis	1916–1939	22	1856–1941
John A. Campbell	1853–1861	8	1811–1889	John H. Clarke	1916–1922	6	1857–1945
Nathan Clifford	1858–1881	23	1803–1881	*William H. Taft*	1921–1930	8	1857–1930

	Term of Service	Years of Service	Life Span		Term of Service	Years of Service	Life Span
George Sutherland	1922–1938	15	1862–1942	Charles E. Whittaker	1957–1962	5	1901–1973
Pierce Butler	1922–1939	16	1866–1939	Potter Stewart	1958–1981	23	1915–1985
Edward T. Sanford	1923–1930	7	1865–1930	Byron R. White	1962–1993	31	1917–
Harlan F. Stone	1925–1941	16	1872–1946	Arthur J. Goldberg	1962–1965	3	1908–1990
Charles E. Hughes	1930–1941	11	1862–1948	Abe Fortas	1965–1969	4	1910–1982
Owen J. Roberts	1930–1945	15	1875–1955	Thurgood Marshall	1967–1991	24	1908–1993
Benjamin N. Cardozo	1932–1938	6	1870–1938	*Warren C. Burger*	1969–1986	17	1907–1995
Hugo L. Black	1937–1971	34	1886–1971	Harry A. Blackmun	1970–1994	24	1908–1998
Stanley F. Reed	1938–1957	19	1884–1980	Lewis F. Powell Jr.	1972–1987	15	1907–1998
Felix Frankfurter	1939–1962	23	1882–1965	*William H. Rehnquist*	1972–2005	33	1924–2005
William O. Douglas	1939–1975	36	1898–1980	John P. Stevens III	1975–2010	35	1920–
Frank Murphy	1940–1949	9	1890–1949	Sandra Day O'Connor	1981–2006	25	1930–
Harlan F. Stone	1941–1946	5	1872–1946	Antonin Scalia	1986–	—	1936–
James F. Byrnes	1941–1942	1	1879–1972	Anthony M. Kennedy	1988–	—	1936–
Robert H. Jackson	1941–1954	13	1892–1954	David H. Souter	1990–2009	19	1939–
Wiley B. Rutledge	1943–1949	6	1894–1949	Clarence Thomas	1991–	—	1948–
Harold H. Burton	1945–1958	13	1888–1964	Ruth Bader Ginsburg	1993–	—	1933–
Fred M. Vinson	1946–1953	7	1890–1953	Stephen Breyer	1994–	—	1938–
Tom C. Clark	1949–1967	18	1899–1977	John G. Roberts	2005–	—	1955–
Sherman Minton	1949–1956	7	1890–1965	Samuel A. Alito, Jr.	2006–	—	1950–
Earl Warren	1953–1969	16	1891–1974	Sonia Sotomayor	2009–	—	1954–
John Marshall Harlan	1955–1971	16	1899–1971	Elena Kagan	2010–	—	1960–
William J. Brennan Jr.	1956–1990	34	1906–1997				

Note: Chief justices are in italics.

*Appointed and served one term, but not confirmed by the Senate.

Index